Michael L. Butterworth (Ed.)
Communication and Sport

Handbooks of Communication Science

Edited by
Peter J. Schulz and Paul Cobley

Advisory Board
Klaus Bruhn Jensen (University of Copenhagen)
Min-Sun Kim (University of Hawaii at Manoa)
Denis McQuail † (University of Southampton)
Katherine I. Miller (Arizona State University)
Daniel O'Keefe (Northwestern University)
Frans H. van Eemeren (University Amsterdam)
Jürgen Wilke (Johannes Gutenberg University, Mainz)

Volume 28

Communication and Sport

Edited by
Michael L. Butterworth

DE GRUYTER
MOUTON

Università
della
Svizzera
italiana

Faculty of Communication Sciences

The publication of this series has been partly funded by the Università della Svizzera italiana – University of Lugano.

ISBN 978-3-11-125783-9
e-ISBN (PDF) 978-3-11-066088-3
e-ISBN (EPUB) 978-3-11-065715-9
ISSN 2199-6288

Library of Congress Control Number: 2021933300

Bibliographic information published by the Deutsche Nationalbibliothek
The Deutsche Nationalbibliothek lists this publication in the Deutsche Nationalbibliografie; detailed bibliographic data are available on the Internet at http://dnb.dnb.de.

© 2023 Walter de Gruyter GmbH, Berlin/Boston
This volume is text- and page-identical with the hardback published in 2021.

Cover image: Oliver Rossi/Photographer's Choice RF/Gettyimages
Typesetting: Dörlemann Satz, Lemförde
Printing and binding: CPI books GmbH, Leck

www.degruyter.com

Preface to *Handbooks of Communication Science* series

This volume is part of the series *Handbooks of Communication Science*, published from 2012 onwards by de Gruyter Mouton. When our generation of scholars was in their undergraduate years, and one happened to be studying communication, a series like this one was hard to imagine. There was, in fact, such a dearth of basic and reference literature that trying to make one's way in communication studies as our generation did would be unimaginable to today's undergraduates in the field. In truth, there was simply nothing much to turn to when you needed to cast a first glance at the key objects in the field of communication. The situation in the United States was slightly different; nevertheless, it is only within the last generation that the basic literature has really proliferated there.

What one did when looking for an overview or just a quick reference was to turn to social science books in general, or to the handbooks or textbooks from the neighbouring disciplines such as psychology, sociology, political science, linguistics, and probably other fields. That situation has changed dramatically. There are more textbooks available on some subjects than even the most industrious undergraduate can read. The representative key multi-volume *International Encyclopedia of Communication* has now been available for some years. Overviews of subfields of communication exist in abundance. There is no longer a dearth for the curious undergraduate, who might nevertheless overlook the abundance of printed material and Google whatever he or she wants to know, to find a suitable Wikipedia entry within seconds.

'Overview literature' in an academic discipline serves to draw a balance. There has been a demand and a necessity to draw that balance in the field of communication and it is an indicator of the maturing of the discipline. Our project of a multi-volume series of *Handbooks of Communication Science* is a part of this coming-of-age movement of the field. It is certainly one of the largest endeavours of its kind within communication sciences, with almost two dozen volumes already planned. But it is also unique in its combination of several things.

The series is a major publishing venture which aims to offer a portrait of the current state of the art in the study of communication. But it seeks to do more than just assemble our knowledge of communication structures and processes; it seeks to *integrate* this knowledge. It does so by offering comprehensive articles in all the volumes instead of small entries in the style of an encyclopedia. An extensive index in each *Handbook* in the series, serves the encyclopedic task of find relevant specific pieces of information. There are already several handbooks in sub-disciplines of communication sciences such as political communication, methodology, organizational communication – but none so far has tried to comprehensively cover the discipline as a whole.

https://doi.org/10.1515/9783110660883-201

For all that it is maturing, communication as a discipline is still young and one of its benefits is that it derives its theories and methods from a great variety of work in other, and often older, disciplines. One consequence of this is that there is a variety of approaches and traditions in the field. For the *Handbooks* in this series, this has created two necessities: commitment to a pluralism of approaches, and a commitment to honour the scholarly traditions of current work and its intellectual roots in the knowledge in earlier times.

There is really no single object of communication sciences. However, if one were to posit one possible object it might be the human communicative act – often conceived as "someone communicates something to someone else." This is the departure point for much study of communication and, in consonance with such study, it is also the departure point for this series of *Handbooks*. As such, the series does not attempt to adopt the untenable position of understanding communication sciences as the study of everything that can be conceived as communicating. Rather, while acknowledging that the study of communication must be multifaceted or fragmented, it also recognizes two very general approaches to communication which can be distinguished as: a) the semiotic or linguistic approach associated particularly with the humanities and developed especially where the Romance languages have been dominant and b) a quantitative approach associated with the hard and the social sciences and developed, especially, within an Anglo-German tradition. Although the relationship between these two approaches and between theory and research has not always been straightforward, the series does not privilege one above the other. In being committed to a plurality of approaches it assumes that different camps have something to tell each other. In this way, the *Handbooks* aspire to be relevant for all approaches to communication. The specific designation "communication science" for the *Handbooks* should be taken to indicate this commitment to plurality; like "the study of communication", it merely designates the disciplined, methodologically informed, institutionalized study of (human) communication.

On an operational level, the series aims at meeting the needs of undergraduates, postgraduates, academics and researchers across the area of communication studies. Integrating knowledge of communication structures and processes, it is dedicated to cultural and epistemological diversity, covering work originating from around the globe and applying very different scholarly approaches. To this end, the series is divided into 6 sections: "Theories and Models of Communication", "Messages, Codes and Channels", "Mode of Address, Communicative Situations and Contexts", "Methodologies", "Application areas" and "Futures". As readers will see, the first four sections are fixed; yet it is in the nature of our field that the "Application areas" will expand. It is inevitable that the futures for the field promise to be intriguing with their proximity to the key concerns of human existence on this planet (and even beyond), with the continuing prospect in communication sciences that that future is increasingly susceptible of prediction.

Note: administration on this series has been funded by the Universita della Svizzera italiana – University of Lugano. Thanks go to the president of the university, Professor Piero Martinoli, as well as to the administration director, Albino Zgraggen.

Peter J. Schulz, Universita della Svizzera italiana, Lugano
Paul Cobley, Middlesex University, London

Acknowledgments

As the interest in "communication and sport" or "sports communication" has grown in recent years, so too has the attempt to define the scope of the field. Although I had been involved in the organizational efforts to establish the Communication and Sport division with the National Communication Association and to launch the International Association for Communication and Sport, I did not imagine jumping into the conversation by assembling a handbook. What a daunting task, I might have thought, to attempt to capture the range of theories, methods, and topics informing communication and sport scholarship from around the world.

It is often the case, however, that we aren't aware of our interest in something until it is presented to us. So, when Paul Cobley and Peter Schulz invited me in the fall of 2017 to take on this project, it did not take long for me to respond affirmatively. I want to begin, then, by thanking both of them for giving me the opportunity in the first place and for endorsing the vision for the handbook that I established over the ensuing months and years. They have been patient, supportive, and enthusiastic throughout this entire process.

It will have been nearly four years from the time of that initial invitation to the time of publication, so there are many people at DeGruyter Mouton who have been involved in this project. The editorial team has been professional, encouraging, and responsive throughout, and I am grateful for the guidance they have provided. In particular, thanks to Natalie Fecher, Barbara Karlsson, Michaela Göbels, Liz Nichols, Monika Pfleghar, and David from IndexBusters.

I am extremely fortunate to be a part of the faculty of the Department of Communication Studies and to direct the Center for Sports Communication & Media in the Moody College of Communication at The University of Texas at Austin. UT-Austin is a remarkable institution, and it is a rich environment for research and teaching. I am surrounded by accomplished and generous colleagues, and my work with the Center connects me to a wide range of intellectual pursuits and industry practices. I am so grateful to be a part of this incredible community. In addition, as the Governor Ann W. Richards Chair for the Texas Program in Sports and Media, I benefit greatly from endowed funds that support my work, including this handbook project.

This book itself would be of little interest if not for the contributions of a spectacular group of scholars. I thank them all not only for their talent and time, but also for their patience and professional courtesy. Everyone has helped to make this a rewarding experience. I also want to acknowledge the work of those not included in this volume, in particular the many scholars in communication, media, sociology, cultural studies, and related fields who have made something called "communication and sport" possible.

Finally, I thank my spouse, Gina, and children Emily and James. What an experience it has been to navigate a project of this scope in the midst of a global pandemic and its repercussions for school, work, and family life. You all are the best fans a sports scholar could wish for.

https://doi.org/10.1515/9783110660883-202

Contents

I Introduction to communication and sport

Michael L. Butterworth

1 Communication and sport: an emergent field

Abstract: The field of communication and sport has expanded rapidly in the past two decades, bringing together related traditions in communication studies, mass communication, journalism, and cultural studies. The field's legitimacy has been confirmed by the growth of representation in academic associations and a growing body of research. Yet, the coherence of "communication and sport" as a field remains in question. This book makes the case that a shared emphasis on messages and meaning brings sometimes divergent interests under one "big tent." Given scholarly trends and contemporary issues in sport, the time is ideal for the *Handbook of Communication and Sport*.

Keywords: communication and sport; sport media; sport journalism; sport culture; social media and sport; sport nationalism

1 Introduction: contextualizing the field

It is fair to claim that never has the relationship between communication and sport been more relevant. On the one hand, this observation merely acknowledges well-established trends emergent in the late 20th and early 21st centuries. Such trends include: (1) the continued expansion of mega-events such as the Olympic Games and FIFA World Cup; (2) the reconfiguration of media industries adjusting to the advent of interactive and social media; (3) the fluidity of national affiliation and identity in the global sport marketplace; (4) the use of sport as a means of identification for political candidates and officials; (5) the proliferation of multi-year sport media contracts, often valued in the billions of USD; (6) the legitimization of industries adjacent to sport, including legal gambling, fantasy sports, and eSports; and (7) the transformation of youth sport worldwide, much of which has depended on economic shifts that have exacerbated the disparities of opportunity among those with financial resources and those without. Surely, there are other important developments one might add to this list.

On the other hand, any assessment of contemporary sport must also contend with the (re)emergence of more specific issues affecting the landscape of communication and sport. Specifically, three events at the beginning of the 21st-century's third decade have spotlighted both the scope of sport's global significance as well as the precarious balance between sport and other social structures. Among the largest sporting events at the beginning of 2020 was tennis' Australian Open, the first of four major tournaments shared by the men's and women's tours. During the event's qualifying rounds, smoke from nearby catastrophic bushfires made the air quality in Melbourne "the worst in the world" (Murray 2020), causing physical distress for several players.

https://doi.org/10.1515/9783110660883-001

The Australian fires were perhaps the most important news story as the year began, prompting much commentary about the effects of global climate change and sport's environmental footprint. The crisis in Australia spotlighted ongoing concerns about the environmental consequences of hosting mega-events (Karamichas 2015) and reminded observers of the effects on competition of increasing temperatures during hot weather months or decreasing snowfall in the winter (Zirin 2020).

The concerns about sport's effect on the environment were not new, but they momentarily became centered in conversations about how to manage the relationship between climate change and an industry with such global reach. That moment was short-lived, however, as a different global crisis eventually brought all of sport to a halt. There will be much written in the coming years about the effect of the coronavirus named COVID-19. Although it emerged in late 2019, the severity of the problem became apparent on March 11, 2020 when the World Health Organization officially declared the virus a pandemic ("Coronavirus confirmed" 2020). Even before that announcement, the major European football leagues – Ligue 1 (France), the English Premier League (UK), Serie A (Italy), La Liga (Spain), and the Bundesliga (Germany) – had all suspended play. The launch of the Basketball Africa League was postponed ("Basketball Africa League" 2020), professional baseball leagues in Japan (Conway 2020) and South Korea (Yonhap 2020) made similar decisions, and South America's 2020 Copa America was pushed back until 2021 (Gonzalez 2020). By the end of March, every US league had come to a halt (Mather 2020) and the 2020 Summer Olympic Games in Tokyo were moved to 2021 (Talmazan 2020).

Over the course of 2020, sports leagues around the world gradually found ways to start or resume their seasons. The Korean Baseball Organization began play on May 5 and the German Bundeslinga returned on May 16. Both proceeded with strict testing protocols and without fans in the stands. The absence of live spectators provided organizations and broadcasters with new opportunities for fan participation and digital engagement, including virtual attendance, simulated crowd noise, and inventive new camera angles (Newman 2020). In spite of these mediated innovations, the lack of in-person contact created a potentially awkward atmosphere for athletes and diminished the social experience for fans (Chau 2020). How sport organizations, leagues, media, and related institutions managed the crisis and anticipated which changes would become permanent was arguably the most significant communication priority of the time.

If the pandemic revealed several vulnerabilities, a third crisis in 2020 spotlighted additional tensions within sport industries. When a Minneapolis police officer killed George Floyd on May 25, many athletes joined the voices of outrage being heard across the United States. Floyd's murder was the latest in a tragically long string of incidents in which white law enforcement officers have responded with deadly force against unarmed Black men. Such cases had prompted protests among athletes in 2016 and 2017, but the injustice of Floyd's death sparked an unprecedented response, in part because it was dramatized by a graphic video widely shared on social media and also because the suspension of sports during the pandemic led to more intense scrutiny regarding police violence in the United States (Bebernes 2020). In addition to Floyd, the high profile stories detailing the deaths of innocent Black citizens Ahmaud Arbery and Breanna Taylor fueled a resurgence of the Black Lives Matter movement, much of it driven by athletes (Radnofsky and Beaton 2020).

Although the particulars of racial violence in the United States may have been the impetus for athlete activism in 2020, it was quickly apparent that the movement resonated around the world. Athletes in association football, auto racing, cricket, surfing, and tennis echoed anti-racism expressions that proliferated within US leagues ("In photos" 2020). As tempting as it may be to attribute the resurgence of activism only to the incidents that took place in 2020, it is important to note the increased attention given to the intersection of politics and sport in recent years. Since the killing of Trayvon Martin in 2012, athletes in the United States have used sport as a platform for protest, most notably in the case of National Football League (NFL) quarterback Colin Kaepernick. As I have noted elsewhere, "the visibility of Kaepernick's actions and the intensity of subsequent commentary seem to have galvanized the communication and sport community" (Butterworth 2020: 453–454). Meanwhile, protests have erupted in conjunction with the staging of the Olympic Games, sport's ultimate mega-event and one that all too often exacerbates social inequalities and enables corruption (Boykoff 2020; Zirin 2016).

Pro-democracy protests in Hong Kong illustrate the developing commitment to activism in the sport community. Political unrest emerged in response to proposed legislation that would have changed extradition laws between Hong Kong and mainland China. Outrage over the bill led to massive public demonstrations, some of which turned violent. Although the bill was eventually withdrawn, protestors continued to press for reform ("Hong Kong formally" 2019). Athletes were among those following the situation in Hong Kong. In a particularly newsworthy case, eSports star Ng Wai Chung, known better by his player name "Blitzchung," expressed solidarity with the pro-democracy activists during a live interview associated with a *Hearthstone* tournament. After putting on a ski mask and gas mask that looked like those worn by protestors, he said, "Liberate Hong Kong. Revolution of our age." The Hong Kong native later explained his commitment to the protest and acknowledged his actions "could cause me a lot of trouble." *Hearthstone* developer, Blizzard Entertainment, responded by rescinding Blitzchung's prize money and banning him from the game's tournaments for a year (Clark 2019).

The dispute between Blitzchung and Blizzard echoed the fallout in the National Basketball Association (NBA) after Houston Rockets general manager Daryl Morey tweeted his support of the Hong Kong demonstrators, stating, "Fight for Freedom, Stand with Hong Kong." Criticism from China was swift, and Morey and league officials tried to minimize the damage (Greer 2019). Given the NBA's enormous investment in the Chinese market, the economic implications were significant. Moreover, the subsequent discourse regarding the propriety of US citizens commenting on Chinese politics spotlighted the ambiguities and contradictions of "free speech" advocacy among US politicians, including President Donald Trump (Burns 2019). In each case – both Blizzard and the NBA – the intersections of sport, media, and political communication were immediately apparent.

My aim here is not to recount every detail of these developments; rather, it is to use them as snapshots to dramatize the various and intensifying entanglements of communication and sport. The earth's climate, global health, and political activism are perhaps the most obvious contexts in which we can assess the interconnections of sport and media production, journalism, technological innovation, intercultural interactions, organizational statements, political speech, interpersonal dynamics, and much more, but they are not the only ones. Indeed, we are inundated daily with reminders of sport's social importance, economic impact, and political symbolism. In short, it is an ideal moment for the *Handbook of Communication and Sport*, one in which scholars must assess and evaluate the practices and processes of communication in sporting contexts. What does it mean, however, to identify "communication and sport" as our domain? It is to that question I turn next.

2 Defining the field

As may be apparent, I have been careful to frame the above issues in terms of "communication and sport." This is not a simple reflection of the book's title; rather the title is a reflection of the disciplinary commitments found within this volume. In short, as a rhetorical scholar educated and employed in the United States, I have been enculturated into the discipline of "communication" or "communication studies." Around the world, academic approaches to "communication" are sometimes equated with "media" or "journalism." In addition, the study of communication behaviors is often located within other scholarly traditions, including management, philosophy, and psychology. In the United States, the discipline represents a mid-20th-century merger between the rhetorical tradition – rooted in ancient Greece and Rome – and the post-war expansion of government-sponsored research to understand and counteract forms of mass persuasion popularized by fascism. Although distinct traditions in speech and journalism/mass communication remained, the broader convergence of these overlapping interests led to the emergence of "communication studies" as a modern discipline in the US academy (Simonson and Weimann 2003).

In subsequent decades, the field consolidated around the National Communication Association (NCA) and incorporated related disciplinary interests in areas such as intercultural, interpersonal, and organizational communication, among many others. As communication studies matured, its interdisciplinarity became both an asset and a liability. Although drawing from multiple traditions enabled innovative academic inquiry, disputes about method and theory reinforced a certain fragmentation. By the end of the 1960s, scholars frustrated by the influence of rhetorical studies within NCA broke away to form the International Communication Association (ICA) (Weaver 1977). Rhetoric, meanwhile, responded to the political unrest of the 1960s and 1970s with a shift of focus away from the "great speakers and speeches" (Gehrke and Keith 2014) model and to a focus on social movements, ideology, and continental philosophy (Lucaites and Condit 1998). This shift meant that rhetorical scholars within communication studies often held more in common with cultural studies, literary studies, and philosophy than their counterparts in media and social scientific researchers influenced by psychology and sociology.

This is, of course, a truncated version of the discipline's history and, for a more comprehensive narrative, I defer to those who have traced these developments with great care and sophistication (Gehrke and Keith 2014; Katz et al. 2003; Peters 1999). What is important here is that these scholarly intersections and divides have affected the study of sport. Disciplines in the humanities and social sciences were not quick to accept sport as a legitimate site of inquiry. Scholars who began studying sport in the 1970s and 1980s surely recall the skepticism of their colleagues about the necessity or rigor of sport-based research. Although some doubts remain today, the study of sport increased in earnest in 1990s (Trujillo 2003) and, as Wenner details in the next chapter, became normalized through organizations and publications in the first two decades of the 21st century. Yet, the fragmented nature of "communication studies" has often meant that scholars with shared intellectual commitments have pursued their work independently, sometimes unaware of larger conversations taking place within their subfield or in other parts of the world.

As I noted above, one of the virtues of the communication discipline is its interdisciplinary scope. Thus, I have no interest in trying to find a magic formula to unify these overlapping traditions. Nevertheless, there is value in recognizing that "communication" provides a useful organizational focus. That focus is most evident, I argue, in the shared emphasis on messages and their meaning. Returning to the primary examples of the previous section, consider the following:

(1) In the days before the 2020 Australian Open began, tournament officials insisted it was safe to play. The head of Tennis Australia, Craig Tilley, declared, "We have committed substantial extra resources to analysis, monitoring and logistics to ensure the health and safety of all players, staff and fans throughout the summer." Defending champion Novak Djokovic, ranked second in the world at the start of 2020, met privately with Tilley on behalf of the Association of Tennis Professionals (ATP) Player Council to discuss the well-being of the participants (Phillips 2020). In this case, *interpersonal communication* between Tilley and Djokovic (and others) intersected with *organizational statements* assuring the public the tournament was being held under safe conditions.

(2) As the effects of the coronavirus pandemic became apparent in the spring and summer of 2020, competing constituents argued over the viability of continuing or returning to sport. Among the most visible sports in the United States is college

football, which traditionally begins in late August. As momentum built to postpone or cancel the upcoming season, some players advocated it be preserved. Perhaps most noteworthy was Clemson University quarterback Trevor Lawrence, a favorite for the sport's coveted Heisman Trophy award and presumptive first pick of the 2021 NFL draft. On August 9, Lawrence tweeted "#WeWantToPlay," accompanied by a list of health and safety conditions agreed upon by the major conferences in the National Collegiate Athletic Association (NCAA). Lawrence's tweet went viral (Lawrence 2020), influencing other athletes on *social media* and setting the agenda for more traditional *sport media* as the story progressed.

(3) As athlete activism intensified in 2020, various sport institutions struggled with efforts to appear supportive of social justice causes while also seeking to minimize disruptions to their events. Earlier in the year, the International Olympic Committee (IOC) had already clarified rules to ensure that the Olympic Games (presumably to be held that summer) would be free from "any form of political, religious or ethnic demonstrations" (Armour 2020). In his June speech to the organization, IOC President Thomas Bach reiterated his concerns about politics in the Olympics, what he termed "the growing misuse of sport for political purposes" (Bach 2020a). He emphasized this argument once more in an October editorial in which he declared, "The Olympic Games are not about politics," even adding that the IOC "is strictly politically neutral at all times" (Bach 2020b). In addition to leveraging the credibility of the IOC and mainstream media outlets in these cases, Bach also relies on the conventions of *public address* (rhetoric) in order to reach multiple audiences.

The connections among and between these examples may seem obvious enough, but it is worth highlighting the shared emphasis on *persuasion*. In each context – organizational, interpersonal, mediated, public – communicators seek to influence attitudes, beliefs, and behaviors. Yet, it is not sufficient to identify only these instrumental aims; indeed, communication outcomes are based as much if not more so on the interpretations made by audiences and by unintended meanings constituted by these messages. In short, *communication is a practice and process*, not simply the dissemination of a message. We can therefore understand communication in many contexts and through various media, as is evident in the range of approaches found in this volume.

As Wenner suggests in the subsequent chapter, this expansive definition of communication requires scholars to see themselves sharing space under a single "big tent." I find that metaphor appropriate; the more open question is whether or not we spend our time mostly under the tent of "communication," or if we find ourselves moving among and between others. Wenner notes the valuable contributions of sports sociologists and psychologists to the discipline of communication. Those contributions are inarguable and they have both informed the work done by communication scholars and eased the legitimization of sport-based scholarship. That said, I think it is safe to conclude that a uniquely *communicative* approach to the study of sport is both possible and present, and that the subfield of "communication and sport" must assert itself more assuredly. This is not an argument about drawing disciplinary lines in the sand; rather, it is about advancing an intellectual project that offers unique and important insights into one of the world's most universal and influential institutions.

There are plenty of signs that the field has "arrived." Wenner's chapter offers a sterling history of its emergence, so I will not repeat it here. But it is worth noting that among each of the discipline's primary associations – NCA, ICA, the International Association for Media and Communication Research (IAMCR), the Association of Educators of Journalism and Mass Communication (AEJMC), among others – there now exists a division or interest group to represent work on sport. The launch of the International Association for Communication and Sport (IACS), an organization for which I served as founding Executive Director, confirms that sport-based research can sustain an entire academic enterprise. In addition, journals such as the *International Journal of Sport Communication* and *Communication & Sport* have emerged alongside a flurry of special issues and a growing number of scholarly books to add legitimacy to the area. Nevertheless, as a member of several editorial boards and as an ad hoc reviewer for numerous journals and book proposals, I all too often read scholarship by authors who remain ambivalent or uncertain about the discipline's status. This is most commonly exemplified by citations of work in the sociology of sport that may be 20 or 30 years old at the expense of engaging with much more current work that comes from a different area of communication (studies). I am neither arguing that all citations must be within a given discipline nor that they must meet some arbitrary standard of currency; rather, I am noting that, in many cases, when current and compelling work is available within the discipline, communication scholars instead look elsewhere. One of my aims for this handbook, then, is to advance the argument that communication and sport *is* a subfield of its own, and it is one that can stand on its own merits.

As I hope is clear, the disciplinary emphasis on communication does not mean that I do not welcome other disciplines *to* the subfield. To the contrary, I encourage it and hope that the interest communication scholars have shown in other areas can be reciprocated. Indeed, some of the contributors to this volume may identify primarily with sociology or a related field, yet their chapters here are contextualized by the commitments of communication inquiry. This communicative focus is one of four guiding assumptions that I had in mind as I assembled this book. To clarify further, I have consciously featured communication as both the "big tent" term (thus subsuming "media" beneath it) and as the dominant term in the phrase, "communication and sport." I prefer this order to the oft-used "sport communication," if only because it places the emphasis on the disciplinary framework as opposed to the site of study. There are good reasons to reverse the order, however, and I generally accept the terms as interchangeable. I am insistent, however, on avoiding the plural, "communications," as this connotes particular technological or industry-specific interests. With that distinction in mind, the book is designed to account for a wide range of communicative phenomena, including studies that are empirical, interpretive, and critical.

A second assumption I have made is that a handbook on communication and sport ought to be as expansive as possible with respect to topics and approaches. It is tempting, of course, to be pulled in particular directions. The explosion of social media in the past 10–15 years warrants substantial attention, as does the proliferation of athlete activism more recently. Or it might seem appropriate to isolate mediatization or social identity theory to account for the growth of those approaches. To be sure, each of these examples is accounted for in the book. Nevertheless, I curated chapters with a more open-ended approach, soliciting authors based on clear areas of expertise while also allowing the latitude for each of them to contribute as they saw fit. That approach undoubtedly leaves some gaps and produces occasional points of overlap, but I am confident the following 38 chapters capture the essence of the field. In allowing for author flexibility, I also chose not to prescribe whether each chapter should attempt a summary or meta-analysis of a given area of study. Some of the chapters here do take that approach, but many of them are original research designs or case studies. Previous handbooks, such as the *Routledge Handbook of Sport Communication* (Pedersen 2015) and *Defining Sport Communication* (Billings 2016) take different approaches. The former is similarly ambitious, but I would suggest retains the emphasis on "media" that often defines the field. The latter has a more inclusive orientation to communication but favors descriptive approaches to sport rather than demonstrations of original research. The current project owes much to both excellent collections but seeks to capture a wider range of communicative approaches while still introducing new work.

Third, I sought to include a diverse collection of authors from around the world. Although some contributors had to bow out of the project along the way (for perfectly fair and legitimate reasons), and others who were invited were unable to commit in the first place, I am pleased with the roster of contributors that follows. Counting myself, the book includes a total of 58 authors, representing a clear international scope. Thirty of the authors are based outside of the United States and many are writing in English even though that is not their native language. There are many identity characteristics about which I cannot comment with credibility – e. g., race, ethnicity, sexual orientation – yet there are clear indications that the book is inclusive. That said, there remain limitations. Communication studies as a whole continues to lack racial diversity (Chakravartty et al. 2018), and communication and sport scholarship has long been dominated by men. Further, my own location within the United States and its higher education structure undoubtedly influenced the network of scholars with whom I have engaged. I made conscious efforts to recruit contributions that could address these shortcomings, but I recognize the field must continue to expand those it invites under the "big tent."

Fourth, the chapters collected here reflect both established trajectories and current (and future) trends in the field. Communication and sport scholars have long attended to media representations or political ideologies, for example, and it is clear such work remains vital. At the same time, we should be prepared to assess newer areas, such as the impact of eSports or the relationship between sport and the environment. Doing so means acknowledging the voices of both senior scholars and those newer to the field. With that in mind, I am especially pleased to have a number of graduate students and junior scholars included in the volume.

3 Previewing the book

The *Handbook of Communication and Sport* is organized in five sections. Section I, "Introduction to Communication and Sport," consists only of this introductory chapter and the subsequent overview of the field. Wenner's assessment draws on his experience as a scholar and editor, as well as his role as an ambassador for communication and sport research. As he has noted in recent essays (2015, 2017), questions remain as to whether or not "communication and sport" can be considered a distinct field. He provides a compelling historical review of the disciplinary intersections that have brought us to the contemporary moment. He then articulates three scholarly dispositions – (1) Media, Sports, and Society; (2) Sport Communication as a Profession; and (3) Communication Studies and Sport – that he sees as defining the field as we know it. Wenner's chapter is part exposition, part exhortation – i. e., he acknowledges the value of what communication and sport has become, but also wants scholars to push for more. I agree with him, and I see this book as an effort to meet that call.

Section II, "Communication Studies of Sport," reflects many of the approaches that fall under Wenner's third scholarly disposition and the disciplinary accommodations between the rhetorical tradition and studies of mass communication noted above. Admittedly, these chapters largely reflect North American traditions in intercultural, interpersonal, organizational, and rhetorical communication. This is a conscious choice, consistent with my effort to foreground communication practices and processes. It begins with Gantz, Lewis, and van Driel's effort in Chapter 3 to expand our understanding of sport fan identity. Noting that fan scholarship too often simplifies the way people understand the intensity of their commitments, the authors develop a typology isolating 17 different categories of fan identity. In doing so, they provide a comprehensive survey of extant sport fan literature and add nuance to an already robust area of scholarship. In Chapter 4, Danielle Sarver Coombs extends the discussion of fan identity with a focus on non-local fan communities. Using a model she has developed previously– the Psychological Continuum Model – Coombs identifies three kinds of non-local fans: satellite, displaced, and distant. To develop these categories further, she encourages scholars to embrace interdisciplinary approaches, investigate fans and collaborate with scholars in regions such as the Global South, and evaluate non-local fanship in relation to media.

Gregory Cranmer turns our attention in Chapter 5 to organizational communication, specifically focusing on processes used by athletic coaches. He situates the chapter with an overview of organizational communications scholarship, and then focuses on the ways coaches socialize athletes, enact leadership, and manage athlete dissent. Cranmer's approach helps to ground sport scholarship specifically in organizational communication, an area that remains under-developed in the subfield. He also offers applied recommendations for coaching practices that emerge from his empirical observations. In Chapter 6, Kim Bissell and Tyana Ellis focus on the influence of media on youth participation in sport. Like Cranmer, they are invested in practical outcomes for improved youth behaviors. Integrating scholarship in communication with kinesiology and public health, Bissell and Ellis offer insights about barriers to physical activity for children as well as social support concerns. The intersection of sport, health, and interpersonal communication provides a compelling roadmap for future expansion of communication studies of sport. Chapter 7, by Jimmy Sanderson, complements the preceding chapter with a continued focus on family dynamics. Here, Sanderson provides an overview of the ways family relationships are affected by participation in sport, including family identity, parent–child interactions, parental behaviors, and the influence of technology. Acknowledging the relative lack of communication research in these areas, Sanderson draws from fields such as human movement and psychology to dramatize why the family context should motivate more work in communication and sport.

Hatsuko Itaya makes the first contribution from outside of North America in Chapter 8, with her study of baseball interpreters in Japan. Itaya interviewed current and former interpreters for the Nippon Professional Baseball Organization to identify their communication objectives. Grounding the chapter in the intercultural differences between Japan and western nations such as the United States, she notes that interpreters prioritize social and interpersonal roles over linguistic roles. They enact these roles by shifting their "footing" in order to optimize the connections between players and fans. The chapter offers insights both into communication differences between cultures and the particular communication practices of a unique role in the sporting context.

In Chapter 9, Abraham Khan theorizes the "ethos of the activist athlete," both revisiting historical exemplars from the United States such as Curt Flood and responding to contemporary political expressions by athletes such as Colin Kaepernick. Khan integrates African American history with rhetorical theory to identify four attributes that reveal the potency of athlete activism: double-consciousness, risk, solidarity, and poetry. In addition, he assesses the calls for racial justice that define sport in the summer of 2020 in the context of these attributes as they have evolved over time. Chapter 10 explores similar spaces, as Daniel Grano evaluates the pardon granted to former boxer Jack Johnson by President Donald Trump in 2018. Grano notes the irony of a president who trades in racist and white supremacist discourse issuing a pardon to Black athlete who had provoked racial resentment among whites at the turn of the 20th century. He further explains the constraints of respectability politics that prevented President Barack Obama, the nation's first Black president, from being able to pardon Johnson instead. Together, chapters 9 and 10 reveal the communicative intersections of rhetoric, race, and politics.

Courtney Cox's study of Muslim women in international basketball spotlights additional cultural and racial dynamics in Chapter 11. Specifically, she analyzes the Fédération Internationale de Basketball's (FIBA) policy banning athletes from wearing the hijab. Featuring media accounts and an interview with soccer player-turned-journalist Shireen Ahmed, Cox interrogates the relationship between sport's governing bodies, financial interests, and the regulation of identity. She especially notes how Muslim women athletes face a "dual hijabophobia," as they are subjected to scrutiny from both Islamic and non-Islamic actors alike. Despite these concerns, Cox also notes that Muslim women athletes may find new opportunities to forge a transnational community through online interactions.

No other nation tethers athletics to colleges and universities like the United States, and that system faces an increasing number of challenges. In Chapter 12, Katie Lever attends to one of those challenges – discussions about ways athletes may earn compensation beyond their scholarships. Through a close reading of the NCAA's policy manual, Lever, a former college track and field athlete, determines that the term "student-athlete" functions as an "ideograph," a term rhetorical scholars use to describe specific phrases that condense influential ideologies. This ideograph depends on the myth of amateurism, and Lever concludes that its use enables the NCAA to control, exploit, and subjugate college athletes.

The final chapter of this section, Chapter 13, comes from Jeffrey Kassing, who assesses the relationship to sport's local and global influences. The specific object of his analysis is FC Barcelona, one of the most recognizable and influential sport organizations in the world. Kassing explores both internal and external organizational communication that have shaped the club throughout its history, connecting these efforts to the specific demands of Catalan nationalism. He also builds on previous work to demonstrate the (re)producing, consuming, enacting, and organizing communication processes (Kassing et al. 2004). The chapter summarizes many of the themes found within this section and forecasts the forthcoming sections featuring more particular studies of media and national identity.

Section III, "Sport and Media," presents a series of chapters focused on media institutions and their cultural impact. It is safe to conclude that "media" has received more attention from communication and sport scholars than any other context. Yet, consistent innovation and the expansion of the "MediaSport" (Wenner 1998) nexus requires that studies of media remain central to the field. The authors in this section examine the evolving media landscape through both theoretical overviews and case-driven inquiries. The first two chapters capture snapshots of the overall media landscape, charting historical developments as well as contemporary trends. In Chapter 14, David Rowe and Toby Miller feature a comparison of sport media between Australia and the United States to take stock of MediaSport's ongoing influence. They focus in particular on the processes of production and consumption in an examination of both nations' efforts to expand the sport media marketplace. These pursuits often exhibit imperialist impulses and risk exploiting economic and political inequalities. Much of this is rooted in corporate influences, and David Andrews extends this discussion through his concept of "Uber-Sport" in Chapter 15. Working through the intellectual foundations of the Frankfurt School and cultural studies, Andrews proposes Uber-Sport as the hegemonic form of sport media's convergence. He organizes the chapter around four processes characteristic of late capitalism: corporatization, commercialization, spectacularization, and celebritization. Together, these two chapters provide a critical vocabulary for making sense of sport media's economic and political influence.

Moving to more specific case studies, John Kelly and Jung Woo Lee offer a comparative study of sport media and militarism in Chapter 16. Noting the influence of militaristic discourse in the United States in the years after the 9/11 terrorist attacks, Kelly and Lee note how similar symbolism is present in the United Kingdom and South Korea. In the UK, sport militarism has echoed many of the commitments found within the US, while also advancing a unique form of remembrance linked to British freedom and sacrifice. Meanwhile, in South Korea, where military service for men is compulsory, militarism enacts a kind of celebritization that favors entertaining spectacles over solemn ceremonies of remembrance. In both cases, sport militarism validates existing military policy and legitimizes "ideological righteousness" in response to emergent political concerns.

In Chapter 17, Lindsey Meân and Beth Fielding-Lloyd turn to the world's most popular sport, football. More specifically, they address the growth of the women's game and related television coverage. The chapter offers an overview of persistent sexism in media coverage and within the sport's governing bodies before turning its attention to British television coverage of the 2017 Women's Euros. Despite an increase in coverage, Meân and Fielding-Lloyd find continued patterns that treat the women's game in diminished terms. The authors question, therefore, the common refrain that women's soccer has somehow "arrived." Staying in the UK, Chapter 18, by Michael Silk, Emma Pullen, and Daniel Jackson, focuses on television coverage of the Paralympic Games. They argue that the visibility of Paralympic athletes articulates with discourses of nationalism in ways that reinforce "preferred" images of disability and national identity. In particular, they identify the emphasis on inspirational stories – embodied by the notion of the "supercrip" – that actually reinforce discourses of ableism. In Chapter 19, Jennifer McClearen and Brett Siegel similarly trace NBC's Olympic coverage that celebrates LGBTQ athletes. Noting NBC's emphasis on "inclusion" and "diversity," the authors argue the positive attention given to US Olympians Adam Rippon and Gus Kenworthy is filtered through a post-identity politics frame that denies ongoing struggles. Although this coverage provides important visibility to LGBTQ athletes, it defaults to story frames that emphasize the comfort of conventionally liberal and straight viewers.

Another issue often framed in progressive political terms is attention to the environment. In Chapter 20, Brett Hutchins, Libby Lester, and Toby Miller examine the "greening" of MediaSport. They acknowledge that sport media are more actively attending to environmental concerns, which in turn enhances audience awareness of pro-environmental messages. Nevertheless, sport media depend on an energy-intensive infrastructure, thus complicating any commitment to sustainability initiatives. Capturing an impressive range of sport and geographical contexts, Hutchins, Lester, and Miller hint at a "post-carbon" future for sport media in which communication and sport scholars may play an important role. Section III concludes with a shift to the context of eSports, with Markus Stauff and Travis Vogan in Chapter 21. Stauff and Vogan suggest that eSports may be the fastest growing segment of the entire sport industry, demonstrating its popularity across genres and continents. Their focus is specifically on the NBA 2K League, a partnership between the league and the makers of the popular *NBA 2K* video game, Take-Two Interactive. Although the growth of eSports is a potential challenge or even threat to traditional sport media forms, Stauff and Vogan contend that such partnerships may ultimately help reinforce the centrality of sport in commercial media.

The chapters in Section IV, "Communicating Nationalism(s) in Sport," reflect many of the topics raised in the first two sections. However, each chapter here features a primary focus on expressions of national identity and nationalism. This section includes historical assessments of sport within a given nation, as well as specific case studies that illustrate particular principles of nationalism. It begins with an assessment that might reasonably contribute to the previous section, as well. In Chapter 22, Andrew Billings and Elisabetta Zengaro survey scholarship about sport media coverage of the Olympics. Although they focus on several variables, including gender and race, their attention to national identity helps frame this section. Through a literature review that accounts for multiple Olympic Games and varying national perspectives, Billings and Zengaro note that Olympic media coverage often translates feelings of patriotism into more problematic notions of nationalism, and that the representation of nations too often is reduced to the medal count.

Richard Haynes provides an account of British sport media history in Chapter 23, demonstrating the ways that technological innovations in British television influenced European sport media broadly. The chapter is a study in diffusion and collaboration, but it also speaks to efforts by the BBC to assert a particular vision of sport media practice. Writing against the backdrop of the Cold War and the growth of the Olympics, Haynes provides a careful account of the ways one nation's media landscape can affect the global sport media ecosystem. Karsten Senkbeil then focuses on German sport media practices in Chapter 24. Senkbeil uses coverage of the national football team to identify four distinct post-war phases. Noting the ambivalence felt in Germany with regard to assertive displays of nationalism, he demonstrates the ways Germany's World Cup performances have allowed collective expressions of national identity. Senkbeil also features important dynamics of intercultural communication, using Mesut Özil's controversial departure from the national team to illustrate ongoing contradictions in the German "imagined community" (Anderson 1983).

Shifting to Asia, Younghan Cho assesses discourses of globalization and multiculturalism in Chapter 25. He begins by outlining the efforts to use multiculturalism to bolster myths of nationalism in South Korea. By focusing on the case of Tang Ye-seo, an immigrant from China who competed in the Olympics for South Korea, Cho illustrates the challenges presented when official discourses of inclusion encounter entrenched regional rivalries with complicated histories. Despite these challenges, he concludes that there is promise in the story of Tang, as it helps expand ideas about national identity and citizenship. In Chapter 26, Lee Thompson surveys the development of sport media in Japan. Thompson's focus is primarily historical, noting the dearth of awareness of Japanese sport in the western world. By focusing on the trajectories of specific media forms, as well as the influence of the two most significant sports in Japan – sumo and baseball – Thompson demonstrates points of overlap and divergence from similar developments in western sport media.

Much like Thompson observes about Japan, Chuka Onwumechili notes in Chapter 27 a lack of attention on the entire continent of Africa. Drawing on his own experiences, Onwumechili combines autoethnography with analysis of media coverage of football in Nigeria. In particular, he focuses on the Igbo ethnic nation within Nigeria, thus making an important distinction between civic nationalism and ethnic nationalism. As he details, Igbo nationalism has influenced sport culture in Nigeria, especially through the emergence of the Enugu Rangers football club. In addition to illuminating the particular dynamics in Nigeria, Onwumechili also points to the potential of future scholarship that isolates ethnic nationalism in sporting contexts. Mahfoud Amara and Kamal Hamidou focus their attention on political identity across the Middle East and North Africa (MENA) region in Chapter 28. They begin by situating sport in the regional context, providing a necessary foundation for making sense of claims to national identity and unity. Amara and Hamidou then assess the developments in sport television, particularly in the Arabian Gulf. As they note, sport in the region has been strongly influenced by state ideologies, something reflected in developments in broadcasting. Nevertheless, they also identify prospects for social media to allow citizens to have more influence in the discourses of sport nationalism. In Chapter 29, Ilan Tamir looks to the behaviors of fans in Israel and their expressions of identity through crowd chants at soccer matches. Although the chants add to the atmosphere of the game, Tamir demonstrates problematic attitudes that exploit national histories and gender stereotypes. In doing so, he reveals important tensions between cultivating loyalty to a team and creating enemies out of divisions of "us" and "them."

In Chapter 30, Toby Miller and Alfredo Sabbagh Fajardo detail the competing efforts in Colombia to "own" football on behalf of the nation. Detailing Colombia's complicated history of drug trafficking and para-military intervention, Miller and Sabbagh argue that violence has served as the organizing principle in the development of a "national popular" (Gramsci 2000). Their chapter articulates militarism with masculinity, showing the ways football has been used to both acquire and assert power and control. Section IV concludes with Chapter 31, by Pablo Alabarces, which traces the historical parallels between the state and sport media in Argentina. Alabarces describes the "Suarez Syndrome," referring to the former head of the Argentine Football Association, Valentin Suarez, whose influence is still felt in sport media today. As the chapter reveals, the availability of sport on television in Argentina has long been political, and Alabarces notes the particular tendencies to use football broadcasts to enhance nationalism. Thus, the chapter concludes this section with an important reminder – i. e., sport media, like sport itself, is a continued site of political contestation.

The book concludes with Section V, "Communicating in Applied Sport Contexts." This section returns to a focus primarily on media; however, these chapters attend more to professional practices and industry trends than cultural and political factors. This is not a perfectly clean distinction, I realize, but it does allow for a more precise focus on practices in sport journalism, social media, and public relations. The section begins with Natalie Brown-Devlin and Sabitha Sudarshan's overview of crisis communication in sport in Chapter 32. They identify two primary traditions – Image Repair Theory and Situational Crisis Communication Theory – as the most influential approaches in communication and sport scholarship. The chapter includes discussions of organizations, athletes, and fans as the primary actors in sport crises. In addition to providing a roadmap to this landscape, they offer important suggestions for scholars to acknowledge commercial influences and question the ethical implications of reputation management. Chapter 33, by Brody Ruihley, also offers a survey of extant scholarship, in this case focusing on fantasy sports. Ruihley focuses on the United States and Canada to trace the origins and developments of one of the most robust sectors of the sport industry. In addition to the rich historical context, the chapter animates the many influences fantasy sports have had on sport media practices and consumption.

The next two chapters provide comprehensive summaries of what has been arguably the most studied context in the past decade – sport and social media. Although Chapters 34 and 35 ostensibly cover similar ground, their authors provide notable different points of focus and survey different bodies of scholarship. First, Norm O'Reilly and Gashaw Abeza isolate the growth of social media in professional sport by categorizing "other," "I," and "we" as distinct domains. Their review establishes the professional practices that have become normalized, and it concludes with a recommendation that "social media platform" is the most useful unit of analysis for sport industry professionals and sport marketing scholars. Ann Pegoraro and Katie Lebel's chapter follows with a similarly comprehensive review of literature. They, too, are focused primarily on sport management and marketing conversations, but their attention is more on fandom and sponsorship opportunities. They also give considerable attention to gender imbalances present in sport social media. Together, these two chapters help catalog and clarify the rapidly expanding scholarship on social media and sport.

Social media's impact on journalistic practices characterizes the next set of chapters. In Chapter 36, Galen Clavio and Brian Moritz detail the changing landscape of US sport media since the turn of the 21st century. It offers a highly accessible overview of this modern history and assesses the state of contemporary sport journalism. They note the integration of social media with current practices, noting the ethical and professional challenges this presents to journalists. Haim Hagay and Alina Bernstein note the growing influence of social media for sport journalists around the world, especially through Twitter. With a focus on sport journalism in Israel, Hagay and Bernstein identify differences between men and women on Twitter – interaction, personal life, sports fandom, and professional commentary. In this analysis, they reveal that gendered norms in sport media persist on Twitter, even at time reinforced by women subjected to gender hegemony. In Chapter 38, Thomas Horky and Robin Meyer look to social media's influence on sport mega-events. Through an analysis of the 2016 Rio Summer Games and the 2018 FIFA World Cup, Horky and Meyer observe the integration of Facebook and Twitter in sport journalism. The explosive growth of social media coverage, they argue, raises questions about access and credibility, as well as the relationship between journalists and fans and organizations.

The final chapter of book retains the focus on sport journalism, examining the distinct practice of ghostwriting. Amber Roessner's treatment in Chapter 39 includes a rich archival examination of ghostwriting's origins in the US in the early 20th century. These early efforts expanded sport journalism's "gee whiz" ethos and assisted in the production of athletes as mythic heroes. As journalistic standards shifted and athletes offered more candid assessments of sport culture in the 1960s and 1970s, ghostwriting provoked conversations among journalists about ethics and propriety. Today, with the rise of social media and publications such as *The Players' Tribune*, ghostwriting has returned in earnest. Roessner concludes that, although it still presents ethical challenges, ghostwriting can assist in contesting dominant narratives in sport and sport journalism.

In sum, the chapters collected here offer a comprehensive and substantial assessment of communication and sport as a unique field. Of course, it cannot claim to address every context, theory, or controversy. Nevertheless, communication and sport scholars should benefit from the specific case studies, the reviews of literatures, and the provocations and questions asked across these contributions. My sincere hope is that the book answers the call to address major issues in the field, to provide useful examples in classrooms around the world, and to invite more research regarding the topics addressed here as well as those not included.

References

Anderson, Benedict. 1983. *Imagined communities: Reflections on the origin and spread of nationalism*. New York: Verso.

Armour, Nancy. 2020. International Olympic Committee's ban on political protests is the height of hypocrisy. *USA Today*, 9 January. https://www.usatoday.com/story/sports/columnist/nancy-armour/2020/01/09/tokyo-olympics-ioc-political-protests/4424333002/ (23 November 2020).

Bach, Thomas. 2020a. Opening speech to the 136th IOC session. *International Olympic Committee*, 17 July. https://stillmedab.olympic.org/media/Document%20Library/OlympicOrg/IOC/Who-We-Are/IOC-Sessions/136-IOC-Session/136-IOC-Session-President-Bach-opening-speech.pdf#_ga=2.143764981.1723501523.1606250741-1231718209.1606152555 (23 November 2020).

Bach, Thomas. 2020b. The Olympics are about diversity and unity, not politics and profit. *The Guardian*, 23 October. https://www.theguardian.com/sport/2020/oct/24/the-olympics-are-about-diversity-and-unity-not-politics-and-profit-boycotts-dont-work-thomas-bach (23 November 2020).

Basketball Africa League postpones start of inaugural season. 2020. *NBA.com*, 3 March. https://www.nba.com/news/basketball-africa-league-postpones-start-inaugural-season (23 November 2020).

Bebernes, Mike. 2020. Why was George Floyd's death the breaking point? *Yahoo!Sports*, 7 June. https://sports.yahoo.com/why-was-george-floyds-death-the-breaking-point-143440621.html (23 November 2020).

Billings, Andrew C. (ed.). 2016. *Defining sport communication*. New York: Routledge.

Boykoff, Jules. 2020. *Nolympians: Inside the fight against capitalist mega-sports in Los Angeles, Tokyo and beyond*. New York: Fernwood Publishing.

Burns, Max. 2019. The NBA and Activision Blizzard are one thing – but Trump's silence on China is downright eerie. *The Independent*, 14 October. https://www.independent.co.uk/voices/trump-china-hong-kong-protests-nba-activision-blizzard-a9155806.html (23 November 2020).

Butterworth, Michael L. 2020. Sport and the quest for unity: How the logic of consensus undermines democratic culture. *Communication & Sport* 8 (4–5). 452–472.

Chakravartty, Paula, Rachel Kuo, Victoria Grubbs & Charlton McIlwain. 2018. #CommunicationSoWhite. *Journal of Communication* 68(2). 254–266.

Chau, Danny. 2020. Athletes during the pandemic are learning what fans have always known. *The Atlantic*, 20 May. https://www.theatlantic.com/culture/archive/2020/05/bundesliga-sports-return-pandemic-athletes-fans-shared-imagination/611857/ (23 November 2020).

Clark, Peter Allen. 2019. What to know about Blizzard, Hong Kong and the controversy over politics in Esports. *Time*, 21 October. https://time.com/5702971/blizzard-esports-hearthstone-hong-kong-protests-backlash-blitzchung/ (23 November 2020).

Conway, Tyler. Japan's Nippon Professional Baseball delays season because of coronavirus fears. *BleacherReport.com*, 9 March. https://bleacherreport.com/articles/2880007-japans-nippon-professional-baseball-delays-season-because-of-coronavirus-fears (23 November 2020).

Coronavirus confirmed as pandemic by World Health Organization. 2020. *BBCNews.com*, 11March. https://www.bbc.com/news/world-51839944 (23 November 2020).

Gehrke, Pat J. & William M. Keith (eds.). 2014. *A century of communication studies: The unfinished conversation*. New York: Routledge.

Gonzalez, Roger. 2020. Coronavirus: Copa America 2020 postponed to 2021 by CONMEBOL over COVID-19 pandemic, report says. *CBSSports.com*, 19 March. https://www.cbssports.com/soccer/news/coronavirus-copa-america-2020-postponed-to-2021-by-conmebol-over-covid-19-pandemic-report-says/ (23 November 2020).

Gramsci, Antonio. 2000. *The Antonio Gramsci reader: Selected writings 1916–1935*. David Forgacs (ed.). New York: New York University Press.

Greer, Jordan. 2019. The Daryl Morey controversy, explained: How a tweet created a costly rift between the NBA and China. *The Sporting News*, 23 October. https://www.sportingnews.com/us/nba/news/daryl-morey-tweet-controversy-nba-china-explained/togzszxh37fi1mpw177p9bqwi (23 November 2020).

Hong Kong formally scraps extradition bill that sparked protests. 2019. *BBCNews.com*, 23 October. https://www.bbc.com/news/world-asia-china-50150853 (23 November 2020).

In photos: The sports world has been taking a stand. 2020. *CNN.com*, 1 October. https://www.cnn.com/2020/08/27/world/gallery/sports-protests/index.html (23 November 2020).

Karamichas, John. 2015. Sport mega-event hosting and environmental concern: From Sydney to Rio. *Aegean Journal of Environmental Sciences* 1(1). 22–39.

Kassing, Jeffrey, Andrew Billings, Robert Brown, Kelby Halone, Kristen Harrison, Robert Krizek, Lindsey Meân & Paul Turman. 2004. Communication in the community of sport: The process of enacting, (re)producing, consuming, and organizing sport. In Pamela Kalbfleisch (ed.), *Communication Yearbook* 28, 373–409. Mahwah, NJ: LEA Publishers.

Katz, Elihu, John Durham Peters, Tamar Liebes & Avril Orloff (eds.). 2003. *Canonic texts in media research*. Cambridge: Polity.

Lawrence, Trevor. 2020. *Twitter*, 9 August. https://twitter.com/trevorlawrencee/status/1292672300152758273?lang=en (23 November 2020).

Lucaites, John L. & Celeste M. Condit. 1998. Introduction. In Celeste M. Condit, John L. Lucaites & Sally Caudill (eds.), *Contemporary rhetorical theory: A reader*, 1–18. New York: Guilford.

Mather, Victor. 2020. Updates on sports canceled by coronavirus. *New York Times*, 13 March. https://www.nytimes.com/2020/03/13/sports/sports-canceled-coronavirus.html (23 November 2020).

Murray, Jessica. 2020. Australian Open players affected by bushfire smoke. *The Guardian*, 14 January. https://www.theguardian.com/australia-news/2020/jan/14/australian-open-in-doubt-as-bushfire-smoke-endangers-players (23 November 2020).

Newman, Daniel. 2020. How the pandemic is fueling the digital transformation of sports. *Forbes.com*, 15 October. https://www.forbes.com/sites/danielnewman/2020/10/15/how-the-pandemic-is-fueling-the-digital-transformation-of-sports/?sh=6565f7e85e22 (23 November 2020).

Pedersen, Paul M. 2015. *Routledge handbook of sport communication*. London: Routledge.

Peters, John Durham. 1999. *Speaking into the air: A history of the idea of communication*. Chicago: University of Chicago Press.

Phillips, Sam. 2020. Organisers insist Australian Open show will go on despite smoke hazard. *Sydney Morning Herald*, 6 January. Nexis Uni (23 November 2020).

Radnofsky, Louise & Andrew Beaton. 2020. A broad array of sports stars rush to embrace "Black Lives Matter." *Wall Street Journal*, 2 June. https://www.wsj.com/articles/a-broad-array-of-sports-stars-rush-to-embrace-black-lives-matter-11591123204 (23 November 2020).

Simonson, Peter & Gabriel Weimann. 2003. Critical research at Columbia: Lazarsfelds' and Merton's "mass communication and popular taste, and organized social action." In Elihu Katz, John Durham Peters, Tamar Liebes & Avril Orloff (eds.), *Canonic texts in media research*, 12–38. Cambridge: Polity.

Talmazan, Yuliya. 2020. New dates announced for Tokyo 2020 Olympics postponed over coronavirus concerns. *NBCNews.com*, 30 March. https://www.nbcnews.com/news/world/new-dates-announced-tokyo-2020-olympics-postponed-over-coronavirus-concerns-n1171871 (23 November 2020).

Trujillo, Nick. 2003. Introduction. In Robert S. Brown & Daniel O'Rourke, III (eds.), *Case studies in sport communication*, xi–xv. Westport, CT: Praeger.

Weaver, Carl H. 1977. A history of the International Communication Association. In Brent D. Ruben (ed.), *Communication yearbook*, vol. 1, 607–618. New Brunswick, NJ: Transaction.

Wenner, Lawrence A. (ed.). 1998. *Mediasport*. London: Routledge.

Wenner, Lawrence A. 2015. Communication and sport, where art thou? Epistemological reflections on the moment and the field(s) of play. *Communication & Sport* 3. 247–260.

Wenner, Lawrence A. 2017. Anniversaries, trajectories, and the challenges for the communication of sport. *Communication & Sport* 5. 399–406.

Yonhap. 2020. Pro baseball league postpones start of regular season over coronavirus. The *Korean Herald*, 10 March. http://www.koreaherald.com/view.php?ud=20200310000750 (23 November 2020).

Zirin, Dave. 2016. *Brazil's dance with the devil: The World Cup, the Olympics, and the fight for democracy* (Olympics edn.). Chicago: Haymarket Books.

Zirin, Dave. 2020. The Australian Open is just the tip of a melting iceberg. *The Nation*, 17 January. https://www.thenation.com/article/environment/australian-open-fires-climate-change/ (23 November 2020).

Lawrence A. Wenner

2 Playing on the communication and sport field: dispositions, challenges, and priorities

Abstract: This chapter considers the origins, development, and epistemological contexts undergirding the study of communication and sport as an emergent and growing field of inquiry. Early in the chapter, the contexts underlying the development of studying sport in communication and media studies are considered and woven into a brief chronology of the area's maturation towards disciplinary legitimacy. This is followed by an analysis of the challenges presented by competing and complementary interests at play in three disciplinary and epistemological dispositions seen in the study of communication and sport. The closing section of the chapter considers key challenges that need to be met in further developing the study of communication and sport along with some priorities that need to be focused upon for the area to extend its impact.

Keywords: sport communication; mediated sport; media studies; sociology of sport; sport management; communication studies; epistemology

1 Introduction

There have been many indicators over the last few years that the study of communication and sport has become one of the new "hot areas" in communication and media studies. Foremost, with three scholarly journals – the *Journal of Sports Media*, the *International Journal of Sport Communication*, and *Communication and Sport* – now being published in this academic space and with all of the major communication and media scholarly organizations (Wenner 2015a) now recognizing the nexus of communication and sport in their infrastructures, the time has come for taking communication *in* and *about* sport seriously. Yet, for some of us who have long endeavored to make the case to the communication and media studies scholarly communities that the communicative contexts of sport are integral, rather than peripheral, to any broad understandings of communication and culture, this has been a decidedly slow journey, one that has required overcoming a tepid reception and some resistance from the discipline's mainstream (Wenner 2006).

Still, it is clear that ignition has taken place recently in enough places such that a tipping point has been reached about the worthiness of studying the nexus of communication and sport. While the answers as to why sport has only recently been "discovered" by mainstream communication and media studies are complex, its long and winding road to disciplinary acceptance begs the joking observation that it has only

https://doi.org/10.1515/9783110660883-002

taken thirty or forty years for the study of communication and sport to have become an overnight success. This chapter offers some reflections on this "overnight success" and its outfall in the resultant state of affairs. As we experience this newfound legitimacy, what does the study of communication and sport look like? What is the state of play on the communication and sport field(s)? What are its contours and who is on the playing field and why? Can there be coherence amidst the competing dispositions that have taken shape in approaching communication and sport? What challenges do scholars have in moving forward on a meaningful research agenda? What should our priorities be? In offering answers to questions such as these, this chapter aims to clarify thinking about some fruitful pathways for the future study of communication and sport.

2 Contexts

Today, it is obvious that the business of sport and its cultural and social impacts are huge, not just in developed countries, but throughout the world. In hindsight, it is easily recognized that much of the drive towards this "hugeness" was facilitated through the symbiotic marriage of sport and television, a foundational building block of what is more broadly recognized as the "media-sport-culture complex" (Jhally 1989) or, more simply, "mediasport" (Wenner 1998). Indeed, it is easy to make the argument that there could be no truly big-time sport without big-time media. The rise of professional sports leagues, the professionalization of "amateur" athletics, the creation of today's outsized sporting mega-events (Wenner and Billings 2017), and the routine imbuing of sports heroes with the cachet of celebrity (Smart 2005) are all attributable to what Jackson (2013) has called a "circuit of commodification and communication model" where marketing and promotional communication plays a central role.

While today it seems unimaginable that any meaningful study of sport and society could be possible without understanding the workings of communication and media, sport studies across the academy developed in disparate quarters with only occasional, usually isolated, study in communication (Bryant, Comisky, and Zillmann 1977; Parente 1977; Real 1975; Zillmann, Bryant, and Sapolsky 1979). As a stable component in maturing articulations of physical education in the 1960s and 1970s, rebranded under the guise of kinesiology, exercise and sport science, human movement studies, and the like, the socio-cultural study of sport developed in ways that paralleled approaches to sport in society that were gaining legitimacy in sociology. During that same period of time, the study of sport saw niche development that remains to this day across the social sciences and humanities. Much developed beyond a sociology of sport approach, which itself evolved to be both "more than sociology" and "more than sport" (Wenner 2017b). Sustained attention on engagement with sport came from psychology where a substantial line of research on fanship (Wann et al. 2001) built on early inquiry on spectator experience (Hasdorf and Cantril 1954) developed alongside a more pragmatic focus on how to stimulate motivation in a way that would optimize athletic performance. Other pragmatics, those having to do with the growing of the sport marketplace, came from other quarters of the academy. Here the study of sport business, economics, leadership, and organization coalesced into sport management with contributions from business schools, economics, and early articulations of sport administration in physical education. And, while the study of sport gained early toeholds across a host of disciplines that included history, philosophy, ethics, law, politics, policy, literature, and other fields, it struggled to find its footing in communication and media studies. As a result, as late as the 1980s and 1990s, communication and media studies researchers looking to find a warm reception for their nascent work on sport necessarily engaged with scholarly societies in the sociology of sport, such as the North American Society for the Sociology of Sport and the International Sociology of Sport Association, and scholarly journals such as the *Sociology of Sport Journal*, the *International Review for the Sociology of Sport*, and the *Journal of Sport and Social Issues*, which were welcoming to research recognizing the increasing importance of media in shaping and experiencing contemporary sport (Wenner 2015b).

Even as sport studies gained standing across the academy in the last third of the twentieth century, inquiry concerning sport failed to gain meaningful momentum in communication and media studies until the new millennium. Even as late as the 1990s, resistance came from received sensibilities in "mass communication research" (the normative precursor to the now more broadly defined "media studies" that includes critical entailments), while there was seeming indifference to the sporting context across disparate quarters of "communication studies" (Kassing et al. 2004; Wenner 1989). This tepid reception was in some sense an understandable example of communication and media studies, as relatively new disciplines, looking to establish their credentials in the social sciences by focusing on what normatively seemed more important matters. In the 1960s and 1970s, the study of communication, although having long antecedents in study of rhetoric, was striving to establish its own legitimacy through using empirical social science methods to study processes and impacts of communication and media. Towards that goal, priorities were focused on more appropriate "serious" matters (media effects, socialization, political influence, agenda-setting, cultivation, stereotypes, psychological, and group processes amongst them) than sport as a way for communication scholars to more swiftly advance their legitimacy (Wenner 2015b).

With the coming of cultural studies (and the influence of Stuart Hall and the Birmingham school) to communication (which lagged in being embraced in U.S. communication and media studies), cases were made for the importance and legitimacy of studying the popular (including sport) in communicative contexts (Buscombe 1975; Jhally 1989; Whannel 1983). Thus, it may be said that it took until the study of the popular actually became popular in communication and media studies for the sporting nexus to begin to draw meaningful interest. In the mid- to late-1980s, key publications by Whannel (1983) and Wenner (1989) laid important groundwork for legitimizing the study of mediated sport from both cultural-critical and empirical social science perspectives. The 1990s saw both the continued interest in the communication and sport nexus by a growing set of scholars in the sociology of sport community and a blossoming of interest in communication and media studies that was fueled by influential book-length treatments such as those by Whannel (1992), Trujillo (1994), Wenner (1998), and Rowe (1999). Importantly, the early 1990s also brought the first example of institutionalized legitimacy for mediated sport inquiry within communication as the International Association for Media and Communication Research established its media and sport section (Wenner 2015b).

The new millennium brought important "tipping point" publications in premier handbooks. Key amongst those, published in a benchmark sport studies handbook, Whannel (2000) advanced a strong case for studying mediated sport as essential to socio-cultural understandings of sport. Even more influential to the broader terroir of communication was a landmark treatise coming from a diverse group of early career scholars from across communication and media studies (Kassing et al. 2004) that made a case for the importance of studying communicative processes and settings entailed in "enacting, (re)producing, consuming, and organizing sport" in ways that reached beyond the mediated contexts that had dominated inquiry up to that point. A pattern of other markers signaled that communication and sport inquiry was coming of age. Important handbooks were published (Raney and Bryant 2006; Pedersen 2013; Billings and Hardin 2014) and the area's first textbooks (Billings, Butterworth, and Turman 2012; Kennedy and Hills 2009; Rowe 1999) facilitated curricular development.

Following on efforts by a group of scholars to find a "place to call home," a series of informally organized Summits on Communication and Sport began in 2002, stimulating institutional legitimacy and the formation of interest groups and divisions in mainstream communication and media studies organizations. First in 2008 came the Broadcast Communication Association, with a parade of formations following in the Association for Education in Journalism and Mass Communication in 2010, the International Communication Association in 2013, and the National Communication Association in 2015. In the midst of this signing of institutional legitimacy, in 2012, the scholarly community that came together by necessity around a series of Summits on Communication and Sport made a home of its own by establishing a freestanding scholarly society, the International Association for Communication and Sport (Wenner 2015a, 2015b).

Paralleling these institutional formations, scholarly journals focused on the communication and sport nexus were launched. First published on a limited schedule in 2007, the *Journal of Sports Media* tended towards a focus on journalism and public relations practice. In 2008, the publication of the area's first quarterly scholarly journal, the *International Journal of Sport Communication* was driven, in part, by rising interest about communication and sport in sport management and, while publishing diverse work, maintained a focus on strategic sport communication and professional practice.

In 2013, with a focus on the social and cultural dynamics of communication and sport, and explicitly looking to include research on interpersonal, group, and organizational communication in addition to work focused on mediated sport, *Communication and Sport* began quarterly publication. The reception of that journal, signaled by a 2017 expansion of its production schedule to six issues a year to accommodate blooming interest in the area and garnering recognition with a PROSE Award as the Best New Journal in the Social Sciences, suggests that the study of communication and sport had both come of age and achieved long sought-after disciplinary legitimacy (Wenner 2017a). Taken in light of the contextual chronology presented here, it is clear that communication and sport has "come a long way, baby." Yet, while we have arrived, where are we exactly? What follows is an assessment of where we seem to be on the playing fields of communication and sport.

3 Dispositions

Having made progress along a number of fronts to gain standing, the "mo" is no longer slow for the study of communication and sport. The moment, however, begs a good look in the mirror to assess where things stand. Is the area on a "sustainable path" to facilitate growth and influence? Is it heading on a trajectory towards becoming a coherent field of inquiry? Or does "the field" really just consist of epistemologically different "fields of play" with offset objectives, priorities, and levels of development? Earlier analyses (Wenner 2015a, 2017a) suggest that three disciplinarily distinct dispositions co-exist within the communication and sport scholarly space: (1) Media, Sports, and Society, (2) Sport Communication as a Profession, and (3) Communication Studies and Sport. While certainly some points of overlap may exist in a Venn diagram rendering of the three areas, they may be sufficiently epistemologically distinct enough to pose risks to broader dialogue and disciplinary coherence. An analysis of the state of each of these three dispositions, their epistemological core, and the issues they confront in development follows.

3.1 Media, Sports, and Society

The Media, Sports, and Society disposition is both the most longstanding and widely adopted orientation to study of communication and sport. Serving as an early port of entry for sociology of sport inquiry into the sport and media nexus and as a driver for the first forays into studying sport in communication and media studies (Wenner 1989; Wenner 2006), the main practitioners today come from those domains, along with some seated in sport management. The disposition necessarily requires engaging interdisciplinarity and understandings of both sport's organization and socio-cultural functioning and communication processes and effects. Indeed, early work may be seen as a mashup of the social problems orientation that underlies much sociological inquiry and the once dominant mass communication research tradition that embraced a social-psychological orientation in studying the processing of media content and its impacts. More recently, with the coming of cultural studies, the disposition has expanded to include diverse critical-cultural lenses and qualitative approaches seen across the humanities and social sciences.

Most researchers using this disposition tend to situate their work within one of the three classic components used to characterize the communication process: (1) senders/institutions/production/encoding, (2) messages/content/texts/representation/signification, and (3) receivers/audiences/fandom/consumption/decoding, and it is not unusual to see compendiums of work in this area to be organized into sections reflecting these foci (Wenner 1989, 1998). Speaking to a deficiency seen more broadly across media studies and mass communication research, critiques of the area often cite a need for research to bridge two or more of these areas in individual studies, to adopt what Hall (1973) has advocated for in his more holistically dynamic encoding/decoding model or engage Giddens' (1984) structuration model to gain a more fluid understanding of the dynamism inherent in communication processes, but the pragmatics of research design have limited how often this is done (Wenner 2015a).

A good deal is shared under the relatively large umbrella of the Media, Sports, and Society disposition. Much of its thrust has grown from a core concern, initiated in early sociology of sport inquiry, about the outsized role that media seemed to be making in the social and cultural dynamic *in* and *around* sport. The area continues to be dominated by overarching concerns about the impacts of sports media on individual and societal levels, including the ways in which mediated sport sets the agenda for thinking about sport and how media and sport "logics" (Altheide and Snow 1979) intermix to influence a set of issues central to understanding identities and politics. Perhaps understandably, much inquiry in the Media, Sports, and Society disposition is driven by fundamental concerns over issues of fairness, equity, and the power to shape beliefs and cultural priorities. Issues given attention from this disposition include stereotyped or imbalanced gender and racial/ethnic portrayals, narratives that stress tilted nationalistic biases, and harms that may come from the inappropriate wielding of power in a political economy that seeks to leverage advantage from the "marriage" of sport and media organizations and institutions. Derivative of that marriage, other key foci include examinations of the cultures of sport and media workers and the pressures to produce product that will heighten significance and influence meanings. A key target of that political economy, the engagement (both functions and dysfunctions) of and selling to audiences and spectators in mediated sport, has similarly been a longstanding concern from this disposition.

While much is shared within the Media, Sport, and Society disposition, its coherence is challenged by being comprised of two distinct epistemological "houses" with very different sensibilities, tendencies, and shortcomings. One house features a media studies/cultural studies orientation, focusing critical lenses on the "media-sport-culture complex" (Jhally 1989). Seated in social theories of cultural power and relying on qualitative methods, particular attention in given to inequities in representation, problematics in hyper-commodification, and the political repercussions of mediated sport on lived experience. Key shortcomings in a cultural/critical approach to mediated sport stem from the challenges of accessibility that come with reliance on obtuse (and too often poorly understood and/or unpacked) continental social theory, showy but sometimes amorphous jargon, simplistic and pre-ordained political sensibilities that cloud dispassionate analysis, and qualitative methods that offer little generalizability.

A contrasting house of inquiry within the Media, Sports, and Society disposition relies on the traditions of "mass communication research" and social psychology in a more "scienticized" and detached approach to many of the same social and cultural issues of concern to critical scholars. Here there is a distancing (often to the point of obliviousness and avoidance) from the arguably necessarily politicized contexts of mediated sport in pursuit of process-oriented answers about uses and effects. While such distancing is perhaps necessary in the employ of the tools and tactics of empirical social science, both distancing and tactics come with shortcomings. Empirical measurement and generalizability are both experiencing challenging times. Building standardized scales in a fluid media and sport ecosystem ripe with technological change and disruptions, obtaining clearances from institutional review boards for experimental manipulations, and challenges of garnering the truly random samples in survey research remain considerable obstacles. The latter matter portends to destabilize much that undergirds generalizability and replicability. With increased pressures on publishing, pragmatic reliance on "convenience" samples, from undergraduate student populations to the self-selecting (and often paid) respondents polled through online services such as Survey Monkey and Amazon Turk, is understandable. Unfortunately, along with such "conveniences" come breaches in reliability and validity as stable statistical inference is predicated on random sampling.

While the differences between the two houses within the Media, Sports, and Society disposition, and the challenges they face, are not unique to the study of communication and sport, the fissure they demarcate between scholars working from the cultural/critical humanities and the empirical social sciences can be considerable. There is no question that this induces a bit of "babble" into potentially fruitful dialogue between different scholarly communities working within the Media, Sports, and Society disposition, even though they may share much in common in terms of interests. Beyond tendencies to stay in one's "comfort zone," these are competing houses, with different epistemological foundations that may fuel antipathies. As a result, dialogue between them may be elusive, taking place instead within the silos of each house, and magnifying risks of side-by-side communities *talking past* rather than *talking to* each other.

Beyond these fundamental fissures, work from the Media, Sports, and Society disposition features other tendencies that need some redress. Understandable, given the pragmatics and increased pressures of publishing in scholarly careers, has been the disproportional focus on mediated sport content. Given the appeal of "doing the easy stuff first," ready access to abundant mediated sport content has resulted in a plethora of studies analyzing and critiquing mediated sport content and texts. As low-hanging fruit, the draw to texts that so often vividly illustrate socio-cultural inequities and harms evident in sport is understandable. Still, more difficult work that reveals the leap from content to its negotiation and effect, and most particularly, on research that reveals how that content comes to be as it is, has notably lagged.

Studies of the forces at play in the "why and how" of producing mediated sport content are infrequently seen. Done well (Billings 2008; Serazio 2019) such studies can reveal much about the dynamics and values that drive the mediated sport marketplace and shape its institutions, professional climate, and received practices. Similarly, research on audiences, spectatorship, and fanship, which requires overcoming more obstacles than content-centered analysis, has lagged. Gaining access, garnering samples that support generalizability, and doing sufficiently broad and deep observation and interviewing in qualitative work are all more challenging than making something of content alone. Clearly, more and more meaningful work needs to be done on the reception and interpretation of mediated sport content and the range of effects to be explored needs to be broadened. Beyond these structural challenges, work emanating from the Media, Sports, and Society disposition, driven as it is from heartfelt concerns with fairness, inequities, effects and abuses of power and anchored in both social and social-psychological theories, can struggle with having "real-world" sensitivities to pragmatics and applications. The "real-world," at least as seen through the lens of the marketplace, drives the Sport Communication as a Profession disposition is considered next.

3.2 Sport Communication as a Profession

With very different priorities, the Sport Communication as a Profession disposition is very much anchored in valuing a real-world orientation. Yet, in having core concerns with the pragmatics of practice, strategies, and effectiveness in the sport marketplace, the disposition risks having structural blinders that can tint priorities in the search for knowledge and limit interpretation of findings. Anchored as it is in professionalism and the functioning of sport communication in the marketplace, the "real-world" that that is often assumed comes from a received view of the world as a given. In this worldview construction, the marketplace is preeminent, seen as both normal and valuable, worthy of advancement, and a place where citizens are often more likely to be framed as consumers. This seems an inescapable epistemological characteristic of most marketplace-focused professional disciplines and is evident in the two strains that comprise the Sport Communication as Profession disposition.

The roots of this disposition can be seen arising from two quarters of the academy. One, from the communication and media studies side of the house, developed in professionally oriented programs in journalism and broadcasting and their concerns with standards of practice and effectiveness in sports reporting, broadcasting, public relations, and advertising. Second, with development largely coterminous with those in sport-focused media education, came a focus on strategic sport communication (Pedersen et al. 2016). Seated primarily in programs in sport administration and management, which have had recent burgeoning success within academic units conceptualized as physical education, kinesiology, exercise and sport science and the like, there is conceptual overlap with the sport-focused promotional communication concerns as situated within media education.

Still, there are inflection-point differences that may make a difference between these two variants. In the articulation of strategic sport communication as seated in the domain of sport management, sport and its strategic management, of which communication is a part, are chief concerns. As seated in communication and media studies programs, the processes of effective and appealing communication, applications of which may be focused on sport settings, serve as the chief points of departure. Although what is shared between the two is a focus on professional practice, as seated in sport management, the lens foremost puts administrative, managerial, professional effectiveness and their service to sport and media organization atop priorities. Certainly, a focus on such priorities in the context of the norms of professional education may be eminently defensible.

Yet, while studies from the vantage point of the Sport Communication as a Profession disposition obviously need to engage the dynamics of "communication processes," and there is room to be sure for theoretical engagement, even to the point of using critical lenses on engaging studies of professional cultures and questions of social impact, as seated in sport management, there is an overarching concern with "effectiveness." It is inescapable at a foundational level that sport management as a field is about the institutional and marketplace advancement of sport, the building of organizations, brands, franchises, and ultimately, profit. This is not to say that there is no room from this disposition to consider matters of social harm and inequity that are central to a Media, Sports, and Society disposition, but these are clearly secondary concerns. These are most typically dwarfed by the posited value of research to sport and media organizations and its relevance to developing skills and strategies to advance professional practices in a way that will be well received in and grow marketplaces around sport and its communication.

Herein lies a key conundrum underlying sport management research, including work focused on sport communication. Too often the rationale or mandate used to justify inquiry is centered, in many cases exclusively so, on the goal of helping sport managers and marketers advance the reach and reception of their wares. And, while this may at times seem to be anchored in achieving a more enjoyable or "better" spectator, fan, or customer experience, even that end goal is almost always at one with advancing the yield of those holding power in the sport marketplace. Thus, in a fundamental sense, a quiet and seemingly little questioned political world view underlies research from the Sport Communication as a Profession disposition as it is most likely to be approached from sport management. Beyond being a seemingly inadequate and arguably debased theoretical posture from which to pursue scholarly knowledge, it has, hegemonically, resulted in scholars willingly serving as *de facto* unpaid research assistants for sport and media organizations in their search to capitalize on sport communication. And, while that "helping the industry rationale" is a common driver of inquiry, it may be specious as there is scant evidence to suggest that the sport or media industry has asked for help through these studies or actually used their findings in marketplace applications.

Sport communication, as situated in sport management, may be seen as part of a larger toolkit wielded to gain more information that can aid in strategically growing sport. Sport is seen not so much as a socio-cultural practice, but rather as a given, a naturalized product to be advanced rather than interrogated. This is true also in sport public relations and advertising coursework seated in communication and media studies units. Here training comes in using the tools of the trade to advance the interests of sport organizations and events, and of course those of its "sponsors" and partners, including media organizations.

This disposition to be "friendly" to sport, a posture that makes the everyday doing of sports coverage a bit easier, can be a pervasive received logic in sport journalism and broadcasting academic sensibilities as well. Certainly, in the doing of day-to-day sports reporting, there is little time or place to question the importance and heralded values of sport which are perceived to be shared by fans that comprise readership and audiences. Indeed, reporters or broadcasters who regularly question or criticize the sporting *status quo* may risk compromising their access to the insider information and gossip that both brings value to and fans the flames of fanship. In a very basic sense, fanning those flames enables the market for sport journalism to be well-received and grow, which of course, is in the self-serving best interests of reporters and broadcasters, with side benefits extending to academics building careers through research focused on growing the sport marketplace. A bottom line truism is that there can be no sport journalism without sport, and bigger, stronger, more important, and well-received sport is also good for the health of sport journalists and academics alike.

This "friendliness" to sport and an entrenched *de facto* fanship orientation that pervasively underlies much sports reporting has undoubtedly contributed to frequent "toy department" characterizations of sport journalism (Rowe 2007). Yet, in sport broadcasting, the orientation frame advances from one of merely just being in a "toy department" stocked with sport to becoming partners with sport entities. Having paid increasingly exorbitant rights to air sport contests, broadcast and cable companies look to sell their productions to both consumers and marketers for the highest price possible. This brings a structural imperative to polish the sports product they are offering and avoid diminishing its appeal in any way that can "soil" its marketability. For broadcasters, the resultant necessity of "being in bed" with sport organizations facilitates a "sports first" obligation as this mutual benefice drives value and profit.

Implicit in this climate is an expectation for broadcast announcers to "stick to sports" rather than raise questions about injustices or the tenor of political-economic dynamics in the contemporary world of sports. The structural improprieties that yield close and friendly bedfellows is magnified further when the broadcasters who "cover" sport are actually paid by a sport organization rather than the media entity, a state of affairs common in professional sports. In sum, the pressures and conflicts rife in the professional and marketplace relationships between sport and media are considerable and they necessarily extend to logics in academic milieus where a Sport Communication as a Profession disposition focuses on the pragmatics of "successful" professional practice and/or growing the sport marketplace.

3.3 Communication Studies and Sport

Coming into definition in the new millennium, a third discernable but clearly less developed disposition, anchored in traditions and concerns central to "communication studies," has evolved to broaden what heretofore has been a media-centric focus undergirding the first two dispositions. Although at first glance, the Communication Studies and Sport disposition may seem to share little with the Sport Communication as a Profession disposition, the approach may be seen in many ways as a complementary extension of the Media, Sport, and Society disposition, focusing on the communicative dynamics *in* and *about* sport that are not explicitly anchored in or driven by the media interface. In this sense, this disposition begs for what is really an "impossible" modifier – non-mediated – to distinguish its framing and focus. The scholarly community forming around the Communication Studies and Sport disposition tend to bring a "personal" or "human," rather than "media," orientation to the study of communication. Stemming from speech acts, speech communication, and communication sciences traditions, core concerns with interpersonal, group, organizational, and other communication settings, along with the communicative dynamics of leadership and management, come to the fore (Kassing et al. 2004).

As well, the Communication Studies and Sport disposition distinguishes itself from the other two dispositions by heightened concerns over the use of language and symbols in sport settings and to frame cultural assertions and societal understandings about sport and its meanings. As the employ of language and symbols are necessary to fashioning rhetoric in sporting contexts, a key component within the Communication Studies and Sport disposition is genealogically anchored in rhetorical studies and criticism. As the study of rhetoric has always been relatively agnostic as to forms of delivery, rhetorical criticism has long left its mark on the critical-cultural studies side of the Media, Sports, and Society disposition as it is inescapable that a goodly amount of rhetoric in the sporting context reaches public view through the media. This reality, along with unavoidable reality that "personal" communication in dyadic, group, organizational, and other "human-centered" settings may be influenced by or transmitted through media, often make the "non-mediated" modifier to the Communication Studies and Sport disposition spoken to above technically "impossible."

As human communication contexts and processes are central to approaching sport from this disposition, its more laggardly development is in some sense understandable. After all, there are many contexts for human communication study, from political, health, familial, organizational settings that may be seen to have broader significance for society for researchers schooled in communication studies traditions. Here, sport settings may be viewed as a more delimited communicative context. In contrast, the institutionalization, growth, and impacts of outsized industries for the Media, Sport, and Society disposition and facilitating interest in and the robustness of those industries for the Sport Communication as a Profession disposition, writ proportionally larger on the disciplinary landscapes of media studies and sport management. That mediated sport was seen as "big time" and influential drew early attention across sport studies, both in the sociology of sport and in sport management, and while this laid track for legitimacy in media studies, it didn't stimulate the study of human communication processes in sport.

Yet, the focus on the human communication contexts and processes that is central to approaching sport from the Communication Studies and Sport disposition has much to offer to enrich and extend work not only from the two more established dispositions but also, more broadly, in sport sociology and psychology. For example, as approached from communication studies, core starting point concerns with human communication processes can facilitate the study of leadership, organization, management and their cultures without being preoccupied by overarching concerns with effectiveness, the bottom line, and the strategic advance of enterprise. While these are matters that are central to the Sport Communication as a Profession disposition, they may draw the ire of critical-cultural scholars, as well as those embracing a social-scientific paradigm for its standpoint of detachment, for tainting too much of the drive of research by prioritizing the beneficences to the marketplace.

Similarly, in obvious ways, advancing the interface of the Communication Studies and Sport disposition with core concerns in the sociology of sport and sport psychology holds considerable promise. For the sociology of sport, engaged focus on the processes of the non-mediated communicative dynamics within and about sport (Billings et al. 2012; Kassing et al. 2004) will deepen understandings of sport organizations, leadership, cultures, and subcultures. Similarly, for an area such as sport psychology, which has a goodly interest in how to optimize athletic performance, better understandings of communication processes will undoubtedly yield improvements in mindset and motivation that can help advance competitive results. Bringing a Communication Studies and Sport disposition to other areas such as coaching or how communication in and about sport is transacted within particular contexts, such as between members of a family or an athletic team, can help meld research lines in diverse areas. It is easy to see how communication is at the heart of the coaching enterprise (Cranmer 2020) with its effectiveness a chief concern of sport psychology

(Nicholls 2017) and an understanding of its cultures and values central to inquiry in the sociology of sport (Potrac, Gilbert, and Denison 2015).

Still, at this juncture, while research stemming from the Communication Studies and Sport disposition holds much promise to shine light across broad swatches of communicative contexts that intersect with sport, interest is comparatively nascent, with coherent lines of inquiry far less developed when compared to the relative robustness of bodies of work stemming from the other two dispositions with longer standing interests in sport. While foundational to the speech acts traditions undergirding communication studies, rhetorical criticism focused on sporting contexts (Brummett 2009) has seen the most development, but because the most available sporting rhetorics in contemporary times are mediated and because rhetorical criticism and critical lenses in cultural studies often come together, much rhetorical criticism of sport can be seen as (or more) relevant to the Media, Sports, and Society disposition. Similarly, a related area that has received attention, the communicative dynamics of athlete image repair (Blaney, Lippert, and Smith 2012), because of its bridged focus on communication process and rhetoric used within that frame, would seem at its core to fit best within the Communication Studies and Sport disposition. But, as another example of what Geertz (1973) has called "blurred genres," in practice, research on athlete image repair, as easily fits the Media, Sports, and Society disposition as rhetorical attempts at repair are necessarily reliant on media to sway public sympathies or the Sport Communication as a Profession disposition as repair strategies reside clearly in the crisis management toolkits of public relations practitioners. This is all to say that while the Communication Studies and Sport disposition has seen lesser development, its potential to fill gaps in understanding and reach across the aisles to bridge established lines of inquiry is considerable.

4 Challenges and priorities

The meta-level analyses here of the three dispositions at play across the fields of communication and sport inquiry point to a number of challenges that need to be met to advance a growing and inherently interdisciplinary area. Addressing these challenges and prioritizing some matters within the scholarly communities will be key in the area being able to broaden its impact and engage meaningful dialogues about the roles that communication in and about sport may play in larger social, cultural, and political power dynamics. In the following sections, an analysis of both those challenges and matters that need prioritization is structured by considering four "Cs": (1) coherence, (2) core, (3) community, and (4) contagion.

4.1 Coherence

This essay began by asking series of questions about the state of development of communication and sport as a new "hot area." Clearly, inquiry about this nexus has accelerated and most notably gained long sought-after acceptance and legitimacy across a swatch of communication and media studies scholarly organizations. Three dedicated research journals and a handful of academic book series now populate this scholarly space. With such development thus advanced, what can be made of the "there" that is "there"? Fundamental questions undergirding this essay asked whether there can be coherence amidst the competing dispositions at play on the communication and sport academic field. Are we headed on a trajectory towards becoming a coherent field of inquiry or is the area really just comprised of three different epistemological fields of play?

The most honest, but of course ultimately unsatisfying, answer to the latter question is "yes." But this is true also of correct "all of the above" answers to multiple choice questions and probably the best that can be done in responding to the problematics inherent in any double-barreled question such as this. The state of play, simply put, is "complicated." The dispositions at play in the study of communication and sport are both interlocking and competing. Thus, their ultimate compatibility remains an open question. Presently, there are ever-changing points of overlap in any Venn diagram rendering of their intersections. Each point of intersection brings opportunities for defining core priorities and, over time, the largest points of intersection will likely come to define a center for "a" or "the" scholarly field of play around communication and sport.

As spoken to in the analysis above, fundamental epistemological and ontological differences amongst the dispositions present real challenges to coherence. The Media, Sports, and Society disposition, centered in inquiry from media studies and the sociology of sport, is ultimately anchored in its view of denizens of the world as "citizens." Shared amongst its two houses, using both critical/cultural and social scientific approaches, are foundational concerns over the social and cultural priorities and effects of mediated sport. With focus on propriety and equity, the disposition features a fundamental "ethical impulse" seated in philosophical concerns over "how best to live," the greater good, virtuous action, fairness, and the duties of mediated sport to limit harm.

In contrast, the Sport Communication as a Profession disposition, as seated both in sport management and in professional communication education's approach to sport journalism, broadcasting, public relations and advertising, tends to see denizens of the world as "consumers." Here, key overarching concerns, such as those over "optimizing" the consumer experience with mediated sport or practicing sport communication more "effectively," foundationally service larger goals of advancing the market reception for sport as a product and growing the influence and bottom lines of sport and media entities in the marketplace. Thus, in fundamental ways, this disposition is both epistemologically and ontologically distinct.

The third disposition, that of Communication Studies and Sport, has more in common with, and in a sense, may be seen as an extension of, the Media, Sports, and Society disposition. Still, anchored as it is in a communication sciences orientation with its focus on interpersonal, group, and organizational "actors" and the processes and dynamics at play in such "non-mediated" sport-centric communication settings, the Communication Studies and Sport orientation might best be characterized as a "persons" disposition, seeing denizens of the world as human beings rather than in more delimited roles as citizens or consumers. While seating rhetorical criticism largely within this disposition admittedly raises complications of the "persons" orientation more easily seen in the communication sciences, some core foci, on the rhetor and speech acts, reinforce this assessment. While less developed than the other two dispositions, the Communication Studies and Sport disposition can serve as a bridge to both the processes and effects concerns of the Media, Sports, and Society disposition and those over pragmatics and effectiveness at the heart of the Sport Communication as a Profession disposition.

4.2 Core

Given some fundamental differences, finding a core amongst these epistemologically distinct dispositions will be challenging. Yet, ultimately, we are, all at once, citizens, consumers, and persons in our transactions with communication and sport. While recognition of this may help in putting these together in some kind of coherent whole, the present state of affairs does not a field make. At the present moment, as suggested above, a focus on key points of overlap amongst the dispositions may be the most promising way to find the evolving centers that define a more coherent field of play for the study of communication and sport.

In this search, it is worthwhile noting that the most promising points of overlap are between the more established Media, Sports, and Society disposition and the more nascent Communication Studies and Sport disposition. The reason for this is obvious. At their cores, both put communication first, media communication in the former and "non-mediated" communication in the latter. There is more shared here between these two dispositions, both by putting communication first and also by overarching concerns with communication processes, than either share with the Sport Communication as a Profession disposition where clearly sport, and the role that sport communication plays in the health of that larger marketplace comes first. Certainly, there can be points of intersection between the two "communication first" dispositions and concerns over the functioning of sport communication to support the larger sport marketplace. But just as social and cultural concerns over sport communication are approached from time to time by those with a professionally-centered disposition, we can expect that pragmatics, especially those aimed at market health or expansion, will remain secondary concerns of the "communication first" dispositions.

In finding a core to scholarly inquiry on communication and sport, we need to realize as well that some attractive "shiny pennies" can be blinding to the point of disruption and disorientation. Here, two infatuations, one with sport and the other with new technology, need to be recognized as potential problems that may decenter what might otherwise be at the heart of communication and sport inquiry. Perhaps as sport had long been subject *non grata* in communication and media studies, new scholars who are "sport fans" may understandably be drawn to the relatively new research opportunities opened by legitimacy for communication and sport. But, when scholars enter the communication and sport scholarly terrain fueled by avid fanship or a received view of sport that is too "rose-tinted" about its virtues, the lack of scholarly dispassion can cloud understandings. For communication and media studies-centered scholars this can be blinding to the point of not being able to see, in an unfettered way, social and cultural effects that may be problematic. For those bringing a Sport Communication as a Profession disposition, such blinders can often be seated alongside a larger received view of sport that is little questioned. In each instance, such endemic underlayments can compromise knowledge production with structural biases.

A second "shiny penny" that holds risks for decentering inquiry on communication and sport has to do with overestimating the impacts of new digital and social media. In recent times, the combination of techno-smitten researchers stimulated by the potential of Twitter and other emerging social media forms alongside pathways to "fast and easy" digital data collection (Wenner et al. 2014) has resulted in a flood of studies seated in overestimates of the power and influence of new media on communication about sport. While the "newness" of new media forms is often greeted as a "game changer," the larger body of evidence suggests that McLuhan (1964) was right that the content and logics of new media are most often seated in old media and we underestimate their lasting power (Wenner 2014) and the nimbleness of legacy media to "remediate" (Bolter and Grusin 1999) by incorporating and re-appropriating the new in reimagined older structures. Often, the evidence suggests, the influence of dominant media remains as a rock that hits the water with new digital and social media functioning as ripples emanating from its splash serve as an echo chamber departing from the mainstream (Wenner 2014).

4.3 Community

Now that the study of communication and sport has achieved a base level of legitimacy with area-specific research journals and is recognized by institutional formations across a set of scholarly organizations, a chief challenge will be how to best grow the community of scholars that hold interest in the area. At the end of the day, even though its social-cultural, economic, and political significance is now beyond dispute, a focus on the sporting context will never be the 800-pound gorilla on the scholarly agenda of communication and media studies. The community of scholars, within communication and media studies, while growing, is destined to be comparatively small.

Because of this, a key to the area's viability and expanded impact depends on the creation of a big tent that is proactively welcoming to communication and media studies scholars across the world on one hand and to scholars from key areas across sport studies on the other. On the former matter, the field is fortunate. There is good evidence that sport and its communication is growing. As a media product, the "liveness" of sport contests, has enhanced its value to legacy broadcasters and new media platforms as well. As the sport industries grow, understanding communicative contexts from marketing to organizational leadership to coaching to familial dynamics hold more value.

Still, for the area to truly succeed and grow that big tent it cannot be contained by a communication and media studies fence. For the area to succeed, its center and core in communication and media studies needs to reach across sport studies most notably to the sociology of sport and sport psychology where interest, in mediated sport in the former and in motivation and the psychology of engagement in the latter, resides. For communication and media studies scholars first approaching inquiry, engaging the sociology of sport is essential. Often scholars with interests in sport think they know a good deal about it, but much evidence suggests that they don't know what they don't know and what they often don't know is much about both the sport marketplace and substantial established lines of inquiry in the sociology of sport and other areas that bear on their interests. Thus, the challenges at this nexus are two-fold. First, there is a need to cross disciplinary lines to engage with the sociology of sport and its scholarly formations. Second, there is a need to proactively invite those who share interests in communication and media in adjacent scholarly communities, in the sociology of sport, sport management, and other areas of sport studies, to share some time in our tents and to learn more about communication and media studies and their disciplinary traditions.

4.4 Contagion

The last matter to be considered in this essay is perhaps the most important as the concept is central to the ways that "logics" about sport and mediated sport are diffused through communication to be adopted, spread, and come to be seen to have value across diverse sites in culture and the marketplace. Simply put, this last "C" that needs to be prioritized on the communication and sport scholarly agenda is contagion. At the heart of any communication inquiry is the circulation and control of meanings. The former is about process, while the latter is about power and influence.

A key idea about how mediated communication wields a quiet power is anchored in the notion of "media logic" first put forward in the late 1970s (Altheide and Snow

1979). The notion is simple but robust. As adopted and developed more recently in theoretical development as "mediatization" (Hepp 2013; Hjarvard 2013; Lundby 2009) the notion broadens how media effects are conceptualized by focusing on how the "logics" of media have been strategically integrated into diverse institutional and organizational practices. Thus, the lens seeks to reveal how media effects may leak into virtually every crevice of the cultural fabric. This is easily seen when real life events like a sporting contest are changed to make them more media-friendly or when non-mediated events mimic the structure and values embraced in mediated articulations.

This contagion process is mirrored in theoretical development about "sportification" (Heere 2018; Ingham 2004). Here the focus is on how diverse non-sporting activities embrace the logic and values of sport. An easy example here is in the cultural framing of political campaigns as sporting contests replete with the use of sporting language to describe and understand political jousting. For communication scholars interested in how sport and its communication come together to have broad social and cultural influences, the conceptual marriage of mediatization and sportification processes and the following of their processes of contagion seems most promising (Frandsen 2014). In the hyper-commodified settings of mediated sport in the particular, an understanding of core processes of "consumer sociality" seem essential (Bauman 2007). There is much evidence that contagion from the "dirty logics" (Wenner 2007) of the mediated sport marketplace extends to everyday communication and broadly to lived experience. For these reasons, the processes of contagion offer a promising center to communication and sport inquiry.

References

Altheide, David L. & Robert P. Snow. 1979. *Media logic*. Newbury Park, CA: Sage.
Bauman, Zygmunt. 2007. *Consuming life*. Cambridge: Polity.
Billings, Andrew C. 2008. *Olympic media: Inside the biggest show on television*. London: Routledge.
Billings, Andrew C. & Marie Hardin (eds.). 2014. *Routledge handbook of sport and new media*. London: Routledge.
Billings, Andrew C., Michael L. Butterworth & Paul D. Turman. 2012. *Communication and sport: Surveying the field*. Thousand Oaks, CA: Sage.
Blaney, Joseph R., Lance R. Lippert & Scott J. Smith (eds.). 2012. *Repairing the athlete's image: Studies in sports image restoration*. Landham, MD: Lexington.
Bolter, Jay D. & Richard Grusin. 1999. *Remediation: Understanding new media*. Cambridge, MA: MIT Press.
Brummett, Barry (ed.). 2009. *Sporting rhetoric: Performance, games, and politics*. New York: Peter Lang.
Bryant, Jennings, Paul Comisky & Dolf Zillmann. 1977. Drama in sports commentary. *Journal of Communication* 27. 140–149.
Buscombe, Edward. 1975. *Football on television*. London: British Film Institute.
Cranmer, Gregory A. 2020. *Athletic coaching: A communication perspective*. New York: Peter Lang.

Frandsen, Kirsten. 2014. Mediatization of sports. In Knut Lundby (ed.), *Mediatization of communication*, 525–543. Berlin: Mouton de Gruyter.
Geertz, Clifford. 1973. *The interpretation of cultures*. New York: Basic Books.
Giddens, Anthony. 1984. *The constitution of society: Outline of the theory of structuration*. Cambridge: Polity.
Hall, Stuart. 1973. *Encoding and decoding in the television discourse*. Birmingham, UK: Centre for the Study of Contemporary Cultural Studies.
Hasdorf, Albert H. & Hadley Cantril. 1954. They saw a game: A case study. *Journal of Abnormal and Social Psychology* 2. 129–134.
Heere, Bob. 2018. Embracing the sportification of society: Defining e-sports through a polymorphic view on sport. *Sport Management Review* 21. 21–24.
Hepp, Andreas. 2013. *Cultures of mediatization*. Cambridge: Polity.
Hjarvard, Stig. 2013. *The mediatization of culture and society*. London: Routledge.
Ingham, Alan G. 2004. The sportification process: A biographical analysis framed by the work of Marx, Weber, Durheim and Freud. In Richard Giulianotti (ed.), *Sport and modern social theorists*, 11–32. New York: Palgrave Macmillan.
Jackson, Steven. 2013. Reflections on communication and sport: On advertising and promotional culture. *Communication & Sport* 1. 100–112.
Jhally, Sut. 1989. Cultural studies and the sports/media complex. In Lawrence A. Wenner (ed.), *Media, sports, and society*, 70–93. Newbury Park, CA: Sage.
Kassing, Jeffrey, Andrew Billings, Robert Brown, Kelby Halone, Kristen Harrison, Robert Krizek, Lindsey Meân & Paul Turman. 2004. Communication in the community of sport: The process of enacting, (re)producing, consuming, and organizing sport. In Pamela Kalbfleisch (ed.), *Communication Yearbook* 28, 373–409. Mahwah, NJ: LEA Publishers.
Kennedy, Eileen & Laura Hills. 2009. *Sport, media, and society*. Oxford: Berg.
Lundby, Knut (ed.). 2009. *Mediatization: Concept, changes, consequences*. New York: Peter Lang.
McLuhan, Marshall. 1964. *Understanding media: The extensions of man*. New York: McGraw-Hill.
Nicholls, Adam R. 2017. *Psychology of sports coaching: Theory and practice*, 2nd edn. London: Routledge.
Parente, Donald. 1977. The interdependence of sports and television. *Journal of Communication* 29. 94–102.
Pedersen, Paul M. (ed.). 2013. *Routledge handbook of sport communication*. London: Routledge.
Pedersen, Paul M., Pamela C. Laucella, Edward M. Kian & Andrea N. Guerin. 2016. *Strategic sport communication*, 2nd edn. Champaign, IL: Human Kinetics.
Potrac, Paul, Wade Gilbert & Jim Denison (eds.). 2015. *Routledge handbook of sports coaching*. London: Routledge.
Raney, Arthur A. & Jennings Bryant (eds.). 2006. *Handbook of sports media*. Mahwah, NJ: Erlbaum.
Real, Michael R. 1975. The Superbowl: Mythic spectacle. *Journal of Communication* 25(1). 31–43.
Rowe, David. 1999. *Sport, culture, and the media: The unruly trinity*. Buckingham, UK: Open University Press.
Rowe, David. 2007. Sports journalism: Still the 'toy department' of the news media? *Journalism: Theory, Practice & Criticism* 8. 385–405.
Serazio, Michael. 2019. *The power of sports: Media and spectacle in American culture*. New York: NYU Press.
Smart, Barry. 2005. *The sport star: Modern sport and the cultural economy of sporting celebrity*. London: Sage.
Trujillo, Nick. 1994. *The meaning of Nolan Ryan*. College Station, TX: Texas A&M University Press.
Wann, Daniel L., Merrill J. Melnick, Gordon W. Russell & Dale G. Pease. 2001. *Sports fans: The psychology and social impact of spectators*. New York: Routledge.

Wenner, Lawrence A. (ed.). 1989. *Media, sports, and society*. Newbury Park, CA: Sage.
Wenner, Lawrence A. (ed.). 1998. *Mediasport*. London: Routledge.
Wenner, Lawrence A. 2006. Sport and media through the super glass mirror: Placing blame, breast-beating, and a gaze to the future. In Arthur A. Raney & Jennings Bryant (eds.), *Handbook of sports media*, 45–60. Hillsdale, NJ: Lawrence Erlbaum.
Wenner, Lawrence A. 2007. Towards a dirty theory of narrative ethics. Prolegomenon on media, sport and commodity value. *International Journal of Media and Cultural Politics* 3. 111–129.
Wenner, Lawrence A. 2014. On the limits of the new and the lasting power of the mediasport interpellation. *Television & New Media* 15. 732–740.
Wenner, Lawrence A. 2015a. Communication and sport, where art thou? Epistemological reflections on the moment and the field(s) of play. *Communication & Sport* 3. 247–260.
Wenner, Lawrence A. 2015b. Sport and media. In Richard Giulianotti (ed.), *Routledge handbook of the sociology of sport*, 377–387. London: Routledge.
Wenner, Lawrence A. 2017a. Anniversaries, trajectories, and the challenges for the communication of sport. *Communication & Sport* 5. 399–406.
Wenner, Lawrence A. 2017b. On the *International Review for the Sociology of Sport*, the field of play, and six years of more "more than less". *International Review for the Sociology of Sport* 52. 903–909.
Wenner, Lawrence A. & Andrew C. Billings (eds.). 2017. *Sport, media, and mega-events*. London: Routledge.
Wenner, Lawrence A., Andrew C. Billings, Marie Hardin, David Rowe, Brett Hutchins, Jimmy Sanderson, Ann Pegoraro & Paul M. Pedersen. 2014. Twitter research forum. *Communication & Sport* 2. 103–142.
Whannel, Gary. 1983. *Blowing the whistle: The politics of sport*. London: Pluto.
Whannel, Gary. 1992. *Fields in vision: Television sport and cultural transformation*. London: Routledge.
Whannel, Gary. 2000. Sport and the media. In Jay Coakley & Eric Dunning (eds.), *Handbook of sport studies*, 291–308. London: Sage.
Zillmann, Dolf, Jennings Bryant & Barry S. Sapolsky. 1979. The enjoyment of watching sports contests. In Jeffrey H. Goldstein (ed.), *Sports, games and play: Social and psychological viewpoints*, 297–335. Hillsdale, NJ: Erlbaum.

II Communication studies of sport

Walter Gantz, Nicky Lewis, and Irene I. van Driel

3 Through the kaleidoscope: all the colors of sports fanship

Abstract: This chapter is guided by the view that sports fanship is not a monolithic block – fans are fans – but rather is characterized by shades of intensity and gradations of interest. Relying on data collected from nearly 1,000 Amazon Mechanical Turk participants, we found that sports fanship is quite nuanced, coming in a variety of shapes and forms. Many adults do reside on polar opposites of the sports fanship typology we created – they either have just about no interest in following sports or they follow teams across leagues and enjoy following other sports. Nonetheless, a majority were situated in mid-point locations that would otherwise get lost in easy-to-measure and describe single item measures of the concept. Gender, perceived knowledge and interest in sports as well as emotional responsiveness to sports and overall competitiveness were linked to where participants were located on the typology whereas age did not. In all, our study points to the value of using multi-item measures of sports fanship.

Keywords: sports fanship; fan typology; gender; age; competitiveness; emotional responsiveness

1 Introduction

Sports fans are not a monolithic group. Besides rooting for different teams and caring about different sports, sports fanship varies in intensity, with some fans more emotionally invested in their favorite players and teams than others. Yet, other than acknowledging shades of intensity, academic researchers and marketers of sport fans – those in the popular press as well – tend to use a one-size-fits-all approach to fans: Fans are fans. We disagree. Instead, we believe fanship includes those who only care about individual athletes such as LeBron James or Megan Rapinoe; those who only follow a favorite college such as Notre Dame or Alabama; those who love a single team and their coach such as the New England Patriots and Bill Belichick or the Golden State Warriors and Steve Kerr; and those who only pay attention when the Olympics or the Women's World Cup is on. We believe there are gradations of fanship ranging from those who could not care less about sports to those who follow multiple teams and leagues and, overall, love every game and match sports has to offer. This chapter was guided by the view that sports fanship is not a monolithic block and offers a study of sports fans in the United States of America designed to assess that premise. It is our hope that the findings also speak to sports fanship globally.

https://doi.org/10.1515/9783110660883-003

2 Literature review

Sports fanship has been thoroughly examined by scholars and marketers alike. Scholars have focused on the origins of sports fanship (Gantz et al. 2008; Dietz-Uhler et al. 2000; Wann 2006); motivations for following, attending, and watching sporting events (Harris 1972; Madrigal 1995); sports media consumption, including second-screens (Earnheardt and Haridakis 2008; Rubenking and Lewis 2016); the cognitive, affective, and behavioral correlates of sports exposure (Billings and Ruihley 2013; Cummins 2009; Gantz and Wenner 1995); and the impact fanship has on self-esteem, friendships, and family life (Cialdini et al. 1976; Gantz et al. 1995; Hirt et al. 1992).

This wide range of scholarship explains a great deal about sports fans. For many, fanship starts at an early age, driven by a mix of environmental factors such as family and peer interest in sports, as well as personality factors such as competitiveness (Gantz et al. 2008; Wann et al. 2001). We also know that exposure to mediated sports is the result of an array of cognitive, affective, and social motivations (Raney 2006), many centering on eustress, and that mediated sports consumption is generally an active and social activity, enhanced by the use of second screens and social media (Gantz 2013; Lewis and Gantz 2018). The sports viewing experience can be riveting, with fans experiencing the emotional highs and lows that go along with victory and defeat (Cialdini et al. 1976; Schramm and Knoll 2017), as well as effects on their outlook and self-esteem, at least temporarily, which are largely dependent on how their favored teams and athletes fare in the arena (Hirt et al. 1992). There is also evidence that leisure time, more broadly speaking, can be shaped by the day's schedule of televised sporting events (Gantz 1985). In recent years, the rise of online gambling (in its various forms), fantasy sports, and esports have further increased the consumption of sports media (Brown et al. 2018; Brown, Billings, and Ruihley 2012) and are especially attractive for younger audiences, thanks to the development of interactive digital technology and social media platforms.

Marketing-oriented studies have also examined the connection between sports fanship, brand loyalty, and purchase intentions (Bristow and Sebastian 2001; Levin, Beasley, and Gamble 2004; Madrigal 2000), while marketers themselves, from sports leagues and teams to corporations considering sports sponsorships, have examined what it takes to attract and keep fans in stadiums (Dimensional Innovations 2018; Spanberg 2019). These efforts tell us that fans are likely to have higher brand recognition and affinity for brands that sponsor major sports leagues and teams, even if they are not always accurate in identifying the brands that are associated with major sports sponsorships (Biscaia et al. 2014; Sports Business Journal 2018). Networks airing sports content work to keep viewer attention and interest, in part by using multiple platforms (e. g., websites, apps) to showcase content and provide information relevant to viewers. With the near-ubiquitous availability of large, high-definition screens and interactive technology at fan fingertips, teams have had to redouble their efforts to attract fans to stadia and arenas (Arkenberg, Giorgio, and Deweese 2019).

There are a variety of parties interested in understanding the role of sports fanship in our lives, albeit for different reasons. For scholars, much of the interest centers on understanding the psychology of sports fans and their associated behaviors. For those working in the sports industry, understanding sports fanship is a key part of their bottom line. By getting fans to sit in the stands, devote time on media platforms, and purchase merchandise, more money and profits can be made. In the years ahead, sports media consumption looks to increase among audiences (Verna 2019) and understanding sports fanship as a ubiquitous phenomenon in society seems more important now than ever. There is likely to be a kaleidoscope of fans, comprised of individuals expressing different shades of fanship, that a simple yes/no or 0–10 scale cannot capture.

Existing unidimensional measures of fanship (e. g., self-identifying as a fan) fall short in capturing all of the ways in which sports fanship can manifest across individuals and society. Beyond avidity or intensity of fanship, which is how it is usually measured, we suggest that there are a variety of fans who care, support, and only root for individual athletes, or only follow a favorite college, or only love a single team and coach, or only care when a sports mega-event like the Olympics or World Cup is taking place. This chapter will present the ways that sports fanship actually varies – and will look at how that variation intersects with demographic attributes such as gender and age, personality attributes such as competitiveness, fanship correlates such as sports interest and perceived knowledge of sports, and outcomes such as emotional responses to sports content.

2.1 Measuring sports fanship

One major complication in the existing literature on sports fanship involves the myriad of ways scholars and marketers have labeled and measured sports fanship. Along with other scholars (e. g., Funk et al. 2001; Reysen and Branscombe 2010; Wann 1995), we have spent a good deal of time thinking and writing about this. At the heart of our concern is this key question: What does it mean to be a sports fan? The challenge in answering that question lies in determining how we go about capturing that meaning. Our studies have demonstrated that the meaning and core of sports fanship varies across individuals (e. g., Gantz et al. 2006; van Driel and Gantz 2019; van Driel, Gantz, and Lewis 2019). For some, it involves deep emotional investment; for others, it is longstanding loyalty or putting in the time to follow their favorite team throughout the season; and for some, fanship is the unintended byproduct of familial connections, of enjoying time with one's spouse or children. Sports fans tend to spend more time consuming mediated sports content than fans of other content genres (e. g., drama, reality). In addition, mediated sports content tends to hold greater cognitive, emotional, and moral weight for strong sports fans as compared to weak sports fans (e. g., Cummins 2009; Lewis and Hirt 2019; Lewis and Weaver 2015).

As the concept of fanship is central to what so many of us study, we have long argued for studies validating its measurement. Does a single, simple item – Are you a fan? – capture what we are trying to measure? If intensity of fanship matters, where is the cut-off? Do avid fans reside at 8, 9, or 10 on a 11-point, 0–10 scale or at some other point? Truth be told, it may be that at least for some purposes, a single measure may suffice, but with others, it simply will not do.

When asked, most adults say they are sports fans (Gough 2020). Yet, some of those who say they are not sports fans engage in behaviors that actually reflect fanship – they follow a team, player, or sport – and for those who say they are fans, a small number do not appear to reflect that in what they do (van Driel, Gantz, and Lewis 2019). We are unwilling to accept some of the shortcomings of this single-item measure and instead, see the value of creating a typology of fans, one that perhaps rests on an underlying continuum of fanship. We want to explore what may be hidden when people say they are – or are not – fans. That is: *What are they sports fans of*? For some, the answer is, "Nothing!" These people are not fans. At the other end of the spectrum, we have those whose answer is, "Everything!" They follow and deeply care about multiple sports. Sports form a central focus in their lives. We believe a typology of fanship better reflects variations across fans than a score on a single item scale – all the while potentially serving the same purpose of a single-item scale if points on the typology correlate with scales of fanship intensity. Moreover, we believe self-report measures can be used for fans and non-fans to place themselves on the typology and that such placement will enhance our understanding of the sports fanship phenomenon.

2.2 Correlates of sports fanship

Previous research has established the relationships among key individual differences (gender, age, competitiveness) with sports fanship and mediated sports consumption (e. g., (Dietz-Uhler et al. 2000; Gantz et al. 2008; van Driel and Gantz 2019). Men are more likely to identify as a sports fan than women, but women hold stronger feelings of pride toward their favored university teams than men (Ridinger and Funk 2006). Furthermore, the social dimension of sports fanship is important to women (Gantz and Wenner 1991; Osborne and Coombs 2016), while men engage in more sports fan behaviors (Dietz-Uhler et al. 2000). This suggests that sports fanship can vary for individuals in ways much more complex than just the avidity of their fanship. While fanship intensity may be equal, men and women express their fanship in different ways.

The proposed relationship between age and sports fanship is an emerging area of research (e. g., Brown, Billings, and Ruihley 2012; van Driel and Gantz 2019). Evidence suggests that sports fanship and sports media use can decrease over the course of the life cycle (ESPN 2009; Gantz and Lewis 2016), likely as a result of changing life roles, shifting priorities, and less time available to spend on the activity. Beyond this, competitiveness has demonstrated to be a predictor of sports fanship (Gantz et al. 2008) as well as associated with fantasy sports participation (Lewis 2012), but its influence has gone relatively untested as it relates to the various dimensions of sports fanship.

Other correlates of fanship also have been identified (Cialdini et al. 1976; Funk et al. 2001; Raney 2006; Wann 1995), many centering on cognitive and affective domains. The cognitive component of sports fanship includes sports interest in and perceived knowledge of sports, while the affective component often focuses on the emotional outcomes of sporting events themselves. Those who are driven to acquire as much sports information as possible, such as statistics, wagering lines, and historical facts are likely to be a different type of fan than those who get caught up in the emotional experience of sporting events, with all of the dramatic suspense and excitement it can hold. All these correlates may influence how individuals describe and define their sports fanship.

2.3 Research questions

Other than anticipating a wide range of fanship levels, we had no specific expectations, hence our study was guided by these research questions rather than a specific hypothesis:

RQ1: Where do adults place themselves within a sports fanship typology?

RQ2: To what extent does this typology reflect an underlying continuum of sports fanship?

Because more men self-identify as sports fans, we anticipated male and female participants would array themselves differently across our typology. We also wondered if age and competitiveness might intersect with where participants placed themselves. Finally, we expected interest in sports and perceived sports knowledge, as well as how much wins and losses affect one's emotions would tie in with self-placement. With this in mind, we asked:

RQ3a: To what extent do gender, age, and competitiveness influence where participants place themselves within a sports fanship typology?

RQ3b: To what extent do interest in sports, perceived knowledge of sports and exposure to mediated sports influence where participants place themselves within a sports fanship typology?

RQ3c: To what extent does sports fanship and how one emotionally responds to sports align with where participants place themselves within a fanship typology?

3 Method

3.1 Procedure and participants

Data were collected from a sample of Amazon's Mechanical Turk (MTurk) online workers. Only US residents at least 18 years old were eligible to complete our questionnaire. Those who did received a US $1 reward provided through the MTurk platform. Our call for participants noted our study was for sports fans as well as nonfans. Those who participated needed, on average, 20 minutes to complete the survey although, because they had more questions to address, it took sports fans a bit longer than non-fans to complete our questionnaire. We deleted data from over 200 participants either because their questionnaires were incomplete, blank, completed in less than five minutes (which we considered too fast to read through the questions and provide valid answers), or because participants failed our attention-checks. That left us with responses from 984 participants.

Participants ranged in age from 18 to 73, the average age for those in our sample was 35.9 (SD = 11.4). A slight majority of our sample (53 percent) was female and a majority (55 percent) was married. Most (78 percent) were White; 7 percent were Black, 6 percent were Asian, 6 percent were Latino, while 2 percent checked off "other." A large majority (85 percent) said they had at least some college education. Just about as many participants self-identified as fans (49 percent) as non-fans. Compared to women, a larger proportion of men identified as fans (64 percent to 36 percent). Fans were more likely to have a college degree than non-fans (61 percent to 47 percent). Beyond that, fans and non-fans were quite similar, at least in terms of the demographic attributes we assessed.

3.2 Measures

3.2.1 Sports fanship typology

We created this typology, central to this study, based on personal observations, answers to open-ended questions, and conversations with sports fans and non-fans over many years. We saw the typology as a potential continuum, with at least the bookends clear: One end consisted of non-fans who had no interest at all in following any sports. Those at the opposite end followed more than one team in more than one league and, overall, simply enjoyed following sports. In between, but not necessarily in ordinal order, we placed those with varying types of interest in following sports, including those who did so primarily for its social function; those whose interest seemed more team or player-specific than global; and whose interest seemed by the standings and an accompanying groundswell of interest among others. Our typology made one further differentiation by including interest and enjoyment of following sports beyond their specific focus of their fanship to each item. We anticipated that fanship scores would be higher for those who "also enjoy following sports" than for those who followed something "but otherwise have no interest in following sports." In all, our typology had 17 fanship descriptors:

I have just about no interest in following sports
I enjoy following or watching sports when my friends or family watch but otherwise I have no interest in following sports
I enjoy going to games or matches with my friends or family but otherwise I have no interest in following sports
I'm a fair-weather fan – I'll follow a team or player that's doing great but otherwise I have no interest in following sports
I follow the big sports events like the Super Bowl, the World Cup, or the Olympics but otherwise I have no interest in following sports
I follow a particular athlete, manager, or coach or two but otherwise have just about no interest in following sports
I follow a particular team but otherwise have just about no interest in following sports
I follow my college's teams but otherwise have just about no interest in following sports
I follow my city's teams but otherwise have no interest in following sports
I follow a particular team and league but otherwise have just about no interest in following sports
I follow at least one team in more than one league but otherwise have just about no interest in following sports
I primarily follow a particular athlete, manager, or coach or two and also enjoy following sports
I primarily follow a particular team and also enjoy following sports
I primarily follow my college's teams and also enjoy following sports
I primarily follow my city's teams and also enjoy following sports
I follow more than one team in a league and also enjoy following other sports
I follow at least one team in more than one league and also enjoy following other sports

Participants were instructed to select the descriptor (item) that most closely reflected their sports fanship.

3.2.2 Competitiveness

Competitiveness was measured with 16 items. Using our 0–10 agreement scale, participants were asked how much they agreed with each item. The following four items illustrate those contained in the scale: "I perform best when I compete with others," "Winning is the only thing that matters," and "I work hard at being the best." Mean responses ranged from 2.04 to 6.16. The overall mean response on this index was 4.51 ($SD = 2.14$). Cronbach's alpha for the index was .93.

3.2.3 Interest in and perceived knowledge of sports

Participants were given a list of 29 sports: Major League Baseball; college baseball; NFL football; college football; high school football; NBA basketball; WNBA basketball; men's college basketball; women's college basketball; men's or women's high school basketball; European soccer; professional [NASL] soccer in the US; men's or women's World Cup soccer, college soccer; NHL hockey; college hockey; esports; men's or women's professional tennis, track and field, swimming, gymnastics, professional skiing, martial arts; the participant's high school teams; the participant's city's high school, college or pro teams; their own college's teams if they went to college; and other men's or women's sports aired during the Olympics. For each sport, participants were asked, in separate sets of questions, to indicate how (1) interested and (2) knowledgeable they were. We used 11-point 0–10 scales here with the end points "no interest at all" and "a great deal of interest" for the interest items and "just about no knowledge at all" and "a great deal of knowledge." Cronbach alpha for our interest index was .94 [M = 2.14 (range = .91 to 4.96); SD = 1.80]; for our perceived sports knowledge index, the corresponding alpha was .95 [M = 2.21 (range = 1.08 to 4.93); SD = 1.85].

3.2.4 Sports media exposure behaviors

We used a set of 11 items to assess time spent following sports. If participants indicated to have a favorite sport, the questions were prefaced by asking participants to think about when their sport was in season. For participants who indicated not to have a favorite sport, but a favorite team or player were asked to think about when that sport was in season. Subsequently, all of those participants were asked to go through those items again, thinking about when their favorite sport, or when their favorite team or player's sport was *not* in season. Participants who did not have a favorite sport, team, or athlete were asked to estimate their time following sports using the same 11 items.

Our 11 items consisted of: hours per day spent watching sports on TV or on line on weekdays and weekends; minutes per day watching sports news on TV or online, reading about sports in print or online, reading about sports on team sites and blogs, following sports on social media, following sports on sports news and talk radio, exchanging messages about sports with others, talking about sports with one's family, and spending time on fantasy sports. Each item was open-ended, giving participants the opportunity to provide the number of hours or minutes that best fit their sports media use. A small number of participants – mostly fans – offered estimates for individual questions using hours that were quite high (e. g., 10+ hours daily watching sports) or simply impossible (>24 hours). We chose to be conservative here and replaced responses that were greater than two standard deviations from the mean with the group mean. Responses across items were totaled and averaged per day. Total minutes using sports media (or talking about sports) ranged from 0 to 2414 per day. These higher estimates are likely due to multitasking, such as watching sports on TV while talking to friends. The mean response across participants was 125 (*SD* = 187). Cronbach's alpha for this index ranged between .75 and .86 depending on whether the sport was in season and whether respondents had a favorite sport or athlete/team.

3.2.5 Sports fanship

We measured sports fanship in two ways. In our first measure, participants were asked a single question – Do you consider yourself a fan? – and given two response options (yes/no). Our second measure used an 11-point, 0–10 agreement scale. Here, participants were asked how much they agreed with each of 13 statements. Five of those statements should illustrate our intent and focus: I consider myself a sports fan; my friends see me as a sports fan; my family sees me as a sports fan; my life would be less enjoyable if I were not able to follow sports; being a sports fan is important to me; being a sports fan provides added meaning to me life. The mean response for this index was 3.97 (*SD* = 3.33). Means ranged from 2.78 to 6.16 on our 11-point scale. The Cronbach alpha for our fanship index was .99.

3.2.6 Emotional responses to sports content

This measure assessed the emotional rollercoaster that fans experience as their favorite players or teams play through wins and losses. We used six items here, three for their favorite athlete and three for their favorite team. The items were "I feel great when my favorite athlete (team) wins or does well," "I feel lousy when my favorite athlete (team) loses or does poorly," and "I take my favorite athlete's (team's) wins and losses personally." Participants used our 0–10 agreement scale for these items. The mean response on the scale was 3.45 (*SD* = 3.19); mean responses ranged from 2.36 to 4.91. Cronbach's alpha was .95.

4 Results

4.1 Sports fanship typology

A plurality of our participants (39.3 percent) placed themselves at our bookend descriptors, with a similar proportion (19.8 percent) selecting "I follow at least one team in more than one league and also enjoy following other sports" to those (19.5

percent) selecting "I have just about no interest in following sports (see Table 1)." Beyond this, roughly equal proportions of our sample aligned themselves on the non-sports and widespread sports fan sides. For many, interest and enjoyment appeared to be swayed by social connections: 13.7 percent noted they "enjoy following or watching sports when my friends or family watch but otherwise I have no interest in following sports"; an additional 5.3 percent selected "I enjoy going to games or matches with my friends or family but otherwise I have no interest in following sports." Yet, 40.5 percent (collectively) noted that in addition to following a particular team, their college's teams or their city's teams, they enjoyed following sports.

Few (1.8 percent) described themselves as fair-weather fans, only following and interested in sports when a team or player is "doing great." More (7.5 percent) acknowledged following major sports events like the Super Bowl, World Cup, or the Olympics even though they had no interest in sports. And, there were those (2.0 percent) who followed a particular team or league but otherwise had no interest in following sports. It was rare, though, to find anyone who followed a particular athlete, manager or coach but otherwise did not care for sports (0.5 percent) or also enjoyed following sports (0.5 percent).

4.2 Differences based on gender, age, and competitiveness

Female participants were more likely than male participants to cast themselves among those with limited interest in following sports. Indeed, they were almost twice as likely as men (24 percent vs. 15 percent) to say they had "just about no interest in following sports" and were more than twice as likely (18 percent vs. 9 percent) to select "I enjoy following or watching sports when my friends or family watch but otherwise I have no great interest in following sports" (see Table 1). They also were twice as likely as men (10 percent vs. 5 percent) to acknowledge following major events like the Super Bowl, the Olympics, and the World Cup – or following a particular team (6 percent vs. 3 percent) – even though they had just about no interest in following sports generally. On the other hand, men were far more likely (30 percent vs. 11 percent) to select the option that they followed teams and leagues and enjoyed following sports beyond those teams and leagues.

Age did not appear to meaningfully distinguish types of fans from one another. Other than small spikes in age for several items in our typology where the *n* was quite small, the average age for those who selected each item hovered within three years of the average age for our entire sample.

Competitiveness appeared related to where participants situated themselves on our sports fanship typology with those following multiple teams and sports more competitive than those generally disinterested in sports. The mean competitiveness score for those who selected "I have just about no interest in following sports" was 3.6. The corresponding score for those who selected that they followed "at least one

Tab. 1: Distribution of respondents by demographics, fanship measures, and correlates of fanship (N = 984) across the fanship typology

	N (%)	Gender (%)		Age (*M*)	Comp (*M*)	Fan (%)		Fanship (*M*)	Know (*M*)	Interest (*M*)	Emo (*M*)	Media (*M*)
Fan description that fits me best		male	fem			yes	no					
I have just about no interest in following sports	192 (19.5)	14.9	23.6	35.20	3.61	0.4	37.9	0.22	0.87	0.56	0.26	12.89
I enjoy following or watching sports when my friends or family watch but otherwise I have no interest in following sports	135 (13.7)	9.3	17.6	34.86	3.87	4.6	22.6	1.22	1.83	1.82	1.79	50.32
I enjoy going to games or matches with my friends or family but otherwise I have no interest in following sports	52 (5.3)	4.1	6.3	32.31	4.07	2.3	8.2	1.47	1.53	1.71	1.61	49.98
I'm a fair-weather fan – I'll follow a team or player that's doing great but otherwise I have no interest in following sports	18 (1.8)	1.5	2.1	37.61	4.64	1.4	2.2	3.03	1.98	1.71	3.05	74.98
I follow the big sports events like the Super Bowl. the World Cup or the Olympics but otherwise I have no interest in following sports	74 (7.5)	5.2	9.6	34.81	3.59	2.5	12.4	1.63	1.63	1.85	2.08	53.36
I follow a particular athlete, manager or coach or two but otherwise have just about no interest in following sports	5 (.5)	0.2	0.8	44.20	5.20	0.6	0.4	3.89	2.43	2.11	4.67	134.49
I follow a particular team but otherwise have just about no interest in following sports	45 (4.6)	2.6	6.3	34.93	3.79	2.7	6.4	2.52	1.64	1.63	2.95	69.52
I follow my college's teams but otherwise have just about no interest in following sports	8 (.8)	0.0	1.5	31.13	4.45	0.8	0.8	2.80	1.98	1.76	2.58	44.96

Tab. 1: (continued)

	N (%)	Gender (%)		Age (*M*)	Comp (*M*)	Fan (%)		Fanship (*M*)	Know (*M*)	Interest (*M*)	Emo (*M*)	Media (*M*)
I follow my city's teams but otherwise have no interest in following sports	10 (1.0)	0.9	1.1	33.60	4.28	0.6	1.4	2.06	1.52	1.53	2.58	32.32
I follow a particular team and league but otherwise have just about no interest in following sports	20 (2.0)	2.8	1.3	46.50	5.03	1.7	2.4	3.89	1.17	1.17	3.43	91.50
I follow at least one team in more than one league but otherwise have just about no interest in following sports	26 (2.6)	2.4	2.9	37.58	4.88	2.5	2.8	3.63	1.89	2.01	3.75	164.84
I primarily follow a particular athlete, manager or coach or two and also enjoy following sports	5 (.5)	0.2	0.8	49.80	3.86	0.8	0.2	4.08	3.39	2.96	4.20	102.13
I primarily follow a particular team and also enjoy following sports	86 (8.7)	11.3	6.5	36.55	5.12	16.4	1.4	6.36	3.05	2.96	5.63	199.11
I primarily follow my college's teams and also enjoy following sports	18 (1.8)	1.9	1.7	39.61	5.07	3.7	0.0	7.24	3.48	3.26	6.06	177.69
I primarily follow my city's teams and also enjoy following sports	39 (4.0)	5.6	2.5	35.21	5.07	7.5	0.6	7.10	2.85	2.94	6.29	204.88
I follow more than one team in a league and also enjoy following other sports	56 (5.7)	6.9	4.6	36.71	5.05	11.2	0.4	6.69	3.62	3.51	5.64	236.45
I follow at least one team in more than one league and also enjoy following other sports	195 (19.8)	30.1	10.7	36.51	5.78	40.4	0.0	7.92	3.45	3.40	6.51	268.11
Total/Average	984 (100)	100	100	35.91	4.51	100	100	3.76	2.20	2.14	3.45	124.52

team in more than one league and also enjoy[ed] following other sports" was 5.8. Competitiveness repeatedly increased as participants moved from being disinterested to interested in following sports. To illustrate: The mean competitiveness score for those who "follow a particular team and also enjoy following sports" was 5.1. In contrast, the mean score for those who "follow big events like the Super bowl, the World Cup or the Olympics but otherwise [I] have no interest in following sports" was 3.6.

4.3 Differences based on sports interest, perceived sports knowledge, and sports media use

Interest as well as perceived sports knowledge appeared related to placement on our typology. Overall, the means for our interest and perceived sports knowledge indices were low (2.2 for each), a reflection of the range of sports covered in the indices. Despite that, we again saw a linkage between location on our fanship typology and mean responses. Those who followed teams and leagues and enjoyed following other sports had higher interest and perceived sports knowledge levels than those who selected a location that pointed to low interest in following sports. In both cases, the extremes illustrate the point. Those who checked off "I have just about no interest in following sports" average 0.6 on our interest index and 0.9 on our perceived sports knowledge index. In comparison, the respective means for participants who selected "I follow at least one team in more than league and also enjoy following other sports" were both 3.4.

The difference in time spent following sports between those who indicated to have just about no interest in sports (M = 22.48, SD = 75.09) and those who follow at least one team in more than one league and enjoy following other sports is telling (M = 422.40, SD = 260.57) and further supports the value of our typology. However, in line with the previous sports fanship characteristics, the increase is not linear – at least with this sample of participants. For example, those who follow a particular athlete or coach indicated to follow sports for a total of 208 minutes, whereas those who follow their college's or city's team did not come close to 100 minutes of following sports.

4.4 Differences based on sports fanship and emotional responses to sports content

We examined differences based on fanship in two ways. First, we relied on self-designation, with fans stating if they were – or were not – fans. Not surprisingly, those who identified as fans or were included in our avid fan group were much more likely to select typology options commonly linked with sports fanship. One example clearly illustrates this finding: All of those who selected "I follow at least one team in more than one league and also enjoy following other sports" defined themselves as sports fans. On the other hand, almost all who said they were not sports fans (190 of 192 participants) checked off that they had "just about no interest in following sports." Yet, only 38 percent of the self-identified non-fans picked that option as the one that fit them best. The linkage between other locations on our typology and sports fanship were also less clear-cut, especially as we move from the end points on our typology to those closer to the center. So, while almost all of those (92 percent) who selected "I primarily follow my city's teams and also enjoy following sports" said they were sports fans, 28 percent of those who followed a particular team but otherwise had just about no interest in following sports self-identified as a sports fan. Similarly, 46 percent of those who selected following at least one team in more than one league but otherwise had just about no interest in following sports self-identified as sports fans.

Our second assessment made use of our fanship index. Here too, we see a clear overall pattern: The mean fanship score among those who selected "I have just about no interest in following sports" was 0.2 (see Table 1). At the other end of our typology, the mean fanship score for those who picked "I follow at least one team in more than one league and also enjoy following other sports" was 7.9. Mean fanship scores for those with limited interest in following sports (e. g., they enjoyed watching or going to games and matches with friends or followed a particular team, player, big sports event but otherwise had no interest in following sports) ranged between 1.2 and 3.9. Mean fanship scores for those who followed at least one athlete, coach or team *and* enjoyed following sports ranged from 4.1 to 6.7 (with, as noted, the mean topping out at 7.9 for those at the highest point on our typology).

Emotional responsiveness increased as participant placement moved from "I have just about no interest in following sports (M = 0.3) to "I follow at least one team in more than one league and also enjoy following other sports (M = 6.5). As seen in Table 1, the mean score for almost all of those who enjoyed following something but otherwise had just about no interest in sports was no higher than 3.8 on our 0–10 scale. The apparent lone exception here was for those few who followed a particular athlete, manager, or coach or two; the mean score for this group was 4.7. Among those who followed something (at least a single team or league) but also enjoyed following other sports, means were no lower than 5.6.

The relationship between self-placement on our fanship typology and competitiveness, our fanship index, and emotional responses to wins and losses can be seen in Figure 1. Because some of the data points reflect small *ns* (and large variation around them), we suspect the pattern that emerged would be more linear with a larger sample of participants. Yet, it also may be that there are no meaningful fanship score differences across some of the points in our typology.

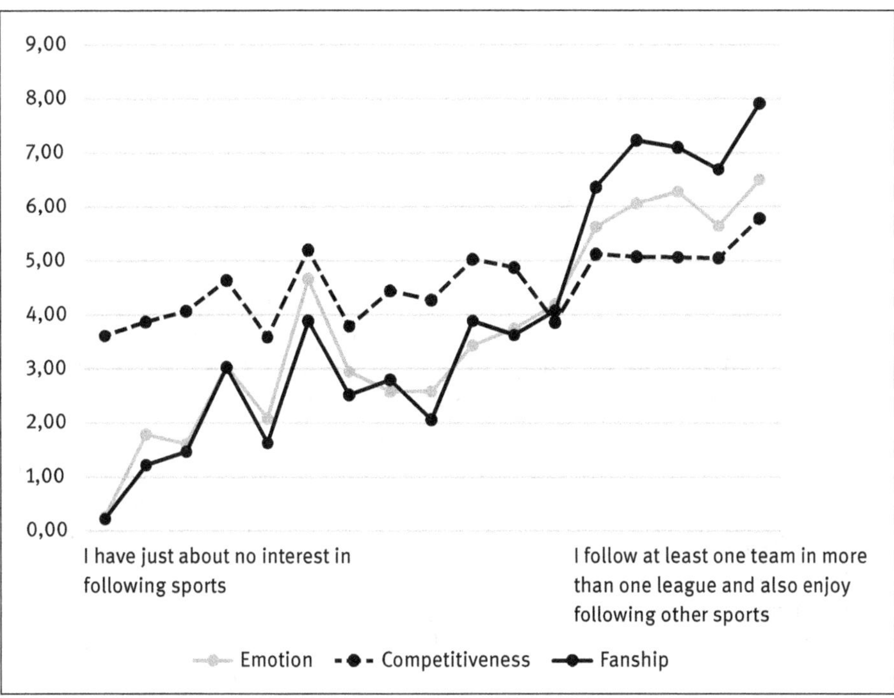

Fig. 1: Fanship and fanship correlates across the fanship continuum

5 Discussion

This study demonstrated that sports fanship is considerably more nuanced than the often used binary distinction of non-fan/fan or the threefold distinction of non-fan/fan/avid fan. Instead, it is clear that sports fanship comes in many shapes and forms, in typologies that somewhat follow the lines of a continuum. Adults occupy a place on that continuum based on their particular interests and tastes. Our study tested a value and fit of a descriptive, 17-point typology of fans and, using existing measures of fanship, correlates of fanships, and personality characteristics, assessed how each of those points would fall on an underlying fanship continuum. While many adults chose either one or the other of our two polar opposites, a majority of our sample situated themselves in locations that would otherwise get lost in some easy-to-measure and as easy-to-describe dichotomous or threefold assessment of sports fanship. Those who follow sports are more than just non-fans, fans, or avid fans. They follow and are fans of a player, a coach, or manager; a team or league; a school or city; a major sporting event; they are fair-weather or die-hard; there for companionship and along for the ride or focused on the action on and off the field; passionate or detached; they are not of one demographic, one voice, or one set of exposure patterns or one set of outcome behaviors.

Our proposed correlates of gender, age, and competitiveness informed our typology in several ways. Women were less interested in following sports. Indeed, they were twice as likely to have no interest in following sports than men. Here, and as demonstrated in previous research, women reported social motivations for watching sports (e. g., Dietz-Uhler et al. 2000). Age was not a strong predictor in distinguishing different types of fans. It is possible that as we age, the intensity of our fanship simply fades without affecting the number of players, teams, and leagues one follows (Gantz and Lewis 2016). As expected, competitiveness was high for those who reported following multiple teams and sports. It appears that sports consumption can serve as an avenue for manifesting one's drive for competition (Gantz et al. 2008). Affective and cognitive correlates (perceived interest and knowledge) were also associated with following multiple teams and sports, which aligns with previous research (e. g., Raney 2006). Clearly, many of the correlates of sports fanship proposed in past research were relevant to our typology.

As social scientists, we look for underlying commonalities and are comfortable grouping like-minded individuals. So, while it is true that we created a typology to demonstrate differences, we also were comfortable asking individuals to fit themselves into a grouping that may not perfectly or best reflect their own level of sports fanship. It is unlikely that any finite set of points will perfectly capture individuality. But, we argue that even with a finite – and realistically limited – set of points or descriptors, we can come close enough to capturing the essence of sports fanship for the typology to be more inclusive of all types of fans, while still having descriptive and predictive value. Here, we face three challenges.

The first challenge is to determine the level of specificity assigned to each group. Scholars and marketers will pick a level of specificity that meets their interests and needs (e. g., ESPN 2009; Madrigal 2000). For leagues, owners, media platforms, and manufacturers, the level of specificity needs to serve marketing purposes – that is, getting people to attend matches, follow them on the media, or purchase sponsored products. For them, many divisions may not be needed. Knowing who are avid fans, measured by a single item, may be sufficient to predict the bottom-line behaviors marketers seek. We argue that at least for scholars, where full description is a valued outcome, specificity matters. But, we also recognize that specificity has its limits, that a fine-grained typology loses value when each point fits only a few, and that some clustering around each point is inevitable. There is no magic number here. We arrived at 17 options on our own but we quickly concede that a comprehensive sports fanship typology may depend on its purpose.

The second challenge deals with ordering each position so it reflects differing levels of fanship – a typology linked with fanship intensity. It remains to be seen if that is possible. At least conceptually, there may be no intensity differences between two different types of fans – for instance, those just interested following their college teams and those who just follow their local (professional) teams.

Our third challenge is that our typology reflects traditional, US-centric sports and the one-way flow of sports content. On social media sites and blogs related to sports, people share their views. Those who contribute are likely to be fans but it is possible that they are more interested in the exercise of free expression (especially their points of view!) than sports. Perhaps they merit a separate designation. In somewhat related fashion, we need to consider those who participate in fantasy sports leagues. Most fantasy sports players are sports fans (Billings and Ruihley 2013). Yet, fantasy league participation has taken on a life of its own: Participants may be more vested in their fantasy teams than their home town or college squads and may have little interest in following sports beyond checking to see how their lineup is doing. A comprehensive fanship typology may need one or more places to situate those who participate in fantasy sport activities.

Finally, we need to deal with the increasing popularity of esports, particularly among adolescents and young adults (Brown et al. 2018). We are prepared to include esports as a sport, although other scholars may not be (e. g., Hallmann and Giel 2018): It contains clear rules, formal competitions, winners and losers, competitors who train rigorously, and massive audiences and fans of players. For those who agree with our position, studies of sports fans will need to explicitly tell participants that, for the study underway, esports is considered a sport. We suspect this will increase the proportion of those who say they are sports fans, especially among those who grew up with multiplayer video games. It could be that esports fans will be like those who follow a specific athlete, team, or sport and have little interest beyond that. But, since esports are every bit as competitive as traditional sports, esports fans may be those who enjoy many sports, this merely one of them.

This discussion suggests there is still much to be done for those interested in carefully defining and measuring sports fanship. Like those who look forward to the next season of their favorite sport, we think that is terrific.

References

Arkenberg, Chris, Pete Giorgio & Chad Deweese. 2019. Redesigning stadiums for a better fan experience. *Deloitte*. https://www2.deloitte.com/us/en/insights/industry/telecommunications/in-stadium-fan-experience.html (27 June 2019).

Billings, Andrew C. & Brody Ruihley. 2013. Why we watch, why we play: The relationship between fantasy sport and fanship motivations. *Mass Communication and Society* 16. 5–25.

Biscaia, Rui, Abel Correia, Stephen D. Ross & António Fernando Rosado. 2014. Sponsorship effectiveness in professional sport: an examination of recall and recognition among football fans. *International Journal of Sports Marketing and Sponsorship* 16. 2–18.

Bristow, Dennis N. & Richard J. Sebastian. 2001. Holy cow! Wait 'til next year! A closer look at the brand loyalty of Chicago Cubs baseball fans. *Journal of Consumer Marketing* 18. 256–275.

Brown, Kenon A., Andrew C. Billings, Breann Murphy & Luis Puesan. 2018. Intersections of fandom in the age of interactive media: eSports fandom as a predictor of traditional sport fandom. *Communication & Sport* 6. 418–435.

Brown, Natalie, Andrew C. Billings & Brody Ruihley. 2012. Exploring the change in motivations for fantasy sport participation during the life cycle of a sports fan. *Communication Research Reports* 29. 333–342.

Cialdini, Robert B., Richard J. Borden, Avril Thorne, Marcus R. Walker, Stephen Freeman & Lloyd Sloan. 1976. Basking in reflected glory: Three (football) field studies. *Journal of Personality and Social Psychology* 34. 366–375.

Cummins, R. Glenn. 2009. The effects of subjective camera and fanship on viewers' experience of presence and perception of play in sports telecasts. *Journal of Applied Communication Research* 37. 374–396.

Dietz-Uhler, Beth, Elizabeth A. Harrick, Christian End & Lindy Jacquemotte. 2000. Sex differences in sport fan behavior and reasons for being a sport fan. *Journal of Sport Behavior* 23. 219–231.

Dimensional Innovations. 2018. Reinventing the sports experience: Sports + fan experience trends 2017 analysis and 2018 forecast. *Dimin.com*. https://dimin.com/wp-content/uploads/2016/11/DI_2018-TrendsInSports_02-2018.pdf (27 June 2019).

Earnheardt, Adam C. & Paul M. Haridakis. 2008. Exploring fandom and motives for viewing televised sports. In Lawrence W. Hugenberg, Paul M. Haridakis, & Adam C. Earnheardt (eds.), *Sports mania: Essays on fandom and the media in the 21st century*, 158–171. Jefferson, NC: McFarland & Company.

ESPN. 2009. *The life cycle of the sports fan – 2008*. Bristol, CT: Author.

Funk, Daniel C., Daniel F. Mahony, Makato Nakazawa & Sumiko Hirakawa. 2001. Development of the sport interest inventory (SII): Implications for measuring unique consumer motives at team sporting events. *International Journal of Sports Marketing and Sponsorship* 3. 38–63.

Gantz, Walter. 1985. Exploring the role of television in married life. *Journal of Broadcasting & Electronic Media* 29. 65–78.

Gantz, Walter. 2013. Reflections on communication and sport: On fanship and social relationships. *Communication & Sport* 1. 176–187.

Gantz, Walter & Nicky Lewis. 2016. Fleeting or forever: Changes in fanship across the lifespan. Presented June 2019 at the meeting International Communication Association, Fukuoka, Japan.

Gantz, Walter & Lawrence A. Wenner. 1991. Men, women, and sports: Audience experiences and effects. *Journal of Broadcasting & Electronic Media* 35. 233–243.

Gantz, Walter & Lawrence A. Wenner. 1995. Fanship and the television viewing experience. *Sociology of Sport Journal* 12. 56–73.

Gantz, Walter, Zheng Wang, Bryant Paul & Robert F. Potter. 2006. Sports versus all comers: Comparing TV sports fans with fans of other programming genres. *Journal of Broadcasting & Electronic Media* 50. 95–118.

Gantz, Walter, Lawrence A. Wenner, Christina Carrico & Matt Knorr. 1995. Televised sports and marital relationships. *Sociology of Sport Journal* 12. 306–323.

Gantz, Walter, Brian Wilson, Hyangsun Lee & David Fingerhut. 2008. Exploring the roots of sports fanship. In Lawrence W. Hugenberg, Paul M. Haradakis, & Adam C. Earnheardt (eds.), *Sports mania: Essays on fandom and the media in the 21st century*, 68–77. Jefferson, NC: McFarland & Company, Inc.

Gough, Christina. 2020. Sports fans share in the US 2020. *Statista*, 24 March. https://www.statista.com/statistics/300148/interest-nfl-football-age-canada/ (27 June 2019).

Hallmann, Kirstin & Thomas Giel. 2018. eSports – Competitive sports or recreational activity? *Sport Management Review* 21. 14–20.
Harris, Harold A. 1972. *Sport in Greece and Rome.* Ithaca, NY: Cornell University Press.
Hirt, Edward R., Dolf Zillmann, Grant A. Erickson & Chris Kennedy. 1992. Costs and benefits of allegiance: Changes in fans' self-ascribed competencies after team victory versus defeat. *Journal of Personality and Social Psychology* 63. 724–738.
Levin, Aron M., Fred Beasley & Tom Gamble. 2004. Brand loyalty of NASCAR fans towards sponsors: The impact of fan identification. *International Journal of Sports Marketing and Sponsorship* 6. 7–17.
Lewis, Nicky. 2012. *Trait and motivational differences in fantasy football participation.* Doctoral dissertation, Indiana University.
Lewis, Nicky & Walter Gantz. 2018. An online dimension of sports fanship: Fan activity on NFL team sponsored websites. *Journal of Global Sport Management* 4. 257–270.
Lewis, Nicky & Edward R. Hirt. 2019. Sacred sports: Moral responses to sports media content. *Journalism & Mass Communication* Quarterly 96. 579–597.
Lewis, Nicky & Andrew J. Weaver. 2015. More than a game: Sports media framing effects on attitudes, intentions, and enjoyment. *Communication & Sport* 3. 219–242.
Madrigal, Robert. 1995. Cognitive and affective determinants of fan satisfaction with sporting event attendance. *Journal of Leisure Research* 27. 205–227.
Madrigal, Robert. 2000. The influence of social alliances with sports teams on intentions to purchase corporate sponsors' products. *Journal of Advertising* 29. 13–24.
Osborne, Anne C. & Danielle S. Coombs. 2016. *Female fans of the NFL: Taking their place in the stands.* New York: Routledge.
Raney, Arthur A. 2006. Why we watch and enjoy mediated sports. In Arthur. A. Raney & Jennings Bryant (eds.), *Handbook of sports and media*, 313–329. Mahwah, NJ: Erlbaum.
Reysen, Stephen & Nyla R. Branscombe. 2010. Fanship and fandom: Comparisons between sport and non-sport fans. *Journal of Sport Behavior* 33. 176–193.
Ridinger, Lynn L. & Daniel C. Funk. 2006. Looking at gender differences through the lens of sport spectators. *Sport Marketing Quarterly* 15. 155–166.
Rubenking, Bridget & N. Lewis. 2016. The sweet spot: An examination of second-screen sports viewing. *International Journal of Sport Communication* 9. 424–439.
Schramm, Holger & Johannes Knoll. 2017. Effects of women's football broadcastings on viewers' moods and judgments: Investigating the moderating role of team identification and sex. *Communication Research* 44. 54–76.
Spanberg, Erik. 2019. The push to get fans to arrive early. *Sports Business Journal*, 8 July 2019. https://www.sportsbusinessdaily.com/Journal/Issues/2019/07/08/In-Depth/Concessions.aspx (27 July 2019).
Sports Business Journal. 2018. What resonated with fans among NHL sponsors? *Sports Business Journal*, 8 October 2018. https://www.sportsbusinessdaily.com/Journal/Issues/2018/10/08/Research-and-Ratings/Turnkey-Research-NHL.aspx (27 June 2019)
van Driel, Irene I. & Walter Gantz. 2019. The role of emotion regulation and age in experiencing mediated sports. *Communication & Sport.* Advance online publication. doi: 10.1177/2167479519861704.
van Driel, Irene I., Walter Gantz & Nicky Lewis. 2019. Unpacking what it means to be – or not be – a fan. *Communication & Sport* 7. 611–629.
Verna, Paul. 2019. Sports OTT landscape 2019: How viewing sports is shifting to streaming, social and OTT services. *Emarketer*, 24 January 2019. https://www.emarketer.com/content/sports-video-2019 (27 June 2019)

Wann, Daniel L. 1995. Preliminary validation of the sport fan motivation scale. *Journal of Sport and Social Issues* 19. 377–396.
Wann, Daniel L. 2006. The causes and consequences of sport team identification. In Arthur A. Raney & Jennings Bryant (eds.), *Handbook of sports and media*, 331–352. Mahwah, NJ: Erlbaum.
Wann, D. L., M. J. Melnick, G. W. Russell & D. G. Pease. 2001. *Sport fans: The psychology and social impact of spectators*. New York: Routledge.

Danielle Sarver Coombs

4 Moving beyond the local: media, marketing, and "satellite" sports fans

Abstract: Widespread mediated access to sports means fandom is no longer bound by geography. Fans can develop affinity for teams around the world, and this phenomenon has only become more important as sports teams and leagues seek to expand globally. Despite these shifts in how professional sports organizations see their audience, most academic literature continues to operationalize fans (whether implicitly or explicitly) as local. To help bridge this gap, this chapter explores the ways non-local fans are conceptualized and operationalized in the literature (satellite fans, displaced fans, and distant fans) as well as how the Psychological Continuum Model (PCM) can be used to understand this fan group. It then explores the various roles media plan in non-local fan engagement and experience in terms of digital media, traditional media, and marketing. This literature is then considered in the context of communication and sport.

Keywords: sport fandom; satellite fans; distant fans; Psychological Continuum Model; sport media

1 Introduction

Each year, millions of fans from around the world use media to engage with their favorite sports teams. These fans' teams of choice often are geographically based – a hometown team with connections to a proximate community, allowing for both face-to-face opportunities for engagement as well as mediated. That is not always the case, however. Fans often find themselves following a team from afar. In some cases, a move to a new town means the fan is no longer in close range of her favorite club, yet their loyalty remains firmly entrenched despite geographic distance. For others, some outside variable – family connections, a new favorite player, a long-term track record of success, an exhibition game played nearby in a local stadium, or even an appealing name or logo – engender an initial connection with a team that eventually might develop into a long-term emotional connection to and investment in a sports team from a different city, country, or even continent.

Through media, geographic proximity is no longer a prerequisite to fandom. A young Nepalese refugee in Akron, Ohio, USA can stay connected to her national cricket team, watching with her parents and carrying on the traditions established through years of fandom in their homeland. A Londoner with a vague awareness of American football can decide to attend one of the annual National Football League (NFL) games held at Wembley Stadium, determining which team they will root for

https://doi.org/10.1515/9783110660883-004

based on nothing more than the color of their uniforms – and then develop a lifelong affiliation with the franchise, joining in on discussion boards and social media with fans from around the world. Fans no longer need to be right next door to be part of a team's fandom. Time and space barriers have diminished as media – both traditional and digital – allow for fans to be part of a sports team's broader fandom, no matter where in the world they are.

This interest has led to significant financial benefits for some of the biggest teams in the world. Teams like Barcelona (La Liga, Spain), Manchester United (Premier League, United Kingdom), the New York Yankees (Major League Baseball, United States), and Dallas Cowboys (National Football League, United States) boast significant international audiences. While some may never be able to attend a game in person, they can – and do – buy jerseys, t-shirts, hats, and more. And the more these sports grow in popularity around the world, the more leagues want to invest. In just 2019, for example, Major League Baseball opened its season in Japan with a two-game series; the NFL played three regular-season games over a three-week period; and the National Hockey League sent teams to play in Finland. For Britain's Premier League, international audiences are a huge business; researchers found that a substantial number of teams have the majority of their fans located outside of their home cities (Kuzma, Bell, and Logue 2014). Building international audiences for your product – and fans for your teams – is now recognized as an essential component of strategic growth for a top-tier side.

Despite the global nature of sports fandom in the twenty-first century, most academic work in this area continues to focus – whether explicitly or by default – on local fans. Participants often are recruited from season ticket holder lists or at the stadium or arena on gamedays; or, for university-related research, students at a particular class take part in a fan survey, often for extra credit. While these studies are valuable for making sense of sports fandom, they often do not account for the large body of fans around the world who can only dream of being there in person. Furthermore, scholars focused specifically on sport communication often are unaware of the work being done in this area in other disciplines – and vice versa. Since media are a required component to allow for this sort of global fandom to develop and thrive, it is essential that we consider the ways non-local fans are operationalized and understood in other bodies of literature.

With that goal in mind, this chapter centers on exploring three key areas. First, I examine the ways non-local sports fans are conceptualized and operationalized in the literature (satellite fans, further operationalized as displaced fans, and distant fans). Second, in an effort to better connect work being done in other disciplines with sports communication, the Psychological Continuum Model (PCM) is reviewed. The third section explores the various roles media play in non-local fan engagement and experience, particularly in terms of traditional media, digital media, and marketing. Finally, this body of work is considered specifically in the context of communication and sport, including recommendations for future areas of study.

2 Satellite fans

While there generally is a dearth of academic research on non-local fans, recent evidence indicates that this is starting to change. This is in part driven by the globalization of professional sports organizations and teams. Local markets offer little opportunity for continued growth or audience development; most would widely be considered saturated, leaving teams looking for new territories to conquer. While the origin stories of most modern teams involved naming around the city or neighborhood (e. g., Cleveland Browns in Cleveland, Ohio; Aston Villa Football Club in the Aston catchment of Birmingham, England) or representative of the local industry or employer (e. g., Pittsburgh Steelers, nicknamed in recognition of the city's dominant industry; Arsenal Football Club in North London, home of the Royal Arsenal armaments factory and storehouse), teams are no longer as closely tied to their localities. Today, "the shifting consumption culture in the context of late capitalism has at times diluted the salience of geography in the formation of sport fandom. The role of sport organizations as embodiments of local communities consisting of certain ethnic groups, classes, and nationalities is redefined by the logic of capitalism" (Pu and James 2017: 420). Teams have recognized the necessity of going global, and they have made significant investments in building international fan bases to support their clubs and – perhaps more importantly – invest in team-related memorabilia and merchandise.

To help facilitate this study of non-local fans among sport communication scholars, it is essential to start with a clear, shared understanding of key terms. Unfortunately, but not unusually for an emerging topic of study, extant literature has not been entirely consistent. In this section, I will examine three general categories of non-local fans: satellite, displaced, and distant. The broadest of the three – satellite fans – is the most encompassing, including all fans who live out of market; in fact, "out of market" (OOM) is another term encapsulating this group. Unlike displaced or distant fans, satellite fans can have any point of origin in their relationship with their team of choice. Perhaps they lived in the town in the past, or maybe they just loved a certain player in their youth. The incentive for following is immaterial; satellite fans just need to live someplace else. The name itself is derived from the ways remote fans could choose to engage with the team, by watching games (or matches, depending on the sport) via satellite television. As Kerr and Gladden (2008) note:

> The rise of communication technology in recent years has given fans unprecedented access to their favorite teams and players regardless of geographic location. This has led to fans forming or continuing bonds with teams in other countries, hereafter referred to as "satellite fans." These fans maintain an emotional bond with a foreign-based team, despite the absence of a shared geography. From the comfort of their living rooms, these fans can marvel at their heroes' athletic exploits content in the knowledge they are part of a community of fans worldwide. (Kerr and Gladden 2008: 59)

These fans can be an important part of a team's fan base. While they may not be able to go to games and spend money in-stadium, remote supporters can account for substantial percentage of merchandising sales, particularly for teams with a large global fanbase. For example, the NBA's Los Angeles Lakers are one of the most popular basketball teams around the world; as far back as 2008, 94 percent of their games were distributed internationally, and their star player Kobe Bryant's jersey was the top seller in China and Europe (Daily News 2008). Their international appeal has only grown in the ensuing decade. This offers a significant incentive for sports teams to expand their international audience.

In the same article where they first coined the term "satellite fans," Kerr and Gladden (2008) identified three categories of antecedents in their conceptual framework for understanding brand equity among this population: *team-related* (success, star player [ambassador, magician, icon], and head coach); *organization-related* (conference or league, stadium/arena, sponsor, and reputation/tradition); and *market-related* (geographic location, competitive forces, existing brand community, and international media arrangements). Grounded in the sports marketing tradition, Kerr and Gladden's work foregrounds the importance of satellite fans in building brand equity. Ultimately:

> The capacity for a professional sport team to generate media coverage, highlights packages, newspaper, magazine or internet, outside its home market is an excellent indicator of the brand equity that the organization has abroad. Greater exposure results in greater brand equity and can boost the bottom line as media rights fees increase or advertising rates rise for club-controlled properties. (Kerr and Gladden 2008: 71)

It is important to note that the term "satellite fans" still does not have shared agreement. While some include domestic fans outside of the local market (Kerr and Gladden 2008), others specifically operationalize satellite fans to include only foreign fans abroad (Behrens and Uhrich 2019). In the United States, an emerging parameter for establishing out-of-market fans is a 100-mile radius (Collins et al. 2016; Scola, Stensland, and Gordon 2018), a distance slightly farther than the NFL's defined primary market. Much of the work in this area has been grounded in psychology, often building on the work of Wann and his colleagues (including Wann and Branscombe 1990; Branscombe and Wann 1991; Wann, Tucker, and Schrader 1996) in examining the benefits of social connections. Through this research, we are beginning to understand how satellite fans may "reap the psychological and social benefits" (Scola, Stensland, and Gordon 2018: 12), enhancing their fandom through both online and face-to-face supporters' groups. As we continue to explore both the unique and common experiences of these remote fans from the local counterparts, it is useful to further break down what we know about the two types of fans that can be understood as subsets under the broader "satellite" umbrella: *displaced* and *distant*.

2.1 Displaced fans

While the phrase *satellite fans* comprises all non-local fans, the term *displaced fans* specifically refers to those who once lived in close geographic proximity to a team but have since moved. Earlier literature in this area often used displaced and distant interchangeably, leading to some operational confusion over the specific audience under examination. Scholars recognized the challenges these imprecise definitions created, noting, "Future researchers may also want to better articulate what is meant by a displaced/distant fan" (Wann, Polk, and Franz 2011: 200). Taking on this charge, Collins et al. (2016) studied the importance of new media (defined as that which allows for active audience participation) on fans who have moved away from their hometowns yet remained loyal to their hometown teams. They were particularly interested in those who moved to a place with a competing NFL team – in other words, fans who now had two potential "home" teams to support. The importance of studying displaced fans was tied to media access, since

> our society also is characterized by increasing access to technology, which in the context of sports means that people have access to their favorite teams regardless of their location. This allows for the emergence of "displaced fans," a term reserved for people who moved away from the city they grew up in yet still support the team associated with that city. (Collins et al. 2016: 656)

In this context, media is an essential part of being a displaced fan – it is only through access to media content that supporters can maintain their fandom, even when no longer local. Thanks to the increase in televised broadcast of matches (such as NBC's Saturday morning Premier League block, featuring matches played in England in real time), the introduction of league-specific premium packages (NFL Red Zone, NBA Pass) and advances in streamed content of live sports (Hulu Live), it is now easier than ever to remain actively engaged with your team. A London transplant living in the Midwestern United States no longer has to give up the opportunity to watch their beloved Tottenham Hotspur play; in fact, not only can they watch the match live on American television, they can use telephones, tablets, or laptops to offer their armchair analysis and celebrate (or commiserate) with other Spurs fans around the world, maintaining active membership in the Spurs fan community.

This Spurs' fan's experience reflects what Collins et al. discovered in their study of displaced fans. Their results identified three significant factors that affected displaced fans' identification with the hometown team: the level of identification with the hometown community; use of social media; and use of Internet streaming for viewing sports. As they noted, "with new media options making it more convenient to follow the results of one's hometown team and remain part of a community of like-minded fans without ever leaving the comfort of one's living room, it seems likely that this trend will continue in the future" (Collins et al. 2016: 668). It is particularly critical to note the importance of remaining part of one's community. Team fandom provides a meaningful way to remain engaged with and connected to the family and friends left behind during a long-distance move, and media help facilitate those connections.

2.2 Distant fans

The final category of satellite fans reviewed in this chapter are characterized as *distant fans*. While they have no geographical connection to the team's home base, these fans have discovered an affiliation and fandom for unrelated reasons. As noted by Pu and James, "With the technological means available, it is possible for sports teams to work with fans, particularly distant fans, which literally are around the world" (2017: 418). Their research with Chinese fans of the National Basketball Association was the first to treat distant fans as a specifically defined audience, one with its own set of distinctive attributes, values, and behaviors. In this study, significant differences were found among distant fans at each of the four stages of the Psychological Continuum Model (discussed further below): Awareness, Attraction, Attachment, and Allegiance. Perhaps most importantly for sports media and communication scholars, their findings indicated that a purely mediated experience was sufficient to develop a strong connection with a distant team and that the more intense that connection, the more time was spent on media consumption:

> The examination of a group of distant fans of the NBA provides an example for us to rethink the role of "place" in the creation of fandom and the appealing of culture, tradition, and spectacles as sophisticatedly refined commodities sold to a global marketplace. We conclude that the integration of sport into global consumption culture has reproduced the ways that people are identified with sport teams. More attention is called for to recognize distant fans as a unique focal object and the geography of sport fandom in general in future studies of sport consumer behavior. (Pu and James 2017: 435)

While the Pu and James (2017) study was the first to explicitly identify and operationalize the distant fan as one who has never lived or spent significant time in the location of a fan, it builds on Hyatt and Andrijiw's (2008) study of Ontario natives and residents who became fans of non-local National Hockey League teams. Their research was in response to the overwhelmingly dominating local orientation found in most fan studies. After all:

> Socializing agents, in the form of family, friends, and members of the local community and the media, readily promote the adoption of a local team as a favorite. When considering all these mutually reinforcing socializing factors, one must wonder how anyone growing up in such an environment could possibly reject the local option and become a fan of a distant team. Fans who do just that form the basis of this study. (Hyatt and Andrijiw 2008: 340)

Using qualitative, semi-structured interviews, the investigators explored the discovery and process of developing fandom with a remote team using the Psychological Continuum Model. They found that their participants generally formed an attachment to hockey first, and through that developed an awareness of a distant team that caught their attention. Their research uncovered several factors that played a role in turning away from their local club and instead bonding with a distant team (Hyatt and Andrijiw 2008: 353):

- A specific player
- The team's colors and uniforms
- The team's logo
- Meeting the team's players in person
- The team's underdog status

While these two studies were selected to give an initial understanding of how we currently understand distant fans, this is the least studied of the three (all of which suffer from a dearth of research and theorization). Because of the role media can – and must – play in developing fandom toward a non-local team, it is a ripe area of study for scholars in our field.

3 Psychological Continuum Model (PCM)

As noted in the introduction, a vast majority of research done in sport communication has focused either explicitly or implicitly on local fans. As our field continues to evolve, it is essential that we begin to explore the ways non-local fans – whether displaced or distant – are similar to and different from those who are local. The extant work in this area largely has been centered in sports marketing. These studies often are presented in ways that focus on how findings can help the marketing and communications arms of professional sports teams engage with their fans from afar. This does not mean they are atheoretical, however. As evidenced above, the Psychological Continuum Model (PCM) is one of the most prominent models for understanding the ways non-local fans move through various stages of fandom. As part of my stated effort to better integrate the academic conversations between sports communication scholars and those in other related disciplines, it is important to establish at least a baseline understanding of PCM and the role it plays in this emergent body of research.

Despite the importance of media to understanding the experiences of non-local fans, PCM has not yet made significant inroads in communication and sport literature. Originally developed by Funk and James in 2001, the model was clarified and revised in their 2006 article. Explicitly multi-disciplinary, the model draws from a range of sports-related areas of study, including psychology, consumer behavior, sociology, and marketing. According to Funk and James in their initial establishment of the model, PCM "represents a cognitive approach that places existing fan behavior theory and research under one conceptual umbrella" (2001: 121). The model identifies four levels along a vertical axis, representing the psychological connections fans establish and sustain with particular sports and teams:

> The initial floor, **Awareness**, denotes when an individual first learns that certain sports, and/or teams, exist, but does not have a specific favorite. The second floor, **Attraction**, indicates when an individual acknowledges having a favorite team or favorite sport based upon various social-psychological and demographic-based motives. On the third floor, **Attachment**, a psychological connection begins to crystallize, creating various degrees of association between the individual and the sport object (e. g., a favorite team). Attachment represents the degree or strength of association based upon the perceived importance attached to physical and psychological features associated with a team or sport. Finally, on the fourth floor, **Allegiance**, an individual has become a loyal (or committed) fan of the sport or team. Allegiance results in influential attitudes that produce consistent and durable behavior. (Funk and James 2001: 121)

In the 2006 revision of the model, Funk and James clarified that the first three floors (now called hierarchical areas or stages) – Awareness, Attraction, and Attachment – should be considered processes, while the fourth stage – Allegiance – is better understood as "outcomes of commitment and behavior based upon the strength of attitude formation and the collective meaning placed upon the [Attraction] outcomes" (2006: 207–208); or, as McClung et al. defined it, "this allegiance is basically brand performance on steroids" (2012: 183). The process a fan would go through as they move through this vertical continuum is artfully explored in de Groot and Robinson's 2008 case study of an Australian football league fan. As this case illustrates, key points in a fan's movement from Awareness through to Allegiance are influenced and informed by various types of media and news engagement, including the dissemination and sharing of:

> symbols, organizational heroes, and rituals. This leads to strong loyalty and identification. It is as if there is an almost "unspoken understanding" between the fans. The enthusiasm and passion of sports fans is fed by a pool of memories that connects them to a sports team or other fans. The nostalgic memories of the good experiences ... make sure the attachment will last because people cherish these positive emotions to create balance in their lives. (de Groot and Robinson 2008: 135)

While news and media usage certainly are not the sole variables involved in these processes, they play an important role that should be foregrounded and understood in the context of this model.

Despite the lack of research related to or grounded in PCM in the communication and sport corpus, this framework merits inclusion in this chapter due to its tremendous potential for helping understand the roles media play in non-local fandom. As evidenced in de Groot and Robinson's case study, media likely have a substantial impact across all three levels and in the context of Allegiance outcomes. Fans often are exposed to new teams – and new sports and leagues – through television and the Internet. A team's media and public relations can increase Attraction and a well-orchestrated campaign can cement Attachment. Allegiance outcomes must be reinforced through media messages, whether online or via more traditional media (particularly television and radio). Evidence suggests "it is possible that indirect consumption, through various types of media, may serve to create and strengthen internal links between the team and other important attitudes, values, and beliefs" (McClung et al. 2012: 174). Because this model does not explicitly draw from communication literature, however, media and media effects have not been centered in most extant PCM research. Incorporating this model into research conducted in our branch of this discipline will both help strengthen the model and likely offer substantial explanatory value as we seek to understand how to engage with fans.

The most likely bridge between PCM and communication and sport research is through sports marketing and management, two areas that often feature research with explicit practical applications included in the publications. These articles often touch on the role media can play in establishing Awareness, building Attraction, developing Attachment, and cementing Allegiance, including outlining "the role of news and media as a socialization agent" (Lock et al. 2012: 291) and a means for fans to demonstrate expertise, "a core manifestation of identity based on intragroup evaluation and team success" (Lock et al. 2012: 290). The importance of this is foregrounded as smaller, local leagues struggle to remain financially viable. In professional and semi-professional team "deserts," areas where there *are* no local clubs to support, those who want to follow a sport are driven to look elsewhere. This phenomenon also comes into play during off-seasons; after all, if you can't watch your own team play, why not watch further afield – including international leagues that might operate on different schedules? These opportunities for expanding audiences both domestically and globally are appealing for teams, and PCM offers a useful framework for considering how to reach these potential fans – and keep them.

4 Media, marketing, and satellite fans

As demonstrated above, media are an essential component of maintaining engagement between distant fans and their team of choice. Being able to watch games on television or through streaming, follow the organization and its coaches and players online, and engage with fellow fans via online discussion boards or social media channels gives fans the opportunity to be part of their team's community, even if they can rarely – or never – make it to the grounds to see the team in person. While our focus in communication and sport tends to center on how this happens and why it matters, it is important to remember that the business case for this is clear. Ultimately, the array of media available helps maintain sports' status as one of the most effective means of reaching audiences:

> Advances in technology have made it possible for sports fans to follow their favorite athletes, teams, and sports 24/7 – and in ways that expand and enrich the fanship experience. Traditional and newer digital media offer an enticing array of content and platform options designed to attract and retain sports fans who remain, in part because they are predominantly male, a highly desirable audience for advertisers. (Gantz and Lewis 2014: 760)

Furthermore, a savvy marketing team will be able to utilize media to maximize remote fans' engagement with the team and leverage this to increase merchandise sales and boost attendance for games played out of market.

In this section, I explore the importance of media for non-local fans through three areas: traditional media (radio and television); digital media (Internet and social media); and the role of marketing in building and maintaining remote fan bases. While the third clearly stands on its own, the first two categories – traditional and digital media – are blurring as technology continues to advance. I have used these categories to reflect how much of our scholarship has historically considered these options, but it is important to note that "Discussion of old and new media is largely redundant in the digital age. While even the term *digital media* is becoming superfluous, we simply have a media environment with various platforms, screens, and the content on those screens" (Boyle 2014: 747). Ultimately, media usage for remote fans often is similar to that of local fans, using multiple screens and options to get the information they need and want, when they need and want it. Rather than picking just one, fans will find what works for them, selecting from an ever-growing list of options:

> From reading newspaper articles, magazines, and books about the team and players to watching television broadcasts of games; listening to radio commentaries; logging on to sports Web sites, forums, and blogs; playing fantasy sports; and using mobile phones to get the latest stats and updates, sports fans continually engage with their team and players, as well as with other fans. (Phua 2010: 199)

While this range of media are important to understand, television remains central to the fan experience.

4.1 Traditional media

As evidenced by the term "satellite fans," traditional media – notably television and radio – have historically been and continue to be primary channels for non-local fans to maintain engagement with their team. For many fans, television remains the medium of choice for live events. Producers have incorporated high-end technology that enhances the viewing experience, offering "clear, crisp pictures, motion that is unbroken, and sound that covers the expanse of human hearing" (Gantz and Lewis 2014: 761). Rather than watching a static broadcast or squinting to see what happened, today's viewers are treated to some of the most exciting and innovative presentations available: "Content providers incorporate all the advances in technology, too, to deliver arresting coverage of the activity on the field of play. In turn, sports fans with cable or satellite connections and reasonably new TV sets have grown to expect a viewing experience that may be more intense than being at the stadium or arena" (Gantz and Lewis 2014: 761).

The importance of television in particular is evidenced by the vast sums of money paid for broadcasting rights. In the United States alone, Fox reportedly paid $400 million for the English-language rights to broadcast the 2018 and 2022 men's World Cup tournaments, and Telemundo shelled out $600 million for the Spanish-language broadcasts of the same tournaments (Lafayette 2018). The National Football League's television contracts are staggering, with CBS, NBC, and Fox paying an estimated $3.1 billion per year for Sunday games, ESPN paying an estimated $1.9 billion per year for "Monday Night Football," and Fox separately paying around $650 million per year for "Thursday Night Football" (Steinberg 2019). Clearly, broadcasters still consider television to be a primary medium for communicating with their audiences, particularly as audiences otherwise become increasingly fragmented:

> Against this backdrop, the premium nature of live sports events as "event television" continues to develop. In an age when technological change, in part unleashed through a lighter regulatory framework, is restructuring how people watch and think about TV, the ability of sports at major events to pull together fragmented audiences remains compelling, even if they disagree over what they appear to be watching and are engaging in second or even third screen activity and conversations. (Boyle 2014: 749)

The recency of research focused on distant and displaced fans as specific audiences has paralleled a (perhaps problematic) overwhelming focus in sports communication and media research on digital and social media. As such, we do not have much understanding of how these audiences might differ from others in terms of traditional media usage. Because these fans are not local and thus are less likely to be able to actively engage with a community of fans around them, however, it is likely that television and other forms of traditional media play an increased role in their engagement with their team of choice when compared to local fans.

4.2 Digital media

Research clearly demonstrates the importance of understanding the role of digital media and fandom in general, and this is amplified when it comes to displaced fans. Despite often not having access to local news broadcasts, the "global availability of sports information and analysis via digital networks is transforming the way in which breaking news about sport is gathered, selected, and disseminated" (Boyle and Haynes 2002: 96). In addition to changing the ways we access news, both in terms of time and medium, the rise of digital media has opened the door to interactivity. No longer do teams and broadcasters control what we see and when; now, fans have the opportunity to initiate conversations, draw attention to topics, and share information and opinions with each other. While they may not be able to engage with a local fan community, interactive media and engagement with team materials online allow for a continued sense of community.

Prior to the Internet, teams generally relied on mass media to disseminate their messages to audiences. While mailers and game-day giveaways were not uncommon, information about who was playing, statistics, histories, and compelling stories relied on finding a reporter willing to cover that information. Now, team websites allow an organization to share the content they want, in the way they want to share it, when they want to share it. This can be a powerful tool in developing Allegiance in the PCM model (McClung et al. 2012). As a medium, a website is

> interactive, non-linear, and on-demand. Fans can choose the time when they use the medium. They have the ability to spend as little or as much time as they choose in the interaction with the website. They have the ability to access video, audio, and information when they choose and as many times as they want. It could be said that the team website is a strong instrument in developing fan attachment. (McClung et al. 2012: 182)

To be most effective, websites should contain a variety of current, regularly updated content to meet a range of cognitive, affective, and behavioral needs of the fans visiting the site (McClung et al. 2012).

Of particular importance to the study of non-local fans is the use of social media. This is one of the most widely researched areas of investigation among sports media scholars in recent years, albeit often not isolating that group for study. In his study of Turkish sports fans, Özsoy (2011) highlighted the importance of Facebook for following sports news, discovering that platform was used as frequently as the Internet for information gathering. Beyond news, Smith et al. found that Twitter could offer a social connection to other fans of their team; "that virtual social interaction may be fulfilling the emotional need of enjoyment that they may not otherwise derive when watching the game alone, or with a very small group of people" (Smith, Pegararo, and Cruikshank 2019: 105). Beyond allowing fans to communicate with each other during a game, Twitter also has allowed for more effective communication between fans and the players they support (Özsoy 2011). Building and maintaining relationships with remote fans through social media is possible, but it requires specific effort on the part of organizations. To maximize interactivity, Clavio and Walsh recommend organizations "should continue to provide the informational sources that their social media users are seeking, while at the same time providing more incentives (i. e., promotions, giveaways, exclusive chat opportunities with coaches, athletes, etc.) to encourage a higher level of interactivity" (2013: 276).

Continued exponential advances in technology make it difficult to predict what sports media will look like in a decade, but increasingly scholars believe that audiences will continue using a variety of media and platforms to meet their viewing needs. As Boyle eloquently writes:

> Sports fans will always use different media for differing reasons and situations, many of the online and mobile media services will remain add-ons for some time to come with regard to live sports watching. In reality, we are in a period of ongoing evolution rather than revolution, and events such as the World Cup remind us of this as we connect with the narratives of previous tournaments and histories while engaging with technology that facilitates our access to an event that most of us will not attend in person. (Boyle 2014: 750)

This multi-media approach is not limited to live viewing audiences, however; it has important implications for marketing as well.

4.3 Marketing

For most professional teams, local fan bases no longer provide an easy target for audience expansion. Most people would be aware of the team already, and only a championship run is likely to bring more into the fold. With this in mind, teams have increasingly begun seeking distant fans to continue growth of the fan base. Marketing is essential to this process, both in terms of shoring up local fan bases as well as establishing pathways for non-local audiences to begin to identify with the team and its brand. This can be made more difficult, although not impossible, when teams are not winning championships. Without adept communications and a cohesive strategy to attract far-away fans, a team is unlikely to build its global audience – or its local one: "The marketing and communication functions of a sports team cannot directly influence on-field success. Therefore, fan identification is an important concept because it may minimize the effects of team performance on long-term fiscal success and position in the sport entertainment hierarchy of its community" (Sutton et al. 1997: 15).

Of particular importance to this area of study is emphasizing the ways we need to reconceptualize fandom and team identification. The concept of community typically has been operationalized in terms of geography; the surrounding environs, often within 100 miles of the team's home grounds – community as a common physical space, even if covering a large area. With advances in media, this definition needs to be extended. In that vein, Heere and James (2007) make a compelling argument that:

> sports teams serve not only as a source of group identity but also provide a symbolic representation of other aspects of social or community life (e. g., geography, ethnicity, vocation, gender, etc.). We refer to these other aspects as external group identities. We further argue that sports franchises place little emphasis on tapping into these external group identities that characterize the larger community when looking for salient targets on which to build team identification. By emphasizing these external group identities, sports teams have the potential to strengthen a fan's overall team identification. In effect, loyalty to a sports team can be reinforced by membership in a larger community. (Heere and James 2007: 320)

In this conceptualization, the authors "propose to shift the focus from fans as consumers to fans as community members" (Heere and James 2007: 321) and encourage organizations to build connections to external group identities that will "provide extra meaning to the community around a team (so) the team serves as a symbol for the external group identities" (Heere and James 2007: 331). For a marketing team working to maximize awareness among distant fans or reinforce attachment or allegiance among distant or displaced fans, building a connection between these external group identities – the city, the history, traditions, or even the fan base itself – can be an important means of engaging with non-local fans and building a global brand. For example, the combination of Manchester United's success on the pitch, storied history, and inclusion of global superstars – including Cristiano Ronaldo and David Beckham – certainly has helped facilitate global awareness of the organization. In their years of success, the team's merchandise was sold (and worn) around the world, providing a lucrative revenue stream for the club.

Global attention is not limited to teams who have continued success on the field, however. With appropriate marketing and communications strategies, even teams with limited success can maintain strong relationships with displaced fans. In their study of Cleveland Browns supporters in the late 1990s (in the wake of former owner Art Modell's decision to move the team to Baltimore), Sutton et al. recommended four strategies for maximizing fan identification that fit through marketing. Two are of particular importance when considering remote fans, specifically (1) reinforcing the team's history and tradition to increase the sense of belonging; and (2) create opportunities for group affiliation and participation, including organizing fan clubs and using media effectively to promote affiliation and participation (1997: 21). For sports organizations, these efforts can pay dividends. While local markets may be saturated – or, in places like Cleveland, decreasing population figures lead to smaller potential local audiences – a solid strategy combined with effective execution can lead to a meaningful non-local audience, even without continued success on the field.

5 Opportunities for continued research

As teams continue to build their brand presence in global markets, understanding the unique experiences of distant and displaced fans becomes more and more important. As demonstrated in this chapter, the work in this specific area remains underdeveloped when compared to fan studies broadly and media-related fan studies more specifically. There are three key opportunities for scholars interested in studying satellite fans: engaging in interdisciplinary or cross-disciplinary research; diversifying the type of work done in this area in terms of both geography and methodology; and centering media as a primary variable in newly developed work.

5.1 Interdisciplinary research

While some theories have crossed boundaries between and among sports- and fandom-related work in various disciplines, most of this work remains siloed in specific disciplines. Unfortunately, this often means that theoretical work that could hold substantial explanatory value in sports media and communication research is not considered. While I acknowledge the difficulty of truly integrating the work of scholars in other disciplines, the theoretical frameworks and models presented earlier in this chapter offer valuable perspectives for communication and sport scholars. Engaging in a much-needed scholarly conversation with those working in sports psychology, sociology, and marketing will strengthen work done in our field, both in terms of academic goals – including conceptualization and theoretical development – as well as reinforcing the practical relevance of our work to sports organizations. This dual purpose is an important means of reiterating the importance of our field and body of work at a time when resources for academic scholarship continue to decline.

While encouraging interdisciplinary research is a commonly stated goal, communication and sport scholars are particularly well positioned to embrace this approach. Work done by prominent sports psychologists, including the widely influential series of studies by Wann and his colleagues, are foundational readings for most budding communication and sport scholars. Theories developed by sociologists (including the commonly utilized Situational Identity Theory) are often used in sports communication studies. However, more recent work seems to be running on a more parallel track rather than truly intersecting. By broadening our work to better include other disciplines exploring fandom – particularly the experiences of distant, displaced, and satellite fans – we can advance our knowledge and understanding in a meaningful way.

5.2 Diversify scholarship

Beyond the call to better engage with and integrate theoretical developments and models from other disciplines, the work being done in this area would benefit from a broader range of methods and geography. Most of the work in English-language journals centers on the global north – Western Europe, Canada, the United States, and more economically advanced parts of Asia (notably China, Japan, and South Korea). While this certainly is reflective of the vast majority of work in sports studies, the topic of non-local fandom – particularly when operationalized as satellite or distant fans – is ripe for study in countries in other parts of the world. As more and more players from around the world are moving to ply their trade in professional leagues abroad, the potential for growth is notable. Fans from smaller nations often are overjoyed when their players sign on to prominent teams, leading to substantial engagement and affiliation with their hometown player's new club. For example, in July 2019, England's Aston Villa Football Club signed Egyptian player Mahmoud Ahmed Ibrahim

Hassan (almost always referenced among fans, the team, and media by his nickname, Trézéguet). Passionate Egyptian fans immediately bombarded Villa's official and fan pages, celebrating the signing and reassuring Villa fans that he was going to be a huge success. This type of signing provides an exciting opportunity to expand research into newer geographic areas, particularly in terms of testing the efficacy of the Psychological Continuum Model.

It is important that this call for more geographical diversity is not limited simply to coverage, however. Academics in the global north must work to better engage with peers in areas where sports research is less prevalent in order to support, mentor, and encourage interested scholars. This type of work is essential in diversifying the voices and experiences represented in our discipline and cannot be papered over by Western scholars simply shifting focus to new areas. As witnessed in other areas of writing, publishing, and scholarship, sports communication's academic community needs to actively support and amplify "own voices" work.

5.3 Media as a primary variable

Because much of the work done to understand the experiences of satellite or non-local fans has been centered in other disciplines, media often is treated as an ancillary variable rather than a primary focus. As more sports communication scholars begin to parse the experiences of non-local fans from those in closer geographic proximity, the role of media will be centered. This expansion of the current body of work will play an important role in better understanding the ways fans engage with remote teams and how these forms of engagement satisfy needs and provide benefits. As demonstrated in the media section above, this means both exploring traditional media (which, as operationalized here, includes streaming services that utilize the formats and structures of traditional broadcasts) and social media. While much of sports media research has centered on Twitter in recent years – often to the detriment of theoretical development and expansion, unfortunately – this two-pronged approach will allow for a more robust understanding of how media allow and support remote fans in their building and maintaining of sports team allegiances.

6 Conclusion

As the world becomes smaller, both through immigration and media and technological expansion, it correspondingly becomes more important for sports communication scholars to understand how non-local fans engage with their teams of choice. By better understanding the unique experiences of satellite, distant, and displaced fans – studying them as discrete categories with clear differences from local fans –

sports scholars will be positioned to expand how we conceptualize fandom, media, and communication. It is clear that media are central to these phenomena and relationships, and this is an area ripe for study.

References

Behrens, Anton & Sebastian Uhrich. 2019. Uniting a sport teams' global fan community: Prototypical behavior of satellite fans enhances local fans' attitudes and perceptions of groupness. *European Sport Management Quarterly*, http://doi.org/10.1080/16184742.2019.1643384 (11 November 2020).

Boyle, Raymond. 2014. Television sport in the age of screens and content. *Television & New Media* 15(8). 746–751.

Boyle, Raymond & Richard Haynes. 2002. New media sport. *Sport in Society* 5(3). 96–114.

Branscombe, Nyla R. & Daniel L. Wann. 1991. The positive social and self concept consequences of sports team identification. *Journal of Sport & Social Issues* 15(2). 115–127.

Clavio, Galen & Patrick Walsh. 2013. Dimensions of social media utilization among college sport fans. *Communication & Sport* 2(3). 261–281.

Collins, Dorothy R., Bob Heere, Stephen Shapiro, Lynn Ridinger & Henry Wear. 2016. The displaced fan: The importance of new media and community identification for maintaining team identity with your hometown team. *European Sport Management Quarterly* 16(5). 655–674.

Daily News. 2008. Lakers have universal appeal. *Los Angeles Daily News*, 18 May. https://www.dailynews.com/2008/05/18/lakers-have-universal-appeal/ (11 November 2020).

Funk, Daniel C. & Jeff James. 2001. The Psychological Continuum Model: A conceptual framework for understanding an individual's psychological connection to sport. *Sport Management Review* 4. 119–150.

Funk, Daniel C. & Jeff James. 2006. Consumer loyalty: The meaning of attachment in the development of sport team allegiance. *Journal of Sport Management* 20. 189–217.

Gantz, Walter & Nicky Lewis. 2014. Sports on traditional and newer digital media: Is there really a fight for fans? *Television & New Media* 15(8). 760–768.

Groot, Marieke de & Tom Robinson. 2008. Sport fan attachment and the psychological continuum model: A case study of an Australian football league fan. *Leisure/Loisir* 32(1). 117–138.

Heere, Bob & Jeffrey D. James. 2007. Sports teams and their communities: Examining the influence of external group identities on team identity. *Journal of Sport Management* 21(3). 319–337.

Hyatt, C.G. and Andrijiw, A.M. (2008), "How people raised and living in Ontario became fans of non-local National Hockey League teams",International Journal of Sport Management and

Hyatt, C. G. and A. M. Andrijiw. 2008. How people raised and living in Ontario became fans of non-local National Hockey League teams. *International Journal of Sport Management and Marketing* 4(4). 338–355.

Kerr, Anthony K. & James M. Gladden. 2008. Extending the understanding of professional team brand equity to the global marketplace. *International Journal of Sport Management and Marketing* 3(1–2). 58–77.

Kuzma, Joanne, Viv Bell & Ciaran Logue. 2014. A study of the use of social media marketing in the football industry. *Journal of Emerging Trends in Computer and Information Sciences* 5(10). 728–738.

Lafayette, Jon. 2018. World Cup coming to Americas in 2026. *Broadcasting & Cable*, 13 June. https://www.broadcastingcable.com/news/world-cup-coming-to-americas-in-2026 (11 November 2020).

Lock, Daniel, Tracy Taylor, Daniel Funk & Simon Darcy. 2012. Exploring the development of team identification. *Journal of Sport Management* 26. 283–294.

McClung, Steven, Vicki Eveland, Daniel Sweeney & Jeffrey D. James. 2012. Role of the Internet site in promotion management of sports teams and franchise brands. *Journal of Promotion Management* 18(2). 169–188.

Özsoy, Selami. 2011. Use of new media by Turkish fans in sport communication: Facebook and Twitter. *Journal of Human Kinetics* 28. 165–176.

Phua, Joe J. 2010. Sports fans and media use: Influence on sports fan identification and collective self-esteem. *International Journal of Sport Communication* 3(2). 190–206.

Pu, Haozhou & Jeffrey James. 2017. The distant fan segment: Exploring motives and psychological connection of international National Basketball Association fans. *International Journal of Sports Marketing and Sponsorship* 18(4). 418–438.

Scola, Zach, Peyton J. Stensland & Brian S. Gordon. 2018. Steeler Nation in the Midwest: Exploring membership benefits of an out-of-market Pittsburgh Steelers fan club. *Journal of Global Sport Management* 4(4). 352–370.

Smith, Lauren Reichart, Ann Pegararo & Sally Ann Cruikshank. 2019. Tweet, retweet, favorite: The impact of Twitter use on enjoyment and sports viewing. *Journal of Broadcasting & Electronic Media* 63(1). 94–110.

Steinberg, Brian. 2019. NFL, networks mull Sunday-afternoon shake-up for TV football. *Variety*, 5 March. https://variety.com/2019/tv/news/nfl-sunday-afternoon-football-cbs-fox-1203155658/ (11 November 2020).

Sutton, William A., Mark A McDonald, George R. Milne & John Cimperman. 1997. Creating and fostering fan identification in professional sports. *Sport Marketing Quarterly* 6(1). 15–22.

Wann, Daniel L. 1995. Preliminary validation of the sport fan motivation scale. *Journal of Sport & Social Issues* 19(4). 377–396.

Wann, Daniel L. & Nyla R. Branscombe. 1990. Die-hard and fair-weather fans: Effects of identification on BIRGing and CORFing tendencies. *Journal of Sport & Social Issues* 14(2). 103–117.

Wann, Daniel L., Josh Polk & Gentzy Franz. 2011. Examining the state social psychological health benefits of identifying with a distant sport team. *Journal of Sport Behavior* 35(2). 188–205.

Wann, Daniel L., Kathleen B. Tucker & Michael P. Schrader. 1996. An exploratory examination of the factors influencing the origination, continuation, and cessation of identification with sports teams. *International Journal of Sport Psychology* 24(1). 1–17.

Gregory A. Cranmer

5 The organizational processes of athletic coaching

Abstract: Throughout the past two decades, a body of scholarship on coach communication has emerged from the intersections of coaching science and communication studies. Much of this literature has forwarded that coaches act as managers who utilize their communication and influence to guide athletes and teams toward successful performances. The current chapter considers three organizational process around which teams function: socializing athletes into teams, enacting leadership, and managing athlete dissent. These processes encompass issues such as the career transitions of athletes, team social dynamics and culture, the exchange of organizational resources, power and influence, organizational policies and procedures, and athlete voice. The empirical record provides communicative strategies by which coaches manage these processes, as they seek to accomplish team goals. Upon the foundation of this chapter, more complex, holistic, and applied coach communication research is not only needed but possible.

Keywords: athletic coaching; dissent; leadership; organizational communication; organizational socialization

1 Introduction: athletic coaching as an important communicative and organizational endeavor

Sport has become an increasingly important context of social discourse throughout the 20th and 21st centuries, and its existence is dependent upon a complex web of interaction between sporting stakeholders, known as *the community of sport* (Billings, Butterworth, and Turman 2018: 21). Sport communication scholars seek to understand this web of interaction as they consider the "process by which people in sport, in a sport setting, or through a sport endeavor, share symbols as they create meaning through interaction" (Pedersen et al. 2007: 196). Although the origins of sports communication date back at least half a century – depending on if one considers Riding's (1934) examination of slang in sport journalism or Real's (1975) examination of the spectacle of the Super Bowl as the foundational piece of sport communication research – there are many important aspects of human interaction within sport that remain underexplored. An apparent and important example of a growing but often-overlooked area of research is that of coach communication. To date, scholarly interests in media (social and mass) and cultural/rhetorical studies have dominated the field of sport communication (Wenner 2015: 255), with coaching receiving no acknowledgement within pre-

https://doi.org/10.1515/9783110660883-005

vious handbooks (e. g., the *Routledge Handbook of Sport Communication*: Pedersen 2013) and little journal space within the *International Journal of Sport Communication* (Abeza, O'Reilly, and Nadeau 2014: 301). Such pursuits have instead occurred within sport psychology, sociology, and management.

However, athletic coaching has a central role within sport and shapes much of human interaction within the context. Coaching is at the heart of *enacting sport*, which is the central communicative process that considers sport performance and "everyday practices and habits of language" (Kassing et al. 2004: 376), and determines how sport is organized at the interpersonal and team levels (Kassing and Matthews 2017: 138). Cranmer (2019: 12–13) argued:

> Coaches are the conduits of information that connect sport organizations and structures to athletes, teach skills and team strategy, manage interactions and disputes between teammates and opposition, set and model appropriate forms of interaction with sources of authority, and influence the life-lessons taken from sport. In other words, by examining coaching, scholars learn about the everyday interactions through which sports are taught, structured, maintained, and performed. Without these interactions, the organized and skilled versions of sports featured within sport media and popular culture would not exist.

Coaches also are important sources of the physical, social, moral, and cognitive development of athletes, as athletes' positive affect, competence, confidence, character, life skills, psychological capacities, connections to others, and team climates are within coaches' purview (Vella, Oades, and Crowe 2011: 37). Two realities further underscore the significance of coaches' impact on athletes and within the sporting environment. First, most participants within organized sport are in crucial developmental stages throughout childhood and early adolescence, during which they are being socialized into adulthood (Atkinson 2009). Second, there are millions of athletes across the globe who participate in organized sport (Duffy et al. 2011: 94–95), with estimates suggesting that there are more than 21.5 million child athletes (i. e., aged 6–17-year-olds) within the United States alone (Kelley and Carchia 2013). Together, these realities suggest that coaches are important figures who shape the sporting environment and influence the development of a large portion of the human population.

It is not surprising that since the late 20th century the academic pursuit of athletic coaching has garnered increased interest from scholars throughout the western world and across social scientific fields, including sport psychology, sociology, and management (Gilbert and Trudel 2004: 391, 394–395; Potrac, Denison, and Gilbert 2013: 1). These scholars largely focus on the role of cognitive states and abilities, demographic patterns, and educational programs in promoting effective sporting environments. Coach communication scholars contribute to this research by seeking to understand how coaches promote improved performances and human development directly via verbal and nonverbal messages or indirectly through the strategic management of sporting environments (Cranmer 2019). These scholars contend that the effectiveness of coaches is dependent upon how they interact with athletes and structure sporting environments (Turman 2017: 166–169). Simply, coach communication scholars offer prescriptive knowledge regarding what effective coaches say or do. Thus, this scholarship is relevant to the efforts of numerous institutions and nonprofit organizations that seek to promote knowledge of effective coaching behaviors and techniques, such as the Coaching Association of Canada, European Coaching Council, Positive Coaching Alliance, and the National Association for Sport and Physical Education (Duffy et al. 2011: 95–96). Literature reviews and handbook chapters are ideal locations to contribute toward the advancement of such knowledge through synthesizing, contextualizing, and easing the integration of research into applied settings (Gilbert and Trudel 2004: 388). The current chapter seeks to meet this aim by overviewing coach communication literature that addresses the efficient management of organizational processes within sport.

Organizing teams and sporting environments is a fundamental role of coaches (Cranmer 2019; Cranmer and Myers 2015: 101) and one of the four central communicative processes within sport (Kassing et al. 2004: 376). Organizational perspectives are especially apt for understanding athletic coaching for three reasons. First, sport teams are organizations that feature the specialized and coordinated efforts of a collective toward the achievement of short- and long-term goals (Cranmer and Myers 2015: 101–102; Kassing and Matthews 2017: 137–138). Second, within these organizations athletes and coaches form relationships that parallel those of supervisors and subordinates (Jablin 1979: 1202). In addition to being separated by formal hierarchy and having direct authority over athletes, coaches share information and feedback about sporting skills and techniques such as footwork, assign tasks and roles, outline team functioning and strategies, and set team objectives (Cranmer 2019; Cranmer and Myers 2015: 102). In return, athletes share information about themselves and teammates (e. g., self-disclosures about experiences and difficulties), provide feedback about organizational functioning, and seek information or resources for completing tasks and fulfilling roles (Cranmer 2019). Third, coaching features numerous processes that underlie supervising organizations. Three specific organizational processes have garnered considerable attention from communication scholars, including socializing team members, leading teams toward goals, and managing athlete dissent. To navigate such a variety of processes requires a diverse array of professional, interpersonal, and intrapersonal knowledge (Côté and Gilbert 2009: 309–312), as well as communication competence (Turman 2017: 166–169). The communicative means through which coaches successfully manage these organizational processes are considered below.

2 Socializing athletes

A central role of coaches is to help athletes become fully functioning team members and adjust to organizational realities, including performing their tasks, learning their roles, socially integrating among peers, and assimilating to team culture (Cranmer 2019). This progression is encompassed within *organizational socialization*, which refers to "the process by which an individual acquires the social knowledge and skills necessary to assume an organizational role" (Van Maanen and Schein 1979: 211). The successful socialization of athletes is imperative, as it determines athlete "well-being, organizational attitudes and behaviors, and the performance of their organizations" (Cranmer 2018: 350). The degree to which athletes are successfully socialized is dependent upon their acquisition of the needed knowledge, attitudes, behaviors, and values of their teams via interactions with a variety of stakeholders. Coaches are particularly important conduits of information during this process, as they oversee and shape much of the sporting environment, team dynamics, and individuals' sporting experiences (Cranmer and Myers 2017: 127–128). As such, coaches are central figures throughout athlete socialization.

The socialization process begins with a period known as *anticipatory socialization*, which includes all of athletes' interactions and experiences before joining a team (Cranmer and Myers 2017: 126). For example, previous sports participation in other sports, leagues, or teams, as well as interactions with sporting culture are important sources of knowledge within this period. During anticipatory socialization, athletes form interests, attitudes, motivations, and expectations for future team membership (Cranmer 2019). Put differently, this period determines the starting point for athletes' subsequent periods of socialization (Cranmer 2017: 243–248). Coaches participate in anticipatory socialization by communicating information that is meant to prepare athletes to join their or another's team. Brief but enduring and influential messages – known as *memorable messages* – are one means through which this information is communicated (Knapp, Stohl, and Reardon 1981). These early interactions with coaches have lingering effects as athletes retain and use their memorable messages throughout their careers to make sense of novel situations and relationships, evaluate their own behavior, and guide interactions during times of uncertainty (Cranmer 2017: 245–248; Cranmer 2019). Coaches utilize these messages to communicate two types of information. First, these messages address the characteristics needed to be a successful athlete, including being loyal, responsible, honest, or sportsmanly; enjoying sports participation; and working diligently and with persistence (Cranmer and Myers 2017: 132–136; Kassing and Pappas 2007: 541–543). Such messages inform athletes' mindsets prior to joining their teams, as they are sources of motivation, confidence, and optimism, as well as reframe sport as a means of self-improvement and opportunity (Cranmer 2017: 243). Much of this information is consistent across athlete populations and indicates that coaches rely upon communicative scripts or macro-narratives within sporting culture to socialize athletes (Cranmer and Myers 2017: 137).

Second, athletes' memorable messages may address the experiences that come with athletic participation on specific teams or at particular levels of athletics. For example, the opportunities to make new friends or unique memories, challenges and time demands, or significance of participation are referenced within these messages (Cranmer and Myers 2017: 132–136). The scope of topics fit within those discussed during periods of recruitment in elite athletics, including athletic routines, social implications of membership, and ancillary roles that accompany athletic participation (Cranmer, Yeargin, and Spinda 2019: 79). Messages that address team specific experiences aid athletes' participative decision-making – whether and with which team to participate in sports – and set specific expectations for membership, including the anticipation of new relationships and time demands (Cranmer 2017: 244–245). Put differently, these messages directly inform expectations for specific organizational settings, rather than an understanding of the general role of athlete. Together, athletes' anticipatory socialization experiences form the initial benchmark from which their experiences upon joining a team will be assessed and negotiated.

Once athletes join a team, they begin a period known as *entry*, which encompasses their initial efforts to learn their tasks and roles, as well as socially integrate among their teams (Cranmer 2019). Entry centers on athletes' attempts to resolve stress and uncertainty, as their initial expectations and understandings of membership adjust to match their organizational realities. Although individuals naturally inflate expectations for future organizational experiences, receiving information that is inaccurate or inefficient during anticipatory socialization can prolong entry (Cranmer 2017: 245–246). Unfortunately, such a scenario is quite common within athletics and anticipatory socialization is rife with impression management and restricted forms of communication (Kilger and Jonsson 2017: 116–125). The demands for talented athletes across levels of competitive athletics – such as youth all-star, AAU, middle and high school, and collegiate athletics – fosters cultural norms of deception within athlete recruitment. Deceptions may be blatant and severe, such as explicit promises of playing time at specific positions, or more subtle suggestions about future roles. For instance, Cranmer, Yeargin, and Spinda (2019: 79–81) noted coaches' use of strategic ambiguity during recruiting pitches with American, college football players, including the provision of limited insight into daily athletic routines, a de-emphasis on the importance of academics, and an avoidance of the detrimental aspects of becoming a public figure. Similarly, Posteher (2019: 62–63) documented patterns of deception and half-truths within recruitment that are meant to make future team experiences more attractive to athletes. Unfortunately, these realities make entry within sport teams especially pronounced and potentially tumultuous, as they increase the disparity between expectations and the eventual organizational reality of athletes.

Coaches can ease athletes' socialization into their tasks and roles in three ways. First, coaches may provide a realistic job preview by sharing relevant and accurate information during anticipatory socialization. Such information allows athletes to self-select into teams that fit their personality, abilities, or expectations. When athletes join teams with accurate and shared understandings for team functioning, they report better social integration among their peers (Cranmer 2017: 245–246). In turn, the building of new relationships with teammates further aids in their socialization, as peers inform their understandings of tasks and roles.

Second, upon entry, coaches may directly address organizational realities with athletes. In particular, coaches are important sources of organizational knowledge regarding macro-team structures, including team history, values, and goals (Cranmer 2018: 358–360). Coaches also delegate roles prescribed within the nature of the sport, such as formal positions and duties (e. g., leadoff batter in softball or baseball) and sometimes leadership positions, like team captain (Benson, Surya, and Eys 2014: 232–234). This information provides fundamental understandings for team functioning and individual athletes' responsibilities within the team structure. From these understandings, athletes are then able to create and individualize informal roles, such as spark plug, mentor, cancer, comedian, enforcer, distractor, or leader – among others (Cope et al. 2011: 24). The nature of role identification and acceptance speaks to the dualistic influence of coaches and athletes on the socialization process.

Third, coaches can provide additional organizational resources and support to athletes. Cranmer (2018: 364) argued that head coaches of large teams indirectly influence athlete socialization through the environments and cultures that they create, the structures that the put in place, and the individuals that they include within their teams. For instance, the provision of newcomer orientations, teammate mentoring programs, and team building exercises can serve as socialization resources (Cranmer 2019; Saks and Gruman 2012: 48). Coaches may also offer support staff (e. g., sport psychologists or professional development personnel) to help athletes socialize into their teams. Cranmer, Yeargin, and Spinda (2019: 82) demonstrated the effectiveness of such a staffer in helping athletes resolve uncertainties and manage the stresses of transitioning into collegiate athletics. The availability of organizational documents – including playbooks, coaching philosophies, or team manuals – are also good resources that aid socialization. Athletes may consult these documents as needed and utilize them to self-socialize without the face threats that accompany seeking information publicly.

Coaches indirectly influence athletes' social integration into their teams through cultivating cohesion and prosocial climates via engaging behaviors (Turman 2008). The ability to socially integrate athletes is imperative for inspiring commitment and keeping athletes engaged in team efforts (Cranmer 2019). *Cohesion* refers to "an individual's sense of belonging to a particular group and his or her feelings of morale associated with membership in groups" (Bollen and Hoyle 1990: 482). Coaches may build cohesion through numerous communicative strategies, including addressing teams collectively (e. g., motivational speeches), participating in team prayer, encouraging social integration (e. g., team social events or study hall), building up the quality of future opponents, or highlighting the abilities and accomplishments of position groups or teammates (Turman 2003b: 94–99). These communicative strategies create and reinforce shared experiences – including objectives, accomplishments, or opponents – that allow athletes to develop a sense of belonging with teammates. In contrast, coaches' mistreatment of athletes or behaviors that create detrimental emotions – like jealousy of teammates, anger, or shame – hinder team cohesion and the development of functional social dynamics. Specifically, demonstrations of favoritism (Turman 2003b: 93) and use of verbal aggression (Kassing and Infante 1999: 116) are especially destructive. These strategies and behaviors create secondary resources upon which athletes can rely and from which they can seek information.

Once athletes view themselves as fully integrated members of their teams, they begin a period of *metamorphosis*. A psychological sense of belonging defines this period and may be observable via athletes' successful performances, possession of organizational knowledge, acceptance of team culture, or demonstration of desirable attitudes, such as commitment and satisfaction. Improperly socialized athletes will engage in displays of disinterest, have poor relationships with teammates, resist coaching, and experience burnout or turnover (Cranmer 2019). Nevertheless, sources of uncertainty and stress persist within this period but become associated with specific events that alter team functioning and require continued adjustment, including cohorts of new athletes, injuries among teammates, or coach turnover. For example, Fontana, Cranmer, and Sollitto (2019) demonstrated that in the wake of roster turnover athletes continue to socialize into new tasks, roles, and team dynamics. Coaches assist in said socialization through providing extra support and feedback, as well as by being transparent regarding the antecedents and consequences of turnover (Fontana, Cranmer, and Sollitto 2019). Coaches must be mindful of the continuous changes their teams may experience and mitigate the stress and uncertainties associated with these changes.

The metamorphosis period continues until athletes terminate their team membership – at which point they begin a period of *exit*. Exit is a transitionary period that features new psychological changes and relationships that result from ceasing membership among a team. Athletes may exit a particular team or eventually a sport entirely. Coaches assist in this process by preparing athletes and offering support to manage the difficulties associated with these changes, including a loss of identity, relationships, or sense of purpose (Lavallee and Andersen 2000: 249). These efforts will be effective if they promote additional identities and provide a perception of completion. Collectively, socialization literature indicates that coaches are central figures throughout athletes' joining, integrating into, and leaving teams. Through providing shared and accurate information about the knowledge, attitudes, behaviors, and values needed for team membership, coaches promote functional team dynamics and athletic performance.

3 Leading and goal accomplishment

Coaching is a task-oriented role that seeks to set and accomplish team goals – most notably winning or a predetermined proficiency in performance (Cranmer 2019). Kassing and Matthews (2017: 139) contended that – like traditional organizations – athletes are best able to accomplish team goals when coaches ensure that they are motivated and committed. *Leadership* considers the organizational process of influence through which one directs another's behavior toward the accomplishment of an objective (Hackman and Johnson 2009: 5). Coaches are widely noted as leaders, who exert influence over athletes as a means of getting them to adopt needed attitudes, perform specific behaviors, or gain compliance. Leadership manifests in numerous ways – as evident by trait, behavioral, contingency, or interactional approaches to leadership – and to varying extents. Coach communication scholars have traditionally placed an emphasis on the role of relationships, behaviors, and messages within the leadership process. This emphasis has fostered a diverse body of scholarship that provides multiple mechanisms through which coaches lead athletes toward goal accomplishment.

An emergent body of literature on athlete–coach Leader-Member Exchange considers how coaches strategically invest their interpersonal and organizational resources to better their teams' performance. As an interactional approach, Leader-Member Exchange theory (LMX) (Dansereau, Graen, and Haga 1975) forwards that leadership functions through dyadic relationships that form between leaders (i. e., coaches) and followers (i. e., athletes). These relationships vary in quality, with high-LMX relationships (i. e., in-group relationships) characterized by mutual respect, influence, trust, affect, and degrees of professionalism. In contrast, low-LMX relationships (i. e., out-group relationships) feature the absence of these qualities (Graen and Uhl-Bien 1995: 226–227). LMX literature underscores that coaches' influence stems from their interpersonal relationships with athletes (Turman 2017: 166). Quality relationships can be leveraged toward the aims of leadership because athletes are more satisfied with sporting experiences (Cranmer and Sollitto 2015: 259–260) and easier to motivate, assure, and make perseverant when they have close relationships with coaches (Jowett 2017: 156–157).

Although dispositions and homophily arguably influence the formation of LMX (Cranmer, et al. 2019: 522), coaches strategically invest in the athletes who are most capable of contributing to a team's performance (Cranmer and Myers 2015: 102). Data across multiple studies have confirmed that starting athletes report higher-quality LMX with coaches (Case 1998: 392; Cranmer 2016: 52). To encourage and reinforce quality performances, in-group athletes have more voice in team functioning (Cranmer and Buckner 2017: 46; Cranmer and Myers 2015: 109–110). They also receive more developmental resources, such as confirmation (Cranmer, et al. 2019: 518–519) and organizational knowledge (Cranmer 2018: 358–360). These incentives further athletes' abilities to assist in the execution of team strategy or sporting skills.

Other approaches toward leadership focus on the behaviors that coaches enact to influence athletes. The Multidimensional Leadership Model (MDLM) is one such example and suggests that leadership is comprised of a set of general behaviors that coaches enact toward their teams (Chelladurai and Saleh 1980). These behaviors manifest in five distinct styles of coaching that concern organizational pursuits (Chelladurai and Saleh 1980: 37–44). Two of the coaching styles address the motivational climates of teams via coaches' recognition and expression of appreciation for athletes' efforts (*positive feedback*) and attempts to meet the interpersonal needs of athletes (*social support*). These behaviors function through positive reinforcement and the promotion of prosocial team environments. Coaches may also directly influence athletes' efforts by developing and guiding their sporting knowledge and abilities (*training and instruction*). The final two sets of coaching styles address athlete involvement in team decision-making, including diagnosing problems, selecting solutions, and implementing those resolutions. These styles differ in the degrees of cooperation and reciprocity and range from inviting athletes to collaborate in team decision-making (*democratic behaviors*) to reinforcing coaches' authority (*autocratic behaviors*).

An application of the MDLM as a behavioral approach to leadership indicated that coaches' independent use of positive feedback, social support, training and instruction, and democratic behaviors create productive sporting environments that promote athletes' internalization of positive attitudes toward coaches – making them more suggestable and compliant (Turman and Schrodt 2004: 136). Yet, the use of autocratic behaviors in conjunction with positive feedback was comparatively the most effective combination of leadership styles (Turman and Schrodt 2004: 137). Such findings indicate that coaches can be authoritative if they also reinforce athletes' desirable efforts. Other applications have employed a contingency approach to leadership that forwards the importance of the contexts in which specific aspects of the MDLM are preferred. These scholars suggest that coaches should: (a) give greater degrees of positive feedback at the beginning of season when team dynamics are forming and the significance of competition is lower (Turman 2003a: 79), (b) provide more training and instruction throughout a season when their teams are successful (Turman 2001: 585), and (c) exert more control over decision-making as seasons progress (Turman 2003a: 80).

The use of power is another behavior that is relevant to coach leadership. *Power* addresses "an individual's capacity to influence another person to do something he/she would not have done had he/she not been influenced" (Richmond and McCroskey 1984: 125). Jones (2006) argued, "Coaching is an activity primarily based on social interaction and power" (3). When coach power use is applied toward goal accomplishment, it constitutes leadership (Hackman and Johnson 2009: 136). Power rests within five bases of influence (French and Raven 1959). Coaches' power derives from the belief that they (a) possess expertise or competence regarding strategies, styles of play, specific techniques, or training methods (*expert power*); (b) are admirable and worthy of compliance (*referent power*); (c) can provide psychological, social, or tangible benefits (e. g., praise, recognition, or playing time) (*reward power*); (d) are able to assign psychological, social, or tangible punishments (e. g., scold them, assign punitive tasks, or take away their playing time) (*coercive power*); and (e) are imbued with formal authority and require respect because of their position (*legitimate power*).

These power bases provide coaches with opportunities to influence or gain compliance from athletes. For example, the cultivation and reliance on one's expert and reward power underscore the utility of coaching efforts and further athletes' retention of instruction (Cranmer and Goodboy 2015: 624). Likewise, these bases of power also motivate athletes (Martin et al. 2009: 234) and render them more satisfied with sporting experiences (Turman 2006: 278) – factors that contribute to athlete engagement and continued efforts. In contrast, the reliance on punishments – while not detracting from affective evaluations of coaches and sport (Turman 2006: 278) – strain the flow and reciprocity of athlete–coach communication (Cranmer and Goodboy 2015: 624). Collectively, power research indicates that demonstrating knowledge, creating rewarding environments, and relating to athletes are the best means of influencing athletes to accept coaching efforts and strive toward specific goals.

Another means of coaches' leadership is through emotional appeals that direct performance, especially messages that address athletes' feelings of regret or guilt. Simply, coaches utilize athletes' desires to avoid feelings of regret or guilt for the purpose of task accomplishment (Turman 2005: 125–131) – at which point these messages fulfill the function of leadership. Coaches may influence athletes via connecting their performances with the accomplishment of team goals (*accountability regret*) or their emotional states immediately following games (*individual performance regret*) and in the distant future (*future regret*). These strategies recognize that athletics are a source of athlete identity and gratification, and that the lingering implications of poor performance are strong motivators. Further, coaches can attribute the emotions of coaches and teammates (*collective failure regret*) or communities (*social significance regret*) to athletes' poor performances. These messages leverage the social nature of sport and accountability to others to influence performance in a desirable manner.

Coaches implement regret inducing messages strategically to maximize team performance. For example, the potential of experiencing future regret and disappointing others are utilized prior to games, with the social significance and long-term implications of games being emphasized more during post-season play (Turman 2007: 342). Midgame adjustments feature messages that connect athletes' performances to a team's future failure or the disappointment of team members. However, effective coaches also carefully manage the emotional states of athletes to mitigate potential feelings of regret (*regret reduction*) (Turman 2005: 130), especially after poor performances (Turman 2007: 342). Reducing regret, in conjunction with encouragement, keeps athletes engaged and relieves experiences of regret and guilt associated with past performances (Sagar and Jowett 2012: 159). Overall, regret message research indicates that coaches manipulate the real and potential negative affective states of athletes via strategic messages to increase their performance in the present and future.

4 Managing athlete dissent

All collectives, including sport teams, feature some level of disagreement about instituted organizational policies, practices, and procedures; such disagreements are ubiquitous to organizations (Kassing 2011: 16–19). When expressed to another, these disagreements constitute *organizational dissent* (Kassing 1997: 313–315). Recent scholarship has extended organizational dissent to the context of team sports and revealed that the efficient management of dissent is necessary for coaching effectiveness. It is noteworthy that this chapter is concerned with dissent about team functioning, not social or political issues that define research on athlete activism (Frederick, Pegoraro, and Sanderson 2019; Sanderson, Frederick, and Stocz 2016). Athlete dissent allows coaches to acquire feedback regarding team functioning and provides opportunities for redress and innovation. In other words, valid and well-articulated dissent may result in the changing of team operations, whereas misguided dissent can be rectified through explaining or justifying the existence of specific policies, practices, and procedures (Cranmer et al. 2018: 539). As such, under the right conditions, dissent is a means of leveraging the intelligence and motivation of athletes toward bettering their teams – a notion consistent with a human resources approach to management (Kassing and Matthews 2017: 140). Coaches are fundamental within the dissent process as they oversee many of the organizational realities that trigger dissent, influence its expression, and determine its reception.

The process of organizational dissent begins with a triggering event – sometimes referred to as an agent – that fosters feelings of discomfort or distance from a team and serves as the impetus for voicing disagreement (Kassing 1997: 322). Dissent triggering events are contextual and associated with specific policies, practices, or procedures of a coach or team. Most triggering events broadly address team performance, the distribution and use of power and influence amongst a team, the requirements and logistics of membership, and team cultures and climates (Cranmer et al. 2018: 524–525). Specific triggers among college and high school athletes include the distributions of playing time, assignments of roles, selections of strategies, use of dangerous training techniques, the inconsistent application of rules and policies, the prevalence of parental involvement, failure to exercise authority appropriately, restrictions on educational or social activities, hostile social climates (e. g., verbal aggression or gossip), and team dysfunction (Cranmer et al. 2018: 533–536; Rey 2019: 25–42).

The scope and contradictions within dissent triggering events are potentially overwhelming for practitioners and coaches. Cranmer et al. (2018) noted several contradictions within their research findings: "participants dissented about (a) not having their own voice but also about others having influence in the management of their teams, (b) coaches not correcting teammate behavior but punishing other behaviors, and (c) not training enough but training too much on weekends or during the offseason" (539). Moreover, such events were inclusive of nearly "every aspect of athletic experience, including those that may seem perfectly normal to most sporting stakeholders," including running during practice, weekend practices, or mandated uniforms (Cranmer et al. 2018: 539). Therefore, it would be naïve and counterproductive for coaches to believe that they can prevent every instance of athlete dissent. Instead, the recognition of common triggering events should inform coaches' efforts to prevent unnecessary or excessive amounts of dissent by preemptively establishing expectations for team functioning or justifying the existence of policies, practices, or procedures. These efforts may save coaches time and effort over the course of a season. The use of codified documents, including philosophies, team handbooks, or player contractions, or team/parent meetings would be ideal resources through which coaches can address how their teams are to function and why.

Coaches also influence to whom athletes express dissent. Athletes dissent to three distinct audiences. Athletes may engage in (a) *upward dissent* to those above them in their team hierarchy, such as coaches or athletic directors, (b) *lateral dissent* to their teammates, or (c) *displaced dissent* to those outside of their team organizations, including parents or displaced peers (Cranmer and Buckner 2017: 38–39; Rey 2019: 42–43). It is desirable for coaches to be the recipients of athlete dissent because "they possess the power to alter and the knowledge to further explain team policies, procedures, or practices" (Cranmer and Buckner 2017: 38). In contrast, teammates and displaced others are less able to resolve athlete dissent, as they are often unable to change or explain the underlying reasons for modes of team functioning to the same degree as a coach (Cranmer and Buckner 2017: 39). Failure to resolve athlete dissent is of consequence because it contributes to quitting, absenteeism, or defiance to coaching (Hirschman 1970). Moreover, excessive lateral dissent may create a milieu of rumination that furthers dissatisfaction and disengagement among athletes (Cranmer and Buckner 2017: 39). Thus, coaches' awareness of dissent among athletes is a necessity.

Research examining high school athletes indicated that coaches may encourage upward dissent through consulting starters, whose positions within the team enable expressions of disagreement to coaches (Cranmer and Buckner 2017: 46–47). Scheduled interviews or individual meetings with these individuals to go over team concerns could be beneficial. Additionally, coaches' expressions of openness to feedback and abilities to foster climates in which teammates support each other empower athletes to dissent directly to coaches (Cranmer and Buckner 2017: 46–47; Kassing and Anderson 2014: 180). The importance of teammate support – essential to the dissent strategy of coalition building – is especially important within sporting environments because of the cultural resonance of top-down approaches to coaching (Cranmer and Buckner 2017: 48). On the contrary, when coaches are disinterested in athletes' concerns or have impersonal relationships with athletes, lateral dissent was found to increase among high school athletes (Cranmer and Buckner 2017: 46–47; Kassing and Anderson 2014: 180–181). The level of athletics in which athletes compete may explain some deviation in audiences of dissent. For example, collegiate athletics, which is noted for its classical management approaches, hinders student-athletes' abilities to express disagreement either publicly or to their superiors (Romo 2017: 503). Consequently, lateral dissent is especially common among college student-athletes (Rey 2019: 42–43). Coaches must effectively manage dissent through formal team policies that facilitate the expression of disagreements to coaches (e. g., team councils), the promotion of social cultures that emphasize coaches' concern for athletes' experiences, and the reduction of power distances with athletes.

The encouragement of rational expressions of disagreement is another means of properly managing dissent. Garner (2009: 200) forwarded eleven types of dissent messages. These messages include expressions that feature: (a) offers of quid-pro-quo (*exchange*), (b) appeals to morals or ethics (*inspiration*), (c) demands for compliance (*pressure*), (d) descriptions of emotions (*venting*), (e) resolutions (*solution presentation*), (f) reasons for disagreement (*direct-factual appeal*), (g) jokes and witty remarks (*humor*), (h) references to the support of others (*coalitions*), or (i) efforts to make the receiver of dissent feel important (*ingratiation*). Further, messages may be repeated (*repetition*) or expressed to the superior of a coach (*circumvention*).

The selection of dissent message strategies is paramount, as their effectiveness is independent of triggering events – meaning, "the success or failure of dissent is dependent on *how it is expressed* rather than *what it is about*" (Cranmer et al. 2018: 540). Of these messages, those that clearly articulate why dissent is occurring and offer potential remedies (i. e., direct-factual appeal and solution presentation) provide coaches with the best chance to address athlete disagreement (Cranmer et al. 2018: 537). These types of messages allow coaches to address what athletes find objectionable about their policies, practices, and procedures and contemplate alternative modes of functioning. Encouragingly, solution presentation, followed by direct factual appeals, are the most utilized dissent messages among high school athletes (Cranmer et al. 2018: 536). Coaches may further encourage the use of such messages by instituting team policies through which athletes are required to articulate explanations for disagreement and realistic solutions when dissenting. Collectively, it is in the best interest of coaches and their teams to foster conditions that (a) minimize unnecessary or excessive amounts of dissent, (b) direct disagreements to coaches, and (c) encourage rational and articulate expressions of disagreement.

5 A future scholarly agenda

Despite the establishment of the aforementioned bodies of research, several opportunities to advance and refine scholarly and applied understandings of the organizational processes that underlie athletic coaching remain. Although countless behaviors, concepts, theories, issues, etc. could be incorporated into extent literature, three pressing issues may benefit the growth of coach communication research. The first opportunity is the need for increased complexity in the representations of sports teams as organizations. Much of the cited literature within this chapter operates from a managerial bias and focuses on athlete–coach interaction in isolation. Athlete–coach relationships are somewhat reciprocal – although rarely symmetrical – and athletes are capable of self-socializing, self-leading, and taking autonomy within dissent expression. Sport teams are often comprised of multiple levels of authority, including head coach, various assistant coaches, captains, and support or training staff. Studies that have recognized this reality have underscored the comparative importance of mid-level management (Cranmer 2018: 358–360) and peers (Cranmer and Buckner 2017: 46) in altering organizational functioning, which undermines previous assertions about the supremacy of head coaches. As such, systems theory is a fruitful and relatively underutilized contemporary framework for understanding such complexity within sport teams – especially that which spans hierarchy or occurs between teammates (Kassing and Matthews 2017: 140).

To date, organizational communication within sports has dichotomized as either external communication, such as marketing, or internal communication, like that between athletes and coaches. In addition to utilizing systems theory for understanding internal communication within sport teams, as Kassing and Matthews (2018) encourage, an open systems approach may better encompass how coaches optimize external stakeholders' contributions and involvement with their teams to acquire appropriate degrees of investment, boundaries, cooperation, resources, and relationships (Washington and Reade 2013: 297). Sports teams operate within larger social communities (e. g., towns, states, nations, or international leagues) that are comprised of various stakeholders – including parents, peers, and fans – that influence athletes' attitudes, behaviors, and involvement in athletics. For example, many sport teams within the United States are under the oversight of larger institutions – such as athletic departments, school districts, universities, conferences, and leagues – that set rules and guidelines for teams and coaches and act as regulatory bodies. It is necessary to recognize the indirect influence of these external stakeholders may be cultivated to improve the functioning of a team, often through tangible support.

A second opportunity is the need for the continued integration of literature toward a holistic understanding of coaching. A holistic approach is beneficial when it balances the incorporation of diverse components and perspectives with applicability; such frameworks run the risk of being overly burdensome for coaches and practitioners to integrate into their coaching efforts. Cranmer (2019) articulated that a holistic approach within communication would incorporate athlete and coach characteristics and the nature of sporting environments, as well as bridge multiple perspectives of coaching, including those that utilize instructional, organizational, group, and interpersonal frameworks. Consequently, such an approach would yield insight regarding which behaviors and messages are effective, for what coaches, with what athletes, and in which contexts. Furthermore, a holistic approach would allow scholars to find the intersections between how coaches structure and manage their teams with their teaching styles, grasp of group dynamics, and their interpersonal relationships. Some early examples of these efforts link coaches' organizational and interpersonal goals.

For instance, coaches are more likely to validate and socially develop athletes who start; thus, distributing psychological and personal benefits that transcend sport and building interpersonal bonds based on athletic ability (Cranmer et al. 2019: 519; Cranmer and Brann 2015: 202–203).

A third opportunity is the need to *emphasize the application of scholarly research*, with acknowledgement that an increased emphasis on application is not mutually exclusive of rigorous study designs, diversity in methodology, nor theory building. Coaching research, in general, has the explicit aim of improving coach effectiveness – a ready-made and applied purpose. To date, scholars have struggled to balance both application and scientific inquiry. For some scholars, the rigor of study designs and the ability to test theories is restricted as access to elite sports programs and teams can be challenging and when granted requires non-interference. Not surprisingly, such research is often observational and descriptive, rather than explanatory (Becker 2009; Turman 2005; Webster 2009). The ability to provide coaches with prescriptive advice regarding what they should say or do while coaching uniquely positions communication scholars to assist in the translation of scholarship into practice. Other researchers prioritize their control over study designs and theoretical testing and often utilize convenience or network sampling (Cranmer and Myers 2015; Turman 2003a), which decontextualize findings from specific sporting situations. These scholars should seek out more opportunities to work with intact teams and in live sporting situations, which will provide more contextualized insight.

Further, our scholarship needs to be accessible in language, location, and takeaways. Scholars should be intentional and strategic with sharing their work. There are numerous professional conferences (e. g., The United States Center for Coaching Excellence annual summit) and journals (e. g., *Strategies: A Journal for Physical and Sport Educators*) that would be appropriate outlets for sharing our research with coaches. Even within articles published in traditional communication journals (e. g., *Communication & Sport*), scholars should make a serious effort to emphasize the practical implications of their research by illustrating how findings are to be implemented. Cranmer (2019) forwarded, "It is not sufficient to encourage the replication of a particular behavior in a general sense; how to implement a behavior and under what conditions are relevant" (134). Such issues of accessibility also require the consideration of the US-centric focus of coach communication research, which presents numerous opportunities to become an intercultural pursuit. Interdisciplinary pursuits with coaching science scholars from across the western world provide convenient avenues for addressing this concern.

The organizational approach to athletic coaching allows for the consideration of issues of formal authority and power, the creation and alteration of team structures, the flow of information, and the negotiation of task and relational concerns. Simply, it is useful for understanding how coaches manage their teams and guide the efforts of athletes toward successful performances. To date, the establishment of multiple lines of research on the organizational processes of coaching are not only foundational but encouraging. Likewise, the emergence of the many opportunities that are available to future scholars is promising and speaks to the potential development of this important aspect of sport communication. These observations confirm Kassing et al.'s (2004: 383) initial prognostication that coach communication "has limitless potential" as an area of specialization.

References

Abeza, Gashaw, Norm O'Reilly & John Nadeau. 2014. Sport communication: A multidimensional assessment of the field's development. *International Journal of Sport Communication* 7(3). 289–316.

Atkinson, Jaye. 2009. Age matters in sport communication. *The Electronic Journal of Communication* 19. http://www.cios.org/EJCPUBLIC/019/2/019341.html (1 July 2019).

Becker, Andrea. 2009. It's not what they do, it's how they do it: Athlete experiences of great coaching. *International Journal of Sports Science & Coaching* 4(1). 93–119.

Benson, Alex, Mark Surya & Mark Eys. 2014. The nature and transmission of roles in sport teams. *Sport, Exercise, and Performance Psychology* 3(4). 228–240.

Billings, Andrew C., Michael L. Butterworth & Paul D. Turman. 2018. *Communication and sport: Surveying the field*, 3rd edn. Los Angeles: Sage.

Bollen, Kenneth & Rick Hoyle. 1990. Perceived cohesion: A conceptual and empirical examination. *Social Forces* 69(2). 479–504.

Case, Robert. 1998. Leader member exchange theory and sport: Possible applications. *Journal of Sport Behavior* 21(4). 387–396.

Chelladurai, Packianathan & S. Saleh. 1980. Dimensions of leader behavior in sports: Development of a leadership scale. *Journal of Sport Psychology 2(1)*. 34–45.

Cope, Cassandra, Mark Eys, Mark Beauchamp, Robert Schinke, & Grégoire Bosselut. 2011. Informal roles on sport teams. *International Journal of Sport and Exercise Psychology* 9(1). 19–30.

Côté, Jean & Wade Gilbert. 2009. An integrative definition of coaching effectiveness and expertise. *International Journal of Sports Science & Coaching* 4(3). 307–323.

Cranmer, Gregory. 2016. A continuation of sport teams from an organizational perspective: Predictors of athlete-coach leader-member exchange. *Communication & Sport* 4(1). 43–61.

Cranmer, Gregory. 2017. A communicative approach to sport socialization: The functions of memorable messages during Division-I student-athletes' socialization. *International Journal of Sport Communication* 10(2). 233–257.

Cranmer, Gregory. 2018. An application of socialization resources theory: Collegiate student-athletes' team socialization as a function of their social exchanges with coaches and teammates. *Communication & Sport* 6(3). 349–367.

Cranmer, Gregory. 2019. *Athletic coaching: A communication perspective*. New York: Peter Lang.

Cranmer, Gregory & Maria Brann. 2015. "It makes me feel like I am an important part of this team": An exploratory study of coach confirmation. *International Journal of Sport Communication* 8(2). 193–211.

Cranmer, Gregory & Marjorie Buckner. 2017. High school athletes' relationships with head coaches and teammates as predictors of their expressions of upward and lateral dissent. *Communication Studies* 68(1). 37–55.

Cranmer, Gregory & Alan Goodboy. 2015. Power play: Coach power use and athletes' communicative evaluations and responses. *Western Journal of Communication* 79(5). 614–633.

Cranmer, Gregory & Scott Myers. 2015. Sports teams as organizations: A leader-member exchange perspective of player communication with coaches and teammates. *Communication & Sport* 3(1). 100–118.
Cranmer, Gregory & Scott Myers. 2017. Exploring Division-I student-athletes' memorable messages from their anticipatory socialization. *Communication Quarterly* 65(2). 125–143.
Cranmer, Gregory & Michael Sollitto. 2015. Sport support: Received social support as a predictor of athlete satisfaction. *Communication Research Reports* 32(3). 253–264.
Cranmer, Gregory, Emily Arnson, Andrew Moore, Alexander Scott & Joshua Peed. 2019. High school athletes' reports of confirmation as a function of starting status and leader-member exchange. *Communication & Sport* 7(4). 510–528.
Cranmer, Gregory, Marjorie Buckner, Niki Pham & Brandon Jordan. 2018. "I disagree": An exploration of triggering events, messages, and effectiveness of athletes' dissent. *Communication & Sport* 6(5). 523–546.
Cranmer, Gregory, Richard Yeargin & John Spinda. 2019. Life after signing: The recruiting process as a resource of college football players' socialization. In Terry Rentner & David Burns (eds.), *Case studies in sport communication: You make the call*, 77–84. New York: Routledge.
Dansereau, Fred, George Graen & William Haga. 1975. A vertical dyad linkage approach to leadership within formal organizations: A longitudinal investigation of the role making process. *Organizational Behavior and Human Performance* 13(1). 46–78.
Duffy, Patrick, Hazel Hartley, John Bales, Miguel Crespo, Frank Dick, Desire Vardhan, Lutz Nordmann & Jose Curado. 2011. Sport coaching as a "profession": Challenges and future directions. *International Journal of Coaching Science* 5(2). 93–123.
Fontana, Joseph, Gregory Cranmer & Michael Sollitto. 2019. "Next person up": Understanding collegiate student-athletes' socialization experiences with teammate exit. *Communication & Sport* (Advance Online) (15 November 2020).
Frederick, Evan, Ann Pegoraro & Jimmy Sanderson. 2019. Divided and united: Perceptions of athlete activism at the ESPYS. *Sport in Society: Cultures, Commerce, Media, Politics* 22(12). 1919–1936.
French, John & Bertram Raven. 1959. The bases for social power. In Dorwin Cartwright (ed.), *Studies in social power*, 150–167. Ann Arbor: University of Michigan Press.
Garner, Johny. 2009. When things go wrong at work: An exploration of organizational dissent messages. *Communication Studies* 60(2). 197–218.
Gilbert, Wade & Pierre Trudel. 2004. Analysis of coaching science research published from 1970–2001. *Research Quarterly for Exercise and Sport* 75(4). 388–399.
Graen, George & Mary Uhl-Bien. 1995. Relationship-based approach to leadership: Development of leader-member exchange (LMX) theory of leadership over 25 years: Applying a multi-level multi-domain perspective. *The Leadership Quarterly* 6(2). 219–247.
Hackman, Michael & Craig Johnson. 2009. *Leadership: A communicative perspective*, 5th edn. Long Grove: Waveland.
Hirschman, Albert. 1970. *Exit, voice, loyalty: Response to decline in firms, organizations, and states*. Cambridge: Harvard University Press.
Jablin, Fredric. 1979. Superior–subordinate communication: The state of the art. *Psychological Bulletin* 86(6). 1201–1222.
Jones, Robyn. 2006. *The sports coach as educator: Reconceptualizing sports coaching*. New York: Routledge.
Jowett, Sophia. 2017. Coaching effectiveness: The coach–athlete relationship at its heart. *Current Opinion in Psychology* 16(1). 154–158.
Kassing, Jeffrey. 1997. Articulating, antagonizing, and displacing: A model of employee dissent. *Communication Studies* 48(4). 311–332.
Kassing, Jeffrey. 2011. *Dissent in organizations*. Malden: Polity.

Kassing, Jeffrey & Rachael Anderson. 2014. Contradicting coach or grumbling to teammates: Exploring dissent expression in the coach–athlete relationship. *Communication & Sport* 2(2). 172–185.

Kassing, Jeffrey & Dominic Infante. 1999. Aggressive communication in the coach–athlete relationship. *Communication Research Reports* 16(2). 110–120.

Kassing, Jeffrey & Robyn Matthews. 2017. Sport and organizational communication. In Andrew Billings (ed.), *Defining sport communication*, 137–149. New York: Routledge.

Kassing, Jeffrey & Micah Pappas. 2007. "Champions are built in the off season": An exploration of high school coaches' memorable messages. *Human Communication* 10(4). 537–546.

Kassing, Jeffrey, Andrew Billings, Robert Brown, Kelby Halone, Kristen Harrison, Robert Krizek, Lindsey Meân & Paul Turman. 2004. Communication in the community of sport: The process of enacting, (re)producing, consuming, and organizing sport. In Pamela Kalbfleisch (ed.) *Communication Yearbook* 28, 373–409. Mahwah, NJ: LEA Publishers.

Kelley, Bruce & Carl Carchia. 2013. Hey, data data – swing! The hidden demographics of youth sports. *ESPN.com*, 11 July. http://espn.go.com/espn/story/_/id/9469252/hidden-demographics-youth-sports-espn-magazine (1 July 2019).

Kilger, Magnus & Rickard Jonsson. 2017. Talent production in interaction: Performance appraisal interviews in talent selection camps. *Communication & Sport* 5(1). 110–129.

Knapp, Mark, Cynthia Stohl & Kathleen Reardon. 1981. Memorable messages. *Journal of Communication* 31(4). 27–41.

Lavallee, David & Mark Andersen. 2000. Leaving sport: Easing career transitions. In Mark Andersen (ed.), *Doing sport psychology*, 249–260. Champaign: Human Kinetics.

Martin, Matthew, Kelly Rocca, Jacob Cayanus & Keith Weber. 2009. Relationship between coaches' use of behavior alteration techniques and verbal aggression on athletes' motivation and affect. *Journal of Sport Behavior* 32(2). 227–241.

Pedersen, Paul (ed.). 2013. *Routledge handbook of sport communication*. New York: Routledge.

Pedersen, Paul, Pamela Laucella, Kimberly Miloch & Larry Fielding. 2007. The juxtaposition of sport and communication: Defining the field of sport communication. *International Journal of Sport Management and Marketing* 2(3). 193–207.

Posteher, Karlee. 2019. *Winning the recruiting game: The student-athlete perspective*. Tempe, AZ: Arizona State University Dissertation.

Potrac, Paul, Jim Denison & Wade Gilbert. 2013. Introduction. In Paul Potrac, Wade Gilbert & Jim Denison (eds.), *Routledge handbook of sports coaching*, 1–2. New York: Routledge.

Real, Michael. 1975. Super Bowl: Mythic spectacle. *Journal of Communication* 25(1). 31–43.

Rey, Rikishi. 2019. *College student-athlete dissent*. Fullerton, CA: California State University-Fullerton MA thesis.

Richmond, Virginia & James McCroskey. 1984. Power in the classroom II: Power and learning. *Communication Education* 33(2). 125–136.

Riding, J. Willard. 1934. Use of slang in newspaper sports writing. *Journalism Quarterly* 11(4). 348–360.

Romo, Lynsey. 2017. College student-athletes' communicative negotiation of emotion labor. *Communication & Sport* 5(4). 492–509.

Sagar, Sam & Sophia Jowett. 2012. Communicative acts in coach–athlete interactions: When losing competitions when making mistakes in training. *Western Journal of Communication* 76(2). 148–174.

Saks, Alan & Jamie Gruman. 2012. Getting newcomers on board: A review of socialization practices and introduction to socialization resources theory. In Connie Wanberg (ed.), *The Oxford handbook of organizational socialization*, 27–55. New York: Oxford University Press.

Sanderson, Jimmy, Evan Frederick & Mike Stocz. 2016. When athlete activism clashes with group values: Social identity threat management via social media. *Mass Communication and Society* 19(3). 301–322.
Turman, Paul. 2001. Situational coaching styles: The impact of success and athlete maturity level on coaches' leadership styles over time. *Small Group Research* 32(5). 576–594.
Turman, Paul. 2003a. Athletic coaching from an instructional communication perspective: The influence of coach experience of high school wrestlers' preferences and perceptions of coaching behaviors across a season. *Communication Education* 23(2). 73–86.
Turman, Paul. 2003b. Coaches and cohesion: The impact of coaching techniques on team cohesion in the small group sport setting. *Journal of Sport Behavior* 26(1). 86–104.
Turman, Paul. 2005. Coaches' use of anticipatory and counterfactual regret messages during competition. *Journal of Applied Communication Research* 33(2). 116–138.
Turman, Paul. 2006. Athletes' perception of coach power use and the association between playing status and sport satisfaction. *Communication Research Reports* 23(4). 273–282.
Turman, Paul. 2007. The influence of athlete sex, context, and performance on high school basketball coaches' use of regret messages during competition. *Communication Education* 56(3). 333–353.
Turman, Paul. 2008. Coaches' immediacy behaviors as predictors of athletes' perceptions of satisfaction and team cohesion. *Western Journal of Communication* 72(2). 162–179.
Turman, Paul. 2017. Sports as interpersonal communication. In Andrew Billings (ed.), *Defining sport communication*, 165–177. New York: Routledge.
Turman, Paul & Paul Schrodt. 2004. New avenues for instructional communication research: Relationships among coaches' leadership behaviors and athletes' affective learning. *Communication Research Reports* 21(2). 130–143.
Van Maanen, John & Edgar Schein. 1979. Toward a theory of organizational socialization. In Barry Staw (ed.), *Research in organizational behavior*, 209–264. Greenwich: JAI Press.
Vella, Stewart, Lindsay Oades & Trevor Crowe. 2011. The role of coach in facilitating positive youth development: Moving from theory to practice. *Journal of Applied Sport Psychology* 22(1). 33–48.
Washington, Marvin & Ian Reade. 2013. Coach: The open systems' manager. In Paul Protrac, Wade Gilbert & Jim Denison (eds.), *The Routledge handbook of sports coaching*, 297–306. New York: Routledge.
Webster, Collin. Expert teachers' instructional communication in golf. *International Journal of Sport Communication* 2(2). 205–222.
Wenner, Lawrence. 2015. Communication and sport, where art thou? Epistemological reflections on the moment and field(s) of play. *Communication & Sport* 3(3). 247–260.

Kim Bissell and Tyana Ellis

6 Are children getting outplayed? Examining the intersection of children's involvement in physical activity, youth sports, and barriers to participation

Abstract: Involvement in and participation in sports and physical activities can literally be one of the most positive types of experiences children, adolescents, and adults can have. This involvement can come in the form of direct participation in a sporting event or physical activity or can come in the form of viewing a sport in a live or mediated context. Regardless of what form the involvement may come in, barriers exist that represent a gap in those who can be involved and those who cannot. The following chapter examines children's involvement in physical activity and youth sports and the factors – social, interpersonal, and environmental – that threaten their involvement. This chapter explores some of the threats to involvement by examining access issues as well as social support issues. While it is known that roughly one-third of American children do participate in formalized youth sports, two-thirds do not, and this percentage drops as children get older. Since involvement in physical activity and youth sports has a positive association with children's health and well-being, it is important to examine the potential barriers that might result in children getting outplayed.

Keywords: sports participation; children; physical activity

1 Introduction

> "It doesn't matter what your background is or where you came from. If you have dreams and goals, that's all that matters."
> – Serena Williams, professional tennis player

At the young age of five, Serena Williams picked up a tennis racquet for the first time and headed to the court with her dad and older sister, Venus. From that time on, she watched Grand Slam tournaments and professional matches, looking up to idols that came before her – Monica Seles and Steffi Graf – and saw herself, one day, following in their footsteps: "Everyone's dream can come true if you just stick to it and work hard." Fast-forward several years, and Serena Williams hit the pro circuit at the age of 14 and won her first Grand Slam just a few years later. Williams' story is not unlike many of those that professional athletes across sports could tell – a sporting event was watched, idols were identified, and big dreams started forming. In some cases, children are exposed to individual or team sports at young ages and then begin viewing

https://doi.org/10.1515/9783110660883-006

the collegiate or professional level of that sport in a mediated context. In other cases, younger children are exposed to individual or team sports, find themselves loving the sport and engage directly with the sport, and then get hooked. Regardless of the route children take into organized team or individual sports, sports – in all contexts – undoubtedly have played an important role in the development of children not only physically, but socially and emotionally. In Serena Williams' case, her experience with sports and physical activity was facilitated by having access to the game itself along with having strong social support from family and peers. This chapter examines these factors, along with others, to identify how and why a gap may exist in children's abilities to be involved in sports and physical activity.

The present chapter will synthesize the literature as it relates to children's involvement in sports and physical activity. The overarching goal is to identify the initial possible impediments or threats to children's involvement in physical activity (PA), or factors that lead to them not continuing that involvement. Throughout this chapter, we will review the literature as it relates to individual and interpersonal factors that may influence how much a child is involved in sports or physical activities as well as review the literature that focuses more on environmental attributes and children's physical activity levels. This chapter also considers these topics through a public health lens while keeping in mind the balance between time spent with the media, time spent at school, and time spent at home. In short, we consider the daily lives of children and youth and examine the role of sport participation within this broader context.

State of Play: 2018 reported that by the end of 2017, 35 percent of high school-aged kids participated in a team or individual sport, comprising of activity at least "one day during the year".[1] This percentage indicates a slight increase in youth participation in sports from the previous year but a decline of four percent over the last four years. Aspen Project Play conducted a 10-year analysis of youth participation in sports by sport type and noted, not too surprisingly, a decline in youth involvement in contact sports such as tackle football and soccer but an increase in sports like track and field, lacrosse, and volleyball.[2] Despite the increase in several youth sports, fear of injury remains an important issue for parents and players alike (The Aspen Institute 2017).[3] Overall, participation in a sporting activity is still beneficial for most children for health and social reasons alone; however, the gap is starting to widen between those who have the opportunity and access to participate and those who do not. Ultimately, the effect of this could lead to long-term negative effects related to children's health and well-being. While injuries could be one factor that are ultimately related to the slight decline in children's involvement in physical activity and sports, other factors within the home and social environment may also be important to consider.

1 See https://www.aspenprojectplay.org/kids-sports-participation-rates.
2 See https://www.stanfordchildrens.org/en/topic/default?id=sports-injury-statistics-90-P02787.
3 See https://www.aspenprojectplay.org/youth-sports-facts/challenges.

Younger children spend approximately 25 percent of their time awake watching television and are consequently exposed to television programming that may deemphasize the importance of exercise for health and participation in sport for competition or recreation. Children are said to form many of their attitudes, beliefs, and perceptions about their health and ways to live a healthy lifestyle during this same time. Given the sedentary nature of television viewing and other types of media consumption, it is quite possible that children today are choosing not to play a sport or engage in exercise in lieu of engaging with some form of media (Bissell and Birchall 2008). However, over an individual's lifespan, babies, toddlers, children, teens, and adults spend much of their time doing two key activities: consuming media and playing some form of sport or game, even if the time spent with the media is greater than their participation in sport. From infancy on, babies are exposed to different forms of media via television, movies, music, hand-held devices, books, and video games, and concurrently, young children are socialized to play a sport or play a game. Both of these key variables become agents of socialization as children learn about themselves and the world around them from either their consumption of media or their involvement or activity in a sport. According to the Center for Kids First, 75 percent of American families with school-aged children have at least one child involved in an organized sport. While involvement in some form of organized sports at a minimum remains steady, several factors may be relevant in keeping those same children actively involved in sports for a longer period of time, and we may also be reaching a point when the sedentary lifestyles associated with media use and media consumption may be the driving force behind other children getting involved or not.

2 Overview of childhood health and well-being

According to the Centers for Disease Control and Prevention (CDC), approximately 18.5 percent of children and adolescents are obese, with obesity being defined as having a body mass index (BMI) at or above the 95th percentile in the respective sex-specific growth chart (Centers for Disease Control and Prevention 2019). Childhood obesity has been a topic of conversation among health educators, public health officials, teachers, and parents for several decades, and now, children themselves. Childhood obesity is a complex health issue because the causes of weight gain in younger children can be attributed to many factors such as the child's health behaviors, the home environment, genetics, and, increasingly, a child's social environment (Centers for Disease Control and Prevention 2019). When looking at the statistics by race and age, several trends emerge: the prevalence of obesity is highest among Hispanic and non-Hispanic African American children (21.9 percent and 19.5 percent respectively); furthermore, the prevalence of obesity among preschoolers is 13.9 percent but climbs to 18.4 percent for those between 6 to 11, and even higher at 20.6 percent for those 12 to 19 (Centers for Disease Control and Prevention 2019).

Media scholars have analyzed the potential influence of the media in the context of eating behaviors and obesity concerns and have examined the media as one correlate that relates to passive or sedentary activities and the promotion of unhealthy food fare through food advertising. For example, the "couch potato" hypothesis has asserted that when children integrate television watching into daily routines, weight gain or childhood obesity may follow (Rideout et al. 2010). Common Sense Media reported in its 2019 census of tween and teen use of the media that tweens spent an average of four hours and 45 minutes a day exposed to a screen and teens spent more than seven hours a day in front of a screen (Rideout and Robb 2019). One could argue that this amount of time spent in front of a screen is detracting from engaging in physical activity along with interpersonal interactions. However, the counterargument seems to hold some truth, that if the screen time decreases, it is more likely that obesity can be prevented (Maniccia 2011). In this regard, many studies using physical video games to promote physical activity seem to offer hope (Zhang et al. 2016).

Another reason why media use may potentially increase the likelihood of obesity is through snacking behaviors associated with screen time. It has been suggested that viewing TV while eating suppresses satiety cues, introducing a tendency to overeat (Blass, Anderson, Kirkorian et al. 2006). Snacking during media use has been observed to increase consumption of soda and fast food (Sargent and Heatherton 2009), which predicts long-term consequences if the habit is adopted (Barr-Anderson et al. 2009). Prolonged screen time has also been proposed as negatively impacting sleep quality, with shorter sleep durations at very young ages leading to childhood obesity as children age (Taheri 2006).

While time spent with media and media content is certainly an important factor potentially related to the expanding waistline of children, researchers have also noted other social factors of importance such as the home environment. In a longitudinal study of the relationship of the home environment and obesity, Strauss and Knight (1999) found that maternal obesity was the most significant predictor of childhood obesity; however, children with lower cognitive stimulation also had significantly elevated risks of developing obesity. It is important to note that this study dates back more than 20 years and that the media landscape has changed significantly since. However, the home environment certainly could be influential as it related to involvement in sports and physical activity as Social Cognitive Theory (Bandura 1999) suggests because children will observe and model behavior seen at home and in other contexts.

3 Overview of PE programs, organized sports, participation numbers and potential gaps

According to the CDC, physical activity (PA) is considered an important way of maintaining lifelong health and wellbeing in children and adolescents. Both children and adolescents are encouraged to get 60 minutes of PA each day. Oftentimes, kids are expected to get this hour of activity while at school. However, even though physical education (PE) is considered an academic subject in K-12 curriculum, these requirements are not always being met nationwide (McKenzie and Lounsbery 2009).

Researchers in Georgia investigated physical activity environments throughout the state and studied all 1,333 public elementary schools by administering an online questionnaire to school officials. The results showed that 30 percent of Georgia elementary schools were classified as rural, and while most schools had access to either gyms or fields, fewer schools had access to more advanced equipment including blacktops, playgrounds, tracks, and classrooms. Schools identified as lower socioeconomic status (SES) schools had limited access to this equipment and were less likely to give the kids access to the PE/PA equipment during recess periods (Van Dyke et al. 2018). Other schools have moved away from recess and other forms of "free play" because of the increasing emphasis on academics and standardized test scores (Pellegrini and Bohn 2005).

As the formalized and structured access to physical education during school-time declines, many children and adolescents often turn to organized and team sports as a way to get PA in a fun way. In 2016, approximately 36.9 percent of children (ages 6–12) played a team sport on a regular basis and the number only decreased slightly for high school-aged students (35 percent), which is a slight decrease from the previous year (38.6 percent). Additionally, the participation rates were lower for individuals with a lower socioeconomic status (34.6 percent, under $25,000) in comparison to more affluent counterparts (68.4 percent, $100,000 or more) (The Aspen Institute 2017). However, not all children and adolescents are participating in organized and team sports in the same way that other children can. Physical and financial deficits could be the reason for this problem. As this chapter explores later, several factors predict children's ability or inability to be involved in physical activity and organized sports, and these factors could be key variables in understanding children's overall health and wellbeing.

Academic endeavors have slowly become more important in the eyes of school and state boards, with annual standardized testing guiding lesson planning and school days (Pellegrini and Bohn 2005). With children spending large parts of their days in the school setting, plenty of opportunities to engage in PA and have children meet their exercise goals for the day should exist, and in some cases, this built-in time for physical activity and free play have proven to have positive social and physical outcomes. In one study, physical activity breaks were built into a preschool curriculum in a school located in the rural Southeast of the United States. Children engaged in two activity breaks that lasted for ten minutes each, with a warm-up and cool-down session included into the exercise. The study showed that instances of moderate-to-vigorous physical activity (MVPA) were more frequent, with the breaks leading to more time spent in MVPA compared to regular unstructured and unplanned activity outside of the classroom (Wadsworth et al. 2011). While data generally support the notion that involvement in physical activity or physical education within the school environment can be a positive experience for children, several factors exist that prove to be strong influencers in determining children's involvement *outside* of the classroom or school environment.

Access plays a crucial role in determining a child's participation in sports and engagement in physical activity. Barriers to access are often out of a child's control and can have negative effects on their health and wellbeing. Some barriers that inhibit children from playing sports and being physically active include geographical location (Frost et al. 2010), socioeconomic status (SES) (Mutz and Albrecht 2017), and limited access to healthy foods (Bhargava and Lee 2016). Taking a closer look at the various barriers to access can help us understand why children may not be participating in sports and physical activity.

3.1 Geographical location and built environment

Neighborhood environments are likely to influence a child's decision to engage in PA (Roemmich et al. 2007) and can have negative and/or positive effects on a child's PA levels and their overall health and well-being. For example, a lack of availability of organized sports and/or considerable distance to sports and recreational facilities are thought to have negative influences on a child's PA (Niclasen, Petzold, and Schnohr 2012). Furthermore, infrastructural components such as a lack of sidewalks and streetlights have been found to be significantly related to adolescent PA because the diminished walkability creates unsafe environments for children to go outside and play (Norman et al. 2006). High crime levels also create unsafe environments and "might act as a barrier for sports participation" (Beenackers et al. 2011: 3) because children are less likely to leave their houses to play sports or engage in PA if the neighborhood is perceived as dangerous (Beenackers et al. 2011). While pleasant scenery, safe neighborhoods, and sidewalks are positively related to individuals being physically active (Frost et al. 2010), these characteristics are not reflected in areas with poor infrastructure, causing many children to stay indoors and engage in more sedentary activities like consuming media.

Rurality, another kind of geographical characterization, is an additional barrier that can exacerbate the issue of a child's physical inactivity (Frost et al. 2010). Research comparisons have found that "rural youth are less likely to engage in physical activity [when] compared to urban and suburban kids" (Roemmich et al. 2018: 1), and that children in rural areas have the fewest PA and sports resources (Frost et. al 2010) "even when controlling for race, education, and income" (Roemmich et al. 2018: 1). National surveys have found differences in PA behavior in relation to geographical location (Martin et al. 2005) and that children in rural areas are "less likely to meet physical activity guidelines" (Patterson et al. 2004: 152) which can largely be attributed to the limited resources in rural areas. It is fairly straightforward that "people with greater access to recreation facilities engage in more physical activity" (Abercrombie et al. 2008: 9) and that less access in rural areas results in less physical activity. Therefore, a factor as simple as living in a rural area can easily become a difficult barrier for any child to overcome in order to participate in PA or sports.

3.2 Socioeconomic status (SES)

Similar to geographical location, SES is another barrier to physical activity that is out of the control of children yet can greatly affect their health outcomes and overall well-being. Families with low SES are particularly reliant on low-cost or free recreational opportunities so youth centers or gyms where membership fees are required are not always helpful resources. However, playgrounds are free and easily accessible resources that "encourage physical and social activity among children ... and therefore represent a low-threshold health care resource for socially disadvantaged minors" (Buck, Bolbos, and Schneider 2019: 397). Unfortunately, playground access is found less in low SES neighborhoods (Abercrombie et al. 2008) and even when they are present, low SES communities have higher rates of crime and less money to allocate toward the upkeep of playgrounds, which can greatly reduce the utilization of them. The likeliness of a child using a playground is very much "dependent on the [playground's] condition, amenities, design characteristics" (Roemmich et al. 2018: 2), and perceived safety. If resources are present yet failing to meet societal standards, they are essentially nonexistent in the eyes of potential users. If playgrounds are present yet are not deemed fun, clean, and safe, they hold relatively no value to children.

Playing outside at a playground is not the only way that children can be physically active as sports participation has long been an avenue for keeping children physically active if available and affordable. But it is in this area where the gap seems to widen. Having children involved in sports can prove to be a problem for families with low SES as "many sports require a considerable financial investment for on-going participation" (Witt and Dangi 2018: 194). Families have to purchase uniforms and equipment (Mutz and Albrecht 2017), pay for gas in order to transport children to and from practices and games, and pay for general registration fees (Shen et al. 2018). With studies showing that parents spend an average of $1,500 a year on outside sports, children from low SES families often do "not participate initially or cease participation if costs cannot be covered" (Witt and Dangi 2018: 194). If families are struggling to pay bills and purchase food, often additional activities such as sports are the first cuts to be made. While this is financially beneficial for the families, a lack of participation in sports can create poor health outcomes for children in low SES families.

3.3 Healthy foods

Healthy eating goes hand in hand with physical activity. Both are often used in interventions to combat overweight and obesity and "have been shown to decrease body mass index (BMI) in children and adolescents" (Eisenberg et al. 2013: S442). In addition to being partners in fighting the childhood obesity epidemic, healthy eating greatly influences a child's ability to be physically active. "Healthy eating behaviors, such as increased fruit and vegetable consumption and decreased sugary beverage consumption" (Eisenberg et al. 2013: S442) ensure that children have the energizing nutrients needed for them to be physically active. However, accessing the healthy foods that are necessary to have an active lifestyle can prove to be challenging for some children and their families. Some children live in food deserts which are areas with poor access to healthy and affordable foods (Wrigley et al. 2002) leaving their families with the option of getting food from fast food restaurants and convenience stores, locations not famous for nutritious food options (Mader and Busse 2011). With children needing nutritious foods in order to engage in an adequate amount of PA, the issue of food access must be considered when addressing potential childhood PA barriers.

4 Social support

"Social and environmental factors [both] play a role in shaping PA practices" (Gill et al. 2018: 208), and in addition to physical inactivity and food insecurity influencing physical well-being is social support. Walen and Lachman report that studies "frequently find a link between social support and increased ... physical health, generally demonstrating beneficial effects" (2000: 6). With regard to PA among youth, a "great number of research [reveals] that support from parents and peers is positively correlated with higher levels of PA" (Milošević and Tubić 2018: 29). According to Albert Bandura's Social Cognitive Theory (SCT), "other people [can] affect [an individual's] behavior by sharing their thoughts, advice, and feelings and by the emotional support and assistance they provide" (Hayden 2014: 3). Children are especially susceptible to having their behaviors influenced because they have a tendency to "learn and do what they see" (Hayden 2014: 177) from their parents, friends/peers, and other authority figures in their lives. The social support received from a child's interpersonal domain, their parents, friends, peers, coaches, etc., can therefore play a major role in their PA habits. Unfortunately, the behaviors that children witness and the messages that they receive from their interpersonal domain are not always positively associated with PA and do not always lead to healthy behaviors (Hayden 2014).

With an understanding of how SCT affects children's learned behavior and perspective on physical activity, a child's family, peers, and coaches can greatly influence their engagement in PA, with positive social support serving as a major mechanism for increased PA (Gill et al. 2018). Furthermore, the "inter-relationship between social support and the level of PA is strongly influenced by the age of the [child]" (Milošević and Tubić 2018: 29). When a child is pre-teen age (12 and under), the social support of their parents is the greatest influence on their PA. During the teenage years (13–18), the support of both friends and family "strongly influences the level of physical activity" (Milošević and Tubić 2018: 29), and for children of all ages, the support of coaches greatly influences their PA and sport participation (Wiersma and Sherman 2005: 325). Knowing that social support plays such a crucial role in influencing the physical activity levels among children, it is important to evaluate the different kinds of social support separately.

4.1 Parents

Many studies have found correlations between parental support and child and adolescent PA (Yao and Rhodes 2015) identifying social support from parents as an "especially important factor related to children's participation in PA" (Shen et al. 2018: 346). Parents can provide social support to children in relation to sports and PA in a multitude of ways, one being instrumental support. Instrumental support is foundational in a child even having the opportunity to participate in sports or PA as it encompasses many logistical aspects surrounding sports or PA. Parental instrumental support includes "organizing PAs, paying activity fees" (Shen et al. 2018: 347), and "investing into equipment" (Mutz and Albrecht 2017: 3027). As addressed earlier, financial support can be difficult for families lower in SES, which can inevitably cause children of lower social classes to have less access to PA or sports simply because their parents cannot provide the vital instrumental support needed for their participation. Instrumental support also includes providing transportation (Shen et al. 2018), which does not matter as much for children who can walk to nearby sports fields or gyms. However, for children in rural communities or those in socially disadvantaged communities that do not have nearby opportunities for sports or PAs, transportation plays an integral role in them having the ability to participate in sports or PA.

Other forms of parental social support include emotional support and informational support. Emotional support is conveyed through parents supporting their child's individuality through warmth, encouragement, praise, and reinforcement which is correlated with greater child participation in PA and better overall health (Courtney et al. 2019; Gill et al. 2018). SCT also becomes relevant within emotional support because a child's interpersonal domain can influence his or her own perceptions and behaviors meaning that if their parents display positive emotions toward sports and PA as a whole in addition to positive emotions about them participating in PA, children may feel personally encouraged to pursue sports or PA themselves. Building on emotional support is informational support, which can provide "reasoned communication" by explaining the benefits of PA in addition to having a positive attitude (Courtney et al. 2019). An understanding of the health benefits associated with PA is important for both children and adults and for some children reasoned communication is just as, if not more, important than positive feelings.

Companionship and validation are two more forms of parental support that go hand in hand. Validation is characterized by parents "serving as role models" (Shen et al. 2018: 347), and companionship involves children and parents "being active together" (Vander et al. 2012: 277), "going for a walk together" (Bakalár, Kopčáková, and Gecková 2019: 17), and "accompany[ing] them to competitions" (Mutz and Albrecht 2017: 3027). SCT tells us that children are encouraged to do what they are seeing and through companionship and validation, children are shown that they are not alone in their PA endeavors and they feel validated in their choice to participate in sports (Mutz and Albrecht 2017).

4.2 Coaches

In addition to parents, "coaches may become authority figures to whom children can turn to for guidance and support" (Kirkpatrick et al. 2020) and thus play a critical role in "positively or negatively influencing youths' sport experiences" (Fraser-Thomas and Côté 2006: 15). Coaches' attitudes, beliefs, expectations, and emotional reactions to both sports and how children perform during sports can significantly affect children's sport experiences (Kirkpatrick et al. 2020). Considering the vital role that coaches play in "establishing an active environment" (Cohen, Bovbjerg, and Wegis 2020: 136), it is important to understand how coaches provide social support for children and adolescents.

Similar to parents, "coaches provide the instrumental support crucial for the existence of children's sport programs [such as] money, time, [and] transportation" (Wiersma and Sherman 2005: 324). As key organizers of youth sports, coaches can also provide emotional support through encouragement and positive reinforcement, and informational support can be provided through technical instruction (Fraser-Thomas and Côté 2006). However, coaches also run a high risk of negatively affecting "children's enjoyment, self-concept, and continued participation in sport and other PA opportunities" (Cohen, Bovbjerg, and Wegis 2020: 136) if they heavily focus on winning rather than recognizing that children are still in developmental stages (Fraser-Thomas and Côté 2006). Therefore, coaches play an especially prominent and delicate role in shaping children's perspective on PA and sports.

4.3 Peers

As part of their interpersonal domain, social support from peers also plays a crucial role in a child's PA behaviors, and "become[s] more influential in adolescence" (Gill, et al. 2018: 208). "Children live in peer-rich worlds" (Stearns et al. 2019: 1) and as they grow older and "spend increased time with peers" (Fitzgerald, Fitzgerald, and Aherne 2012: 942) the likelihood of their peers having an influence over their norms and behaviors, including their PA levels, drastically increases (Fitzgerald, Fitzgerald, and Aherne 2012). In regard to PA, studies have found support "from peers [to be] a consistent predictor of PA across [both] gender and age groups" (Gill et al. 2018: 208). Therefore, investigating and understanding friendship patterns and forms of support for PA "can provide insights into why some children are more active than others" (Stearns et al. 2019: 1).

Peers and friends may influence how physically active an adolescent is in a wide variety of ways. One form of support that is particularly important is instrumental/direct support (Bakalár, Kopčáková, and Gecková 2019). This type of support is characterized by "peers or friends participating in PA with an adolescent" (Bakalár, Kopčáková, and Gecková 2019: 17) and plays a strong role as children themselves have "described their friends as influencing their PA [through] co-participation" (Stearns et al. 2019: 1). Studies have found that children prefer engaging in PA with friends rather than by themselves so much so that the "presence of [just one] single peer or friend appears to be beneficial for children's physical activity" (Sanders et al. 2014: 95) demonstrating how influential instrumental support can be.

Another way in which children have stated that their peers are able to influence their PA is through encouragement or praise, which is known as emotional/motivational support (Fitzgerald, Fitzgerald, and Aherne 2012; Stearns et al. 2019). Emotional/motivational support ties directly into instrumental/direct support in that "engaging in physical activity with friends has been associated with increased motivation for being active" (Jago et al. 2009: 2). Engaging in PA with peers does more than keep a child from feeling lonely during the activities, but also provides emotional support through reassurance and a sense of relatedness because their peers are at the same stage of life as they are (Jago et al. 2009). Additionally, peers can provide observational support through their modeling of PA (Bakalár, Kopčáková, and Gecková 2019) which again creates a sense of relatedness and aligns with SCT in that children are inspired to do what they see. While access and social support are key factors that may predict children's involvement in PA and/or sporting activities, individual factors such as self-efficacy could be equally important.

5 Self-efficacy

Many factors outside of a child's control such as barriers to access and social support can affect a child's participation in sports and PA. However, children can also experience intrapersonal interactions within themselves that can influence their PA levels. According to Feltz and Magyar, "one belief central to navigating positive and negative experiences in sport and PA is self-efficacy" (2006: 161). Self-efficacy, which is a "person's beliefs in their own capabilities to achieve something" (Reverdito et al. 2017: 571) is an intrapersonal construct that can greatly affect whether or not a child chooses to engage in PA. Generally, people only like to do things that they believe they can do well (Hayden 2014) and children in particular are more likely to be active if they feel confident and competent in the sports or physical activities that they have the opportunity to participate in (Jago et al. 2009). Additionally, children's perception of their competence and skills can greatly influence the fun and enjoyment that they should have while participating in sports and PA (Shen et al. 2018).

Children's self-efficacy can be influenced in both negative and positive ways, which in turn influences their willingness to engage in sports and PA. For children who are beginning a new sport, they may be self-conscious that they are not doing it right and may worry that their peers and coaches are watching them, which creates a negative emotional arousal (Hayden 2014). The negative feelings created by a combination of high levels of arousal and fear may lead to a child rating his or her self-efficacy as low (James and Harding 2018). This then becomes a vicious cycle as studies have found that children with lower self-efficacy are more likely to have poorer athletic performance (Feltz and Magyar 2006) and poorer performance leads to lower self-efficacy. Oftentimes, children who find themselves in this seemingly never-ending cycle see one way out: quit playing sports. They do not feel confident or competent about being active, and they do not believe in their ability to be successful and subsequently, they lack motivation to be physically active (Gao, Lochbaum, and Podlog 2011).

On the contrary, positive self-efficacy can serve as a driving factor for increased participation in sports and PA. In fact, the emotional arousal that children may experience while playing a sport is not always a negative thing; if the arousal is interpreted as excitement rather than fear, a child may rate his or her self-efficacy as being high (James and Harding 2018). The high self-efficacy can in turn serve as a reason that a child may be motivated to participate in sports even if the odds are not favorable and/or the conditions are not the best (i. e., bad weather) (Dinç 2011). With self-efficacy serving as a positive predictor of PA levels (Feltz and Magyar 2006) and being regarded as one of the most significant contribution to PA literature (Young et al. 2014) it is important to have a general understanding of what factors may positively influence a child's self-efficacy in relation to sports and PA.

6 Decreasing the gap and helping all children have access to PA and sports

There are several intervention programs designed to help kids of all socioeconomic backgrounds gain access to physical activity and sports as one means to bridge the existing gap and address the possible threats as outlined above. Michelle Obama's "Let's Move" campaign was launched in 2010 as a means of increasing awareness about the growing issue of childhood obesity and encouraging children to be more physically active. While the campaign itself had its share of critics (Johnson 2016), the premise behind it was one to increase awareness about a global health issue. Black and Macinko (2008) reported that an important determinant for involvement in physical activity resides in what they call the "built environment," which consists of all human-made elements of the physical environment such as buildings, sidewalks, play spaces, sporting facilities, streets, and trails. While these solutions are less likely to take hold without the support of local governments, other researchers have examined home environmental factors as a way to get children moving and more physically active. Bissell, Zhang, and Meadows (2014) tested the effectiveness of using Wii exercise games as a way to engage children in PA while also keeping enjoyment levels up. In this study, children played a variety of games on a Wii, including exercise and fitness games, and their respective heart rates were measured as they engaged with each game. The findings indicated that all games involving movement resulted in an increase in each child's heart rate, and some of the more challenging exercise games like running or tennis elevated children's heart rates into a target heart rate. However, children were less likely to enjoy playing the games that involved greater physical exertion, so the researchers reported that games such as *Dance Dance Revolution* were the most likely to keep children exerting themselves while they also reported having fun. In a similar study, Gao, Chen, and Stodden (2013) compared children's exertion levels while participating in a physical education program, while playing at recess, and while playing an exergame. The authors report that school-based physical activity programs could utilize exergames, especially those that could involve entire classes, as a means for helping children be physically active. This general question about ways to get children involved and keep children involved in PA has been a topic under consideration by researchers in health education and health promotion for decades.

A more comprehensive look at health promotion requires an examination of the connections between the many relationships in the socio-physical environment that are related to a specific health behavior and the designing of programs that address them (Stokols 1996). Ecologically oriented frameworks for school health include the well-recognized Coordinated School Health Program and the more recent Whole School, Whole Child, Whole Community Model, both of which address the need for strong partnerships among schools, parents, and communities for effective change (Lewallen et al. 2015). Research shows that schools following guidelines from coordinated, school-based healthy eating programs have students with lower rates of overweight and obesity and higher dietary intake scores than schools that simply offered healthy menu alternatives (Veugelers and Fitzgerald 2005). As involvement in sporting activities is considered, several studies note the importance of peers and parents in the form of social support. Patrick and colleagues (1999) reported that peer influence was a stronger factor for girls dropping out of sporting activities and/or team sports than it was for boys, and further noted that as girls became more involved with a specific sport, their available time to socialize with friends decreased, which led to more fluid dynamics within peer and friend groups. While there may not be any one right way to increase or at least maintain children's involvement in sports and physical activity, research supports the notion that involvement leads to positive social outcomes including positive self-perception as well as positive health outcomes (Neely and Holt 2013).

Last, Common Sense Media reported in its 2019 Census that "more than twice the number of young people watch videos every day compared to 2015" and the amount of time spent watching videos has almost doubled since that time. While some of the screen time could be spent being physically active with one of many online fitness programs now available, it could easily be argued that kids and teens are not spending the bulk of their time in front of a screen being active. This raises the question of how to reduce screen time with a population that has grown up in front of some sort of screen for entertainment and educational purposes. Tang, Darlington, Ma, and Haines (2018) suggest that one way to teach younger children better media use practices is to model better media use practices for them. The authors found a significant correlation between mothers' screen-time modeling, media use during meal time, and the use of a device to occupy young children and young children's daily use of screens. Twenge and colleagues (2017) found increases in depressive symptoms and suicidal ideation among teens who spent more time using media as they found in this study that media use displaced in-person social interaction, sports and exercise, and homework. Changing adolescent and teen behavior related to screen time and media use could be challenging; however, scholars and health advocates suggest that it starts with adults modeling appropriate behaviors in both contexts – media use and physical activity. As noted above, social support from family and peers in the context of sports is another one to keep children engaged in physical activity. Additionally, the more support and positive reinforcement a child gets from a coach or physical education teacher, the more likely it is the child will feel supported doing the activity and will continue. Future research should continue to examine the ways in which these environments – home and social – interact with social support in the context of children's engagement in sports and PA. Furthermore, studies should continue to examine these barriers addressed above and ways these barriers can be eliminated to keep more children involved in sports.

While not all teenagers will wind up winning a Grand Slam event like Serena Williams or striking up a MLB deal at the age of 18, exposure to sports and physical activity is one way that children and youth can come together for a shared experience that ultimately leads to improved health and wellbeing. The research examined for the present chapter suggests that ultimately the key comes down to awareness – awareness of the benefits of participation in sports and involvement in physical activity and then working collectively to give children as many opportunities as possible to stay involved.

References

Abercrombie, Lauren C., James F. Sallis, Terry L. Conway, Lawrence D. Frank, Brian E. Saelens & James E. Chapman. 2008. *Income and racial disparities in access to public parks and private recreation facilities* doi://doi.org/10.1016/j.amepre.2007.09.030 (11 November 2020).

The Aspen Institute. 2017. State of Play: Trends and Developments 2017. https://assets.aspeninstitute.org/content/uploads/2017/12/FINAL-SOP2017-report.pdf (27 July 2020).

Bakalár, Peter, Jaroslava Kopčáková & Andrea M. Gecková. 2019. Association between potential parental and peers' correlates and physical activity recommendations compliance among 13–16 years old adolescents. *Acta Gymnica* 49(1). 16–24.

Bandura, Albert. 1999. Social cognitive theory of personality. In Daniel Cervone & Yuichi Shoda (eds.), *The coherence of personality: Social-cognitive bases of consistency, variability, and organization*, 185–241. New York: Guilford.

Barr-Anderson, Daheia J., Nicole I. Larson, Melissa C. Nelson, Dianne Neumark-Sztainer & Mary Story. 2009. Does television viewing predict dietary intake five years later in high school students and young adults? *International Journal of Behavioral Nutrition and Physical Activity* 6(7). doi.org/10.1186/1479-5868-6-7.

Beenackers, Mariëlle A., Carlijn B. M. Kamphuis, Alex Burdorf, Johan P. Mackenbach & Frank J. van Lenthe. 2011. Sports participation, perceived neighborhood safety, and individual cognitions: How do they interact? *The International Journal of Behavioral Nutrition and Physical Activity* 8. 76.

Bhargava, Vibha & Jung Sun Lee. 2016. Food insecurity and health care utilization among older adults in the United States. *Journal of Nutrition in Gerontology and Geriatrics* 35. 177–192.

Bissell, Kim & Kathy Birchall. 2008. Through the hoop: How sports participation displaces media use and is related to body self-esteem in competitive female athletes. *Journal of Sports Media* 3(2). 25–59.

Bissell, Kim, Cui Zhang & Charles Meadows III. 2014. A Wii, a Mii, and a new me? Testing the effectiveness of Wii exergames on children's enjoyment, engagement, and exertion in physical activity. *International Journal of Child Health and Human Development* 7(1). 37–47.

Black, Jennifer L. & James Macinko. 2008. Neighborhoods and obesity. *Nutrition Reviews* 66(1). 2–20.

Blass, Elliott M., Daniel R. Anderson, Heather L. Kirkorian, Tiffany A. Pempek, Iris Price & Melanie F. Koleini. 2006. On the road to obesity: Television viewing increases intake of high-density foods. *Physiology & Behavior* 88(4–5). 597–604.

Buck, Christoph, Anca Bolbos & Sven Schneider. 2019. Do poorer children have poorer playgrounds? A geographically weighted analysis of attractiveness, cleanliness, and safety of playgrounds in affluent and deprived urban neighborhoods. *Journal of Physical Activity & Health* 16(6). 397–405.

Centers for Disease Control and Prevention. 2019. Childhood obesity facts: Prevalence of childhood obesity in the United States. Centers for Disease Control. https://www.cdc.gov/obesity/data/childhood.html (27 July 2020).

Cohen, Alysia J., Viktor Bovbjerg & Heidi Wegis. 2020. Does coaching experience and coaching efficacy of untrained volunteer youth sport coaches influence children's moderate-to-vigorous physical activity? *International Journal of Sports Science & Coaching* 15(2). 135–145.

Courtney, Jimikaye B., Haley E. Moss, Brian D. Butki & Kaigang Li. 2019. Parent support, perceptions, and child attributes affect child activity. *American Journal of Health Behavior* 43(2). 311–325.

Dinç, Zeynep. 2011. Social self-efficacy of adolescents who participate in individual and team sports. *Social Behavior & Personality: An International Journal* 39(10). 1417–1424.

Eisenberg, Christina M., Luz María Sánchez-Romero, Juan A. Rivera-Dommarco, Christina K. Holub, Elva M. Arredondo, John P. Elder & Simón Barquera. 2013. Interventions to increase physical activity and healthy eating among overweight and obese children in Mexico. *Salud Publica De Mexico* 55. 441–446.

Feltz, Deborah, L. & T. Michelle Magyar. 2006. Self-efficacy and adolescents in sport and physical activity. In Frank Pajares & Tim Urdan (eds.), *Self-efficacy beliefs of adolescents*, 161–180. Greenwich, CT: Information Age Publishing.

Fitzgerald, Amanda, Noelle Fitzgerald & Cian Aherne. 2012. *Do peers matter? A review of peer and/or friends' influence on physical activity among American adolescents* 35. 941–958.

Fraser-Thomas, Jessica & Jean Côté. 2006. Youth sports: Implementing findings and moving forward with research. *Athletic Insight* 8(3). 12–27.

Frost, Stephanie S., R. Turner Goins, Rebecca H. Hunter, Steven P. Hooker, Lucinda Bryant, Judy Kruger & Delores Pluto. 2010. Effects of the built environment on physical activity of adults living in rural settings. *American Journal of Health Promotion* 24(4). 267–283.

Gao, Zan, Senlin Chen & David Stodden. 2013. A comparison of children's physical activity levels in physical education, recess and exergaming. *Journal of Physical Activity and Health*. 12(3). 349–354.

Gao, Zan, Marc Lochbaum & Leslie Podlog. 2011. Self-efficacy as a mediator of children's achievement motivation and in-class physical activity. *Perceptual & Motor Skills*. 113(3). 969–981.

Gill, Monique, Alec Chan-Golston, Lindsay N. Rice, Sarah E. Roth, Catherine Crespi, Brian L. Cole, Deborah Koniak-Griffin & Michael L. Prelip. 2018. Correlates of social support and its association with physical activity among young adolescents. *Health Education & Behavior* 45(2). 207–216.

Hayden, Joanna. 2014. *Introduction to health behavior theory*, 2nd edn. Burlington, MA: Jones and Bartlett Learning.

Jago, Russell, Rowan Brockman, Kenneth R. Fox, Kim Cartwright, Angie S. Page & Janice L. Thompson. 2009. Friendship groups and physical activity: Qualitative findings on how physical activity is initiated and maintained among 10–11 year old children. *International Journal of Behavioral Nutrition and Physical Activity* 6(4). 1–9.

James, Ian A. & Michael Harding. 2018. Self-belief in youth sport: How the relation-inferred self-efficacy (RISE) model can be used to improve the communication skills of physiotherapists and coaches. *Sport & Exercise Psychology Review* 14(2) 53–61.

Johnson, Steven R. 2016. Gauging the public health value of Michelle Obama's 'Let's Move' Campaign. *Modern Healthcare*. https://www.modernhealthcare.com/article/20160823/NEWS/160829986/gauging-the-public-health-value-of-michelle-obama-s-let-s-move-campaign.

Kirkpatrick, Alison, Linda Rose-Krasnor, Laura L. Ooi & Robert Coplan. 2020. Coaching the quiet: Exploring coaches' beliefs about shy children in a sport context. *Psychology of Sport and Exercise* 47. https://doi.org/10.1016/j.psychsport.2019.101640 (11 November 2020).

Lewallen, Theresa C., Holly Hunt, William Potts-Datema, Stephanie Zaza & Wayne Giles. 2015. The whole school, whole community, whole child model: A new approach for improving educational attainment and healthy development for students. *Journal of School Health* 85(11). 729–739.

Mader, Erin & Heidi Busse. 2011. Hungry in the heartland: Using community food systems as a strategy to reduce rural food deserts. *Journal of Hunger & Environmental Nutrition* 6(1). 45–53.

Maniccia, Dayna M., Kirsten K. Davison, Simon J. Marshall, Jennifer A. Manganello & Barbara A. Dennison. 2011. A meta-analysis of interventions that target children's screen time for reduction. *Pediatrics* 128(1). e193–e210.

Martin, Sarah L., Gregory J. Kirkner, Kelly Mayo, Charles E. Matthews, Larry J. Durstine & James R. Hebert. 2005. Urban, rural, and regional variations in physical activity. *The Journal of Rural Health* 21(3). 239–244.

McKenzie, Thomas L. & Monica A. F. Lounsbery. 2009. School physical education: The pill not taken. *American Journal of Lifestyle Medicine* 3(3). 219–225.

Milošević, Živan N. & Tatjana Tubić. 2018. Social support and physical activity level of elementary school students. *Physical Culture* 72(2). 29–36.

Mutz, Michael & Peggy Albrecht. 2017. Parents' social status and children's daily physical activity: The role of familial socialization and support. *Journal of Child & Family Studies* 26(11). 3026–3035.

Neely, Kacey C. & Nicholas L. Holt. 2013. Parents perspectives on the benefits of sport participation for young children. *The Sport Psychologist* 28(3). 255–268.

Niclasen, Birgit, Max Petzold & Christina Schnohr. 2012. The association between high recreational physical activity and physical activity as a part of daily living in adolescents and availability of local indoor sports facilities and sports clubs. *Scandinavian Journal of Public Health* 40(7). 614–620.

Norman, Gregory J., Sandra K. Nutter, Sherry Ryan, James F. Sallis, Karen J. Calfas & Kevin Patrick. 2006. Community design and access to recreational facilities as correlates of adolescent physical activity and body-mass index. *Journal of Physical Activity & Health* 3. 118–128.

Patrick, Helen, Allison M. Ryan, Corinne Alfeld-Liro, Jennifer A. Fredericks, Ludmilla Hruda & Jacquelynne Eccles. 1999. Adolescents' commitment to developing talent: The role of peers in continuing motivation for sports and the arts. *Journal of Youth and Adolescence* 28(6). 741–763.

Patterson, Paul D., Charity G. Moore, Janice C. Probst & Judith Ann Shinogle. 2004. Obesity and physical inactivity in rural America. *The Journal of Rural Health* 20(2). 151–159.

Pellegrini, Anthony D. & Catherine M. Bohn. 2005. The role of recess in children's cognitive performance and school adjustment. *Educational Researcher* 34(1) 13–19.

Reverdito, Riller S., Humberto M. Carvalho, Larissa R. Galatti, Alcides J. Scaglia, Carlos E. Gonçalves & Roberto R. Paes. 2017. Effects of youth participation in extra-curricular sport programs on perceived self-efficacy: A multilevel analysis. *Perceptual and Motor Skills* 124(3). 569–583.

Rideout, V. & Michael. B. Robb. 2019. *The Common Sense census: Media use by tweens and teens, 2019*. San Francisco, CA: Common Sense Media.

Rideout, Victoria J., Ulla G. Foehr & Donald F. Roberts. 2010. *Generation M^2: Media in the Lives of 8- to 18-Year-Olds*. Menlo Park, CA: Henry J. Kaiser Family Foundation.

Roemmich, James N., Leonard H. Epstein, Samina Raja & Li Yin. 2007. The neighborhood and home environments: Disparate relationships with physical activity and sedentary behaviors in youth. *Annals of Behavioral Medicine* 33. 29–38.

Roemmich, James N., LuAnn Johnson, Grace Oberg, Joley E. Beeler & Kelsey E. Ufholz. 2018. Youth and adult visitation and physical activity intensity at rural and urban parks. *International Journal of Environmental Research and Public Health* 15(8). 1760.

Sanders, Gabriel J., Corey A. Peacock, Megan Williamson, Kayla Wilson, Andrew Carnes & Jacob E. Barkley. 2014. The effect of friendship groups on children's physical activity: An experimental study. *Journal of Behavioral Health* 3(2). 95–100.

Sargent, James D. & Todd F. Heatherton. 2009. Comparison of trends for adolescent smoking and smoking in movies, 1990–2007. *Jama* 301(21). 2211–2213.

Shen, Bo, Erin Centeio, Alex Garn, Jeffrey Martin, Noel Kulik, Cheryl Somers Cheryl & Nate McCaughtry. 2018. Parental social support, perceived competence and enjoyment in school physical activity. *Journal of Sport and Health Science* 7(3). 346–352.

Stearns, Jodie A., Jenny Godley, Paul J. Veugelers, John P. Ekwaru, Kerry Bastian, Biao Wu, & John C. Spence. 2019. Associations of friendship and children's physical activity during and outside of school: A social network study. *SSM – Population Health* 7. doi:10.1016/j.ssmph.2018.10.008 (11 November 2020).

Stokols, Daniel. 1996. Translating social ecological theory into guidelines for community health promotion. *American Journal of Health Promotion* 10(4). 282–298.

Strauss, Richard S. & Judith Knight. 1999. Influence of the home environment on the development of obesity in children. *Pediatrics* 103(6). e85. doi.org/10.1542/peds.103.6.e85.

Taheri, Shahrad. 2006. The link between short sleep duration and obesity: we should recommend more sleep to prevent obesity. *Archives of Disease in Childhood* 91(11). 881–884.

Tang, Lisa, Gerarda Darlington, David W. L. Ma & Jess Haines. 2018. Mothers' and fathers' media parenting practices associated with young children's screen-time: a cross-sectional study. *BMC Obesity* 5. 37.

Twenge, Jean M., Thomas E. Joiner, Megan L. Rogers & Gabrielle N. Martin. 2018. Increases in depressive symptoms, suicide-related outcomes, and suicide rates among US adolescents after 2010 and links to increased new media screen time. *Clinical Psychological Science* 6(1). 3–17.

Vander, Kerry A., Katerina Maximova, Stefan Kuhle, Aline Simen-Kapeu & Paul J. Veugelers. 2012. The importance of parental beliefs and support for physical activity and body weights of children: A population-based analysis. *Canadian Journal of Public Health* 103(4). e277–e281.

Van Dyke, Miriam E., Patricia C. Cheung, Padra Franks & Julie A. Gazmararian. 2018. Socioeconomic and racial/ethnic disparities in physical activity environments in Georgia elementary schools. *American Journal of Health Promotion* 32(2). 453–463.

Veugelers, Paul J. & Angela L. Fitzgerald. 2005. Prevalence of and risk factors for childhood overweight and obesity. *CMAJ* 173(6). 607–613.

Wadsworth, Danielle D., Leah E. Robinson, Karen Beckham & Kip Webster. 2011. Break for physical activity: Incorporating classroom-based physical activity breaks into preschools. *Early Childhood Education Journal* 39. 391–395.

Walen, Heather R. & Margie E. Lachman. 2000. Social support and strain from partner, family, and friends: Costs and benefits for men and women in adulthood. *Journal of Social and Personal Relationships* 17(1). 5–30.

Wiersma, Lenny D. & Clay P. Sherman. 2005. Volunteer youth sport coaches' perspectives of coaching education/certification and parental codes of conduct. *Research Quarterly for Exercise and Sport* 76(3). 324–338.

Witt, Peter A. & Tek B. Dangi. 2018. Why children/youth drop out of sports. *Journal of Park & Recreation Administration* 36(3). 191–199.

Wrigley, Neil, Daniel Warm, Barrie Margetts & Amanda Whelan. 2002. Assessing the impact of improved retail access on diet in a "food desert": A preliminary report. *Urban Studies* 39(11). 2061–2082.

Yao, Christopher A. & Ryan E. Rhodes. 2015. Parental correlates in child and adolescent physical activity: A meta-analysis. *The International Journal of Behavioral Nutrition and Physical Activity* 12. doi:10.1186/s12966-015-0163-y.

Young, M. D., R. C. Plotnikoff, C. E. Collins, R. Callister & P. J. Morgan. 2014. Social cognitive theory and physical activity: A systematic review and meta-analysis. *Obesity Reviews* 15. 983–995.

Zhang, Xueying, Bijie Bie, Lindsey Conlin, Dylan McLemore, Kim Bissell & Perrin Lowrey. 2017. Active video game play in African American children: The effect of gender and BMI on exertion and enjoyment. *Howard Journal of Communications* 28(3). 280–296.

Jimmy Sanderson

7 From the living room to the ball field: a communicative approach to studying the family through sport

Abstract: This chapter examines the role of communication in the family context. The family has been largely overlooked by communication and sport scholars and this chapter explores how communication plays a significant role in understanding family dynamics and relationships through sport. It examines family identity and sport, parent–child interaction, parent behavior, the parent dyad, and the growing presence of technology and sport and how this impacts the family. It concludes by providing directions for future research in the hopes that communication and sport researchers will more actively explore this fertile area.

Keywords: family communication; parent–child interaction; youth sports; parents and technology; parent behavior and sport

1 Introduction

This chapter covers a compelling, yet understudied area within communication and sport scholarship, the family (Nussbaum and Worthington 2017: 179). Scholars have noted the lack of communication and sport research that goes beyond media analyses (Butterworth and Kassing 2015), and the family represents a promising domain that can help balance the communication and sport literature. Indeed, this lack of attention is surprising given how central sport is to the lived experience of many families (Nussbaum and Worthington 2017: 181), the 60 million children who participate in youth sport annually in the United States (Sage and Eitzen 2013: 62), and the estimated $17 billion (USD) youth sport market (Jimenez 2018). The purpose of this chapter is to highlight the need for communication and sport scholarship anchored in the family and to invite communication and sport scholars to participate in enhancing this area of the communication and sport literature.

A few examples will suffice to demonstrate the significance and scope of sport in the family unit. Families gather together to consume both mediated and live sport, engaging in rituals such as parties around their favorite sporting events. Parents socialize their children to follow certain sports and not others (Spaaij and Anderson 2010), and children can shift course and influence parents' fandom as well (Hyatt et al. 2018). Many children participate in youth sports and in some cases, family dynamics revolve around youth sport schedules, particularly when children are involved in travel/club or competitive sport (Smits, Jacobs, and Knoppers 2017). Accordingly, as

https://doi.org/10.1515/9783110660883-007

children begin participating in sport, family communication and interaction plays out in varied ways. Parents may engage in problematic behavior while watching their children participate (Knight, Neely, and Holt 2011; Ross, Mallett, and Parkes 2015), actions which have been argued to contribute to declining sport participation rates among children (Corbin 2019). Indeed, a Google search about parent behavior and youth sports reveals headlines such as "How parents are ruining youth sports" (Atkinson 2014), and, "Overbearing parents can take the fun out of youth sports" (Mercogliano 2018). Such headlines are emboldened by incidents such as a 2019 parent brawl that occurred at a 7-year-old youth baseball game in Colorado that received national news coverage. The brawl erupted as parents were angered by the calls of the umpire – who was 13 years old (Sylte and Gutierrez 2019). Reports indicated that five people were cited for disorderly conduct and local police suggested more arrests could follow (Sylte and Gutierrez 2019). In another example, the father of a North Carolina high school wrestler was arrested after he intervened in his son's match and threw his son's opponent to the floor (Li and Syed 2020).

Parents behavior also manifests through pressure placed on their children to maximize their performance in sport, which has led to an increasing number of children specializing in one sport (Livingston, Schmidt, and Lehman 2016). Some parents also act as their child's coach and this dual role can influence family dynamics and relationships (Nussbaum and Worthington 2017: 183) as children may be unsure when parents are acting as parents and when they are performing as coaches (Prewitt-White et al. 2016). Additionally, when a child becomes injured, parents face decisions about how to handle the injury. Should the child continue to play? How does communication influence what decisions parents make in this scenario? Gender roles also play important roles in how children experience sport (Bowker et al. 2009; Dorsch, Smith, and Dotterer 2016). However, much family and sport research is often centered on nuclear families, and emerging research is beginning to understand the experiences for LGBTQ parents and families (Trussell, Kovac, and Apgar 2018). Finally, technology such as social media have become dominant communication mediums in our society, and young people consume this technology at exceptional rates (Anderson and Jiang 2018). In the realm of sport, this presents challenges for parents to monitor what their children are posting on social media, as coaches have rescinded scholarship offers and stopped recruiting young athletes because of social media content (DiVeronica 2017; Potkey 2017). Moreover, there are an unfortunate number of sexual abuse cases involving coaches and young athletes that are facilitated through technology such as Snapchat (Sanderson and Weathers 2020). These outcomes reinforce the need for parents, school administrators, and youth sport organizations to be vigilant in digitally safeguarding young athletes.

Certainly, the examples mentioned above are not exhaustive, which illustrates the richness this area of inquiry possesses. Unfortunately, despite communication's prominent role in family experiences around sport, most work that looks at communication-centric topics – for example – parent–child interaction during car rides home after games is not located in the communication discipline (Nussbaum and Worthington 2017: 179). Instead, scholars in sport psychology, exercise science, and leisure studies have done much of this inquiry. While this work is instructive and beneficial to our understanding of how sport influences family dynamics and relationships, communication research needs, in sporting parlance, to step up to the plate. Accordingly, this chapter discusses how communication underpins family communication and sport in the following areas: (a) Family Identity and Sport; (b) Parent-Child Interaction and Sport; (c) Parent Behavior; (d) The Parent Dyad and Sport; and (e) Family Communication, Technology, & Sport. The chapter then outlines directions for future research in hopes that this area of inquiry will blossom in the communication and sport literature.

2 Family identity and sport

Sport is a common experience that many families share, and it can be a significant factor in constructing and maintaining family identity (Nussbaum and Worthington 2017: 180–181). There are several ways in which sport becomes a featured family identity that is cultivated and perpetuated. Nussbaum and Worthington (2017: 182) discussed how sport functions as a form of intergenerational family exchange. For instance, parents can pass on their love or disdain for a particular sport or a sport organization to their children, which can then influence how their children develop their own sport fandom. It is not uncommon to hear a person talk about a sport team they have followed since they were a child, and parents, grandparents, or other family members can influence a child following a particular team. Yet, it is possible that children may develop an independent sense of fandom and such outcomes can potentially strain family relationships. Tamir (2019) interviewed fathers whose son supported a different soccer team than the one espoused by the father. Results indicated that fathers perceived their son's deviation as an: (a) offense to family heritage, which they felt disrupted family cohesion and complicated the family spending time together; (b) offense to team heritage, as fathers recognized that their son's choice represented a lost opportunity for the father's team to gain a fan, and threatened the existence of the father's team; (c) offense to masculinity, which involved fathers believing that they had failed in their duty to raise their son, as he had deviated from the father's expectations; and (d) offense to religious beliefs, as fathers felt the son's fandom compromised the family spirit and their ability to participate in sport ceremony and rituals.

Family identity and sport also manifests through sport participation (Boneau, Richardson, and McGlynn 2020). Sport participation is something that many children are socialized into while growing up as parents believe that sport participation possesses multiple benefits for their children such as, "maintaining mental and physical health, (b) giving them something to do; (c) teaching dedication and discipline; and

(d) benefiting their social lives" (Nussbaum and Worthington 2017: 181). For some parents, allowing a child to participate in as many sports as possible to expose them to a diverse range of sport activities may be the goal, while for other parents, they may have firm views on what sports their child will play, which could be driven by their individual sport preferences. Whatever the motivation, at young ages, parents are making unidirectional decisions about the sports in which their child will participate (Billings, Butterworth, and Turman 2015: 219).

To further illustrate the role that family identity can play in sport socialization for children, Boneau, Richardson, and McGlynn (2020) interviewed parents who allowed their children to play tackle football, a topic that has become prominent in recent years in the United States (Larned 2017). They found that some parents' decision was rooted in being a "football-first" family (9). For these parents, football was central to their family identity and dominated their time, conversations, and resources. In some of these families, the football spirit was so strong that parents enrolled their child in tackle football, despite the child not having a desire to participate. In addition, results revealed that these parents also had a historical longevity with football that guided their decisions (for example, parent was a football coach) and that these families were more likely to focus on the benefits of football, prioritizing them over the risks of the sport. These researchers also found other parents who were safety-oriented, who were characterized by a concern for the safety risks of tackle football, but who allowed their children to play and rationalized their decision to do so. Finally, some parents were classified as laissez-faire parents, who allowed their children to play because the child enjoyed the sport, but these parents did not view football as central to the child's or family identity.

Sport also is central to family identity through the parents seeking to derive status or validation from their child's athletic participation (Billings, Butterworth, and Turman 2015: 211). For some parents, this may be the result of not achieving success in their own athletic endeavors; consequently, they seek to live vicariously through their child (Hirschhorn and Loughead 2000), which can make it difficult for a parent to separate their goals from those of their child's. Further, some parents seek validation and status as a "good parent" through placing their child in sport or by their child excelling in sport (Coakley 2006; Trussell and Shaw 2012). Meân and Kassing (2008) examined parent behavior during athletic contests and found that parents enact multiple identities at youth sporting events that are "complex, conflicting, and often paradoxical" (63). They further observed that talk and identity performance tended to be more about the parents than the children. Meân (2015: 344) also discussed that parents who have a strong identity component vested in their child's athletic performance can contribute to children becoming burned out with the sport and potentially dropping out altogether. Parents also may seek to establish identity through how early they expose and socialize their children to a sport. For example, when parents give infants a baseball glove, or basketball, is there a pressure to perform that begins to matriculate in the parent's mind? Skolnikoff and Engvall (2014: 42) observed that parents who engage in competitive practices early in a child's development see those competitive desires escalate if a child begins to show athletic talent at a young age.

Identity is a salient function in how families experience sport. It can guide parental decision-making about what sport their children will play, when they will do so, and what kinds of sports children will be exposed to, both through media consumption and participation. Identity operates as a foundational mechanism that serves as the springboard for family decision-making around sport. One pathway emanating from this base includes parent–child interaction and the influence it has on the family sport experience.

3 Parent–child interaction and sport

Parents have multiple opportunities to communicate with their children about sport. Sport can be a positive way for parents to engage their children and spend time with them (Baker et al. 2016), and positive parent–child interaction predicts sport enjoyment for child athletes (Bailey, Cope, and Pearce 2013). Yet sport often becomes a source of conflict and contention that can dissuade children from further participation in sport. Parental involvement is one element that influences parent–child interaction in sport contexts. Parental involvement seems to have increased from previous generations, as parents view involvement as a mechanism to stay connected to their children and aid in their development, thereby normalizing sport involvement (Stefansen, Smette, and Strandbu 2018). Parental involvement ranges and the level at which parents are involved can impact a child's athletic experiences and manifests as support-oriented or pressure-oriented. For instance, parents who are moderately involved tend to create the most ideal sporting experience, as they balance competition and enjoyment goals (Billings, Butterworth, and Turman 2015: 224). Parents who show low involvement create uncertain environments for child athletes, and highly involved parents can cause their children to feel stress resulting from not wanting to let parents down (Billings, Butterworth, and Turman 2015: 224). Some child athletes view parental involvement as entirely undesirable (Strandbu et al. 2017).

Turman (2007) interviewed young athletes to investigate factors that contributed to conversations with parents about sports participation. His results indicated four themes: (a) playing time; (b) sport politics; (c) negative coaching behaviors; and (d) sport competitiveness. The playing time theme involved parents talking to their children about their frustration with playing time, encouraging them to see the issue from the coach's perspective, which helped the athlete focus on what she/he could control, such as his/her effort. Parents in this category also expressed to the child that his/her athletic contribution also included being a good teammate and having a positive attitude. With respect to sport politics, communication centered on coaching decisions that were outside the athlete's control, such as the coach showing favoritism to the coach's child, or to those who attended extra practices. Negative coaching behaviors included parents questioning the coach's behavior and discussed with their child how these behaviors were inappropriate. Finally, with sport competitiveness, parents felt that winning had become overemphasized at the expense of the child's enjoyment. These parents talked with their children about continuing to participate in sport while focusing less on winning.

Whereas parent–child communication on sport can take place in a variety of contexts, the car ride home is a particularly rich area to understand these interactions. Elliott and Drummond (2017) interviewed both Australian youth football players and their parents to understand their experiences with discussing the athlete's performance in the car ride home after athletic events. They found that parents felt that this time was important to "debrief" (2017: 396) by discussing their child's performance, reinforcing performance aspects, while also suggesting where improvements could be made. Parents reported making mental notes or recording notes on their iPads or mobile phones in preparation for the car ride home and further discussed using a "sandwich" strategy (2017: 397) wherein they would provide some positive comments, before offering critique, and concluding with a positive comment. Parents also acknowledged that these interactions could upset their children but viewed such communication as instrumental for the child's development in the sport and as indicative of being a "good parent" (2017: 398). For the athletes, they reported that parental comments that were perceived to be critical enhanced their anxiety and dissatisfaction. For example, one participant shared, "Sometimes where you are really pissed off at yourself and they're going like 'you could have done this, you could have done that' they make you feel worse" (2017: 400). The athletes suggested that parents could improve by asking the child how the child perceived his/her performance or by waiting for the child to ask for feedback.

Tamminen, Poucher, and Povilaitis (2017) also interviewed youth athletes to determine how they perceived parent communication in the context of the car ride home. They found that athletes reported either enjoying the ride home or perceiving it as an unpleasant event they had to endure. Athletes further reported using coping strategies such as employing sarcasm to upset their parents or engaging in avoidant behaviors such as being selective about where they sat on the car ride home and watching content on a mobile device. Athletes also reported that they appreciated getting critique privately rather than in a public setting. These researchers noted that the car ride home functions as a way for parents and athletes to become socialized and come to understand the youth sport experience. They further discussed that conversations in the car ride home may be more/less productive based on the degree of power/agency a parent seeks. For instance, child athletes may be more willing to open up if the parent gives them the space to do, whereas if a parent seeks to exert control, the athlete may engage in avoidant behaviors.

There also appear to be gender differences in parent–child communication centered on sport. Prewitt-White and colleagues (2016) interviewed female Division I athletes in the United States and discovered that athletes reported that their relationships with their fathers were centered on their sport participation. These athletes also discussed wanting to spend more alone time with their fathers, yet they realized that such time would be dominated by conversation about their performance, with an emphasis on what they had done wrong. These athletes also reported that their mothers were mediators between the athlete and her father, often serving as a communicative bridge to pass on information the daughter or father shared with the mother, but not with the intended recipient. Athletes believed their mothers filled this role as their mothers were more lenient and understanding of the athlete's performance and they also believed that their mothers did not understand the sport as well as their father. Dorsch and colleagues (2016) also found that youth sport fathers reported higher conflict and pressure suggesting that athletes might experience more conflict with their fathers than mothers.

Parent–child interaction can be further complicated when the parent is also the child's coach. Witt and Dangi (2018) discussed that parent-coaches can be beneficial as parents get to spend more time with their child and can create shared experiences with them. However, parent-coaches also can experience increased conflict both at the sporting venue and at home (Lauer 2016). Parents also may be more likely to lose their temper with their own children, which can impact family routines, and they also can fracture relationships with family friends if the parent-coach engages in conflict with parents of other children on the team (Witt and Dangi 2018). Children also may have difficulty separating parent roles from coach roles, which can lead to conflict in situations as the car ride home after games (e. g., is this parent time or coach time) (Witt and Dangi 2018).

Prewitt-White and colleagues (2016) in their study of female Division I athletes found that participants felt their fathers coached them harder than other athletes and that they were not granted the same opportunity to make mistakes and grow as their teammates. Although these athletes ultimately disclosed appreciating how their fathers had coached them, this parental duality role, "created a sense of split personality where daughter-athletes had to remember when Dad was "Dad" versus when he was "Coach" (2016: 154). Researchers have suggested that parents who elect to be coaches should be mindful of their child's sports goals and be cautious about continuing coaching at home (e. g., extra practice) (Witt and Dangi 2018).

Although family experiences with sport are greatly influenced by parent–child interaction, they also are impacted by how parents behave at games. Many young athletes are wary of how their parents behave at athletic events which can cause undue stress on child athletes (Reeves, Nicholls, and McKenna 2009) and fracture their relationships with their parents (Knight, Boden, and Holt 2010; Knight, Neely, and Holt 2011).

4 Parent behavior

Arguably, the most visible aspect of family communication and sport centers on parents' behavior while watching their children participate in sport. Indeed, researchers have discovered that most people can recall an incident of problematic parent behavior at a youth sporting event (Elliott and Drummond 2015). Parent feedback during games has been classified as either positive, negative, or neutral (Billings, Butterworth, and Turman 2015: 227). Positive comments are conceptualized as those that reinforce or support athlete performance ("Good Job"), while negative comments include statements toward the child or his/her team that attempt to correct or scold behavior ("I can't believe you did that!"). Neutral comments encompass statements that reinforce coaching tactics or elements of the sport ("Be a good teammate") (Blom and Drane 2009). Parents often give children multiple forms of feedback which can confuse a child (Blom and Drane 2009). Moreover, parents may provide inaccurate appraisals of a child's play which can prompt negative self-esteem in the child athlete (Mach 1994). The child also may give more weight to parental messages about their athletic ability than those provided by the coach (McCullagh et al. 1993).

How parents behave at sporting events may be a function of socialization. Dorsch, Smith, and McDonough (2009) discussed that parents learn acceptable spectator behavior through feedback from their children, by modeling other parents' behaviors, and adapting their behavior based on the cues they observe. Parents goals for their child's sport activity also can influence their behavior (Dorsch et al. 2015). For instance, parents may state that their goal is for their child to win, and if the child does not, they may react aggressively. Additionally, some parents may change their goals, such that their behavior may not align with the goals (for example, a parent whose goal is for child to have fun but who acts aggressively) (Dorsch et al. 2015). Some parents also may change their behaviors if they perceive that their actions are socially unacceptable (Dorsch et al. 2015). Parental behavior at youth sporting events also may reflect vicarious involvement (Siekańska 2012) or reflect a parent's overemphasis on winning and competitive success (Elliott and Drummond 2015). Social and cultural factors also may contribute to parental behavior (Elliott and Drummond 2015). For instance, if a sport is characterized as violent and abusive, parents may become acculturated to perform in that manner while watching their child play that sport (Elliott and Drummond 2015). Gender roles and norms may influence behavior as well, as research has indicated that female parents tend to make more positive comments than male parents (Bowker et al. 2009). Children also may mimic the behavior they see enacted by their parents as they participate in sport (Billings, Butterworth, and Turman 2015: 226).

Parental behavior also might be guided by uncertainty, particularly if their child is an elite athlete (Elliott, Drummond, and Knight 2017). Some parents report having stress because they do not know how to act before, during, and after games (Knight, Boden, and Holt 2010). Thus, there may be divergence in how parents think they should behave and how children would prefer them to behave. Knight, Neely, and

Holt (2011) interviewed young female athletes to determine how they wanted parents to behave during competition. Their results indicated that during competition, athletes desired parents to encourage the team, focus on the athlete's effort rather than the outcome, interact positively with other athlete participants, and maintain control of their emotions. The athletes reported that they desired parents to avoid drawing attention to themselves or to their child, to refrain from coaching from the stands, and to avoid arguing with the officials. Knight, Boden, and Holt (2010) interviewed junior tennis players regarding their preferences for parental behavior during competition and found that athletes reported that parents should avoid providing tactical or technical advice, instead providing practical advice (e. g., reminders to eat before competition, or to warm up before competing), respecting the etiquette of the sport, and matching non-verbal behaviors with supportive comments.

Parent behavior is one of the most visible indicators of family communication in the sport context. Parent behavior is shaped by a variety of factors and gender may influence how parents act and how the family experiences sport.

5 The parent dyad and sport

Parents play a crucial role in shaping their children's relationship with sport. At least early in life, parents are primarily responsible for enrolling their children in sports and determining what sports they will play. Consequently, parents must communicate about a number of topics related to sport participation, including when a child will begin playing sport, what sport he/she will play, and how much money will be spent on the sport. Nussbaum and Worthington (2017: 181) noted that families with higher income levels tend to embrace sport more than those with lower income levels. With the growth in the youth sports market, parents are confronted with an endless supply of private coaches, facilities, travel/club teams, and equipment costs that can shape the degree to which a child will participate in sport, or at least how much of the family budget will be spent on sport.

There also may be differences in how each member of the parent dyad views sport and the sphere of their influence in making decisions about sport. Historically, research has indicated that fathers have more influence over male children, while mothers fulfill the same function with girls (Billings, Butterworth, and Turman 2015: 229). Stein, Raedeke, and Glenn (1999) observed that fathers were more likely to elicit feelings of stress in both male and female athletes and Leff and Hoyle (1995) discovered that male athletes perceived their fathers to use more pressure than mothers, while female athletes reported similar amount of pressure from both mothers and fathers.

Parents invest a great deal of time and money into their children's sporting activities (Gould et al. 2008), particularly if their child is playing travel or elite sports. For example, Post et al. (2018) found that parents in the United States spend an average of $1,500 yearly on club sports, with most club sport parents having an income of over $100,000 annually. Researchers have noted the ways in which club sports affect families financially as well as socially, with the club sport schedules dominating the family calendar (Smits, Jacobs, and Knoppers 2017). In cases where parents have committed to their children playing travel or club sports, a family decision has clearly been made. However, what is often missing in these examinations is the communication process by which parents and families make these choices.

6 Family communication, technology, and sport

Technology is a major force in family structures (McDaniel and Radesky 2018; Nelissen and Van den Bulck 2018). In many homes, parents and children are active consumers of technology ranging from smart home devices, to social media, to gaming, to personal assistants like Amazon's Alexa. As technology continues to grow at rapid pace, it has become ensconced into the family sport experience, as parents and children are now confronted with a variety of technological tools that are marketed to help enhance performance (Sanderson and Baerg 2020). For example, consider products like Blast Baseball, which uses a sensor placed on the baseball bat to track a host of statistical metrics that young players can use to improve hitting accuracy. Or products like Motus Global, which makes wearable technology in the form of compression sleeves that young baseball player wear, which tracks multiple statistical metrics designed to both enhance performance and protect young players from the increasing rate of arm injuries. Sanderson and Baerg (2020) discussed the use of another technology, the GameChanger app, which is used to score baseball and softball games (among other sports) and which provides a host of metrics to parents and coaches that can be used to evaluate performance. Sanderson and Baerg (2020) discussed how these tools are transforming the youth sport experience, shifting it into a more calculative, predictive model based on data. Another dynamic to this emerging technology is that it requires investment in the form of time to understand the application and money, to purchase items from among the plethora of technology related tools. These technologies may only enhance the performance of those who can afford them and whose parents can master the technological sophistication associated with deploying them successfully. Not surprisingly, many of these tools are used by elite/travel teams, further advantaging those who can afford to participate in this realm of youth sports.

Social media also warrants discussion in this section. Researchers have noted that teens and children may be more experienced with technology such as social media, in some cases teaching their parents how to use these platforms (Nelissen and Van den Bulck 2018). While this outcome is perhaps not surprising, it raised concern when it comes to safeguarding children from sexual abuse. Sanderson and Weathers (2020) examined news reports of coaches arrested for sexual crimes involving the use of social media platform Snapchat. They found that coach perpetrators used Snapchat to groom victims by communicating with them in seemingly harmless ways, which opened the doors for further communication that escalated in severity. For example, one coach perpetrator began by sending a topless picture to a victim, then a picture with only a towel around his waist, before finally sending a nude picture (2019: 7). They also discovered that coach perpetrators often created fake accounts, posing as a member of the opposite sex to entice victims to send them nude pictures and videos via Snapchat. They also found that coach perpetrators took advantage of Snapchat's location feature to approach victims at their homes and find out where the victim was in the community. Sanderson and Weathers (2020) argued that parents needed to be aware of their children's Snapchat activity and establish guidelines to help safeguard their children. These recommendations are helpful, but also require investigating what parents know about sexually abusive behaviors occurring on social media platforms like Snapchat, along with understanding how parents are talking to their children about rules and guidelines to protect them (for example, encouraging children to report any attempt from another Snapchat user to request nude photographs or videos, coaches requesting the child to add him/her on Snapchat).

7 Future directions

This chapter has outlined some of the ways that communication is prominent to understanding sport and the family. In doing so, I recognize that what I have covered is not exhaustive. I contend that communication within the family is a rich scholarly area that holds many promising directions for scholarly inquiry. In this section, I briefly discuss some pathways related to the focal areas discussed in this chapter, along with some additional areas that can be pursued. In doing so, I also draw upon some personal experiences that may help illustrate how these topics might play out in people's lived family experiences.

With respect to family identity and sport, one potential avenue to pursue pertains to spouse/partner socialization. For example, when people enter a relationship, and one is a sports fan or consumer, and the other is not, how is the relationship navigated with respect to sport? It would be fruitful for researchers to look at how spouses and partners with little affinity for sport are socialized to sport when they enter a relationship with a passionate sports fan and consumer. Another area of family identity that researchers can investigate is the experience of siblings who do not participate in sport, or at least, who are carted around to a sibling's tournaments multiple weekends out of the year. How does this impact their sport experience? Does this create tension between family members with those who "have" and those who "have not?"

In terms of parent–child interaction, there are multiple directions to pursue here. Researchers who have investigated the car ride home phenomenon (Elliott and Drummond 2017; Tamminen, Poucher, and Povilaitis 2017) have argued that more research is needed across different sport and geographic locations, and communication and sport researchers could certainly answer this call. Researchers could also test gender roles and parent–child interaction. Do athletes feel more pressure from mothers or fathers? Additionally, more diversity is needed in samples to reflect the changing family structures in society. For example, it would be beneficial to look at parents in same-sex relationships and marriages and examine how their behavior aligns or differs in with parents in heterosexual marriages and relationships. Here, it also may be helpful to look at children who grow up in single parent households or who are raised by other family members such as grandparent. Broadening sample diversity would help inform our collective understanding of parent–child interaction and sport. With respect to parent behavior at youth sporting events, much of the research, understandably, has focused on negative behaviors. Certainly though, there is room to examine parental behavior that is positive and supportive in nature. Having a better picture of parental positive and the outcomes that has on family relationships would help to balance out the literature. Additionally, media framing would be a useful framework to investigate. How the mainstream media covers parent behavior in youth sports, and framing mechanisms like headlines are likely to impact how societies view cultural norms around parental behavior and interaction in sport.

In terms of dyadic interaction between parents and partners, one direction that would be worth pursing is how parents talk about and decide to let a child specialize in a sport at an early age. Much research discusses the problematic nature of sport specialization (Russell and Limle 2013; Stewart and Shroyer 2015), but how do parents/partners arrive at this decision? Similarly, do parents/partners decide how much money to spend on children's sporting activities? Does conflict arise? If so, how is it handled? With respect to technology and the family experience around sport, it would be fruitful to examine how parents monitor their children's activity on social media, particularly in light of athletes losing scholarships over social media content, or in the case of some professional athletes, having their archival social media content from high school become a major news story (Hartwell 2018). Further, to what extent are parents aware of sexually predatory behavior that can occur from coaches via social media? How do they discuss this topic with their children?

Finally, it would be worthwhile to engage in cross-cultural examination of family communication and sport topics. Much of the research around parental interaction in sport has been done by scholars outside the United States. Working collaboratively, researchers could investigate similarity and differences in family sport experiences while simultaneously promoting more globally connected scholarship. Additionally, family communication and sport would benefit from critical research. What are the impacts of those in higher socioeconomic groups being able to afford the increasing costs of youth sports, particularly at the club/travel level? Does the ability to access resources such as private coaches, the latest equipment, and technological applications lead to children in lower socioeconomic groups losing interest and dropping out of sport? Additionally, what are the outcomes of parents feeding vast amounts of information about their child into statistical applications? What do we make of predictive analytics and calculate assessments of players tricking down to Little League (Sanderson and Baerg 2020).

8 Conclusion

This chapter has explored communication and sport in the context of the family. Much of what we know about the family and sport concerns outcomes. For example, we know that parents allow their child to specialize in sport, despite evidence that this may be harm the child long-term. We know that parents elect to spend significant time and monetary resources on sport. What we know less about is how parents and families arrive at these decisions. As scholarly interest in communication and the sport through the family increases, we will not only bring much needed diversity to this body of scholarship, but also learn more about the process that families use to reach outcomes related to sport participation and sport consumption.

References

Anderson, Monica & Jingjing Jiang. 2018. Teens, social media, & technology 2018. *Pew Research Center*, 31 May. http://www.pewinternet.org/2018/05/31/teens-social-media-technology-2018/ (30 July 2019).

Atkinson, Jay. 2014. How parents are ruining youth sports. *Boston Globe Magazine*, 3 May. https://www.bostonglobe.com/Magazine/2014/05/03/how-parents-are-ruining-youth-sports/vbR1n8qYXkrrNFJcsuvNyM/story.html (30 July 2019).

Bailey, Richard, Edward J. Cope & Gemma Pearce. 2013. Why do children take part in, and remain involved in sport? A literature review and discussion of implications for sport coaches. *International Journal of Coaching Science* 7(1). 56–75.

Baker, Timberly L., Jillian Wise, Gwendolyn Kelley & Russell J. Skiba. 2016. Identifying barriers: Creating solutions to improve family engagement. *School Community Journal* 26(2). 161–184.

Billings, Andrew C., Michael L. Butterworth & Paul D. Turman. 2015. *Communication and sport: Surveying the field*, 2nd edn. Thousand Oaks, CA: Sage.

Blom, Lindsey C. & Dan Drane. 2009. Parents sideline comments: Exploring the reality of a growing issue. *Online Journal of Sport Psychology* 10(3). 12.

Boneau, Rebecca D., Brian K. Richardson & Joseph McGlynn, 2020. "We are a football family": Making sense of parents' decisions to allow their children to play tackle football. *Communication & Sport* 8(1). 26–49.

Bowker, Anne, Belinda Boekhoven, Amanda Nolan, Stephanie Bauhaus, Paul Glover, Tamara Powell & Shannon Taylor. 2009. Naturalistic observations of spectator behavior at youth hockey games. *The Sport Psychologist* 23(3). 301–316.

Butterworth Michael L. & Jeffrey W. Kassing. 2015. Introduction to "mapping the terrain": Shaping the landscape of communication and sport scholarship. *Communication & Sport* 3(1). 3–7.

Coakley, Jay. 2006. The good father: Parental expectations and youth sports. *Leisure Studies* 25(2). 153–163.

Corbin, Cristina. 2019. Experts cite "bully parents" in decline in youth sports participation world-wide. *Fox News*, 31 May. https://www.foxnews.com/sports/experts-cite-bully-parents-in-decline-in-youth-sports-participation (30 July 2019).

DiVeronica, Jeff. 2017. Don't let one bad tweet ruin an athlete's future. *Democrat & Chronicle*, September 6. https://www.democratandchronicle.com/story/sports/2017/09/06/cyber bullying-social-media-student-athletes-scholarships/464543001/ (30 July 2019).

Dorsch, Travis E., Alan L. Smith & Aryn M. Dotterer. 2016. Individual, relationship, and context factors associated with parent support and pressure in organized youth sport. *Psychology of Sport and Exercise* 23. 132–141.

Dorsch, Travis E., Alan L. Smith & Meghan L. McDonough. 2009. Parents' perceptions of child-to-parent socialization in organized youth sport. *Journal of Sport and Exercise Psychology* 31(4). 444–468.

Dorsch, Travis E., Alan L. Smith, Steven R. Wilson & Meghan H. McDonough. 2015. Parent goals and verbal sideline behavior in organized youth sport. *Sport, Exercise, and Performance Psychology* 4(1). 19–35.

Elliott, Sam & Murray Drummond. 2015. The (limited) impact of sport policy on parental behaviour in youth sport: A qualitive inquiry in junior Australian football. *International Journal of Sport Policy and Politics* 7(4). 519–530.

Elliott, Samuel Kim & Murray J. N. Drummond. 2017. Parents in youth sport: What happens after the game? *Sport, Education and Society* 22(3). 391–406.

Elliott, Sam, Murray J. N. Drummond & Camilla Knight. 2017. The experiences of being a talented youth athlete: Lessons for parents. *Journal of Applied Sport Psychology* 30(4). 437–455.

Gould, Daniel, Larry Lauer, Cristina Rolo, Caroline Jannes & Nora Pennisi. 2008. The role of parents in tennis success: Focus group interviews with junior coaches. *The Sport Psychologist* 22(1). 18–37.

Hartwell, Darren. 2018. Brewers' Josh Hader apologizes after racist, homophobic old tweets surface. *NESN*, 18 July. https://nesn.com/2018/07/brewers-josh-hader-apologizes-for-racist-homophobic-tweets/ (30 July 2019).

Hirschorn, Douglas Kamin & Teri Olisky Loughead. 2000. Parental impact on youth participation in sport: The physical educator's role. *Journal of Physical Education, Recreation, & Dance* 71(9). 26–29.

Hyatt, Craig, Shannon Kerwin, Larena Hoeber & Katherine Sveinson. 2018. The reverse socialization of sport fans: How children impact their parents sport fandom. *Journal of Sport Management* 32(6). 542–554.

Jimenez, Abdel. 2018. The big business of youth sports. *Business Journalism*, 4 December. https://businessjournalism.org/2018/12/business-of-youth-sports/ (30 July 2019).

Knight, Camilla J., Candice M. Boden & Nicholas L. Holt. 2010. Junior tennis players' preferences for parental behaviors. *Journal of Applied Sport Psychology* 22(4). 377–391.

Knight, Camilla J., Kacey C. Neely & Nicholas L. Holt. 2011. Parental behaviors in team sports: How do female athletes want parents to behave? *Journal of Applied Sport Psychology* 23(1). 76–92.

Larned, Victoria. 2017. Would you let your child play football? *CNN.com*, 8 November. https://www.cnn.com/2017/11/02/health/youth-football-parent-curve/index.html (11 November 2020).

Lauer, Larry. 2016. Should I coach my child? https://appliedsportpsych.org/resources-for-parents-should-i-coach-my-child/ (30 July 2019).

Leff, Stephen S. & Rick H. Hoyle. 1995. Young athletes' perceptions of parental support and pressure. *Journal of Youth and Adolescence* 24(2). 187–203.

Li, David K. & Mohammed Syed. 2020. Video shows North Carolina dad tackling son's wrestling match opponent. *NBC News*, 21 January. https://www.nbcnews.com/news/us-news/video-shows-north-carolina-dad-tackling-son-s-wrestling-match-n1119296 (11 November 2020).

Livingston, Jennifer, Christopher Schmidt & Sharon Lehman. 2016. Competitive club soccer: Parents' assessments of children's early and later sports specialization. *Journal of Sport Behavior* 39(3). 301–316.

Mach, F. 1994. Defusing parent-coach dissidence. *Scholastic Coach* 63(10). 5–6.

McCullagh, Penny, Karen T. Matzkanin, Susan D. Shaw & Marcela Maldonado. 1993. Motivation for participation in physical activity: A comparison of parent–child perceived competencies and participation motives. *Pediatric Exercise Science* 5(3). 224–233.

McDaniel, Brandon T. & Jenny S. Radesky. 2018. Technoference: Parent distraction with technology and associations with child behavior problems. *Child Development* 89(1). 100–109.

Meân, Lindsey J. 2015. The communicative complexity of youth sport: Maintaining benefits, managing discourses, and challenging identities. In Paul M. Pedersen (ed.), *Routledge handbook of sport communication*, 338–349. New York: Routledge.

Meân, Lindsey J. & Jeffrey W. Kassing. 2008. Identities at youth sporting events: A critical discourse analysis. *International Journal of Sport Communication* 1. 42–66.

Mercogliano, Vincent Z. 2018. Overbearing parents can take the fun out of sports for their kids. *Lohud*, 12 December. https://www.lohud.com/story/sports-high-school/2018/12/12/misbehaving-sports-parents/2240082002/ (30 July 2019).

Nelissen, Sara & Jan Van den Bulck. 2018. When digital natives instruct digital immigrants: Active guidance of parental media use by children and conflict in the family. *Information, Communication & Society* 21(3). 375–387.

Nussbaum, Jon F. & Amber K. Worthington. 2017. Sport as family communication. In Andrew C. Billings (ed.), *Defining sport communication*, 178–189. New York: Routledge.

Post, Eric G., Nicole E. Green, Daniel A. Schaefer, Stephanie M. Trigsted, Alison M. Brooks, Timothy A. McGuine, Andrew M. Watson & David R. Bell. 2018. Socioeconomic status of parents with children participating on youth club sport teams. *Physical Therapy in Sport* 32. 126–132.

Potkey, Rhiannon. 2017. Don't tweet that, University of Tennessee may pull your scholarship offer. *USA Today*, 6 March. https://sports.usatoday.com/2017/03/06/dont-tweet-that-university-of-tennessee-may-pull-your-scholarship-offer/ (30 July 2019).

Prewitt-White, Tanya R., Leslee A. Fisher, Eleanor F. Odenheimer & Rebecca R. Buchanan. 2016. "He just wanted everything to be perfect, me to be perfect": U.S. NCAA Division I daughter-athletes experiences of the father–daughter relationship. *Sport, Exercise, and Performance Psychology* 5(2). 144 –160.

Reeves, Clive W., Adam R. Nicholls & Jim McKenna. 2009. Stressors and coping strategies among early and adolescent Premier League Academy soccer players: Differences according to age. *Journal of Applied Sport Psychology* 21(1). 31–48.

Ross, Anthony J., Clifford J. Mallett & Jarred F. Parkes. 2015. The influence of parent sport behaviours on children's development: Youth coach and administrator perspectives. *International Journal of Sports Science & Coaching* 10(4). 605–621.

Russell, William D. & Ashley N. Limle. 2013. The relationship between youth sport specialization and involvement in sport and physical activity in young adulthood. *Journal of Sport Behavior* 36(1). 82–98.

Sage, George H. & D. Stanley Eitzen. 2013. *Sociology of North American sport*. New York: Oxford University Press.

Sanderson, Jimmy & Andrew Baerg. 2020. Youth baseball and data analytics: Quantifying risk management and producing neoliberal responsible citizenship through the GameChanger app. Communication and Sport, 8, 72–91.

Sanderson, Jimmy & Melinda R. Weathers. 2020. Snapchat and child sexual abuse in sport: Protecting child athletes in the social media age. Sport Management Review, 23, 81–94.

Siekańska, Małgorzata. 2012. Athletes' perception of parental support and its influence in sports accomplishments – a retrospective study. *Human Movement* 13(4). 380–387.

Skolnikoff, Jessica & Robert Engvall. 2014. *Young athletes, couch potatoes, and helicopter parents: The productivity of play*. Lanham, MD: Rowman & Littlefield.

Smits, Froukje, Frank Jacobs & Annelies Knoppers. 2017. Everything revolves around gymnastics: Athletes and parents make sense of elite youth sport. *Sport in Society: Cultures, Commerce, Media, Politics* 20(1). 66–83.

Spaaji, Ramon & Alastair Anderson. 2010. Psychosocial influences on children's identification with sport teams: A case study of Australian Rules football supporters. *Journal of Sociology* 46(3). 299–315.

Stefansen, Kari, Ingrid Smette & Åse Strandbu. 2018. Understanding the increase in parents' involvement in organized youth sports. *Sport, Education and Society* 23(2). 162–172.

Stein, Gary L., Thomas D. Raedeke & Susan D. Glenn. 1999. Children's perceptions of parent sport involvement: It's not how much but to what degree that's important. *Journal of Sport Behavior* 22(4). 591–601.

Stewart, Craig & Josh Shroyer. 2015. Sport specialization: A coach's role in being honest with parents. *Strategies: A Journal for Physical and Sport Educators* 28(5). 10–17.

Strandbu, Åse, Kari Stefansen, Ingrid Smette & Morten Renslo Sandvik. 2017. Young people's experiences of parental involvement in youth sport. *Sport, Education, and Society* 24(1). 66–77.

Sylte, Allison & Sonia Gutierrez. 2019. 13-year-old umpire describes what led to brawl between parents at youth baseball game. *KUSA News*, 3 June. http://www.9news.com/article/news/local/13-year-old-umpire-describes-what-led-to-brawl-between-parents-at-youth-baseball-game/73-25981be6-40ef-49e9-b965-2b7a147450c6 (30 July 2019).

Tamir, Ilan, 2019. I love you kid but ...: Intergenerational soccer fandom conflict. *Men and Masculinities*, advance online publication. doi: 10.1177/1097184X19859393 (11 November 2020).

Tamminen, Katherine A., Zoe A. Poucher & Victoria Povilaitis. 2017. The car ride home: An interpretive examination of parent–athlete sport conversations. *Sport, Exercise, and Performance Psychology* 6(4). 325–339.

Trussell, Dawn E. & Susan M. Shaw. 2012. Organized youth sport and parenting in public and private spaces. *Leisure Sciences* 34(5). 377–394.

Trussell, Dawn E., Laura Kovac & Jen Apgar. 2018. LGBTQ parents' experience of community youth sport: Change your forms, change your (hetero) norms. *Sport Management Review* 21(1). 51–62.

Turman, Paul D. 2007. Parental sport involvement: Parental influence to encourage young athlete continued sport participation. *Journal of Family Communication* 7(3). 151–175.

Witt, Peter A. & Tek B. Dangi. 2018. Helping parents be better youth sport coaches and spectators. *Journal of Park & Recreation Administration* 36(3). 200–208.

Hatsuko Itaya

8 The sports interpreter's role and interpreting strategies: a case study of Japanese professional baseball interpreters

Abstract: This chapter investigates two things: the role of sports interpreters and their interpreting strategies. The researcher conducted fieldwork with the Pacific League of the Nippon Professional Baseball Organization (NPB) and interviewed incumbent and former baseball interpreters, some of whom had had interpreting experiences with Major League Baseball (MLB) in the United States as well. In addition, the researcher analyzed recordings of interpreted media interviews with players in order to compare the source language (SL) with the interpreted or target language (TL). The research results reveal that, in the case of baseball interpreters, more importance is attached to interpersonal or social roles than to cognitive or linguistic roles. Moreover, regarding interpreting strategies, the research results show that baseball interpreters adopt various interpreting strategies by shifting their "footing" from an "animator" to an "author" or "principal" in order to create an optimal environment for players and fans. This study also suggests that sports interpreters regard the *spokos*, or purpose, of sports interpreting as the achievement of victory rather than communication itself, and they aim to fulfill this function in a *spokos*-oriented manner, playing multiple roles and shifting their footing according to different situations.

Keywords: sports interpreting; baseball interpreter; roles of interpreters; interpreting strategies; intercultural communication; foreign language; footing; *spokos*

1 Introduction

We often hear it said that sports know no boundaries. Indeed, the act of running as fast as you can or passing a ball to your teammates does not require any common language. Players and athletes, therefore, move from one country to another to train and play. As sports have been mediated and become an increasingly interconnected industry, however, the role language plays has become increasingly significant. For one thing, athletes and supporting staff accumulate and analyze enormous amount of data, then discuss and devise a strategy using language. In team sports, communication among teammates is vital for producing desired results. In addition, athletes, often obliged to pose as role models, are expected to inspire the public with their messages. Therefore, when athletes do not speak the same language as their teammates and fans, they communicate through interpreters.

https://doi.org/10.1515/9783110660883-008

This chapter discusses the roles that interpreters play in sports and the sport-specific interpreting strategies they employ. Mediated sports attract tremendously large audiences across the globe (Billings and Brown 2015: 155), and interpreters are an indispensable part of international sports events. In the case of the 2012 London Olympics and Paralympics, for example, approximately seven hundred volunteers provided language assistance in thirty or so different languages (Nishikawa 2018: 47–48). In professional sports, players cross national boundaries to find the best possible environment for their performance, even without knowing other countries' languages. For example, in the time since the first non-Japanese player joined a Japanese professional baseball team in the NPB in 1936, numerous overseas players have come to Japan to seize opportunities (Nakajima 1994: 80). In 2015 alone, approximately eighty overseas players participated in twelve professional baseball teams in the Central and Pacific Leagues (Nakajima 2015: 8). Each team employs three to five interpreters so that players and their families from abroad can smoothly adjust to their teams and lives in Japan (Nakasone 2019). When these overseas athletes are exposed to the public by the media, interpreters play a significant role in determining how they are portrayed.

Despite this reality, little academic attention has been given to sports interpreting (Itaya 2017a: 23, 2017b: 1, 2019: 111). One reason for this lack of empirical research may be the difficulty of gaining access to the research field. As athletes devote their lives to intense training, it is highly unlikely that permission will readily be given for a researcher to enter the field. Despite such difficulties, however, research on sports interpreting is necessary because modern spectator sports are increasingly globalized and mediated, and they therefore have a greater impact on people's lives (Roche 2000: 168). Viewers are not only concerned about the outcome of the game, but they also take an interest in players' thoughts and remarks (Harris 2015: 388). When fans and athletes speak different languages, a sports interpreter becomes a bridge. Revealing how an interpreter fulfills his or her role in the arena of sports, therefore, will not only benefit future sports interpreters but fans and athletes as well. To this end, the following chapter presents research conducted on professional baseball interpreters to examine the sports interpreter's role and sport-specific interpreting strategies.

2 Background

2.1 History of Japanese baseball interpreters

The Japanese government ended its seclusion policy in 1854, after more than two hundred years of voluntary isolation from the rest of the world. Shortly thereafter, in 1869, professional baseball was accepted in the United States (Butterworth 2010: 9), and American missionaries and teachers introduced baseball to Japan during the Meiji Era (1868–1912) (Whiting 2009: 27). Before the Meiji Era, the European concept of sports was foreign to Japanese people. The few sports-like events that took place in Japan, including Sumo, were conducted for military training, not for enjoyment; so unfamiliar was the concept of sports that there was no equivalent word for sports in the Japanese language. The word sports, therefore, entered into the Japanese language and culture along with the concept of sports, and the new Japanese word *supottsu* was born (Whiting 2009: 28); thus, historically, baseball marked the dawn of sports in Japan.

Japanese professional baseball began in 1934 (Tachibanaki 2016: 14), and the first overseas player, Bucky Harris, joined a Japanese professional baseball team in 1936 (Whiting 2006: 43). Since then, numerous players from overseas have come to Japan to play baseball with neither knowledge of the Japanese language nor the intention to speak it, since they only plan to stay in Japan for a limited period of time (Ikei 1991: 117). Such players, then, must communicate through interpreters. Because Japanese baseball has historically borne this intercultural aspect, it can safely be said that baseball interpreters were the first sports interpreters in Japan, and perhaps in the world, making them appropriate research subjects for initiating a probe into sports interpreting.

Records of early Japanese baseball interpreters are limited; it can only be speculated that various people have been interpreting since 1936, the year Bucky Harris joined a Japanese team. One relatively early account comes from, Ushigome, who stated that he became an interpreter in 1964 for a team called the Taiyo Whales (1993: 4). What can definitively be said, therefore, is that the history of baseball interpreters extends to at least more than half a century.

When we compare the beginning of baseball interpreters and professional interpreters in general in Japan, we can see the history of Japanese baseball interpreters is at least as long as, if not longer than, that of other professional interpreters. Other events that confirmed the importance of interpreters included the 1964 Tokyo Olympics (Torikai 2007: 62) and the live TV broadcast of the Apollo 11 moon landing in 1969 (Torikai 2013: 26–27). Given the timing of these events, it is clear that baseball interpreters were among the pioneer professional interpreters in post-war Japan.

2.2 Interpreter's role

The notion of a role stems from the field of sociology. Goffman writes, "Role consists of the activity the incumbent would engage in were he [*sic*] to act solely in terms of the normative demands upon someone in his [*sic*] position" (2013: 85). With respect to speech, Goffman (1981: 144) grouped speakers into three categories: an "animator," who only produces utterances; an "author," who selects the sentiments and the words in which they are encoded; and a "principal," who is committed to what the words say. To alternate between an "animator," an "author," and a "principal" is to change one's footing. He also introduced the notion of "role conflict" and "role distance."

"Role conflict" arises when an individual is faced with different roles that contradict each other (Goffman 2013: 91). "Role distance" occurs when the individual and his or her putative role separate (Goffman 2013: 108). Sato (1976: 35) claims that the satisfaction of needs and wants is the fundamental motivation for committing to a given role. What constitutes a source of motivation for baseball interpreters will be examined below in section 4.2.7.

The basic role of an interpreter is to facilitate communication (Angelelli 2004: 7). It has been widely accepted that, in theory, when facilitating communication, the interpretation should be faithful to the original utterance (Herbert 1952: 4; Harris 1990: 118). Historically in Europe, an interpreter was conceived as a machine that produces literal translation. Based on this comparison, metaphors have emerged to describe the interpreter's role, such as "faithful echo," "channel," "conduit," "switching device," "transmission belt," "modem," or "input-output robot" (Pöchhacker 2004: 147). Similarly, in Japan, the interpreter has been compared to an "invisible man [*sic*]" (Nishiyama 1970: 33) or "*kuroko*," meaning a stagehand in *Kabuki*, dressed in black who is not supposed to be seen. Nagai (2014: 104) agrees with this concept of an interpreter as necessarily "invisible" in order to be truthful to the original statement, claiming that an interpreter has no authority to edit the interlocutor's utterance, even when it is politically controversial. Empirical studies have suggested, however, that many interpreters, in practice, perceive their role as visible (Angelelli 2004: 98). Komatsu's utterance affords a good illustration of this perception. He defines an interpreter as a "visible but highly efficient machine" (Torikai 2007: 326) who intentionally deviates when necessary. Komatsu is known to have modified excessively humble utterances by the former Prime Minister of Japan to make it sound more appropriate to foreign listeners. In this particular instance, Komatsu changed his footing from an "animator" to an "author."

Such judgment by an interpreter can also be considered in accordance with *spokos* theory. *Spokos* is the Greek word for "aim," "function," or "purpose." *Spokos* theory, which was established by the functionalist Hans Josef Vermeer (2004), asserts that translation should be conducted in order to fulfill the aim pursued by the target culture and language (Pöchhacker 2004: 76–77). Komatsu intended for the message to be acceptable and understandable in listeners' cultural context. Thus, some linguistic deviation, including omissions, additions, or alterations, may be unavoidable in order to interpret messages more relevantly for listeners (Gile 1992: 188; Hale 1997: 211). How interpreters themselves view their role depends more on the work setting than on their social identity, age, or social or economic status (Angelelli 2004: 83).

2.3 Cultural differences between Japan and America

Numerous studies have identified cultural differences between Japan and the United States since the 1970s. In fact, the number of communication studies between Japan and the United States is larger than that of any other two cultures (Ito 1992). One of the foundational concepts of intercultural communication is high-context/low-context cultures (Hall 1976). In high-context cultures, people share a higher degree of common experiences, feelings, and values in their background for communication, raising the extent of implicit communication and nonverbal cues. In low-context cultures, communication heavily relies on direct verbal language. Japan is categorized in high-context culture, while the United States is low-context (Hall 1976). Americans regard Japanese "lack of verbal clarity," "lack of verbal specificity," and "verbal indirection" as the sources of communication difficulties, whereas Japanese listed Americans' "lack of intuitive understanding," "focus on speaking," "poor listening," "emotional communication," and "need for detailed instruction" (Kim and Paulk 1994: 124–127). Some of the similar sentiments echoed by baseball players from overseas playing in Japan and their interpreters will be shown later in 4.3.2.

3 Research method

3.1 Participants

Participants consisted of twelve incumbent or former baseball interpreters in the Nippon Professional Baseball Organization (NPB) and Major League Baseball (MLB). In addition, three former MLB players in the NPB and one of their family members were interviewed. Although the research was only conducted in Japan, some of the former baseball interpreters had had the experience of working in MLB. The longest work experience for an interpreter was twenty-five years, while the shortest was one year; of the seven incumbent interpreters, three were in their twenties, two were in their thirties, and two were in their forties.

3.2 Intensive interviews

Intensive interviews were conducted with sixteen participants, as described in 3.1. The nature of an intensive interview is quite different from that of an informational interview (Charmaz 2006: 25–35). In the latter, an interviewer asks questions to obtain specific information while, in the former, the objective is to "elicit each participant's interpretation of his or her experience" (Charmaz 2006: 25). For that purpose, the author devised broad, open-ended questions to encourage unanticipated statements and stories to emerge (Charmaz 2006: 26). The interview lengths ranged from seventeen minutes to four hours, with an average of two hours for interpreters and thirty minutes for overseas players.

The interview transcripts were analyzed by a qualitative-research method called Modified Grounded Theory Approach (M-GTA), developed by Kinoshita (1999, 2003,

2007). M-GTA is a type of qualitative analysis known as Grounded Theory Approach (GTA), the aim of which is the generation of unique theories. In conventional GTA, text data is coded line-by-line or often word-by-word. In M-GTA, in order to avoid destroying the context of the data, it is not sliced into small pieces for coding (Kinoshita 2003: 154–172). Instead, similar kinds of utterances are grouped together into a concept on an analytical worksheet, and then similar concepts are classified into a category. In general, ten or so similar utterances are enough to create one concept. The procedure of M-GTA is illustrated in Figure 1. In this analysis, twenty-two concepts and seven categories were created out of one hundred and four pages of analytical worksheets. In M-GTA, the result is exhibited in a diagram and explained (Kinoshita 2003: 240).

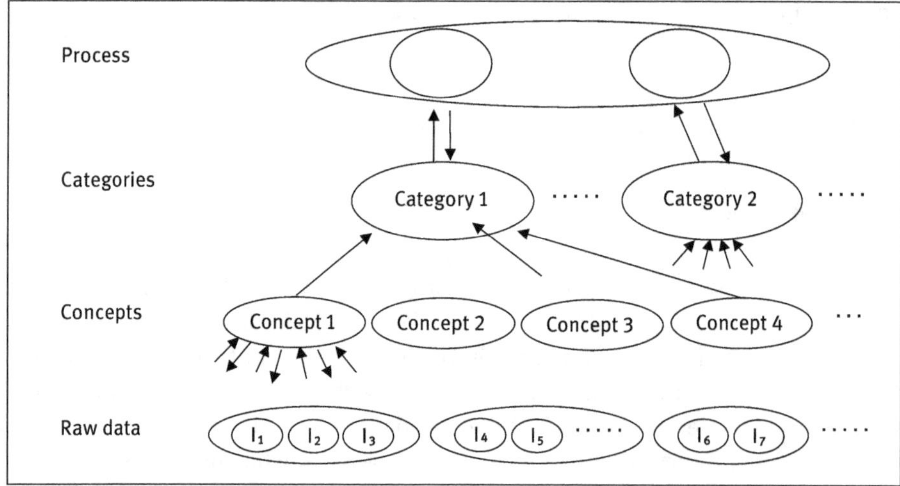

Fig. 1: Procedure of M-GTA (Kinoshita 2003: 214)

3.3 Comparison between hero interview SL and TL

In Japanese professional baseball, the winning team's key player is called the hero of the day, and the hero is interviewed by a TV announcer right after the game in front of excited fans. The hero interview is the highlight of the day in Japanese professional baseball and it is broadcast on TV. When an overseas player is a hero, the player's answer is interpreted by an interpreter, who stands right next to the player. In this research, all Pacific League hero interviews source language (SL), or the original speech, and the target language (TL), or the interpreted speech, from 2016 were compared by the researcher. In addition, the time spent on SL and TL was measured and compared.

3.4 Observation of interpreters at work

Observations of four teams in the NPB were made during practice hours before night games. In the NPB, most home teams practice between two and four o'clock on the field and the visitor team practices after that. Observations were conducted eleven times in front of the dugout, where the press and TV crews stay during practice. With permission, press and TV after-practice interpreted interviews of overseas players were videotaped. How interpreters interact with players was also monitored.

4 Results and discussion

This section presents both results and discussion, as qualitative research requires interpretation by a researcher to produce data analysis. As stated in the introduction, this research aims to describe mainly two things: the roles played by sports interpreters and their interpreting strategies. First, based on the results of M-GTA analysis, baseball interpreter roles are discussed. Subsequently, interpreting strategies are explained. Note that because there have only been male baseball interpreters in NPB, they will be referred to as "he" when described in a singular form.

4.1 Categories of baseball interpreter roles

In M-GTA, results are illustrated with a conceptual diagram (Figure 2). Although it is usually not required to show an analytical worksheet used for research, an example is provided here in order to demonstrate the M-GTA analytic process (Table 1). On the worksheet, interviewees' utterances representing similar thoughts and feelings are listed in the "variation" section, and the researcher examines variations to develop a "concept" ("Role Distance" in Table 1) and its definition ("Stagehand vs Actor" in Table 1). Exceptions or any comments by the researcher are listed in the "Note" section. Table 2 indicates categories, concepts, and their definitions. Figure 2 demonstrates the various roles played by baseball interpreters. Note that the word "stagehand" and "actor" in Tables 1 and 2 and in Figure 2 are used figuratively. A "stagehand" signifies a worker who works behind the scenes and who is not supposed to be seen or heard. An "actor" represents a person who can voice his or her opinions. Note also that the interviews conducted in Japanese were translated into English by the author.

Tab. 1: Example of an analytical worksheet

Concept 21	⟨Role Distance⟩ : Stagehand vs Actor
Definition	Most of baseball interpreters feel the distance between what he or she is (stagehand) and what he or she wishes to be (actor). They wish to reflect their opinions in the operation of the team.
Variation	

No. 1: I had an ambition, an ambition of becoming an executive of this team or climbing up the corporate ladder. So, I had to succeed in this business of interpreting first; otherwise, no one would recognize me, no matter how ambitious I was.
No. 2: If I speak honestly, truly honestly, when interpreting in this same enclosed environment year after year, unlike professional interpreters who get to work in different situations, I come to lose sight of my own existence. Take a meeting, for example. If everybody spoke the same language, my presence would not have been required. I was not in a position to voice my own opinions. The longer I worked for the team, however, the more opinions I began to form on the improvement of the team. I must say that toward the end of my interpreting career, I felt the frustration of not being able to express myself. I admit I was doubting my raison d'être. I'm not sure if this metaphor would express the feelings, but I think many of the baseball interpreters have the desire to cast dice.
No. 3: This position of an interpreter, I'm not saying that it is unimportant, but I would like to assume a more responsible post.
No. 4: I think there is a limit to this job in terms of the scope of the work.
No. 5: As an interpreter, I draw a clear line between what I can do and cannot do. In order to go above the power of an interpreter, I need to add on more experiences and impress my boss. I would like to be someone who can make a decision, or at least, whose opinion is reflected in the decision-making process, or who can at least witness the process of decision-making. You cannot attain that by being an interpreter.
No. 6: I would like to hang on to this world of baseball, and hopefully, move up to a position of more importance.
No. 7: The role of an interpreter is more or less passive. We work on the assumption that we do not state our opinions. In this sense, I have witnessed a few cases where other interpreters asked for different positions with the team. They said they wanted to engage in something more productive.
No. 8: I was not sure if staying where I was as an interpreter was what I wanted.
No. 9: When people find out I was an interpreter for a famous MLB player, that's all they become interested in, not in me. So, I intend to do something larger than be a baseball interpreter.
No. 10: There is another occupation I would like to take up in the future, not this one.
No. 11: In the future, I would still like to work in the baseball world, but not as an interpreter, I hope.

Note: One interpreter out of twelve expressed his hope to stay as an interpreter.

Tab. 2: Categories, concepts, and definitions

Category	Concept	Definition
View on Baseball Interpreters (B.I.)	1. Gateway	B.I. is a gateway to a baseball world.
	2. Lay Interpreter	Self-view is a lay interpreter.
	3. Halfway Point	Current job is a halfway point to the goal.
	4. Low Self-Esteem	B.I. is replaceable.
Linguistic Role	5. Immediacy	Immediacy is imperative.
	6. Creativity	Creative delivery may be necessary.
Social Role	7. Stagehand	B.I. is a stagehand.
	8. Public Relations	B.I. is a public relations staff.
	9. Mediator	B.I. is a mediator for coaches and teammates.
	10. Listener	B.I. lets players vent.
	11. Manager	B.I. manages players' schedules.
	12. Glue	B.I. connects overseas players with the team.
	13. Family's Caretaker	B.I.'s main job is the care of the family.
	14. Mastermind	B.I. could pull strings behind the scenes.
Susceptibility	15. Taking a Hint	Good B.I. can read between the lines.
	16. Neutrality	B.I. should not take anyone's side.
	17. Giving Space	Not too close to nor too far from players.
	18. Trustworthiness	Winning trust from players is a must.
Role Conflict	19. Sandwiched	Anger from all sides is directed to B.I.
	20. No Private Life	24/7 work, both physically and mentally.
Role Distance	21. Stagehand vs. Actor	Desire to reflect one's opinion in workplace.
Fulfillment	22. Fulfillment	Fulfillment comes from social roles.

4.2 Discussion of baseball interpreters' roles

In M-GTA, after categories are made, a diagram (Figure 2) illustrating the connections between each category is explained (4.2.1 through 4.2.7). A title of each section (e. g., 4.2.1 View on baseball interpreter job) corresponds to the same or similar title in Figure 2 (e. g., <View on B.I.>); words or phrases in Figure 2 (e. g., Gateway) and other essential words and phrases are shown in quotation marks (e. g., "gateway") in the discussion.

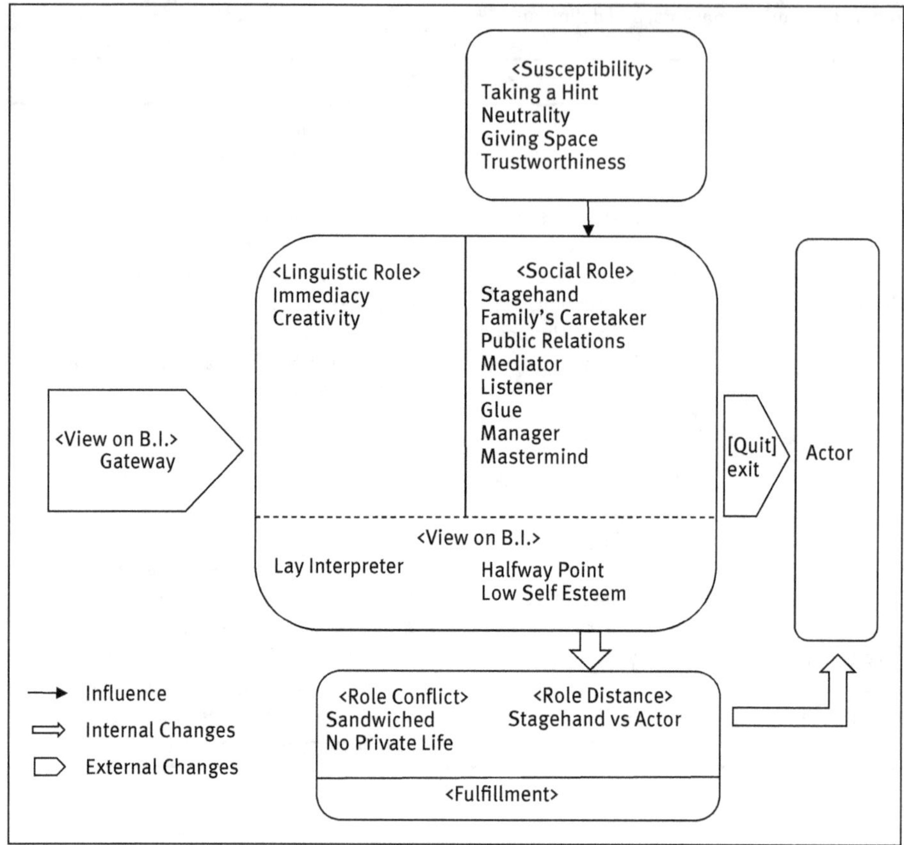

Fig. 2: Process of baseball interpreters' role changes

4.2.1 Views on baseball interpreter job

Eleven out of twelve interpreters confessed that the job of baseball interpreter was merely a "gateway" into the world of professional baseball and that they were at their "halfway point" to their end. They considered themselves "lay interpreters," as they had had no official interpreting training. Their "self-esteem" was far from high, as demonstrated with such utterances as "I am replaceable," "My translation will never move anybody's heart," or "No matter how hard I try, I cannot be a factor in the player's success." Notably, early baseball interpreters in the NPB expressed the opposite view: "whether an overseas player can succeed in Japan or not depends on the interpreter" (Nakajima 1994: 104). This difference in self-view may be the result of the different time periods. When overseas players first came to Japan, the difference between American and Japanese baseball and culture was striking to them. For example, Bob Horner confessed in his book, "Because of the differences in culture and language,

I found myself in some difficult situations from time to time" (Horner 1988: 7). He wrote that the anxiety he had felt could only be understood by someone who had lived in a different cultural environment (Horner 1988: 54). Therefore, baseball interpreter pioneers devoted much time and energy to helping players adjust to the Japanese environment (Nakajima 1994, 2015). Because players who did not get used to Japanese baseball and the Japanese lifestyle had a tendency to be unsuccessful, early interpreters were told by coaches that the success of overseas players was on their shoulders. Nowadays, however, most overseas players have some knowledge of Japanese baseball and culture before they come to Japan. In addition, Japanese teams make a point of scouting only those players who would likely fit in with Japanese society. Accordingly, one of the early roles of bridging the gap between Japanese and American baseball and culture has been lessened (Tachihara 2015: 69), which explains the self-esteem discrepancy between early and current baseball interpreters.

4.2.2 Linguistic role

Nine out of twelve baseball interpreters interviewed referred to "immediacy" as one of the most important aspects of baseball interpreting. Three interviewees used the same word – "speediness" – to explain the importance, while others expressed their opinions with utterances such as "in the sports world, time is limited and everybody is in a rush," "lengthy interpreting irritates athletes," or "it's a warzone here." That immediacy is sometimes attained by "creativity" will be discussed in section 4.3.1.

4.2.3 Social role

The self-view of baseball interpreters is that of a "stagehand." Interestingly, many interviewees talked about their social roles using negative expressions, such as "*shinai yo ni*" or "try not to," to express their social role as a *kuroko* or stagehand: "try not to stand out," "try not to be in the way of players," "try not to be photographed with players," "try not to have my existence felt," "try not to reveal my feelings," and so on. These wordings are indicative of how interpreters make a conscious effort to stay as low-profile as possible.

Each interpreter responded that he feels his social role comprises 90–99.5 percent of his responsibilities. "Family caretaker" was the role most of them mentioned first and foremost as the most crucial. Other concepts created were a player's "public relations" representative, a "mediator" between players and coaches or other teammates, a "listener" who lets players vent, a "manager" or administrative assistant who manages a player's schedule, and the "glue" that connects a player with his teammates. From the player's point of view, having a listener is of great importance. The following are excerpts from interviews with two overseas players:

> Player 1: "... so he just listens you know, he is a listener, sometimes I get mad, and he just tries to 'Yeah, yeah, yeah, I know, just take it easy,' but yeah, he listens to a lot of my frustrations, he handles it pretty good, you know, he, he is always there ..."
> Player 2: "I get angry, letting my anger come out which you know, you shouldn't, or it's the coaches that piss me off, it's not interpreter's fault, and they do pretty good, just listening, and just letting us vent, getting it off my chest, and so it's been awesome ..."

All these aforementioned roles are in a sense powerless or passive in nature, but one role with unique power was identified: the role of "mastermind" (Anderson 2002). Because the interaction does not readily occur without the interpreter's presence and because the interpreter is the only person that understands everything in both languages, he possesses a unique power to manipulate the situation. In this study, some interviewees reported cases of other interpreters giving favorable information about their favorite overseas players to monolingual coaches. In addition, some interviewees said that interpreters sometimes played the role of mastermind on the pitcher's mound. In this situation, when a pitching coach goes to the pitcher's mound to give advice during a game, the interpreter might not interpret the coach's advice because he judged it would only aggravate the pitcher. One interpreter reported he had pretended to interpret but had actually said to the pitcher, "I will buy you a drink after the game. Hang in there." According to this interpreter, upon hearing this encouragement, the pitcher's tense expression softened in a heartbeat, and his pitching was much improved. Other interpreters shared similar stories with the researcher as well. In the above example, the interpreter deviated from his role of interpreting and acted in accordance with his own judgment without being conspicuous. Although an interpreter is an "animator" in principle, by neglecting the coach's utterance and talking directly to the player, the interpreter in the above example changed his footing from "animator" to "principal." It has been established that interpreters change the way they interpret to meet the *skopos*, or aim, of the interpreting (Pöchhacker 2004: 76; Takeda 2013: 123). In the case of sports interpreting, the ultimate *skopos* is to maximize the performance of the players, which in turn could lead to victory and the satisfaction of fans. In the above example, the interpreter made an effort to achieve the *skopos* of winning the game by changing his footing to "principal." An example of an interpreter changing his footing to that of an "author" will be cited in section 4.3.

4.2.4 Susceptibility

Social roles cannot be satisfactorily fulfilled without sufficient susceptibility to others' feelings. According to a NPB team, this is the trait they value most when hiring an interpreter. In communication in Japan, it is assumed that each party understands and anticipates the needs of the other and fills them before any verbal communication becomes necessary (Clancy 1985). Therefore, a good interpreter is expected to "take a hint" and acts before a player makes a request. Remaining "neutral" between a player and a coach and "giving space" to players are also important abilities. With regard to space, some overseas players confessed that sometimes they became tired of being so close to the same interpreter all the time and wanted to be left alone. From the interpreters' point of view, there are mainly three types of overseas players when the "space" is concerned: the one who wants his interpreter at hand at any time, the one who wants to be left alone, and the one who says he does not need so much attention but looks very lonely when actually left on his own. Most of the interpreters the researcher interviewed vocalized that *kyori kan* or "the ability to discern appropriate space" for each player is vital for their job. Interpreters reported that they often make a conscious effort not to be too close to their players in order to facilitate direct communication between overseas and Japanese players. "Trustworthiness" was a trait that was highly valued by overseas players. One of the players the researcher interviewed, for instance, reiterated the word "trust" six times in one minute to explain what he treasured most about his interpreter.

4.2.5 Role conflict

Role conflict occurs when having contradicting roles at once (Goffman 2013: 91). For instance, a baseball interpreter often gets "sandwiched" between a coach and a player (Whiting 1987: 37–102). In other words, when a coach and a player disagree on certain issues, anger is projected at an interpreter from both sides. In addition, concerning the concept "no private life," a Japanese doctor (Abe 2013: 25) coined the term *zen-jinkaku-roudou* or "the whole-self work," to describe the kind of work that demands that workers devote their whole life and self. The job of baseball interpreters falls into this category. Multiple baseball interpreters made confessions such as "It's 24/7 work for ten months," "I have my phone switched on 24/7," "I often go to bed with my clothes on, in case I get called by players in the middle of the night," and "I don't have my own private life." Because they recognize the importance of being ready at any time for overseas players and their families, they are unable to balance their work and private lives. In one instance, for example, an interviewee explained that he had accompanied one player to dinner after a night game and did not get home until early the next morning; he slept for a few hours and then had to take another player's family sightseeing for the day. He rarely had time to see his own family.

4.2.6 Role distance

Role distance is the extent of separation between the individual and his or her putative role (Goffman 2013: 108). As seen in Table 1, most interpreters voiced some kind of dissatisfaction about their raison d'être. After being a "stagehand" for some time, the desire to voice or reflect one's opinion in the organization began to emerge; in other words, this was the moment when a baseball interpreter wished to be an "actor" instead of a "stagehand." The majority of baseball interpreters quit after several years to be an "actor"; some started sports-related businesses, while others became scouts for MLB, and yet others became freelance interpreters.

4.2.7 Fulfillment

While being torn between the reality of being a stagehand, or voiceless supporter, and the ideal of being an actor, or someone with a voice, there indeed was a moment when baseball interpreters achieved spiritual "fulfillment." Not a single baseball interpreter talked about the linguistic aspect as the most fulfilling experience. Nor, surprisingly, did anyone mention the team's victory or superb play as the source of their satisfaction. They said, instead, things like, "Job satisfaction comes from the joy and honor of being a part of overseas players' lives," "When overseas players leave Japan, they often tell me they are happy about the decision to come to Japan. That is the moment when I feel I have been of some help," or "I felt the utmost pleasure when the wives and children of the players said to me that they couldn't have survived without me." Satisfaction of needs and wants is the fundamental motivation for committing to a given role (Sato 1976: 35), and these utterances lead us to presume that baseball interpreters gain more motivation from the mental satisfaction such as being recognized by players and their families than from physical achievement such as good interpreting or the victory of the team. In other words, motivation was found mostly to come from social roles. This finding agrees with the result stated in 4.2.3 that baseball interpreters attach higher importance to social roles than to linguistic roles.

4.3 Interpreting strategies employed by baseball interpreters

4.3.1 Strategy to reduce interpreting time

As explained in 4.2.2, baseball interpreters consider "immediacy" as essential to sports interpreting. They explained, "Players want to focus on their play, so lengthy interviews are in their way," "Professional players are often under a burst of adrenaline, so words do not always enter their ears," "Fans prefer as little interpreting lagtime as possible," and "Because of the time limitations of TV broadcasts, interpreters are required to waste as little time as possible."

The researcher examined how much the "immediacy" was attained in hero interviews by measuring time spent on interpreting. A hero interview is the occasion when a player who has contributed the most to a team's victory is interviewed by a TV announcer; the interview takes place on the field right after a game and is broadcast live. This is a festive moment when victorious fans cheer every time the player utters a word. When a hero is an overseas player, a baseball interpreter stands right next to the player and interprets. When interpreting the interviewer's questions into a foreign language, the interpreter whispers to the player, so fans can see him interpreting but cannot catch every word. The overseas player then answers the question into a microphone, and then an interpreter interprets into a microphone. Table 3 indicates the percentage of interpreting time compared to the time length of the original speech for eleven interpreters in hero interviews in the NPB Pacific League in 2016. The number of hero interviews is different for each interpreter. As just explained, interpreted foreign language is mostly inaudible. Even so, the time spent interpreting was measured when lip and mouth movement were clearly observed on the TV screen. The time spent on translation into Japanese was measured seventy times, while translation into foreign languages was measured thirty-nine times.

Tab. 3: Percentage of interpreting time compared to utterance time in hero interviews in the NPB Pacific League in 2016

Interpreters	Delivery time compared to time of players' utterances	Delivery time compared to time of interviewers' utterances
#1	69 %	39 %
#2	98 %	31 %
#3	111 %	32 %
#4	85 %	58 %
#5	103 %	54 %
#6	84 %	98 %
#7	88 %	49 %
#8	87 %	30 %
#9	96 %	87 %
#10	119 %	90 %
#11	87 %	41 %
Average	93 %	55 %

With the exception of interpreter #6, all the baseball interpreters spent more time on interpreting players' words than interviewers' words, with averages of 93 and 55 percent, respectively. As for interpreting players' utterances into Japanese, although the ideal interpreting time is considered to be 75 percent of the original utterance (Herbert 1952: 71), considering the fact that interpreting from English to Japanese tends to take longer than interpreting from Japanese to English (Matsuyama 2008: 3) as well as interpreters' plausible efforts to convey players' full intention to fans, 93 percent is a likely result. How, then, do baseball interpreters interpret interviewers' utterances in almost half the time?

One of the simplest ways to shorten interpreting time is to interpret the question at double-speed to players. Although analysis of speed was not conducted in this research, instances of baseball interpreters speaking very quickly to players were not prominent. Naturally, interpreters do not want to place the unnecessary burden of attentive listening on players. If interpreting very quickly to players is not the way to shorten the interpreting time, then the next likely means is to reduce the amount of information. In the researcher's interviews, all the baseball interpreters admitted that they selected the information to be conveyed to players. In particular, they omitted long statements that preceded the actual question unless such statements were relevant. The following is a typical example of such a hero interview. Note that the interviewer's utterances were translated into English by the author and the same holds true for all the other Japanese sentences in this chapter:

> Interviewer: You hit two consecutive game-ending home runs yesterday and today. It was truly brilliant. Did the idea of another game-ending home run occur to you when you were approaching the batter's box?
> Interpreter: You thought you could hit a home run today, too?

In this example, the interviewer's first two sentences were not interpreted, as they were not questions. Even in the interpreted question, the additional phrase "when you were approaching the batter's box" was eliminated.

Another way to shorten interpreting time is through creative rendering. The following hero interview demonstrates such shortening (Itaya 2017b: 13) by means of creative rendering:

> Interviewer: When you connected for a timely two-base hit, you didn't start to run, did you? (6.3 seconds)
> Interpreter: Inaudible. (less than 1 second)
> Player: Sorry, uh ... sorry.
> Interviewer: If you compare today's winning two-base hit to sushi, what kind of sushi would it be? (6.1 seconds)
> Interpreter: Inaudible. (less than 1 second)
> Player: Tuna and salmon. I love sushi.

In this example, the interpreter spent less than one second translating a 6.3-second Japanese utterance into English, and again less than one second translating a 6.1-second Japanese utterance. The interpreter later explained to the researcher how he shortened the time. The first question was interpreted as "You pimped it. Why?" "Pimp" is baseball slang meaning "standing at home plate watching the ball." This example shows that to be well-versed in sports terminology is fundamental to immediate delivery. The second question was interpreted as "What's your favorite sushi?" According to the interpreter, players often get confused by such irrelevant questions and therefore ask back to confirm the intent of the question or give odd answers. In order to avoid an awkward moment of that sort, when a question does not directly pertain to the play itself, the interpreter explained that he crafts a simpler question, the answer to which would meet the needs of the audience. As was explained at the beginning of this section, spectators do not usually catch the interpreted words. Therefore, the answer "Tuna and salmon" made sense, and fans cheered with little time-lag. This is one example of how creativity generates immediacy and may ultimately meet the *skopos* of creating a happy moment for fans. The ability to interpret selectively or creatively to achieve a goal is an added value of interpreters (Kimura 2017: 197–198). Professional sport is a form of entertainment that could not exist without fans or spectators (Kawashima 2013: 29). In the above two examples, interpreters can be said to put the *spokos* of fan satisfaction before the accuracy of the words.

Table 4 illustrates another sports interpreting strategy. As mentioned in 3.4, the researcher observed and videotaped some backstage interviews when players, surrounded by reporters in the designated area, are asked questions. The remarks of overseas players were, of course, interpreted. Table 4 indicates that interpreter #2 shortened the interpreting time for the interviewer's question to one-third (31 percent) in the hero interview, while spending more time than the original speech (113 percent) for the backstage interview. When interpreting players' utterances, this interpreter spends about the same length of time, even in different situations (98 and 96 percent, respectively).

Tab. 4: Difference of interpreting time for Interpreter #2 in different situations

	Delivery time compared to time of players' utterances	**Delivery time compared to time of interviewers' utterances**
Hero interview	98 %	31 %
Back stage interview	96 %	113 %

Interpreter #2 explained to the researcher that, during the hero interview, he was conscious of minimizing the interpreting time for the sake of fans cheering in the field or in front of their TV screens. He said that, during the backstage interview, he intentionally took a longer time to interpret in order to avoid misinterpretation. He added that the risk entailed by misinterpretation is higher in backstage press interviews, because questions are more serious and interpreted words will be in newspapers and on web sites the next day. This phenomenon of a growth in interpreting time in the context of a riskier situation agrees with recent research showing that, when the risk is higher, interpreting time tends to lengthen (Matsushita 2015: 1–16).

4.3.2 Strategy to fill the cultural gap

Some former MLB players expressed feelings of frustration in this research about the way members of the Japanese press ask questions. These interviewees complained that Japanese press members made statements when they were supposed to ask questions. For example, in a hero interview in 2015 in the Pacific League, an interviewer said, "Today's game was the game from which a determined will to win by Laird and the whole team was fully conveyed to us." The interviewer then thrust a microphone at a player. This kind of statement puts a player in a difficult situation, as the player bears the burden of hammering out what to say out of countless options. All the interpreters interviewed by the researcher said that, in a situation like this, they put appropriateness before accuracy and changed statements into closed questions that could be answered by a simple "yes" or "no." Mr Dabadie, the former interpreter for the French manager of a Japanese national football team, echoed this sentiment. He complained that TV announcers made statements like, "In today's match against Brazil, you lost zero to five." This clearly was not a question, and so the manager became infuriated and the rest of the interview was a mess. He added that this held true when the team won, too. According to Mr Senda, an interpreter for the manager of another Japanese national football team from the Republic of Bosnia and Herzegovina, when faced with a similar situation, the manager calmly but sarcastically answered, "I am also aware of the fact" (Japan Broadcasting Corporation 2012). A former baseball interpreter shared a similar anecdote with the researcher. He said that an American manager constantly complained about members of the Japanese press making statements rather than asking questions and admitted that he often changed the statement into question form so as not to upset the manager.

Clearly, negative opinions about how members of the Japanese press form questions exist. According to Mr Dabadie, in the Western world, it is rare for an interviewer from the press to make statements rather to ask questions. This dissatisfaction toward the way the Japanese press communicate resonates with sources of communication difficulties raised by Americans toward their Japanese co-workers: "lack of verbal clarity," "lack of verbal specificity," and "verbal indirection" (Kim and Paulk 1994: 124–127). As mentioned in 2.3, Japan is a country with a high-context culture, where tacit understanding is widely treasured. A baseball interpreter the researcher interviewed made an interesting comment on the plausible reason for the way interviewers form questions. He thinks vague expressions by the Japanese press is due to their expectation toward interviewees to anticipate the intention of the question and answer accordingly. By not narrowing down the question, they hope that versatile answers will come out. In case the interview is interpreted, they expect interpreters to put the question in the way players would be willing to talk. However, this is still a supposition based on anecdotal evidence, which deserves further exploration.

Another instance where baseball interpreters made conscious efforts to adjust intercultural differences is when players include religious words or phrases in their utterances. Players from Western cultures, for instance, may occasionally mention "God" in hero interviews. Research shows that around 80 percent of Japanese people, while not necessarily against religion, either have no religion or do not practice a particular religion (Kaneko 1997: 297–298). Therefore, it is very rare, or it would at least sound strange, to mention God in everyday life, let alone at sporting events. When Christian players uttered words like "God" or "prayer," interpreters deviated from the principle of accuracy by using non-religious Japanese words in order to fill the cultural gap. In the following hero interview, the player was asked to give an encouraging message to residents of Kumamoto prefecture, which had been hit by a severe earthquake. Note that two words related to religion are underlined and that the interpreter's Japanese utterances were translated by the researcher:

> Player: God is the way, and we're gonna get through this with you with prayer, and we are gonna just focus on our future, and keep our heads up and we're gonna get through this.
> Interpreter: I know it's hard, but we will be with you to get through this hardship. Let us keep our heads up to move forward.

The interpreter explained to the researcher that this player was committed to God and frequently touched upon God in hero interviews. The interpreter did not interpret the word God every time the player mentioned it. According to the interpreter, for every four times the player mentioned God, perhaps, he interpreted it once. This way, the interpreter tried to balance accuracy and appropriateness.

Yet another gap, although not linguistic aspect, is found in collectivism/individualism (Condon and Saito 1974, 1976; Barnlund 1975; Samovar, Porter, and Stefani 1998). Japan and the United States, where the MLB operates, are "almost diametrically separated" on this dimension (Donahue 1998: 12). For some former MLB players, some aspects of Japanese culture are frustrating. The following remark by a former MLB player, originally from South America, seems to convey how he feels about how things are done in Japan:

> [O]f course you come from different culture ..., for us, it's like sometimes too many rules, so many things they do, they do like, very very, how do you say, very right, very formal, so for us, it's not wrong but kind of like weird, like, we don't get used to being so right, so formal, you know like a soldier, so that's what I mean like him [his interpreter], he grows up over there [America], so he knows, what, how, what we like, like you know ... so I think, for me, the interpreter is the guy who knows how we grow up, you know, how we live in the States ...

In the interview, this player complained how standardized Japanese team training was and how it is not catered for individual needs, but complemented his interpreter for understanding his frustration and helping the player skip some of the "meaningless" routine inconspicuously. It seems that the ability to detect and bridge cultural differences is one very important trait of baseball interpreters.

Differences of culture and communication styles in the context of sports are in and by themselves a worthwhile subject to be investigated, when sports have been witnessing rapid globalization. As this chapter can only provide some anecdotal evidence, further studies on this subject need to be conducted.

5 Conclusions

Sports and language are inseparable, as sports are increasingly mediated by language on TV and social media, and the globalization of sports has made the presence of sports interpreters essential. By discussing the outcomes of research on baseball interpreters, this chapter has attempted to reveal how sports interpreters negotiate this critical role. It has been demonstrated that baseball interpreters believe social roles are no less important than linguistic roles in sports interpreting. It has also been found that baseball interpreters fulfill multiple social functions, despite experiencing role conflict and role distance. This is not to say, however, that the linguistic aspect is trifling. Baseball interpreters employ different interpreting tactics according to various situations in order to meet the *spokos*, often by shifting their "footing," moving between "animator," "author," and "principal." This chapter demonstrates that the *spokos* of sports interpreting is not solely communication: interpreters strive to let players demonstrate their maximum power and to interpret under the media's rigid time constraints. In order to achieve a sports-specific *spokos*, sports interpreters perform multiple functions, both linguistically and socially.

References

Abe, Masao. 2013. *Kaiteki Shokuba no Tsukuri Kata* [How to create a comfortable work environment]. Tokyo: Association for Workers Education of Japan.

Anderson, R. Bruce W. 2002. Perspectives on the role of interpreter. In Franz Pöchhacker & Miriam Shlesinger (eds.), *The interpreting studies reader*, 209–217. London: Routledge.

Angelelli, Claudia V. 2004. *Revisiting the interpreter's role: A Study of conference, court, and medical interpreters in Canada, Mexico, and the United States*. Amsterdam: John Benjamins Publishing Company.

Barnlund, Dean. 1975. *Public and private self in Japan and the United States*. Tokyo: Simul Press.

Billings, Andrew C. & Natalie Brown. 2015. Understanding the biggest show in media: What the Olympic Games communicates to the world. In Paul M. Pedersen (ed.), *Routledge handbook of sport communication*, 155–164. London/New York: Routledge.

Butterworth, Michael L. 2010. *Baseball and rhetorics of purity: The national pastime and American identity during the war on terror*. Tuscaloosa, AL: University of Alabama Press.

Charmaz, Kathy C. 2006. *Constructing grounded theory: A practical guide through qualitative analysis*. Thousand Oaks, CA: Sage.

Clancy, Patricia M. 1985. The acquisition of Japanese. In Dan I. Slobin (ed.), *The crosslinguistic study of language acquisition*, Vol. 1, 373–524. Hillsdale, HJ: Lawrence Erlbaum.

Condon, John C. & Mitsuko Saito (eds.). 1974. *Intercultural encounters with Japan: Communication – Contact and Conflict*. Tokyo: Simul Press.

Condon, John C. & Mitsuko Saito (eds.). 1976. *Communication across cultures for what? A symposium on humane responsibility in intercultural communication*. Tokyo: Simul Press.

Donahue, Ray T. 1998. *Japanese culture and communication: Critical cultural analysis*. Lanham, MD: University Press of America.

Gile, Daniel. 1992. Basic theoretical components for interpreter and translator training. In Cay Dollerup & Anne Loddegaard (eds.), *Teaching translation and interpreting*, 185–194. Amsterdam: John Benjamins Publishing Company.

Goffman, Erving. 1981. *Forms of talk*. Philadelphia: University of Pennsylvania Press.

Goffman, Erving. 2013. *Encounters: Two studies in the sociology of interaction*. CT: Martino Publishing.

Hale, Sandra. 1997. The interpreter on trial: Pragmatics in court interpreting. In Silvana Carr, Roda P. Roberts, Aideen Dufour & Dini Steyn (eds.), *The critical link: Interpreters in the community*, 201–214. Amsterdam/Philadelphia: John Benjamins Publishing Company.

Hall, Edward T. 1976. *Beyond culture*. Garden City, NY: Doubleday.

Harris, Brian. 1990. Norms in interpretation. *Target* 2(1). 115–119.

Harris, John. 2015. Sport, celebrity, and the meaning of style. In Paul M. Pedersen (ed.), *Routledge handbook of sport communication*, 388–397. London: Routledge.

Herbert, Jean. 1952. *The interpreter's handbook: How to become a conference interpreter*. Geneva, Switzerland: Georg.

Horner, James R. 1988. *Eureka! Different baseball across the globe*. Tokyo: Hinode Publishers.

Ikei, Masaru. 1991. *Yakyu to Nihonjin* [Baseball and the Japanese]. Tokyo: Maruzen.

Itaya, Hatsuko. 2017a. The roles expected of sports interpreters: From a study employing M-GTA on professional baseball interpreters. *Interpreting and Translation Studies* 17. 23–43.

Itaya, Hatsuko. 2017b. Interpreting strategies in the field of sports: From a study of professional baseball interpreters. *Studies in Sports and Language* 2. 1–19.

Itaya, Hatsuko. 2019. *Kyujo de Tsuyakusha wo Otta Ichinenkan* [One year of research on interpreters at ballparks]. *Tsuyaku Honyaku Journal* 30(3). Tokyo: Ikaros Publications.

Ito, Youichi 1992. Theories on intercultural communication styles from a Japanese perspective: A sociological approach. In Jay Blumler, Jack M. Mcleod & Karl Erik Rosengren (eds.), *Comparatively speaking: Communication and culture across space and time*, 238–268. Thousand Oaks, CA: Sage.

Japan Broadcasting Corporation. 2012. *Deep people: Interpreters for Japan national football team*. Aired on December 24, 2012.

Kaneko, Satoru. 1997. *Nihonjin no Shukyo Sei* [Religiousness of the Japanese]. Tokyo: Shin yo-sha.

Kawashima, Norimoto. 2013. *Supottsu Gyokai no Arukikata: Supottsu wo Shigoto ni Shitai Hito, Supottsu no Chikara wo Shinjiru Hito he* [How to work in the field of sport: To those who wish to make sport your occupation and who believe in the power of sport]. Tokyo: Paru Shuppann.

Kim, Young Y. & Sheryl Paulk. 1994. Intercultural challenges and personal adjustments. A qualitative analysis of the experiences of American and Japanese co-workers. In Richard L. Wiseman & Robert Shuter (eds.), *Communicating in multinational organizations*, 117–140. Thousand Oaks, CA: Sage.

Kimura, Gorō. Christoph. 2017. Tsunagari Kata wo Saguru: Doitsu Porando Kokkyo Chiiki Ibunka Komyunikeshon no Shohoryaku [Probe into how to be connected: Intercultural communication strategies in the border region of Germany and Poland]. In Fumiya Hirataka & Gorō Christoph Kimura (eds.), *Tagengo Shugi Shakai ni Mukete*. [Toward the society of multilingualism]. Tokyo: Kuroshio Publishers.

Kinoshita, Yasuhito. 1999. *Guraundedo Seori Apurochi: Shitsuteki Jissho Kenkyu no Saisei* [Grounded theory approach: Reproduction of empirical research]. Tokyo: Koubundou.

Kinoshita, Yasuhito. 2003. *Guraundedo Seori Apurochi no Jissen: Shitsuteki Kenkyu heno Sasoi* [Practice of grounded theory approach: Invitation to qualitative research]. Tokyo: Koubundou.
Kinoshita, Yasuhito. 2007. *Raibu Kogi M-GTA: Jissenteki Shitsuteki Kenkyu Hou: Shuseiban Guraundedo Seori Apurochi no Subete* [Live lecture on M-GTA: Practical method of qualitative research: Everything on modified grounded theory approach]. Tokyo: Koubundou.
Matsushita, Kayo. 2015. Risk management in political interpreting: Case study of a press conference held in Japan. *Interpreting and Translation Studies* 15. 1–16.
Matsuyama, Shoko. 2008. English-Japanese consecutive interpreting and note-taking: A study looking into the time needed for renditions. *Interpreting and Translation Studies*, 8. 1–18.
Nagai, Mariko. 2014. *Tsutaeru Gokui* [The secret of communication]. Tokyo: Shueisha.
Nakajima, Kuniaki. 1994. *Puro Yakyu Tuyaku Funtou Ki – Namida to Warai no Ibunka Kouryu* [A record of a struggle of a professional baseball interpreter – Intercultural communication with tears and laughs]. Tokyo: NHK Publishing.
Nakajima, Kuniaki. 2015. *Puro Yakyu Saikyo no Suketto Ron* [Theory on the best foreign power suketto players in professional baseball]. Tokyo: Kodansha.
Nakasone, Shun. 2019. Welcome to the ballpark! *Japan Interpreters*, 5 March. https://www.japan-interpreters.org/news/baseball-nakasone1/ (20 April 2019).
Nishikawa, Chiharu. 2018. *Tokyo Orinpikku no Borantia ni Naritai Hito ga Yomu Hon* [A book for those who want to be volunteers in Tokyo Olympics]. Tokyo: Ikaros Publications.
Nishiyama, Sen. 1970. *The art of interpretation.* Tokyo: Jitsugyo no Nihon Sha.
Pöchhacker, Franz. 2004. *Introducing interpreting studies.* London: Routledge.
Roche, Maurice. 2000. *Mega-events and modernity: Olympics and expos in the growth of global culture.* London: Routledge.
Samovar, Larry, Richard E. Porter & Lisa A. Stefani. 1998. *Communication between cultures.* Belmont, CA: Wadsworth Publishing Company.
Sato, Tsutomu. 1976. Shakai no Kiso Riron [Basic theory of society]. In Kouhei Honma, Aiko Tanosaki, Toshiyuki Mitsuyoshi & Tsutomu Shinohara (eds.), *Shakaigaku Gairon* [An introduction to sociology], 33. Tokyo: Yuhikaku Publishing.
Tachibanaki, Toshiaki. 2016. *Puro Yakyu no Keizai Gaku* [Economics of professional baseball]. Tokyo: Toyo Keizai Inc.
Tachihara, Tomohiro. 2015. *Kyudan Tsuyakusha ni Motomerareru Yakuwari ni Kansuru Kenkyu: Nihon Yakyu to Amerika Yakyu ni Okeru Bunka no Sa wo Umeru Sonzai* [Research on roles required of Professional baseball interpreters: An existence to fill the gap between Japanese baseball and American baseball]. A Master's Thesis at Graduate School of Intercultural Communication, Rikkyo University, Tokyo.
Takeda, Kayoko. 2013. Kino Shugiteki Apurochi (Supokosu Riron) [Functionalist approach (*Spokos* theory)]. In Kumiko Torikai (ed.), *Yokuwakaru Honyaku Tsuyaku Gaku.* [Easy-to-understand translation and interpreting studies], 122. Kyoto: Minerva Shobo.
Torikai, Kumiko. 2007. *Tsuyakusha to Sengo Nihon Gaiko* [Interpreters and postwar Japan diplomacy]. Tokyo: Misuzu Shobo.
Torikai, Kumiko (ed.). 2013. Aporo Douji Chukei to Douji Tsuyaku [Television broadcast of Apollo moon-landing and simultaneous interpreting]. In Kumiko Torikai (ed.), *Yokuwakaru Honyaku Tsuyaku Gaku* [Easy-to-understand translation and interpreting studies], 26. Kyoto: Minerva Shobo.
Ushigome, Tadahiro. 1993. *Samurai Yakyu to Suketto Tachi* [Samurai baseball and foreign power Suketto Players]. Tokyo: Sanseido.
Vermeer, H. J., trans. Andrew Chesterman. 2004. Spokos and commission in translational action. In Lawrence Venuti (ed.), *The translation studies reader*, 2nd edn., 221–232. London: Routledge.

Whiting, Robert. 1987. *Nippon Yakyu ha Eien ni Fumetsu Desu* [Japanese baseball will never perish]. Tokyo: Chikuma Shobo.
Whiting, Robert. 2006. *Yakyu ha Besuboru wo Koeta Noka* [Has yakyu surpassed baseball?] Tokyo: Chikuma Shobo.
Whiting, Robert. 2009. *You gotta have wa*. New York: Vintage Books.

Abraham I. Khan

9 The ethos of the activist athlete

Abstract: Since at least 1969, when Harry Edwards wrote that "the sports world is not a rose flourishing in the middle of a wasteland" but "is part and parcel of that wasteland," sport's capacity to reflect its sociopolitical surroundings has served as an assumption that guides scholarly practice in communication studies and its cognate disciplines. This chapter explores this familiar axiom from the opposite direction by considering sport's unique contributions to social and political life. Edwards once led the "revolt of the Black athlete," and as the phenomenon of Black athlete activism has returned in the 2010s, I borrow the concept of ethos from rhetorical studies in order to identify the communicative practices that render athlete activism durable across space and time. Four attributes, I argue, bind the past and the present in constituting the ethos of the activist athlete: double-consciousness, risk, solidarity, and poetry.

Keywords: athlete activism; protest; rhetoric; ethos; race

1 Introduction

Following a sequence of racist incidents at the University of Missouri in 2015, a protest group named Concerned Student 1950 attempted to press the university's administration into remedial action. On October 27, 2015, the group presented a list of demands to President Tim Wolfe, including a demand for his resignation. Wolfe dismissed the group as a nuisance and invited the students into a "dialogue." On November 2, Jonathan Butler, a graduate student in journalism who had come to occupy the protest group's moral center, announced the beginning of a hunger strike intended to carry on "until either Tim Wolfe is removed from office or my internal organs fail and my life is lost" (Horn 2015). Over the next few days, the English department delivered a no-confidence vote on University Chancellor R. Bowen Loftin, student protesters remained unmoved, and Wolfe issued an apology that, while recognizing the existence of "long standing, systemic" racism at Mizzou, asked students to "move forward in addressing" it (Williams 2015). On November 7, Missouri's football team declared its refusal to "participate in any football related activities until President Tim Wolfe resigns or is removed due to his negligence toward marginalized students." On November 9, both Wolfe and Loftin resigned (Belkin and Horn 2015). This narrative can be written in a variety of ways, but in a click-bait media landscape, one *USA Today* headline rang true: "Missouri president, chancellor quit after football team walks out" (Son and Madhani 2015). Neither a critical mass of disaffected Black students, nor months of demonstrations, nor a hunger strike could effectuate a change in the university's lead-

https://doi.org/10.1515/9783110660883-009

ership. The loss of faculty support certainly could not. But when the football team threatened to strike? Wolfe's firing took 36 hours.

Events at the University of Missouri punctuated a resurgence of media interest in sport's significance to American political culture. Black athletes inhabit a rich tradition of protest speech both drawn from and brought to bear on larger social and political struggles in the United States. Sport's political significance is made obvious in the patriotic rituals that structure its spectacular presentation (Butterworth 2008), but when sport's political inflection takes the form of protest or dissent, we often hear that sport is a "mirror of society." This notion has been repeated since at least the 1960s, when Harry Edwards wrote in *Revolt of the Black Athlete* that "the sports world is not a rose flourishing in the middle of a wasteland" but "is part and parcel of that wasteland, reeking of the same racism that corrupts other areas of our society" (1969: 34). When spectators at Boston's Fenway Park spewed racist invective at Baltimore Orioles outfielder Adam Jones in 2017, Kevin Blackistone (2017) described the incident as "the refrain that sport reflects society come to life." Without modifying any part of that axiom, I want to explore its inverse. Sport not only reflects society, it refracts its light back to society. Black athlete activism generates novel possibilities by modeling creative forms of protest, dissent, and resistance. In this chapter, I argue that "the activist athlete" is more than just a useful shorthand for what Howard Bryant (2018) calls "The Heritage" of politically courageous Black athletes extending back through the 20th century, but is also an *ethos*, a communal mode of social existence constituted by identifiable commitments to political action and public communication.

Both communication scholars and sport scholars working within communication's traditions have long taken an interest in the political behavior and expression of Black athletes. Scholarly treatments of attempts to organize an international Black boycott of the 1968 Olympics in Mexico City are almost too numerous to mention, and as the legacy of activism once crystallized in those events seems to have been revived in the 2010s, scholars working at the intersection of communication and sport have taken a renewed interest, particularly as Black athlete activism has been shaped by new media technologies. In a recent special issue of *Communication and Sport* dedicated to the study of social justice movements, the issue editors point out that "participatory platforms and user-generated content have the potential to disrupt traditional relationships between important constituencies including athletes, sports teams, governing bodies, the news media, and fans" (Jackson et al. 2020: 438). As urgent as this work seems to be, I offer two caveats: first, the field of communication and sport is unique in its interdisciplinarity. As those same editors note, their work is "drawn from differing disciplines: sociology, gender studies, disability studies, (physical) cultural studies, political communication, and journalism studies." My own history of the study of race and sport makes a similar claim, namely that "the field of scholarship marked by the specific relation of race to sport has become thoroughly interdisciplinary" (2016: 109). Such interdisciplinarity means not only that the field is structured in epistemological diversity, but also that it attracts the kind of scholarship that renders the field irreducible to a single mode of inquiry (e. g., social science) or single object of inquiry (e. g., journalism or social media). Second, to attend to sport communication's cutting edge does not mean that we must all become Twitter scholars. It would surely be an error to ignore the role social media play in shaping political protest, but the tradition called "media studies" does not exhaust the study of sport communication.

Following Michael Butterworth (2016), who invites sport scholars to see sport as a "rhetorical artifact," I have elsewhere argued that "rhetorical scholarship defines its object domain in ways from which the study of race and sport would benefit, and the historical development of the interface of society and sport contains texts, images, and events that rhetorical critics are bound to find provocative" (Khan 2016: 116). In proposing the ethos of the activist athlete, I draw on the rhetorical tradition in order to grasp the meaning of the moment in which we as sport communication scholars find ourselves and, perhaps more importantly, in which Black athletes find themselves. I focus here on athlete expression in the United States, not because anti-racist speech is unnecessary or insignificant in other parts of the world, but because of the influence of African American political speech on sport's global protest landscape. For example, as the killings of Breonna Taylor, Ahmaud Arbery, George Floyd, and Elijah McClain reignited waves of anti-racist protest around the U.S., not only did the world take notice, but so did athletes in the world's most popular sports. In July 2020, Lewis Hamilton, the only Black driver in Formula 1 racing and the reigning world champion, wore a Black Lives Matter t-shirt and took a knee before the Austrian Grand Prix. Hamilton was joined by several other drivers, including many who did not kneel but who wore t-shirts saying "End Racism" (Lynch 2020). A month earlier, when European soccer re-started after its pause for the COVID-19 pandemic, players in both the English Premier League and the German Bundesliga demonstrated with public statements, slogan-bearing t-shirts, and more kneeling (Bumbaca 2020). It is not that these gestures are less impactful than those occurring in the U.S., but that it is U.S. athletes that have historically modeled the ethos of the activist athlete. If the repetition of Colin Kaepernick's signature gesture from 2016 – taking a knee during the national anthem – is any indication, it seems clear that the ethos of the activist athlete continues to emerge from a North American context.

S. Michael Halloran reminds us that "the most concrete meaning given for [ethos] in the Greek lexicon is a 'habitual gathering place'" (1982: 60). Nedra Reynolds takes the spatial and social dimensions of ethos to designate a "location" which helps to "reestablish ethos as a social act and product of community's character" (1993: 327). As the memories of activist athletes from the 1960s are summoned in public discourse as templates for political conduct in the present, the location in which activist athletes congregate acquires a temporal dimension. Accounts of Black athlete activism are replete with invocations of figures like Tommie Smith, John Carlos, and Muhammad Ali. The repetition of those names is habitual inside a gathering place shaped by the competing vectors of continuity and change in racial politics. The conditions imposed by structural racism in the U.S., as many have argued, amount to a "changing same." Moreover, says Stephen White, "ethos is animated by a given set of ontological 'figures,'" and "a constellation of such figures sustains an ethos in the sense of prefiguring its cognitive perspective, moral bearing, and aesthetic-affective sensibility" (2009: 4). Perhaps in the way that a lighthouse orients approaching ships to the shoreline, ethos marks a communal orientation to public affairs. Lighthouses, to adopt a metaphor, communicate their differences from one another by distinctive patterns of illumination called "light signatures." We might discover "character" in ethos not simply as credibility, but as a light signature, as a constellation of attributes that emerge in public address as a collective disposition durable across space and time. In naming the "ethos of the activist athlete," I draw attention to a pattern of four beacons, four interdependent dimensions of public political expression: double-consciousness, risk, solidarity, and poetry.

2 Dimensions of the activist athlete

2.1 Sport and double-consciousness

Owing to its frequent circulation for over fifty years, the photograph of American sprinters Tommie Smith and John Carlos (along with Australian silver medalist Peter Norman) on the Olympic medal podium in 1968 is among the most recognizable images in sports history. As individuals like Kaepernick, groups like the Missouri football team, and organizations like the WNBA herald the return of the activist athlete, the Mexico City photograph continues to circulate as evidence of their historical precedent, as a touchstone for the collective memory that makes Black athlete activism possible in the present. The image is often called the "Black Power salute," a label which tends to conceal its context. Harry Edwards had sown the seeds for the Olympic Project for Human Rights (OPHR) in San Jose, CA in 1967. He had been a track and field athlete at San Jose State University in the early sixties, and returned with an advanced degree in sociology from Cornell a few years later, when he encountered Carlos and Smith, individuals with whom he had shared experiences with, as he put it, "racism in the fraternities and sororities, racism in housing, racism and out-and-out mistreatment in athletics, and a general lack of understanding of the problems of Afro-Americans by the college administration" (Edwards 1969: 43). By the Fall of 1967, Edwards had organized 60 of San Jose State's 72 Black students (out of a student body of approximately 12,000) into a protest group, effectively causing the cancellation of the school's opening football game. This experience was formative. Edwards said, "we had learned the use of power – the power to be gained from exploiting the white man's economic and almost religious involvement in athletics" (1969: 47).

Edwards communicated his awakening to a Black youth conference in Los Angeles on November 23, 1967. The most provocative idea to emerge from the workshop on athletics was the OPHR, conceived originally as an international Black boycott of the Mexico City Olympics. Drafted with the help of Louis Lomax, the OPHR's demands included the restoration of Muhammad Ali's boxing titles, the removal of Avery Brundage (a notorious anti-Semite) from the head of the International Olympic Committee, and the expulsion of South Africa and Rhodesia from Olympic competition (Edwards 1969: 58–59). On December 15 in New York, Edwards held a meeting with Lomax, Floyd McKissick, and Martin Luther King, each of whom agreed to serve the project in an official advisory capacity. For understandable reasons – a divisive press, a looming backlash, and the fact that Black athletes around the world had committed their lives to Olympic competition – the boycott itself failed, but the actions of Carlos and Smith, the "Black power salute," emerged from the atmosphere of protest generated over the previous year.

By 1969, Edwards was out of the day-to-day business of running a social movement and had set his attention to writing his first book, *Revolt of the Black Athlete*. Part manifesto, part scholarship, *Revolt* spends three chapters theorizing the social conditions of Black athletes, and the following hundred pages or so documenting the events of 1967 and 1968, revealing a language and strategy for Black militant organization in rich detail. On the whole, *Revolt* was an account of how the experiences of Black athletes had manifested a revolutionary consciousness. *Revolt* expresses what W. E. B. DuBois in 1903 called double-consciousness, which arises out of the unique standpoint of Black identity in America. This is a familiar passage, but worth repeating: "The Negro is a sort of seventh son, born with a veil and gifted with second sight in this American world," Du Bois said, "It is a peculiar sensation, this double consciousness, this sense of always looking at one's self through the eyes of others. One ever feels his two-ness – An American, a Negro; two souls, two thoughts, two unreconciled strivings; two warring ideals in one dark body, whose dogged strength alone keeps it from being torn asunder" (1903: 9). Edwards's *Revolt* testified to that dogged strength, to the rebellious impulses born of understanding the way he was regarded by others. Double-consciousness, for Du Bois, was perhaps a gift not worth the cost, but it was a gift nonetheless, its benefit consisting in the ability to see things that others cannot, to identify states of affairs that dehumanize and oppress. At its core, double-consciousness refers to a critical aptitude arising out of the difference between Black self-perception and white mistreatment. As a form of public address, double-consciousness involves, as it did in *Revolt of the Black Athlete*, accounts of Black experience as lived in close proximity to white society.

Edwards' central rhetorical strategy was to disclose the circumstances of Black athletes, link them to the circumstances of Black people in the U.S., and enact the reckoning produced by these circumstances. "In this book, we will analyze the newest phase of the Black liberation movement in America," Edwards wrote in the preface. "The statements we will make are ... the documentary facts of the movement from the perspective of a man who was himself victimized by the American athletic structure, who helped plan, direct, and implement the revolt, and who intends to continue to fight until the goals of that revolt have been achieved" (1969: xvii). Edwards, moreover, claimed to speak not merely for himself, but for Black athletes who were "for the first time reacting in a human and masculine fashion to the disparities between the heady artificial world of newspaper clippings, photographers, and screaming spectators and the real world of degradation, humiliation, and horror that confronts the overwhelming majority of Afro-Americans." Edwards's revolt would never materialize in the way he had hoped, but his disclosures regarding Black social experience charged the symbolic atmosphere surrounding Carlos and Smith on the medal podium in 1968.

2.2 Athlete activism and risk

The second dimension of the ethos of the activist athlete is risk, or more precisely, the willingness to risk oneself in the pursuit of justice. Like Muhammad Ali before them, about whom I will say more below, Carlos and Smith held conscience above reward. Both received death threats for years after their medal podium demonstration, but when the willingness to risk oneself is a component of one's ethos, backlash is the cost of doing business, so to speak, and when it comes, it reveals the righteousness of the cause. Provocation is the point. Following the demonstration in Mexico City, Carlos and Smith were ejected from Olympic Village, banned from Olympic participation for life, and called "Black skinned stormtroopers" by Brent Musburger, now a well-known sports announcer, then a columnist for the *Chicago American* newspaper (Zirin 2012). The manner in which Carlos and Smith were vilified illustrated the truth of their claims. They provoked the powers-that-be into doing and saying what powers-that-be do and say.

2.3 The solidarity of athletes

The third dimension of the ethos of the activist athlete is solidarity, and I mean solidarity in two senses: first, in the sense that the activist athlete's gathering place draws its energy from collective protest, and second, in the sense that individuals and groups with dissimilar problems find in each other sources of recognition and support. It is worth noting that Peter Norman, the white Australian in the famous photo, was also vilified when he returned home. For the crime of wearing the OPHR patch, Norman, the second fastest man in the world, was excluded from Australia's Olympic delegation to Munich in 1972 (Posnanski 2012). It is perhaps more important to remember that the demonstration in Mexico City was the expression of a critical mass of Black athletes bearing witness to mistreatment, injustice, and violence. Edwards saw the revolt of the Black athlete as the cumulative outcome of preceding events, including the political protests of Muhammad Ali, whom Edwards called, "the patron saint" of the revolt (1969: 59). Refusing to be drafted and sent to Vietnam in 1967, Ali was sentenced to five years in prison, stripped of his boxing titles, and blacklisted from fighting for three years. He never served any prison time, but at only 25 years old in 1967, Ali lost the prime of his career.

Ali's stand was supported by some of the best Black athletes in the world, but not before holding a day-long meeting with him in Cleveland to determine his intentions. Brokered by Browns running back Jim Brown, the meeting is now known to history as the "Ali Summit." Its proceedings were off limits to the papers, but it concluded with a press conference attended by Ali, Brown, the Boston Celtics Bill Russell, Lew Alcindor (who would later change his name to Kareem Abdul-Jabbar), and a number of other notable NFL players. John Wooten was a Browns offensive lineman whose Black Economic Union hosted the meeting. "We didn't care about any perceived threats," Wooten said. "We weren't concerned because we weren't going to waver. We were unified. We all had a real relationship with each other and we knew we were doing something for the betterment of all" (Wright 2012). The moment captured the way that solidarity finds a home within the ethos of the activist athlete. As the winds of revolt blew, they shared in each other's risks and embraced the virtues of collective action.

2.4 Politics and poetry

If we are to understand the fourth dimension of this ethos, poetry, we would be wise to learn more from Ali. Of course, Ali is well known for his poetry. Whether it was to promote himself or to trash talk his opponent, Ali was a wordsmith. He spoke publicly in verse, evoking artistic traditions of Black oratory with cleverness and depth (Grano 2009). His tempo and ingenuity make an easy home in our memory, which is certainly what I mean by poetry, but I also mean more than that. By poetry, I also mean that Ali demonstrated a gift for speaking into existence a world that looked like the one he saw. As he once admitted, "I am the greatest. I said that even before I knew I was. I figured that if I said it enough, I would convince the world" (Martin 2016). Ali's artistry consisted not only in the symmetries of rhyme, but in the asymmetries in power his rhyme could so creatively reveal. I want to call this aptitude poetry in order to highlight Ali's ability to alter the terms in which he and others like him were received. But poetry need not require rhythm and meter. Describing the poetic-expressive function of public address, Michael Warner contends that public address "says not only 'let a public exist,' but 'let it have this character, speak this way, see the world in this way.' It then goes in search of confirmation that such a public exists. ... Run it up the flagpole and see who salutes. Put on a show and see who shows up" (2002: 114). The whole world showed up for Muhammad Ali in both life and in death. Ali offered Black political culture a poetic ethos, a brightly burning beacon of creativity and self-love that drew forceful attention to the gathering place of protest. Few public figures, athletes or otherwise, possessed the same capacity to bring a public into existence. He is the patron saint of the revolt for exactly this reason. Without Ali's rhetorical gifts, without the enticement to join him in his world, there might not have been a revolt for Harry Edwards to theorize.

3 Rhetorical constructions of the activist athlete

These four dimensions of social and political engagement characterize the ethos of the activist athlete: double-consciousness, risk, solidarity, and poetry. Ali embodied these, as did Carlos, Smith, and Edwards. But the sixties would end, Ali would get his titles back, and Harry Edwards would take his wisdom to the academy. The ethos of the activist athlete did not disappear in 1970, but neither did the competing vectors of continuity and change in the nation's racial order. Put simply, athlete salaries would begin to soar in the 1970s and 1980s, and to understand how this period altered athlete activism, it is worth considering a lesser known figure, one whose attempts to inhabit an activist's ethos were frustrated when an aversion to risk took hold.

Curt Flood was an all-star centerfielder for the St. Louis Cardinals from 1958 to 1969. He played in three World Series, helping the Cardinals win two, and by 1968 had acquired a reputation as the best player in baseball at his position. Despite a decade of success, the Cardinals finished a disappointing fourth in 1969, and team management attempted to trade Flood to the Philadelphia Phillies at the end of the season. At the time, all Major League Baseball players were subject to a contract condition called the reserve clause, which in essence bound a player to work in perpetuity for his original team unless that team traded him for another player or sold him for cash. This left Flood with two choices. He could report to Philadelphia, or he could retire. There was no such thing as "free agency" (a complete account of Flood's lawsuit is available in Snyder 2006). Baseball owners publicly claimed that this arrangement was necessary to protect an equitable economic order, since without it, the wealthiest owners could purchase the best players at the highest prices and undermine league competition. Fearing the result if players could negotiate for their wages, the owners cried infamously that free agency would bring about, "the end of baseball as we know it" (Korr 2002: 1). Flood and others countered that this economic order relied on a collusive labor practice that unlawfully limited wages, unfairly curtailed careers, and bore a striking resemblance to slavery. Flood sought a third option. He filed a lawsuit in Federal court, claiming first, that Major League Baseball was in violation of the Sherman Antitrust Act (colluding to depress wages), and second, that league owners were in violation of the 13th amendment's prohibition of involuntary servitude. In a letter to baseball commissioner Bowie Kuhn effectively announcing his lawsuit, Flood said, "I do not feel that I am a piece of property to be bought and sold irrespective of my wishes" (Khan 2012: 11).

Flood lost his case twice, first in federal court in 1970, and again at the U.S. Supreme Court in 1972. Put simply, the lawsuit ruined him. He escaped to Europe beaten and broke, never to play organized baseball again. The owners were determined to defeat

Flood's challenge. They called him ungrateful and greedy, maligned his character and labeled him a mortal threat. But the legal momentum his case generated resulted in a system of free agency in 1975, a system from which Flood never benefited. Today, he is regarded as a lonely rebel, as a sad casualty crushed in history's pivot, a martyr to the wealth contemporary athletes now command. The 13th amendment claim never had a chance in court, but the suggestion that baseball was slavery was a confrontational gesture drawn from the ethos of the activist athlete. And Flood didn't only say it in court. Explaining his lawsuit on television to a doubting nation, Curt Flood said infamously, "a well-paid slave is nonetheless a slave" (Khan 2012: 11).

Flood's success in the courts of both law and public opinion, depended on the support of the emerging Players Association, a labor organization composed of 24 white players, each representing one major league team. They helped him secure legal representation, but not a single one testified on his behalf at his trial. They feared two things: reprisal from the owners, who were likely to blacklist Flood's confederates, and poor treatment from the sports press, who were, as historians have noted, firmly in the owners' pocket. Flood's attempt to transform the clubhouse into a gathering place for activist athletes short-circuited on double-consciousness's relation to both solidarity and risk. Getting white players to see themselves as slaves meant producing a kind of double-consciousness deprived of racial identity. And the term "slave" in the context of the late 1960s and early 1970s, sounded to his colleagues like a racial expression bound to draw the owner's wrath. As Tom Haller, the LA Dodgers player representative put it years later, "I didn't want it to be just a Black thing. ... I wanted it to be a baseball thing" (Snyder 2006: 76). The language of slavery was an invitation to backlash. White players simply could not abide the analogy. For them, the risks were too costly to bear.

Two things happened to Flood's slave analogy. On the one hand, it was taken up by radicals. A special issue of *The Black Scholar* (then a very new journal) in 1971 devoted itself to "the Black athlete." The third article was titled "The Struggle of Curt Flood," by Charles Aikens, who inserted Flood directly into the revolt of the Black athlete. Likening Flood to Dred Scott, Aikens said, "Flood's suit is among many events in the Black struggle that have heightened awareness of a brutal system where people are still treated as chattel" (Aikens 1971: 15). Black radicals and intellectuals may have seen the wisdom of calling baseball slavery, but Black newspapers, on the other hand, did not. The largest Black newspapers, including the *Baltimore Afro-American*, had earned their sportswriting credentials narrating the career of Jackie Robinson, who, in 1947, had desegregated the Major Leagues. Black newspapers had oriented their understanding of sports toward the question of inclusion. They advocated for Flood, to be sure, but they were quick to take the confrontational sting out of his claim. The "well-paid slave," as these papers understood it, was a dangerous gambit, and the "end of baseball as we know it" a credible threat. Like the national sports press, Black newspapers softened Flood's point. Baseball's reserve clause didn't need to be abolished, they insisted. It needed to be altered, adjusted, and reconfigured to new economic realities (Khan 2012: 108–113). Sport's economic modernization was seen as inevitable, and the reformist argument blunted the slave metaphor's razor-sharp edge.

Curt Flood stood at the fault line of competing models of Black political rhetoric in the early 1970s. He stood between a deeply racialized mode of civic engagement committed to a militant confrontation with socioeconomic injustice, and a liberal mode of civic engagement in search of the compromises and reforms that might unlock the doors segregation had sealed shut. Straddling a fault line is hazardous to one's health, of course, especially when the tremors begin. And in sport, the economic changes amounted to an earthquake. In 1950, twenty years before Flood filed suit, baseball's highest paid player was Joe DiMaggio, who made an even $100,000. When a Federal Court ruled against Flood in 1970 (twenty years later), the highest paid player in baseball was Willie Mays, who made $135,000, a 35 percent increase. By 1995 (twenty years after free agency was adopted in baseball), the highest paid player was Detroit first baseman Cecil Fielder, who made $9.24 million, a 6300 percent increase (Haupert 2012).

By the mid-2000s, a new narrative emerged in popular culture regarding the activist athlete, most notably in Bill Rhoden's (2006) *$40 Million Slaves*. Using the ascendance of Michael Jordan and Tiger Woods as exhibits A and B, the story went that the activist athlete has been sold to Nike, and that contemporary athletes have been etherized by wealth – too rich, too soft, too disconnected from the communities that produce an activist's conscience. Rhoden offers an insightful read of the way athletes are socialized in youth and amateur sports to concentrate on a path to financial reward. Not only has the incentive to act on the courage of one's convictions been lost, but convictions never develop in the first place. Sport produces celebrities, not activists. There is wisdom here, but Rhoden lands in a confounding place. He writes, "Black athletes seem most at a loss, lacking purpose and drive. Given the journey that has led to this point, contemporary Black athletes have abdicated their responsibility to the community with treasonous vigor" (2006: 8). *Treasonous vigor*, says Rhoden. The picture that had developed of Black athletes in the late 2000s was one animated by selfishness, indifference, and betrayal. There are a variety of reasons to doubt this line of thinking. First, of course, it leaves us in no better position than to wag our fingers at spoiled children, a paternalistic attitude not unlike wishing your kids had it as badly as you once did. Second, it ignores Black liberalism's triumph over radicalism in the 1970s, a process visible in Curt Flood. The vocabulary of Black power lost the struggle for control of Black political culture. By the 1980s, progress was tracked in increments, and rich Black athletes became vibrant reflections of integration's greatest achievements. Finally, Rhoden's line of reasoning misses larger shifts in American political culture, particularly those marked by seismic changes in global capitalism.

Upon learning, for example, that American athletes were asked to sign a no-protest pledge in advance of the 2008 Olympics in Beijing, ESPN television personality Stephen A. Smith was apoplectic. Admittedly, sanctimonious befuddlement seems to be Smith's default rhetorical setting, but in a column on *ESPN.com*, Smith wondered, "Today's athletes show very little interest in standing up for something bigger than themselves – whether it's war, tyranny, economic deprivation, global warming. Think about it!," shouted Smith, "The African American stars of the 1930s through the 1960s ... met the obligations of their time" (2008). This, ultimately, is my concern. The cry to wake the echoes of the past rings hollow without a lucid diagnosis of the new conditions. The obligations of our time – if they are in fact obligations to begin with – are far from self-evident.

Despite the nefarious return of Olympic speech restrictions in 2020, Smith could not anticipate the revival of athletic activism that would begin in the next decade. When this revival began is not entirely clear, but according to *Washington Post* sportswriter Cindy Boren (2018), "the Trayvon Martin killing in Florida in 2012 is a good place to start." That moment, she writes, "offered athletes the chance to use their platform when the Miami Heat, for whom LeBron James then played, stepped up with James, Dwyane Wade, Chris Bosh, and others posing for a photo wearing hoodies." Six years later at his Pro Football Hall of Fame induction ceremony, Randy Moss wore a necktie bearing the bearing the names of Black people killed by police. Between the Heat in hoodies and Moss's tie lie enough examples of outspoken athletes to identify a surge in the number of Black athletes identifiable as social or political activists and an expansive media discourse dedicated to narrating it. As Boren writes, "When it comes to political and social activism, athletes of all colors and genders are finding their voice and refusing to remain silent, whether in vocal, physical or social media demonstrations." In 2013, for example, Seattle Seahawks cornerback Richard Sherman pointed out, live on CNN, that "thug" is code for "the n word" (Boren 2014). The following summer, the Los Angeles Clippers hid their team logos from fans in symbolic protest of owner Donald Sterling's shockingly offensive racial attitudes (Markazi 2014). Following the police killings of Michael Brown and Eric Garner, St. Louis Rams wide receivers took to the field with their hands up, and a number of NBA stars appeared in their arenas with T-shirts bearing the inscription, "I Can't Breathe" (Adande 2014). And in 2016, of course, Kaepernick took a knee to draw attention to racist violence, was blackballed by NFL owners from ever playing again, settled a lawsuit accusing the owners of discriminatory collusion, and announced a multi-million-dollar partnership with Nike (Cobb 2018).

4 The dynamics of contemporary activism

I want to invoke "neoliberalism" here without belaboring the point. Recognizing the contested nature of the term, with respect to both its critical and historiographic utility, I hope it is enough to say that neoliberalism is what Angela Davis (2013) calls "market fundamentalism." "Neoliberalism," she says, "sees the market as the very paradigm of freedom, and democracy emerges as a synonym for capitalism." It is a constitutive dimension of public life to the extent that it articulates the liberalism of 20th-century social movements to the 21st-century market's promise to deliver liberty and social mobility. Instead of indexing sources of conflict and grievance, racial difference has become the site of celebratory expression, and notions like diversity and tolerance work as easy corporate slogans, urging us to believe that colorblind markets can be trusted to allocate the common good. This is the seismic shift in the global economy to which I earlier referred. This is what was happening in the 1980s and 1990s while Bill Rhoden was shaking his head at Michael Jordan. Jordan was not plotting treason but availing himself of the dynamic processes through which global capitalism had learned to commodify Blackness and market racial progress.

The myth of the so-called post-racial era relies on a naive colorblind wager that trades the moral irrelevance of race for a reluctance to talk about race. So it is both significant and true for Richard Sherman to point out that "thug" is racial code, but such an insight does not an activist athlete make. Sherman now sells Chunky Soup on television. It is not just that the risks are not the same as they were in 1968, it is that the market colonizes risk, repackages it, sells it back to us, and then asks us to call the purchase our politics. Neoliberalism's trick, as critics like Davis remind us, is to bury our understanding of structural and historical racism beneath the spectacle of diversity. Racism names a variety of dubious practices in a variety of political contexts, including education, housing, and criminal justice. Within the places where athletes gather, institutional racism refers not necessarily to racist coaches (though sometimes it does refer to that), but to a sporting plantation in which universities extract unpaid labor from athletes, and then asks them to be grateful for their opportunity. Coach Nick Saban earns a salary in excess of $8 million from the University of Alabama but calls the sports agents who approach his players with financial opportunities "no better than pimps" (Rosenthal 2010). Television networks pay the NCAA over $1 billion annually for the right to broadcast the NCAA basketball tournament, but as University of Connecticut point guard Shabazz Napier revealed in 2014, even All-Americans go to bed hungry at night (Ganim 2014). The racialization of labor in college sports illustrates that markets are miserable tools for allocating the common good.

The intense and polarized responses to Kaepernick's 2016 protests ignited a debate the following spring over whether sportswriting had become "a liberal profession," a contention to which *The Ringer*'s Bryan Curtis (2017) enthusiastically assented. Identifying a journalistic tradition in a kind of historical parallel to the ethos of the activist athlete, Curtis recalls the work of Lester Rodney, the legendary communist sportswriter at the *Daily Worker* whose columns against baseball's color line in the 1930s and 1940s worked as a form of print activism in sport. To make his case for the present, Curtis cites civil rights historian Taylor Branch's influential essay in *The Atlantic* in 2011, "The Shame of College Sports." Branch did extraordinary damage to idea that the NCAA protected "amateurism" and the notion of the "student-athlete," calling them "cynical hoaxes, legalistic confections propagated by the universities so they can exploit the skills and fame of young athletes." Though Branch's piece would become famous for its money quote, that college sports produced "an unmistakable whiff of the plantation," it would take a few years before so-called "liberal sportswriting" issued an extended racial analysis. In 2016, about four months before Kaepernick's kneel spread around the nation, Patrick Hruby wrote in *Vice Sports* that though NCAA rules are race-neutral on their face, "in the revenue sports of Division I football and men's basketball, where most of the fan interest and television dollars are, the athletes are disproportionately Black." As neoliberal rationality enriches coaches, administrators, universities, and the advertisers on which they depend, it carves Black athletes out of its circuits, establishing a racialized, two-tiered system in which athletes are expected to dwell, but not gather.

The commercialized symbolic gestures originating from professional athletes like Kaepernick are certainly welcome developments. If sports merchandise makes political arguments, then those arguments leave little with which to quibble. But it is in intercollegiate athletics where Black athletes are becoming increasingly resistant to exploitive commodification. When a regional Labor Relations Board ruled that college football players at Northwestern University qualify as employees under federal guidelines in 2014, Tennessee Senator Lamar Alexander said, "This is an absurd decision that will destroy intercollegiate athletics as we know it" (Farrey 2014). That is the *exact same thing* baseball owners said about Curt Flood, and, I might add, what a slave-owner might have said about abolition's effect on his crops. College sports is where slavery might find redemption as an expression of socioeconomic injustice, and where the ethos of the activist athlete illuminates its beacons once again.

To close the case, I return to Missouri, which reveals, upon close examination, a complex connection between race and labor. In Concerned Students 1950s protests we hear new narratives of racial injustice which, despite being some 50 years removed from Harry Edwards's formative experiences, bespeak "a general lack of understanding of the problems of Afro-Americans by the college administration." These narratives enact double-consciousness's gift for second sight, but the parallax image which comes into view in Missouri is not only Black, *it is at work*, building the institutions which confer the social and economic advantages we now call white privilege. A common protest t-shirt read, "1839 was built on my Black" (Kingkade 2015) a reference to the date on which the University of Missouri was founded, built with the help of slave labor.

Curt Flood was not the first to import the plantation's repugnant social dynamic into the discourse of sport, and Missouri's football team proved he would not be the last. Their promise to strike recognized "the power to be gained from exploiting the white man's economic and almost religious involvement in athletics," as Harry Edwards had put it, and modeled the withholding of unwaged labor as an effective political strategy. Moreover, it is not a strategy confined to situations like Missouri's. The following week, the Georgetown University basketball team concealed the logos on their sneakers with white tape to protest Nike's use of sweatshop labor (Miller 2015). They did not produce results like Missouri's football did, but it was an activist expression derived from a kind of double-consciousness which sees labor as raced.

Nike's sweatshop labor is comprised of poor people of color, of course, a point made eagerly by skeptics of Kaepernick's corporate partnership. The Georgetown basketball players, however, saw that *they* were *also* Nike workers. Covering the swoosh withheld unwaged labor.

Erik Doxtater suggests that "An appreciation of ethos shows that the dissident's challenge involves self-risk. It invites shunning, sanction, and punishment. The communicative transgression of the law places the voice and body of the dissident in danger" (2000: 360). College athletes living under the regulatory regime of the NCAA certainly know this well, but we should not overlook the broader ways in which the ethos of the activist athlete calculates risk. Columbia, MO is not far from Ferguson, where racist violence, we now know, became institutionalized in law enforcement. The threat of a strike exposed athletes not only to that violence, but also to official punishment (such as in the revoking of scholarships), and to the same social forces that see Black labor speaking for itself as ungrateful. That is what baseball said about Curt Flood in 1970 in order to destroy him. And in our contemporary context, where democracy seems generally unreliable, police shoot Black people with impunity, and the President of the United States promotes the kinds of moral equivalences that support the contention that neo-Nazis are "very fine people," unpaid Black university labor, already precarious, courts grave peril in righteous protest. Moreover, intercollegiate athletes seem to be increasingly aware that they are not alone in *confronting* risk. The power to be gained from exploiting the white man's economic and almost religious involvement in athletics meant that the university was in peril as well. Sports agent Don Yee derived a broader lesson from Missouri's strike. As he told Howard Bryant (2018), "The players, I'm telling you, have no idea how much power they really have. If they wanted to, they could take the whole thing down." The ethos of the activist athlete is, above all, a mechanism for discovering, harnessing, and expressing the power to take the whole thing down.

There is, in any case, security, and perhaps even strength, in solidarity. This, ultimately, is why I regard the ethos of the activist athlete as a gathering place. Contrast the Missouri football boycott with what happened at the University of Virginia not long before. In the spring of 2011, a football player at UVA was persuaded in a political science class by members of the living wage campaign to join a hunger strike in support of a wage and benefit increase for the school's custodial staff. He was pressured by coaches to "find a better way of making a difference" (Smith 2012) and warned that his hunger strike was actually an act of selfishness toward his teammates. His name is Joseph Williams, and few people have ever heard of him, despite the fact that his story made the cover of *Sports Illustrated*. But at Missouri in 2015, the gathering included the speech and images of #Blacklivesmatter, the symbolic energy of Ferguson, fresh memories of violence and protest in Charleston, Cleveland, and Baltimore. It also included Jonathan Butler, Concerned Students 1950s' hunger striker. The arrival of the football team heralded the ethos of the activist athlete, its beacon of solidarity reflecting off televisions and smartphone screens with furious urgency.

5 Ethos as a rhetorical resource

In naming the ethos of the activist athlete, I hope that those working at the intersection of race and sport are able to appreciate that the relationship between contemporary athletic protests and those of earlier eras depends on an intergenerational memory, the kind that gives substance to axiom that history never repeats itself, but it does rhyme. As racism is a changing same, so goes opposition to it. The ethos of the activist athlete and its four constituent elements are resources for discovering what binds the past to the present, and for tracing the legacies of resistance that continue to place Black athletes at the center of struggles for social justice. Double-consciousness, risk, solidarity, and poetry are conceptual resources not only for drawing historical connections, but for making sense of how those connections appear within the instruments of public communication. There is no question that new media technologies provide novel means of circulation and organization and that those means accelerate the pace of protest movements. One wonders, for instance, what might have become of the international Black boycott of the 1968 Olympics had Harry Edwards been armed with Twitter. Contemporary acts of athletic protest work through quicker temporalities, a fact which scholars of sport communication might bring to bear on how political consciousness spreads, how risk is embraced and shared, how and with whom solidarities are formed, and what kinds of creative energies are required to generate new publics and modes of publicity. But temporality is not our only path to studying the ethos of the activist athlete. When Black athletes protest today, their speech is neither purely spontaneous nor purely derivative. We might wonder how the shifting routines of journalism alter calculations of risk, or how hiring Black coaches changes the interpersonal communication patterns that give rise to political consciousness, or how athletes' own media consumption habits drive novel forms of allyship, or even how media literacy among young athletes drives their poetic invention. The ethos of the activist athlete is an elastic concept with a variety of heuristic possibilities.

In November 2015, protestors who had mobilized over the police shooting of Jamar Clark *were themselves shot* in Minneapolis, and video of the Chicago police murdering Laquan McDonald saw the light of day after a full year. Nearly five years after the Mizzou protests, a Minneapolis police officer choked the life out of George Floyd. Nearly four years after Kaepernick called attention to bodies in the street, Louisville police shot and killed Breonna Taylor in her own home. So, I don't want to overstate the case. Athletes cannot prevent racist violence with protest speech alone. The police also have to stop killing Black people. But in their communal orientation, the hope is that they offer a source of poetic invention, that they help us, as scholars or activists or those of us who think of ourselves as both, rewrite the scripts that narrate injury and demand redress.

References

Adande, J. A. 2014. Purpose of "I Can't Breathe" t-shirts. *ESPN.com*, 10 December. https://www.espn.com/nba/story/_/id/12010612/nba-stars-making-statement-wearing-breathe-shirts (28 July 2020).

Aikens, Charles. 1971. The struggle of Curt Flood. *The Black Scholar* 3. 10–15.

Belkin, Douglas & Melissa Horn. 2015. University of Missouri system president Tim Wolfe resigns. *Wall Street Journal*, 9 November. http://www.wsj.com/articles/university-of-missouri-system-president-tim-wolfe-resigns-1447086505 (28 July 2020).

Blackistone, Kevin. 2017. Sports are not a sanctuary from racism. They are reflections of society. *Washington Post*, 5 May. https://www.washingtonpost.com/sports/sports-are-not-a-sanctuary-from-racism-they-are-a-reflection-of-society/2017/05/05/d012fbfa-3198-11e7-8674-437ddb6e813e_story.html (28 July 2020).

Boren, Cindy. 2014. Richard Sherman frustrated by reaction, equates "thug" with racial slur. *Washington Post*, 23 January. https://www.washingtonpost.com/news/early-lead/wp/2014/01/23/richard-sherman-frustrated-by-reaction-equates-thug-with-racial-slur/ (28 July 2020).

Boren, Cindy. 2018. When Trump attacked LeBron James, it had an unintended effect: Other athletes speaking out. *Washington Post*, 15 August. https://www.washingtonpost.com/news/early-lead/wp/2018/08/05/when-trump-attacked-lebron-james-it-had-an-unintended-effect-other-athletes-speaking-out/ (28 July 2020).

Branch, Taylor. 2011. The shame of college sports. *The Atlantic*, October. https://www.theatlantic.com/magazine/archive/2011/10/the-shame-of-college-sports/308643/ (28 July 2020).

Bryant, Howard. 2018. *The heritage: Black athletes, a divided America, and the politics of patriotism*. Boston: Beacon Press.

Bumbaca, Chris. 2020. Soccer players wear "Black Lives Matter" kits, kneel at start of games as EPL returns. *USA Today*, 17 June. https://www.usatoday.com/story/sports/soccer/europe/2020/06/17/english-premier-league-soccer-return-black-lives-matter-protest-kneel/3208109001/ (28 July 2020).

Butterworth, Michael L. 2008. Fox sports, Super Bowl XLII, and the affirmation of American civil religion. *Journal of Sport & Social Issues* 32. 318–323.

Butterworth, Michael L. 2016. Sport as rhetorical artifact. In Andrew C. Billings (ed.), *Defining sport communication*, 11–25. New York, Routledge.

Cobb, Jelani. 2018. Behind Nike's decision to stand by Colin Kaepernick. *New Yorker*, 4 September. https://www.newyorker.com/news/daily-comment/behind-nikes-decision-to-stand-by-colin-kaepernick (28 July 2020).

Curtis, Bryan. 2017. Sportswriting has become a liberal profession – Here's how it happened. *The Ringer*, 16 February. https://www.theringer.com/2017/2/16/16042460/how-sportswriting-became-a-liberal-profession-dc7123a5caba (28 July 2020).

Davis, Angela. 2013. Recognizing racism in the era of neoliberalism. https://truthout.org/articles/recognizing-racism-in-the-era-of-neoliberalism/ (29 July 2020).

Doxtader, Eric. 2000. Characters in the middle of public life: Consensus, dissent, and ethos. *Philosophy and Rhetoric* 33. 336–369.

Du Bois, W.E.B. 1903. *The souls of Black folk*. New York: Barnes & Noble Classics.

Edwards, Harry. 1969. *Revolt of the Black athlete*. New York: Free Press.

Farrey, Tom. 2014. NW union reps off to Congress. *ESPN.com*, 31 March. https://www.espn.com/espn/print?id=10695272 (28 July 2020).

Ganim, Sara. 2014. UConn guard on unions: I go to bed "starving." *CNN*, 8 April. https://www.cnn.com/2014/04/07/us/ncaa-basketball-finals-shabazz-napier-hungry/index.html (28 July 2020).

Grano, Daniel A. 2009. Muhammad Ali versus the "modern athlete": On voice in mediated sports culture. *Critical Studies in Media Communication* 26. 191–211.

Halloran, S. Michael. 1982. Aristotle's concept of ethos, or, if not his, someone else's. *Rhetoric Review* 1. 58–63.

Haupert, Michael. 2012. MLB annual salary leaders since 1874. *Society for American Baseball Research*, Fall. https://sabr.org/research/article/mlbs-annual-salary-leaders-since-1874/ (28 July 2020).

Horn, Leslie. 2015. What's going on at the University of Missouri? All your questions, answered. *Deadspin*, 9 November. http://deadspin.com/whats-going-on-at-the-university-of-missouri-all-your-1741447807 (28 July 2020).

Hruby, Patrick. 2016. Four years a student athlete: The racial injustice of big-time college sports. *Vice*, 4 April. https://www.vice.com/en_us/article/ezexjp/four-years-a-student-athlete-the-racial-injustice-of-big-time-college-sports (28 July 2020).

Jackson, Daniel, Filippo Trevisan, Emma Pullen & Michael Silk. 2020. Towards a social justice disposition in communication and sport scholarship. *Communication & Sport* 8. 435–453.

Khan, Abraham I. 2012. *Curt Flood in the media: Baseball, race, and the demise of the activist athlete*. Jackson, MS: University Press of Mississippi.

Khan, Abraham I. 2016. Sport and race: A disciplinary history and exhortation. In Andrew C. Billings (ed.), *Defining sport communication*, 107–120. New York, Routledge.

Kingkade, Tyler. 2015. The incident you have to see to understand why students wanted Mizzou's president to go. *Huffington Post*, 12 November. https://www.huffpost.com/entry/tim-wolfe-homecoming-parade_n_56402cc8e4b0307f2cadea10 (28 July 2020).

Korr, Charles P. 2002. *The end of baseball as we knew it: The players union, 1960–1981*. Champaign, IL: University of Illinois Press.

Lynch, Kieran. 2020. Lewis Hamilton speaks out after kneeling in support of Black Lives Matter movement alongside 11 other drivers. *Daily Mail*, 13 July. https://www.dailymail.co.uk/sport/sportsnews/article-8514737/Lewis-Hamilton-kneels-support-Black-Lives-Matter-movement-alongside-11-drivers.html (28 July 2020).

Markazi, Arash. 2014. Clippers stage silent protest. *ESPN.com*, 27 April. https://www.espn.com/los-angeles/nba/story/_/id/10848577/los-angeles-clippers-stage-silent-protest-donald-sterling-hide-team-logo (28 July 2020).

Martin, Brian. 2016. Power rankings: Inspiration from the greatest. *WNBA.com*, 7 June. https://www.wnba.com/news/power-rankings-060716/ (10 November 2020).

Miller, Ryan. 2015. Student-athletes cover up Nike logo on university-provided equipment. *Georgetown Voice*, 11 November. http://georgetownvoice.com/2015/11/11/student-athletes-cover-up-nike-logo-on-university-provided-equipment/ (11 November 2020).

Posnanski, Joe. 2012. The forgotten story of Peter Norman. *Sports on Earth*, 27 August. http://www.sportsonearth.com/article/36921250/the-forgotten-story-of-australian-olympian-peter-norman (28 July 2020).

Reynolds, Nedra. 1993. Ethos as location: New sites for understanding discourse. *Rhetoric Review* 11. 325–338.

Rhoden, William C. 2006. *$40 million slaves: The rise, fall, and redemption of the Black athlete*. New York: Crown.

Rosenthal, Gregg. 2010. Saban Compares NFL agents to pimps. *NBC Sports*, 22 July. https://profootballtalk.nbcsports.com/2010/07/22/saban-compares-nfl-agents-to-pimps/ (28 July 2020).

Smith, Gary. 2012. Why don't more athletes take a stand? *Sports Illustrated*, 9 July. http://www.si.com/vault/2015/07/10/106211227/why-dont-more-athletes-take-a-stand (28 July 2020).

Smith, Stephen A. 2008. Remembering when Olympians had the guts to speak up. *ESPN.com*, 15 July. http://sports.espn.go.com/espnmag/story?id=3487980 (28 July 2020).

Snyder, Brad. 2006. *A well-paid slave*. New York: Viking.
Son, Covey & Aamer Madhani. 2015. Missouri president, chancellor quit after football team walks out. *USA Today*, 10 November. http://www.usatoday.com/story/news/2015/11/09/mizzou-faculty-walks-out-student-association-calls-presidents-removal/75448392/ (28 July 2020).
Warner, Michael. 2002. *Publics and counterpublics*. New York: Zone Books.
White, Stephen K. 2009. *The ethos of a late-modern citizen*. Cambridge, MA: Harvard UP.
Williams, Mará. 2015. University of Missouri system president says he handled protests poorly. *Kansas City Star*, 6 November. https://www.kansascity.com/news/politics-government/article43438974.html (28 July 2020).
Wright, Branson. 2012. Remembering Cleveland's Muhammad Ali summit, 45 years later. *Cleveland.com*, 3 June. http://www.cleveland.com/sports/index.ssf/2012/06/gathering_of_stars.html (28 July 2020).
Zirin, Dave. 2012. After forty years, it's time Brent Musburger apologized to John Carlos and Tommie Smith. *The Nation*, 4 June. http://www.thenation.com/article/after-forty-four-years-its-time-brent-musburger-apologized-john-carlos-and-tommie-smith/ (28 July 2020).

Daniel A. Grano

10 Forgivable blackness: Jack Johnson and the politics of presidential clemency

Abstract: In 2018, President Donald Trump pardoned Jack Johnson, the first black heavyweight boxing champion in history, for a conviction in 1913 under the Mann Act. The pardon came after Barack Obama, the first Black president in US history, had declined previous clemency petitions on behalf of the fighter. This chapter demonstrates how Obama's refusal and Trump's approval mark differences in privilege and propriety that constitute public forgiveness as both conditional and racialized. I analyze how the Johnson pardon represents interdependencies between black violation and white institutional redemption that are both produced within, and contestable through, sport.

Keywords: forgiveness; presidential pardon; race; respectability politics; boxing; Donald Trump

1 Introduction

Jack Johnson, the first black heavyweight boxing champion in history, successfully defended his title against a white challenger, Frank Moran, in Paris in 1914. In the August 1914 issue of *The Crisis* magazine, the official publication of the National Association for the Advancement of Colored People (NAACP), W. E. B. DuBois contextualized the "shivery horror" with which the white press in the US had received news of Johnson's victory (1914: 181). Boxing had "fallen into disfavor," DuBois argued, because of Johnson's blackness:

> The cause is clear: Jack Johnson ... has out-sparred an Irishman. He did it with little brutality, the utmost fairness and great good nature. He did not "knock" his opponent senseless. Apparently he did not even try ... Why then this thrill of national disgust? Because Johnson is black. Of course, some pretend to object to Mr. Johnson's character. But we have yet to hear, in the case of white America, that marital troubles have disqualified prize fighters or ball players or even statesmen. It comes down, then, after all to this unforgivable blackness (1914: 181–182).

Here DuBois identifies the two general historical bases for Johnson's "unforgivability": his effortless dominance of white fighters, and his sexual relationships with white women. Both of these "offenses" led to Johnson's conviction in 1913 under the White Slave Traffic Act (more commonly known as the Mann Act) for transporting a white woman across state lines. The conviction is widely regarded today as a racist miscarriage of justice, a belief that generated support for a presidential pardon beginning in the early 21st century.

https://doi.org/10.1515/9783110660883-010

In 2004, the celebrated documentary filmmaker Ken Burns helped to form the Committee to Pardon Jack Johnson (referred to hereafter as the Committee), along with a bipartisan group of politicians from the US Senate and House of Representatives, as well as several prominent boxers and entertainers. DuBois's "unforgivable blackness" framework figured prominently in the Committee's efforts. Burns directed and produced a documentary titled *Unforgivable Blackness* for release on PBS in 2005 (Schaye, Barnes, and Burns 2005). This was a companion film to Geoffrey C. Ward's book *Unforgivable Blackness: The Rise and Fall of Jack Johnson*, praised widely as the definitive Johnson biography (2004). The Committee filed its first petition for a pardon in 2004 during President George W. Bush's administration but failed to persuade officials to act. The Committee also failed in efforts with President Barack Obama's administration in 2009 and 2013, before ultimately succeeding with President Donald Trump in 2018.

How, then, did one of history's great antiracist icons come to be pardoned not by America's first Black president, but by Trump, a racist who made his political career on appeals to white nationalism, xenophobia, and a "law and order" platform? The answer lies, I argue, in differences of racial privilege and propriety inherent to acts of public forgiveness in both sporting and political contexts. Accordingly, I demonstrate how the Johnson pardon dramatizes an interdependency between black violation and white institutional redemption that is both produced within, and contestable through, sport.

This essay analyzes the problems of Johnson's forgivability within a rhetorical framework. Michael Butterworth notes that a rhetorical approach to communication and sport accounts for how symbolic actions exert influence in public, democratic contexts, where meanings are contingent and thus subject to contestation and change. Rhetoric is engaged, then, with problems of political struggle, and brings to light the inherently political character of sport (Butterworth 2017: 11–13). Rhetoric engages with politics or "the political" in at least two important ways. First, it recognizes *as political* a broad range of sport cultural activities, from the obvious examples of athlete-activism to the most mundane institutional routines. Second, it frames sport as a site for consequential action, where communication practices constitute notions of value, order, and identity that shape possibilities for broader social change (Grano and Butterworth 2019).

Rhetorical critics assume that meaning takes shape through interrelationships between texts and contexts. My approach to the Johnson case is rhetorical insofar as I analyze how terms for Johnson's forgiveness were established through the production of public texts – news reports, White House ceremonies, legal decisions – and how these terms became influential within particular cultural and historical moments. By focusing on text-in-context relationships, communication and sport scholars can closely read the practices composing a specific case of sport cultural production while simultaneously accounting for the broader modes of cultural production that the case represents. This is, as Butterworth and I argue, one of the basic aims of rhetorical analyses of sport: to demonstrate how a multitude of social forces (in the Johnson case, for example, clemency, celebrity culture, respectability politics) "take *particular shape* within, through, and around sport," so we can better appreciate how sport constitutes distinctive formations of power that influence the broader culture (Grano and Butterworth 2019: 11).

I support my argument in four parts. First, I provide a brief summary of Johnson's career, with a specific focus on the racial politics of offense and forgivability that he has come to represent. Second, I critique the Obama administration's refusal to pardon Johnson through the lens of respectability politics. Third, I analyze the politics of Trump's pardon in contradistinction to Obama's refusal, situating the act within Trump's record of appropriating sport for reputational and racially opportunistic ends. Finally, I consider how confrontational athlete-activism and politicized sport journalism represent the capacity to resist the authority of public forgiveness within sport.

2 Jack Johnson's unforgivable legacy

Full histories of Johnson's career are available elsewhere (Runstedtler 2012; Hietala 2004; Ward 2004) so I will not offer a detailed biography. My focus will be more precisely on the events and images that have constituted Johnson's "unforgivable blackness" as a problem for contemporary pardoning efforts. Johnson won the heavyweight title in 1908 when he beat Tommy Burns in Australia, but the victory that made him an antiracist and civil rights icon, despite Johnson's own hesitations to identify with these struggles (Teresa 2017: 250), came in the 1910 "Fight of the Century" against James Jeffries. Jeffries was a beloved former heavyweight champion who retired from boxing with an undefeated record in 1905. In retirement Jeffries remained a mythic representation of white masculine power (Young 2010: 95) and all eyes turned immediately to him after Burns fell.

Johnson defeated the heavily favored Jeffries easily, bruising him for 15 rounds before the referee awarded him a knockout. In the aftermath of Johnson's victory, racial violence broke out across the United States (Hietala 2004: 39–47). Theatres were pressured to suppress the Johnson–Jeffries fight film, as images of Johnson's domination were deemed too dangerous for public circulation (Vogan 2010: 400–406). Black newspapers, which had covered Johnson as a representation of collective black identity and aspiration (Young 2010: 93–95), celebrated the Jeffries victory as a positive "reflection on the race itself" (Teresa 2015: 29). For many whites, conversely, Jeffries's fall exploded the mythologies of white superiority popularly invested in his body (Young 2010: 97–98).

So, the first historical basis for Johnson's "unforgivable blackness" comes from his role in establishing prizefighting as a stage for black countercultural politics. As heavyweight champion, Johnson held a title that, as Phillip Hutchison writes, had come to represent "tenuous discourses of whiteness, civilization, and masculinity" (2014: 233). Successful black boxers threatened turn-of-the-century social and scientific theories that posited black fighters as deferent, while representing the white male body as the evolutionary product of the fittest human traits (Alderman, Inwood, and Tyner 2018: 229). Theresa Runstedtler situates Johnson as a particular threat to white insecurities over civilizational ascendancy and social control expressed in late 19th-century imperialism and early 20th-century racial segregation. Boxing seemed an ideal setting for addressing these insecurities through direct, racialized competition, but became instead a stage for disproving supremacist claims at the level of mass consumer spectacle (2012: 5–7, 18–22, 32–33). Johnson established himself on this stage as a uniquely brash, arrogant, dominant black man.

The second historical basis for Johnson's "unforgivable blackness" comes from his relationships with white women and the related series of events that led to his conviction under the Mann Act. Specifically, the suicide of Johnson's wife Etta Duryea in September 1912 and his subsequent marriage to Lucille Cameron less than three months later intensified public anger over Johnson's personal life and mobilized efforts to have him criminally prosecuted (Gilmore 1973: 18–19). Duryea, a well-educated socialite from a wealthy family, was credited as an "elegant" public and personal presence in Johnson's life, but their relationship was turbulent. In December 1910, Johnson beat Duryea over suspicions she was having an affair, and she had to be hospitalized (Ward 2004: 176–180, 251–254). The couple reconciled and married weeks later, but Duryea's struggles with depression, Johnson's infidelity and abusiveness, and isolation from her family and friends all contributed to her suicide.

Weeks after Duryea's funeral, Johnson showed up with Cameron, a young white prostitute, on his arm at his popular Chicago night club the Café de Champion. Alarmed by the relationship, Cameron's mother accused Johnson of abducting Lucille and subjecting her to his "hypnotic powers." At the time, there was a growing national panic over white women being coerced into prostitution (or "white slavery") by immigrant-run underground trafficking rings. James Robert Mann, a Republican Congressman from Illinois, had drafted the "White Slave Traffic Act" (or Mann Act) in 1909 to prohibit the interstate or foreign transportation of women for the purposes of "debauchery," prostitution, or "any other immoral purposes"; the law went into effect in 1910, shortly before the Fight of the Century (Ward 2004: 296–305; Gilmore 1973: 18–19).

The effort to convict Johnson for abducting Cameron failed, mainly because Lucille emphatically denied the charges. A second effort succeeded, however, as the federal government leveraged the vague language of the Mann Act to charge Johnson for travelling across state lines with Belle Schrieber, a white prostitute with whom he had a romantic relationship. The government convicted Johnson in May 1913 and sentenced him to one year in prison (Teresa 2017: 251–252). Johnson fled the country and lived in exile in Europe and the Americas before surrendering to US authorities in 1920 (Runstedtler 2012: 2).

3 Pardoning rhetoric and problems of public forgiveness

The pardon clause of the Constitution, which appears in Article II, section 2, provides the president the power "to grant reprieves and pardons for offenses against the United States." Pardons are just one of five total forms of executive clemency. The two most common forms granted today are a full pardon, which provides broad remission (lifting both the penalty and the legal stigma behind the offense) and a commutation, which reduces the offender's sentence. The other three forms – remittance, reprieve, and amnesty – are less common. The Constitution limits pardons to federal crimes and does not allow them in cases of impeachment. Otherwise, "the presidential pardon power is – on its face – unlimited" (Crouch 2009: 9, 20). One implication of this unfettered power is an investment of considerable rhetorical authority over clemency and the public good in the institution of the presidency. Presidents must seek an opportune moment to grant a pardon, and they typically provide some level of public justification, but pardons are most commonly cast "in the rhetoric of assertion and declaration." In pardoning, presidents claim the authority to enact mercy under "special circumstances," on behalf of worthy candidates, and for the advancement of collective values (Campbell and Jamieson 1990: 169–174). These are all importantly *conditional* powers, calculated around normative notions of offense and worthiness.

Jacques Derrida insists that forgiveness can only occur between two unique "singularities" – the guilty and the victim, otherwise the right to forgive becomes transferred to a "tertiary institution" and appropriated to political ends (2001: 31–45). These ends might include calls for closure that release governments or organizations from their responsibilities to address past injustices, or (as in the case of pardoning) moral authorizations for state authority (Derrida 2001: 31–39, 59; Ricoeur 2004: 488; Doxtader 2004: 383–384). These problems are evident in the Department of Justice pardon guidelines, which characterize a presidential pardon as "a sign of forgiveness" granted by officials who determine that applicants have accepted responsibility and demonstrated "remorse" and "atonement" (DOJ 2018). For prospective applicants the most important questions surround how officials in a particular administration establish standards for remorse or atonement, and according to what relevant social norms. In the Johnson case, these standards took shape around the overlapping interests of sporting and political institutions and their interrelated capacities to police black masculinity.

Sport serves as a context for the repetitive display of black, male offense and white institutional authority over forgiveness. This is due primarily to the construction of black male athletes as criminal types "naturally" prone to dispositional instability, and thus dependent upon the disciplinary structures of institutions (e. g., teams, leagues, the criminal justice system, or in this case, the presidency) as mechanisms for restoring public status (Grano 2014, 2010). League officials may coordinate elaborate public forgiveness campaigns around processes of surveillance, therapeutic intervention, and confession aimed at testing and displaying the "genuine remorse" of offending black, male athletes, but only when such campaigns represent the interests of their organizations (e.g., labor production, image restoration) (Grano 2014). In these ways forgiveness reinforces popular investments in sport as an institution that both pathologizes and disciplines blackness in order to reinstate the controls of a white, patriarchal, and commercial order (Griffin and Calafell 2011; Enck-Wanzer 2009; Dickinson and Anderson 2004).

In the Johnson case, the pardon power encapsulated the authority to forgive vested in both sporting and political institutions, and their overlapping capacities to enforce a racialized social order. This was especially evident because of the dramatic differences in how Obama and Trump approached clemency in general, and Johnson in particular. Trump's disregard for precedent, and his right to ignore the politics of respectability – as irrelevant to both his race and to his political brand – left him unencumbered. For Obama, conversely, the politics of respectability were more binding, both inherent to his political brand and especially applicable to a figure like Johnson.

4 Obama declines: forgiveness and respectability politics

In April 2009 John McCain, Republican Senator of Arizona, and Peter King, Republican Representative of New York, introduced a resolution requesting a pardon for Johnson. McCain expressed confidence that Obama, the first Black president in US history, would be "the last person" he would have to convince about Johnson's case. King added that it would be historically significant "to have the first African-American president granting a pardon to the first African-American heavyweight champion" (Frommer 2009a) and that the act would finally "remove a cloud that has been over the American sporting scene" (McCain seeks 2009). Congress approved the resolution in July 2009 (Congress seeking 2009). In December 2009, however, the Justice Department issued a letter to McCain and King informing them that it was general policy to not process posthumous pardon requests, so that resources could be reserved for individuals who could "truly benefit" from clemency (Associated Press 2009).

King and McCain responded by insisting that a pardon was necessary for rectifying the past and restoring Johnson's damaged reputation. In a letter back to the Justice Department they wrote that "a posthumous pardon would represent a final vindication to Mr. Johnson's family and to the ignominious stain on our nation's history" (Frommer 2009b). After another resolution filed in 2013 went unanswered, McCain wondered again at the president's refusal to "correct history" (Washington 2016). Journalists similarly lamented the lost opportunity of Obama's corrective agency. William C. Rhoden noted in *The New York Times* that when Obama took office, many hoped

Johnson had finally gained "an ally in the White House"; instead, Obama's inaction represented the nation's general "reluctance to look back, to do the work" of fixing America's racist foundations (2015).

Posthumous pardons are very rare. Johnson would be only the third person posthumously pardoned in US history, and the other two cases were recent (Clinton in 1999, and Bush in 2008) (Korte 2018). In addition, Obama's acts of clemency were focused less on pardons than on commutations of prison sentences, part of his administration's larger effort to address the injustices of mass incarceration. By the end of his second term, Obama had commuted more prison sentences (1,715 in total) than any president in history; this included 330 commutations for nonviolent drug offenders on his last full day of office in 2017 (Smart 2017). As Kevin Blackistone argued, Obama's focus on the present was more consequential for problems of racial injustice than the ceremonial historical cleansing that a pardon for Johnson would have performed (2018).

Yet Obama's focus on commutation did not necessarily preclude consideration of a pardon for Johnson, and some observers wondered about a connection between his refusal and the politics of respectability. One reason for this suspicion was the centrality of respectability to Obama's political career. Commonly traced to the work of Evelyn Brooks Higginbotham, respectability emphasizes Black peoples' conformity to and assimilation of dominant society's racial norms as a pathway to self-improvement and as an accommodationist approach to reforming American race relations (1993: 187, 197). As Frederick Harris argues, respectability serves the politics of neoliberalism in the 21st century – the idea that "virtues of self-care and self-correction" will lift up poor, black Americans by helping them to operate strategically in a market economy. This idea was especially powerful in the Obama era, as Obama himself relied often upon respectability appeals in speeches that called upon black listeners to be "honest" with themselves and to take responsibility for "stalling their own progress" (2014: 33–37). While authors have traced a gradual disappearance of respectability from Obama's rhetoric in the latter part of his presidency (Coates 2017) the idea remains associated with his presidency and was on the minds of journalists pondering Johnson's chances at a pardon.

In a piece for *The Undefeated*, Jesse Washington opined that Johnson's "moral character" would likely preclude a pardon from Obama. Johnson, after all, "was no Jackie Robinson": "As heavyweight champ from 1908 to 1915, the most famous black man in America loved fast cars, white women, flashy jewelry and racy nightclubs. He taunted, gloated, and lived by his own rules" (2016). Washington's reference to Robinson is illustrative. As Abraham Khan argues, Robinson has long served as an icon for racial respectability and integration within and beyond sport (2017: 331–351; 2012: 55–86). In offering Johnson as the antithesis to Robinson's mythologized image, Washington points to the difficulties of pardoning a figure who does not fit within the white hegemony of sport and race progress narratives. Indeed, Johnson's historical importance is tied to his status as an anti-respectability figure. He brazenly defied the boundaries established in the early decades of Jim Crow, driving expensive cars through white neighborhoods and appearing in public with his white girlfriends and wives (Hutchison 2014: 233). He self-consciously played upon the fears and insecurities of whites, characterizing his boxing dominance as an inversion of master/slave relations (Young 2010: 95–99). Gerald Early claims Johnson as "an early prototype of the New Negro" (1991: 25), a trope associated historically with a new capacity to see and depict an image of *modern* blackness that displaces the caricatured figures of white supremacy and Jim Crow paternalism (Watts 2002: 25).

This was not the image of Johnson put forward by the Committee. Rather, the Committee's case for a pardon rest on what Carrie Teresa characterizes as a "white-washed" version of Johnson's legacy. Modern revisions of the Johnson story have cast Johnson as humble and passive in order to appeal to white sympathies, and have erased his history of womanizing and domestic violence (2017: 255–256). Outside of a brief "renaissance" during the 1960 and 1970s – when the Black Power movement and Muhammad Ali's career temporarily revived his legacy – Johnson had largely disappeared from public memory. It took a celebrated white documentarian like Burns to bring Johnson back into the American public consciousness (Runstedtler 2012: 2–3), and Burns insisted upon de-racializing the pardon effort, arguing that it was about "justice, which is not only blind, but color-blind" (Frommer 2009a). As Khan argues, respectability commonly underwrites narratives of racial progress in sport, reducing the unique racial and sexual contradictions embodied by a given athlete to generic images of inclusivity and redemption (2017: 333). The Committee needed this respectable, whitewashed version of Johnson both to meet the conditional demands of presidential forgiveness, and to advance their narrative of historical repair.

The broader complexity of Johnson's anti-respectability would, conversely, complicate the Committee's official narrative. As Runstedtler argued, the practical possibility and social importance of a pardon both turned on a basic interconnection between respectability and selective memory. Runstedtler wrote that while Johnson clearly deserved a pardon, she was concerned the motives behind the campaign – the *correction* of history as McCain and others had stated – would foster celebrations of American post-racialism and colorblindness (2013). To meaningfully embrace Johnson's legacy would require acknowledging him as a leading figure in an emerging black, subcultural expression of "New Negro masculinity" that "embraced conspicuous consumption and outspoken bravado" as means for combating dehumanization and exploitation. This was, Runstedtler continues, "the hip-hop culture of its day, widely associated with black criminality and black masculine pathology," and "much like hip-hop today," it was condemned for its lack of respectability both by whites and by some in the black middle class (2013).

Teresa notes that the African American newspapers that covered Johnson had redefined their institutional missions around "the importance of racial progress, pride, and uplift as ... components in the fight for civil rights." These papers largely depicted Johnson as a source of racial pride throughout his boxing career, but as his personal and legal troubles eclipsed his accomplishments in the ring, "black journalists began to re-evaluate Johnson's role as a positive representative for the community." Cameron was a particular source of anger, as journalists claimed that Johnson's relationship with such a "fallen girl" violated the decorum of "sensible colored men" and would be used by white audiences to condemn "the entire colored race" (2015: 24–37). Booker T. Washington – an advocate for black advancement through accommodation and entrepreneurialism – argued similarly that Johnson's legal troubles represented "the almost irreparable injury that a wrong action on the part of a single individual may do to a whole race" (1982: 43–44).

For black authors and public figures invested in respectability, then, Johnson has historically represented problems for forgivability bound up in debates over collective representation and personal comportment. Runstedtler predicted that Johnson's connections to an "underground culture that was outside the lines of respectability" would make a pardon from Obama impossible; Johnson was difficult to narrate "into a clean-cut story of racial uplift and respectability," the very framework that Obama had "banked his whole career on" (Washington 2016). Whatever the ultimate basis for Obama's decision to not pardon Johnson, popular suspicions about the role of respectability brought to light the inequitable privileges of forgiveness for black and white institutional authorities, a reality that became all the more evident as popular focus shifted from the disappointment of Obama's inaction, to the surprise of Trump's approval.

5 Trump approves: forgiveness as a political weapon

In March 2017, two months into the Trump presidency, McCain and King, along with Democratic Senator Corey Booker of New Jersey and Democratic Representative Gregory Meeks of New York, reintroduced a resolution urging a posthumous pardon for Johnson (States News Service 2017). Trump announced on Twitter roughly a year later, in April 2018, that he was considering a pardon, but not in response to the resolution:

> Sylvester Stallone called me with the story of heavyweight boxing champion Jack Johnson. His trials and tribulations were great, his life complex and controversial. Others have looked at this over the years, most thought it would be done, but yes, I am considering a Full Pardon! (Trump 2018)

The tweet summarized at least two patterns behind Trump's pardons: he was influenced significantly by the recommendations of celebrities; and he viewed pardons as ways to settle political scores or goad opponents (as became apparent eventually, "others" likely referred to Obama). Stallone became a Hollywood star after his 1976 film *Rocky* started a commercially successful franchise. Stallone based that film – which tells the fictional story of Rocky Balboa, a white boxer who gets an unlikely chance to challenge the black heavyweight champion of the world Apollo Creed – on a 1975 fight between Muhammad Ali and Chuck Wepner. Ali said about the ending of *Rocky II* (where Rocky defeats Creed in a rematch) "I have been so great in boxing they had to create an image like Rocky, a white image on the screen, to counteract my image in the ring" (Ebert 1979). Thus, Stallone mediated the effort to pardon Johnson through an iconic representation of boxing's racial hopefulness: the idea that a white underdog can overcome a physiologically superior black man, and then (as happens in the later movies) form an affectionate bond with him.

Johnson's great-niece Linda Haywood, who had campaigned for years for a pardon, was surprised by the president's tweet. She and Burns both expressed hope that there might finally be an official act of clemency. Posthumous pardons had been the main barrier to previous efforts, but Trump had already proven a disregard for precedent (Andrews 2018). Applications for clemency are typically screened by the Office of the Pardon Attorney in the Department of Justice (Crouch 2009: 21) but Trump bypassed that system, ignoring thousands of applications sitting with the pardon attorney in favor of cases brought to his attention by celebrities and conservative news media, cases related to his past endeavors in the private sector and reality television, cases where he could help political allies, and cases where he felt a shared sense of grievance with the individual (Baker 2018; Cillizza 2018; Blake 2019).

Journalists at *The Washington Post* argued that for Trump, who came to the presidency expecting to wield the kind of "monarchical" power he had grown accustomed to in running his own company, the pardon power held a "special resonance ... representing the one area where he [had] almost unchecked power ..." (Costa, Dawsey, and Parker 2018). That power made it possible for Trump to treat the pardon as "an everyday tool of the culture war," operating (as he had in other abuses of executive authority) within the strict legal limits of his power but outside the boundaries of propriety (Graham 2018).

A pardon for Johnson would provide an opportunity to apply this newfound power to sport, a context where, Thomas Oates and Kyle Kusz write, Trump had long worked to cultivate his "identity as a dominant white male figure." In 1983, for example, Trump purchased a majority share of the United States Football League (USFL) franchise The New Jersey Generals. In 1985 (after the USFL went under) he began a series of investments in combat sports promotions, including boxing, professional wrestling, and mixed martial arts (MMA). Both football and combat sports allowed Trump to associate himself with hypermasculine, violent figures, and to "publicly exercise control over the bodies of people of color, a hallmark of his later political appeal" (Oates and Kusz 2019: 208–212).

During his 2016 presidential campaign Trump recruited dominant white, male sports figures as surrogates who reinforced his promises to "re-center white masculinity in American socio-cultural life" (Oates and Kusz 2019: 213–214). David Andrews notes that Trump relied consistently upon sport as a foil for the "nostalgic masculinism" and whiteness of his campaign slogan "Make America Great Again." Trump paralleled the supposed "softness" of modern-day football to a more general feminization of American society and approached sporting issues from the perspective of an "indignant fan," using sport to depict a nation in crisis needful of his restorative populism (2019: 119–121).

As president, Trump continues to capitalize upon sport as a context for advancing the nostalgic, white nationalist politics of his campaign. While other presidents have certainly leveraged sport as a context for militant patriotism and nationalist appeals (Butterworth 2005, 2007, 2010, 2019), Trump has been uniquely preoccupied with athletes and sport-related conflicts. Best known are his responses to the national anthem kneeling protests started by former National Football League (NFL) quarterback Colin Kaepernick, particularly his infamous direction of a misogynistic slur toward protesting NFL players at a 2017 rally (Serwer 2017). Complaints about championship teams refusing to visit the White House, or criticisms of athlete-activism, allow Trump to weaponize patriotism (Lockhart 2018) in narratives about a lost white cultural order, to play the role of a dominant white leader reminding "arrogant young millionaires" about the supposed illegitimacy of their case for social justice (Fox News Insider 2017).

As a counterpart to the open, seething grievance represented in anti-activist criticism, clemency allowed Trump to exercise the privileges of selective forgiveness through the language of historical redemption and postracial healing. Trump presided over the pardoning ceremony in the Oval Office on May 24, 2018. In his official statement, he said, "I've issued an executive grant of clemency, a full pardon, posthumously, to John Arthur 'Jack' Johnson," a "truly great fighter" who was treated in the case of the Mann Act conviction "very, very rough." Trump characterized his action in line with the Committee's claims about historical and reputational repair: "I am taking this very righteous step ... to correct a wrong that occurred in our history" and to honor a historically consequential black athlete who was "treated unfairly as a human being and unfairly as a champion." Though different in tone, the pardon still served as a reminder of Trump's desired dominion over black status, an extension of his long-standing efforts at dominance in sport now actualized through the power of the presidency.

Celebrity influence is a particularly telling expression of that dominance, as it simultaneously illustrates the constitutive influence of elite power interests over forgivability *and* the potential arbitrariness of its determinations in the person of an institutional authority. John Ziegler argued that Trump's sole regard for the "rich and/or famous" aligned pardoning with a cultural condition where it was "*far* more important to have a celebrity take up your cause than for your cause to be just ..." (2018). The corruptibility of the power, and its broader racialized and conditional character, were evident in Trump's selection of only those cases of racial injustice brought to his attention through the circuits of fame, celebrity, and popular culture – spaces where he had established personal and economic interests.

Aside from the official pardoning statement, the Oval Office ceremony proceeded as a series of affectionate exchanges between Trump and the celebrities assembled around him. Stallone was present, as were the current heavyweight champion of the world Deontay Wilder, and the former heavyweight champion Lennox Lewis. Trump referred to Stallone as "my friend for a long time." He jokingly asked Lewis "if I really ... started working out, could I take Deontay in a fight?" (*The New York Times* 2018). Trump had long connected himself with sporting figures to enhance his own (insecure) masculine image (Oates and Kusz 2019). The approval of two dominant Black fighters provided him the benefits of "Black friends" commonly claimed by white men – supplemental coolness, colorblind bona fides. Just as important, their physical presence suggested that Trump could, as president, *summon* Black bodies to participate in engineered political spectacles, a process that played out in other episodes such as a bizarre and widely covered 2018 Oval Office visit from the rapper Kanye West and the Hall of Fame running back Jim Brown (Wolf 2018).

Trump's abuses of the clemency power did little to devalue the meaningfulness of the Johnson pardon, at least within the space of the Oval Office ceremony. Each participant spoke to prevailing popular associations between pardons and absolution, lending credence to Trump's power through deferential statements of thanks and admiration. Lewis cited Johnson as a "great inspiration" and told Trump "everyone will thank you, and I'll thank you" for an action that would be felt around the world. Haywood expressed relief that clemency had come at last, as her family had been "deeply ashamed" about her uncle's conviction. "The most important person that decided to do this," she continued, "is sitting here ... President Trump. ... I appreciate you rewriting history" (*New York Times* 2018). These affirmations of the president's official authority over Johnson's status, articulated by a black former heavyweight champion and a black blood relative, lent credence to presumed *necessity* of executive clemency for purging experiences of personal shame and public condemnation, even for convictions recognized in retrospect as racist and illegitimate.

Mary Stuckey argues that pardons offer presidents the means to distinguish themselves from predecessors, establishing their own "rhetorical legitimacy" in contradistinction to the actions of previous administrations (1992: 28). As with the pardon power more generally, Trump weaponized this process. Prior to his official pardoning statement, Trump noted that Congress had supported multiple resolutions calling for Johnson's pardon, and claimed that the Congressional Black Caucus supported the measure enthusiastically. Yet "the last administration" had let everyone down, an action he was there to correct (*New York Times* 2018). Hours before the pardon ceremony, Trump appeared on Fox News and said that NFL players who refused to stand for the national anthem "maybe ... shouldn't be in the country" (Eligon and Shear 2018). Shortly after he was in the Oval Office mocking Obama as an impotent failure to his own race for refusing to pardon one of history's most controversial black athletes. Qasim Rashid identified this hypocrisy as basic to the racialized, conditional character of Trump's clemency: "Jack Johnson is a reminder that Black athletes are free to protest racial injustices in America as long as they have already died" (2018). What Trump's pardon displayed, above all else, was the raw authority of white institutional forgiveness: the right to bypass procedure, disregard norms, openly ridicule political opponents, and *still* act upon history in a way deemed by at least some representatives of the forgiven as both legitimate and necessary.

Yet in goading Obama, Trump also made the racial politics of his clemency obvious. Washington noted that "[e]xonerating Johnson would have opened Obama up to racial repercussions unique to the first black president," particularly due to the politics of respectability and the standard that "holds African-Americans accountable for all black sins ..." (2018b). Trump, of course, had no such concerns. In fact, a pardon represented considerable upside: he could offer a mostly symbolic (posthumous) gesture that reinforced familiar sport and race progress narratives, while also leaving in place (unlike Obama's commutation decisions) the systems for criminalizing and punishing Blackness that he had promised his supporters he would uphold. In addition, Trump's history of sexual assault allegations, hush money payments to mistresses, and other offenses are largely "baked into" his popular support (Bruni 2019), effectively relieving pressure to consider Johnson's infidelity or abusiveness on either political or personal grounds. As Washington argued, it should have come as no surprise that it took a white president, one himself accused of sexual misconduct, to pardon "the first black heavyweight champion ... for having sex with white women" (Washington 2018a, 2018b).

As a figure unconcerned with the pieties traditionally associated with his office, Trump was uniquely positioned to suspend the ordinary standards for historical and legal precedent surrounding the pardon power. Trump also represented how white forgivers can constitute the politics of respectability – which had previously blocked Johnson's case – as conditionally irrelevant. Even so, the Johnson pardon drew popular attention to the racialized conditions of public forgiveness, and generated confrontations over problems of respectability associated with the re-emergence of athlete-activism and the increasing politicization of sport journalism in the Trump era. I conclude by considering how these confrontations might challenge frameworks for forgivable blackness.

6 Confronting public forgiveness and sport in the Trump era

The current revival of athlete-activism brings back to the surface long-standing discussions in sport and civil rights circles about respectability versus radicalism as approaches to change (Bryant 2018: 47). Insofar as sport culture conflates respectability and forgivability, these debates may prove particularly relevant for addressing and critiquing standards for forgivable blackness. Black athletes increasingly cite respectability as a basis for integrationist versus resistive activism (Starr 2018) and those athletes who advocate for anti-respectability approaches represent, in my estimation, the most productive and directly relevant counterargument to conditional public forgiveness.

We might consider this potential within the context of what Khan cites as the growth of "confrontational rhetoric" among athlete-activists in the Trump era. Khan argues that athletes' confrontational rhetoric represents the "threat" of "exposing the truth," of "revealing that which mystifies a clear understanding of the order of things." When Trump condemns black athletes, he obscures truth and reveals nothing more than the capacity to exercise raw power. By way of contrast, activist athletes "practice a confrontational rhetoric, clarifying the social divisions that impede our moral progress, inviting us into a view of exploitation and injustice" (2019: 30, 35; see also Scott and Smith 1969). Trump's dependency upon sport as a site for engendering white grievance has produced extended social media exchanges with black athletes, and while these exchanges allow the president opportunities to delight his supporters by goading "arrogant," wealthy black men they also provide athletes opportunities to criticize Trump as racist, unfit for office, and all bluster (Reid 2017), the final charge issuing a direct blow to the soft, insecure underbelly of Trump's sport-supplemented machismo. So, as Trump appropriates sport he invites, as Khan suggests, the "threat" of athletes' confrontational rhetoric: the capacity to reveal truths that authority figures would prefer to hide (2019: 30).

In addition to athlete-activism, sport and news journalism may also prove essential to challenging the racialized authority of public forgiveness. In fact, some of the most direct attacks on the legitimacy of the Johnson pardon came from journalists and commentators with extensive backgrounds on problems of race and sport. Harry Edwards, for example, pointed to the "abject fraud" at the center of Trump's pardon. Pardons are for criminals, and the only "crimes" Johnson committed were "arrogance" and "audacity"; the government owed Johnson an *apology*, and an unconditional expunging of the "slander" of his conviction "from official records" (2018). Dave Zirin argued similarly that a pardon would do little more than reflect the "hollow conceit" of claims to postracial healing that divert attention from ongoing systemic racism, anti-immigrant sentiment, and Islamophobia – the tactics of white grievance that many of Johnson's presumed forgivers benefit from politically (2017). As sportswriting becomes a more "liberal" profession in the age of Trump (Curtis 2017) commentaries like these will likely become more commonplace. When Trump engages sport – as he cannot help but do – he provokes an intensification of confrontational forms of athlete-activism and of politicized sport media, thus positioning sport as a central context for challenging the terms and conditions of forgiveness on a larger social scale.

Communication and sport scholars have a role to play in advancing these activist, confrontational modes of analysis. Contemporary rhetoric embraces a characteristically critical/cultural mission dedicated to interrogating inequitable power structures and proposing alternative, more just ideas and practices. This is, as Butterworth argues, the "attitude" that rhetoric brings to the broader area of communication and sport: a commitment to "*take sides*" in moments like our own, when pervasive inequality and oppression warrant academic intervention. Butterworth clarifies that one need not adopt rhetorical theories or approaches to "embrace a rhetorical *attitude*." Rather, one must simply move from an observational stance to a critical stance by refusing to accept messages proffered by sport institutions at face value (Butterworth 2014: 5–8).

Consider the Johnson case as an example. Accepting official discourses from the Committee or from President Trump about the requirements for Johnson's "redemption," and about the standards by which that redemption could be realized, would foreclose critique of the racial injustices and institutionalized power interests implicated in the very idea of "forgiving" Johnson. The resulting analysis would likely focus on how pardon supporters met the presumed requirements of redemption through a series of strategic steps (as we often see, for example, in communication scholarship on image repair or apologia). The rhetorical approach I take in this chapter suggests an alternative: to consider whether the question of forgiving or redeeming a public sport figure is just in the first place, or whether it is founded upon inequitably racialized, gendered, classed, nationalistic, or ethnic standards for offense and inclusion. Given the prominent role that sport plays in shaping ideas about redemption and forgiveness, these are pressing questions that communication and sport scholars are uniquely positioned to address.

References

Alderman, Derek H., Joshua Inwood & James A. Tyner. 2018. Jack Johnson versus Jim Crow: Race, reputation, and the politics of Black villainy: The fight of the century. *Southern Geographer* 58. 227–249.

Andrews, David L. 2019. *Making sport great again: The uber-sport assemblage, neoliberalism, and the Trump conjuncture.* Cham, Switzerland: Palgrave Pivot.

Andrews, Malika. 2018. A relative wages Jack Johnson's biggest fight: To clear his name. *The New York Times*, 8 May. https://www.nytimes.com/2018/05/08/sports/jack-johnson-pardon.html (27 May 2020).

Associated Press. 2009. Justice Dept. nixes Johnson pardon. *ESPN.com*, 10 December. https://www.espn.com/sports/boxing/news/story?id=4732473 (11 November 2020).

Baker, Peter. 2018. Trump wields pardon pen to confront justice system. *The New York Times*, 31 May. https://www.nytimes.com/2018/05/31/us/politics/dsouza-pardon.html (27 May 2020).

Blackistone, Kevin. B. 2018. A pardon for Jack Johnson would be symbolic but living opportunities abound. *The Washington Post*, 26 April. https://www.washingtonpost.com/sports/a-pardon-for-jack-johnson-would-be-symbolic-but-living-opportunities-abound/2018/04/26/3ce142d6-48fa-11e8-8b5a-3b1697adcc2a_story.html (11 November 2020).

Blake, Aaron. 2019. The very political pattern of Trump's pardons. *The Washington Post*, 16 May. https://www.washingtonpost.com/politics/2019/05/16/very-political-pattern-trumps-pardons/ (27 May 2020).

Bruni, Frank. 2019. Donald Trump's outrageous 2020 advantage. *The New York Times*, 7 August. https://www.nytimes.com/2019/08/07/opinion/donald-trump-2020.html (27 May 2020).

Bryant, Howard. 2018. *The heritage: Black athletes, a divided America, and the politics of patriotism*. Boston, MA: Beacon Press.
Butterworth, Michael L. 2005. Ritual in the "church of baseball": Suppressing the discourse of democracy after 9/11. *Communication and Critical/Cultural Studies* 2. 107–129.
Butterworth, Michael L. 2007. The politics of the pitch: Claiming and contesting democracy through the Iraqi national soccer team. *Communication and Critical/Cultural Studies* 4. 184–203.
Butterworth, Michael L. 2010. *Baseball and rhetorics of purity: The national pastime and American identity during the war on terror*. Tuscaloosa, AL: University of Alabama Press.
Butterworth, Michael L. 2014. Introduction: Communication and sport identity scholarship, and the identity of communication and sport scholars. In Barry Brummett & Andrew W. Ishak (eds.), *Sports and identity: New agendas in communication*, 1–16. New York: Routledge.
Butterworth, Michael L. 2017. Sport as rhetorical artifact. In Andrew C. Billings (ed.), *Defining sport communication*, 11–25. New York: Routledge.
Butterworth, Michael L. 2019. George Bush as the "man in the arena": Baseball, public memory, and the rhetorical redemption of a president. *Rhetoric & Public Affairs* 22. 1–31.
Campbell, Karlyn Kohrs & Kathleen Hall Jamieson. 1990. *Deeds done in words: Presidential rhetoric and the genres of governance*. Chicago: The University of Chicago Press.
Cillizza, Chris. 2018. Another day, another clemency: What Trump's pardons are really saying. *CNN.com*, 6 June. https://www.cnn.com/2018/06/06/politics/donald-trump-alice-johnson-pardon/index.html (27 May 2020).
Coates, Ta-Nehisi. 2017. My president was Black. *The Atlantic*, January/February. https://www.theatlantic.com/magazine/archive/2017/01/my-president-was-black/508793/ (27 May 2020).
Congress seeking pardon for Jack Johnson. 2009. *New York Times*, 30 July. https://www.nytimes.com/2009/07/30/sports/30sportsbriefs-johnson.html (27 May 2020).
Costa, Robert, Josh Dawsey & Ashley Parker. 2018. Pardons become a Trump fixation. *The Washington Post*, 5 June. https://www.washingtonpost.com/politics/trump-fixates-on-pardons-could-soon-give-reprieve-to-63-year-old-woman-after-meeting-with-kim-kardashian/2018/06/05/37ac6cb6-683d-11e8-bbc5-dc9f3634fa0a_story.html (27 May 2020).
Crouch, Jeffrey. 2009. *The presidential pardon power*. Lawrence, KS: University of Kansas Press.
Curtis, Bryan. 2017. Sportswriting has become a liberal profession – here's how it happened. *The Ringer*, 16 February. https://www.theringer.com/2017/2/16/16042460/how-sportswriting-became-a-liberal-profession-dc7123a5caba (27 May 2020).
Derrida, Jacques. 2001. *On cosmopolitanism and forgiveness* (trans. Mark Dooley and Michael Hughes). New York: Routledge.
Dickinson, Greg & Karrin Vasby Anderson. 2004. Fallen: O.J. Simpson, Hillary Rodham Clinton, and the re-centering of white patriarchy. *Communication and Critical/Cultural Studies* 1. 271–296.
Doxtader, Eric. 2004. The potential of reconciliation's beginning: A reply. *Rhetoric & Public Affairs* 7. 378–390.
DuBois, W. E. B. 1914. The prize fighter. *The Crisis* 8. 181–182.
Early, Gerald. 1991. Introduction. In Gerald Early (ed.), *My soul's high song: The collected writings of Countee Cullen, voice of the Harlem Renaissance*. New York: Anchor Books.
Ebert, Roger. 1979. Watching Rocky II with Muhammad Ali. *Roger Ebert.com*, 31 July. https://www.rogerebert.com/interviews/watching-rocky-ii-with-muhammad-ali (27 May 2020).
Edwards, Harry. 2018. The abject fraud of presuming to 'pardon' Jack Johnson. *San Francisco Chronicle*, 23 April. https://www.sfchronicle.com/opinion/openforum/article/The-abject-fraud-of-presuming-to-pardon-12858633.php (27 May 2020).
Eligon, John & Michael D. Shear. 2018. Trump pardons Jack Johnson, heavyweight boxing champion. *The New York Times*, 24 May. https://www.nytimes.com/2018/05/24/sports/jack-johnson-pardon-trump.html (27 May 2020).

Enck-Wanzer, Suzanne M. 2009. All's fair in love and sport: Black masculinity and domestic violence in the news. *Communication and Critical/Cultural Studies* 6. 1–18.

Fox News Insider, 2017. Gingrich to NFL: "Arrogant young millionaires" who feel oppressed "need a therapist not a publicity stunt." *Fox News*, 24 September. https://insider.foxnews.com/2017/09/24/gingrich-rips-nfl-anthem-kneelers-arrogant-young-millionaires-who-need-therapy (27 May 2020).

Frommer, Frederic J. 2009a. McCain seeks pardon for first Black champ. *The Associated Press*, 1 April. https://www.foxnews.com/wires/2009Apr01/0,4670,BoxingPardon,00.html (27 May 2020).

Frommer, Frederic J. 2009b. Obama asked to pardon legendary boxer; Jack Johnson was victim of "bigotry and prejudice." *Pittsburgh Post-Gazette*, 20 December. https://www.post-gazette.com/sports/other-sports/2009/12/20/Obama-asked-to-pardon-legendary-boxer/stories/200912200131 (27 May 2020).

Gilmore, Al-Tony. 1973. Jack Johnson and white women: The national impact. *The Journal of Negro History* 58. 18–38.

Graham, David A. 2018. Trump is weaponizing pardons. *The Atlantic*, 31 May. https://www.theatlantic.com/politics/archive/2018/05/trump-is-weaponizing-the-pardon-power/561617/ (27 May 2020.

Grano, Daniel A. 2010. Risky dispositions: Thick moral description and character-talk in sports culture. *Southern Communication Journal* 75. 255–276.

Grano, Daniel A. 2014. Michael Vick's "genuine remorse" and problems of public forgiveness. *Quarterly Journal of Speech* 100. 81–104.

Grano, Daniel A. & Michael L. Butterworth. 2019. Rhetoric, sport, and the political: An introduction. In Daniel A. Grano & Michael L. Butterworth (eds.), *Sport, rhetoric, and political struggle*, 1–22. New York: Peter Lang.

Griffin, Rachel A. & Bernadette M. Calafell. 2011. Control, discipline, and punish: Black masculinity and (in)visible whiteness in the NBA. In Michael G. Lacy & Kent A. Ono (eds.), *Critical rhetorics of race*, 117–136. New York: New York University Press.

Harris, Fredrick C. 2014. The rise of respectability politics. *Dissent* 16. 33–37.

Hietala, Thomas R. 2004. *The fight of the century: Jack Johnson, Joe Louis, and the struggle for racial equality*. New York: Routledge.

Higginbotham, Evelyn B. 1993. *Righteous discontent: The women's movement in the Black Baptist church 1880–1920*. Cambridge, MA: Harvard University Press.

Hutchison, Phillip J. 2014. Usually white, but not always great: A journalistic archaeology of white hopes, 1908–2013. *Journalism History* 39. 231–240.

Khan, Abraham I. 2012. *Curt Flood in the media: Baseball, race, and the demise of the activist-athlete*. Jackson: University Press of Mississippi.

Khan, Abraham I. 2017. Michael Sam, Jackie Robinson, and the politics of respectability. *Communication & Sport* 5. 331–351.

Khan, Abraham I. 2019. Curt Flood, confrontational rhetoric, and the radical's constellation. In Daniel A. Grano & Michael L. Butterworth (eds.), *Sport, rhetoric, and political struggle*, 25–37. New York: Peter Lang.

Korte, Gregory. 2018. A Trump pardon for boxer Jack Johnson would be just the third posthumous pardon in history. *USA Today*, 26 April. From https://www.usatoday.com/story/news/politics/2018/04/25/trump-pardon-boxer-jack-johnson-would-just-third-posthumous-pardon-history/539030002/ (27 May 2020).

Lockhart, P. R. 2018. Trump's reaction to the NFL protests shows how he fights the culture war. *Vox*, 4 February. https://www.vox.com/identities/2018/2/4/16967902/nfl-protests-patriotism-race-donald-trump-super-bowl (27 May 2020).

McCain seeks pardon for first Black heavyweight champ. 2009. *Times Herald-Record*, 1 April. https://www.recordonline.com/article/20090401/news/90401016 (11 November 2020).

Oates, Thomas P. & Kyle W. Kusz. 2019. "My whole life is about winning": The Trump brand and the political/commercial uses of sport. In Daniel A. Grano & Michael L. Butterworth (eds.), *Sport, rhetoric, and political struggle*, 207–222. New York: Peter Lang.

Rashid, Qasim. 2018. *Twitter*, 24 May, 11:33 a.m. https://twitter.com/QasimRashid/status/999720094522642433 (27 May 2020).

Reid, Jason. 2017. Trump pokes at Black players in the NFL and NBA – and many poke back. *The Undefeated*, 24 September. https://theundefeated.com/features/trump-pokes-at-black-players-in-the-nfl-and-nba-and-many-poke-back/ (27 May 2020).

Rhoden, William C. 2015. A century later, Jack Johnson awaits a nation's absolution. *The New York Times*, 3 December. https://www.nytimes.com/2015/12/04/sports/a-century-later-jack-johnson-awaits-a-nations-absolution.html (27 May 2020).

Ricoeur, Paul. 2004. *Memory, history, forgetting* (trans. Kathleen Blamey & David Pellauer). Chicago: The University of Chicago Press.

Runstedtler, Theresa. 2012. *Jack Johnson, rebel sojourner: Boxing in the shadow of the global color line*. Berkeley, CA: University of California Press.

Runstedtler, Theresa. 2013. Op-ed: Jack Johnson and the racial politics of a presidential pardon. *thefeministwire*, 17 March. https://www.thefeministwire.com/2013/03/op-ed-jack-johnson-and-the-racial-politics-of-a-presidential-pardon (27 May 2020).

Schaye, David, Paul Barnes & Ken Burns. 2005. *Unforgivable Blackness: The rise and fall of Jack Johnson*. PBS Home Video.

Scott, Robert L. & Donald K. Smith. 1969. The rhetoric of confrontation. *Quarterly Journal of Speech* 55. 1–8.

Serwer, Adam. 2017. Trump's war of words with Black athletes. *The Atlantic*, 23 September. https://www.theatlantic.com/politics/archive/2017/09/trump-urges-nfl-owners-to-fire-players-who-protest/540897/ (27 May 2020).

Smart, Charlie. 2017. Obama granted clemency unlike any other president in history. *FiveThirtyEight.com*, 19 January. https://fivethirtyeight.com/features/obama-granted-clemency-unlike-any-other-president-in-history/ (27 May 2020).

Starr, Terrell J. 2018. Serena Williams says everyone should be 'grateful and honored' for Colin Kaepernick, Eric Reid. *The Root*, 1 September. https://www.theroot.com/serena-williams-says-athletes-should-be-grateful-and-ho-1828762134 (27 May 2020).

States News Service, 2017. McCain, Booker, King and Meeks reintroduce resolution calling for posthumous pardon of boxing legend Jack Johnson, 2 March. https://meeks.house.gov/press-release/meeks-king-booker-and-mccain-reintroduce-resolution-calling-posthumous-pardon-boxing (27 May 2020).

Stuckey, Mary. 1992. Legitimating leadership: The rhetoric of succession as a genre of presidential discourse. *Rhetoric Society Quarterly* 22. 25–38.

Teresa, Carrie. 2015. "We need a Booker T. Washington … and certainly a Jack Johnson": The Black press, Johnson, and issues of representation, 1909–1915. *American Journalism* 32. 23–40.

Teresa, Carrie. 2017. A "varied or intense existence": Public commemoration of boxing champion Jack Johnson. *Howard Journal of Communications* 28. 249–262.

The New York Times. 2018. Trump pardoning Jack Johnson: The official transcript from the Oval Office, 24 May. https://www.nytimes.com/2018/05/24/sports/trump-jack-johnson-pardon-transcript.html/ (27 May 2020).

The United States Department of Justice. 2018. *Pardon information and instruction*, 23 November. https://www.justice.gov/pardon/pardon-information-and-instructions (27 May 2020).

Trump, Donald. 2018. *Twitter*, 21 April 2018, 12:02 p.m. https://twitter.com/realdonaldtrump/status/987768453338673152?lang=en (27 May 2020).

Vogan, Travis. 2010. Irrational power: Jack Johnson, prizefighting films, and documentary affect. *Journal of Sports History* 37. 397–413.

Ward, Geoffrey. C. 2004. *Unforgivable Blackness: The rise and fall of Jack Johnson*. New York: Alfred A. Knopf.

Washington, Booker T. 1982. A statement on Jack Johnson for the United States Press Association. In Louis R. Harlan & Raymond W. Smock (eds.), *Booker T. Washington Papers Volume 12*, 43–44. Champaign, IL: University of Illinois Press.

Washington, Jesse. 2016. Jack Johnson, still unforgivable? *The Undefeated*, 29 December. https://theundefeated.com/features/will-obama-pardon-heavyweight-boxing-champ-jack-johnson/ (27 May 2020).

Washington, Jesse. 2018a. Why a Jack Johnson pardon would be easier for Trump than Obama. *The Undefeated*, 23 April. https://theundefeated.com/whhw/why-a-jack-johnson-pardon-would-be-easier-for-trump-than-obama/ (27 May 2020).

Washington, Jesse. 2018b. The irony of Trump's Jack Johnson pardon. *The Undefeated*, 24 May. https://theundefeated.com/whhw/the-irony-of-trumps-jack-johnson-pardon/ (27 May 2020).

Watts, Eric. K. 2002. African American ethos and hermeneutical rhetoric: An exploration of Alain Locke's *The New Negro*. *Quarterly Journal of Speech* 88. 19–32.

Wolf, Z. Byron. 2018. Donald Trump, Kanye West and Jim Brown in the Oval Office, Annotated. *CNN*, 12 October. https://www.cnn.com/2018/10/12/politics/donald-trump-kanye-west-and-jim-brown-annotated/index.html (27 May 2020).

Young, Harvey. 2010. *Embodying Black experience: Stillness, critical memory, and the Black body*. Ann Arbor: University of Michigan Press.

Ziegler, John. 2018. Why Trump's pardon policy tells us everything we need to know about our president. *Mediaite*, 2 June. https://www.mediaite.com/online/why-trumps-pardon-policy-tells-us-everything-we-need-to-know-about-our-president/ (27 May 2020).

Zirin, Dave. 2017. Why Jack Johnson's family should refuse any exoneration. *The Nation*, 2 January. https://www.thenation.com/article/why-jack-johnsons-family-should-refuse-any-exoneration/ (27 May 2020).

Courtney M. Cox

11 Haram hoops? FIBA, Nike, and the hijab's half-court defense

Abstract: Over the last twenty years, legislation in the West designed to control the attire of Muslim women continues to reinforce the limits of the appropriate as well as access to public space, including sport. This chapter investigates FIBA's (the global governing body of basketball) ban on the hijab and the various forms of resistance by Muslim girls and women to carve out space on the court despite this policy. Focusing on the simultaneous marketability and marginalization of Muslim women in sport, this chapter considers how Sarah Banet-Weiser's *economies of visibility* framework might inform how governing bodies and corporations interact with athletes in the service of their own financial interests. It also interrogates how Muslim women's attire and actions remain continuously subjected to scrutiny through what Manal Hamzeh defines as a *dual hijabophobia*, a gendered form of Islamophobia directed towards Muslim women by both Islamic and non-Islamic factions. In using FIBA's hijab ban as a case study, this research also examines how new possibilities for transnational community form in online spaces for Muslim women athletes and advocates.

Keywords: FIBA; basketball; intersectionality; economies of visibility; sporting activism; Islamophobia; sport governance

1 Introduction: governing bodies that govern bodies

> "You have to look back to when and how these sports were created and invented. And the rules were written ... by men for men. They didn't understand that women, Muslim women in particular, wanted to access it. I think you've got the same issues with all of the other governing bodies ... sport is meant to be this microcosm of society, but sport was originally designed by men for men and done by men."
> – Dana Abdulkarim (Day 2: Session 1: Innovation in Modest Sportswear 2018)

In the epigraph above, netball athlete Dana Abdulkarim notes how the foundational principles of Global Sports Organizations (GSOs) such as the International Olympic Committee (IOC) and other international sport federations such as FIFA (football) or FIBA (basketball) do not take into account the variety of cultures and bodies that play sport. While these transnational organizations operate outside of government regulation, they remain bound by the political climate and systems in which they exist. International sport becomes a mechanism connected to a broader global system and the nation-states that regularly take part in mega-events such as the Olympics or World Cup.

https://doi.org/10.1515/9783110660883-011

This chapter interrogates how athletes maneuver through the policies and profit margins of sport governance and corporations. It also argues that contemporary social media platforms offer new ways of forming resistance and solidarity across borders for athletes and advocates. For scholars, it offers new opportunities to center their voices in research. Using FIBA – the global governing body of basketball – and their ban on religious headwear as a case study, I consider how advertising, activism, and agency circulate within the broader sports-media complex.

FIBA dictates how the game is played, who can take the court, and how the sport is officiated. "We are basketball," their motto declares, an apt statement given the role of the organization in shifting the rules, values, and culture of the game on a global level. A ban on religious headwear, dictated by FIBA's article 4.4.2 states that:

> Players shall not wear equipment (objects) that may cause injury to other players. The following are not permitted:
> - Finger, hand, wrist, elbow or forearm guards, casts or braces made of leather, plastic, pliable (soft) plastic, metal or any other hard substance, even if covered with soft padding.
> - Objects that could cut or cause abrasions (fingernails must be closely cut).
> - Headgear, hair accessories and jewellery [*sic*].

The implementation of this policy disproportionately affected Muslim women athletes who found themselves relegated to the sidelines following the enforcement of this policy. As Abdulkarim states above, global governing bodies are always already exclusionary based upon the guiding structures of a white masculine Christianity, one that Richard Gruneau argues is based on the discourses the West has written about itself (2017: 10).

Basketball emerges as yet another vivid example of the ways in which the Muslim world is torn between its fascination with Western modernity and its struggle against colonial and neocolonial dominance (Amara 2008: 67). Mahfoud Amara writes that for female Muslim athletes in particular, "The international sports arena has become a privileged space where they can regain their status as full citizens and as role models," while also acknowledging that within the public sphere, these women are embodied proof of progress (in Muslim societies) and integration (in the West) (2008: 71–72). It would then seem that sport serves as less of space of freedom, but rather as a site of cultural tension, debate, and forum about these women's perceived status. Amara believes that sport can serve as a negotiating space for Muslim and non-Muslim fans and athletes alike to traverse national and cultural borders (2008: 73), but who stands to benefit (or lose) from these crossover moments? For sports institutions such as FIBA, these crossovers are defended through regulations that aim to contain hijabi hoopers, governing their bodies as they attempt to compete on the court. Additionally, companies like Nike often find new ways to commodify difference in the service of their own corporate interest. FIBA's ban on the hijab is a case study that offers the opportunity for sport communication researchers to move beyond analysis focused on mere representation to a more intersectional approach that interrogates the sports–

media nexus as it relates to how power and performance operate across race, gender, and religion.

In the sections that follow, I analyze the inaugural Muslim Women in Sport Summit, centering the voices of Muslim women, especially those who wear hijab, in order to explore how those who campaigned against FIBA created space for one another in the white Christian heteronormative patriarchal industry of sport. I take up Aarti Ratna's call for critical sport scholarship, which moves beyond cultural tropes of difference and speaks directly to the alternative knowledges produced by those experiencing racial and gendered forms of violence (2018: 197–206). In "Not Just Merely Different: Travelling Theories, Post-Feminism and the Racialized Politics of Women of Color," Ratna laments the white, Western framings of sport research which too often fail to take into account how people of color (especially women) use sport as a site of resistance and pleasure. Ratna details the urgency of critical scholarship focused on the complex relationship between women of color and sport. She calls for renewed attention to writings and recordings from women of color, valuable sources I utilize here to contribute additional voices and perspectives across time and space. She also calls for more work addressing racist and Islamophobic sport governance and emphasizes the importance of scholarship attending to acts of resistance and places these figures within more extensive dialogues/ontologies of women of color. This chapter addresses some of these gaps through this case study.

2 The Muslim Women in Sport Network and Summit

To document Muslim women athletes and activists' response to FIBA's hijab ban and Nike's Pro Hijab, I attended the Muslim Women in Sport Network's inaugural online summit in 2018. Established in March 2017, the Muslim Women in Sport Network is comprised of athletes, journalists, coaches, researchers, and executives dedicated to influencing policy, programming, and engagement involving Muslim women. Their website's mission declares, "It is time Muslim women instruct decision and policy-makers on what it means to be a Muslim woman in sport and shed light on the diversity of Muslim women" (About us 2018). The online conference focused on issues such as athlete activism, sport for development, and sports leadership. Over three days, the virtual summit featured thirteen speakers across six time zones and viewers from 22 countries. During the conference, journalist Shireen Ahmed said that one of the reasons the organization was developed is "because we were tired of people talking about us, we want to talk for ourselves" (*Day 1: Session 1: Athlete Activism* 2018).

The analysis that follows is structured by the notion that digital media continues to shift how we relate to ourselves and others in a myriad of ways. The Muslim Women in Sport Summit represents how relationships and group memberships cross physical boundaries and have the potential to shape new opportunities for self-expression and organizing (Baym 2015). I consider the Muslim Women in Sport Summit (and its affiliated network) as a cybercommunity (Jones 1998: 211), where shared value systems, norms, and a sense of identity bind these various women together and through these shared experiences, generate knowledge production often rendered invisible in mainstream discourses surrounding Muslim women. "Cybercommunity is not just a *thing*; it is also a *process*," Jan Fernback writes. "It is defined by its inhabitants, its boundaries and meanings are renegotiated, and although virtual communities do possess many of the same essential traits as physical communities, they possess the 'substance' that allows for common experience and common meaning among members" (Jones 1998: 217).

3 Legal, sporting, and media representation of Muslim women

Sporting regulations surrounding the attire and covering of Muslim women mirror larger societal and political shifts across North America and Europe. Since 2003, the West's obsession with legislation controlling the attire of Muslim women has expanded, with Germany banning teachers from wearing headscarves, to France and Belgium banning the burqa and niqab in 2011. Austria and Germany have followed suit, albeit with partial bans. And in 2017, Quebec adopted new legislation, Bill 62, which forbids anyone from giving or receiving public services while wearing a face covering (Weaver 2018; Lowrie 2017; Levine 2015). Around the world, from the individual to the institutional, discourses surrounding Muslim women's attire continue to frame policies that constrict their movements within public spaces. Whereas Islam has been depicted as a symbol of female oppression in Western culture (Eid 2014: 1902), recent Islamophobic policies within Europe and North America seemingly restrict Muslim women in particular more than any religious text or leader.

These policies shifted to sport in 2007, when FIFA, soccer's global governing body, instituted a ban on the hijab. Law 4 of the federation's laws of the game states that, "The basic compulsory equipment must not contain any political, religious or personal statements. ... The team of a player whose basic compulsory equipment contains political, religious or personal slogans or statements will be sanctioned by the competition organizer or by FIFA" (FIFA 2007). The federation's policy on the hijab would later change to one of safety, arguing that the hijab posed a strangulation risk to athletes should they take the pitch to play while covered. Eventually, following a two-year provisional period, FIFA was forced to acknowledge that no medical research exists confirming any risk or incident of injury for athletes wearing headscarves. However, the influence of FIFA instituting the ban impacted other sports who had originally followed suit, including FIBA. Carolyn Prouse, in analyzing discourses surrounding the FIFA hijab ban, writes that:

> Through FIFA and IFAB's codifications, the Muslim Female Footballer materializes as at risk of strangulation by her cultural choices while entrenching the centuries-old colonial and imperial structures of benevolence that celebrates male saviours ... In an ironic yet unsurprising twist, FIFA's regulation of the hijab as a safety concern strangles Muslim women's voices in a continuing coloniality of racialized and gendered power. (2015: 32)

Here she argues that FIFA positions itself as a benevolent governing body allowing the hijab only if it passes a safety test, a self-congratulatory stance which frames the organization as both culturally sensitive and invested in player safety (2015: 29). The FIFA ban on the hijab can read as a microcosm of larger anti-Muslim sentiments and cultural battles waged across Europe and North America, shrouded in a neocolonial paternalism which reflects the white patriarchal structures imposed on these women as it does in other economic and political spaces.

When FIBA failed to lift their ban after FIFA's ended in 2014, debates and petitions began to circulate in support of hijabi hoopers. These discourses challenged notions that essentialized Muslim women as "backward," passive subjects donning a dangerous head covering, which was later used by FIBA and other governing bodies to legitimize Islamophobic policies as protective measures (Prouse 2015: 26). The implementation of FIBA's discriminatory policy affects not only international play, but competition at the local, state, and national levels as well. The continued ban at the federation affected leagues and teams not only in majority-Muslim countries, but also countries such as the United States, seeping into sporting regulations at even the elementary and secondary school level (see Dougherty 2017).

Reina Lewis writes that, "matters of Muslim self-presentation have come to operate as the litmus test in debates about citizenship and belonging, secularity and modernity, for both the majority non-Muslim (or, in Turkey, non-religious) public and often for Muslim (religious) communities themselves" (2015: Introduction, Section 1, para. 10) In this case, the hijab's place in basketball postmodernity – as well as the girls and women who choose to wear it – is constantly marketed, contested, and resolved through both corporate and institutional entities.

This also reverberates across media representations of Muslim women, where scholars such as Evelyn Alsutany detail how hijabi women are largely rendered invisible, and when they are depicted in US media, they are read through what she calls *simplified complex representations* – strategies that give the impression they are producing complex racial representations designed to supposedly challenge former stereotypes and create a multicultural post-racial landscape (2012: 38). When Muslim women wearing hijab do appear on TV, they are typically framed as victims of hate crimes or require saving from the patriarchal constraints of their faith (2012: 71). Tropes of the "oppressed Muslim woman" or the gendered "good Muslim" are frequently positioned opposite the "bad Muslim," most often depicted as a (Brown, male) terrorist (2012: 71).

As Alsutany and others have written, both the "good Muslim" and "bad Muslim" tropes are read through a post-9/11 Orientalism which shape different Muslim and non-Muslim publics as utterly Other, culturally illegible and unable to cross over into Western cultural forms (2012: 92; Mamdani 2002). Women in the West who choose to wear the hijab seem to be accused in both subtle and obvious ways of false consciousness, while Muslim women who play basketball in Muslim-majority countries are accused of participating in what is considered forbidden, or *haram*, submitting to the influence of secular American culture, one dribble at a time. Sociologist Paul Eid asks, "If the hijab is politically instrumentalized, both in the West and in the Muslim world, what room is left to Muslim women in the production of the social meanings embedded in veil wearing?" (Eid 2014: 1903).

The various forms of meaning attached to Muslim women's decision to cover (or not) results in what Manal Hamzeh defines as a dual hijabophobia – a gendered form of Islamophobia directed towards Muslim women – by both Islamic and non-Islamic factions. The racist, colonialist discourses of the West are defined as *Islamophobic hijabophobia*, while Hamzeh defines *Islamist hijabophobia* within the constraints of nationalist and religious groups who use hijabophobia to blatantly police women's bodies in specific countries and contexts (2015: 519). "These two hijabophobias," Hamzeh writes, "construct the body of the Muslim woman as a threat to the nation's unity and the purity of Islam, as well as a threat to the secular notion of freedom, the security of the West, and playing sports or 'the game'" (2015: 519). These Islamophobic policies cross over into sport through hijab bans, most notably within FIFA and FIBA, the global governing bodies of football and basketball, respectively.

Throughout the virtual conference, several women argued that at the highest level, FIBA's hesitancy to revoke the hijab ban is rooted in a hijabophobia which failed to consider Muslim women's ability to play basketball a matter of importance. In her presentation, Bilqis Abdul-Qaadir, a US-based basketball player denied the opportunity to play internationally following her collegiate career because she wears a hijab, said, "it was on the back burner the whole time." Part of this failure to prioritize the rights of these players is due to the lack of diversity at the hoops headquarters. In an interview I conducted with journalist Shireen Ahmed before the summit, she told me, "My critique of FIBA is that they had nobody on the inside, and they made this policy and it was ridiculous and had no basis, but they also didn't feel moved to change it. FIBA have all men on their executive committee, they don't give a shit if Muslim women in hijab play. They also sadly didn't give a shit if men in turbans didn't play ... so for me, this is not only rooted in misogyny it's rooted in xenophobia because heads of federations are all in Switzerland." For these women, they are caught between not only the federations and lower organizations that dictate if they can take the court, but their own communities which seek to contain them.

At the online summit, Bilqis Abdul-Qaadir clearly defines a dual hijabophobia of Islamaphobic and Islamic hijabophobic within sport. In her keynote address, she asserted:

> The prophet, Prophet Muhammad peace be upon him, who we follow, played sport. And he said, teach your children sports. Of course, back then they didn't have basketball and soccer and things of that nature but he wanted that for our people. So it's important that we number one, teach them or give them the opportunity so that if they do fall in love with it, they can go play. So that's number one. And number two, I think the people outside of our communities need to accept us.

Here, she addresses both the internal and external barriers to accessing sport for those within Muslim communities. Other speakers noted how the actions and attitudes of fellow Muslims as well as non-Muslims contributed to challenges in pursuing an active role within sports.

Abdul-Qaadir also provided several examples of the types of external pressures and problematic discourses surrounding her decision to cover, even thought it would jeopardize her career as a professional athlete. "Many people would come up to me saying, 'Well why don't you just take your scarf off and then put it on after the game.'" She often found herself defending wearing the hijab or explaining how it was more than a scarf, more than material which she wore each day. The lack of knowledge surrounding the hijab and Islamic law is not contained to everyday dialogues; it also resonates across the field of play, where ignorance surrounding athletes' modest apparel decisions affects how they are perceived as competitors. More broadly, it also extends to formal political institutions, which too often reaffirms these misconceptions. In another Muslim Women in Sport summit session on modest sportswear, Dana Abdulkarim, a netball athlete, described external judgment due to the additional layers she wore during a local tryout in the United Kingdom:

> I'm there in my tracksuit bottoms, my multi-layered long sleeve top that I fashioned to be covering most of my hair ... a high-necked top, my netball bib, and there I was trying to keep up with everybody else, be as fit as everybody else, thinking I'm playing really well. Little did I know, the selectors had already put a cross by my name assuming I was too lazy to get changed, too lazy to take it seriously, because netballers didn't look like that ... my quite arbitrary innovation to get on the court almost took me out in that scenario.

Both Abdul-Qaadir and Abdulkarim pointed to gatekeepers who failed to understand both the significance of the hijab as well as the additional labor and ingenuity required to take the court.

In my interview with Ahmed, I defined dual hijabophobia and asked her if she could provide examples over the course of her career as a sports journalist or an athlete. She became animated as she began to describe a question she received from a fellow Muslim in the crowd during a recent SXSW panel Q&A session. He asked, "What do you think of Muslim women not being covered modestly because you can see the shape of their legs when they wear tights?" The question was obviously directed towards athletes like Ahmed (a former soccer player) and Abdul-Qaadir, who wears tights underneath her basketball shorts for modesty. She described her emotions in the moment:

> I was so frustrated. I was like, after all this shit. My face is legitimately like – I'm not good at poker face – I was like scowling at the man ... So then I get to him and I'm like, "Wait a minute, who do you mean by people, do you mean Muslim men? Who is asking these questions about what Muslim women are wearing? First thing, stop asking these questions. What Muslim women wear is not your business." I was so pissed off. But that is a perfect example of what happens in our community and I'm not going to lie about it ... they're not off the hook.

In this case, "after all this shit" refers to the struggles against regulations such as the FIFA and FIBA bans, where Islamophobic hijabophobia dominated. After all of the structural oppression the panel had just discussed, she had to also contend with the misogyny of the man's question. She expressed hesitancy in addressing Islamist hijabophobia in front of a primarily white, Western audience because of the way that Islam is vilified as misogynistic within a Western context, but felt she had to speak up given that:

> Every community suffers from misogyny ... issues in Nigeria of women not getting paid there – the national team after Nigeria won the African Cup, they hadn't played in one year. The women had to do a sit in to get the money they were owed. Let's fast forward to Denmark – the women went on strike and almost missed a World Cup qualifying match. Okay, let's go to Ireland and talk about how the women had to wear tracksuits and take them off in the airport to hand the back to the federation. Let's talk about Pakistan, how the federation there was blocking women from trying out overseas because they didn't want them to ... so my point is that there's issues and instances of misogyny all across the world, but they way that it's written up it's easy for white people to point at folks and say "look at the Global South, they're a mess." No, look at all of y'all; the U.S. women's team just sued U.S. Soccer. You're not immune to these systems, it's literally misogyny everywhere.

As she rattled off the variety of sexist practices across geography and sport, she pointed to the hypocrisy of many of the experiences in light of how Islam is often portrayed within the media. In this quote, she also invokes how women of color are perceived as disadvantaged through a white, Western lens, illustrating the various intersections within Muslim women's identities.

4 Sporting economies of visibility

In February of 2017, sporting goods giant Nike announced a multi-year partnership with FIBA, providing the apparel, footwear, and equipment for all men's, women's, and youth competitions, as well as the title partner for the governing body's World Rankings and licensing rights (Nike News 2017). Days later, Nike debuted the Pro Hijab, a Dri-Fit head covering emblazoned with the company's logo, and released an ad titled "What Will They Say About You?" featuring Muslim women competing in an array of sports. At the time of the Nike Pro Hijab announcement, *ESPNw* columnist Kavitha A. Davidson wrote, "Now that Nike has released this line of headgear, the hope is that FIBA, and the sports world at large, will start making Muslim women a priority, too" (2017). Nike, in producing the ad and athletic hijab in a particularly volatile political moment for Muslim visibility, seemingly takes the activist branding framework one step further. In partnering with FIBA, it interjects the market into this discursive colonization, where the massive swoosh becomes a symbolic planted flag across the profile of the produced Muslim Woman Athlete. Nuraan Davids argues the Pro Hijab has legitimized the hijab across two very different platforms. The first addresses the "hostile liberal democracies" which seek to "modernize" the Muslim woman by removing her hijab. The second responds to interpretations of Islam which renders the attire and actions of Muslim women incompatible with sport (2017).

As corporations continue to appropriate social movements and cultural expression in order to create niche markets for consumption, this current moment consistently capitalizes on what feminist scholar Sarah Banet-Weiser defines as "economies of visibility" in her book *Empowered: Popular Feminism and Popular Misogyny* (2018). Whereas the politics of visibility highlight the marginalization of raced, gendered, or classed bodies, she argues that economies of visibility privilege and give value to individuals capable of participating in that economy (Banet-Weiser 2018). There is inherently a buy-in element within these economies – one "invests" in their cause of choice through both financial support and/or by circulating media related to a particular cause. Retweets, hashtags, and online petitions all reflect the proliferation of these economies of visibility. Recent sports-related examples include the Ice Bucket Challenge (an online viral fundraiser for Lou Gehrig's disease, or ALS), the National Football League's Crucial Catch campaign (for breast cancer), and the Always #LikeAGirl campaign (an attempt to reclaim the sexist understandings of what it means to play sports "like a girl").

Nike consistently builds their brand through the economies of visibility, specifically as it relates to gender equity and access in sport. Their 1995 ad, "If You Let Me Play," captured the affective appeal of young girls competing in sports, as viewers receive a range of statistics read by young athletes detailing the positive physical and mental health outcomes of "letting them play." Other marketing ploys include a reactionary campaign following conservative radio host Don Imus's infamous "nappy-headed hos" commentary referring to the 2007 Rutgers University women's basketball team and more recently, their "Dream Crazier" ad, where tennis legend Serena Williams voices over a response to the sexist, ableist phrase of outspoken women described as "crazy." Nike and other advertisers' human interest marketing strategies circulate more rapidly and persuasively than their more straightforward campaigns, especially with today's new media platforms (Turow 2013: 6). What becomes clear is that Nike is now in the "equality and empowerment" business, which simultaneously opens up opportunities for athletes to speak in support of or against a variety of causes while reproducing these notions of consumption within a rabid capitalist framework. As Nike's massive swoosh marks the Pro Hijab, what is taken? What is lost? Naomi Klein calls this "branding's cruelest irony – the co-optation of authentic scenes and sacred spaces in order to make their companies or brands *mean something*" (Klein, 2000: 33). More often than the original holders of these cultural relics would like (and even perhaps at times the corporations behind the brand creation), the consumption corrupts the original beauty, the realness towards what was once so cherished. Companies move along to the "next thing" to restock their cultural and economic resonance (Klein 2000; LaFeber 1999).

During the interview with Ahmed, she expressed frustration that the Nike Pro Hijab was heralded as the premiere modest headwear given that so many hijabi athletes had innovated their own for years prior, noting women and hijabi-run companies such as ResportOn and Capsters who have created athletic hijabs for years. "I was so fucking frustrated at how media kept saying, 'Oh, the first sports hijab' I'm like nooooooo ... it's like I'm literally shouting into the bro abyss of sports media," she told me. A variety of women were already innovating modest sportswear for themselves decades before the Pro Hijab, she argues, and both the design and price point of Nike's version were a cause of concern for her. She said:

> It's forty bucks for a hijab. Let me tell you, I've never paid forty bucks for a hijab in my life ... I just think it's important to know there is a name brand to things. And yeah, there's women that definitely want this. My own daughter is like "Can I get a Nike hijab?" and I'm like yes, you can get a Nike hijab ... I'm not a big fan of the swoosh on the side of the head, I think that's a little tacky personally ... but that's fine. And I get how brands and sport are really important ... I also want people to understand that corporate culture. I don't consider Nike to be allies of Muslim women in sport necessarily.

She created a distinction between the early innovators of modest sportswear creating for themselves and other Muslim women and Nike as a corporate entity capitalizing on a moment, which she argues is driven by the partnership with FIBA. She also questioned how the production of the Pro Hijab also exploits women, questioning the labor practices of Nike, asking:

> Is it made in a Rana Plaza-type place in Bangladesh? Where is this hijab being stitched? Is it women that are stitching it and do the young kids know that it's going to be sold for exorbitant prices to Muslims around the world? It's a $40 hijab, that's expensive. So I have all of these questions. And I said this to my daughter – do you know where it's made? Why don't you write the company? Because sustainable fashion should be a part of how Muslims live.

In considering the material realities of the Pro Hijab, Ahmed's comments reveal the contradictions created by the hijab's current visibility and promotion in sporting and retail culture. She compared the creation of Olympian fencer Ibtihaj Muhammad's Barbie doll to the Pro Hijab announcement – both operating as highly visible objects of consumption hailed as innovative despite the creativity of marginalized women who have produced athletic hijabs or diverse representations of dolls for decades.

In a particularly passionate moment in our interview, she compared the release of the Pro Hijab and FIBA's ban with that of FIFA:

> FIFA at least went through the ruse and the "let's do medical testing to make sure the safety is fine." FIBA didn't even do that shit. They literally were contacted by Nike and were like "Hey, we're going to make a sports hijab." Oh, let's announce our partnership deal that FIBA and Nike are doing together and suddenly, poof, hijab is allowed and hey, there's a Nike hijab. And I'm like, okay so if you sincerely had safety concerns IFAB actually mandated that the hijabs that the women wear while playing sports they're not any name brand at all. They're Capsters, they're like, maybe $20 they just have to have Velcro. It doesn't even have to be a specific company they just have to be removable with Velcro ... and they have to be tucked into the kit. Those are the rules for IFAB so they went through the motions, they went through that research, they have to be removable with one tug. Like FIBA, if you were sincerely concerned about safety ... the Nike hijab doesn't have Velcro, it's a slip on.

In this response, she addresses the frailty of the "safety" argument posed by FIBA given the federation's failure to invest in scientific testing and argues the timing of the FIBA/Nike partnership and Pro Hijab announcement was transactional more than transformational.

During a panel on modest sportswear innovation, Aheda Zanetti, the inventor of the burkini, offered a different perspective on the impact of Nike's entrance into more diverse designs:

> There's only one of me ... compared to a big major brand that can do something with a click of a finger like that. That can change a completely new concept and market and thoughts. Which I should be thanking ... I should be thanking Nike for that Nike hijab. In a way, it's going to be lot easier for me to find these athletes that need my products because I believe that my garment is better ... I'm a producer because I'm the market. I wear it.

Zanetti viewed Nike's entrance into the market as a positive, convinced there might be some trickle-down effect to her own business. The other panelist, Dana Abdulkarim, a former England Rounders member and physical education teacher, saw the heightened visibility of Muslim athletes and new apparel as a sign of more inclusion within sporting spaces:

> I really hope that the likes of Nike might be listening to this summit this weekend, because actually, then they'll see more than ever, people are asking for it, we are asking for it. As a community, we are expecting it, and instead of feeling inferior to our non-Muslim counterparts, who maybe have a plethora of opportunity. Work with us, collaborate with us, and then it doesn't become this token one item, it becomes as many and as varied items of sporting wear, of modest sportswear for every woman that chooses to wear it.

In each instance, these women read Nike's entrance into modest sportswear differently, considering both the problems and potential of corporate intervention. Abdulkarim's statement that she hopes that Nike is listening also connects how the summit and the Muslim Women in Sport Network aspires to cross over into policy and product development to move beyond mere economies of visibility.

5 Economies of (in)visibility

In a short film titled *FIBA Allow Hijab* (produced by *Uninterrupted*, an online media venture co-founded by the NBA's LeBron James), there is a scene where former basketball player Bilqis Abdul-Qaadir is told before speaking in front of the US State Department that many are unaware of FIBA's hijab ban, even fellow athletes who would join in advocating with her as allies. Shireen Ahmed mentioned a moment where she realized the ban and resulting campaign hadn't reached non-hijabi athletes, even players such as WNBA player Essence Carson, who competed overseas in Turkey during the offseason. Much of this invisibility can be attributed to the lack of legibility within post-9/11 narratives which situate Muslim women as either victims of their religion or success stories after "escaping" the confines of Islam. Evelyn Alsutany writes that if a story fails to fit one or both of these molds, it is unlikely to gain any meaningful traction (Alsutany 2012: 105). In fact, in responding to the stereotypical categories these women are placed within, there is little room to articulate their own experiences and agendas (Alsutany 2012: 102).

For Bilqis Abdul-Qaadir and Asma Elbadawi, the lack of knowledge regarding the FIBA ban became a significant barrier to their activism. In the Athlete Activism session, Elbadawi recounted the lack of knowledge surrounding the ban and resulting campaign:

> Even 'til now, I'll have conversations with people and they'll be like 'oh, we didn't even know there was a ban' ... in many ways, there was lots of signs that there was something in place that maybe isn't allowing Muslim women to progress as high as the other women. Because we couldn't see them on TV, they weren't in the WNBA, they weren't in the [overseas] professional leagues, and so no one really questioned why that was the case. And for me, I just thought "oh maybe it's just a religious thing" like a lot of these girls think you know it's forbidden for us Muslim girls to play and it's difficult for us maintain our modesty at the same time so it's just best not to play at those levels and then suddenly it all made sense the moment that I realized there's an actual ban ... that's why they're not being seen.

The lack of visibility was also attributed to the FIBA ban protest lacking the support of a significant political presence. During the FIFA hijab ban, the advocacy and financial support of Prince Ali bin Hussein of Jordan elevated activists' voices to new levels; the FIBA ban lacked an equivalent supporter within the federation. This speaks to both the dearth of diversity within FIBA (geographically as well as in terms of gender) as well as the need to procure a wealthy, well-connected male insider to ensure change within the organization. Without any inside support, the resulting Change.org campaign, #FIBAAllowHijab, relied upon grassroots advocacy, a strategy that Asma Elbadawi, the creator of the campaign's petition believes showed the range of global support and challenged notions of where Muslim women live. During the Athlete Activism panel she said, "I think what helped was the fact that there was so many of us from completely different locations in the world. We had Nigeria, Indonesia, Saudi Arabia, and they're supposed to be ... doing [anything] at the moment." In alluding to the perception of Saudi women as unable to advocate for themselves, Asma speaks to both the potential of these virtual campaigns to reach a global audience, but the efficacy and appropriation of these strategies within various economies of visibility is also an important aspect of online activism. One of the primary fears Dana Abdulkarim mentioned for GSOs is change – changing the sport, as well as its white, Western, male roots. The inclusion of non-white Muslim women from around the world competing on the court would significantly challenge the hegemonic norms of who the game is for and how it can be accessed. The lack of knowledge surrounding barriers to entry for hijabi athletes is obscured from the policymakers at the top of the game, Abdulkarim said. The athletes themselves are seemingly restricted from view as well.

Bilqis Abdul-Qaadir eventually met with FIBA officials following the lifting of the ban in 2017, and during her presentation told the conference:

> It was terrible. I was in a room full of men – no other women in this meeting. And after coming out of the meeting, I know exactly why it took so long [to end the FIBA ban]. These two representatives they had were very insensitive. They didn't care about a Muslim girl trying to play basketball, it was evident. You know when I shared my story with them and you know, what the goal was to try to get them in the future to maybe use a different process or different protocols to help these rules get removed faster if they ever came upon something similar to this situation. And they were like, "Why are we going backwards? What's the point? The rule is gone, now get out of our face," basically. And I was just like I actually broke down in tears not because I was sad but because I was so angry I wanted to really slap all of them in the room.

Her attempts to remedy the exclusionary policy-making protocols of FIBA failed to resonate with leadership within the basketball federation and rendered her helpless in efforts to prevent future marginalization by the governing body.

6 Intersectional Islamic identities

Throughout the Muslim Women in Sport Summit, the speakers represented a diversity of sporting interests, career paths, nationalities, race and ethnicity, as well as age, all joined under a shared religious identity. During the Q&A portion of Bilqis Abdul-Qaadir's keynote address, a viewer asked, "What would you say were the key lessons of this journey?" She replied:

> I learned that we cannot measure our success or our identity in the eyes of society because through that journey there were three things that I began to question about myself that I couldn't change. Number one, that I was a woman. Number two, that I'm a Black woman, and number three, that I'm a Black Muslim woman. And in society's eyes, I'm looked at as the bottom. We're looked at as if we are not going to succeed at anything. It was a time where, you know, I didn't want to be those three things. It's really a disadvantage, you know, but I learned very fast to not measure my success or who I am in the world's eyes.

In her response, Abdul-Qaadir acknowledges the racialized, gendered, and religious hierarchies which render her at "the bottom." In order to defend against the perceptions placed on her as a person read through these three identities simultaneously, she self-identifies how success appears for her as an athlete pushed to the periphery of the hoops habitus. A follow-up question posed by a viewer asked her, "How do you balance these identities in relation to sport? Do these identities ever challenge each other?" Abdul-Qaadir responded by providing examples of a racialized Islamic hijabophobia where other Muslims would question if she was a revert or convert, certain that she couldn't have been born Muslim. When she pronounces Arabic words correctly, other Muslims are at times surprised. "I've been taking Quran classes and Arabic classes since day one. Even within [Muslim communities], as an African American Muslim there aren't places that we necessarily fit into so that's definitely a struggle within itself." In both of these responses, Abdul-Qaadir is articulating her position "in the world's eyes," through both Muslim and non-Muslims who read her as Other through a racialized dual hijabophobia. Ahmed noted that when she interviewed Elbadawi previously, "she was very clear to say that she experienced far more racism and anti-Blackness when she moved through Muslim communities as opposed to living in a white majority when she was younger." Abdul-Qaadir and Elbadawi speak of their Black Muslim womanhood as interlocking, not additive, a distinction Patricia Hill Collins notes as key to considering how power and privilege operate. Collins defines the matrix of domination through axes which may include (but are not limited to) race, gender, sexuality, religion, and class. The experience and resistance of oppression operates on three levels, according to Collins – personal biography (Abdul-Qaadir's experiences as an athlete and Muslim), the group or community level (the Muslim Women in Sport Network or a local mosque), and the systemic level of social institutions (FIBA's hijab ban) (2000). Each of these levels has the potential to either push women to the periphery or create space for resistance.

7 Discussion

Near the end of my interview with Ahmed, she noted her biggest frustration with Nike positioned as a sports savior for Muslim women:

> My thing with modest sportswear specifically is that it was born out of a resistance of women who wanted to help women and that's where we know activism comes from. We know political activism is on the backs of Black women ... we know this. We know that women of color organized and mobilized since the beginning of our existence because that's how we do, we know this.

In connecting this particular case to larger societal and historical norms which obscure the labor and activist practices of women of color, here she diagnoses commodity activism – the melding of social action onto corporate profits (Mukherjee and

Banet-Weiser 2012) – as yet another way marginalized women are rendered (in)visible solely in the interest of capital. I would argue the Muslim Women in Sport Network and its accompanying summit disrupt dominant discourses surrounding Muslim women and allow for community engagement and knowledge production which could serve as a disruptive organizational mechanism in the future. While unable to solely force change within FIBA, the end of the hijab ban in 2017 signals new openings for hijabi hoopers in the future. Online strategies to challenge structural inequality are complicated by the fact that, as a group of Muslim women (primarily of color), they are utilizing platforms built upon a social and technological structure that has historically maintained "white, masculine, bourgeois, heterosexual and Christian culture through its content" (Brock 2011: 1088). To create space for one another in a hostile environment which either obscures their activism or leaves them open to dual hijabophobic attacks is in itself a form of resistance. The creation of the Muslim Women in Sport Network and its resulting summit open up online platforms where these women can share experiences and strategize against dual hijabophobia within sport. On the other hand, as new technological forms capitalize off of discriminatory policies and resulting outrage from users, platforms such as Change.org, Twitter, and Facebook (and their affiliates) continue to profit off of protest with every click. Compounded with multinational corporations such as Nike cashing in on the economies of visibility, this reflects yet another example of the confinements and negotiations present within the cultural logics of late capitalism.

There is significant literature dedicated to revealing the contradictions of commodity activism and the invisibility of women's sporting practices. However, I would argue an opportunity exists within this area of study to contribute scholarship focused on (1) the intersecting identities of athletes, (2) organizing strategies of athletes engaged in activism, and (3) centering athlete voices in conversation with existing literature. In aligning this project with Ratna's call for more intersectional research, especially as it relates to the study of women in sport, I suggest avoiding the monolithic "women in sport" category, given that even in a case study concerning the experiences of Muslim women in sport, there exist vastly different experiences based upon one's sport, nationality, racial identity, and class. Whereas this case study could have focused solely on the actions/inactions of FIBA in regards to the hijab ban, avoiding the interrogation of power from a top-down approach provides new insights into how athletes organize within their communities and advocate for change. It also allows scholars to bridge the political thought of athletes with current literature; they can "talk back" to this very scholarship (whether concurring or contradicting) that examines the lived experiences of athletes, activists, and advocates within a larger global sports–media nexus.

References

About us. n.d. *Muslim Women in Sport Network*. https://mwisn.org/about-us/ (10 April 2018).

Alsutany, Evelyn. 2012. *Arabs and Muslims in the media: Race and representation after 9/11*. New York: New York University Press.

Amara, Mahfoud. 2008. The Muslim world in the global sporting arena. *The Brown Journal of World Affairs* 14(2). 67–75.

Banet-Weiser, S. 2018. *Empowered: Popular feminism and popular misogyny* (Kindle edition). Durham, NC: Duke University Press.

Baym, Nancy K. 2015. *Personal connections in the digital age*, 2nd edn. Cambridge: Polity.

Brock, André. 2011. Beyond the pale: The Blackbird web browser's critical reception. *New Media & Society* 13(7). 1085–1103.

Collins, Patricia H. 2000. *Black feminist thought*. London: Routledge.

Davids, Nuraan. 2017. How Nike's hijab sports gear is taking on Islamophobia and patriarchy. *The Conversation*, 2 November. https://theconversation.com/how-nikes-hijab-sports-gear-is-taking-on-islamophobia-and-patriarchy-86700 (3 December 2017).

Davidson, Kavitha A. 2017. Nike Pro Hijab gives important validation to Muslim women athletes, *ESPNw*, 7 May. http://www.espn.com/espnw/voices/article/18845880/nike-pro-hijab-gives-important-validation-muslim-women-athletes (24 March 2017).

Day 1: Session 1: Athlete activism. 2018. *Muslim Women in Sport*, 4 May. https://www.youtube.com/watch?v=ZCLh6AgnMwE&t=295s

Day 2: Session 1: Innovation in modest sportswear. 2018. *Muslim Women in Sport*, 5 May. https://www.youtube.com/watch?v=VvVjlwsa3o0&t=12s

Dougherty, Jesse. 2017. After playing all season, Maryland girl held out of basketball game for wearing a hijab. *Washington Post*, 13 March. https://www.washingtonpost.com/sports/highschools/after-playing-all-season-maryland-girl-held-out-of-basketball-game-for-wearing-a-hijab/2017/03/13/63fe82be-0767-11e7-8884-96e6a6713f4b_story.html (3 December 2017).

Eid, Paul. 2014. Balancing agency, gender and race: How do Muslim female teenagers in Quebec negotiate the social meanings embedded in the hijab? *Ethnic and Racial Studies* 38(11). 1902–1917.

Gruneau, Richard. 2017. *Sport and modernity*. Malden, MA: Polity Press.

Hamzeh, Manal. 2015. Jordanian national football *Muslimat* players: Interrupting Islamophobia in FIFA's *hijab* ban. *Physical Education and Sport Pedagogy* 20(5). 517–531.

Jones, Steve. 1998. *Doing internet research: Critical issues and methods for examining the net*. Thousand Oaks. CA: Sage.

Klein, Naomi. 2000. *No logo: Taking aim at the brand bullies*. London: Picador.

LaFeber, Walter. 1999. *Michael Jordan and the new global capitalism*. New York: W.W. Norton.

Laws of the Game. 2007. FIFA. https://www.fifa.com/mm/document/affederation/federation/laws_of_the_game_0708_10565.pdf (17 June 2016).

Levine, Marianne. 2015. Supreme Court rules against Abercrombie in hijab case. *Politico*, 1 June. https://www.politico.com/story/2015/06/ambercrombie-fitch-hijab-case-supreme-court-ruling-118492 (1 June 2018).

Lewis, Reina. 2015. *Muslim fashion: Contemporary style cultures*. Durham, NC: Duke University Press.

Lowrie, Morgan. 2017. Quebec women who've worn niqabs discuss controversial neutrality bill: "It's part of who I am, my identity." *National Post*, 22 October. https://nationalpost.com/news/canada/quebec-women-whove-worn-niqabs-discuss-provinces-controversial-neutrality-bill (15 June 2018).

Mamdani, Mahmood. 2002. Good Muslim, bad Muslim: A political perspective on culture and terrorism. *American Anthropologist* 104(3). 766–775.

Mukherjee, Roopali & Sarah Banet-Weiser, S. 2012. *Commodity activism: Cultural resistance in neoliberal times*. New York: New York University Press.

Nike and FIBA partner to grow basketball around the world. *Nike News*, 27 February 2017. https://news.nike.com/news/nike-fiba-partnership (5 June 2018).

Prouse, Carolyn. 2015. Harnessing the hijab: The emergence of the Muslim Female Footballer through international sport governance. *Gender, Place & Culture* 22(1). 20–36.

Ratna, Aarti. 2018. Not just merely different: Travelling theories, post-feminism and the racialized politics of women of color. *Sociology of Sport Journal* 35. 197–206.

Turow, Joseph. 2013. *The daily you: How the new advertising industry is defining your identity and your worth*. New Haven, CT: Yale University Press.

Weaver, Matthew. 2018. Burqa bans, headscarves and veils: A timeline of legislation in the west. *The Guardian*, 31 May. https://www.theguardian.com/world/2017/mar/14/headscarves-and-muslim-veil-ban-debate-timeline (25 June 2018).

Katie Lever

12 “Ideology in practice”: conceptualizing the NCAA’s <student-athlete> as an ideograph

Abstract: This chapter conducts an ideographic analysis of the term <student-athlete> as it is used in NCAA policy and in recent legislation pertaining to the financial rights of college athletes. Specifically, I argue that the ideograph <student-athlete> functions as a control mechanism centered around three main ideological elements: control, exploitation, and subjugation. I further argue that the NCAA’s use of <student-athlete> in its policy and public addresses is an ongoing ideological effort to solidify the mental schema surrounding what college athletes are allowed to do and the conditions under which they are required to perform. However, in spite of decades of the term’s use, no academic writing exists to frame <student-athlete> as an ideograph. This chapter aims to outline the problematic history of the term <student-athlete>, with an emphasis on its ideographic elements, discuss the term in its newest context, and address future directions. To do this, I will first trace the history of <student-athlete>, cover the ideological underpinnings that persist in the use of <student-athlete>, even in legislation designed to emancipate college athletes then outline the NCAA’s most recent fight over use of the term.

Keywords: ideograph; ideology; Marx; student-athlete; NCAA

1 Introduction: the NCAA and its fight against fair pay

The National Collegiate Athletic Association (NCAA) is the largest governing body of collegiate sports in the United States. Divided into three divisions and made up of 1,098 universities across the country, the NCAA describes itself as a “member-led organization dedicated to the well-being and lifelong success of college athletes (National Collegiate Athletic Association 2020a). However, the association also receives a fair amount of scrutiny, as it has been commonly likened with a “plantation” (Hruby 2016), and a “cartel” (Schauffer 2014). These descriptors are largely because college athletes, in spite of generating billions of dollars in revenue for their universities and the NCAA itself, cannot receive payment for use of their names, images, likenesses, or skills because of NCAA policies that require college athletes to uphold their status as amateur athletes.

Although popular wisdom might suggest that “amateurism is the original, pure state of sport” (Pope 1990: 290), it is, at best, both a myth and a social construct. Contrary to popular belief, athletic amateurism did not originate in ancient Greece.

https://doi.org/10.1515/9783110660883-012

Rather, it developed in England in the late nineteenth century, when sports such as football (soccer) and cricket became more accessible and popular, and "the English apostles of amateurism created a myth and sanctioned their new practice in timeless tradition by connecting their new ideas to the ancient Greeks" (Pope: 295–296). The reason amateurism developed in these circles is because upper-class English athletes found themselves competing against the lower-class, which was a reality they found difficult to accept. "More importantly," adds Young, "they found it difficult to win" (1984: 18). Thus, the English began dividing "amateurs" from "professionals" based on socioeconomic class – those who had to earn money from their athletic labor to make a living were considered professionals, while the "gentlemen amateurs" could afford to compete uncompensated, and therefore treated athletics as an avocation. According to Weiss (1969), the English distinction between professional and amateur athletes was "mainly a line between the unpaid members of a privileged class and the paid members of an underprivileged class" (192), and Smith purports "it may be that amateurism can never succeed in a society which has egalitarian beliefs. It may be that amateur athletics at a high level of expertise can only exist in a society dominated by upper-class elitists" (1990: 172).

Perhaps, then, it is fitting that the NCAA's current amateurism requirements, which mandate that college athletes cannot be paid or receive compensation in any way, further contribute to scandals, corruption, and inequity within collegiate athletics. Elite college football and basketball players – most of whom are Black men – subsidize not only the paychecks of their predominately white coaches, but also the many (mostly white) Olympic sports that their universities sponsor. With this dynamic in mind, Branch (2014) notes, "Slavery analogies should be used carefully. College athletes are not slaves. Yet to survey the scene – corporations and universities enriching themselves on the backs of uncompensated young men, whose status as 'student-athletes' deprives them of the right to due process guaranteed by the Constitution – is to catch an unmistakable whiff of the plantation." Extending on Branch's emphasis on Constitutional rights, I will later discuss the fact that even when college athletes are represented by the U.S. legal system, they are still subject to ideologies forced upon them by the NCAA, in large part due to their aforementioned status as <student-athletes>. For now, it is worth noting that although athletic amateurism is highly romanticized in the U.S., it is a fairly recently developed social construct with a strong historical emphasis on elitism and class division.

Although the construct of athletic amateurism and the NCAA's model of elite athletics within the realm of higher education are both familiar to American audiences, the college sports complex as it is carried out in the United States is unique from an international perspective, and not necessarily for the better. For example, the NCAA requires college athletes to maintain high educational standards as both full-time college students and elite athletes, committing anywhere from 30 to 60 hours per week to their sport (National Collegiate Athletic Association 2020a; National Collegiate Athletic Association 2016; Nocerra and Strauss 2014). Ridpath (2018) contrasts this to European sport, using the example of Dennis Schröder, a European basketball player who started his elite career in the German club system before playing professionally for the Atlanta Hawks in the United States' National Basketball Association. Ridpath notes that, because of the flexibility of the German model, Schröder was "able to focus on basketball at a time when his skills were at their peak" (12) because European models of collegiate-level athletics provide college-aged athletes a means to reach both their educational and athletic goals without imposing strict limits on their economic rights or hindering their educational pursuits. Furthermore, as college athletes in the United States are oftentimes pushed toward easier degrees of study, or have to sacrifice time spent on their studies to keep up with their athletic pursuits (National Collegiate Athletic Association 2016), Ridpath observes of the aforementioned German model of elite athletics: "the main difference from the US model is that [Schröder] was not constrained by arbitrary academic standards that could have limited his ability to compete, or that could have led him to a substandard educational experience just to maintain his eligibility" (2018: 12), a concern that is all too common for American athletes.

In this chapter, I discuss other ways in which amateurism and the label of <student-athlete> negatively impacts over 400,000 young adults, over 20,000 of whom are international students (National Collegiate Athletic Association 2020b). To do so, I first I discuss the ideological underpinnings of <student-athlete> through an ideographic analysis. Next, I discuss the NCAA's use of the term, and how it contributes to the exploitation, control, and subjugation of college athletes in NCAA policy. Finally, I trace the legislative process of NIL reform using California's "Fair Pay to Play Act" as a case study, in which I argue that the ideological emphasis of <student-athlete> is still present, even in policies designed to emancipate college athletes.

2 Student-athlete as ideograph

Borrowing from Karl Marx's assumption that ideology determines mass belief, Michael Calvin McGee coined the term "ideograph" to describe how ideology is "transcendent, as much an influence on the belief and behavior on the ruler as the ruled" and states that "social control is as much in its essence control of the consciousness" (1980: 5). Using war as an example, McGee argues that "the state's insistence on some degree on conformity of behavior and belief is ... a rhetoric of control, a system of persuasion presumed to be effective on the whole community" (1980: 5) Thus, social control is by nature rhetorical. Enter the ideograph, or "ideology in practice ... a political language preserved in rhetorical documents, with the capacity to dictate decision and control public belief and behavior" (McGee 1980: 8). Condit and Lucaites also describe ideographs as argumentative, noting that they represent "in condensed form, the normative, collective, commitments of a general public and they typically appear in public argumentation as the necessary motivations or justifications for action performed in the name of the public" (1993: xi–xiii).

Examples of ideographic terms include <freedom>, <liberty>, and <property>, and they function in American society to condition individuals to yield to the ideologies implicit in these words. Ideographs, McGee argues, turn individuals toward social laws and are "more pregnant than propositions ever could be. They are the building blocks of ideology" (1980: 5). Such ideographs "define a collectivity ... because such terms do not exist in other societies or do not have precisely similar meanings" (1980: 8). By these standards, the ideograph <student-athlete> functions to subjugate over 400,000 college athletes to negligent policy that undermines both their financial interests, and overall health.

Cloud adds that ideographs have both utopian and scapegoating elements, noting "utopian rhetorics often elide material constraints and determination in posting a set of ideal solutions to structural problems" (1998: 391). Like Cloud's <family values> ideograph, <student-athlete> contains both utopian and scapegoating elements. "Student" in <student-athlete> is the remedy to the structural problem of the "athlete" side of collegiate athletics. Framing college athletes as <student-athletes> draws the NCAA's "line of demarcation" between collegiate and professional athletics, therefore, "privatizing an idealist approach to a social crisis" (Cloud 1998: 392), that is, the rampant commercialism of college sports.

"Student" in <student-athlete> solves a second structural problem associated with collegiate sports: injuries. Because <student-athletes> are students, rather than university employees, the NCAA is not liable for injuries these athletes accrue. NCAA policy works to define <student-athletes> in terms of what they are not: professional athletes covered with comprehensive healthcare, able to profit from use of their NIL, and able to unionize when their financial and healthcare-related needs are not meet. This delineation between <student-athletes> and professional athletes/university employees has been a cornerstone argument since the NCAA's inception.

2.1 Building blocks of ideology

McGee acknowledges that ideographs are significant, both at fixed points in time and over extended periods of time because "each has a history, an etymology, such that current meanings of the term are linked to past usages of it diachronically. The diachronic structure of an ideograph establishes the parameters, the category, of its meaning" (1980: 16). <Student-athlete> is no different, and its usage is strategic. In 1947, Walter Byers became the National Collegiate Athletic Association's first-ever executive director and retained the role until 1987. In the beginning of his tenure, he notes, "I was charged with the dual mission of keeping intercollegiate sports clean while generating millions of dollars each year as income for the colleges (Byers 1995: 5). To manage this tension, Byers coined the term "student-athlete" in 1951, which soon “was embedded in all NCAA rules and interpretations as a mandated substitute for such words as ‘players’ and ‘athletes’” (1995: 69). Byers notes that his reframing of the amateur athlete was in response to mounting legal pressure that threatened to identify NCAA athletes as university employees, and to deflect from “the issue of workmen’s [sic] compensation for players” (1995: 69), and the same argument surrounding worker’s rights of college athletes persists today.

2.2 Exploitation

Byers’ strategic reframing of <student-athlete> is ideologically significant because it is used exclusively to describe NCAA college athletes as it pertains to them following NCAA rules. All college athletes, as well as potential college athletes, are subject to NCAA amateurism restrictions, and the ideograph thus defines “a collectivity ... because such terms either do not exist in other societies or do not have precisely similar meanings” (McGee 1980: 8). Although athletic amateurism has existed for decades as a monetary restraint outside of the NCAA, it currently does not function in the same way anywhere else as it does within the realm of American collegiate athletics. Thus, <student-athlete> defines a collective by labeling college athletes as “amateurs,” and subsequently restricts what over 400,000 current college athletes are allowed to do. Similarly, the term “student-athlete” is only monetarily relevant to NCAA athletes, which is why it functions as an ideograph: it is a phrase that has little meaning outside of American college sports, and its use is strategic and relentless in policy-making. Although <student-athlete> implies mythic images of purity, amateurism, and a “playing for the love of the game” mentality, in reality, <student-athlete> functions as a control mechanism and a methodology for mass exploitation of the very people the NCAA purports amateurism protects.

2.3 Control

Furthermore, among rhetorical devices, “it is the ideograph that is the most resistant to change. Whereas other components of the public vocabulary tend to disappear from public view, once their meaning calcifies, ideographs rarely disappear, even though their particular meanings and usages change” (Condit and Lucaites 1993: 2). The term “student-athlete” fits the framework of a “discursive constant,” as it is used 3,686 times in the 2019–20 *Division 1 Manual*, which is the most recent version of the NCAA’s enforceable policy book. The term is loosely defined as a “student who choose[s] to participate in intercollegiate athletics as a part of their educational experience and *in accordance with NCAA bylaws* [emphasis mine], thus maintaining a line of demarcation between student-athletes who participate in the Collegiate Model and athletes competing in the professional model.” NCAA policy mandates that “student-athletes shall be amateurs in an intercollegiate sport, and their participation should be motivated primarily by education and by the physical, mental and social benefits to be derived" (4), which means that, as of this writing, college athletes are not allowed to benefit from their names, images, and likenesses (NIL), and are bound to NCAA legislation to maintain their eligibility.

Fittingly, <student-athlete> is strategically imbedded into NCAA policy and practice as a control device, and the reiteration of the term <student-athlete> is significant, not only in NCAA policy, but also in maintaining the mythic purity of elite collegiate athletics. Grano notes that "by constantly restating 'student-athlete,' or 'amateurism,' as defenses for the current system, administrators and officials might still appeal to fans who want these ideals retained as symbolic reserves and points of nostalgic return, but they also express a discontinuity between expressed faith and actual practice" (2017: 199). In sum, <student-athlete> allows fans of college sports and NCAA officials to return to a nonexistent, but highly desired, amateur model of collegiate athletics, while also allowing the NCAA to control its athletes, especially those who threaten the purity of the "collegiate model."

<Student-athletes> who disrupt this desire for nostalgia are harshly punished. Much like the rhetoric of <family values> "has vilified feminists alongside gays and lesbians for disrupting 'traditional' family values" (Cloud 1998: 395), so too does <student-athlete> vilify athletes who break any number of the NCAA's amateurism rules. Several notable college athletes were suspended for amateurism violations over the course of the 2019–2020 athletic season, even amid the conversation about NIL rule enhancement. For example, University of Memphis basketball player James Wiseman and Ohio State University football player Chase Young both received suspensions from the NCAA for amateurism violations and were publicly vilified by the head office for these rule violations (Boone 2019; Rittenberg 2019). These suspensions also frame athletes as autonomous agents to a structural problem, and therefore, their economic actions threaten the amateur ideal that serves as the NCAA's organizational foundation.

2.4 Subjugation

The term <student-athlete> is "agent-centered, rather than scene-centered" (Cloud 1998: 391), placing the responsibility of athletic purity on the same athletes that amateurism subdues, thus emphasizing "personal responsibility rather than social context as an explanation, excuse, or otherwise apparently destructive individual actions, such as looting, participation in an underground economy, or violence" (1998: 391). When such actions occur, athletes disproportionately carry the weight of violations, as evidenced in the case studies of both Wiseman and Young, thus subjugating them to the NCAA's wishes, as no standard for penalties currently exists in the *Division 1 Manual*. Even when coaches violate NCAA recruiting rules, their athletes are still punished via title-stripping and scholarship reductions rather than salary reductions or suspensions for coaches, further placing the responsibility of athletic purity and the mythic amateurism ideal on college athletes (Johnson 2018; Carino 2019). This responsibility is difficult to displace, especially when prominent athletes reference nostalgia to support the NCAA’s ideology and further subjugate athletes to NCAA policy.

2.5 The “model athlete”

Former University of Florida and National Football League quarterback Tim Tebow’s reaction to SB-206 passing through the California state Senate (which I address in the next section) clearly illustrates the ideological underpinning of the ideographic use of <student-athlete>. On a September 13, 2019 episode of ESPN’s *First Take*, Tebow discussed his time at the University of Florida, when his “jersey was one of the top-selling jerseys around the world. It was like Kobe, LeBron, and then I was right behind them. And I didn’t make a dollar from it, but nor did I want to because I knew going into college what it was all about,” implying that college athletes should not be paid, because payment corrupts the purity of the game. Tebow went on to say “I know going to Florida, my dream school, where I wanted to go, the passion for it, and if I could support my team, support my college, support my university, that’s what it’s all about” (West 2019).

Ideographs such as <student-athlete> are “loci of structured tensions, in their meaning representing public contestation over society’s key commitments” (Cloud 1998: 389) which Tebow argues is the tension between amateur and professional athletes, where amateurism represents all that is pure about collegiate athletics. According to Butterworth, Tebow achieved a borderline god-like status, bolstered by American sports media who constructed him “as a heroic figure of (almost) religious significance, a perfect leader, and an embodiment of faithful dedication” (2013: 31). This dynamic makes him both a logical supporter of “purity” narratives and a dangerous messenger when he overlooks systemic inequity in such discourse. Essentially, the NCAA’s concept of amateurism is what Tebow describes as “what it’s [college sports is] all about” (West 2019). By this logic, athlete compensation corrupts the “purity” of amateurism. Ironically, Division 1 athletics are shrouded in commercialism – the NCAA is a billion-dollar industry that derives the vast majority of its revenue from marketing (National Collegiate Athletic Association 2019), so athletic amateurism does not protect student athletes from commercial corruption – it merely subjugates them to policy that controls their access to monetary resources, and ensures they can be exploited by those who profit from them, a dynamic that disproportionately affects Black men.

2.6 Ideology in practice and policy

In spite of these contradictions, the NCAA still roots its ideology in amateurism and athletic purity through the wording of its policy. Decades after Walter Byers left the NCAA, the *Division I Manual* never refers to college athletes simply as "athletes," but rather as <student-athletes> or simply "students" to uphold its organizational framework and prevent <student-athletes> from being considered university employees. Furthermore, this phrasing is consistent outside of the *Manual* as well. For example, during the 2014 National Labor Relations Board ruling in which the Northwestern University football team won the legal right to be considered employees and to unionize (a ruling that eventually was reversed), the NCAA released a statement claiming, "[W]e frequently hear from *student-athletes*, across all sports, that they participate to enhance their overall college experience and for the love of their sport, not to be paid" (Khan 2019: 33–34, emphasis mine). Such romantic descriptions crystallize the myth of the amateur Division 1 athlete in court, even though civil rights historian Taylor Branch (2014) describes the NCAA's notion of "amateurism" and the concept of the <student-athlete> as "cynical hoaxes." Branch argues that the term <student-athlete> "is meant to conjure the nobility of amateurism, and the precedence of scholarship over athletic endeavor" and to aid the NCAA's "fight against workmen's compensation insurance claims for injured football players," a battle that still persists years after Branch published his piece.

3 The Fair Pay to Play Act

In spite of recent pushback, the association has been historically resistant to change, and its strict athletic amateurism policies coupled with its lax regulations pertaining to athletic health and safety make it a popular target for sports critics both inside and outside of the academy. Because the NCAA has historically been reluctant to modify its policies, it has also become a target within the U.S. judicial system, as athletic activists strive to promote change within college sports from the outside. On February 4, 2019, California Senator Nancy Skinner introduced the Fair Pay to Play Act (SB-206) to the California State Senate (California Legislative Information 2019). The bill, authored by Skinner and co-sponsored by the National Collegiate Players' Association, was designed to counter the NCAA's principle of athletic amateurism at the state level, and allow college athletes to profit from use of their names, images, and likenesses (NIL). SB-206 moved through the legislative process swiftly, was set for its first hearing on March 27, and passed through committee on May 17. Throughout the legal process, the NCAA worked to counteract the bill's efforts just as quickly as the bill advanced.

On May 14, 2019, the NCAA set up a working group to examine its name, image, and likeness rules. Dubbed the NCAA Board of Governors and Federal and State Legislation Working Group, the collection of individuals was formed to "bring together diverse opinions from the membership – from presidents and commissioners to student-athletes – that will examine the NCAA's position on name, image and likeness benefits and potentially propose rule modifications tethered to education" (Hosick 2019). The NCAA's working group was headed by two staunch amateurism defenders: Big East commissioner Val Ackerman and Ohio State University athletic director Gene Smith. The Board also included a collection of other athletic directors, commissioners, compliance directors, and university presidents, as well as three unnamed college athletes.

Meanwhile, SB-206 continued through the legislative process, and was read in the California State Assembly on May 22, 2019. In June, NCAA president Mark Emmert sent letters to the chairs of the arts, letters, and entertainment committees that were overseeing the bill in an effort to postpone it, arguing that "when contrasted with current NCAA rules, as drafted the bill threatens to alter materially the principles of intercollegiate athletics and create local differences that would make it impossible to host fair national championships. We humbly ask that the California legislature provide NCAA member schools the time and opportunity to thoroughly assess issues surrounding student-athlete name, image, and likeness, including potential unintended consequences that might arise if SB 206 is passed as written" (Emmert 2019). On September 30, 2019, California Governor Gavin Newsom signed the Fair Pay to Play Act into law (Murphy 2019), which sparked an immediate reaction from the NCAA. Stacey Osburn, NCAA Director of Public and Media Relations, said in a statement that "the NCAA agrees changes are needed to continue to support student-athletes, but improvement needs to happen on a national level through the NCAA's rules-making process ... [the NCAA] will consider next steps in California while our members move forward with ongoing efforts to make adjustments to NCAA name, image and likeness rules that are both realistic in modern society and tied to higher education" (Osburn 2019a).

The NCAA's next step was described as unprecedented by many, when its Board of Governors announced a plan to enhance NIL opportunities on October 29, 2019, to be drafted through April of 2020, and promised to go into effect no later than January 2021. According to the statement, "in the Association's continuing efforts to support college athletes, the NCAA's top governing board voted unanimously to permit students participating in athletics the opportunity to benefit from the use of their name, image and likeness in a manner consistent with the collegiate model." Notably, the Board of Governors emphasized the NCAA's desire to ensure that any new NIL rules will "assure student-athletes are treated similarly to non-athlete students unless a compelling reason exists to differentiate ... maintain the priorities of education and the collegiate experience to provide opportunities for student-athlete success ... make clear the distinction between collegiate and professional opportunities ... make clear that compensation for athletics performance or participation is impermissible ... [and] reaffirm that student-athletes are students first and not employees of the university" (Osburn 2019b), thus drawing a line between college athletes and university employees.

3.1 Rule modifications

Even when considering rule modifications in regard to amateurism, the NCAA reverted to the <student-athlete> ideograph in its response to the passing of SB-206 to maintain its mythic amateurism ideal and deny college athletes workers' rights. Specifically, its statement on enhancing NIL opportunities read that any rule modifications would "assure student-athletes are treated similarly to non-athlete students unless a compelling reason exists to differentiate ... maintain the priorities of education and the collegiate experience to provide opportunities for student-athlete success ... [and] reaffirm that student-athletes are students first and not employees of the university" (Osburn 2019b). Thus, the term <student-athlete> functions as an ideograph even in discussions of rule modifications, in that it shapes collective consciousness, monetary activity, and even the health and safety of those it labels.

3.2 Reclaiming the student athlete

Interestingly, the text of the Fair Pay to Play Act (SB-206) also uses the term "student athlete," but in a way the NCAA never has. While the separate words "student" and "athlete" are used in reference to college athlete's educational, athletic, and monetary pursuits, <student-athlete> as a combined term is used almost exclusively to describe the bill's intent to allow college athletes the right to profit from their NIL, which is the opposite of the NCAA's ideographic intent. For example, the second paragraph of the Fair Pay to Play Act states that "the bill would prohibit a team contract from preventing a *student athlete* from using the *athlete's* name, image, or likeness for a commercial purpose when the *athlete* is not engaged in official team activities, as specified" (California State Legislation 2019, emphasis mine). Conversely, the words "student" and "athlete" in isolation are used relatively interchangeably.

Furthermore, section 1, subheading (b) of SB-206 states the legislation will "continue to develop policies to ensure appropriate protections are in place to avoid exploitation of student athletes, colleges, and universities" (California State Legislation 2019). The use of the word "exploitation" in this context is interesting, considering that the NCAA uses the same term to defend amateurism. According to the *Division 1 Manual*'s Principle of Amateurism, "student participation in intercollegiate athletics is an avocation, and student-athletes should be protected from exploitation by professional and commercial enterprises." Thus, I argue that the use of the term "student athlete" in the context of SB-206 is intentional: the California State Legislature is attempting to reclaim the ideological underpinnings of <student-athlete> and the NCAA will have to fight for its control of the term moving forward.

4 Exploitation, control, and fair pay

The passing of SB-206 was met with widespread praise from the media, athletes, and fans of college sports. However, a close reading of the text and its surrounding discourse imply this optimism is premature for two reasons: (1) SB-206 implies that athletes will still be exploited by the state of California, rather than the NCAA, and (2) the conversation surrounding the bill’s passing suggests that college athletes are only viewed positively in terms of their monetary value. Thus, the ideological nature of <student-athlete> perpetuated by the NCAA persists, even in legislation shrouded in equality and emancipation. Under SB-206, athletes will still be vulnerable to the NCAA’s ideology of exploitation, control, and subjugation, but under state actors rather than the NCAA itself.

4.1 Exploitation

According to the text, SB-206 “would require professional representation obtained by student athletes to be from persons licensed by the state.” Thus, revenue garnered by college athletes in the state of California would be taxable by the state, meaning that athletes will still be exploitable by a governing entity, just not the NCAA. Furthermore, California’s proposal of the bill led several other states, including Ohio, New York, and Florida to begin passing similar bills (Carroll 2019). Other governments clearly see the monetary and extractive potential of college athletes by passing NIL legislation at the state level, including North Carolina senator Richard Burr. One hour after SB-206 was passed, Burr tweeted: “if college athletes are going to make money off their likenesses while in school, their scholarships should be treated like income. I’ll be introducing legislation that subjects scholarships given to athletes who choose to ‘cash in’ to income taxes” (Burr 2019).

It is important to note that SB-206 was proposed in February of 2018, just before South Carolina representative Mark Walker proposed The Student-Athlete Equity Act to Congress in March, which would make fair pay more equitable than requiring individual states to mandate policy (West 2019). However, instead of rallying behind Walker’s bill, states have made efforts to pass bills similar to SB-206, likely in hopes of keeping athletic revenue in state, as Burr implies, rather than at the federal level. Should this momentum continue, the exploitation of college athletes will continue at the state level, rather than by the NCAA.

4.2 Control

Although the Fair Pay to Play Act offers promise to college athletes looking to earn money from their NIL, there are several ways in which the bill will control the financial activities of college athletes. For example, SB-206 prohibits “a student athlete from entering into a contract providing compensation to the athlete for use of the athlete’s name, image, or likeness if a provision of the contract is in conflict with a provision of the athlete’s team contract,” and “the bill would prohibit a team contract from preventing a student athlete from using the athlete’s name, image, or likeness for a commercial purpose when the athlete is not engaged in official team activities, as specified” (California Legislative Information 2019).

The first excerpt, although a significant leap forward from current amateurism legislation, still regulates the financial activities of college athletes: they cannot sign contracts with sport brands not associated with their current universities. For example, Stanford University is a Nike-sponsored program, but if a college athlete wanted to sign an endorsement contract with Adidas, the legislation outlined in SB-206 would prohibit this from happening. The second excerpt, which prohibits a team from interfering with an athlete’s economic activities when the athlete “is not engaged in official team activities” is promising, but vague. The bill does not define what constitutes “official team activities,” thus leveraging power to universities and coaches to control their athletes’ monetary pursuits. Thus, although SB-206 is certainly loosening the grip the NCAA holds over the financial activities of student athletes, its use of the ideograph <student-athlete> still implies that these athletes are under the control of those who oversee them.

4.3 Subjugation

Furthermore, even in the NCAA’s language in enhancing NIL rules, the use of <student-athlete> still functions as a control mechanism, because the NCAA reiterates that student-athletes are not university employees. Here it is clear that <student-athlete> is being used to draw a clear line between college athletes and university employees. The societal emphasis on pay for play ultimately reiterates the ideology behind <student-athlete> especially in terms of what the argument does not cover. Although SB-206 is aimed to grant college athletes freedom from amateurism, the bill still does not consider athletes as employees. This law, although generating productive conversation about athletic rights and fair compensation, does not uproot the deeply entrenched ideology that subdues college athletes, as evidenced in other court battles. For example, the ninth circuit court, which covers the state of California, has repeatedly ruled in favor of the NCAA’s conceptualization of student-athletes as *not* university employees, and antitrust lawsuits have resulted in similar outcomes (Baker 2019; Tracy 2019). Even if the NCAA enhances athletes’ economic rights in the future, it appears that the battle over ideology will continue as long as the courts favor the NCAA. For now, the ideology behind <student-athlete> remains, and is even evident in legislation designed to emancipate them.

5 Conclusion

The Fair Pay to Play Act, although generating constructive conversation about the rights of college athletes does not dismantle the ideology that subjugates college athletes to harm, and the consequences of this ideology are staggering, in terms of the faulty policy college athletes are constrained to. Thus, the ideology behind the NCAA's ideal <student-athlete>, one that is contingent on exploitation, control, and subjugation, causes real physical and mental harm to hundreds of thousands of athletes who compete under the NCAA. Although the passing of the Fair Pay to Play Act is generating productive conversation, even the text of legislation designed to emancipate athletes does little to provide actual benefits to college athletes. Until college athletes are granted employee status, they will remain victims of the NCAA's ideology. To quote Elizabeth Warren (2019): passing SB-206 "is a good start. Now it's time to allow [college athletes] to join a union – and get paid" (Daugherty 2019).

It appears that public discourse may be (slowly) shifting in that direction. In addition to the Fair Pay to Play Act, dozens of state and several federal-level NIL bills are currently in circulation across the U.S., and although they closely mirror the California bill in drawing a line between college athletes and employees, other available evidence has recently called that distinction into question. The coronavirus pandemic was widely cited as a catalyst for highlighting many of the aforementioned issues surrounding collegiate athletics, and it also cast doubts over the lack of employment status afforded to college athletes. Many universities, largely dependent on football revenue, continued to conduct athletic competitions during the pandemic, even as outbreaks occurred on campuses across the country. For example, in August 2020, the University of North Carolina moved to an online learning format after the first week of in-person classes due to outbreaks. In light of this news, the UNC football team did not alter its plan to forge ahead with its season (Blinder 2020). In late October, after the Big Ten Conference controversially reversed its decision to cancel its fall sports season, the University of Michigan played in its season opener against the University of Minnesota even as students were subject to a statewide stay-in-place order (VanHaaren 2020). As universities emphasized their need to conduct football seasons, the line between "students" and "employees" was increasingly blurred.

Additionally, it appears that college athletes are slowly realizing the immense labor power they hold, and they began to flex that power in the summer of 2020. Although several player movements have taken place in the past, including the aforementioned 2014 Northwestern labor union push and the University of Missouri football strike in 2015 (Nocerra and Strauss 2014; Peralta 2015), more recently athletes have made demands on behalf of entire conferences. In July, three player groups represented by the Pac-12, Big Ten, and Mountain West conferences, respectively, tweeted lists of demands to be met by their conferences and the NCAA – including increased safety protocols, racial justice initiatives, and, perhaps most controversially, revenue sharing, some accompanied by threats of player boycotts if their conferences did not comply (Players of the Pac-12 2020; Players of the Big Ten 2020, Mauss 2020). These groups sparked the #WeWantToPlay movement in August, in which athletes made clear that they wanted to play football amid the pandemic, but only under safe conditions (Arias 2020). The hashtag was accompanied by a list of requests similar to the aforementioned movements, including enhanced efforts to ensure player safety, but omitted the racial justice initiatives. Most notably, however, was the added request to form a players' association in collegiate athletics. For the first time in history, athletes from multiple around a single labor-based cause.

Ironically, the #WeWantToPlay movement ultimately served (temporarily) to discontinue the Pac-12 and Big Ten football seasons, as conferences announced season cancellations within days of the hashtag's circulation. Only the conferences whose players released unified statements prior to the #WeWantToPlay movement chose to postpone their seasons, leading some to believe the season postponement served as a union-busting effort, rather than a health and safety measure (Silva, Kalman-Lamb, and Mellis 2020). The failed #WeWantToPlay movement highlights a key issue within organization in collegiate athletics: college athletes have immense labor power, but little actual agency because they lack union leverage. This is ideology in practice – since college athletes are not employees, they are therefore subject to the aforementioned ideologies of their <student-athlete> label: control, exploitation, and subjugation, and these forces actively serve to silence them.

As the coronavirus pandemic and its long-term effects continue to reveal power imbalances and corruption in elite athletics, it is important for scholars to assess language use in sport. Specifically, the validity of athletic labor as legitimate work has yet to be realized fully, and this is a reality outside of collegiate athletics. For example, when professional baseball and men's and women's basketball players sat out games during the 2020 season in response to the murder of Jacob Blake, many news outlets referred to the movement as a "boycott" rather than a "labor strike" (Wimbish 2020; Stein 2020). Additionally, words such as "play" and "game" may very well have ideological underpinnings that downplay the real labor that goes into elite athletics, and thus, they deserve critical attention. As common words such as these have the proclivity to slip into casual vernacular, future writings should critically assess the ideological underpinnings of common language used in all areas of elite sport, and further explore conceptualizations of athletic work as valid labor. As for the NCAA, we should resist the ideograph of <student-athlete> and use language that more accurately describes who these people are, including "athlete," "college athlete," "athletic laborer," or even "employee."

References

Arias, Greg. 2020. #WeWantToPlay, but is anyone listening? *Sports Illustrated*, 10 August. https://www.si.com/college/vanderbilt/football/wewanttoplay-but-is-anyone-actually-listening (20 October 2020).

Baker, Thomas. 2019. Narrow decision favoring NCAA and Pac-12 fails to resolve whether college athletes are employees. *Forbes*, 15 August https://www.forbes.com/sites/thomasbaker/2019/08/15/narrow-ninth-circuit-decision-favoring-the-ncaa-and-pac-12-fails-to-resolve-whether-college-athletes-are-employees/#24b10855312a (1 December 2019).

Blinder, Alan. 2020. U.N.C. moved classes online. The football games are still on, for now. *The New York Times*, 17 August. https://www.nytimes.com/2020/08/18/sports/ncaafootball/unc-football-acc-online-classes.html (10 October 2020).

Boone, Kyle. 2019. James Wiseman suspension: NCAA upholds 12-game punishment for Memphis star freshman. *CBS Sports*, 27 November. https://www.cbssports.com/college-basketball/news/james-wiseman-suspension-ncaa-upholds-12-game-punishment-for-memphis-star-freshman/ (1 December 2019).

Branch, Taylor. 2014. The shame of college sports. *The Atlantic*, October. https://www.theatlantic.com/magazine/archive/2011/10/the-shame-of-college-sports/308643/ (20 November 2019).

Burr, Richard. 2019. *Twitter* post. 29 October. https://twitter.com/SenatorBurr/status/1189262863552208896?ref_src=twsrc%5Etfw%7Ctwcamp%5Etweetembed&ref_url=https%3A%2F%2Fwww.cnbc.com%2F2019%2F10%2F29%2Frichard-burr-proposes-taxing-scholarships-of-student-athletes-who-cash-in.html (15 November 2020).

Butterworth, Michael L. 2013. The passion of the Tebow: Sports media and heroic language in the tragic frame. *Critical Studies in Media Communication* 30(1). 17–33.

Byers, Walter. 1995. *Unsportsmanlike conduct: Exploiting college athletes*. Ann Arbor, MI: University of Michigan Press.

California Legislative Information. 2019. *Senate Bill No. 206*, by Nancy Skinner. Sacramento, California, 30 September. https://leginfo.legislature.ca.gov/faces/billNavClient.xhtml?bill_id=201920200SB206 (30 October 2019).

Carino. Jerry. 2019. Seton Hall basketball: NCAA imposes penalties for transfer tampering. *The Associated Press*, 15 November. https://www.app.com/story/sports/college/2019/11/15/seton-hall-basketball-ncaa-penalty/4201849002/ (1 December 2019).

Carroll, Charlotte. 2019. Tracking NCAA fair pay legislation across the country. *Sports Illustrated*, 2 October. https://www.si.com/college/2019/10/02/tracking-ncaa-fair-play-image-likeness-laws#:~:targetText=filed%20a%20bill%20in%20the,of%20their%20likeness%20or%20name (1 December 2019).

Cloud. Dana. 1998. The rhetoric of <family values>: Privatization of social responsibility. *The Western Journal of Communication* 62(4). 387–419.

Condit, Celeste M. & John Louis Lucaites. 1993. *Crafting equality*. Chicago: The University of Chicago Press.

Daugherty, Owen. 2019. *The Hill*, 29 October. https://thehill.com/blogs/blog-briefing-room/news/468037-warren-says-college-athletes-should-be-able-to-unionize-after (10 November 2020).

Division 1 Manual. 2019. *The National Collegiate Athletic Association*. http://www.ncaapublications.com/productdownloads/D120.pdf (20 October 2019).

Emmert, Mark. (2019). NCAA President Mark Emmert’s letter to the California Assembly. *Washington Post*, 25 June. https://www.washingtonpost.com/context/ncaa-president-mark-emmert-s-letter-to-the-california-assembly/9189935d-3282-4046-88f7-abee191f8d4c/ (25 June 2019).

Grano, Daniel A. 2017. *The eternal present of sport: Rethinking sport and religion*. Philadelphia, PA: Temple University Press.

Hosick, Michelle B. 2019. NCAA working group to examine name, image and likeness. *National Collegiate Athletic Association*, 14 May. http://www.ncaa.org/about/resources/media-center/news/ncaa-working-group-examine-name-image-and-likeness (14 May 2019).

Hruby, Patrick. 2016. Four years a student-athlete. *Vice*, 4 April. https://www.vice.com/en_us/article/ezexjp/four-years-a-student-athlete-the-racial-injustice-of-big-time-college-sports (10 October 2019).

Johnson, Richard. 2018. Louisville loses NCAA appeal and becomes the 1st men's basketball program to have an NCAA banner taken down. *SB Nation*, 21 February. https://www.sbnation.com/college-basketball/2018/2/20/17032440/louisville-basketball-2013-title-banner-stripped-taken-down. (1 December 2019).

Khan, Abraham I. 2019. Curt Flood, confrontational rhetoric, and the radical's constellation. In Daniel A. Grano & Michael L. Butterworth (eds.), *Sport, rhetoric, and political struggle*, 25–37. New York: Peter Lang.

Mauss, Jeremy. 2020. Mountain West athletes come together for COVID-19 protections in #MWUnited letter. *Mountain West Wire*, 6 August. https://mwwire.com/2020/08/06/mountain-west-athletes-come-together-for-covid-19-protections-in-mwunited-letter/ (10 October 2020).

McGee, Michael Calvin. 1980. The "ideograph": A link between rhetoric and ideology. *Quarterly Journal of Speech* 66. 1–16.

Murphy, Dan. 2019. California defies NCAA as Gov. Gavin Newsom signs into law Fair Pay to Play Act. *ESPN.com*, 30 September. https://www.espn.com/college-sports/story/_/id/27735933/california-defies-ncaa-gov-gavin-newsom-signs-law-fair-pay-play-act (30 September 2019).

National Collegiate Athletic Association. 2016. NCAA GOALS Study of the Student-Athlete Experience Initial Summary of Findings, January. http://www.ncaa.org/sites/default/files/GOALS_2015_summary_jan2016_final_20160627.pdf (10 October 2020).

National Collegiate Athletic Association. 2019. Where does the money go? http://www.ncaa.org/about/where-does-money-go (1 December 2019).

National Collegiate Athletic Association. 2020a. What is the NCAA? http://www.ncaa.org/about/resources/media-center/ncaa-101/what-ncaa (1 August 2020).

National Collegiate Athletic Association. 2020b. International Student-Athletes. https://www.ncaa.org/student-athletes/future/international-student-athletes (16 January 2021).

Nocerra, Joe and Ben Strauss. 2014. Fate of the Union: How Northwestern football union nearly came to be. *Sports Illustrated*, 24 February. https://www.si.com/college/2016/02/24/northwestern-union-case-book-indentured (12 October 2020).

Osburn, Stacey. 2019a. NCAA statement on Gov. Newsom signing SB-206. *NCAA.org*, 30 September. http://www.ncaa.org/about/resources/media-center/news/ncaa-statement-gov-newsom-signing-sb-206 (30 September 2019).

Osburn, Stacey. 2019b. Board of Governors starts process to enhance name, image, and likeness opportunities. *NCAA.org*, October 29. http://www.ncaa.org/about/resources/media-center/news/board-governors-starts-process-enhance-name-image-and-likeness-opportunities (16 January 2021).

Peralta, Eyder. 2015. Missouri football players strike to demand ouster of university President. *National Public Radio*, 8 November. https://www.npr.org/sections/thetwo-way/2015/11/08/455216375/missouri-football-players-strike-to-demand-ouster-of-university-president (15 October 2020).

Players of the Big Ten. 2020. #BigTenUnited. *The Players Tribune*, 5 August. https://www.theplayerstribune.com/articles/big-ten-covid-19-football-season (10 October 2020).

Players of the Pac-12. 2020. #WeAreUnited. *The Players Tribune*, 2 August. https://www.theplayerstribune.com/articles/pac-12-players-covid-19-statement-football-season (10 October 2020).

Pope, Steven W. 1996. Amateurism and American sports culture: The invention of an athletic tradition in the United States, 1870–1900. *The International Journal of the History of Sport* 13(3), 290–309.

Ridpath, B. David. 2018. *Alternative models of sports development in America: Solutions to a crisis in education and public health*. Athens, OH: Ohio University Press.

Rittenberg, Adam. 2019. Buckeyes' Chase Young suspended vs. Rutgers, then can return. *ESPN.com*, 13 November. https://www.espn.com/college-football/story/_/id/28072754/buckeyes-chase-young-suspended-vs-rutgers-return (1 December 2019).

Schauffer, Zachary. 2014. Does the NCAA rule college sports like a "cartel?" *PBS*, 11 June. https://www.pbs.org/wgbh/frontline/article/does-the-ncaa-rule-college-sports-like-a-cartel/#:~:text=%E2%80%9CThe%20NCAA%20is%20a%20cartel,typically%20to%20maximize%20joint%20profits.%E2%80%9D (10 October 2020).

Silva, Derek, Nathan Kalman-Lamb & Johanna Mellis. 2020. Cancelling the college football season is about union busting, not health. *The Guardian*, 12 August. https://www.theguardian.com/sport/2020/aug/12/cancelling-the-college-football-season-is-about-union-busting-not-health (20 October 2020).

Smith, Ronald A. 1990. *Sports and freedom: The rise of big-time college athletics*. New York: Oxford University Press.

Stein, Marc. 2020. Led by N.B.A., boycotts disrupt pro sports in wake of Blake shooting. *The New York Times*, 24 September. https://www.nytimes.com/2020/08/26/sports/basketball/nba-boycott-bucks-magic-blake-shooting.html (20 October 2020).

Tracy, Marc. 2019. The N.C.A.A. lost in court, but athletes didn't win, either. *New York Times*, 11 March. https://www.nytimes.com/2019/03/11/sports/ncaa-court-ruling-antitrust.html (10 October 2019).

VanHaaren, Tom. 2020. University of Michigan stay-in-place order won't impact Wolverines athletics. *ESPN.com*, 20 October. https://www.espn.com/college-football/story/_/id/30155430/university-michigan-stay-place-order-impact-wolverines-athletics (22 October 2020).

Warren, Elizabeth. 2019. *Twitter* post. 29 October, 4:19 pm. https://twitter.com/ewarren/status/1189320974560321537?ref_src=twsrc%5Etfw%7Ctwcamp%5Etweetembed%7Ctwterm%5E1189320974560321537&ref_url=https%3A%2F%2Fthehill.com% (11 November 2020).

Weiss, Paul. 1969. *Sport: A philosophical inquiry*. Carbondale, IL: Southern Illinois University Press.

West, Jenna. 2019. Tim Tebow on Fair Play Act: It changes what's special about college sports. *Sports Illustrated*, September 13. https://www.si.com/college/2019/09/13/tim-tebow-fair-pay-play-act-playing-college-players-video (16 January 2021).

Wimbish, Jasmyn. 2020. WNBA announces games will resume Friday night after players boycott in solidarity with NBA players. *CBS Sports*, 28 August. https://www.cbssports.com/wnba/news/wnba-announces-games-will-resume-friday-night-after-players-boycott-in-solidarity-with-nba-players/ (22 October 2020).

Young, David C. 1984. *The Olympic myth of Greek amateur athletics*. Chicago: Ares.

Jeffrey W. Kassing

13 Connecting local and global aspirations and audiences: communication in, around, and about Football Club Barcelona

Abstract: Football Club Barcelona has developed into a modern sports juggernaut achieving global influence while protecting a celebrated past, local sentiment, and a set of core values. This chapter explores the communication practices (both internal and external) that have shaped the club and its role and place in modern sport. Examination of the communicative processes tied to (re)producing, consuming, enacting, and organizing the club reveal how it attempts to manage tensions created by pursuing global aspirations while embodying Catalan nationalism.

Keywords: transnational; Football Club Barcelona; Barça; Catalonia; Catalan nationalism; soccer

1 Introduction

Football Club Barcelona (FCB), commonly known as Barça, is a transnational sports organization with global reach and an historic and entrenched connection to the region it represents. As such it negotiates the demands of the local and global simultaneously and consistently. That is, the club aspires and pushes to be recognized worldwide, cultivating an international fan base, while also attending closely to its Catalan roots and association. Perhaps no other sport club in the world exists in this binary with the tug of two powerful forces constantly in play. For this reason, the communication practices that facilitate the club moving ostensibly in two different directions warrant examination.

Giulianotti and Robertson characterized football/soccer clubs that transcend regional and national boundaries as transnational clubs. They stipulated that "leading clubs have retained strong legal, financial and symbolic ties to their home cities and surrounding cultures while building competitive success and supporter markets internationally" (2004: 561). Undeniably FCB "has transformed into a transnational organization attracting many supporters from around the world" (Rabassó, Rabassó, and Matere 2013: 46). Specific localities benefit when global audiences observe spectator cultures embracing particular symbols like colors, songs, and flags. Accordingly, football exports local traditions to global audiences and in doing so becomes a manifestation of globalization.

Football and nationalism are linked in several ways (Shobe 2008a). "Nationalism can be understood as both a political ideology and a feeling of belonging to a

https://doi.org/10.1515/9783110660883-013

community, a nation, formed by a group of people with a consciousness of being part of that community, claiming a distinctive common history, culture, attachment to a delimited territory and the right to rule itself" (Berdún 2019: 105). Football fosters collective identification because "global and local understandings of place draw upon football" and "fans construct the team as an extension or embodiment of a people and/or place" (Shobe 2008a: 331). This is certainly true for FCB, which has become a mechanism for asserting Catalan nationalism (Berdún 2019; Kassing 2019; Shobe 2008a, 2008b). While this connection is manufactured and reinforced at the organizational and cultural level, it also plays out in "social life through everyday experiences that significantly shape fans' identities" (Berdún 2019: 105).

This chapter explores the communication practices necessary to navigate the complex global/local nexus that FCB occupies. This is accomplished by utilizing the framework provided by Kassing and colleagues (2004), which compartmentalizes the community of sport into four overlapping and corresponding domains of activity: (re) producing, consuming, enacting, and organizing sport. (Re)producing concerns how media represent sport generally and those who participate and support it. Consuming refers to how people consume sport and its cultural representations. Enacting references how everyday communication practices and language use contribute to the performance of sport among and between individual athletes, teammates, and fans. And organizing captures how teams, governing bodies, fan clubs, players unions, and the like operate communicatively including activities related to marketing, public relations, brand imaging, and merchandising.

2 FCB and Catalan identity/nationalism

The inception of FCB in 1899 coincided with a period of prosperity and modernity in Catalonia, evidenced by rapid population growth and industrialization (McFarland 2013; Shobe 2008a). During this period there was a movement (*Catalanisme*) dedicated to "advancing the political, economic, social and cultural interests of Catalonia" (Shobe 2008a: 334). This entailed popularizing the notion that Catalonia was a discrete place with its own people, language, and institutions that deserved to be autonomous. At the same time, sport had become a symbol of modernization. Thus, the middle class' embrace of FCB as a representation of Catalonia signaled an outward looking populous ready to integrate with the rest of Europe (McFarland 2013; Shobe 2008a). In the years that followed FCB "became an increasingly important part of the Catalan experience of modernity" (Shobe 2008a: 335).

In 1910 the club's original crest, a simple replication of the city's coat of arms, was redesigned to include clear symbols of Catalan nationalism in the form of the cross of St. Jordi (one of the patron saints of Catalonia) and the Catalan flag (Shobe 2008a). The club crest remains essentially the same to this day. A few years later, in

1917, FCB adopted Catalan as the official language of the club, publicly backed *La Diada* (the National Day of Catalonia established in 1886), and campaigned visibly for Catalan independence. "Club documents claim that for a majority of supporters of that era to actively follow the club was to express a form of Catalan patriotism" (Shobe 2008a: 336). The club hymn, unveiled in 1923, reflected a strong civic, political, and social association with Catalonia. Hence, in the first two decades of its founding, FCB emerged as an early symbol of Catalan nationalism. Positioned as such, it would play an instrumental role in preserving and representing Catalan identity during the repressive regimes that followed.

During the dictatorship of Miguel Primo de Rivera (1923–1930) the local Catalan government was abolished, political and cultural institutions were repressed, and the Catalan language was banned. This meant that Castilian Spanish had to be used in FCB announcements, membership records had to be shared with authorities, and the presence of the Catalan flag was forbidden. Interestingly, these repressive tactics only seemed to strengthen the Catalan resolve as membership in the club increased dramatically (Shobe 2008a). The second and more sustained period of repression came with General Francisco Franco's rise to power after the Spanish Civil war ended in 1939. The fascist dictatorship he fashioned would span almost four decades stretching into the mid-1970s. Franco uncompromisingly pursued a policy of Spanish unification that involved centralizing power and authority in Madrid. This resulted in prohibition of the Catalan language and institutions. On the sporting front, Franco replaced club officers with his own appointees, changed club badges, and required that all clubs use the Castilian equivalent of their name (Lowe 2014). As a result, FCB became *Club de Fútbol Barcelona*. Moreover, Franco's uninhibited patronage of Real Madrid Club de Fútbol during this period amplified and politicized the rivalry with FCB.

Despite the name change and authoritarian practices, FCB remained, and again intensified, its standing as an important Catalan cultural institution (Barcelo, Clinton, and Sero 2015; Shobe 2008a). The club ground was in fact the only public place where Catalans could gather to sing and chant in their native language, the place where they could express their pride and identity as Catalans (Barcelo, Clinton, and Sero 2105; Xifra 2008). As Franco's regime wound down in the early 1970s due to his failing health, FCB members took active steps to reassert Catalan identity back into its formal practices. They once again began flying the Catalan flag, reinstated Catalan as the official language of the club, and reclaimed the original club name (Shobe 2008a). It was during this same period that the now axiomatic club motto *mes que un club* (more than a club) emerged. As the country transitioned to democracy, Barça evolved into an economic and sporting behemoth with global appeal, while keeping close connections to Catalan identity and nationalism intact (Kassing 2019; Shobe 2008b).

Against this historical backdrop, the following sections examine the different communication activities that constitute and surround FCB. Unpacking the (re)production, consumption, enactment, and organization of Barça contributes to understanding how it historically has and currently continues to navigate the "place-based tension" (Shobe 2008b: 103) that accompanies FCB's aspiration to be both local and global.

3 (Re)producing Football Club Barcelona

Media is the primary mechanism by which people symbolically connect with the community of sport. The activity of (re)producing sport mainly considers the role media plays in representing sport and those who participate in it. This can happen at the level of individual athletes, specific teams, and even nations (Kassing et al. 2004). This section explores how media have (re)produced FCB with regard to sponsorship, global expansion, and sporting rivalry.

Barça is the main object of news coverage in Catalonia, routinely receiving more attention than the activities of the regional government and city affairs (Xifra 2008). There is a robust media network covering FCB that includes four public Catalan television channels, 20 daily sports programs on the radio, and two sport-focused daily newspapers (*Sport* and *El Mundo Deportivo*). In addition, there are media outlets affiliated directly with the club – the monthly newsletter (*Revista Barça*), the newspaper available at each game (*Diari del Partit*), and the satellite television channel *Barça TV*. The monthly newsletter, according to club sources, has the largest circulation of all press written in Catalan including the daily Catalan papers. Given the media apparatus available to the club it is not surprising that it takes "advantage of its immense global prestige and following" by participating "actively in the global media-sport complex'" (de San Eugenio, Ginesta, and Xifra 2017: 837).

Ginesta and de San Eugenio (2014) explore how global popularity and extensive media coverage affords political actors the possibility of using sports organizations to address social, national, and international public relations concerns via place branding. Place branding occurs when "citizens, tourists, and companies purchase the image of the places and not the places themselves" (2014: 229–230) and the FCB partnership with the Qatar Foundation provides a case for examining how Catalan media addressed this practice. During the 2011–2012 season, the Qatar Foundation became the first paying sponsor to appear on the front of FCB's jersey. The Qatar Foundation, founded in 1995, focuses on education, science, solidarity, and community development. It was globally unknown before the sponsorship agreement with FCB. At that point in time, the partnership resulted in the largest sponsorship agreement (30 million euros per annum for 6 years) for a European club in history. It also introduced the world to Qatar's passion for sports, particularly football. The media applauded the move for demonstrating appreciation for FCB's growing Arabic fan base and recognized the importance of choosing a nonprofit entity for the first major shirt sponsor. However, as part of the larger agreement, Qatar Airways replaced the foundation for the final two years of the contract – marking the club's first for-profit shirt sponsor (Filizöz and Fişne 2011). The deal was not renewed due to mounting concerns about Qatar's treatment of women, gays, and foreign laborers, accusations of financing terrorist groups, and revelations about corruption in the bidding process for the 2022 World Cup (Filizöz and Fişne 2011; Ginesta and de San Eugenio 2014).

In other work, media scholars consider how international press covered the opening of the FC Barcelona office in New York City (Ginesta et al. 2018). An analysis of stories appearing across print, radio, and television news indicated that the majority of those derived from US media outlets (65 percent), yet 24 different countries reported about the event. In terms of story content, the main theme concerned extending the Barça brand internationally in order to capitalize on new markets and partnerships. The tenth anniversary event commemorating the club's partnership with UNICEF that occurred as part of the larger string of activities leading to the opening of the New York office also received significant coverage. Media linked it to the club's track record of on-going social outreach efforts. Interestingly, media reports overlooked political and social associations between FCB and Catalan nationalism. They also excluded, despite being regularly mentioned in club press releases, the connection with and representation of the city and region. This suggests that the economic implications of the opening overpowered the club's attempt to act as representatives for Catalonia.

El Clásico (the name given to matches between Real Madrid and FCB), receives abundant media coverage since the contestations pit not only two of the biggest, best supported, and richest football clubs in the world but also ones whereby "the 'Catalanness' and the 'Spanishness' are situated at the very epicenter of the conflict" (Lopez-Gonzalez, Guerrero-Sole, and Hayes 2014: 691). Indeed, the intense rivalry has become "symbolic of the struggle between separatists and advocates of the central state" (Gómez-Bantel 2016: 699). Lopez-Gonzalez, Guerrero-Sole, and Hayes (2014) characterize the conflict narratives evident in media coverage of these matchups. Front pages of online news outlets covered the match for a cycle of 35 days prior to and after the game accounting for roughly 7 percent of the reportage in general periodicals and up to 42 percent in sport-specific ones. Moreover, the conflict narratives occurred over three stages. The first stage featured assessments and foretelling from previous coaches/managers, former players, or others connected with the clubs and players. In the second stage, which led up to the actual match, emphasis shifted to direct assertions made about or by managers, players, current teams, and clubs generally. Opinions and expertise of third parties evaporated as the media featured the main actors and their opponents. In the final stage, which stretched for 10 days after the match, media celebrated and lauded the victors for two days before refocusing on the vanquished and the implications of the loss.

Unquestionably, FCB garners significant media attention that the club attempts to leverage as part of its efforts to become a global enterprise – generating goodwill through social action and representing Catalonia as a cultural envoy. These aspirations though are not always clear-cut and seemingly on occasion eclipse one another.

The New York City events depicted Barça as a club with a history of being socially active, but one that also clearly sought economic gain. Similarly, the association with Qatar transformed over time from a social one to something more commercial. These difficulties point to the challenge of balancing support for Catalonia while pursuing global exposure, which in turn affects how the public consumes FCB.

4 Consuming Football Club Barcelona

This domain of activity considers how fans and audience members consume sport and its cultural representations (Kassing et al. 2004). With regard to FCB, the prolonged association with the region and the recent revitalization of that connection leads many to "see membership of the club as a form of Catalan nationalism" (Berdún 2019: 112) or as a form of civil religion (Xifra 2008), the commodification of which can be seen on match day whereby a plethora of Catalan nationalist symbols are made available to consumers including but not limited to pro-Catalan independence party leaflets, flags that blend the club badge with the *Senyera*, (the national flag of Catalonia), and even Senyera-striped donuts (Berdún 2019). This section surveys some of the major objects of consumption related to FCB and their significance to the club and its supporters.

Consumer goods, like wearing the team's current or previous seasons' jersey, represent a connection to the club for many fans. The club has adopted "specific nationalist iconography for their merchandizing, worn and displayed by fans across the world" (Berdún 2019: 113). In his first term as club president Joan Laporta inscribed the Catalan flag on the neck of Barça's jersey. FCB and their uniform sponsor Nike have partnered in recent years to introduce a series of jerseys that celebrate the cultural aspects of the city. For example, in 2017–2018 the team's third kit celebrated the city's architecture with a subtle pattern in the shirt that resembled the use of mosaics popularized in the work of architect Antoni Gaudí. The following year the third kit featured a subtle pattern that reproduced an aerial view of the cyclic housing blocks in the *Eixample* neighborhood of Barcelona. The imagery in these designs is fairly concealed and comparatively esoteric. In contrast, the 2013–2014 away jersey was a full replication of the *Senyera* flag. The gold shirt with red stripes commemorated the 300th anniversary of 1714 (the year commonly understood to connote the end of Catalan sovereignty). Reputedly the club's best-selling jersey, a more subtle version was revisited as the pre-match training top for the 2017–2018 season. Merchandising that incorporates Catalan iconography symbolically represents the merging of team and nation and "presents this tie as indissoluble through displaying a simultaneous commitment to both communities" (Berdún 2019: 114).

The rivalry between Real Madrid and Barça, and *El Clásico* matchups between the two, have become another object of consumption. Both nations and clubs need one another as reference points to define and give meaning to their national sensibilities and contrasting communities. "Barça playing Madrid symbolizes and reinforces the political clash between separatism and centralism, two opposing interpretations of Spain which the clubs themselves are deeply interested in exploiting" (Berdún 2019: 111). Shobe (2008a: 339) recognized that instances of bias seldom get interpreted "so explicitly along political lines as they have been time and time again in the case of FC Barcelona and Real Madrid." This is due to the fact that for many FCB supporters Real Madrid became affiliated and synonymous with Franco's regime. A litany of events contributes to this orientation including claims that referees were bribed, players coerced to lose, and key transfer deals manipulated – all with the intention of producing favorable outcomes for the Franco-backed, capital club Real Madrid (Lowe 2014). Indeed, "Franco sought to demonstrate the power of his centralized control through the support of and his association with Real Madrid" (Shobe 2008a: 339). The positioning of the two clubs as such meant that "Increasingly, on-field occurrences were seen through a lens of political conflict" (2008a: 339).

El Clásico, then, has been consumed by Barça fans through a political and nationalist lens. Nationalist symbols like the *Senyera* and *Estelada* (the Catalan independence flag) surface at Barça rallies (Ortega 2016). But given the globalization of the two clubs the political dimensions of the rivalry may be waning. *El Clásico* definitely "has been mercilessly exploited in recent years to expand into a global fandom based on merchandising, sponsorship and the realization of imagined communities" (O'Brien 2013: 326). Through web technology both Real Madrid and Barça have "merged into focal points of global fandom and football tourism" (2013: 326), exporting the values and traditions of each club. Yet this level and type of consumption, fueled by a global media focus, may have denationalized FCB (O'Brien 2013).

Another point of consumption for FCB is its popularized club motto: *mes que un club*. First uttered by incoming club President Narcis de Carreras in 1968, the expression has become an axiom for the club suggesting that much more than sport is at stake (Shobe 2008b). It did not enter fully into the club's vocabulary until the 1970s, but the organization insists that it has always been more than a club. In a recent case study, Kassing (2019) reasons that the term served the club well as a mechanism of strategic ambiguity utilized to promote unified diversity. That is, as a means for the club to pursue multiple goals simultaneously without specifically defining objectives, tactics, or strategies necessary for achieving those goals. The ambiguity of the club motto allowed for supporters to consume the club as one that promoted Catalan identity and values, achieved athletic success through home-grown talent, and practiced social outreach via charitable partnerships.

A final mechanism of consumption is the stadium tour and museum. Fans from all over the world come to visit the *Camp Nou* stadium and FCB museum throughout the year. For many this is an important pilgrimage that acknowledges their standing as full-fledged fans of the club (Kassing and Nyaupane 2019). In fact, the FCB Museum is the most popular museum in Catalonia (Xifra 2008). The museum and stadium tour capture the complexity of the global/local nexus. For example, in the tunnel leading to the pitch there is the small chapel dedicated to the Black Madonna of Montserrat (one of two patron saints of Catalonia). Opposite the chapel is a broadcasting room used for interviewing the Man of the Match (Crawford 2013). Inside the stadium the club motto features prominently, composed of yellow seats against a backdrop of the more prevalent blue ones. At the same time, the corporate logos of the team's two key sponsors (Rakuten and Nike) are prominently displayed via offsetting seats on each end of the cavernous venue (Kassing 2019). The museum is a combination of historical artifacts and multi-media displays, which also combine to mix both the local origins and global reach of the club. Thus, consuming the museum and stadium indicates how the club works to maintain a Catalan connection while clearly striving to be a global powerhouse.

Consuming FCB entails attending to the significant symbols of the club – that is, the jersey, motto, stadium, and so on. These symbols inculcate fans with regard to what it means to be a Barça supporter – accordingly fans can enjoy the sporting appeal of the club but also appreciate its socio-historical roots and cultural legacy. The symbolism, however, is layered, which allows supporters to consume and represent the club at varying levels of intensity. Fans can simply wear the club's jersey to games, or they can bring and wave the Catalan flag during matches. Both realities are possible with regard to enacting FCB fandom.

5 Enacting Football Club Barcelona

Enactment concerns everyday communication practices and language use and how those function explicitly or implicitly to shape identity, ideologies, and discourses, as well as behavior and beliefs (Kassing et al. 2004). At a fundamental level enactment includes interactions between participants in the sporting environment – for example, coaches, athletes, fans – but also involves the discourses that articulate access to and inclusion in the community of sport. This section explores some of the common practices by which supporters communicatively enact their identities and membership in the community of FCB.

One particular practice that surfaced in October of 2012 during a match against Real Madrid, which has become customary at home matches since, is the *Independencia!* (Independence!) chant (Berdún 2019; Chopra 2014; Gómez-Bantel 2016). This comparatively new tradition, which stands as a public and symbolic reminder "that Catalonia was once an independent territory" (Berdún 2019: 112), coincides with a resurgence in Catalan identity and the politicization of the club. The chant occurs at the 17 minute and 14 second mark of home matches to signal the ongoing desire for Catalan independence from Spain. This action commemorates the year (1714) that "marks the symbolic date of the end of self-government of Catalonia after Barcelona's fall during the Spanish War of Succession" (Berdún 2019: 112), which for all intents and purposes "meant the end of the Catalan autonomy and the integration of Catalonia into the Spanish Kingdom" (Gómez-Bantel 2016: 699).

Claret and Subirana (2015) provide an in-depth look at another customary practice enacted by Barça fans – whistling (the equivalent of booing in other parts of the world). A tradition of whistling in defense of Catalan identity and nationalism has persisted throughout the history of the club. For example, there was an incident in 1925 during the dictatorship of Primo de Rivera, at the original *Les Corts* stadium. At halftime a visiting British Royal Navy band played several tunes before beginning the Spanish national anthem "only to find, to their bewilderment, that the crowd started to whistle and shout unanimously, completely drowning out the music" (2015: 82). The intention of the crowd became evident when the band proceeded to a rendition of God Save the King and "the whistling gave way to respectful silence followed by loud applause" (2015: 82). The result of this rebellious act was swift and punitive. The club was closed for six months and President Joan Gamper was forced to resign his post and return to Switzerland. In response to the financial threat these retaliatory actions produced, club members donated funds, paid their dues and renewed their memberships, and in some cases offered personal loans to the club.

In 1970 Franco planned to visit Barcelona to attend the final of the *Copa del Generalísimo* (i. e., the domestic cup during his regime). His visit was complicated, however, by a controversial quarterfinal match that was riddled with several questionable refereeing decisions. The result of the seemingly partial affair saw Barça knocked out the competition by Real Madrid. In response, FCB supporters organized a movement to whistle the dictator during his appearance at the final in Barcelona, which was apparent in a publicly distributed flyer uncovered in the city archives that had triggered an investigation by Franco's police (Claret and Subirana 2015). The handbill framed the refereeing decisions as a mere continuation of "the marked preference for Madrid, the club that represents central power" and of "the unequal treatment we Catalans receive" at the hands of the centralist state (2015: 75). It also made an impassioned appeal to "put an end to our silent acceptance of this disgraceful situation of abuse. Against injustice not just on the football pitch but everywhere to which we are subjected" (2015: 76). The flyer concluded with a direct request to "come and whistle this Sunday" (2015: 76). Franco managed to avoid being whistled at the match, but only after extreme measures were taken to ensure the crowd was comprised of supporters of the two clubs playing and neutral fans who posed no threat to the dictator. In the end, there was no whistling despite the strident call for such action.

With the resurgence of separatism movements in the early 2000s, whistling returned as a form of protest against the national anthem and the Spanish state. Both occurrences involved the final of the *Copa del Rey* (Spain's annual domestic cup competition) and featured two clubs most closely associated with regional identities – Athletic Bilboa representing Basque nationalism and FCB representing Catalan nationalism. Interestingly, both occurred in neutral venues, Valencia (2009) and Madrid (2012) respectively. In the first instance, the crowd whistling overpowered the playing of the Spanish national anthem, but Spain's public television channel (RTVE) manipulated both the images and soundtrack to disguise the occurrence. In anticipation of a similar reaction in 2012, match organizers produced a 27-second abridged version of the Spanish anthem that played at full volume to drown out the whistling protests captured on television.

With regard to identity, it is clear that Barça "is not only an object of identification but at the same time also the voice of a separatist tradition" (Gómez-Bantel 2016: 699). Over time support for FCB has become a proxy for representing Catalonia whereby "their theatre of protest is FC Barcelona's stadium, the *Camp Nou*, and their methodology entails a passionate lifelong support of their football club" (Chopra 2014: 16). Backing FCB leverages several inherent and longstanding Catalan cultural values like working steadfastly over time to achieve objectives, taking a measured and balanced approach, and practicing commonsense (Hargreaves 2000). Their sport-affiliated political activism (patronage of FCB) exists as an extension of these cultural values, which differentiates their resistance against a centralized government and unified Spain from the more violent and aggressive tactics adopted by the Basque separatist movement (Chopra 2014). Filtering resistance peacefully through the football club has not meant less notoriety though as global media broadcast the Catalan struggle for independence to a worldwide audience (Chopra 2014).

Yet not all fans of FCB are politically active or in support of independence from Spain. The Catalan press, various political organizations, and the local government have used FCB as a vehicle for promoting Catalan nationalism – creating "a full nationalist communion" between the club and its supporters which winds up "constantly exploited for political purposes" (Garcia 2013: 560). This connection overlooks fans that affiliate with the club for nonpolitical reasons. For example, for many migrants from other parts of Spain supporting Barça facilitated assimilation into Catalan culture. This cohort of fans tends not to question the politicization of the club because "understanding nationalist sentiment, even if they do not share it, is overall an aspiring, positive, and ultimately necessary quality for integrating into Catalan society" (Garcia 2012: 10). Fans in other parts of Spain simply adopt the club because of its massive popularity, world-class players, and track record of success.

An overstated, highly politicized perception of Barça fans neglects the social and individual identities that also dictate support for the club (Garcia 2012). For instance, a recent examination of FCB fans' use of internet memes in response to *El Clásico* victories reveals that they relied upon juxtaposing images and text, as well as knowledge of specific matches and the larger context of the rivalry, to accomplish diminution of their rivals and idolization of FCB players (Kassing 2020). This was accomplished without calling upon specifically political or nationalistic references. Nonetheless FCB "has maintained its base of supporters despite a political radicalization that does not please a significant part of its social base" (Garcia 2012: 9).

Intergenerational differences, between those who lived through Franco's dictatorship and those who were born and raised after Spain transitioned to a democracy, also influence and reflect the identities of Barça supporters (Barceló, Clinton, and Sero 2015). While both groups understood Barça "as an arena in which they could express their Catalan identity" (2015: 474), they construed the political/social dimensions of the club differently. The older generation valued FCB's role as an active "vehicle to express alternative views to the dictatorship of General Franco" (2015: 474), emphasized solidarity, and spoke of the club anthem as testament to "the cohesiveness of the Barça identity" (2015: 476). In contrast, the younger generation understood the club's history and Catalan affiliation not as a pronounced value, but rather as a latent one. They, in turn, highlighted the quality of football and placed little emphasis on the club anthem. Both generations recognized the significance of the Real Madrid/Barça rivalry. The younger audience construed it as an intercity competition, whereas the older generation viewed it as a national contest between Catalonia and Spain. Finally, the relevance of Barça's *mes que un club* motto migrated from representing Catalan nationalism and identity to accessing and accommodating a global fan base.

Whether chanting *Independencia!* at the 17:14 mark of matches or whistling the Spanish national anthem, some FCB supporters have embraced the dualism of doing local politics on a global stage. The club's history and affiliation with Catalan culture and its sporting prowess that draws multinational media attention facilitate this dualism. But not all fans identify as such. Supporters affiliate with the club as a mechanism for assimilation into Catalan culture and according to their generational mores. There are multiple options for enacting support for and allegiance to Barça, which the organizing practices of FCB influence.

6 Organizing Football Club Barcelona

Sport organizations include teams, governing bodies, fan clubs, players' unions, etc. These organizations engage in both internal and external communication to facilitate sporting endeavors and thereby affect the experience of sport. The organizing function considers communication emanating from and within organizations and how it shapes experiences within the community of sport. Of particular interest are the practices of marketing, public relations, brand imaging, and merchandising (Kassing et al. 2004). This section explores the communicative actions that FCB takes to promote Catalan identity and nationalism, balance local and global audiences, and manage social responsibility and community outreach.

The communication deriving from FCB clearly "captures and monopolizes definitions of Catalan identity" (Xifra 2008: 193). In addition to conducting all official business in Catalan, FCB displays both the club flag and the Catalan one at private and public events and promotes Catalonia as a tourist destination when embarking on international tours (Garcia 2012). All of these practices contribute to a patriotic Catalan hegemonic discourse that passes "as natural in FCB to a large extent without difficulty" (Berdún 2019: 112). Indeed, Barça has become a dominant symbol, alongside the national day and flag, of Catalonia – "drawing together complex notions of vital experiences such as Catalonia, Catalan nationalism, national sentiment, a common past, shared grievances, family tradition, festive celebrations, and so on" (Xifra 2008: 195).

During the post-Franco years, messaging coming from the club regarding its Catalan cultural connection waned considerably due to the presidential orientation of Luis Núñez. He conducted the club's business with little regard for its role in the social context of Catalonia by avoiding associations with political parties and isolating the club from any references to the pro-independence movement. As a result, FCB "ceased to be an important Catalan political/cultural institution and became more of a business" (Shobe 2008b: 94). By contrast, the organization began emitting clear signals of reconstituting its long-standing affiliation with Catalonia with the presidential election of Joan Laporta. During his tenure (2003–2010) the club promoted and used the Catalan language, adopted Catalan symbols, and officials spoke "openly about FC Barcelona as necessarily linked to Catalanism and Catalonia" (Shobe 2008b: 100), practices that continue to this day. In addition, Laporta pushed nationalist themes in his public speeches both at home and abroad because he "understood that a team with one of the largest numbers of members in the world could help the Catalan nationalist cause to obtain international legitimization" (Berdún 2019: 109). Laporta also hired Josep (Pep) Guardiola (a native Catalan and former player/club legend) to coach the team. Guardiola, who orchestrated the most prolific and successful period of sporting success in Barça's history, was a staunch proponent of Catalan nationalism evidenced by his use of Catalan in press conferences, public activism, and evocation of Catalan independence through cultural and historical references in his public remarks (Berdún 2019).

FCB aspires uncompromisingly to be an international brand, but "is faced with a challenge: how to juggle its strong Catalan identity with its willingness to transcend its regional cachet and become a global brand" (Richelieu, Lopez, and Desbordes 2008: 40). Barça is unique symbolically in the world of soccer in that it has the largest number of members (cresting 177,000 in 2018) and the largest stadium in Europe. Moreover, there are three major daily sporting papers in Catalonia that routinely fill their pages with stories about Barça (Gil-Lafuente 2007). These attributes assure a strong connection to the local community, but also provide the apparatus by which the club can build upon and extend its global reach. One way in which FCB negotiates the local/global tension is by revisiting its genesis story and former periods of success, recognizing that the club was founded by a multicultural group of expats who had emigrated to Catalonia and that it historically has and continues to welcome and depend on foreign players (Rabassó, Rabassó, and Matere 2013).

Club efforts to showcase the connection between FCB and Catalonia can be quite pronounced when the organization leverages its sizeable fan base and global audience. Consider, for instance, the events that transpired during a match against Real

Madrid in October of 2012. The club engineered a stadium-wide mosaic (i. e., a design revealed when each individual in attendance holds up a colored card) that displayed the red and yellow stripes of the Catalan flag. A single word (Barça) appeared overlaid on the flag. This display unfolded in front of a global television audience of 400 million and led to an a cappella rendition of the team's anthem by those in the stadium – with supporters singing in unison about how "a flag unites us" because "we are strong all together." The mosaic and anthem combined to conflate Catalan nationalism with FCB in front of a worldwide audience despite the fact that "not everyone identifies simultaneously with the team and the nation" (Berdún 2019: 112).

The challenge of attending concurrently to global and local audiences surfaced in a crisis the club confronted in fall 2017 (Kassing 2019). On October 1, the semi-autonomous Catalan government held an independence referendum that resulted in disturbing images of voters being beaten and restrained by Spanish police who were deployed to prevent what the state had deemed an illegal vote. FCB had issued a statement a few days earlier supporting Catalans' rights of self-determination and freedom of expression but stopped short of endorsing independence. Recognizing the mounting tension, the club also requested a postponement of their home match that was scheduled for the same afternoon as the referendum. The league denied their request and insisted that the match be played. After violence broke out that morning a second appeal was made to the league which triggered another denial accompanied by a rather punitive sanction. If FCB chose not to play the game the team would receive a six-point deduction in the league table (three points for the forfeit and an additional three). The situation thrust the club into the very difficult position of finding a solution that would show support for the local Catalan community, but also protect the global sports brand tied to success on the field. After deliberating for several hours and consulting players, the club took the unusual step of playing the match behind closed doors (i. e., in front of an empty stadium devoid of supporters). Club statements assured the public that this unorthodox decision was in fact symbolically meant to signify its discontent with the Spanish government's response to Catalans exercising their right to freedom of expression. It also claimed that by playing the match in front of an empty stadium the club drew attention to the day's events from its global audience and international media.

In a case study examining public reactions to the club's decision, Kassing (2019) concedes that playing the match behind closed doors proved to be a contentious choice. Former president Joan Laporta and former coach Pep Guardiola both made strident public statements that the club, given its avowed Catalan allegiance, should have cancelled the game in a show of solidarity. Moreover, the decision proved problematic for both local and traveling fans. Many locals expected the match to be played in front of a home crowd given the history of the club and its legacy of supporting Catalonia in times of repression, whereas others felt that cancelling it and incurring the points deduction would have produced a more powerful statement. Being a global brand, it is not unusual for fans to travel to Barcelona for games from all over the world, which meant that the club's customary offer to refund tickets fell short of not only the financial but the emotional investment traveling fans had made in coming to the *Camp Nou*. The symbolic intent of the gesture, then, was neither universally accepted nor endorsed by the multiple stakeholders it engaged.

Rabassó, Rabassó, and Matere (2013: 51) characterize FCB as a caring organization – one that develops "an organizational identity that encompasses concern for those outside the organization." The club's social responsibility derives from a felt obligation to respond to the growing international passion for Barça (Hamil, Walters, and Watson 2010). The FC Barcelona Foundation is sizeable, serving 400,000 beneficiaries in 70 locations and 30 countries through partnerships with other entities like UNICEF, the Bill and Melinda Gates Foundation, and the International Olympic Committee. The foundation strives to empower youth through sports-related and educational programs that foster creativity, confidence, self-respect, and entrepreneurship while addressing poverty, childhood disease, gender inequality, and universal education (Rabassó, Briars, and Rabassó 2015; Rabassó, Rabassó, and Matere 2013). As the club's charitable arm, the foundation operates under the slogan "Football is not everything" and has matured from a local entity into a global one that functions to "institutionalize community involvement at the club" (Hamil, Walters, and Watson 2010: 492).

While many football clubs demonstrate corporate social responsibility through their respective foundations, FCB deploys additional methods as well. For example, the club also engages in sports diplomacy through activities like the FC Barcelona Peace Tour 2013 (de San Eugenio, Ginesta, and Xifra 2017). In this instance FCB traveled to the Middle East as ambassadors of freedom and democracy (two key values espoused by the club) with the primary intention of "taking advantage of the symbolic value that FC Barcelona carries for both of the opposed communities in this region of the Middle East: Israelis and Palestinians, Jews and Muslims" (2017: 838). Based on having large fanbases in these communities the club sought to function "as a banner for peace and freedom in a region of conflict" by appealing specifically to Jewish and Muslim adolescents (2017: 840). The club also understood that its established position in the sports-media complex would equate to considerable attention with 450 national and international journalists following its tour activities. As part of the peace tour FCB held training sessions open to the public and coaching clinics for youth. The success of the effort was apparent in comments shared by Palestinian youth who described thinking about football and not the occupation as a result of the training alongside Israeli youth. Overall the effort substantiated the persistent claim that Barça is more than a club and boosted its position in the global media sports complex.

Another widely publicized endeavor illustrates Barça's efforts to construct a socially relevant impression (Filizöz and Fişne 2011; Hamil, Walters, and Watson 2010; Richelieu, Lopez, and Desbordes 2008). This was the decision in September of 2006 to sign a five-year collaborative agreement with UNICEF. The agreement was remarkable for several reasons (Filizöz and Fişne 2011). First, Barça "was alone among the top clubs in the world in spurning lucrative offers to sell advertising space on its shirts" (2011: 1413). Second, Barça would instead pay for the privilege of wearing UNICEF on their jerseys by donating €1.5 million to its humanitarian projects over the next five years. And third, it was the first time in the club's history that they wore the name of another organization on the front of their jerseys. This action signaled "a tangible expression that somehow FC Barcelona was different, not just another entertainment brand" (Hamil, Walters, and Watson 2010: 493). The unusual decision indicated that the club preferred co-branding and merchandising outcomes compared to outright sponsorship (Richelieu, Lopez, and Desbordes 2008). It proved to be an astute choice as popular press, industry leaders, and academics praised the agreement as an exemplary act of corporate social responsibility (Filizöz and Fişne 2011; Hamil, Walters, and Watson 2010; Richelieu, Lopez, and Desbordes 2008).

Over the course of its history messages from FCB have embraced or downplayed its affiliation with Catalonia, with the emphasis fluctuating in response to historical incidents, political crises, and club administrations. As such, communication from the club continually revisits and reimages how it connects locally to the region of Catalonia and its people. More recently, FCB has embarked on efforts to associate its global brand with large-scale corporate social responsibility and public sports diplomacy efforts. Through these activities the organization signals its intention to be a transnational force in sport. Accordingly, FCB manages to tack communicatively between local and global orientations as it pursues apparently incongruent global and local objectives.

7 Conclusion

Barça is not alone as a transnational club with global appeal and a strong local connection. The same can be said for the likes of Manchester United, Liverpool, and Bayern Munich – clubs whose representations "are available in all corners of the world" (Silk and Chumley 2004: 254). Given that fans can vary from locally rooted and highly affiliated supporters to distant ones connected primarily through communication technology (Guilianotti 2002), transnational clubs deploy a network of symbols to link existing fans and to attract new ones. Increasingly, associations with these clubs can be arbitrary and wholly dependent on the transmission and diffusion of club images broadly enough that they wind up "within easy and immediate reach" of probable fans (Silk and Chumley 2004: 254). At the same time, dispersion of symbols can facilitate connection for longstanding fans dislocated through sports diaspora. Thus, widespread representations of transnational clubs can activate affiliation for prospective fans and cement attachment for disconnected ones (Silk and Chumley 2004).

Yet doing so does not guarantee the accurate translation or authentic appropriation of these symbols. This happens when "the club's traditions become gradually and partially de-localized and increasingly dependent on mediated forms of communication for their maintenance" (Silk and Chumley 2004: 256). When symbols detach from their local origins they resurface as commodified manifestations that signify "differing degrees of belonging among different types of peoples" (Silk and Chumley 2004: 257). Unmoored symbols, then, morph and reconstitute as something resembling, but fundamentally different from their original expressions. As transnational sports organizations extend their brands globally, they benefit by increasing their followership, but risk diluting their fellowship with supporters in the process.

Examining the communication in and around FCB provides a sense of how transnational sports organizations achieve global success while staying meaningfully connected to their local origins. This involves understanding media construals of Barça as both a socially conscious club and as an outright expansionist one; identifying the various and significant symbols of FCB that consumers adopt; considering the more-or-less political identities supporters implement and enact; and examining the communicative practices FCB uses to promote Catalan nationalism/identity, social responsibility, and public diplomacy. While there are many transnational sports organizations available to examine, exploration of Barça proves particularly informative due to the acute contrast between global and local expectations and the communicative implications and challenges of navigating that divide.

References

Barceló, Joan, Peter Clinton & Carles Sero. 2015. National identity, social institutions and political values: The case of FC Barcelona and Catalonia from an intergenerational comparison. *Soccer & Society* 16(4). 469–481.

Berdún, Silvia. 2019. Much "more than a club": Football Club Barcelona's contribution to the rise of a national consciousness in Catalonia (2003–2014). *Soccer & Society* 20(1). 103–122.

Chopra, Rakshit. 2014. The role of FC Barcelona in fueling Catalan nationalism: Football and regional identity. *International Journal of Sport and Society* 4. 11–22.

Claret, Juanme & Juanme Subirana. 2015. 1970, 1925, 2009: Whistling in the stadium as a form of protest. *Journal of Iberian and Latin American Studies* 21(1). 75–88.

Crawford, Scott. 2013. Football Club Barcelona museum. *Journal of Sport History* 40(3). 480–482.

De San Eugenio, Jordi, Xavier Ginesta & Jordi Xifra. 2017. Peace, sports diplomacy and corporate social responsibility: A case study of Football Club Barcelona Peace Tour 2013. *Soccer & Society* 18(7). 836–848.

Filizöz, Berrin & Mücahit Fişne. 2011. Corporate social responsibility: A study of striking corporate social responsibility practices in sport management. *Procedia Social and Behavioral Sciences* 24. 1405–1417.

García, César. 2012. Nationalism, identity, and fan relationship building in Barcelona Football Club. *International Journal of Sport Communication* 5. 1–15.

García, César. 2013. Strategic communication applied to nation building in Spain: The experience of the Catalan region. *Public Relations Review* 39. 558–562.

Gil-Lafuente, Jaime. 2007. Marketing management in a socially complex club: Barcelona FC. In Michel Desbordes (ed.), *Marketing in football: An international perspective*, 186–207. Oxford: Butterworth-Heinemann.
Ginesta, Xavier & Jordi de San Eugenio. 2014. The use of football as a country branding strategy. Case study: Qatar and the Catalan sports press. *Communication & Sport* 2(3). 225–241.
Ginesta, Xavier, Jordi de San Eugenio, Pau Bonet & Martí Ferrer. 2018. Global football in the US market. The internationalization of FC Barcelona and its media coverage. *Soccer & Society*. https://doi.org/10.1080/14660970.2018.1556645 (15 November 2020).
Giulianotti, Richard. 2002. Supporters, followers, fans and flaneurs: A taxonomy of spectator identities in football. *Journal of Sport and Social Issues* 26(1). 6–24.
Giulianotti, Richard & Roland Robertson. 2004. The globalization of football: A study in the glocalization of the "serious life." *British Journal of Sociology* 55(4). 545–568.
Gómez-Bantel, Adriano. 2016. Football clubs as symbols of regional identities. *Soccer & Society* 17(5). 692–702.
Hamil, Sean, Geoff Walters & Lee Watson. 2010. The model of governance at FC Barcelona: Balancing member democracy, commercial strategy, corporate social responsibility and sporting performance. *Soccer & Society* 11(4). 475–504.
Hargreaves, John. 2000. *Freedom for Catalonia? Catalan nationalism, Spanish identity and the Barcelona Olympic Games*. Cambridge: Cambridge University Press.
Kassing, Jeffrey. 2019. "Mes que un club" and an empty Camp Nou: A case study of strategic ambiguity and Catalan nationalism at Football Club Barcelona. *International Journal of Sport Communication* 12. 260–274.
Kassing, Jeffrey. 2020. Messi hanging laundry at the Bernabéu: The production and consumption of Internet sports memes as trash talk. *Discourse, Context & Media*. https://doi.org/10.1016/j.dcm.2019.100320 (15 November 2020).
Kassing, Jeffrey & Pratik Nyaupane. 2019. "I just couldn't believe I was there": An exploration of soccer pilgrimage. *International Journal of Sport Communication*. https://doi.org/10.1123/ijsc.2018-0165 (15 November 2020).
Kassing, Jeffrey, Andrew Billings, Robert Brown, Kelby Halone, Kristen Harrison, Robert Krizek, Lindsey Meân & Paul Turman. 2004. Communication in the community of sport: The process of enacting, (re)producing, consuming, and organizing sport. In Pamela Kalbfleisch (ed.), *Communication Yearbook* 28, 373–409. Mahwah, NJ: LEA Publishers.
Lopez-Gonzalez, Hibai, Frederic Guerrero-Sole & Richard Hayes. 2014. Manufacturing conflict narratives in real Madrid versus Barcelona football matches. *International Review for the Sociology of Sport* 49(6). 688–706.
Lowe, Sid. 2014. *Fear and loathing in La Liga: Barcelona, Real Madrid, and the world's greatest sports rivalry*. New York: Nation Books.
McFarland, Andrew. 2013. Founders, foundations and early identities: Football's early growth in Barcelona. *Soccer & Society* 13(1). 93–107.
O'Brien, Jim. 2013. 'El Clasico' and the demise of tradition in Spanish club football: Perspectives on shifting patterns of cultural identity. *Soccer & Society* 14(3). 315–330.
Ortega, Vincente. 2016. Soccer, nationalism and the media in contemporary Spanish society: La Roja, Real Madrid & FC Barcelona. *Soccer & Society* 17(4). 628–643.
Rabassó, Carlos, Martin Briars & Francisco Rabassó. 2015. Royal family business in Qatar and the Emirates through sports club management: "Green washing" or a sustainable model? The cases of FC Barcelona and Manchester City. *International Journal of Employment Studies* 23(2). 5–25.
Rabassó, Carlos, Francisco Rabassó & Saku Matere. 2013. Cultural diversity as a tool for caring and productive resistance. The case of FC Barcelona: A responsible perspective. *International Journal of Employment Studies* 21(2). 44–61.

Richelieu, André, Sibylle Lopez & Michel Desbordes. 2008. The internationalization of a sports team brand: The case of European soccer teams. *International Journal of Sports Marketing & Sponsorship* 10(1). 29–44.
Shobe, Hunter. 2008a. Place, identity and football. Catalonia, Catalanisme and Football Club Barcelona, 1899–1975. *National Identities* 10(3). 329–343.
Shobe, Hunter. 2008b. Football and the politics of place: Football Club Barcelona and Catalonia, 1975–2005. *Journal of Cultural Geography* 25(1). 87–105.
Silk, Michael & Emma Chumley. 2004. Memphis United? Diaspora, s(t)imulated spaces and global consumption economies. In David L. Andrews (ed.), *Manchester United: A thematic study*, 249–264. London: Routledge.
Xifra, Jordi. 2008. Soccer, civil religion, and public relations: Devotional-promotional communication and Barcelona Football Club. *Public Relations Review* 34. 192–198.

III Sport and media

David Rowe and Toby Miller

14 MediaSport: over production and global consumption

Abstract: Sport and media ("MediaSport") are deeply co-dependent in reaching, developing, and exploiting their intersecting audiences. In major MediaSport markets, the outcome has been over production and consequent consumption saturation, especially in the United States, which pioneered the commercialized co-development of MediaSport. As a result, US sports – many of which, like baseball and American football, have been determinedly parochial and inward-looking – are seeking to cultivate new consumers, especially those in the more affluent parts of Europe. This strategy highlights the increasing inability of single nation-state markets to thrive in a globalizing MediaSport environment. For example, in Australia's congested market (which includes four competing codes of football), sports are turning to Asian consumers (who are also being actively courted by the US's National Basketball Association and association football's English Premier League). This chapter addresses, in particular, US and Australian consumer "outreach" strategies in analyzing the global dynamics of contemporary MediaSport.

Keywords: MediaSport; over production; consumption; globalization; TV; USA; Australia; environment

1 Introduction: producing and consuming MediaSport

In addressing global sport consumption, professional (pro) sports, especially in the Global North, cannot be understood without considering the media. The consumer practices of the two domains are deeply entwined, to the point where the neologism "MediaSport" (Wenner 1998) was created to describe their interpenetrating production and consumption. MediaSport production and consumption occur at the intersection of two fields (Bourdieu and Wacquant 1992). The sporting field is internally subject to struggles over various forms of capital, such as for economic supremacy between different sports in pursuing audiences or proposing the symbolic superiority of one over another. The same could be said of the media field (for example, between news producers and content distributors over programs, or between film and literature over cultural prestige). There are also struggles between the two fields – over, for example, proprietary rights and scheduling – that see them converge and overlap without mutual absorption (lisahunter, Smith, and emerald 2015; Rowe 2019).

https://doi.org/10.1515/9783110660883-014

The Global North's pivotal live sports experience is located within a massive supporting media apparatus – the "media sports cultural complex" (Rowe 2004). Media-related consumption practices within this complex range from TV sport subscriptions to advertising-stimulated online gambling on sport outcomes. Audiences consume professional sports performance both in the conventional role of spectator and fan and via a range of products and services associated with it. Media coverage of sports can take many forms, including print and online journalism, video gaming, sports-themed film and literature, radio commentary, professional and amateur web pages, and online exchanges. They interact to accommodate and stimulate consumption. Sports audiences have frequently been built up by state broadcasters, then exploited by capitalist companies that are too unimaginative and indolent to innovate themselves. This predatory practice is evident in the history of basketball in the United States, which was pioneered on television by San Francisco's public station; cricket and rugby union around the world (developed as spectator sports by public networks in Ireland, Britain, Australia, India, South Africa, France, and Aotearoa/New Zealand); and association football across Europe. Public culture bore the cost of developing what became commercially exploited culture.

Screened live, sport has become an especially valuable commodity because it can attract audiences in numbers ranging from the respectable to the staggering (Tomlinson and Young 2006). Media rights to the most popular sports and biggest events are sold by their governing organizations or individual teams at a considerable premium. Audiences pay to watch via subscription and on-demand services, and/or their presumed attention span is sold to advertisers and sponsors (Smythe 2004). Alongside the live competitive reality television shows that have in various ways mimicked sports, the fragmentation of free-to-air (FTA) television audiences in the deregulated satellite and subscription era has given them a strong position within the contemporary broadcast environment (Hutchins and Rowe 2012). However, the increasingly desperate search for audience-friendly sports and sporting formats within national MediaSport contexts has led to a cost-price squeeze in the acquisition of rights and a certain overproduction in multi-channel environments. Derek Thompson (quoted in Lotz 2014: 14) has captured these problems well: "Without live sports, the TV business could fall apart; and because of live sports, the TV business could fall apart."

In this chapter, we concentrate on two rather different, but comparable, MediaSport environments – the United States and Australia – to analyze the contrasting ways in which MediaSport consumption is organized and enacted under different conditions of production and consumption. In the quest for, and cultivation of, the Global North's MediaSport consumers, the principal agents within these convergent "field[s] of struggles" (Bourdieu and Wacquant 1992: 101) seek to mold the choices and practices that they claim to serve. In the process, the consumer – sometimes also figured as the citizen – takes on an abstract quality that is conventionally defined more by extravagant, expansionist marketing rhetoric than by concrete, demonstrable practices of consumption.

As a consequence, we emphasize how MediaSport's capitalist expansionism creates conditions that must be negotiated by sport aficionados and casual viewers alike in everyday forms of consumption, with significant ramifications for cultural citizenship (Miller 2007). In addition, sometimes the MediaSport audience needs to be understood not as central in itself, either to fantasies of belonging or advertising, but as a means of struggling for business or contributing to social problems.

To give two examples, in 2015, the English Premier League (EPL) of men's association football announced that two subscription TV companies, BT and Sky, had committed to spend US $7.9 billion between them for the right to televise matches over three seasons. That was 70 percent more than the previous contract costs. It put the EPL's TV value ahead of Major League Baseball, comparable to the National Basketball Association (NBA), and behind only the National Football League (NFL) in domestic rights deals – this in a country with a population one-fifth the size of the United States. The deal is bigger than all three when foreign territories are added (an additional US $4.3 billion) (Bonesteel 2015). In the same week, sports' share of television viewing in the UK was just 6.23 percent, well behind hobbies, news, documentaries, and other genres (Broadcasters' Audience 2015a). Sky Sports 1 had just 0.99 percent of the TV audience. All its channels combined, from drama to news to football to cricket and so on, "commanded" a mere 8.3 per cent of the total audience. For its part, BT Sport secured 0.39 percent of viewers (Broadcasters' Audience 2015b). At the same time, the UK's National Grid was promoting its management of peak electricity usage based on audience activity during half time in major football matches, when people race to the kettle. Power use surges by as much as 10 percent in what is known as the "TV pick-up," with the Carbon Trust showing that people watching football via mobile telephony multiply their footprint tenfold in comparison with television or Wi-Fi signals. The drain on power sources in other countries broadcasting the Cup is huge – and rarely acknowledged (Miller 2017).

How can we explain these two phenomena – the extraordinary valuation of the EPL, given its rather inconsequential domestic viewing numbers, and the blithely extravagant energy use associated with consuming sport through the media? Despite sports' importance in television history, the EPL deal is not about gigantic ratings, but a struggle between competing capitalist interests to obtain consumer subscriptions for broadband and telephony – a contest between wealthy corporations set on decimating the other's core business: broadband and telephony subscriptions. MediaSport is the signifier, not the referent. In our second example, the environmental impact of sports consumption is part of a wider issue of consumer ignorance of such problems when not directly articulated by public policy via domestic recycling programs or awareness campaigns. Confronted by such questions, we seek to look sideways as well as directly at MediaSport, so that their rhetoric does not distract us from the real political economy that both animates them and arises from their excesses.

2 The United States: subsidy, over production, and overflow

The world's historically largest MediaSport market, the United States, has tended towards a rather inward-looking "exceptionalism" (Miller et al. 2003, 2011). Its world of MediaSport is distinctive in terms of media and sport systems, consumer preferences, flows of texts, and degrees of market saturation. In addition, unlike most other nations, the internal United States audience for TV can be as fixated on high-school football, in small markets, and college basketball, in national ones, as on their professional (pro) equivalents. Such dynamics are relatively immune to international tendencies. They relate, instead, to the decentralized nature of the United States population by contrast with most industrial and post-industrial nations, and the lack of pro teams outside major urban agglomerations.

From the earliest days of United States television, sports were crucial programming sources. Before World War II, baseball was screened live to wealthy New Yorkers. The first network broadcast was a 1945 football game that featured President Harry S. Truman in the stadium, thereby binding sport, politics, and corporate power in a symbolic whirl that presaged the central role of sports in an emergent TV system. A decade later, the development of a coaxial-cable link connecting the coasts brought the first movement of sports teams across the country, when the Brooklyn Dodgers and Giants headed to California. As pro ball on TV took off, Congress protected college sports by insisting that Saturdays be kept free for college American football for much of the season, a *quid pro quo* after the courts found that TV rights exclusives breached anti-trust rules (Florio 2014).

The United States basked in the breakthrough television coverage of the 1964 Olympiad – the first color broadcast of the Games and the first to be available live internationally via satellite (NHK n.d.). Ever since, the fabulous riches bestowed on the International Olympic Committee (IOC) and craven local hosts by United States broadcast networks have seen NBC and its forebears take prime position for the coverage of events, determine starting times and locations, muscle out other broadcasters, and dominate proceedings in every imaginable way. NBC's 2014 contract with the IOC guaranteed that corrupt, unrepresentative, undemocratic body US $7.7 billion (Armour 2014). The London Games of 2012, which were not especially popular, paled by contrast with Rio in 2016, when NBC more than doubled its 2012 Games profits to US $250 million (Crupi 2016a). Such expenditures and receipts are inconceivable from any other broadcaster in world history. They are predicated on tricking watchers into believing that events are covered as actuality rather than being delayed to suit ratings' needs – the notorious "plausibly live" policy that stands in stark contrast to non-Anglo TV – and focusing on virtually nothing where the United States team is unlikely to succeed. Univisión, which regularly attracts more viewers than NBC in general, is more cosmopolitan in addressing viewers than its English-only counterpart (Moreno 2014).

United States residents frequently outnumber other nations' tourists at the men's World Cup of football, and the nation is coming to exert similar pressure on the Fédération Internationale de Football Association (FIFA), the game's governing body – this time via the state. The Justice Department has made remarkable strides towards reforming that decadent body through swift and profound interdiction (United States of America 2015). Pitiful European, Asian, and Latin American courtiers to FIFA, such as the UK government and its public service broadcasters ITV and the BBC, have signally failed to achieve – or even attempt – such reforming tasks. Complicit networks and states remained largely silent as their money made FIFA wealthy, and vice versa (Bean 2016; Clarke 2016; Bayle 2015).

In terms of its own major leagues, the New International Division of Cultural Labor (NICL) has become a means of ensuring that the United States has a high standard of both athletic ability and global spectator appeal (Miller et al. 2001, 2003). So, for example, having saturated the domestic supply of good, cheap, obedient athletes and affluent consumers, the NBA went overseas in search of cheap talent and likely customers, opening offices in Switzerland, Spain, Australia, Hong Kong, and Mexico during the 1990s. Needless to say, this internationalism extends to imperialism. The domestic United States consumer is always-already addressed as a militarized patriot – so the Association headlines its "green" credentials as part of corporate social responsibility, even as it disports its commitment to the military-industrial complex (NBA Green n.d.; Hoops for Troops n.d.). United States "football" and the media have specialized in interpellating consumers' nationalistic fervor through coordination with the military since the American War in Việt Nam, and there is now even an Armed Forces Bowl. College "football" was sponsored by Bell Helicopter-Textron from 2006 to 2013, and, since 2014, by Lockheed Martin, two of the vast array of "private-enterprise" companies whose livelihoods rely on public sector welfare via the development and purchase of murderous technology. In this instance, promotional activities are not about selling products to fans, as per most sports underwriting. Instead, they are dedicated to creating public goodwill towards corporate militaristic welfare through homologies between sport, nation, and *matériel*, via a contest that is televised – and owned – by ESPN. It features opportunistic recruiters looking to prey on young spectators and the presentation of a "Great American Patriot Award." For its part, baseball offers "Welcome Back Veterans" and "Military Appreciation" events (Butterworth and Moskal 2009).

The Women's National Basketball Association (WNBA) *began* with use of the NICL, rather than turning to it once the domestic market in players and fans had become super-saturated in, respectively, cost/quality and wealth/quantity. In 2002, five All-Stars were foreign nationals (WNBA players 2005). By 2017, unlike their male counterparts, players were not just encouraged to play elsewhere – it was headlined as a League initiative (Maloney 2017). And in place of the NBA's address of environmentalism and militarism to attract viewers, the WNBA highlighted queerness (WNBA pride n.d.).

These tendencies reflected media-audience targeting. The NICL references fiscal crises for the national sports system at the level of both demand and supply, necessitating an outreach that undermines the hermetically sealed domestic world and the college sports system's services in recruiting and training talent internationally (Bale 1991) as well as nationally, prior to serving it up for the delectation of the pros. The NICL runs counter to a potent brand of amateur intellectualism and reactionary academia that celebrates a putative "American exceptionalism," which supposedly makes United States sports part of an export rather than an import culture. So we encounter claims that "foreignness" can make a sport unpopular in the United States, and that the media will not accept practices coded as "other" (Brown 2005; Willis 2005). But by 2005, the United States had English- and Spanish-language TV networks dedicated to association football, covering leagues in Britain, Germany, Asia, Africa, France, Spain, the Netherlands, Australia, Latin America – and the United States (men's *and* women's four years later). In Los Angeles in 2009, 93,000 people turned up to watch an association football match. NBC's 2012 purchase of EPL coverage from the minor obstacle of the lapsed-Australian Rupert Murdoch showed how far the sport had come – renewed three years later for a billion dollars (Sandomir 2015).

There is considerable debate about whether MediaSport is immune to recession. Premium sports claim that their brands will protect them from general reductions in TV rights and sponsorship when media companies confront balance sheets with reduced advertising and subscription revenue. In barely two decades, over-bidding for TV rights, fueled by Murdoch's dual ambition of creating a global sporting television service while achieving hegemony in its foundational market, helped turn broadcast sports from a prized commodity to a valued loss leader, and finally into a contractual liability. As one commentator put it, during the largest slump in spending on advertising since the Second World War, but before the debt-driven crisis of five years later, "[t]he U.S. media market is glutted with more sports and entertainment properties than there is ad money to go round" (McCarthy 2002: 2B).

This century clearly shows that the protectionism of the United States sports market has produced a domestic over-supply. Morgan Stanley estimates that the major TV networks lost US $1.3 billion on sports between 2002 and 2006. The NFL's TV ratings fell 13 percent in the five seasons to 2002. Disney dispatched *Monday Night Football* from ABC to ESPN in 2006 due to falling audience numbers. In 2009, NBC was unable to sell all its advertising slots for the Super Bowl. By 2016, the numbers were catastrophically down on even the previous year (Hiestand 2002; Solomon 2002; Crupi 2016b). This over-supply led to write-downs of billions in the value of rights to TV sport paid by United States media companies (Chenoweth and O'Riordan 2002). News Corporation lost US $5.4 billion in 2008–09, partly because of declining advertising revenue for regional cable sports networks and increased marketing and sports rights costs, such as the National Association for Stock Car Racing (NASCAR). Spectators stream to raceways – to watch college ball. Since 2012, NASCAR has mysteriously declined to circulate the spectatorship statistics that it once so arrogantly trumpeted (Is it Recession-Proof? 2009; Caldwell 2016).

When rights come up for renegotiation, television's losses are passed onto sports. Competition for shrinking resources between owners, administrators, coaches, elite players, and other fractions of the sporting industries was exacerbated by the post-2007 global financial crisis. By 2009–10, the NBA needed a US $200 million line of credit to subsidize bankrupt teams. Under these circumstances, smaller sports (including many Olympic and United States college sports and the WNBA) and media companies vulnerable to a credit squeeze have been in jeopardy (Arango 2009; News Corporation 2009; Sherlock 2008; Zirin 2009).

Along the way, pretensions to a working-class base of consumption for pro sports have been eroded. In the five years from 1997, the proportion of NFL fans earning below US $30,000 decreased by more than 7 percent, while the proportion earning over US $100,000 increased by 30 percent. In keeping with this gentrification, banks moved into the center of United States sports sponsorship (including of the Armed Forces Bowl by PlainsCapital Bank between 2003 and 2004), even as they were dealing with the public opprobrium resulting from their role in the Great Recession and subsequent reward of corporate welfare. The 2009–10 NFL season saw ticket prices soar and attendances crash, as average prices for the hour or less of actual action per match went to around US $100 (Goetzl 2008). For 2017–18, the predictions went as high as US $250 a regular-season fixture.

The NBA Commissioner euphemized the drastic impact of domestic over-expansion as a sign that "[t]he American sports market is mature," as he unveiled plans to draw 50 percent of the league's revenue from overseas (Hiestand 2002). This movement from provincial protectionism to a NICL that addresses the crisis of domestic overproduction is the key to the future of United States basketball, with white European stars an added "advantage" via racialized marketing both internationally and at home. Basketball's use of Yao Ming and other leading players to attract audiences in their countries of origin and diasporic contexts is a conspicuous example of global sport marketing (Rowe and Gilmour 2008). When he retired, the media reaction was as much about his marketing impact in China as his playing career (Fan 2011).

NBA TV began in 1999, and within ten years was available in 79 countries and territories. Africa recently became not only a site for producing talent, but of attracting viewers (Category: NBA Africa n.d.), with the Basketball Africa League designed to launch in 2019 (delayed until 2021 because of COVID-19) by means of a collaboration between the NBA and the international governing body, Fédération Internationale de Basketball (FIBA) (Spears 2019). ESPN, a series of sports television cable channels owned by Disney that modestly styles itself the "worldwide leader in sports," has 26 networks outside the United States, in addition to related interests in promotions and other media. Its texts are on sale in 61 countries and territories, across 15 language groups. The Latin American network, which began in 1989, operates alongside three sub-regional hubs, and there are networks in Canada, several European Union (EU) channels, and stations across Asia. Its programming in the Arab world and Africa has ended for financial reasons, and some outlets are joint ventures. ESPN customizes programs established in the United States for foreign viewers, notably its highlights show *SportsCenter*, and emphasizes local interests in materials devised for particular audiences, especially football. At issue here are the expropriation of profit and consolidation of already-dominant sports, while the network's domestic parochialism is mirrored in regional hubs (for example, South American viewers must accept Argentine accents, looks, and interests (Miller 2010; Esensten 2013; Szalai 2012).

To summarize, sporting cartels in the United States are endeavoring, through the NICL, to avoid paying the price of their overproduction. Protectionism has consequently eased somewhat in terms of player origins and even rules of the game, in the case of basketball, but major barriers remain to truly international exchange. Massive resources are dedicated to importing and exporting players and exporting tastes, but few to importing the latter. The empire wants to expropriate and buy human capital and develop audiences from elsewhere. It does not seek an open market. Viewers are figured into calculations of everything from player costs and culture to media platforms. Next we turn to a southern hemisphere context for the purposes of comparison and contrast.

3 Australia: regulation and return

Sport has a particularly important place in Australian culture. Within a settler-colonial nation formed in 1901, sports developed as key signifiers of Australianness *avant la lettre*. Levels of participation in sport are not especially high – a recent national survey of adults found that 61.2 percent played no organized sport but 84.9 per cent watched it on television (Gayo and Rowe 2018), while organizations like Cricket Australia have been criticized for heavily inflating how many people play rather than spectate (Knox and Gladstone 2019). Live sports television is heavily represented in the highest-rating programs in Australia, accounting for 16 of the top 20 metropolitan TV programs this century (Mediaweek 2016). This combination of nation-state endorsement of sport and the popularity of its mediated spectatorship has given the TV sports viewer the dual status of citizen-consumer. For this reason – along with the political power of commercial FTA networks, which dominate sports broadcasting in Australia historically – the country has the most stringent anti-siphoning regime in the world (in the United States, attempts to create lists of sports and events that must be made available on free-to-air media have been ruled unconstitutional – Smith, Evens, and Iosifidis 2015). As a result, many major sport events in Australia, and some international events involving Australian teams, are protected by legislation from being acquired exclusively by subscription television on the grounds that they are "events of national importance and cultural significance" (Australian Communications and Media Authority 2015). Nonetheless, subscription television carries a great deal of sport, and recent legislative changes have reduced the anti-siphoning list and its enforcement (Tiffen 2018).

Unsurprisingly, any intervention by the state in MediaSport on behalf of citizen-consumers has been resisted (Tonagh 2016a) by those who see it as an unwarranted distortion of the market, predominantly the oligopolistic pay-TV provider Foxtel (owned by the Murdoch-controlled News Corp Australia and Telstra, the dominant, former state-owned, telecommunications company). The lack of coercive power to require that viewers pay to watch many major Australian sporting events has limited the proportion of subscribing households to around 30 percent. Nonetheless, international sports competitions such as the NBA, NFL, and UEFA Champions League appeal to Foxtel viewers, who can watch them alongside the main domestic sports on its twelve dedicated sports channels (which include Fox Sports, beIN, ESPN, and Eurosport). Although there are signs that telecommunications companies are moving into the Australian MediaSport market – for example, in 2016 Optus seized the rights to the EPL from Foxtel for its mobile and broadband platforms – at present these are only tentative developments (Tucker 2016).

Australia has two dominant commercial FTA networks, both of which have regional affiliates. They hold the rights to the main national sporting "properties": Channel Seven (for example, Australian rules football, The Olympics, test cricket) and Nine (rugby league, tennis, golf). The third, Ten, has limited sports content (A-League association football, rugby union, Melbourne Cup horseracing). These commercial entities co-exist with public service broadcasters: the Australian Broadcasting Corporation (ABC), which takes no advertising and mostly offers less commercially lucrative sports (such as Women's Australian Open golf), and the Special Broadcasting Service (SBS). SBS is funded by a mixture of public funding and advertising, and has a limited, mega-event sport roster (Tour de France, FIFA World Cup). A significant rise in women's sport is beginning to challenge male supremacy within the country's sport field (Jeffrey 2016; McLachlan 2019). There is insufficient space to discuss the growth of professional women's leagues here, but it should be noted that there is more TV sport coverage, greater internationalization (except in the case of Australian rules) and intensified positional competition within the media and sport fields (Mark 2019).

This part of the chapter focuses on the four, male-dominated forms of football in Australia, although as noted there has been a recent "surge" in women's sport in the country that includes football forms and other sports. Football is the focus here because it has strong historical resonance and contemporary prominence in Australia; although much of the analysis, including of mediation, can be applied by way of illustration to other sports, including cricket (the so-called "national sport"), tennis, swimming, and various Olympic sports (Rowe and Gayo 2020).

Australian rules, a distinctive local form that incorporates elements of other sports such as Gaelic, association, and rugby football, is the largest of the "codes" (the conventional term in Australia describing the various forms of football, all of which often claim the singular name for themselves) but is largely restricted to a single country. Its player and fan base is strongest in Victoria, South Australia, Tasmania, and Western Australia. The dominant Victorian Football League expanded to incorporate other major states from the late 1980s, notably News South Wales and Queensland, and formed the Australian Football League (AFL) in 1990. The 2015 AFL Chairman's Report detailed its latest broadcast contract (including FTA, subscription, and digital rights, the last acquired by Foxtel co-owner Telstra). This six-year (2017–22) AU $2.508 billion sale represented the "biggest broadcast rights deal in Australian sporting history" (AFL 2015: 23). Although the focus of the announcement was predominantly on the national market, the AFL also broadcasts "to more than 250 countries and territories worldwide by rights holders Australia Plus, ESPN, Fox Sports/Fox Soccer Plus, Eurosport, Orbit Showtime Network, Over the Line Sports Media, Sky New Zealand, Super Sport, TSN and Claro Sports," with new rights holders RDS (Quebec) and TVNZ (New Zealand), and a live and on-demand digital streaming service on desktop, mobile, and tablet available only outside Australia, thereby ensuring that "fans outside Australia received the greatest possible access to the game across all media platforms" (AFL 2015: 44). It should be noted, though, that such boasts may not be very meaningful, as deregulation and satellites have seen sport networks around the world seek 24-hour-a-day content; and some of these deals have involved the AFL providing free programming in return for a portion of any advertising sales.

In the national media market, the record rights contract was struck at a time when gross national and key metropolitan audiences viewing for the AFL had diminished by 1.1 per cent from the previous year, "a marginal decline compared to the decline in Australian free-to-air television ratings generally" (AFL 2015: 44). One reason for this seemingly anomalous arrangement is that, as the above quotation indicates, the fall in the AFL's FTA metropolitan television audience was less than that of the general metropolitan and regional and pay-TV audience. In other words, AFL was less affected than other programming by the slow, general downturn in advertiser-supported television (Hutchins and Rowe 2012). But there is an additional, important explanation: the AFL rights negotiations occurred when its chief rival, the National Rugby League (NRL – the premier rugby league competition) was also in the marketplace. The NRL declined to sell its FTA TV rights (acquired by Nine in 2015 for a record AU $925 million) at the same time as its subscription and digital rights, with the former previously held by (the Murdoch-owned) Fox Sports.

Rugby league competes directly with Australian rules in the sports and media markets. Each claims superiority in audience size, engagement, spread, and potential, and the significance and scale of specific TV events. AFL asserts that a larger audience (4.1m vs. 3.7m) watches its longer game over more time (an average of 102 of the 160-minute match telecast [64 percent] versus 67 of the 120-minute match telecast [56 percent]). These large audiences, though, remain concentrated in different parts of the country, despite attempts to make both sports uniformly national: "the AFL derived 70 per cent of its metropolitan audience from heartland markets (Melbourne, Adelaide,

Perth) while the NRL similarly derived 67 per cent of its audience from Sydney and Brisbane" (Fujak 2016). The NRL ultimately concluded a subscription TV rights deal with News Corporation and its subsidiary Fox Sports and with naming-rights sponsor Telstra for digital mobile rights (the NRL took back other digital assets). There was a familiarly triumphant tone to the NRL's announcement of a deal that, in the context of competition between sports and broadcasters, had laid bare the ruthless nature of the struggle over MediaSport intellectual property in the name of improved consumer viewing experiences and opportunities: "Rugby League will reach more fans than ever before – both in Australia and globally – under a massive new NRL broadcast deal unveiled today" (NRL 2015).

The contract also stipulated that there be a dedicated Rugby League channel on Fox Sports, "giving the game more exposure than any time in the game's history." Unlike Australian rules football, rugby league is played professionally in other parts of the world (mainly northern England, southern France, Papua New Guinea, Wales, and Aotearoa/New Zealand), giving it a stronger base for international playing expansion (for example, in Fiji) and international competitions, including a four-nations tournament (involving Australia, Aotearoa/New Zealand, England, and one other qualifier) and a 14-nation World Cup (including the United States, Italy, and Samoa, but with lax national qualification rules). Although international rights are currently worth less than AU $10 million of an almost AU $2 billion multi-year contract, they have been struck across the globe, largely though the existing relationship with Fox Sports (NRL 2017). As is the case with the AFL (2017), which has contracts with BT Sport and ESPN, the NRL uses a combination of local broadcasters and live/video on demand streaming, either free or by subscription. Although these dispersed international audiences may be small, and in many cases negligible, they enable claims to be made for league's global status and reach (Rowe 2011: 38–41).

It is apparent from the discussion above that Australia's major football codes have difficulty establishing themselves as fully national, let alone international. Their primary media consumption is domestic. Rugby union (which suffered rugby league's secession in 1908 over the question of player payment) is similarly concentrated in only some parts of the country (like rugby league, the eastern states of New South Wales and Queensland, and the Australian Capital Territory). It is also historically marked in sectarian terms – dominated by ruling-class Anglo Protestants versus league's more proletarian Irish Catholicism. In terms of rules, league might be considered in relation to union as the Canadian Football League is to the NFL. Until 2021, it appears on FTA only when the national team, the Wallabies, is playing, but has a much more extensive international presence than Australian rules or rugby league, through its membership of SANZAAR, an entity involving South Africa, New Zealand and Australia responsible for Super Rugby and The Rugby Championship (which has admitted Japanese and Argentine teams since 2016). The lack of FTA presence, except, as noted, for the main Wallabies matches (the most important of which involve the Rugby World Cup, one of the world's largest sport events, the annual Bledisloe Cup competition with New

Zealand, and tours involving the British and Irish Lions), has severely limited viewer access. It is historically dependent on Fox Sports (which also broadcasts the lower tier domestic National Rugby Championship) although the 2016–20 media rights contract enabled more games to be available in replay and highlight format on FTA: "The ARU [now Rugby Australia] will receive a total of AUD $285m in media rights revenue from the total package of SANZAAR agreements – a 148 % increase on revenue achieved from the previous media rights arrangements (2011–15)" (Rugby.com.au 2015).

Fox Sports retained live Australian rights for Test matches played in Australia, New Zealand, and South Africa and the expanded 18-team Asteron Life (an insurance-company sponsor) Super Rugby competition, and all Qantas (the naming-rights national airline) domestic Wallabies Tests, New Zealand and South Africa domestic Tests, and matches in The Rugby Championship. Network Ten, by contrast, can only simulcast domestic Wallabies Tests, the Bledisloe Cup, and matches played by the Wallabies in The Rugby Championship. Reliance on simulcasts, replays, and highlights packages indicates FTA's weak position in the rugby union media market (Ten has the lowest level of rights purchase of the commercial networks), especially given that Australia also plays in the World Rugby Sevens, which is on subscription television. This form of the game was available live on FTA during the 2016 Rio Olympics. Rugby fans may, therefore, use virtual private networks (VPNs) to avoid geo-blocking or access pirate websites if they do not subscribe to pay-TV channels or rely on last-minute arrangements made by FTA broadcasters (Zavos 2016). By 2020, though, in the light of Foxtel's financial problems and Rugby Australia's search for greater competitive tension among bidding rights holders, its long-term relationship with Fox Sports had declined. The Covid-19 pandemic, though, interrupted the 2021–25 media rights negotiation round (Rugby Australia 2020), which ultimately resulted in a deal with the Nine-owned pay-TV provider Stan Sport.

There is apparently an inverse relationship between the strength of FTA TV provision and the international orientation of these codes, with the most "global", association football, also having little FTA TV presence. Unlike Australian rules and the rugby codes, football's A-League is nowhere near the apex of the sport in world terms, although it has the highest level of participation (partially because of its popularity with women – AusPlay 2016). Association football also has a difficult history in Australia, being often characterized as, in contrast to the other football codes, "foreign" (echoing gridiron's and baseball's assertion of their American "roots" in contrast to football's cosmopolitan Otherness, as noted above). The deep connection at ethnic community level between the game and the post-World War II wave of southern and eastern European migration to Australia accentuated this "foreignness" of football (Hallinan and Hughson 2010).

European football leagues have long had a strong following on subscription television in Australia, especially the EPL, La Liga, and Serie A. Like Super Rugby, the new competition was not protected by anti-siphoning legislation, and there was little FTA domestic presence for football apart, belatedly, for a single match on SBS (now on Network Ten). Football became a more desirable commercial proposition as the A-League, originally founded on a one-team, one-town basis, became more established. The men's national side appeared in the 2006 World Cup and has qualified for every one since (the Matildas, the national women's team has, like their American counterparts, been much more successful – Thomas 2018). It left the small Oceania Confederation to join the much larger Asian Football Confederation (AFC), which is responsible for major competitions in the AFC Champions League (won in 2014 by the Western Sydney Wanderers) and the AFC Asian Cup (hosted and won by Australia in 2015). Also of significance is the increased targeting of Asia by major European leagues and clubs (such as Manchester United, Arsenal, and Real Madrid) for marketing and promotion and as a base for club development, with Manchester City's Arab and Chinese owners in a financial and governmental marriage of convenience purchasing the A-League team Melbourne City (formerly Melbourne Heart), overseas entities bidding for new A-League franchises, and Liverpool FC setting up a training base in New South Wales. These developments are occurring alongside migration from countries, such as China, Vietnam, and India, where football is far more important than the rugby codes and Australian rules. These recent migrants prefer to watch the major European leagues on FTA television (Rowe 2016). Association football in Australia has benefited from the general increase in broadcast rights, from a much lower base. Its six-year agreement (2017–22) totals "$346 million, which on a like for like comparison is more than double the current arrangements" (Football Federation Australia 2016).

Fox Sports' then-Chief Executive Officer, Patrick Delany, has affirmed his organization's power over all kinds of football: "Today's deal sees FOX SPORTS home to every major Australian football code until 2020. That's your team, every round live, no compromises" (quoted in FFA 2016). Fox Sports gained virtual exclusivity in Super Rugby and the A-League. Through a series of contracts involving simulcasts and match sharing with FTA networks, it has maintained a strong position across the spectrum. When Fox Sports lost mobile and broadband rights to the EPL to Optus, its carrier Foxtel contracted with beIN to carry some premium European football and games on delay and other material from six EPL clubs at no cost to subscribers (Tonagh 2016b). The strain of securing inflated rights and competition from streaming services is showing, with Foxtel, having lost AU $417 million in 2018, pledging to "reduce spending on 'non-marquee' sporting content" (Perry 2019) and, as noted, losing some rights to sports like football and rugby.

MediaSport consumers in Australia (as elsewhere) must, therefore, negotiate varying payment arrangements, production and reception quality, and exposure to advertising. While access to these cultural texts is maximized by providing them for "free," it is evident that, with regard to the citizen-consumer dyad, the latter is more rigorously interpellated in a dual "field of struggles" of the sporting and the mediated.

4 Conclusion: consuming the MediaSport citizen

Our brief comparison between the US and Australia is as limited as it may be illuminating. It tells us little about most other countries, notably those in the Global South, both in terms of the extraordinary wealth of these two countries and their comparative failure to connect with the only really important world sport, association football. Their vicious and vapid TV business contests have minor corollaries in less-wealthy nations, while their chronic over-consumption – and valorization of the fact – are meaningless to most of the world's peoples. That said, the triumphant march of consumerism as a citizen's responsibility that has impelled these two countries' economies since World War II has been enormously telling, as is the rhetoric, both popular and scholarly, that undergirds it. Yet, even the prelates of consumption have begun to see through the scrimshaw veil that they have woven.

In his cautious welcoming of "the practice turn" in the study of consumption, Alan Warde (2014: 297) emphasized that:

> Practice theories may need supplementing with other frameworks, particularly to capture macro-level or structural aspects of consumption. This does not mean a return to the old economism, but probably entails some recovery of political economy and re-articulation of the link between consumption and economic production.

It is important to take into account the practices that constitute how consumption is enacted in a manner that is not reduced to individual choice or agency (Bourdieu [1972] 1977). But it is equally impossible to understand MediaSport consumption without a grasp of political-economic forces. This does not mean that decisions taken in the boardrooms of sport and media organizations automatically produce specific consumption practices and disciplined MediaSport consumers. The state also remains capable of mitigating the oligopolistic power of markets by intervening to maintain wide public access to nationally significant mediated sport texts in the name of cultural citizenship.

A site of convergent or overlapping fields, MediaSport is characterized by struggles over practices of consumption that extend well beyond it. Across a range of cultural fields, there are myriad opportunities to consume culture in high, middlebrow, and popular forms. The development of digital technologies has intensified this competition for audience attention.

As a form of physical culture, sport has progressively professionalized and corporatized, moving from a once-dominant amateur ethos to what can be termed "sportainment" or the "sportsbiz." In a crowded cultural marketplace, it has become increasingly dependent on the media, especially television, to expand its principal consumer base beyond attendees at intermittent sports contests in a physical stadium. At the same time, sporting television (after, as noted, being pioneered in many countries by public service broadcasters in constructing a national popular) became an increasingly attractive (though expensive) source of viewers for commercial FTA broadcasters and subscription-based companies. It became even more attractive as broadcast sports' liveness helped stave off the splintering of TV audiences by online and mobile services. It could attract many consumers otherwise little interested in sport through spectacular "event television," also using the social media platforms that were once believed to distract viewers from scheduled television on large screens to create a "buzz," amplified by multi-screen uses (Hutchins and Rowe 2012).

This sedulous hunt for audiences and their "eyeballs" has created an excessive supply of "domestic" MediaSport and efforts to cultivate consumer interest and sports brand loyalty. We have shown that commercial interests are consolidating and extending their power in two selected national MediaSport consumption environments through the use of various platforms and international markets in labor and consumption. In the process, we touched on certain problematic consequences – environmental, budgetary, and ideological – that arise alongside struggles over production, distribution, and access. A combination of deregulatory fervor, corporate over-reach, consumer saturation, and new technologies makes mass audiences all the more difficult to corral. Those sports that appear to guarantee either niche fascination or national and international appeal become the objects of intense capital desire, their consumers adored and fetishized in just the way that those consumers approach their beloved sports.

References

Arango, Tim. 2009. News Corporation posts a loss on MySpace charge. *New York Times*, 5 August. http://www.nytimes.com/2009/08/06/business/global/06news.html (2 March 2020).

Armour, Nancy. 2014. NBC Universal pays $7.75 billion for Olympics through 2032. *USA Today*, 7 May. http://www.usatoday.com/story/sports/olympics/2014/05/07/nbc-olympics-broadcast-rights-2032/8805989/ (2 March 2020).

AusPlay. 2016. Participation data for the sport sector. December. http://apo.org.au/files/Resource/34648_ausplay_summary_report_accessible_final_7.12.2016.pdf (2 March 2020).

Australian Communications and Media Authority. 2015. Sport (anti-siphoning), 9 October. http://www.acma.gov.au/Industry/Broadcast/Television/TV-content-regulation/sport-anti-siphoning-tv-content-regulation-acma (2 March 2020).

Australian Football League. 2015. Annual report 2015. http://s.afl.com.au/staticfile/AFL%20Tenant/AFL/Files/Annual%20Report/AFLAnnualReport2015.pdf (2 March 2020).

Australian Football League. 2017. International broadcast partners – television. https://www.afl.com.au/matches/broadcast-guide/international-broadcast-partners (2 March 2020).

Bale, John. 1991. *The brawn drain: Foreign student-athletes in American universities*. Urbana, IL: University of Illinois Press.

Bayle, Emmanuel. 2015. "FIFA-Gate": An opportunity to clean up international sports governance. *Soccer & Society* 21(5). 622–623.

Bean, Bruce W. 2016. An interim essay on FIFA's World Cup of corruption: The desperate need for international corporate governance at FIFA. *ILSA Journal of International & Comparative Law* 22. 1–27.

Bonesteel, Matt. 2015. Massive new English Premier League TV deal has the rest of European soccer worried. *Washington Post*, 13 February. http://www.washingtonpost.com/blogs/early-lead/wp/2015/02/13/massive-new-english-premier-league-tv-deal-has-the-rest-of-european-soccer-worried/ (2 March 2020).

Bourdieu, Pierre. 1977 [1972]. Outline of a theory of practice (trans. Richard Nice). Cambridge: Cambridge University Press.

Bourdieu, Pierre & Loïc J. D. Wacquant. 1992. *An invitation to reflexive sociology*. Chicago: University of Chicago Press.

Broadcasters' Audience Research Board. 2015a. Weekly viewing by genre. December. https://www.barb.co.uk/?s=2015+weekly+viewing+by+genre (2 March 2020).

Broadcasters' Audience Research Board. 2015b. Weekly viewing by channel, December. https://www.barb.co.uk/?s=2015+weekly+viewing+by+genre (2 March 2020).

Brown, Sean F. 2005. Exceptionalist America: American sports fans' reaction to internationalization. *International Journal of the History of Sport* 22(6). 1106–1135.

Butterworth, Michael L. & Stormi D. Moskal. 2009. American football, flags, and "fun": The Bell Helicopter Armed Forces Bowl and the rhetorical production of militarism. *Communication, Culture & Critique* 2(4). 411–433.

Caldwell, Dave. 2016. "I don't think it can recover": What's behind Nascar's nosedive? *The Guardian*, 16 September. https://www.theguardian.com/sport/blog/2016/sep/16/nascar-decline-struggles-auto-racing (2 March 2020).

Category: NBA Africa. n.d. NBA.com. http://pr.nba.com/category/nba-africa/ (2 March 2020).

Chenoweth, Neil & Bernard O' Riordan. 2002. The sick business of sport. *Australian Financial Review*, June 4.

Clarke, Gerard. 2016. Governance and transnational civil society: The problem of transnational rent-seeking. *Journal of Civil Society* 12(1). 82–100.

Crupi, Anthony. 2016a. Laughing all the way to the bank: Rio Olympics make NBC $250 million richer. *AdAge*, 14 September. http://adage.com/article/special-report-the-olympics/nbc-rio-olympics-quarter-billion-profit/305859/ (2 March 2020).

Crupi, Anthony. 2016b. Buyers take a wait-and-see approach to NFL ratings slide. *AdAge*, 7 October. http://adage.com/article/media/heaven-hell-preacher-a-respectable-start/306209/ (2 March 2020).

Esensten, Andrew. 2013. American sports fans cry foul as ESPN yanks Israeli broadcasts. *Haaretz*, July 23. http://www.haaretz.com/israel-news/1.537323 (2 March 2020).

Fan, H. 2011. Yao Ming retirement press conference. *Shanghaiist*, 20 July. http://shanghaiist.com/2011/07/20/yao_ming_retirement_press_conferenc.php (2 March 2020).

Florio, Mike 2014. Antitrust exemption limits NFL's window for Saturday games. *NBC Sports*, 6 February. http://profootballtalk.nbcsports.com/2014/02/06/antitrust-exemption-limits-nfls-window-for-saturday-games/ (2 March 2020).

Football Federation Australia. 2016. Football Federation Australia announces new broadcast deal, 20 December. http://www.footballaustralia.com.au/article/football-federation-australia-announces-new-broadcast-deal/1wq000eodlga51v54sh1hp3dvr (2 March 2020).

Fujak, Hunter. 2016. AFL and NRL grand final TV ratings show codes still rely on their traditional heartlands. *The Conversation*, 4 October. https://theconversation.com/afl-and-nrl-grand-final-tv-ratings-show-codes-still-rely-on-their-traditional-heartlands-66485 (2 March 2020).

Gayo, Modesto & David Rowe. 2018. The Australian sport field: Moving and watching. *Media International Australia* 167(1). 162–180.

Goetzl, David. 2008. ESPN: "Monday Night Football" top '08 cable series. *MediaDailyNews*, 30 December. http://www.mediapost.com/publications/article/97357/espn-monday-night-football-top-08-cable-series.html (2 March 2020).

Hallinan, Christopher & John Hughson. 2010. The beautiful game in Howard's "Brutopia": Football, ethnicity and citizenship in Australia. In Christopher Hallinan & John Hughson (eds.), *The containment of soccer in Australia: Fencing off the world game*, 1–8. London: Routledge.
Hiestand, Michael. 2002. U.S. sports increasingly looking to international market. *Sports Business Daily*, 30 April. https://www.sportsbusinessdaily.com/Daily/Issues/2002/04/30/Sports-Society/US-Sports-Increasingly-Looking-To-International-Market.aspx (11 November 2020).
Hoops for troops. n.d. NBA.com. http://hoopsfortroops.nba.com/ (2 March 2020).
Hutchins, Brett & David Rowe. 2012. *Sport beyond television: The internet, digital media and the rise of networked media sport*. New York: Routledge.
Is it recession-proof? 2009. *Economist*, 12 February. https://www.economist.com/international/2009/02/12/is-it-recession-proof (11 November 2020).
Jeffrey, Nicole. 2016. AFL women's competition sparks arms race for best female athletes. *The Australian*, 23 October. http://www.theaustralian.com.au/sport/afl/afl-womens-competition-sparks-arms-race-for-best-female-athletes/news-story/a44e6224bda47bc1054e494ce7a5d4cd (2 March 2020).
Knox, Malcolm & Nigel Gladstone. 2019. Caught out: Cricket's inflated playing numbers revealed. *Sydney Morning Herald*, 21 July. https://www.smh.com.au/sport/cricket/caught-out-cricket-s-inflated-playing-numbers-revealed-20190720-p5292s.html (2 March 2020).
lisahunter, Wayne Smith & elke emerald. 2015. Pierre Bourdieu and his conceptual tools. In lisahunter, Wayne Smith & elke emerald (eds.), *Pierre Bourdieu and physical culture*, 3–24. Abingdon: Routledge.
Lotz, Amanda D. 2014. *The television will be revolutionized*, 2nd edn. New York: New York University Press.
Maloney, Jack. 2017. WNBA overseas report. *WNBA.com*, 23 January. http://www.wnba.com/news/wnba-overseas-report-january-23/ (2 March 2020).
Mark, David. 2019. With big bash, A-League, AFLW and the NBL competing for viewers, there is such a thing as too much sport. *ABC News*, 10 February https://www.abc.net.au/news/2019-02-10/too-much-sport-ratings-attendance-cricket-football-basketball/10792710 (2 March 2020).
McCarthy, Michael. 2002. Bowl, Olympics compete for gold. *USA Today*, January 31.
McLachlan, Fiona. 2019. It's boom time! (again): Progress narratives and women's sport in Australia. *Journal of Australian Studies*. 43(1). 7–21.
Mediaweek. 2016. Live sport still most watched TV in Oz, data confirms. *Mediaweek*, 16 August. http://www.mediaweek.com.au/live-sport-most-watched-tv/ (2 March 2020).
Miller, Toby. 2007. *Cultural citizenship: Cosmopolitanism, consumerism, and television in a neoliberal age*. Philadelphia: Temple University Press.
Miller, Toby. 2010. *Television studies: The basics*. London: Routledge.
Miller, Toby. 2017. *Greenwashing sports*. London: Routledge.
Miller, Toby, Geoffrey Lawrence, Jim McKay & David Rowe. 2001. *Globalization and sport: Playing the world*. London: Sage.
Miller, Toby, Geoffrey Lawrence, Jim McKay & David Rowe. 2003. The over-production of US sports and the new international division of cultural labor. *International Review for the Sociology of Sport* 38(4). 427–440.
Miller, Toby, David Rowe & Geoffrey Lawrence. 2011. The new international division of cultural labour and sport. In Joseph Maguire & Mark Falcous (eds.), *Sport and migration: Borders, boundaries and crossings*, 217–229. London: Routledge.
Moreno, Carolina. 2014. Univision trumps English-language network giants, again. *Huffington Post*, 1 August. http://www.huffingtonpost.com/2014/08/01/unvision-number-1-network_n_5642872.html (2 March 2020).
NBA Green. n.d. NBA.com. *NBA.com*. https://green.nba.com/ (2 March 2020).

News Corporation. 2009. 4th quarter fiscal 2009 earnings release, 5 August. http://newscorp.com/news/index.html (2 March 2020).

NHK. n.d. Color TV broadcasts and the Tokyo Games. http://www.nhk.or.jp/strl/aboutstrl/evolution-of-tv-en/p12.html (2 March 2020).

NRL. 2015. NRL broadcast rights deal announced, 27 November. http://www.nrl.com/nrl-broadcast-rights-deal announced/tabid/10874/newsid/91023/default.aspx (2 March 2020).

NRL. 2017. Rugby League Reference Centre. https://www.nrl.com/watchlive/watchoverseas/internationalbroadcast/tabid/10443/default.aspx (2 March 2020).

Perry, Kevin. 2019. FOXTEL axes 3 Sports Channels as cuts to premium programming continues. *TV Blackbox*, 21 May. https://tvblackbox.com.au/page/2019/05/21/2019-5-22-foxtel-axes-3-sports-channels-as-cuts-to-premium-programming-continues/ (2 March 2020).

Rowe, David. 2004. *Sport, culture and the media: The unruly trinity*, 2nd edn. Maidenhead: Open University Press.

Rowe, David. 2011. *Global media sport: Flows, forms and futures*. London: Bloomsbury Academic.

Rowe, David. 2016. We're all transnational now: Sport in dynamic socio-cultural environments. *Sport in Society*. 20(10). 1470–1484.

Rowe, David. 2019. Sport, media ownership and control. In Joseph Maguire, Mark Falcous & Katie Liston (eds). *The business and culture of sport*, 155–166. Farmington Hills, MI: Macmillan Reference USA.

Rowe, D. & Modesto Gayo. 2020. Contesting national culture: The sport field. In Tony Bennett, David Carter, Modesto Gayo, Michelle Kelly & Greg Noble (eds.), *Fields, capitals, habitus: Australian culture, inequalities and social divisions*, 100–116. London and New York: Routledge.

Rowe, David & Callum Gilmour. 2008. Contemporary media sport: De- or re-Westernization? *International Journal of Sport Communication* 1(2). 177–194.

Rugby Australia suspends broadcast negotiations. 2020. *The Australian*, 17 March. https://www.theaustralian.com.au/sport/rugby-union/rugby-australia-suspends-broadcast-negotiations/news-story/1fccd61d2e140828898d5c44894589e68 (2 March 2020).

Rugby.com.au. 2015. Australian Rugby announces new media rights arrangements for 2016–2020. *Rugby.com.au*, 17 December. http://www.rugby.com.au/en/news/2016/01/31/australian-rugby-announces-new-media-rights-arrangements-for-2016-2020 (2 March 2020).

Sandomir, Richard. 2015. NBC retains rights to Premier League in six-year deal. *New York Times*, 10 August https://www.nytimes.com/2015/08/11/sports/soccer/nbc-retains-rights-to-premier-league-in-six-year-deal.html (2 March 2020).

Sherlock, Miriam. 2008. Downturn could offer sporting opportunity. *Sport Business*, 19 November https://www.sportbusiness.com/news/downturn-could-offer-sporting-opportunity/ (11 November 2020).

Smith, Paul, Tom Evens & Petros Iosifidis. 2015. The regulation of television sports broadcasting: A comparative analysis. *Media, Culture & Society* 37(5). 720–736.

Smythe, Dallas. 2004. The consumer's stake in radio and television. In John Durham Peters & Peter Simonson (eds.), *Mass communication and American social thought: Key texts, 1919–1968*, 318–328. Lanham: Rowman & Littlefield.

Solomon, John D. 2002. The sports market is looking soggy. *New York Times*, 21 April. http://www.nytimes.com/2002/04/21/business/the-sports-market-is-looking-soggy.html (2 March 2020).

Spears, Marc J. 2019. Basketball Africa League: "A dream come true for all of us." *The Undefeated*, 16 February. https://theundefeated.com/features/basketball-africa-league-dikembe-mutombo-a-dream-come-true-for-all-of-us/ (2 March 2020).

Szalai, Georg. 2012. News Corp to buy out ESPN's stake in Asian TV venture. *Hollywood Reporter*, 6 June. http://www.hollywoodreporter.com/news/news-corp-buy-espn-asia-stake-334177 (2 March 2020).

Thomas, Stuart. 2018. The Matildas keep showing the Socceroos how it's done. *The Roar*, 1 August. https://www.theroar.com.au/2018/08/02/matildas-keep-showing-socceroos-done/ (2 March 2020).

Thompson, Derek. 2013. Sports could save the TV business – or destroy it. *The Atlantic*, 17 July. https://www.theatlantic.com/business/archive/2013/07/sports-could-save-the-tv-business-or-destroy-it/277808/ (2 March 2020).

Tiffen, Rodney. 2018. It's not (just) cricket. *Inside Story*, 7 July. https://insidestory.org.au/its-not-just-cricket/ (2 March 2020).

Tomlinson, Alan & Christopher Young (eds.). 2006 *National identity and global sports events: Culture, politics, and spectacle in the Olympics and the football World Cup*. New York: State University of New York Press.

Tonagh, Peter. 2016a. Media reform needed to protect our culture and society. *The Australian Business Review*, 17 October. http://www.theaustralian.com.au/business/media/opinion/media-reform-needed-to-protect-our-culture-and-society/news-story/029b96eb3fe44ae8ae372b23507ee85c (2 March 2020).

Tonagh, Peter. 2016b. EPL on Fox Sports: Foxtel CEO's open letter to fans about Optus/Fox deals. *Fox Sports*, 6 May. http://www.foxsports.com.au/football/epl-on-fox-sports-foxtel-ceos-open-letter-to-fans-about-optusfox-deals/news-story/9a26b28b92aad4bc596104dadb3efae1 (2 March 2020).

Tucker, Harry. 2016. How Optus stole the English Premier League from Foxtel. *Business Insider Australia*, 5 May. http://www.businessinsider.com.au/how-optus-stole-the-english-premier-league-from-foxtel-2016-5 (2 March 2020).

United States of America against various. 2015. DSS: EMN/AH/DAL/SPN/MKM/PT/KDE/TH/BDM F. #2015R00747. United States District Court. Eastern District of New York, 25 November. https://www.justice.gov/opa/file/796966/download (11 November 2020).

Warde, Alan. 2014. After taste: Culture, consumption and theories of practice. *Journal of Consumer Culture* 14(3). 279–303.

Wenner, Lawrence A. (ed.). 1998. *MediaSport*. London: Routledge.

Willis, Oliver. 2010. As the World Cup starts, conservative media declare war on soccer. *MediaMatters for America*, 11 June. http://mediamatters.org/research/2010/06/11/as-the-world-cup-starts-conservative-media-decl/166099 (2 March 2020).

WNBA players from around the world. 2005. *WNBA.com*, 20 May. http://wnba.com/players/international_roster.html (2 March 2020).

WNBA pride. n.d. *WNBA.com*. http://www.wnba.com/pride/ (2 March 2020).

Zavos, Spiro. 2016. The Wallabies could win a Grand Slam and angry fans might not see it. *The Roar*, 3 November. http://www.theroar.com.au/2016/11/03/wallabies-win-grand-slam-angry-fans-might-not-see/ (2 March 2020).

Zirin, Dave. 2009. Big league blues. *The Nation*, 16 November. https://www.thenation.com/article/big-league-blues/ (2 March 2020).

David L. Andrews

15 *Uber-sport*

Abstract: This chapter introduces and develops the concept of *uber-sport*, which describes the hegemonic form of contemporary elite/professional sport structure, delivery, and experience. Shaped by, and simultaneously, reinscribing the late capitalist processes of corporatization, commercialization, spectacularization, and celebritization, *uber-sport* represents a highly rationalized, diversified, yet integrated phenomenon, generating mass audiences/markets, and thereby popularity/profits, across an array of culturally and economically multiplying streams (products, bodies, services, events, spectacles, and spaces). Drawing theoretical formulations from, amongst others, Theodor Adorno, Herbert Marcuse, Frederic Jameson, Guy Debord, and Manuel DeLanda, this chapter offers a synthetic (derived from an accumulative synthesis) theoretical framework for understanding the contextual nature and influence of *uber-sport*'s infrastructural dynamics. The discussion concludes with a critical explication of *uber-sport* as assemblage: a mass mediated and spectated performance event which is itself a non-repeatable and momentary confederation of multi-scaled and multi-sited assemblages.

Keywords: *uber-sport*; spectacle; culture industry; assemblage

1 Introduction

Previously I have utilized the term "corporate sport" (Andrews 2006, 2009) as a means of delineating the nature and influence of sport within the late capitalist moment. Having discovered the boundaries of the term's usefulness, I no longer find "corporate sport" sufficiently prescient as a means of capturing the operational and experiential complexities of "professional sports as primarily entertainment businesses" (Szymanski 2010: xii). In light of this conceptual deficiency, I turned to the somewhat unwieldy, yet hopefully suggestive term, *uber-sport*. *Uber-sport* encompasses the concerted reformation of elite/professional level physically based contests by the late capitalist processes of: replicative *corporatization* (institutional and management reorganization designed to realize profit-driven structures and logics); expansive *commercialization* (sport brand diversification and non-sport brand promotion across multiple sectors); creative *spectacularization* (entertainment-focused delivery of popular sport spectacles, realized through a combination of structural reformation and cross-platform mass mediation); and, *celebritization* (sporting contests constructed around, and a site for the embellishment of, specific public persona). *Uber-sport* thus describes a highly rationalized, diversified, yet integrated popular sport phenomenon designed to generate mass audiences/markets, and thereby popularity/profits, across an array of

https://doi.org/10.1515/9783110660883-015

culturally and economically multiplying streams (products, bodies, services, events, spectacles, and spaces). As with any acentered assemblage, *uber-sport* is constituted by "multitudinous subsystems" (Jameson 2009: 359) or sub-assemblages, most notably the sport media, which plays a pivotal role in the corporatized, commercialized, spectacularized, and celebritized formation that is *uber-sport*. Of course, the very term *uber-sport* is in all probability an anathema to many, but at the very least my intention is to challenge the abstracted empiricism implicit within much sport communication research. Utilizing the term *uber-sport* announces the artificial and inadequate nature of the default sport media abstraction that dominates certain sections of the field, and implores the utilization of an empirically heterogenous relational ontology whichever aspect of the *uber-sport* assemblage is being engaged.

Yet, what is uber about *uber-sport*? Utilizing uber- as a prefix, and invoking über's German meaning (the umlaut consciously dropped to denote the American Anglicization of the term [as in Uber Technologies Inc., the self-styled leader in the so-called sharing economy] and the Americanized nature of *uber-sport* itself), *uber-sport* signifies the highest, superlative, or consummate sport form (in its literal German sense, above the rest). If sport in its most generic sense refers to the structure and practice of physically based contests between individuals or collectives, *uber-sport* is the term utilized within this project to refer to the currently idealized model of corporatized-commercialized-spectacularized-celebritized sport culture; the hegemonic blueprint for the structure, delivery, and diversified consumptive experience of elite/professional sport. Cast as the consummate/superior mode of sport organization, *uber-sport* possesses a cultural authority prescribed by dutiful industry advocates as a matter of course, in a manner that effectively renders other modes of sport structure and delivery as sub-optimal/inferior. As a consequence, *uber-sport* is (re)created as "its own object" (Gruneau 2017: 63) – and as the way elite/professional sport formations are expected to operate and exist within late capitalist society – by those working within the industry. Moreover, the material and representational instantiation of *uber-sport* has, in a tautological sense, become a normalized and normalizing agent in the lived experience of spectators, viewers, and consumers alike. So, within the United States, which provides the primary context for this discussion, the prevalence of the *uber-sport* form and function is evident across major sport organizations, leagues, and events (such as those linked to the ATP, LPGA, NASCAR, MLB, MLS, NBA, NFL, NHL, PGA, UFC, WNBA, and the WTA).

Pointing to its ubiquity, *uber-sport* is clearly a trans-sport mode of institutional structure and delivery. However, its ubiquity is not restricted to sport within the US *Uber-sport* is also a trans-national phenomenon: the spread of culturally oriented late capitalism propelling the global diffusion of the *uber-sport* model across national (i. e., Australian National Rugby League, English Premier League, and Indian Premier League) and transnational sport organizations (i. e., the IOC, FIFA, ATP, IAAF, FIBA, or FIA) (Andrews and Grainger 2007). Through the global circulation, exchange, and surveillance of *uber-sport* products, information, and expertise, *uber-sport* has been established as the sport industry standard around the world. As such, the architecture, values, and practices of *uber-sport* are every bit in evidence in the hyperbolically named Chinese Super League, Super Rugby, or Australian Suncorp Super Netball League, as they are in the NFL, WNBA, or NASCAR. While the global diffusion of the *uber-sport* model brings with it a semblance of American-derived homogenization – specifically in terms of institutional objectives and infrastructure – it is far from a universal monolith. The shape of the ball, the nature of the physical contest, cast of characters on display, or litany of corporate sponsors differ even if the mode, means, and relations of *uber-sport* production remain unerringly similar. In this manner, *uber-sport* has emerged as a truly trans-national phenomenon, existing simultaneously in multiple settings around globe, yet operating in each of these within the language of the sporting local. *Uber-sport* institutions consciously mobilize the particularities of the local sport marketplace (be they metropolitan, regional, or national scales), in looking to engage and animate consumer consciousness and behavior at the local level. *Uber-sport* thus represents a condition of formulated ubiety: a state of being or existence derived from location in a given time or space, a whereness. Hence, *uber-sport* is both global and local, ubiquitous and ubietous.

Within the contemporary US context, a vibrant alchemy of corporate capitalism, commercial media culture, mass consumerism, neoliberalism, and nationalism frame the reified constitution, delivery, and experience of elite/professional sport as a mass entertainment and widely diversified commercial product: *uber-sport*. *Uber-sport* is plainly not a term used by either producers or consumers of sports (as it is generally referred to in the American vernacular), even though there is a widespread recognition of many of the constituent processes and elements underpinning the *uber-sport* configuration. As such, the reader may very well question *uber-sport*'s descriptive or interpretive value as the empirical frame for this project. In a Saussurean (Saussure 1959) sense, advancing the concept of *uber-sport* is a conscious attempt to identify an "object of study" for critical sport scholars, that renders visible its structure and function as a "structured assemblage of practices," revealing many of the complexities of the "context in which it is constituted" (Grossberg 2010: 25). Drawing theoretical formulations from, amongst others, Theodor Adorno, Herbert Marcuse, Frederic Jameson, Guy Debord, and Manuel DeLanda, this chapter offers a synthetic (derived from an accumulative synthesis) theoretical framework for understanding the contextual nature and influence of *uber-sport*'s infrastructural dynamics.

2 One-dimensional *uber-sport*

The work emanating from the Frankfurt School (and, by implication, various sport-focused derivatives: Alt 1983; Brohm 1978; Grano 2017; Gruneau 2017; Inglis 2004; McDonald 2009; Morgan 1998; Perelman 2012) has long been criticized for its cultural elitism, intellectual pessimism, and political impotence; exponents of the project were famously described by Hungarian Marxist philosopher György Lukács as residing complacently in the "Grand Hotel Abyss" (Lukács 1971: 22). Nonetheless, despite its perception among certain circles as a haughty and anachronistic intellectual backwater, there is considerable value in revisiting, and subsequently extending, the theoretical insights of the Frankfurt School as a starting point for this critical explication of *uber-sport*.

Founded in 1923, and affiliated with the University of Frankfurt am Main, the Frankfurt Institute for Social Research (Institut für Sozialforschung) developed as an intellectual response to the cultural, economic, and political evolution of post-World War I Germany (Arato, Gebhardt, and Piccone 1982), Frankfurt School theorists examined the myriad ways modern capitalism led to the enslavement of populations by commingled and ensnaring economic, political, technological, social, and cultural institutions, forces, and logics. Any potentially disruptive mass mobilizations against economic, political, and/or social unfreedoms (Adorno 1978) are effectively defused by the consumer freedoms (needs and desires) constructed within and satiated by the culture industries (film, television, new media, advertising, popular music, and *uber-sport*). In political terms, the pacifying capacities of culture industries thus contribute to the stability, and largely unquestioned continuation, of the democratic capitalist formation. Here is the "mass deception" of the culture industries to which Horkheimer and Adorno (2002) famously referred.

Published in 1964, Herbert Marcuse's *One-dimensional Man: Studies in the Ideology of Advanced Industrial Society* (2002) furthered the Frankfurt School indictment of the cultural politics of consumer capitalism in general, and the culture industries more specifically, and so informs this examination of the *uber-sport* culture industry. Marcuse identified the mechanisms of domination and social control, whereby individual thoughts and behaviors become integrated into consumer capitalism's domineering cultural institutions and logics (Kellner 2002). Rather than finding individualized self-actualization through consumption, Marcuse (1998: 48) argued the illusionary freedom to consume hid the "mechanics of conformity" underpinning a system of collective domination and control. These modern "mechanics of conformity" originated in the workplace, but subsequently spread to all realms of existence, such that they came to "govern performance not only in the factories and shops, but also in the offices, schools, assemblies and, finally, in the realm of relaxation and entertainment" (Marcuse 1998: 48), where *uber-sport* resides in all its putatively benign and populist glory. Marcuse thus depicted a "one-dimensional society" centered around the technologies and rationalities of the marketplace, that created an epoch defining ontology: "one dimensional man [*sic*]" referring to the nature of being within this new phase of civilization, wherein individual freedom and happiness are created and satiated by needs and desires generated by the complex consumerist incitement that is contemporary society. The proliferating and fortifying outpourings of the culture industries propagate the dominion of the capitalist system by integrating individuals into the ideology and practices of consumer society, such that the normalization of its consumptive expressions contributes to the stabilization of the political order underpinning it.

Conjoining Adorno and Marcuse's understandings, this chapter advances *uber-sport* as a contemporary culture industry and, as such, an oppressively conformist one-dimensional institution: a one-dimensional sport (indeed, one-dimensional sport and *uber-sport* can be considered synonymous and are treated as such herein). The concept of one-dimensional sport was first advanced by revolutionary Marxist sociology of sport scholar and documentary film maker, Ian McDonald (2009), who provided a brief yet suggestive outline for a Marcusian analysis of contemporary sport. Yet, more than any other Frankfurt School theorist, Adorno discussed sport as a facet of industrialized mass culture, acknowledging it as an important aspect of modern society (Adorno 1981). Regarding spectator sport, Adorno similarly considered it a venue wherein the "subjected celebrate their subjection" (Adorno 2001: 89), an ironic observation providing insight into his frequently cited statement that "athletic events were the models for totalitarian mass rallies" (Adorno 1981: 80). McDonald (2009) highlighted a related irony of the modern sport formation, namely sport's appeal to the masses initially derived from its function as a cathartic release – a source of escape and diversion – from the harsh realities of rapidly industrializing and urbanizing capitalist existence. However, the industrialization of sport itself subsequently led to its wholesale co-optation into the logics of one-dimensional society; *uber-sport* may appear to be a venue of pleasurable liberation from capitalist existence when, in actuality, it is a site imbued with its oppressive and alienating aspects, and thereby culpable in the passive and indeed enjoyable reproduction of the capitalist status quo. In a Marcusian sense, through sport the populace may find joy and contentment in their perceived ability to temporarily abscond from the constraints of one-dimensional society. However, the influence of one-dimensional sport as a covert proxy for one-dimensional society makes their escape little more than a comforting illusion. According to McDonald (2009) the institution and culture of high-performance sport is fully integrated into the logics of consumer capitalism, such that it acts as a buttress to one-dimensional society's dominant productivist and consumerist ideologies, and an effective suppressant of any resistance or alternatives to them. Hence, as an institutional expression of one-dimensional society, one-dimensional sport/the *uber-sport* culture industry produces highly rationalized, entertainment-driven sport spectacles subject to continual purposeful reformulation, as prompted by the perpetual pursuit of maximizing audience/market share, and thereby profit, across an array of corroborating revenue streams (products, bodies, services, events, spectacles, and spaces).

In a fashion inimitable with other culture industries, *uber-sport* is manufactured as a "species of canned and neutralised demotic populism" (Hall 1981: 233): it is an important source of the entertaining and pleasurable democratic unfreedoms (Marcuse 2002) that neutralize the critical energies of the consuming masses and contribute to the political pacification of one-dimensional society. This point was later elaborated upon in Baudrillard's commentary on the French populace's indifference toward the treatment of the German lawyer, Klaus Croissant, a far-left militant who had his application for political asylum rejected by the French government. Despite garnering high-profile support for his case – including from Michel Foucault and Jean-Paul Sartre – Croissant's subsequent extradition back to Germany in November 1977, generated little more than a few hundred demonstrators. On the same evening, more than twenty million of the French populace watched a crucial qualifying game for the 1978 World Cup between France and Bulgaria. According to Baudrillard's (1983: 12) rationalization, "Not a single query about the mystery of this indifference. One same reason is always invoked: the manipulation of the masses by power, their mystification by football." So, within the contemporary US, the economic, political, and cultural power of *uber-sport* – and that of the culture industries more generally – mystifies the masses, creating a climate of political indifference enabling the operation – if not securing the unquestioned authority – of the US' neoliberal democratic formation (Andrews and Silk 2012).

In Adorno's (1981: 80–81) terms, *uber-sport* is a "pseudo-activity" involving the "channelling of energies which could otherwise become dangerous" through the "endowing of meaningless activity with a specious seriousness and significance." He continued, "mass culture is not interested in turning its consumers into sportsmen as such but only into howling devotees of the stadium" and, by inference, passive advocates of the capitalist order in toto (Adorno 2001: 90). Updating this position through reference to Marx's understanding of religion as a site of "illusory happiness" and "oppression," Brohm (1978) and Perelman (2012) speak to *uber-sport* as a new opiate of the masses that: absorbs, diverts, and neutralizes the discontents of the mass; is constituted as an "ideological bloc" and site of popular acclamation and stabilization; and, positions spectators and viewers as an undifferentiated mass of "cheering machines" for sport, and more importantly, for the established socio-politico-cultural order (Perelman 2012: 125, 127). In Althusser's neo-Marxist terms (Althusser informing both Brohm and Perelman's analyses), the *uber-sport* culture industry consequently functions as part of the ideological state apparatus (ISA): those relatively autonomous, but nonetheless ideologically unified institutions (Althusser cites the mass media, religion, the family, the political system, schools, and sport as examples of ISAs), which individually, and combined, express and reinforce the values and beliefs of the dominant capitalist classes (Althusser 1971).

3 The *uber-sport* integrated spectacle

Despite its interpretive value, an exclusively Frankfurt School-informed approach fails to provide an understanding of the architecture of *uber-sport*. Such an empirical, and indeed ontological, deficit was identified by Jameson when pointing to the problem with Frankfurt School approaches in "passing from a study of commodified forms to the infrastructural dynamics of this or that industry or technology" (2009: 334). In developing an understanding of *uber-sport*'s infrastructural dynamics – a precise conceptualizing or detailing of *uber-sport*'s multivalent state of being and becoming – this section places Jamesonian understanding of late capitalism in conversation with Debord's understanding of the society of the spectacle.

Taking a broad overview of his transdisciplinary scholarship, Jameson's work encompasses both vertical (synchronic) and horizontal (diachronic) frames of textual interpretation (Kellner and Homer 2004) which, when combined, significantly inform the dialectic analysis of *uber-sport* as a symptom of late capitalist conditions, forces, and relations. Along the vertical axis, a Jamesonian approach acknowledges how cultural texts/products are exhibited in different forms and dimensions. *Uber-sport* is manifest in myriad ways (visual, aural, digital, textual, material), each of which offers numerous dimensions of experiential engagement (i. e., physical, affective, ideological, discursive, expressive, symbolic, psychoanalytic). Moving up and down *uber-sport*'s vertical axis, the immediacy of experience tends to lead to a reifying of the engaged cultural form; to a focus on the *uber-sport* event, broadcast, digital content, material space, or physical commodity, as if it were somehow isolated from the various other forms which coalesce to create *uber-sport*'s organic unity. A Jamesonian approach thus recognizes the co-constitutive vertical (synchronic) structure of *uber-sport* as an aggregated empirical whole (Jameson 2008). However, it also emphasizes, as he has done in his later work, the importance of horizontal (diachronic) analysis as a means of escaping the textualism of literary and cultural criticism. Jameson (1992) stressed the necessary relationality of cultural objects, which exist, and have to be understood in coexistence with, various interrelated historical, sociopolitical, and economic dimensions. As Hardt and Weeks (2000: 2) note, Jameson's later commitment to the diachronic practice of historical contextualization exhorted against the interpretive limits of textual myopia, arguing "you will not understand the texts and objects you read and interpret unless you work simultaneously to understand the large social whole in which they are organically embedded." Similarly, *uber-sport* can only be understood in dialectic relation to what Jameson (1991) variously describes as postmodern, late, or consumer capitalist society.

Over the decades spanning the late 20th and early 21st centuries, *uber-sport* has matured into a culture industry every bit as culturally and economically significant as the film, television, internet, and advertising sectors with which it is productively enmeshed (late capitalism's dedifferentiation of fields making rigid delineation little more than a self-affirming heuristic illusion/device for those working in, or studying, a specific industrial sector). *Uber-sport* represents the sum of a series of interdependent sectoral elements, whose "constituent parts appear increasingly naturalized and indispensable" (Rowe 1995: 115). However, *uber-sport*'s readily apparent conflation of culture, the economy, and mass media represents the interpenetration of but three of the late capitalism's "multitudinous subsystems" (Jameson 2009: 359). Clearly, other subsystems exist (include politics, judiciary, military, religion, technology, and various other cultural spheres, such as fashion, music, dance), any or all of which are potential contributors to *uber-sport*'s subsystemic amalgam. As such, *uber-sport*'s contingent variegated complexity, as determined by the specificities of time and space, cannot be ignored.

Jameson's understanding of late capitalism clearly owes a considerable debt to French Situationist, Guy Debord's (1990 [1988]; 1994 [1967]) rather abstract and fragmentary, yet simultaneously suggestive and influential, treatise on the mass media's role in (re)producing contemporary society. Debord provided a framework for understanding how late capitalist existence is subject to the cycles, circuitry, and control (Dyer-Witheford 1999) of spectacular society, broadly construed. For Jameson, as for Debord, the spectacle represents both the system and "historical moment by which we happen to be governed" (Debord 1994 [1967]: 15).

In his later reflection upon the society of the spectacle, Debord's (1990 [1988]) notion of the integrated spectacle provides a useful conceptual frame for delineating the multidimensional interdependence of *uber-sport*'s economy of spectacles. The integrated spectacle synthesized Debord's earlier dichotomous understanding which positions the "concentrated" spectacle/spectacular power as distinct from the "diffuse" spectacle/spectacular power (Debord 1994 [1967]). By "concentrated" spectacle, Debord referred to the condensed expression of ideology and power "around a dictatorial power" be it fascist or communist (Debord 1990 [1988]: 8). This contrasted with the "diffuse" form of spectacular power communicated through the proliferating array of mass mediated commodities and commodified experiences associated with the "Americanisation of the world" (Debord 1990 [1988]: 8). For Debord, the second half of the 20th century witnessed the triumph of the diffuse spectacle, and the incorporation of the concentrated "mass multimedia spectacle" as the "indispensable adjunct of the spectacle of the commodity," and vice versa (Roberts 2003: 65). Simultaneously concentrated and diffuse, for Debord there is no escape from the integrated spectacle, since it has "never before put its mark to such a degree on almost the full range of socially produced behaviour and objects" and has "spread itself to the point where it now permeates all reality" (Debord 1990 [1988]: 9). In this manner, *uber-sport*, typifies important ontological elements of the integrated Debordian spectacle. While *uber-sport* may be subject to spectacularizing mass mediation, it cannot simply be reduced to being "a collection of images." Rather, as an integrated spectacle, *uber-sport* comprises a complex economy of spectacular forms (comprising mass mediated events, bodies, products, spaces, and services) facilitating social relationships with and between consumers, and fashioning the lived "real unreality" of postmodern or late capitalist society (Debord 1994 [1967]: 12, 13).

Having positioned *uber-sport* as an integrated spectacle one is compelled to offer a delineation of its multiple and interpenetrating constitutive formations. Despite its popular perception as a coherent and concrete (reified) whole, the *uber-sport* integrated spectacle is a sectorally indistinguishable nexus of complexly interrelated constitutive elements pervading seemingly all aspects of contemporary life. The generative cross-contamination between the multifarious nodes of *uber-sport* render any interpretive dissection inescapably arbitrary, yet hopefully illuminating. Hence, the following represents an attempt to capture the mutually implicated sub-spectacles that coalesce to form the complex spectacular composite that is *uber-sport*:

Performative Spectacle: The mass mediation of the athletic performances or contests, between teams or individuals, that constitute the *uber-sport* event. Generated across the full range of media technologies (from print to digital, traditional to social), the mediation of *uber-sport* includes the a priori narrative positioning and promotion of the event, live broadcast coverage of the event, and post-event analysis and reportage.

Embodied Spectacle: Derived from various sanctioned and unsanctioned sources of media representation, the accumulated symbolic meaning of celebrated individuals (players, coaches, owners, or fans), synonymous with *uber-sport* events.

Commodity Spectacle: The mobilization of resonant *uber-sport* referents (most frequently individual athletes, involved teams, and/or competitions) within multi-platform advertising and marketing campaigns, designed to enhance brand identity and market appeal of sport and non-sport related commodities and services.

Virtual Spectacle: The digitally generated creation of virtual *uber-sport* environments and experiences. These include competitions between virtual *uber-sport* teams assembled using quantified aspects of player performance in actual games (fantasy sports), and virtual recreations of sporting events within *uber-sport* computer game environments based on predictive algorithmic models of team and player performance (eSports).

Ceremonial Spectacle: The ritualistic and symbolic elements performed around the *uber-sport* event, i.e., national anthems, anti-racism announcements, dignitary presentations, torch relays, opening and closing ceremonies, and award ceremonies.

Spatial Spectacle: The symbolic contribution of the event location, landscape, and/or built environment to the constitution of the *uber-sport* spectacle. Invokes different spatial scales based on the nature of the event, i.e., nation-based FIFA World Cups; city/region-based Olympic Games; city/stadium-based teams; sport-themed restaurants, museums, or commercial spaces.

Pernicious Spectacle: The outpourings of the sensationalist sectors of the mass culture industries, looking to further their readership/viewership through tabloid coverage of *uber-sport* bodies, themes, and issues.

Social Spectacle: The contributions from the various forms of new social media technologies, involving the contribution of disparately located, and differentially invested, institutions and individuals, to the representation and experience of the *uber-sport* event.

This model of the *uber-sport* formation as integrated spectacle complementary alternative to Debord's abstract and generalized spectacle-based cosmology, through an analytically expedient, empirically speculative, yet hopefully suggestive, deconstruction of *uber-sport*'s compound structure and influence as an integrated spectacle. This is not to assert some unchanging *uber-sport* universalism; the dictates of spatial and temporal specificities coalesce to form what are necessarily contingent *uber-sport* amalgams (contextually specific forces, relations, and permutations of sub-spectacle). Although possessing a degree of mutually manufactured consistency linking its various constituent parts, the loose amalgam that is *uber-sport* is subject to perpetual instability and change. Hence, *uber-sport* is a phenomenon always in the process of becoming, continually being made and remade, established and disestablished, by the shifting intensities of its constituent elements, as moderated by the equally fluid forces and networks forging the broader contexts with which *uber-sport* is mutually implicated.

4 *Uber-sport*'s assemblages of assemblages

Through the integrated spectacle, Debord offers a conceptualizing of *uber-sport* foregrounding its compound and contingent structure. However, Debord only takes the theorizing of *uber-sport*'s "multitudinous subsystems" (Jameson 2009: 359) so far, leaving a degree of empirical and ontological ambiguity needing to be addressed. To this end, there is much to be gained through engaging DeLanda's Deleuze-Guattari informed social ontology, variously referred to as "'neo-assemblage theory', 'assemblage theory 2.0', or some other name" (DeLanda 2006: 4). DeLanda (2006, 2016) developed a conceptualizing of the social whole/society based around the assemblage, countering what he perceived as the totalizing and linear evolutionary tendencies of dialectic materialism. For DeLanda (2016), an assemblage is a heterogeneous coalescence whose diverse components exhibit different forms of content, scale, temporality, and affectivity: "humans, materials, technologies, organizations, techniques, procedures, norms, and events" (Baker and McGuirk: 428). In developing this heterogeneous relational ontology, assemblage theory disrupts nature/culture, material/non-material, human/non-human, subject/object, structure/agency, surface/depth, and elemental/expressive binaries (Fox and Alldred 2017). Such variegated empirical composition means assemblages possess multi-scalar and multi-temporal enactments: the constituent elements of an assemblage exhibit contrasting scales (i. e., the geographic range of individual human existence operates at a different level than that of an organization, or energy source) and temporalities (i. e., differing rates of change exist between technological, architectural, and human elements). An assemblage is a totality comprised of the relationships between its separate parts, the precise properties of each individual element, and hence of the greater whole, are neither necessary nor transcendent. Rather, the assemblage and its constituent elements are formed through generative and ever-changing interactions, the assemblage being a phenomenon occupying the fluid space created by its protean relationality (DeLanda 2016).

Invoking Farias (2010: 15), assemblages such as *uber-sport* do not possess a pre-existent, coherent, and stable essence: an "out-there reality." Rather, an assemblage comes to have "presence" by being provisionally "stitched into place by fragmented, multi-scaled and multi-sited networks of association" (Jacobs 2006: 3) within itself and with other assemblages, whether larger, comparable, or smaller in scale. Assemblage theorizing similarly explains how assemblages "come into being in multiple ways" – are made and re-made, affected and affecting – through manifold collisions, overlapping, and interference with one another (Farias 2010: 15). As a result, despite giving the appearance of stasis and stability, assemblages – including that of the human subject, and indeed *uber-sport* – are devoid of any transcendent essence. They are always characterized by the condition of perpetual (dis/re)assembly; always incorporating either internally and/or externally derived states of contradiction; always subject to potential transformation; always in a state of becoming.

Although routinely engaged as if they possessed some singular, stable, and essential capacities transcending temporal and spatial differences, the mass spectated *uber-sport* "performance events" (individual game/match/contest) (Martin 1997: 188), are nonrepeatable and momentary confederations of multi-scaled and multi-sited assemblages (including athletes/players, teams, coaches, medical staff, apparel and footwear technologies, game-related equipment, playing surfaces, officials, rules, spectators, service workers, retail spaces, sponsors, security personnel, stadia, cities, leagues, media broadcast operatives, and viewers, to name but a few). Importantly, each of the variously scaled and sited components of the *uber-sport* event assemblage, possesses their own generative relation with external assemblages (i. e., the economy, media, fashion, technology, nation, religion, military, and politics, amongst myriad others), rendering *uber-sport*, as with any assemblage, always open to the potential for externally derived transformative change. For those in physical attendance, and certainly for the viewing masses, the *uber-sport* performance event is never an unfiltered "interface between performers and public" (Martin 1997: 188). Layers of pre-game media positioning, in-game narrativization, and post-game rumination, generated by traditional and social media, means any *uber-sport* event is unavoidably subject to preemptive, instantaneous, and retroactive mediated becomings: it is a complex outgrowth of the productive convergence between *uber-sport* and various media assemblages operating within a given cultural context.

In Malins' (2004) terms, *uber-sport*'s function and meaning is dependent on those sub- and supra-, internal and external, assemblage relations which combine to inform its assemblage being and becoming. All of which corroborates DeLanda's (2016: 3) observation that "at all times we are dealing with assemblages of assemblages." The *uber-sport* assemblage is not an essential, necessary, or transcendent category. Instead, as an interstitial phenomenon, its form, meanings, properties, and capacities, exist and endure within the spaces created by its multifarious generative elements and relations (both internal and external): to underscore, with *uber-sport* we are once again "dealing with assemblages of assemblages." As an assemblage comprised of a multiplicity of multi-scaled and multi-sited network of assemblage relations, *uber-sport* is thus materially and expressively sutured into situated place, from which it derives its socio-cultural presence, identity, and influence (DeLanda 2006; Jacobs 2006: 3).

Despite the possibility for ambiguity and incoherence derived from *uber-sport*'s heterogeneous assemblant formation, an expressive consistency exhibited across its "nested set of assemblages" (DeLanda 2016: 4) frequently provides (codes) *uber-sport* with a tacit semblance of homogeneity that delineates, or territorializes, its boundaries (DeLanda 2016: 3). That should not infer the erasure of localized differences within and between *uber-sport* assemblages, which are always susceptible to de-territorialization (de-coding of boundaries). For instance, widely referred to in universalizing terms as the global game, association football is in fact a mobile technology (Ong 2007): the global sport is an assemblage of nationally localized football, futebol, fútbol, calcio, sokker, soka, or soccer assemblages, each of which is potentially (there is no necessary relation) articulated to, and becomes an expression of, the situated cultural, historic, aesthetic, political, and/or economic regimes of the nation in question. Hence, the game can, and indeed has, variously been articulated as a material-expressive enactment of neoliberal capitalist, social democratic, socialist, state capitalist, communist, absolute monarchist, and theocratic national assemblages.

As an assemblage, the performance-based *uber-sport* event and/or its hypermediated representation cannot be assumed to be an integrative ontological fulcrum of *uber-sport*, from which ancillary elements are derived. There is no macro-to-micro, top-down hierarchy of influences shaping *uber-sport*. Rather, as a rhizome, *uber-sport* is a "chaosmosis, a chaotic osmosis of varied and variable connections rather than an ordered cosmos" (Conley 2009: 33). As such, *uber-sport* is flattened multiplicity of connections between heterogenous component elements (including athletes/coaches/animals, teams/franchises, performances events [games/matches/contests], media broadcasts and content, products, services, spectators, viewers, consumers, sponsors, retail spaces, natural and/or built environments, leagues, competitions, tournaments, multi-sport events organizations, and governing bodies), wherein no element is guaranteed affecting ascendancy, and all elements possess the potential for securing a position of empirical dominance and ontological influence, as determined by the myriad articulations which (in)form the *uber-sport* assemblage at any given moment. In this state of perpetual becoming, *uber-sport* is not only "continually produced by the day-to-day interactions" between its material and expressive assemblant parts, but also through its multiple "relations of exteriority" – points of engagement and influence – with inveterately fluid economic, political, cultural, and technological assemblages (DeLanda 2016: 19, 73).

As an "open-ended collective, a 'non-totalizable sum'" (Bennett 2010: 24), the *uber-sport* assemblage is always already susceptible to externally derived contraventions (decodings) of previously established delineating parameters, potentially leading to a state of assemblage irregularity or incoherence. This comes to the fore where the generative dynamism of economic, political, cultural, media, and technological assemblages destabilizes a period of *uber-sport* stasis. For instance, at the present time, the ontological primacy previously ascribed to the performance event, and subsequently the televisual representation thereof, as the primary manifestations of (and gateways into) *uber-sport*, are increasingly challenged by the encroachment of social media and digital gaming technologies into the sporting realm. These externally generated agents of change – what some within the sport industry describe as its "disruptors" (Gray 2018) – contribute to the on-going mutation of the structure, delivery, and experience of *uber-sport*. Examples of such disruption include: the phenomenon whereby individuals are introduced to professional football (soccer) – and often teams choose their favorite team – through the virtual universe of computer gaming (i. e., products such as EA Sports FIFA Soccer becoming the gateway to more traditional engagement with the performative spectacle); the increasing convergence of *uber-sport* and gaming cultures (NFL players celebrating touchdowns with dances mirrored from Fortnite emotes, and Fortnite gamers being able to purchase NFL jerseys for their avatars); the licensed live streaming of *uber-sport* events via web (YouTube, Amazon) or social media (i. e., Twitter, Facebook) platforms; the evolution of social media platforms as *uber-sport* originators (i. e., YouTube's 2018 promotion and pay-per-view coverage of the boxing match between vloggers Logan Paul and KSI); and, the proliferation of user generated content on social media outlets (i. e., Twitter, Facebook, Instagram, Snapchat, and Periscope) enabling unsanctioned individuals and groups to become prosumers of *uber-sport* media discourse (Andrews and Ritzer 2018). Although such disruptions to the *uber-sport* landscape may be perceived as largely contained within particular empirical realms, or sub-assemblages, they are nonetheless consequential to *uber-sport* assemblage in its entirety. The intra/inter-connective nature of rhizomes dictates that alterations can never be wholly discrete or bounded, they always and unavoidably result in modifications to the whole (Buchanan 2009). *Uber-sport* may advance the appearance of reified stasis, yet this merely masks the influence of social, cultural, political, economic, and/or technological changes. In Deleuze and Guattari's (1987: 262) terms, the "individuated aggregate" of the *uber-sport* rhizome renders it a haecceity (individual or unique entity), inexorably subject to, and occupying space created by, the "always-emergent condition of the present" (Marcus and Saka 2006: 101–102).

5 Conclusion

This discussion has engaged Adorno's understanding of culture industries, Jameson's periodizing of late capitalism, Debord's concept of the integrated spectacle, and DeLanda's assemblage theory, as a means of rendering visible the *uber-sport* assemblage as the heterogenous confluence of a series of contextual forces and articulations (economic, political, technological, social, and cultural). Despite its habitual reification, the *uber-sport* assemblage is an interstitial phenomenon framed and operating within the spaces formed by complex, and contextually specific, relations of assemblant interiority and exteriority. Innumerable "relations of exteriority" (DeLanda 2016: 11, 73) are responsible for the provisional nature of the *uber-sport* formation, since externally situated transformations with external assemblages (i. e., media, economic, fashion, technology, nation, religion, military, or political assemblages) have, both subtly and profoundly, altered the very being of the *uber-sport* assemblage. A truly comprehensive explication of the *uber-sport* assemblage would therefore necessarily consider its relations with a broad range of external assemblant formations.

Not that all assemblages or assemblage relations are equally impactful. Assemblage theorizing's flat ontology does not "flatten all realities ... singularize every territory ... [make] every system of relationality equivalent" (Grossberg 2006: 4). Conversely, an assemblage approach recognizes there is no pre-ordained, necessary hierarchy of assemblage influences; each assemblage possesses the same ontological possibility to become a more, or less, powerful agent (McFarlane 2011). DeLanda (2006, 2016) developed a conceptualizing of the social whole/society based around the assemblage, countering what he perceived as the totalizing and linear evolutionary tendencies of dialectic materialism. As Bennett (2010: 24) noted, and unlike more economically determinist models of society, according to assemblage theorizing no single entity possesses the "competence to determine consistently the trajectory" of an assemblage. That is not to say the economic (for one instance) cannot be a determining force upon/within an assemblage. Rather, DeLanda's social ontology asserts there is no guarantee of the primacy of economic, or indeed any other determinant influences: as Fernand Braudel reminded us, it is "important not to imagine a priori that a single sector may achieve permanent superiority over another, or over all the others" (Braudel 1982: 460). The varied constituents of the *uber-sport* assemblage (materials, symbols, persons, non-persons, spaces, values, architecture, technology, and energies) are complexly interwoven with those of the other assemblages that combine to form a society as a contingent assemblage of assemblages (DeLanda 2016). The aim of any approach to the *uber-sport* assemblage is therefore to discern and engage the most determinant, or affecting, internal and external assemblant relations within a given spatial and temporal context. With this assemblage approach in mind, the study of the sport media as a discrete entity would, at best, appear ontologically inadvisable. Constituted by/constitutive of myriad assemblage relations that are themselves contextually specific, *uber-sport*'s empirical heterogeneity, scalar complexity, and temporal reach render its boundaries so permeable, that any essentializing or universalizing coherence ascribed to it is assemblage/sub-assemblage formations are little more than managerial/epistemological illusions. Hence, any truly contextual study of the sport media assemblage as a heterogenous entity, is compelled to acknowledge the multitudinous sub-assemblages, as well as the inter-assemblages relations, with which it is constitutively linked, or articulated, in constituting the broader *uber-sport* assemblage. As E. M. Forster implored within *Howard's End* – albeit speaking to a very different context and constituency – for sport communication it is time to "Only connect! ... Live in fragments no longer."

Acknowledgement: This chapter summarizes a number of the arguments made in Andrews (2019). The material is used with the permission of the copyright holder.

References

Adorno, Theodor. 1978. *Minima moralia: Reflections from damaged life*. London: Verso.
Adorno, Theodor. W. 1981. *Prisms*, 1st MIT Press edn. Cambridge, MA: MIT Press.
Adorno, Theodor. 2001. *The culture industry*. London: Routledge.
Alt, John. 1983. Sport and cultural reification: From ritual to mass consumption. *Theory, Culture and Society* 13. 93–107.
Althusser, Louis. 1971. *Lenin and philosophy and other essays*. London: New Left Books.
Andrews, David L. 2006. *Sport-commerce-culture: Essays on sport in late capitalist America*. New York: Peter Lang.
Andrews, David L. 2009. Sport, culture, and late capitalism. In Ben Carrington & Ian McDonald (eds.), *Marxism, cultural studies and sport*, 213–231. London: Routledge.
Andrews, David L. 2019. *Making sport great again: The* uber-sport *assemblage, neoliberalism, and the Trump conjuncture*. Cham, Switzerland: Palgrave Pivot.
Andrews, David L. & Andrew D. Grainger. 2007. Sport and globalization. In George Ritzer (ed.), *The Blackwell Companion to Globalization*, 478–497. Malden, MA: Blackwell.
Andrews, David L. & George Ritzer. 2018. Sport and prosumption. *Journal of Consumer Culture* 182. 356–373.
Andrews, David L. & Michael L. Silk (eds.). 2012. *Sport and neoliberalism: Politics, consumption, and culture*. Philadelphia: Temple University Press.
Arato, Andrew, Eike Gebhardt & Paul Piccone. 1982. *The essential Frankfurt School reader*. New York: Continuum.
Baker, Tom & Pauline McGuirk. 2016. Assemblage thinking as methodology: Commitments and practices for critical policy research. *Territory, Politics, Governance* 5(4). 425–442.
Baudrillard, Jean. 1983. *In the shadow of the silent majorities ... or the end of the social and other essays*. New York: Semiotext(e).
Bennett, Jane. 2010. *Vibrant matter: A political ecology of things*. Durham, NC: Duke University Press.
Braudel, Fernand. 1982. *The wheels of commerce (civilization and capitalism, 15th–18th century – Volume II)*. New York: Harper & Row.
Brohm, Jean-Marie. 1978. *Sport: A prison of measured time*. London: Pluto Press.
Buchanan, Ian. 2009. Deleuze and the internet. In Mark Poster & David Savat (eds.), *Deleuze and new technology*, 143–160. Edinburgh: Edinburgh University Press.
Conley, Verena A. 2009. Of rhizomes, smooth space, war machines and new media. In Mark Poster & David Savat (eds.), *Deleuze and new technology*, 32–44. Edinburgh: Edinburgh University Press.
Debord, Guy. 1990 [1988]. *Comments on the society of the spectacle* (trans. Malcolm Imrie). London: Verso.
Debord, Guy. 1994 [1967]. *The society of the spectacle* (trans. Donald Nicholson-Smith). New York: Zone Books.
DeLanda, Manuel. 2006. *A new philosophy of society: Assemblage theory and social complexity*. London: Continuum.
DeLanda, Manuel. 2016. *Assemblage theory*. Edinburgh: Edinburgh University Press.
Deleuze, Gilles & Félix Guattari. 1987. *A thousand plateaus: Capitalism and schizophrenia*. Minneapolis: University of Minnesota Press.
Dyer-Witheford, Nick. 1999. *Cyber-Marx: Cycles and circuits of struggles in high-technology capitalism*. Urbana, IL: University of Illinois Press.
Farias, Ignacio. 2010. Introduction: Decentring the object of urban studies. In Ignacio Farias & Thomas Bender (eds.), *Urban assemblages: How actor-network theory changes urban studies*, 1–24. New York: Routledge.

Fox, Nick J. & Pam Alldred. 2017. *Sociology and the new materialism: Theory, research, action*. London: SAGE Publications.

Grano, Daniel A. 2017. *The eternal present of sport*. Philadelphia, PA: Temple University Press.

Gray, Robert. 2018. Jed York, 19 April. https://www.sportsbusinessdaily.com/en/Daily/Issues/2018/04/19/World%20Congress%20of%20Sports/Disruptors.aspx (11 November 2020).

Grossberg, Lawrence. 2006. Does cultural studies have futures? Should it? (or what's the matter with New York?): Cultural studies, contexts and conjunctures. *Cultural Studies* 20(1). 1–32.

Grossberg, Lawrence. 2010. *Cultural studies in the future tense*. Durham, NC: Duke University Press.

Gruneau, Richard S. 2017. *Sport and modernity*. Cambridge: Polity Press.

Hall, Stuart. 1981. Notes on deconstructing "the popular." In Raphael Samuel (ed.), *People's history and socialist theory*, 227–241. London: Routledge & Kegan Paul.

Hardt, Michael & Kathi Weeks. 2000. Introduction. In Michael Hardt & Kathi Weeks (eds.), *The Jameson reader*, 1–30. Oxford: Blackwell.

Horkheimer, Max & Theodor W. Adorno. 2002. *Dialectic of enlightenment: Philosophical fragments*. Stanford, CA: Stanford University Press.

Inglis, David. 2004. Theodor Adorno on sport: The jeu d'esprit of despair. In Richard Giulianotti (ed.), *Sport and modern social theorists*, 81–95. New York: Palgrave Macmillan.

Jacobs, Jane M. 2006. A geography of big things. *Cultural Geographies* 13. 1–27.

Jameson, Frederic. 1991. *Postmodernism, or, the cultural logic of late capitalism*. Durham, NC: Duke University Press.

Jameson, Frederic. 1992. *The geopolitical aesthetic*. Bloomington, IN: Indiana University Press.

Jameson, Frederic. 2008. *The ideologies of theory*. London: Verso.

Jameson, Frederic. 2009. *Valences of the dialectic*. London: Verso.

Kellner, Douglas. 2002. Introduction to the second edition. In Herbert Marcuse (ed.), *One dimensional man: Studies in the ideology of advanced industrial society*, xi–xxxviii. London: Routledge Classics.

Kellner, Douglas & Sean Homer. 2004. Introduction. In D. Kellner & S. Homer (eds.), *Frederic Jameson: A critical reader*, xii–xxii. Basingstoke: Palgrave/Macmillan.

Lukács, Georg. 1971. *The theory of the novel: A historico-philosophical essay on the forms of great epic literature* (trans. Anna Bostock). Cambridge, MA: MIT Press.

Malins, Peta. 2004. Machinic assemblages: Deleuze, Guattari and an ethico-aesthetics of drug use. *Janus Head: Journal of Interdisciplinary Studies in Literature, Continental Philosophy, Phenomenological Psychology, and the Arts* 7(1). 84–104.

Marcus, George E. & Erkan Saka. 2006. Assemblage. *Theory, Culture & Society* 23(2–3). 101–106.

Marcuse, Herbert. 1998. Some social implications of modern technology. In Douglas Kellner (ed.), *Technology, war, and fascism*, 39–66. London: Routledge.

Marcuse, Herbert. 2002. *One dimensional man: Studies in the ideology of advanced industrial society*. London: Routledge Classics.

Martin, Randy. 1997. Staging crisis: Twin takes in moving performance. In Peggy Phelan & Jill Lane (eds.), *The ends of performance*, 186–196. New York: New York University Press.

McDonald, Ian. 2009. One-dimensional sport: Revolutionary Marxism and the critique of sport. In Ben Carrington & Ian MacDonald (eds.), *Marxism, cultural studies and sport*, 32–48. London: Routledge.

McFarlane, Colin. 2011. On context: Assemblage, political economy and structure. *City* 15(3–4). 375–388.

Morgan, William J. 1998. Adorno on sport: The case of the fractured dialectic. *Theory and Society* 17(6). 813–838.

Ong, Aihwa. 2007. Neoliberalism as a mobile technology. *Transactions of the Institute of British Geographers* 32(1). 3–8.

Perelman, Marc. 2012. *Barbaric sport: A global plague*. London: Verso.
Roberts, David. 2003. Towards a genealogy and typology of spectacle: Some comments on Debord. *Thesis Eleven* 75(1). 54–68.
Rowe, David. 1995. *Popular cultures: Rock music, sport and the politics of pleasure*. London: Sage.
Saussure, Ferdinand de. 1959. *Course in general linguistics* (trans. Wade Baskin). New York: Philosophical Library.
Szymanski, Stefan. 2010. *The comparative economics of sport*. New York: Palgrave Macmillan.

John Kelly and Jung Woo Lee

16 Sport, media and the promotion of militarism: theoretical inter-continental reflections of the United Kingdom and South Korea

Abstract: The relationship between sport, popular culture, and western militarism is well established with the United States and its western allies witnessing a plethora of popular culture events being co-opted into providing platforms for citizens to "support" their governments' respective armed forces. Central to such events has been the relationship between sport and the media, with sport having long been a fruitful cultural arena utilized to enable and encourage citizens to support and "thank" national military actors. The mediated spectacle of sport combined with its sacred symbolic significance offers both governments and disparate individuals the sanctuary of the imagined ("democratic") nation and its accompanying ideological righteousness in the face of an uncertain global political world of "wars on terror," economic crises, and "fake news."

Keywords: United Kingdom; South Korea; remembrance; CDA; ideology; militarism

1 Introduction

The current phase of the sport–media–military nexus, precipitated and sustained by the US-led "war on terror," has a fascinating history (for example, see Jansen and Sabo 1994; Silk and Falcous 2005; Butterworth 2005, 2008, 2010, 2017; Stempel 2006; King 2008; Scherer and Koch 2010; Jenkins 2013; Kelly 2013, 2017a, 2017b; Penn and Berridge 2016; Cree and Caddick 2019). The American and Canadian governments developed propaganda departments designed to use the mediatization of popular cultural activities to elicit, manufacture, and communicate consent for their respective military actors and actions, the latter of which consisted largely of two controversial wars in the Middle East (an invasion of Iraq and an occupation of Afghanistan) (see Stempel 2006; Butterworth and Moskal 2009; Scherer and Koch 2010). Operation Tribute to Freedom (USA) and Operation Connection (Canada) emerged in 2003 and 2004 respectively and have placed sport and other such patriotism-inducing cultural events at the center of their "support the troops" initiatives. Part of the power of such events is that the coordinated activities are highly mediated spectacles communicating to (and crucially) *via* the public that the events and the ideological causes they underpin are normalized and deeply embedded into the everyday culture of society. They become the militarized wing of the "banal nationalism" Billig (1995) so clearly

https://doi.org/10.1515/9783110660883-016

has outlined. The spectacle of military fighter planes flying over a major sports arena, military tanks being used as background props for promotional photos of sporting mascots, or uniformed military personnel entering the sports field to adulation and applause are just three examples of the everyday fusion of mediated sport and militarism in US and allied countries. The hidden governmental orchestration of such practices in the US emerged in 2015 when – after freedom of information requests – it was revealed that its government paid sports clubs more than US $9 million (combined) in return for military appreciation events; events which appeared at the time to be organically supported rather than manufactured by the government using the money of the taxpayers it sought support from (Aljazeera 2015).

Given there has been much work written on the US, this chapter extends its analysis to consider two (contrasting) allies of the United States – the United Kingdom (UK) and South Korea. The UK offers a European, western, and NATO perspective. South Korea's status as a non-western and Indian Pacific Strategy ally of the US further extends our understanding of the sport–military–media nexus to Asia. Due to its military tensions with North Korea and universal conscription for men over the last seven decades, South Korea's military culture is embedded uniquely in civil society (Moon 2005; Song 2014). One may therefore expect different relationships and patterns to develop with regard to civil–military relations and indeed the associated sport–media–military nexus. Yet, as we reveal, in common with the US and UK, in the last decade major sporting occasions have been increasingly occurring and mediated in ways which communicate consent for militaristic ideology in South Korea in the last decade. One such example is the Korean professional baseball league, the most popular and culturally significant spectator sport in the country. We discuss this illustrating the potency of the sport–media–military nexus in South Korea with its forms of militaristic and patriotic discourse being infused with baseball matches and their mediated coverage.

First, however, we discuss the UK and its most culturally symbolic and universally mediated sport, football. In 2016, FIFA reprimanded the UK's football associations (FAs) for placing remembrance poppies on playing kits (FIFA investigates 2016; Royson, Davidson, and de la Mare 2017).[1] Despite FIFA's judgement that these acts of remembrance had breached Law 4.4 relating to "political, religious or personal slogans" (IFAB 2016), commentators in the UK universally defended these acts of remembrance as unequivocally non-political.[2] To analyse this case study and the sig-

1 The Earl Haig (red) poppy, named after First World War British military general, is the primary symbol of UK and Commonwealth military-related remembrance.

2 For example, Scottish secretary David Mundell asserted "this isn't a political gesture; it's a gesture about paying respect." He condemned FIFA's application of its own rules as "inexplicable" rejecting the world governing body's authority to legislate its own sport, adding they "should duck out of the issue" (FIFA completely 2016). British Prime, Minister Theresa May described the ruling as "utterly outrageous" (Elgot 2016) and, through her official spokeswoman, noted: "We continue to believe that footballers and fans should be able very clearly to show their support for all that our armed forces do" (FIFA fines 2016).

nificance of communication in (and of) sport, we locate the everyday lived intersections between language, power, and society as they relate to UK military-related remembrance. While the chapter's focus is sport, we avoid viewing the sport–media–military nexus as a de-contextualized abstraction. It is vital to contextualize that sport's power to communicate such ideological messages is *because* it reinforces identical messages communicated across a range of other national settings. In other words, sport acts in harmony across a multitude of socio-cultural settings to normalize and legitimize identical ideologically laden messages of banal militarism camouflaged as apolitical spectacle. After illustrating some of these sporting settings in which banal militarism occurs, we analyze the alleged (and refuted) politics of the red poppy and remembrance in British sport by outlining the wider national meanings of remembrance to illustrate the ways in which it is ubiquitously and officially interpreted. This involves first offering a critical discourse analysis (CDA) of the live television coverage of the 2016 Remembrance Sunday event by the British Broadcasting Corporation (BBC1) and Sky News. Understanding the ideological representation of the UK's primary remembrance-focused event by the official British state's national broadcaster and the UK's most prominent commercial broadcaster enables a fuller contextual understanding of communicating consent for militaristic violence on behalf of the UK government. We reveal a common set of ideological discursive articulations that are almost universally accepted in Britain, eliciting few critical comments or acts of dissention. We suggest that these televised productions and their articulations represent a trustworthy barometer with which to judge accepted and common interpretations of British remembrance and, consequently, contextualize the FIFA "poppy controversy" more fully.

We conclude that, despite being quite different types of US ally with very different historic and political civil–military relationships, the sport–media–military nexus in both the UK and South Korea functions similarly as part of an overarching cultural reproduction process that serves to use sport to both normalize and communicate consent for US-allies' foreign policy, military violence, and wars.

2 UK remembrance

The United Kingdom has witnessed many of the American and Canadian "support the troops" campaigns being replicated. Beauty contests, prime time Saturday night television shows, military-related music albums, military branded food products, newly formed charities, recently invented traditions such as Armed Forces Day, and homecoming parades have all combined to ensure a multi-agency hero-ification and celebritization of the British military occurs (see Kelly 2013). Britain's Invictus Games has joined the American Warrior Games to offer a sporting platform for injured military personnel to compete and elicit public support. British football clubs such as Bolton Wanderers FC, Raith Rovers FC, and Millwall FC have honored the military by sporting playing kits that resemble military uniforms and/or include military camouflage designs. There has also been a growth in military charities partnering sporting organizations in providing platforms for ideological and financial support. For instance, the recently invented *Tickets for Troops* charity offers free tickets for serving soldiers for a range of high-profile sports occasions, each serving to increase military visibility, social acceptance and public support through the vehicle of sport. Such examples exist as part of a wider sport–media–military nexus. Accompanying these events and partnerships are quite explicit political messages communicated via media platforms. For example, in describing the Football League and Help for Heroes partnership in 2010, Football League chairman Lord Mawhinney was cited in the popular UK daily newspaper *The Sun* as incorporating Britain's football supporting public into showing "appreciation." He stated:

> [t]he contribution being made by our armed forces around the world is truly humbling. The football for heroes week will provide an excellent opportunity for supporters to show their appreciation for the outstanding work being done (see Footie clubs 2010).

Understanding that sport and popular culture events have been used as stages to incorporate citizens by proxy into showing support and appreciation for the military violence of nation-states (euphemistically sanitized as "contribution" and "outstanding work") is important because it exposes the intimate – yet often less-than-explicit – ideological overlap between government, foreign policy makers, military figures, and sporting governing bodies. Moreover, the role of the media is central to such events. For without widespread media coverage, sporting and political figures would be unable to inform supporters and citizens of how they are expected to ideologically internalize and interpret such activities. It is within this context that the aforementioned British football governing bodies' fine occurred for making political statements, and it is events such as these which raise questions around the politics of sport, the ideological interpretations of military-related remembrance, and the function of the media. We now turn to the UK's remembrance activities in order to further consider such questions.

The UK's (and wider Commonwealth's) Remembrance Sunday event occurs annually on the nearest Sunday to Armistice Day, November 11, incorporating senior members of the British establishment such as the hereditary head of state – i. e., the Queen – and other senior royal family members, the Prime Minister, leaders of opposition parties, senior religious clergy, and military groups (including bands and British military personnel). The event has traditionally been perceived by many as a mark of remembrance for those who have suffered as a result of military conflict – most commonly connected to the two world wars – but its meaning remains fluid and open to interpretation with debates around its meaning occurring as far back as the immediate aftermath of World War I (Basham 2015; Iles 2008). In recent times, remembrance has signified a conflation of sorrow, pride, and gratitude towards both past and present military actors and actions. It is increasingly being connected to supporting those

British military actors recently engaged or currently engaging in military violence in locations such as Iraq, Afghanistan, Libya, and Syria. For example, in 2016 – the same year of the FIFA controversy – the official custodians and coordinators of UK remembrance, The Royal British Legion, officially re-branded their annual campaign as "Rethink Remembrance" stating:

> There's a new generation of veterans that need your support. This year, The Royal British Legion is asking the nation to *Rethink Remembrance* by recognising the sacrifices made not just by the Armed Forces of the past, but by today's generation too. ... For many people, Remembrance is associated with the fallen of the First and Second World Wars. While we will always remember them, the Legion wants to raise awareness of a new generation of veterans and Service personnel that need our support. (Rethink remembrance 2016)

Thus, the shift from a symbol of sorrowful remembrance to symbolizing *current* (and living) military actors has now been widely acknowledged and forms a central focus of the official branding strategy of UK remembrance. Furthermore, this marketing campaign extends sorrowful remembrance to include seeking recognition, support, and awareness of the sacrifices of British military actors.

The Remembrance Sunday event always places primary focus and importance on the British military – as an institution and on military individuals – with marching soldiers, military insignia, military-infused nostalgia, and military-centered performances for (and by) dignitaries who stand attentive in deference to militarism and who behave with a ceremonial solemn demeanor to the "sacrifices" of British and Commonwealth military. Such practices – and their ideological articulations – constitute historical and contemporary events that are both open to political interpretation and involve particular power interests such as the state, foreign policy, and militarism. Remembrance in Britain, therefore, has functioned as part of a broader civil–military relationship, and in understanding its political significance (and/or meaning) in and beyond sport, these relationships and discourses should be acknowledged and understood.

In considering the political potency of UK military-related remembrance and how sport is utilized as an extension of the state's militaristic public relations, the starting point is the centerpiece institutional representation of British remembrance at the political, cultural, and mediated levels, Remembrance Sunday. This day is marked annually by a televised event broadcast live on the state-funded BBC and commercial channel Sky News. Post-ceremony, it is treated as nationally significant news to be covered in local and national news sites in all modes of British media. We provide a critical discourse analysis (CDA) of the live BBC1 and Sky News broadcast coverage of Remembrance Sunday 2016.[3] As Machin and Mayr stress:

---

3 2016 was selected because it was the same year of the Royal British Legion's noted re-branding campaign to "re-think Remembrance" and it was also the year the debates surrounding the political nature of remembrance in the UK emerged (largely due to the aforementioned FIFA decision to fine the UK football governing bodies for breaking the rule on political advertising).

> CDA assumes that power relations are discursive. In other words, power is transmitted and practised through discourse ... exposing strategies that appear normal or neutral on the surface but which may in fact be ideological and seek to shape the representation of events and persons for particular ends. The term "critical" therefore means "denaturalizing" the language to reveal the kinds of ideas, absences and taken-for-granted assumptions in texts. This will allow us to reveal the kinds of power interests buried in these texts (2012: 4–5).

In analyzing the live television coverage, we hope to reveal and critique the strategies and representations of these events and de-naturalize the language, revealing those ideas, absences, and taken-for-granted assumptions in the discourses. When understanding the relationship between sport, language, power, and UK society, it is reasonable, therefore, to situate the discussion in its broader contexts around language, communication, and symbolism. By doing this, more trustworthy analyses of meaning and symbolism within sport can be achieved. We recorded two live broadcasts (Remembrance Sunday Live, BBC1 2016; Remembrance Sunday Live, Sky News 2016) from beginning to end and watched the entire broadcasts numerous times each, noting thematic articulations until saturation point was reached and no new themes emerged. This allowed us to isolate and categorize major themes from each broadcast. We only include a major theme if it was obvious in both broadcasts. Four inter-related themes emerged as key articulations of the event and its media representation in almost parallel fashion on both national channels:

(1) Remembrance is continually connected to current military conflicts/violence as well as the traditional two world wars.
(2) Remembrance Day is framed as a day to venerate some or all of the British Empire, the United Kingdom (and its constituent nations), and the monarch/crown.
(3) Remembrance Day is articulated as being about remembering those who "protected" and continue to "protect" "freedom." Freedom here is represented as an apolitical matter of fact that is undisputed and the desired property of every (presumably virtuous) human being. The possibility that this freedom is a British state version contested by some citizens (of the United Kingdom and other nation-states) is overlooked.
(4) Remembrance Day is utilized as an opportunity for "the nation" to pay homage to the British military. This includes "the nation" honoring, thanking, and showing gratitude (and is mirrored in the BBC and Sky broadcasts' editorial approaches which both involve presenters positioning themselves as being grateful, thankful, and in deference to military actors and actions).

These four themes are briefly discussed in turn.

2.1 Connecting remembrance to current military conflict/violence

In apparent harmony with the Royal British Legion's re-branding of remembrance, both the BBC and Sky television broadcasts articulated the "Rethink Remembrance" unambiguously as paying respect to current military actors. In distinguishing between the conscripts of two world wars and current military actors, BBC anchor David Dimbleby discussed the latter early on in the three-hour broadcast stressing, "we have a moment to remember *those* men and women and their families too and the sacrifices they've made" (original emphasis). Connecting such sentiments of recent and current military personnel as being integral to the meaning of remembrance and framing this as the "nation's collective remembrance," the BBC production supplemented its live coverage with a series of pre-recorded interviews of current and recent soldiers or their bereaved families discussing the more recent "wars" in Afghanistan, Iraq, and Argentina. Sky News anchor Alistair Bruce made a similar connection in the opening three minutes of Sky's coverage, acknowledging the 100 years anniversary of the Battle of the Somme before lexically connecting this to today commenting, "and so many other things come to mind, and not least more recent memories of loss in battle [pause] here at the cenotaph." During these comments, Sky's on-screen strap line header reinforced a similar message reading: "PM: Remembrance Day should honour UK forces fighting Islamic State as well as those killed in previous conflicts." Continuing the theme of re-thinking remembrance, Sky's coverage turned to their female presenter Rebecca Williams who was among the marchers. The main studio anchor (Alistair Bruce) introduced Williams as having a better understanding of the meaning of the event (insinuating this was due to her being among the participants of the ceremony). Williams then began:

> Yes, very emotional here. As you can see so many people have turned out as [pause] as far as the eye can see, to pay tribute to those who've made the ultimate sacrifice, not just in the first and second world war but in conflicts in between, and now, as Theresa May has said, also those who continue to fight the threat of Islamic State and Daesh.

Reproducing a conservative Prime Minister's request as though it is presenting neutral news, the Sky News presenter informed viewers that this request is being fulfilled by those present – and by extension, one may assume, she was encouraging viewers to do likewise. It is also significant at this point to note that Williams framed the attendees' presence and involvement in the event as representing them "paying tribute" (as opposed to alternative interpretations such as showing regret and/or sorrow or representing a never again attitude to war and military violence).

2.2 Remembrance as celebration of empire, nation-state, and monarch

The second main theme to emerge from the BBC1 and Sky News coverage involved Remembrance Day acting as a quasi-celebration of the British Empire, the United Kingdom, and monarchy. Displaying a musical "united" Kingdom of the nations of the UK, the BBC broadcast military bands playing "Rule Britannia," "The Minstrel Boy," "Men of Harlech," and the "Skye Boat Song." At Sky, Alastair Bruce commented on the significance of the music, noting, "everything means something and [he chuckles] and the music says something too. There'll always be an England."[4] Bruce then informed viewers of the meaning of the cenotaph, stating it means "an empty tomb" before encouraging viewers to begin considering who they would think about during the approaching two-minute silence. He then instructed, "The concept is that whoever you are, whoever you may be thinking about, place your thoughts in that empty tomb and it will be your personal memorial as well as one for a British Empire that stretched all across the world."

Bruce demonstrates the ease with which the personal becomes the national while representing the national as constituting the British Empire. Here we see how British remembrance works to make a person's existence as an individual indissoluble from her/his existence as a patriotic citizen of the nation (and Empire). The clear insinuation without being explicit is that remembrance (and its symbols) represents a connection with (or even longing for) a lost Empire and as a memorial to those who secured it. The possibility of contested versions of empire is absent as is the notion that remembrance may be detached from this (or any) ideologically framed version of national identity or nationhood.

Both channels reinforced a British state identity. The BBC incorporated an identical production practice as Sky, having a main (male) anchor (David Dimbleby) commentating from the studio while intermittently moving to their (female) presenter (Sophie Rayworth) located on the streets of London among the procession participants. Rayworth was shown interviewing two serving soldiers who had received injuries in Iraq. One of the soldiers noted the connection between public support and remembrance, framing this combination as increasing his pride in his national identity: "When you march out those gates to all those wonderful people who have supported us and tens of thousands who line the streets, it just (pauses emotionally) it just makes me proud to be British."

The United Kingdom (and its constituent nations) and the British Empire were joined by the crown and monarchy in being remembered and honored both as part of the official ceremony and its mediatization. Sky's coverage showed the Church of England's the Right Reverend Richard Chartres addressing the audience: "Almighty God,

4 The band was playing the tune "There'll Always be an England" at the time this comment was made.

grant we beseech thee, that we who here do honor to the memory of those who have died in the service of their country and of the Crown." This plea was followed by the military band playing the United Kingdom national anthem, God Save the Queen. At this point, the ceremony is clearly invoking the Christian God, framing remembrance as being about honoring the memory of people who died "for a country" and an unelected, hereditary monarch.

2.3 Remembrance "remembers" those protecting "freedom"

The next main theme to emerge in the coverage involved framing it as about remembering those who protected and continue to protect "freedom." This freedom in turn was framed as universal rather than a British state[5] (or British media) interpretation of freedom. Freedom here is represented as an undisputed, apolitical matter of fact that is the desired property of every (presumably) virtuous human being. One such illustrative example capturing this involved an interviewed soldier commenting, "I'll be thinking about Brett [recently deceased soldier] and about all those who have served, who have given me and my country and family the freedom and opportunities that we are able to have today because of them" (BBC1, 13/11/16).

On Sky, Alistair Bruce sought to frame the viewers' reflection for them as inextricably involving freedom and sacrifice, noting, "we reflect on much this year. ... through all of it, we have to understand the cost of freedom." He then informed viewers of what the day's events should mean for them, adding, "it's a day for you (viewer) to value your family and to value the freedom in which you live and to say thank you through poppies to those who have given the final sacrifice. We think of them here."

Remembrance is used here to symbolize a politically infused narrative consisting of two related ideological assertions:

(1) That military violence and death resulted from a fight for freedom rather than for economic, political, geographical, or ideological reasons/gain.
(2) That this alleged fight for freedom necessarily required physical violence and its predictable outcomes (death and injury to soldiers and civilians) as opposed to other peaceful diplomatic actions.

Moreover, sorrowful remembrance and/or regret is/are supplanted by "thanks" and viewers are informed that thanks should be given by them through the red poppy. With an air of foreboding, Bruce adds, "we are always having to fight or to defend ourselves to protect freedom." Thus, not only is British military violence represented by remembrance (and the poppy) as a defensive apolitical act securing universal freedom, but

5 Of course, a "British state" version is really the version of the political party in government at the time and may not be shared by other political parties or individual members from that state.

the viewer is primed for future military violence, and viewers' acquiescence for it is subtly built-in to the discourse. This example of "ideological squaring" (Machin and Mayr 2012) leaves viewers in little doubt as to how they should evaluate the participants and their most visible symbolic signifier, the red poppy. Without being explicit, British violence is articulated as a defensive response to foreign aggression with the former protecting freedom and the latter violating it. Understanding such ideological work and UK remembrance more broadly is necessary because its cumulative effects build on and extend official political leaders' mediated messages which occur simultaneously and function as a compounding and self-fulfilling political message – that British military violence is necessary for freedom. British Prime Minister Theresa May further revealed political interpretations of British remembrance when promoting the 2016 Remembrance Sunday event, commenting:

> The way of life we enjoy today depends upon the service offered by members of the armed forces and their families. Across generations and in every corner of the UK, today we remember those who gave so much for our values, our democracy and our nation. At this time of reflection, we must not forget those members of the armed forces who are currently away from loved ones, whether taking the fight to Daesh, assisting UN peacekeeping efforts in Africa or fighting piracy on the high seas. As we are united in remembrance of those who have made sacrifices for our freedom, so we are united in our gratitude to those who continue to keep us safe (Sky News 2016).

Way of life, values, democracy, sacrifice, freedom, safety, British unity, and nation (state) are all invoked as integral to remembrance, and sorrowful remembrance elides into proud gratitude. May extends remembrance further still to include remembering those who may not be dead or even injured to include soliciting gratitude to military personnel who are "away from loved ones." Re-articulating remembrance as being about current military actors and action and presenting such action as representing a quest for freedom, democracy, and nationhood are furnished in multiple ways and Remembrance Sunday offers high profile and politically potent stages for such undeniably ideological messages to be promoted.

2.4 Remembrance is opportunity to honor British military

The final narrative emanating from the BBC and Sky broadcasts underpins the previous three in that it involves framing Remembrance Sunday as a UK military venerating event mixing nostalgia, fun, and personal support from the individual presenters, revealing a combined message of unquestioning loyalty and support for the British (and Commonwealth) military and its actions. Honor, thanks, and gratitude were all used during the broadcasts. Framing the event as fun, Sky News' Rebecca Williams interviewed a serving female soldier with an explicit carnivalesque tone and related questions, encouraging the soldier to enunciate on the "great atmosphere" and how wonderful military life/career is. Williams ended the interview by telling the soldier to "enjoy the rest of today." Reproducing a similar carnivalesque tone, Williams' colleague Bruce used the military band's live tune to break into song before pausing to suggest, "you can almost hear them singing on their way to the battlefields. It must have been extraordinary." These representations combine to expurgate the reality and horror of boys and men leaving home to fight in World War I with a romanticized version of invented nostalgia that seamlessly connects to contemporary times and its 21st-century personification of the female soldier carrying on the tradition by soaking up the "great atmosphere" during what has historically been perceived to be a solemn ceremony of remembrance.

This analysis of the television coverage of Remembrance Sunday 2016 emphasizes that, in conjunction with the long-standing military-centered commemoration of loss and sacrifice, there is a shifting emphasis in the way remembrance and the red poppy are being represented and re-articulated in Britain. This re-articulation – which gathered momentum after the invasion/liberation of Iraq in 2003 – maintains the long-standing constituents of regret and sorrow for damaged or lost lives from two world wars. However, of critical importance for the current debate, the re-articulation explicitly "incorporates British citizens by proxy" (Kelly 2013) into showing "appreciation and support" for currently serving military personnel, whilst simultaneously extending military-related tributes to ideologically position British military as "heroes" "serving the country," "fighting for freedom," and "keeping us safe" by carrying out current military violence in the cause of the British government's foreign policy objectives.

This reveals the official and accepted narratives around the red poppy and remembrance in the UK allowing us to contextualize the use of sport for "support the troops" initiatives in the UK. Utilizing sport, these narratives are reinforced and widely used to communicate consent for British militarism. Yet in understanding FIFA fining British football governing bodies for its act of remembrance (displaying the red poppy on football shirts), further contextualization can enable even deeper insights. Football was used during a period of increasing concerns from senior British state officials about dwindling public support for both military actors and their (violent) actions. For example, in 2007, senior British military commander General Dannatt lamented that the British public don't support the troops enough, commenting:

> Soldiers are genuinely concerned when they come back from Iraq to hear the population that sent them being occasionally dismissive or indifferent about their achievements ... As operational commitments have become more intense, so has the need for support from the nation (Army chief warns 2007).

Repeating a corresponding message in 2009, the British Chief of Defense Staff Jock Stirrup complained that the Taliban's bombs were less threatening to the morale of British troops than "declining will" among the public to see the war won (cited in Gee 2014: 29). He added, "support for our servicemen and women is indivisible from support for this mission" (cited in Gee 2014: 29). British Prime Minister, Tony Blair made similar pleas for the public to make seamless connections between support for soldiers and support for military violence stressing "the armed forces want public opinion not just behind them but behind their mission; [we should] understand their value not just their courage" (cited in Gee 2014: 29). In the UK, therefore, connection is continually made between the ontologically separate *support for troops* and *support for military action*, which includes politically opposed/supported military violence (described by both public figures as "mission") carried out to fulfill the British state's politically infused foreign policies. The umbilical connection between incorporating citizens by proxy into connecting *support for troops* seamlessly with *support for military action* alongside such action being represented as necessary for securing "freedom" and "way of life" is difficult to escape. Such interpretations are inherently political and ideological, yet when they are intimately connected to and expressed through the apparently non-political world of sport, they become de-contextualized to the extent the political is rendered invisible. Such political articulations compound wider remembrance acts – such as those that FIFA judged broke its rules on political statements – serving to promote and justify British foreign policy (and wars) through what Basham calls the "everyday embodied and emotional practices of remembrance and forgetting" (2015: 883). In other words, sacrifice is remembered while its political contexts are forgotten (or more accurately airbrushed out).

3 South Korean celebritization of militarism

We now turn to the sport–media–military nexus in South Korea, another close ally of the United States. South Korea maintains an important defense partnership with the US as its Indo-Pacific strategy report highlights (Panda 2019). Indeed, the alliance between the two countries is claimed to be the "lynchpin of peace and prosperity of Northeast Asia" (The Department of Defense 2019: 24). As we illustrate, the sport–media–military nexus relating to South Korea's armed forces, reveals close practical and ideological overlaps with that of the UK (and US and its allies).

South Korea is still technically at war with North Korea and there are occasional military confrontations between them. For both the US and South Korea, communist Korea represents a serious military threat, and the allied forces' regular military exercises in the South are alleged to be "provocative" by the North (Landay 2019). Unlike the UK, South Korea operates a mandatory (two-year) national service for its male citizens. Because of this near-universal conscription for men, a (male-centered) legacy of national service is deeply embedded in South Korean society (Moon 2005) and compulsory service is often featured as one of the most sacred devotions to the nation (Song 2014).

With this prevalence of militaristic social practice, it is no surprise that South Korean cultural commodities often romanticize and normalize a rather rigid (and gendered) army culture (Baek 2018). Sport is no exception. In common with the UK (and US), a range of remembrance rituals take place in environments frequently associated with major sporting competitions. Sport is also actively exploited to reinforce civil–military relations. Our media analysis examines the intersection between South Korean professional baseball and the South Korean military.[6]

3.1 The South Korean army and its community relations

Professional baseball is the most widely circulated sport-media product in South Korea (Yi and Lee 2011). The Korean Baseball Organization (KBO) league is arguably the most popular spectator sport league in the country. Almost every match is broadcast live, and national television runs daily and weekly magazine programs. KBO league news is a major feature of sport pages in most South Korean newspapers. It is therefore unsurprising that in South Korea the baseball field is where the fusion of sport, media, and militarism frequently occurs. With parallels to the US, in 2015 the KBO and the South Korean army signed a memorandum of understanding, with the stated aim of improving the image of the armed forces via professional baseball. As part of this military PR campaign, the army headquarters dispatches its ceremonial regiment to a number of high-profile baseball matches. The KBO All-Star Game is one of the most popular baseball matches in the season. This annual one-off match is often imbued with carnivalesque elements because it is largely organized to entertain baseball fans including children. Understandably, a range of cultural events also take place in association with the annual baseball festival. Since the MoU agreement in 2015, the performance of a ceremonial army regiment has become a regular feature of this baseball event.[7] An army orchestra plays the national anthem before the match and its soldiers perform rifle drills and hand-to-hand combat skills to the spectators during the pre-game show. A special-forces parachute display team also parachutes over the stadium. It is worth noting the similarities here between the US's practices as part of its Operation Tribute to Freedom.

In sport, the stadium spectators are increasingly becoming secondary to their social (and traditional) media-consuming spectators. Therefore, such patriotic and militaristic performances would be unlikely to occur and would certainly not have the propaganda potential unless they were highly mediated productions. Moreover, in common with the overwhelming majority of their US and UK counterparts, the

---

6 All media reports (TV and newspapers) being discussed in relation to South Korea are originally published in Korean. As native speakers of English and Korean respectively, we carefully checked our translation in order to be sensitive to subtle cultural meanings when the Korean text was translated into English.

7 There have been occasional military performances like this before, but these never used to be an annual performance.

media productions are universally supportive and ideologically framed to endorse the military actions of its government. For instance, when almost 100 soldiers entered the stadium at the 2016 All-Star Game (to perform a taekwondo demonstration), the SPOTV (16/07/16) commented that, "the Korean Army demonstration team are brave soldiers who, being equipped with a must-win spirit, train their battle skills *against enemies* day and night. *We should support them*!" (italics added).

Such commentary is illuminating because it reveals that despite those servicemen performing in the stadium as part of a carnivalesque celebration of a special sporting occasion, they were essentially represented as warriors prepared and ready to fight against "enemies." Although the media do not explicitly name North Korea, few are likely to doubt the identity of the imagined "enemy." The communicative power of such imagined enemies is that it further facilitates, if not explicitly instructs, the sport fan and media consumer to "support the troops." These developments are not unrelated to the fact that since the end of the Cold War and subsequent termination of a military dictatorship in the 1990s (Lee 2020), the social status of the armed forces in South Korea has diminished. In this context, the Ministry of Defense (MoD) seeks to manufacture support from the public in order to boost the morale of the South Korean armed forces. It should be noted that unlike the respective civic domains in the US and UK, pro-military public campaigns such as "support our troops" and charities such as Help for Heroes are not widespread in South Korean society. Sport, especially baseball, is one of the few windows through which the Korean armed forces undertake community relations programs. This media commentary can be understood as the media publicity of the MoD.

Despite these subtle differences, such celebration and pride in the nation's military has, in common with the US and UK, become normalized even when the event is sport-focused (rather than for explicit military purposes). When honor guards performed a rifle demonstration before the 2017 event, the SPOTV (15/07/17) also proclaimed that "the army honor guards are showing remarkable drills! They must have trained a lot, and their hard work finally makes this amazing performance. It is really spectacular, indeed."

Here, we can see the media celebrate the appearance of the army unit in the stadium. Various national newspapers also published a series of photographs depicting the army displaying meticulous drills on the diamond with positive undertones. By disseminating these texts, the media naturalizes, if not glorifies, the presence of the military personnel at the All-Star Games. Such practices can, therefore, be interpreted as supporting the South Korean and American military alliance in order to protect geo-political and economically motivated ideological desires (articulated as safeguarding peace and prosperity in the Korean peninsula). In common with the UK and US, the fusion of sport and the military has become more visible and pronounced over recent years. The following two episodes aptly reveal this.

3.2 The Korean Series

The Korean Series is the grand finale of the Korean professional baseball league, which is KBO equivalent of the MLB World Series. In 2015, the sport governing body decided that each game should be given a special theme. The showcase opening match of the 2015 Korean series was given the theme of national defense and security. A game logo was created containing an army camouflage outline, and players wore camouflaged baseball caps and uniforms during this game. The reason for this militaristic branding of sport was to pay respect to two South Korean soldiers who were maimed by North Korean land mines while patrolling the border area in August 2015 (Choe 2015). The tensions between the two Koreas was high at that time (relating to North Korea's missile tests and its alleged attempt to develop a nuclear warhead) creating a situation whereby a particular form of anti-North Korea patriotism emerged as a major political and cultural discourse (North Korea missile tests 2017). The Korean series, especially the opening game, was clearly reflecting and reproducing this mood.

The KBO invited the seven servicemen who were on duty with the two maimed soldiers to the Korean series along with more than 100 members of the armed forces. A military band played the national anthem and the army honor guards performed rifle drills as a tribute to the two amputees. Additionally, a retired military man (Colonel Lee) who had lost his two legs while saving a wounded soldier in the demilitarized zone 15 years previously was also invited to the series. The retired officer opened the competition by pitching the ceremonial ball. The involvement of Colonel Lee at the series was particularly noteworthy because he is regarded as a military hero for losing both legs while protecting junior infantry members. Colonel Lee has become a symbol of South Korean patriotic militarism in the 21st century.[8] The YNA, a major news agency in South Korea, reported, "The retired Colonel Lee was walking towards the mound, *relying on his prosthesis*. He waved back to the fans who welcomed his entrance to the stadium, and pitched the ball to the catcher. The sound of applause was getting louder" (26/10/15, italics added). *Kukmin Ildo*, a daily newspaper in the country, added that, "Colonel Lee ... stepped into the baseball ground wearing a military uniform. He was a *true military man* who lost his two legs due to a mine explosion while trying to save wounded soldiers" (26/10/15, italics added).

Such media discourses demonstrate Lee's heroic status in South Korean society. It is important to note that these newspapers highlighted his military injury despite it having no relevance to the sporting occasion. Hence, the overall meaning that these media discourses disseminate is that as a "true military man," Colonel Lee becomes a role model for patriotic South Korean servicemen and citizens. Significantly for us, this occurred as a result of the fusion of sport, media, and militarism.

---

8 A measure of Colonel Kim's elevated national status is that a musical commemorating his military actions was produced in South Korea.

3.3 Busan Giants' military series

The final example to illustrate this increasingly close sport–media–military alliance in South Korea involves the Busan Lotte Giants baseball club, which, since 2017, has devoted one weekend in June to organize an annual military series. In this military weekend, the Giants' players wear a camouflaged baseball uniform and several hundred soldiers are invited to the matches. Additionally, cheerleaders sing patriotic songs and battle hymns during the matches and a large electric screen in the stadium shows a short film that honors war veterans. Interestingly, the overall festive and light-hearted atmosphere of this military series contrasts with the more solemn and traditional June remembrance rituals. Fans, specially invited solders, and athletes joyfully watch and participate in this military-themed competition. Given the majority of adult male spectators would have completed military service, many of them participate by wearing their vintage army uniform. In short, this baseball series offers a stage on which deeply seated South Korean civic militarism is widely performed and accepted without dissention.

Because this is a regional event in Busan, the second-largest city in South Korea, national television networks tend not to cover the Giants' military series though some national newspapers publish a preview of it. However, Giants TV, the online channel run by the club, released a short video featuring the key moments of the military series (02.06.17). In this respect, three distinctive elements emerge from this media production. First, wearing a semi-military uniform, the captain of the cheerleaders is shown standing on a podium in the grandstand. Then he salutes the spectators, calling out his rank and identification number as if he was a soldier on duty. Then, with military terminology, he ordered the fans to follow his gestures. The spectators cheered joyfully at the captain. Second, female cheerleaders, dressed in sexualized military uniforms, were shown dancing provocatively while the camera captured the military dressed male fans visibly entertained and gazing at the cheerleaders. Third, the video also showed male fans who wore a camouflage outfit performing a humorous dance and mimicking military demeanor. After these light-hearted gestures, they saluted back to the captain and the cheerleaders.

This short video clearly reveals the deeply seated military culture in South Korea. So much so that, the fusion of sport and militarism is freely circulated without much if any public dissension. The case of the Giants' military series is particularly interesting in that unlike other war commemorations which are rather serious and solemn, militarism in this occasion is actively celebrated as a form of popular culture. Notably, the rather comical performance of the male fans seems to represent a common perception in South Korea that, insofar as they do not physically harm others, sexist and misogynistic actions of servicemen within civic society are generally accepted and easily pardoned because they sacrifice their youth for the country. This is indicative of the permeation of military culture in the daily life of most Korean people (Moon 2005). Moreover, the power and significance of the sport–media–military nexus is further revealed.

4 Conclusion

The media-focused campaigns briefly outlined here in the UK and South Korea cannot be viewed in a de-contextualized vortex. Nor can the sport, media, and military relationship be considered in isolation from wider geo-political processes. As Philo (2007) acknowledged:

> [L]anguage [is] linked to wider social processes and how individual meanings and communications relate to conflict and divisions within society as a whole. [Therefore] the issue then [is] not to look simply at the descriptions which were offered of the world in a specific text, but to look at the *social relations* which underpinned the generation of these descriptions (Philo 2007, 5, our emphasis).

These examples contextualize civil–military relations in Britain as political, exposing official concerns of dwindling public support for military action/violence, and leave no room for doubt that senior British state officials were aware of the need to expose the British public to "support the troops" public relations/propaganda. When assessing the political symbolism and utility of sport – for example, the FIFA poppy controversy – such political contexts expose the world of sport as a site for communicating consent for militaristic violence on behalf of nation-state governments' foreign policy objectives as part of geo-political processes.

The increasing celebritization of civil–military relations in South Korea has also occurred in tandem with wider geo-political processes, notably increasing tensions between North and South Korea (and the US and China). Thus, when baseball competitions and teams celebrate and "honor" military personnel and incorporate baseball fans and the wider public by proxy via media platforms to "support" them, it becomes difficult to detach the geo-political desires and conflicts of nation-states from sport. The nature of civil–military relations in South Korea is different from the UK and the US, with the former still enforcing military service for its men while still being "at war" with its northern counterpart. This inevitably impacts on the culturally embeddedness of military life and appreciation for military personnel in the country. Perhaps South Korea requires less manufacturing of military consent as the US and UK, but it still utilizes the sport–media–military nexus to promote and normalize everyday militarism in ways that are often ideologically aligned with US foreign policy and militaristic dogma.

Sport is a powerful propaganda tool for a number of intersecting reasons: it represents a sacred site of national expression and identity; it is viewed and presented as pure, heroic and virtuous in and of itself; it is articulated as separate from the serious elements of life such as the political. Sport's everyday apolitical façade offers effective camouflage for those using it for political purposes. As a sacred site of popular culture in both the UK and South Korea, sport continues to be a primary media product. Indeed, it is this intersection of the sport–media–militarism nexus that facilitates such rich "public relations" opportunities. In a period of so-called fake news, wars on terror, and dynamic international movements such as #MeToo and #BlackLivesMatter, critical readers of media productions capable of situating media re-presentations and their communicated events in broader socio-political contexts, have seldom, if ever, been more necessary.

References

Aljazeera 2015. Pro teams 'paid millions' to promote US military. *Aljazeera online*, 6 November. http://www.aljazeera.com/news/2015/11/pro-teams-paid-millions-promote-military-151105065531488.html (6 November 2015).

Army chief warns of social gulf. 2007. *BBC*, 22 September. http://news.bbc.co.uk/1/hi/uk/7006720.stm (11 November 2015).

Baek, Tae-hyun. 2018. The meanings of militarism masculinities represented in Major Kang Jae-gu and Sanai UDT. *The Journal of Korean Studies* 67. 139–168.

Basham, Victoria M. 2015. Gender, race, militarism and remembrance: The everyday geopolitics of the poppy. *Gender, Place and Culture* 23(6). 883–896.

Billig, Michael. 1995. *Banal nationalism*. London: Sage.

Butterworth, Michael L. 2005. Ritual in the 'church of baseball': Suppressing the discourse of democracy after 9/11. *Communication and Critical/Cultural Studies* 2(2). 107–129.

Butterworth, Michael L. 2008. Fox Sports, Super Bowl XLII, and the affirmation of American civil religion. *Journal of Sport and Social Issues* 32(3). 318–323.

Butterworth, Michael L. 2010. Major League Baseball, Welcome back Veterans, and the rhetoric of "support the troops." In Ron Briley (ed.), *The politics of baseball: Essays on the pastime and power at home and abroad*, 226–240. Jefferson, NC: McFarland.

Butterworth, Michael L. (ed.). 2017. *Sport and militarism: Contemporary global perspectives*. London: Routledge.

Butterworth, Michael L. & Stormi D. Moskal. 2009. American football flags, and "fun": The Bell Helicopter Armed Forces Bowl and the rhetorical production of militarism. *Communication, Culture and Critique* 2. 411–433.

Choe, Sang Hun. 2015. South Korea accuses the north after land mines maim two soldiers in DMZ. *The New York Times*, 10 August. https://www.nytimes.com/2015/08/11/world/asia/north-korea-placed-mines-that-maimed-2-south-korean-soldiers-at-dmz-seoul-says.html (11 November 2015).

Cree, Alice & Nick Caddick. 2019 Unconquerable heroes: Invictus, redemption, and the cultural politics of narrative. *Journal of War and Cultural Studies* 13. 1–21.

Elgot, Jessica. 2016. Theresa May attacks FIFA over "utterly outrageous" poppy ban. *The Guardian*, 2 November. https://www.theguardian.com/uk-news/2016/nov/02/theresa-may-attacks-fifa-over-utterly-outrageous-poppy-ban-remembrance-day (2 November 2015).

FIFA completely wrong on poppies ban, insists David Mundell. 2016. *Herald Scotland*, 3 November. https://www.heraldscotland.com/news/14842291.fifa-completely-wrong-on-poppies-ban-insists-david-mundell/ (11 November 2015).

FIFA fines English, Scottish, Welsh and Northern Irish FAs for poppies. 2016. *ESPN.com*, 19 December. https://www.espn.com/soccer/blog-fifa/story/3023352/fifa-fines-home-nations-over-poppy-displays (6 November 2015).

FIFA investigates Welsh and Northern Irish fans over poppy displays. 2016. *BBC*, 23 November. http://www.bbc.co.uk/sport/football/38077727.

Footie clubs unite for heroes. 2010. *Sun Newspaper*, 2 March.
Gee, David. 2014. *Spectacle, reality, resistance: Confronting a culture of militarism*. London: Forces Watch Press.
IFAB. 2016. Laws of the Game 2016–17. 1 June. https://intheopinionofthereferee.files.wordpress.com/2012/06/ifab-laws-of-the-game-2016-17.pdf (6 November 2015).
Iles, Jennifer. 2008. In remembering the Flanders poppy. *Mortality: Promoting the interdisciplinary study of death and dying* 13(3). 201–221.
Jansen, Sue C. & Don Sabo. 1994. The sport/war metaphor: Hegemonic masculinity, the Persian Gulf War, and the New World Order. *Sociology of Sport Journal* 11(1). 1–17.
Jenkins, Tricia. 2013. The militarization of American professional sports. *Journal of Sport & Social Issues* 37(3). 245–260.
Kelly, John. 2013. Popular culture, sport and the "hero"-fication of British militarism. *Sociology* 47(4). 722–738.
Kelly, John. 2017a. Western militarism and the political utility of sport. In Alan Bairner, John Kelly & Jung Woo Lee (eds.), *Routledge handbook of sport and politics*, 277–292. London: Routledge.
Kelly, John. 2017b. The paradox of militaristic remembrance in British sport and popular culture. In Michael L. Butterworth (ed.), *Sport and militarism*, 149–162. London: Routledge.
King, Samantha. 2008. Offensive lines: Sport-state synergy in an era of perpetual war. *Cultural Studies – Critical Methodologies* 8(4). 527–539.
Landay, Jonathan. 2019. US-South Korean military exercise to proceed: Top South Korean official. *Reuters*, 20 July. https://www.reuters.com/article/us-usa-southkorea-military/u-s-south-korean-military-exercise-to-proceed-top-south-korean-official-idUSKCN1UF0OV (6 November 2015).
Lee, M. R. 2020. *The state and the army*. Seoul: E-pubple.
Machin, David & Andrea Mayr. 2012. *How to do critical discourse analysis*. London: Sage.
Moon, Seungsook. 2005. *Militarized modernity and gendered citizenship in South Korea*. Durham, NC: Duke University Press.
North Korea missile tests: a timeline. 2017. *CBS News*, 6 September. https://www.cbsnews.com/news/north-korea-missile-tests-a-timeline/ (6 November 2015).
Panda, Ankit. 2019. South Korea and the US Indo-Pacific strategy: At an arm's length? *The Diplomat*, 7 July. https://thediplomat.com/2019/07/south-korea-and-the-us-indo-pacific-strategy-at-an-arms-length/ (6 November 2015).
Penn, Roger & Damon Berridge. 2016. Football and the military in contemporary Britain: An exploration of invisible nationalism. *Armed Forces & Society*. 44(1). 116–138.
Philo, Greg. 2007. Can discourse analysis successfully explain the content of media and journalistic practice? *Journalism Studies* 8(2). 175–196.
Remembrance Sunday Live Broadcast, 2016. *BBC1. November* 13.
Remembrance Sunday Live Broadcast, 2016. *Sky News*. November 13.
Rethink remembrance – poppy appeal. 2016. *Gomer Junior School*, 4 November. https://gomer.gfmat.org/2016/11/04/rethink-remembrance-poppy-appeal/ (11 November 2020).
Royson, Jack, Lynn Davidson & Tess de la Mare. 2016. 3 Lions led by donkeys. *Sun Online*, 31 October. https://www.thesun.co.uk/sport/2088817/fury-as-cold-blooded-fifa-chiefs-ban-england-and-scotland-players-from-wearing-poppies-on-shirts-during-world-cup-qualifying-match/ (11 November 2020).
Scherer, Jay & Jordan Koch. 2010. Living with war: Sport, citizenship and the cultural politics of post-9/11 Canadian identity. *Sociology of Sport Journal* 27. 1–29.
Silk, Michael & Mark Falcous. 2005. One day in September/a week in February: Mobilizing American (sporting) nationalisms. *Sociology of Sport Journal* 22. 447–471.

Song, Sang-ho. 2014. Military culture in Korean society. *The Korea Herald*, 9 April. http://www.koreaherald.com/view.php?ud=20140409000974 (6 November 2015).

Stempel, Carl. 2006. Televised sports, masculine moral capital, and support for the US invasion of Iraq. *Journal of Sport & Social Issues* 30(1). 79–106.

United States Department of Defense. 2019. *Indo-Pacific strategy report: Preparedness, partnerships, and promoting a networked region*. Washington, DC: United States Department of Defense.

Yi, J. Y. & Lee, Y. W. 2011. A preliminary study on changes in Korean baseball spectators' culture. *Korean Journal of Sociology of Sport* 24(2). 169–198.

Lindsey J. Meân and Beth Fielding-Lloyd

17 Football, gender, and sexism: the ugly side of the world's beautiful game

Abstract: The last 10–15 years have seen substantive claims of an apparent shift in the institutional support for women's football by the sport's governing bodies, a shift that is being somewhat echoed in more recent commitments from some major television broadcasters of the sport. However, while the women's game has seen increasing audiences and more media attention, research suggests that a deeply embedded antipathy to it continues to permeate throughout the sport. In this chapter, we discuss some of the major factors and practices that serve to maintain the traditional gendered order of football (aka soccer), how these connect to football as a powerful and global ideological site, and the extent to which a shift in gendered representation was evident in the British television coverage of the 2017 Women's Euros.

Keywords: gender; ideology; football; soccer; discourses; narratives; FIFA; UEFA; World Cup; Euros

1 Introduction: football, women's football, and the world's most powerful sport

This chapter explores sport and gender through the lens of international football. Sport generally and football specifically are powerful, often Euro-centric, white, male dominated, global sites, which makes them particularly significant for understanding the intersection of gender with sexuality, race, and nation. In this chapter, our focus is primarily on gender as it is managed, organized, and represented by the mainstream institutions that regulate and report football. While we restrict our present analysis to gender, we encourage readers to consider the implications of football beyond these connections.

Across the globe, football – or soccer – is *the* most watched, followed, and played sport. Known as *The Beautiful Game*, football is the sport that represents nation and national identity in most countries making it, arguably, the most powerful and influential sport in the world. This power is wielded effectively by football's governing institutions, notably the Fédération Internationale de Football Association (FIFA), an acknowledged global socio-economic and cultural force (Sklair 1991). But, as for all sports, the significance of football has become increasingly connected to the power of the media. The unmitigated influence and impact of the sport-media complex over cultures, identities, and understandings has been widely acknowledged (Jhally 1989; Rowe 2004; Wenner 1989). Accordingly, football takes up a large share of the sport-me-

https://doi.org/10.1515/9783110660883-017

dia market while its governing bodies and club teams have become major producers of media content.

Football is thus best understood as a powerful global *mediated* force, and an established ideological site for the (re)production (i.e., production and reproduction) of key identities, cultural formations, and discourses, particularly in relation to gender, sexuality, and race. That is, football shapes wider understandings of masculinity, gender, sexuality, and race, and serves as a key site for the development of traditional heterosexual, male identities. Football's governing bodies and key institutions (including sport-media) serve as authoritative and dominant forces in the construction of gendered understandings in local cultures and across the globe through multiple levels of action and inaction; including the consistent construction and framing of women's football, female players, coaches, and officials as sub-standard and "other." Football remains the quintessential "men's game" and the epitome of traditional heterosexual masculinity, meaning the incursion of women into football has been strongly resisted (e.g., Caudwell 1999; Meân 2001). Indeed the hegemony of football as a male site is so deeply entrenched that even those directly involved in women's football can be subject to these discourses, effectively (re)producing the men's game as naturally superior and positioning the women's game, players, and coaches as different and deficient (Fielding-Lloyd and Meân 2008; Meân and Kassing 2008). Scholars have also observed comparative hegemonic consequences in sports journalism given the dominance of similarly gendered ideologies in sport-media and sport news (Hardin and Shain 2005).

The global dominance of men's football is manifest in its prominence across levels of competition. The flagship international men's football competition, the FIFA World Cup (hereafter the World Cup), draws the largest global audiences of all sports. Across the world, domestic and local levels of competition permeate life in mundane and everyday ways as people watch, play, and consume (men's) football in multiple forms. A number of top domestic clubs and club leagues also have global audiences and fans, notably England's Premier League, Germany's Bundesliga, and Spain's La Liga. Consequently, while major international tournaments and competitions garner massive global media attention and audiences, European club football holds a substantive share of the global sport-media market throughout the year (seasons typically run August to May while the summer transfer window keeps audiences engaged with off-season news or "gossip"). Although fandom of globally distant football clubs has been evident for decades, the proliferation of ways to consume sport has led to burgeoning global audiences (Hutchins, Li, and Rowe 2019) including football-resistant markets like the United States (Nalbantis and Pawlowski 2016).

In contrast, women's football is still working to establish itself at the international and domestic levels. There has been recent progress in this, such as bigger global audiences for FIFA's 2015 and 2019 Women's World Cups, but suggestions that these achievements indicate the women's game has reached a turning point and is finally established belies the facts and such claims have been made many times before. The myth of a flourishing women's game is evident in some obvious ways: the lack of basic access for girls and women in many football nations across the globe; the lack of or slow building of (national) youth development programs for girls; and even countries with successful women's national teams, like the USA, struggle to establish stable, economically viable professional women's leagues (Meân 2015). All of these are essential requirements before we can herald the successful establishment of women's football. Indeed the recent demise of US Soccer's elite Development Academy (DA) (Scavuzzo 2020), in part due to contentiousness over the costs of adding a girl's program in 2017, reveals an underlying issue regarding investment in the women's game that resonates with the USWNT national team pay dispute. The immediate announcement of Major League Soccer's plan to sponsor a new elite replacement league for most of the boy's clubs while most of the female players and clubs were left in an uncertain place in uncertain times (a pandemic) compounds this disparity. Thus, while men's football is the most popular and powerful game in the world, the professional women's game is still emerging despite, or in spite of, the continued failure of football's governing bodies to effectively promote and manage the women's game and youth development.

2 Governing bodies and gendered organization(s)

As a powerful collection of global and local organizations, FIFA and its subordinate affiliates are uniquely placed to be a force for progress or a force that maintains the gendered status quo. Historically, the governing bodies of football resisted, and even outlawed, the women's game. Women's football was only incorporated into these organizations comparatively recently, arguably because the women's game was taking off without their sanction and external commercial operators were beginning to make profits from the game (Dunn 2018; Williams 2013). However, deeply embedded gendered and racialized orientations remain prominent in the management, representation, and regulation of football. The legacy of the colonial history of the modern game is manifest in FIFA's structure, including the dominance of Europe's confederation. For example, only one of FIFA's eight Presidents has not been from Europe (Havelange from Brazil, 1974–1998) and all have been white males.

Regarding the 211 affiliated national associations, FIFA states, "As representatives of FIFA in their countries, they [national associations] have obligations to respect the statutes, aims and ideals of football's governing body and promote and manage our sport accordingly" (fifa.com n.d. para.1). As an institution FIFA explicitly claims to support the development and promotion of the women's game, yet it rarely exerts its influence over explicit gendered practices by affiliate associations, not even in response to the abuse and exclusion of women (Ahmed 2019). Indeed FIFA continues to promote major myths and problematic framing of the women's game for the wider global community. FIFA's President Blatter (1998–2015) was widely known for his problematic views on women's football despite declarations of support. For example, to attract men to watch the women's game Blatter suggested, "They [women players] could, for example, have tighter shorts. Female players are pretty, if you excuse me for saying so, and they already have some different rules to men – such as playing with a lighter ball. That decision was taken to create a more female aesthetic, so why not do it in fashion?" (Christenson and Kelso 2004). Beyond the obvious problems with eroticization of athletes to attract (heterosexual) men, Blatter also inaccurately claimed women played with a lighter ball. This untruth – from one of the most authoritative figures in football – perpetuates the false difference between the men's and women's game, framing the women's game as not "real" football but a (literally) lightweight substandard version. The idea that the beauty of women's football lies primarily in their aesthetic embodiment was evident in the first official Women's World Cup song in 2007: "You Are The Most Beautiful in the World" (Meân 2010a).

UEFA has made some commitments to developing the women's game, including a 50 percent increase in funding (to start in 2020). Notable also was the appointment of the first female referee, Frappart of France, to officiate (with female assistants) a major European men's showcase match for the UEFA Super Cup in August 2019. This was groundbreaking as women officiating men's games remains rare, and women officials are still subject to hostile criticism as they directly challenge basic sexist assumptions about women's ability to "master" the rules of the game. However, it is in the mundane and ordinary that the gendered inclusion and exclusion, othering and standardizing, advocating and undermining all occur, often simultaneously. Consequently, studying the everyday and routine action of inclusion/exclusion remains relevant, especially in mediated spaces – like the websites of the governing bodies (e. g., Meân 2010a).

A glance at uefa.com's homepage provides scant evidence of the systemic inclusion of women. In August 2019, the first three (of five) main menu selections were for men's leagues and tournaments, unmarked for gender (UEFA Champions League, UEFA Europa League, UEFA Super Cup). The fourth was "Member associations" and the fifth, "Equal Game" (promoting a range of players and issues related to health and diversity and the assertion that "Everyone Can Play"). Arguably more insidious than the primacy of the unmarked men's competitions was the explicit categorization of the men's game as nation in the "Competitions" section as the last item on the homepage. As shown in Table 1, UEFA categorized the (unmarked) men's games as "National" while the women's and youth/amateur competitions were under separate category headings linguistically marked for gender but not as nation. Additionally, youth/amateur was actually an unmarked male category since the parallel Women's "Under-19" and "Under-17" competitions were listed under the "Women" category heading. Linguistic marking is significant as unmarked forms denote the standard meaning and, as such, who is represented and included. In contrast marked forms denote deviation from norms and standards, functioning to naturalize and reify these cultural patterns. Such discursive action (in representing and organizing) routinely (re)produce the men's game as central, standard, and as nation, and the women's game as peripheral (Fielding-Lloyd and Meân 2008; Meân 2001; 2010a, 2014).

Tab. 1: Reproduction of 'Competitions' first four columns from uefa.com homepage

Clubs	National	Women	Youth & Amateur
UEFA Champions League	European Qualifiers	UEFA Women's Euro	Under-19
UEFA Europa League	UEFA EURO 2020	FIFA Women's World Cup	Under-17
UEFA Super Cup	UEFA Nations League	UEFA Women's Champions League	UEFA Regions' Cup
UEFA Youth League	Under-21	Women's Under-19	
		Women's Under-17	

Source: Adapted from uefa.com (2019)

3 International competition and the (re)production of gender asymmetry

The (men's) World Cup is the biggest global sport event, over 3.5 billion watched in 2018 (fifa.com). Held every four years, it is the final play-off stage of a larger tournament with regional qualifiers played during the interim years. The Women's World Cup uses the same model, albeit smaller in terms of national participation, media coverage, and audience figures. It runs one year behind the men's (e. g., 2018 World Cup and 2019 Women's World Cup). Reflecting the significance of Europe in football, the next largest international competition is arguably the men's UEFA European Championship or Euros, scheduled every four years in an oppositional cycle to the World Cup; that is, a Euros or World Cup occurs every two years. The Women's Euros is similarly scheduled against the Women's World Cup. However, for women's football the Olympics has been a major competition, although it is significant for its *irrelevance* to the men's game.

The significance of the Olympics for women's football in part reflects its historical irrelevance to the men's game. At a time when the women's game was not fully sanctioned by football's governing bodies, the Olympics offered an international competition that did not overtly resist women's incursion into the men's game. However, the Olympics is becoming challenged as a key football site because teams from significant submerged footballing nations are excluded, notably England, Northern Ireland, Scotland, and Wales (alphabetically listed). These nations can only compete in the Olympics as a unified Great Britain and Northern Ireland (GBR) team. This caused major political fall-out during the 2012 London Olympics as host nations are required to enter all events and the GBR football teams did not include all four "home" nations.

Consequently, for many countries the World Cup and Euros comprise the key international events for football as a sport and for the performance of football as a nation. Equally, despite the secondary positioning of the women's game, the significance of football in Europe is evident in the strength of the emerging women's teams. Indeed nine of the 24 nations in the 2019 Women's World Cup and three of the teams in the semi-finals were European. As such, the Euros provide useful parallel tournaments for gender analysis.

3.1 Nation and ideology

Given their power to engage audiences of millions in ritualistic and celebratory displays of nation, major sport events are well established sites of "hot nationalism" deployed through banal forms (Billig 1995) inextricably rooted in maleness and masculinity (Bowes and Bairner 2019). Indeed men's football is amongst the most powerful sites for nation-building and the playing out of wider historical, ideological, and political events. Routine media constructions reify the bond between sport, nationalism, and masculinity, with negative events and poor performances often described as national disasters. For example, Italy's failure to qualify for the 2018 men's World Cup was described as "a national shame," as "the apocalypse," and equated to a disastrous World War I battle (Dwyer 2019). Political and ideological factors can render almost any men's sport a potent representation of nation as evidenced in the temporary suspension of American antipathy towards football for the 1998 World Cup US–Iran match (Delgado 2003).

In contrast, the women's game is rarely deployed as nation (Bowes and Bairner 2019; Fielding-Lloyd and Meân 2013; Meân 2010b, 2015; Meân and Herrera 2017). The characterizations, rivalry narratives, and banal routines necessary for communicating national identity and pride are habitually missing from coverage, branding, and audience-building of women's international sports. Even the highly successful US women's national team are primarily framed through domestic narratives and mythologies of women's progress rather than via the typical sporting, political, and ideological rivalries of men's sport (Meân 2010b, 2015; Meân and Herrera 2017).

Similarly, England's women's team does not engender the same historical rivalries and performativity as the men. Referred to as the "Lionesses" by the English Football Association (FA), fans, and media, this moniker is a gendered modification of the "Three Lions" branding of the FA worn on the men's team shirt since 1872 (Ingle 2002). However, the England women's team are not potent signifiers of nation and "Lionesses" is more of an endearment that is not matched to parallel use of "Lions" for men's football. Nonetheless the Three Lions branding does have significance for the men's team, amplified by the hugely popular song "Three Lions [on a Shirt] ('It's

Coming Home')" released for the men's 1996 Euros.[1] This song continues to be played and sung by fans when the England men are competing in the World Cup or the Euros, but it has not been played/sung for the women. The song, its continued use, and the enactment of the "three lions on a shirt" (rather than the players) are powerful symbolic forms of patriotism. As such, the asymmetry in performativity and deployment for the men's and women's teams is significant.

3.2 Branding and promotional content

One of the gendered issues that permeates football (and sport generally) is the framing and marketing of women's sport to families with young girls rather than wider adult audiences including the established and knowledgeable fans of the men's game. At both national and international levels women's football has been explicitly marketed for young girls and families, positioning the women's game in direct contrast to men's football. Efforts to garner family audiences have often focused on traditional heterosexualization of players while also failing to acknowledge and appeal to lesbian and queer fans. In England this has led to the marginalization of existing lesbian and adult audiences, particularly those adults without children who are viewed with suspicion (Allison 2018; Fielding-Lloyd, Woodhouse, and Sequerra 2018).

The dominant assumptions about the fans and audiences of women's football exclude them as "serious" consumers of sport in terms of travel, media, and merchandizing. This also impacts other decisions by governing bodies, such as the drawing of national teams for international competitions according to their time zone, rather than their competitive standing, as the means to increase television viewing figures (Dunn 2018). This can effectively (re)produce the women's game as less competitive than it actually is, especially given inevitable comparisons to the men's game. This framing also hides the historic and continuing impacts on audience building of the common failure to broadcast high quality production of women's games on accessible mainstream channels and/or during primetime hours. Accordingly, the legitimacy of women's football as a sport in its own right is undermined by repositioning it as a convenient form of family entertainment (Allison 2018; Fielding-Lloyd, Woodhouse, and Sequerra 2018), with the explicit sexualization of women athletes now replaced with a form of "gender blind sexism" (Musto, Cooky, and Messner 2017). With lower production values and restricted coverage, women's sport cannot readily compete with the spectacularized, extensive coverage of men's sport. Equally, those responsible for regulating and branding women's football appear to take an apologetic stance that

1 The song "Three Lions" was written and performed by Ian Broudie (from The Lightning Seeds) together with David Baddiel and Frank Skinner, two comedians who co-hosted a popular comedic football punditry British television show.

assumes audiences will not be attracted to women's football in its own right, especially without peripheral distractions or concessions that distinguish it from the more serious ones provided around the men's game.

Nearly every successful major women's football event has been heralded as a "watershed moment" or turning point in terms of grassroots participation, elite success, professional status, and media coverage (Brewster and Brewster 2019; Meân 2015); from the limited successes of the first unofficial Women's World Cup in Mexico in 1971 (Brewster and Brewster 2019), through the 1999 US Women's World Cup (Longman 2000), the 2005 European Championships in England (House of Commons 2006), through to the current tournaments. Yet behind the headlines and celebratory claims, many have consistently accused FIFA and its affiliates with ambivalence towards women's football, which remains evident in the questionable conditions, poor organization, and lack of ambition apparent in the execution and basis of promotional opportunities in the major women's competitions. Notably, the 2015 Women's World Cup saw women players required to risk injuries by playing on artificial turf (Dubois 2015). The 2019 Women's World Cup also attracted criticism regarding its secondary status based on the direct scheduling conflict with the CONCACAF (Men's) Gold Cup and intended exclusion of the Video Assistant Referee (VAR) system successfully implemented at the men's 2018 World Cup. Succumbing to pressure to use VAR shortly before the tournament, officials were insufficiently trained especially given the implementation of major new rules. Other criticisms of the 2015 and 2019 Women's World Cups include: lack of visible promotion in major host cities, poorly planned transportation, low profile "fan zones," and highly problematic ticketing procedures (Dunn 2018; Kassouf 2019).

While the narrow branding of the women's game (re)produces restricted understandings, the game is a powerful vehicle for the myth of women's empowerment. This is apparent in FIFA's branding of #LiveYourGoals for the 2015 Women's World Cup, and #Daretoshine for the 2019 tournament – similar to US Soccer's #SheBelieves. Such branding focuses on inspirational messages that position the tournaments and players as tools for female empowerment, and (re)produce neo-liberal discourses of individual responsibility that fail to recognize wider restrictions on women's progress. The irony of this is paramount given the consistent substandard framing, organization, and promotion of women's football (including current equal pay disputes), rendering the messaging, slogans, and mythic empowerment ironic. In stark contrast, the branding and marketing for men's international football celebrate the highest levels of skills and competition. As Clarke (2019) argued, "Sadly, FIFA has never embraced the brutal, brilliant athleticism of women's soccer – much less celebrated or adequately rewarded it. For decades, FIFA has treated women's soccer as if it's some sort of exercise in self-esteem for female players and young girls. *Real* soccer is what men play."

FIFA's #Daretoshine is reminiscent of England's #wecanplay campaign. Initiated after the England team placed third at the 2015 Women's World Cup, this campaign sought to inspire young girls to take up football and encouraged their fathers to support them (Dads urged 2015).

Of course, female representation and participation in many sports across the world need to be increased and their achievements celebrated. However, the (re)production of discourses that foreground the players as role models and their message as "empowerment" places the responsibility of engagement on individual women and frame success as simply requiring girls and women be "inspired" and "believe" in themselves. At the same time, these render invisible the role of wider socio-political, cultural, and structural issues in ways that absolve sport's governing organizations of responsibility and diminish pressure to invest and change the infrastructure to effectively tackle these problems.

4 British media and broadcasts of the 2017 Women's Euros

The rest of this chapter focuses on findings from our research into the British television broadcasts of the 2017 Women's Euros. We analyzed the broadcasts of all 32 matches, which were produced by two different providers reflecting recent practices that split media rights to tournaments. This does not mean wider access as the broadcast rights to specific matches remain the property of one provider (audiences switch between channels to watch). The matches were broadcast by Eurosport and Channel 4 (and its digital affiliate More4). This meant different presenters, production values, etc., across matches depending upon who aired each match. Our analysis covered the main broadcasts of the two primary channels which are quite distinct in provision and access for audiences: Channel 4 is a free-to-air national channel (equivalent to US "cable"), Eurosport is a dedicated sport channel available via subscription packages through the main cable television providers in Britain.

The structure that follows separates out topics for discussion; in reality, these practices work together to build and construct women's football as a gendered form in contrast to the men's game as the standard. Such analysis does not require direct comparison with data from the men's game as the key components of media and news coverage of women's and men's sport are well-established. Thus, the analysis below focuses on identifying deviations and differences in normative patterns of representation and production and how these serve to naturalize the gender differences they simultaneously create.[2]

---

2 Transcriptions have been simplified, but necessarily reflect some of the complexities required for a discursive and rhetorical focus. There are four key notations used in this chapter: (1) Underline denotes emphasis on the word or syllable; (2) (.) noticeable pause, but not a substantive pause (1 second plus); (3) [overlapping talk; (4) [additional contextualization or omitted words].

4.1 Promotion and audience building

Sports (media) audiences do not emerge organically or naturally but are constructed through socialization within and outside media practices. Therefore, dominant media discourses and associated narratives play a central role in shaping audience understandings of sport values, history, and meanings. The audience learns about the rivalries, national identities, and profiles of a few selected individual players, which are formulaic tropes in the building of interest and narratives in sport generally. This includes meta-narratives – historic and current – intertwined with specific narratives deployed to enable audiences to consume the event. This is important given that audiences for many major events may not be regular consumers of the sport or fans of the nation (or team), meaning these narratives enable points of engagement and meaning-making to build audience interest and involvement (e. g., individual and team/ nation rivalries). The dominant discourses deployed in such narratives and action are then crucial as they shape, challenge, resist, and (re)produce the dominant "commonsense" understandings of football. Most notably for women's football this concerns the deployment, or not, of conventional constructions of heteronormative femininity in contrast to the heteronormative masculinity of men's football.

Media economy means that not all tournaments or football events have journalists or commentators present at the live event or offer consistent levels of media production (replays, slow-motion, graphics, studio settings with expert analysis) from the broadcast feed provided from the tournament. The broadcast feed itself also varies (number of cameras and placement) depending upon the investment of the organization that purchased the rights to the event. This is significant for audiences because consumers of the dominant sports, like men's football, are used to high production values that reinforce the sport's status and importance but also "spectacularize" it to appear more exciting. Thus, while there may have been an increase in the broadcasting of women's football tournaments, the quality of the broadcasts and the promotional content is crucial to audience building and perceptions of the women's game more generally.

British television coverage of the Women's Euros 2017 showed some improvement in the routine elements of audience building during the tournament. For Channel 4, the team presenting the coverage were led by the senior, widely respected female sport presenter Clare Balding, albeit her first-time as a host for football. Balding was primarily accompanied by Eni Aluko, formerly of England's women's team and current club player, and Jermaine Jenas, a retired men's club player and current television pundit (expert) for men's football. Very occasionally joined by higher status pundits from men's football, the team conveyed a much higher status that has been missing from previous coverage; although the "in the stands" setting for the team did not convey the level of production typically afforded to the men's game.

Channel 4's pre- and post-match segments also provided team profiles, details on tactical strategies, and the key attributes of selected individual players for discussion and narrative building purposes. Frequent detail of player's domestic club season provided a broader context and positively connected the international event to the wider professional women's game. Such details and connection serve to promote and legitimize the professional women's game, simultaneously build the authenticity and status of the players, and (re)produce the audience as legitimate (i. e., interested and knowledgeable) consumers of football. This type of action may seem mundane and ordinary, but coverage of women's football has not consistently provided such formulaic content in turn failing to build interest and narrative or construct the audience as serious fans (Fielding-Lloyd and Meân 2013).

In contrast, Eurosport's coverage had no pre- or post-match content and, consequently, such audience building and narrative construction was almost entirely missing. Equally, the Eurosport coverage provided little visual representation of the commentators or in-studio footage indicative of low investment and production values. In some ways the Eurosport commentators' coverage appeared to assume that audiences were informed, but the wider failure to provide time to build narratives around the current and up-coming matches suggested an institutional indifference to the tournament and a lack of long-term investment in the women's game. As an authoritative and influential major sport channel, such low production values and lack of investment are problematic. The typical production of the men's Euros meant that – regardless of the level of commentary – Eurosport's failure to build narratives, guide audience consumption, or provide match analysis (re)produced the women's game as sub-standard, secondary, and undeserving of airtime.

A recurring narrative of the Women's Euro 2017 broadcast coverage was the subject of friendships between players from opposing teams. Camaraderie between players of different nations was emphasized and several broadcasts showed footage of players from opposing teams greeting and embracing each other prior to matches. While this may be an important part of the current women's game, the editorial choice to focus on friendships is significant and in contrast to the prevailing narratives of the men's game where individuals that play on the same club team are often acknowledged but not commonly discussed in terms of friendships. This was much more evident in Channel 4's coverage given that Eurosport had such restricted coverage typically commencing to broadcast very shortly before kickoff and finishing almost immediately after the final whistle blew. Nonetheless, the emphasis on friendships and camaraderie within and across women's teams serves to contrast and naturalize gender differences. This is especially notable in constructions around competitiveness and aggression. These constructions are evident in the Channel 4 commentary accompanying footage of England and Scotland players embracing each other on the pitch before their match:

> *Female:* Watching the players earlier as they greeted each other there was-there was no Braveheart about it (.) there was no roaring in each other's faces (.) they looked genuinely pleased to see each other (.) and-and it seemed very- you know amicable.

This is especially significant given the historical, colonially infused, national rivalry and sport–war intertext in the reference to "Braveheart," positioning the women as disconnected from aggressive and geopolitical rivalry and instead invoking a more genteel disposition with the use of "amicable." Perceptions of women's football as morally good and more refined are reified by such coverage and this may be interpreted as a positive alternative to the men's game, particularly in Europe where the celebrification of football at the elite level, and perceived deviance of its players, can be represented as immoral and a negative influence on young fans. However, the dominance of the friendship theme within the routine coverage of an elite women's tournament delegitimizes and feminizes the women's competition especially in the absence of the geo-political, national, and soap-opera style rivalries typical of men's sport. Indeed, we found a marked absence of (historic or current) rivalry (or grudge) narratives throughout coverage including in pre-match content that focused on the record of previous matches. The only significant stories of the tournament were the "toppling" of Germany from their 22-year reign as European champions and the "dark horse" Austrian newcomers who exceeded expectations by reaching the semi-finals.

4.2 Gendered representation

Linguistic gender marking and its asymmetry remain a concern within discourses of contemporary women's sport. This is significant because the gender marking of women's sports paired with unmarked men's sports (i. e., absence of gender marking) (re)produces male players and men's sports as the standard and the norm, naturalizing male forms as central and women's as peripheral and lesser in comparison. Consequently, it was interesting to observe a decrease in linguistic gender marking throughout the coverage of the 2017 Women's Euros of both Eurosport and Channel 4 that was fairly consistent on both channels. This lack of gender marking is evident in the Eurosport male commentator's deployment of a key narrative for the second half during a semi-final:

> *Male*: The first time that Germany since we've had a Euros final tournament have fail̲e̲d to reach (.) the semifinal (.) their 2̲2̲ year reign is over (.) who will take their crown though and who will get through out of France and England the second half coming up very shortly. [cut to commercial].

Given the linguistic norms, this can be argued to be a purposive effort to avoid gender marking to include the women as standard; so, even if the context assumes the audience already know it is women's football, this is a linguistic shift. The avoidance of gender marking was also evident in some discussion of how England as a nation was progressing in this major tournament as this excerpt from the Channel 4 commentary team demonstrates:

> *Female*: We are all looking forward to this Ian. First of all you (.) how impressed were you with England against Scotland and did you watch all of that at home?
> *Male*: Absolutely (.) very impressed erm (long pause) I- look the thing is I-I always said (.) I don't thi- I don't think I'll see England win one in my lifetime but I-I believe I will (pause) it might be – it might be this one it might be (.) it might be the women erm (.) we saw the guys (.) we saw the under-20s, we saw the under-21s do very well, but there's a determination and a ruthlessness and erm a professionalism about the way they dealt with Scotland the other day.

Here we can see that England's progression is being described in gender neutral terms, until the habitual unmarked forms of referral to the men's game start to make tricky work of extending the discussion to national performance that includes the men's teams. The inclusive connection of the women to the men as nation in a positive discussion of national performance is progress in many ways as the commentator builds on the initial reference to how impressed he was by the women's previous game and starts to connect this to the recent impressive performances by the under-21 men's team, (re)producing them within the same category. However, the hesitation, repetition, reparation, and changes in footing (e. g., point of view) in the statement reveal the tension and tricky work of navigating around gender and the politics of making a gender comparison, while also managing the normative patterns of representation of the men's and women's games. Nonetheless, as he reverts to talking just about the women, we also see descriptions that mark the women's competitiveness marked by the descriptors "determination" and "ruthlessness" with only a brief "erm" to indicate the slightly less than fluid association with "professionalism."

We also observed a tension in the use of "inspirational" messages from heroes of the male game as while this accords a shared category and construction as nation it simultaneously frames the men and the men's games as the aspirational figures and historical for women's football. For example, in the build-up to the 2017 semi-final against France, Channel 4 broadcast a short pre-match, pre-recorded segment profiling the England striker Jodie Taylor as the first female to score a hat-trick (score three goals in one game) for England at a major international tournament. In the segment Geoff Hurst and Gary Lineker, the first and second strikers respectively to score hat-tricks for the England men's team at major tournaments, appeared as floating heads above Taylor's shoulders as the more experienced players to bestow their inspirational messages of congratulations on the younger player. This segment was then followed by another which profiled Fran Kirby, England forward, as a "mini Messi" (referencing the prominent Argentinian male forward, Lionel Messi). The celebratory integration of the men's and women's games provided by the segment on Taylor can be welcomed as an equitable recognition of achievement in international football for nation regardless of gender. But tension is apparent in the humorous and somewhat unusual animation and depiction of the floating heads, in many ways trivializing and infantilizing the audience and Taylor herself. The problem with the use of male authoritative and heroic figures in the second segment is arguably more straightforward, despite the flattering comparison with Messi. Using male figures suggests there are no great female players to compare Kirby with in terms of the same skills and (re)produces the men's game as the more established, credible, and highly achieving standard. It can be argued that the use of Messi also suggests an assumption that the audience knows men's football and not women's, or perhaps the use of a male player by media producers themselves unfamiliar with the women's game. However, the (sole) use of a male player fails to grasp the opportunity to build audience knowledge about an established female player for the longer term.

Directly comparing female players to their male counterparts is a common trope in sports media coverage including football (Black and Fielding-Lloyd 2019) and is argued by some as an understandable "quick fix" to address the audience's probable lack of familiarity with women's football (Petty and Pope 2019). But building audiences and narratives for sports includes providing useful and historic points of comparison for new and existing audiences. Thus, we would argue that knowledgeable and informative content could easily be integrated into future coverage using content from women's football to build new audiences and satisfy established ones. But failure to provide information and build heroic narratives in the ways that are typical of the men's game, especially in terms of nation, have been observed in both the USA and England (Meân 2015; Woodward 2016); inaction that has been observed to miss out on the powerful opportunities, including the soap-opera narratives, that could build audiences and stars (Woodhouse, Fielding-Lloyd, and Sequerra 2019).

Knowledgeable and informative content also requires analysis which, to be effective, needs to include fair criticisms of perceived weaknesses in play or tactical strategy as expected tropes. Such analysis and criticism have typically been lacking in previous coverage of women's football which instead has included patronizing surprise at any level of skill. In contrast, coverage of the Euros evidenced authentic analysis and criticism of the women's game. This is demonstrated in the criticism exampled below:

> I have to say I think Toni Duggan has been one of the only players out on the pitch today for England that's err actually <u>shown</u> the level of quality that she possesses. The rest of the England team I think need to buck their ideas up. I think their attitude's been poor erm and it's why they find themselves in the situation that they're in now [1–1 at half time].
> Jermaine Jenas, England vs Portugal, Channel 4

To provide decent analysis requires a former knowledge of the players – as individuals and a team – given that criticism requires a realistic expectation of performances and this was fairly evident throughout the coverage, offering a positive finding for the representation of women's sport. However, while informed commentary teams were provided by both channels, Channel 4's coverage included substantive pre-, post-, and half-time analysis offered by pundits who appeared to know the women's game.

As noted earlier, a prominent feature of women's sport generally and football in particular is the recurring myth that heralds women's sport as having "arrived" with any major achievement (McLachlan 2019; Meân 2015). The (re)production of this myth typically deploys narratives that obscure histories of sexism and related inequalities while simultaneously framing the achievement as self-congratulatory evidence of an equal and progressive culture (Meân 2015). This is often reflected in efforts to represent women's football as making progress towards gender equity in sport, with a focus on the present without giving credence to the sociopolitical history of the sport, which means that failure to capitalize on the visibility can then be easily accounted for by a failure of the women to grasp their opportunity. In the excerpt below, the male and female Eurosport commentators discuss the opportunity for women's football in Austria based on the response to their unexpectedly good performance:

> *Male*: And Denmark had lost all five of their previous semifinals (pause) but s- bad luck's got to end some time and theirs was going to end today and these were the penalties that the Austrians missed (pause) but what a great learning curve for (.) women's football that (.) in (.) Austria they'll take this back all of the (.) headlines and all the media interest that it's generated (.) [a-and they build on it
> *Female*: [Aaah yes (Big pause) And they were actually saying that the media (.) in Austria (.) it was on front page of-of newspapers [it was on the radio and the tv
> *Male*: [coz let's be honest I mean with men's team it's not ah-uh [uses name] was the last time [they had a decent men's team
> *Woman*: [laughs (pause) yeah (pause) But they really got behind them and I think (.) you-you just hope that they-they will get more investment because (.) this is a team that potentially (.) could do really really well

In the excerpt we see the usual claims that the women can simply "take this back" and "build on it" without any consideration of why the media were not interested before. The only moment that there is any acknowledgement of the barriers faced by the women's team is when the female observes that "... you-you just hope that they-they will get more investment" the repetition indicating potentially tricky socio-political content as it hints to the underlying lack of structural support. However, it is also interesting that the male commentator humorously, but seriously, suggests that the support might also be related to the lack of a "... decent men's team" arguably suggesting that the interest would not be the same if the men were good. This dig at the men's team also serves to evoke nation and, in turn, some patriotism and comparative building of the England men's team by comparison. The conversation as a whole serves to position England as more progressive and advanced in its equitable treatment of women's football than Austria and obscures the fact that the women's game has only very recently been embraced by the English media which otherwise has a lamentable history of its inclusion and promotion.

5 Concluding remarks

There is a long history of claims that women's sport has finally arrived and that the institutional support for women's sport has shifted. Yet these claims have typically proved false given the failure of key institutions to recognize the deeply embedded social, cultural, and institutional barriers that continue to restrict the progress and representation of women's sport and female athletes. This is especially notable in sports, like football, that are most ideologically connected to nation and masculinity. In this chapter we noted evidence of efforts by some media to address some of the ways that women's football can be positioned as peripheral, alongside the continued asymmetry and embedded practices that maintain many of the disparities that (re) produce men's football as the standard.

There is a continued need for analytical attention to the ways in which the traditional gendered order of sport is deeply embedded into routine cultural practices. Minor positive changes in sport are often deployed as self-congratulatory, progressive narratives that simultaneously obscure the continued problematic practices or recent histories of exclusion. This is relevant given the tendency to quickly make claims of substantive and utopian change (Woodward 2016). But the ideological significance of sport makes such narratives even more pernicious when they function to frame "us" and our nation as progressive and "better." This can occur with direct or indirect contrasts with the lack of progression in other nations, but the comparison is not required (Meân 2015). These progressive narratives also serve the discourses that construct sport as an idealized site of equal opportunity, open access, and as a force for good; mythologies that often belie the truth of sport as a major site for the problematic construction of gender, sexuality, race, and so forth.

Thus, while our analysis showed some signs of a positive shift in the ways that women were (re)presented it also revealed the deeply entrenched and subtle ways the gender order is maintained and, we hope, the complexities of and resistance to shifting these embedded formations. We encourage scholars to continue to scrutinize the routine action of sport and sport-media, to consider the ways in which "things are done" across a range of sports sites and contexts to provide analytical and theoretical insights and ideally facilitate and guide real change – and not just in relation to gender. But at the most basic level change requires a willingness on the part of key governance and media organizations (or rather their members) to actively engage with such analysis, to explicitly acknowledge and accept the power and responsibility to address the processes, asymmetries, and problematic ways of thinking, understanding, and categorizing that underpin disparities. Equally, to be wary of succumbing to self-congratulatory claims and marketing gimmicks that feign positive progress rather than substantive change. Policies, pledges, and marketing campaigns are meaningless without attention to the subtle and underlying action and enactments that resist change, perpetuate disparities, and – in the case of neoliberal accounts of success and failure – ultimately blame the victims.

References

Ahmed, Shireen. 2019. This is the most anticipated Women's World Cup Ever. But corruption and abuse still block women from soccer. *Time*, 5 June. https://time.com/5601154/women-world-cup-abuse-sexism/ (11 November 2020).

Allison, Rachel. 2018. *Kicking center: Gender and the selling of women's professional soccer.* Piscataway, NJ: Rutgers University Press.

Billig, Michael. 1995. *Banal nationalism.* London: Sage.

Black, Jack & Beth Fielding-Lloyd. 2019. Re-establishing the "outsiders": English press coverage of the 2015 FIFA Women's World Cup. *International Review for Sociology of Sport* 54. 282–301.

Bowes, Ali & Alan Bairner. 2019. "Three Lions on her shirt": Hot and banal nationalism for England's sportswomen. *Journal of Sport and Social Issues* 43. 531–550.

Brewster, Claire & Keith Brewster. 2019. "A lesson in football wisdom"? Coverage of the unofficial Women's World Cup of 1971 in the Mexican press. *Sport in History* 39. 147–166.

Caudwell, Jayne. 1999. Women's football in the United Kingdom. *Journal of Sport & Social Issues* 23. 390–402.

Christenson, Marcus & Paul Kelso. 2004. Soccer chief's plan to boost women's game? Hotpants. *The Guardian*, 15 January. https://www.theguardian.com/uk/2004/jan/16/football.gender (11 November 2020).

Clarke, Liz. 2019. Women's World Cup misses the mark with patronizing "dare to shine" slogan. *The Washington Post*, 7 June. https://www.washingtonpost.com/sports/2019/06/07/womens-world-cup-misses-mark-with-patronizing-dare-shine-slogan/?noredirect=on&utm_term=.654bffbb1092 (11 November 2020).

Dads urged to support the FA's we can play campaign. 2015. TheFA.com, 19 June. http://www.thefa.com/news/2015/jun/19/the-fas-we-can-play-campaign-19062015 (11 November 2020).

Delgado, Fernando. 2003. The fusing of sports and politics: Media constructions of U.S. versus Iran at France '98. *Journal of Sport & Social Issues* 27. 293–307.

Dubois, Laurent. 2015. Artificial turf controversy a constant in backdrop of Women's World Cup. *Sports Illustrated*, 23 June. https://www.si.com/planet-futbol/2015/06/23/womens-world-cup-artificial-turf-canada (11 November 2020).

Dunn, Carrie. 2018. Canada 2015: Perceptions and experiences of the organisation and governance of the Women's World Cup. *Sport in Society* 21. 788–799.

Dwyer, Colin. 2017. Powerhouse Italy copes with the 'indelible stain' of missing the World Cup. *NPR*, 14 November. https://www.npr.org/sections/thetwo-way/2017/11/14/564050540/powerhouse-italy-copes-with-the-indelible-stain-of-missing-the-world-cup (11 November 2020).

Fielding-Lloyd, Beth & Lindsey Meân. 2008. Standards and separatism: The discursive construction of gender in English football coach education. *Sex Roles* 58. 24–39.

Fielding-Lloyd, Beth & Lindsey Meân. 2013. Soccer and "Team GB": Managing nation and gender in the media coverage of the London Olympics 2012. *Sixth Summit on Communication and Sport, International Association for Communication and Sport*, 22–24 February, Austin, TX, USA.

Fielding-Lloyd, Beth, Donna Woodhouse & Ruth Sequerra. 2018. "More than just a game": Family and spectacle in marketing the England women's super league. *Soccer and Society* 21. 166–179.

Fifa.com. n.d. Fifa member associations. https://www.fifa.com/associations

Fifa.com. 2018. More than half the world watched record-breaking 2018 World Cup. https://www.fifa.com/worldcup/news/more-than-half-the-world-watched-record-breaking-2018-world-cup (11 November 2020).

Hardin, Marie & Stacie Shain. 2005. Strength in numbers? The experiences and attitudes of women in sports media careers. *Journalism and Mass Communication Quarterly* 82. 804–819.

House of Commons Culture, media and sport – fourth report. 2006. *Parliament.uk*. https://publications.parliament.uk/pa/cm200506/cmselect/cmcumeds/1357/135703.htm#a4 (11 November 2020).

Hutchins, Brett, Bo Li & David Rowe. 2019. Over-the-top sport: Live streaming services, changing coverage rights markets and the growth of media sport portals. *Media, Culture & Society* 4. 975–994.

Ingle, Sean. 2002. Why do England have three lions on their shirts? *The Guardian*, 18 July. https://www.theguardian.com/football/2002/jul/18/theknowledge.sport (11 November 2020).

Jhally, Sut. 1989. Cultural studies and the sports/media complex. In Lawrence A. Wenner (ed.), *Media, sports, and society*, 70–93. Newbury Park: Sage.

Kassouf, Jeff. 2019. Logistics were a real problem in France. *The Equalizer*, 10 July. https://equalizersoccer.com/2019/07/10/france-womens-world-cup-logistics-problem-travel-transport/ (11 November 2020).

Longman, Jeré. 2000. *The girls of summer. The U.S. women's soccer team and how it changed the world*. New York: Harper Collins.

McLachlan, Fiona. 2019. It's boom time! (again): Progress narratives and women's sport in Australia. *Journal of Australia Studies* 43, 7–21.

Meân, Lindsey J. 2001. Identity and discursive practice: Doing gender on the football pitch. *Discourse & Society* 12. 789–815.

Meân, Lindsey J. 2010a. Making masculinity and framing femininity: FIFA, soccer and World Cup websites. In Heather Hundley & Andrew C. Billings (eds.), *Examining identity in sports media*, 65–86. Thousand Oaks, CA: Sage.

Meân, Lindsey J. 2010b. "Dare to dream": U.S. women's soccer vs. the world. In David K. Wiggins & R. Pierre Rodgers (eds.), *Rivals: Legendary sport matchups that made sports history*, 359–381. Fayetteville, AR: University of Arkansas Press.

Meân, Lindsey J. 2014. Sport websites, embedded discursive action, and the gendered reproduction of sport. In Andrew C. Billings & Marie Hardin (eds.), *The Routledge handbook of sport and new media*, 331–341. London/New York: Routledge.

Meân, Lindsey J. 2015. The 99ers: Celebrating the mythological. *Journal of Sports Media* 10. 31–43.

Meân, Lindsey J. & Raquel Herrera. 2017. Gendered nations: Media representations of the men's and women's U.S.–Mexico soccer rivalry. In Jeffrey W. Kassing & Lindsey J. Meân (eds.), *Perspectives on the U.S.-Mexico soccer rivalry: Passion and politics in red, white, blue, and green*, 99–122. London/New York: Palgrave Macmillan.

Meân, Lindsey & Jeffrey Kassing. 2008. "I would just like to be known as an athlete": Managing hegemony, femininity, and heterosexuality in female sport. *Western Journal of Communication* 72. 126–144.

Musto, Michaela, Cheryl Cooky & Michael A. Messner. 2017. "From fizzle to sizzle!" Televised sports news and the production of gender-bland sexism. *Gender & Society* 31. 573–596.

Nalbantis, Georgios & Tim Pawlowski. 2016. *The demand for international football telecasts in the United States*. Cham, Switzerland: Palgrave Macmillan.

Petty, Kate & Stacey Pope. 2019. A new age for media coverage of women's Sport? An analysis of English media coverage of the 2015 FIFA Women's World Cup. *Sociology* 53. 486–502.

Rowe, David. 2004. *Sport, culture, and media*. Maidenhead, UK: Open University Press.

Scavuzzo, Diane. 2020. Seismic changes to rock the youth soccer landscape. *Soccer Today*, 15 April. https://www.soccertoday.com/u-s-soccer-development-academy-to-close/ (11 November 2020).

Sklair, Leslie. 1991. *Sociology of the global system*. London: Harvester Wheatsheaf.

Wenner, Lawrence A. 1989. Media, sports, and society: The research agenda. In Lawrence A. Wenner (ed.), *Media, sports, and society*, 13–48. Newbury Park, CA: Sage.

Williams, Jean. 2013. *A beautiful game: International perspectives on women's football.* Oxford: Berg.
Woodhouse, Donna, Beth Fielding-Lloyd & Ruth Sequerra. 2019. Big brother's little sister: The ideological construction of women's super league. *Sport in Society* 22. 2006–2023.
Woodward, Kath. 2016. Women's time? Time and temporality in women's football. *Sport in Society* 20. 689–700.

Michael Silk, Emma Pullen, and Daniel Jackson

18 Communication, sport, disability, and the (able)national

Abstract: Given the accelerated commodification of the Paralympic spectacle and the shift to what we have previously termed a "hyper-visibility" of disability, our focus within this chapter is on the media's role in the social construction of disability and the production of Paralympic media texts as those through which political/national discourse can be traced. In so doing, we point to the state of play in understandings of, and relationships between, disability politics, Paralympic mediation, the contemporary neoliberal nation, and gender. Subsequently, through a focus on recent academic work, we look at the role of Paralympic media in defining which athletes are important, which disabilities/bodies are made hyper-visible – and thereby those which are marginalized or hypo-visible – through production practices that present productive, neoliberal, national disability icons who inculcate particular, preferred, notions of disability and the (re-)imagined nation.

Keywords: Paralympics; disability; nationalism; media; sport; gender; technology; able-nationalism

1 Introduction

The complex relationships between various forms of sport, communication, nations, and nationalism have been well established in academic debate (see, e. g., Bairner 2001; Andrews and Jackson 2001; Silk, Andrew, and Cole 2005). Of particular interest has been the role of sport mega-events (SME) in mediating national narratives and imagined communities around normative discourses of race, ethnicity, and citizenship (e. g., Robins 1997; Silk, Andrews, and Cole 2005). However, there has been a relative absence of these discussions in the context of disability and para-sport. Here, debate about the mediation of nationalism in Paralympic sport has been all but absent, a particularly telling omission given the recent, but significant, shift of the Paralympics from pastime to global spectacle (Howe 2011). Given the accelerated commodification of the Paralympic spectacle (Silva and Howe 2012) and the shift to what we have previously termed a "hyper-visibility" of disability (Pullen et al. 2018), our focus within this chapter is on the media's role in the social construction of disability and the production of Paralympic media texts as those through which political/national discourse can be traced (Whannel 2013). In so doing, we point to the state of play in understandings of, and relationships between, disability politics, Paralympic mediation, the contemporary neoliberal nation, and disability politics. Subsequently, through a focus on recent academic work, we look at the role of Paralympic media in

https://doi.org/10.1515/9783110660883-018

defining which athletes are important, which disabilities/bodies are made *hyper-visible* – and thereby those which are marginalized or *hypo-visible* – through production practices that present productive, neoliberal, national disability icons who inculcate particular, preferred, notions of disability and the (re)imagined nation.

2 Sport, the nation, and nationalism

The staging of exhibitions, expositions, and later sporting events – what Roche (2000) calls event ecology – paralleled the growth and spread of modernity and nation-state consciousness; they were (and still are) cultural occasions in which to tell the story of a country, a people, and a nation. They offer a space in which to construct national images for recognition in relation to other nations and the eyes of the world; they offer space for contouring a national past, present, and future and for reaffirming common tradition and community (see also Gellner 1983). For Anderson ([1983] 1991), over any other cultural form, it is perhaps sport that represents a truly compelling and seductive agent of cohesive commonality – a (symbolic) collective glue – that creates the imagined community of nation. That is, sporting events, international competition, and the hosting of SMEs are particularly lustrous and affective cultural forms (see Silk 2012) constituting part of what Stuart Hall (1992) termed narratives of nation. Sporting discourse is also inextricably articulated with what Hall (1981) referred to as the "state of play" in cultural and power relations. Concretely grounded in material relations of the temporal juncture, (mediated) sporting forms and spectacles often simplify, amplify, (de)politicalize, and (re)invent a nation; acting as spaces for the assertion and affirmation of particular discursive constructions of nations that reflect and reproduce social hierarchies and offer particular constructions of the character, culture, and the historical trajectory of people – constructions that by their very nature are acts of inclusion and exclusion (cf. Bairner and Molnar 2009; De Cillia, Reisigl, and Wodak 1999; Silk 2012). Thus, and as an element of the cultural terrain within a wider cultural politics, critical interrogation of the national can aid understanding of which discourses are adopted, and by whom, in regard to the organization of daily life in the service of particular corporo-political agendas (Giroux 2001; Grossberg 1992).

Of course, the power dynamics underlying the responsibility for contouring the nation are not static. In recent years, we can identify a tilting away from national governing elites (states) as sole auteurs of national sensibilities, towards nationally resonant discursive systems and materialities dictated by the impulses of transnational capital (Silk and Andrews 2001). As such, the locus of control in influencing the manner in which the nation and national identity are represented becomes exteriorized through, and internalized within, the promotional strategies of transnational corporations and the economic logics of neoliberalism. As Hardin (2014) argues, the form, position, ethos, structures, and sensibilities of corporations (what Hardin calls *corporism*) are a defining mechanism through which national identities and popular cultural products, forms, and experiences – including SMEs such as the Paralympics – become infused, intertwined, and embedded. We have previously termed this process, *corporate nationalisms* (Silk, Andrews, and Cole 2005), as transnational organizations seek, quite literally, to capitalize upon the nation as a source of collective identification and differentiation through *negotiating* with the local. Modestly updating Eric Hobsbawm's classic tome (1983: 11), the "badges of membership" have been increasingly brought under the control of corporate entities (e. g., global media companies and sporting brands) who have developed symbolic campaigns and cultural products as part of their relationship with specific (sporting) locales.

Importantly, we ground our understandings of the corporate nation and the negotiation of sporting locales alongside the role of *affect* in mediating sources of collective identification. Affect can be understood as a feeling of existence where "things become significant and relations are lived" (Anderson 2016: 735). Not only a property of the material body, affect works through the sites, networks, articulations, and representations of neoliberalism as dispersed qualities, sensibilities, climates, and atmosphere. In such a way, we can identify the *affective nationalism* that is *felt* through SMEs such as the Paralympics as an *atmosphere* that is both directed and orchestrated as well as working passively through micropolitical circulations (Stephens 2016). As the primary vehicle for delivering SMEs to national audiences, television broadcasters semi-conduct affective nationalism through spectacularized production values and associated promotional campaigns (Pullen, Jackson, and Silk 2020). As such, they provide an important site of study for the relationship between sporting and national cultures.

3 The mediation of the Paralympics

In the above, we have addressed the contemporary, corporatized, state of play in the mediation of nation through sport, specifically through SMEs. As previously mentioned, the Paralympics has recently become bound within the dictates of an accelerated commodification. It is thus important to think about the relationships between the Paralympics, the media, and the production of nation. Mediated representations of disability have historically been largely negative and drawn on a limited number of stereotypes, in particular those of: helpless, passive victims who are dependent on others; as vulnerable and pitiable and childlike dependents; as "supercrips" with an emphasis on inspirational stories of determination and personal courage to overcome adversity (see Cherney and Lindemann 2019); as less than human, often presented as villain, freak shows, or exotic; or, defined by their disability rather than other aspects of their identity, presented as unable to participate fully in everyday life (Ellis 2009; Hodges, Scullion, and Jackson 2015; Shakespeare 1999). Indeed, Briant and colleagues (2013) suggest that there has been a marked and relatively recent shift in the mediation of disability from sympathetic towards positioning the disabled as a new folk devil (fraudulent, not disabled, benefit scroungers) and less deserving (especially regarding mental health over physical disabilities, with invisible impairments where the severity cannot be visually demonstrated being most demonized). This is especially the case amidst a context (at least in the UK) of austerity, benefits cuts for the disabled, and increasingly polarized labor markets.

Given this context, there remain pressing concerns about everyday lives for disabled people and with respect to public attitudes/perceptions towards disability (Goodley 2011). Indeed, according to the World Health Organization (2011), the lived experiences of many disabled people are linked to negative attitudes, beliefs, and prejudices that constitute a multitude of barriers to education, employment, and participation in everyday life. Access to employment is a particularly pronounced issue facing disabled people despite the passing of legislation and policy focused on disability inclusion in the workplace (Barnes and Mercer 2010). This is particularly the case in a visual medium such as television where a "preferred" body politic holds significant capital, and where disabled people have been historically underrepresented (Ellis and Goggin 2017). Given the important role of mediation in the *construction of disability* (Barnes and Mercer 2010; Cherney and Lindemann 2019), we turn our attention to a cultural form – para-sport – in which disability, albeit for ephemeral moments during major competitions, is heightened, if not, hyper-visible.

The media representation of para-athletes has not been extensively studied, described as being in its infancy (Pappous, Marcellini, and de Léséleuc 2011; Ellis and Goggin 2017).[1] Indeed, in a commercial media culture that celebrates the pleasure derived from cultivated and enhanced embodiment (healthy, fit, sexual, hetero-normative, attractive), the principal challenge to the production of an idealized aesthetic comes from ageing, death, and *disability* (Turner 1996). This is perhaps exacerbated in sport; sports journalists – whose professional habitus is to produce pictures of perfect, (gendered) idealized neoliberal bodies (Cooky, Messner, and Hextrum 2013) – have, it is argued, reacted negatively towards disability (see, e. g., Schantz and Gilbert 2001). Indeed, the Paralympic Games itself has transitioned from pastime to global spectacle (Howe 2008); accompanied by the need for advertising and sponsorship revenues, celebrity performers, and the dictates of the mega-event marketplace. Thus, and at this juncture, as the profile of Paralympics/para-athletes has increased, Paralympic stakeholders possess a variety of competing, albeit not mutually exclusive, tensions regarding the ways in which sport and disability are and/or should be represented via the Paralympic Games. While some stakeholders position the Games as an elite sports event, others prefer to highlight the role disability plays in giving meaning and value to disabled bodies (Purdue and Howe 2013).

1 The argument in the balance of this section is a revised and condensed excerpt from: Pullen, Jackson, and Silk 2020: copyright © 2019 by Emma Pullen. Reprinted by Permission of SAGE Publications, Ltd.

Those scholars investigating Paralympic and para-sport coverage (e.g., Bruce 2014; Cherney, Lindemann, and Hardin 2015; Howe and Silva 2017; Pappous, Marcellini, and de Léséleuc 2011; Purdue and Howe 2013), have pointed to the marginalization or inferiority of elite disabled athletes, comparative lack of interest, and the reinforcement of medicalized, individualized, and stereotypical understandings of disability, often presenting disabled athletes as having triumphed over adversity (Cherney, Lindemann, and Hardin 2015; Hardin and Hardin 2005). In particular, Paralympic coverage has been critiqued for a dominant narrative of heroic achievement and disability bravely overcome, and as non-representative of everyday life with disability (Howe and Silva 2017).

Particular attention, in part relational to the IPC's own classification system (see Howe 2008), has been paid to how coverage tends to reinforce established hierarchies of disability. Based on hierarchies of acceptance or acceptance hierarchies (see Westbrook, Legge, and Pennay 1993), these are structures of preferences among the general population regarding disabled people or other perceived differences. In Paralympic coverage, such hierarchies have been clearly manifest, especially through a technocratic ideology that privileges cyborgified athlete-prosthetic hybrids (see Silva and Howe 2012) often in the guise of the supercrip or superhuman. Whilst the prefix "super" – superhuman, superathlete, supercrip – offers apparent positive narratives of people who "overcome" their own personal tragedy through courage, dedication and hard work (Ellis and Goggin 2017; Hardin and Hardin 2005; Silva and Howe 2012), it implies a stereotyping process that requires an individual to fight against his/her impairment in order to conquer it and achieve unlikely success (Berger 2008). In this way, "super" narratives can serve to distance and disconnect athletes from the lives and perceived lives, of many (non-athlete) disabled people (Cherney and Lindemann 2019).

4 The Paralympics, nationalism, and the gendered constitution of nation

Despite the Paralympic movement's historical links with the nation through the rehabilitation of injured military personnel, the mediation of nationalism through the Paralympic Games has been given limited scholarly attention (see Batts and Andrews 2011; Bruce 2014). This is surprising in the context of the recent commodification of the Paralympics and the associated focus on athlete backstories representing heroic soldiers (often fast-tracked into para-sport through, for example the USA's Paralympic military program and Battle Back program in Great Britain). Such representations position para-sport bodies as symbols of national, military, and sporting constituencies as a fertile site upon which contemporary cultural meanings of nation and the political and economic trajectories of neoliberalism are inscribed and mobilized (Batts and Andrews 2011).

Prior to our recent work, a small number of studies examined the relationship between the nation and the Paralympics, although this has tended to be a secondary focus of the analysis. For instance, analysis of newspaper coverage conducted across a number of countries has demonstrated a focus on home nation medal winning athletes (see, Schantz and Gilbert 2001; Chang and Crossman 2009; Pappous, Marcellini, and de Léséleuc 2011; Solves et al. 2018). Through a focus on newspaper coverage of the Paralympics in New Zealand, Bruce (2014) found that dominant and familiar representational norms continue to structure coverage, yet a number of representational devices were used to promote home nation para-athletes within a nationalist discourse. This included, for instance, storied coverage of home nation para-athletes compared to foreign competitors; use of rhetorical devices such as "Kiwi"; coverage of home nation athletes against a backdrop of national cultural symbolism, and, presenting home nation athletes in dominant sporting positions, all of which served to align home-nation para-athletes as part of the national community and are reminiscent of discourses applied to non-disabled sport.

Further, there exists a clearly established body of work that understands the place of sport/communication forms and technologies in the gendered constitution of nation (see, e. g., Rowe, McKay, and Miller 1998); this is however far less established when considering the place of para-sport. Scholars working at the intersection of disability and gender have explored the ways intersecting discourses of able-bodiedness, compulsory heterosexuality, and normative corporeal aesthetics and sexual functioning have led to the representational exclusion of disabled gendered bodies across the cultural industries (McRuer 2006, 2017). Certainly, disability has been viewed as incompatible with notions of both masculinity and femininity; with the construction of masculinity grounded on ideologies of physicality, strength, autonomy, and power (Shuttleworth, Wedgwood, and Wilson 2012) and femininity to "normative" – and able-bodied – aesthetics of beauty, both mediated by functionality with regard to sexual practices (Shakespeare 1999). Unsurprisingly, disability's representational history is marked by "asexual objectification" (Hahn 1988); one that could not be further from the dominant research narratives assigned to able-bodied sport (see Bruce 2013). Indeed, able-bodied sport coverage is comprised of gender *marking* and gender *making*; articulating compulsory heterosexuality (privilege afforded to those who fulfill heterosexual gender rules while silencing lesbian identity), appropriate femininity (physical and emotional characteristics that mark women as different from men), infantilization (representation as nonthreatening girls), sexualization (idealized sexual attractiveness), a focus on non-sport related aspects (wife, personality, physical appearance), and ambivalence (representations that oscillate between valorization and trivialization) (Bruce 2013).

In contradistinction, limited research has been conducted on the representation of gender and disability, particularly at the intersection of technology, disability politics, and nation. In concert with disability studies per se, there has been a modicum of para-sport research that points to the asexual objectification (Hahn 1988) of the para-athlete (Léséleuc, Pappous, and Marcellini 2010; Schell and Rodriguez 2001; Schell and Duncan 1999; Hardin and Hardin 2005). These scholars have demonstrated the extent the asexual/genderless disabled body is typically framed via a process of infantilization or trivialization with portrayals of a passive child-like dependency, lack of autonomy (Léséleuc, Pappous, and Marcellini 2010; Ferri and Gregg 1998) and ambivalence (Ferri and Gregg 1998). In line with an absence of gendered identity, the emphases on corporeal aesthetics and modes of beautification associated with the representation of able-bodied athletes are, it is argued, all but absent in the images of para-athletes reflective of a cultural industry that views femininity and disability as incompatible (see Claydon 2014).

Yet, and in concert with the encroaching commodification of the Paralympic spectacle alluded to above (Howe 2008), anecdotal evidence from the London 2012 and Rio 2016 Paralympic Games is more suggestive of an emerging economy of gendered/celebrity para-athlete bodies (at least in the UK). There appears to be an emerging media culture; for example, with *FHM* magazine's "Hottest Female Paralympians," the *Daily Mirror*'s "Sexiest Female Paralympians," and social media sites Pinterest and Facebook displaying "Paralympian Babes" and Paralympian and "Paratriathlon Babes" respectively, that points to shifting narratives of disability, sport, and sexuality. Whilst as academics, we (and the disciplines we represent) have long been attuned to the invisibility and marginalization of sexual pleasure/disability (e. g., Tepper 2000) and wider representational history, we need to pay greater attention to the mediation of (selected, commodified) disabled female bodies through the Paralympic spectacle and the intersection of this emerging economy with forms of technology and gendered/sexual relations.

There exists a more complex representational history of the gendering of the male para-body due, in part, to the long affinity between war, militarization, disability, and the Paralympic Games leading to a greater *visibility* of the male disabled body (Batts and Andrews 2011). In the contemporary moment, through rehabilitation programs such as the USA's Paralympic military program and Wounded Warriors, Canada's Soldiering On, and the Australian Defence Force Paralympic Program (and the emergence of the Invictus games for wounded service personnel), soldiers injured in conflict have been fast-tracked into their country's Paralympic training programs – sport once again (as it was when Guttman rehabilitated soldiers with spinal cord injuries following World War II) being seen as important in attempting to re-build the lives of military personnel who have endured life-changing trauma (Brittain and Green 2012). Narratives of cyborgified heroic returning soldiers and "terror" victims have dominated recent coverage (see Crow 2014). With Batts and Andrews (2011), the new subjectivity of the elite male soldier/athlete – as a symbol of both military and sporting constituencies – is far from benign and apolitical; it is a malleable site upon which contemporary cultural meanings and political demands are inscribed and mobilized.

Indeed, compounded by the relationship between masculinity, military, and disability, the elite male solider/athlete is as much more a cultural and national display of a new military masculinity to accommodate the increasing number of *male* military bodies becoming disabled through military intervention. Following Barounis (2009), disability sustained through high-risk masculinizing activities (such as war) increasingly operates as the "logical extension of masculinity's excess" (Barounis 2009: 55). Like the military, the masculinizing space of sport is framed as an alternative site to perform exceptional physicality and, in doing so, reclaim and re-embody a form of resilient heroic masculinity (see also Barounis 2009). This is further compounded by the historical use of high-tech prosthetic technology in both the rehabilitation of injured servicemen and para-sport that can be read as a surface extension of masculine discourse. Indeed, with the increasing visibility of the elite male soldier/athlete, prosthetic technology is symbolic of strength, power, domination, competition, and technohumanity; military/sporting properties re-inscribing militarism and athleticism back onto the disabled (typically male) body.

The Paralympic spectacle, then, provides a compelling cultural space through which to explore technology, gender, nation, and contemporary disability body politics. It has been the case that recent shifts in para-sport media coverage could present a challenge to stereotypical representations of gender and disability. Certainly, the relatively recent and palpable shift in the style of broadcasting, promotion, and popularity of the Paralympics (in some cultural contexts) in the last decade could challenge such representations and increase the visibility of disability, both on television through increased coverage (Walsh 2015), and the wider print media. Indeed, there exists a number of iconic disabled bodies that have emerged across popular culture as a result of the cultural platform provided by the Paralympic spectacle. For example, Aimee Mullins, a successful model and former track and field athlete celebrated for her feminine identity constructed through her use of prosthesis (Dolezal 2017), the Dutch sprinter Marlou Van Rhijn, and South African sprinter Oscar Pistorius (prior to his famed conviction in 2016), all with a recognized disability celebrity status, in part, down to a disability transcendence via carbon fibre prosthetic technology – and the embodiment of a celebrity supercrip.

The embodiment of prosthetic technology has received much attention by disability scholars (see Balsamo 1996; Kirkup 2000; Cherney 2001; Siebers 2008; Howe 2008; Haraway 1991), particularly how the prosthetically enhanced body articulates within biopolitical boundaries at the intersection of environments, practices, and the forces (or agency) of material objects themselves (Siebers 2008). This has been echoed by critical disability scholars who remind us that the disabled body is always materially and discursively (re-)constituted in response to its position within a *biopolitical* context that shapes evolving infrastructure and definitions of accessibility and cultural and national inclusionary discourses (Mitchell and Snyder 2015; Puar 2017).

Certainly, for scholars Mitchell and Snyder (2015), disability, in the context of neoliberalism, has been shaped by contemporary inclusionary discourses alongside other (select) – previously marginalized – bodies and identities are invested with forms of cultural citizenship through their regulation, inclusion, and visibility across the cultural industries. Following the logics of neoliberal inclusionary discourses, disabled bodies that can access and embody forms of prosthetic technology and supplementation, thereby aligning with the aesthetics, productivity, and functionality of normatively able neoliberal bodies, and of which can successfully navigate ableist structures and environments, are successfully absorbed within the flows of cultural–economic exchange. The fracturing of discursive binaries of inclusion/exclusion and able/disabled in neoliberal economies, and the material, cultural, and social transformation of disabled identities, is perhaps best surmised by Puar (2017). In mobilizing the terms *debility* and *capacity* alongside disability, Puar (2017) highlights how some disabled bodies can be viewed as disabled *capacitated* by virtue of their ability to be increasingly able through technological supplementation become absorbed into neoliberal economies. Termed able-disabled bodied by Mitchell and Snyder (2015), disabled capacitated bodies can be viewed as the supercrips of contemporary disability representation. However, and relatedly, for many disabled bodies, who are unable to transcend their disability for reasons such as uneven distribution of resources, form of impairment, lack of access to healthcare, and social support, they remain disabled *debilitated*. This fluid theorization, toggling between capacitation, debilitation, and disablement, allows scholars such Mitchell and Snyder (2015) and Puar (2017) to consider the ongoing generative properties disabled bodies and identities and the conditions that make forms of disabled embodiment – and disability transformation – possible for a select few disabled bodies.

It is at this juncture we can begin to explore the gendered and technologized representations of para-bodies and the role of the Paralympics as a unique, if not pre-eminent, site for the celebration of neoliberal inclusionary discourses. Following from Snyder and Mitchell (2015) who highlight the extent able-disabled supercrip bodies perform "representational work as a symbol of expansive neoliberal inclusion efforts" (Snyder and Mitchell 2010: 116) via a process they term "able-nationalism," we can begin to read the Paralympics as popular and potent cultural space of able-nationalism. Indeed, the Paralympics is an extremely important, pedagogic pervasive, political and powerful vehicle through which to explore disabled body-politics and the contemporary nation. Situated as a global sporting *and* national disability inclusion project, Paralympic success is driven by the increasing approximation to able-bodied sporting norms often manufactured through the *technologicalization* of disability (Howe 2011) made possible by expanding neoliberal economies. Whilst scholars focusing on Paralympic representations have identified the extent the technologically capacitated body is viewed as the hallmark of Paralympic representation, especially those deemed supercrips who tell inspirational stories of overcoming dis-ablement gaining the most media attention (Howe 2011), there has yet to be adequate scholarly focus on *how* such hierarchies operate within, and are mobilized through, the biopolitical management of the disabled body-politic as it intersects with the materiality of the body; gender, nation, and technology. This is an area of work that is not only much needed in studies focusing on communication forms, gender, disability, technology, and the nation; but formed the essence of much of our recent work on the mediation of the Paralympics.

In the balance of this chapter, we thus offer a brief window into our own ongoing work.[2] We are focused on the UK context at this juncture, although certainly hopeful we can expand our focus. Whilst previous work has focused on NBC's coverage in the United States (see Cherney and Lindemann 2019), the UK context however is important; not least due to the entry of Channel 4 (C4) – a public service broadcaster – as the UK Paralympic rights holders in 2012. C4 brought a level of ambition for Paralympic broadcasting that was, in the words of their former Disability Executive Alison Walsh, at "a whole new level" from previous events; the ambition centering on creating a nation "at ease with disability" (Walsh 2015: 27). Under the auspices of broadcasting regulation in the UK, this included fostering both on- and off-screen disability talent by recruiting presentation and production staff with impairments, giving unprecedented exposure to para sport (a 400 percent increase in coverage from the 2008 Beijing Paralympic Games), and pursuing a "no-holds-barred approach to portrayal of disabled people" (Walsh 2015: 49). C4's engagement with the Paralympics offered us a distinct contextual moment from which to understand the representation of disability. This was a moment defined by the increased commodification of the Paralympic spectacle, a heightened, if fleeting, visibility of disability on television – which we termed the hyper-visibility of disability – and oft (although far from exclusively) historically embedded stereotypical representations of disability. This maelstrom provided a telling contextual moment from which to address representations of disability, especially in its most (hyper)visible vehicle, the Paralympics. Thus, in what follows, we present a mere sketch of some of the observations gleaned from a recent project that focused on the circuit of Paralympic cultural production in the UK. The project followed an integrative methodological approach, concentrating on the televisual production of the 2016 Paralympics, the content of all broadcasts (in the UK) that went to air, audience engagement, responses and attitudes towards coverage, and national attitudes towards the Paralympics.[3]

2 See especially Jackson, Pullen, and Silk 2020; Pullen and Silk 2020; Pullen, Jackson, and Silk 2020; and Pullen et al. 2018.

3 Full detail of the project (AH/P003842/1: Re-presenting parasport bodies: Disability and the cultural legacy of the Paralympics) can be found here: https://gtr.ukri.org/projects?ref=AH%2FP003842%2F1 The final report from the project can be located here: http://pasccal.com/pasccal-final-project-report/.

5 The hyper-visibility of disability: the ablenational body politic

Perhaps the most overarching observation to be made from our recent work relates to the strategic approach by the UK-based Paralympic rights holder to narrate the Games through *good sport* and *big stars* so as to engage audiences with their coverage (Pullen, Jackson, and Silk 2020). Whilst this approach is consistent with the logics of the general sport-media landscape and aligned to the dictates of corporate nationalism, it was also essential so as to hook audiences and serve the broadcaster's wider public service remit. To successfully achieve this strategy meant a particular focus on the events deemed to be most *accessible* to audiences. These events are where the largest proportion of British medals were expected to be won, and those where disabled bodies that most approximate ableist sporting norms (swimming, athletics, and tennis) through mobility enhancing technology are present. Here, leaning on Mitchell and Snyder (2015), we read Paralympics broadcasting as a cultural space through which technological-enhanced disabled bodies – the "able-disabled" – gain entrance into a sporting neoliberal celebrity economy. This works through perceived widening circuits of bodily inclusion; celebrated and valorized as symbols of successful national disability inclusion (Pullen, Jackson, and Silk 2020. In this sense, with celebrated and "cyborgified" bodies as "representative subjectivities" of the nation (Marshall 1997), the Paralympics serves as an exemplar of ablenationalism (Mitchell and Snyder 2015); a cultural strategy that promotes equality and makes visible hyper-capacitated bodies within the national cultural sphere.

Successfully displacing otherness through alignment to normative frameworks of nationalism and ableism (Mitchell and Snyder 2015), these bodies can meet the demands of a neoliberal citizenship (productive, functional, and aesthetically pleasing) (Puar 2017). Yet, we argue, disabled bodies that are most visible and celebrated as national icons are distant to the bodies of most *othered* Paralympians and non-athletes living with an array of impairments. As such, Paralympic representations may contribute to the continuation of many ableist structures by using national attractors to ideologically serve the national disability imaginary – narrating universal ideas around disability and cultivating progressive discourses around a country's commitment to inclusivity – than they do make visible the wider politics of disability that have a very real impact on the lives of disabled people (see Mitchell and Snyder 2015; Pullen, Jackson, and Silk 2020. Questions thus remain over athletes with more severe forms of impairment who participate in events that are considered more inaccessible to audiences and are thereby less able to *transcend* their debility (Puar 2017), and thus become excluded from the national normative neoliberal disabled body (Pullen et al. 2019).

Through connecting (primarily) able-bodied audiences to para-athletes – to get behind Paralympics GB – required displacing perceived otherness and making *national attractors* out of the most successful, palatable, disabled bodies with the capacity for transcendence (Pullen at al. 2019). We argue that while this may serve to "create a nation at ease with disability" (Walsh 2015: 27), it also, problematically, favors a productive neoliberal disability aesthetic. Thus, the Paralympics makes a hyper-visible and nationally normative privileged form of disability representation centered on the most able-disabled technologically enhanced, white, and upwardly mobile disabled body. This results in important questions remaining over how the Paralympics might serve to marginalize and disempower those at the intersections of disability, racial, ethnic, and classed identity politics (see also Crow 2014). Indeed, as in able-bodied sport, powerful and affective invocations of nation are often highly gendered (see, e. g., Rowe, McKay, and Miller 1998).

6 Gendering the nation: technological capacitation

Within our work, we have argued that contemporary representations of celebrated and spectacularized able-national para-sport bodies (in the UK at least) form part of a seductive apparatus of neoliberal micro-governance suggestive of an emerging ecology of disability–gender relations. This is a sexualized/celebrity disability culture where the *technologicalization* of disability (Howe 2011) invests certain disabled bodies with forms of citizenship – a process of able-nationalism (Mitchell and Snyder 2015) – that facilitate *some* modes of heteronormative gendering for *some* select disabled bodies. Holding together contemporary representations of disability through perhaps its most hyper-visible form – the Paralympics – with extant knowledge and recent contributions to disability theorizing from Puar (2017) and Mitchell and Snyder (2015), we have been exploring a more nuanced interpretation of the disabled body politic, suggesting how both *hyper-* and *hypo*-visible Paralympic bodies are indicative of an affective ablenationalism that privileges certain bodies as effectively and normatively (Mitchell and Snyder 2015) disabled and manifests *gendered* disability icons that serve the nation ideologically under the guise of inclusion.

Through an emphasis in coverage, certain (gendered) bodies – via carbon fiber prosthetic technologies – become presented as cyborgified hyper-capacitated transformative bodies: the "*buffed, muscular yet technologically supplemented*" (Mitchell and Snyder 2015: 56) or the heteronormative prosthetic aesthetic body of the national disability imaginary. These are typically the male (ex-service personnel) disabled bodies or male bodies who demonstrate an increased functionality, form, and feature of technological integration and corporeal aesthetics, manifesting a carbon-fiber masculinization. These bodies are often presented through affective national frames curated via high production value backstory features. Comparatively, other bodies – by virtue of their condition or form of debilitation –lack the potential for hyper capacitated forms of technological augmentation. As such they concomitantly lack the capacity for (re-)claiming masculinity and femininity in an emergent neoliberalized disability body politics in which technological transformation is seemingly deemed central to the gendered national disability body politic. As such, other(ed) bodies become hypo-visible, represented through dominant disability representations as a body of asexual objectification; regulated via a narrative of infantilization or marginalization, and lacking the affective dimensions of able-national narratives and high value production aesthetics. Such bodies thereby remain marginalized in the emerging ecology of gender–disability–neoliberal relations. Whilst the cyborg body is clearly a body marked other through the visible and specific form of technological augmentation, the able-national form of gendering of these bodies acts, paradoxically, to *naturalize* such a body, reinforcing the grounds of its inclusion by making it increasingly and affectively knowable across a media sphere – and wider cultural industry – dominantly framed on the pleasure derived through a fit, sexual, and heteronormative (ableist) corporeal body politic.

In sum, and at this conjunctural moment, we can understand the representation of the Paralympics (at least in the UK) as a site of "national recognition" (Puar 2017: 70); a particularly powerful, potent, and popular space that serves to nourish gendered able-national representations and narratives through the privileged bodies of highly capacitated nationally normative cyborgs. On the surface, this cultivates an illusion of greater, more diverse and inclusive disability representation that seemingly challenge stereotypes. Yet, able-national frameworks that structure such representations inherently nourish extant neoliberal power structures where the representation of *some, selected*, normatively gendered disabled bodies is based on the regulated exclusion of others. In this regard, the Paralympics can be understood as another, and we would aver hyper-visible, disability site that engenders the "*contradictions of neoliberalism*" (Sothern 2007: 146) creating a greater disparity between disabled bodies; between those who are folded into the biopolitical vectors for life (Puar 2017) at the expense of debilitated-disabled bodies deemed redundant against the demands of neoliberal economies and left for "slow death" (Berlant 2007). Thus, as Paralympic representations aim to *normalize* disability (see Pullen et al. 2018), they may conversely act to *exceptionalize*; they not only obscure the conditions that debilitate bodies and make inclusion within and outside of sport tangible, but they reproduce, sustain, nourish, and propagate wider conditions of debilitation via highly affective but limited mediation of technologically capacitated privileged bodies marketed to the masses under the wider universal category of disability.

7 Concluding comments

The celebrated Paralympic body, bound with the cult of neoliberal individualism and technological enhancement, is suggestive of contemporary Paralympic broadcasting serving as an important site for the national celebration of disability inclusion and a form of neoliberal disabled embodiment (Mitchell and Snyder 2015). Inclusion, however, appears contingent on, and extended only to, the most privileged able-disabled bodies reflective of normative (able-)national corporeality. We would argue that more nuanced analysis of para-sport communications can enable our field to develop more sophisticated reading of narratives as they are produced, mediated, and consumed within a specific cultural and political context. Indeed, a supercrip narrative has provided important contributions thus far and dominated understandings of Paralympics and Paralympians. However, in concert with Schalk (2016), its largely uncritical and singular use across Paralympic studies limited entirely to media content and read outside of important shifting cultural context, has rendered it conceptually limited as a tool for nuanced future analysis. We propose that scholars offer more careful analysis of narrative logics and performance; context and power relations; disabled corporeality and affect; and the reception, internalization, and (re-)production of stories by audiences, so as to better understand the hyper-visibility of the most able-disabled, often technologically enhanced, para-bodies and by virtue, the relative hypo-visibility of more severe disabled para-bodies – and the important representational work such bodies do as national sporting national icons on behalf of disability. Such an approach requires carefully weaving together neoliberal discourses of disability equality, sporting legacy, celebritization, militarization, gender relations, and technologization through the visible and storied representation of particular para-athletes.

Of course, we are cognizant that our research is based in a particular national context, however, it is likely, given their broad appeal, that the types of narratives we allude to above are present, to differing degrees and intensities according to cultural, social, and media conditions, in other national contexts. Therefore, important cross-cultural work has yet to be done, particularly in providing knowledge as to how Paralympic media may perform and produce different cultural knowledge and structure shifting inequalities. Collectively, it is hoped that a sophisticated body of knowledge across an array of different communication forms and mediums will provide a compelling body of evidence that can be used to shape industry practice and thereby make a progressive social impact.

References

Anderson, Ben. 2016. Neoliberal affects. *Progress in Human Geography* 40(6). 734–753.

Anderson, Benedict. 1991 [1983]. *Imagined communities: Reflections on the origin and spread of nationalism* London: Verso.

Andrews, David & Steven J. Jackson. 2001. *Sports stars: The cultural politics of sporting celebrity*. London: Routledge.

Bairner, Alan. 2001. *Sport, nationalism, and globalisation: European and North American perspectives*. Albany, NY: State University of New York Press.

Bairner, Alan & Gyozo Molnar. 2009. *The politics of the Olympics: A survey*. London: Routledge.

Balsamo, Anne M. 1996. *Technologies of the gendered body: Reading cyborg women*. London: Duke University Press.
Barnes, Colin & Geof Mercer. 2010. *Exploring disability*. Cambridge: Polity Press.
Barounis, Cynthia. 2009. Cripping heterosexuality, queering able-bodiness: Murderball, Brokeback Mountain and the contested masculine body. *Journal of Visual Culture* 8(1). 54–75.
Batts, Callie & David L. Andrews. 2011. "Tactical athletes": The United States Paralympic military program and the mobilization of the disabled soldier/athlete. *Sport in Society* 14(5). 553–568.
Berger, Ronald J. 2008. Disability and the dedicated wheelchair athlete: Beyond the supercrip critique. *Journal of Contemporary Ethnography* 37(6). 647–678.
Berlant, Lauren. 2007. Slow death (sovereignty, obesity, lateral agency). *Critical Inquiry* 33(4). 754–780.
Briant, Emma, Nick Watson & Gregory Philo. 2013. Reporting disability in the age of austerity: The changing face of media representation of disability and disabled people in the United Kingdom and the creation of new "folk devils." *Disability & Society* 28(6), 874–889.
Brittain, Ian & Sarah Green. 2012. Disability sport is going back to its roots: rehabilitation of military personnel receiving sudden traumatic disabilities in the twenty-first century. *Qualitative Research in Sport, Exercise and Health* 4(2). 244–264.
Bruce, Toni. 2013. Reflections on communication and sport: On women and femininities. *Communication & Sport* 1(1–2). 125–137.
Bruce, Toni. 2014. Us and them: the influence of discourses of nationalism on media coverage of the Paralympics. *Disability & Society* 29(9). 1443–1459.
Chang, Ik Young & Jane Crossman. 2009. "When there is a will, there is a way": A quantitative comparison of the newspaper coverage of the 2004 summer Paralympic and Olympic Games. *International Journal of Applied Sports Sciences* 21. 16–34.
Cherney, James L. 2001. Sexy cyborgs: Disability and erotic politics in Cronenberg's crash. In Christopher R. Smit & Anthony Enns (eds.), *Screening disability: Essays on cinema and disability*, 165–180. Lanham, MD: University Press of America.
Cherney, James L. & Kurt Lindemann. 2019. Ableism and Paralympic politics: Media stereotypes and the rhetoric of disability sport. In Daniel A. Grano & Michael L. Butterworth (eds.), *Sport, rhetoric, and political struggle*, 143–157. New York: Peter Lang.
Cherney, James L., Kurt Lindemann & Marie Hardin. 2015. Research in communication, disability, and sport. *Communication & Sport*. 3(1). 8–26.
Claydon, E. Anna. 2014. Framing the difference(s): Analysing the representations of the body of the athlete in the 2012 Olympics' and Paralympics' official programs. In Daniel Jackson, Caroline E. M. Hodges, Mike Molesworth & Richard Scullion (eds.), *Reframing disability? Media, (dis) empowerment, and voice in the 2012 Paralympics*, 79–94. London: Routledge.
Cooky, Cheryl, Michael A. Messner & Robin H. Hextrum. 2013. Women play sport, but not on TV: A longitudinal study of televised news media. *Communication & Sport* 1(3). 203–230.
Crow, Liz. 2014. Scroungers and superhumans: Images of disability from the summer of 2012: A visual inquiry. *Journal of Visual Culture* 13(2). 168–181.
De Cillia, Rudolf, Martin Reisigl & Ruth Wodak. 1999. The discursive construction of national identities. *Discourse & Society* 10(2). 149–173.
Dolezal, Luna. 2017. Representing posthuman embodiment: Considering disability and the case of Aimee Mullins. *Women's Studies* 46(1). 60–75.
Ellis, Katie. 2009. Beyond the aww factor: Human interest profiles of Paralympians and the media navigation of physical difference and social stigma. *Asia Pacific Media Educator* 19. 23–36.
Ellis, Katie & Gerard Goggin. 2017. Disability, global popular media, and injustice in the trial of Oscar Pistorius. In Elizabeth Ellcessor & Bill Kirkpatrick (eds.), *Disability media studies*, 197–222. New York: NY University Press.

Ferri, Beth A. & Noël Gregg. 1998. Women with disabilities: missing voices. *Women's Studies International Forum* 21(4). 429–439.
Gellner, Ernest. 1983. *Nations and nationalisms*. Ithaca, NY: Cornell University Press.
Giroux, Henry. 2001. Private satisfactions and public disorders: "Fight club," patriarchy, and the politics of masculine violence. *JAC: A Journal of Composition Theory* 21(1). 1–31.
Goodley, Dan. 2011. *Disability studies: An interdisciplinary introduction*. London: Sage.
Grossberg, Lawrence. 1992. *We gotta get out of this place: Popular conservatism and postmodern culture*. London: Routledge.
Hahn, Harlan. 1988. Can disability be beautiful? *Social Policy* 18. 26–31.
Hall, Stuart. 1981. Notes on deconstructing the popular. In Raphael Samuel (ed.), *People's history and socialist theory*, 21–33. London: Routledge.
Hall, Stuart. 1992. Cultural studies and its theoretical legacies. In Lawrence C. Grossberg, Cary Nelson & Paula Treichler (eds.), *Cultural Studies*, 277–294. London: Routledge.
Haraway, Donna. 1991. *Simians, cyborgs, and women: The reinvention of nature*. London: Routledge.
Hardin, Carolyn. 2014. Finding the "neo" in neoliberalism. *Cultural Studies* 28(2). 199–221.
Hardin, Marie & Brent Hardin. 2005. Performance of participation ... pluralism or hegemony? Images of disability & gender in Sports 'n Spokes magazine. *Disability Studies Quarterly* 25(4). https://dsq-sds.org/article/view/606/783 (11 November 2020).
Hobsbawm, Eric. 1983. Introduction: Inventing traditions. In Eric Hobsbawm and Terence Ranger (eds.), *The invention of tradition*, 1–14. Cambridge: Cambridge University Press.
Hodges Caroline E. M., Richard Scullion & Daniel Jackson. 2015. From aww to awe factor: UK audience meaning-making of the 2012 Paralympics as mediated spectacle. *Journal of Popular Television* 3(2). 195–212.
Howe, P. David. 2008. *The cultural politics of the Paralympic movement: Through the anthropological lens*. London: Routledge.
Howe, P. David. 2011. Cyborg and supercrip: The Paralympics technology and the (dis)empowerment of disabled athletes. *Sociology* 45(5). 869–882.
Howe, P. David & Carla F. Silva 2017. Challenging normalcy: Possibilities and pitfalls of Paralympic bodies. *South African Journal for Research in Sport, Physical Education and Recreation* 39(1–2). 191–204.
Jackson, Daniel, Emma Pullen & Michael Silk. 2020. Watching disability: UK audience perceptions of the Paralympics, equality, and social change. *European Journal of Communication* 35. 469–483.
Kirkup, Gill. 2000. Introduction to part one. In Gill Kirkup, Linda Janes, Fiona Hovenden & Kathryn Woodward (eds.), *The gendered cyborg: a reader*, 3–10. London: Routledge.
Léséleuc, Eric, Athanasios Pappous & Anne Marcellini. 2010. The media coverage of female athletes with disability: Analysis of the daily press of four European countries during the 2000 Sydney Paralympic Games. *European Journal for Sport and Society* 7 (3–4). 283–296.
Marshall, David. 1997. *Celebrity and power: Fame in contemporary culture*. Minneapolis, MN: University of Minnesota Press.
McRuer, Robert. 2006. *Crip theory: Cultural signs of queerness and disability*. New York: New York University Press.
McRuer, Robert. 2017. Compulsory able-bodiedness and queer/disabled existence. In Lennard J. Davis (ed.), *The disability studies reader*, 396–406. London: Routledge.
Mitchell, David & Sharon L. Snyder. 2015. *The biopolitics of disability: Neoliberalism, ablenationalism and peripheral embodiment*. Ann Arbor, MI: University of Michigan Press.
Pappous, Athanasios, Anne Marcellini & Eric de Léséleuc. 2011. Contested issue in research on the media coverage of female Paralympic athletes. *Sport in Society* 14(9) 1182–1191.

Puar, Jasbir K. 2017. *The right to maim: Debility, capacity, disability*. Durham, NC: Duke University Press.

Pullen, Emma & Michael Silk. 2020. Gender, technology and the ablenational Paralympic body politic. *Cultural Studies* 34. 466–488.

Pullen, Emma, Daniel Jackson & Michael Silk. 2020. (Re-)presenting the Paralympics: Affective nationalism and the "able-disabled". *Communication & Sport* 8(6). 715–737.

Pullen, E., D. Jackson, M. Silk & R. Scullion. 2018. Re-presenting the Paralympics: (Contested) philosophies, production practices and the hypervisibility of disability. *Media, Culture and Society* 41(4). 465–481.

Purdue, David & P. David Howe 2013. Who's in and who is it? Legitimate bodies within the Paralympic Games. *Sociology of Sport Journal* 30(1), 24–40.

Robins, Kevin. 1997. What in the world is going on? In Paul D. Gay (ed.), *Production of culture/ cultures of production*, 11–66. London: Routledge.

Roche, Maurice. 2000. *Mega-events and modernity: Olympics and expos in the growth of global culture*. London: Routledge.

Rowe, David, Jim McKay & Toby Miller. 1998. Come together: Sport, nationalism and the media image. In Lawrence A. Wenner (ed.), *MediaSport*, 119–133. London: Routledge.

Schalk, Sami. 2016. Reevaluating the supercrip. *Journal of Literary & Cultural Disability Studies* 10(1). 71–86.

Schantz, Otto J. & Keith Gilbert. 2001. An ideal misconstrued: Newspaper coverage of the Atlanta Paralympic Games in France and Germany. *Sociology of Sport Journal* 18. 69–94.

Schell, Lee Ann & Margaret Carlisle Duncan. 1999. A content analysis of CBS's coverage of the 1996 Paralympic games. *Adapted Physical Activity Quarterly* 16 (1). 27–47.

Schell, Lee Ann & Stephanie Rodriguez. 2001. Subverting bodies/ambivalent representations: Media analysis of Paralympian, Hope Lewellen. *Sociology of Sport Journal* 18. 127–135.

Shakespeare, Tom. 1999. Art and lies? Representations of disability on film. In Marian Corker & Sally French (eds.), *Disability discourse*, 164–172. Buckingham: Open University Press.

Shuttleworth, Russell, Nikki Wedgwood & Nathan J. Wilson. 2012. The dilemma of disabled masculinity. *Men and Masculinities* 15(2). 174–194.

Siebers, Tobin. 2008. *Disability theory*. Ann Arbor, MI: University of Michigan Press.

Silk, Michael. 2012. *The cultural politics of post 9/11 American sport: Power, pedagogy and the popular*. New York: Routledge.

Silk, Michael & David Andrews. 2001. Beyond a boundary: sport, transnational advertising, and the reiminaging of national culture. *Journal of Sport & Social Issues* 25(2). 180–202.

Silk, Michael, David Andrews & C. L. Cole. 2005. Corporate nationalism(s)? The spatial dimensions of sporting capital. In Michael Silk, David Andrews & C. L. Cole (eds.), *Corporate nationalisms: Sport, cultural identity and transnational marketing*, 1–12. Oxford: Berg.

Silva, Carla F. & P. David Howe. 2012. The (in)validity of supercrip representation of Paralympic athletes. *Journal of Sport & Social Issues* 36(2). 174–194.

Snyder, Sharon L. & David T. Mitchell. 2010. Introduction: Ablenationalism and the geo-politics of disability. *Journal of Literary and Cultural Disability Studies* 4(2). 113–125.

Solves, Josep, Athanasios Pappous, Immaculada Rius & Geoffrey Z. Kohe. 2018. Framing the Paralympic Games. A mixed-methods analysis of Spanish media coverage of the Beijing 2008 and London 2012 Paralympic Games. *Communication & Sport* 7(6). 729–751.

Sothern, Matthew. 2007. You could truly be yourself if you just weren't you: Sexuality, disabled body space, and the (neo)liberal politics of self-help. *Environment and Planning: Society and Space* 25(1). 144–159.

Stephens, Angharad C. 2016. The affective atmospheres of nationalism. *Cultural Geographies* 23(2). 181–198.

Tepper, Mitchell S. 2000. Sexuality and disability: The missing discourse of pleasure. *Sexuality and Disability* 18(4). 283–290.

Turner, Bryan S. 1996. *The body and society: Explorations in social theory*, 2nd edn. London: Sage.

Walsh, Alison. 2015. Out of the shadows, into the light? The broadcasting legacy of the 2012 Paralympics for Channel 4. In Daniel Jackson, Caroline E. M. Hodges, Mike Molesworth & Richard Scullion (eds.), *Reframing disability? Media, (dis)empowerment, and voice in the 2012 Paralympics*, 26–36. London: Routledge.

Westbrook, Mary T., Varoe Legge & Mark Pennay. 1993. Attitudes towards disabilities in a multicultural society. *Social Science & Medicine* 36(5). 615–623.

Whannel, Gary. 2013. On mediatization and cultural analysis. *Communication & Sport* 1(1–2). 7–17.

WHO. 2011. World report on disability. Available at: http://www.who.int/disabilities/world_report/2011/report.pdf (accessed 20 June 2018).

Jennifer McClearen and Brett Siegel

19 NBC's diversity Olympics: promoting gay athletes in PyeongChang

Abstract: The US-based television network NBC distinctly branded the 2018 Winter Olympic Games in PyeongChang "the most diverse ever" while promoting the international sporting mega-event to its American audience. In this chapter, we examine the discourse surrounding NBC's branding of diversity with a specific focus on the network's promotion of two openly gay Olympic athletes, Adam Rippon and Gus Kenworthy. While the network's celebration of Rippon and Kenworthy appears progressive on the surface, we argue that these discourses of inclusion operate through ambivalent dialectics, which are pairs of discourses that seem opposite one another but work together in tandem to temper radical societal change. In this case, ambivalent dialectics give the outward projection of the US Olympic team as progressive, novel, and new while coupling them with embedded regulatory discourses that encourage a return to the harmony of post-identity politics – a liberal political ideology that contends that inequalities based on gender, race, and sexuality have been overcome. NBC's branding of diversity is ironically a regressive political stance that seeks to restore American politics to a cultural climate where homophobia, racism, and sexism were largely invisible, but political discourse was more comfortable for liberal, straight, White identities.

Keywords: Olympics; ambivalent dialectics; LGBTQ athletes; NBC; American exceptionalism; post-identity; post-gay

1 Introduction

In 2018 the United States Olympic Committee (USOC) proudly declared its Winter Olympic team representing the US in PyeongChang, South Korea as the "most diverse ever." Following the USOC's lead, NBC – the network broadcasting the Games in the US – overtly celebrated the diversity of American athletes, including Maame Biney as the first Black woman to make the US speed skating team, Chloe Kim as a Korean-American snowboarding phenom, and figure skater Adam Rippon and freestyle skier Gus Kenworthy as the first openly gay male athletes on the US Winter Olympic team. NBC's emphasis on stories of racial diversity, queer athletes, and inclusion produced the impression that the Winter Games had made major progress towards rectifying longstanding trends towards White supremacy and queer invisibility at the Olympics. Despite fervently declaring that these Games were exceptionally diverse, only 8 percent of the US Winter Olympic Team were athletes of color and just three were out LGBTQ athletes (Minsberg 2018; 2018 Olympics will 2018). All the while, the American

https://doi.org/10.1515/9783110660883-019

broadcast of the 2018 Winter Olympics portrayed the US team as more diverse on television than in real life (Minsberg 2018).

In this chapter, we examine NBC's earnest representation of the American team as diverse even as the current political climate in the US is decidedly in turmoil around a whole host of issues relating to racial justice and LGBTQ inclusion. We narrow from a focus on the discourses of diversity more broadly to considering how NBC represented Adam Rippon and Gus Kenworthy as the first two openly gay male athletes at the Winter Games. To do so, we deploy discourse analysis of NBC's interviews with and commentary about Rippon and Kenworthy to examine how the network contributes to a long history of US exceptionalism that attempts to prove to the world that Americans have overcome social injustice. We argue that progressive discourses of inclusion in the NBC brand operate through ambivalent dialectics, which are pairs of discourses that seem opposite one another but work together in tandem. In this case, ambivalent dialectics give the outward projection of the US Olympic team as progressive, novel, and new while coupling those discourses with embedded regulatory discourses that temper radical change. NBC can profit on the attention-grabbing nature of political disruption while providing an avenue to return to the harmony of post-identity politics – a liberal political ideology that contends that inequalities based on gender, race, and sexuality have been overcome (Bell 2019; McClearen 2015). This allows identity politics to enter the presumed apolitical athletic space of the Olympics while also having a built-in mechanism to control those politics at the same time.

Ambivalent dialectics are pairs of discourses that "appear to be opposite but in fact work together in problematic ways" and ultimately "gain definition and meaning through their interrelationship" (Ono and Pham 2009). German philosopher George Hegel argues that the internal conflict between ideas that appear to be opposites generates feelings of discomfort among people who seek a resolution to those tensions as a result (Hegel and Inwood 2018). Hegel sought a rationalized truth that stemmed from the conflict and eventual compromise between the seemingly antithetical binaries of right/wrong and conservative/liberal. Hegel views the resolution of conflict through dialectics as a desirable outcome for civil society while Kent Ono and Vincent Pham use the concept of ambivalent dialectics to consider how stereotypes maintain systems of inequality. They theorize that two seemingly contradictory media stereotypes of Asian-American women such as the dragon lady (deceitful, dangerous, and sensual) and the lotus blossom (docile, subservient, but also sexy) may seem opposite on the surface but actually work together to emphasize the sexual availability of Asian women (2009). Following Ono and Pham, we assert that the conflict between two opposing discourses does not necessarily produce a desirable resolution as Hegel would contend. In the case of NBC's treatment of Rippon and Kenworthy, the embedded compromise in the discourse pairs maintains the status quo when it comes to issues of gay rights.

Ambivalent dialectics allow us to consider how seemingly opposite discourses about Rippon and Kenworthy gain definition and meaning when considering three discourse pairs circulating around them: political and apolitical, unique and universal, and disruptive and harmonious. Our discourse analysis focuses on a range of content produced or co-produced by NBCUniversal, the parent company that owns properties such as NBC, NBC Sports, MSNBC, Telemundo, and co-owns the Olympic Channel with the USOC. We examine electronic media, social media, and content that originally aired on television but was later shared online; however, NBC Sports declined our request to secure recordings of full broadcasts of the Olympic events. Consequently, our study is limited to the content with an afterlife since the 2018 Games.

2 Diversity at the Olympics

In order to understand how and why the ambivalent dialectics surrounding Rippon and Kenworthy developed, it is important to consider the historical context for diversity at the Olympics. We need look no further than the origin story of the modern Olympics to uncover a heritage of exclusion. Pierre de Coubertin, the "father" of the modern Olympics, believed that European and American athletes were far superior to those outside Western nations and developed the modern Games with these beliefs ingrained. He "spoke in clear terms about the superiority of Europeans, in contrast with the unrefined, lazy, and libidinal subject peoples in Africa and to a lesser extent Asia" (King 2007: 90). The legacy of Coubertin's vision of the games has resulted in an overwhelmingly Eurocentric competition with a focus on European and American sports, especially for the Winter Games. Winter Olympics events are typically those that are popular in the US and Europe, necessitate copious amounts of snow, and require large financial commitments to train. For example, in the US, most ski and snowboarding training takes place outside urban centers, requires travel to mountain regions, and demands expensive equipment and passes to practice even at the recreational level. These conditions ensure that people of color and people from lower socio-economic classes have difficulty accessing these sports.

While the sporting space of the Games has long been overwhelmingly Eurocentric, White, and/or presumed heterosexual, the US as a nation has long touted its diversity on the international sporting stage while simultaneously struggling to fully enfranchise queer people and people of color back home. American runner Jesse Owens' participation at the 1936 Summer Games in Berlin is one of the most famous examples of this trend. The US almost boycotted Adolf Hitler's games due to the growing awareness of the Führer's treatment of Jewish-German citizens. In the end, the US decided to send its delegation, which allowed the Black athlete to win multiple gold medals in front of the dictator. Numerous American journalists framed Owens' victories as a direct challenge to Hitler's belief in the superiority of the Aryan race (The United States Holocaust Museum n.d.). As Damion L. Thomas notes, the US State Department and other government agencies used Black athletes as evidence that US race relations were improved to a greater extent than the Civil Rights movement might suggest (2012). They regularly sent Black athletes on global tours during the Cold War in order to assert that the United States was indeed racially progressive even while the fight for racial justice raged on American soil.

More recently the Olympics has become a venue for various Western nations to claim cultural superiority by citing the inclusion of queer athletes even as there are relatively few out athletes who compete (Travers and Shearman 2017; Hubbard and Wilkinson 2015). Only fifteen – of the nearly 3000 athletes at the Winter Games – were publicly out during the competition (2018 Olympics will 2018). For comparison, there were just seven out athletes (all women) at the 2014 Winter Games in Sochi and 56 at the much larger 2016 Summer Games in Rio de Janeiro, which included 11 out men (7 out LGBT 2014; A record 2016). The relatively few out athletes at the Olympics mirrors other sporting spaces, which many perceive to be the "final closet" for gay rights in the US (Billings and Moscowitz 2018). Despite a relatively small number of out athletes, the desire to prove US exceptionalism through the visibility of queer athletes is reminiscent of highlighting athletes of color in the lead up to World War II and during the Cold War. The visibility of queer identities becomes a marker of progress and tolerance that simultaneously become part of the identity of the nation. Jasbir Puar describes this discourse as "homonationalism" (2018), a form of nationalism that positions Western nations as progressive states in contrast with regressive ones – states portrayed as culturally debased due to conservative or even violently homophobic stances on gay rights. Western homonationalism, then, remains fixed within a binary of "us" vs. "them." Several sports scholars have examined international sporting mega-events as sites where homonationalist rhetoric is pronounced (Sykes 2016; Travers and Shearman 2017). Phil Hubbard and Eleanor Wilkinson scrutinize the efforts to brand cities as inclusive of LGBTQ identities, arguing that the London Olympics "represented a moment when particular ideas of sexual cosmopolitanism were deployed to regulate, order and normalize the variegated sexual landscapes of a world city" (2015: 598). Likewise, the US projected an inclusive image to the world when President Obama chose out LGBTQ athletes such as Billie Jean King and Brian Boitano as delegates to the 2014 Sochi Olympics after Russia passed anti-LGBTQ laws. Obama declared "that when it comes to the Olympics and athletic performance, we do not make distinctions on the basis of sexual orientation" (Kiley 2013). While the US has an abysmal record of diversity at the Winter Games, the nation has simultaneously used athletes of color and queer athletes to prove its exceptionalism. We now consider how NBC regulates discourses of diversity through the first of three ambivalent dialectics: political and apolitical.

3 Political and apolitical

Team USA presented the opportunity to celebrate America's ostensible commitment to diversity on a global stage. Rippon and Kenworthy proved to be a relatively safe and palatable emblem of progress that lent the network a socially conscious veneer while still foregrounding White, cisgender identities. Their status as openly gay athletes representing the United States allowed NBC to broach political issues without explicitly critiquing the Trump administration or challenging the familiar dogma that "sport transcends politics" (Travers and Shearman 2017). Throughout the 2018 Winter Olympics, the narratives circulating around Rippon and Kenworthy demonstrated an ambivalent dialectic that negotiated political and apolitical sentiments, ultimately striking a balance that capitalized on the athletes' unique personalities and perspectives without offending audiences in the political middle.

This dynamic emerged most prominently in the discourses surrounding Vice President Mike Pence, who was chosen to lead the US Olympic delegation to PyeongChang. When *USA Today* asked Rippon about the selection, the skater voiced his dissent by replying, "You mean Mike Pence, the same Mike Pence that funded gay conversion therapy? I'm not buying it" (Brennan 2018). With a long-running political career built in part on anti-LGBTQ policies, Pence ran for the US House of Representatives in 2000 on a platform insisting that federal dollars should no longer be "given to organizations that celebrate and encourage the types of behaviors that facilitate the spreading of the HIV virus" (Mike Pence for Congress n.d.). Further stating, "Resources should be directed toward those institutions which provide assistance to those seeking to change their sexual behavior," this point has been interpreted as advocating for gay conversion therapy. Combined with his documented opposition to same-sex marriage and gay anti-discrimination protections, Pence's politics clashed with NBC's project of branding Team USA, and by extension the nation itself, as inclusive and diverse. As two of the obvious candidates to express an opinion about Pence's involvement, Rippon and Kenworthy gave NBC an edge without jeopardizing claims to journalistic objectivity.

Much of the discourse surrounding Pence's ceremonial position at the Winter Games concerned whether or not Rippon would decide to meet with the Vice President. In his initial comments to *USA Today*, the skater maintained, "If it were before my event, I would absolutely not go out of my way to meet somebody who I felt has gone out of their way to not only show that they aren't a friend of a gay person but that they think that they're sick" (Brennan 2018). When the Vice President's office reportedly reached out to the USOC to set up a formal meeting between Pence and Rippon, the skater again declined (Brennan 2018). While acknowledging the political platform that the Olympics provides and occasionally activating that potential to critique the Trump administration and its policies, Rippon prioritized his role as an athlete over his capacity as an activist. "I'm trying to train for the biggest competition of my life," he declared. "I'm not trying to pick a fight with the Vice President of the United States" (Olympian Adam 2018). In an effort to discredit Rippon's remarks and manufacture a semblance of unity between the country's government and its team, Pence attempted to save face on Twitter. "Headed to the Olympics to cheer on #TeamUSA," he posted. "One reporter trying to distort 18 yr old nonstory to sow seeds of division. We won't let that happen! #FAKENEWS. Our athletes are the best in the world and we are for ALL of them!" (Pence 2018a). In a more targeted tweet minutes later, Pence wrote, "@ Adaripp I want you to know we are here FOR YOU. Don't let fake news distract you. I am proud of you and ALL OF OUR GREAT athletes and my only hope for you and all of #TeamUSA is to bring home the gold. Go get 'em!" (Pence 2018b). By publicly repudiating Rippon's concerns and proclaiming his support for the athlete, Pence performed superficial gestures of egalitarianism that ultimately belied his continued efforts to disenfranchise LGBTQ identities. NBC did not avoid the political implications of enlisting Pence to represent a national team with queer athletes, but its coverage of the controversy indicated an overarching tendency to contain the revolutionary potential of these discourses.

Rippon especially was often compelled to engage with Pence, and the onus was frequently placed on the skater to cooperate with the Vice President in reaching some sort of compromise. For example, when the figure skating events concluded, reporters again approached Rippon with inquiries about a potential meeting with Pence. In a *Today* interview with Rippon and Kenworthy, NBC's Craig Melvin asked Rippon, "Why wouldn't you at least talk to the VP?" (Adam Rippon & Gus 2018). The phrasing of the question implies that accepting a phone call from Pence would be small but significant gesture of goodwill, consequently making Rippon seem petty for refusing the call and minimizing the depth of the skater's objections to a man that has sought to endanger LGBTQ rights. When Rippon indicated that he didn't take the call because he "needed to focus on the competition," Melvin prompted, "You would take the phone call now," to which the skater confirmed, "Totally" (Adam Rippon & Gus 2018). In an *NBC News* YouTube channel video from *NBC Out*, Rippon explained, "I always said I would be open to talking with [Pence] after the Olympics. Mike Pence has had a lot of anti-LGBTQ views in the past and if that opportunity was still available, I would like to take advantage of it" (U.S. Olympic medalist 2018). The discourses surrounding the Pence controversy suggested that it was important, if not crucial, for Rippon eventually to meet with the Vice President, while the framing of Pence's anti-LGBTQ sentiments as "in the past" evokes faith in a harmonious future that could be achieved by simply putting aside differences and finding a middle ground.

NBC's embrace of Rippon and Kenworthy functioned to reconstitute the Olympics as a sacred space that eclipses politics by bringing people from different backgrounds and experiences together. The coverage of the Pence controversy, then, fulfilled an ambivalent dialectic by drawing attention to divisive political issues while simultaneously proposing that these issues could be resolved in the spirit of "peace and goodwill" that the Olympics embodies (Travers and Shearman 2017). In an *NBC News* interview with Gus Kenworthy, Kate Snow asked what the freestyle skier thought "the administration needs to know about gay athletes" (Olympics 2018). Kenworthy replied, "I didn't really want to get super political. I know that's not what the Olympics is about. It's about sport and the greater good of sport and the entire world coming together for it, but I also think that the Olympics is about inclusion and I feel like Pence hasn't necessarily stood up for inclusion." Both athletes acknowledged and accepted the political stakes of their position as out gay men, but they also cast the Pence controversy as a distraction to the inherent spirit of the Games, compartmentalizing their politics and reaffirming sport as a space that could and should be separated from these issues. Rippon opined, "The Olympics are about the competition and the athletes involved. I talked to you about how I felt before the games [and] it's brought a lot of attention and questions to my other teammates. I don't want to distract from their Olympic experience, and I don't want my Olympic experience to be about Mike Pence" (US Skater 2018). Rippon and Kenworthy's radical potential was ultimately limited by discourses, including the athletes' own comments on the subject, that relegated their activism outside of sport. When Kate Snow asked Kenworthy if he would want to talk to Pence, the skier answered, "Maybe after the Olympics, but I think right now I just want to focus on my sport and I don't want to be too distracted." As with Rippon, the discussion orbits around the possibility of a meeting between the athlete and the Vice President as a symbol of compromise between the two parties, even though only one has attempted to infringe upon the other's basic human rights.

NBC exploited the entertainment value of attractive and normative queer identities (i. e., White, cisgender, and favoring monogamous same-sex relationships), while still containing their potential resistance to hegemonic discourses. For instance, a pair of *Access* videos on NBC's website stripped the Pence controversy of its substance and urgency, instead displaying a commitment to post-identity politics that positions social inequalities as mostly transcended. Depicting "several cute pics" of the two athletes at the Opening Ceremony posted by Kenworthy on his Instagram, the text in the video remarked, "Gus even added a little jab at Vice President Pence in his caption: 'Eat your heart out, Pence. #TeamUSA #TeamUSGay.'" (2018 Winter Olympics 2018). After the skier broke his thumb in practice, another *Access* video took a similar approach, observing, "[Kenworthy] took a jab at VP Mike Pence [on Twitter]: 'But it does prevent me from shaking Pence's hands so ... silver linings.'" The video then recounted the ensuing interaction between the skier and a Twitter user who posted, "Your obsession with Pence is creepy." Evidently siding with the athlete, the text in the video exclaimed, "But Kenworthy had an epic clapback!: 'This was literally my first Tweet ever that mentioned him. You tweeted more about me than I have about him. Soooo actually it looks like YOU'RE the one who is obsessed with ME! And while I'm flattered I'm really just not interested. K thx bye!'" (Gus Kenworthy takes 2018). Deeming Kenworthy's posts "little jabs" and highlighting his "epic clapbacks" with Twitter trolls minimizes the impact of his and Rippon's objections to Pence and downplays the threat that the Vice President represents to the LGBTQ community. In so doing, NBC exhibited an ambivalent dialectic that managed the athletes' political potential by rendering them playful, harmless, and apolitical.

4 Unique and universal

NBCUniversal's choice for the 2018 Winter Olympic theme song exemplifies the next ambivalent dialectic: a focus on Rippon and Kenworthy's uniqueness and a corresponding claim that uniqueness is actually a universal characteristic of humanity. The network selected the song "This Is Me" from the film *The Greatest Showman* (2017) as the soundtrack for the promotion and broadcast of the events. The emotional score includes the declarations, "I am who I'm meant to be, this is me," "I'm marching to the beat I drum," and "I'm not scared to be seen," espousing individual uniqueness and the social obstacles that come with standing out. Reading the song's meaning intertextually reveals the anthem's discursive significance further. In the film, which is set amidst a traveling circus, "This is Me" is sung by a bearded woman and a chorus of non-normative performers, including a woman with albino skin, a little person, an extremely tall man, among others. The song's message is clear: be uniquely you and be proud of it. Kevin Weaver, the President of Atlantic Records and owner of the rights to the soundtrack stated, "The song's messages of celebrating diversity and individual uniqueness couldn't be more well suited for the themes and spirit of what the Olympics stand for" (quoted in NBC to use 2018). NBC shared similar sentiments. Jenny Storms, CMO of the NBC Sports Group, said, "'This Is Me' is the perfect song to connect viewers with Olympic athletes on a human level" (quoted in NBC to use 2018).

Like the song, the ambivalent dialectic of uniqueness and universality surrounding Rippon and Kenworthy claims that each person is special, and regardless of the precise flavor of uniqueness, the fact that individuals are different from one another is universal. Adam Rippon, in particular, couched much of the description of his life experience in this dialectic and NBC readily represented soundbites that reflected uniqueness and universality when portraying the figure skater. Consider how Rippon describes the country's fascination with him during the Games (Browne 2019). He does not consider himself as embodying what people would typically consider "America's sweetheart" and instead thinks he is awarded that designation because he is atypical. He proclaims during a press conference, "My story is different. I'm different. I think that on some level we all feel different and when we're embraced for being who we are and speaking our minds, it's awesome." He asserts that it is his difference that makes him relatable to the American public. In this soundbite, Rippon never specifies what actually makes him different. He does not explicitly discuss his sexuality and instead makes broad sweeping statements that could be interpreted to mean multiple different things. He talks about feeling different as a child and being afraid of being exposed, but he speaks in more generalized terms. The malleability of the uniqueness discourse better allows it to be applied universally because Rippon can vaguely refer to his sexuality or other aspects of his identity while allowing those in the audience to relate it to their own personal brand of difference. He echoes NBC's theme song for the Olympics by saying "Honestly, it's really fun to be yourself. It's fun to be me," i. e., this is me.

When Rippon discusses his sexuality explicitly, he tends to return to the refrains of his difference as ultimately universal. In an interview with NBC reporter Kate Snow, Rippon describes his experience growing up as a "young gay kid from the middle of nowhere Pennsylvania" and feeling like he "didn't belong anywhere" (Adam Rippon 2018). He acknowledges that as he became more comfortable with his sexuality, he translated that confidence into his training and his life more broadly. He emphasizes, "I felt so much power in just being myself." Snow then asks Rippon what he would say to "LBGT kids" who look up to the figure skater as an openly gay athlete. Rippon says "I would say to those kids: it doesn't matter where you came from. It doesn't matter who you are ... no matter what happens ... stay true to yourself. You can do anything." The language again shifts from explicitly speaking to gay youth and becomes applicable to identity and difference more broadly. Likewise, one of the most repeated interviews across NBC platforms was a moment when Rippon called himself a relatable "hot mess," which is slang for a disheveled but alluring person (Browne 2019). He says, "I'm just me and I'm just a hot mess. And I think on some level everybody can relate to that. ...you can be a hot mess, but as long as you work hard, and you treat everybody with respect ... you can do anything." Rippon repeats several phrases common within American discourse – hard work, respect, and ability to achieve one's dreams – which are universalizing ideas presumably applicable to all Americans despite their differences. NBC produced numerous soundbites of Rippon declaring that he was uniquely "himself" while repeatedly returning to the aspects of himself that "everybody can relate to." Rippon can be America's sweetheart because his queerness is just edgy enough to be palatable and contained through ambivalence.

The tensions between unique and universal appear inclusionary on the surface, but ambivalent dialectics are essentially a compromise that reaffirms the status quo. I analyze a similar strain of discourse in my work on the representation of difference in the mixed-martial arts promotion, the Ultimate Fighting Championship (UFC) (McClearen 2017). The UFC promotes fighters by vacillating between a homogenizing discourse, "we are all fighters," and a strategic emphasis on individual difference, such as gender, race, sexuality, or nationality. Effectively, the discourse pairs assert that we are all different and we all face adversity, which is a human characteristic that we share. Yet, I contend that this ambivalence between difference and sameness flattens power relations and fails to consider how the adversity facing a woman of color from a developing nation and the adversity facing a White man from the US are drastically different.

Gus Kenworthy's trip to a Ugandan refugee camp prior to the 2016 Summer Games in Rio de Janeiro exemplifies NBCUniversal's and the International Olympic Committee's (IOC) commitment to reasserting universalizing discourses without an earnest consideration of the broader structural barriers facing athletes from around the globe. Kenworthy serves as a guide for viewers on a trip to the Nakivale refugee camp in a short film called *Camps to Champs: The Power of Sport for the Displaced*, which was sponsored by the IOC and co-produced by the Olympic Channel to promote refugee athletes in the lead up to the first ever refugee delegation to the Olympics during the Rio Games (Silver medalist 2018). The film was also edited into shorter promotional spots and distributed across various NBCUniversal and Olympic social media accounts. Kenworthy tours the camps and meets several athletes who have been displaced by conflicts in central Africa. The film focuses on the individual refugee stories of war, displacement, and loss of loved ones; yet the primary message of the film is the connection Kenworthy finds with the refugees through sport.

Consider an exchange between the skier and the refugee basketball player Estella Muhunguti Fughaa. Kenworthy describes playing sports as "a way to escape my everyday life" and stressors. He then asks Fughaa if she understands sports similarly. She replies, "When I am playing basketball, I forget about everything. I forget all my problems and everything in the Congo." Kenworthy reaches the conclusion that people from all over the world and from all sorts of backgrounds play sports for similar, universal reasons even as he has struggled with the realities of the circumstances facing refugee athletes in the camp. In the ambivalent dialectics of unique and universal, an American, cisgender, White, gay athlete and a refugee female athlete from the Global South are distinct from one another but still share a common humanity that becomes the main takeaway. In the final line of the film Kenworthy says, "A lot of the time we can't speak, but it doesn't really matter. Sport, music, and the different things we got to enjoy here are just universal." The ambivalent dialectic of uniqueness and universality emphasizes the athletes' personal brand of uniqueness – be that background, life experience, or identity category – but connects Kenworthy and the refugees via discourse of universalism thereby lessening the impact of their plight for the viewers.

The documentary generates discomfort for viewers as Kenworthy somberly faces each of the refugees' stories but solves this tension through discourses of universality. He sheds tears as he grapples with the refugees' stories of pain and loss. Yet, true to the ambivalent dialectic, the audience gains catharsis through a tempering discourse of the universality of sport. Kenworthy reflects on his own learning from visiting the camp and considers his horizons broadened even while he asserts that the refugees have little light at the end of the tunnel and seem to be "okay with it." He smooths over the tensions generated from what the viewers see and hear in the camps and reduces the extent of the refugees' trauma as granting him perspective about his privilege and giving him "motivation to go to the gym." The film ultimately flattens Fughaa's experience as a refugee in order to connect her with Kenworthy through sports. Yet, as Michael Serazio reminds us, nations with the largest GDP are the nations with the largest medal count at the Olympics, a fact that correlates athletic success with a form of wealth and opportunity that Fughaa and her fellow refugees in Uganda have little hope to achieve (2019). Additionally, the dialectic shirks any real consideration of the structural barriers, and in the case of Nakivale, geopolitical conflict, that individual athletes face to compete as Olympians. The film does not, for example, address the role that the extraction of natural resources from the Democratic Republic of the Congo by Western companies has played in the conflict causing Fughaa's displacement to Uganda. The discussion of violence and war is decontextualized for the viewers thereby allowing Kenworthy's incursion into the camp to remain benevolent as he simultaneously resolves the tensions produced as he hears each athlete's story.

It is interesting that the IOC and the Olympic Channel chose Kenworthy to guide the audience through Nakivale. The film never mentions Kenworthy's sexuality explicitly, but he notes briefly that the persecution of homosexuality might be one of the many reasons why refugees may have fled their home countries. A few years after the trip in 2019, the Olympic Channel includes Kenworthy and his trip to Uganda as part of an article on Olympic LGBTQ athletes and Pride month. Rory Jiwani, the article's author, describes Kenworthy as a humanitarian committed to LGBTQ rights and note that his trip to Uganda came with some "personal risk" (2019). He emphasizes that "Uganda had only recently rescinded its Anti-Homosexuality Act but, to this day, LGBT+ people remain vulnerable to violent attacks." This framing of Kenworthy's trip to Uganda shows there was an explicit understanding of what it meant to send an openly gay man to the African nation. Whether the IOC intentionally sent Kenworthy because he was out or not, the freestyle skier transforms into a political symbol of homonationalism in the aftermath. Kenworthy becomes the White savior who broadens his own horizons while heroically navigating the destitution of the refugee camp thereby reasserting Western cultural dominance because he is American *and* gay.

5 Disruptive and harmonious

The same regulatory impulses that render uniqueness a universal phenomenon and temper political potential with apolitical sentiments intersect with the last ambivalent dialectic surrounding Rippon and Kenworthy, one which folds the athletes' disruptive nature into more harmonious and conservative discourses. For NBC, controlling the disruption that the openly gay Olympians embodied functioned to ensure their widespread marketability, benefitting from the buzzworthy appeal of the "new" and the novel while still ensuring that any progressive inclinations could be made comfortable for straight, White, moderately liberal audiences. The result is a renewed commitment to post-identity politics that relegates the "true" period of inequality to an amorphous past, allowing NBC to applaud the team, the country, and ultimately itself for leading the world on matters of diversity. The suggestion that America always has and continues to carry the proverbial human rights torch belies the continued threats faced by the LGBTQ community, particularly in the context of a regressive and reactionary political landscape.

The majority of discourses involving Rippon and Kenworthy emphasized their status as the "first two openly gay athletes to compete for Team USA in the Winter Games" (2018 Winter Olympics 2018), further evincing "the mass media's invention of perpetual newness in the case of gay male athletes" (King 2017: 373). NBC's coverage of the Olympians insisted that Rippon and Kenworthy were "making history" (Get to know 2018). By incessantly highlighting the historic nature of the athletes' feat, NBC strategically positioned itself within that history, lending further credence to the network's claims to innovation and newsworthiness as well as their attempts to capitalize on the apparently unprecedented diversity of the team as a whole. This focus on "firsts" led Craig Melvin, in a *Today* interview with Rippon and Kenworthy, to identify Rippon as "the first openly gay American athlete to win a medal at the Olympic Games," later clarifying that Kenworthy "could have claimed that first back in Sochi when he took home the silver in Men's Slope Style, but he wasn't ready ... yet" (Adam Rippon & Gus 2018). Melvin's declaration frames the skier's journey to coming out as an individual struggle devoid of societal context, pressures, and limitations. Yet upon receiving the Human Rights Campaign (HRC) Visibility Award in 2017, Kenworthy explained, "Action sports was a totally different world. I would hear snowboarders refer to skiers as skier fags. Everybody in the industry said anything that was bad or disappointing was gay, and there was an almost unspoken rule that you had to say, 'no homo' before anything sensitive, complimentary, or kind" (Gus Kenworthy receives 2017). Reducing the skier's process of coming out to just being "ready" elides the unique cultural conditions that shaped and at times hindered the athlete's relationship to his sport and his sexuality. In the *Today* interview, Kenworthy also pushed back on the tendency to assign and celebrate "firsts," confirming, "There are definitely other athletes before us and other athletes currently and other athletes that will be after us that are gay" (Adam Rippon & Gus 2018). Intercut with images of other (straight) Olympians representing a variety of sports and countries, the interview contains the disruption that Rippon and Kenworthy introduced by implicitly connecting them to a broader community and tradition believed to transcend both identity and difference. The ambivalent dialectic thus relies upon discourses that are malleable enough to accommodate the appeal of historic firsts without upsetting the presumed utopia of the Olympics or dismantling the status quo that it maintains.

Part of NBC's balancing act included more provocative aspects of the athletes' personas with reassurances that Rippon and Kenworthy were ultimately innocuous and wholesome. In an *Access* video on NBC's website, Kit Hoover proclaimed that Rippon's "bold personality is already making him a fan favorite. He's unapologetically outspoken" (2018 Winter Olympics 2018). Referring to an interview in which Rippon admitted to NBC's Mike Tirico, "I want to throw up. I want to go over to the judges and say, 'Can I just have a Xanax and a quick drink?'" Hoover noted how "refreshing it was" for someone to "just say what's on his mind." Seemingly out of nowhere, co-host Scott Evans responded, "I wonder if he took his brow pencil with him," to which Hoover then replied, "Remember he told us he has great brows and lashes." The brief exchange downplays Rippon's promise as an agitator and all but erases his status as an elite and accomplished athlete, instead favoring a sanitized portrayal that elevates the skater's role as "America's Sweetheart" while minimizing his disruptive potential. Similarly, another *Access* video provides a montage of Rippon and Kenworthy posing together at the Opening Ceremony, notably registering delight when "Gus even planted a big kiss on the figure skater's cheek!" (2018 Winter Olympics 2018). The video positions the "smooch" between the two "pals" as an exciting and significant act, but the image's symbolic capacity is ultimately undercut by infantilizing verbiage that renders Rippon and Kenworthy adorable and harmless. The platonic display of affection between two openly gay White athletes was assimilated with relative ease when considering other instances of gay intimacy in sports media. When Michael Sam kissed his boyfriend at the 2014 NFL Draft, for example, "the startling image of a large Black athlete passionately locking lips with a much smaller White man imperiled the proximity to Whiteness Sam would need to remain positioned within gay respectability's rhetorical frame" (Khan 2017: 340). As the *Access* video demonstrates, Rippon and Kenworthy are not policed in the same ways, nor to the same extent, as someone like Sam. The Olympians become a promotional strategy that gestures towards progressive ideals without acknowledging the disparate struggles faced by queer people of color. Thus, the *Access* video's inclusion of a Kenworthy tweet stating, "We're here. We're queer. Get used to it," trivializes the LGBTQ community's enduring fight for equality, erases the intersectional identities involved in this fight, and promotes the USOC and NBC as allies to a vaguely inferenced cause.

Resilience in the face of adversity has long been a popular narrative in Olympic mythmaking, consequently granting the struggles and triumphs of openly gay athletes an irresistible human-interest quality that could further publicize Team USA's diversity. The hardships overcome by Rippon and Kenworthy were frequently deployed as incontrovertible evidence of progress for gay athletes, for which NBC could notably take credit in providing a platform. In an Olympic Channel video with Kenworthy and Canadian figure skater Eric Radford, Kenworthy shared, "As a kid watching sports, I didn't really feel like I totally fit in, and I hope that you (Radford) being here and me and Adam and all these other athletes that are here and out and proud encourage younger kids to find a reflection of themselves in us" (Gus Kenworthy and 2018). The skier addresses persistent issues of invisibility, marginalization, and condemnation of gay athletes as belonging to a more discriminatory past, envisioning a harmonious future that would one day look back on PyeongChang as a watershed moment for queer representation and opportunity.

Looking back on his Olympic experience in Sochi, Kenworthy told Craig Melvin in the *Today* interview, "I was very much in the closet and very much ashamed of who I was, and I actually didn't get to appreciate the medal that I won because of that. I didn't know if the gay skier would be an image that anyone wanted to get behind and wanted to support" (Adam Rippon & Gus 2018). Through voiceover, Melvin intimates that Kenworthy's reservations and fears were largely unfounded, claiming, "When Kenworthy came out in 2015, sponsors didn't just stick with the skier. They grew exponentially." Transitioning to a Head & Shoulders advertisement in which the athlete declares, "My shoulders carry more than my country's pride. They carry my community's pride," the segment confirms that the athlete's sexuality would not jeopardize his market value, much less his popularity. The organization and structure of the interview, along with its accompanying images and clips, seems to interpret America's embrace of Kenworthy as natural and obvious, a foregone (homonationalist) conclusion that relegates regressive ideologies to a less accepting and inclusive past. The eagerness to elevate Kenworthy as a symbol of American exceptionalism recalls the experience of Black athletes such as Jesse Owens, who continue to be celebrated as exemplars of democracy and nationalism when competing on the global stage only to be denied basic human rights in their own country. Eliding the urgency of continued struggles for social justice and equality, Melvin concluded that the support for Kenworthy reflected a "broader cultural shift that has not only allowed these talented athletes to come out, but also stand up as advocates." NBC thus negotiated the ambivalent discourses of disruption and harmony by affirming the apparent sea change that Rippon and Kenworthy represented while simultaneously taking progress for granted and presenting it as common sense.

While NBC acknowledged the divisive political climate surrounding the Winter Games, and often highlighted Rippon and Kenworthy's unique position within this landscape, the discourses involving the gay Olympians reconsolidated notions of America as an emblem of progress and human rights. In their attempts to accentuate the historic diversity of Team USA, NBC devoted substantial coverage to the two athletes, offering a platform to potentially disruptive personalities who openly critiqued the Trump administration and its vision for America. With Rippon and Kenworthy, NBC had to reconcile the threat that Trump's America poses to minoritized groups with the lingering belief that this moment of crisis is an anomaly in a broader pattern of otherwise linear progress. The latter, of course, represents a far more palatable strain of discourses for mainstream audiences who identify as liberal. Embracing the Olympic success of Rippon and Kenworthy allows NBC and its viewers to uncritically celebrate the outward signs of (American) progress while re-burying the ongoing realities of homophobia, racism, and sexism that continue to plague the country.

These discourses worked to translate their potential as disruptive, unruly Americans to those that represent everything America purportedly stands for and symbolizes. In an Olympic Channel video, Rippon claimed, "I've always sort of been unabashedly myself and I've always spoken my mind and from the heart, and you know what? I think America's just catching on" (Browne 2019). The skater's comments further validate the sentiments that America is ultimately headed in the right direction, even as his entanglement in the Pence controversy points to the many remaining barriers to progress for LGBTQ individuals. In an Olympic Channel video filmed in the Canada Olympic House at PyeongChang, Kenworthy talks about the inclusion of a "Pride House" hosting LGBT athletes, volunteers, and visitors, observing: "Canada's been so incredibly open and supportive of all members of their country, and the US has too ... I think that it just shows the next chapter for the world and especially for sports" (Gus Kenworthy and 2018). While Kenworthy praises Canada specifically for its commitment to LGBTQ communities, he also reconsolidates North America and the West more broadly as the global standard for progress on issues related to human rights. Evoking the "winds of change," as Radford puts it, Kenworthy acknowledges a pronounced and positive cultural evolution, but he also credits that change to a belief that Western nations are capably orchestrating and ushering in this harmonious future.

This utopian thinking clashes with the reality of regressive politics that continues to endanger the basic rights of LGBTQ people, particularly non-normative and racialized queer identities who have not been as readily assimilated into the myths of American exceptionalism as Rippon and Kenworthy. NBC attempted to manage the potential disruption of out, outspoken Olympians by framing their popularity as evidence of America's "true" character, implicitly contrasting these ethics, and by extension the network's, with those held by Pence and the Trump administration. But while the athletes at times attest to a progressive shift in cultural attitudes towards LGBTQ individuals and issues, they also point out that the fight for equality, safety, and acceptance is not over. In the *Today* interview, Craig Melvin wondered, "Have we all made too much of this?", vaguely referencing the ways in which NBC and the public at large seemed to latch on to Rippon and Kenworthy as groundbreaking figures. Rippon replied, "I think there's a lot being made of it because people still, on some level, have a problem" (Adam Rippon & Gus 2018). Kenworthy concurred, recalling, "My boyfriend and I had a kiss at the bottom of the contest and people were like, 'We get it. We don't need to see it though. I don't care what you do behind closed doors but don't put it in my face.'" Rippon and Kenworthy presented a notable disruption in the overrepresentation of heterosexual athletes representing Team USA at the Winter Olympics, and many of their comments challenged audiences to consider not only the damaging politics of those in power, but also to reflect on the more subtle discourses that disparage and dehumanize members of the LGBTQ community in everyday life. Melvin's suggestion that NBC had perhaps blown the athletes' revolutionary capacity out of proportion works to contain the possibilities of their resistance, reconstituting a harmonious, post-identity politics that precludes radical progress.

6 Conclusion

NBC's representation of the first two out gay American athletes at the Winter Olympics is ironically a regressive political maneuver that elevates a diversity discourse that is more comfortable for liberal, straight, White identities. The network accomplishes this feat by tempering protests against homophobia, racism, and sexism through ambivalent dialectics that facilitate a return to post-identity politics and American exceptionalism. NBC bolsters discourses of Rippon and Kenworthy as political, unique, and disruptive in order to distance themselves from the overt homophobia and racism of the Trump Administration. At the same time, the network pairs representations of these athletes with a discourse that can control and contain their symbolism. NBC simultaneously pairs the depiction of these athletes with the apolitical, the universal, and the harmonious in order to soften their meanings and make them more palatable for an American audience that is uncomfortable with too much political disruption. Rippon and Kenworthy become malleable and contained symbols that allow the American viewing public to again feel comfortable at their country's place on the world stage even as the nation's daily political news provides stark evidence to the contrary.

References

7 out LGBT Winter Olympians in Sochi. 2014. *Outsports*, 5 February. https://www.outsports.com/2014/2/5/5382406/gay-winter-olympians-lesbian-bisexual-lgbt-athletes (29 July 2019).

2018 Olympics will have a record 15 out LGBTQ athletes. 2018. *Outsports*, 14 February. https://www.outsports.com/2018/2/6/16924846/2018-winter-olympics-pyeongchang-out-gay-lesbian-bisexual-athletes (29 July 2019).

2018 Winter Olympics: Gus Kenworthy & Adam Rippon share a smooch at the Opening Ceremony. 2018. *NBC.com*, 9 February. https://www.nbc.com/access/video/2018-winter-olympics-gus-kenworthy-adam-rippon-share-a-smooch-at-the-opening-ceremony/3666254 (13 November 2020).

A record 56 out LGBT athletes compete in Rio Olympics. 2016. *Outsports*, 11 July. https://www.outsports.com/2016/7/11/12133594/rio-olympics-teams-2016-gay-lgbt-athletes-record (29 July 2019).

Adam Rippon & Gus Kenworthy Today Show Olympic interview. 2018. *Today Show from YouTube*, 24 February. https://www.youtube.com/watch?v=jtHvw6v4-5M (30 July 2019).

Adam Rippon on being a role model and his advice to kids. 2018. Adam Rippon on being a role model and his advice to kids. *NBC News*, 21 February. https://www.nbcnews.com/nightly-news/video/adam-rippon-on-being-a-role-model-and-his-advice-to-kids-1166549571709 (29 July 2019).

Bell, Katherine M. 2019. "This is not who we are:" Progressive media and post-race in the new era of overt racism. *Communication, Culture and Critique* 12(1). 1–17.

Billings, Andrew C. & Leigh Moscowitz. 2018. *Media and the coming out of gay male athletes in American team sports*. New York: Peter Lang.

Brennan, Christine. 2018. Gay Olympian Adam Rippon blasts selection of Mike Pence to lead U.S. delegation. *USA Today*, 17 January. https://www.usatoday.com/story/sports/christine brennan/2018/01/17/gay-olympian-adam-rippon-blasts-selection-mike-pence-lead-u-s-delegation/1040610001/ (30 July 2019).

Browne, Ken. 2019. How figure skating star Adam Rippon became "America's Sweetheart." *Olympic Channel*. Retrieved https://www.olympicchannel.com/en/stories/news/detail/adam-rippon-olympics-america-sweetheart/ (30 July 2019).

Get to know Olympic figure skating stars Mirai Nagasu, Adam Rippon and the Shib sibs. 2018. NBC.com, 16 February. https://www.nbc.com/access/video/get-to-know-olympic-figure-skating-stars-mirai-nagasu-adam-rippon-and-the-shib-sibs/3669928 (13 November 2020).

Gus Kenworthy and Eric Radford on being out and proud Olympians. 2018. *Olympic Channel*. https://www.olympicchannel.com/en/video/detail/gus-kenworthy-and-eric-radford-on-being-out-and-proud-olympians/ (30 July 2019).

Gus Kenworthy receives visibility award. 2017. *Human Rights Campaign from YouTube*, 16 June. Retrieved https://www.youtube.com/watch?v=Rfe9iZj-35A (30 July 2019).

Gus Kenworthy takes jab at Mike Pence after breaking his thumb & injures his bum. 2018. *NBC.com*, 16 February. https://www.nbc.com/access/video/gus-kenworthy-takes-jab-at-mike-pence-after-breaking-his-thumb-injures-his-bum/3669701 (13 November 2020).

Hegel, Georg Wilhelm Friedrich & Michael Inwood. 2018. *Hegel: The phenomenology of spirit*. Oxford: Oxford University Press.

Hubbard, Phil & Eleanor Wilkinson. 2015. Welcoming the world? Hospitality, homonationalism, and the London 2012 Olympics. *Antipode* 47(3). 598–615.

Jiwani, Rory. 2019. Celebrate pride with Olympic Channel! *Olympic Channel*. https://www.olympicchannel.com/en/stories/features/detail/celebrate-pride-content-olympic-channel/ (29 July 2019).

Khan, Abraham Iqbal. 2017. Michael Sam, Jackie Robinson, and the politics of respectability. *Communication & Sport* 5(3). 331–351.

Kiley, Jocelyn. 2013. Obama had strong support from LGBT adults even before stance on Sochi Olympics. *Pew Research Center*, 26 December. https://www.pewresearch.org/fact-tank/2013/12/26/obama-had-strong-support-from-lgbt-adults-before-stance-on-sochi-olympics/ (13 November 2020).

King, C. Richard. 2007. Staging the Winter Olympics: Or, why sport matters to white power. *Journal of Sport & Social Issues* 31(1). 89–94.

King, Kyle R. 2017. Three waves of gay male athlete coming out narratives. *Quarterly Journal of Speech* 103(4). 372–394.

McClearen, Jennifer. 2015. Gladiator in a suit?: *Scandal*'s Olivia Pope and the post-identity regulation of physical agency. In Kumarini Silva & Kaitlynn Mendes (eds.), *Feminist erasures: Challenging backlash culture*, 150–163. London: Palgrave Macmillan.

McClearen, Jennifer. 2017. "We are all fighters": The transmedia marketing of difference in the Ultimate Fighting Championship (UFC). *International Journal of Communication Systems* 11. 3224–3241.

Mike Pence for Congress. n.d. The Pence agenda for the 107th Congress. http://web.archive.org/web/20010519165033fw_/http://cybertext.net/pence/issues.html (30 July 2019).

Minsberg, Talya. 2018. Online, a diverse Winter Olympics. But on the ground? *The New York Times*, 12 February. https://www.nytimes.com/2018/02/12/sports/olympics/olympics-diversity-Maame-Biney-Fenlator-Victorian-Adigun.html (29 July 2019).

NBC to use Keala Settle's "This Is Me" to spark attention for Winter Olympics. 2018. *Variety*, 3 February. https://variety.com/2018/tv/news/this-is-me-winter-olympics-greatest-showman-1202686512/ (29 July 2019).

Olympian Adam Rippon has "no interest" in fight with Pence. 2018. *USA Today*, 29 January. https://www.usatoday.com/story/sports/olympics/2018/01/29/olympian-adam-rippon-has-no-interest-in-fight-with-pence/109910240/ (30 July 2019).

Olympics 2018: Gus Kenworthy on his criticism of Vice President Mike Pence in PeyongChang. 2018. *NBC News*, 11 February. https://www.nbcnews.com/video/olympics-2018-gus-kenworthy-on-his-criticism-of-vice-president-mike-pence-in-pyeongchang-1159209027564 (29 July 2019).

Ono, Kent A. & Vincent Pham. 2009. *Asian Americans and the media*. Cambridge: Polity.

Pence, Mike. 2018a. *Twitter* post. https://twitter.com/vp/status/961465775444971521?lang=en.

Pence, Mike. 2018b. *Twitter* post. https://twitter.com/vp/status/961466229671284736?lang=en.

Puar, Jasbir K. 2018. *Terrorist assemblages: Homonationalism in queer times*. Durham, NC: Duke University Press.

Serazio, Michael. 2019. *The power of sports: Media and spectacle in American culture*. New York: New York University Press.

Silver medalist Gus Kenworthy visits refugees at Uganda's Nakivale Camp. 2018. *Olympic Channel*. https://www.olympicchannel.com/en/original-series/detail/camps-to-champs/camps-to-champs-season-season-1/episodes/silver-medallist-gus-kenworthy-visits-refugees-at-uganda-s-nakivale-camp/ (29 July 2019).

Sykes, Heather. 2016. Gay pride on stolen land: Homonationalism and settler colonialism at the Vancouver Winter Olympics. *Sociology of Sport Journal* 33(1). 54–65.

Thomas, Damion L. 2012. *Globetrotting: African American athletes and Cold War politics*. Urbana, IL: University of Illinois Press.

Travers, Ann & Mary Shearman. 2017. The Sochi Olympics, celebration capitalism, and homonationalist pride. *Journal of Sport & Social Issues* 41(1). 42–69.

United States Holocaust Museum. n.d. African American athletes. https://www.ushmm.org/exhibition/olympics/?content=aa_athletes&lang=en (27 July 2019).

U.S. Olympic medalist Adam Rippon says he will talk to VP Mike Pence. 2018. U.S. Olympic medalist Adam Rippon says he will talk to VP Mike Pence. *NBC News YouTube*, March 8. https://www.youtube.com/watch?v=az3luH3Kkpl (29 July 2019).

US Skater Adam Rippon doesn't want Olympic experience "to be about Mike Pence." 2018. IBTimes UK from *YouTube*, February 13. https://www.youtube.com/watch?v=EkzPY-W6Lfg (30 July 2019).

Brett Hutchins, Libby Lester, and Toby Miller

20 Greening media sport: sport and the communication of environmental issues

Abstract: This chapter examines the contested role of media sport as a "platform" for communicating pro-environmental messages. The potential of media sport in this regard is informed by its longstanding role in the popular communication of political, social, and cultural issues, including race, ethnicity, gender, sexuality, politics, commercialism, nationalism, and citizenship. It is argued that environmentalism and sustainability represent a vital new frontier in this context, especially given the threat posed to the planet by climate change. The role of media sport in this regard is conflicted, involving the promotion of environmental awareness through popular events, activities, technologies, and infrastructures that inevitably generate their own ecological footprints. A range of original examples and evidence is presented throughout the chapter that demonstrate how the uneven process of "greening" media sport is occurring, including a case study of a global mega-event, the postponed 2020 Tokyo Olympics and Paralympics. The evidence presented demonstrates both the growing use and significance of media sport for the communication of environmental messages, and the tensions involved in conducting social activities within carbon- and energy-intensive systems and economies. In building on our analysis, an urgent next step is to imagine what a *post-carbon* media sports cultural complex looks like, and to assess how media sport might contribute to a fundamental transformation in the resource and energy foundations of global society.

Keywords: climate change; environment; green; Olympics and Paralympics; pro-environmental; post-carbon; sustainability

1 Introduction: sport and climate action

Held in Katowice, Poland in December 2018, the United Nations (UN) Climate Change Conference, COP24, witnessed the endorsement and launch of the first-ever international Sports for Climate Action Framework (Sports for climate 2018). Signatories include the International Olympic Committee (IOC), the Fédération Internationale de Football Association (FIFA), Formula E Motor-racing, the National Basketball Association (NBA), the World Surf League, the New York Yankees, and Fukushima United Football Club.[1]

1 The research and analysis presented in this chapter is supported by the Australian Research Council Discovery Program (DP200103360 Fields of Green? Sport as a Communications Platform for Environmental Issues and Sustainability, 2020–2023).

https://doi.org/10.1515/9783110660883-020

The Framework articulates the impact of climate change on sporting activities and the ability of sport to "undertake systematic efforts to promote greater environmental responsibility" by engaging "billions of fans" (Sports for climate 2018: 3, 5). Communication through broadcast channels, social media, events, associations, venues, clubs, teams, and athletes forms a key plank of the Framework and underpins the assertion that "sports' global interest for billions of fans, and the media coverage generated in response, provide a strong platform for the sport sector to play an exemplary role in meeting the challenge of climate change, and inspire and engage large audiences to do the same" (Sports for climate 2018: 3). In recognizing this role, however, the Framework highlights a significant dilemma in the deployment of this power. Sport events and activities generate their own "considerable" environmental and climate impacts through "associated travel, energy use, construction, catering, and so on" (Sports for climate 2018: 3). It is a timely observation that corresponds with the growing profile and work of sport and environment advocacy groups such as the Green Sports Alliance (US based), Sport and Sustainability International (Switzerland based), and the Sports Environment Alliance (Australasian based). The Framework also represents long-overdue action, given the recognized impacts of extreme heat and drought on summer sporting activities and calendars, and warmer winters on outdoor snow and ice sports (Kay 2019; Martin 2019).

The UN's reference to sport as "a strong platform" is significant, particularly when this platform is used to communicate the parlous state of the physical world and widespread environmental risks in an age of ecological crisis. It is difficult to understate what is at stake in the use of this platform, given that environmental degradation and risks can be observed globally across an array of ecosystems, animal and insect species, wilderness areas, forests and plant systems, aquatic environments, food productions chains, weather conditions, and urban conglomerations (Hutchins and Lester 2015; Lester and Hutchins 2013). The idea that there is a *strong* platform with an *exemplary* ability to highlight and address these problems demands examination. Drawing on scholarship in media studies, environmental communications, and sociology, our chapter offers such an examination by presenting original evidence about how media sport is used to communicate pro-environmental messages, and the different dimensions of "greening" contemporary media sport (Maxwell and Miller 2012: 1; Miller 2018: 93).

2 Platforms and communication

Reflecting the symbiotic relationship that exists between sport and media – encapsulated in the term "MediaSport" (Wenner 1998: 3) – professional and elite-level sport has long been a popular site for the promotion of progressive, conflicted, and reactionary positions on race, ethnicity, gender, sexuality, disability, politics, commercialism, nationalism, and citizenship (Grano and Butterworth 2019; Rowe 2004). Built on the cultural potency of sporting symbols, rituals, and myths, this history can be observed through a variety of examples, including the profile of the Olympic Project for Human Rights, the use of fascist salutes by spectators in Italian football, and confused media responses around the world to South African middle-distance runner Caster Semenya because she embodies the complexities of sex, gender, race, the body, and biology (Edwards 1979; Kassimeris 2011; Montañola and Olivesi 2016; Serazio 2019). There are also many radical attempts both to transform and analyze sport. Consider the Gramscian fans of Livorno in Italy; the anti-fascist, pro-feminist supporters of FC St. Pauli in Hamburg, Germany; and Sócrates' leading followers and fellow-players of Corinthians in their memorable movement, Democracia Corinthiana, against Brazil's military dictatorship. Academically, progressive sports scholarship draws on political economy, counter-hegemonic analysis, feminism, and post-colonialism.

As the UN's Sports for Climate Action Framework and its various signatories highlight, environmentalism and sustainability represent a vital new frontier in the communication work performed in and by sport, capitalizing on sport's "projective power" both within nations and around the globe (Barthes 1977: 40). Being seen as environmentally aware and responsible – or green – has fast become a primary form of "symbolic capital" in the communication of corporate and social responsibility by sport leagues, teams, events, venues, and athletes (Bourdieu 2013: 171). This is a change that has also led to an environmental sport movement dedicated to influencing the business and governance affairs of sport organizations and industries (McCullough and Kellison 2018).

The UNCC's positioning of sport as a "platform" for climate action involves two interrelated issues. The first is the term "platform," which if it is to foster pro-environmental attitudes and practices, must be approached in a specific and purposeful fashion. As Tarleton Gillespie (2010) observes about the semantics of the term and the history of its use in computing, architecture, politics, and media, "platform" is a word that implies neutrality of function and agnosticism of purpose. Acting as a "neutral conduit," a platform facilitates activity for those who stand or operate on it, but presupposes no causal relationship with the values or politics that animate this activity (Gillespie 2010; Gillespie 2018: 14). This inference is a problem in the case of sport because positive environmental change cannot be achieved passively under the conditions of "carbon capitalism" (Klein 2014; Murdock 2017: 207). Neutrality must be avoided because sport has long served as a site for significant greenwashing by extractive corporations in the petroleum, chemical, gas, and technology industries (in conjunction with the socially extractive gambling, alcohol, fast food, and media industries), with "the everyday pleasures of sport" offering effective symbolic cover for sponsorship and branding (Miller 2018: 2). Sport offers a powerful means to project an image of being green and committed to environmental sustainability while drawing negative attention away from activities and industries that are neither.

The combination of neutral language and greenwashing fails to confront a fundamental challenge. Hyper-commodified sporting forms and commercial sporting markets at all levels make major impacts on landscapes and environments – for example, stadium construction, energy use, waste disposal, use of non-recyclable materials, player and spectator travel, equipment and clothing production chains, animal mistreatment, the altering of landscapes for competitions, and media coverage and reception (Miller 2018). One need only contemplate carbon emissions generated by flying over 15,000 athletes and multiple horses (for equestrian events) to and from the 2016 summer Olympics and Paralympics in Rio de Janeiro to comprehend the scale of the challenge at hand, and what it might mean to transition from high-carbon to low-carbon systems (ICAO carbon 2019; Urry 2011). The IOC has finally confronted the material reality of this problem, releasing a Carbon Footprint Methodology for the Olympic Games that will inform "effective carbon reduction strategies" for forthcoming Olympiads (Carbon footprint 2018: 11). Given the urgent need to address such challenges, the question of how best to communicate and use sport as a site for positive environmental actions and outcomes must be confronted actively and directly, not passively or neutrally. A clear and activist pro-environmental agenda in sport is essential if it is to contribute to lasting environmental justice.

The second issue is the need to analyze sport's capacity to serve as a pro-environmental communications platform. This requires an appreciation of sport's relationship with nature over the course of modernity. In his book *Landscapes of Modern Sport*, cultural geographer John Bale (1994) pinpoints how sport and leisure pastimes have functioned as simultaneously natural and cultural categories over time. In both drawing on and (occasionally) contesting Bale's arguments, we contend that sport's capacity to communicate environmental messages is grounded in its uniquely ambiguous position "between nature and culture" (Bale 1994: 39). Sport is a product of the cultivation, adaptation, reimagining, and/or exploitation of natural environments, and is constituted by the deep interrelationships that exist between nature, land- and waterscapes, weather, atmosphere, human and animal physiology, materiality, objects, human-created social orders, and dynamic cultural practices (cf. Bale 1994; Peters 2015). Modern sport events and activities perpetuate a clear tendency towards "extravagance and wastefulness" (Bale 1994: 43), but even at their most grandiose (World Cups, Olympic Games) and artificial (indoor stadiums, synthetic surfaces), they never transcend their historical and ecological connections to the natural world by virtue of their carbon footprints and lineage in "traditional" outdoor settings and pastimes. The compelling strength and fragility of sporting bodies and human biology also underline a confronting existential reality articulated by Friedrich Engels almost a century ago: "nature does not just *exist*, but *comes into being and passes away*" (Engels 1946: 9, emphasis in original; Miller 2018: 4). Given the catastrophic effects of climate change, the threat of such a "passing" is hinted at by the social media tagline of the Sports Environment Alliance: #noplanetnoplay.

Bale (1994: 43) uses the term "sportscapes" to capture the refashioning of nature and landscapes for the social, economic, and cultural needs of sport. In conjunction with wider developments in science and politics, this process is now changing the way fans, spectators, and sporting organizations approach their relationship to the environment due to the risks and degradation caused by sporting activities. Yet, as Bale's historically informed examination of sport and leisure forms shows, this relationship has been evident for some time to anyone willing to look closely. Sporting activity and practices have always been reliant on and affected by the environment, and have actively changed it, which underpins an arguably unique – or at least under-utilized – capacity to communicate pro-environmental messages. The relationship between sport and environmental impacts is, for example, apparent in the effects of golf course development in terms of land clearance and chemical and water usage. These impacts have led to pro-environmental initiatives and programs in many contexts, including chemical-free golf courses, the activism of groups such as the Global Anti-Golf Movement, and opposition to Donald J. Trump's efforts to alter Scottish landscapes through course-building (Millington and Wilson 2016, 2017). A complex ecological sensibility among surfers and beach communities is, as Clifton Evers (2019: 425) identifies, grounded in the felt and swallowed experience of polluted water. The image of a "pristine nature" is a "delusion" because of this routine experience:

> Going surfing in Australia has long been shaped by pollution. There is a close relationship between sewage and surfing at the world-renowned Bondi Beach in Australia. Surfers in England go surfing among raw sewage, and media reports show that surfers in Scotland, New Zealand, South Africa, Brazil, and the United States do as well ... Surfers in Bali, Indonesia, face a "plastics crisis" ... Their experience is backed up by how the seas, oceans, and their dwelling animals are now entangled with plastic.

Fortunately, there are civil society groups such as Los Angeles-based Heal the Bay that step in with both science and labor to understand, monitor, and ameliorate these situations.

Environmental degradation and pro-environmental advocacy are interlinked phenomena, with the first setting the conditions for the emergence and operation of the second. Similar relationships with land, sea, snow, and air can be observed in rowing and sailing (pollution, waste, and ocean plastics), alpine sports and ice-skating (reduced snow cover and ice-formation as a result of warming temperatures), and sports such as cricket, baseball, football, and tennis (drought and flood and their impact on grass and playing fields, extreme weather events, and high temperatures and air pollution effecting athletes' wellbeing in games and during training). In stadium- and arena-based spectator sports such as basketball and handball, challenges center on waste reduction and management, water consumption and recycling, and the carbon footprint left by energy intensive lighting, heating and cooling, electricity consumption, and in-stadium wireless communications networks and cloud computing. These challenges have led to widely publicized environmental ratings systems in the building, renovation, and operation of venues, including differing types of LEED (Mercedes-Benz Stadium in Atlanta), BREEAM (Luzhniki Stadium in Moscow) and ISO (Principality Stadium in Cardiff) certification (Bullock 2017). There is no "neutrality" to be found in sport's relationship with the environment in any of this – only impacts, consequences, and responses.

The next section centers attention squarely on media sport because of the crucial role performed by the media and communications in constructing definitions of environmental risk and impact, as well as the social, commercial, and policy responses that flow from them (Beck 2009; Cottle 2013).

3 Communicating about nature through media and culture

Media sport is constituted by the messages, texts, representations, discourses, practices, screens, technologies, infrastructures, and industries that create the "media sports cultural complex," as well as the audiences, users, and communities that form the "broad, dynamic field of contemporary sports culture" (Rowe 2004: 4, 216). It is the vibrancy and reach of this field into other fields and formations, including politics, the market, popular culture, and the nation, that create the potential for its use as a strong pro-environmental communications platform. It is also a strength grounded in an ability to communicate about nature through media and culture.

While we have identified problems with the term "platform," our preferred course of action at this point in time is to appropriate its meaning, given that the UN has embedded it in its Sports for Climate Action Framework (Sports for climate 2018). The arguments of Monroe E. Price (2008) are helpful in attempting to eliminate the neutrality inferred by this term. In examining the Olympics and the 2008 Summer Games in Beijing in particular, Price (2008) draws on Daniel Dayan and Elihu Katz's (1992) widely cited Durkheimian examination of broadcast media events and their role in the formation of audiences and national publics. With an eye on the history of the Olympic Games as a media setting where social change and politics are made visible on a global scale, Price uses "the term *platform* in a special way" (Price 2008: 88, emphasis in original). He regards the Games as a platform especially suited for the communication of social and political messages because it reaches "large, indeed massive, audiences" and presents "new opportunities to deliver messages and pathways to persuade" (Price 2008: 87–88). This emphasis on the power of the Games to persuade and influence, combined with the fact the messages sent through the event are subject to constant contestation and renewal over time, positions media sport as a platform that can contribute positively to pro-environmental discourses and outcomes. This capacity is further enhanced by the historical role performed by popular culture forms in entertaining audiences *and* contributing to the conditions that make social change possible by increasing citizen awareness (Singhal and Rogers 1999). Influence exercised by and through media sport as a platform is based on the scale of mediatized spectacle, and the intensity of viewer, spectator, and fan attention focused on sporting events, and the social and media rituals surrounding them. Within the realm of popular culture, these characteristics distinguish media sport from many fictional entertainment texts (e. g., science fiction, drama, soap operas, video games, novels) because it offers routine access to shared and richly affective social realities (Couldry and Hepp 2017; Serazio 2019; Singhal and Rogers 1999; van Es 2017).

In the effort to green media sport, the challenge is to understand how sport connects with the foundational "big picture" environmental discourses of our age (Murphy 2017: 17). Distinct discourses emphasize both contending and interrelated priorities, including the market and entrepreneurship, conservation and human problem-solving, citizens and the public sphere, science and industry efficiencies, activism and community, and nature and environmental collapse (Dryzek 2013; Murphy 2017). These naturalized and self-perpetuating emphases are grounded in "particular knowledge systems" and "cultural story lines" that frame how environmental and sustainability are thought about individually and collectively, and as a result influence the actions taken in the face of environmental challenges (Murphy 2017: 8). The question then becomes how media sport reflects and alters these discourses and actions through messages communicated from the local through to the global.

Our chapter sits within a larger project that traces the many ways in which media sport communicates environmental and sustainability issues, and the features, problems, impacts, and conflicts revealed by these uses. The greening of media sport requires an understanding of the following six overlapping categories and the various actors, interests, and agencies with which they connect:

(1) *Sport teams, clubs, leagues, and associations*, including the official media communications, policies and programs (e. g., recycling, travel, waste reduction and disposal, carbon neutrality initiatives, etc.), sponsorship arrangements, promotional activities, and news coverage of sport leagues, associations, and teams in relation to environmental and sustainability practices. For instance, the UK League Two football team, Forest Green Rovers, has been labelled the "world's greenest" sports team and football club by *The New Yorker* magazine and FIFA respectively (Elder 2017; The greenest 2017; League Two is the fourth highest division in the pyramid of UK football). It is a label certified by the UN, given that it declared the Rovers the world's first "carbon neutral club" in 2018 (Warshaw 2018). Owned by the founder of a renewable energy company, Dale Vince, the club plays on an organic grass pitch, mows the grass with a solar-powered lawn mower, recycles rainwater, serves only vegan food at games, and is planning to build a 5,000-seat capacity stadium made almost entirely of wood. Promotional environmental initiatives are also occurring at higher levels of UK football. An unofficial English Premier League (EPL) "Sustainability Table" now ranks clubs according to eight measures, including clean energy generation, waste management, single use plastic reduction or removal, and the availability of plant-based/low-carbon food options at games (EPL sustainability 2020). Arsenal, Manchester City, Manchester United, and Tottenham Hotspur all rank equal first on this table, while Southampton and Crystal Palace sit at the bottom.

One example of a competition-wide sustainability program is the North American National Hockey League's "NHL Green" program, which features a sustainability report articulating the relationship between hockey and nature:

Hockey depends on a healthy natural environment and, like most sports, it is resource-intensive. Changing climates, increasing resource constraints, and upcoming regulation impact the hockey industry. The NHL, as a leader in the sports world, seeks to reduce its impact and protect the roots of the sport. NHL Green works to improve the natural and built environments where hockey is played by championing sustainable innovation and community development. (Play it forward 2018)

Up until April 2018, this program saw the NHL listed as the only North American sport league in the Environmental Protection Agency's "National Top 100" for "green power users" (admittedly appearing alongside some decidedly suspect friends of the earth and/or people, such as Boeing, Lockheed Martin, Goldman Sachs, and the World Bank) (EPA Green Power Partnership 2018).

(2) *Major sport events and tournaments*, including the official media communications, policies (e.g., waste production and diversion, recycling, energy consumption, water use, transport networks, etc.), sponsorship, and news coverage of major sport events – particularly in terms of environmental sustainability claims-making, carbon footprints, promised event legacies, and "social licences" for the hosting of events (Lester 2016: 542; Miller 2018: 17). An expanding number of environmental and sustainability policies and measures have, for instance, produced increased demand for "carbon footprint accounting" that can be used by event organizers to assess and ameliorate the environmental impacts of events (Blaustein 2018a). The result is the entry of companies like South Pole into the ancillary media sport industries, offering climate impact assessments and working with organizers to measure, minimize, and offset carbon emissions. Headquartered in Switzerland, this company has partnered with the Union of European Football Associations (UEFA) since 2012. South Pole administered carbon credit programs for the 2016 UEFA European Championships in France ("the Euros," won by Portugal), including the provision of an online carbon calculator for those fans who wished to offset the carbon produced by their travel to the host country (Blaustein 2018a). While admirable, such measures appear to have done little to influence scheduling for the 2020 European Championships (or Euro 2020 as it is commonly known). This tournament is organized in "a new transcontinental format" that will leave a massive "carbon bootprint" as football fans journey to Germany, Hungary, Scotland, England, Azerbaijan, Holland, Italy, Denmark, Russia, Ireland, and Spain (McKie, Savage, and Cornwall 2019). The forced postponement of Euro 2020 for twelve months because of COVID-19 is also unlikely to reduce this "bootprint" given that the transcontinental format is to be maintained at the time of writing.

(3) *Sport stadiums and venues*, including the promotion of sustainable planning, venues and stadiums, as well as issues of land use, urban development, funding and construction, environmental ratings and certification systems, community wellbeing, and government decision-making (Kellison and Hong 2015). Able to host 100,024 spectators, the Melbourne Cricket Ground (MCG) in Australia is an example of a stadium that has invested significantly in recycling and waste-diversion programs (Cuthbertson 2018). Once one of the city's top 100 water users, the installation of an on-site water recycling plant has seen the venue reduce its water consumption by 50 percent. Food waste scraps left behind after matches are now fed into industrial recycling machines and turned into organic fertilizer, which is distributed in the gardens surrounding the MCG. Invoking both the symbolic power of sport and a discourse of environmental justice, the language of moral responsibility is used by the venue's facilities general manager, Peter Wearne, to justify these investments: "I think the

MCG, because of its iconic nature, has a responsibility to reduce its environmental footprint, consumption and waste to landfill. We have a moral obligation" (Cuthbertson 2018).

(4) *Environmental claims-makers, protest and activism*, including the activities of athletes, non-governmental organizations (NGOs), campaign-based groups, and activists, all of whom occupy an increasingly visible and varying range of positions. The growing prominence of the "eco-athlete" and an identifiable environmental sport movement are important developments that serve different functions (Blaustein 2018b). United by a sense of environmental awareness, these functions include image branding, symbolic protest, the building of social movements, and activism and civil disobedience. Examples of each continue to emerge, including the clever branding of US stock-car driver Leilani Münter as "a vegan hippie chick with a race car" (Münter 2019). The globally focused NGO Protect Our Winters is building a worldwide movement that claims over 130,000 supporters dedicated to turning "passionate outdoor people into effective climate advocates" (Protect Our Winters 2019). Activism targeted at the extractive industries is also evident. Australian Rugby Union representative David Pocock was arrested for chaining himself to a digger during a 2014 protest against a coal mine in northern New South Wales. In explaining his actions, Pocock said, "I believe it's time for direct action on climate change, standing together as ordinary Australians to take control of our shared future" (Former Wallabies 2014).

A poignant case of symbolic protest is that of Kiribati weightlifter David Katoatau at the 2016 Summer Olympics in Brazil. Competing in the 105-kilogram men's group, Katoatau danced on stage to draw international media attention to the catastrophic impact of rising sea levels on his small island home in the central Pacific Ocean (Friedman 2016). A public letter released by Katoatau prior to the Games reads:

Every day my people fear for their lives as their homes are lost to rising sea levels. We live on an atoll with nothing but flat land and ocean surrounding us. We have nowhere to climb and nowhere to run to. As a sporting representative of my country, I am begging you to save us ... Kiribati will be wiped off the face of the earth in less than 30 years ... I beg the countries of the world to see what is happening to Kiribati. The simple truth is that we do not have the resources to save ourselves. We will be the first to go. It will be the extinction of a race. Open your eyes and look to the other low-lying level islands around the Pacific – they will soon fall with us. In the not too distant future, we will all drown. (Katoatau 2016)

In addition to the obvious physical threat, the tragedy for citizens of small island states is their positioning as a perverse "evidentiary test" that demonstrates the consequences of changing weather patterns and rising sea levels to the rest of the world (Nash and Bacon 2013: 258).

(5) *Apparel, equipment and objects* are the always present but sometimes little noticed material artefacts required to make sporting activity possible, including specialist clothing, uniforms, balls, bats, racquets, boards, helmets, apparatus, and vehicles (cf. Lievrouw 2014). Each of these items is made possible by the processing of raw materials, design technologies, production systems, supply chains, and logistical media (Rossiter 2016). Again, initiatives in this category range from the local through to the global, with an emphasis on "the plastics crisis" (Vidal 2018). For example, Nube is a Seattle-based clothing company that makes athletic wear out of recycled plastic bottles (About Nube 2019). The origin story of this company stems from the founder's experience of attending junior basketball tournaments with her daughters and the enormous amount of waste created by young players purchasing single-use plastic water bottles (Blaustein 2017). At the national level, Major League Soccer's LA Galaxy promoted its support for sustainability initiatives by playing in an "upcycled" limited-edition jersey, which was manufactured with plastic recovered from Californian beaches and coastal communities (Wentworth 2018).

(6) *Energy and resource intensive technologies, digital devices and screens,* including telecommunications infrastructures, cloud computing, and e-waste. It is essential to consider the environmental impact of the technologies used to communicate media sport to audiences and users, and how users communicate with each other across multiple screens, devices, and telecommunications networks. This is an issue irrespective of whether broadcast, internet-based, or mobile communications are considered (although it can be mitigated if citizens are powering their screens and devices from renewable energy sources). The UK's National Grid Electricity System Operator (ESO) reports that demand for electricity spiked by 600 megawatts during England's opening match of the 2018 men's FIFA World Cup against Tunisia. Identified as "TV pick-up," this demand is caused by people opening fridge doors, boiling kettles, and turning lights on at the same time and was particularly noticeable during the half-time break (Miller 2018: 62; National Grid experience 2018). Furthermore, The Carbon Trust reports that the electricity required to watch live football in standard definition on a smartphone via a mobile network is 40 times more carbon intensive than a LED smart television using a digital terrestrial signal. This figure grows up to 180 times when watching a high-definition stream on a tablet computer (The "carbon bootprint" 2016). These sport-related issues contribute to a wider problem, given that global data traffic increased about "30 times" between 2005 and 2015 (Malmodin and Lundén 2018: 11). The marketing of streamed content, data centers, and cloud computing may offer the promise of connectedness, immediacy, and flow to the user, but extraordinary demands are made on resources and the environment as a result of their operation (Mosco 2014).

The afterlife of devices and computing equipment and the extraordinary proliferation of e-waste globally need to be considered when calculating the environmental cost of "exciting" new consumer technologies (Gabrys 2011; Maxwell and Miller 2012, 2020). For instance, the organizers of the Tokyo Olympics are drawing attention to the proliferation and toxic legacy of e-waste in Japan, while also indirectly highlighting the country's reputation for consumer technology innovation (Morris-Suzuki 2011). The Tokyo 2020 Medal Project will see the medals awarded to Olympic and Paralympic athletes – around 5,000 gold, silver, and bronze medals – manufactured from materials recycled from old mobile phones and electronic devices (Tokyo 2020 medal 2019).

4 The Tokyo 2020 Olympics and Paralympics

We now examine the postponed (and potentially cancelled) Tokyo 2020 Olympics and Paralympics because of their combined status as a global mega-event that, to differing degrees, complicate and expand the six categories nominated above. As with Euro 2020, the postponement of the Games until 2021 due to COVID-19 is a problem, causing significant disruption to the plans of the Tokyo Organizing Committee of the Olympic and Paralympic Games (Framework 2020). It is, however, likely that the combined global crises of climate change and COVID-19 are intensifying the Committee's promotional focus on sustainability. This likelihood is consistent with the Olympic Movement's recognition and endorsement of all 17 UN Sustainable Development

Goals, which, among a host of objectives, encompass health and well-being alongside climate change and life on land and in water (IOC sustainability 2017: 18). A strong emphasis on public health messages and measures in Tokyo would, therefore, fit comfortably alongside the existing environmental sustainability claims of organizers.

The Tokyo 2020 Games, as the Olympic and Paralympic events are collectively known, carry the "sustainability concept" of "Be better, together, for the planet and the people" (Sustainability n.d.). Along with statements on human rights, labor practices, and diversity and equality, the sustainability concept incorporates environmental ambitions that include the use of existing venues, public transport, renewable energy, recycled rainwater, and the reuse or recycling of 99 percent of items and goods procured for the Games. As previous Olympic and Paralympic Games have shown, the sustainability goals of the Tokyo 2020 Games also provide unparalleled opportunities for those activists working transnationally to upscale the impact of their messages via communication media. This has been evident in numerous ways leading up to the Games. For example, in September 2018, the Japan Sailing Federation was forced to make a widely shared apology after a local organizing committee of an Olympics "test run" sailing competition took international participants to a dolphin display at the popular seaside resort of Enoshima, south of Tokyo (McCurry 2018). Including the hashtag #sorrynature, British sailor Luke Patience tweeted from the aquarium, "Couldn't be more embarrassed with what I'm witnessing. We are sailing and apparently a 'green' sport" (@patience_luke 9 September 2018). Governing body World Sailing, which uses the tag line "sport/nature/technology," joined the chorus of condemnation, citing its 2030 sustainability agenda with specific targets linked to marine life. In its apology, the Japan Sailing Federation acknowledged that the decision to include live dolphins showed "a lack of consideration." However, it also highlighted a key difficulty faced by "global" green initiatives when the Federation's head, Hirobumi Kawano, pointed to different attitudes towards the treatment of dolphins "among countries and individuals" (McCurry 2018).

The scrutiny experienced by the Japan Sailing Federation hints at the complex interaction between international sport, communication media, cultural expectations, national pride, and commercial brands that now routinely plays out in the lead-up to each Olympics and Paralympics. That the expectation of such scrutiny changes corporate activities is undoubted. What is questionable is whether, or in what combination, this change is contained in the realm of strategic communication and public relations activities, and largely functions as greenwashing, or contributes meaningfully to achieving environmental sustainability goals in both the short and long term, or in fact causes further environmental harm. In Japan, the opportunity for financial gain (through being selected as a contractor for Tokyo 2020 medal) and/or brand enhancement (via association with the Olympics) has quickly been embraced by Japanese corporations, many of which have highly developed processes and products designed over decades, if not centuries, specifically for global trade and markets (Lester 2019).

During a series of interviews with major corporations in Japan between 2015 and 2017,[2] corporate representatives spoke of the strategic opportunity to promote their green credentials through the Tokyo 2020 Games. They also, unprompted, presented an acute awareness of the international scrutiny of environmental and other corporate practices they expected in the lead-up to the Games. Speaking specifically about sustainable seafood procurement practices, a corporate and social responsibility executive from one of Asia's largest retailers said:

> We had many contacts from NGOs because of the scarcity of the [seafood] resource ... we started a responsible seafood eco-label. But then we started to think maybe this is not the right thing. Ten years ago we thought [this] could be very strategic but then we felt maybe we are missing something. Then suddenly the Olympic Games happened, one, two years ago, then we started to think maybe it could be some opportunity ... We discussed and we decided maybe we should act more proactively and we should act more strategically ... (Interview with author 2016 Tokyo)

The understanding of the relationship between the staging of the Games and the opportunity this presents to international NGOs operating within global communication media flows is made clear:

> Of course, there is some shift toward 2020 for sustainability ... but also there are risks because [of the] international NGOs' investment is now put into Japan because we have the Olympic Games. They want a shift in Japan and they want to have some shift starting from Japan and toward Asian companies because we procure lots of products from Asian countries ... So they are big risks if we don't do anything. (Interview with author 2016 Tokyo)

This investment of resources into transnational activism by NGOs in the lead-up to the Tokyo Games has been particularly evident in the targeting of the timber trade. Japanese corporations have long been under scrutiny for their timber procurement practices and the increasingly complex supply chains they support (e. g., Dauvergne 1997). The companies have often pleaded ignorance about what happens at some links in these supply chains – for example, about illegal logging, dispossession of lands, and violence against locals protesting the activities (Lester 2019). In the lead-up to the Games, international NGOs such as Global Witness, the Environmental Investigation Agency, and the Rainforest Action Network have developed campaigns with local Japanese environmental groups to produce reports and hold workshops aimed squarely at Japanese corporate buyers of these timbers, ensuring that claims of ignorance are no longer valid (e. g., Global Witness 2016).

NGOs have also specifically targeted the Games, and in particular the construction of the symbolic and physical heart of the event – the New National Stadium – which

2 These interviews, and the evidence produced by them, were supported by the Australian Research Council Discovery Program (DP150103454 Transnational Environmental Campaigns in the Asia-Australia Region 2015–2018).

began in Shinjuku in 2016. Accusations have been made that Japanese construction companies have used cheap, unsustainable, uncertified, and even illegally sourced timber from the rainforests of Borneo for concrete formwork in building the stadium, and that they have entered into business deals with Malaysian and Indonesian timber companies known for their poor environmental and human rights records (Sim 2018). When these accusations are widely circulated in international news stories, their "shareability" is ensured by accompanying images of an orangutan mother and baby (Neslen 2018). Such images undermine the carefully constructed narratives of sustainability constructed by the Games organizing committee. Indeed, the organizing committee's statement that construction practices meet the "sustainability criteria specified in our sustainable sourcing code" (Neslen 2018) suffers from what counter-claims and responses to media scandal have long experienced: being buried down story or at least one click away.

5 Conclusion: imagining a post-carbon media sports cultural complex

There is an inescapable problem in the use and operation of media sport as a platform for pro-environmental communication. *As currently organized and constituted, media sport crystallizes the dilemma of promoting environmental awareness through popular events, activities, technologies and infrastructures that also generate their own significant ecological footprints.* This is the material and mediatized reality of social life lived in carbon-intensive systems, economies, and societies, and we are all a part of the problem, given the entanglement of human activity, capitalist modes of production, globalized markets, media technology and communications networks, symbolic power, and the environment (Maxwell and Miller 2012; Peters 2015; TePoel 2017). This chapter has demonstrated that it is essential to trace how these entanglements operate in the context of media sport and to identify where and how progress is being gained and lost.

The harder step is to begin imagining what a *post-carbon* media sports cultural complex looks like and assess how media sport might contribute to a fundamental transformation in the resource and energy foundations of global society (Rowe 2004; Urry 2011). Given their expertise and interests, scholars and students working across the various sub-fields of sport communication and media are well-positioned to reimagine the relationship between sport and nature, explain the significance and consequences of their deep interconnectedness, and communicate arguments and stories that both reflect and lead to pro-environmental actions and change. As hinted at earlier in this chapter, nothing less than the future of sport on our planet is at stake – #noplanetnoplay.

References

About Nube. 2019. *Nube*. https://nubeusa.com/pages/about (1 August 2019).
Bale, John. 1994. *Landscapes of modern sport*. Leicester: Leicester University Press.
Barthes, Roland. 1977. *Image music text*. London: Fontana.
Beck, Ulrich. 2009. *World at risk*. Cambridge: Polity Press.
Blaustein, Lew. 2017. Green-sports startups: Nube9 and the circular economy. *Green Sports Blog*, 15 June. https://greensportsblog.com/green-sports-startups-nube-9-and-the-circular-economy/ (19 June 2018).
Blaustein, Lew. 2018a. South Pole measure carbon footprint for FIFA World Cup, UEFA Euro Championships; helps members of auto racing's FIA offset emissions. *Green Sports Blog*, 21 March. https://greensportsblog.com/south-pole-measures-carbon-footprint-for-fifa-world-cup-uefa-euro-championships-and-fia-motorsports (21 March 2018).
Blaustein, Lew. 2018b. GSB eco-scorecard #3: Catching up with green-sports leaders on the field. *Green Sports Blog*, 9 January. https://greensportsblog.com/gsb-eco-scorecard-3-catching-up-with-green-sports-leaders-on-the-field (3 February 2018).
Bourdieu, Pierre. 2013 [1977]. *Outline of a theory of practice* (trans. Richard Nice). Cambridge: Cambridge University Press.
Bullock, Graham. 2017. *Green grades: Can information save the earth?* Cambridge, MA: MIT Press.
Carbon footprint methodology for the Olympic Games. 2018. International Olympic Committee. https://library.olympic.org/Default/doc/SYRACUSE/184686/carbon-footprint-methodology-for-the-olympic-games-international-olympic-committee?_lg=fr-FR (1 April 2020).
Cottle, Simon. 2013. Environmental conflict in a global, media age: Beyond dualisms. In Libby Lester & Brett Hutchins (eds.), *Environmental conflict and the media*, 19–33. New York: Peter Lang.
Couldry, Nick & Andreas Hepp. 2017. *The mediated construction of reality*. Cambridge: Polity Press.
Cuthbertson, Debbie. 2018. How the MCG got ahead of the recycling game. *The Age*, 4 May. https://www.theage.com.au/environment/sustainability/how-the-mcg-got-ahead-of-the-recycling-game-20180503-p4zd5f.html (5 May 2018).
Dauvergne, Peter. 1997. *Shadows in the forest: Japan and the politics of timber in Southeast Asia*. Cambridge, MA: MIT Press.
Dayan, Daniel & Elihu Katz. 1992. *Media events: The live broadcasting of history*. Cambridge, MA: Harvard University Press.
Dryzek, John S. 2013. *The politics of the earth: Environmental discourses*, 3rd edn. Oxford: Oxford University Press.
Edwards, Harry. 1979. The Olympic Project for Human Rights: An assessment ten years later. *The Black Scholar* 10(6–7). 2–8.
Elder, Adam. 2017. The world's greenest sports team is a century-old football club in a tiny English town. *The New Yorker*, 21 September. https://www.newyorker.com/sports/sporting-scene/the-worlds-greenest-sports-team-is-a-century-old-football-club-in-a-tiny-english-town (22 September 2017).
Engels, Friedrich. 1946 [1925]. *The dialectics of nature* (trans. & ed. Clemens P. Dutt). London: Lawrence and Wishart.
EPA Green Power Partnership national top 100. 2020. *US Environmental Protection Agency*, 19 October. https://www.epa.gov/sites/production/files/2018-06/documents/top100_april2018.pdf (14 November 2020).
EPL sustainability table. 2020. Sport Positive Summit. https://www.sportpositivesummit.com/epl-sustainability-table/ (1 April 2020).
Evers, Clifton W. 2019. Polluted leisure. *Leisure Sciences* 41(5): 423–440.

Former Wallabies captain David Pocock arrested at NSW coal mine protest in Leard State Forest. 2014. *ABC/Reuters*, 29 November. https://www.abc.net.au/news/2014-11-30/former-wallabies-captain-pocock-arrested-at-coal-mine-protest/5929024 (14 November 2020).

Framework for the preparation of the Olympic and Paralympic Games following postponement. 2020. *Tokyo 2020*, 16 April. https://tokyo2020.org/en/news/framework-for-the-preparation-of-the-olympic-and-paralympic-games-following-post (16 April 2020).

Friedman, Uri. 2016. The saddest Olympic celebration. *The Atlantic*, 17 August. https://www.theatlantic.com/international/archive/2016/08/david-katoatau-olympics-kiribati/496175 (4 June 2018).

Gabrys, Jennifer. 2011. *Digital rubbish: A natural history of electronics*. Ann Arbor, MI: University of Michigan Press.

Gillespie, Tarleton. 2010. The politics of "platforms." *New Media and Society* 12(3). 347–364.

Gillespie, Tarleton. 2018. *Custodians of the internet: Platforms, content moderation, and the hidden decisions that shape social media*. New Haven, CT: Yale University Press.

Global Witness. 2016. Wilful ignorance. *Global Witness*, 21 April. https://www.globalwitness.org/en/reports/wilful-ignorance (12 February 2018).

Grano, Daniel A. & Michael L. Butterworth (eds.) 2019. *Sport, rhetoric, and political struggle*. New York: Peter Lang.

Hutchins, Brett. & Libby Lester. 2015. Theorizing the enactment of mediatized environmental conflict. *International Communication Gazette* 77(4). 337–358.

ICAO carbon emissions calculator. 2019. International *Civil Aviation Organization*. https://www.icao.int/environmental-protection/CarbonOffset/Pages/default.aspx (2 June 2019).

IOC sustainability strategy. 2017. International *Olympic Committee*. https://www.olympic.org/sustainability (1 April 2020).

Kassimeris, Christos. 2011. Fascism, separatism and the *ultràs*: Discrimination in Italian football. *Soccer & Society* 12(5). 677–688.

Katoatau, David. 2016. Save our country. http://www.climate.gov.ki/wp-content/uploads/2015/09/ANNEX-2-David-Katoatau.pdf (4 June 2018).

Kay, Stanley. 2019. Winter is going: How climate change is imperiling outdoor sporting heritage. *Sports Illustrated*, 22 April. https://www.si.com/nhl/2019/04/22/climate-change-canada-winter-sports-hockey-backyard-rinks (26 April 2019).

Kellison, Timothy. B. & Sungil Hong. 2015. The adoption and diffusion of pro-environmental stadium design. *European Sport Management Quarterly* 15(2). 249–269.

Klein, Naomi. 2014. *This changes everything: Capitalism vs the climate*. New York: Simon & Schuster.

Lester, Libby. 2016. Media and social licence: On being publicly useful in the Tasmanian forests conflict. *Forestry* 89(5). 542–551.

Lester, Libby. 2019. *Global trade and mediatised environmental protest: The view from here*. London: Palgrave Macmillan.

Lester, Libby & Brett Hutchins (eds.) 2013. *Environmental conflict and the media*. New York: Peter Lang.

Lievrouw, Leah A. 2014. Materiality and media in communication and technology studies. In Tarleton Gillespie, Pablo J. Boczkowski & Kirsten A. Foot (eds.), *Media technologies: Essays on communication, materiality, and society*, 21–51. Cambridge, MA: MIT Press.

Malmodin, Jens & Dag Lundén. 2018. The energy and carbon footprint of the global ICT and E&M sectors 2010–2015. *Sustainability* 10(9). 3027–3058.

Martin, Lisa. 2019. Climate change set to disrupt Australia's summer sports calendar. *The Guardian*, 6 February. https://www.theguardian.com/environment/2019/feb/06/climate-change-set-to-disrupt-australias-summer-sports-calendar (7 February 2019).

Maxwell, Richard & Toby Miller. 2012. *Greening the media*. Oxford: Oxford University Press.

Maxwell, Richard & Toby Miller. 2020. *How green is your smartphone?* Cambridge: Polity Press.

McCullough, Brian P. & Timothy B. Kellison. 2018. An introduction to environmental sustainability and sport. In Brian P. McCullough & Timothy B. Kellison (eds.), *Routledge handbook of sport and the environment*, 3–10. London: Routledge.

McCurry, Justin. 2018. Japan apologises for captive dolphin show during Olympic sailing test run. *The Guardian*, 12 September. https://www.theguardian.com/sport/2018/sep/12/tokyo-2020-organisers-apologise-for-taking-sailors-to-captive-dolphin-show (1 September 2019).

McKie, R., M. Savage & P. Cornwall. 2019. As English fans get set to cross Europe, anger rises at football's carbon bootprint. *The Guardian*, 12 May. Available: https://www.theguardian.com/environment/2019/may/11/anger-carbon-bootprint-english-football-finals-champions-league-europa-league (accessed 12 May 2019).

Miller, Toby. 2018. *Greenwashing sport*. London: Routledge.

Millington, Brad & Brian Wilson. 2016. *The greening of golf: Sport, globalization and the environment*. Manchester: Manchester University Press.

Millington, Brad & Brian Wilson. 2017. Contested terrain and terrain that contests: Donald Trump, golf's environmental politics, and a challenge to anthropocentrism in physical cultural studies. *International Review for the Sociology of Sport* 52(8): 910–923.

Montañola, Sandy & Aurélie Olivesi (eds.) 2016. *Gender testing in sport: Ethics, cases and controversies*. London: Routledge.

Morris-Suzuki, Tessa. 2011. *Beyond computopia: Information, automation and democracy in Japan*. Abingdon: Routledge.

Mosco, Vincent. 2014. *To the cloud: Big data in a turbulent world*. Boulder, CO: Paradigm.

Münter, Leilani. 2019. Official site of Leilani Münter. http://www.leilani.green (4 June 2019).

Murdock, Graham. 2017. Conclusion: One month in the life of the planet – carbon capitalism and the struggle for the commons. In Benedetta Brevini & Graham Murdock (eds.), *Carbon capitalism and communication: Confronting climate crisis*, 207–219. New York: Palgrave Macmillan.

Murphy, Patrick D. 2017. *The media commons: Globalization and environmental discourses*. Chicago, IL: University of Illinois Press.

Nash, Christopher & Wendy Bacon. 2013. "That sinking feeling": Climate change, journalism and small island states. In Libby Lester & Brett Hutchins (eds.), *Environmental conflict and the media*, 245–259. New York: Peter Lang.

National Grid experience 600MW "pick up" during England's World Cup opener. 2018. *Network*, 19 June. https://networks.online/gphsn/news/1001102/national-grid-experience-600mw-%E2%80%98pick-%E2%80%99-england%E2%80%99-world-cup-opener (2 August 2019).

Neslen, Arthur. 2018. Tokyo Olympics venues built with wood from threatened rainforests. *The Guardian*, 30 November. https://www.theguardian.com/environment/2018/nov/29/tokyo-olympics-venues-built-with-wood-from-threatened-rainforests (1 September 2019).

Peters, John D. 2015. *The marvelous clouds: Towards a philosophy of elemental media*. Chicago, IL: University of Chicago Press.

Play it forward: Innovating for the next generation. 2018. *NHL.com*. http://sustainability.nhl.com/report/#!/home/index (2 February 2019).

Price, Monroe E. 2008. On seizing the Olympic platform. In Monroe E. Price & Daniel Dayan (eds.), *Owning the Olympics: Narratives of the new China*, 86–114. Ann Arbor, MI: University of Michigan Press.

Protect Our Winters. 2019. About POW. https://protectourwinters.org/about-us (3 February 2019).

Rossiter, Ned. 2016. *Software, infrastructure, media: A media theory of logistical nightmares*. New York: Routledge.

Rowe, David. 2004. *Sport, culture and the media: The unruly trinity*, 2nd edn. Maidenhead: Open University Press.
Serazio, Michael. 2019. *The power of sports: Media and spectacle in American culture*. New York: New York University Press.
Sim, Walter. 2018. Environment group accuses Tokyo Olympics organisers of using illegally sourced wood. *Straits Times*, 12 November. https://www.straitstimes.com/asia/east-asia/environment-group-accuses-tokyo-olympics-organisers-of-using-illegally-sourced-wood (1 September 2019).
Singhal, Arvind & Everett M. Rogers. 1999. *Entertainment-education: A communication strategy for social change*. Mahwah, NJ: Lawrence Erlbaum.
Sports for climate action framework. 2018. *United Nations Climate Change*. https://unfccc.int/sites/default/files/resource/Sports_for_Climate_Action_Declaration_and_Framework.pdf (19 January 2019).
Sustainability. n.d. *Tokyo 2020*. https://tokyo2020.org/en/games/sustainability (1 September 2019).
TePoel, Dain. 2017. Digital sport history, with costs: An ecocentric critique. *Journal of Sport History* 44(2). 350–366.
The "carbon bootprint" of Euro 2016. 2016. The Carbon Trust. https://www.carbontrust.com/news/2016/06/the-carbon-bootprint-of-euro-2016-carbon-trust-reveals-which-nations-fans-have-lowest-carbon-footprint (19 August 2016).
The greenest football club in the world? 2017. *FIFA.TV*, 11 May. https://www.youtube.com/watch?v=BHErK7J9aAo (13 March 2019).
Tokyo 2020 medal project: Towards an innovative future for all. 2019. *Tokyo 2020*. https://tokyo2020.org/en/games/medals/project (1 August 2019).
Urry, John. 2011. *Climate change and society*. Cambridge: Polity Press.
van Es, Karin. 2017. *The future of live*. Cambridge: Polity Press.
Vidal, John. 2018. The plastics crisis is more urgent than you know: Recycling bottles won't fix it. *The Guardian*, 29 March. https://www.theguardian.com/commentisfree/2018/mar/28/plastic-crisis-urgent-recycling-bottles-no-fix (30 March 2018).
Warshaw, Andrew. 2018. Doing the right thing. Forest Green Rovers are world's first UN-certified carbon neutral club. *Inside World Football*, 1 August. http://www.insideworldfootball.com/2018/08/01/right-thing-forest-green-rovers-worlds-first-un-certified-carbon-neutral-club (2 August 2018).
Wenner, Lawrence A. 1998. Playing the MediaSport game. In Lawrence A. Wenner (ed.), *MediaSport*, 3–13. London: Routledge.
Wentworth, Adam. 2018. LA Galaxy and MLS aim to fight plastic waste with recycled jersey. *Climate Action*, 12 April. http://www.climateaction.org/news/la-galaxy-aims-to-fight-plastic-waste-with-recycled-jersey (12 April 2018).

Markus Stauff and Travis Vogan

21 Legitimizing and institutionalizing eSports in the NBA 2K League

Abstract: Launched in 2018, the NBA 2K League is a National Basketball Association eSports subsidiary centered on the popular *NBA 2K* video game series. The 2K League enables the NBA, an organization that has more aggressively embraced trends in emerging media than its North American peers, to infiltrate new markets and platforms through investing in eSports. Meanwhile, the 2K League helps to legitimize eSports by attaching the niche activity to an established sports brand. This chapter uses the 2K League to explore how eSports' development and institutionalization are changing sports organizations' relationship to media while preserving – and even strengthening – sports' significance and role in commercial media culture.

Keywords: eSports; video games; National Basketball Association; media convergence; branding

1 Introduction

> "Think of the eBulls against the eKnicks."
> – Adam Silver, NBA commissioner (Needleman 2017)

> "When you see 200 million-plus eSports viewers worldwide, if that doesn't get your attention, you should go into another business; maybe the Salvation Army, Kris Kringle at Christmas ringing a bell on a corner."
> – Peter Guber, Golden State Warriors owner (Youngmisuk and Wolf 2018)

In April 2018, the athlete who ranked highest in the world in "social interactions" – a measurement of social media attention – was not LeBron James, Lionel Messi, or Serena Williams. It was Tyler "Ninja" Blevins, who is most famous for playing the video game *Fortnite*. *Forbes* reported that Blevins was making approximately $500,000 a month by streaming his *Fortnite* sessions and competing in tournaments (Heitner 2018; Paumgarten 2018).

Arguably the fastest growing segment of the sport industry, eSports expands on and formalizes competitive video gaming, which has been around as long as gaming itself.[1] Like golf and poker, eSports is a "participant sport" in which consumers

1 As arcade gaming emerged in the 1970s, high scores allowed gamers playing on the same machine to outperform each other. Networked computing extended these competitions, and the Internet allowed

https://doi.org/10.1515/9783110660883-021

partake in the same games as professionals. The professional gamers' relatability is amplified by the interactivity of eSports' streamed presentation on platforms like the Amazon-owned Twitch, which includes chat overlays that enable viewers to comment and garner responses from the gamers, exchanges that are as important to building gamers' valuable personal brands as their gameplay. Twitch and other livestreaming platforms allow anybody to share their gameplay, build a community, and learn from others. For the most prominent gamers, these interactive platforms offer income through advertising revenue and donations. Organized tournaments reach global audiences that rival established mega sport events. In 2017 and 2018, for instance, the *League of Legends* World Championship attracted around 100 million viewers compared to the Super Bowl's respective 111 and 103 million (Mickunas 2019).

Far from online-only events, such prominent eSports tournaments are now also regularly broadcast by traditional TV networks and staged in stadiums that otherwise house traditional sports. An August 2016 *League of Legends* tournament sold out Toronto's Air Canada Centre in 34 seconds, faster than any event – sports or not – in the venue's history. As Brett Hutchins claims, eSports uniquely redefines sport's traditional and symbiotic relationship with media. Unlike media that represent sports or sports that media represent, eSports constitutes "sport as media" and is the "production of the logic of media" (Hutchins 2008: 857).

The eSports industry – an economy composed of media rights, advertising, ticket sales, and merchandise – generated $865 million in 2018 and the Amsterdam-based market research firm Newzoo estimates that it will grow to more than US $1.5 billion by 2021 (Pannekeet 2019; Webster 2018; Cioletti 2018). Beyond their escalating profitability, eSports are uniquely positioned to attract the coveted young male demographic that is becoming "harder to reach with conventional TV advertisements" (Wingfield 2014). What's more, Kenon A. Brown and colleagues (2018) found that eSports consumers are unusually devoted to their favorite sport, and potentially to those brands that attach themselves to it. After all, in eSports participants both purchase games and provide "free labor" through their play that helps to build the community and attracts other participants, who purchase more games and provide their own playful and community-building labor (Johnson and Woodcock 2019; N. T. Taylor 2016). As Tobias Sherman, head of eSports at the talent agency WME-IMG, bluntly put it, "If you are a CMO [Chief Marketing Officer] and you are not in eSports in 2017, you are going to risk getting fired" (Schultz 2017: 12).

Amid this combination of growing popularity, increasingly professional competition, and new interactive infrastructures, eSports developed an ambivalent relationship to the established sports industry and its long running efforts to adapt to the

---

for real-time competitions. By the 2000s gaming tournaments were organized that allowed for professional and sponsored careers. This happened first in South Korea, where gaming was harnessed as a tool of governmental and industrial IT initiatives, but quickly became a global phenomenon (see T. L. Taylor 2006: 19–26).

transforming media landscape. On the one hand, eSports imitates audience building strategies from traditional sports – the serialized and hierarchized system of competitions, big live events with stars and branding, and so forth – and aggressively adapts them to a convergent media environment geared toward a younger, tech-savvy audience. The interactive, participatory features of streaming platforms and the constant innovation of game play contrast the organizational and cultural inertia of established sports. As such, eSports threatens to lure consumers away from legacy sports. On the other hand, the traditional media sport industry increasingly enrolls eSports as an extension to complement and intensify existing cross-media branding strategies. While the competitive playing of first-person shooter and action-oriented real-time strategy games have encountered difficulty integrating into sports culture, sports-themed games blur the boundaries between the traditional sports media industry and eSports. Moreover, eSports is organized, branded, and culturally legitimized through its entanglement with famous teams, leagues, and broadcasters. It thereby remediates established narratives and visual forms into streaming media platforms.

Launched in 2018, the National Basketball Association's NBA 2K League illustrates this ambivalence and eSports' evolution from marginal to mainstream. The 2K League is an NBA subsidiary centered on Take-Two Interactive's popular *NBA 2K* video game series, the second-most popular sports video game franchise after EA Sports' *FIFA*. The 17 NBA franchises that participated in the inaugural season have parallel *NBA 2K* teams that compete in front of live audiences and on Twitch, which partnered with the NBA for the effort. The 2K League enables the NBA, an organization that has more aggressively embraced trends in emerging media than its North American peers, to infiltrate new markets and platforms.[2] Meanwhile, the NBA 2K League helps to legitimize eSports by attaching the niche activity to an established sports brand. Beyond simultaneously fueling the NBA's growth and fostering eSports' mainstreaming, the 2K League illustrates how eSports' development and institutionalization are changing sports organizations' broader relationship to media while preserving – and even strengthening – sports' significance and role in commercial media culture.

2 Sporting legitimacy in eSports

While its reputation is changing, eSports is still often marginalized in mainstream sports culture and beleaguered by stereotypes of gamers as antisocial misfits neglecting healthier and more serious pursuits (Li 2016: 41; Crawford and Gosling 2009: 51). The prevalence of violent and war-oriented games in eSports does not help its reputa-

2 The NBA began distributing game highlights on Twitter in 2013, using Instagram as a "storytelling platform" in 2015, and experimenting with virtual reality coverage in 2017 (Popper 2013; O'Kane 2015; Sarconi 2017).

tion. Traditional sports organizations – suppressing their own histories of corruption, violence, and exclusion – often promote themselves as peacemaking and edifying sites of cultural production. These purist and dubious discourses further fuel traditional sports' denigration of eSports as artificial and depraved. Reinhard Grindel, president of the German Football Association (DFB), derided eSports as an impoverishment of traditional sports (Krempl 2018). Similarly, International Olympic Committee (IOC) president Thomas Bach sanctimoniously rationalized excluding eSports from the vaunted Olympic Games by asserting, "We cannot have in the Olympic program a game which is promoting violence or discrimination" (Wade 2018).[3]

Reflecting these turf wars, the little scholarship yet produced about eSports has focused mostly on whether and under what circumstances it might be considered a legitimate sport (Hallmann and Giel 2018; Jenny et al. 2017). These questions, however, seem unproductive and old-fashioned to those involved in eSports. "The industry is asleep at the switch," said Lee Trink, owner of the eSports team FaZe Clan. "For people my age and older who control a lot of the zeitgeist, the vibe is still 'gamers must be nerds in their parents' basements'" (Bowles 2018). As Alex Lim, secretary of South Korea's International eSports Federation (IESF) added, "Broadcasters, traditional sports, advertisers they are all going to have to get used to the idea that these games and these tournaments are not just a niche activity, but the way that a generation that grew up with very different choices [...] thinks about entertainment" (Lewis and Bradshaw 2017: 9). Ted Leonsis, owner of the NBA's Washington Wizards, even predicted that eSports will eventually become the world's biggest spectator sport. "It will dwarf the NFL [National Football League], it will dwarf the NBA," he declared, "because first and foremost, it is a global phenomenon" (Schuster 2017). These accounts of an economic and symbolic rivalry notwithstanding, eSports and traditional sports are interrelated not only because of the audience attention for which they compete and the similar target groups they aim to attract, but also because of the increasingly similar ways they organize and mediate competitive events.

Investment analysts for the London-based firm J. Stern likened eSports' growth potential to soccer in the 1990s, but maintained that "for eSports to track a similar path [...] it needs to be more professionally structured, starting with an organized calendar of events and leagues" (Yu 2017). Similarly, Seth E. Jenny and colleagues (2017) identified eSports' lack of familiar institutional characteristics as a key barrier to its acceptance as a bona fide sport. Media ethnographer T. L. Taylor, however, tracks how eSports throughout the past decade has successively established legitimacy through a combination of rhetorical and structural measures that align with traditional sport and media coverage of it (T. L. Taylor 2012: 17, 2018: 138–139).

---

3 In 2016, the Finnish eSports Federation became the first eSports organization to be accepted as an associate member of its national Olympic Committee (Turtiainen, Friman, and Ruotsalainen 2020).

Increasingly, eSports is organized in leagues with unified rules and seasonal schedules that reflect mainstream sports calendars (N. T. Taylor 2016: 298; Roettgers 2011). This follows the pattern of sportification, a process by which leisure activities "assume the structural characteristics of 'sports'" (Elias and Dunning 1986: 151; see also Turtiainen, Friman, and Ruotsalainen 2020). This dynamic impacted more and more playful activities throughout the later 20th century and continues to characterize activities such as skateboarding and snowboarding, which occupy a precarious cultural position somewhere between legitimate, competitive (e. g., Olympic) sport and a lifestyle activity that, in fact, subverts several basic ideas of sports (discipline, etc.).

Additionally, eSports establishes an increasingly rigid demarcation between players and spectators, another characteristic of sportification, and aims more and more at a mediated audience instead of a community of fellow players. This also implies that the actual competitions are augmented by media practices imitating traditional sports coverage (from draw events to post-game interviews) and that the interfaces of computer games are adapted to display relevant knowledge for a broader audience (T. L. Taylor 2018: 159–160).

As eSports emerged, the competitions mainly drew TV coverage from marginal broadcasters that could not afford the rights to marquee sport events. ESPN, for instance, hesitated to give eSports attention. But ESPN's attitude shifted once it noticed the valuable audience eSports was attracting. "Those were young, predominately male consumers," former ESPN president John Skipper remarked, "and that's what matters to us, so we entered the business" (Li 2016: 103–104). Thus, eSports is part of a longer history of using sports to create and address a principally male audience. Ironically, though, gaming – because of the lack of physical toughness associated with it – is at once a stereotypical symbol of emasculation and an instrument that broadcasters use to capture young male audiences.

ESPN began covering eSports competitions in 2014 on its less prominent appendages like ESPN2 and the streaming service ESPN3. While ESPN's eSports coverage drew some backlash from traditionalists, this content, as Skipper surmised, tapped into a growing and devoted audience that overlapped with its primary viewership. Consequently, *ESPN.com* launched a permanent eSports section in 2016 (Gaudiosi 2016). In 2018, ESPN made the *Overwatch* League Grand Finals the first eSports event to be carried live in prime time on its flagship channel. Beyond courting the elusive young male demographic, ESPN's coverage further legitimizes eSports by placing it into the context of the conventional sports ESPN typically covers and building recognition as such among its viewers and advertisers.

In part because of these shifts, eSports is slowly gaining acceptance from institutions that confer sporting status. As early as 2013, the US State Department began granting visas to professional gamers under the same program that covers traditional athletes. Shortly thereafter, a smattering of American universities created eSports teams, some of which award scholarships to top gamers, and some that create academic courses and programs on eSports (Anderson 2019). Though the university eSports teams are not sanctioned by the NCAA (National Collegiate Athletic Association), in 2017 the NCAA's ruling board of governors began to discuss potentially including eSports (Schonbrun 2017). Along these lines, the global eSports community identified the need to augment South Korea's IESF by forming the World eSports Association (WESA) in 2016, which approves teams, ensures players are fairly compensated, and works with anti-doping agencies to curb the use of performance-enhancing drugs. Subsequently, the 2018 Asian Games in Indonesia – the second largest multisport competition after the Olympics – included eSports as a demonstration sport, which means the medals earned in the competitions do not register on official medal counts. Extending this gradual trend toward acceptance, the 2022 Asia Games in Hangzhou, China will feature eSports as an official medal event. Despite Thomas Bach's stated aversion toward eSports' violence, the IOC is beginning to consider whether eSports may someday have a future in the Olympics (Crook 2018).

3 Sports organizations and the gaming industry

Sports organizations and the gaming industry share a longstanding commercial entanglement through the sports-themed games that publicize leagues and offer them additional income through licensing. Sports organizations provide the game industry a "built-in audience" and help to convince consumers to buy updated games each year that reflect seasonal cycles. Likewise, sports video games cultivate fan engagement with the organizations they simulate.

Often, though, the biggest video game tournaments were organized around non-sports themed games. Nevertheless, some traditional sports organizations quickly identified eSports as a convenient and profitable way to diversify and expand their audience and started investing in eSports by acquiring pre-existing teams that mainly competed in a broad variety of non-sports games. In 2015, the Turkish club Besiktas JK bought Aces High eSports Club and renamed it Besiktas eSports Club. Besiktas was quickly joined by soccer clubs like Brazil's Remo and Santos, Germany's VfL Wolfsburg and FC Schalke, France's Paris Saint-Germain, England's Manchester City, and the Netherlands' Ajax.

American sports executives followed the lead of their European counterparts and similarly focused their initial attention on eSports teams that competed in non-sports games. Los Angeles Rams owner Stan Kroenke, New England Patriots owner Robert Kraft, and New York Mets COO Jeff Wilpon bought separate *Overwatch* teams in 2017. NBA owners and executives were even more bullish on eSports than their peers in football and baseball. The Philadelphia 76ers, Miami Heat, Houston Rockets, Milwaukee Bucks, Washington Wizards, and Golden State Warriors all invested in eSports between 2016 and 2017. "We see great asset appreciation quickly," observed Wizards owner Ted Leonsis, who bought Team Liquid in partnership with Warriors owner Peter

Guber in October 2017. "To put that in perspective, when Peter Guber and I bought Team Liquid, it was valued higher than when I bought the [National Hockey League's] Washington Capitals in 1999. At that time, the Caps were 30 years old, and the NHL was 70 years old. These were established brands" (Aldridge 2018). Philadelphia 76ers CEO Scott O'Neill compared eSports' emergence to the Ultimate Fighting Championship in the 1990s – "coming almost out of nowhere, very quickly" (Yu 2017: A12).

By now, sports organizations' investment in eSports has been more systematically applied to sports-themed games that simulate and complement their primary products. In 2016, the top Dutch soccer league, the Eredevisie, formed the eDevisie, an eSports league based on *FIFA*. The Eredevisie obliged each of its member clubs to participate in the eDevisie by creating corresponding eSports teams that would compete via *FIFA* during the 2016–2017 season (Zantingh 2017). Such expansion to eSports was not always welcomed by fans of the traditional sport. Supporters of Switzerland's Berner SC, for instance, protested the club's entry into eSports by heaving game controllers onto the pitch and displaying a banner that read "Pull the plug on eSports" (Holland 2018). Yet, the institutionalized convergence of eSports and traditional sports composes a promising strategy to cope with a changing media landscape.

4 "Our fourth league"

Arguably the most ambitious eSports concern run by a professional sports organization, the NBA 2K League expands on the eDevisie and builds on its owners' earlier investment in various eSports. The 2K League complements the NBA's gradual expansion through the past decade by staging exhibition games across the globe, nurturing the WNBA and the developmental G-League, and venturing into virtual reality. "When you are able to aggregate that kind of audience," 76ers CEO Scott O'Neill said of eSports, "I think certainly there's a business to be had. In a nutshell, we have an organization that looks to be innovative and progressive. We have an ownership group that always likes to explore new and exciting opportunities" (Chin 2018). 2K League managing director Brendan Donohue suggests the upstart will specifically cater to the NBA and *NBA 2K*'s increasingly global following. "What I would say is the reason we think we have a chance with all our demographics is our game, more than any other in eSports, is globally recognizable," he explained. "Whether you're in Texas or in Africa, you know the NBA" (Aldridge 2018).

As with sports video game franchises like *FIFA* and *Madden NFL*, *NBA 2K* has driven younger fans to the professional league since its launch in 1999. Dallas Mavericks owner Mark Cuban acknowledges the vast number of NBA fans who built lasting attachments to the league through playing *NBA 2K* and views the 2K League as an obvious way to deepen that connection. "I can't tell you how many fans know and love the Mavs because they play *2K*," he says (Aldridge 2018). Speaking on behalf of the NBA, Cuban told *USA Today*, "We think we can take traditional NBA fans, *2K* fans and strengthen the bond they have to the NBA" (Game On! 2018).

The 2K League's partnership with the streaming and social media platform Twitch expands on the interactivity common in eSports – a quality the NBA's broadcast partners have attempted to develop with practices like in-game interviews and sideline microphones but are not able to reproduce through traditional TV coverage and the protocols that guide it. The 2K League streams include split-screen displays that show both the game and the players as they compete and collaborate. Rather than farming out broadcasting duties, the NBA has hired its own Twitch commentators – called "casters" in eSports lingo. Here, eSports adds to a broader trend in which leagues and federations aim to gain greater control by producing "their own 'approved' television coverage of their signature events, including the Olympics and [FIFA] World Cup Finals" (Milne 2016: 5). These in-house commentators are as involved in promoting the 2K League as they are in explaining its events.

Additionally, the streams include chat overlays that allow viewers to remark on the competitions and interact with the casters. "That's what attracts the millennial audience," said marketing executive Dario Raciti of the interactive Twitch streams (Katz 2018). The NBA's partnership with Twitch offers the 2K League competitions for free across the globe and in places where telecasts of the basketball games might be difficult to access. "The Twitches and YouTubes are unwired, available to people throughout the world," Ted Leonsis remarked (Aldridge 2018). This is particularly valuable in the Asian market, which is both the center of professional eSports and the region where the NBA's fanbase is most rapidly expanding. While the spread of US sports brands is dependent on facilities and access to media coverage (and susceptible to international political tensions), the availability of game consoles and platforms like Twitch make these global ambitions easier to realize.

The NBA carefully brands the 2K League as a vital part of the organization rather than an experimental gimmick. "From the NBA's standpoint, this is our fourth league," remarked commissioner Adam Silver. "Of course, we have the NBA, the WNBA and the G League, and now this is the fourth league in our family, and that's exactly as we're treating it: one more professional league" (Aldridge 2018; Rasetti 2018). The NBA organized a worldwide competition to recruit eligible 2K League players that started with roughly 72,000 gamers – a process that both reproduces the meritocratic ideology of competitive sports and courts media coverage in the different countries the players represent.[4]

The 2K League winnowed the competitors down to 250 hopefuls and invited them to a league combine that consisted of skills tests, scrimmages, and other competitions. Finally, it shaved that group of 250 down to 102 – enough for each of the league's 17

4 For instance, an interview with a German gamer who made it to the 2K league was published in Germany's most important weekly news magazine, *Der Spiegel* (Zander and Klitzsch 2018).

teams to draft six players. The 2K League draft mimicked the NBA's ritzy annual ceremony. Like the NBA draft, the 2K League draft took place at New York City's Madison Square Garden and Adam Silver announced the picks. The players in attendance, like their NBA counterparts, wore formal attire and joined Silver on the podium for a photo op after being selected. While the 2K League draft resembled the NBA's annual ritual, the players' salaries are appreciably lower. 2K Leaguers earn between $32,000 and $35,000 plus benefits with the opportunity to make additional money through tournaments that occur over the course of the season. The NBA also houses teams together in the city where their franchises are based to maximize synergies between 2K League teams and their NBA affiliates.

While 2K League players make less over the course of an entire season than many NBA players earn in a single game, Knicks Gaming point guard Adam Kudiemati, who plays under the handle "iamadamthe1st," maintains that "the NBA is constantly letting us know that we're part of the family."[5] The 2K League instituted a multifaceted infrastructure for teams that includes coaches, general managers, scouts, and trainers. It also claims to offer gamers the same professional resources it gives NBA, WNBA, and G-League players. "We'll treat them with the respect that they deserve," said Washington Wizards executive Zach Leonsis. "We'll give them access to our facilities and trainers. We want them to be comfortable, we want them to be healthy, we want them to be professionals so that they can play at the very top skill level" (Schuster 2017). The new league instituted a rookie transition program similar to the NBA's required orientation that teaches incoming players about the challenges professional athletes face, such as living away from home, dealing with fame, handling social media, and keeping healthy. The 2K League program added a component devoted to vision and eye care, which pose the greatest physical risks to eSports athletes. Donohue suggested this professional training was particularly important for the 2K Leaguers, who, unlike players entering the NBA, have not received the same degree of media attention elite amateur athletes attract prior to turning professional. "We have 102 players that really didn't have the path to professional sports that many athletes have," he stated. "Playing at a major college or university, or being on TV previously, or talking to the media – all those types of things probably help with the transition" (Darcy 2018). The NBA, then, works to treat its 2K League members as bona fide athletes and accommodates the unique needs that come along with the nascent profession.

The 2K League further reflects its parent organization by having the teams adopt names and logos that mirror their sister franchises. The Golden State Warriors 2K League affiliate, for instance, is called Warriors Gaming Squad, and the Miami Heat affiliate is named Heat Check Gaming. The team logos combine the affiliated franchises' color schemes and emblems with a computerized look that evokes the mechanized culture of eSports. NBA.com also created webpages for the teams and players

5 Adam Kudeimati, interview with author, 24 August 2018.

that – like the NBA's main website – include league news, schedules, standings, and statistics. The logos ensure the 2K League resembles the NBA while the webpages filter it through the familiar quantitative frameworks that organize traditional sports.

The 2K Leaguers compete as the individualized avatars they established before joining the league. The Twitch casts display a combination of the virtual world of the game play and the people playing the game. During matches small close-ups of all ten players and their nicknames are inserted on the upper edge of the frame. Their avatars – with each gamer only controlling one corresponding player in the game – are also marked with their respective handles. This allows clear accountability of each player's performance. Additionally, the audience sees the gamers' focused faces while playing. During short game breaks, the players are displayed full screen and can be observed communicating with each other, including, in rare cases, conflicts between the competing teams. The casters also switch between commenting on the moves of the virtual players and the performance and behavior of the actual players. Of course, the players are also asked to comment on replays after the games. This mimics the visuals and rhetoric of traditional sports coverage and increases the relatability and authenticity of the gamers, who otherwise tend to become invisible behind the spectacle of the simulated game play.

Most 2K League players were obscure, even within the eSports and *NBA 2K* community, before being drafted. Their branded connection to the NBA, in the words of *SportsBusiness Journal*'s Ben Fischer, provides "legitimacy and clarity" to otherwise unfamiliar consumers (Fischer 2018). The NBA, for example, secured each 2K League player a verified Twitter account immediately after the draft, a marker of prestige in social media reserved only for celebrities determined to be in danger of potential impersonation. In doing so, it suggests these players have social status on par with mainstream athletes. As Taylor found, eSports "fandom is often regarded either quizzically or suspiciously" in contrast to the acceptance that mainstream sports fandom – and performances of it like wearing gear and purchasing memorabilia – commonly enjoys in popular culture (T. L. Taylor 2012: 193). The 2K League works against this stigmatized fandom by enveloping an eSports product into a traditional sports league and making sure it is recognized as authentic by that established organization.

Pistons GT point guard Fred "I'm So Far Ahead" Mendoza considers the 2K League to be similar to the original NBA. "We're doing the same thing, it's just in a virtual aspect," he insists.[6] These apparent resemblances, however, are not obvious to those unacquainted with eSports. But the NBA's affiliation with the 2K League imbues the eSports athletes with the organization's identity and symbolic capital. Heat Check Gaming small forward Carlos "Sharpshooterlos" Zayas-Diaz said his friends and family responded to his choice to become a professional eSports athlete differently given the 2K League's formal connection to the NBA and he recounted impressing

6 Fred Mendoza, interview with author, 22 August 2018.

people he meets by telling them he works for the NBA.[7] Other 2K League players left more lucrative and stable careers to join the league in large part because of its relationship to the NBA. Mendoza had a comfortable IT job and Zayas-Diaz worked at a bank. Jazz Gaming small forward Jaishon "Smoove" Scott secured a position working for the United Parcel Service just before learning that he earned a spot in the 2K League.[8] Without hesitation, he declined the permanent job to join the upstart eSports venture. The 2K League, as Kudiemati put it, "legitimized eSports across the board" by affiliating with the NBA.[9]

The 2K League's casters deliberately align its competitions with traditional sports in their Twitch coverage – part of their intersecting efforts to explain the league's competitions and promote the upstart. The stream of the 2K League finals between Knicks Gaming and Heat Check Gaming, a three-game series that Knicks Gaming won, repeatedly used popular sports references to make sense of the teams and their competition. The casters likened Knicks Gaming's surprising late-season run into the championship to the English Premier League soccer team Leicester City's improbable 2016 league title. They also said the championship "feels like those old Knicks–Heat rivalries in the '90s," drawing a direct comparison between the 2K League teams and the decades-long histories of the basketball franchises on which they are based. The coverage augments the effort to legitimize the 2K League by placing it into dialogue with mainstream sports.

Amid its legitimizing alignment with the NBA, the 2K League participates in the less formal and structured culture of eSports. Taylor indicates that authenticity in eSports is characterized in part by players adopting unpolished personas detached from traditional institutions (T. L. Taylor 2012: 189). NBA 2K League publicity fosters this brand of authenticity by stressing players' backstories as regular folks. Reflecting Mendoza's work in IT and Zayas-Diaz's job in banking, the first pick of the 2K League draft, Mavericks Gaming's Artreyo "Dimez" Boyd, drove a tractor trailer before entering the league and Kudiemati was a student at Penn State University. The 2K League uses these biographies to emphasize the players' similarity to those who play video games in their spare time and might aspire to turn professional. "Certainly, we will help amplify our teams through the game competition," Donohue explains, "but in addition, we think where the teams are going to have a huge advantage is growing a large grass roots audience as well. We think there's a huge opportunity, and we've seen it in eSports, growing content around the practice house, where they're living, how they came to be great players" (Aldridge 2018). A 2K League-produced video centering on Portland's Blazers Gaming, for instance, has the team going on an outing after practice to pal around, sample snacks from downtown Portland's food trucks, and

7 Carlos Diaz-Zayas, interview with author, 31 August 2018.

8 Jaishon Scott, interview with author, 5 September 2018.

9 Adam Kudiemati, interview with author, 28 August 2018.

mingle with locals. Similarly, the New York-based Madison Square Garden Network produced a series that offers behind-the-scenes coverage of Knicks Gaming, such as a trip the team took to the Brooklyn Bridge. The theme that unites these promotional videos is the players' status as normal people who are employed by the NBA but do not exhibit the unapproachability and entitlement often associated with wealthy and famous athletes. They are down-to-earth folks who have turned their hobbies into a profession. "I'm just like you," Mendoza modestly says of his fans. "It puts me in awe that someone is in awe of me."[10]

Before the 2K League launched, Silver speculated that the upstart would ensure players' relatability by broadening the range of participants beyond the NBA's decidedly limited horizons. "There's a global pool of players," he told *USA Today*. "They come in all ages and sizes and ethnicities and sexes" (Amick 2017). The 2K League communicated this inclusivity by adopting a variation of the NBA's logo that abandons the silhouette of Jerry West. As Donohue explains, "The absence of that silhouette is important to us because it actually represents the fact that there is no prototypical NBA 2K athlete. Man, woman, tall, short, young, old, domestic, or international" (Yeboah 2017). But only one of the 250 hopefuls the 2K League selected for its draft pool was a woman – Wendy "ALittleLady87" Fleming – and she did not make the final cut to the 102 draft-eligible players. The NBA expressed astonishment at this result and created a task force to guarantee greater diversity in subsequent seasons. We expected there to be women in the draft," said Oris Stuart, the NBA's chief diversity and inclusion officer. "We know women play the game and that they do play and compete at an elite level" (Peterson 2018). The next season, only two women qualified for the 2K League draft, which had more spots than the previous season once the league expanded from 17 to 21 teams. Just one of these players, Chiquita Evans, was drafted when Warriors Gaming selected her in the fourth round.

But the 2K League's exclusively male debut season, and almost entirely male sophomore campaign, reflects a broader gender disparity across traditional and eSports. Taylor indicates that while women participate in eSports, the competitions are "deeply segregated, with women and men generally playing on different teams and in separate tournaments" (T. L. Taylor 2012: 125). The 2K League perpetuates this separation by extending a culture of eSports competitions composed almost solely of male gamers, basing itself on a sports organization constituted entirely of men, and using a video game that exclusively had male avatars until *NBA 2K18* began including WNBA teams. Although this gender segregation characterizes eSports as a whole, the 2K League in particular encourages even fewer women participants than other popular games like *Fortnite* and *Overwatch*, which have included female avatars since their inception.

The 2K League works to build legitimacy – and contributes to the broader effort to legitimize eSports – by simultaneously participating in mainstream sports' branded

10 Fred Mendoza, interview with author, 22 August 2018.

corporatism and eSports' relatable populism. The upstart organization's efforts to establish itself across these spheres illustrate Sarah Banet-Weiser's theorization of how authenticity is constructed and exploited in commercial culture. Banet-Weiser indicates that the concept of authenticity traditionally distances itself from corporate commercial culture. However, she asserts that corporate brands are increasingly engaged in the work of conveying authenticity – often by suppressing their corporate identities and commercial motives. Authenticity, in contemporary brand culture, is characterized by ambivalence and exists both within and outside corporate commercialism (Banet-Weiser 2012). Along these lines, Taylor claims the "public performance of a professional athletic identity sits uneasily within e-sports" and can potentially diminish pro gamers' perceived legitimacy (T. L. Taylor 2012: 220). The 2K League accommodates this sort of sporting identity while still ensconcing it within the NBA's authenticating corporate image. The 2K players represent the NBA – and the traditional sporting culture it signifies – while maintaining the down-to-Earth personas that deliver cultural capital in the context of eSports.

Similar eSports leagues tethered to established professional sports organizations emerged to reproduce the 2K League's synergistic recipe. Major League Soccer founded the eMLS in 2018, which, like the Dutch eDevisie, focuses on *FIFA*. MLS senior director of properties and events James Ruth says that more MLS supporters become fans of soccer through *FIFA* than by watching or even playing the sport. "It's only natural for the MLS to use gaming as a conduit to create great content or different touch points with fans," he explains. Similarly, the National Hockey League established the NHL Gaming Championship in 2018 – an eSports tournament based on EA Sports' *NHL* series. The MLS and NHL follow the NBA's lead by using eSports to broaden their audience beyond traditional sports fans. They also participate in eSports' legitimization through attaching to legacy sports organizations.

Sports institutions have a long history of reinventing themselves and cultivating new fans through emerging media. To do this, they steadily accommodate the shifting media platforms' imperatives to capitalize on the exposure they provide and the audiences they gather. Baseball, for instance, gained its "National Pastime" status by collaborating with print journalists and football became "America's Game" through suiting television's needs. More recently, mainstream sports organizations have become media outlets themselves that administer their own robust, cross-platform, and promotionally-driven media infrastructures. The NBA 2K League continues this longstanding trajectory by extending the National Basketball Association's aggressive engagement with emerging media to stoke its growth into new global markets and demographics. The 2K League marks an important moment in sport's gradual transformation from relying on media to becoming media that drives economic and technological innovation across the industry. It also shows how the new and historically marginalized practice of eSports is legitimized through connecting to traditional sports organizations, the marketing practices surrounding them, and the media coverage they receive.

References

Aldridge, David. 2018. Not just a game: NBA 2K quickly becoming a serious business for all, *NBA.com*, 9 April. http://www.nba.com/article/2018/04/09/morning-tip-nba-2k-league-draft-serious-business-players-owners-fans (15 June 2019).

Amick, Sam. 2017. NBA to announce partnership for first competitive esports gaming league. *USA Today*, 9 February. https://www.usatoday.com/story/sports/nba/2017/02/09/nba-first-competitive-esports-gaming-league-nba2k/97668832/ (15 June 2019).

Anderson, Greta. 2019. Roses and thorns. *Inside Higher Ed*, 5 November. https://www.insidehighered.com/news/2019/11/05/institutions-introduce-undergraduate-degree-programs-esports (16 February 2020).

Banet-Weiser, Sarah. 2012. *Authentic: The politics of ambivalence in a brand culture*. New York: New York University Press.

Bowles, Nellie. 2018. All we want to do is watch each other play video games. *New York Times*, 2 May.

Brown, Kenon A., Andrew C. Billings, Breann Murphy & Luis Puesan. 2018. Intersections of fandom in the age of interactive media: eSports fandom as a predictor of traditional sport fandom. *Communication & Sport* 6(4). 418–435.

Chin, Daniel. 2018. NBA tips off NBA 2K League with first-ever basketball draft. *New York Daily News*, 10 April. http://www.nydailynews.com/sports/basketball/nba-tips-nba-2k-league-first-ever-basketball-draft-article-1.3926338# (16 May 2019).

Cioletti, Amanda. 2018, All eyes on e-sports. *License Global*, 20 April. https://www.licenseglobal.com/magazine-article/trendwatch-all-eyes-esports (30 August 2018).

Crawford, Garry & Victoria K. Gosling. 2009. More than a game: Sports-themed video games and player narratives. *Sociology of Sport Journal* 26(1). 50–66.

Crook, Jordan. 2018. The International Olympic Committee is curious about esports. *Techcrunch.com*, 28 June. https://techcrunch.com/2018/06/28/the-international-olympic-committee-is-curious-about-esports (30 August 2018).

Darcy, Kieran. 2018. 2K League gives players the NBA Rookie Camp experience. *ESPN.com*, 16 August. http://www.espn.com/esports/story/_/id/24168748/nba-2k-league-players-go-same-rookie-camp-their-nba-counterparts (30 August 2018).

Elias, Norbert & Eric Dunning. 1986. *Quest for excitement. Sport and leisure in the civilizing process*. Oxford: Blackwell.

Fischer, Ben. 2018. NBA 2K focused on building star power. *SportsBusiness Journal*, 7 May. https://www.sportsbusinessdaily.com/Journal/Issues/2018/05/07/esports/NBA-2K.aspx (30 August 2018).

Game on! NBA makes esports entry with NBA 2K League debut. 2018. *USA Today*, 4 May. https://www.usatoday.com/story/sports/nba/2018/05/04/game-on-nba-makes-esports-entry-with-nba-2k-league-debut/34543765 (30 August 2018).

Gaudiosi, John. 2016. Why ESPN is investing in esports coverage," *Fortune*, 22 January. http://fortune.com/2016/01/22/espn-invests-in-esports-coverage/ (16 May 2019).

Hallmann, Kristin & Thomas Giel. 2018. eSports: Competitive sports or recreational activity? *Sport Management Review* 21. 14–20.

Heitner, Darren. 2018. Esports legend Ninja confirms he is earning over $500,000 per month. *Forbes*, 20 March. https://www.forbes.com/sites/darrenheitner/2018/03/20/esports-legend-ninja-confirms-he-is-earning-over-500000-per-month/#69d1df266652 (16 May 2019).

Holland, Martin. 2018. Schweiz: Fußballfans protestieren gegen E-Sport. *Heise online*, 25 September. https://www.heise.de/newsticker/meldung/Schweiz-Fussballfans-protestieren-gegen-E-Sport-4172125.html (16 May 2019).

Hutchins, Brett. 2008. Signs of meta-change in second modernity: the growth of e-sport and the World Cyber Games. *New Media & Society* 10(6). 851–869.
Jenny, Seth E., R. Douglas Manning, Margaret C. Keiper & Tracy W. Olrich. 2017. Virtual(ly) athletes: Where eSports fit within the definition of "sport." *Quest* 69(1). 1–18.
Johnson, Mark R. & Jamie Woodcock. 2019. The impacts of live streaming and Twitch.tv on the video game industry. *Media, Culture & Society* 41(5). 670–688.
Katz, A. J. 2018. Why the NBA, NFL and MLS are trying to compete with established esports leagues. *AdWeek*, 30 April. https://www.adweek.com/tv-video/why-the-nba-nfl-and-mls-are-trying-to-compete-with-established-esports-leagues/ (15 June 2019).
Krempl, Stefan. 2018. DFB-Chef Grindel: E-Sport ist eine "absolute Verarmung." *Heise online*, 5 March. https://www.heise.de/newsticker/meldung/DFB-Chef-Grindel-E-Sport-ist-eine-absolute-Verarmung-3986893.html (16 May 2019).
Lewis, Lew & Tim Bradshaw. 2017. Esports move into big league. *Financial Times*, 6 November. 9.
Li, Roland. 2016. *Good luck, have fun: The rise of eSports*. New York: Skyhorse Publishing.
Mickunas, Aaron. 2019. How does League's Worlds viewership compare to the Super Bowl? *Dot Esports*, 4 February. https://dotesports.com/league-of-legends/news/league-of-legends-vs-superbowl-viewer-numbers (16 February 2020).
Milne, Mike. 2016. *The transformation of television sport: New methods, new rules*. Houndsmills: Palgrave Macmillan.
Needleman, Sarah E. 2017. NBA, take-two to create professional videogame league. *Wall Street Journal*, 9 February. https://www.wsj.com/articles/nba-take-two-to-create-professional-videogame-league-1486616461 (16 May 2019).
O'Kane, Sean. 2015. How the NBA became the first major sport to embrace VR. *The Verge*, 17 February. https://www.theverge.com/2015/2/17/8052163/nba-all-star-virtual-reality-samsung-mobile-gear-vr (16 February 2020).
Pannekeet, Jurre. 2019. Global esports economy will top $1 billion for the first time in 2019. *Newzoo*, 12 February. https://newzoo.com/insights/articles/newzoo-global-esports-economy-will-top-1-billion-for-the-first-time-in-2019/ (16 February 2020).
Paumgarten, Nick. 2018. Weaponized. *The New Yorker*, 21 May 21.
Peterson, Latoya. 2018. Can the NBA 2K League tackle gender diversity in gaming. *ESPN.com*, 3 April. http://www.espn.com/esports/story/_/id/23014746/can-nba-2k-league-tackle-gender-diversity-gaming (16 May 2019).
Popper, Ben. 2013. TV tweets: Twitter partners with networks to make live TV fun ... and profitable. *The Verge*, 23 May. https://www.theverge.com/2013/5/23/4358730/twitter-advertising-tv-brands-amplify (16 February 2020).
Rasetti, Jérôme. 2018. Virtual championship, real ambition as NBA launches esport league. *Yahoo! Sports*, 1 May. https://sports.yahoo.com/virtual-championship-real-ambition-nba-launches-esport-league-222736011--nba.html (15 June 2019).
Roettgers, Janko. 2011. Video gamers: the secret stars of live streaming. *Gigaom*, 28 June. http://gigaom.com/video/video-gamers-the-secret-stars-of-live-streaming/ (16 May 2019).
Sarconi, Paul. 2017. Why Instagram is suddenly the place for sports highlights. *Wired.com*, 16 March. https://www.wired.com/2017/03/instagram-sports-highlights/ (16 February 2020).
Schonbrun, Zach. 2017. An NCAA for esports? *New York Times*, 6 October.
Schultz, E. J. 2017. Are you game? *Advertising Age*, 3 April. https://adage.com/article/news/e-sports/308447 (28 August 2018).
Schuster, Blake. 2017. 'It will dwarf the NFL': The NBA's going all-in on eSports with the NBA 2K League. *Yahoo! Sports*, 6 December. https://sports.yahoo.com/will-dwarf-nfl-nbas-going-esports-nba-2k-league-202943490.html?guccounter=1 (28 August 2018).

Taylor, Nicholas Thiel. 2016. Now you're playing with audience power: the work of watching games. *Critical Studies in Media Communication* 33(4). 293–307.
Taylor, T. L. 2006. *Play between worlds: Exploring online game culture*. Cambridge, MA: MIT Press.
Taylor, T. L. 2012. *Raising the stakes: e-sports and the professionalization of computer gaming*. Cambridge, MA: MIT Press.
Taylor, T. L. 2018. *Watch me play: Twitch and the rise of game live streaming* (Princeton Studies in Culture and Technology). Princeton, NJ: Princeton University Press.
Turtiainen, Riikka, Usva Friman & Maria Ruotsalainen. 2020. "Not only for a celebration of competitive overwatch but also for national pride": Sportificating the Overwatch World Cup 2016. *Games and Culture* 15(4). 351–371.
Wade, Stephen. 2018. Bach: No Olympic future for esports until "violence" removed." *AP News*, 1 September. https://apnews.com/3615bd17ebb8478ab534691080a9a32a (16 May 2019).
Webster, Andrew. 2018. Why competitive gaming is starting to look a lot like professional sports. *The Verge*, 27 July. https://www.theverge.com/2018/7/27/17616532/overwatch-league-of-legends-nba-nfl-esports (16 May 2019).
Wingfield, Nick. 2014. In e-sports, video gamers draw real crowds and big money. *New York Times*, 20 August.
Yeboah, Kofie. 2017. Feast your eyes on the sleek new 'NBA 2K' league logo! *SB Nation*, 11 December. https://www.sbnation.com/2017/12/11/16751964/nba2k-league-logo-released-e-sports (16 May 2019).
Youngmisuk, Ohm & Jacob Wolf. 2018. How Adam Silver made his mark on esports in North America. *ESPN.com*, 3 April. http://www.espn.com/esports/story/_/id/23006808/how-adam-silver-made-mark-esports-north-america (16 May 2019).
Yu, Fan. 2017. Investors eyeing esport as growth soars. *The Epoch Times*, 15 September. A12.
Zander, Catrin & Michael Klitzsch. 2018, Profi in der NBA-E-Sport-Liga [Professionals in the NBA eSports league]. *Spiegel Online*, 4 April. http://www.spiegel.de/sport/sonst/e-sport-nba-2k-spieler-jannis-neumann-im-interview-a-1200918.html (15 June 2019).
Zantingh, Peter. 2017. Vier vragen over de E-Divisie [Four questions about the E-division]. *NRC*, 6 February. https://www.nrc.nl/nieuws/2017/02/06/virtueel-voetballen-6539472-a1544657 (16 May 2019).

IV Communicating nationalism(s) in sport

Andrew C. Billings and Elisabetta Zengaro

22 The biggest double-edged sword in sport media: Olympic media and the rendering of identity

Abstract: The Olympics features the most prolonged global media exposure in all of sport; over 3.6 billion people witness the Summer Olympics over 18 saturating days of coverage. This chapter explores both the opportunities and inherent dangers of conveying the Games to the masses, specifically focusing on how issues of identity (gender, nationality, race, and beyond) are shaped and received during the mediated Olympic process.

Keywords: Olympics; media; gender; nationality; race; ethnicity

1 Introduction

Mediated sports events occur in non-stop programming fashions; there is always something on. However, very few of them rise to the moniker of sport mega-event, matching all four of Muller's (2015) lofty markers of mega-event status, including high visitor attractiveness, cost, mediated reach, and transformative impact. Yet, one event, the Olympic Games, clears these lofty markers with such ease that Muller (2015: 636) argues for a new distinction: the sports "giga-event." Such a classification appears warranted, as 3.6 billion people tuned in to the 2016 Rio Summer Olympics (Chapman 2016). Even the Winter Olympics reaches a viewership of nearly two billion (Global Broadcast and Audience Report 2018). From the continents hosting/participating to the collective impact on each national sporting culture, no other event possesses the depth and breadth of the Olympics.

Of course, the overwhelming majority of people witnessing the Games do so via media devices rather than watching first-hand, meaning the manner in which Olympic media is rendered has some of the most forceful senses of cultivated impact (Billings, Angelini, and MacArthur 2018). Some media renderings of the Games are so overwhelming in their scope that no one could ever watch each competition in their entirety. To wit, NBC offered 6,755 hours of coverage for the 2016 Rio Summer Olympic Games (McAdams 2016); if one were to treat watching the Rio Summer Games as a 40-hour per week job, that job would have extended beyond three years, to the point that one could seamlessly transition to preview and trials for the next Summer installment. And that is just the Summer Games.

Thus, there is a ubiquity to Olympic media that simply is unmatched. One can be a fan of Manchester United or the Dallas Cowboys and, fairly easily, say that they

https://doi.org/10.1515/9783110660883-022

have never missed a game, but such a statement is not feasibly possible for a fan of the Olympics. No network can properly render it all within the time period. No human can watch it all within that same time period. The result is that the Games are viewed in snippets, doled out via myriad devices, platforms, and networks, with network hierarchies placed on sports that achieve the largest and most desirable audiences and individuals customizing their viewership to best match their interests. This chapter will explore the ramifications of this cultivated ubiquity, showing how the Olympics (broadly defined) offer the highest level of gender, national, and racial diversity in all of sports media all while necessitating that the fan opts for one rendering of the Games over another, with certain identity groups being elevated or relegated in that process of individualization. Ultimately, a double-edged sword is argued to be occurring where women athletes finally receive media exposure commensurate to their achievements, yet only through the bolstering of patriotism and nationalism through nationalized sports renderings.

2 Conveying issues of gender and biological sex

Overviews of identity in the Olympics often start with notions of gender, partly because of the plentiful numbers of studies in the area (e. g., Bissell and Smith 2013; Broch 2016; Davis and Tuggle 2012; Greer, Hardin, and Homan 2009; Poniatowski and Hardin 2012) and partly because of the stark contrast between what audiences expect in an Olympic telecast (complete or near gender equity) and what audiences have grown accustomed to outside of these Olympic parameters (ubiquitous men's coverage paired with scant women's coverage). Indeed, non-Olympic sports media often proportionally render women's sports in single-digit percentages (Billings and Young 2015; Cooky, Messner, and Musto 2015) while the Olympic telecast, says US Olympic media producer Molly Solomon, offers gender equity as "happenstance" as it naturally produces women who are "some of the most popular and most influential athletes in American sports history" (Billings 2008: 47). In sum, while sports media could avoid the biggest stories in women's sports and mostly do so without large-scale criticism, this has never been possible in modern media renderings of the Olympics because, as Antunovic (2016: 1551) contends, "you *had* [emphasis added] to cover Nadia Comaneci."

However, the expectancy of equity in terms of *amount* of coverage is sometimes used to pre-empt or blunt the differences found in the *type* of coverage devoted to men and women athletes. The former is largely a function of agenda-setting theory (McCombs and Shaw 1972) with the key premise being the belief that media does not tell people what to think, but can be effective in telling people what to think *about*; the latter is largely a function of framing (Goffman 1974), specifically the narratives that are present, absent, and inordinately emphasized (Tankard 2001). To varying extents across the globe, the amount of coverage devoted to women in the Olympics has always been higher than any other form of sports media, and the gap between men's and women's coverage has dwindled to the point that some would argue it no longer exists (DeLorme 2014). For example, American coverage of the Games has now reached the point that the proportion of coverage by gender regularly mirrors the proportion of medals won by American men and women athletes; women won the majority of medals for the United States in the 2012, 2016, and 2018 iterations of the Games and, consequently, received the majority of the US telecast focus as well (Billings and Angelini 2019).

The depiction of the women athletes within such clock-time offers a more nuanced story, however. Most scholars conclude that the characterizations of women athletes are better in the Olympics than in other sports mega-events such as the World Cup (Ravel and Gareau 2016), yet differences still pervade – some generally justified and others not. Items such as Olympic media guides disproportionately emphasize the personal information of women athletes, minimizing the focus on athletic achievement (Carter, Casanova, and Maume 2015), while other depictions occur directly when the athletic performance is being mediated, with men more likely to be depicted as aggressive, while women were more apt to be spoken of in terms of communal traits (Jones and Greer 2012). Some trends have dissipated over time (e. g., focus on women athletes' appearance was found in three consecutive Olympic analyses in the 1990s, while largely disappearing in 21st-century studies: Billings, Angelini, and MacArthur 2018) while other trends sporadically appear in datasets without consistent trend (e. g., disproportionate emphasis on women athletes' inexperience/youth: Billings Angelini, and MacArthur 2018).

Often, such tendencies to highlight one set of qualities over another could be argued to be founded in elements endemic to the athletic performance itself. For instance, when telecasting gymnastics coverage in a Summer Olympics, the average age of a female gymnast is significantly lower than the average age of a male gymnast, making a focus on youth or inexperience of a female gymnast more apt to occur. Similarly, some personal stories play out differently for one gender than another. While one could certainly argue that fatherhood causes disruption to a male athlete's training and competitiveness, it would be difficult to claim this disruption is remotely akin to that a pregnant/new mother experiences while attempting to succeed at the highest Olympic levels. As McGannon and colleagues (2015) uncovered, mentioning motherhood resulted in two macro-level narratives about women athletes: the athlete and mother in conflict and athlete and mother as superwoman, each part of the transformative journey. Moreover, the scholars wrote that "when portrayed as separate and polarized, athlete mother identities had associated meanings that downplayed an athletic career, forcing women to choose between an athletic career and good mother ideals" (McGannon et al. 2015: 58). A good exemplar happened in the 2016 Rio Games, with Hungarian swimmer Katinka Hosszu and her husband, Shane Tusup, who was also her coach. In the moments after Hosszu won a gold medal in the 400-meter individual medley, NBC announcer Dan Hicks referenced Tusup as "the man responsible" for the incredible performance.

The other element that can blunt notions of gender equity can be the laser-like focus on national identity as the lead element of any athletic achievement. Thus, when a woman earns a medal in the Games, the gendered narrative that could be empowering for women's sports can be trumped by a nationalized one which focuses on the glory earned for one's nation (Jaworska and Hunt 2017; Xu, Billings, and Fan 2018). Instead of witnessing women at the pinnacles of athletic performance, one receives mediated discourses promoting "patriots at play" (Vincent and Crossman 2012: 87). As a result, "these patterns in turn reflect and reinforce dominant discourses of social hierarchies" (Jaworska and Hunt 2017: 359).

More recent studies of the Games and the media surrounding them have shown that Internet-based offerings are more likely to exhibit equitable coverage than traditional/legacy forms of media. Eagleman, Burch, and Vooris (2014: 465) advance the argument that this is largely because "the Internet allows for more equitable coverage, at least in terms of the amount of coverage provided, because of its expanded spatial allowances." Any ability to move beyond one central channel of media conveyance certainly has expanded the types of sports one could witness, advancing both men's and women's sports alike (Arth et al. 2019), with Internet options – particularly with its mobile and user-generated components – augmenting this breadth substantially more, even shifting the uses and gratifications one attains from being an "Olympic fan" (Billings et al. 2020).

In sum, the double-edged sword of gender is advanced in Olympic media by illuminating how women athletes are shown at an unprecedented mediated level all while having different types of narratives being advanced within that heralded coverage. Because of its relative unicorn status in relation to virtually all other sports media offerings, single comments about women athletes – either positive or negative – can carry substantial weight in terms of influence on society. As Amara (2012: 648) explains in an analysis of veiled athletes and the subsequent impact on developing Muslim and Arab identities, the "Olympics was an opportunity for certain media to debate internal societal problems such as the increasing demand among Muslim communities in the West to accommodate sport practice to Islamic religious principles, or as in the case of Al Qaniir, to underline the issue of girls' rights to practise sport in schools in Saudi Arabia." These debates can be useful, yet are often originated without full-formed contexts for understanding the evolution and dynamics of women's sports and the histories and understandings that must surround them to advance informed conversations.

3 Olympic media via national foci

Arguably even more powerful than the role gender plays within Olympic media, national identity permeates virtually every aspect of the Games. From the impact on the host city (Jovanovic 2017; MacRury and Poynter 2010) to political and social entanglements between and among countries (Yoon and Wilson 2016) to local news coverage and beyond (King 2007a; Vincent et al. 2018), the Games are imbued with notions of "differentiation and identification" (Jovanovic 2017: 778). Even events such as a torch relay preceding the Games have conceptions of national identity endemic to their media renderings, dating back to the 1936 Berlin Games, hosted under German dictator Adolf Hitler. Notes Papa (2010: 1459) in analyzing the 2008 Beijing torch relay coverage, "The torch relay also gave the media as a whole the opportunity to represent and to give a shape to the vision of the Chinese political regime that the democratic Western countries share, and, in so doing, they reinforced their own representation as defenders and a part of fundamental rights and freedoms." Hence, there are nationalized heuristics of comparison inherent to many ways one views the Olympics: winner/loser, good/bad, home/foreign, and us/them. The result, argue Yoon and Wilson (2016: 520), is that "western media representations ... offer an easy 'us versus them/Other' comparison that would potentially prompt a hierarchical, binary value-judgment."

Scholars have focused on various forms of national identity that seemingly are tinged with notions of whether such concepts are good or bad for society. For instance, two of Kosterman and Feshbach's (1989) conceptions are frequently invoked in different terms, with patriotism ("I'm proud of my country") a generally positive aspect to advance and nationalism ("my country is better than your country") a generally negative aspect to embody. Their other conceptions range from the overtly positive (advancing of civil liberties, internationalism) to overtly negative (smugness). Each of these elements permeate an Olympic media rendering, with scholars finding that, for instance, a relationship persists between the number of medals won and the likelihood that a nation's viewers will exhibit notions of smugness (Billings et al. 2013), while also uncovering dramatic differences in core measures depending on the nation in which one nation resides. Table 1 indicates mean scores on four of Kosterman and Feshbach's (1989) measures (patriotism, nationalism, internationalism, smugness) among a six-nation composite (Australia, Bulgaria, China, the Netherlands, Slovenia, and the United States).

As Table 1 shows, nations could score relatively similar on measures of, for instance, patriotism and nationalism (as was the case in Bulgaria), or these can function with considerable deviation (as was the case in Australia and China). However, even more pertinently, the study highlighted that while relationships existed between Olympic media consumption and likelihood to score more highly on these measures, the *ordering* still necessitated clarification.

Such clarity was offered in later work from Brown and colleagues (2016), who utilized structural equation modeling to determine the best fit for the manner in which

Tab. 1: Mean scores for nationalism qualities by country in 2012 Summer Olympics (Billings et al. 2013)

	AUS	BUL	CHN	NED	SLO	USA	Overall*
Patriotism	5.32	5.85	6.04	4.97	5.81	6.11	**5.74**
Nationalism	3.95	5.78	4.82	4.06	4.98	4.93	**4.80**
Smugness	3.1	4.11	4.61	2.55	3.41	5.23	**3.76**
Internationalism	5.33	4.78	4.35	4.78	4.74	3.88	**4.68**

* Based on 7-point scales (1 = Low; 7 = High)

these concepts unfold as well as the placement of one's fan involvement as a mediating variable. Ultimately, national qualities were found to be antecedents rather than subsequent effects of Olympic media consumption. Figure 1 illustrates the relationships uncovered within the context of the 2014 Winter Olympics.

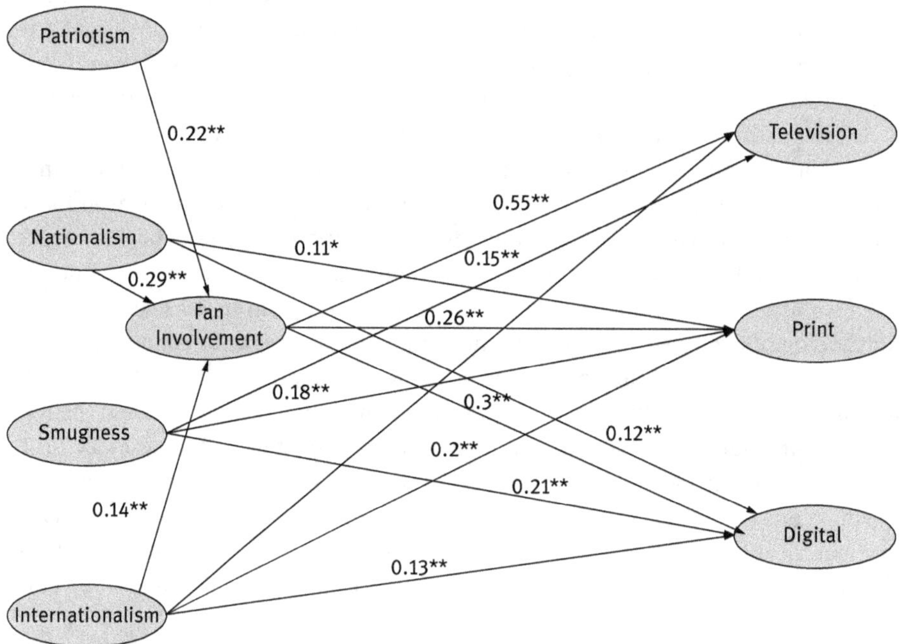

Fig. 1: Structural equation model for 2014 Olympic media consumption (Brown et al. 2016)

Thus, what this study found was that the best summarization of the relationship between Olympic media (A) and the bolstering of one's national qualities (B) was not that A caused B but, rather, than people high in B (national qualities) were predisposed to seek out more of A (Olympic media content). Given the ubiquity of media choices now offered in an Internet-enabled world, such relationships are less surprising. Whatever content people most enjoy (whether crime dramas, politics, crude cartoons, or international battles in sporting competitions) can now be found in more abundance than ever before; no one need "settle" for content that they do not find highly appealing, meaning that the people consuming the Olympics in large quantities are canvassing all media options like anyone else and consistently choosing the content with nationalized binaries and comparisons, replete with anthems and flag-waving cheerleading.

This is precisely where the double-edged sword of national identity appears, when patriotism (pride in one's country) has the tendency to beget nationalism (believing one's nation is superior to another country). Thus, questions unfold regarding how to render (and receive) a nationalized product in which both producers and viewers feel the inherent bond Benedict Anderson (1983: 1) refers to as the "imagined community," one in which the nation is the in-group and all others are the out-group within any conceptions of social identity (Tajfel and Turner 1986) or social comparison (Festinger 1954). Consider, for instance, the problematizing of the medals table, a regular feature in the majority of Olympic media productions. There appears an innate desire (this is a sports competition, after all) for a macro-level contest – one that could name overall "winner" and "loser" nations when aggregating over two weeks of competition. Nevertheless, this aggregation is truly an apple to oranges comparison quandary. For instance, there are six total medals available to be won in soccer (women's and men's gold, silver, and bronze) and no nation, no matter how successful in soccer it may be, could win more than two medals. In contrast, there are 108 possible medals to win in swimming (18 different events for both women and men to compete) and nations can (and do) win multiple medals in many of these events. Placing two sports like these into an aggregated table will inevitably elevate the strong swimming nations and demote the strong soccer nations. As a result, Starr (2008: 42) notes that the medals table represents a competition "contested primarily on an abacus, not in a sports arena." Thus, principles of upward contact (bonding with a nation because it is doing well on the medals charts) and downward derogation (feeling ambivalence or disassociation with a poor medal-performing nation) come into play in the form of Basking in Reflected Glory (BIRGing, for the former case: Cialdini et al. 1976) and Cutting Off Reflected Failure (CORFing, for the latter case: Wann and Branscombe 1990).

This becomes more problematic when considering Olympic effects; Chen (2012) utilized a panel survey in China where Chinese participants were asked to rate 18 countries' Olympic performances over the 2004 and 2008 Olympic Games according to three criteria: athletic ability, strength, and favorable attitude of the country. Results indicated that performance, the number of medals a country won, was positively correlated to national image of the country in Chinese audiences, but not in third-world nations. Chen (2012: 763) concludes:

> The winning medal list represented a media agenda that ranks the issues (countries), and perceived national image scores of each country were measured as indicators of public agenda towards the issues (countries). The "sport superpower" countries (i. e. USA, China and Russia) that were highly publicized by the media during the games were considered by the Chinese audience to be countries with greater athletic ability, more general strength, and these countries also attracted more favorable feelings.

In the end, it is the representation of nations that is problematic in that it is shaded by many elements including – but not limited to – the medals table. Sometimes these images are shaped by the narrative a host nation seeks to advance (Thomas and Antony 2015; Zhou et al. 2013); other times narratives are shaped for a home nation's preferred viewing pleasure (Bie and Billings 2015; Jiang 2013; Yan and Watanabe 2014). Hence, the Olympics can help to expand one's national horizons (Wang, Guo, and Shen 2011), yet it is important to acknowledge that Olympic media "representational strategies are not neutral but rather ideological, and they connect to broader discourses, social practices, and power relations" (Mostafa 2018). The pomp and circumstance offered in any Olympics can tend to blunt schisms and "overtly idealize" conceptions of unification and commonality (Lee and Maguire 2011: 863). Olympic media literacy in the context of national identity thus becomes crucial in such contexts because, as Vessey wisely asserts "ideologies are normally embedded and naturalised, they are not usually openly contested" within the backdrop of Olympic media content renderings (Vessey 2013: 676).

4 Footnoting more than analyzing: racial and ethnic depictions

Given the complexity that the concepts of race and ethnicity entail in any discussion (Carrington 2010) and, in particular, mediated environments, it is no surprise that Olympic media is fraught with questions on how one advances societal discussions while maintaining its light-hearted entertainment role. Questions within this double-edged sword enter the conversation both immediately and awkwardly: How does a media entity separate race (traditionally unpacked based on skin/appearance) from ethnicity (traditionally unpacked in terms of one's historial heritage) within sport? How does one briefly mention an issue of race without doing so clumsily? How does one gently insert race into a mediated dialogue without making it the main/only conversation within that dialogue? How does one use Olympic media to forge racial and ethnic ties that bind while simultaneously acknowledging the severing of these ties in a variety of problematic historical and societal circumstances?

Even talking about racial diversity in the Olympics is a dicey prospect, as the Summer Games inherently has more breadth of representation than the Winter Games, most notably due to strong participation from athletes in African and South American nations, leading King (2007b) to conclude that the Winter Games are racist upon their origination. Moreover, each event is imbued with a sense of historical context that is different depending on the nation in which they compete and the manner in which opportunities unfolded within that given sport in years far preceding the highlighted athlete's birth.

Some exemplars of these nuances include the 1968 medal stand protest by Tommie Smith and John Carlos that can only be adequately or even rudimentarily understood by understanding both America's racial history predating the salute as well as a sense of where that racial history stood at that given moment in time (Bass 2002). Moreover, because sports media is often seen as not only separate but also a respite from "hard" news stories in which race, ethnicity, and historical context are most likely to appear, such moments are difficult for many sportswriters to advance because of their own lack of familiarity with the issues. Thus, Peterson (2009: 115) notes that "the one-fist black power protest was one of the first times that political action and sports intersected on such a grand stage, a complexity that left many writers angry and confused." These moments are powerful and important as they become key points of racial resistance (Hartmann 1996), yet they often are conveyed within an Olympic media product seeking to celebrate more than problematize, only embracing protests in the decades following when activism has proven to stand the test of time.

Another example of this struggle to adequately handle issues of race and ethnicity occurred in the 2000 Sydney Summer Olympic story of Aboriginal runner Cathy Freeman, who lit the Olympic torch to start the Games and then won the 400-meter gold medal 10 days later, celebrating by carrying both the Australian and Aboriginal flags simultaneously (even when the latter was not formally recognized as a national flag by the International Olympic Committee and technically banned). As is the case in many Olympic narratives, themes of reconciliation and unity overwhelm stories of resistance and, in this case, feelings of forced assimilation by indigenous peoples in Australia. Media seemingly allows such triumphant storylines to percolate because they more closely represent the Olympic ideal – as well as being good television. As Mayeda (2001: 178–179) asserts, "television media forces will take significant measures to redirect the athletes' presentation, making these athletes appear less disrespectful and/or critical of their respective nation."

Thus, race gets reduced to popular narratives of overcoming obstacles – which are important – yet often then reduce the conveyance of race and/or ethnicity in the Olympics to skin tone and letting the camera do the work (Billings 2008) or only inserting race into the discussion when a valid "first" occurs (see Bass 2002), such as speed skater Shani Davis becoming the first Black athlete to win gold in a Winter Games in 2006. These discussions of race are often done post-hoc, as a way of noting the racial significance of the moment that has just unfurled within media. For instance, once American gymnast Gabby Douglas won the all-around gold in the Summer 2012 Olympics, her race (other than what the viewer could note visually on-screen during her performances) became a context cue provided later in the studio by NBC anchor

Bob Costas, who offered on-air after the performance: "It's a happy measure of how far we've come that it doesn't seem all that remarkable but still is noteworthy: Gabby Douglas is, as it happens, the first African American to win the women's all-around in gymnastics. The barriers have long since been down, but sometimes there can be an imaginary barrier based on how one sees oneself."

This is a lofty, useful moment that needed to be acknowledged, yet the lack of the ability or willingness to do so more directly during the athletic performances could be seen as a missed opportunity for some while being a welcome diversion from the rest of the racially troubling stories one witnesses in other forms of media for others. Hence, the double-edged sword. Consider, for instance, how one could note overrepresentation of Black athletes in many forms of sport preserves notions of their "innate" ability or, as Hoberman (1997: 1) labels them, "Darwin's athletes." Using the Olympics as backdrop, scholars have argued that "Blacks are overrepresented in sports media to preserve power relations in U.S. society" (Hardin et al. 2004: 223).

Thus, race becomes problematic to render in the fact that both over and underrepresentation could cause public outcry, as can either mentioning it (purposely inserting race into a conversation) or muting it (failing to acknowledge the racial histories embedded with the stories Olympic media aspires to tell). Racial stacking thus becomes pertinent to understanding Olympic athlete participation and successes as it involves both the overt and covert legacies that cause an athlete to opt for one sport over another, as well as the encouragement to participate in one position or event above another (e. g., sprinting vs. distance running).

The Summer Olympics are racially diverse, yet less so within each sport as they are when taken as a whole. Swimmers are mostly White/Caucasian; track athletes are mostly Black/African American. Acknowledging the encouragements as well as the impediments is necessary to provide a useful heuristic for understanding why one could, for instance, cheer for a Jamaican bobsledding team, or find the last-place swimming finish of Equatorial Guinea's Eric Moussambani inspiring. Moussambani swam the 100 meters in 1:52:72, the slowest time in Olympic history – yet did so as a Black athlete from a nation with only one swimming pool (a hotel pool) in which to train. Those stories are intricate and nuanced, but help to shape the way one understands obstacles within the Olympic experience.

Similarly, the troubled racial history of Black swimmers in America (Chen 2010) must be told in a manner in which people understand that there were significant swaths of time in which Black people were not permitted to swim in pools, lakes, or ocean beaches. Generations of Black Americans without the opportunity to swim led to legacies of their children not having family members to teach them to do so themselves. Those histories must be explained and acknowledged so that the Olympic media audience understands the significance of an American Black athlete doing well in a swimming event at the Games.

5 Olympicized identity: beyond gender, nationality, and race

Of course, there are sub-elements within each of these aforementioned areas, whether pertaining to the manner in which sex testing (Cooky, Dycus, and Dworkin 2013) and transgender athletes (Harper et al. 2018) create new spaces for challenging traditions of binary biological sex distinctions, discerning differences between borders of nations, territories, and continents (such as Taiwan's relationship with China or understanding Great Britain's relationship with Europe post-Brexit vote), or even the often in-group/out-group elements of race with all non-White participants being problematically amalgamated as "other."

Even beyond these distinctions, many other aspects of identity should and must be unpacked with a gaze to Olympic media, most notably including the manner in which Paralympics should be unpacked in regard to disability narratives (Butler and Bissell 2015; Hardin and Hardin 2009). However, other studies should focus upon relatively lightly trodden scholarly pursuits such as depictions of age/aging, which is likely difficult to unpack at least partly because of the differential lifespans of careers depending on the sport being enacted, or sexual orientation, which is difficult to convey to the masses in sports media because it bears no direct influence on the performance and yet speaks considerably about the context in which that athlete challenged particular heterosexual assumptions (Billings and Moscowitz 2018). These aspects – and many more – make Olympic media ripe for future studies in a variety of identity-oriented ways pertaining to production, content, and effects.

6 Conclusion

As witnessed with a keen focus on issues of gender, nationality, and race/ethnicity, the clear metaphor of the double-edged sword appears. Opportunities abound for exploring how a global audience understands people that they might not interact with on a regular basis, if at all. Simultaneously, the Olympics also provides a venue in which such narratives can be blunted or minimized. Consider, for a moment, the roughly one minute given to a nation like Kazakhstan within an Opening Ceremony. Then ponder the influence of NBC host Matt Lauer's decision to use those 60 seconds to make an illusion to the popular Sasha Baron Cohen comedy *Borat* rather than offering dialogue about the nation's actual culture or history.

In the end, we witness Olympic media being embraced for the gender equity it provides, yet also rejected by the racial and national characterizations it also typically advances. However, rarely is the yin/yang of this relationship truly established. The double-edged sword can advance women athletes in exponentially higher proportions than any other sport media property, yet that comes at a cost for other in-groups and out-groups that this elevation inherently creates. The Olympic media presents a mammoth opportunity: one that can be embraced or squandered in equal measure. Finding a way to maintain the high levels of gender equity while alleviating some of the other problematic portrayals within the Olympics should be a primary endeavor for any media company fortunate enough to have the rights to render the biggest show on television.

References

Amara, Mahfoud. 2012. Veiled women athletes in the 2008 Beijing Olympics: Media accounts. *The International Journal of the History of Sport* 29(4). 638–651.

Anderson, Benedict. 1983. *Imagined communities*, 2nd edn. New York: Verso.

Antunovic, Dunja. 2016. "You had to cover Nadia Comaneci": "Points of change" in coverage of women's sport. *The International Journal of the History of Sport* 33(13). 1551–1573.

Arth, Zachary W., Jue Hou, Stephen Rush & James R. Angelini. 2019. (Broad)casting a wider net: Clocking men and women in the primetime and non-primetime coverage of the 2018 Winter Olympic Games. *Communication & Sport* 7(5). 565–587.

Bass, Amy. 2002. *Not the triumph but the struggle: The 1968 Olympics and the making of the Black athlete*. Minneapolis: University of Minnesota Press.

Bie, Bijie & Andrew C. Billings. 2015. "Too good to be true?": U.S. and Chinese media coverage of Chinese swimmer Ye Shiwen in the 2012 Olympic Games. *International Review for the Sociology of Sport* 50(7). 785–803.

Billings, Andrew C. 2008. *Olympic media: Inside the biggest show on television*. London: Routledge.

Billings, A. C. & J. R. Angelini. 2019. Equity achieved?: A longitudinal examination of Biological sex representation in the NBC Olympic telecast (2000–2018). *Communication & Sport* 7(5). 551–564.

Billings, Andrew C. & Leigh M. Moscowitz. 2018. *Media and the coming out of gay male athletes in American team sports*. New York: Peter Lang.

Billings, Andrew C. & Brittany D. Young. 2015. Comparing flagship news programs: Women's sport coverage in ESPN's *SportsCenter* and FOX Sports 1's *FOX Sports Live*. *Electronic News* 9(1). 3–16.

Billings, Andrew C., James R. Angelini & Paul J. MacArthur. 2018. *Olympic television: Inside the biggest show on earth*. London: Routledge.

Billings, Andrew C., Natalie A. Brown-Devlin, Kenon A. Brown & Michael B. Devlin. 2020. When 18 days of coverage is not enough: A six-nation composite of motivations for mobile media use in the 2018 Winter Olympic Games. *Mass Communication & Society* 22(4). 535–557.

Billings, Andrew C., Natalie A. Brown, Kenon A. Brown, Guoqing, Mark A. Leeman, Simon Ličen, David R. Novak & David Rowe. 2013. From pride to smugness and the nationalism between: Olympic media consumption effects on nationalism across the globe. *Mass Communication & Society* 16(6). 910–932.

Bissell, Kim & Lauren R. Smith. 2013. Let's (not) talk about sex: An analysis of the verbal and visual coverage of women's beach volleyball during the 2008 Olympic Games. *Journal of Sports Media* 8(2). 1–30.

Broch, Trygve B. 2016. Intersections of gender and national identity in sport: A cultural sociological overview. *Sociology Compass* 10(7). 567–579.

Brown, Kenon A., Andrew C. Billings, Christiana Schallhorn, Holger Schramm & Natalie A. Brown-Devlin. 2016. Power within the Olympic rings?: Nationalism, Olympic media consumption, and comparative cases in Germany and the United States. *Journal of International Communication* 22(1). 143–169.

Butler, Sim & Kim Bissell. 2015. Olympic effort: Disability, culture, and resistance in the 2012 London Olympic Games. *Journalism & Communication Monographs* 17(4). 228–273.

Carrington, Ben. 2010. *Race, sport, and politics: The sporting black diaspora*. London: Sage.

Carter, J. A., Erin Casanova & David J. Maume. 2015. Gendering Olympians: Olympic media guide profiles of men and women athletes. *Society of Sport Journal* 32(3). 312–331.

Chapman, Ben. 2016. Rio 2016: The richest Games in 120 years of Olympic history. *The Independent*, 5 August. https://www.independent.co.uk/news/business/analysis-and-features/rio-2016-olympic-games-richest-ever-usain-bolt-mo-farah-a7171811.html (16 November 2020).

Chen, Huailin. 2012. Medals, media and myth of national images: How Chinese audiences thought of foreign countries during the Beijing Olympics. *Public Relations Review* 38. 755–764.

Chen, Michelle. 2010. Black women don't swim? *Color Lines*, 21 July. https://www.colorlines.com/articles/black-women-dont-swim (16 November 2020).

Cialdini, Robert B., Richard J. Borden, Avril Thorne, Marcus Randall Walker, Stephen Freeman & Lloyd Reynolds Sloan. 1976. Basking in reflected glory: Three (football) field studies. *Journal of Personality and Social Psychology* 34(3). 366–375.

Cooky, Cheryl, Ranissa Dycus & Shari Dworkin. 2013. "What makes a woman a woman?" versus "our First Lady of sport": A comparative analysis of the United States and the South African media coverage of Caster Semenya. *Journal of Sport & Social Issues* 37(1). 31–56.

Cooky, Cheryl, Michael A. Messner & Michela Musto. 2015. "It's dude time!": A quarter century of excluding women's events in televised news and highlight shows. *Communication & Sport* 3(3). 261–287.

Davis, Kelly K. & C. A. Tuggle. 2012. A gender analysis of NBC's coverage of the 2008 Summer Olympics. *Electronic News* 6(2). 51–66.

DeLorme, Nicolas. 2014. Were women really underrepresented in media coverage of Summer Olympic Games (1984–2008)? An invitation to open a methodological discussion regarding sex equity in sports media. *Mass Communication & Society* 17(1). 121–147.

Eagleman, Andrea, Lauren M. Burch & Ryan Vooris. 2014. A unified version of London 2012: New-media coverage of gender, nationality, and sport for Olympics consumers in six countries. *Journal of Sport Management* 28(4). 457–470.

Festinger, Leon. 1954. A theory of social comparison processes. *Human Relations* 7(2). 117–140.

Global Broadcast and Audience Report. 2018. Olympic Winter Games PyeongChang 2018. *Publicis Media*, June. https://stillmed.olympic.org/media/Document%20Library/OlympicOrg/Games/Winter-Games/Games-PyeongChang-2018-Winter-Olympic-Games/IOC-Marketing/Olympic-Winter-Games-PyeongChang-2018-Broadcast-Report.pdf (16 November 2020).

Goffman, Erving. 1974. *Frame analysis: An essay on the organization of experience*. Cambridge, MA: Harvard University Press.

Greer, Jennifer D., Marie Hardin & Casey Homan. 2009. "Naturally" less exciting? Visual production of men's and women's track and field coverage during the 2004 Olympics. *Journal of Broadcasting & Electronic Media* 53(2). 173–189.

Hardin, Marie & Brent Hardin. 2009. Elite wheelchair athletes relate to sport media. In Keith Gilbert (ed.), *The Paralympic Games: Empowerment or side show?*, 25–33. Aachen: Meyer & Meyer Verlag.

Hardin, Marie, Julie E. Dodd, Jean Chance & Kristie Walsdorf. 2004. Sporting images in black and white: Race in newspaper coverage of the 2000 Olympic Games. *The Howard Journal of Communications* 15(4). 211–227.

Harper, Joanna, Giscard Lima, Alexander Kolliari-Turner, Fernanda R. Malinsky, Guan Wang, Maria Jose Martinez-Patino, Siddhartha S. Angadi, Theodora Papadopoulou, Fabio Pigozzi, Leighton Seal, James Barrett & Yannis P. Pitsiladis. 2018. The fluidity of gender and implications for the biology of inclusion for transgender and intersex athletes. *Current Sports Medicine Reports* 17(12). 467–472.

Hartmann, Douglas. 1996. The politics of race and sport: Resistance and domination in the 1968 African American Olympic protest movement. *Ethnic and Racial Studies* 19(3). 548–566.

Hoberman, John. 1997. *Darwin's athletes: How sport has damaged Black America and preserved the myth of race.* Boston: Houghton-Mifflin.

Jaworska, Sylvia & Sally Hunt. 2017. Differentiations and intersections: A corpus-assisted discourse study of gender representations in the British press before, during and after the London Olympics 2012. *Gender and Language* 11(3). 336–364.

Jiang, Qiaolei. 2013. Celebrity athletes, soft power and national identity: Hong Kong newspaper coverage of the Olympic champions of Beijing 2008 and London 2012. *Mass Communication and Society* 16. 888–909.

Jones, Amy & Jennifer Greer. 2012. Go "heavy" or go home: An examination of audience attitudes and their relationship to gender cues in the 2010 Olympic snowboarding coverage. *Mass Communication and Society* 15(4). 598–621.

Jovanovic, Zlatko. 2017. The 1984 Sarajevo Winter Olympics and identity-formation in late socialist Sarajevo. *The International Journal of the History of Sport* 34(9). 767–782.

King, Christopher R. 2007a. Media portrayals of male and female athletes: A text and picture analysis of British national newspaper coverage of the Olympic Games since 1948. International *Review for the Sociology of Sport* 42(2). 187–199.

King, Christopher R. 2007b. Staging the Winter White Olympics. *Journal of Sport & Social Issues* 31. 89–94.

Kosterman, Rick & Seymour Feshbach. 1989. Toward a measure of patriotic and nationalistic attitudes. *Political Psychology* 10(2). 257–274.

Lee, Jung Woo & Joseph Maguire. 2011. Road to reunification? Unitary Korean nationalism in South Korean media coverage of the 2004 Athens Olympic Games. *Sociology* 45(5). 848–867.

MacRury, Ian & Gavin Poynter. 2010. "Team GB" and London 2012: The paradox of national and global identities. *The International Journal of the History of Sport* 27(16–18). 2958–2975.

Mayeda, David. 2001. Characterizing gender and race in the 2000 Summer Olympics: NBC's coverage of Maurice Greene, Michael Johnson, Marion Jones, and Cathy Freeman. *Social Thought & Research* 24(1–2). 145–186.

McAdams, Deborah D. 2016. NBC 2016 Rio Olympic coverage by the numbers. *TV Technology*, 4 August. https://www.tvtechnology.com/news/nbc-2016-rio-olympics-coverage-by-the-numbers (16 November 2020).

McCombs, Maxwell & Donald Shaw. 1972. The agenda-setting function of mass media. *The Public Opinion Quarterly* 36(2). 176–187.

McGannon, Kerry R., Christine A. Gonsalves, Robert J. Schinke & Rebecca Busanich. 2015. Negotiating motherhood and athletic identity: A qualitative analysis of Olympic athlete mother representations in media narratives. *Psychology of Sport and Exercise* 20. 51–59.

Mostafa, Rasha Mohammad Saeed. 2018. Online newspapers portrayal of Arab female athletes in Rio 2016 Olympics: A multimodal critical discourse analysis. *International Journal of Arabic-English Studies* 18. 49–70.

Muller, Martin. 2015. What makes an event a mega-event?: Definitions and sizes. *Leisure Studies* 34(6). 627–642.

Papa, Françoise. 2010. France: A conflict of values? The Olympic torch relay in Paris – the mass media were on cue. *The International Journal of the History of Sport* 27(9–10). 1452–1460.

Peterson, Jason. 2009. A "race" for equality: Print media coverage of the 1968 Olympic protest by Tommie Smith and John Carlos. *American Journalism Historians Association* 26(2). 99–121.

Poniatowski, Kelly & Marie Hardin. 2012. "The more things change, the more they ...": Commentary during Women's ice hockey at the 2010 Winter Olympic Games. *Mass Communication and Society* 15(4). 622–641.

Ravel, Barbara & Marc Gareau. 2016. 'French football needs more women like Adriana'? Examining the media coverage of France's women's national football team for the 2011 World Cup and the 2012 Olympic Games. *International Review for the Sociology of Sport* 51(7). 833–847.

Starr, Mark. 2008. The U.S.-China gold rush: Get out your abacus. *Newsweek*. 42.

Tajfel, Henri & John C. Turner. 1986. The social identity theory of inter-group behavior. In Stephen Worchel & William G. Austin (eds.), *Psychology of Intergroup Relations*, 7–24. Chicago: Nelson-Hall.

Tankard, James W. 2001. The empirical approach to the study of media framing. In Stephen D. Reese, Oscar H. Gandy & August E. Grant (eds.), *Framing public life*, 95–106. Mahwah, NJ: Lawrence Erlbaum.

Thomas, Ryan J. & Mary Grace Antony. 2015. Competing constructions of British national identity: British newspaper comment on the 2012 Olympics opening ceremony. *Media, Culture & Society* 37(3). 493–503.

Vessey, Rachelle. 2013. Too much French? Not enough French?: The Vancouver Olympics and a very Canadian language ideological debate. *Multilingua: Journal of Cross-Cultural and Interlanguage Communication* 32(5). 659–682.

Vincent, John & Jane Crossman. 2012. "Patriots at play": Analysis of newspaper coverage of the gold medal contenders in Men's and Women's ice hockey at the 2010 Winter Olympic Games. *International Journal of Sport Communication* 5(1). 87–108.

Vincent, John, John S. Hill, Andrew C. Billings, John Harris & Dwayne Massey. 2018. We are GREAT Britain: British newspaper narratives during the London 2012 Olympic Games. *International Review for the Sociology of Sport* 53(8). 895–923.

Wang, Ning, Zhongshi Guo & Fei Shen. 2011. Message, perception, and the Beijing Olympics: Impact of differential media exposure on perceived opinion diversity. *Communication Research* 38(3). 422–445.

Wann, Daniel L & Nyla R. Branscombe. 1990. Die-hard and fair-weather fans: Effects of identification on BIRGing and CORFing tendencies. *Journal of Sport & Social Issues* 14(2). 103–117.

Xu, Qingru, Andrew C. Billings & Minghui Fan. 2018. When women fail to 'hold up more than half the sky': Gendered frames of CCTV's coverage of gymnastics at the 2016 Summer Olympics. *Communication & Sport* 6(2). 154–174.

Yan, Grace & Nicholas M. Watanabe. 2014. The Liancourt Rocks: Media dynamics and national identities at the 2012 Summer Olympic Games. *International Journal of Sport Communication* 7. 495–515.

Yoon, Liv & Brian Wilson. 2016. "Nice Korea, Naughty Korea": Media framings of North Korea and the inter-Korean relationship in the London 2012 Olympic Games. *International Review for the Sociology of Sport* 51(5). 505–528.

Zhou, Shuhua, Bin Shen, Cui Zhang & Xin Zhong. 2013. Creating a competitive identity: Public diplomacy in the London Olympics and media portrayal. *Mass Communication and Society* 16. 869–887.

Richard Haynes

23 "For the good of the world": the innovations and influences of the UK's early international televizing of sport

Abstract: British television's early experiments in pan-continental exchanges of programming were heavily reliant on sharing live coverage of sport events with other nations. This led the BBC's post-War Controller of Television Cecil McGivern to proclaim such international exchanges of television were "for the good of the world." These formative explorations in pan-European exchanges are explored in order to understand the motivations for such innovations, the operational challenges that needed to be overcome and the ideological underpinnings for the national prestige some of these broadcasts brought to both television broadcasters and audiences. Through case studies of the BBC's international sport broadcasts and the pan-European coverage of the 1954 FIFA World Cup from Switzerland, the chapter explains how the BBC's public service mission and technological know-how were influential in the development of the European Broadcasting Union and the prominence of sport in its "Eurovision" broadcasts. The chapter explores the development of unilateral opt-outs from the multilateral broadcasts of the 1958 World Cup and how such innovations continue to shape contemporary coverage of major sport events on television. In conclusion, the chapter urges scholars to recognize the importance of broadcast history to help explain the cultural and technological transformations of television's relationship to sport.

Keywords: television sport; BBC; FIFA World Cup; Eurovision; unilateral broadcasts

1 Introduction: for the good of the world

> "There is something very much deeper in Eurovision than, shall we say, Wimbledon being seen by various countries. There is the B.B.C.s purpose of using broadcasting for the good of the world. There is the gratifying fact that when I go to an E.B.U. conference I meet friends. Not only friends, but good friends. We have learned to know one another, to respect each other. This fundamentally, is Eurovision."
> – Cecil McGivern (cited in Ross 1961: 134)

In the mid-1950s the BBC's Controller of Television, Cecil McGivern, remarked that the prospect of European viewers watching live coverage from the Wimbledon Lawn Tennis Championships would be "for the good of the world" (Ross 1961). McGivern's chief point was to suggest that broadcasting of live events on television brought people

https://doi.org/10.1515/9783110660883-023

together, and with the advent of international transmissions, could potentially bring people from different nations and cultures together to share in the same moments of international sport. The BBC had first televized the Wimbledon Championships in 1937 as it sought to exploit the cultural value of big public occasions, especially major sporting events. From 1951 the BBC had begun trials to transmit programmes to the south of England from France and in 1954 the first major trans-continental exchange of broadcasts, labelled "Eurovision" by the journalist George Campey of the London *Evening Standard* newspaper, led the way in the development of international television in Europe. By the end of the 1950s the European Broadcasting Union, which oversaw such broadcasts, included twelve nations and sixteen television services. Many of these broadcasts included live outside broadcasts (known as telecasts in North America) from sport. In some cases, they set the mould for future collaboration of broadcasters in the coverage of major sport mega-events such as Olympic Games and the FIFA men's World Cup among others (Billings and Wenner 2017). This chapter explores some of the BBC's early interventions in the pan-continental exchanges in order to understand the motivations for such innovations, the operational challenges that needed to be overcome and the ideological underpinnings for the national prestige some of these broadcasts brought to both television broadcasters and audiences.

The BBC's innovations and legacies in international broadcasting from sport, much of which continue to echo in the global sport broadcasting landscape of the 21st century, sought to bring the world of sport under its influence and control in order to ensure both a sense of realism and entertainment for its viewers (Whannel 1992). The immediacy of television, showing what happens as it happens, has consistently made for thrilling spectacles from sport. However, in the formative period of the medium such exchanges were frequently hampered by the constraints of technology and geography. Nevertheless, the drive of television's pioneers to bring such moments to the television screen arguably remains a continuing driver of contemporary television sport production with all its sophisticated technologies and global reach. This chapter is based on archival research from the BBC's Written Archives and a set of oral history interviews with a key pioneer of outside broadcasting, Peter Dimmock. Dimmock, the former General Manager of BBC Outside Broadcasts who joined the BBC in 1946, was a leading figure in negotiating television access to sport and championing the development of shared European transmissions. In this sense, the chapter gives a voice to someone who was involved at a senior level of decision making at the time. Capturing Dimmock's memories prior to his death in 2016 is also worthy of methodological note, as the need to capture the memories of sport communications professionals of the middle period of the 20th century is now an issue of extreme historical importance and urgency.

Investigating the immediate post-war coverage of sport up to the late 1950s provides knowledge on the place of sport in the BBC's public mission as well as its formative role in the development of international television exchanges. The historical analysis focuses on the organizational structures and cultures of sports production at the time, as well as the wider relationships the BBC had with governing bodies of sport and other European broadcasters. The late 1940s and the 1950s represent a period of intense innovation in the medium and one that arguably casts a shadow on the production practices and principles of today. What the chapter does not account for is the social and cultural impact televized sport had on its audience. Although contemporary evidence from the BBC's Audience Research can provide insights on the reception of television in the past, far more evidence survives of the institutional practices of the BBC outside broadcast department.

The chapter is shaped around key developments in the Eurovision project and the role of sport in the 1950s. This is significant not only because of the eventual growth of Olympic television (Billings et al. 2018) which was eventually driven by the leading American networks and the mediatization of sport-mega events more generally (Frandsen 2015), but also because it was happening at a time of the emergent ideological battle between Soviet and Western sport as a backdrop to the Cold War. I begin with an overview of how sport broadcasting fitted into, and became a central showcase of, the BBC's public mission to inform, educate, and entertain. Much of the vision for how the BBC approached its sports coverage came from the firebrand leadership of its General Manager of Outside Broadcasting, Peter Dimmock, which began to transform the range of television's ambitions to bring live events to the small screen. Secondly, the focus turns to innovations in the geographical and technical boundaries of what television engineers could develop in order to bring the first trans-national live outside broadcasts. Driven mainly by technocratic and symbolic motivations for linking the television systems of European nations, these innovations led to the Eurovision experiment in 1954, where coverage of the FIFA World Cup finals from Switzerland was a fortunate happenstance. The remainder of the chapter focuses on the preparations and planning for the coverage of the 1958 FIFA World Cup held in Sweden, which saw the rise of attempts to produce nation-specific coverage, commonly known as unilateral coverage, as a complimentary source of coverage from multi-lateral broadcasts of Eurovision. This latter development has remained a significant feature of global broadcast sport, particularly at Olympic Games and FIFA World Cups. It is part of the local–global nexus of how broadcasting continues to remain wedded to national norms and cultures.

2 Why sport mattered to BBC Television

One of the central issues raised by the BBC's coverage of sport has been the role it has played in the BBC's mission as a public service broadcaster. From its inception in 1936, the BBC Television service was adventurous in spirit but heavily constrained by resources in comparison to radio broadcasting (Briggs 1979). This was partly because radio had established itself as an affordable and immediate medium for news and entertainment, but also because the BBC's own public service mission, imbued by its first Director General John Reith, created an environment among its senior management that television was to be contained, not least to ward off the encroachment of commercial interests of advertisers that was driving the expansion of American television networks. Therefore, in Britain by 1950 there were 12 million radio-only licenses and a mere 350,000 joint radio and television licenses (Briggs 1979).

In the 1930s, outside broadcasts from sport were already well established in the mix of programming in radio at both national and local levels. It would, therefore, have seemed natural for television programming to simply follow suit. As Mark Aldridge (2011) has suggested, why television emerged as it did in the pre-war years was largely due to bureaucratic reasons, of how the BBC was institutionally established and operationally run. The great difference in the reality of producing outside broadcasts in radio and television, however, was the scale of the technology required to achieve this. Television outside broadcasts required significant investment in equipment and personnel compared to radio, and producers also faced enormous logistical problems to resolve, both on site and in relaying the pictures back to BBC Television's first home at Alexandra Palace in North London.

The need for resources, in technology and skilled employees, as well as in time and energy to set things up, meant that meeting the BBC's core value of serving the public interest through televized coverage of major national sporting events required a far greater investment than many forms of broadcasting. Sport was central to the public service mission to inform and entertain, with live coverage of national sporting occasions drawing interest from across Britain, producing some of the BBC's largest audience ratings. Sport has been central to the BBC's public service identity. It brought households and the UK nations together, in doing so defining the boundaries of what constituted a "national community" (Born 2005: 512). The BBC's monopoly of some sports and events both cemented its position as the nations' favored sports broadcaster and invented broadcast traditions that were culturally and politically difficult to challenge. When commercial television was launched in 1955 it found the doors to sport either firmly closed or, at the very least, firmly established with the BBC way of doing things (Whannel 1992. It arguably brought what would now be considered minor sports to the screen from a very early stage. In the 1950s, the BBC brought sports such as show jumping, ice hockey, motor sport, snooker, and skiing to new audiences. As the reach of television grew, it also brought sport from beyond the UK to British audiences, opening up opportunities to see international sports stars and competitions for the first time.

In 1950, the BBC's Television Outside Broadcasting (OB) department began to gain new impetus and a sense of adventure following the appointment of a new Assistant Head of OBs, Peter Dimmock. A former RAF flight-lieutenant flying instructor during World War II and a post-war horse-racing correspondent for the Press Association, Dimmock quickly rose to prominence in the modest-sized OB department. As the Head of Television Outside Broadcasts, a role he later designated as General Manager,

Dimmock oversaw the first live broadcast from an aeroplane, the first trans-continental television transmission, the first international satellite transmission, presented the first regular television sports magazine program *Sportsview*, was the first on British television to use a "teleprompter" (autocue), and the first to negotiate television coverage of the Grand National horse race and many other sporting events on television. At one time, in the late 1960s, he was arguably among the most experienced and most powerful people in the BBC and British broadcasting more broadly. His own modesty, however, would not allow him to concede he held such a position, but his international reputation in brokering deals for the Olympic Games and the FIFA World Cup ultimately led him to be head hunted by American networks keen to capitalize on the Dimmock charm.

In an oral history interview with Dimmock in 2009, he revealed why sport and outside broadcasts became so important to the BBC:

> With OB, dash it, they depended on us enormously for the overall audience figures. *Sportsview*, I suppose when you think about it now and it may sound ridiculous, but we had a regular audience of about 11 million. Which in those days was huge. All our events, our royal events and things in those days, they all got enormous audiences.[1]

Through the late 1950s and into the 1960s, Dimmock's role as negotiator became vital to keeping the BBC ahead of its commercial rival ITV. Following the launch of Eurovision in 1954, Dimmock became the head of sports negotiations on behalf of the European Broadcasting Union, frequently travelling the globe to meet and smooth-talk international administrators of sport. Again, his modesty in opening the way for global television coverage of sport shone through in his praise for the institution he worked for: "When I travelled all round the world, it was so wonderful. It was the fact that I was from the BBC that they gave me a great deal of respect, and help, and courtesy. Which was entirely because I was BBC, nothing to do with me."[2] Dimmock's professional achievements in internationalizing televized sport are not only evidence of a broadcasting pioneer, but also offer an insight into the discourse of modernity which was driving the motivation to push television technology to its limits and bring both European, and subsequently international, populations together through the shared experiences of viewing sport. The remainder of the chapter focuses on specific instances of this process and based on the BBC's written archives and Dimmock's memories, explores how innovation and professional ideologies of public service began to globalize television sport.

1 Peter Dimmock, interview with the author, 2009.

2 Dimmock interview, 2009.

3 Origins of Eurovision sport

The pan-European broadcasts to the allied forces and European populations during World War II had cemented the notion that European broadcasters could collaborate to deliver multi-lateral content (Stourton 2017). Although pan-continental broadcasts had featured since the origins of radio services in the 1920s with the formation of the International Broadcasting Union (IBU) in 1925, the harm caused to pan-continental relations created by conflict with Nazi Germany and, post-war, subsequent mistrust from the Allies of the emerging influence of the Soviet Union meant attempts to create new international broadcasting unions were heavily politicized and full of mistrust. Following a Constitutive Conference at Torquay in February 1950 chaired by the BBC's Director of external broadcasting services, Ian Jacob, it was decided to create a new entity, the European Broadcasting Union (EBU), which would be formed by representatives from West European broadcasters, with Jacob as its first President (Ross 1961: 128).

Early negotiations between emerging television services across Europe focused on how best to standardize television frequencies. Different nations used different frequencies and according to Fickers and O'Dwyer (2012: 69) there was "a hidden techno-political conflict" masking the *entente cordiale* being developed under the banner of the EBU. Underlying the technical conflict were industrial trade wars: British television manufacturers were keen for the BBC to work with European partners to help serve their commercial interests in competition with American rivals. The BBC were also keen to be viewed as the standard-bearer of television production practices having launched the world's first public television service in 1936. Therefore, the "techno-political bargaining" of pan-European broadcasts was also inflected by protectionist industrial policies and hegemonic struggles for cultural leadership as to what a European network would look like and how programs under its remit would be produced (Fickers and O'Dwyer 2012: 69).

In August 1950, the BBC instigated a series of Franco-British experiments to transmit television signals across the Channel using new portable radio links stationed across the south coast of England ideally positioned by BBC engineers pick up transmissions from Calais. In the BBC listings magazine, the *Radio Times*, the BBC's Controller of Television Programmes, Cecil McGivern recalled the moment the first flickering images came through in early engineering trials:

> For several hours we have been staring at the pictures on the screen. At seven o'clock it was black. Then light flickered across it, then turned blackness again. We knew that our outside broadcast engineers in Calais had switched on their gear, that cameras were alive, that pictures were struggling to reach us in Alexandra Palace. No one was sure if they would come. Then slowly a picture formed. It was L'Hôtel de Ville, the Town Hall of Calais. The picture settled. The building became clear. [...] all thoughts of the suffering of Calais were pushed in to the background by the excitement of this moment. (McGivern 1950: 35)

McGivern's report of the first cross-channel experiment captures the genuine sense of awe in the power of television to bring live images across the continent. Live outside broadcasts were key to television's aesthetic in developing a sense of "co-presence" with the audience: essentially giving them a sense of being somewhere else or, in the sporting context, a front row seat at the stadium (Ellis 2000). As the BBC sought new sites and events from which to broadcast, Dimmock's experience as a pilot proved efficacious in the speedy reconnaissance of new locations and European partners.

In January 1951, Dimmock travelled to the United States to learn how they had begun to transmit television over hundreds of miles. While on his visit, he watched live scenes of a large fire in Chicago from his hotel room in New York (Cannel 1951). Throughout the 1950s, Dimmock's work-life became increasingly driven by the desire to stretch the horizons of television technology and the distance it could relay live images from across the world. Further exchanges were planned between the BBC and Radiodiffusion-Télévision Française (RTF), such as "Paris Week" in July 1952 with Dimmock working closely with his French counterpart Jean d'Arcy for an entire week of broadcasts from the French capital including cycling from Velodrome d'Hiver. Frequently held as a television visionary, d'Arcy became integral to the success of the EBU and pan-European broadcasts from sport. In their analysis of d'Arcy during this period of innovation Fickers and O'Dwyer (2012: 70) conclude he "clearly saw the potential of television as a tool of rapprochement between people and nations and developed into an ambassador of this vision all around the world." The Paris transmissions were important for promoting further uptake of television in the UK, with 1.5 million homes reported to have access to the coverage, but technical issues bedevilled the broadcasts as viewers received sound without images, images without sound, pictures that wobbled or split the screen.[3] Nevertheless, some standards in how to transmit television across longer distances from mainland Europe to the UK, and vice versa, were beginning to take shape ahead of the largest outside broadcast of the era: the Coronation of Queen Elizabeth II in 1953. The scale of the Coronation broadcast, shared with five European countries, gave a further fillip to the confidence of the BBC explore further experiments with European broadcasters and in 1954 a major breakthrough for the EBU came with plans for the first major "Television Continental Exchange."

3.1 Eurovision and the 1954 World Cup

The first televizing of the World Cup came in 1954 from Switzerland from 16 June to 4 July. By 1953, with the prospect of the finals in Switzerland, the possibility of linking up a number of European countries as part of a "Television Continental Exchange" were being discussed by the EBU. A series of programs were transmitted between June

3 Unknown cutting from Peter Dimmock's private scrapbooks.

and July 1954, and the Swiss contribution from Berne included ten matches from the World Cup Finals. This represented the largest contribution to the exchange by any single country. The EBU exchange relied upon some four thousand miles of connecting landlines, with forty-four transmitters spread across the continent. The ideological motivation for the exchange, at least from a British perspective, is identifiable in the following quote from the BBC's chief engineer Michael Pilling (1954) in the *Radio Times*: "We have tried to advantage the universality of the picture as a way of overcoming the language barrier. This has led us to develop much more along the lines of shared programmes." The modern rhetoric of "universality" is quite striking in this statement, and represents a cultural politics cast in the shadow of the post-War international relations, cemented in organizations like the United Nations, but also identifiable in collaborative schemes to share knowledge and resources in organizations like UNESCO and the EBU.

Each participating national broadcaster – many of them less than one year in operation, many borrowing equipment and expertise from the BBC – had their own commentator for the same pictures, situated either at the stadium or in a remote studio. The technique of segregating background sounds or "effects" from commentary had first been used during the Coronation in 1953, with telerecordings exported to North America and Australia. British manufacturers supplied much of the technical apparatus to European broadcasters: for example, Pye sold outside broadcasting units to Belgium and Switzerland, and Marconi sold microwave links to enable transmitters to link up across national boundaries (British equipment 1954).

The "Eurovision" experiment represented the beginning of a new standard broadcasting format for the delivery of global sporting events, which later combined "unilateral" and "multilateral" feeds. In September 1953, EBU members met in London to discuss the 1954 summer season of television exchanges, which would act as a prelude to regular Eurovision programming (Fickers and Johnson 2012: 35). The concept of Eurovision enabled nations with modest resources to sustain a regular television service. The exchange worked on principles of reciprocity, independence of program selection, and voluntary participation.

The BBC started planning their coverage of the World Cup in December 1953 in the knowledge that both England and Scotland would be involved in the tournament. Initial correspondence with the Swiss revealed their lack of outside broadcasting technology and experience, and the BBC's premier producer of televized football Alan Chivers was dispatched to Geneva to work with Swiss producer (Regisseur) Frank Tappolet to help establish the best camera positions in the World Cup stadia and provide advice on how to cover a football match (Haynes 2016: 79). By 1954, the Swiss had only produced one outside broadcast of any note, so the European link-up from the World Cup hosts came with considerable risk. Chivers produced coverage of a friendly international between Switzerland and Holland on 30 May, the match being relayed live to audiences in the Netherlands. The coverage of the World Cup was an early experiment in production knowledge exchange, with the BBC sharing both equipment and, perhaps more crucially, its technical expertise of outside broadcasting. Production of the World Cup coverage was handled by the Swiss following Chivers' tuition who stepped aside following his mentoring of Swiss producers. The only exception was the main camera operator Bill Wright from the BBC, who as an experienced hand with the zoom lens was brought in to provide the close-up shots of the players.

The *Radio Times* (21 May 1954) previewed the broadcasting experiment under the heading "Television in Europe Today" noting that "between June 6 and July 4 viewers in Britain will be able to see a series of programmes relayed from seven European countries." Alongside British television were RTF from France (launched in March 1945), NTS from Holland (October 1951), ARD from (West) Germany (December 1952), RTB from Belgium (October 1953), SRG from Switzerland (November 1953), RAI from Italy (January 1954) and DR from Denmark (January 1954). The BBC transmitted eight live games in total starting with France versus Yugoslavia from La Pontaise Stadium, Lausanne, subsequently followed by England's opening group game against Belgium and Scotland's second group game against the then World Champions Uruguay.

Scotland had entered the World Cup Finals for the first time and following defeat to Austria in their opening game the Scots fell to a heavy defeat in their first live televized game on 19 June 1954, with ignominious defeat to Uruguay by seven goals to nil in Basle. Commentator Kenneth Wolstenholme was highly critical of the Scotland players and he later reflected the broadcast had emphasized the revelatory power of television which was "giving the British public its first real view of the might of world soccer" (Wolstenholme 1958: 77). Wolstenholme's commentary had caused controversy back in the UK, with some television critics suggesting his role was to "comment and not to criticize." In Scotland, the Glasgow newspaper the *Evening Citizen* published an open letter from Wolstenholme on its front page under the headline "Stop Your Crying, Scotland," explaining why his commentary had been so disparaging. This further fanned the flames of criticism of the BBC's coverage, but McGivern sent a telegram to Wolstenholme congratulating him on a "first-class job" (Wolstenholme 1958: 77). The episode revealed the way in which television was not simply a "window on the world" of international sport, but increasingly engaged within its discursive cultures. The controversy also revealed the tensions apparent for television when navigating the cultural politics of Britishness, Englishness, and Scottishness. Television became part of the national conversation on football, and as future World Cups would reveal, the passions associated with the tournament ran deep for all nations involved. Television played a compelling role in fostering strong emotions around international sport, at the same time revealing a need for more localized coverage. By the end of the 1950s the demands for more "unilateral" coverage, either live or recorded, from major international sporting events became increasingly apparent.

4 From multilateral to unilateral television sport: the 1958 World Cup

At an EBU conference in July 1954, M. Eduard Haas, the Program Director for Swiss Television announced to members that the next World Cup would be held in Sweden. The 1958 Finals were something of a landmark for the World Cup as a global tournament, not least because it was the first time Brazil became world champions, but principally because it was extensively filmed and televized for more nations than ever before. FIFA, ostensibly governed by post-colonial Europeans were, nevertheless, expanding their membership and reach following the relative success of the 1954 World Cup. By the time of the World Cup in Sweden, FIFA had 84 affiliated member associations, and from June 1956 an English president in Arthur Drewry (Rollin 1978). Grimsby born Drewry, a former President of the Football League and selector of England's losing side against the USA in 1950, had been hostile to television in the early 1950's (Briggs 1979: 856). In 1958, television had emerged from its relative infancy and was now playing an increasingly important role in gelling the international profile of FIFA and its event, delivering an emergent global consciousness to national audiences.

The World Cup was certainly high on the agenda of the BBC's outside broadcast department. Although accessing live coverage of the Finals via Eurovision was given highest priority, the BBC's *Sportsview* team under the leadership of Paul Fox (Editor) was key to the BBC's coverage of the event. The *Sportsview* team had invested time in covering some of the qualifying round matches, including England's game with the Republic of Ireland, Scotland's fixture with Spain, live Eurovision coverage of Northern Ireland's first-leg qualifier against Italy in Rome, capped by filmed highlights of a deciding qualifying match between one of the favorites for the Cup, Czechoslovakia versus Wales in May 1957.

The 1958 finals offered an opportunity for British football to redeem its international standing, as well as reverse a noticeable decline in aggregate attendances at English League matches from the high of the immediate post-war years; down from 41.3 million in 1948–49 to 33.2 million in 1955–56 (Rollin 1979). Calamitous defeats in previous World Cups for both England and Scotland had been sobering for British football, but according to Wolstenholme, it required "a road back" to prosperity, and to his mind the fault lay at the door of the poor standard of British football. Wolstenholme (1958: 61) conjectured: "is it not conceivable that the public, realizing that our standard of football has dropped to third rate, has decided to look elsewhere for its pleasures?" With all four home nations present at the 1958 Finals in Sweden the mounting pressure on British teams to succeed was growing in the face of immense criticism in certain quarters of the British press. Wolstenholme's pleas for improved standards and forethought against international competition was representative of a broader shift in the British sports media, which perceived home nation success as being crucial for national morale.

Radiotjänst, Sweden's first public television service, began in September 1956, and the prospect of relaying live football matches, in some cases simultaneously, from Malmo, Gothenburg, Norrkoping, and the capital Stockholm required significant investment (3.9m Swedish Krona) in telecommunications by the Swedish state. The Swedes planned to use twelve stadia for the finals, and it was viewed as impossible to get live relays from them all. Instead, EBU members would be supplied with 15-minute edited 16mm films of games where live transmission via microwave and landlines was not feasible.[4] There were two major issues: first, there were concerns that the landlines to connect the major cities of Malmo, Gothenburg, Norrkoping, and Stockholm would not be ready in time; and secondly, that Svenska Fotbollförbundet (the Swedish Football Association) were stalling on negotiations over television rights in fear that television would affect ticket sales.

The logistical and commercial issues compounded a number of issues facing the BBC, which created tension between senior managers and the *Sportsview* unit. Interest in the 1958 World Cup had up-scaled considerably since 1954, and Dimmock, ever conscious of the threat of losing out on a rights deal to commercial rivals ITV in either television or film, purposefully built an alliance with the host broadcaster Radiotjänst, visiting their offices in May 1957. The Swedish FA had given Radiotjänst the final option on the World Cup coverage, and thereby by default the BBC.[5]

4.1 Unilateral *Sportsview* film

With the logistical issue unresolved the BBC began to explore the idea of having their own unilateral *Sportsview* Unit film crews covering matches. This meant eschewing the Swedes' 15-minute 16mm film, which would have to be dubbed back in England, by substituting their own footage of entire games filmed with unilateral sound and running commentary. The consequences on resources were significant: flying out a whole production crew of camera operators, sound engineers, electricians, editors, commentators; producers and couriers to transport the film; purchasing enough film for at least 3000 feet per match; a motor pool of motorcyclists to transport film from stadia to laboratories for development; finding suitable editing facilities near to transmission facilities; facilities for redubbing German-built "Mayhak" tapes the Swedes were using into transmittable magnetic tape; finding suitable telecine transmission facilities; and studio facilities for introducing and analyzing the film.[6] The other problem associated with filmed matches was the likelihood they could not be screened on the same day as the matches, so an enforced 24-hour delay in transmis-

4 Letter from Henrik Hahr to Peter Dimmock, 4 April 1957, BBC Written Archives Centre.

5 Letter from Gert Engstroom to Peter Dimmock, 28 May 1957, BBC WAC.

6 Paul Fox to Peter Dimmock, World Cup Championships, no date given but likely October 1957, BBC WAC.

sion would occur, losing much of the power of immediacy created by live Eurovision feeds. It was not the solution Dimmock's team had anticipated but the pressure to have BBC coverage alongside the multilateral feed was felt to be paramount to meet the demands of British viewers.

Controller of Television Programmes, McGivern, was not keen on sending the *Sportsview* Unit to Sweden for fear of jeopardizing the production of *Sportsview* itself scheduled to run through June 1958. Relaying the disappointing news to editor Paul Fox and producer Brian Cowgill, Dimmock revealed McGivern did not feel "that the interest of a World Cup will be sufficient to warrant a late night placing of expensive film material unless we can provide overwhelming and concrete evidence to the contrary."[7] The editor Fox was unequivocal in his belief the BBC required a *Sportsview* unit out in Sweden, both because the Swedish football films he had seen were "most unsatisfactory" but primarily because all four United Kingdom nations were likely to be represented. In January 1958 he wrote a strong plea in favor of sending a BBC crew:

> All our soccer coverage throughout the winter is building up towards the World Cup. Football interest is enormous because of the approach of the World Cup. A million people – a potential three million audience – are going to soccer each Saturday. I feel that we have a duty towards them, and to the millions more who regularly follow our sports programmes, to provide the best possible World Cup reports.[8]

Fox knew the British press would be giving full attention to the Finals and would therefore be a major talking point of the nation. The divergent views revealed a discord between the BBC's senior and middle management about the status the World Cup, its popularity and why it should matter to the BBC's public mission. While those working in televized sport completely understood the emergent international kudos associated with the World Cup, senior management could not appreciate its broader appeal. Fox clearly thought the BBC would look out of pace with the nation if they didn't provide extensive coverage, going so far as to suggest: "England could win this World Cup – and wouldn't we look silly if we weren't on the spot!"[9]

With all four home nations represented, one further issue for the BBC to overcome was the scheduling of matches. FIFA had scheduled many of the games on the same date and the same time, and in an attempt to relax this policy Dimmock wrote to Drewry requesting FIFA revise the timetabling of significant fixtures. It was the first time television had attempted to interfere with the organization of the World Cup, but Dimmock's request fell on deaf ears. The reluctance to move fixtures meant Eurovision could only televize one quarter-final and one semi-final. With the high possibility of fixture clashes, the BBC were concerned at the prospect of limited live feeds of rele-

7 Dimmock to Fox and Cowgill, 20 December 1957, BBC WAC.
8 Paul Fox to Peter Dimmock, 3 January 1958, BBC WAC.
9 Paul Fox to Peter Dimmock, 3 January 1958, BBC WAC.

vant games for British viewers. Jack Oaten, the BBC's "Sports Organizer" spelt out the consequences to Dimmock:

> It could well be that the BBC would not get any of the British teams in a "live" relay and I would have thought more study should be given to the prospect of alternative routes for relays, although obviously Germany hold the key to this. The combinations of the various matches will greatly affect the issue. Regretfully these may not be known in time to do much about it.[10]

In the event, live coverage was complemented by *Sportsview* crews filming the British nations in action and Fox worked on the logistics of access and resources with the EBU representative Kirk Bergoten. There were therefore three sources of coverage: Eurovision live transmission, Radiotjänst non-dubbed pooled edited film highlights, and BBC dubbed filmed material with commentary. Both un-dubbed pooled film and dubbed *Sportsview* film were flown from Stockholm at 8.30am arriving in London at 1.30pm. The pooled material was sent to Television News, who inserted no more than two minutes of film in the evening news bulletin, and the latter produced for *Sportsview*, was included in a television news feature called *World Cup Report* transmitted during the early evening topical magazine program *Tonight* presented by Cliff Michelmore. The *Tonight* feature enabled the BBC to provide some filmed highlights of the British national teams in action, including England's matches against the USSR and Austria, Scotland's matches against Yugoslavia, Paraguay, and France, Wales against Hungary and Mexico, and Northern Ireland against Czechoslovakia and Argentina as well as a roundup of the first week's events. Fox again, detailed the reasoning for the BBC's singular approach: "We have evolved our own, highly specialized system of football reporting on film and since the World Cup is a highlight that occurs only every four years, we hope to be given the facilities to use our own reporting methods."[11]

The BBC had arranged editing facilities on a Steinbeck machine, unilateral telecine transmission, and unilateral studio facilities. This set up had first been trialed on a smaller scale during the Winter Olympics from Cortina, Italy in 1956, but Sweden was a new departure in combining pooled and BBC shot footage. The film shot by two BBC crews led by Alan Prentice and Jimmy Balfour would also form part of the EBU pooled content. FIFA had insisted no more than ten minutes of film could be televized from any one day, which had to be transmitted as "news" rather than sports content per se. Any contravention of the contract would be met with a hefty fine from FIFA.[12] The *Sportsview* film for the *Tonight* program, was cut in Sweden, with commentary recorded and synchronized on 16mm sprocketed-sound-film, before being flown back and transferred to 35mm magnetic tape at the BBC's Television Film Studio in Ealing.[13] The dubbing of commentary in Sweden was shared by Wolstenholme, Peter

10 Jack Oaten to Peter Dimmock, 21 October 1957, BBC WAC.
11 Paul Fox to Imlay Newbiggin-Watts, 3 January 1958, BBC WAC.
12 Paul Fox to Donald Baverstock, 27 May 1958, BBC WAC.
13 Ronnie Noble to Jack Oaten, 30 May 1958, BBC WAC.

Thompson who described Scotland's games against Paraguay and France, and by a new voice of the time, David Coleman. Where the *Sportsview* crews were filming the game, commentary was produced live on to the recording, where pooled material was used the commentary was dubbed afterward. Coleman's cooption in to the *Sportsview* team did not go down well with his superior the Head of Programmes in the Midland Region, Denis Morris, who agreed the experience would help Coleman's career but would leave a group of "hard pressed people" to produce a daily television bulletin, radio, and sports output at "tremendous strain."[14]

Dimmock thought the inclusion of World Cup football in *Tonight* would give its producer Donald Baverstock "an invaluable ingredient to his programme in terms of audience size and appreciation."[15] His assumption was premised on the ratings boost *Tonight* received when it televized the FA Cup draw in 1958. On 18 June, at the mid-point of the World Cup, Fox attempted to arrange a live feed from Sweden during the weekly edition of Sportsview. The idea of hosting the entire program from Sweden would, Fox argued, "mount another audience-puller by the very fact that the *Sportsview* desk has been moved to Stockholm, where the big sports news is being made."[16] The Swedes could not release the lines required at that time in the evening and the idea was sunk. Broadcasters now invest huge resources on locating their studio to showcase their presence at the host nation of a major sporting event. Fox's idea reveals the early imagination of such global possibilities for live sports coverage, which he considered important for the viewer. In the end, the cost of sending two *Sportsview* crews to film the games was £3527, a modest investment for maximum impact of having World Cup football across ten evenings.[17]

4.2 Eurovision, live rights and competition

In March 1958, FIFA and the Swedish FA established a small working group to negotiate live television rights, which included Sir Stanley Rous. Rous promptly wrote to the BBC's Director General, Sir Ian Jacob, who was also the President of EBU, in order to ascertain where the matter stood so that he may "know where to begin negotiations."[18] However, negotiations for the live television rights took a new, and for the BBC alarming, turn later in the same month when Bill Ward at commercial franchise Associated Television (ATV) directly offered £103,500 for an exclusive deal to the Swedish FA to televize and distribute the European rights for the World Cup. The Swedes notified the EBU, and Jean d'Arcy issued a stern warning to ATV via Bernard

14 Denis Morris to Peter Dimmock, 2 May 1958, BBC WAC.
15 Peter Dimmock to Seymour de Lotbiniere, 22 May 1958, BBC WAC.
16 Paul Fox to S.P.A.Tel II, 28 May 1958, BBC WAC.
17 J. Mair to de Lotbiniere, 27 May 1958, BBC WAC.
18 Sir Stanley Rous to Sir Ian Jacob, 12 March 1958, BBC WAC.

Sendall at the commercial regulator the Independent Broadcasting Authority. Ward and other commercial television managers were invited to an EBU Bureau meeting in Brussels where they were asked to put their case. The Bureau pronounced the deal was contrary to all EBU agreements and ATV retracted their offer. The episode alerted BBC senior managers, including Seymour de Lotbiniere and Cecil McGivern of the threat the ITV companies now posed to the BBC's position in covering major sporting events. The contract Ward had offered to the Swedish FA had mentioned using transmission lines to "Swingate or any other point suitable to ITA," and McGivern concluded, "ITA can be disconcertingly successful in its aims and methods."[19] The late intervention from commercial television emphasized the poor management of the rights process by the Swedish FA and FIFA. On 7 May 1958 the Swedish FA in conjunction with FIFA representatives agreed a television and sound deal with the Swedish Broadcasting Corporation for 1.5 million Swedish Kronar (£104,000). The BBC's estimated share of the rights fee was £20,000, and the total cost of sending Kenneth Wolstenholme (covering eight matches), Wally Barnes (covering two matches), Peter Dimmock and a producer was £1473. When added to the *Sportsview* crew costs, this brought the total cost of televizing the World Cup to approximately £25,000. When the negotiations were finalized, Dimmock admitted to de Lotbiniere:

> All in all it has been a most frustrating negotiation, and I am still bitterly disappointed that by leaving things so late we have been landed with – comparatively speaking – an unsatisfactory contract. At the same time, although it is not financially outrageous, it would have been unthinkable had negotiations finally broken down altogether on the live side, in view of the participation of four teams from the British Isles.[20]

Dimmock's concerns were clearly born of the delays to signing the contract which had left the door open to the late-comer ITV to join the Eurovision feed, and adversely affect the aspiration of the BBC to schedule coverage of more games involving British teams. The BBC ultimately televized ten live transmissions including the opening ceremony which kick-started the event with a fly-past by the Swedish Royal Air Force. ITV transmitted three group matches including games involving England and Wales, as well as one quarter-final, semi-final, third-placed play-off, and the final. Special dispensation was given by the EBU for two English-speaking commentators to be present in the stadium, where other language groups could only have one. The BBC's live coverage from Sweden was as follows:

> 2.00pm, 8 June, Mexico vs Sweden, Stockholm.
> 7.00pm, 8 June, Germany vs Argentina, Malmo.
> 7.00pm, 11 June, England vs Brazil, Gothenburg.
> 7.00pm, 12 June, Sweden vs Hungary, Stockholm.

19 Cecil McGivern to C.Tel.S.Eng, 24 March 1958, BBC WAC.
20 Peter Dimmock to Seymour de Lotbiniere, 22 May 1958, BBC WAC.

2.00pm, 15 June, Sweden vs Wales, Stockholm.
7.00pm, 15 June, Northern Ireland vs Germany, Malmo.
7.00pm, 19 June, Quarter-Final, Sweden vs USSR, Solna.
7.00pm, 24 June, Semi-Final, Brazil vs France, Solna.
7.00pm, 28 June, 3rd Place Play-Off, France vs West Germany, Gothenburg.
7.00pm, 29 June, Final, Sweden vs Brazil, Stockholm.

The BBC also made contingencies to take live feeds of any replayed matches, though none were required. Noticeably absent from the list of live games were Scotland, which for a nation of football enthusiasts must have been deeply disappointing to many viewers. Although all three of Scotland's games were filmed, most Scots were left with the option of listening to live running commentaries or eyewitness reports on the BBC's Light Programme. England's only live transmission was against Brazil and produced the first ever 0–0 draw in World Cup Finals history.

British audiences had never been exposed to so much football on television, and the BBC's competition with ITV had heightened the promotional battle to capture viewers. ITV had proposed alternating the coverage, to avoid both channels covering the same event, but Dimmock had refused claiming the BBC had "9,000,000 viewers not served by commercial." Moreover, the BBC had "paid a big fee" and it "would be unfair to cut some of our licence fee payers off from some of the matches."[21] For some, as the *Daily Express* critic James Thomas put it, "duplicated soccer relays are killing any idea of choice in live television."[22] It was a scenario that would perpetuate for decades to come, until genuine alternation of World Cup games was agreed between the two rival broadcasters. Nevertheless, on another front, the experiment of mixing unilateral with multilateral coverage showed quite convincingly that televizing large-scale international sports events needed to be contextualized for the home audience.

5 Conclusion

The BBC's coverage of the World Cups in 1954 and 1958 reveal both material and symbolic dimensions of television technology and the role of sport within it. There were technical challenges: the logistical problems of transmission across the continent; the incommensurable technical standards and capacities of different EBU partners; the limits of technology to provide live coverage from every location; and innumerable resource constraints of material and human kind. But there was an optimistic, pioneering will to overcome these challenges, even in the face of cultural differences. Televizing the World Cup also had symbolic meaning, which transformed over the

21 World Cup TV "Double" Sparks Row, *Daily Express*, 17 June 1958.
22 World Cup TV "Double" Sparks Row, *Daily Express*, 17 June 1958.

decade from near ignorance and willing indifference, to greater public awareness and mass appeal to share the World Cup televisual experience. This sense of the World Cup as a mediated experience was still new, contested and unstable.

The BBC's approach to the coverage of sport in the 1950s was central to the consumption and appropriation of television in the UK, which had changed from a monopoly service when relaunched in 1946 to a hard-fought competition for viewers following the launch of Independent Television regional franchises in 1955. The BBC under the leadership of Peter Dimmock used its leverage as the established national broadcaster, built on the foundations of public service, to secure access to sport events and competitions and lay the foundations among the British public that sport was wedded to the BBC's national identity. It is an identity the BBC has attempted to maintain, even under severe pressure from dedicated sport channels delivered by Sky, BT, and others which have massively undermined the BBC's ability to obtain rights to television sport.

Where the BBC has been able to maintain its position as a public broadcaster of sport has been major international competitions such as the Winter and Summer Olympic Games and coverage of the FIFA World Cups for men and women. This is partly due to the protected status of such events to be freely available under the UK's Listed Events legislation, but it is also arguably part of a legacy which stretches back to the BBC's formative role in the development of televizing such events, organized through its collaboration with the EBU and Eurovision project, naturalizing the BBC's place in the coverage of certain sport mega-events for the British public. Ultimately, the economic and technological environment in public broadcasting shall dictate the ability for the BBC to sustain its position in this respect, but what this chapter has also revealed is that the cultural importance of how television brings a nation together during moments of major sporting competition, something which has been maintained even in the face of the digital disruption to global television industries, had its roots in the innovations in sports programming of the 1950s.

Such continuities in television sport, which cut across the impulse in communications research to recognize every new technological revolution which is changing our society and culture, are important to recognize and also study historically. As Michael Pickering (2015: 16) has persuasively argued regarding the devaluation of history among media and communication scholars, we need to be "more receptive to slower processes of cultural change and adaptation, longer-term institutional formations and resilient structural continuities." In the context of international television sport, the BBC, the EBU, and other public television networks of the world represent such resilient forms as they adapt to new global and local economic, cultural, and political circumstances.

The growth of new television services across Europe in the 1950s and the pioneering work achieved by engineers and producers at the BBC and their counterparts across the Eurovision enterprise in the coverage of sport continues to shape the mechanics of how major sporting events are covered, distributed, and viewed across the world. The development of satellite technology in the early to mid-1960s obviously transformed the technological reach and immediacy of televized sport into homes across the world. Nevertheless, the combination of multilateral with unilateral feeds continues to feature strongly in the coverage of major sports, combining as it does, both shared images of momentous moments of sport with the localized narratives of national sport stars and teams. The BBC's inroads to deliver unilateral coverage from the FIFA World Cup in 1958, and subsequently from the Olympic Games in Rome 1960 (Haynes 2014) and subsequent sport mega-events, represent a particular approach to global television sport which the broadcaster felt was its duty to deliver for British audiences.

One key to this process has been the availability of technical know-how and resources to do so, something not all international public broadcasters have been able to do. To this extent it must be recognized that the world of global televized sport continues to have economic and cultural discrepancies between nations in how televized sport is distributed and received by different audiences. Moreover, as public broadcasters across the globe have receded in the face of inroads in local television markets by global media conglomerates, so free public access to major sport mega-events like the FIFA World Cup and the Olympic Games have been privatized behind subscription pay-walls. Again, this is where historical research on what such coverage of global events has meant to both public broadcasters and their audiences provides useful counterpoints to contemporary economic decisions on sports broadcasting which do not always meet with public favor. The cultural politics of global televized sport, therefore, can benefit from a knowledge of previous generations of sports broadcasters and their motivations for marrying the interests of sport and television, as Cecil McGivern suggested, "for the good of the world."

References

Aldridge, Mark. 2011. *The birth of British television: A history*. London: Palgrave.

Billings, Andrew C. & Lawrence A. Wenner. 2017. The curious case of the megasporting event: Media, mediatization and seminal sports events. In Lawrence A. Wenner & Andrew C. Billings (eds.), *Sport, media and mega-events*, 3–18. New York: Routledge.

Billings, Andrew C., James R. Angelini & Paul J. MacArthur. 2018. *Olympic television: Broadcasting the biggest show on earth*. New York: Routledge.

Born, Georgina. 2005. *Uncertain vision: Birt, Dyke and the reinvention of the BBC*. London: Vintage.

Briggs, Asa. 1979. *The history of broadcasting in the United Kingdom: Sound and vision (1945–1955)*. Oxford: Oxford University Press.

British equipment for Eurovision. 1954. *Financial Times*. 8 June 1954. 1.

Cannel, R. 1951. 100-mile TV in summer. *Daily Express*, 20 January 1951 (no page, cutting from Peter Dimmock scrapbooks).

Ellis, John. 2000. *Seeing things: Television in the age of uncertainty*. London: Bloomsbury.

Fickers, Anders & Catherine Johnson (eds.). 2012. *Transnational television history: A comparative approach*. London: Routledge.

Fickers, Anders & Andy O'Dwyer. 2012. Reading between the lines: A transnational history of the Franco-British "Entente Cordiale" in post-war television. *View Journal of European Television History and Culture* 1(2). 56–70.

Frandsen, Kirsten. 2015. Sports organizations in a new wave of mediatization. *Communication & Sport* 4(4). 385–400.

Haynes, Richard. 2014. The maturation of Olympic television: The BBC, Eurovision and Rome 1960. *Stadion* 38/39. 163–182.

Haynes, Richard. 2016. *BBC Sport in black and white*. London: Palgrave.

McGivern, Cecil. 1950. Calais en Fête. *Radio Times*. 25 August 1950.

Pickering, Michael. 2015. The devaluation of history in media studies. In Martin Conboy & John Steel (eds.), *The Routledge companion to British media history*, 9–18. Abingdon: Routledge.

Pilling, Michael. 1954. *Radio Times*. 21 May 1954.

Rollin, Jack. 1978. *The Guinness book of soccer facts & feats*. London: Guinness.

Ross, Gordon. 1961. *Television jubilee: The story of twenty-five years of BBC Television*. London: W.H. Allen & Co.

Stourton, Edward. 2017. *Auntie's war: The BBC during the Second World War*. London: Doubleday.

Whannel, Garry. 1992. *Fields in vision: Television sport and cultural transformation*. London: Routledge.

Wolstenholme, Kenneth. 1958. *Sport special*. London: Sportsmans Book Club.

Karsten Senkbeil

24 Sports and the media in Germany: lessons in nationhood and multiculturalism

Abstract: The history of German sports culture and media communication shows parallels to other Western countries – e. g., in terms of commercialization and internationalization – but also some remarkable differences. In particular, the German ambivalence with its own nationhood and history has repeatedly become topical around the most popular soccer event, the FIFA World Cup, which continues to be organized around nationality and understood as a venue of intercultural contact. The Germans' problematic relationship with their own nation(s) and historical legacy has made sports fandom and sports patriotism around international contests involving a German team ambiguous and controversial. This chapter recapitulates how the German sports media has discursively framed international success and failure of the German male national soccer team at FIFA World Cups since the 1950s as yardsticks of Germany's status in the world, and as expressions of cultural and sociopolitical change within. One particular recent event, Mesut Özil's retiring from the national soccer team on the grounds of perceived racism and discrimination in 2018, may represent a rupture of a theretofore relatively continuous process. Therefore, a case study analysis of the "Özil crisis" will shed light not only on the status quo of sports communication in Germany, but also how this event may be indicative for future developments in society in general.

Keywords: nationality; multiculturalism; ethnicity; Germany; media communication; soccer; FIFA World Cup; discourse analysis

1 Introduction

Almost 40 years after Anderson's foundational observation that nations are, first and foremost, "imagined communities" (Anderson 1983), the nation state has indeed lost much of its meaning when it comes to the dispersion of cultural, particularly popular cultural practices. While politically the nation state has recently seen a renaissance in the rhetoric of right-wing movements in many European countries, many (though of course not all) citizens of the EU have come to embrace the idea of a "supra-" or "post-"national organization of social and cultural life. This includes the most important and most profitable soccer competition on the continent: the UEFA Champions League. In this light, it must appear anachronistic that the other most popular soccer event, the FIFA World Cup (taking place less often, but then largely outshining the UEFA CL), remains organized around nationality and understood as a venue of "old-fashioned" nation-vs-nation clashes. The general trend in soccer-friendly countries today is that the international and multicultural day-to-day of city-based club

https://doi.org/10.1515/9783110660883-024

teams is superseded every four years by the FIFA World Cup, in which the countries' national (men's) teams are celebrated as a seemingly reliable measurement of the nation's prowess and skill. This is true for Germany as much as for all other larger European (and also South American and African) nations.

In Germany, however, the meaning of the national football team has been further complicated by the nation's highly ambiguous relationship with its own history. Whereas people in many other countries have found it fairly easy to gather behind their national teams with an air of benevolent, sportsmanlike patriotism in times of peace, the German public's love–hate relationship with its own nation(s) and cultural roots has made sports fandom around international contests a controversial topic (see Senkbeil 2017).

This chapter recapitulates how the German sports media has rhetorically framed international success and failure (particularly of the German male national football team, the single most important team in the country) as yardsticks of Germany's status in the world, as examples of intercultural contact, and as expressions of sociodemographic and cultural change within. It identifies four phases since 1949, in which the German public tackled questions of nationhood and cultural diversity in and around sports rather differently. It argues that the cultural history of soccer in Germany is an exemplary case of the struggle between the forces of transnationalism and multiculturalism and older, yet still prevalent yearnings for clear-cut nation states, ethnic homogeneity, and a seemingly simpler, more orderly world.

The latest of these four phases is still under way, or may be currently ending. To discuss its status quo in Germany, this chapter will examine a particular media event, which represents a turning point in a theretofore rather continuous process. In July 2018, Mesut Özil, one of the most talented German players and previously a public figurehead of multiculturalism and integration of Germans with foreign family roots, retired from the national football team on the grounds of perceived racism and discrimination. This event became the most prevalent topic in soccer journalism in Germany in that year. This chapter will analyze the media discourse about this recent event to shed light not only on the status quo of sports communication in Germany, but also to discuss in how far Özil's case may be indicative for future developments in European societies in general.

Naturally, as the phases that this chapter defines describe cultural and ideological developments, which obviously take time and are rarely unidirectional, these phases cannot have clear and precise start or end points. Instead, I hold that they can be roughly organized *around* (rather than *before* or *after*) four climactic events in German soccer history, specifically the four times when the German national team won the world championship (1954, 1974, 1990, 2014). So, without claiming to account for the entirety of socio-culturally relevant events or trends during these four phases, I hold that these four years and successful teams in particular represent pinnacles, but hence also decisive turning points in the German understanding of itself as a (sports) nation and culture.

2 Phase 1: 1954 – steps towards a "normal" nation

Immediately after World War II, the German nation was militarily, politically, and economically practically non-existent: it had started and then been defeated in the most destructive war in history, occupied by four world powers, then split into two halves, and politically and economically fully dependent on decisions made elsewhere. In the social, cultural, and sports sphere, Germans were internationally ostracized for understandable reasons.

Their fascination for soccer, however, had survived the war, and club games amid the city ruins were welcome distractions from the rough life in post-war Germany. When in 1950, a West German soccer team was allowed to play its first international game (against Switzerland) after World War II, this carried large symbolic value, as many understood this as a first step of the humbled sinner back into the ranks of civilized nations (Beck 2010). In 1954, West Germany was admitted to the FIFA World Cup (also in Switzerland), and, again, this was largely seen as an important step towards becoming a "normal" nation, able to peacefully and sportsmanly measure forces with other countries, and a chance to mitigate the image of the "ugly German" (Brüggemeier 2006).

Video footage (though it is comparably scarce) shows how the German players were apparently aware of the touchy political context in which they returned to the world stage and were thus on their best behavior: fair play was emphasized, and when scoring a goal, the German players avoided overly triumphant celebrations (see video footage at: 1954: Das Wunder 2011). The historiography of the 1954 World Cup is full of anecdotes that display the politically sensitive situation. For example, the lyrics of the German national anthem from before 1945 had, at this point, been "tainted" by their usage by the Nazi government, its aggressive militarism, racism, and nationalism, and thus been exchanged with "tamer" lyrics in 1952, while keeping the melody the same. The problem in 1954 was that the German players – just as most other citizens – only knew the old lyrics, and had not memorized the new verse yet, so they (players and Germans in the audience) did not know what exactly to sing when their anthem played (Brüggemeier 2006). Film documents (e. g., *Forschungsstelle NS und Pädagogik* 2012) show that German fans sung the old version – which was, technically speaking, illegal – and were shushed by others; some players timidly moved their lips, pretending to sing, others tenaciously chewed gum, many kept their mouth tightly shut. As mentioned, it was a socially awkward and, at the same time, politically explosive situation.

In what has come to be known as the "Miracle of Bern," the German team was able to beat Hungary 3–2 in the final game against all odds, surprising themselves just as much as most sports journalists. The highly ambivalent role that this victory played in the political climate of 1954 for Germans and how they saw themselves can be exemplarily seen in the moment of receiving the Jules Rimet trophy after the game: video footage shows Fritz Walter, the German captain, being handed the trophy, and, in a stark contrast to today's trophy celebrations, strongly curbing his emotions, smiling shyly, shaking hands with officials and the Hungarian team captain, and then, as he quite obviously had no idea about what to do with the shiny statue in his hand, walking over to his coach, the soft-spoken, friendly authority figure Sepp Herberger, attempting to hand over the trophy to him, hoping to put an end to this obviously embarrassing moment. This mix of positive emotions (happiness, pride, thankfulness) coupled with self-consciousness and insecurity about how to behave on the world stage can be regarded as emblematic for the national self-understanding of Germany in the 1950s: this is, after all, the happiest moment in Walter's career, and at the same time it is the first time in decades that Germans have a reason to honestly and innocently celebrate and be proud of something. But quite symbolically, Walter had no idea what to do. Rather than behaving wrongly – according to the stereotypical image of the triumphant, arrogant German – with the eyes of the world on him, he chose to "hide" his joy and pride, and get it over with as soon as possible.

It would be too early to speak of any obvious "multicultural" element in this first phase, though this term will become central in the discussion of later phases. However, this first climactic event in German soccer history displays one key element that cannot be overemphasized for all developments that were to follow: the German national soccer team has meant and still means much more than merely a sports team. It carries the weight of the central symbol for the nation's self-understanding, and its stance towards its neighbors.

3 Phase 2: 1974 – young, smart, talented Germans

The sociopolitical and ideological transformation of the 1960s counter-culture movements in the United States had arrived in Germany with a slight time lag. After 1968 though, Western German culture and public life changed just as drastically towards a more liberal, progressive lifestyle. What had started at universities had filtered into youth culture and sports by 1972 and 1974, when West Germany hosted the two most important international sport events (the Olympic Games in 1972 and the FIFA World Cup in 1974). The Olympic Games of Munich 1972 are a key element for the German collective memory around sports (Butterworth 2016), and the soccer tournament of 1974 (also with the final game in Munich) is today widely remembered as a source of joy and pride, as – finally – Germany felt it had shed its Nazi personality and acquired an air of hospitality, fun, and youthful modernity (for example, in terms of fashion and stadium architecture). The German team won on its home turf against a strong Dutch side, and most Germans felt that even though they should not (yet, or anymore) feel proud about their nation, they could be proud of the remarkable skills of world class players such as Franz Beckenbauer, Gerd Müller, Paul Breitner, and Günter Netzer. Following the general zeitgeist, this generation of players was the first to actively and consciously look and act differently to their stiff and soldierly predecessors (Gizinski

2014). They let their hair grow longer, wore colorful designer fashion off the pitch, questioned and occasionally disobeyed authorities, and tentatively tested rock-star-like identity performances, most notably Günter Netzer, driving to team practice in his Ferrari. Others, such as Paul Breitner, were politically active and supported Mao Zedong and the anti-war movement. Though they were not without critics at the time these new representatives of "young Germany" appeared to the media public decidedly cooler, smarter, and generally much more interesting than the post-war generation of the 1950s and 60s.

Also, the team's success and the two sport events in general functioned as door-openers for international contact and raised awareness for interculturality to a new level. The West German population took pride in the role of the friendly and competent host to their foreign guests in 1972 and 1974, and then was surprised and fascinated by their favorite soccer players owning Italian sports cars and fashion, discussing Che Guevara's legacy with journalists, traveling across Europe (for UEFA cup games), or signing contracts with Spanish world class teams.

Still, celebrating this new, lighter version of Germanness was by no means without emotional downsides: any international sport event during the Cold War also served as a reminder that the German people remained separated into two nations that, ideologically, were locked in enmity. In 1974, the Federal Republic of Germany in fact had to play against the German Democratic Republic in a relatively meaningless first-round game. Not only did the later champions lose 1–0 after a weak performance against "the Other Germans," but such politically touchy confrontations on the sports pitch also curbed much of the lighthearted patriotism that other European national teams embodied for their countries. This situation only resolved itself 16 years later.

4 Phase 3: 1990 – petit bourgeois sports in times of tremendous change

The years 1989 and 1990 were tumultuous for German nationhood for obvious reasons. Right between two momentous events – the fall of the Berlin Wall in November 1989 and the reunification of East and West in October 1990 – the (then still exclusively West) German national team won its third world championship in Italy in June 1990. Interestingly, while the political developments of the time went stunningly quickly, culturally the late 1980s in West Germany had been remarkably conservative. Similar to Reaganism in the USA and Thatcherism in the UK, Kohlism (after Helmut Kohl, chancellor 1982–1998) in West Germany was a time in which much of the progressivist energy of the 1970s had given way to a form of petit bourgeois conservatism, based on its pride in hard work, productivity, orderliness, and social and cultural stability.

Since the 1950s, a booming economy had needed a workforce that the German labor market could not provide, so the government had initiated so-called "guest worker" programs with Southern European countries. Between 1955 and 1973, 14 million people, particularly from Italy, Greece, Turkey, and from many other countries in smaller numbers had migrated to West Germany to work. About three million of them stayed, spent the rest of their lives there, brought their families, and had children.

So, even though demographically Germany must be considered a multicultural society by 1990, politically and culturally this process was largely a non-issue. A person's national identity was widely equivocated with their ethnic identity (stemming from an autochthonous family), and the fact that German cities and factories were full of men with slightly darker skin, black hair, and foreign names, whose children now went to school side-by-side with native German kids, did not yet fully register as a central issue for the future of society, culture – or sports for that matter.

The 1990s football team and its public representation largely mirrored this cultural conservatism and lack of awareness about a quickly changing society. Not a single player on the roster had a migration background; instead, the media of the time stressed the players' petit bourgeois or working-class roots ("Klinsmann ... the son of a baker from Stuttgart ...," "Völler ... the son of a lathe machinist and a seamstress,"[1] Nolte 2000) to emphasize the down-to-earth character of their stars. German soccer players were nationally known for their simple language and single-mindedness towards sports, and internationally ridiculed for their mullet-and-moustache style (see, for example, the parody by the British pop group The Lightning Seeds, *LightningSeedsVEVO* 1998). Meanwhile, some German fans watched in disbelief, some even found it unfair, that their rivals from England or the Netherlands had players with black skin among their rosters. Given the colonial history of these countries, this was not surprising, and reflective of their earlier embrace of an ethnicity-independent definition of nationhood: *ius soli*, as practiced in most liberal Western countries vs. *ius sanguinis*, which remained in place in Germany until 2000 (Conrad and Kocka 2001).

When the German sports public stepped in contact with "foreign" cultures, they did so with the perspective of the fascinated tourist, exoticizing the Other with the air of the benevolent, yet distanced observer. For example, almost all the best German players on the 1990 championship team played for top teams of the Italian *Serie A*, then the strongest and most lucrative league in the world. When German television visited these stars for "home story"-type reports, they presented them as boys from simple backgrounds who now, all of a sudden, wore designer sunglasses, drove Italian sports cars to their favorite restaurants, meeting beautiful women and ordering *antipasti* in fluent Italian. In other words, these "documentaries" recycled traditional stereotypes of the Italian *dolce vita* in a tourist-style version, enjoyed by the rich and famous soccer stars, serving as proxies for the fascinated public back in Germany (Köhler and Rubenbauer 1990). Actual transcultural contact, which was

---

1 These and all other translations from German are by the author of this chapter.

in fact taking place in German neighborhoods, workplaces, and on amateur soccer pitches on a daily basis, was rarely topical around 1990. Again, the public perception of the German national team reflected larger trends in society, in this case ignoring multiculturality at home, while portraying foreign travels as exotic fun for the privileged, meeting "spectacular Others."

5 Phase 4: 2014 – victory of the "colorful republic of Germany"

After weak performances during the 1990s and early 2000s, German soccer went through a renaissance of its technical and tactical skills and modern play style in the mid-2000s. Again, a FIFA World championship in Germany (2006) served as a door-opener towards a new self-understanding of the nation as a "friend of the whole world" (Schwier 2006). The German population was enthusiastic to welcome other nations' representatives with open arms, curious about their guests' mentality, food, and language, and took pride in its own surprising friendliness. The German team lost its semi-final against Italy, but the 2006 World Cup remains locked in the collective memory as an amazingly joyful multicultural party, a "midsummer fairy tale" ("Sommermärchen") (Wortmann 2006).

This new-found strength of the soccer team and open-mindedness of its fans coincided with the quickly growing presence and acceptance of Germany's internal multiculturalism in society, and – again quite symbolically – in the team roster between 2006 and 2014. Two of the most popular German strikers of the time were born in Poland and had migrated to Germany as children (Miroslav Klose and Lukas Podolski). Others were naturalized children of "guest workers" (Mesut Özil) and several had black skin, such as Gerald Asamoah, David Odonkor, Patrick Owomoyela, and Jérôme Boateng (all born and raised in Germany, but with parents stemming from Africa). By 2010, 11 out of 22 German national players had family roots in foreign countries (Krusch 2010), and only very few voices from far-right political movements found this problematic. By 2014, anti-racism and a positive stance towards multiculturalism had become the hegemonic mainstream in German popular culture, including sports. Mainstream rock music, for example, celebrated the "Colorful Republic of Germany," a word play based on the phonetic similarity between "Bundesrepublik"/ "Federal Republic" and "bunte Republik"/ "colorful Republic" (50.000 rocken gegen Rechts 2011).

In athletic terms, the 2014 World Cup marks the climax of a positive development: a highly skilled and evidently multi-ethnic German national team dominated the tournament, among other things beating soccer heavyweight Brazil 7–1 on its own turf, and won its fourth championship title. Because most Germans felt that this public version of their nation was so decidedly "not ugly" anymore and so far removed from the shameful legacy of German history, they allowed themselves to be joyfully patriotic (Wagener 2014). Waving the German flag, or decorating gardens, balconies, and cars with the German colors was suddenly not interpreted as a sign of questionable ultra-conservative political views anymore, but merely a sign of fandom for a likeable, multicultural team. The term "party patriotism" ("Partypatriotismus") (Moritz and Sternburg 2018) was coined by media commentators to describe the new zeitgeist. Only a few left-leaning intellectual voices warned that "party patriotism" could be considered a first step towards a new, but just as harmful form of nationalism, of which German society should consciously steer clear as stringently as possible (Schulte von Drach 2012; Senkbeil 2017). Considering later developments, they were not entirely wrong.

6 Recent developments: disillusionment and debate

One year after Germany's victory in Brazil, the European Union faced a stern international crisis, as millions of refugees from the Syrian civil war sought refuge in Europe in 2015, many of them heading towards Germany, a country known for its wealth and comparably well-funded social welfare system. Chancellor Angela Merkel's decision to avoid a humanitarian crisis in south-east Europe by letting the largest caravans into the country, circumventing the usual processes of immigration and asylum applications, was answered by a resurgence of xenophobic and nationalistic sentiment in parts of society, and a stronger political right wing, not only in Germany. The political climate since 2015 has become rougher and more confrontational, as anti-Islamic and anti-immigration voices repeatedly succeeded in their agenda setting. For the first time since the World War, an extreme right-wing party (Alternative für Deutschland, AfD) was elected to the German parliament in 2017.

This background (the refugee crisis of 2015/16 and the subsequent renaissance of the extreme right) is important in understanding a particular "crisis" of the German national soccer team in 2018. During 2018, it became clear that some of the seemingly positive atmosphere in and around the multi-ethnic and transcultural German soccer team was based on a rather fragile consensus equilibrium, and that reactionary, xenophobic forces were not as negligible as they may have seemed during the fourth phase discussed in the prior section. Because the "soccer crisis" of 2018 is still not resolved, neither athletically nor culturally, it appears worthwhile to analyze some of the media discourse that has attempted to frame its meaning in the form of a media discourse analysis.

7 Case study: Özil's retirement from the national team in 2018

So what exactly happened? The "Özil crisis" started on May 13, 2018, when two current German national players with family roots in Turkey, İlkay Gündoğan and Mesut Özil, met with the Turkish president Recep Tayyip Erdoğan in a hotel in London, giving and receiving gifts, chatting, and using the meeting as a photo-op for social media accounts. As Erdoğan was currently campaigning for a presidential election in June, this was widely interpreted as a political statement and campaign aid by the two star players, who have a large fan base among Turkish youth (both in Turkey and in the diaspora). Meanwhile, the relationship between the German government and public and the Turkish president was tenser than ever: on the one hand, Chancellor Merkel needed Erdoğan's cooperation in managing the continued flow of refugees from the Middle East to Europe. On the other hand, Erdoğan was heavily criticized for his attempts at restructuring the Turkish republic into an authoritarian state, infringing on free speech and free press, imprisoning critical academics and journalists (including German citizens) on the grounds of shady claims to "terroristic propaganda," and pressuring the EU (and particularly Merkel) into unsavory "deals" (Huggler 2018). In other words, President Erdoğan was one of the most unpopular foreigners in Germany at that moment.

The media echo after the meeting of Özil, Gündoğan, and Erdoğan was accordingly vehement. Right-wing and nationalistic voices labeled Özil and Gündoğan "traitors" to the German nation and demanded that they be fired from the national soccer team. Moderate conservative voices remarked that Gündoğan, who had signed and given a jersey to Erdoğan including the dedication "for my honored president – with compliments," should re-think his use of possessive pronouns, as "his" president, as a representative of the German nation on the soccer pitch, was, by definition, the German Frank-Walter Steinmeier (Huggler 2018). Left-leaning voices in Germany were logically more critical of nationalistic backlashes in this situation, and rather in favor of German multiculturalism and thus generally content with the players' hybrid national identity. They, however, also criticized Özil and Gündoğan for publicly supporting an increasingly anti-liberal politician and for (mis)using their role-model status for anti-democratic purposes. Cem Özdemir, leader of the German Green Party, serves as a prominent example, arguing that "to pose with the autocrat Erdoğan is disrespectful to all those who have their rights infringed upon and who are arbitrarily imprisoned [in Turkey]. One should pay respect only to Democratic leaders" (quoted in Vor Özil-Rücktritt 2018). In short, nobody in Germany thought that a photo-op of German national players with president Erdoğan had actually been a good idea.

What has come to be known as a "shitstorm" seemed to subside temporarily once the FIFA World Cup started in June 2018. Gündoğan and Özil remained on the roster and were part of a historically weak performance of the German team, ousted from the tournament after the first round, a huge embarrassment for the self-proclaimed "soccer giant" Germany, losing against comparably "dwarvish" teams (Hanke 2018) from Mexico and South Korea.

As is common in developed sports media societies, the "blame game" ensued immediately. Team officials (coach Joachim Löw, team manager Oliver Bierhoff, and the president of the German soccer association DFB, Reinhard Grindel) self-critically pondered tactical mistakes and their own "arrogance" against supposedly small teams (Löw, quoted in Das war fast schon arrogant 2018), but they also made headlines with public critical remarks directed at one particular player: Mesut Özil. President Grindel, who had had a career in politics as a conservative hardliner before becoming president of the DFB, was "disappointed" in Özil, and demanded "an explanation" from him, and insinuated that the coach should plan the future of the team without Özil (Grindel 2018). Bierhoff said in an interview that Özil "could not be convinced" (quoted in Gartenschläger 2018), and that therefore, in hindsight, it had been a mistake to have him on the team that summer. What these statements had in common was, firstly, their ambiguity of what exactly they criticized. Grindel was not fully clear whether Özil's explanation or apology should concern his political stance (renouncing his support of Erdoğan?) or his sub-par athletic feats that summer. And should Özil "be convinced" of the correct political perspective, or to be more loyal to Germany, or rather of the coach's ideas in terms of team tactics? This remained vague, maybe intentionally so. Secondly, the DFB's public statements were surprising in that they singled out one player from the team collective (which journalists are prone to do, but team officials usually forego), to blame his public activities for the "irritations in the team" (Bierhoff, quoted in Gartenschläger 2018), and thus indirectly for the bad team spirit and, ultimately, failure.

As mentioned, the public and particularly social media landscape in Germany had undergone a hefty swerve to the political right since 2015. Anti-immigrant, xeno- and Islamophobic utterances, which would have been deemed unacceptable hate-speech and socially sanctioned before 2015, had now become uncomfortably common in the German online world (and in stadiums), had entered the mainstream, and even become legitimized by the extreme right AfD on the political level. In that climate, the official statements mentioned above – though not intrinsically racist – fed into a wave of anti-Turkish and anti-immigrant sentiment. If even the usually soft-spoken, diplomatic, and "politically correct" soccer officials blamed "the Turk" for his lack of loyalty and for destroying the German team spirit, the German version of the alt-right concluded that this must be proof that Özil – and all other "foreigners" –could not be trusted, did not and would never fully belong to the German national team, i. e., Germany. Among others, the popular conservative pundit Claus Strunz stated on national television that "Özil does not belong to Germany" (Strunz spricht 2018). Later, Özil recalled yet another "shitstorm" during this period, consisting of racist slurs, "hate mail, threatening phone calls and comments on social media" (Özil 2018) against himself and his family.

Left-liberal commentators, vice versa, were dismayed by the DFB's communication strategy, understood the connection between the renaissance of nationalism, the growth of "acceptable racism" in parts of the population, and this "pathetic attempt" (Tretbar 2018) to find a "scapegoat" (Spörl 2018) for structural dysfunction and individual incompetence in this influential sports organization.

At this point, the Özil crisis had become a "state affair" (Stolz and Schulze 2018), in which even the president of the German parliament Wolfgang Schäuble pitched in, asking for more professionalism in the DFB, and worrying about the damaging effect that this whole affair might have on the German nation.

Interestingly, the discussion soon received another dimension, which added to the complexity and multi-layeredness of the Özil case: gender, or rather masculinity. Mesut Özil is physically rather small and slender; his playing style is highly technical and based on quick action with the ball rather than pace or force without it. Also, he is known to occasionally jog across the pitch with his shoulders slouched forward, his face relatively expressionless even in tense game situations, as if the heated activity around him does not concern him much. Throughout his career, Özil was never known to grit his teeth, get in fights with opponents, yell at referees, thump his own chest, or perform any other public display of his masculinity, which are so common among other players. When things went well, this was mostly interpreted as a sign of his "artistry," his aloofness, and confidence in his talent: Özil did not need to match the hyper-masculine performances of his opponents, he just needed the ball at his feet to show who was boss (Gumbrecht 2012; Heiser 2018). But now that things had stopped going well, Özil's body language became an issue, and weirdly intermingled with the abovementioned categories of nationality and ethnicity. For example, Lothar Matthäus, himself a former star player and world champion of 1990, commented in the leading tabloid newspaper in Germany that, "[when I look at his body language], I often have the feeling that Özil does not feel well in the German jersey, that he is not free, even: that he does not want to play in it at all. ... No heart, no joy, no passion" (Matthäus quoted in Özil fühlt sich nicht wohl 2018).

One might remark that this is quite obviously nonsense, considering that Özil shows the same body language wearing any other jersey as well, and that he had successfully played for Germany for nine years at that point, among other things winning a world championship, with the exact same body language. But Matthäus's remark vividly show how different levels of identity markers were mixed and clumsily matched in this escalating discussion: on the surface, he feigns concern ("poor Özil, he does not feel well"), then connects his criticism to a politically highly charged term – freedom – without clarifying what kind of freedom he means ("free" from what, or to do what exactly?), to conclude as a lay-psychologist that, deep down, Özil does not want to play for Germany – that is: to be German – after all. The logical result could only be that the jersey should be taken away from Özil, the "unwell," "not-fully German" player, in favor of a "real German" without such psycho-emotional conflicts.

Other formerly big names in German soccer chimed in similarly. Mario Basler, a simple-minded pundit for tabloid newspapers and TV stations, remarked that Özil had the body language of a "dead frog" (Basler, quoted in Wie ein toter Frosch 2018). Uli Hoeneß became agitated in an interview and ranted that "Özil has been playing crap for years. He won his last defensive tackling before 2014. And now he is hiding his crappy play behind this photo [with Erdoğan]," adding a snide and potentially homophobic remark on Özil's "35 million follower boys" on social media. When asked whether this word choice and his criticism was not overly harsh in the currently heated debate over perceived racism, Hoeneß justified his statements by pointing out that his criticism was decidedly *not* based on race or religion, and *not* based on politics; he wanted "to boil it down to what it is: sports." The current intermixing of politics and sports was "a disaster in our country" (Hoeneß, quoted in Uli Hoeneß übt vernichtende Kritik 2018).

In other words, commentators such as Matthäus and Hoeneß attempted to actively steer clear from politics and from Özil's ethnic or religious background, and instead chose to attack him on the grounds of un-masculine body language, weak tackling, and popularity with social media users (as a shorthand for superficial, effeminate showboating). What this analysis shows, however, is that these levels (masculinity, nationality, ethnicity) are not simply separable, particularly in a country in which the default expectation of an athlete representing the country is still that of a tall, broad-shouldered, physically strong, latently aggressive, and usually blond athlete (Senkbeil 2017), while Özil is none of these things.

Özil himself remained silent for a while and took his time to react. In a four-page written statement published via Twitter on July 22, 2018, he heavily criticized the German media, DFB president Grindel, and announced he would never play for Germany again, as he felt unwelcome. In a rather long text – formulated not in German or Turkish, but in flawless English, performing the role of a true cosmopolitan – Özil made several statements that can be considered programmatic for the difficult situation of mixed-heritage Germans, for everyday racism around them, but also referring to his own feelings of conflict and in-betweenness. He argues that his meeting with the Turkish president was about family rather than about politics, about "respecting the highest office of my family's country," because "my mother never let me lose sight of my ancestry, heritage and family traditions," so that "not meeting the president would have been disrespecting the roots of my ancestors, who I know would be proud of where I am today" (Özil 2018).

His alienation from the German fan base has deeper roots than the current Erdoğan affair, Özil clarifies:

> Despite paying taxes in Germany, donating facilities to German schools and winning the World Cup with Germany in 2014, I am still not accepted in society. I am treated as being 'different'. ... Are there criteria for being fully German that I do not fit? ... Is it because it is Turkey? Is it because I'm a Muslim? I think here lays an important issue. By being referred to as German-Turkish, it is already distinguishing people who have family from more than one country. I was born and educated in Germany, so why don't people accept that I am German? (Özil 2018)

From an academic perspective, Özil's insights into his hybrid national identity – including the internal and external conflicts it implies – are of course not spectacularly new. Özil's argument vindicates the accepted wisdom of sociological and anthropological studies, that migration and globalization bring forward cultural hybridity, which may occasionally be publicly celebrated as a sign of progressivism and a peaceful post-racist future (as in phase 4), while also producing emotional pains and frustrations among those who actively live this hybridity (Werbner 2015). Özil mentions heritage and ancestry as reasons for his choices, which, he claims, autochtonous Germans would never be able to fully understand. Families who live in the diaspora are known to have stronger emotional ties to those than most indigenous families, independently of where and when (Gilroy 1997).

He concludes in one of the most often quoted passages from this document that, for parts of the German public, "I am German when we win, but I am an immigrant when we lose" (Özil 2018). This is insofar remarkable as very similar complaints with very similar wording had been made by soccer stars from other European countries, such as Romelo Lukaku ("When everything went well, [in newspaper articles] I was 'the Belgian striker'. When it didn't go well, I was 'the Belgian striker with Kongolesian roots'") and Karim Benzema ("When I score, I am French, when I don't, I am an Arab") (quoted in Parallelen zwischen 2018). Capitalistic and meritocratic societies celebrate "pure" meritocracy in sports, which is why sports appear to be the perfect sphere for emancipatory and anti-racist messages. What culturally hybrid Europeans note on a regular basis, however, is that there exists a double-standard in the evaluation of their achievement – in sports and elsewhere. Again, this is no new insight, academically speaking. One of the most important results of the Özil case is that, for the first time, the feeling of being treated unfairly, which so many Germans with foreign family roots know all too well, was made accessible, even understandable to the broad public.

As the last act of the drama about the weak World Cup of 2018 and Özil's departure, one of the recurring replies to Özil's statements was that he, of all people, should not complain and that the role of the victim would not befit a celebrated multi-millionaire with a luxurious cosmopolitan lifestyle, who lived and played in Madrid and London. Grindel attempted to change the discussion away from racism towards the personal level and asked whether Özil should not be "more thankful" towards the people in German soccer (and German society in general), who had made his shining career possible (Grindel, quoted in Kein Ende 2018). So even this final part of the play-by-play of the Özil scandal is reminiscent of similar discussions elsewhere: the accusation of ungratefulness appears to be a standard move of conservative voices towards sports stars from a minority background who formulate uncomfortable truths about racism and discrimination (see for example the Colin Kaepernick case in the USA, Cobb 2017).

What are the results of the soccer crisis of 2018 and the heated debates about Özil's withdrawal? Athletically, the situation has not resolved itself so quickly, of course. The German national team has continued to play weakly without Özil in 2019 and 2020, but it has remained (and certainly will remain) a multi-ethnic and multicultural enterprise, mirroring the factual demographics among young Germans, particularly in big cities and sports clubs.

Many media critics said, in hindsight, that the discussions about Özil had become "horribly out of joint" (Köster 2018), that they displayed "malignity without inhibitions" on the political right, and a "baleful tug-of-war" (Müller 2018) between political ideologies. Others concluded that that Özil's withdrawal was a "disastrous sign in worrisome times" and that, in the end, "the populists won" (Spiller 2018). Schulze-Marmeling and colleagues' book *Der Fall Özil* (2018) comes to a similar conclusion.

On the other hand, less pessimistic voices from the academic sphere have attempted to put the case in a historical perspective. El-Mafaalani argues that the public argument and Özil's self-confident display of anger and disappointment with Germany, are, paradoxically, positive signs (El-Mafaalani 2018; Schenk 2018). Only when minorities are already halfway accepted and participating in mainstream society are their demands and complaints publicly heard and taken seriously, he points out. As opposed to the 1980s–90s, when immigrants in Germany were much more heavily discriminated against, but public discourse all but ignored that they existed (see phase 3), in 2018, Özil's case was symptomatic for the newfound self-confidence of the so-called "third generation" in immigrant families. Discussions such as these only take place on a societal scale, El-Mafaalani claims, when the minorities begin to self-confidently demand respect and "a piece of the cake," but also only when a large part of the majority culture agree that they actually deserve it (El-Mafaalani 2018). Despite the negativity of the moment in 2018, El-Mafaalani and colleagues (Kayikci 2018) argue that in the long run, Özil's case, and the controversial discussion about who and what is "German," are signs that society is "heading in the right direction" (El-Mafaalani, quoted in Schenk 2018). The future will show whether this evaluation is accurate.

8 Conclusion

In sports, as in society as a whole, liberal-progressive, multicultural sentiment and reactionary yearning for a homosocial and homoethnic society seem to alternate in waves. These waves take years, even decades to come and recede. In German sports history, such sociocultural and political developments have been in a dialogic relationship with soccer, particularly with the German national team as the prime figurehead of the German self-image as a nation among nations. Relatively continuous processes towards an increasingly open mindset and interest in other nations and cultures found their expression in enthusiastic celebrations around soccer in the 1970s and 2006–2014, for example. Vice versa, backsliding into more conservative, migration-critical discourses has been observable in around the German national team as well, for example in the 1980s–90s, and in 2018. Even though this has not been the central focus of this text in particular, it has also become clear that in all phases, soccer was and is the center stage for negotiations about (German) masculinity, ranging from the timid, shy, post-war generation, via long-haired, cocky hippies in the 1970s, to the mustachioed petit bourgeoisie of 1990, all the way to the ambivalence of the slender, minimalistic "artist" Mesut Özil in 2014/2018.

Thus, Germany's strained relationship with its own history, nationhood (and, we may add, manliness) has repeatedly found its way into communication about sports. The centrality of sports (and of the men's soccer team in particular) may be even more pronounced in Germany than in comparable nations, because other potentially symbolic institutions do not exist (such as aristocracy/royalty), or play little or no role in popular culture (such as the military) to connote the woes and virtues of the nation. Soccer is highly emotional (not only in Germany, of course), and success and failure at the quadrennial FIFA World Cup are often surrounded by tears of either joy or despair, which is not all that trivial given that German culture is not known to be overly eccentric or prone to public displays of emotions. So, when public discourse frames athletic success, failure, or internal conflict (such as in the soccer crisis of 2018) as reliable sources to deduce what is currently brewing in the country, we should of course critically remark that, rationally and objectively, sports are not immediately and causally connected to politics or socio-demographics. But through sports communication, we can catch a glimpse at the emotional, sub-conscious part of the collective mindset of Germans at a certain point in time, particularly in terms of their fleeting and ambivalent sensation of togetherness as a nation, as a quite literally "imagined" community.

References

1954: Das Wunder von Bern. 2011. *Zeitzeugen-portal*, 26 August. https://www.youtube.com/watch?v=pB9t9DQyEZo (23 May 2019).

50.000 rocken gegen Rechts. 2011. *Spiegel.de*, 3 December. https://www.spiegel.de/panorama/gesellschaft/konzert-in-jena-50-000-rocken-gegen-rechts-a-801447.html (23 May 2019).

Anderson, Benedict. 1983. *Imagined communities: Reflections on the origin and spread of nationalism*. New York: Verso.

Beck, Oscar. 2010. Als der DFB auf die internationale Bühne zurückkam. *Welt.de*, 22 November. https://www.welt.de/sport/fussball/article11105464/Als-der-DFB-auf-die-internationale-Buehne-zurueckkam.html (17 November 2020).

Brüggemeier, Franz-Josef. 2006. Das "Fußballwunder" von 1954. Auswirkungen des WM-Gewinns. *Bundeszentrale für politische Bildung*, 4 May. http://www.bpb.de/izpb/8767/das-fussball wunder-von-1954?p=1 (23 May 2019).

Butterworth, Michael L. 2016. Public memory and morality at Munich's Olympiapark. Paper presented at the Rhetoric Society of America conference, Atlanta, GA, 27–29 May.

Cobb, Jelani. 2017. From Louis Armstrong to the N.F.L.: Ungrateful as the new uppity. *The New Yorker*, 24 September. https://www.newyorker.com/news/news-desk/from-louis-armstrong-to-the-nfl-ungrateful-as-the-new-uppity (13 February 2020).

Conrad, Christoph & Jürgen Kocka (eds.). 2001. *Staatsbürgerschaft in Europa: Historische Erfahrungen und aktuelle Debatten*. Hamburg: Edition Körber-Stiftung.
Das war fast schon arrogant. 2018. *Spiegel.de*, 29 August. https://www.spiegel.de/sport/fussball/joachim-loew-ueber-wm-debakel-das-war-fast-schon-arrogant-a-1225474.html (23 May 2019).
El-Mafaalani, Aladin. 2018. *Das Integrationsparadox: Warum gelungene Integration zu mehr Konflikten führt* (2nd edn.). Cologne: Kiepenheuer & Witsch.
Forschungsstelle NS und Pädagogik. 2012. Die erste Strophe des Deutschlandliedes nach Sieg bei der Fußballweltmeisterschaft 1954. *NSundPaedagogik*, 5 August. https://www.youtube.com/watch?v=2CAR3NfQpCg (23 May 2019).
Gartenschläger, Lars. 2018. "Man hätte überlegen müssen, ob man auf Özil verzichtet". *Die Welt*. 5 July. https://www.welt.de/sport/fussball/wm-2018/plus178838920/Oliver-Bierhoff-Man-haette-ueberlegen-muessen-ob-man-auf-Oezil-verzichtet.html (17 November 2020).
Gilroy, Paul. 1997. Diaspora and the detours of identity. In Kath Woodward (ed.), *Identity and difference* (Culture, Media, and Identities), 299–346. Thousand Oaks, CA: Sage.
Gizinski, M. 2014. *Unsere Geschichte – Als die WM in den Norden kam*. NDR, June 12. https://programm.ard.de/programm/sender/unsere-geschichte---als-die-wm-in-den-norden-kam/eid_2822612311874178?sender=28226&datum=12.06.2014&list=main&archiv=1 (23 May 2019).
Grindel: "Özil sollte sich öffentlich äußern." 2018. *kicker*, 8 July. https://www.kicker.de/grindel_oezil-sollte-sich-oeffentlich-aeussern-727105/artikel (17 November 2020).
Gumbrecht, Hans. U. 2012. Eleganz des Minimalismus. *11Freunde*, 22 June. https://11freunde.de/artikel/eleganz-des-minimalismus/427489 (17 November 2020).
Hanke, Sebastian. 2018. Nach Blamage gegen Südkorea: Die DFB-Kicker in der Einzelkritik. *90min.de*, 27 June. https://www.90min.de/posts/6102068-nach-blamage-gegen-suedkorea-die-dfb-kicker-in-der-einzelkritik (13 February 2020).
Heiser, Jörg. 2018. Minimalism, masculinity and Mesut Özil. *Frieze*, 23 September. https://www.frieze.com/article/minimalism-masculinity-and-mesut-ozil (17 November 2020).
Huggler, Justin. 2018. Arsenal star Mesut Ozil criticised by German football association after posing with Turkey's Erdogan. *The Telegraph*, 15 May. https://www.telegraph.co.uk/news/2018/05/15/arsenal-star-mesut-ozil-criticised-german-football-association/ (17 November 2020).
Kayikci, Merve. 2018. Wir undankbaren Deutschtürken. *ZEIT Campus*, 24 July. https://www.zeit.de/campus/2018-07/mesut-oezil-deutschtuerken-fussball-kopftuch?utm_referrer=https%3A%2F%2Fwww.google.com%2F (17 November 2020).
Kein Ende in Özil-Causa – Grindel: Gespräch gehört sich. *Welt.de*, 28 September. https://www.waz.de/sport/fussball/grindel-hofft-auf-persoenliches-gespraech-oezils-mit-loew-id215435763.html (17 November 2020).
Köhler, Uli & Gerd Rubenbauer. Italia 90: Der Rückblick auf die XIV. Fußball-WM. 1990. Bayrischer Rundfunk, 7 July. https://www.br.de/mediathek/video/italia-90-der-rueckblick-auf-die-xiv-fussball-wm-av:585d9d5d3e2f29001293cdf9 (22 May 2019).
Köster, Philipp. 2018. Integrationsmaskottchen zum Buhmann degradiert. *Übermedien.de*, 29 June. https://uebermedien.de/29417/integrationsmaskottchen-zum-buhmann-degradiert/ (17 November 2020).
Krusch, Hendrik. 2010. Elf deutsche WM-Spieler haben Wurzeln in acht Ländern. *Stuttgarter Nachrichten*, 17 June.
Moritz, Rainer & Juri Sternburg. 2018. Wenn die schwarz-rot-goldenen Fahnen wehen, 16 June. *Deutschlandfunk Kultur*. https://www.deutschlandfunkkultur.de/pro-contra-party-patriotismus-wenn-die-schwarz-rot-goldenen.2165.de.html?dram:article_id=420547 (17 November 2020).
Müller, Jan Christian. 2018. Der Irrsinn mit Mesut Özil. *Frankfurter Rundschau*, 22 July. https://www.fr.de/meinung/irrsinn-mesut-oezil-10955485.html (17 November 2020).

Nolte, Georg. 2000. Aus Tante Käthe wird das Mädchen für alles. *Die Welt.com*, 23 October. Munich. https://www.welt.de/print-welt/article539955/Aus-Tante-Kaethe-wird-das-Maedchen-fuer-alles.html (17 November 2020).

Özil, Mesut. 2018. III / III. *Twitter.com*, 22 July. https://twitter.com/mesutozil1088/status/1021093637411700741?lang=en (23 May 2019).

"Özil fühlt sich nicht wohl im DFB-Trikot." 2018. *Waz.de*, 19 June. https://www.waz.de/sport/matthaeus-oezil-fuehlt-sich-im-dfb-trikot-nicht-wohl-id214630831.html (17 November 2020).

Parallelen zwischen Özil, Lukaku und Benzema. 2018. *Süddeutsche Zeitung*, 23 July. https://www.waz.de/sport/fussball/parallelen-zwischen-oezil-lukaku-und-benzema-id214910575.html (17 November 2020).

Schenk, Arnfried. 2018. Integration gelingt heute besser als je zuvor. *Die Zeit*, 19 September. https://www.zeit.de/2018/39/aladin-el-mafaalani-gelungene-integration-paradox-thilo-sarrazin (17 November 2020).

Schulte von Drach, Markus C. 2012. Party-Patriotismus ist Nationalismus. *Sueddeutsche.de*, 29 June. https://www.sueddeutsche.de/wissen/fahnenmeere-zur-em-party-patriotismus-ist-nationalismus-1.1394854 (17 November 2020).

Schulze-Marmeling, Dietrich, Robert Claus, Ilker Gündoğan & Diethelm Blecking. 2018. *Der Fall Özil: über ein Foto, Rassismus und das deutsche WM-Aus*. Göttingen: Verlag Die Werkstatt.

Schwier, Jürgen. 2006. Die Welt zu Gast bei Freunden – Fußball, nationale Identität und der Standort Deutschland. In Jürgen Schwier & Claus Leggewie (eds.), *Wettbewerbsspiele: die Inszenierung von Sport und Politik in den Medien*, 79–104. Frankfurt am Main: Campus.

Senkbeil, Karsten 2017. "Blood warriors" and "polite Siegfrieds": Militarism and neo-nationalism in German media discourse after the 2014 World Cup. In Michael L. Butterworth (ed.), *Sport and militarism: Contemporary global perspectives*, 163–177. New York: Routledge.

Spiller, Christian. 2018. So viel mehr als ein Rücktritt. *Zeit Online*, 23 July. https://www.zeit.de/sport/2018-07/mesut-oezil-fussball-rassismus-kommentar-ruecktritt (17 November 2020).

Spörl, Gerhard. 2018. DFB-Boss Grindel nimmt der AfD die Arbeit ab. *t-online.de*, 25 May. https://www.t-online.de/sport/fussball/id_84163540/mesut-oezil-als-suendenbock-dfb-boss-grindel-nimmt-der-afd-die-arbeit-ab.html (17 November 2020).

Stolz, Christopher & Katrin Schulze. 2018. Der Fall Özil wird zur Staatsaffäre. *Der Tagesspiegel*, 26 July. https://www.tagesspiegel.de/sport/grindel-erklaert-sich-der-fall-oezil-wird-zur-staatsaffaere/22846042.html (17 November 2020).

Strunz spricht Klartext: Wie politisch ist der Fußball? 2018. *Sat.1 Frühstücksfernsehen*, 15 May. https://www.sat1.de/tv/fruehstuecksfernsehen/video/strunz-spricht-klartext-wie-politisch-ist-der-fussball-clip (22 May 2019).

The Lightning Seeds – Three Lions '98. 2009. *LightningSeedsVEVO*, 25 November. https://www.youtube.com/watch?v=oyoy2_7Fegl. (23 May 2019).

Tretbar, Christian. 2018. Özil ist gescheitert an der populistischen Stimmung im Land. *Der Tagesspiegel*, 23 July. https://www.tagesspiegel.de/politik/ruecktritt-des-weltmeisters-oezil-ist-gescheitert-an-der-populistischen-stimmung-im-land/22831642.html (17 November 2020).

Uli Hoeneß übt vernichtende Kritik an Mesut Özil. *Welt.de*, 23 July. https://www.welt.de/sport/fussball/article179800484/Uli-Hoeness-ueber-Mesut-Oezil-Spielt-seit-Jahren-Dreck.html (22 May 2019).

Vor Özil-Rücktritt aus Nationalmannschaft: Grünen-Politiker Özdemir mit deutlicher Kritik. *DerWesten.de*, 22 July. https://www.derwesten.de/sport/fussball/vor-oezil-ruecktritt-aus-nationalmannschaft-gruenen-politiker-oezdemir-mit-deutlicher-kritik-id214908763.html (23 May 2019).

Wagener, Volker. 2014. Kommentar: Von wegen hässliche Deutsche – Sie lieben uns! *Deutsche Welle*, 15 July. https://www.dw.com/de/kommentar-von-wegen-h%C3%A4ssliche-deutsche-sie-lieben-uns/a-17786361 (17 November 2020).
Werbner, Pnina & Tariq Modood (eds.). 2015. *Debating cultural hybridity: Multicultural identities and the politics of anti-racism* (Critique, Influence, Change 8). London: Zed Books.
Wie ein toter Frosch: Mario Basler ledert gegen Mesut Özil. 19 June. https://www.stern.de/sport/fussball/wm-2018/mesut-oezil-wie-ein-toter-frosch--mario-basler-pestet-gegen-weltmeister-8131378.html (22 May 2020).
Wortmann, Sönke. 2006. *Deutschland. Ein Sommermärchen*. Kinowelt Filmverleih.

Younghan Cho

25 Sport celebrity and multiculturalism in South Korea during the 2008 Beijing Olympic Games

Abstract: Since the new millennium, the idea of multiculturalism has become a trend within government policies and mass media in South Korea. While the state actively implemented multicultural policies, state-led multicultural policies have been characterized by the method of inclusion. For the 2008 Beijing Olympics, Tang Ye-seo, a migrating Chinese athlete in table tennis was selected to be part of the national team after becoming naturalized as a Korean citizen. As the first naturalized Korean to lead a national Korean sports team, she won the bronze medal in the women's team event. From the selection procedure to the briefing session after the Olympics, she attracted huge attention from the media and people and elicited extensive debates on migration, citizenship, and the changing regional relations. While she was in part welcomed as a national heroine, she often received criticism both from South Korea and China. In the contexts of East Asia, sport celebrities do not always represent mobility, flexibility, and transnationalism, but often manifest inflexibility, regional rivalry, and even conflict of national interests. By analyzing news reporting on Tang, this study examines the complex, contradictory roles of migrant sport celebrities in cultural policy and regional relations in South Korea.

Keywords: sport celebrity; Olympics; news media; multiculturalism; South Korea; East Asia

1 Introduction

As globalization has been extensively facilitating the diverse routes of international migration, the topic of sport migrants has attracted some scholarly attention since the 1990s, which inevitably led to "focus on migration to ask questions about the impact of global sport more broadly" (Maguire and Falcous 2011: 1). In the contexts of South Korea and East Asia, sport and particularly sport migration do not always represent mobility, flexibility, and transnationalism, but often manifest inflexibility, regional rivalry, and even conflicts of national interests. As Rowe succinctly argues in his work on sport and the repudiation of the global, sport celebrities "may be constitutionally unsuited to accomplish globalization in its fullest sense" (2003: 281).

This study examines the roles of a sport athlete in the era of globalization with a focus on a migrating Chinese athlete and her dual engagement within the cultural policy of multiculturalism in South Korea during the 2008 Beijing Olympics. By exam-

https://doi.org/10.1515/9783110660883-025

ining South Korean media coverage, this study suggests that the media representation of a migrating sport celebrity serves both to reify and to expand the idea and scope of multiculturalism in South Korea that has been extensively becoming more globalized and neoliberalized since the late 1990s. In so doing, this research also thinks of the possibilities and limitations of sport culture in the era of multiculturalism in South Korea as well as East Asia.

In the new millennium, the idea of multiculturalism has become more than a trend in the society and governmental policies of South Korea as the number of the migrating population came to exceed one million. For a long period of time, South Korea strove to hold on to the idea of being a single-race nation, which consists of one-blood and a homogeneous population. However, such a myth was no longer tenable once the South Korean governments allowed long-term migration and the naturalization of foreigners in the late 1990s in an attempt to solve issues of low birthrate, an aging population, and a decrease in manpower, particularly in so-called 3D (difficult, dangerous, and dirty) jobs that native South Koreans would not want. While the state actively implemented multicultural policies, state-led multicultural policies have been characterized by the method of inclusion. Furthermore, the government tends to pursue multiculturalism as a symbol of an advanced society or as a tool for reaching the level of advanced countries. In this vein, Ahn argues that "the multiculturalism agenda is more than a governmental policy to regulate Korea's growing immigrant population," and that it is part of a "larger social transformation into a neoliberal, global Korea" (2018: 3). Then, two key questions are worth addressing in the emergence of multiculturalism as seen in South Korea. First, what are the specific significances of sport celebrities in multiculturalism? And second, how might sports celebrities contribute to reinforcing or dismantling state-led multiculturalism in South Korea where the notion of a single-race nation was prevalent?

Simultaneously, the 2008 Beijing Olympics is an important spectacle that not only attracted global attention, but also reinforced a complex interplay of nationalism and internationalism at the same time (Brownell 2011). While China attempted to demonstrate its economic development and culture to global societies, the 2008 Beijing Olympics also fueled regional tensions and rivalries. In this sense, the 2008 Beijing Olympics became an arena of competition among "local agents, nationalist sentiments, regional rivalries and global ambitions" (Kelly 2011). As such, the 2008 Beijing Olympics was an important venue in which the South Korean government could advertise its societal transition to multiculturalism and its governmental efforts in this process both to domestic and international audiences. In particular, Tang Ye-seo,[1] a migrating Chinese athlete who became a naturalized South Korean, was selected as a member of the national team in women's table tennis. As the first natu-

1 In this paper, Korean and Japanese names are ordered with family names first followed by given names in accordance with their convention.

ralized Korean to represent a South Korean national team in the Olympics, she led the South Korean national women's table tennis team and won the bronze medal in the women's team event. From the selection procedure to the briefing session after the Olympics, she attracted huge attention from the public and media and elicited extensive debates on migration, citizenship, and the changing regional relations to China. While she was in part welcomed as a national heroine, she often received criticism from both South Korea and China, labeled as being a mercenary without a sense of national belonging and as betraying national loyalty for personal gain. While sport mega-events and sport celebrities often become harbingers of globalization, neoliberalism, and even multiculturalism, in South Korea, they also instigate multiple debates and unexpected controversies around state-led multiculturalism. In South Korea, multiculturalism is a ramification of globalization as well as a national desire through which South Korea strove to emulate so-called "advanced" countries. By situating a migrating sport celebrity in the domestic and regional relations of South Korea, this study examines the complex, contradictory roles of sport celebrities both in Korea's policies of multiculturalism and in its globalizing desires.

2 Approach and methodology

Following Turner (2004), this study deals with the discourses on celebrities not only as a discursive litmus that is reflective of social values and cultural standards, but also as a collective battleground on which collisions and negotiations among diverse social values and voices take place. Specific media representations and their semiotic meanings as well as the social implications of sports celebrities in media discourse will be considered. Tang Ye-seo, a migrating Chinese athlete who obtained South Korean citizenship and competed as a member of the Korean national team during the 2008 Beijing Olympics, provides a unique lens for exploring issues such as national identities, multiple citizenships, and regional relationships, which are more or less connected with the multicultural agenda in South Korea.

The interdisciplinary methodology used in this study combines qualitative methods, including discourse analysis and archival research. The major data come from mass media representations of sport celebrities and the Olympics. To trace the media representation of sport celebrities during the 2008 Beijing Olympics, this study collected South Korean news media coverages between 2008 and 2012. I searched through the news reportages using the keywords Tang Ye-seo and naturalized table-tennis athlete using KINDS (Korean Integrated News Database System, www.kinds.or.kr). While the 2008 Beijing Olympics were held in August 2008, related news reportages on Tang continued to appear in 2012 when Tang also prepared to participate in the 2012 London Olympics. After identifying the meaningful reportages, I was left with a collection of 526 news articles on Tang. Critical discourse analysis

(Fairclough 1992) was employed to analyze the news coverage on Tang and to categorize the meaningful social discourse around her. Fairclough (1992) suggests that the examination of discourses will show how discourse is articulated within a structure, power, and ideology in order to generate a set of knowledge and beliefs. In particular, to approach news coverages as a process of social construction is useful for revealing the ideological function of news media and for explicating news consumption in an integrated context (Kang 1994). Critical discourse analysis "effectively shows how each discourse is produced, distributed and interpreted in a particular conjuncture" (Cho 2009: 350).

By adopting a combination of these qualitative methods, this study also advocates the position of approaching sport celebrities as emblematic individuals who act for the negotiation of cultural struggles so that they are closely positioned within the changes of surrounding societies (Andrews and Jackson 2001). The media discourses of migrating sport celebrities provide ample clues for tracing the changes of the government's policies and public responses on multiculturalism in South Korea. Analyzing the discourses of sport celebrities, hence, "reveals the deeper transformations of social structures and public sentiments that are occurring as South Korea becomes both more interconnected and also more regionalized" (Cho 2015: 6).

3 Sport celebrities, multiculturalism and globalization in South Korea

3.1 Sport celebrities and their ambiguity toward globalization

Described as "the universal language of entertainment" (Andrews 2004: 100), sport and sport celebrities seem to be capable of crossing spatial, linguistic, cultural, and racial boundaries, but at the same time, they are compelled to keep accommodating to the local, national, and even regional cultures and tastes (Maguire 1999). This section illuminates the ambiguous engagements of sport celebrities within the larger process of globalization.

On the one hand, sport and its celebrities are replacing the pioneering roles that American pop culture, including films, television shows, and pop music, have been playing in the procedures of cultural globalization (Miller et al. 2001). According to Marshall (1997), the film star is located at the pinnacle of the celebrity hierarchy and the television star is constructed as more common and more related to the everyday. In contrast, sport celebrities are distinguished by their excellence in records and physical performance in games, which in turn propel their fans to assign them authenticity (Andrews and Jackson 2001). Though the concept of celebrity had already become systemized within film in early 20th-century America (Gamson 1994), sport celebrity has also "become an indispensable element of specific sports as sport figures have become integral parts of the entertainment industry and the broadcasting business" (Cho 2015: 3). Sport celebrities have become one of the most powerful worldwide audience magnets, particularly propelled by the development of telecommunication technology, the transformation of the media environment, and the globalization of broadcasting networks. As mass media and representation is the key principle in the formation of celebrity culture (Rojek 2011), sport celebrities have become an integral part of the entertainment industry and broadcasting business. The nexus between Michael Jordan, Nike, and the National Basketball Association of the US is a compelling and influential case: Michael Jordan was not simply the best player of the NBA but also functioned as a powerful vehicle for globalizing the NBA and associated transnational corporations. Besides the broadcasting and promotion business, according to Andrews (2001), Michael Jordan is also an embodied exaltation of the twinned discourses of late modernity such as neo-liberal democracy and consumer capitalism. Recently, the ubiquitous natures of internet technology and Wi-Fi networks through smartphones have further enhanced global audiences' capacity to enjoy vivid images of sport celebrities and to watch live broadcasting of sporting events and celebrities' performances at any time and place.

On the other hand, sport and sport celebrities remain closely connected to local, national, and regional sentiments. Compared to the significance of actors in film or television, the influential identities produced by popular sport are often explicitly linked with definitions of nationality and ethnicity. In Asia, the configurations of sport celebrities are often attached to fixed nationalities associated with citizenship, nationalist discourse, and often postcolonial desires (Kobayashi and Cho 2019).[2] In the cases of international sporting events such as the Olympics and the football World Cup, it is obvious that sports invoke a nation as an enduring space of identity and provoke nationalism in sports fans, audiences, and even general populations. Mega-sporting events such as the 2002 Korea–Japan World Cup, the 2008 Beijing Olympics and, most recently, the 2018 PyeongChang Winter Olympics brought about inter-Korean and inter-Asian issues within short spans of time. In the 2010 Winter Olympics, the rivalry between two famous female figure skaters, Kim Yuna (from Korea) and Mao Asada (from Japan), exemplifies a case in which sport celebrities evoke nationalism and regional tensions within their fans. In this vein, several Asian athletes who successfully made it to the US professional leagues in basketball, baseball, and golf also emerge both as global celebrities and as national heroes. For example, many Korean female golfers who have dominated the Ladies Professional Golf League in the US are represented "as an important symbol of a global Koreanness – one that travels across borders, a figure caught up in circuits of corporate capital, and an idealized

2 For detailed discussions of Asian sport celebrities, see the special issues in *The International Journal of Sport of History* 37(7–8).

representation of the neoliberal Korean subject" (Joo 2012: 18). Furthermore, several sport mega-events mediate the regional and the global: for instance, the Asian Football Confederation Asian Cup is "simultaneously continental and global" and "marks itself variously in terms of nation, continent, regional and the globe" (Rowe 2017: 186).

As a multi-textual and multi-platform promotional entity, high-profile sport celebrities have the ability to cross spatial, linguistic, cultural, and racial boundaries. Symbiotic relations between media and sports in particular enable the mobility of sport celebrities, specifically the cross-border flourishing of their fame and images. Nonetheless, in Asia, the configurations of sport celebrities are by and large attached to fixed nationalities associated with citizenship, nationalist discourses, and post-colonial desires. In addition, sport celebrities are also habitually deployed in the government's projects and policies as well as in domestic and international sporting events.

3.2 Sport celebrities and multiculturalism in global Korea

It is beyond the scope of this study to assess the whole history and development of multiculturalism in South Korea. Nonetheless, for a better understanding, this section locates multiculturalism in South Korea within a longer process of national development under globalization.

The globalization project was pursued as a nation-state project in South Korea in the mid-1990s, but it was quickly followed by the East Asian economic crisis in the late 1990s. During and after undergoing extensive structural transformation under the guidance of the International Monetary Fund between 1997 and 2001, South Korean government exalted the idea of a multicultural Korea to renew Korea's national identity. As briefly mentioned in the introduction, the changing period of the new millennium was the moment that South Korea accepted a large population of foreign immigrants and many cases of naturalization. While the extensive process of globalization contributed to deconstructing the essentialist understanding of nationalism as well as the long-standing mono-ethnic/racial/national myth (Cho 2009), South Korea began to live everyday life with a great influx of immigrants. That is to say, Korean multiculturalism is employed to respond to the increasing number of foreigners residing and working in South Korea as well as to control the possible risks. Korean multiculturalism is not only employed to handle the social changes, but also to be pursued as a national project (Ahn 2014, 2018).

The Korean government also advertises the term multiculturalism as another symbol of advanced countries, similar to the ways in which the government pursued globalization as a way to self-proclaim itself an advanced country. Under such a rationale, both the Korean society and Koreans not only accept, but also seek to accomplish the goals of multiculturalism in order to become a first-world society and global citizens, respectively. Korean multiculturalism by and large repeats a rhetoric similar to developmentalism,[3] which had functioned as the hegemonic ideology during the past decades. Multiculturalism was represented as an unavoidable path through which South Korea would be able to become more globally competitive and accomplish continuous economic success. Meanwhile, multiculturalism has often been perceived economically rather than culturally, and for the sake of national interest, not human rights. To put simply, multiculturalism is advertised as a magical tool for accomplishing the national goal, i. e., national development, which will make Koreans rich. It is no wonder that Korean public officials and the press habitually mention representative cases of multiculturalism from several advanced countries such as the US, Australia, and Canada.

In so doing, Korean multiculturalism is often characterized as state-led, where the government still functions as a central initiator or orchestrator. In order to understand the details of its characteristics, this study refers to the procedure of state-led multiculturalism as multiculturalism from above. In this model, Korean multiculturalism is best characterized as a top-down project where the government actively and voluntarily installs major policies and projects under the umbrella idea of multiculturalism. Initiated either by the government or by NGOs, Korean multiculturalism is operated based on public or semi-public projects, in which the major targets are mostly foreign brides and guest workers. Consequently, Korean multiculturalism operates mostly as top-down programming, and many programs are installed in a compressed way within short periods of time. Furthermore, Korean multiculturalism's ultimate goal is to contribute to the continual (economic) success and development of Korea. Under the scheme of multiculturalism from above, multiculturalism is deployed to recognize the issues of cultural diversity or, at most, tolerance toward minorities and subordinate groups, but it rarely deals with issues of citizenship. Also, Korean multiculturalism and its policies mostly target immigrants and naturalized citizens but do not concern themselves with changing perceptions and attitudes towards migrants in South Korea.

---

3 Developmentalism refers to a dominant ideology in the rapid industrial periods (between the 1960s and 1980s) which prioritized national economic development along with enforcing the sacrifice of individuals and other values (Cho 2010).

4 Sport celebrities and Korean multiculturalism: the case of Tang Ye-seo during the 2008 Beijing Olympics

4.1 Tang Ye-seo, a Chinese migrant athlete at the 2008 Beijing Olympics

It is no longer unusual to observe the transnational mobility of sports athletes via various sports mega-events and professional sports leagues. As Kelly (2013) mentions, such foreign athletes are the subject of extensive news coverage, which often follows a predictable messiah-scapegoat cycle in the Asian society. Contrary to the increasing number of foreign athletes in South Korea, it is still rare for migrating athletes to obtain Korean citizenship in order to represent South Korea as members of the national sports teams. Compared to foreign players who are usually regarded as mercenaries or temporary players, such migrating athletes provoke public debate surrounding their loyalties, dual citizenship and eligibility for being selected for the national team as new citizens.

The 2008 Beijing Olympics became a unique avenue for discussions surrounding migrating athletes and their changing citizenships both in South Korea and East Asia. For the 2008 Beijing Olympics, it was in the table tennis events in particular where many ethnic Chinese athletes, who had migrated to different countries, could be seen competing for different national teams. In the women's table tennis team, for an instance, 16 among the 55 participant countries included ethnic-Chinese players in their national teams, and 33 out of a total of 172 players were Chinese ethnics (almost 20 percent).[4] In particular, among the nine winners (three players each with gold, silver, and bronze medals), seven were ethnically Chinese. As a by-product, in 2008, the International Table Tennis Federation (ITTF) drafted a new rule that prohibits migratory players from participating in international games if the players changed their nationalities after the age of 21.

South Korea is not an exception to this trend: Tang Ye-seo, a migrating Chinese athlete, became naturalized and was then selected as a member of the women's table tennis team. Tang is one of the migrating Chinese players who began to play in South Korea since 2001, as partnered players for a South Korean commercial team. After spending eight years playing for a Korean team, she finally achieved Korean citizenship in early 2008, and was selected to be in the Korean national team for the world championship tournament in the same year. It took overcoming a couple of contro-

4 *Munhwa-ilbo*, Passions for the 2008 Olympics: Athletes change their nationalities. 6 August 2008; *Segye-ilbo*, The 2008 Olympics have become a party of mercantile. 15 August 2008. Unless noted otherwise, news articles that are written in Korean are translated into English by the author.

versies regarding her eligibility, but she was then finally selected as a member for the 2008 Beijing Olympics. Due to her excellent skills, she is often called the ace of the national team. During the Olympics, she led the national team who then won the bronze medal in the women's team event. In so doing, Tang became not only a celebrity who attracted media attention, but also a heroine who contributed significantly to winning a bronze medal for South Korea. Furthermore, the media attention on Tang and ensuing controversies enforced South Korean society to think about nationality, citizenship, migration, and a multi-ethnic society. Such issues, which are important to multiculturalism but had rarely been discussed before, would be critical for the broadening or even dismantling of the hegemonic discourses of multiculturalism in South Korea. As introduced, it was in the first decade of the new millennium that the idea of multiculturalism emerged as an important policy in South Korea, but it was still new and unfamiliar to most of Korean people.

4.2 News media discourses on Tang: multiculturalism from below

By exploring various debates on Tang from media coverage, this section investigates both the limits and possibilities of the news media discourses on Tang in terms of multiculturalism. The news media discourses are effective at tracing the changing structures of feeling toward the emerging trend and policies of multiculturalism (Williams 1977). Compared to state-led multiculturalism as a prototype of Korean multiculturalism (Ahn 2018), the examination of the news media discourses on Tang would provide a useful hint towards illuminating the dimension of public perceptions and attitudes on multiculturalism, which is heuristically called multiculturalism from below. This section divides the news media discourses on Tang into two trends (terrains) in order to underscore the similarities and differences to state-led multiculturalism – multiculturalism from above – in South Korea.

4.2.1 News media discourses as the extensions of state-led multiculturalism

On the one hand, the news media discourses on Tang, or the Tang discourses, tend to reconsolidate the characteristics of state-led multiculturalism, which is a hegemonic form of multiculturalism in South Korea. This trend among the Tang discourses can be categorized into three focuses: 1) a national project, 2) the Korean dream, and 3) the myth of success.

Firstly, the Tang discourses treat the case of Tang as another useful resource for achieving the national goal – that is, the South Korean goal. Most obviously, the news coverage advocates the inclusion of Tang as a Korean team member because her inclusion would boost the Korean team's possibility of winning a medal in the 2008 Olympics. In early 2008, when the competition for being selected for the national team was ongoing, Tang was already naturalized as a Korean, so she was eligible to be selected for the national team. While Tang was still regarded as the best asset for the Korean team, the selecting committee of women's table tennis seemed to prefer adding an "original" Korean athlete as a supplementary player before the Olympics. However, there were increasing voices both from the press and the people that the best athletes, irrespective of their origins, should be selected for the Olympics.[5] In particular, the news media often advocated that the committee needed to consider Tang seriously.[6] Soon after the controversy emerged, the selecting committee changed its position and held a special event for selecting the last player. Without this event, Tang would not have been eligible for participating in the Olympics, and as expected, Tang eventually won the event and came to represent South Korea in the 2008 Olympics. The process of selecting Tang shows that Tang was invited as a special unit for the national team for the purpose of achieving the national goal – that is, to win a medal. After the Olympics, Tang was represented as an exemplary player who "accomplished her dream of naturalization" by providing an "Olympic medal to her second mother country" (*Segye-ilbo* 2008).

Furthermore, the news media suggested advertising Tang as a symbol of multiculturalism in South Korea. News coverage also urged people to embrace her as a "true Korean" who now represents her new motherland, which shows that South Korean society was, at this point, no longer adhering to the perpetuation of the myth of being a single-race or one-blood nation. The news media even advocated that the Korean society or Koreans ("we") needed to advertise Tang as evidence of a multicultural Korean society to the eyes of the world throughout the Olympics:[7]

> I was able to witness this ambitious dream from sports [Tang in the 2008 Olympics]. I could see a new understanding of nation-state with a sound rationale beyond the unity of blood only. Youths come to accomplish their goals in a country where their abilities are recognized, and in so doing, the concepts of nation-state are transformed. (*Kookmin-ilbo*, 21 August 2008).[8]

A multicultural society was often identified as a criterion of advanced countries. In short, the Tang discourses underscore that Tang could contribute to achieving national goals either in winning a medal or in upgrading the national reputation during the 2008 Olympics.

Secondly, news coverage represented Tang as a person who strove to accomplish the Korean dream. Before the Olympics, the news coverage highlighted how difficult it

5 *Kookmin-ilbo*, Still controversies over the selecting committees ... just before the 2008 Beijing Olympics. 27 June 2007; *Hankuk-ilbo*, The stepping down of the President of Table Tennis can lead to a gold medal! 7 July 2008.

6 *Hankyoreh*, A Chinese migrant athlete came to represent South Korea? 23 January 2008.

7 *Munhwa-ilbo*, Future of South Korea, multi-culture and multi-nation toward global Korea. 14 August 2008.

8 *Kookmin-ilbo*, Table tennis singles, defeated by Chinese. 21 August 2008.

was for Tang to pass the test for becoming a Korean national as well as how hard Tang tried to acquire Korean citizenship. By detailing the various obstacles and difficult procedures of acquiring citizenship, the media discourses underscored her unyielding desire to become a Korean. Although Tang spent eight years in South Korea, she had to pass the nationalization test in order to be eligible for the national team. Tang pointed out the tests on early modern Korean history and lyrics of Korean anthem as especially difficult (*Kyunghyang-shinmoon*, 29 February 2008).[9] According to media interviews, Tang confessed that "the naturalization test was too difficult, so I had to stop practicing for three months just to prepare for the test" (*SBS* 27 August 2008).

Throughout the Olympics, the news coverage continued to call Tang a true Korean player. By highlighting her relentless training and work ethics, the media often described her as "performing more like Koreans than real Koreans" (*Hankyoreh* 2008).[10] When Tang contributed to earning an Olympic medal, the news coverages repeated the same rationale that Tang finally recognized the significance of representing South Korea in the international events and that she was so happy to accomplish her duty as a Korean – i. e., to win a medal:

> Tang Ye-seo cried over [winning a bronze medal] [...] 'Korean dream' *(Financial-times*, 17 August 2008)
> Tang: I really put my all into preparing for the Olympics because it is very hard to win a medal. I was so happy to win a medal with the help of the coaches of the Korean national teams. (*SBS*, 17 August 2008)

As Kelly (2013) aptly explains from the case of transnational athletes in Japan, cultural nationalism is about being Korean, which is much more about doing Korean-ness and about performing Korean-ness rather than being legally Korean. The Tang discourses intentionally overstate her "Korean-ness" and continuously repeat her responsibility as a Korean.

Thirdly, the Tang discourses demonstrate that the myth of success is a central criterion of embracing a migrant as one of "us" – that is, "true" Koreans in South Korea. Although it was not a legal issue for naturalized athletes to be selected as national team members, public sentiment partly expressed feelings and thoughts of discomfort against the idea of having Tang as a national representative. One of the main criticisms was that her choice of becoming a Korean was simply an individual decision to fulfill her own ambitions, i. e., to participate in the Olympics and to be an Olympic medalist. Because she had not been competitive enough to be selected as a member of the Chinese national team, it was highlighted that Tang abandoned her native country, China, in favor of pursuing her personal goals. Others pointed out that her decision of becoming Korean had nothing to do with Korea itself: rather, her

9 *Kyunghyang-shinmoon*, Naturalized table tennis player from China is suspended, 29 February 2008.
10 *Hankyoreh*, Tang pledges to win a medal in the Olympics. 15 August 2008.

change of citizenship was simply an accidental outcome of her personal ambitions. In this sense, her decision of becoming a Korean was often regarded as a selfish decision. However, such criticism by and large lost any traction once Tang contributed to winning a bronze medal in the women's table tennis team event for South Korea. Instead, the news coverage bestowed her with the title of the first naturalized Korean medalist, calling it a great honor:

> "Congratulations to the first naturalized athlete ... Bronze medal from the women's table tennis," (*Kookmin-ilbo*, 17 August 2008)
> "Tang Ye-seo, the honor of being the first medalist as a naturalized Korean," (*Segye-ilbo*, 17 August 2008)
> "Naturalized Korean, Tang Ye-Seo's tear on bronze medal," (*Hankuk-ilbo*, 18 August 2008).

Along with the news of the bronze medal, the disputes over Tang's allegedly selfish decisions were no longer a focus in the media coverage surrounding her. Such a change seems to repeat the myth of success, in which good outcomes always supersede the intention of the events. In the era of multiculturalism, the government's policies of accepting foreign workers for lower skilled areas or foreign brides are justified with the rationale that these migrants are useful for continuing the development of the South Korean economy. Such a rationale is another basis for maintaining the myth of success, which could also be easily observed in the accepting of naturalized athletes as national team members in South Korea.

This dimension of the news discourses on Tang tends to reify a hegemonic ideology of Korean multiculturalism as state-led by highlighting Tang as a national project, the Korean dream, and an example of success. These elements are also the central pillar of the mode of inclusion of Korean multiculturalism (Kim 2011; Hwang 2011). In the dominant discourse of Korean multiculturalism, most immigrants are treated as subjects who should be fully included into the norms of Korean society. The Tang discourse similarly applied this mode of inclusion in describing Tang and her efforts to be a member of the national team.

4.2.2 News media discourses as the expansions of state-led multiculturalism

On the other hand, the Tang discourses of the news media contribute to broadening the hegemonic ideology of Korean multiculturalism by repeatedly emphasizing three issues: (1) changing citizenship, (2) eligibility of representing the nation, and (3) embedded regionalism. Despite their close connections with multiculturalism, these three issues had not been seriously discussed in South Korea before this point.

Firstly, the news media on Tang made the issue of acquiring Korean citizenship visible in South Korea. Contrary to many Western countries that underwent heated discussions over granting citizenships or residencies to immigrants, South Korea was, at the time, a country with a non-immigrant policy. The governmental policies on multiculturalism were adopted under the flows of globalization, but issues of granting permanent residency or citizenship to immigrants had rarely become the heart of multicultural debates in South Korea. In the arena of sports, Hines Ward, a Korean American football player in the National Football League, elicited nationwide media discussion when he visited South Korea along with his Korean mother after becoming a celebrity in the United States, having earned the MVP in the 2006 Super Bowl XL. His visit to Korea in 2007 brought up the issues of mixed-race identity and multiculturalism in South Korean discourse, but his temporary stay had nothing to do with changing citizenship or naturalization (Ahn 2014, 2018). As mentioned, however, the news coverages on Tang's strenuous effort of gaining Korean citizenship around the same time forced South Korea to face the issues of granting citizenship to foreigners and the difficult procedures of being naturalized in South Korea. Accordingly, news articles covered the notoriously difficult procedures and excessive requirements of being naturalized as a Korean previously unknown to the general public, including details such as minimum period of stay, Korean proficiency, immigration tests. and so on (*Donga-ilbo*, 25 January 2008).[11]

Tang's naturalization process was also contrasted with those of Guss Hiddink and Brian Orser,[12] both of whom are white and Euro-Americans, and who were openly embraced in South Korea with much celebration and conferred with honorary citizenships (Lee, Jackson and Lee 2007). As sport sociologist Jung comments, "the notion of naturalization along with acquisition of citizenship or changes of nationalities is never neutral in South Korea" (2001: 267). Such starkly different procedures of naturalization were vividly observed in the news media in which hierarchal perceptions of global order based on race, class, and skin color seem to reflect the stereotypes of South Korea in general. Immigrants and children of multicultural families from Southeast Asia, China, or even North Korea who usually belong to lower economic classes are often the targets for such stereotypical representation (Kim 2014; Kwon 2015).

Secondly, the Tang discourse dealt with the question of who deserves to represent South Korea, which is related but not limited to a legal issue. As a naturalized Korean, Tang was eligible for being selected as a member of the national team for the Olympics. Seeing that she was one of the top athletes in women's table tennis, as shown, the news coverages rarely called into question whether Tang was qualified to be part of the national team. However, there still existed a tendency of voicing some discomfort with having a naturalized athlete as a representative of South Korea. For instance, several news articles still regarded Tang as a kind of mercenary in the sporting world who plays for any team that pay her rather than as a legitimate Korean

11 *Donga-ilbo*. "Korean Dream", Tang will challenge the gold medal for the Beijing Olympics. 25 January 2008.

12 Guss Hiddink, a former manager of the Korean national football team and Brian Orser, a former coach of Korean sport celebrity Kim Yuna.

member of the team.[13] For example, "Regardless of nationalities, the world for mercenaries has arrived. Athletes changed their nationalities for the sake of money and personal ambitions. The Olympics, which were once an arena for national competition, have changed." (*Kyunghyang-shinmmon*, 21 August 2008)

Tang's real intention for being nationalized was sometimes scrutinized even after she contributed to winning a bronze medal for the 2008 Olympics. By pointing out that her husband still lived in Shanghai and was doing business as a real estate agent,[14] some doubted Tang's sincerity in her reason for acquiring Korean citizenship. While Tang was represented as a symbol of ending the myth of single-nation and one-blood nation,[15] Tang's intention of being nationalized into Korean was not fully embraced by the media.

Lastly, the Tang discourses demonstrate that multiculturalism in South Korea is explicitly embedded with regionalism, which includes China–Korea relations, history, rivalry, and East Asian relations to the West. While Tang played as a member of the Korean national team in the international events, including the 2008 Olympics, the Korean news media paid special attention to how China and the Chinese media responded. In particular, news articles closely reported Chinese responses when the Chinese media said something negative about Tang's naturalization, and about her competing as part of the Korean national team.

In February 2008, when Tang played as part of the Korean team in Guangzhou, China in the World Championship of Table Tennis events, she was frustrated by the severe criticism she received from the Chinese media. The Chinese media ridiculed her, saying that Tang chose to represent South Korea because she had failed to become China's representative because of her lack of skill. In addition, the Chinese crowd shouted out jeers, calling her "traitor" (*Munhwa-ilbo*, 8 August 2008).

The news media pointed out that the Chinese media mocked and criticized Tang among many Chinese migrant athletes who participated in the 2008 Olympics in different national teams. The media reports often described how much the Chinese media heavily quoted the interviews of Tang with the Korean news media, then utilized parts of them to criticize Tang for betraying her original home country.[16] The Korean news coverage the proceeded to praise Tang for "not only acquiring Korean citizenship but also overcoming the Chinese voices of 'traitor' during the 2008 Olympics" (*Kyunggi-ilbo*, 18 August 2008). Such a tendency in Korean news media is also related to the

13 *Kyunghyang-shimoon*, Peoples who exploits Sports. 3 September 2008.

14 *Munhwa-ilbo*, Lunar new year vacation in China lasts about 20 days, but in South Korea: Interview with Tang Ye-seo. 19 January 2012.

15 *Munhwa-ilbo*, Ending of Mono-culture and Single nation state through migrating athletes. 14 August 2008.

16 *Kookmin-ilbo*, Athletes changed their nationalities for their dreams for the Olympics. 15 August 2008; *Chosun-Ilbo*, Tang interview: "I will become part of the Korean national team and win the Olympic gold medal." 21 January 2008.

historic and regional issues over territorial and historical disputes among East Asian countries. The case of Tang effectively shows that trans-border mobility among East Asian countries does not necessarily lessen the regional tensions and rivalries. Furthermore, the Tang discourse hints that South Korea and other East Asian countries have to pay serious attention to embedded regionalism in relation to public perception on both migration and multicultural policies.

As discussed, the Tang discourses in the news media do not simply reinforce the hegemonic ideology of Korean multiculturalism, but rather, they contribute to expanding the realm of Korean multiculturalism by initiating discussions on citizenship, eligibility, and embedded regionalism. During the 2008 Olympics, Tang and her performance attracted a great amount of attention from Korean audiences, which attests to the pervasiveness of sport celebrities during sport mega-events in various kinds of locations in daily life (Turner 2004).

5 Concluding remarks

The case of Tang and its related discourses illuminate both the limits and the possibilities in Korean multiculturalism, which is heavily invested in as a major government policy in the era of globalization. While the Tang discourses in part repeat the dominant discourses of Korean multiculturalism, they also are "broadening the realm of the possible and extending the horizon of expectations" in relation to the further development of Korean multiculturalism (Kelly 2013: 1243). In particular, the issues of changing citizenship, eligibility and embedded regionalism were seriously taken into consideration for a better future of Korean multicultural society. In South Korea and East Asia, the mobility of sport athletes and celebrities does not always guarantee transnational identities or trans-border sensibilities in their local and regional publics. Such configurations of Tang both in South Korea and China exemplify even sport celebrities as part of a global–local–regional nexus (Cho 2016). As much as sport celebrities might contribute to decoupling the governance of citizenship from the nation-state, they also rekindle issues of citizenship and prompt people to re-imagine the regional relationships and regional history. In so doing, migrating sport celebrities enable people to be engaged with issues of mobility, nationality, and citizenship in the era of multiculturalism and globalization.

Tracing the discourses of sport celebrities in South Korea, furthermore, reveals deeper transformations of social structures and public sentiment which are occurring as this region becomes both more interconnected and more regionalized. Because sport celebrities function as a potent, multifaceted source of cultural identification, they are reflective of public sensibilities – even as individual celebrities provide desirable role models. These media discourses are "cultural sites for the production and contestation of mixed-race Koreans whose presence demands a new imagining of what it means to be a Korean in the era of globalization" (Ahn 2018: 4). This suggests that the primacy of celebrities within the media-sport complex might provide a unique opportunity for developing multiculturalism from below, which is to change the public perception or consciousness on multicultural issues. The analysis of the Tang discourses shows that Korean multiculturalism needs to go beyond the issues of tolerance, donation, dispensation, and top-down programming. The pervasiveness and popularity of sport culture, celebrities, and fandom may invite people to reconsider the essentialist understanding of national identity and citizenship, and to be engaged with multicultural issues in daily conversations and activities. Because such possibilities are never guaranteed, the ongoing attention on and academic reassessment of such a case are necessary for making this possibility a reality.

The 2008 Beijing Olympics are particularly significant within the context of the changing relationships in East Asia as the Chinese and Korean governments pursued their national goals in front of a global audience. The sporting event and several athletes thus played the role of enhancing national unity and power as part of the governments' soft power. As discussed, the fluctuating discourses on migrating sport celebrities during the 2008 Beijing Olympics highlight the importance and necessity of seriously considering sport celebrities and their relations to cultural policy in East Asia. Sport celebrities also stimulate cross-spatial, linguistic, and cultural transformations: they are both global and regional, and also local and particular. In East Asia, the influential identities produced by sport celebrities are often explicitly linked with the definitions of nationality, ethnicity, and even citizenship. Mega-sporting events as well as the proliferation of global sports fandom in East Asia make it not only opportune, but also imperative, to investigate the causes and effects of sport celebrities in this region. The collaborative efforts of understanding sports and related culture through the Olympics and migrant athletes can be another momentum for highlighting the importance of sport in the governments' policies and regional relations in Asia. This study investigates the complex, contradictory ways that sport celebrities are articulated among global sport discourse as well as the regional and national identities in relation to the emerging discourses of multiculturalism in South Korea. This effort aims to make a unique contribution to understanding the roles of sports in multiculturalism as well as cultural diplomacy both in South Korean and East Asian contexts.

References

Ahn, Ji-Hyun. 2014. Rearticulating black mixed-race in the era of globalization: Hines Ward and the struggle for Koreanness in contemporary South Korean media. *Cultural Studies* 28(3). 391–447.

Ahn, Ji-Hyun. 2018. *Mixed-race politics and neoliberal multiculturalism in South Korean media.* Cham, Switzerland: Palgrave Macmillan.

Andrews, David L. 2001. Introduction: Michael Jordan matters. In David L. Andrews (ed.), *Michael Jordan, Inc.: Corporate sport, media culture, and late modern America*, xiii–xx. New York: State University of New York Press.

Andrews, David L. 2004. Speaking the "universal language of entertainment": News Corporation, culture and the global sport media economy. In David Rowe (ed.), *Critical readings: Sport, culture and the media*, 99–128. Maidenhead: Open University Press.

Andrews, David L. & Steven Jackson. 2001. Introduction: Sport celebrities, public culture, and private experience. In David L. Andrews & Steven Jackson (eds.), *Sport stars: The cultural politics of sporting celebrity*, 1–19. London & New York: Routledge.

Brownell, Susan. 2011. The Beijing Olympics as a turning point? China's first Olympics in East Asian perspective. In William W. Kelly & Susan Brownell (eds.), *The Olympics in East Asia: Nationalism, regionalism, and globalism on the center stage of world sports*, 189–203. New Haven, CT: Yale University Press.

Cho, Heeyon. 2010. *Mobilized modernity: Duplicity of the developmental regime of Park Jung-hee.* Seoul: Humanitas (in Korean).

Cho, Younghan. 2009. Unfolding sporting nationalism in South Korean media representation of the 1968, 1984 and 2000 Olympics. *Media, Culture & Society* 31(3). 347–364.

Cho, Younghan. 2015. Sport celebrity in South Korea: Park, Tae-Hwan from new generation to fallen angel. *Asian Pacific Journal of Sport and Social Science* 4(3). https://doi.org/10.1080/21640599.2015.1127943.

Cho, Younghan. 2016. Toward the post-westernization of baseball? The national-regional-global nexus of Korean Major League Baseball fans during the 2006 World Baseball Classic. *International Review for Sociology of Sport* 51(6). 752–769.

Fairclough, Norman. 1992. *Discourse and social change.* Cambridge: Polity Press.

Gamson, Joshua. 1994. *Claims to fame: Celebrity in contemporary America.* Berkeley, CA: University of California Press.

Hwang, Jung-Mee. 2011. Transnational migration and new issues in women's citizenship, *Korean Gender Studies* 27(4). 111–143 (in Korean).

Joo, Rachael Miyung. 2012. *Transnational sport: Gender, media and global Korea.* Durham, NC: Duke University Press.

Jung, Hee-Joon. 2001. Conditions of sport heroes. *Journal of Korean Sport Sociology* 14(1). 257–272 (in Korean).

Kang, Myungkoo. 1994. *Theory of Korean journalism: News, discourse and ideology.* Seoul: Nanam (in Korean).

Kelly, William W. 2011. East Asian Olympics, Beijing 2008, and the globalization of sport. *The International Journal of the History of Sport* 28(16). 2261–2270.

Kelly, William W. 2013. Japan's embrace of soccer: Mutable ethnic players and flexible soccer citizenship in the new East Asian sports order. *The International Journal of the History of Sport* 30(11). 1235–1246.

Kim, Hyun Mee. 2014. *We are leaving home: Immigrants strive to live in South Korea.* Seoul: Dolbegea (in Korean).

Kim, Jung-Sun. 2011. The critical study of 'Korean style' multiculturalism as welfare policy excluding citizenship. *Economics and Society* 92. 205–246 (in Korean).

Kobayashi, Koji & Younghan Cho. 2019. Asian sport celebrity: The nexus of race, ethnicity and regionality. *The International Journal of the History of Sport* 36(7–8). 611–625.
Kwon, June Hee (2015). The work of waiting: Love and money in Korean Chinese transnational migration. *Cultural Anthropology* 30(3). 477–500.
Lee, Nammi, Steven J. Jackson & Keunmo Lee. 2007. South Korea's "glocal" hero: The Hiddink syndrome and the rearticulation of national citizenship and identity. *Sociology of Sport Journal* 24. 283–301.
Maguire, Joseph. 1999. *Global sport: Identities, societies, civilizations*. Cambridge: Polity Press.
Maguire, Joseph & Mark Falcous 2011. Introduction: Borders, boundaries and crossings: Sport, migration and identities. In Joseph Maguire & Mark Falcous (eds.) *Sport and migration: Borders, boundaries and crossings*, 1–12. Abingdon: Routledge.
Marshall, P. David. 1997. *Celebrity and power: Fame in contemporary culture*. Minneapolis: University of Minnesota Press.
Miller, Toby, Geoffrey A. Lawrence, Jim MacKay & David Rowe. 2001. *Globalization and sport: Playing the world*. Thousand Oaks, CA: Sage.
Rojek, Chris. 2001. *Celebrity*. London: Reaktion Books.
Rowe, David. 2003. Sport and the repudiation of the global. *International Review for the Sociology of Sport*. 38(3). 281–294.
Rowe, David. 2017. The AFC Asian Cup: Continental competition, global disposition. In Lawrence A. Wenner & Andrew C. Billings (eds.), *Sport, media, and mega-events*, 185–198. Abingdon: Routledge.
Turner, Graeme. 2004. *Understanding celebrity*. London: Sage Publications.
Williams, Raymond. 1977. *Marxism and literature*. Oxford and New York: Oxford University Press.

Lee Thompson

26 Communication and sport in Japan

Abstract: Communication and media studies of sport in Japan are not well-known in the English-speaking world. Nonetheless, paralleling the more well-known situation in Europe and the Americas, communication and sport have been intricately linked in Japan. Sport and sport-like activities are represented in the earliest written and archaeological records. Managing communication played an important role in the development and transmission of the various martial arts. Spectator sports such as sumo were advertised through the medium of woodblock printing. The mass media, introduced in the 19th century, played an integral role in the development of modern sports in Japan. Newspapers established and sponsored competitions that have become important dates on the national calendar, and, along with railway companies, established the first professional baseball teams, making baseball the most popular sport throughout the 20th century. The ostensibly traditional sport of sumo has been strongly shaped through its encounter with newspapers, radio, and television. The digital media have followed in this trend of becoming owners of professional teams themselves and infusing money into sport through acquisition of broadcast rights. The example of Japan is an important contribution to the study of sport and communication in general.

Keywords: Japanese sports; martial arts; sports media; manga; anime; baseball; sumo; Olympics

1 Introduction

Communicating about sport and sport-like activities has a long history in Japan, and this communication has played an integral part in the development of sport in that country. That is to say, Japan is no different from other countries; but because of language and academic barriers, that history is perhaps not so well known outside of Japan. In this chapter I would like to acquaint readers with this long and fascinating relationship, to both present Japan as another sector in which communication and sport can be fruitfully studied, and to demonstrate that Japan perhaps has something unique to contribute to that study.

The structure of this chapter is chronological, starting with the communication of sport before the advent of mass media, and then taking up various media roughly in the order that they made their impact on sport. Exceptions were made for baseball and sumo, two sports with particularly rich relationships with the media that warranted their own treatment. The story of the communication of sport can be told from the perspective of how a particular medium communicated sport, or how a particular

https://doi.org/10.1515/9783110660883-026

sport was communicated in the media. To make a good story it is sometimes necessary to switch perspectives. I hope this is not too jarring.

2 Premodern Japan and the martial arts

Sport and sport-like activities in Japan have been communicated for as long as there is a written record. Tales of archery, swordsmanship, horsemanship, and barehanded martial arts appear in the myths and legends of Japan, compiled some 1300 years ago in the *Kojiki* (Records of Ancient Matters) and *Nihonshoki* (The Chronicles of Japan) (Guttmann and Thompson 2001: 14–15, 42; Hurst 1998: 28–29; Nitta 2010: 29–36). Sports such as *kemari* (literally "kick-ball") also feature in classical poetry (*waka*) from the 10th century CE (Sasaki 2008: 178). Sports have been depicted in paintings and other works of art throughout Japanese history (The Tokugawa Art Museum, Nagoya 1994; Sakai sumōten jikkōiinkai 1998). The technique of woodblock printing made mass production possible to a certain degree, and from the early 18th century sumo tournaments were advertised through printed ranking sheets called *banzuke*. Indeed, the prevalence and familiarity of these printed *banzuke* led to the compilation of similar rankings of other phenomena using the form and terminology of sumo. Subjects thus ranked include restaurants, brands of sake, tourist spots, mountains, and prostitutes (Ishikawa 2001). Sumo matches and wrestlers were popular subjects of *ukiyo-e* woodblock prints as well (Bickford 1994). Although all of these representations were created under specific social, economic, and cultural conditions, for distinct communicative purposes and to meet specific needs, they serve another communicative purpose by transmitting to us today the only information we have about the activities depicted and the societies in which they were held.

One can also focus on communication within sport. Communication can be managed and controlled as a means to acquire and maintain power. In pre-modern Japan, there were a plethora of martial arts schools (*ryūha*), most claiming authority for their esoteric techniques based on transmission from a prestigious deity, emperor, or some other respected historical figure. These schools carefully guarded their purportedly superior techniques, and only after an appropriate period of tuition would a master transmit these secrets to a deserving disciple. Although the secret techniques were often transmitted orally, some written acknowledgement – a *kudensho* – was often provided. If so specified, this document authorized the disciple to take on students and offer training in the school's techniques himself. The certified disciple in turn presented his master with a *kishōmon*, a pledge not to reveal the secrets, written on special paper in a peculiar calligraphy, and often sealed with blood (Hurst 1998: 177–189).

There is thus a certain mysticism associated with the Japanese martial arts and their associated sports, probably best expressed in *Zen in the Art of Archery* by Eugen

Herrigel. In that book, Herrigel wrote about his experiences studying archery while in Japan in the 1920s to teach philosophy. Herrigel was perplexed with many of his teacher's instructions, such as "[y]ou must not draw the bow with your physical strength; you must do it with your mind," and "[s]ince an arrow shot in the proper way naturally hits the target, you need not, or rather should not, aim at the target" (quoted in Inoue 2006: 229, 230). As the title of his book indicates, Herrigel associated these comments with the philosophy of Zen. In a brief exposition of Pierre Bourdieu's concept of "embodied habitus," Inoue offers a more contemporary interpretation of Herrigel's disorientation, arguing that it demonstrates that "techniques of the body" such as archery cannot be transmitted verbally (2006: 230). Yamada Shoji, on the other hand, makes the more prosaic case that Herrigel's spiritual interpretation of his teacher's comments was in large part due to a lack of communication exacerbated by mistranslation (2001: 24–26). Yamada writes, "the complex spiritual episodes related in the book occurred either when there was no interpreter present, or were misinterpreted by Herrigel via the interpreter's intentionally liberal translations" and "the personal desire of Herrigel to pursue things Zen" (2001: 1). The book, Herrigel's interpretations of his teacher's instructions, and Inoue and Yamada's analyses of Herrigel's interpretations, all provide different examples of or angles from which to approach the communication of sport.

The founder of the modern martial arts, Kanō Jigorō, developed his own system of unarmed combat, which he named "judo," by synthesizing a variety of martial arts codes. He first studied the Tenjin Shin'yō and the Kitō schools of jujutsu, but was also able to find at secondhand bookstores "previously closely guarded martial arts instructional manuals" (Inoue 1998: 165). He then selected their "best elements" for incorporation into judo, which he founded in 1882. From the standpoint of communication, Kanō broke away from the tradition of guarding these "secrets" and using them as the source of his authority. Instead, he broke open the code of secrecy and wrote openly about the techniques he had synthesized and developed. Unlike the archery teacher described by Herrigel, Kanō believed that these techniques could and should be rationally explained, which he did in numerous books and lectures (Inoue 1998: 164–165; Inoue and Nishiyama 1996: 124–129).

3 Newspapers

The mechanical printing press with movable type was introduced to Japan in the 19th century, and sports were among the topics taken up in the resulting books and newspapers. In 1883 English educator Frederick W. Strange wrote the book *Outdoor Games* as a reference to the fairly new world of Western sports. It was translated into Japanese in 1885 and was influential in popularizing these exotic activities (Guttmann and Thompson 2001: 73).

Modern newspapers have been published in Japan since the 1870s. From their beginnings, the newspapers have covered modern sports imported from the West (as well as traditional sports) and, as in other countries, this coverage has played a central role in the development of sports. Newspapers established and sponsored contests and tournaments in many sports. For example, in 1901 the newspaper *Jiji shimpō* sponsored a 12-hour running race around the perimeter of a lake in Tokyo. In 1905, another newspaper, the *Osaka Mainichi Shimbun*, sponsored a 10-mile swimming race in Osaka Bay (Guttmann and Thompson 2001: 73, 76).

Some of these races and competitions have become established features not only of the sports scene in Japan but also of the yearly cycle of national life. One of these races is the Hakone Ekiden, a long-distance relay race held annually over two days on January 2 and 3. The Hōchi Shimbun instituted the race in 1920 as a collegiate race competed in by universities from the area around Tokyo. The more than 100-kilometer course stretches between Tokyo and the mountain resort of Hakone and is divided into five stages of around 20 kilometers each. Teams of student-athletes representing their universities run up to Hakone on the first day of the race, and then back down to Tokyo on the second. Live radio broadcasts of the entire two days began in 1953. Commercial broadcaster Nippon Television started broadcasting the entire race (six hours per day for two days) in 1987. Ratings in the Tokyo area for these broadcasts are regularly around 30 percent, peaking at 38.4 percent in 1995, meaning that four out of ten households were tuned into the race (Guttmann and Thompson 2001: 74; Havens 2015: 6, 76–77).

Regional newspapers followed suit. In 1952 the *Nishi-Nippon Shimbun* established a long-distance relay race that circled the island of Kyushu. This event, the Round-Kyushu Ekiden, featured runners from the seven prefectures in Kyushu plus the adjacent prefectures of Yamaguchi and Okinawa. The more than 1,000 kilometer course was divided into 72 stages, and the race took ten days to complete. At its peak over 2 million spectators gathered at numerous points along the course to watch the runners pass. The event was held annually for over 60 years but was discontinued after 2013 as the logistics became too overwhelming (Yamamoto 2002).

4 Radio

Radio also had an important role in popularizing sports, including the Olympic Games. Japan Broadcasting Corporation (NHK) broadcast the 1932 Los Angeles Olympics, but, according to Hashimoto, the US Olympic committee would not allow live coverage of the Games because they could not come to terms over the rights with the American network NBC. Unable to broadcast live from the stadium, NHK resorted to something they dubbed "lifelike" broadcasts (*jikkan hōsō*) to cover the events participated in by Japanese athletes. That is, the announcer watched the event at the stadium, taking notes, then rushed by car to the studio of a local NBC affiliate, where, referring to his notes, he announced the event as if he was watching it live. Supposedly it took renowned sports announcer Matsuuchi Norizō almost one full minute to recreate from start to finish the final heat of the 100-meter dash featuring Japanese runner Yoshioka Takayoshi (Hashimoto 1992: 45–49). (Kobayashi [2017: 43, 45–46] points out that the listeners back in Japan had been informed that the events were not actually being broadcast live, and that in the early days of radio there was precedent for this kind of after-the-fact recreation of live events.)

The 1936 Berlin Olympics are famous for the live broadcast of the women's 200-meter breaststroke final, won by Japan's Maehata Hideko. In the final lap, Maehata was in a dead heat with a German swimmer, and in his excitement veteran announcer Kasai Sansei could only keep shouting into the mike, "*Maehata gambare! Maehata gambare*! (Come on, Maehata! Come on, Maehata!)" (Hashimoto 1992: 74 –77). The merits of this broadcast in particular, and the style in general, in which the announcer forgoes describing the action and instead becomes a member of the cheering section, have been debated ever since. (Different countries or groups produce their own stories of the Olympics; for many Americans, the Berlin Olympics were where Jesse Owens vanquished the Nazi myth of Aryan supremacy.)

Radio was also enlisted to promote "nationality through physical drills and calisthenics" (Shimizu 2007: 60) by means of "radio exercises" (*rajio taisō*), a set of calisthenics performed to a simple piano accompaniment and shouted instructions broadcast over the radio. NHK began radio exercise broadcasts in 1928, and from 1931 the practice was popularized through "clubs" in which people gathered in the early morning, usually in the summer, at open public spaces such as the grounds of shrines, temples, and schoolyards to perform the prescribed exercises in unison with the radio. This project was sponsored by the Ministry of the Interior and the Ministry of Education and Culture. By 1937, some 122 million people were taking part in this mass exercise: millions of people all over the country, young and old, simultaneously going through the same motions. NHK still broadcasts the exercises, and, although they are not as prevalent as before, people still regularly gather to perform them at "kindergartens, schools, factories, corporations, hospitals, prisons, meetings and festivities." Shimizu quotes Kuroda (1999): "Radio Taisō is the means of mobilizing an individual's body for society as a blind effort towards modernity, decorated with such key words as health, rationality, efficiency and home" (Shimizu 2007: 61).

5 Baseball

Baseball has arguably been the most popular and influential sport in Japan for more than one hundred years, and its trajectory is inextricable from the successive introduction of the various mass media. One of the most prominent events of the annual sports calendar is the national high school baseball tournament, which was inaugurated by the *Asahi Shimbun* newspaper in 1915. Paradoxically, this came only a few years after a campaign by the Tokyo edition of the newspaper reviling the sport of baseball as an unsuitable pastime for young men. Preliminary tournaments are held in each of the country's 49 prefectures to select a school to represent it at the two-week final stage, held during the summer break at the venerable Kōshien Stadium in Nishinomiya (owned by Hanshin Electric Railway). The 102nd annual tournament was scheduled for 2020, but was cancelled because of the COVID-19 pandemic, the first peacetime cancellation of the event. The tournament was such a success that in 1924 a rival newspaper, the *Mainichi Shimbun*, started its own tournament held during the spring break, also at Kōshien Stadium (Guttmann and Thompson 2001: 83, 88, 131; Ariyama 1997).

The national high school baseball tournament has been taken up by each subsequent "new medium." The tournament has been broadcast on the radio since 1927, only two years after radio broadcasting started in Japan. Needless to say, live radio broadcasts of sporting events were unprecedented, and announcers had to develop a style and norms. Live broadcasts presented a particular problem for the Ministry of Communication, which pre-censored all radio content. This was dealt with by having an official from the Ministry sit next to the announcer with a breaker in front of him with which he could switch off the live broadcast at any time to prevent "agitating or immoral" material from being disseminated over the airwaves (Guttmann and Thompson 2001: 134). The tournament was broadcast nationwide from 1929. A nationwide relay network had been rapidly assembled the year before to broadcast to the nation the enthronement ceremony of Emperor Hirohito. Ariyama remarks that the live broadcast of the enthronement ceremony was intended to create a sense of unity throughout the dispersed population, and the live broadcasts of the national baseball tournament had the same effect (1997: 129–137).

The popularity of the high-school tournament surpasses that of college baseball. Many people prefer the "innocent" and supposedly unadulterated motives of the high school players to the suspect motives of professional baseball. Newspapers and television broadcasts provide their readers and viewers with stories that support this perception (Komuku 1994). The amateur nature of high school baseball, however, provided a shaky foundation for the commercial interests of the newspapers. In 1934 the *Yomiuri* newspaper, one of the "big three" newspapers in Japan along with the *Asahi* and the *Mainichi*, and Japan's largest daily newspaper in terms of circulation – and the only one of the three not to have its own high school baseball tournament – responded by forming the first successful professional baseball team, the Yomiuri Giants. A professional league with seven teams was established in 1936. Four of the teams were sponsored by newspapers, and three by railway companies, all of which saw the potential for symbiosis between baseball and their enterprises. (The railway companies built stadiums, serviced by their train lines. Hanshin Electric Railway, who already owned the Kōshien Stadium, formed the Hanshin Tigers professional baseball team. Guttmann and Thompson 2001: 137–138).

The Yomiuri Giants have had a gigantic influence on professional baseball in Japan, due largely to the fact that their owner is a national newspaper and can "sell" its product nationally. This influence was compounded when television began broadcasts in 1953. Like the other newspapers, the Yomiuri became a media conglomerate with radio and television stations, also with a national reach. The team's games were broadcast nationally and covered in the nationally distributed newspaper, establishing Yomiuri Giants fans all over the country. Other teams were broadcast only regionally; the only national exposure they got was via their games with the Giants. The Yomiuri conglomerate used this power to control the league to their advantage. For many years this influence was wielded by the outspoken and autocratic Watanabe Tsuneo, who worked his way up from a business reporter to the head of the conglomerate and baseball team (Whiting 2004: 92–94).

The tensions between the spirit of amateurism ideally embodied by high school players and the commercial pressures of professional baseball were depicted in the 1956 novel *Anata kaimasu* ("We buy you") by Ono Minoru, based on a real incident, and made into a movie later that year produced by the Shōchiku movie studio and starring popular actors Sada Keiji and Kishi Keiko. A promising young college player is being wooed by a pack of pro scouts, and his family and an enigmatic patron are also hoping to cash in on his talents. In the end he betrays them all, and the woman he loves. The novel and movie lament the corruption of an innocent youth through the commercialization of a putatively bucolic pastime, a theme that perhaps resonates beyond Japan's borders.

6 Sumo

The seemingly traditional sport of sumo has also been impacted by its relationship with the modern media, starting with the newspapers. From the middle of the 18th century sumo tournaments were held regularly in the main cities of Kyoto, Osaka, and Edo (present-day Tokyo). Each wrestler had one match on each of the ten days of the tournament, but records were not compared over the course of a tournament to determine a champion. What you saw in the ring was what you got. From around 1890, newspapers began to award prizes to wrestlers based on their record over the course of a tournament. The purpose of these prizes of course was to create increased interest in the tournament, interest that would hopefully be translated into higher sales. The newspapers stimulated this interest by publishing daily tables, called *hoshitorihyō*, summarizing the records of the wrestlers to date. These initial attempts to recognize and reward performance based on a quantified record were formalized into the current championship system in the year 1909, when the newspaper *Jiji Shinpō* announced its intention to designate a single champion at all future tournaments. For the next seventeen years, the championship was maintained solely on the initiative of the newspaper, but in 1926 the Sumo Association, the governing body for professional sumo, finally gave their imprimatur. The introduction of the championship necessitated other changes in the operation of the tournaments, including the elimination of draws and no-contests, and, later, the introduction of a play-off in the case of a tie for the best record (Guttmann and Thompson 2001: 108–113; Thompson 1998: 178–182).

The influence of the media has of course not been limited to the newspapers. Radio broadcasts also had a subtle but fundamental impact on the management of sumo tournaments. The Sumo Association was initially reluctant to allow radio broadcasts of the tournaments. As has been seen in other national contexts and for other sports, they worried that customers would not pay to see the matches when they could listen for free on the radio. As it turned out, of course, the broadcasts provided free advertising, and the tickets sold out.

A different problem arose for the broadcaster, however. As anyone who has ever watched a sumo tournament knows, there is a fairly long routine performed before each match, known as *shikiri*, during which the contestants alternate between facing off in a crouch, and returning to their respective corners for a handful of salt which they then toss into the ring. Given the short duration of the match proper, these preliminaries give the audience a better look at the two protagonists. In theory, the two opponents can start their match at any time, and before the advent of radio broadcasting the start of the match was left entirely to the two contestants. If one of them did not feel quite ready, the *shikiri* could go on for some time. One match is said to have taken almost an hour to start. The unpredictability of match length presented a problem for the broadcaster, who needs to fit the day's matches into a program schedule and has to move on to the next program at a predetermined time. To accommodate the broadcaster, a time limit of ten minutes was set on the *shikiri* when tournaments began to be broadcast on the radio in 1928 (gradually shortened to the current four minutes: Guttmann and Thompson 2001: 114–115).

The seemingly minor adjustment of a time limit must have had a profound effect both for the wrestlers themselves and for the spectators. Today, it is extremely rare for a match to start before the time is up. No one, neither the wrestlers themselves nor the spectators, expect the match to start before the referee announces that the time is up by calling "*matta nashi!*" This means that the prior *shikiri* have become a mere formality, lacking the emotional tension generated by the expectation of the start of the match. Indeed, during these preliminary *shikiri* many wrestlers crouch in a manner from which it would be difficult or awkward to actually charge their opponent. The spectators know that the match will not start before the time is up, and their attention can wander. The introduction of a time limit on the *shikiri* to accommodate the needs of the radio broadcaster thus fundamentally altered the dynamics of professional sumo performances for the performers, and the experience of watching those performances. Sumo can thus be added to the canon of sports whose nature was altered through its relationship with the media. Sumo's encounter with television will be discussed later.

7 Sports newspapers

Apart from the mainstream press, so-called "sports newspapers" are tabloid newspapers for men. Although they feature mainly sports news, they also cover the state-controlled pari-mutuel sports of horse, bicycle, and speedboat racing, and contain male-oriented gossip about athletes and entertainers. Sports newspapers in general display a particular brand of blatant masculinity in their overly dramatized and sensationalized coverage, and in erotic stories, drawings, and photographs (as in other countries, sports in Japan have long been a male bastion). The first sports newspaper, *Nikkan supōtsu* (Daily Sports) was published soon after World War II, in 1946, followed by *Supōtsu Nippon* (Sports Japan) in 1949 and *Sankei Supōtsu* (Sankei Sports) in 1955. The venerable *Hōchi shimbun* also restructured itself as a sports newspaper in 1949. These papers claim circulations of 500,000 to over one million (Guttmann and Thompson 2001: 165; Fujitake and Takeshita 2018: 34–35; Sato 2018: 130).

8 Sports magazines

Sport-themed magazines have been published in Japan since the early 20th century. One of the first was *Gekkan bēsubōru* (Baseball monthly), which hit the racks in 1908, changing its name to *Yakyūkai* (Baseball world) in 1911, using a translated term for "baseball" (*yakyū*) rather than the transliterated *bēsubōru* (the latter sounding more foreign). *Yakyūkai*, along with *Asahi supōtsu* (Asahi sports), were the leading sports magazines in Japan until the 1930s. At its peak *Yakyūkai* had a circulation of 130,000, the highest circulation by far of all the magazines issued by Hakubunkan, the leading publisher in Japan at the time. The magazine took a somewhat highbrow, literary approach in its pages, partly to counter a simmering hostility to Western sports in sectors of the government and general population. Despite its title, the magazine also covered other sports – especially sumo, which rivaled baseball in popularity.

The magazine's chief editor Ikeda Tsuneo quit Hakubunsha in 1946 to start his own publication, *Bēsubōru magajin* (Baseball Magazine). He was not alone: almost 20 baseball magazines were started in the three years after the war. With the advent of television broadcasting in 1953, Baseball Magazine shifted its emphasis from text to photos. Baseball Magazine Co. and its affiliated publisher, Kōbunsha, started more than 30 sport-related magazines in the 1950s and 1960s, including sumo, golf, track and field, table tennis, professional wrestling, boxing, bowling, and volleyball (Sato 2018: 124–127, 153, 286–289).

The company started *Sakkā magajin* (Soccer magazine) in 1966, the oldest magazine dedicated to soccer still being published. The magazine soon became an important source of information for followers of the sport, since soccer at the time was sparsely covered in the newspapers. News about the European leagues and the

FIFA World Cup was particularly hard to come by. In 1968 Tokyo Channel 12 (the current TV Tokyo) started a weekly broadcast called "Diamond Soccer," which featured selected matches from the World Cup and European leagues. For logistical reasons these matches were usually broadcast weeks or months after the event, and because of time limitations, it took two weeks to broadcast one match, the first half being shown one week, and the second half the next. Of course, by the time of the broadcast the results of the matches had already been reported in detail, along with photos, in *Soccer Magazine*. In any case, Tokyo Channel 12 could only be received in the Tokyo area, and so for most soccer fans in Japan at that time, soccer was something that you read about in *Soccer Magazine*, rather than watched on TV (Sato 2018: 202–209).

One other magazine that should be mentioned is *Sports Graphic Number*, published by Bungeishunjū, a publisher more known for its literary and political output. *Number*, as it is usually known, has been published from 1980, and got its start as the Japanese version of the American sports magazine *Sports Illustrated*. Like its antecedent, *Number* is a "general" sports magazine, covering the gamut, but of course focusing on the more popular sports. It features an attractive design and high-quality photographs as well as engaging journalism.

9 Sports in literature and comics

According to Sandra Collins (2012), sport literature of the 1910s and 1920s "aimed to 'uplift and educate' the modern youth of Japan according to the social values of the day": hard work and discipline (1734). As the country expanded its military activities abroad, "many stories in the late 1930s began specifically to reference the Japanese spirit (*Yamato damashii*) as it related to sport discipline and masculinity" (1735). In the post-war era, the focus on "hard work, dedication, and intensity" remained, but now directed toward postwar recovery (1736).

Since the war, sports have also become an important genre of the manga (comic) and anime (animation) industries. Subjects cover the gamut of sports, with combat sports, baseball, and soccer perhaps being the most common, but also including volleyball, tennis, basketball, and the list goes on. Some of the more popular and influential works include *Kyojin no hoshi* (Star of the Giants, baseball), 1966, written by Kajiwara Ikki and illustrated by Kawasaki Noboru; *Ashita no Jō* (Tomorrow's Joe, boxing), 1968, written by Kajiwara Ikki and illustrated by Chiba Tetsuya; *Atakku No. 1* (Attack No. 1, volleyball), 1968, written by Urano Chikako and illustrated by Ozawa Kanon; *Eisu wo nerae!* (Aim for the Ace!, tennis), 1973, written and illustrated by Yamamoto Sumika; *Kyaputen Tsubasa* (Captain Tsubasa, soccer), 1981, written and illustrated by Takahashi Yōichi; and *SLAM DUNK* (basketball), 1990, written and illustrated by Inoue Takehiko.

Many sports manga have been serialized on television as anime, made into feature anime films, and sometimes films with live actors. The success of these cultural products gave rise to the expression *supokon*, derived from the words *supōtsu* (sports) and *konjō*, the latter meaning the inner strength to overcome adversity and achieve one's goals. The demonstration of *konjō* through single-minded dedication to one's sport has been a common motif in many of these manga, especially up through the 1970s, corresponding with Japan's recovery from the devastation of war and ensuing rapid economic growth (Collins 2012: 1737).

The manga industry in Japan is very gendered, with comics written for either male or female readers. The same is true for sports manga, and most content either plays to or plays off common gender stereotypes. While the authors and protagonists are predominantly male, some manga are written by and/or feature women, including *Attack No. 1* and *Aim for the Ace!* The latter often follow the conventional *konjō* story arc.

The popularity of these manga often coincides with the popularity of the sport depicted, but it is difficult to specify which is the cart and which the horse. Successful athletes have cited comics as a primary motivation for taking up their sport. One of the most famous of these is Nakata Hidetoshi, who represented his country at three FIFA World Cups and two Olympic Games. Nakata has said that he was not interested in soccer as a child until he watched *Captain Tsubasa* (Northcroft 2006).

Many of these comics and their corresponding anime have also been translated into other languages and published or broadcast overseas, and some have become quite popular. Such football luminaries as France's Zinedine Zidane and Thierry Henry, Spain's Fernando Torres, Italy's Alessandro Del Piero, and Argentina's Lionel Messi reportedly were also inspired by Takahashi's creation (Sharp 2018). The character has also been coopted by the government of Japan to project soft power. According to then Foreign Minister Aso Tarō, large stickers of *Captain Tsubasa* were prominently displayed on water supply vehicles when Japan's Self-Defense Forces were conducting "humanitarian and reconstruction assistance" in Iraq in 2006, and The Japan Foundation "concluded an agreement to provide to the largest Iraqi television station free of charge the third season of the Captain Tsubasa anime series – a total of 52 shows – dubbed into Arabic" (Aso 2006).

10 Television

Again, like many other countries, sports broadcasts were among the most popular programming in the early years of television in Japan (Thompson 1986: 67; Hashimoto 1992: 216–218). Baseball, boxing, swimming, and professional wrestling were particularly popular. Indeed, during the first ten years of television broadcasts in Japan (1953–1963) professional wrestling, dominated by the larger-than-life figure of

Rikidōzan, had the highest ratings. This was only the second decade after Japan's defeat in World War II, and the decade immediately following the official end of the UN occupation in 1952 (but with the continued presence of unwelcome US troops). In this context, Rikidōzan enjoyed unparalleled popularity by defeating foreign (often American) opponents in the ring, ultimately vanquishing them with his patent move, the karate chop. After Rikidōzan's untimely death in 1963, the popularity of professional wrestling and its television broadcasts has ebbed and flowed (Thompson 1986; Hashimoto 1992: 219–221).

Baseball was among the most popular programming for many decades, especially games featuring the Yomiuri Giants. From the mid-1970s average ratings for Giants games surpassed 20 percent in the Kanto area around Tokyo (Puro yakyū 2017). However, in 2000 the Giants' ratings started to decline, along with the number of live broadcasts of games (Kawakita 2015: 20, 23). There are many reasons for this. Cable and satellite broadcasts have given viewers more choices of programming. A professional soccer league was formed in 1996, and soccer has become more popular especially among the younger generation.

The Games of the XVIII Olympiad, 1964 Tokyo Games, were perhaps the first "television Olympics" (Hashimoto 1992: 273). They were the first Games to be broadcast overseas via satellite. The Games were the occasion for other innovations in broadcasting, such as the live coverage of the marathon in its entirety, thanks to a helicopter hovering over the broadcast car throughout the course to relay its signal. The Games contributed to the diffusion of television in Japan, and according to surveys 97.3 percent of households with television tuned in to the broadcasts at some point (Guttmann and Thompson 2001: 199–200; Hashimoto 1992: 261–287).

Although the Summer Games are usually held in July or August, the 1964 Tokyo Olympics were held in October, thereby avoiding the hot and humid Tokyo summer. The autumn weather in Tokyo was perfect, both for the athletes and the spectators. When Tokyo won the bid to host the Games of the XXXII Olympiad in 2020, however, they were scheduled for July 24 to August 9. According to news reports, the reason for this athlete-unfriendly scheduling was to accommodate American and European sports seasons, and longtime US broadcast rights-holder NBC in particular. According to Reuters, "In September or October, the Olympics would have to compete for viewers' attention against other events, such as the start of the NFL American football season, Major League Baseball playoffs in the United States and the early months of the soccer season in Europe" (Foster 2018).

Concern for the welfare of the athletes, not to mention spectators, led IOC president Thomas Bach to announce in October 2019 that the marathon would be held in the city of Sapporo, 831 kilometers north of Tokyo and a few degrees cooler (Takahashi 2019). The IOC and the organizing committee had another chance to get it right when the Olympics were postponed because of the COVID-19 pandemic, but, again probably with the interests of their main financial backer in mind, the July–August schedule was retained.

Television broadcasts of sporting events help spur interest and are an important source of income to leagues, teams, and governing bodies. They also present challenges, however. Slow motion replay, in particular, provided the TV viewer with a perspective unavailable to those in the stadium, including the referee. Philosopher Harry Collins (2010: 136) describes this as the loss of the referee's "epistemological privilege" based on his "superior view." That is, slow motion replay gives television viewers at home an apparently more accurate, and definitely more leisurely view of the action than the referee on the field. The loss of the referee's epistemological privilege undermines his "ontological authority": the authority to define what happened in the game.

Governing bodies of sports have faced this problem for years, since the advent of instant replay. Perhaps the first sport to effectively deal with this paradox is the ostensibly traditional sport of sumo. On the second day of the March tournament of 1969 the top-ranking wrestler (*yokozuna*) Taihō was unexpectedly defeated by his unheralded opponent Toda. However, the video replay of the match clearly showed that Toda had inadvertently stepped out of the ring before he pushed Taihō out. Millions of television viewers could see for themselves, live, that Taihō should have won the match. The controversy was complicated by the fact that until that match Taihō had been on a winning streak that extended to 45 straight matches without a loss, at the time the second longest winning streak in the history of sumo. Many fans were outraged, and the newspapers the next day showed photos of Toda's offending foot.

In response to this controversy, the Sumo Association introduced a video review of close calls at the next tournament, which was held in May. An additional judge was installed in a room elsewhere on the premises with a TV monitor and a video replay machine (which in 1969 was still quite rare and expensive). The video referee in the outlying room is in contact with the head judge via earpiece and microphone, and when contacted by the head judge he watches a replay of the match and gives his opinion via the microphone and earpiece to the head judge. The final decision is made by the five judges in the ring. This procedure is still in use today.

So, strange as it may seem, perhaps the first sport in the world to allow judges to consult video replay to rule on close calls was the outwardly traditional sport of sumo. The International Football Association Board (IFAB) approved the use of video assistant referees at its 132nd Annual General Meeting in March 2018, almost half a century after the seemingly traditional sport of sumo (Video Assistant 2019). Sumo, which on the surface appears very traditional, is a pioneer in its use of video technology in refereeing.

11 Movies

Sport has been a common topic for movies in Japan, both fiction and documentary. *Sugata Sanshirō*, a novel by Tomita Tsuneo published in 1942 about the early years of judo in Japan, was made into a movie the following year directed by Akira Kurosawa, his first feature film. Kurosawa later directed such masterpieces as *Rashomon* and *Seven Samurai* and was awarded a lifetime achievement award from the American Academy of Motion Picture Arts and Sciences in 1990.

In the 1950s it was not unusual for sports figures to star in movies about themselves, when they were still at the height of their careers. The professional wrestler Rikodōzan played himself in *The Rikidōzan Story* in 1955, and in 1957 the sumo *yokozuna* Wakanohana played himself in *The Wakanohana Story*.

Sports are often the subject of documentaries. Respected filmmaker Ichikawa Kon directed *Tokyo Olympiad*, the well-received documentary of the 1964 Tokyo Olympics.

Sports are the subject of movies made from novels, as with *Anata kaimasu* described above. Successful sports manga are also often made into live action movies: the manga *Ping Pong* which was serialized in 1996 and 1997 was made into a live-action film in 2002, which was nominated for several Japan Academy Awards. The original film *Waterboys* (2001, written and directed by Yaguchi Shinobu), about a high-school boys' synchronized swimming team, won a Japan Academy Award.

12 Digital media

Internet media companies have taken over ownership of some baseball teams following in the tradition of media and transportation companies. In 2004 an opening in the Pacific League of Japan Professional Baseball was created by the merger of two teams: the Osaka Kintetsu Buffaloes (owned by Kintetsu Railway) and the Orix BlueWave (formerly the Hankyu Braves, owned by Hankyu Railway), for financial reasons. The Internet shopping company Rakuten successfully applied to the commissioner for a franchise for the city of Sendai, and established the Tohoku Rakuten Eagles, who started play from the 2005 season. The Golden Eagles won the Japan Series in 2013.

In 2011, mobile telephone game company DeNA purchased 66.92 percent of the outstanding shares in the Yokohama Baystars of the Central League from Tokyo Broadcasting (TBS) and its satellite broadcasting company BS-TBS, and renamed the team the Yokohama DeNA Baystars. In the press release announcing the move, the company said that it intended to leverage the popularity of its "Mobage" portal and social network to turn its 32 million users into fans of professional baseball. In the process, the press release says, the merger will increase the value of the company's brand and name recognition (DeNA 2011).

In July 2016 Japan Professional Soccer League announced that the Internet streaming company DAZN had purchased the rights to broadcast live all matches of the three divisions of J1, J2, and J3, for ten years, from 2017 to 2026, for 210 billion yen (roughly US $2 billion). In the press release, Japan Professional Soccer League Chairman Murai Mitsuru commented, "We believe that [this] contract demonstrates that Japan's sports industry is perceived as excellent content for investment from overseas" (JRiigu to DAZN 2016). From the 2017 season, the number of cameras covering J1 league matches increased from six to nine (six cameras covered J2 matches and 4 cameras covered J3 matches). Unlike its previous contract with Sky Perfect JSAT, the league retains the copyright to the video of the games, allowing them to use images from the games in their social media marketing (Mayazumi 2018). DAZN also offers streaming of a wide variety of domestic sports in Japan such as volleyball, rugby, and professional baseball, as well as overseas competitions such as MLB, NBA, NFL, PGA, Bundesliga, Seria A, Ligue 1, and FA, and FIFA World Cup matches. However, in a 2018 survey, only 1 percent of respondents subscribed to fee-based DAZN. (7 percent said they watched the free streaming service AbemaTV: Mayazumi 2019: 5.)

13 Concluding remarks

Communicating in and about sport in Japan displays many of the same characteristics that have been demonstrated in other, mainly Western, countries, while at the same time offering unique examples and perspectives. The management of communication in the formation and transmission of diverse schools of the martial arts, and the complicated role of communication in creating and maintaining their mystic aura, are phenomena that may have parallels outside this area. It is well known that newspapers and other media companies were instrumental in establishing sporting events around the world, but their role as owners of baseball and other sports teams is perhaps more characteristic of the development of sports in Japan. The role of the media in shaping the "ancient" sport of sumo as we know it today adds a fresh perspective to the ongoing influence of the media on sports today, and the recognition that the ostensibly traditional sport of sumo was an early, if not the first, adopter of video assisted refereeing technology – by decades – should be a part of introductory courses in this field wherever they are taught.

References

Ariyama, Teruo. 1997. *Kōshien yakyū to Nihonjin: Media no tsukutta ibento* [High school baseball and the Japanese: A media-created event]. Tokyo: Yoshikawa bunkan.

Aso, Tarō. 2006. A new look at cultural diplomacy: A call to Japan's cultural practitioners. *Ministry of Foreign Affairs of Japan*, 26 April. Speech by Minister for Foreign Affairs Taro Aso at Digital Hollywood University. https://www.mofa.go.jp/announce/fm/aso/speech0604-2.html (5 October 2019).

Bickford, Lawrence. *Sumo and the woodblock print masters*. Tokyo: Kodansha International.

Collins, Harry. 2010. The philosophy of umpiring and the introduction of decision-aid technology. *Journal of the Philosophy of Sport* 37. 135–146.

Collins, Sandra. 2012. The imperial sportive: Sporting lives in the service of modern Japan. *The International Journal of the History of Sport* 29(12). 1729–1743.
DeNA Press Release. 2011. Puroyakyū no sannyū nitsuite [Moving into professional baseball], 4 November. https://web.archive.org/web/20111104134002/http://dena.jp/press/2011/11/post-103.php (20 September 2019).
Foster, Malcolm. 2018. Why the summer Olympics are held in July, August despite heat. Reuters, 26 July. https://www.reuters.com/article/us-olympics-2020-heat-explainer/why-the-summer-olympics-are-held-in-july-august-despite-heat-idUSKBN1KG17H (23 September 2019).
Fujitake, Akira & Toshirō Takeshita. 2018. *Zusetsu: Nihon no media (shinpan): Dentō media wa netto de dō kawaruka* [Media in Japan, illustrated (new edition]: How the internet will change traditional media]. Tokyo: NHK Shuppan.
Guttmann, Allen & Lee Thompson. 2001. *Japanese sports: A history*. Honolulu: University of Hawai'i Press.
Hashimoto, Kazuo. 1992. *Nihon supōtsu hōsō shi* [A history of sports broadcasting in Japan]. Tokyo: Taishūkan shoten.
Havens, Thomas R. H. 2015. *Marathon Japan: Distance racing and civic culture*. Honolulu: University of Hawai'i Press.
Herrigel, Eugen. 1953. *Zen in the Art of Archery* (trans. R. F. C. Hull). New York: Pantheon Books.
Hurst, III, G. Cameron. 1998. *Armed martial arts of Japan: Swordsmanship and archery*. New Haven, CT: Yale University Press.
Inoue, Shun. 1998. The invention of the martial arts: Kanō Jigorō and Kōdōkan Judo. In Stephen Vlastos (ed.), *Mirror of modernity: Invented traditions of modern Japan*, 163–173. Berkeley, CA: University of California Press.
Inoue, Shun. 2006. Embodied habitus. *Theory, Culture & Society* 23 (2–3). 229–231.
Inoue, Shun & Nishiyama Tetsuo. 1996. Supōtsu to media ibento: "Budō" no keisei to supōtsu no "budōka" [Sports and media events: The formation of "budo" and the "martialization" of sports]. In Toshihiro Tsuganezawa (ed.), *Kindai Nihon no media ibento* [Media events in modern Japan], 115–139. Tokyo: Dōbunkan shuppan.
Ishikawa, Eisuke. 2001. *Ōedo banzuke zukushi* [All about ranking lists in Edo]. Tokyo: Jitsugyō no Nihon sha.
JRiigu to DAZN ga 10 nenkan no hōeiken keiyaku wo teiketsu [J.League and DAZN sign ten-year broadcast rights contract]. 2016. J. League, 20 July. https://www.jleague.jp/release/post-44293/ (21 September 2019).
Kawakita, Hisashi. 2015. Nihon no terebi to puro yakyū ni tsuite no kenkyū: komyunikēshon to shijō keisei no shiten kara [A study of television and professional baseball in Japan: From the perspective of communication and market formation]. *Hyōgengaku* 1. 20–26.
Kobayashi, Toshiyuki. 2017. "Jikkan hōsō" densetsu no haikei: Nihon hatsu no Orimpikku "jikkyō" wo saikenshō suru [The background to the legend of "lifelike broadcasts": Reconstructing the first "live" Olympic broadcasts in Japan]. *Hōsō kenkyū to chōsa [NHK Monthly Report on Broadcast Research]* May. 42–53.
Komuku, Hiroshi. 1994. *Kōshien to "Nihonjin" no Saiseisan* [High school baseball and the reproduction of the "Japanese." In Shōgo Esashi & Hiroshi Komuku (eds.), *Kōkōyakyū no shakaigaku: Kōshien wo yomu* [The sociology of high school baseball: Reading Kōshien], 161–182. Kyoto: Sekai shisōsha.
Kuroda, Isamu. 1999. *Rajio taisō no tanjō* [The birth of radio exercises]. Tokyo: Seikyūsha.
Mayuzumi, Takerō. 2018. "Tsūshin" ga kaeru puro supōtsu bijinesu [Telecom Is changing professional sports business: A new trend in J. League's media strategy]. Hōsō kenkyū to chōsa [NHK Monthly Report on Broadcast Research]. February. 14–27.

Mayuzumi, Takerō. 2019. "Yūryō dōga haishin wa doko made kakudai suru no ka [How far will fee-based video streaming services expand? Analyzing the results of the survey on media use]. NHK Bunken Forum, August. 1–19.
Nitta, Ichirō. 2010. *Sumō no rekishi* [The history of sumo]. Tokyo: Kōdansha.
Northcroft, Jonathan. 2006. I don't understand why people are football fans. I don't like to watch any kind of sport. *The Sunday Times*, 1 January. https://www.thetimes.co.uk/article/i-dont-understand-why-people-are-football-fans-i-dont-like-to-watch-any-kind-of-sport-7nmdkq5tssl (5 October 2019).
Ono, Minoru. 1956. *Anata kaimasu* [We buy you]. Tokyo, Mikasa shobō.
Puro yakyū naitā shichōritsu no ugoki (suii) [Changes in the ratings for professional baseball night games]. 2017. *VR Digest*, 1 April. https://www.videor.co.jp/digestplus/tv/2017/04/632.html (10 October 2019).
Sakai sumōten jikkōiinkai. 1998. *Sumō no rekishi: Sakai sumōten kiten zuroku* [The history of sumo: Illustrated catalogue commemorating the exhibition on sumo]. Sakai: Sakai City Museum.
Sasaki, Takahiro. 2008. *Kemari wo yomu waka* [On the tradition of "Waka" (classical Japanese lyrics) featuring "Kemari" (classical Japanese football)]. *Geibun kenkyū* [Journal of arts and letters] 95. 177–198.
Sato, Akinobu. 2018. *Supōtsu zasshi no media shi: Bēsubōru Magajinsha to taishū kyōyō shugi* [A media history of sports magazines: Baseball Magazine Co. and the education of the masses]. Tokyo: Bensei Shuppan.
Sharp, Will. 2018. Captain Tsubasa: the anime star who changed the face of Japanese football and inspired Messi, Iniesta and Nakata. *These Football Times*, 11 June. https://thesefootballtimes.co/2018/06/11/captain-tsubasa-the-anime-star-who-changed-the-face-of-japanese-football-and-inspired-messi-iniesta-and-nakata/ (5 October 2019).
Shimizu, Satoshi. 2007. Synchronizing body states: Training the body at school and performing the body in the city. In William W. Kelly & Atsuo Sugimoto, *This sporting life: Sports and body culture in modern Japan*, 55–66. New Haven, CT: Yale University Press.
Takahashi, Ryusei. 2019. IOC planning to move Tokyo Olympic marathon north to Sapporo in bid to avoid heat. *The Japan Times*, 17 October. https://www.japantimes.co.jp/sports/2019/10/17/more-sports/track-field/ioc-planning-move-tokyo-olympic-marathon-north-sapporo-bid-avoid-heat/#.Xa5tWyXgpTY (22 October 2019).
The Tokugawa Art Museum, Nagoya. 1994. *Bijutsu ni miru Nippon no supōtsu* [Japanese traditional sports expressed in works of art]. Nagoya, Tokugawa bijutsukan.
Thompson, Lee A. 1986. Professional wrestling in Japan: Media and message. *The International Review for the Sociology of Sport* 21. 65–81.
Thompson, Lee. 1998. The invention of the *Yokozuna* and the championship system, or, Futahaguro's revenge. In Stephen Vlastos (ed.), *Mirror of modernity: Invented traditions of modern Japan*, 174–187. Berkeley, CA: University of California Press.
Video Assistant Referees. 2019. UEFA.com, 10 February. https://www.uefa.com/insideuefa/news/newsid=2590884.html (20 September 2019).
Whiting, Robert. 2004. *The Samurai way of baseball: The impact of Ichiro and the new wave from Japan*. New York: Warner Books.
Yamada, Shōji. 2001. The myth of Zen in the art of archery. *Japanese Journal of Religious Studies* 28 (1–2). 1–30.
Yamamoto, Norihito. 2002. Insatsu media to spōtsu hōdō: "Kyūshū isshū ekiden" no monogatari [Print media and sports coverage: the story of the Round-Kyushu ekiden]. In Jun'ichi Hashimoto (ed.), *Gendai media supōtsu ron* [Contemporary mediasport], 117–137. Tokyo: Sekai shisō sha.

Chuka Onwumechili

27 Communicating Igbo sports nationalism under military dictatorship and democracy

Abstract: This chapter examines ethnic nationalism within Nigeria, specifically focusing on Igbo nationalism through the lens of Enugu Rangers Football Club. The club was established at the end of the Nigerian civil war in 1970, after the defeat of the breakaway Igbo-dominated state of Biafra. The chapter uses autoethnography and media narratives to examine ethnic nationalism that defined the fervent support of Enugu Rangers post-Nigerian civil war. It notes that Igbo nationalism in sports existed since the 1940s, almost three decades before the civil war, during the annual inter-ethnic competition for the annual Alex Oni Cup. Yet, a fervent Igbo nationalism did not manifest widely until after the Nigerian civil war. Importantly, the post-war Igbo nationalism especially in Igbo media is remarkably different from sport-related ethnic nationalism in places like Spain or elsewhere. Among the Igbos, it was subtler and more clandestine. For instance, the genesis for naming the club remained hidden until much later after military dictatorship in the country. Additionally, the media in Igboland did not overtly report but chose to insinuate oppression of Enugu Rangers by Nigerian football officials during the period of military rule. It was not until the end of military rule, creation of additional states in the Igbo homeland, and increased competitive pressure on Enugu Rangers to recruit players from beyond Igbo homeland, that the support for Rangers and its association with Igbo nationalism began to wane.

Keywords: Igbo nationalism; Enugu Rangers; Nigeria; ethnic nationalism; sport nationalism

1 Introduction

A significant number of sports nationalism studies focus their interest on mega sporting events (Rowe, McKay, and Miller 1998; Maguire and Poulton 1999; Bairner 2014; Wenner and Billings 2017). Several of those studies explore how the media communicate nationalism while reporting sporting events or how spectators, who consume the events, communicate nationalism. However, quite a number of these studies, because they focus on state representations at mega events, default to a study of *civic* nationalism. But, as Bairner (2014) points outs, not all expressions of nationalism are civic. There are expressions that are *ethnic* and understanding this latter type of nationalism can provide valuable insights about aspiration, separatism, and conflict.

Notably, a few scholars have studied communication of ethnic nationalism in sports particularly in two regions of Spain – the Basque Country and Catalonia. Those studies have focused on media and fan communication pertaining to Athletic

https://doi.org/10.1515/9783110660883-027

Bilbao of the Basque Country and FC Barcelona of Catalonia. But expressions of ethnic nationalism differ based on differences in culture, experience, and history. While we have learned about the communication of ethnic nationalism in Spain, that knowledge does not always translate elsewhere such as Africa and Asia.

Unfortunately, there is little scholarship that investigates the communication of ethnic nationalism in Africa even when Africa is a continent that is more likely to be rich in sporting nationalism. Unlike much of the world, African countries are modern states created out of more recent amalgamations of ethnic nations. Moreover, it is also a place for continued ethnic contestations. These contestations cannot be entirely absent in the sporting arena. Yet, few scholars have explored these contestations and how they are communicated in sports in the continent.

This chapter attempts to address this gap. It focuses on the communication of Igbo nationalism in sports. Igbo is a major ethnic nation in the southeast area of Nigeria.[1] Not only do Igbos or *N'digbo* (Igbo people) speak a unique language – Igbo – but they also have a culture and experience that differs from other major ethnic groups in Nigeria. These differences are expressed while communicating Igbo nationalism through sports. Importantly, this examination allows for observation of the communication of sports nationalism, its shift and changes, given that the periods examined were under military dictatorship and democratic governments.

It is important to note that I am Igbo and have experienced, as an insider, many of the things reported here. Thus, while I rely on analysis of relevant media for this research, my experiences are also shared in a process of autoethnography. By this I refer to personal narratives that I share to make the culture and context vivid (Lindemann 2009; Ellis, Adams, and Bochner 2011). This is particularly important not only because of the insider advantages in making vivid some of these issues but also because there is paucity of literature on these matters. As will be pointed out later, this cultural insider perspective makes it possible to interpret subtle media communication used under a military dictatorship within the period of analysis.

Nonetheless, to examine the communication of Igbo nationalism in sports, this chapter shall begin by reviewing extant literature on communication and ethnic nationalism in sports. This is designed to explicate what scholars have accomplished in studying ethnic nationalism in sports and provide the baseline for understanding the communication of Igbo nationalism in sports. The chapter will also describe the Igbos by focusing on their shared culture and shared experiences that differentiate

1 In this chapter, it is important to note the use of words that appear to represent similar concepts. They each have subtle meanings. These include Igbo, Biafra, East or Eastern region, and South East. Igbos, prior to the war, were the majority ethnic group in the Eastern region of Nigeria. It was this Eastern region that seceded from Nigeria and fought a civil war under the name "Biafra" against the rest of Nigeria. After the war, Igbos were mostly restricted to a smaller geographical area established as East Central state. Years after, this state became one of six political zones established in Nigeria and is identified as South East zone of Nigeria.

them from their ethnic rivals in Nigeria. The section that then follows investigates how sport, specifically Association football, is exploited in communicating Igbo nationalism. That will be the core of this chapter and it relies not only on extant literature but also on news reports, particularly those drawn from Nigerian newspapers.

2 Communication and ethnic nationalism in sports

One of the complex social concepts is that of a nation, from which nationalism is derived. Nation refers to a group of people or a large community that has a shared culture and history. It is socially constructed and does not require country borders (Anderson 2006). Anderson describes nations as imagined communities because most members would never know each other but yet share identity as members of a community. This image of identity is shared via mass media and during competitive international sporting events as Butterworth (2017) has argued. Billig (1995) has argued, however, that nationalism or fervent belongingness to a nation can be banal in highly developed countries but "hot" or passionate in other nations. While competitive sports discourse around nations focuses on sovereign modern states, academic discourses go beyond modern states to include ethnic nations. Nonetheless, within modern states exist nations. In some cases, a single ethnic nation may spill across borders of multiple modern states. This differentiation between what a nation is and what it is not can be confusing beyond academic circles. Yet, understanding that difference is critical to a discourse on how nationalism is sometimes communicated in the world of sport.

Much of that discourse occurs in the mass media, which reflects sport nationalism. Nationalism in media coverage of sport loosely refers to both identity with nation and modern state (Horak and Spitaler 2003; King 2006; Ward 2009). Some of the studies have sought to maintain some distinction by differentiating *ethnic* nationalism from *civic* nationalism. *Ethnic* nationalism is situated in support for a nation where citizenship is based on blood relationship, race, and shared history over a long period. One example of this is Scotland or the Basque Country in Spain. Both are ethnic nations within the modern states of the United Kingdom and Spain, respectively. Civic nationalism, however, is based on a modern state with geographical boundaries and is governed by law. For instance, both the UK and Spain are modern states and sports identity with such states is referred to as civic nationalism. In such a state, there may be different ethnic nations. Ultimately, expression of civic nationalism is the case in much of the modern countries today and during mega sporting events.

Notwithstanding, the media's focus on nationalism in sports has been studied widely over a long period of time (Rowe, McKay, and Miller 1998; Maguire and Poulton 1999; Cardoza 2010; Wenner and Billings 2017). Such nationalism is demonstrated in media coverage of international sporting contests and is abundant in global mega sporting competitions such as the Olympics, FIFA World Cup, and the World Athletics Championship. Media broadcast of those events has significant global coverage, according to several scholars. For instance, Karp and Ourand (2018) report, "Among the 100 most-viewed shows on TV in 2017, 81 were sports telecasts." Since sports are among the most watched media events in the world, it is not inconceivable that many people consume the nationalistic perspective presented in media coverage. That relationship between media's nationalistic coverage of international sports and consumption by a large number of people affirms the importance of studying the phenomenon.

However, the focus of this chapter is solely on ethnic nationalism. Communicating ethnic nationalism in sport, although not as ubiquitous as studies of civic nationalism, has been studied by some scholars (see MacClancy 1996; Garcia 2012; Rojo-Labaien 2012; Ortega 2015). Ortega discusses how the Spanish media covered, extensively, the ethnic nationalism demonstrated at the 2009 Spanish Copa del Rey final between Athletic Bilbao representing Basque nationalism and FC Barcelona representing Catalan nationalism. Both the Basque and Catalan regions of Spain are widely studied as separatist and ethnic nations within the Spanish modern state. Feelings and expressions of nationalism in those two regions are reportedly high (Tuñón and Brey 2012). In the Basque Country, for instance, Athletic Bilbao has chosen the English word *Athletic*, instead of the Spanish *Athletico* as a way to differentiate between its ethnic identity and Spanish identity. Additionally, the club has made it policy to recruit and sign players who are Basque (Castillo 2007). The demonstration of ethnic nationalism in sports was strongly communicated by football fans at the 2009 Spanish Cup final. Ortega (2015: 4) points out that "the match (Athletic vs. Barcelona) became one of the most polemical confrontations in the history of the trophy due to the fact that, before it started, both Basque and Catalan supporters furiously booed the Spanish national anthem and King Juan Carlos I." The booing, which was loud and prolonged as the anthem played, demonstrates clearly where the supporters' identity resides. It certainly was not Spain even though most hold official Spanish state citizenship.

O'Brien (2014) argues that increased media coverage of football in Spain is responsible for the ubiquity of Catalan ethnic nationalism demonstrated in media reports about FC Barcelona and particularly its rivalry with Real Madrid. He suggests that ethnic nationalism stories in newspapers, magazines, radio, and television are sometimes based on hype and sensationalism. What cannot be denied, however, is that Catalan nationalism is a fact and that FC Barcelona represents that nationalism, which often leans towards separation from the Spanish state. Catalan-speaking regions, based in both Spain and France, see themselves as a nation bound by language and Catalan identity that goes back to the 11th century (McRoberts 2001). By October 2017, the Catalans declared an independent republic, outside the Spanish state, but has received no international recognition.

Catalan separatist nationalism, communicated through football, goes back to 1925, according to Barcelo, Clinton, and Sero (2015) in a game between Barcelona and a fellow Catalan club – CE Jupiter. The authors write that a large number of nationalists were at the game and they booed the Spanish national anthem. At home games of FC Barcelona, since then, the Catalan flag is flown openly to express identity with an anticipated separatist nation. Barcelo, Clinton, and Sero (2015: 475) write: "Barca fans have begun to repeatedly shout 'independencia' every match at 17 min and 14s, in reference to the defeat in 1714 of the Catalan troops fighting during the War of the Spanish Succession." O'Brien (2014: 38) adds that "the rivalry between *Marca* and *El Mundo Deportivo* (two major sports newspapers/magazines) maintains and promotes the football, cultural and political (nationalistic) rivalry between Real Madrid and FC Barcelona, serving as a benchmark for their respective identities." *Marca* is a nationalist sports media, which includes a newspaper, radio and television channel established in 1938 at the height of the Spanish civil war. Its readership is over 1.7 million and the highest in Spain (Number of daily 2018). It supports Real Madrid, a club associated with civic nationalism of Spain. On the other hand, *El Mundo Deportivo* is a daily sports newspaper based in Barcelona that was established in the early 20th century and supports Catalan ethnic nationalism. It is, currently, the oldest sports newspaper in Spain. FC Barcelona's ethnic and separatist national identity is also advanced through its in-house publications that use the Catalan language and alludes to an independent Catalan nation. The case of Barcelona and Catalan nationality shows how a sporting club can be used for national identity as well as to agitate for a separatist nation. The sporting venue also provides a safe environment for such messages. In the case of the media, reports focused on such nationalism are used to stress historical rivalry and stoke nationalistic support for such rivalry and sensationalizing such events generate high readership/viewership and media audience.

There are few studies of ethnic nationalism in sport, outside those published about Spain. Others include Kusz's (2007) work that alludes to white ethnic nationalism. Kusz's analysis demonstrates how American media used Lance Armstrong's Tour de France victories and the 1980 USA Hockey team's *miracle on ice* victory "to naturalize a connection between whiteness and American national identity (Kusz 2007: 12). There are even fewer ethnic nationalism studies on African cases. One of those is by Waliaula and O'kongo (2014), who show how the Luo ethnic group displays its ethnic nationalism in support of Gor Mahia of Kenya. Although their focus is on music and songs in support of Gor Mahia, they note, "Gor Mahia is not an ordinary football club; it represents the desires and interests of an entire ethnic community" (Waliaula and O'kongo 2014: 88). The music and songs celebrate prowess of Gor Mahia and Luo and places them above all other groups in Kenya. The lyrics to the songs clearly aspire to a separate Luo nation.

3 The Igbos: shared culture and experiences

The previous section introduces us to some literature on ethnic nationalism in sport in Spain as well as in Kenya. This chapter, however, focuses on the Igbos in Nigeria. To understand communication of Igbo ethnic nationalism in sport requires, first, an understanding of Igbos and their experiences, which have stoked the communication of their ethnic nationalism.

There is debate whether Igbo was a unitary nation prior to their first encounter with Christian missionaries in the mid-19th century. However, what is known is that there existed communities of people who share a common Igbo language or a language that had striking similarities with Igbo language in the East of the Niger. These groups were distinctly Igbo and, as Afigbo notes (1980: 311), "the emergence of the Igbo as a distinct people with characteristic language is about 6,000 years ago." However, because there is no history of Igbos fighting or acting together as a nation or under a single ruler prior to the arrival of Christian missions, it is unclear that these Igbo communities shared a distinct culture, beyond language, at that time. The classification or perception of these groups as a single group existed during the Christian missions and the subsequent colonialism that took root after the infamous Berlin conference in 1884/85 where the entire continent of Africa was partitioned into states under colonial control, without any consultation with Africans (Ramutsindela 2007; Chamberlain 2013). According to Chamberlain (2013), only 10 percent of Africa was under European control in 1870 but yet the entire continent (with exception of Ethiopia and Liberia) was partitioned 14 years later and ceded to European countries. This act paid no attention to existing African nations or ethnic groups as borders were drawn wherever the Europeans wanted. The result was that erstwhile African ethnic nations were divided into several of the new modern states. In the case of the Igbos, they were small enough to lie within modern Nigeria but suddenly found themselves sharing a country with other ethnic groups with whom they had little in common. The Igbo nationalism communicated in sport can trace the genesis of its agitation and expression of nationalism directly from this act that is now over a century and a half old.

Today, the Igbos share similar language and cultural practices. The cultural practices often are starkly different from other ethnic groups in several areas including intra-ethnic marriage practices, community leadership, entrepreneurship, affinity to the homeland, and importance of social status (Nwagbara 2007).

Once part of Nigeria, the Igbos had to struggle for resources with other ethnic nations that were part of the country and prominent among those groups are the Yorubas in the West and the Hausa-Fulani in the North. Ikpeze (2000) and Onuoha (2012) point to Igbo experiences in Nigeria, which included the massacres of Igbos by Northern Nigerians in Jos in 1945, in Kano in 1953, and the pogrom of 1966 in Northern Nigeria that led to the civil war (Korieh 2013). The civil war was an attempt by Igbos, under the aspirational state of Biafra, to establish a right to self-determination.

The massacres in Northern Nigeria created a sense, among Igbos, that they were not welcomed in the Nigerian state. This situation mirrors what Joireman (2003) argues leads to heightened nationalism that arises in reaction to an intensified politics of exclusion. She argues that such groups then seek political organization to achieve self-determination via "civil disobedience, lobbying and the public articulation of community goals" (Joireman 2003: 14). That was the case of Igbos, prior to the civil war, as demonstrated in my recollection below:

> I was a child during the period of tension preceding the war. We lived in the university campus in Ibadan, Western Nigeria, where my father was a Professor. Though my recollections of life in the university are hazy, the period of tension remains vivid in my memory, even now in adulthood. In our living room were scores of glass bottles filled with liquid which I was to learn were highly combustible petroleum fuel. They were there so that they would be handy to be used as petrol bombs launched against mobs seeking to kill us – Igbos. Ibadan, after all, is Yoruba land and Igbos as the radio made clear were being lynched in the North, Hausa land. Yorubas may do the same and so it was best to prepare. There were three uncles – Festus, Phillip, and Ogor – who lived with us and would be in charge of this petrol bomb defense. But as a child, it was difficult to fully understand why difference in language – Igbo and Yoruba – would divide us in Ibadan. I had friends who spoke Yoruba, their parents did, and how could they now be possibly enemies? ... We eventually left Ibadan for the safety of the countryside, Inyi, deep in Igboland. Inyi was the birthplace of my father and, thus, we were now among kinsmen and women. But I remember trucks arriving almost daily with loads of other kinsmen and women escaping from the North to safety in Inyi. One of those days remain indelible for me. It was the day a truck arrived and it had the Umeh family whose daughter had a large bandage across her stomach. From time to time, she would wail, in apparent and numbing pain. We learned that the Northern mobs had cut her stomach open with a machete. Fortunately, she and her family escaped the mob and were now back in Inyi. It was clear in our minds, regardless of age, that we (the Igbos) were unloved. The adults around us would talk, over drinks, that Igbos were the strongest group and that a single Igbo could take out five Hausas or Yorubas in a fight. We believed it. The truth was that they were readying, psychologically, for the coming war.

The sense of ethnic nationality was crystallized by being victims of the massacres and then the civil war of 1967–1970 that followed. The period before and during the war also involved defining and demonizing the *Other*, that is, non-Igbo Nigerians. These *Others* were ridiculed through sympathetic media as being unintelligent, beasts, among other demonic creations. On the other hand, Igbos created mythologies that ascribed to their own intelligence, scientific and educational prowess, among others. The war created a bunker mentality among Igbos that helped foster the perception and idea that Nigeria had designs to exterminate the Igbos.

Ikpeze (2000) notes that even after Igbos were defeated in the war, the promise by the Nigerian state that Igbos will be welcomed with open hands turned into a mirage. Ikpeze cites four clear dimensions of Igbo marginalization in post-war Nigeria, which are backed by multiple examples. The dimensions were economic strangulation that included several schemes that financially attempted to deprive Igbos, politico-bureaucratic emasculation that occurred in key appointments made by the state and the drastic reduction in ethnic political power through regional administration creations that limited Igbo political presence and power, military neutralization which involved limiting Igbos from progress and representation in Nigeria's armed forces, and ostracism including neglect of problems that were experienced within Igbo areas:

> After the war, we left the deep forest, behind Inyi, where we mostly lived without several household necessities. No stoves, no pillows, no mattresses, among other missing items. My father was re-employed at the university but it was the one in Nsukka, in Igboland. Going back to Ibadan was not an option because it was clear, in adult conversations, that non-Igbos could no longer be trusted. It was safer to be in Igbo homeland or very close to it. Many other families did the same. Those that lived in the North among Hausas or in the West among Yorubas prior to the war had now made their home in Igbo land. To listen to adults in conversations you would think that the Hausas or Yorubas were non-humans, beasts who were intent on getting rid of all of us. The university house allocated to us, other buildings on campus, and elsewhere were riddled with bullet holes on the walls. Some houses had no roofs and doors were missing in several. These were places that we and other Igbos were to make our homes. Yet, they were much better than those we lived in during the war. Now you could purchase a match box, chewing gum, candies and things that were either luxury or nonexistent in Igbo areas during the war. Clearly, our lives had improved.

4 Communicating Igbo nationalism in sports: incline, decline, and change

The previous section was designed to provide an important background of Igbo marginalization within Nigeria that supports the use of sports to communicate nationalism among Igbos. In this section, I demonstrate how that nationalism was expressed in the sporting arena and then communicated via mass media. The section is divided into three periods that mark heightened sports nationalism in the postwar period, a decline of that nationalism and then its recent re-emergence.

4.1 Incline of Igbo sport nationalism

Igbo sport nationalism was not recorded as part of academic research work until my own publication in 2014. However, earlier newspaper reports make it clear that Igbo sports nationalism had long existed. For instance, the Alex Oni Cup competition that was organized among ethnic groups in the 1940s and 1950s (This year's 1951) was reported in the media and several reports alluded to violence and high levels of emotions exhibited on ethnic lines during the contests. In fact, reports by the *Daily Service* allude to high level of ethnic identification and violence associated with ethnic contests that would eventually lead to the discontinuation of the competition in 1957. Both footballers and fans demonstrated high levels of identity with their ethnic groups and interpreted results as indication of ethnic superiority in an environment where identification with ethnic nations was already high. The ethnic teams that participated in the competition were ad hoc teams selected specifically for the event. Off the field, however, there were periods of high tension amongst the ethnic nations. In an open letter to the country's President published in the *Eastern States Express*, Ikoro asked for the following consideration: "That secession of any region from the Federation is not illegal once that region, with reasons, feels to secede" (1965: 2). The Western regional election of 1965 was largely violent because of politico-ethnic strife. That election was the prelude to military coups, which eventually led to a civil war as the country sought to prevent the Eastern region (predominantly Igbos) from seceding.

However, the same fervor for Igbo nationalism, in political and social circles, was not exhibited in the sporting media or arena, beyond the Alex Oni competition, as far as we can find. The likelihood of such fervor was minimal considering that most top Igbo footballers were not representing any of the teams based in the Eastern region. Most were playing for clubs in Lagos, in the Western part of the country. This was not surprising because the amateurism of football during the mid-20th century in Nigeria led footballers to migrate to areas where employment in other occupations was high and that way they were gainfully employed while also playing football. It is likely that the sporting media would have communicated ethnic nationalism if the more stable football clubs and teams were organized on ethnic basis, at the time. However, they were not. Instead, they were based on state civil service agencies and football players recruited from across ethnic groups.

Therefore, the peak of Igbo sports nationalism did not exist until after the civil war of 1967–1970. There are several reasons for this beyond the civil service factor already mentioned, according to Ajuzie (1999) and Onwumechili (2014). They cite such reasons as top Igbo players choosing to stay in the Igbo homeland right after the war because of security fears associated with seeking residence outside the region at that time. They formed the Rangers Football club that would dominate Nigerian football for slightly more than a decade following the war. The club became associated with *N'digbo* (Igbos) because of its competitiveness and its policy of recruiting only Igbo players at the time (Onwumechili 2014). The club's continued dominance in Nigerian football clearly endeared it to Igbos, according to several writers (Ajuzie 1999; Onwumechili 2014; Ekwowusi 2016; Yusuf 2016). Ajuzie (1999: 13) affirms this by stating: "Because of the circumstances leading to its formation, Rangers symbolized the resilience and dynamism of the Igbos." I observed this ethnic nationalism in the following way:

> I became fanatically involved with football after the war. The name Rangers was on everybody's lips, the Igbo adults that I knew supported them, my friends wanted to be Godwin Achebe, Dominic Nwobodo, Kenneth Abana, or Mathias Obianika all Rangers players. I was different. But there was a reason. My first encounter seeing elite players live was Vasco da Gama players (Enugu rivals of Rangers) practicing in Nsukka at the university grounds. The captain of Vasco, Obed Ariri, took a liking of me. He gave me my first cleats, a puma with yellow stripes. I became

> a Vasco fan. But the reality was that I was the only one in my family. My parents and my brother supported Rangers. My sister just did not care. Supporting Vasco was odd in my community. You felt like an outcast because Igbos followed Rangers like religion. For everyone, it seemed every Rangers' game was a do or die affair especially against Ibadan Shooting Stars. To lose to Shooting Stars was sacrilege because the game was about Igbo versus Yoruba in a challenge of ethnic superiority. Football, it seemed, was an opportunity to show how much better Igbos were over other ethnic groups. It showed, according to several adults, that Igbos could easily have won the war if the super powers (America, Britain, and Soviet Union) had not supported the others against Igbo. Every loss, every Federation decision against Rangers, was a demonstration of why Igbos were disliked by jealous Yorubas or Hausas.

However, communicating nationalism in the case of Igbos and Enugu Rangers differs remarkably from elsewhere. Communication, particularly by the mass media, had to be subtle in several ways because media sympathetic to the Igbo cause or managed by the defeated Igbos were under the control and surveillance of Nigeria's military government dictatorship. The dictatorship banned public assembly, with the exception of sporting competitions, and mounted aggressive censorship with dire consequences for journalists who did not toe the line. The military Head of State, General Gowon justified this by stating, "[R]ecent cases of some of your colleagues (journalists) who have had unfortunate brushes with our security forces. [...] I would like to remind all of you and the Nigerian public in general, that Nigeria is still in a period of national emergency [...] there is no absolute freedom; [...] careless news coverage or comment can lead to untold havoc" (Gowon tells 1971: 1). Brooke wrote, "In the post-war era, Biafra became a taboo word. The Bight of Biafra, a stretch of Nigeria's Atlantic coast, was renamed the Bight of Bonny. Biafra Light, the oil pumped from this area, is now called Bonny Light" (1987). In essence, why *Marca* could write about FC Barcelona and its connections to Catalan nationalism, the *Renaissance* and *Daily Star* in Enugu, Nigeria had to find ways to convey Igbo nationalism without attracting military brutality. They had to write implicitly rather than explicitly.

The *Renaissance* conveyed nationalism in multiple reports on Enugu Rangers without specifically mentioning the words Igbo or Biafra that would have triggered repercussions. In fact, the media never mentioned directly the relationship between Rangers and Igbo nationalism and many Nigerians did not realize the genesis of the club's name until much later when it felt safe to do so, by those who named the club. There was an assumption that the name came from the Queens Park Rangers that visited Nigeria in the 1960s, but it was later learned that the name was a dedication to the Biafran guerilla unit that went by the name "Rangers" during the civil war (Onwumechili 2014). To have made this secret known, at the time, would certainly attract harsh repercussions from the military dictatorship. The *Renaissance* and other media were more clever than that. They conveyed Rangers' relationship with Igbo nationalism in other ways, subtle and implied, in order to avoid repercussion.

The club's first major victory was winning the Amachree Cup in 1971, barely a year after the war, in the hostile capital of Lagos. The *Renaissance* noted that the club "fought against all odds including hostile press, which exhibited such sentimental attachment to Lagos teams" (Congrats, Rangers 1971: 19). The statement by the *Renaissance* symbolized how the media used codes to allude to ethnic cleavages that affirmed the basis for Igbo nationalism. In essence, while the *Renaissance* identified with Rangers, it made it clear that other Nigerian media (hostile press) did not. It was a point the *Renaissance* made about the exclusion of Igbos. Notwithstanding, the media provided space for outside contributors who were less tactful. These contributors were not employed by the media and, thus, any military consequence would be solely the burden of the writer. One of these contributors, Nwogo (1975: 15), directly linked Rangers to Igbo nationalism as follows:

> From the bushes (reference to Civil War scenes) where you (Rangers players) operated as sons of want (Igbo) when the instinct of self-preservation forced you to run for your dear lives, you thought of a soccer club and formed one in June 1970. From the inception of your club you get to exhibit high soccer ideals if the din and clatter of war that preceded the birth of your squad transmitted soccer lessons and messages while in the caves.

Although the statement above was less tactful, it still was not explicit on the issue of Igbo nationalism. These types of communication were expressed publicly during that period. Privately, the expressions were far more direct on the potential of Igbo nationalism and how Rangers' accomplishments demonstrated it.

4.2 Decline of media association of Rangers FC with Igbo nationalism

The decline in media communication of Igbo nationalism, through the accomplishments of Enugu Rangers, occurred in the late 1970s for several reasons. Onwumechili (2014) identifies the creation of additional administrative states within Igboland. Each of those states quickly established elite football clubs that drew from the same pool of top Igbo players. Competing for the same players eventually put a stop to Rangers' domination of Nigerian football by the mid-1980s.

Eastern-based media were no longer associating, even in implicit terms, Igbo nationalism with Enugu Rangers and several of them focused, at least for some time, on the other Igbo-based teams that emerged including Owerri Spartans and Aba Enyimba. These teams had financial backing of their state governments. The financial support is what differentiates these latter-day clubs from Vasco da Gama that also existed in the 1970s when Rangers dominated Igbo support. Vasco Da Gama was based in Enugu and played in the elite division but its support among Igbos was far less than support for Rangers among fans and in the local media. In fact, for years, Vasco was virtually a source of player development for the more popular Rangers with top Vasco players frequently transferring to Rangers. But in the latter era of Enyimba and Spartans, Rangers was considered an equal. This adversely impacted Rangers' ability to attract the cream of Igbo players and as Onwumechili (2014: 117) points out, "In response, Rangers moved to recruit non-Igbo-speaking footballers and this further diminished Igbo identification with the team." This decision had a lasting impact as I recollect below:

> The argument that Igbos were dominant in football could no longer be made, based on accomplishment by Rangers beginning in the mid-1980s. Rangers, unlike in previous years, began to recruit non-Igbos. Even a Brazilian was with the club. Although my friends tried to pass off Adokiye Amaesiemaka (a Rangers' recruit then) as Igbo, how could you explain his first name? That is certainly not an Igbo name. Soon after, even Yorubas and Hausas began to join the club. The myth that Rangers' victories symbolized Igbo superiority was as good as dead. Of course, many of the old fans still supported the club but it was clearly not as fervent as before. I remember being at Akanu Ibiam Stadium at the University of Nigeria (Nsukka), which Rangers used as their home ground in the 1978 league season. This was a couple of years after Imo state was created from the East Central state that Rangers previously represented. Imo state established two strong football clubs in Spartans and Enyimba. Rangers was hosting Owerri Spartans (later renamed Iwuanyanwu Nationale) and it was a tough match. What was surprising is that there was a sizeable support for Spartans from the Igbo-dominated crowd on that day. That was unusual to witness, especially when Rangers was playing anywhere in Igboland, in those days. The Daily Star had replaced the Renaissance as the Enugu daily newspaper at the time. Daily Star still wrote about Rangers but not like Renaissance did. The claim of how the federation or other ethnic groups despised Rangers seemed rarer. Imo state had the Daily Statesman, which paid more attention to the Spartans and did not necessarily share the same narrative as the Daily Star. It was the beginning of change.

The decline in local media support for Enugu Rangers in Igbo states reflects not only a shift, especially among younger fans, for the club but it began to erode the club's dominant position as the premier Igbo club. The club's recruitment of non-Igbo players also affected its unspoken perception as a sole-Igbo club. Nevertheless, the historical position of Rangers as reflection of Igbo nationality persists. This situation reflects somewhat the situation of other ethnically supported clubs elsewhere in the world, especially in an era of increased footballer migrations across the globe.

4.3 Nationalism re-imagined in an era of increased player migration

Although, and increasingly, footballers disregard historical ethnic histories of clubs in determining employment, the ethnic associations that football fans make of clubs persist. Thus, although FC Barcelona recruit footballers from all over the world, a substantive section of their fans continue to associate the club with Catalan nationalism (Barcelo, Clinton, and Sero 2015). At the other end of these ethnically supported clubs is Athletic Bilbao in Spain which persists in recruiting only players who are Basque in origin. Athletic persists in using the English spelling Athletic and has a strict policy of recruiting only players of Basque origin, in essence players from the Basque region of France or Spain (Rojo-Labaien 2017). The club has maintained this policy from its formation in 1903 till now and surprisingly has remained competitive in the Spanish Premier League, being one of only three clubs that have never been relegated. The others being the more popularly known Barcelona FC and Real Madrid.

The Bilbao example, however, is increasingly rare. More common is change in a club's recruitment policy allowing recruitment of players beyond the traditional ethnic catchment regions to areas far beyond. However, ethnic nationalism that the club represents persists such as in the case of Enugu Rangers or FC Barcelona in Spain. This means that ethnic-representative clubs and the historical meaning of the clubs also persist. Thus, while these traditionally ethnic representative clubs now recruit beyond their ethnic homelands, their support remain strongly attached to an ethnic homeland.

In Nigeria, while media association of Enugu Rangers with Igbo nationalism has receded, some sections of Rangers football fans maintain the association of the club with Igbo nationalism. As already mentioned, Rangers increasingly recruit players beyond Igbo homeland. The ethnic support for Rangers persists, in spite of the emergence of equally successful clubs such as Owerri Heartland FC (formerly Spartans) and Enyimba of Aba in the same Igbo ethnic area. In fact, one can argue that Enyimba has been more successful on the field than Enugu Rangers in recent times. Yet, the association of Rangers with Igbo nationalism persists among some sections of its supporters, in spite of its declining success on the field and its increasing recruitment of players whose ethnicity is not Igbo. The club continues to enjoy a substantial followership among Igbos. Recently, in the run up to winning the national league championship in 2018, its home ground was packed regularly with fervent supporters some of whom displayed the proscribed Biafran flag in the stands. In one case, a report by Godwin (2016) mentioned a struggle between security officials and a fan who was displaying the proscribed Biafran flag and had attempted to run around the stadium with it. It is notable that this resurgence of Biafran nationalism in the country has been reflected in the support of this particular football club. Thus, even with the increasing open recruitment of footballers by erstwhile ethnically associated clubs, the fans remain largely entrenched in the past and ethnic support of the clubs.

4.4 Change in use of sports to communicate Igbo nationalism

As noted in the previous section, Enugu Rangers' embodiment of Igbo nationalism waned when other elite level competitors emerged in other Igbo administrative states. However, in recent years the quest for a nation for *N'digbo* has reemerged publicly and explicitly. What previously existed underground and was discussed literally in hushed tones, during the era of military dictatorships, has become explicit under Nigerian democracy that began in 1999. The re-emergence of an agitation for an Igbo nation is led primarily by two groups – Indigenous Peoples of Biafra (IPOB) and the Movement for the Actualization of Sovereign State of Biafra (MASSOB) – with support from Igbo youths (Amamkpa and Mbakwe, 2015; Johnson and Olaniyan 2017).

Johnson and Olaniyan (2017) describe this renewed and intense quest for a separatist Igbo state as a derivative of the unfinished nature of the war and the continued perception by the Igbos of oppression and marginalization in Nigeria. However, communicating the quest through media reports on sports has been remarkably different from communicating sports nationalism in Catalonia or the Basque Country and also different from communicating Igbo nationalism through sports reporting in the period immediately following the war. What are those differences? And what drives them?

First, the democratic environment in Spain and in Nigeria (since 1999) provides space for explicit reports in the newspapers and other media about aspirations of ethnic nations. This is dramatically different from reports that were made under Nigerian maximum military rulers in the period immediately following the war. In essence, reports under maximum rulers needed to be coded, subtle, and disguised. In fact, it was impossible, without repercussion, even to mention the word Biafra as an aspiration at that time (see Brooke 1987). But contemporary sports nationalism among Igbos does not entirely share similar characteristics as that of the Catalans or Basques, either. It is different. While the Catalans and Basques rally around symbols of FC Barcelona and Athletic Bilbao, respectively, the Igbos no longer rally around Enugu Rangers because of the division of Igboland into separate states and the emergence of competing teams in those states. Thus, even media sympathetic to the Igbo cause are unlikely to use one team in their bid to communicate sports nationalism. The question becomes, how do Igbos now communicate sports nationalism?

Most of the media communication of Biafran or Igbo nationalism, as it pertains to sport, focuses on display of Biafran symbols at various games, mostly football games where spectators are significant in number. Moreover, these reports are by several media and not necessarily those sympathetic to the Igbo cause. The reports emphasize the use of symbols such as shirts emblazoned with messages about Biafra and Biafran flags. Several of these types of messages have been reported by KayCee (2015), Obiajuru (2016), and Godwin (2018). These incidences occur both in and outside Nigeria. Most importantly, while media reports focus on incidences, they do not espouse support for it. Instead, they report the events as news or report negative public reactions to it. Nevertheless, the media reports reflect increased agitation for an independent Biafra within South East Nigeria. Some of the media reports of Biafran nationalism involve arrests and removal of individuals involved in displaying such nationalism. For instance, KayCee (2015) reports scores of fans, who attended a Nigerian game in Senegal, wearing shirts with the Biafran flag and logo. These fans displayed the Biafran flag and message banners prominently in the stadium but were expelled thereafter by Senegalese authority. Godwin's (2018) report focuses on a prominent display of a Biafran flag during a game in Austria between Nigeria and the Czech Republic. Although much of media reporting of Biafran nationalism in the sporting arena focuses on events occurring outside Nigeria, at least a few cases have also occurred inside the country. In one of those, fans displaying Biafran flags in a home game of Enugu Rangers fought with police (Godwin 2016). It is important to note that this occurrence in a Rangers' game is not necessarily linked to Rangers as sole symbol of Igbo nationalism. Instead, it most likely occurred because of the large presence of fans in Rangers' games in the 2016 season when Rangers was on a strong run to win the championship that they last won in 1984! Similar scenes could also occur in games involving another Igbo football club or the Nigerian national team where a large crowd is present.

5 Conclusion

This chapter focuses attention on the communication of ethnic nationalism among the Igbos in South East Nigeria. This is an important study because there are few studies of ethnic nationalism in sports, particularly on African cases. Yet, with the way modern states were created in Africa two centuries ago, there are several occurrences of such nationalism and possibilities that sports may be used for communicating such nationalisms. The creation of modern African states ensured the splitting of ethnic nations into multiple modern states but also forced several culturally disparate ethnic nations into a single modern state. This has created a situation where ethnic nationalism, although not exclusive to Africa, is replete in the African continent. These nationalisms spill into sporting teams and their fan base. Thus, in Kenya, Luo ethnic nationality is expressed through Gor Mahia and Abaluhya ethnic nationalism is embedded in AFC Leopards (Waliaula and O'kongo 2014); in Zimbabwe, the Shonas and Ndebeles express their ethnic nationalism via the Dynamos and Highlanders respectively (Ncube 2018); and Onwumechili and Totty (2020) recounted Casa Sport's case in Senegal that denoted the Casamance region's search for a Jola nationalism in a Senegalese state dominated by the Wolof ethnic group. The study of these ethnic nationalisms in African sports can only help a deeper understanding of such nationalism, particularly its utility in both social and political arena.

This chapter's focus on the case of Igbo ethnic nationalism in Nigeria affords a great subject for study in various ways. Igbos have agitated for a separate nation for decades and were involved in a war from 1967 to 1970 in their bid to achieve that goal. Furthermore, the emergence of a strong football club – Enugu Rangers – in Igboland right after the war provided a sports team through which the Igbos could communicate nationalism. While the period after the civil war provided the opportunity to examine the communication of Igbo nationalism through sports, it was also a period that was under a maximum military leader. Importantly, the chapter also examines the period when Igbo nationalism, via sports, waned. This, as the chapter explains, occurred because Enugu Rangers lost its place as the sole focus of Igbo pride. A later period, also explored by the chapter, shows the re-emergence of Igbo nationalism and the media use of sports to convey that nationalism. These periods, examined by the chapter, show different articulations of communicating sports nationalism that is contextualized by the structure of the Nigerian government.

Ultimately, the examination of the communication of Igbo nationalism, through sports, provides us with important insights. A key insight is that the political environment determines how ethnic nationalism is conveyed. A state under dictatorship mutes the extent explicit communication of sports nationalism occurs. The Igbo nationalism case shows how newspapers such as *Renaissance* use codes to communicate sports nationalism because of consequences such as arrests and brutality that can take place when making explicit reports that a military dictatorship frowns upon. The newspaper avoided the use of the words "Biafra" or "Igbo" nationalism. Yet, under democratic Nigerian regimes, newspapers are bolder in publicly expressing and communicating Igbo nationalism. The word "Biafra" is not taboo under a democratic regime.

The above also means that studying sports nationalism should take into consideration the environment where the study takes place. Africa, especially, is a fertile ground for studying sports nationalism and its deeper meanings. Africa is home to states that became politically independent less than a century ago and importantly most were states formed without regard to previous relationships among the communities that formed such newer states. Thus, heightened nationalists' struggles exist and are anticipated. Understanding these situations can emerge from understanding sport, its support, and its conflicts as the Biafran case demonstrates. The Biafran case in post-war Nigeria additionally demonstrates that nationalism and its meanings can be coded beneath explicit remarks beyond a dictatorial or perceived dangerous environment. For instance, merely studying explicit messages related to sports nationalism in dictatorial environments will not lead to discovery of what is actually or intended to be communicated because the meanings are coded. To discover such meanings requires deeper examination of messages and interpreting them within the context in which they are made. To do so requires consideration of appropriate methods. Thus, the use of ethnography, observation, critical analysis is more likely to be effective compared to the use of survey research. Ethnography is particularly effective because it requires presence within the studied culture on an everyday basis to understand the true feelings of the people studied and not just what they self-report. The same applies in the use of observation. Critical analysis requires understanding the social power relations in order to effectively explore the social interaction as well as media communication. On the contrary, survey research depends on what is directly reported by participants and those self-reports may be muted in the case of a dictatorial environment.

References

Afigbo, Adiele. 1980. Prolegomena to the study of the culture history of the Igbo-speaking peoples of Nigeria. In B. K. Swartz & Raymond E. Dumett (eds.), *West African culture dynamics: Archeological and historical perspectives*, 305–325. New York: Mouton Publishers.

Ajuzie, Ogechukwu. 1999. *The field marshall: A biography of Chairman Christian Chukwu*. Enugu: Triple Sports Ltd.

Amamkpa, Anthony W. & Paul U. Mbakwe. 2015. Conflict early signs and Nigerian government response dilemma: The case of increasing agitations for statehood by Indigenous People of Biafra (IPOB) and the Movement for the Actualization of Sovereign State of Biafra (MASSOB). *African Journal of History and Archeology* 1. 10–20.

Anderson, Benedict. 2006 [1983]. *Imagined communities: Reflections on the origin and spread of nationalism*. London: Verso.

Bairner, Alan. 2014. Assessing the sociology of sport: On national identity and nationalism. *International Review for the Sociology of Sport* 50: 375–379.

Barceló, Joan, Peter Clinton & Carles S. Seró. 2015. National identity, social institutions and political values: The case of FC Barcelona and Catalonia from an intergenerational comparison. *Soccer & Society* 16: 469–481.

Billig, Michael. 1995. *Banal nationalism*. London: Sage.

Brooke, James. 1987. Few traces of the Civil War linger in Biafra. *The New York Times*, 14 July. https://www.nytimes.com/1987/07/14/world/few-traces-of-the-civil-war-linger-in-biafra.html (18 November 2020).

Butterworth, Michael L. (ed.). 2017. *Sport and militarism: Contemporary global perspectives*. London: Routledge.

Cardoza, Anthony. 2010. Making Italians? Cycling and national identity in Italy: 1900–1950. *Journal of Modern Italian Studies* 15. 354–377.

Castillo, Juan Carlos. 2007. Play fresh, play local: The case of Athletic de Bilbao. *Sport in Society: Cultures, Commerce, Media, Politics* 10. 680–697.

Chamberlain, M. E. 2013. *The scramble for Africa*. New York: Routledge.

Congrats, Rangers. 1971. *The Renaissance*, 21 March. 19.

Ekwowusi, Sonnie. 2016. The return of Enugu Rangers. *This Day*, 5 October. https://www.pressreader.com/nigeria/thisday/20161005/281603829967990 (18 November 2020).

Ellis, Carolyn, Tony E. Adams & Arthur P. Bochner. 2011. Autoethnography: An overview. *Forum: Qualitative Social Research* 12(1). http://www.qualitative-research.net/index.php/fqs/article/view/1589/3095 (18 November 2020).

Garcia, César. 2012. Using strategic communication for nation-building in contemporary Spain: The Basque case. *International Journal of Strategic Communication* 6. 212–231.

Godwin, Ameh C. 2016. Drama as police man battles fan for openly displaying Biafran flag during football match in Enugu. *Daily Post*, 9 July. http://dailypost.ng/2016/07/09/drama-as-police-man-battles-fan-for-openly-displaying-biafran-flag-during-football-match-in-enugu-photos/ (26 March 2020).

Godwin, Ameh C. 2018. Nigeria vs Czech Republic: Fans storm stadium with Biafra flag. *Daily Post*, 6 June. https://dailypost.ng/2018/06/06/nigeria-vs-czech-republic-fans-storm-stadium-biafra-flag/ (18 November 2020).

Gowon tells the press: We don't detain unnecessarily. 1971. *The Nigerian Observer*, 17 August. 1, 3.

Horak, Roman & Georg Spitaler. 2003. Sport, space and national identity: Soccer and skiing as formative forces, on the Austrian example. *American Behavioral Scientist* 46. 1506–1518.

Ikoro, Reginald. 1965. Open letter to Dr. Zik. *Eastern States Express*, 8 January. 2.

Ikpeze, Nnaemeka. 2000. Post-Biafran marginalization of the Igbo in Nigeria. In Ifi Amadiume & Abdullahi An-Na'im (eds.), *The politics of memory: Truth, healing and social justice*, 90–109. London: Zed Books.
Johnson, Idowu & Azeez Olaniyan. 2017. The politics of renewed quest for a Biafra Republic in Nigeria. *Defense & Security Analysis* 33. 320–332.
Joireman, Sandra F. 2003. *Nationalism and political identity*. New York: Continuum.
Karp, Austin & John Ourand. 2018, January 15. Sports maintains dominant hold on viewership. *Sports Business Journal*, 15 January. https://www.sportsbusinessdaily.com/Journal/Issues/2018/01/15/Media/Sports-Media.aspx (17 November 2019).
KayCee. 2015. Nigerians banished from Senegal stadium for displaying Biafra flags. *Obindigbo*, 6 December. Retrieved 11/15/19. http://obindigbo.com.ng/2015/12/nigerians-banished-from-senegal-stadium-for-displaying-biafra-flags/ (15 November 2019).
King, Anthony. 2006. Nationalism and sport. In Gerard Delantey & Krishnan Kumar (eds.), *The Sage handbook on nations and nationalism*, 249–259. London: Sage.
Korieh, Chima J. 2013. Biafra and the discourse on the Igbo genocide. *Journal of Asian and African Studies* 48. 727–740.
Kusz, Kyle W. 2007. *Revolt of the white athlete: Race, media, and the emergence of extreme athletes in America*. New York: Peter Lang.
Lindemann, Kurt. 2009. Self-reflection and our sporting lives: Communication research in the community of sport. *The Electronic Journal of Communication* 19. 1–16.
MacClancy, Jeremy. 1996. Bilingualism and multinationalism in the Basque Country. In Clare Mar-Molinero & Angel Smith (eds.), *Nationalism and the nation in the Iberian Peninsuala: Competing and conflicting identities*, 207–220. Oxford: Berg.
Maguire, Joseph & Emma K. Poulton. 1999. European identity politics in Euro 96: Invented traditions and national habitus codes. *International Review for the Sociology of Sport* 34. 17–29.
McRoberts, Kenneth. 2001. *Catalonia: Nation building without a state*. NY: Oxford Publishing.
Ncube, Lyton. 2018. 'Highlander Ithimu yezwe lonke!': Intersections of Highlanders FC fandom and Ndebele ethnic nationalism in Zimbabwe. *Sport in Society* 21. 1364–1381.
Number of daily readers of the leading newspapers in Spain between February and November 2018 (in 1,000 readers). 2018. *Statista.com*. http://www.statista.com/statistics/436643/most-read-newspapers-in-spain/ (10 November 2019).
Nwagbara, Eucharia. 2007. The Igbo of Southeast Nigeria: The same yesterday, today and tomorrow? *Dialectical Anthropology* 31. 99–110.
Nwogo, Alozie. 1975. Tomorrow is yet another day. *The Daily Star*, 27 December. 15.
Obiajuru, Nomso. 2016, October 3. Drama as Rangers fans display Biafran flag in Enugu. *Legit*, 3 October. https://www.legit.ng/991622-see-what-happened-when-rangers-fans-displayed-biafran-flag-to-celebrate-photo.html (17 November 2019).
O'Brien, Jim. 2014. Communicating football in the context of Spanish Society. In Florentin Smarandache, Stefan Vladutescu & Alina Tenescu (eds.), *Current communication difficulties*, 26–44. Columbus, OH: Zip Publishing.
Onuoha, Godwin. 2012. Contemporary Igbo nationalism and the crisis of self-determination in Nigeria. *African Studies* 71. 29–51.
Onwumechili, Chuka. 2014. Nigeria: Rangers, Igbo identity and the imagination of war. In Chuka Onwumechili & Gerard Akindes (eds.), *Identity and nation in African football: Fans, community and clubs*, 116–132. Basingstoke, UK: Palgrave MacMillan.
Onwumechili, Chuka & Totty O. Totty. 2020. The state, fans and football politics. In Chuka Onwumechili (ed.), *Africa's elite football: Structure, politics, and everyday challenges*, 19–33. New York: Routledge.

Ortega, Vincente R. 2015. Soccer, nationalism and the media in contemporary Spanish society: La Roja, Real Madrid & Barcelona. *Soccer & Society* 17. 628–643.

Ramutsindela, Maano. 2007. African boundaries and their interpreters. *Geopolitics* 4(2). 180–198.

Rojo-Labaien, Ekain. 2012. The media and the construction of national identities in Basque football: Basques and Catalans booing the Spanish anthem in the 2009 Cup Championship Final. *International Journal of Sport & Society* 3. 31–42.

Rojo-Labaien, Ekain. 2017. Football and the representation of Basque identity in the contemporary age. *Soccer & Society* 18. 63–80.

Rowe, David, Jim McKay & Toby Miller. 1998. Come together: Nationalism and the media image. In Lawrence A. Wenner (ed.), *Mediasport*, 119–133. London, UK: Routledge.

This year's inter-tribal football matches. 1951. *The Daily Service*, 9 February. 4.

Tuñón, Jorge & Elisa Brey. 2012. Sports and politics in Spain – football and nationalistattitudes within the Basque country and Catalonia. *European Journal forSport and Society* 9. 7–32.

Waliaula, Solomon & Joseph Basil O'kongo. 2014. Performing Luo identity in Kenya: Songs. In Chuka Onwumechili & Gerard Akindes (eds.), *Identity and nation in African football: Fans, community and clubs*, 83–98. Basingstoke, UK: Palgrave MacMillan.

Ward, Tony. 2009. Sport and national identity. *Soccer and Society* 10. 518–531.

Wenner, Lawrence A. & Andrew C. Billings (eds.). 2017. *Sport, media and mega-events.* New York: Routledge.

Yusuf, Ganiyu. 2016. Chukwu: Rangers have brought glory to entire South Eastern Nigeria. *Complete Sports*, 28 September. https://www.completesportsnigeria.com/51628-2/ (18 November 2020).

Mahfoud Amara and Kamal Hamidou

28 Sport communication and the politics of identity in the MENA region

Abstract: This chapter examines the sporting context in the MENA region, and the role of media coverage in mobilizing narratives around sport performance, in the construction of collective imagination framed around national unity, and as a tool of political legitimization. Furthermore, the chapter focuses on recent trends in the MENA region, and particularly in the Arabian Gulf states, in investing in sport TV broadcasting as a means for nation and city-state branding. Last and not least, the chapter highlights the role of social media as an emerging and alternative space to challenge state's ownership (and control) of communication around sport.

Keywords: MENA; nation-state; identity; sport media; branding; youth; social media

1 Introduction

The importance of sport as a tool for identity building has not escaped political regimes in places within the Middle East and North Africa (MENA) region.[1] We observe in the region almost identical mechanisms of instrumentalization of sport, that is to say as a tool to mobilize the populace, particularly the youth, and at the same time, an instrument to gain prestige. In this process, the state's media is an instrument for identity construction intended for a local national audience on the one hand, and as an instrument of image making, intended for an international audience, on the other. In opposition to official discourse and communication about and through sport to serve the political and economic agenda of ruling parties, social media offers different forms of communication for the youth to use sport, and football in particular, as a means of political contestation to counter the dominant, top-down, state-owned and controlled/ideological (or business oriented) communication about sport.

In the first part of this chapter, we examine the sporting context in the MENA region, and the role of media coverage in capitalizing on sport performance in the construction of collective imagination framed around national unity (unity around the state) and community cohesion. In the second part, we will focus on: 1) recent trends in the MENA region, and particularly in the Arabian Gulf states in investing in sport TV broadcasting coupled with investment in bidding and hosting interna-

1 The Middle East and North Africa (MENA) region is used here in the chapter to include countries in the Maghreb (Algeria, Tunisia, Morocco, Mauretania, and Libya), and countries in the Mashrek, which include the Levant countries, Iraq, Yemen, and Arabian Gulf states. Between these two regions, there is Egypt and Sudan. We do not consider for this chapter Djibouti, Somalia, Israel, Iran, and Turkey.

https://doi.org/10.1515/9783110660883-028

tional sport events as a means for nation and city branding; 2) the positioning of the region in the global map of sport market and industry. We highlight the emerging role of social media in sport as a new space for youth expression with its own code and audience. The chapter focuses on top-down communication in (and through) sport as an instrument to legitimize state's ideology, while highlighting attempts in societies in the MENA region to challenge state ownership (and control) of communication around sport.

2 Sport communication and the necessity for the construction of collective identity

In the MENA region, sport communication and communication about or through sport has been shaped by discourses of nationalism and ethnicity and, for many years, by the one-party state model of communication, which is top-down and heavily ideological, to serve the political interests of the ruling elite, represented in some countries by the father of the nation (known as *Al-Zaim*). This is characteristic of Nasser and Sadat in Egypt, Bourguiba and BenAli in Tunisia, Gaddafi in Libya, Saddam in Iraq, Assad in Syria, Benbella and Boumedienne in Algeria. The communication in post-independence evolved around nation-state building and participation in regional and international sport events as a showcase for national development and modernization projects (Amara 2012a). This project, which is mainly defined along secular lines to counter so-called conservative movements in society, or at least those labelled as such, is generally represented by the advocates of political Islam (or Islamist) movements. The athletes serve as ambassadors of the nation and bearers of its national identity and sentiments whether it is anti-imperialist, third-worldist, socialist, or Baathist. This has been confronted with few pockets of resistance defined by regional and ethnic minority demands for cultural and sometimes political recognition, such as the demand for the recognition of Berber identity in North Africa and Kurdish autonomy in Syria and Iraq. In most countries of the MENA region, sporting achievements, whether in individual or collective sports, are with rare exceptions exploited for political and identity purposes. Sporting achievements are exploited by the state media to get the maximum political credit for political leaders in place as well as for the dominant ruling parties. These sporting achievements are thus presented as the result of plans and actions, as well as policies undertaken by the ruling elite, by governments, and by the country, under the patronage of head of states. Moreover, sporting achievements are always an opportunity to nourish the feeling of national pride and to recreate the feeling of collective belonging and social bond (Bairner 2011). This is the case even if these are most often shaken by the reality of economic, political, and social failures, with some exceptions in oil rich countries of the Gulf, which are doing relatively better in terms of wealth distribution among their citizens.

In the Arab world where the notion of the state – in the modern sense of the term – was born only a few decades ago, after long periods of colonization, sporting achievements have offered governing elites an opportunity to create the social bond and shared sense of identity beyond tribes or restricted geographical areas, in Benedict Anderson's (1983) sense of nationalism as "an imagined community." It was a question of transferring the center of individuals' belongings from tribes to national belonging, and to global consumers of sport goods. It was therefore crucial for newborn states to push individual citizens to transfer their loyalty from tribes to the national state. The political and media elites understood early on that sporting feasts are an important alibi among others, which the media, schools, and all ideological apparatuses of the state have had to deploy to showcase the greatness of the country and the genius of its citizens. Thus, to build a sense of collective belonging beyond the tribe, in favor of national and regional unity, whether Arab, African, or Islamic, under the umbrella of the Arab league, African Union, and the Islamic Council. Pan-Arab Games, Pan-African Games, and Islamic Solidarity Games are examples of sporting occasions in the region to consolidate national unity and regional solidarity.

Khalidi in his work on national movement and sport in Palestine, highlights the role of local and national newspapers in promoting Palestinian national sentiments and the existence of Palestine and its national sporting structure before the existence of Israel, as an antithesis to Zionist movement ideology which emphasized the role of sport and physical fitness as a tool to fulfilling the goal of forming a "new society." In other words, a Jewish society in the land of Palestine (Khalidi 2014). In the same vein, Tamir Sorek describes in his work on the positioning of Israeli Hebrew sports media toward the selection of Arab Israeli footballers to play for the Israeli national football team; and the qualification of an Arab Israeli team, Sakhnin to Europa League competition, which deconstructed the Jewishness of Israeli nationhood and citizenship. This offered a new space for cultural encounters, or "integrative enclaves" as named by Sorek, between Arab communities, which he describes as a minority that live as formal citizens, although alienated from political power and the dominant Jewish community (Sorek 2003). Amara (2006) discusses in his work this notion of in-betweenness in the study of the Algerian diaspora in France and Algerian media construction of their identity as somehow insider when bearing the Algerian flag and celebrating the victory of the Algerian national football team, which is also made of players with dual French-Algerian nationalities. The same media depict them as outsiders (immigrants) when they are involved in confrontations with French police forces. They are then presented as French with social and economic problems. Algerian-French players selected to play for the national team are also depicted as Algerians in times of victory and less Algerians, not loyal enough to the Algerian flag, in times of underperformance. In a way this process of inclusion and exclusion can be similar (but without the racist connotation) to that of populist discourse of the far right in France which rejects the notion of double loyalty of French of Algerian or Maghrebin descents to their country of birth and that of country of origin.

3 Sport as a popular culture and identity component in the MENA region

After gaining their independence in the 1960s and 1970s, many countries in the MENA region implemented sports reforms and policies aimed at encouraging mass sports and at promoting school sports in particular in schools and amateur private clubs. Due to demography, the history of diffusion of modern sport, and proximity to Europe, countries of North Africa witnessed the development of sporting practices among the populations, whether in collective or individual sports. In Egypt, the most populated country in the Arab world, sport was elitist and individual sports took over, thanks in particular to the proliferation of expensive private clubs offering squash, tennis, swimming, weightlifting, and wrestling. Egypt is still a breeding ground for these disciplines in the region and internationally. Egyptians are among the world's best squash players. Seven of the top-ten ranked players are Egyptian, including the world number one (Al Jazeera 2019). Algeria, Morocco, and Tunisia have relied on popular sports, and have for a long time shown a certain regularity in participating in regional and international competitions, with more or less honorable results, especially for Algeria and Morocco, which manage to make it to the table of medals in the Olympic Games as well as in numerous international competitions in various sports; and Tunisia is ranked among top 10 nations in the Mediterranean Games. Communication about these sports in these countries has been shaped around colonial history, particularly in Algeria where the colonial memory and violence are still vivid, where sport was also defined around the ideological line of socialism, anti-imperialism, and third-worldism, as a counter project to (neo) imperialism coming from the liberal West and their agents in the region. With Tunisia and Morocco choosing to be in the western/capitalist side, communication about sport has been shaped around the development of tourism and the positioning of these two countries as more authentic (untouched by colonial influence) and more open to the liberal world, including a women's rights agenda for Tunisia. Communication around women's bodies was used by countries in North Africa to brand themselves as secular, to counter the rise of political Islam.

In the Middle East, there are two situations, that of the Levant countries and that of the Arabian Peninsula. Iraq and Lebanon have had a more developed sport system with a higher level of sport participation than in the rest of the Middle East. However, these countries find it difficult to place themselves on the regional or world stage, with the exception of basketball for Lebanon, due to its significance as professional sport as well as political significance among different politico-religious movements. As for other countries (Syria, Iraq, Jordan, Palestine), popular sports are football with a recent rise in some combat sports in Jordan, but with results that remain modest, with the exception of Ghada Shuaa and a gold medal in Heptathlon in the 1996 Atlanta Games. She is the first, and to date the only, Syrian woman to win an Olympic title.

All of these countries have had to deal with the question of identity and that of an ethnic minority: Kurdistan in Iraq and Syria, and the important Palestinian refugee community in Jordan. The communication in and around sport is dominated by the discourse of collective identity, national unity, and combating regionalism and ethnic tensions. Sport can become a risky terrain that needs to be carefully managed by different actors as well, demonstrated by Tuastad (2014) in his study of the Jordanian derby between Al-Wehdat Sport Club and Al-Faysali Sport Club. Al-Wehdat SC represents Palestinian Refugee Camp, Al-Wehdat, in Amman; while Al-Faysali SC, named after the Hashemite King Faisal, is supported by native Jordanians. The derby between these two teams is an occasion to debate politics of identity, including the condition of Palestinian refugees and their right of full citizenship in Jordan, or right of return to their motherland:

> Football has thus been an arena for the killing of political taboos in Jordan. Communal instigation initiated at the terraces has led to communal violence, threatening the relative harmony Jordan has experienced since the 1970 civil war. The calls for democratization in Jordan has generated a reaction from nationalist Jordanians who fear democratization as it could imply that Palestinians, a majority in the country, gain political control over the country, marginalizing currently privileged ethnic Jordanians. To know where Jordan is heading, from status quo to democratization or civil war, the next Al-Wehdat and Al-Faysali derby should be closely observed (Tuastad 2014: 383).

We note that in general, apart from football, in which we have experienced some sporadic breakthroughs from countries like Kuwait, Saudi Arabia, and the United Arab Emirates since the 1980s, Arabian Gulf countries have for a long time been almost totally absent from international and regional competitions in almost all sports, whether collective or individual sports. Qatar and Saudi Arabia had to wait until 2012 to have women participating in the Olympic Games, due also to some restrictions from international sport federations regarding the dress code of women athletes and their reservations toward the visibility of the veil on the basis of safety as well as on the basis of ideology. In other words, these efforts presumably preserved the neutrality of sport from religious and other political interventions. Such preservation is hard to achieve considering the political and commercial dimension of sport. We would argue that the prevailing climate in these countries does not help the practice of sport in the outdoors. The heat varies between 35 and 45 degrees centigrade for at least eight months, with only two actual seasonal variations (summer and winter). The rising standard of living of the populations of these countries has led most of them to adopt an extremely sedentary way of life, which reduces the level of physical activity whether in the workplace or at home. It is no coincidence that people in these countries suffer from the highest rates of obesity, diabetes, and hypertension in the world (Alhyas et al. 2011). More effort is being put forth by states and health agencies to alert the population to the dangers of lack of physical activity and in promoting a healthy lifestyle. These themes are becoming central in postmodern architecture and the urban regeneration of cities such as Doha, Dubai, and Abu Dhabi where new "sport cities" and recreation hubs are emerging. Qatar went even further in decreeing the second Tuesday of February each year as a national holiday to promote the practice of sport among citizens and residents in the country. Similarly, the UAE National Sports Day was launched in 2016 following a directive of Sheikh Mohammed bin Rashid Al Maktoum, UAE Vice President and Ruler of Dubai. The aim as stated in the UAE national news agency and in the web pages of other government agencies is "to promote healthy living, sporting competition and positive interaction to create among multi-cultures living in the UAE."

A large number of sports halls and fitness centers have been built, and a new industry of sporting goods and retail is booming, including shops of energy drinks and all sorts of other natural/organic and chemical products. The region, which is moving between tradition and postmodernity, is not immune from global consumer culture, including the commodification of the body. As explained by Al Jenaibi (2011: 67), "The rush to modernity and a service-oriented economy, as in the West, images of women are used and exchanged as metaphors for hospitality and openness. In essence, the Arab and Islamic woman and her body are subject to a process of commodification, both in terms of their image and their entry into workforce."

Having discussed the political and ideological significances of sport in the MENA region as space for nation-state formation, as depicted by the state and ruling elites, and a place to claim different forms of national identity, the following section will focus on sport as a tool of diplomacy and image making in the region.

4 Sports as an element of public diplomacy and international identity building

Historically speaking, Kuwait and Bahrain were the first Arab Gulf countries to encourage youth, including women, to practice sport since the 1970s, typically through the provision of equipment and sports halls. But it is Qatar and the United Arab Emirates that have adopted more direct strategies for the promotion of sport which will open the door to competition and rivalry between them over image making and branding. Qatar has been the forerunner in its ambitions to use sport as a means for the development of the economy and human capital, as well as a diplomatic tool. Qatar focused on the development of its infrastructure and human resources, while engaging in a strategy of hosting major sporting events to ensure international positioning of the country in the world map. Qatar has been associated lately with the 2022 FIFA World Cup but, since 1993, the nation has been hosting the Exxon Mobil Open, a prestigious ATP tennis tournament. Since 2000, Qatar has been hosting a major meeting of the Super Grand Prix for Athletics and, since 2005, the "Oryx Cup" for speed boat racing. In 2004, it launched the "Aspire Academy," with the aim of training the next generation of elite athletes to represent Qatar internationally. This was followed in 2007 by the opening of an orthopedic and sports medicine hospital. The hospital has signed a number of partnerships with top football clubs and other international federations to treat injuries of top athletes, hence transforming the hospital (and Doha as destination) as the place to be for these athletes to rest and to recover. A number of European Clubs now choose Doha for their camps during the winter break to prepare for the second half of the season. Qatar is capitalizing on this opportunity to associate its destination with global sport brands. To this effort, Hamad International airport signed a sponsorship deal with FC Bayern München in 2017.

The press release states:

> The strengthening of this fantastic sponsorship between Qatar's award-winning airport and FC Bayern München, truly demonstrates the State of Qatar's role as a global leader in sports. The HIA-Qatar logo on the sleeve of every FC Bayern München jersey helps display the importance that we as a nation place on sports as a means of bringing people together. The HIA-Qatar enhancement of its sponsorship has also further aligned itself with our nation's ambitious national vision (Hamad International 2017).

Similar trends can be seen in the UAE. Policies have been initiated to promote sport through the organization of major international sporting events. The aim is to draw the attention of its population to the importance of sport on the one hand, as well as to ensure the country's visibility on a global stage, on the other. The UAE and particularly Dubai have become within a short time must-go-destinations for tourists from around the world. The countries have mobilized big national companies such as Emirates Airlines, Emirates Fly, Dubai Duty Free, and DP World to raise the funds necessary to organize major tournaments and competitions as well as to sponsor top sport brands. The Dubai Tennis Championship was launched in 1993, and the Emirates Dubai Rugby Sevens in 1996, which became a major milestone in the World Rugby Sevens Series.

Sensing the shift of the center of World Cricket into the region and East Asia, The World Cricket Association decided to simply move its headquarters to Dubai. A major milestone in the country's international sport strategy is the hosting of Formula 1 Abu Dhabi starting in 2009, following the footsteps of Bahrain, the first Arab country to host a Formula 1 race starting in 2004. In addition, the country has hosted numerous other continental and international football tournaments over the last decade.

For its part, the Kingdom of Saudi Arabia (KSA) still lags behind in comparison to other Gulf countries, with the exception of football. The Saudi professional football league is one of the most lucrative in the region with a solid fan base. Under the ruling of Abdallah Second, the country has begun construction of a massive sports infrastructure, financed by the all-powerful oil company ARAMCO (Le Magoariec 2019). Interestingly, the new influential young Crown Prince of Saudi Arabia Mohammad bin Salman bin Abdulaziz Al Saud, understood the importance of sport for the rebranding of the country as more open to the world. Under the new project of "Vision 2030" and "Neom," KSA has engaged in a new aggressive marketing strategy of hosting regional and international sport events. The country hosted the Dakar Rally in 2020 and will host the 2032 Asian Games, following Qatar in 2030. This policy is also expected to increase the country's attractiveness to foreign investors and tourists, which will help the country in the long run to diversify its economy and reduce its dependency on oil revenue. As in Qatar with PSG and the UAE with Manchester City, KSA is also tempted to get a share of the international sport market through direct investment in top professional clubs in Europe and North America. The other strategic sector for investment in sport is the competition (and even battle) over acquiring sport broadcasting rights, as illustrated in next section.

5 Sport, conventional and new media in the Arab world: another asset to conquer

The Arab world has witnessed a mushrooming of TV channels (free to air, cable, and pay-per-view). MENA's traditional TV industry was worth more than US $3.37 billion in revenue in 2015, composed of more than US $2.39 billion in free-to-air (FTA) advertising and US $0.75 billion in pay TV subscription revenues. Egypt, the UAE, and the KSA continue to be the primary countries for FTA stations (Sakr 1999; Satellite pay TV 2016)

The number of Arab state-run and private FTA and pay TV sports channels has significantly increased in the last ten years. According to Digital Research, pay satellite TV penetration will climb from 6.9 percent in 2010 to 11.8 percent in 2020, with subscriber numbers doubling from 5.01 million to 10.32 million. Interestingly there will be 6.16 million legitimate IPTV subscribers across the whole region by 2020; triple the 2014 total. Turkey will be the IPTV subscriber leader in 2020, while Qatar will lead in penetration terms. These channels offer diverse sports programs, debates, documentaries, and national, regional, and international sports competitions, ranging from traditional sports such as camel and horse racing to extreme sports such as the Offshore Powerboat Championships. Nearly every Arab country has its own state-run sport TV station, including Dubai Sport (UAE), Erriadia (Morocco), Al-Haddaf (Algeria), Iraqiya Sport (Iraq), Bahrain Sport (Bahrain), Saudia Sport (Saudi Arabia), and Nile Sport (Egypt), to name but a few. Interestingly, in contrast to many North American countries where state-owned and commercial FTA networks struggle to compete with satellite and subscription channels, the sport broadcasting market in the Middle East and North Africa is dominated by well-financed state networks such as beIN Sports in Qatar, and Abu Dhabi Sport in the United Arab Emirates.

News Channels and Sport TV broadcasting has become a terrain of intra-state competition and rivalry between countries in the Gulf region. Hamidou (2018) suggested that Qatar's involvement in the media race, and the launch of Al Jazeera News, was first motivated by its desire to thwart Saudi Arabia's plan to monopolize the Arab media to ensure a coherent media discourse that could serve its political and ideological interests in the Gulf region. Al Jazeera has largely contributed to the building of both the Qatari state's reputation and its profile in Arab public opinion. Subsequently, Al Jazeera Channel expanded to become Al Jazeera Media Network, which includes Al Jazeera Sports. To disassociate its growing sport TV content from Al Jazeera's news channel, Al Jazeera sport channels were put under the management of independent holding company, beIN Media Group, and Al Jazeera Sport Channels were rebranded as beIN SPORTS. The channels expanded to different continents, opening branches in France in June 2012 and in North America in August 2012. In 2013, beIN launched Sport Asia and an office in Indonesia, followed by beIN Sport Australia in 2014 and in 2015 in Spain. BeINsport has become the sport TV network to challenge and to encounter either legally by entering the race for the acquisition of TV rights of top sport competitions, which beINSport currently controls, or by tackling its supremacy through state or non-state financed piracy. The Qatari Al Jazeera News channel revealed in an investigative documentary that beoutQ, which has been stealing the signal of BeIN-Sport channels and broadcasting it as its own, is based out of the headquarters of a media company in the al-Qirawan district of the Saudi capital, Riyadh (Location of piracy 2019).

Doidge and Lieserb (2017) suggested, "thanks to global media, social media and increased travel, fans view, engage and interact with a range of fans from across the globe and bring various local dimensions to their fandom." The global phenomenon of social media cannot escape the attention of the youth in the Arab World and is becoming an alternative source of communication about sport for football fans. Virtual communities of Football Ultras groups are being formed to promote different innovative forms of communication about their experience of being football fans, hence defying the dominant state sponsored discourse on national identity, unity, and even morality. Social media and football chanting are becoming opportunities to speak up on behalf of the majority and directly, without intermediates, to decision makers. Offering different narratives to state-owned media or media sponsored by private entities that are close of the cycle of power, social media becomes a new medium to reframe identity, in opposition to the institutionalized discourse (Amara 2012b). Today in the age of global information technology, the Internet is becoming for football fans another terrain to conquer, to echo their demands, and to celebrate their sense of belonging beyond traditional nation-state territory. Fans can now share their views instantly and on multiple platforms. As rightly put by Tuastad (2014: 376), "The role of ultras supporters in the Egyptian revolution and the political role of nationalist supporters in Jordan in killing political taboos are cases where supporters represent more than simply a barometer of political trends. The supporters have initiated struggles crucially affecting political developments in their countries."

Football Ultras and social media have played a significant role in mass protestation movements in Egypt and Tunisia in 2011, and more recently in Morocco and Algeria. Lyrics of football supporters chanting, widely shared in social media and viewed by millions, such as that in Morocco (Fi Bladi Dalmouni)[2] and in Algeria (La Casa del Mouradia)[3] are case in point. The lyrics go as follow:

> Fi Bladi Dalmouni:
> "In this country, we live in a dark cloud. We only ask for social peace," the crowd chanted uproariously. "They left us as orphans, waiting for the punishment of the judgement day. Talents have been destroyed, destroyed by the drugs you provide them. How do you want them to shine? You stole the wealth of our country and shared it with strangers." (Translated by Alami 2018)
> La Casa del Mouradia (in reference to the presidential palace and Netflix series "La Casa de Papel"
> "It is Dawn and I can't Sleep. I am just consuming [drugs] slowly. Who is responsible and who is to blame? We had enough of this life ... who is responsible and who is to blame" (AFP 2019).

One can argue that football chanting, social media, and online streaming service such as Netflix, are offering new platforms of expression (and consumption) among youth in the region and elsewhere. Increasingly, these expressions are replacing the (old) state-centered, rigid, and top-down mode of communication.

6 Conclusion

The study of sport communication (or communication through sport) and the TV broadcasting market and industry in the MENA region offers an interesting terrain for the examination of current political and economic dynamics in the region. Disadvantages in terms of image, sports talents, and sports performance that would help in boosting the collective imagination, the Arab Gulf countries, are distinguished by an increasing desire to invest in the global sport market and industry as a means of nation and city branding as well as to diversify their source of revenues. In the rest of the Arab World, communication through sport has been heavily influenced by state ideology mobilized around the rhetoric of the ruling party and the nation's leader. With the end of the bipolar world, economic crises, and the advancement of global technology, it has become hard to sustain this type of top-down communication. Social media are offering more power to citizens, including sport and particularly football fans, to redefine their sense of belonging and to express their discontent and political opinions, outside the conventional and traditional media. Hence, this chapter offers a general overview and opportunities for future studies on the social, political, and commercial significance of sport in the Middle East and North Africa and the shift from traditional to new media. This does not mean that traditional media are not important. The MENA region offers a fertile context to the study of, for instance:

---

2 Fi Bladi Dalmouni, https://www.youtube.com/watch?v=2Auxpy-OwHE (viewed more than 13 million times).

3 La Casa del Mouradia, https://www.youtube.com/watch?v=kHZviPhZQxs (viewed nearly 9 million times).

1) development of sport media and nation-state formation
2) sport media and globalization
3) media, communication, and politics of language and identity in the region (Arabophone vs. Francophone), in *the Maghreb*, and (Arabophone vs. Anglophone) in *the Mashrek*, including the difference between how newspapers and TV channels publishing and broadcasting in foreign languages report on sport affairs in comparison to that of Arabophone ones.
4) how rivalry between countries in the region in sport is fueled and managed (escalated and deescalated) by state controlled and private media networks.
5) the geopolitics of TV sport broadcasting in the region and the competition between private TV networks over the control of broadcasting rights. The development and expansion of BeINSport internationally and the debate about access to premium sport competitions in the region, and different legal and illegal alternatives to counter BeIN Sport dominance.

This chapter thus contributes to the larger conversation about sport communication and media in the MENA region, offering an explanation of established lines of research and inviting consideration of new directions for the future.

References

AFP. 2019. "La Casa del Mouradia", quand un chant de supporters devient l'hymne des manifestants algériens. Retrieved from https://www.challenges.fr/sport/la-casa-del-mouradia-quand-un-chant-de-supporters-devient-l-hymne-des-manifestants-algeriens_664719 (18 July 2019).

Al Jazeera. 2019. Egypt's squash champions. Al Jazeera, 29 October. https://www.aljazeera.com/program/episode/2019/10/29/egypts-squash-champions/ (1 June 2020).

Amara, Mahfoud. 2006. Soccer, post-colonial and post-conflict discourses in Algeria: Algérie-France, 6 Octobre 2001, "ce n'était pas un simple match de foot." *International Review of Modern Sociology* 32(2). 217–239.

Alami. Aida. 2018. The soccer politics of Morocco. New York Review of Books, 20 December. https://www.nybooks.com/daily/2018/12/20/the-soccer-politics-of-morocco/ (1 June 2020).

Alhyas, Layla, Alisa McKay, Anjali Balasanthiran & Azeem Majeed. 2011. Prevalence of overweight, obesity, hypertension and dyslipidemia in the Gulf: A systematic review. *Journal of Royal Society of Medicine* 2(7). 1–16.

Al Jenaibi, Badreya. 2011. The changing representation of the Arab Woman in Middle East advertising and media, *Global Media Journal* 1(2). 67–88.

Amara, Mahfoud. 2012a. *Sport, politics and society in the Arab world*. London: Palgrave.

Amara, Mahfoud. 2012b. Football sub-culture and youth politics in Algeria. *Mediterranean Politics* 17(1). 41–58.

Anderson, Benedict. 1983. *Imagined communities: Reflections on the origin and spread of nationalism*. London: Verso.

Bairner, Alan. 2011. *Sport, nationalism, and globalization European and North American perspectives*. New York: State University of New York Press.

Doidge, Mark & Martin Lieserb. 2017. The importance of research on the ultras: Introduction. *Sport in Society* 21(6). 833–840.

Hamad International Airport and FC Bayern München enhance their sponsorship. 2017. Hamad International Airport, 14 August. https://dohahamadairport.com/media/hamad-international-airport-and-fc-bayern-münchen-enhance-their-sponsorship (10 August 2018).

Hamidou, Kamal. 2018. Qatar's soft power strategy in shaping its international profile. National University of Singapore, Middle East Institute, 2 July. https://mei.nus.edu.sg/publication/insight-186-qatars-soft-power-strategy-in-shaping-its-international-profile/ (3 July 2018).

Khalidi, Issam. 2014. Sports and aspirations: Football in Palestine, 1900–1948, *Jerusalem Quarterly* 58. 74–88.

Le Magoariec, Raphaël. 2019. Pays du Golfe: Les enjeux diplomatiques des politiques sportives. *Institut de Relations Internationales et Stratégiques*, March. https://www.iris-france.org/wp-content/uploads/2019/03/Obs-sport-Golfe-mars-2019.pdf (15 September 2019).

Location of piracy channel beoutQ headquarters in Riyadh revealed. 2019. *The Peninsula*, 23 September. https://thepeninsulaqatar.com/article/23/09/2019/Location-of-piracy-channel-beoutQ-headquarters-in-Riyadh-revealed (23 September 2019).

Sakr, Naomi. 1999. Satellite television and development in the Middle East. *Middle East Report* 210. 6–8.

Satellite pay TV operators in the Arab world 2016. 2016. Arab Advisory Group. https://arabadvisors.com/product/satellite-pay-tv-operators-in-the-arab-world-2016 (18 November 2020).

Sorek, Tamir. 2003. Arab football in Israel as an "integrative enclave." *Ethnic and Racial Studies* 26(3). 422–450.

Tuastad, Dag. 2014. From football riot to revolution. The political role of football in the Arab world, *Soccer & Society* 15(3). 376–388.

Ilan Tamir

29 "Even when the angel of death will come I will still wear yellow-blue": Israeli soccer fans' chants as a window for understanding cultural and sports reality

Abstract: Fans' chants in sports stadiums have, over the years, become an integral part of the spectator experience. While chants provide color, atmosphere, and a demonstration of fans' support for their team, they also play a significant role in defining fans' perceptions of their team's identity and its differentiation from other teams. Therefore, it is not surprising that the chants have become the showcase of the team and its hallmark. An analysis of football chants will therefore shed light on fans' deep-seated worldviews of their own role, their team, the sport in general, and even life itself. The purpose of this study is to find whether and how the content of the chants changed over the years, as a reflection of wider social and cultural changes of the society. Based on an analysis of Israeli football chants over years, this study identifies key changing and stable perceptions of football fans. Findings point to several values that have remained stable over years, including fans' attitudes toward their team and its rivals, and their attitude toward God, alongside recently emerging phenomena such as radicalization of hatred toward others and attitudes to the commercialization of sport, which reflect social and cultural changes both in the world of sports and without.

Keywords: sport; soccer; fans; chants; loyalty

1 Introduction: sport and society in Israel

Sport is a broad cultural phenomenon with a deep impact on all population groups. Much has been written about the extraordinary global popularity of sport and its influence on the major elements of all layers of society. Due to its unique features, sports is considered a sphere that faithfully reflects, and is even actively instrumental in the formation of historical, social, cultural, economic, and political, and other developments.

The premise that sport teams represent something beyond the game itself (e. g., political ideology, geographic environment, and economic status) creates the distinctions between teams and increases tension during games. In this conception, a game is never merely a game: it is a symbolic, competitive, and emotional struggle between groups (Cleland and Cashmore 2015). Therefore, it is not surprising that live sports broadcasts became so popular and are almost consistently the broadcasts with the highest ratings (Wann and James 2019). For years, fans have demonstrated their

https://doi.org/10.1515/9783110660883-029

loyalty to live broadcasts and have even refused to view delayed broadcasts of their favorite teams (Tamir 2019).

Raney (2006) has pointed to three over-arching categories for understanding sports viewing motivations: emotional (e. g., entertainment and eustress), cognitive (e. g., learning), and social (e. g., companionship and group affiliation) motivations. The sociology of sports has traditionally stressed the role of sports in identity construction. Under this broad notion, a distinction is evident between approaches that focus on the power of sports and its potential function to integrate social groups, and between approaches at the other side of that continuum, which emphasize sports' role in reinforcing the boundaries that separate and differentiate teams (Sorek 2007).

The field of sports in Israel, which predates independence, was established as an undisguised extension of political centers of power, and indeed, politicization was initially a predominant feature of sports. Teams were affiliated with political parties and came to reflect society's sectorial-conflictual structure. Accordingly, all sports decision-making was a function of the political reality. Unions and labor committees, budgets, and even sports delegations and the athletes themselves were divided along political lines (Galily 2007). Sports activities in Israel, as around the world, initially had a definitive masculine orientation (Galily, Kaufman, and Tamir 2015). In general, in that initial period, the face of sports was painted in almost uniform colors. The Jewish, male, Ashkenazi, and white dominance loomed large in all areas of sports.

Over the years, Israeli sports underwent a process of professionalization, and subsequently experienced commodification, or what sociologists prefer to describe as a shift "from games to commodities" (Ben-Porat 2009a). These developments were manifest in a long series of changes that ranged from the structure of ownership of sports teams (where political ownership was replaced by ownership of private businesspersons), through considerations in professional decision-making (e. g., game schedules and locations were decided as a function of broadcasting rights), to even cultural and historical issues (e. g., sports facilities that were initially named after illustrious historical figures, were renamed for brands and companies in response to demands of sponsors or businesspersons).

Technological, media, and cultural changes also affected attitudes toward sports and its role in service of national sentiment. Foreign players and coaches were signed up, broadcasts of international sports events became available in all homes, gradually eroding the hegemony of national sports teams in Israel (Tamir 2014; Tamir, Galily, and Yarchi 2016) to the point that a recent survey of sport fans in Israel found that the most popular soccer team is the Spanish team of Barcelona (Daskal 2016).

At the same time, women's presence in Israeli sports expanded as acceptance gradually increased. In the recent Olympic Games (Rio 2016), female athletes accounted for over 50 percent of the Israeli Olympic team. Women also assumed a more prominent role in sports media, media's final male bastion (Tamir, Galily, and Yarchi 2017), to the point where today women are chief sports editors in Israel's most popular sport websites and channels. Nonetheless, women's presence in Israeli sports remains limited, and women's sports are of secondary significance on an everyday basis (Tamir and Galily 2010). For a variety of reasons, representation of new population groups in sports has expanded, in some cases completely reversing the former situation. For example, in Israeli soccer, the country's most popular sport, the former dominance of Ashkenazi players has been almost completely eliminated by a preponderance of Mizrahi Jews and Israeli Arab players. At the same time, significant changes in the composition and nature of Israeli sports fans can also be identified – from the increasing presence of women in sports stadiums to the structure of organized fan groups. It will be, therefore, interesting to examine whether and how the significant changes in Israeli sports will be expressed from the fans point of view.

2 Sports fandom

Fandom in general and soccer fandom in particular have been the target of comprehensive research efforts. For many, sport is considered an "authorization zone" (Ben-Porat 2014: 179) in which players and, even more so, fans feel sufficiently comfortable to speak and act freely and spontaneously, often in disregard of accepted behavioral norms. In sports stadiums, actions and expressions that are typically considered socially unacceptable and legally prohibited are viewed as legitimate. Sport has therefore become a fruitful ground for research (Sorek 2019) on social studies. The emotional spontaneity inherent in the sport experience suppresses political correctness and transforms sport into a reliable site of research that reveals alternative social realities (Tamir 2019). Studies have focused on topics such as fans' features, lifestyles, and fandom practices. Researchers concur that identification as a fan, in most cases, dictates an entire lifestyle that includes fandom rituals, purchase of team merchandise, massive consumption of sports media, and especially a strong commitment to a team and its community. Consequently, the classic fandom pattern obligates fans to attend games, view them on the media, or at least closely follow developments in the games on other media (Tamir 2016).

Fans' socialization includes the acquisition and assimilation of their appreciation of soccer through admiration of a specific team. Soccer fandom is mainly a function of environmental factors including family, status, and gender, which serve as young fans' agents of socialization (Ben-Porat 2010).

The daily and weekly schedules of "true" fans align with the schedules of their teams. Fans are highly committed to fandom rituals, including going regularly to the stadium with other fans, focusing on soccer as a key topic of conversation, purchasing team merchandise (e. g., shirts, scarves), adopting the team's colors (and avoidance of the colors of opponents), and of course, massive consumption of sports media (Ben-Porat 2014; Giulianotti 2002). For example, a study by Ben-Porat (2007) among soccer fans in Israel found that one half would prefer to go to their team's game if the event clashes with a family event, even though they are aware of the cost of their decision to do so in terms of family relations. This finding may be related to the fact that fans believe that their presence in the bleachers affects the results of the game and increases the chances that their team will win (Moskwitz and Wertheim 2012).

3 Fan chants

Chanting is one of the emblematic fandom practices, which fans believe has the capacity to "propel their team forward." Fans' chants create a unique magical atmosphere at games, but their functions extend beyond this arena. Chants are a key tool for fans to express emotions (Ashmore 2017) and convey messages – to their peers, to the players, to rival fans, and to team management. Furthermore, sport chants have assumed an important role in fandom rituals because of the significant role they play in defining fans' identities toward their own teams and the rival teams (Collinson 2009). In this manner, chants highlight the clear essential and ideological distinctions between a team's fans and everyone else (Armstrong and Young 2008). Protest songs also play an important role in defining fans' "red lines," and as such, chants effectively function as a means of affirmation of community membership (Benkwitz and Molnar 2012) and an act of celebration and carnival (Maffesoli 1996; Knijnik 2018). Chants create a sense of community and shared fate, and serve as a test of fans' loyalty, since fans may elect to be merely passive fans or more active supporters by joining in the chants. To a very large degree, the chants also territorialize the field. Therefore, in some cases, sound intensity is also important in defining the level of sympathy (Kytö 2011). In other cases it was found that the chants sometimes even exacerbate fans' levels of aggression (Bensimon and Bodner 2011). It is therefore unsurprising that chants also assume a focal role in the familiar comparison between sport and religion (Bain-Selbo and Sapp 2016).

Chants are associated with a team's spirit, culture, and ideology, and therefore the premise of the current study is that an analysis of fan chants may reveal meanings related to community boundary setting, beliefs, and basic perceptions.

4 Method

This study examines the fan chants of Maccabi Tel Aviv, an Israeli soccer team, over a period of five decades, and through these chants, analyzes the main perceptions, trends, and values that have driven Israeli soccer fans over this period. The selection of Maccabi Tel Aviv was based on three considerations: it is the most long-standing soccer team in Israel, has the greatest number of fans (Leiba 2017), and is the only team in Israel that has placed only in the First League, throughout its entire history, planted firmly and systematically at the forefront of the sports stage.

For the purpose of the study, chants were collected by extracting chants from the Maccabi Tel Aviv fan's main forum "The Twelfth Player," and through an appeal to forum members to locate older chants (N = 98). The forum comprises several thousand fans of Maccabi's soccer and basketball teams, and for almost a decade has served as the main platform of Maccabi's most loyal fans. The forum was established and administered by the Twelfth Player Fan Organization, and after the organization's liquidation, has been managed by private individuals. In the past, the organization regularly published every new chant before it was heard in the bleachers. Although this custom was discontinued when the organization was dissolved, forum members hold lively discussions on the team's chants, and whenever a new chant comes into use, a new thread is typically opened by fans who ask for the chant's words.

In the first stage of the analysis, the chants were ordered by the year in which they were first heard in the bleachers, and then grouped by decade. Chants from the 1970s and the 1980s were combined into a single group due to the very small number of chants from this period –perhaps as a reflection of the era before the professionalization of Israeli football and its fans (Ben-Porat 2012). In summary, four groups were created: one group covering two decades (the 1970s and the 1980s), two groups covering one decade each (1990s, 2000s), and one group covering nine years (2010–2018). In the second stage of the analysis, based on the features of the chants in these groups, I created two groups of chants by consolidating the two earliest groups and the two more recent groups (covering 1970–1999 and 2000–2018, respectively).

Qualitative content analysis was used to analyze the chants. Qualitative interpretative research seeks to study the meanings of words and gain an understanding of the role of the implicit meanings and worldviews underlying texts (Van Dijk 2001). Meanings are interpreted through thematic organization, which makes it possible to identify and map key themes emerging from the texts of the chants (Berger 2014). An analysis of the text allows an understanding of fans' discourse involving the team's management, the rival teams' fans, and all other individuals and groups outside the team. The aim of this research method is to extract the broad social and cultural meanings underlying these chants.

It is important to note that the analysis in the present study focuses on the words of the chants with no reference to the music, which in itself (from its rhythms to the origins of the melodies) constitutes fertile ground for gaining an understanding of interesting aspects of fandom.

5 Findings and discussion

In general, fan chants highlight fans' deep-seated connection and commitment to their team, and the sacrifices they are willing to make for it ("I would give my life for the team"). Love for the team, which is explicitly stated in erotic terms ("my hearts cries for your beauty," "When you touch me, I'm another person," "You've bewitched me," "Forever me and you, there is no one but you," etc.), is never in doubt, unaffected by the team's achievements or results ("I don't care about the score," "Even when the going was a little tough," "We'll cheer you up in any situation," etc.), and independent of the individual players' identity ("Players may change but I will love you Maccabi Tel Aviv forever"). The words to "Never Walk Alone" are familiar within many stadiums and are repeated among fans around the world (Schoonderwoerd 2011). In this respect, the significant connection between the fans and the team is affirmed through love songs to the team, and no less importantly, through chants expressing their hatred of rival teams. These hate songs are blatantly directed to its municipal rival, Hapoel Tel Aviv, which represents the ultimate "other." The color red, identified with Hapoel Tel Aviv, has become the subject of many chants. At the same time, it seems that the main ideas that fans highlight in their chants are systematically reproduced in both love and hate chants.

An analysis of fan chants points to a fundamental division between stable views and beliefs that appear over the entire study period and developing trends that have emerged in recent years in response to external events outside the stadium.

5.1 Stable values

5.1.1 Larger than life – the team is in the center of the universe and fans remain fans even after their death

Soccer fans consider the game a focal part of the reality of their lives and view the team as the center of their universe. Based on the chants, fans appear to be convinced that the entire world, including God, is preoccupied with what happens on the field, and plays an active role in contributing to the team's success. In this respect, the universe is divided into "us" and "them." This is not merely represented as the subjective experience of the fans, it is a universal, dichotomized picture of reality: "The entire world is Maccabi Tel Aviv" in contrast to "The whole world hates you!" This dichotomous division contains a demarcation between the good guys and the bad guys, and clearly defines which God's favorite children are. As a result, fans feel the need to thank God repeatedly for his intervention in sports and the choices that were made. The fact that most soccer matches in Israel take place on Saturday, which is the day of Jewish Sabbath, does not deter fans from appealing to God and expressing their gratitude to him:

"I thank God for hating the Reds"
"I thank God for giving me life and Maccabi"
"Wait for the revenge that will come from God"

Literature from the sociology of sport and the features of fandom has repeatedly pointed to the team's important role in its fans' lives, yet the analysis of the chants adds a universal and possibly deterministic interpretation to the familiar sports reality.

Much has been written about soccer fans and their commitment to their teams, which leads them to financial, family, and even health-related sacrifices (Bernhardt et al. 1998; Wilbert-Lampen et al. 2008). Nonetheless, fan chants describe the teams in extravagant terms. For its fans, the team is larger than life. Fans' deep connection to the team extends beyond the physical realm, and as a result, a fan's life is only a link in the continuous and never-ending relationship with his team (Kytö 2011). In other words, even death does not part fans from their team.

In the chants, we find numerous phrases that describe fans' absolute connection to their team, which virtually begins at birth or even earlier:

"I was born for you," "Yellow-blue blood courses through my veins," "Only one thing flows in my blood since the day I was born," "My life is yours."

In some cases, fans define their team as their *raison d'être*: "There is no point to my life without you" and "I am willing to die for you." Consequently, even death will not sever this strong tie:

"Even death can't separate you from me"
"Even when God takes me, I will not escape ... this is an eternal blood alliance"
"I will not forget to give [you] all even when God takes me"
"Maccabi –'til the end of all generations"
"Even when the angel of death comes, I will wear yellow-blue"
"Maccabi, even the angel of death can't take me away from you"
"Death will not divide us"
"When I die, bury me with the yellow banner"

At a deep level, fans present their sympathy toward the team as a deterministic relationship: they were born with the blood of the team's colors and will die with it. Moreover, fans describe the team as the most stable thing in their lives: they may move their home or change their spouses, but yellow blood will continue to course through their bodies even after their heart stops pumping. In other words, the team is the key foundation that defines a fan's identity and will even be a large part of the tombstone that he leaves behind.

5.1.2 Undermining rivals' masculinity – humiliation and rape

Despite the significant advances for women in global sports in recent years, male hegemony still dominates Israeli sports, especially soccer (Tamir and Galily 2010). The masculine discourse monopolizes the bleachers, and chants are accordingly all formulated from the perspective of male fans. Moreover, a significant portion of the chants refers to the contest between the fan's team and the fan's girlfriend or wife over the fan's heart. When this is the situation, fans try their best to attack fans of the rival team and undermine the latter's intimate ties to their own teams:

> "My wife says to me it's either her or Maccabi – I told her it's either Maccabi or death" "I'll love only you, there'll never be another," "There's no one but you"

Homophobic slurs are frequently used in sports as a means of undermining rival fans' masculinity (Hughson and Free 2011(. The use of homophobic messages in fan chants is not new. Magrath (2018) even highlights the gap between the true attitude of fans to homosexuality and the songs they sing in stadiums. Yet, Maccabi fans try to undercut the masculine image of the rival fans and their close relationship with their team:

> "Gate 5 [which is the entrance to the bleachers' designated for Hapoel fans] he got it in the ass,"
> "Shavit [Hapoel goalie] get it in the ass"
> "Hapoel vegans ... they only get beaten up and love boys"
> "Everything's ready to fuck the Reds"; "Everything's ready to fuck Hapoel"
> "Hapoel gives blow jobs to the whole neighborhood"
> "Wiping my ass with red scarves"

In some sense, the multiplicity of sexual images used to disrupt the continuity of the rival fans' community is understandable: practices of sexual aggression are frequently described in the literature as part of ethnic cleansing campaigns (Henry 2011) and efforts to destroy a contaminating race or community. By sexually violating the other, group members seek to "infect" the social and historical fabric of their rival and thereby destroy its unifying core. The chants, which are replete with expressions of and allusions to sexual acts may also reflect fans' desire to stress their superiority over the rival team and fans through the use of power and humiliation, but also by penetrating the rival territory and undermining the intimate relationships it contains:

> "We will take your girls, and when we will rape them, we will scream 'today is Hapoel death'"

To a large extent, the steady discourse around women and sexuality in fans chants, casts a shadow on the growing presence of women on the soccer fields. The familiar argument about the relative autonomy (Ben-Porat 2009b) of women in the sport sphere is clearly expressed in the present context.

5.1.3 Old politics in a new reality

The origin of the major rivalry between Maccabi and Hapoel clubs in Israeli sports can be traced to political reality and social attitudes that extend beyond the game itself. The division of local sports into the two clubs occurred against the backdrop of the attitude of the Maccabi sports organization to Hebrew workers in pre-state Israel (Kaufman 2007). Hapoel was established as a socialist alternative to Maccabi's capitalist worldview. Hapoel's slogan "From champs to thousands" (Bell 2003) expressed Hapoel's distaste for Maccabi's sanctity of competition (Hapoel proposed an alternative, essentially non-competitive form of sports for the masses). Despite the dramatic changes over time in teams' ownership and political identification, the slogan continues to feature in current fan chants. Maccabi fans remain loyal to the sanctified values of victory – "Always be first" – and at the same time disparage Hapoel's "loser" image.

Furthermore, Maccabi fans continue to refer to the political symbols and icons of Hapoel sports organization, which represent the organization's original political worldview and role as representative of the labor class:

> "Hate the hammer and the sickle, too"
> "Burn the communists"
> "Go back to the Histadrut" [The Histadrut is the national Labor Union, which was established in 1920 by the socialist parties, and which, in turn, established Hapoel sports organization]
> "All red communists should contract cancer"

Over time, the political identity of the soccer clubs in Israel, which was initially closed and clearly defined, underwent a radical change. If in the past, a player might begin and end his career in one club, which also aligned with his own political ideology, transfers among teams have become routine and legitimate practice. In the past seasons, a large number of players including major players and team captains have transferred from Maccabi to Hapoel and vice versa. Moreover, in the era of commercialization and globalization, in which team ownership is controlled by private businesspersons, some of whom are even foreign citizens (many examples of this can be found in many sports clubs around the world), the connection between sports clubs and political parties has become irrelevant. Interestingly, political attitudes have nonetheless remained embedded deeply in chants and fans' consciousness, even after circumstances have changed. Perhaps in the age of frequent transfers of players between teams, the chants are what defines ideological boundaries and are instrumental in efforts to preserve its traditional symbols.

5.2 Changing trends

Alongside the main themes to emerge from the analysis of all the chants, two new trends can be identified in the more recent group of chants only. The first is the radicalization of hate, which is reflected in previously unacceptable language uses, especially Holocaust symbols and comparisons between rival groups and terrorist operations. This trend is in line with extreme expressions of hatred and racism, which are popular among football fans around the world, and specifically in fan chants (Waiton 2018). The second group of the latest trends focuses on protests against the accelerated commercialization and merchandizing of sports.

5.2.1 Radicalization of hate

5.2.1.1 Holocaust images

Changes in Israeli society have made the Holocaust a part of the Israeli cultural repertoire, to the point of "trivialization of traumatic memory" (Zandberg 2015: 109). As a result, sports fields have also begun to use images from the Holocaust period in their repertoire of chants and cheers. It is interesting to observe the dual role that the Holocaust plays in this context: on the one hand, fans protect its sanctity – the Holocaust is mentioned in chants in order to express fans' revulsion of rival fans' uses of Holocaust-related images in their chants:

> "They [Hapoel fans] chant about the Holocaust – shame on you"
> "Hapoel called me a Nazi ... but I'm proud of the Star of David on my chest"

Yet on the other hand, Maccabi fans also use allusions to the traumatic events of the Holocaust when chanting about the rivalry between the two teams:

> "The train races through rock and mountains, and of all the Germans, it runs over Teomim [former manager of Hapoal Tel-Aviv]"

5.2.1.2 Terror-related images

Possibly it is the security situation in Israel that has, in some periods, transformed terror into an integral part of everyday routine in the country. Confrontations between Israel and terrorist organizations (mainly Hamas and Hezbollah), which increased in intensity in the 2000s (Center of Information on Intelligence and Terror 2006), also permeated sports fields and were adopted into the broad range of slurs hurled against rival teams:

> "Hezbollah, Hapoel Hezbollah," "Maccabi Haifa Hezbollah," "All the Reds are Hezbollah"
> "No Red, no terrorist attacks; Gate 5 are the Muslims ... Salim Tuema [Hapoel player] is a terrorist"
> "Hapoel is like the PLO, giving the Arabs refuge."

In both cases (terror and the Holocaust), chants incorporate what are clear expressions of extreme hatred designed to delegitimize and dehumanize the fans of the rival team. The second case (terror) may also be related to the general attitude of Jews in Israel to Islam and the Arab minority and their representation in sports (Tamir and Bernstein 2015). In any case, it is quite clear that the radicalization of fan chants expresses and inflames the verbal violence prevalent in sports fields (Fields, Collins, and Comstock 2007; Wann and James 2019).

5.2.2 Protesting commodification

Another trend is related to economic developments and their impact on sports. Israeli soccer was not unaffected by the global wave of commodification of sports. Beginning in the 1990s, ownership of Israeli soccer teams shifted to private hands (Ben-Porat 2013) and significant components of the clubs’ identity changed in response. As a result, in recent years, there is evidence of fans’ efforts to restore the team’s fundamental identity and reinstate the team’s true owners (its fans) in a position of power (for example, by establishing “fan groups”). Within these efforts, chants express fans’ objections to private ownership of clubs, yet disparage their rivals for allowing commercialization to erode their traditional symbols:

> “Lonny [former owner of Maccabi Tel Aviv], we ask for your forgiveness. We promise never to curse you … you mother fucker.”
> “My heart is yours and can’t be bought for any price”
> “People say that Usishkin [Hapoel Tel Aviv’s mythological basketball court, which was demolished] is Hapoel’s heart … today it’s a parking lot”

The place of sport as a space of protest has been illustrated many times and discussed in other studies (Henderson 2009; Boykoff and Carrington 2020). Protest chants against commodification and commercialization and the new structure of ownership are certainly a recent trend that reflects changes in the sphere of sports. At the same time, they explicitly and directly correspond to the role that fans assume in protecting their teams’ values and symbols through the chants they sing.

6 Summary

Fan chants constitute a major component in the toolbox of fans’ loyalty and love for their team. Beyond the color and atmosphere that they add, chants play an important role in defining a team’s identity, as perceived by its fans, and in differentiating a team from its rivals. The current study analyzed fan chants in an effort to understand fans’ deep-seated views of their roles, their team, the sport, and life itself.

Findings of the current study significantly reinforce our understanding of what fans consider to be a team's role. For fans, their team is at the top of their priorities. They are totally committed to their team, from the day of their birth until the day of their death and perhaps even beyond. Fan chants also stress the significance that symbols play for fans, despite or perhaps even because of the commercialization surrounding the field of sports. In this respect, chants play an important role in preserving traditions and symbols, even when reality changes, erodes the original function of symbols, and obliterates political differences.

In general, it is interesting to observe that fandom rituals do not necessarily reflect the changes, including political changes that have affected sports. On the contrary, chants continue to resonate ideas and values that were characteristic of Israeli sports in its early days. Chants continue to be masculine in nature and content, despite the growing presence of women in the bleachers. References to minorities are made mainly within context of humiliation and disparagement, despite the fact that almost all teams have Arab, Black, and other minority players. Nonetheless, some changes in the contents of chants are in line with contemporary issues that concern fans.

In other words, fan chants have a dual role. On the one hand, they reflect the zeitgeist of a team's fans, especially all aspects of fans' sense of connectedness to their team, structural changes of ownership of sports teams, and even changes in accepted modes of expression. On the other hand, chants play an instrumental role in preserving team values. Through their chants, fans express their insistence on adhering to their team's original ideological and moral positions.

Even on the deeper political level, the chants play a dual role – within in-group level, the chants have an important integrative role: they set clear criteria for loyalty and a demand for unity and solidarity ("Those who do not jump red," "behind you in every situation ... and the whole stadium is jumping now"). At the same time, on the out-group, this is a particularly significant differentiation agent. The chants set clear boundaries between "us" and "them." They clarify the differences between the groups in a clear manner, of course in terms of good and bad ("La Familia did not understand that a school is compulsory," "Hapoel is like the PLO," "Hapoel Taliban").

Functional theory, which compares society to an organism, made up of many parts, all functioning for the survival and social stability (Delaney 2015), has become very popular among sports scholars (Delaney and Madigan 2015). Researchers have sought to examine the contribution of sport to society and to identify the functions it plays. Based on the present research, it can be argued that the chants have significant social roles, such as psychological and physical release, creating a sense of community membership and even the transmission of intergenerational values and traditions (for example, by referring to the team as an anchor for the stable identity definition). The dismantling of social integration, and the verbal assaults, which is clearly expressed on fan chants (for example, in humiliating the opponents or in the gender distinctions), can be seen as dysfunction or, alternatively, as part of the fans' release pressures process. The fact that most of the sports chants' scene remains on the field and are not covered by the media or beyond is worthy of future research as the chants, as the current study presents, reflect clear trends of the fans, including a radical expression of violence.

References

Armstrong, Gary & Malcolm Young. 2008. Fanatical football chants: Creating and controlling the carnival. *Sport in Society* 2(3). 173–211.

Ashmore, Paul. 2017. Of other atmospheres: Football spectatorship beyond the terrace chant. *Soccer & Society* 18(1). 30–46.

Bain-Selbo, Eric & D. Gregory Sapp. 2016. *Understanding sport as a religious phenomenon*. New York: Bloomsbury.

Bell, Daniel 2003. *Encyclopedia of international games* (vol. 1). Jefferson, NC: McFarland.

Ben-Porat, Amir. 2007. *Oh, what a delightful war! Israeli soccer fans*. Haifa: Pardess Publishing. [Hebrew]

Ben-Porat, Amir. 2009a. Not just for men: Israeli women who fancy football. *Soccer & Society* 10(6). 883–896.

Ben-Porat, Amir. 2009b. Six decades of sport, from a game to commodity: Football as a parable. *Sport in Society* 12(8). 999–1012.

Ben-Porat, Amir. 2010. Football fandom: A bounded identification. *Soccer & Society* 11(3). 277–290.

Ben Porat, Amir. 2012. From community to commodity: the commodification of football in Israel. *Soccer & Society* 13(3). 443–457.

Ben-Porat, Amir. 2013. *The passion, the game, and the exchange value: The commercialization of soccer*. Haifa: Pardess Publishing. [Hebrew]

Ben-Porat, Amir. 2014. Who are we? My club? My people? My state? The dilemma of the Arab football fan in Israel. *International Review for the Sociology of Sport* 49(2). 175–189.

Benkwitz, Adam & Gyozo Molnar. 2012. Interpreting and exploring football fan rivalries: An overview. *Soccer & Society* 13(4): 479–494.

Bensimon, Moshe & Ehud Bodner. 2011. Playing with fire: The impact of football game chanting on level of aggression. *Journal of Applied Social Psychology* 41(10). 2421–2433.

Berger, Arthur A. 2014. *Media and communication research methods: An introduction to qualitative and quantitative approaches*, 3rd edn. London: Sage.

Bernhardt, Paul C., J. M. Dabbs Jr., Julie A. Fieldman & Candice D. Lutter. 1998. Testosterone changes during vicarious experiences of winning and losing among fans at sporting events. *Physiology & Behavior* 65(1). 59–62.

Boykoff, Jules & Ben Carrington. 2020. Sporting dissent: Colin Kaepernick, NFL activism, and media framing contests. *International Review for the Sociology of Sport* 55(7). 829–849.

Center for Information on Intelligence and Terror. 2006. *Suicide terrorists during the years of the Israeli-Palestinian confrontation*, 2nd edn. 1January. http://www.terrorism-info.org.il/Data/pdf/PDF_18891_1.pdf (18 November 2020).

Cleland, Jamie & Ellis Cashmore. 2015. Football fans' views of violence in British football: Evidence of a sanitized and gentrified culture. *Journal of Sport & Social Issues* 40(2). 124–142.

Collinson, Ian. 2009. "Singing songs, making places, creating selves": Football songs & fan identity at Sydney FC. *Transforming Cultures Ejournal* 4(1). http://epress.lib.uts.edu.au/journals/index.php/tfc/article/view/1057 (18 November 2020).

Daskal, O. 2016. The big sport survey. https://newmedia.calcalist.co.il/seker/ (29 May 2020).

Delaney, Tim 2015. The functionalist perspective on sport. In Richard Giulianotti (ed.), *Routledge handbook of the sociology of sport*, 18–28. New York: Routledge.
Delaney, Tim & Tim Madigan. 2015. *The sociology of sports: An introduction*, 2nd edn. Jefferson, NC: McFarland.
Fields, Sarah K., Christy L. Collins & R. Dawn Comstock. 2007. Conflict on the courts: A review of sports-related violence literature. *Trauma, Violence, & Abuse* 8(4). 359–369.
Galily, Yair. 2007. Sport, politics and society in Israel: The first fifty-five years. *Israel Affairs* 13(3). 515–528.
Galily, Yair, Haim Kaufman & Ilan Tamir. 2015. She got game?! Women, sport and society from an Israeli perspective. *Israel Affairs* 21(4). 559–584.
Giulianotti, Richard. 2002. Supporters, followers, fans, and flaneurs: A taxonomy of spectator identities in football. *Journal of Sport & Social Issues* 26(1). 25–46.
Henderson, Simon. 2009. Crossing the line: sport and the limits of civil rights protest. *The International Journal of the History of Sport* 26(1). 101–121.
Henry, Nicola. 2011. *War and rape: Law, memory and justice*. New York: Routledge.
Hughson, John & Marcus Free. 2011. Football's "coming out": Soccer and homophobia in England's tabloid press. *Media International Australia* 140(1). 117–125.
Kaufman, Haim. 2007. Maccabi versus Hapoel: The political divide that developed in sports in Eretz Israel, 1926–1935. *Israel Affairs* 13(3). 554–565.
Knijnik, Jorge. 2018. Imagining a multicultural community in an everyday football carnival: Chants, identity and social resistance on Western Sydney terraces. *International Review for the Sociology of Sport* 53(4). 471–489.
Kytö, Meri. 2011. We are the rebellious voice of the terraces, we are Çarşı: Constructing a football supporter group through sound. *Soccer & Society* 12(1). 77–93.
Leiba, Guy. 2017. Survey of soccer fans. *Ynet*, 7 April. http://www.ynet.co.il/articles/0,7340,L-4946439,00.html (29 May 2020).
Maffesoli, Michel. 1996. *The time of the tribes: The decline of individualism in mass society*. Thousand Oaks: Sage.
Magrath, Rory. 2018. To try and gain an advantage for my team: Homophobic and homosexually themed chanting among English football fans. *Sociology* 52(4). 709–726.
Moskwitz, Tobias J. & L. Jon Wertheim. 2012. *Scorecasting: The hidden influences behind how sports are played and games are won*. New York: Crown.
Raney, Arthur A. 2006. Why we watch and enjoy mediated sports. In Arthur A. Raney & Jennings Bryant (eds.), *Handbook of sports and media*, 313–330. Mahwah, NJ: Erlbaum.
Schoonderwoerd, Pieter. 2011. Shall we sing a song for you? Mediation, migration and identity in football chants and fandom. *Soccer & Society* 12(1). 120–141.
Sorek, Tamir. 2007. *Arab soccer in a Jewish state: The integrative enclave*. Cambridge: Cambridge University Press.
Sorek, Tamir. 2019. Hapoel Tel Aviv and Israeli Liberal Secularism. In Daneyl Reiche & Tamir Sorek (eds.), *Sports, society, and politics in the Middle East*, 55–72. Oxford: Oxford University Press.
Tamir, Ilan. 2014. The decline of nationalism among football fans. *Television & New Media* 15(8). 741–745.
Tamir, Ilan. 2016. Choosing to stay away: Soccer fans' purposeful avoidance of soccer events. *Time & Society* 28(1). 231–246.
Tamir, Ilan. 2019. Digital video recorder dodgers – Sport-viewing habits in the face of changing media reality. *Time & Society* 28(4). 1319–1332.
Tamir, Ilan & Alina Bernstein. 2015. Do they even know the national anthem? Minorities in service of the flag – Israeli Arabs in the national football team. *Soccer & Society* 16(5/6). 745–764.

Tamir, Ilan & Yair Galily. 2010. Women's sports coverage in Israel: Perception versus reality. *International Journal of Sport Communication* 3(1). 92–112.
Tamir, Ilan, Yair Galily & Moran Yarchi. 2016. Here's hoping we get pummeled: Anti-nationalist trends among Israeli sports fans. *Journal of Sport & Social Issues* 40(1). 3–21.
Tamir, Ilan, Yair Galily & Moran Yarchi. 2017. Women, sport and the media: Key elements at play in the shaping of the practice of women in sports journalism in Israel. *The European Journal of Communication Research* 42(4). 441–464.
Van Dijk, Teun A. 2001. Multidisciplinary CDA: A plea for diversity. In Ruth Wodak & Michael Meyer (eds.), *Methods of critical discourse analysis*, 95–120. London: Sage.
Waiton, Stuart. 2018. Criminalizing songs and symbols in Scottish Football: How anti-sectarian legislation has created a new "sectarian" divide in Scotland. *Soccer & Society* 19(2). 169–184.
Wann, Daniel L. & Jeffrey D. James. 2019. *Sport fans: The psychology and social impact of fandom.* London: Routledge.
Wilbert-Lampen, Ute, David Leistner, Sonja Greven, Tilmann Pohl, Sebastian Sper, Christoph Völker, Denise Güthlin, Andrea Plasse, Andreas Kenz, Helmut Kuchnhoff & Gerhard Steinbeck. 2008. Cardiovascular events during World Cup soccer. *The New England Journal of Medicine* 358. 475–483.
Zandberg, Eyal. 2015. Ketchup is the Auschwitz of tomatoes: Humor and the collective memory of traumatic events. *Communication, Culture & Critique* 8(1). 108–123.

Toby Miller and Alfredo Sabbagh Fajardo

30 Colombian football: a national popular of pleasure, violence, and labor

Abstract: The quest for a national popular in Colombia that can articulate class interests with the wider population has been lengthy, winding, and incomplete. The country's *narcotraficantes*, *guerrilla*, and political class have all sought to "own" football for one purpose or another, whether to highlight their power, permit the sport relative autonomy from their struggles, or consolidate the idea of national institutions. Throughout, violence has proven a keynote in this trajectory; the media, coeval partners; and the players, exploited missionaries.

Keywords: national popular; football; Colombia; *narcocultura*; violence

1 Introduction

This chapter draws on various *doxa* from critical communication and area studies, such as cultural history, the political economy of the media, radical criminology, *violentología* [the study of violence], and the labor process.[1] We use these approaches reciprocally, to illuminate and be influenced by a particular instance: the lengthy, winding, and incomplete quest for a national popular in Colombia that can articulate class interests with the wider population through association football. At different times over the last seven decades, the country's *guerrilla*, oligarchs, *narcotraficantes*, and political classes have all sought to "own" football for one purpose or another, whether to highlight their power, permit the sport relative autonomy from their struggles, or consolidate the idea of national institutions. Throughout, violence has proven a keynote in this trajectory; the media, coeval partners; and the players, exploited missionaries (Soto 2017). The sport has been a crucible for expressing the manifold tensions of a country founded and governed through conflict in a more overt way even than the modern horrors of liberal imperialism and state socialism.

Polling data say football is of great interest to 94 percent of the Colombian population. Despite its profound associations with dominant masculinity, the sport is played by a third of adolescent girls and 85 percent of the country's minority Afrocolombian and indigenous populations (Plan decenal 2014: 13). When researchers asked a group of Colombian children to define the country, they replied "un partido de fútbol" [a football game] (quoted in Dávila and Londoño 2005: 135). Colombian attitudes are summed up by the local expression, "en la mesa no se habla de religión,

1 Thanks to the editor, Enrique Uribe Jongbloed, and Nicholas Woodward for their help.

https://doi.org/10.1515/9783110660883-030

ni de política, ni de fútbol" [one doesn't speak about religion, politics, or football over dinner] (quoted in Santos Gómez 2018). Football is that important.

In Gabriel García Márquez's (1996) ficto-critical account of victims of Colombian cocaine cartel kidnappings, *Noticia de un secuestro* [*News of a Kidnapping*], prisoners and their guards connect with one another through the sport, transcending the haze and violence that otherwise characterize their lives together. That story encapsulates our contention here: that football in Colombia has zigzagged between being a force for normalcy, for routine, for pleasure, versus a force of violence and inequality. It has been part of the search for a national popular, a key concept in critical communication studies and the sociology of sport, but of much wider applicability in Latin America.

The idea of a national popular is generally associated with Antonio Gramsci. He noted that the words for "national" and "popular" were similar in several languages, such was their affinity, and called for a closer alignment between everyday concerns and intellectual practice to reflect that linguistic kinship and animate socialism (2000: 366). Across Latin America, the concept has been adopted by left and right, journalists and academics, to describe a process whereby class interests are articulated with popular culture such that they appear to index the needs and hopes of the majority. This is achieved under the sign of nationalism (Massardo 1999).

The scholarly tradition populated by conservative ethno-nationalists argues that nations are constants across history, albeit changing their morphology with time and circumstance (Smith 2000). Such thinking is lapped up by the happy functionalists who lurk in the shadows of sports academia, albeit no longer as dominant as they once were, apart from some devoted denizens of kinesiology. For such folks, the nation is sustained through supposedly indelible ties: origin myths, languages, customs, races, and religions (Herder 2002).

Such "ties" are invented traditions (Hobsbawm and Ranger 2002). Far from being the outcome of abiding mythologies, the materiality and idea of the nation derived from the Industrial Revolution and imperialism, which brought places together that had not previously deemed themselves linked in any way. Relatively isolated, subsistence villages were transformed by the interdependence engendered by capitalist organizations, the commodification of everyday relations, and the sense of unity generated from nation-binding technologies and institutions, most notably print and public education (Gellner 1988). Since that time, states articulate nations as spirits-in-dwelling that give them legitimacy, but which they nonetheless reserve the right to name and monitor. Nations are coterminous with systems of government. Nations are said to be already-extant, authentic essences of polities and personhood, but in reality, they are manufactured.

Like most sovereign-states, Colombia's history has been contoured by the earth-shattering concatenation of political-economic events since the 18th century: the shift from absolute monarchy to parliamentary democracy; the social upheavals of imperialism, colonialism, slavery, war, postcolonialism, industrialization, urbanization, human rights, feminism, and climate change; and the expansion of global capitalism. That violence has been incessant.

Discussions with *campesinos* [peasants] about political violence in Colombia generally return to one point of origin: the clearance of the poor from land by murderous means, at the hands of state, *guerrilla*, and *para* alike (Molano 2001). That suggests the non-essentialist account of nationalism can best help us understand Colombia's history – i. e., in the light of the development and reproduction of national, regional, and global capitalism (Giraldo Durán and Álvarez de Castillo 2018).

Many social actors have sought to establish and control a national popular in their pursuit of hegemony over a country laden with profitable potential, given its educated middle class and natural resources. For a nation like Colombia, falling apart again and again and in danger of achieving the status of a "failed state" (Helman and Ratner 1992–93; but see Ross 2013), the obvious task has been to harness such allegiances and energies towards unity. Throughout its history, football in Colombia has moved from the periphery of that quest to its core and back again, as different forces have sought to harness, pervert, neglect, and resurrect the sport's role for hegemonic purposes.

Narco violence dominated the national game for perhaps two decades from the 1980s. That conjuncture changed when the *mafiosi* ended their provocatively overt control of football; right-wing *paramilitares* ceased formal operation; and a peace accord was signed with the principal *guerrilla*. The state and commerce governmentalized, televised, and commodified football to symbolize a new national popular. Its ties to violence were normalized within the conventional policy and rhetoric of national pride founded in alliances between governments and media. This propelled many players into a world of corruption and violence, with legal consequences for some (¿Por qué algunas 2019). Today, the struggle for a legitimate labor process marks the lives of professional footballers, along with the discreet control of numerous prominent teams by *mafiosi*.

Contemporary football is central to the nation's sense of itself, with local and international victories and losses taken as indices of success and failure. When Wittgenstein problematized the seemingly synonymous use of the word "good" in the formulations "a good football player" and "a good fellow," he was referring to the complexities that arise when words are redisposed to connote ethical value rather than empirical description (1965). Attention hegemonic forces! The efforts of functionalism and public policy to make sports resemble welfare interventions designed to pacify populations routinely perish on such rocky terrain, as we shall see.

2 A little history

It is often suggested that football gained its Colombian foothold in Barranquilla, the port city where many British sailors and businessmen alighted, traded, built – and played football (Ruiz Patiño 2017). The sport's mythic formal origin in Colombia is an 1892 match between teams from a military college. Organized by a US colonel, it was played in front of President Miguel Antonio José Zolio Cayetano Andrés Avelino de las Mercedes Caro Tobar and covered by the press. The participants continued regular matches until the Thousand Days War (1899–1902) (Santos Molano 2016).

Colombian football's links to violence derive from the 20th-century diffusion of football and the railway. They connected residents of the sovereign-state to one another and the capitalist world economy. These journeys into modernity were equally journeys into violence, via attempts to impose centralized authority on peripheral regions, both culturally and economically (Quitián Roldán and Urrea Beltrán 2016a).

Ties between violence and football were therefore present from the beginning. Between the 1900s and 1940, the sport emerged from the governmental and commercial elite to become a national pastime. Its stages shifted from polo, golf, and gun clubs to unpaved streets, aided by radio coverage of matches and associated gossip. Football democratized, even as the state's biopolitical regime institutionalized physical education in schools (Quitián Roldán 2013; Ruiz Patiño 2017). Bio-power brought "life and its mechanisms into the realm of explicit calculations," making "knowledge-power an agent of transformation of human life." Bodies were identified with politics. Managing them equated to running the country, with "the life of the species ... wagered on its own political strategies." Keeping populations fit for purpose involved assaying them and encouraging recreational activity (Foucault 1991: 97, 92–95 and 1984: 143). Football's developing strength as a pastime therefore derived from educational institutions and other elements of civil society dedicated to the idea of recreation as a means of control, preparing young men to be disciplined followers rather than dissolute rebels. This in turn drew approbation and support from governments (Torres Velasco 2019).

But the state's ability to harness football as part of a national popular was limited. It did not withstand the century to come, in terms of administration, finance, or legality. In addition, the relative isolation of the country's distinct climatic regions enabled a racialized discourse of essentialism that tied the power-laden but largely immobile sports of baseball and boxing to the Caribbean and the intense labor of cycling and running to the interior (Fernández L'Hoeste 2015).

The early years of *La Violencia* (the 1946–66 civil war between Liberals and Conservatives, i. e., between Protestants and Catholics, new and old money) were surprisingly propitious for the sport; Colombian football mythologizes 1949–54 as its *El Dorado*. That period saw the formation of federations, codification of laws, professionalization, and the capacity to share scores and highlights via the spread of telex, telephone, and radio. Clubs decided to go beyond the restricted wage norms of world football and become an outlier. *El Dorado* marked the sport's insertion into the emergent New International Division of Cultural Labor (NICL) through the offer of unprecedented salaries (Miller 2018) – albeit without the payment of transfer fees, and the nation's subsequent exile from international football as punishment. Perhaps a thousand players came to the Colombian league from Britain, Italy, Yugoslavia, Hungary, Perú, Paraguay, Argentina, Costa Rica, and Uruguay. One of football's greatest, Alfredo Stéfano Di Stéfano Laulhé, appeared with Bogotá's Azul y Blanco Millonarios Fútbol Club SA for four years (Quitián Roldán and Urrea Beltrán 2016a; Santos Molano 2016). This was globalization of the labor process *avant la lettre*.

Amongst this cornucopia of cosmopolitan talent, football was also popularly celebrated by the media for its political neutrality amidst the polarization of *La Violencia*. It became a core part of newspaper reportage, which had largely ignored it until then. Radio coverage during *El Dorado* and later bipartisan politics helped install football as the national popular between *La Violencia* and the mid-1970s, independently of governments. The process took dialectical form: the sport was the property and design of élites seeking incorporation of the population into their projects through carnival, expressivity, and football's myth of upward mobility (Quitián Roldán and Urrea Beltrán 2016a, 2016b; Santos Molano 2016; Jaramillo Racines 2011).

El Dorado's NICL drew to a close when European leagues began their recovery from the War and scouted talent that had gone overseas; other South American leagues entered the transfer market; and Colombia sought reintegration into the world game (Santos Molano 2016; Fernández L'Hoeste 2015). Meanwhile, the country's new military *junta* adopted a modernizing agenda marked by major infrastructural investments, notably in football stadia. One of these, in Ibagué, was named after *coup* leader Gustavo Rojas Pinilla; another, in Pasto, for the day he seized power. When a different *junta* took control in 1957, the former was renamed "La Libertad" [Freedom] and the latter "10 de mayo" [May 10], for the day Rojas Pinilla left office (Aguilera Peña 1999).

But despite these narcissistic nation-building curios, football was more a matter of regional than national identity, as pros and reporters alike sought legitimacy in the eyes of potential local spectators and readers (Bolívar-Ramírez 2018). And other, pressing issues were brewing. The *Violencia*, and subsequent Cold War bipartisan opposition to the left by Liberals and Conservatives, eventually gave way to the *guerrilla* and *narcos*. Football merged with contraband.

3 Narcofútbol

Since the 1980s, Colombian society has been characterized by putatively progressive *guerrilla* movements, putatively unofficial right-wing *paramilitares*, and putatively populist *narcotraficantes/mafiosi*. At different times they held sway over rural and urban terrain; ran institutions of civil society; harvested, refined, distributed, and sold recreational drugs; were ruthless and violent kidnappers and executioners; corrupted state officials; and trumpeted inconspicuous battle fatigues and conspicuous consumption respectively as signs of legitimacy and triumph.

Narco has become the prefix to much of contemporary Colombian life – narcotrafficking, narco war, narco-state, *narcocultura* (Lezcano 2018). In the 1980s and 90s, many football clubs were dominated by these *mafiosi*, whose imported guns and exported drugs made them both wealthy and dangerous. Their involvement in football was far from clandestine; it was a bizarre form of private rule through showy violence, and the sport afforded them *cachet* with the popular classes. Behind the scenes, football was also a laundering facility for *narcotraficante* cash. Governmental audits were limited and the potential for overstatement of attendance figures immense, so the *narcos* used clubs to secret and cleanse money, to make it appear as though their wealth derived from ticket sales or player transfers. The process emerged into the international media spotlight in 1985 when the US extradited Hernán Botero Moreno, President of Medellín's El Atlético Nacional SA, for wire fraud (Sabbagh Fajardo and Miller, 2017).

The same year, El Movimiento 19 de Abril o M-19 [the 19th of April Movement, or M-19, named after the date of a 1974 electoral fraud] attacked the Palacio de Justicia de Colombia [Palace of Colombian Justice]. Funded by the *narcos* to intimidate the judiciary, the *guerrilla* took hundreds of hostages, from Supreme Court judges to clerks, a third of whom died in the ensuing firefight. A match was scheduled nearby between Millonarios and Club Unión Magdalena SA. Seeking to distract the public, the government mandated that it proceed and be televised (McCausland Sojo 2012; Noemí Sanín 2013).

It is estimated that 80 percent of shares in the nation's leading teams in 1997 were held by *narcos*, with many lesser sides involved in trafficking. Juan José Bellini, chief of the Federación Colombiana de Fútbol (COLFUTBOL) from 1992 to 1995 and President of América de Cali, was convicted of money laundering (Fernández L'Hoeste 2015). Over the two decades since, brazen *nouveau riche* drug traffickers have retreated from football, and public life in general, in the face of sustained Colombian and US interdiction. *Narcos* continue their involvement in the sport, but largely as money launderers – acting clandestinely, quietly, under the radar. *Narcofútbol* has become strictly business, rather than a symbolic show of power aimed at compromising governmental legitimacy and seizing the national popular. And there is a great deal to hide – whereas Colombian coffee sells in the US for four times the cost of production, the profits from cocaine are a hundredfold (Bergman 2018: 27).

Since 1995, the US Treasury's Office of Foreign Assets Control has promulgated a *Specially designated nationals and blocked persons list* (2019). Known colloquially in Latin America as the "*Lista* Clinton," it is a set of names associated with international narcotrafficking. As at early 2019, the *Lista* was 1,261 pages long (Specially designated 2020). Colombian football clubs and proprietors still figure prominently. Their assets are blocked, and US citizens, residents, and businesses are usually outlawed from dealing with them (Quitián Roldán 2013).

In 2014, the US Treasury nominated La Oficina de Envigado [The Envigado Office] as a major trafficker, and El Envigado Fútbol Club and its owner, Juan Pablo Upegui Gallego, as launderers. The club sold James David Rodríguez Rubio to Real Madrid to fund the cost of defending itself. A US indictment of numerous football administrators across the Americas identified Luis Erberto Bedoya Giraldo, a senior office-holder with Confederacíon SudAmericana de Fútbol [South American Football Confederation] (CONMEBOL) and President of COLFUTBOL, as taking bribes to deliver TV and marketing rights. He pled guilty to wire-fraud conspiracy and racketeering and received a life ban from world football (United States of America against various 2015; Soto 2017; Homewood 2016). Meanwhile, twenty years after Bellini's disgrace, he remained involved in player transfers. And when América de Cali returned to the first division for the first time in five years in 2016, Miami-based *Caleños* created banners thanking "Don" Miguel Ángel Rodríguez Orejuela, once joint leader of the Cali cartel, long after he had been imprisoned in the US. On his birthday in 2019, Cali's *hinchas* [fans] hoisted a massive banner that read "¡Siempre gracias por todo #DonMiguel, no nos olvidamos de la historia ni la gloria!" [Eternal thanks to #DonMiguel, we'll never forget the history or the glory] (Allen 2015; Lezcano 2018; El desafortunado 2019).

That said, Colombian clubs have come to rely on youth academies and sponsorship as well as contraband in search of ongoing, cross-generational success (MacKenna 2016). The nation's most famous player, Carlos Alberto Valderrama Palacio ("El Pibe") [The Kid] proposed a football match with the *Fuerzas Armadas Revolucionarias de Colombia* (the FARC) as part of the peace process in 2013. The *guerrilla* promoted themselves as preparing for peace by playing football, supporting the national team, and renewing ties to clubs they had followed prior to self-exile. They issued a *communiqué* stressing that such patriotic fervor united the country in the very way needed for a peaceful future (Farc 2014).

In addition, the state re-emerged into the narcissistic glow of football's floodlights as a means of generating a national popular. In 2009, the government established a Comisión Nacional para la Seguridad, Comodidad y Convivencia en el Fútbol [National Commission for Safety, Comfort, and Togetherness in Football]. It forwards the sport's purported character-building qualities of solidarity, health, social cohesion, and pleasure in diverting young people from violence via a ten-year plan tethering football to peace (2014: 17), as a source of integration (Centro Nacional de Consultoría 2014).

Juan Manuel Santos Calderón's government dispatched the national team to the 2014 men's World Cup with the good wishes of all, as a sign of renewed nationhood (Uribe Aramburo and Castaño Pérez 2014; Watson 2018). Its advertising campaign interpellated the FARC as patriotic fans who were welcome to root for the national team, right alongside the military in helicopters, coffee growers in fields, and supporters at grounds: "Colombia le está guardando el puesto" [Colombia is saving a seat for you]. Santos said that Colombians could bask in peace and prosperity if they worked together "como la Seleccion Colombia – ¡UNIDOS POR UN PAÍS!" [like the national team – UNITED AS ONE COUNTRY!] (Alocución 2014). Football was "el máximo símbolo de la unidad nacional" [our greatest symbol of national unity] (Palabras 2014).

During the Finals, Comunidades con Paz [Communities for Peace], the peak body representing over a hundred groups of Afrodescendant, indigenous, and peasant Colombians, sent an open letter to the team's emergent star, James. It was a poetic paean to football as a potential exemplar of individual beauty and expression harmonized with solidarity, work, discipline, and commitment – a model for what the organization hoped the nation could become via a truly inclusive democratic urge that valued all forms and sources of life, and eschewed violence in ways that were akin to his own public displays of humility in the face of spectacular success (Carta abierta 2014).

But militaristic connotations of football were soon to the fore as part of the emergent national popular. The national TV network RCN (originally Radio Cadena Nacional [National Radio Network]) won non-broadcast rights to the 2016 Copa América, a competition between national teams from the region, over its duopolistic rival Caracol (Cadena Radial Colombiana [Colombian Radio Network]). They shared television coverage. RCN and the Colombian military collaborated on commercials redolent with nationalism and militarism. Promotions used the slogan "Himno Copa América Centenario 2016 #YoCreo" [Copa América Centenary Anthem 2016 #IBelieve]. The navy showcased women and men playing instruments and singing, and a ship with a banner alongside the flag. The presidential guard was adorned as per Colombia's historic mimicry of Prussian uniforms. For a helicopter and parachute commercial, soldiers were draped in the flag. And the military's YouTube channel showed three camouflaged soldiers intoning best wishes to the team (Sabbagh Fajardo and Miller 2017).

This imagery was familiar to viewers. The local Cervecería Bavaria [Bavarian Brewery] was connected to the national team via a marketing campaign designed with corrupt COLFUTBOL official Luis Erberto Bedoya Giraldo (see Sabbagh Fajardo and Miller 2017), and RCN's ownership controls Postobón, which sponsors the professional leagues. It calls itself "¡El sabor del fútbol!" [The flavor of football] and constructs athletes as warriors (Sabbagh Fajardo and Miller 2017). Private and public interests aligned, brokered through identification with the players to essay a national popular. The idea was to identify RCN, Postobón, and the military with Radamel Falcao García Zárate, James, and their compatriots. That association with the armed forces points to the need to consider the sport's links to violence of various kinds: state, *narco*, *guerrilla*, and *hincha*.

4 Violence

The Colombian national team's great triumph, defeating Argentina 5–0 away in a 1993 qualifying match for the men's World Cup, continues to be commemorated as an epochal moment of national pride. But 76 people died and over nine hundred were wounded in the aftermath. And while the team awaited its first game of the 1994 Finals, cartel heads sought and obtained reassurances from its manager that his selections would not be affected by the *Limpieza del Fútbol Colombiano* [Clean Up Colombian Football] movement (which in any event was rumored to be a front for disaffected gamblers). Andrés Escobar Saldarriaga was murdered after his own goal consigned Colombia to defeat against the US – an index of how much the sport meant to people and the cheapness of life. His demise is celebrated today in a chant sung by Millonarios fans: "Andrés Escobar, paisa hijueputa no existes más" [Andrés Escobar, Medellín motherfucker, you don't exist] (quoted in Vélez-Maya and Arboleda-Ariza 2016). In 1996, national team player Felipe Pérez Urrea was killed for his cartel associations.

CONMEBOL chose Colombia to host the 2001 Copa. Conflicts between the government and the FARC prior to the event led to urgent discussions between national federations over public safety. When the FARC kidnapped Hernán Mejía Campuzano, COLFUTBOL's Vice-President, CONMEBOL decided to postpone the Copa until the following year in Brazil. Then the *guerrilla* freed him. President Andrés Pastrana Arango was under pressure from television networks and sponsors and hoped to tie sports to his image in the wake of unpopular deals with the FARC. The Copa proceeded with Colombia as host – and the blessing of the *guerrilla* (Las FARC 2013; Fridman Stalnicovitz 2016; Watson 2018). The promotional geniuses who had nominated the event as *La Copa de la Paz* [the Peace Cup] may have been a tad embarrassed (Celis Hernández 2017).

The country's long history of incipient and brazen violence also has homologies in players' and spectators' conduct, regardless of the conjuncture. Functionalist claims for sport – that it produces a fitter population, better able to work, and a more pacific one, capable of expressing powerful feelings in law-abiding ways – are brought into question by violence on and off the pitch (Salinas Arango 2018). Cross-cultural research indicates that more red- and yellow-card sanctions are issued to players for violent conduct in countries with high levels of violence in general. This applies to Colombians and Israelis above other nationalities, in both domestic and foreign leagues (Orrego Ramírez, Velásquez Restrepo, and Uribe-Lopera 2010; Miguel, Saiegh, and Satyanath 2011).

In Colombia, as elsewhere, women have largely been excluded from this discourse of vibrancy, nationalism, and disorder, despite football's embeddedness in the media as the national pastime and symbol of a virile and skilful unity – and women's fascination for the sport (Orrego Ramírez, Velásquez Restrepo, and Uribe-Lopera 2010; Vélez 2001). This is in keeping with generations of powerful taboos, leavened only recently by a development discourse that stresses physical culture as a route to safety, pleasure – and fewer teen pregnancies – that still shows traces of *macho* culture (Oxford and Spaaij 2019; Oxford 2019). The women's national team has struggled in the face of minimal resources but came to be known as "nuestras guerreras" [our fighters] at the 2015 women's World Cup Finals and the Panamerican games (Watson 2018: 608).

There are disturbing correlations between football fandom and domestic assault: during the 2014 and 2018 men's World Cup Finals, the rate of such attacks rose by 38 and 25 percent respectively during matches involving Colombia. The figure was 50 percent for the 2015 Copa América (Salazar 2018). The men's team has spoken out against gendered violence (Selección 2014), but one of their number, Pablo Estifer Armero, was arrested in 2016 for sexual assault. When the prominent sports journalist Andrea María Guerrero Quintero criticized his selection the following year, she received numerous death threats (Salazar 2018).

Colombia's *barras bravas* [hooligans], who follow teams in an organized presence inside and outside stadia, include many violent men characterized by bellicose frames of mind; use of alcohol, marijuana, and cocaine before, during, and after matches; minimal education; maximal alienation; domestic violence; and racist stadium chants and taunts. Schools are recruitment and training grounds for violent *hinchas* – ironic, given their biopolitical role in disseminating the sport. Many fans have spent time with the *paramilitares* and *narcos*; membership of such groups allows them to establish identities within stadia and feel proudly marked as "same" versus "other. The scholarly literature is split between critiques of this hyper-masculinity and its romanticization as carnivalesque proletarian resistance to middle-class, governmental, and corporate norms (Bermúdez-Aponte et al. 2019; Restrepo Escobar 2015; Uribe Aramburo and Castaño Pérez 2014; Castillo Murillejo and Reyes 2013; Galeano et al. 2015; Clavijo Poveda 2004; Uribe Aramburo 2018; Villanueva Bustos 2013; Castro Lozano 2013, 2019; López-Quintero and Neumark 2012).

To address this problem, the government issued Decreto [Decree] 1007 in 2012, establishing a "Statute of the Football Fan in Colombia." It included the expression "barrismo social" [pro-social fandom] to refer to "acciones encaminadas a redimensionar las formas de expresión y las prácticas de los integrantes de las barras de fútbol que inciden negativamente en los ámbitos individual, comunitario y colectivo, y de potenciar los aspectos positivos que de la esencia del barrismo deben rescatarse" [actions aimed at reforming the expressive styles and practices of some football fans that negatively affect individual, community, and collective spheres, and to enhance the positive aspects of fandom]. Projects of re-socialization, resignification, and new identities and social bonds have been developed, including art projects (Acevedo 2017); mayors have convened dialogues about the issue (Tafur Mangada 2016); and supporters participated in community dining and food donation programs during the Covid-19 pandemic (Barras del fútbol 2020). Although the "barra brava" discourse continues to prevail in the social imaginary, these projects have positively influenced both conduct inside stadia and communities that are adversely affected (Lombana 2020). That said, it would be all too easy to ignore the ongoing violence. When Asociación Deportivo Cali failed to make the playoffs in 2018, a player was shot at; after Club Deportivo Popular Junior FC SA, the Barranquilla team, won a match that year, supporters were bombed as they caroused in a Córdoba night club (Colombian Player 2018; 13 Wounded 2018). That is neither carnivalesque nor functional. Not really.

5 The labor process

What does the newly renovated national popular – and ongoing violence – imply for the workers who make football happen? Players and technical staff in Colombian football's labor process have historically suffered major problems with job stability, working conditions, the right to organize, participation in governance, access to the money flowing from proprietary media sales, and the violence outlined above.

The Asociación Colombiana de Futbolistas Profesionales [Colombian Association of Professional Soccer Players] (ACOLFUTPRO) was created in 2005 to seek better working conditions for its members and secure a percentage of television rights in negotiations with the División Mayor del Fútbol Colombiano [First Division of Colombian Football] (DIMAYOR). When nothing happened, ACOLFUTPRO members voted to strike. The strike failed because only América of Cali complied with the decision. ACOLFUTPRO executives denounced pressures and threats from bosses, such as vetoing future jobs for protest leaders (El último 2019).

Then and now, the players' standing was precarious. DIMAYOR argues that labor issues must be directly addressed with teams as employers, many of whom argue that football players have no right to industrial action. In 2019, ACOLFUTPRO asked DIMAYOR to discuss these topics again, along with consolidating the women's league and revising the tournament calendar. The Colombian professional soccer calendar is one of the most extensive in the world, to the point of having to play matches on FIFA dates and coinciding with world championships. In 2018, Junior played seventy matches, a figure well above international standards (Cadena 2018). A general strike was called and the Ministry of Labor commenced mediation (Reunion de 2019).

Players have also staged performances to make their point through spectacle. These protests have included "sitting" or making only light touches of the ball during the first minute of matches. Such images have been "banned" from broadcasts on WiN (the official league network) and RCN. That generated negative public reaction towards such censorship and encouraged alternative-media coverage (Win y Dimayor 2019; Hablan de veto 2019).

Television contracts and the creation of a premium pay channel have provoked corporate discussion with DIMAYOR over sharing revenue. In 2016, a group of powerful teams requested changes to the rights system, based on audience and investment criteria. That didn't happen, because "smaller" clubs – the majority – were not supportive. It nearly led to a split (La disputa 2016) of the kind often threatened in

Europe's major leagues. In 2018, new tournament regulations prevented teams from participating in international tournaments, which harmed the "bigger" teams (Liga aguila 2019). The players were largely excluded from such discussions.

The process typifies Colombia's tightly knit elite of sports, the media, and politics. The current president of DIMAYOR is Jorge Enrique Vélez, a lawyer who is close to the Radical Change party, which is led by former presidential candidate Germán Vargas Lleras. The same party includes Fuad Char Abdala, owner of Junior, former Governor of the Atlantic province, and father of Alejandro Char, twice mayor of Barranquilla. Despite this apparent political consanguinity, Junior seeks a new formula for distributing profits from television rights (Ruiz Rico 2019). Yet even when the good old boys disagree, their interests consistently militate against a fair labor process – one in which the "talent" benefits from TV deals and a share in decision-making. They collude to disenfranchise workers, regardless of their own intra-class disputes.

6 Conclusion

Colombia's problems arose before the nation itself did, with the horror of imperial dispossession and slavery. They concatenated with the formation under independence of a powerful oligarchy, which continues to this day: obsessed with the rule of law and dependent for its *origins* on stolen lands worked by slaves, and for its *continuation* on clientelism and control of the formal economy and politics.

Colombian football has long attracted those interested in hegemonic display – spectacle with a message rather than for its own sake – as well as shady operators who occupy the informal economy's dark shadows. It is a flashy means of displaying wealth, power, and sovereignty, but equally a way of obscuring the flow of illicit money behind the sport's simultaneously folkloric and glamorous status, as the coevally physiocratic property of players and fans and the capitalistic property of owners.

The conjuncture of the 1980s and 90s overdetermined football. It became a zone of gangster killings, gangster "welfare," and gangster popular culture. Violence was everywhere, from the intimidation of referees to the slaughter of opponents. But the sense of a spectacular sporting challenge to government has passed. Today, football continues its complex movement between pacifying, incarnating, attracting, and repelling violence, embodying the distinction between a world of domination, scientific management, and an artificially generated dislike of others, versus a world of collaboration, spontaneity, and fellowship. The untrammeled ecstasy of a lengthy passing movement or dribble – a perfectly material, utopian, snatched alternative to this seemingly most capitalistic of metaphors – stands against banal competitiveness and disciplinary obsessions.

Hence the paradox at the heart of sports, its simultaneously transcendent and imprisoning qualities and astonishing capacity to allegorize. América Larraín overcame her intense antipathy to football through its associations with dance, in terms of the body encapsulating identity – and how Colombia's national team celebrates on the pitch (2015). There is great potential there, if only it could be harnessed towards progressive purposes; beyond hyper-masculinity and *narco* laundries.

Football must remove the powerful *mafiosi* who still populate it, and end money laundering. Clubs must insist on safe seating and transportation for women and children, prohibit hateful speech, and expel for life anyone indulging in linguistic or physical violence. The cosmic failure of the Colombian oligarchy to produce a substantive and inclusive national popular has seen violence fill that gap, as the seeming essence of the nation and its people. A new national popular must emerge, comprised of real reach, depth, and democracy. It must speak to the country's actual demography – and respect the labor and image rights of football's real talents. It remains to be seen whether the struggle for legitimacy via football is won by the state, corporations, or social movements, such as minorities, players, and women.

References

13 wounded in Colombian nightclub explosion. 2018. *AZERTAC*, 17 December. https://azertag.az/en/xeber/13_Wounded_in_Colombia_Nightclub_Explosion-1225053 (18 November 2020).

Acevedo, María F. 2017. De las barras bravas al barrismo social. *15*, 9 June. https://www.periodico15.com/de-las-barras-bravas-al-barrismo-social/ (18 November 2020).

Aguilera Peña, Mario. 1999. Caida de Rojas Pinilla: 10 de mayo de 1957. *Credencial Historia* 117. https://www.banrepcultural.org/biblioteca-virtual/credencial-historia/numero-117/caida-de-rojas-pinilla-10-de-mayo-de-1957 (18 November 2020).

Allen, Jamie. 2015. Pablo Escobar and the narco-fútbol years. *These Football Times*, 30 May. http://thesefootballtimes.co/2015/05/30/pablo-escobar-narco-futbol/ (18 November 2020).

Alocución del Presidente Juan Manuel Santos de agradecimiento a la Selección Colombia de Fútbol. 2014, 5 July. http://wsp.presidencia.gov.co/Prensa/2014/Julio/Paginas/20140705_04-Palabras-Alocucion-Presidente-Santos-agradecimiento-la-Seleccion-Colombia-Futbol.aspx (18 November 2020).

Barras del fútbol colombiano donan mercados durante la cuarentena. 2020. *El Espectador*, 16 April. https://www.elespectador.com/deportes/futbol-colombiano/barras-del-futbol-colombiano-donan-mercados-durante-la-cuarentena-articulo-914924 (18 November 2020).

Bergman, Marcelo. 2018. *Illegal drugs, drug trafficking and violence in Latin America*. Cham, Switzerland: Springer.

Bermúdez-Aponte, Jose Javier, John A. Buitrago-Media, Bibiana Ávila-Martinez & Abel J. Ortiz-Mora. 2019. *Barras bravas*: Youth violence in football crowds at school. *International Education Studies* 12(5). 17–27.

Bolívar-Ramírez, Ingrid J. 2018. Antioquia's regional narratives and the challenges of professional football in Medellín during the 1950s and 1960s. *Bulletin of Latin American Research* 37(5). 582–597.

Cadena, Joshua Mattar. 2018. El maratón de partidos de Junior en el 2018. *Marca Claro*, 2 December. http://co.marca.com/claro/futbol/junio-barranquilla/2018/12/02/5c030c7be2704e68648b45b2.html (18 November 2020).

Carta abierta a James Rodríguez: Construyamos más esperanza, sumemos voluntades. 2014. Comunidades con Paz, 30 June. https://comunidadesconpaz.wordpress.com/2014/07/01/carta-abierta-a-james-rodriguez-construyamos-mas-esperanza-sumemos-voluntades/ (18 November 2020).

Castillo Murillejo, Norma Constanza & Nelson Enrique Rivera Reyes. 2013. TICS, comunicación humana y violencia de género contra niños y adolescents víctimas de la explotación sexual comercial: Los casos de Bogotá y Cartagena, Colombia. *Actas – V Congreso Internacional Latina de Comunicación Social – V CILCS*, December. http://www.revistalatinacs.org/13SLCS/2013_actas/171_Castillo.pdf (18 November 2020).

Castro Lozano, John A. 2013. El carnaval y el combate hacen el aguante en una barra brava. *Revista Colombiana de Sociología* 36(1). 77–92.

Castro Lozano, John A. 2019. De las rivalidades a la violencia del fútbol en Colombia. *Revista Brasileira de Ciências do Esporte* 41(1). 109–115.

Celis Hernández, Marlon S. 2017. Nación, fútbol e imagen publicitaria: Los significados de la Copa América del 2001 en Colombia. *Revista de Ciencias Sociales* 158. 61–83.

Centro Nacional de Consultoría. 2014. *El poder del fútbol*. Bogotá: Ministerio del Interior.

Clavijo Poveda, Jairo. 2004. Estudio de barras de fútbol de Bogotá: Los Comandos azules. *Universidad Humanística* 31(58). 43–59.

Colombian player survives shooting attack after match. 2018. *Reuters*, 12 November. https://uk.reuters.com/article/uk-soccer-colombia/colombian-player-survives-shooting-attack-after-match-idUKKCN1NH2KY (18 November 2020).

Dávila, Andrés & Catalina Londoño. 2005. La nación bajo un uniforme: Fútbol e identidad nacional en Colombia, 1985–2000. In Pablo Alabarces (ed.), *Futbologías: Fútbol, identidad y violencia en América Latina*, 135–158. Buenos Aires: Consejo Latinoamericano de Ciencias Sociales.

Decreto 1007 de 2012 por el cual sé expide el Estatuto del Aficionado al Fútbol en Colombia. 2012. *Ministerio del Interior*, 16 May. https://www.icbf.gov.co/cargues/avance/docs/decreto_1007_2012.htm#:~:text=Derecho%20del%20Bienestar%20Familiar%20%5BDECRETO_1007_2012%5D&text=Por%20el%20cual%20se%20expide,Aficionado%20al%20F%C3%BAtbol%20en%20Colombia.&text=Que%20en%20el%20citado%20Acuerdo,de%20j%C3 %B3venes%2C%20convivencia%20y%20f%C3 %BAtbol (18 November 2020).

El desafortunado trino de barra brava del América. 2019. *Kien y Ke*, 15 August. https://www.kienyke.com/radark/baron-rojo-sur-mensaje-twitter-miguel-angel-rodriguez-orejuela (18 November 2020).

El último antecedente de un intento de paro en el fútbol colombiano. 2019. *El Tiempo*, 16 October. https://www.eltiempo.com/deportes/futbol-colombiano/cuando-fue-el-ultimo-intento-de-paro-en-el-futbol-colombiano-423844 (18 November 2020).

Farc enviaron mensaje de apoyo a los jugadores de la Selección Colombia. 2014. *El País*, 11 June. https://www.elpais.com.co/judicial/farc-enviaron-mensaje-de-apoyo-a-los-jugadores-de-la-seleccion-colombia.html (18 November 2020).

Fernández L'Hoeste, Héctor. 2015. Race, sports, and regionalism in the construction of Colombian nationalism. In Héctor Fernández L'Hoeste, Robert McKee Irwin & Juan Poblete (eds.), *Sports and nationalism in Latin/o America*, 85–104. New York: Palgrave Macmillan.

Foucault, Michel. 1984. *The history of sexuality: An introduction* (trans. Robert Hurley). Harmondsworth: Penguin.

Foucault, Michel. 1991. Governmentality. In Graham Burchell, Colin Gordon & Peter Miller (eds.), *The Foucault effect: Studies in governmentality*, 87–104. London: Harvester Wheatsheaf.

Fridman Stalnicovitz, Dan. 2016. La Copa América incompleta. *Univision*, 5 June. http://www.univision.com/deportes/futbol/copa-america-centenario-2016/la-copa-america-incompleta-colombia-2001-sufrimiento-dudas-y-jubilo-al-final (18 November 2020).

Galeano, Edgar Antonio, Bettsy T. Cruz Ortiz, Jeffrey S. Cruz Jiménez, Edward F. Escovar Álvarez, Andrés S. Gómez Gómez, Juan D. Nieto Manrique & Luisa F. Rodríguez Lesmes. 2015. Barras bravas: ¿Realización desde la marginalidad y las falencias académicas? *Revista Papeles* 7(14). 31–41.

García Márquez, Gabriel. 1996. *Noticia de un secuestro*. Mexico City: Editorial Diana.

Gellner, Ernest. 1988. *Plough, sword and book: The structure of human history*. Chicago: University of Chicago Press.

Giraldo Durán, Angélica & Adrian G. Álvarez de Castillo. 2018. Violencia y paz en Colombia: Una mirada desde la reproducción del capital en América Latina. *Interdisciplina* 6(15). 61–81.

Gramsci, Antonio. 2000. *The Antonio Gramsci reader: Selected writings 1916–1935* (ed. David Forgacs). New York: New York University Press.

Hablan de veto o censura para transmitir protestas de jugadores del fpc. 2019. *Comutricolor*, 7 October. https://comutricolor.com/futbol-colombiano/hablan-de-veto-o-censura-para-transmitir-protestas-de-jugadores-del-fpc/ (18 November 2020).

Helman, Gerald B. & Steven R. Ratner. 1992–93. Saving failed states. *Foreign Policy* 89. 3–20.

Herder, Johann Gottfried von. 2002. *Philosophical writings* (trans. and ed. Michael N. Forster). Cambridge: Cambridge University Press.

Hobsbawm, Eric & Terence Ranger (eds.). 2002. *La invención de la tradición* (trans. Ornar Rodríguez). Barcelona: Editorial Crítica.

Homewood, Brian. 2016. Life bans for ex-South America FA duo Jadue, Bedoya. *Reuters*, 6 May. http://www.reuters.com/article/us-fifa-chile-ban-idUSKCN0XX0ZF (18 November 2020).

Jaramillo Racines, Rafael. 2011. El fútbol de el Dorado: El punto de inflexión que marcó la rápida evolución del "amateurismo" al "profesionalismo." *Curitiba: Revista de Asociación Latinoamericana de Estudios Socioculturales del Deporte* 1(1). 111–128.

La disputa en la dimayor por los derechos de television. 2016. *Semana*, 30 September. https://pruebas.semana.com/deportes/articulo/la-disputa-en-la-dimayor-por-los-derechos-de-television/496037 (18 November 2020).

Larraín, América. 2015. Bailar fútbol: Reflexiones sobre el cuerpo y la nación en Colombia. *Boletín de Antropología* 30(50). 191–207.

Las FARC querían ver la Copa América del 2001. 2013. *El Espectador*, 14 June. http://www.elespectador.com/deportes/futbolcolombiano/farc-querian-ver-copa-america-2001-nicolas-leoz-articulo-427844 (18 November 2020).

Lezcano, Arturo. 2018. Historias del narcofútbol. *Jot Down*, January. https://www.jotdown.es/2018/01/historias-del-narcofutbol/ (18 November 2020).

Liga aguila hoy decisiones para el campeonato 2020. 2019. *Futbolred*, 31 October. https://www.futbolred.com/futbol-colombiano/liga-aguila/liga-aguila-hoy-decisiones-para-el-campeonato-2020-108860 (18 November 2020).

Lombana, Catalina. 2020. Las barras de los clubes en Colombia se unen por un fútbol en paz. *Marca*, 13 February. https://co.marca.com/claro/futbol/liga/2019/02/13/5c647df6ca4741ea168b45cf.html (18 November 2020).

López-Quintero, Catalina & Yehuda Neumark. 2012. Membresía a barras bravas y su influencia en el uso de drogas. *Revista Peruana de Medicina Experimental y Salud Publica* 29(1). 21–27.

MacKenna, Ewan. 2016. Narco-football is dead: Celebrating a Colombia reborn. *Bleacher Report*, 1 June. http://bleacherreport.com/articles/2642116-narco-football-is-dead-celebrating-a-colombia-reborn.

Massardo, Jaime. 1999. La recepción de Gramsci en América Latina: Cuestiones de orden teórico y político. *International Gramsci Society Newsletter*, March. http://www.internationalgramsci-society.org/igsn/articles/a09_s3.shtml (18 November 2020).

McCausland Sojo, Ernesto. 2012. El partido que no distrajo ni a los hinchas. *El Heraldo* January 31. http://www.elheraldo.co/galeria-fotos/55303/noticias/nacional/el-partido-que-no-distrajo-ni-a-los-hinchas-55303 (18 November 2020).

Miguel, Edward, Sebastian M. Saiegh & Shanker Satyanath. 2011. Civil war exposure and violence. *Economics & Politics* 23(1). 59–73.

Miller, Toby. 2018. *Él trabajo cultural*. Barcelona: Editorial Gedisa.

Molano, Alfredo. 2001. *Desterrados: Crónicas del desarraigo*. Bogotá: El Áncora Editores.

Noemí Sanín: Renuncia la embajadora de Los Millonarios. 2013. *Semana*, 3 September. http://www.semana.com/nacion/articulo/noemi-sanin-renuncia-embajadora-los-millonarios/336309-3 (18 November 2020).

Orrego Ramírez, Lina M., Jorge I. Velásquez Restrepo, & Lucas Uribe-Lopera. 2010. Caracterización psicosocial del futbolista perteneciente a la categoría primera "A" del Fútbol Professional Colombiano. *Pensando Psicología* 6(10). 11–21.

Oxford, Sarah. 2019. "You look like a machito!": A decolonial analysis of the social in/exclusion of female participants in a Colombian sport for development and peace organization. *Sport in Society* 22(6). 1025–1042.

Oxford, Sarah & Ramón Spaaij. 2019. Gender relations and sport for development in Colombia: A decolonial feminist analysis. *Leisure Sciences* 41(1–2). 54–71.

Palabras del Presidente Juan Manuel Santos en la entrega del Pabellón Nacional a la Selección Colombia. 2014. *Presidencia de la República – Colombia, from YouTube*, 23 May. https://www.youtube.com/watch?v=mq-lW3EqLGs (18 November 2020).

Plan decenal de seguridad, comodidad y convivencia en el fútbol 2014–2024. 2014. Comisión Nacional de Seguridad, Comodidad y Convivencia en el Fútbol. https://www.mininterior.gov.co/el-poder-del-futbol-la-gran-encuesta (18 November 2020).

¿Por qué algunas estrellas del fútbol caen en el mundo del narcotráfico? 2019. *Revista Seman,* 23 March. https://www.semana.com/deportes/articulo/futbolistas-y-narcotrafico-una-historia-de-tiempo-extra/606714 (18 November 2020).

Quitián Roldán, David L. 2013. La economía del fútbol colombiano: De la ilegalidad y el crimen al glamur globalizado. *Polémika* 10(1). 60–65.

Quitián Roldán, David L. & Olga L. Urrea Beltrán. 2016a. Fútbol, desarrollo social y patria: La violencia como factor de *lo nacional* en clave de gol. *Revista San Gregorio* especial (2). 162–170.

Quitián Roldán, David L. & Olga L. Urrea Beltrán. 2016b. Fútbol, radio y nación (1946–1974): Una visión antropológica de la violencia en Colombia. *Espacio Abierto: Cuaderno Venezolano de Sociología* 25(2). 51–66.

Restrepo Escobar, S. M. 2015. Violencia en el fútbol, asociada a consume de sustancias psicoactivas. In Ángela Maritza Lopera Jaramillo, César Augusto Jaramillo Jaramillo, Wilson Armando Montaño Pardo & Sandra Lorena Botina Narvaéz (eds.), *Prevención y tratamiento de las adicciones desde lo psicosocial*, 35–44. Medellín: Fundación Universitaria Luis Amigó.

Reunion de acolfutpro y dimayor que pasó en ministerio de trabajo. 2019. *Futbolred*, 1 November. https://www.futbolred.com/futbol-colombiano/liga-aguila/reunion-de-acolfutpro-y-dimayor-que-paso-en-ministerio-de-trabajo-2019-108934 (18 November 2020).

Ross, Elliot. 2013. Failed states are a Western myth. *The Guardian*, 28 June. https://www.theguardian.com/commentisfree/2013/jun/28/failed-states-western-myth-us-interests (18 November 2020).

Ruiz Patiño, Jorge Humberto. 2017. Balance sobre la historiografía del deporte en Colombia: Un panorama de su desarrollo. *Materiales para la Historia del Deporte* 15. 24–44.

Ruiz Rico, María Alejandra. 2019. Fútbol colombiano vendió sus derechos de televisión internacional por los próximos 10 años. *La República*, 19 July. https://www.larepublica.co/empresas/futbol-

colombiano-vendio-sus-derechos-de-television-internacional-por-los-proximos-10-anos-2886697 (18 November 2020).
Sabbagh Fajardo, Alfredo & Toby Miller. 2017. The absence and presence of state militarism: Violence, football, *narcos*, and Colombia. In Michael L. Butterworth (ed.), *Sport and militarism: Contemporary global perspectives*, 95–111. London: Routledge.
Salazar, Miguel. 2018. Soccer and domestic violence: When the beautiful game turns ugly. *The Nation*, 26 September. https://www.thenation.com/article/soccer-and-domestic-violence-when-the-beautiful-game-turns-ugly/ (18 November 2020).
Salinas Arango, Natalia Andrea. 2018. Encrucijada de la violencia asociada al fútbol: Entre el desagrado y la complacencia. *Trabajo Social* 20(1). 49–68.
Santos Gómez, David. 2018. La política a la mesa. *El Colombiano*, 27 February. http://www.elcolombiano.com/opinion/columnistas/la-politica-a-la-mesa-DE8262234. (18 November 2020).
Santos Molano, Enrique. 2016. Fútbol: Una pasión incontenible. *Credencial Historia*, September. http://www.revistacredencial.com/credencial/historia/temas/futbol-una-pasion-incontenible (18 November 2020).
Selección Colombia dice "no" a la violencia contra mujeres. 2014. *El Universal*, 16 April. https://www.eluniversal.com.co/deportes/seleccion-colombia-dice-no-la-violencia-contra-las-mujeres-157227-IWEU249364 (18 November 2020).
Smith, Anthony D. 2000. *The nation in history: Historiographical debates about ethnicity and nationalism*. Oxford: Polity Press.
Soto, Martha. 2017. *Los goles de la cocaína*. Bogotá: Intermedio.
Specially designated nationals and blocked persons list. 2019. *U.S. Department of the Treasury Office of Foreign Assets Control*, 18 November 2020. https://www.treasury.gov/ofac/downloads/sdnlist.pdf (18 November 2020).
Tafur Mangada, Sacha Javier. 2016. El barrisomo social visto desde "los diáolgos urbanos". *Universidad Cooperativa de Colombia*, 12 July. https://www.ucc.edu.co/prensa/2016/Paginas/el-barrismo-social-visto-desde-los-dialogos-urbanos.aspx (18 November 2020).
Torres Velasco, Javier. 2019. Civilization and sport in Colombia's drive to modernization. *Journal of Mediterranean Knowledge* 4(1). 55–77.
United States of America against various. 2015. DSS: EMN/AH/DAL/SPN/MKM/PT/KDE/TH/BDM F. #2015R00747. United States District Court. Eastern District of New York, 25 November. https://www.justice.gov/opa/file/796966/download (18 November 2020).
Uribe Aramburo, Nicolás Ignacio & Guillermo Alonso Castaño Pérez. 2014. Barras de fútbol, consumo de drogas y violencia. *Psicología desde el Caribe* 31(2). 243–279.
Uribe Aramburo, Nicolás Ignacio. 2018. Violencia, psicología de masas y barras de fútbol. *Revista Criminalidad* 61(1). 85–96.
Vélez, Beatriz. 2001. La puesta en escena del género en el juego de fútbol. *Revista Educación Física y Deporte* 21(2). 39–49.
Vélez-Maya, Margarita María & Juan Carlos Arboleda-Ariza. 2016. Memoria social y violencia en fútbol: Recuerdos institucionalizados en la prensa de Medellín, Colombia. *Pensando Psicología* 12(20). 53–63.
Villanueva Bustos, Alejandro. 2013. Hinchas del fútbol, academia y nuevas emergencias urbanas. *Revista Colombiana de Sociología* 36(1). 93–108.
Watson, Peter J. 2018. Colombia's political football: President Santos' national unity project and the 2014 football World Cup. *Bulletin of Latin American Research* 37(5). 598–612.
Win y Dimayor censuran protesta de jugadores que piden mejores condiciones: Acolfutpro. 2019. *Pulzo* October 6. https://www.pulzo.com/deportes/win-sports-dimayor-censuran-protesta-futbolistas-acolfutpro-PP779513 (18 November 2020).
Wittgenstein, Ludwig. 1965. I: A lecture on ethics. *The Philosophical Review* 74(1). 3–12.

Pablo Alabarces

31 Football, television, and the state in Argentina: a tale of monopolies, patrimonies, and populisms

Abstract: Discussions on the relationship between televised sports and politics have regularly focused on "manipulation of audiences" and on issues of access to broadcasting of sports and the civil "rights" of audiences and publics. In Argentina, these questions and debates have been ignited in the context of the new monopolistic structure of a privatized national media sector that threatened access to live, free-to-air reception of 2002 FIFA World Cup. In response to these developments and other contemporary political pressures, in 2009, the government of Argentina (re)nationalized football broadcasting, thus marking the return of all first division matches to the public network, called the Televisión Pública [Public TV]. In 2017, a new government cancelled the experience and (re) privatized the broadcasting of the matches. In 2014 and 2018, the Televisión Pública broadcast the most important sport events for Argentine audiences: the FIFA World Cup Finals of Brazil and Russia, respectively. The broadcasts were made under different governments with opposed political orientations – populist the former, conservative the latter. This chapter works, therefore, on the relationship between soccer, television, and politics and its transformations in the last two decades in Argentina. The radical interventions of the governments conform a new landscape that demands a cultural, social, and political analysis.

Keywords: soccer TV rights; sports TV; populism; sport and politics

1 Introduction

Any serious analysis of the relationship between sport and politics in Argentina must begin with the consideration of two factors.[1] The first is the taken-for-granted mediation of sport via television. That is, of course, the mediation not only of sport – its practices, institutional organization, systems of rules, and its practitioners – but also the wider world that is composed of a host of social, economic, political, and cultural dimensions and power relations. As a result of its mediation and, crucially, its visualization, sport has globally become above all a representation, a show, in which television is presented as the fundamental narrator. These are developments and trans-

1 The first part of this article was published, in an earlier version in collaboration with Carolina Duek, in Alabarces and Duek 2014. I am re-writing some considerations after the changes that have occurred in the last five years, along with an analysis of the two last Football World Cup Finals.

https://doi.org/10.1515/9783110660883-031

formations that are widely understood in the world of the fans, club authorities, and journalists, and notably in Argentina, in literary circles. In a narration of Jorge Luis Borges and Adolfo Bioy Casares (with the pseudonym of H. Bustos Domecq), originally published in 1963 and titled "Esse est percipi," a sports authority confesses, "The last match of football was played in this city on June 24th 1937. From that precise moment, football, as the wide range of sports, is a dramatic genre, in charge of one man in a cabin or actors with a t-shirt in front of a cameraman" (Borges and Bioy Casares 1996: 133).[2]

In the imagination of the authors an incredible possibility is unleashed: sport was socially constructed in the media and did not exist beyond its narration as a television product to be consumed by mass audiences. Together, Borges and Bioy Casares announce a semiotic and a technological possibility: with digitalization, sport in Argentina exists as pure simulacrum and is no longer dependent on a "real event."

To this principal factor – the impossibility of analyzing sport beyond its existence as a mediated show – I add another, localized one that I will call the *Valentín Suarez Syndrome*. In 1967, at the beginning of one of the many dictatorships that dominated Argentina between 1955 and 1983, the military government "occupied" the Association of Argentine Football (AFA) by installing Valentín Suarez as president. Prior to ascending to this position, Suarez had been the President of Banfield, a minor first division football club. That same year, Suarez created a new tournament (in addition to the first division championship) that would allow smaller provincial clubs to compete against the most traditional and powerful clubs from Buenos Aires, Rosario, and La Plata (three of the most important cities in the country). Although the main championship would continue to be played in Buenos Aires and its surrounding areas, the new tournament, simply entitled "National," added a significant number of matches to the football calendar. At the same time, Argentine clubs were also encouraged to participate in the broader continental tournament called "Copa Libertadores" created in 1960 as an imitation of the European Cup. Besides these key developments, though, Suarez pursued contracts for the free-to-air television transmission of all football games, and the sport was soon to be televised four days a week (including local and international matches). For Suarez, the political logic behind these developments was simple: "Football keeps people's minds busy" (Palomino and Scher 1985).

Suarez was, of course, reproducing the slogan that regards sport (televised sport in this instance) as a modern and secular opiate of the people, one that prevents "the masses" from engaging in more dangerous activities such as unionism, political mobilization, or worse, *guerrilla* warfare (in 1967, the Argentine revolutionary Che Guevara was assassinated by the Bolivian army). Suarez's affirmation, I argue, is still relevant today, and actively structures political conceptions of the relationship between football, television, and audiences: the more televised football, the more

2 I use *football* instead of *soccer*, as it is the name that the sport receives globally.

control over audiences, a new expression of the old concept of alienation (see Sebreli 1981). Popular understandings of "bread and circuses," though, remain ideological fallacies. Social mechanisms of control and power relations in the modern world are infinitely more complex than the simple indefinite transmission of sport through television.[3] Nevertheless, throughout this chapter I will argue that, even today, Argentine political decisions in relation to sport and television are regularly organized according to *the Suarez syndrome* and other contemporary political pressures. Thus, the mass mediation of football (with its implications for the analysis of sport as a *mise en scène* and an audiovisual narration, among other elements) must be read as a political phenomenon in which, real or imaginary, the construction of social hegemony is disputed (see Frydenberg and Daskal 2010).

Discussions of the relationship between televised sport and politics have, as a result, regularly focused on audience "manipulation" and, prior to 2000, issues of access to live telecasts of sport and the civil "rights" of audiences and publics (Rowe 2004a, Rowe 2004b; Scherer and Whitson 2009). These questions and debates have, however, only recently been ignited in Argentina, in the context of a new monopolistic structure of a privatized national media sector that threatened access to live, free-to-air reception of 2002 FIFA World Cup. In response to these developments and other contemporary political pressures, in 2009, the government of Argentina (re)nationalized football telecasts, thus marking the return of all first division matches to the public broadcaster Televisión Pública. Two years later, moreover, the viewing rights of sports fans in Argentina were enshrined in a broader list of protected events that mandated live, universal access to sporting events of national significance. And in 2014 and 2018, the state TV, known as Televisión Pública (Public Television) broadcast the greatest sporting events for the Argentine public: the Football World Cup Finals of Brazil and Russia, respectively: each under a government of different political orientation –the former, populist, the latter, conservative.

Yet, as we shall see, even in the new millennium the polemics surrounding the nationalization of football telecasts continue to be oriented to arguments concerning the manipulative capacity of the Argentine government in relation to the audience (i. e., the *Suarez syndrome*). The Argentine case, therefore, must be analyzed with this specific history in mind.

3 In the last five decades, there has been a significant and ongoing discussion about sport and the concept of alienation. In Latin America as elsewhere, the first arguments tended to use the classic metaphor of sport as the opium of the masses (Archetti 1998; Da Matta 1982). Readers can find a balancing history of this discussion in the construction of a Latin American field of social studies of sport in Alabarces 2005.

2 Television and football in Argentina

There has, for many years now, been a close affinity between football and television in Argentina. Briefly, Argentine television was not born *because of* football but *with* football. The first experimental transmission on October 17, 1951 televised a mass rallying celebration of Peronism (the political movement then in power). Historically, this was the only live, televisual appearance of Eva Perón, who would die soon after because of cancer. Only a month and a half later, the second live transmission of *creole television* – as Varela (2005) called it – was of a football match between San Lorenzo and River Plate. Under the direction of Samuel Yanquelevich, who was the head of the new Channel 7 (property of the new national broadcaster), this telecast announced a long and happy marriage between football and television. Perón, of course, used television as both a public service and as an ideological state apparatus to promote the Peronist form of populism. Such an approach maintained strict control over news information, but also sought to provide key elements of national popular culture. The two initial transmissions of television (the political act and the football match), then, were articulated with that ideology. If the close and early relationship between sport and media is not original – as has been described by the concept of sport/media complex (Jhally 1984; see also Wenner 1998), the relation with state broadcasting was unique in Latin America.

The first football telecast was sponsored by YPF (the state oil company). The images of the match were captured by two cameras (one behind each goal) and received by approximately 1,300 television sets. The early telecasts of football followed the visual structure and narratives of cinema, especially the football films of the 1930s (like the pioneering *Los tres berretines*, produced by Lumiton in 1933) and many years would pass before the development of any significant changes to the narrative practices of football telecasts (see Alabarces 2002). In the early days of television, there was an average of fifteen viewers per television set, and the sport audience was situated either in private (family homes that could afford television sets) or in semi-public places (such as in front of electrical appliance stores). Still, in 1951 telecasts of football were events in themselves and not necessarily part of the programming flow or content of the emergent medium. This situation changed, as Varela (2005) has remarked, only after television audiences were more systematically measured and targeted as the industry matured.

Twenty-seven years later, the International Federation of Football Association's (FIFA) World Cup of 1978 constituted the most ambitious and significant television event in Argentine history, one with overt political overtones. Related to this latter point, the World Cup was recognized by the then military dictatorship of General Jorge Rafael Videla (who came to power after a 1976 coup d'état that deposed Argentina's President, Isabel Martínez de Perón) as a major opportunity to help quell local unrest and political instability. The World Cup was also widely regarded as a key moment to present to the world an image of national "efficiency" and politeness to counter criticism in the international community directed at the dictatorship's habitual violation of human rights, detentions, disappearances, torture, and murders. The international televisual transmissions, thus, were considered to be decisive political platforms to consolidate the dictatorship's "preferred" image of Argentina. By then, Argentina had several television networks, but all of them had been nationalized and were controlled by the state (the private networks had been nationalized in 1974 by the previous Peronist government).

To prepare for the FIFA World Cup, the government made the most significant investment in technological equipment in local broadcasting history. On May 19, 1978, in Buenos Aires, Videla inaugurated the Center of Television Programmes that introduced color television to the country (Argentina 78 Televisora S.A.). However, these early color transmissions were unreliable, and local viewers had to watch the World Cup – a tournament that was eventually won by Argentina – in black and white, while the international audience saw the event unfold in color. Nonetheless, as with the birth of television, football was an important influence on the development of television in Argentina. The total cost of the World Cup of 1978 remains unknown but estimates suggest US $520 million. In comparison, the total cost of the following 1982 World Cup in Spain was only US $150 million. The construction of ATC (Argentina Televisora Color, the new name of Channel 7) alone cost US $40 million, with an additional US $30 million for equipment (Gilbert and Vitagliano 1998; see also Alabarces 2014).

The 1980s marked the inception of more reliable color images in Argentina and, from that moment on, football clubs were able to use (and promote) the colors of their shirts unconstrained by the limitations of black and white television transmission. The 1982 FIFA World Cup was the first to be seen in color in Argentina, allowing spectators to appreciate a new visual dimension of the football "show" that was, until then, inaccessible to them. The slow development and spread of new receivers and the growing demand of consumers to watch the tournament in color (the Argentine team was a favorite to win the tournament, but failed) spurred the re-emergence of a residual practice that saw thousands of fans watch the telecasts in front of electrical appliance shops as in the 1950s.[4]

It was also at this time that cable television began to emerge and spread throughout the country. The difficulties of transmission in a very large territory (Argentina is 3,694 kilometers long from north to south and 1,423 kilometers from east to west, with highly variable terrain), and the centralization of television production in Buenos Aires, resulted in innumerable technological difficulties in the reproduction of signals in cities and in remote towns. Crucially, the most important football

4 Besides the 1978 World Cup, viewers may have seen in color the Malvinas (Falklands) War that was happening at the exact same time. However, the dictatorship strictly censored and controlled what was being shown in this context.

matches were played in Buenos Aires, and many households in the provinces simply could not receive these signals. Eventually, though, local cable networks developed the capability to download and distribute satellite signals. Again, football promoted a technological expansion, one that would be perfected in the mid-1990s when football transmissions were increasingly encoded, thereby forcing people to adopt a "pay-per-view" arrangement. The birth of pay-per-view services in Argentina, then, was strictly related to the popularity of football telecasts.

3 Privatization and monopolization

Halfway through the 1980s, a "media empire" called Torneos y Competencias (Tournaments and Competences, TyC) began to emerge. Headed by Carlos Avila, an entrepreneur fascinated by the growing revenue from advertising in televised North American sport, TyC aggressively pursued similar strategies in local television in Argentina. After successfully televising golf, in 1985 Avila made two decisive steps. First, he signed an exclusivity contract with the AFA to broadcast and commercialize first division matches. Therefore, all football content became Avila's "property," forcing the rest of the image producers (for example, news shows) to follow his programming decisions. As a second step, a TV show called *Fútbol de Primera* was created, hosted first on Channel 7 by Enrique Macaya Márquez and Mauro Viale, the latter being replaced by Marcelo Araujo when the program was moved to Channel 9. *Fútbol de Primera* replaced *Todos los Goles*, a program that showed all the goals of the day presented on Sunday nights and was hosted by many journalists who offered their commentary on individual matches. In 1991, *Fútbol de Primera* finally arrived at Channel 13 as a key property of the media conglomerate Clarín, thus widening the dimensions of its production and technology, and transforming its classic narrative structures and aesthetics in accordance with international developments in sport television.

Such a radical overhaul of televised sports production and TyC's exclusive contract with AFA provided an influx of money and cemented the sport's dependency on television revenue in the context of much broader economic reform. From 1989, the new President, the Peronist Carlos Menem, implemented a range of neoliberal policies that included the privatization of all public services (that had been nationalized during the first Peronist regime 1945–1955), including television (that had been nationalized during the second Peronist regime 1973–1976). The government, however, retained the old Channel 7 (ATC) as a public service broadcaster. In addition to these developments, the government eliminated any anti-monopoly legislation related to media, a move that resulted in heightened levels of concentration and the emergence of powerful media conglomerates, the most important of which was Clarín. Until that point, Clarín had been the most important national newspaper but, through a host of takeovers and mergers, formed the apex of an immense media group that included other newspapers, radios, television channels, telephone services, internet services and, crucially, cable television companies throughout the country. Football was the focal point of Clarín's monopolistic position in cable services in Argentina (70 percent of the national market of cable television came under the control of Clarín; see Mastrini and Becerra 2006).

The combination of the production of TyC and the technological emphasis in the institutional image of the new Channel 13 would have new and marked effects over *Fútbol de Primera*. The presentation of the program tended to include a proliferation of futuristic themes, an atmosphere created by the choice of the music of Vangelis (the theme of the movie *Blade Runner*). The multiplication of images and the broader transformation of the show and its narrative structure were further reinforced in the studio by the proliferation of video walls and screens akin to popular North American sports production techniques. These developments signaled a new mode of presentation: the matches could be viewed from all angles, and the most important games began to be shot with up to 18 cameras. Of course, no spectator can see all that television captures, and the cameras condense, in an imaginary way, all points of view, even those that are impossible for a "common spectator" to discern. These new production values tended to focus on "close-up" shots and details (for example, of the referee) that many viewers and critics consider "gimmicky" and hyperbolic (Rowe 2004b: 395).

The expansion of football in Argentine television and, especially, the significant amount of capital that flowed into the sport were, however, not unprecedented. The 1990s were the global peak of televisual transmissions as television developed into the main economic driver of football around the world, as was signaled by Giulianotti (1999), among others. The appearance of new cable technologies and, eventually, the domestic satellite antenna, further commercialized the sport, and merchandising logics soon began to dominate. It became apparent that, from this point, football in Argentina would simply not survive without the income provided by television, even though the exclusive contract between TyC and the AFA was an unequal one that allowed TyC to secure immense profits while many clubs found themselves in economic crisis due to incompetent administration and widespread structural corruption. At the same time, the economic crisis of the clubs meant an absolute dependency on TyC resulting in a weak bargaining position regarding many critical decisions associated with the sport, including even programming schedules.

Still, the commercial expansion of televised football was unstoppable. Paying audiences provided virtually unlimited merchandising opportunities, while sports channels were created allowing viewers to spend an entire day watching sport.[5] Nevertheless, the first signal of resistance to this ascendant model began to appear in

5 By the end of 1990s, it was possible to access four specialty channels that aired sport throughout the day. One of them was owned by Clarín Group, which was also the owner of the cable company through which the matches were seen.

2000 when it was announced that the 2002 FIFA World Cup would be broadcast only by satellite and cable television (Clarín also owned the satellite television company called Direct TV). This was, moreover, the first moment when arguments of cultural citizenship (Scherer and Rowe 2014) and the public's right to watch events of national interest began to be debated. With the impending threat of restricted access to the 2002 FIFA World Cup, the Argentine Congress eventually defended live televisual access to the event as a right of cultural citizenship. The journalist Victor Hugo Morales, a renowned football radio commentator, was prominent in criticizing the AFA and Clarín Group. Finally, Law 25342 was passed in October 2000 obliging owners of the television rights to the matches played by the national team to "commercialize those rights in order to guarantee the live transmission of those matches to all the national territory." The law included international football tournaments organized by FIFA, the International Olympic Committee (IOC), and the South American Football Confederation (*Confederación Sudamericana de Fútbol*, CONMEBOL), but access to local professional football matches and other sporting events did not receive the same protection under the law.[6] Within the decade, though, a challenge to the Argentine television sport monopoly would emerge.

4 Football for everyone (*Fútbol para Todos*)?

On August 11, 2009, the unthinkable happened: the AFA cancelled its exclusive contract with TyC, thus dismantling the monopolistic structure of the televised sport industry. The measure was taken in the context of a wider political crisis: the government, presided over by the Peronist Cristina Fernández de Kirchner, was in a heated dispute with Clarín Group, by then the country's most powerful media conglomerate (the owner of television channels and radio stations, 70 percent of cable television, 85 percent of paper for newspapers and the main newspaper, *Clarín*). Unsurprisingly, the media empire had an impact on public opinion and the Clarín Group had recently criticized official positions and policies, and offered its support to the government's opposition. The Argentine government, then, took the offensive: it put before the Parliament a bill concerning audiovisual communication services that effectively forbade the monopolistic concentration of media. The bill was subsequently passed in October 2009.

---

6 I have reconstructed this process through journalistic sources. The law, for example, is available online at http://www.infoleg.gov.ar/infolegInternet/anexos/60000-64999/64834/norma.htm (accessed 4 May 2012). Academics in Communication Studies have played an active role in recent discussions about the new media law but have not studied the case of sport. They also examined the Clarín Group's monopoly in the media structure, but have not examined the importance of football content in the media conglomerate.

The monopolistic position of the Clarín Group had, until then, permeated all levels of football: it was the AFA's television "partner," and the Group owned the exclusive television rights to local and international football matches on the free-to-air Channel 13 and the specialty cable channel TyC Sports. Importantly, Clarín could deny this content to other cable operators, thus crippling competitors that simply could not survive without the most popular football games. By refusing to share its signal, the Clarín Group was, in turn, able to purchase those companies for a very cheap price. The acquisition of the smaller cable companies, moreover, allowed Clarín to transmit throughout the country, thereby further concentrating its power. Clarín's power, however, extended beyond the delivery of popular sports content. Julio Grondona, the President of the AFA since 1979 and the Vice President of FIFA, had long been suspected of corruption.[7] Through a pact with Clarín Group, all potential criticisms and accusations were silenced in the media, and the relationship between the AFA and TyC was mutually beneficial beyond strict economic matters.

In the context of the broader political confrontation between Clarín and the government, the latter sought to secure the television rights to football. TSC (an associate of TyC) offered the AFA US $60 million per year for the broadcasting rights. The football clubs, however, were reported to be seeking US $180 million. When the government made an offer of US $150 million per year, the AFA quickly accepted it and cancelled its contract with TyC (the contract was due for renewal in 2014). Despite threats of court action, the AFA conceded the monopoly of football broadcasting to the State, and *Fútbol Para Todos* (Football for Everyone) began to air on Televisión Pública. These developments marked the end of the private monopoly of encoded cable and satellite signals, and marked the "return" of all first division matches of local tournaments on the public network,[8] while the Clarín Group maintained control over minor league matches.[9]

On the day that the new contract was announced (August 20, 2009), President Cristina Kirchner described the previous private monopoly of football telecasts as a "confiscation of the goals," and compared those practices with the disappearance of people during the military dictatorship of 1976: "It is not possible that the ones who can pay, can watch a match, moreover that they confiscate the goals until Sunday

---

7 Until his death in 2014, Grondona was suspected of corruption, especially about TV rights at the South American level. The case from the FBI in 2015 against most of the football leaders of the Conmebol and Concacaf demonstrated those facts, but he could not be accused.

8 That is how ATC was renamed after a period as Canal 7. It is the only Argentine open free-to-air channel owned by the state.

9 The television rights to minor league football matches (from National B to D Division) had been in the hands of another company, Trisa, which also, incidentally, belonged to the Clarín Group. In 2011, the relegation of River Plate, the second most important football club in Argentina, forced the government to nationalize the transmissions of the "National B" tournament (an equivalent of a second division championship). All matches of the "National B" were also broadcast by Televisión Pública.

even though you pay, as they confiscate your word or images, as they kidnapped and disappeared 30,000 Argentines" (Kirchner cited in Nos habían 2009).

"Fútbol Para Todos" could be understood as an economic, discursive, and semiotic operation aimed at democratizing mediated reception of the most popular sports content, albeit for populist political purposes. Given that Televisión Pública is accessible to anyone who has a television in any part of the country, live access to all football matches was nearly guaranteed. However, the political slogan that football telecasts were "for everyone" did not imply automatic democratization.

The intervention of the national government in the financing of "Fútbol para todos" implied live access to all the matches and goals (previously restricted and exclusive to Channel 13 and "Fútbol de primera"), while all other sports and news channels were able *instantly* to show goal highlights. However, the new contract simply created a new monopoly of football content and images for the state and the public broadcaster. Other channels (cable channels 26 and Crónica television, and the free-to-air America and Channel 9) that re-transmitted the matches and compete with the state channel were now forced to broadcast official transmissions. Notably, the production of these telecasts was granted to a private company, *La corte*, which was hired by Televisión Pública, while commentary on the football telecasts was provided by Marcelo Araujo, who was, as mentioned earlier, the face of Channel 13 for many years (and in the middle of a court case with the dismantled monopoly).

The decision to retain Araujo – a voice closely associated with the former private monopoly (and with his series of expressions, twists, aggressive statements, and vulgarities) – left some doubt about the democratization process. Was this a new type of state-based, ideological monopoly? The decision that Marcelo Araujo would be the "official" voice of "Fútbol para todos" could be interpreted both as a "declaration of war" to Clarín or as recognition of his skills as a commentator. Aníbal Fernández, Chief of Staff of the President and a football authority (of the club called Quilmes), was the most important negotiator of the new contract between the government and the AFA. Fernandez stated in an interview that the choice of Araujo was related only to ratings, although it was rumored among sports journalists that it was demanded by Julio Grondona, the President of AFA, in a political maneuver against the government (see Hamilton and Hernández 2010). The choice of Araujo was probably a combination of two logics: that of the market (the "popularity" of the journalist) and of individual power and nepotism (Grondona's nickname in the world of football was "The Godfather").[10]

Since the nationalization of the football telecasts there had not been any visual or linguistic innovations in the narration of the sport. The melodramatic narration, (ab)

---

10 After early chaos, the show incorporated the sport journalists identified with the government's progressive populism or the ones who were traditionally conservatives but claimed to be opposed to the Clarín Group. The most important perhaps gestural innovation was the incorporation in 2012 of a female commentator, Viviana Vila, and later, in 2013, of a field journalist, Angela Llerena.

use of close-up images, the technological paraphernalia that shows as many points of view as possible, the colloquial and vulgar language, the strong and sexualized jokes, and even some racist comments sentiments, all persisted. The possibility of constructing a new and more progressive style of broadcasting, one not linked with the mercantile values of the cultural industry, had clearly not been encouraged in that instance. If, as Rowe (2004a: 396) remarks, one of the advantages of public broadcasting is the possibility of innovation and quality, *Fútbol para Todos* had chosen continuity, repetition, and aesthetic conservatism. If there was one innovative aspect, however, it has been the reduction of commercial advertising during telecasts, although government propaganda had easily filled this void. Some sport films aired in place of commercials, showing various historical aspects of football clubs that were not well known by the general audience (almost every First Division club is 100 years old).

Articulating with these developments was unabashed support for the national government. Even though a technical monopoly of transmission was not created (as commercial television sport providers still operate in Argentina), the production dimension was restricted and there were certain choices (such as of the narrator and other personnel) conditioned by ideological affinities. The participation of the government in material terms had been barely criticized by opposition parties, although they maintained that "there are more serious situations to solve with state money than pay per view football" (Piden crear 2010). Those who were against the "de-commercial monopolization" of football argued that it was little more than political posturing aimed at cementing the government's popularity and securing votes. Against these claims, supporters of the decision noted that advertising income will comfortably finance the contract. Nevertheless, since February 2010, all private advertising had disappeared and the only advertisements that aired were exclusively those of the government except for IVECO, the tournament's sponsor. After former President Nestor Kirchner's death in October 2010, though, even this sponsorship disappeared, and the 2011 tournament was named in his honor.

With regard to audiences, a space had been filled that was previously restricted by corporate capital through the purchase of "packages" of encoded and pay-per-view matches. State intervention and the provision of free-to-air football telecasts may or may not had guaranteed future votes, but it had marked a radical change in the sports broadcasting landscape that was once, essentially, completely privatized. These developments appeared to be widely supported among Argentine political parties and the wider population. Thus, for example, in the 2011 and 2015 general elections there were no proposals to eliminate "Fútbol para Todos" and, evidently, all Argentine politicians understood that there remained a significant consensus in favor of the nationalization of football telecasts and against the former private monopoly.

5 The Argentine *crown jewels* and the patrimonialization of sport

At the beginning of 2011, the Federal Authority of Audiovisual Communication Services (AFSCA), a legal entity created to organize and regulate the media, took another step toward enshrining viewing rights of sports fans in Argentina. The AFSCA, in accordance with recently passed media legislation, now regulated what it called "the universal access of informative content of relevant interest," including sport. A list similar to that in the United Kingdom covering national and international sports events was established that mandated live, universal access to a list of events as a right of cultural citizenship while forbidding the exclusive transmission of the most popular sport events via cable or pay-per-view. This decision was announced by President Cristina Kirchner on the program "Deporte para todos" (Sport for everyone) in a press conference, where she was accompanied by the CEOs of the most important sport networks (TyC, Fox, and ESPN).

The list included a series of both local and international sporting events. However, it was limited to the most popular sports and omitted smaller sports such as track-and -field, cycling, or handball that have significant participant numbers, but smaller television audiences. Although this development might be understood as an extension of the democratization of television access to certain cultural goods and sport practices, it was clearly driven by the logic of supply and demand in the cultural industries. This could be called a public patrimonialization of sport events as symbolic goods. These "popular" cultural-political decisions that had established Argentine viewing rights, then, were also constituted by the logic of profit and political calculation: even if, in this case, it is only "profit" measured in audience size and a political "return" for the government.[11]

Thus, a policy of *patrimonialization of sport* was presented – rather, the consideration of certain intangible goods, insomuch cultural and mediated products, as public patrimony. The Argentine government had produced a legal instrument that finally confirmed the relationship between sport and *patria* (fatherland), at least as patrimony of a national-popular culture: a kind of definitive affirmation of the nationalist possibilities of sport. Nevertheless, it limited itself to produce sport – it could only produce it – as a cultural commodity, a kind of ratification that, despite democratic temptations, the dominant logic is that of cultural industry. At this point, there is no patriotism which is more than simply merchandise. The sports that the national

11 In April 2012, a new state program was created: "Automovilismo para todos" [Motoring for everyone]. Once again, a contract was cancelled at the Clarín Group's expense. "Carburando," the company owned by the Clarín Goup that transmitted all the local races, lost the rights and, from that moment, all races were televised on the public broadcaster.

government incorporated as patrimony were, of course, just those with significant television audiences: the rest were not worth worrying about.

In 2014, however, things got complicated. *Fútbol para Todos* had acquired the exclusive broadcast rights for the Football World Cup in Brazil, monopolizing almost the entire voice on television, at least on open access channels (the cable network TyC Sports as well as the satellite network Direct TV also transmitted Argentina's matches). First, the program presented its journalists in a formation like a football team, wearing suits but also with jerseys and boots, singing the national anthem on a pitch while imitating the movements of players with the slogan "a football team and a team of journalists for one unique Argentine passion." In this way, the press coverage resembled the game itself, as though representative. Let me put it this way: the journalists also went for the conquest of the Cup, which could explain why the commentaries were so unbearably patriotic, loudmouthed, xenophobic, and even racist – and homophobic, also. Narrators used words like *negrito* to describe some players, alluded continually to genitals referring to courage, and celebrated with happiness Brazil's defeat by Germany. And all of them were, naturally, men, *machos*.

Alongside the journalistic performances was state advertising. As with the domestic tournament, the state prioritized its own propaganda in the advertising space during the transmissions. Some advertisements condemned human trafficking during major events. Others banalized the supposedly successful state programs of "social inclusion" – obtaining credit to buy a house or graduating from a new university – transforming them into goal celebrations for their beneficiaries (a now explicit turn of the screw regarding the footballization of the social and political realms). However, the climax would be reached with the ad "Nobody wins a World Cup alone," which assimilated all the "achievements" of the Kirchernist government with the avatars of the national team: "in order to win, the country must be united".[12] Even Kirchnerist journalist Horacio Verbitsky admitted that it was a "fallacy directly descended from the rhetoric used by the dictatorship during the 1978 championship and reiterated by the unbearable commentating during the Argentine matches. ... This piece constitutes an insufferable banalization and spurious use of things which are too serious" (Verbitsky 2018). Something similar would occur with the YPF advertisement "Pep talk – Proud of our land," produced by Young&Rubicam, in which a voice with military undertones simultaneously directed oil workers and footballers saying "Men, glory is not found; one must go looking for glory." Even though the enunciator is a company, in reality, it is a state company – which is why it abuses with the display of the light blue and white of the Argentine flag everywhere.[13]

---

12 Nadie Gana 2014. The ad can be seen at http://www.youtube.com/watch?v=vuLxfsy7h5o.

13 Argena 2014. This can be seen at http://www.youtube.com/watch?v=NfdfVtkOiuI.

6 Conclusion: all roads lead to populism

Of course, the resemblance that Verbitsky found with the dictatorship's discourse was just that, a resemblance. It was not about identity. The continuity is in the desire, common to democratic and authoritarian, conservative or populist, governments, to use the supposed benefits of football in their favor: to manipulate or to transfer athletic success to political success. As I have pointed out in other places (e. g., Alabarces 2014), the dictatorship aimed for both the famous "smokescreen" and civil consensus whereas in the case of Kirchnerism, the administration attempted to tie a strong athletic performance to a national-popular narrative of an era.

In 2016, in spite of earlier promises of not to do so, the new Argentine conservative government of President Maruicio Macri cancelled *Fútbol para Todos* and signed a new contract with a joint venture of Fox Sports and Turner Network Television Sports (TNT Sports). Football matches were codified again and broadcast only for paying consumers. There were not popular reactions against the cancellation. In 2018, Televisión Pública broadcast the Russia World Cup with almost the same staff as four years before: they were so unbearably patriotic, loudmouthed, xenophobic, and even racist – and homophobic, also. There were not, as four years before, any women among the journalists.

In the 2018 World Cup, the new conservative administrations of Argentina and Brazil – which replaced the allegedly "populist" and progressive prior administrations – along with the already conservative governments of Colombia, Mexico, Panama, Peru, and Costa Rica, employed the same nationalist rhetoric that associated athletic success with supposed or disputed national grandeur. There were no differences between them, but rather levels: the persistent use of Colombia's national team jersey by President Santos; the systematic utilization of football language by Argentine President Macri; *embanderamiento* ceremonies – the assignment of an official flag – of the Mexican team by President Enrique Peña Nieto. All of them are conservative presidents and opponents of an alleged populism.

Essentially, it involves a combination of two logics, which the literature had tended to describe as opposing or irreducible: on the one hand, the national-popular logic which understands the State as a machine that produces democratic meanings and on the other hand, the neoliberal-conservative logic that trusts the market – which it calls *civil society* – as the only enunciator and narrator. In reality, here we see the points of contact between populism and neoliberalism: populism only adds passion, affectivity, and massiveness to what neoliberalism has already transformed into televisual merchandise. In short, even with the novelty of the patrimonialization of televised Argentine sport – radically original in the context of Latin America, where no other government has dared to interfere with the colossal business of the networks – these processes can be described as another twist: the reconciliation of both political and narrative logics. Both of these logics are populist and convinced that people are cultural fools.

References

Alabarces, Pablo. 2002. *Fútbol y Patria. El fútbol y las narrativas nacionales en la Argentina*. Buenos Aires: Prometeo libros.

Alabarces, Pablo. 2005. Veinte años de Ciencias Sociales y Deporte en América Latina: un balance, una agenda. *Revista Brasileira de Informação Bibliográfica en Ciências Sociais* 58. 159–180.

Alabarces, Pablo. 2014. *Héroes, machos y patriotas. El fútbol, entre la violencia y los medios*. Buenos Aires: Aguilar.

Alabarces, Pablo & Carolina Duek. 2014. Football for everyone? Football, television, and politics in Argentina. In Jay Scherer & David Rowe (eds.), *Signal lost? Sport, public broadcasting and cultural citizenship*, 96–109. London: Routledge.

Archetti, Eduardo. 1998. Prólogo. In Pablo Alabarces, Roberto Di Giano & Julio Frydenberg (eds.), *Deporte y Sociedad*, 9–13. Buenos Aires: Eudeba.

Borges, Jorge Luis & Adolfo Bioy Casares. 1996. *Crónicas de Bustos Domecq*. Buenos Aires: Losada.

Da Matta, Roberto (ed.). 1982. *O universo do futebol. Futebol e sociedade brasileira*. Rio de Janeiro: Pinakotheke.

Frydenberg, Julio & Rodrigo Daskal (eds.). 2010. *Fútbol, historia y política*. Buenos Aires: Aurelia Rivera Libros.

Gilbert, Abel & Miguel Vitagliano. 1998. *El terror y la gloria. La vida, el fútbol y la política en la Argentina del Mundial 78*. Buenos Aires: Norma.

Hamilton, Mariano & Carlos Hernández. 2010. Así como estaba el fútbol iba a la muerte, interview with Aníbal Fernández. *Un caño*, April. 13–19.

Giulianotti, Richard. 1999. *Football: A sociology of the global game*. Cambridge: Polity Press.

Jhally, Sut. 1984. The spectacle of accumulation: Material and cultural factors in the evolution of the sport/media complex. *The Insurgent Sociologist* 12(3). 41–57.

Mastrini, Guillermo & Martín Becerra. 2006. *Periodistas y magnates. Estructura y concentración de las industrias culturales en América Latina*. Buenos Aires: Prometeo Libros.

Nos habían secuestrado los goles. 2009. *La Gaceta*, 20 August. http://www.lagaceta.com.ar/nota/340308/Deportes/Nos_habian_secuestrado_goles.html (14 July 2011).

Palomino, Héctor & Ariel Scher. 1985. *AFA: Pasión De multitudes y de elites*. Buenos Aires: CISEA.

Piden crear una comisión investigadora sobre el programa "Fútbol para Todos." 2010. *Clarín*, 19 August. http://www.clarin.com/politica/Piden-comision-investigadora-programa-Futbol_0_319768241.html (4 May 2012).

Rowe, David. 2004a. Fulfilling the cultural mission: Popular genre and public remit. *European Journal of Cultural Studies* 7(3). 381–399.

Rowe, David. 2004b. Watching brief: Cultural citizenship and viewing rights. *Sport in Society* 7(3). 385–402.

Scherer, Jay & David Rowe. 2014 (eds.). *Signal lost? Sport, public broadcasting and cultural citizenship*. London: Routledge.

Scherer, Jay & David Whitson. 2009. Public broadcasting, sport, and cultural citizenship: The future of sport on the Canadian broadcasting corporation? *International Review for the Sociology of Sport* 44(2–3). 213–229.

Sebreli, Juan. 1981. *Fútbol y masas*. Buenos Aires: Galerna.

Varela, Mirta. 2005. *La televisión criolla. Desde sus inicios hasta la llegada del hombre a la luna. 1951–1969*. Buenos Aires: Edhasa/Ensayo.

Verbitsky, Horacio. 2014. Vamos, Argentina. *Página 12*, 7 June. 10.

Wenner, Lawrence A. (ed.). 1998. *MediaSport*. London: Routledge.

V Communicating in applied sport contexts

Natalie Brown-Devlin and Sabitha Sudarshan

32 Crisis communication and sport: the organization, the players, and the fans

Abstract: This chapter examines the intersection of sports media and crisis communication by reviewing how organizations, athletes, and fans have engaged in the image/reputational repair process during sports-related incidents. This chapter, first, reviews two predominant theories utilized by crisis communication scholars: Image Repair Theory (IRT) and Situational Crisis Communication Theory (SCCT). Next, we examine existing scholarship that utilized these two theories as a theoretical foundation for analyzing the various ways in which sports organizations, athletes, and sports fans have reacted and responded to various sports-related crises. Finally, we offer some concluding thoughts pertaining to how technological innovation, unique ethical considerations, and immense financial and emotional stakes associated with the sporting context, itself, present a host of necessary areas for scholarly attention within sports-related crisis communication research.

Keywords: crisis communication; Situational Crisis Communication Theory; Image Repair Theory; sports media; fan identification

1 Introduction

Sport presents a valuable lens through which to examine crisis communication. For instance, sports organizations' primary stakeholders, their fans, find associations with their preferred team to be a part of their identity (Wann 2006). As such, that close association also contributes to fans feeling personally affected by such crises. Furthermore, for most sports, time is divided into seasons, which provides a natural "reset" and a fresh start that can help to reestablish previously damaged images (Koerber and Zabara 2017: 195). Perhaps most importantly, crises that occur within a sporting context can affect the sports organization, its affiliated athletes, or fans that identify with the team. Each party can either create crises or engage in crisis response when issues arise. Crisis communication scholars have thoroughly examined this unique intersection of associated parties. While scholars have examined crises in a myriad of ways, the focus of this chapter includes a discussion of sports-related crisis communication literature through the lens of two primary theories which have guided sports crisis communication scholarship, namely Benoit's Image Repair Theory (IRT) and Coombs' Situational Crisis Communication Theory (SCCT). First, we discuss a broad overview of each theory. Then, we present a thorough examination of existing scholarship that utilized those theories to provide recommendations results regarding organizations, athletes, and fans impacted by crises.

https://doi.org/10.1515/9783110660883-032

2 An overview of Image Repair Theory and Situational Crisis Communication Theory

2.1 Image Repair Theory

Benoit's (1997a) Image Repair Theory (IRT) is a foundational, theoretical framework used in crisis communication scholarship, and was developed on a foundation of critical works by Burke (1961), Scott and Lyman (1968), and Ware and Linkugel (1973). Image is defined as "the perception of a person (or group or organization) held by the audience, shaped by the words and the actions of that person, as well as by the discourse and behaviors of relevant actors" (Benoit 1997b: 251). Image repair studies primarily work on the assumption that all communication is goal-oriented, and that these goals generally entail maintaining a positive impression of the communicative entity. Consequently, most organizations and individuals are often engaged in either protecting or restoring their image (Benoit 1995, 1997a; Fishman 1999; Zhang and Benoit 2004). The innate human need for others' approval makes image management particularly critical during times of crisis, when one's image is threatened.

IRT's central premise hinges on the fact that a crisis is contingent upon whether an individual/group/organization can be held accountable for an offending action. Salient audiences that perceive the presence of the entity(entities) and disapprove of their action(s) weigh the level of accountability that should be attributed; these audiences are generally also stakeholders with diverse interests, goals, and concerns. More importantly however, Benoit stresses that the veracity of an undesirable event happening and the communicative entity's role in it is irrelevant – it is the *image* that is "more important than reality" (Benoit 1997a: 178). It is the active repair of this image in the case of a threat that informs the overarching framework of this theory, which provides five subcategories, each of which contain particular strategies to mitigate the offensiveness of an unwelcome action. They are detailed below as follows:

I. *Denial.* Denial is a tactic that offers two variants: complete denial that the incident occurred (*simple denial*); or shifting the blame for the offensive act onto another party (*scapegoating/shift the blame*). In the former case, if the audience accepts the denial, the culpability of the accused is reduced or abolished; for the latter, it provides a scapegoat to answer the question, "Well if you didn't do it, who did?" (Benoit and Hanczor 1994: 419).

II. *Evasion of responsibility.* In cases where the involvement of the accused cannot be denied, they must resort to evasion of responsibility, whereby typical responses to accusations include attributing actions to (a) *provocation* that demanded the egregious act to be performed, (b) *defeasibility*, where the "rhetor claims a lack of information about or control over important elements in the situation" (Benoit and Hanczor 1994: 21), (c) *accident*, which could be said to mitigate responsibility due to actions being outside the control of the accused (Semin and Manstead 1983; Tedeschi and Riess 1981); and (d) *good intentions*, which while not necessarily absolving the accused of the offensive act, can at least reduce their accountability since it can be demonstrated that such actions were not committed with any harmful intentions in mind.

III. *Reducing offensiveness of events.* Individuals resort to utilizing this strategy when either denial or evasion of responsibility fail, and they attempt to reduce the perceived offensiveness of a certain act. This strategy has six variants, primary amongst them being (a) *bolstering*, whereby the accused brings up prior positive associations with one's image, hoping to offset negative sentiment and thereby gain a net improvement in perception (McClearey 1983). Yet another such variant is (b) *minimization*, whereby the ill-feeling associated with the act is attempted to be reduced. If the audience is led to believe that the act is not as bad as it first appeared to be, there might be some restoration of positive feeling with respect to the rhetor's image. With the (c) *differentiation* tactic, the accused compares his or her actions with a similar but more offensive action, thereby making it seem less offensive in comparison. (d) *Transcendence* is used much more rarely, given that it involves placing the action in a broader, more positive context, such as directing the audience attention to other, higher values to justify the action in question (Shipley 1995). When the credibility of the source of the accusations can be put in doubt, (e) *attacking the accusers* can work well. In cases where no amount of offensiveness reduction can work, (f) *compensation* via reimbursing the victim can help undermine ill-feelings that could have arisen due to the act in question.
IV. *Corrective action.* The corrective action strategy, along with mortification, comes within the larger framework of "apologia," one whereby the accused promises to rectify the problem, by either undertaking actions to restore the state of affairs before the egregious act or ensuring to prevent the recurrence of such acts, or both simultaneously. Whilst Goffman (2009) mentions this as a form of apology, it can be possible to undertake corrective action without one.
V. *Mortification.* A strategy whereby the accused confesses to the wrongdoing and asks for forgiveness, Schönbach (1980) mentions this as an approach that needs to be coupled with another in order to mitigate the severity of one's actions.

2.2 Situational Crisis Communication Theory

In contrast to IRT, Coombs' Situational Crisis Communications Theory (SCCT) is centered on the role of the audience within crisis management. Stemming from Benson's (1988) call for scholars to address the three key issues of forming typologies of crisis in organizations, their response strategies, and a theoretical framework to link the two, Coombs' SCCT highlighted the need for making sure that the audience's perspective of an organization is improved.

The SCCT holds that not only is a crisis a matter of perception (that is, a crisis is said to have happened when the audience perceives it to be so), but that it is often capricious and violates stakeholders' expectations of organizational operations. As such, any crisis has the potential to cause harm or undesirable outcomes. Given such a context, SCCT stipulates three primary objectives: (a) reconfigure stakeholders' assessment of the crisis, (b) sculpt stakeholders' opinions regarding the organization in question, and (c) diminish the negative effects of the crisis (Coombs 2007). Coombs details three distinct stages of a crisis scenario: (a) *pre-crisis*, whereby he holds that organizations need to safeguard themselves against future crises; (b) *crisis response*, during which time the organization focuses its efforts on responding to the situation at hand, and (c) *post-crisis*, the phase in which an organization needs to fortify its crisis response strategies while making sure that it lives up to the promises made to the public.

Depending on the classification of a crisis, stakeholders ascertain the level to which they will hold an organization accountable for a resulting crisis, which revolves around three crisis types: (a) victim, (b) accidental, or (c) intentional (Coombs 2004). Both the victim and accidental crises types lead to very weak attributions of crisis responsibility, seeing as they do not stem from malevolent purposes and appear to be uncontrollable by an organization. For instance, victim crises types include such instances as natural disasters, rumors, workplace violence, or product tampering; while accidental crises often take the form of technical error accidents or product harm, as well as challenges (Coombs 2007). However, intentional crises types are understandably ascribed to pernicious motivations, and are considered purposeful and preventable (Coombs 2007; Coombs and Holladay 2002; Sisco 2012). These include human-error accidents or product harm, and organizational misdeeds that not only violate the law but also put stakeholders at risk.

Consequently, the first stage of the SCCT involves determining in which cluster the crisis lies (Coombs 2007). In the second stage, crisis managers determine the factors that can vary the intensity of the attributions, such as crisis history, reputational history, and crisis severity (Coombs 2006). These factors inform the way audiences will likely perceive the situation, given that negative crisis history intensifies attributions of crisis responsibility (Coombs 2007), and a higher level of crisis severity results in audiences attributing higher levels of organizational responsibility (Lee 2004). Lastly, crisis managers select an appropriate response strategy (Coombs and Holladay 2002). Response strategies fall into one of four different postures: (a) *denial*, (b) *diminishment*, (c) *bolstering*, and (d) *rebuilding*, and range from the defensive to the accommodating.

The *denial* posture encompasses not just simple *denial* asserting the lack of a current crisis, but also an *attack the accuser* strategy that seeks to threaten the credibility of the ones formulating an accusation against the organization. A third strategy within the purview of this posturing is *scapegoating*, whereby someone else is squarely laid the blame upon for the crisis. Within *diminishment*, not only is an *excuse* used as a strategy to diminish any intention of wrongdoing, but also as a way to provide a way out by resorting to a lack of control over the crisis. Another variant that is widely used is *justification*, whereby the perceived damage is sought to be minimized.

Within *bolstering*, however, crisis management can take shape in the form of *reminders*, seeking to appeal to a past whereby organizational good can be highlighted, or even *ingratiation*, whereby crisis managers can seek a “get into the good books of stakeholders” strategy by praising them. What is less commonly, and more interestingly used, however, is the tactic of *victimage*, whereby the organization also posits itself as a crisis victim. The *rebuilding* posture is akin to the corrective action stance within IRT, manifesting in the form of *compensation* to the victims, or as *apology* tendered to the stakeholders.

3 The organization

Sports organizations, whether they be professional sports leagues like the National Football League (NFL) or the Indian Premier League (IPL), or collegiate athletic departments, are responsible for protecting their image, given that they are powerful and valuable brands. A fragmented media landscape means that organizations must determine how to properly procure the benefits of various media while remaining prepared for potential issues that could arise, particularly in digital spaces. Sports organizations must assess potential issues that could arise from various parties, including owners, coaches, athletes, fans, sponsors, etc. Scholarly examinations of the levels of crisis responsibility attributed to sporting organizations revealed trifurcated levels of crisis severity (Brown-Devlin and Brown 2020: 61). The initial, lowest cluster involved environmental/individual crises, such as natural disasters and athlete-driven issues outside of the purview of the team (controversial statements, lifestyle transgressions, criminal issues, etc.), suggesting that organizations are not held responsible for these types of issues. The next cluster involved rules and norms violations (e. g., rule broken by organization) that posed a moderate threat. The final cluster involved organizational mismanagement issues that "should be located within the organization's realm of control; yet, the organization's mismanagement of that issue led to the crisis" (Brown-Devlin and Brown 2020: 62). These issues pose the highest degree of organizational threat. Organizations must, first, assess the attributed levels of crisis responsibility before deciding *how* and *where* to respond. In this section, we examine how various organizations navigated different crises in the moderate and severe clusters.

When several International Federation of Association Football (FIFA) executives were arrested on corruption charges in 2015, the image of the organization was severely damaged by a crisis that included both rules/norms violations and organizational mismanagement. Onwumechili and Bedeau (2017) examined how FIFA responded and engaged in image repair. The authors discovered that FIFA offered multiple statements in traditional media settings, while strategically attempting to evade responsibility using *defeasibility* strategies. FIFA also promised *corrective action*, despite the fact that this strategy is most often recommended in conjunction with *mortification*, something FIFA refused to do. Furthermore, once FIFA did attempt to engage in structural changes, they placed internal representatives on its Reform Committee. The media harshly responded to FIFA's attempt at image repair, noting "that previous ineffective self-policing by FIFA created its reputation for a corrupt, cronyism-infested, insulated, and opaque organization" (Onwumechili and Bedeau 2017: 423). Clearly, this case study presents a few key learnings for sport organizations. First, organizations must select response strategies based on best practice recommendations that have been derived from extensive scholarly examination. Second, organizations must consider their reputation history and prior reputation before selecting a crisis response strategy and should be more accommodating in their response strategy selection if their history is fraught with infractions (Coombs 2014). Lastly, organizations must be transparent during times of crisis, as the sports media will perform their traditional watchdog role and apply pressure to the organization.

While social media has become a place for organizations to disseminate content, it can also create or heighten additional organizational crises. For instance, during the 2014 FIFA World Cup, player Cristoph Kramer seemingly received a head injury during a match, leading to strong concern among fans on social media regarding rules/norms violations pertaining to player safety and a lack of proper concussion protocols (Hughey 2015: 51). Despite the uproar from fans during the match on July 13, 2014, FIFA did not provide traditional media outlets with a formal comment, and furthermore, FIFA did not formally respond until nearly two months later on September 9. In that time span, influential social media accounts generated awareness of the issue, noting FIFA's callousness regarding the threats that traumatic brain injuries posed to its athletes (Hughey 2015: 59). Thus, this case study underscores the need for proper social media listening programs within modern sports organizations, especially since organizations should be utilizing such channels *before* crises erupt (Coombs 2014). Furthermore, crisis scholars have recommended that organizations "effectively utilize the interactivity of social media by creating dialogues with stakeholders, paying more attention to citizen-generated content, adopting stakeholder desired strategies, [and] cultivating opinion leaders on social media" (Cheng 2018: 65).

This failure to create dialogue with stakeholders is reflected in how the NFL has dealt with the extant problem of domestic violence (Schrotenboer 2014). When Baltimore Ravens star running back, Ray Rice, and his fiancée, Janay Palmer, were initially arrested for assault in the winter of 2014, the NFL cautiously expressed its support of Rice (Richards et al. 2017: 615). It was only when TMZ released a video depicting Rice dragging Palmer from an elevator on the night in question, provoking widespread shock and outrage, that the organization was forced to contend with the fallout of Rice's actions.

Thus, the NFL, the Ravens, and Rice himself, had to decide how to respond to the external criminal transgression. The Ravens choice to resort to *minimization* before the video release was ineffective. Even after the video release, Ravens' head coach John Harbaugh sought a combination of *ingratiation* and *diminishment* by stressing Rice's past community involvement and mentioning that Rice and Palmer had sought counseling. The Ravens maintained their support of the athlete even in the face of overwhelming criticism from other players, seeing as he was a valuable player for the team. The NFL failed initially to release any set of press releases condemning Rice's actions, citing their existing internal policy of refraining from commenting on ongoing criminal investigations. Moreover, the league denied having viewed the TMZ video of Rice's actions, thus neglecting to inform the audience of the crisis in an informative manner and elevating the crisis to organizational mismanagement cluster (Brown-Devlin and Brown 2020: 62). This breach of SCCT recommendations led the public to perceive the league's response as a denial of the crisis (Richards et al. 2017: 619). After a second video showed Rice inflicting extreme violence on his fiancée, both the Ravens and the NFL were spurred into taking more concrete steps. NFL commissioner Roger Goodell suspended Rice indefinitely and announced changes to the league's personal conduct policy. The Ravens terminated Rice's contract and took a corrective stance by offering fans an exchange for Ray Rice jerseys. However, the initial *denial* strategies on the part of both the Ravens and the NFL deviated from SCCT recommendations given the league's history of domestic violence (Richards et al. 2017: 619). Furthermore, the *rebuild* strategies of Rice's banishment and policy changes only came about as an outcome of public uproar rather than good-faith tactics to repair their battered image. As the authors suggest, the NFL's established cultural and reputational capital allowed them to weather the crisis fairly well as it had hardly affected the popularity of the game.

However, social media can also be used to communicate with fans during losing seasons, which may feel like a crisis to those who are highly identified (Compton and Compton 2014: 347). Such digital communication has altered the way that sports organizations engage with their fanbases, including during a crisis response. For instance, Compton and Compton (2014), through the lens of IRT, noted that organizations utilize "open letters" as a method to deliver their crisis response to their fanbase, as the demand for organizations to develop more personalized relationships with fans has increased. While traditional strategies were still utilized by sports organizations, namely *evading responsibility*, *reducing offensiveness*, and *corrective action*, it was important to note that open letters are generally written in a style resembling personal communication while being delivered publicly, especially on social media. Thus, this method of crisis response delivery encourages interactivity among fans and can generate both positive and negative reaction from stakeholders that is, then, publicly shared to their online, personal networks (Compton and Compton 2014: 346).

4 The athlete

While organizations and individuals employ their own strategies to mitigate a crisis, in the domain of sports, the individual actor (the athlete) becomes particularly central to image management. Athletes, themselves, become a "brand," distinct from each other due to their individual names, appearances, and personalities (Arai, Ko, and Ross 2014: 97). Gledhill (1991: xiii), in particular, underscores this rise of the athlete as a brand in modern culture by considering them "social sign(s)," who carry cultural and ideological meanings with entanglements of "individual personality, inviting desire and identification" with the larger phenomenon of the "national celebrity, founded on the body, fashion and personal style." The commodification of sport has ensured that athletes have gained valuable commercial power that is maintained via endorsement deals, forays into mainstream entertainment, merchandise tie-ups, and media rights – to the extent that players' remuneration for endorsements often exceeds their payment for actual sports (Smart 2005). This fiscal power, however, is a double-edged sword, considering that athletes more often than not are not considered "normal" employees of an organization but rather independent contractors who render their services for a fee (Onwumechili and Bedeau 2017). As a result, while "regular" corporate employees are often not the locus of a corporate scandal publicly, sports organizations often leverage the benefit of distancing themselves from their athletes' transgressions (Hearit 1995). Consequently, an athlete's evaluation no longer hinges on their on-field performance, and winning games is no longer the sole objective (Gilbert 2011) – they are brands that need to be developed, nurtured, and managed, much like traditional brands across various industries (Arai, Ko, and Ross 2014: 98). Considering this, the concept of athlete brand image, which refers to "a consumers' perception about athlete brand attributes" (Arai, Ko, and Ross 2014: 99), is a particularly important yet vulnerable component of what constitutes an athlete's brand equity. In the age of social media, the current landscape has led to a proliferation of PR firms devoted solely to athletes' image management; even the scope of a modern sports agent's duties has expanded from managing contractual obligations to proactively managing an athlete's image (Brazeal 2008: 146).

In 2009, professional golfer Tiger Woods was embroiled in a scandal regarding his alleged repeated marital infidelity, contradicting his traditionally "squeaky clean image" (Benoit 2013: 90). Following the scandal, Woods lost numerous sponsorships and was forced to engage in image repair. In order to address the scandal, Woods posted two statements on his website and apologized on television. Benoit (2013: 91–94) rhetorically analyzed Woods' response through the lens of IRT, highlighting the appropriateness of his usage of the mortification and corrective action strategies, given the perceived offensiveness of his actions. Meng and Pan noted that this scandal was a defining moment regarding the journalistic reporting of athlete scandals, as many journalists "abandoned traditional news-gathering methods and standards of fair play and relied primarily on aggressive often inaccurate, 'tabloid reporting'" (2013: 92). Despite the negative coverage, one of Woods' primary sponsors, Nike, continued to support him, as his notoriety in golf circles may have prevented them from ending their sponsorship agreement (Meng and Pan 2013: 98). Overall, scholars remarked that Woods' attempt at image repair was mostly successful (Benoit 2013: 89).

Professional cyclist Lance Armstrong's doping scandal offered the potential for examining the nature of social media in mitigating or worsening image-related scandals. Social media offers users the opportunity to engage with content that is dramatically different from traditional media – via the processes of curation, creation, and collaboration (Evans 2010), and for athletes, it offers an additional avenue to enact image repair wherein they can be in greater control of the narrative. Armstrong's troubles cascaded in 2012 when USADA concluded its investigation regarding his alleged use of performance-enhancing drugs and gave him a lifetime ban, while stripping him of his seven Tour de France medals. He, then, lost key sponsorships with Nike, Trek, and Oakley, and was forced to step down from LiveStrong, his cancer research organization. Hambrick, Frederick, and Sanderson (2015) conducted a thematic content analysis of Armstrong's attempt at crisis response on Twitter.

Armstrong's early tactics included *attacking the accuser*, by attempting to paint USADA's actions "unconstitutional" and a "witch-hunt"; *bolstering*, by portraying himself as a legendary athlete; and *stonewalling*, by shifting the focus to his philanthropic pursuits, endorsements, and personal life. The post-USADA investigation period saw a mirroring of these strategies. Yet, in his interview with Oprah Winfrey, he employed strategies that were in stark contrast to the ones used on Twitter. His tactics included *mortification*, by acknowledging that "the blame here falls on me" (Hambrick, Frederick, and Sanderson 2015: 209); simple *denial*, by claiming that he only doped in his early career; *shifting the blame*, by trying to justify his actions as being part of an elite athletic squad; *provocation*, by contextualizing doping as a consequence of his cancer diagnosis; and *victimization*, by comparing his lifetime ban to those of other athletes' suspensions. The combination of strategies, however, did not fail to stem negative backlash from fans. As Sanderson (2008) and Sanderson and Emmons (2014) suggest, an apologetic stance from the beginning might have helped him appear more contrite. The opportunity to redress his issues by engaging with his fans and supporters was squandered, as his stance on social media and traditional media outlets seemed to be completely at odds with each other.

Sometimes, the magnitude of athlete transgressions can be grossly underestimated not only by the athletes themselves, but also, by their agents, as seen in the case of the National Football League's (NFL) Terrell Owens (Brazeal 2008). Owens' prior churlish behavior left him with little reputation capital to spend (Coombs 2007) and signaled a likely difficult contract dispute with the Philadelphia Eagles in 2005. When the Eagles refused to reinstate him, Owens publicly railed against his coaches, the organization, and his teammates, resulting in immediate backlash. Owens' initial strategy was to hold a televised press conference wherein he sought to *bolster* his image by reframing his transgressions as a sign of his passion and loyalty to the game. Owens, however, was met with continued criticism and, as a result, channeled *mortification* by apologizing to his fans, teammates, coaches, and the organization. While Owens' somewhat contrite strategy might still have worked given sufficient passage of time, his agent Drew Rosenhaus effectively sabotaged his chance at redemption. He utilized similar strategies by bolstering Owens' image and engaging in mortification by calling him "remorseful" while refusing to offer redeeming steps. However, Rosenhaus also *attacked the accusers*, which included both the media and the Eagles organization, referring to their refusal to accept Owens' apology as ungrateful. Unfortunately, Rosenhaus did not consider his client's past misdemeanors, and such aggressive strategies destroyed any remaining goodwill. Thus, Owens was unable to re-negotiate a contract, and he did not play for the remainder of the 2005 season (Brazeal 2008: 147–150).

Unlike Owens, decorated Olympics champion swimmer Michael Phelps had a positive prior reputation when pictures of him smoking marijuana from a bong pipe appeared in the *News of the World* in 2009. In analyzing his situation, Walsh and McAllister-Spooner (2011) note that Phelps quickly issued a statement that included the following image repair tactics: he acknowledged his transgression and chalked it up to his youthfulness (he was 23 at the time) to engage in *mortification*; he *bolstered* his image by recognizing that his behavior violated people's expectations of high caliber athletes; and ensured *corrective action* by emphasizing that he would not engage in such behavior again. Most importantly, however, Phelps received unprecedented support from three powerful entities: his sponsors, the organizations he represented, and the media. Phelps' sponsors (Speedo, Omega, Subway, Visa, and Hilton) used *bolstering* and *reduction of offensiveness* strategies to support him through the crisis, with Omega even calling it a "non-crisis" and Visa mentioning that Phelps had promised not to repeat his actions. Although the United States Olympic Committee (USOC) reprimanded Phelps by withdrawing financial support and his eligibility to compete for three months, it also used *bolstering* and *minimization* strategies by emphasizing that he had not violated anti-doping regulations. Thus, not only was Phelps' statement well-received, but was quickly forgotten as a "boys will be boys" situation (Walsh and McAllister-Spooner 2011: 161).

It is critical to understand within the framework of sports that even in a situation where no egregious acts have been committed, fans can be galvanized to pronounce criticism against an athlete for what they deem to be diva-like or immature behavior. Such is the case of the beloved NBA player LeBron James, who, in deciding to announce his signing with the Miami Heat on "The Decision" in 2010, garnered negative press and accusations of immaturity from both fans and those within the NBA, such as the Cleveland Cavaliers owner Dan Gilbert who pronounced him a "coward" and a "narcissist" (Brown, Dickhaus, and Long 2012: 149). Brown, Dickhaus, and Long (2012) conducted an experiment to see what would likely have been an effective strategy for James in such a unique scenario and found that using the *mortification* strategy significantly improved James' image, while the *shifting the blame* and *bolstering* strategies negatively impacted him. More importantly, however, the experiment established the need to conduct more such image-focused experiments on people who are indifferent to an athlete to give a better understanding of image restoration and apologia strategies, given that the theory makes it clear that they would be the most susceptible to apologia, rather than fans who have a high level of involvement with the athlete in question and therefore have established attitudes (generally).

Overall, there is much to learn from these case studies about athlete image repair. For instance, it is imperative that athletes be transparent and authentic during their crisis response. Furthermore, athletes must plan their response while considering their own crisis history and prior reputation, and determining how those factors may impact stakeholder perceptions. Lastly, once a strategy has been formulated, the response must remain consistent across all media, including all parties associated with the athlete in question (i. e., agents, representatives, and so on).

5 The fans

While a majority of sports-related crisis communication research has examined issues affecting athletes and organizations, recent studies are also paying close attention to their primary stakeholders: sports fans. Perhaps one cannot examine the specialized group of stakeholders that are sports fans without mentioning the concept of fan identification. Team identification is defined as "the extent to which the fan views the team as an extension of his or herself" (Wann 2006: 273), underscoring the personal nature of psychological connection a person has with a sports group. In such a situation, a crisis that affects an organization or athlete will feel *personally* relevant to sports fans that highly identify with them. As such, when a fan's favorite team or athlete is in crisis mode, they, too, feel as though they are also in crisis mode. Research notes that for fans, their collective fan base serves as "an extended family in which they, too, participate. What affects one member of the team affects all" (Kruse 1981: 272).

Smith, Pegoraro, and Cruikshank (2019: 94) note that Twitter use is especially important for sports fans, as it heightens their enjoyment levels when used in conjunction with sports viewing. Given the rise of social media, fans now also have the ability to comment publicly on important issues that affect their preferred teams and athletes. Twitter has also served as an important medium for fans to express themselves emotionally when reacting to crises (Meadows and Meadows 2020). As such, a new type of active stakeholder has shown a willingness not to simply be affected by crises that occur, but rather, publicly comment on the organization/athlete's behalf.

One instance of fans utilizing social media to mitigate a threat to their social identity can be observed in the case of how University of Cincinnati football fans responded to their head football coach Brian Kelly's departure for the University of Notre Dame in 2009 (Sanderson 2013). Given the social and economic prominence of a college football head coach, such a loss can trigger loss of esteem and perceptions of a social identity threat (Tajfel and Turner 1979), making threat management inevitable via asserting group/team uniqueness (Ellemers, Spears, and Doosje 2002: 170). Kelly's departure precipitated feelings of insecurity amongst the fans of a team that had only recently enjoyed success, and the loss of their coach was deemed a blow to their team's reputation.

As a sort of retaliation against Kelly's perceived betrayal and a way to manage apprehensions regarding the team's future, fans sought solace in a Facebook group entitled "Get Out of Our City Brian Kelly." A thematic analysis of 717 posts conducted by Sanderson (2013) revealed that fans pursued five main strategies, including *rallying*, by exhorting the team players to use Kelly's exit as motivation to win future games, and encouraging their peers to demonstrate collective strength; *stigmatizing*, by denigrating their rival teams in an attempt to restore their feeling of superiority (Branscombe and Wann 1994: 654); and *victimization*, with fans framing themselves and the players as victims of Kelly's disloyalty and pillorying him in comments that highlighted what they saw as needless greed and insincerity.

Highly identified team members have also been known to demonstrate aggressive behavior (Ellemers, Spears, and Doosje 2002: 170), and this was true in this case as well, with fans resorting to *intimidation* by engaging in profane, threatening commentary against Kelly that veered towards homophobia and implied violence. A variant of intimidation was carried out in *degradation* tactics, with comments that sought to highlight Cincinnati's superiority by barraging Kelly "with misogynistic and homophobic slurs" (Sanderson 2013: 501). As Sanderson (2013: 497) notes, this is a consequence of "vicarious personalism," which makes in-group members more likely to negatively evaluate an out-group or out-group member, as it induces the perception that the latter's behavior is specifically aimed at the former.

In 2011, the University of Miami football team was accused of several possible NCAA violations, which had the potential for severe repercussions for the Miami athletic department. Brown and Billings (2013) conducted a content analysis of fan responses and found that Miami fans actually engaged in traditional crisis communication response strategies on behalf of Miami, namely ingratiation, attacking the accuser, reminder, and diverting attention. Fans' use of ingratiation was quite powerful, as it provided them the opportunity to unite over their shared bond as Miami football fans, and it strengthened the fan community as they maneuvered through the crisis. In fact, fans rallied together by tweeting a single hashtag (#IStandWithTheU) with enough frequency that it was included on Twitter's list of Trending Topics; thereby, fans helped to insert a positive message amid the flurry of negativity that was seen on Twitter as the Miami news broke (Brown and Billings 2013: 80). Koerber and Zabara (2017: 194) echoed the importance of such fan community formation during times of crisis, noting that they can act as buffers, or mediators between the organization and stakeholders, during the crisis communication response process. Thus, the authors argued that sports organizations and athletes generally, over time, withstand a majority of crises that befall them due to the fact that fan solidarity essentially prevents serious reputational damage.

As noted by Cheng (2018: 67), social media serves as an "interactive platform" for both the organization and its stakeholders during times of crisis, especially when a social identity threat among stakeholders is triggered. Cheng's (2018) interactive crisis communication model notes that stakeholders utilize social media to enact various strategies during a crisis, including providing emotional support, information sharing, remediation, rectification, and diverting attention. Thus, collective fan-enacted crisis communication research showcases a truly unique nature of sport – that stakeholders will engage in crisis response on behalf of their preferred team or athlete. Brown, Brown, and Billings (2015) examined how Penn State football fans responded following the news that former assistant football coach Jerry Sandusky had been charged with sexually assaulting 10 boys during his tenure at Penn State. The scandal ultimately led to the firing of head coach Joe Paterno. There were similarities in how Miami and Penn State fans reacted online, as Penn State fans also utilized the ingratiation strategy and tweeted the hashtag "WeSTILLAre" in an attempt to unify their fan community. However, once Paterno was fired, the Penn State case showcased how important the concept of identification is to fan-enacted crisis response, as fans seemingly sided with Paterno over their own school and administration (Brown, Brown, and Billings 2015: 304–305). No longer were fans simply uniting in support for their school; rather, they were uniting in their sense of loyalty to their head coach.

Thus, it is important to note that social media users may very well seize control of a narrative thanks to the two-way nature of interaction on social media (Chewning 2015: 73), and can in fact, *create* a crisis in the first place. This was experienced by Florida State University (FSU) when they invited fans to engage in a dialogue with beleaguered quarterback Jameis Winston via the Twitter campaign #AskJameis in 2014. Sanderson and colleagues (2016: 32) explained that this campaign showcased the risks of social media, since social media users can choose to mock it. The campaign's strategy was quickly questioned, given Winston's history of legal troubles, which ranged from prior accusations of consuming soda without paying for it, stealing crab legs from a grocery store, and raping a female FSU student.

The themes displayed in the tweets ranged from *outright criticism of FSU* ("Clearly Florida State is out of touch with common sense thinking #askjameis was a good idea. Are you stupid?") to *general sarcasm* with light-hearted humor (@FSU Football are you on a first name basis with the Tallahassee cops? #AskJameis;"), that nevertheless underscored the serious nature of the allegations against Winston (Sanderson et al. 2015: 34). Twitter users also outright *referenced Winston's legal incidents*, in particular the rape allegations and his propensity to engage in criminal behavior (@FSU Football when a girl says no, does she really mean yes? #AskJameis;") (Sanderson et al. 2015: 34). They also questioned the manner in which the Tallahassee Police Department and FSU conducted their investigations into the rape allegations and alleged *preferential treatment being meted out to Winston* ("#AskJameis, How glad are you that you play in Tallahassee where the PD protects the football players #whatgoesaroundcomesaround;") (Sanderson et al. 2015: 34). The implications of this research extend beyond merely acknowledging that the open-access nature of social media makes organizations vulnerable to hijacking of conversations by users who feel underserved by the actions of those they deem accountable to them. Rather, it also underscores the criticality of organizations to have a read of the social climate, and to learn to discern "textbook recommendations" (Sanderson et al. 2015: 35) from real-life applications.

Overall, the examination of fan behavior is a primary component of the crisis response process. As scholars have shown, fan behavior, particularly online, can either aid or be detrimental to organizations and athletes during times of crisis. It is imperative for crisis managers to maintain positive relationships with this key stakeholder group and involve social media managers in crisis planning.

6 Conclusion

Overall, the unique blend of sports organizations, athletes, and fans makes sports a compelling lens to examine and advance crisis communication scholarship. Framed by IRT and SCCT, this chapter considers the theories in relation to sports crises, evaluating not only the theoretical components but how they have been utilized to study and analyze various sporting breaches and dilemmas. Fan identification and fanship literature especially finds a crucial place within the structure of this chapter in understanding stakeholder behavior, given the emotional stakes involved on fans' part. As technology continues to alter the relationship between the three entities (sports organizations, athletes, and fans), crisis scholars should continue to analyze crisis response to formulate best practices that could potentially aid practitioners.

It is also necessary, however, to acknowledge that unlike the more "regular" world of business, organized sports operates by its own set of rules that makes it a particularly challenging arena to bridge the gap between the theory and application of crisis communication practices. As has been noted by scholars previously, the most prominent players involved within the crisis communication focus – owners, players, coaches, organizations themselves – have a level of prominence that is rare in the business world, not to mention that fans primarily buy into the drama of spectatorship that is unusual in other field of consumerism – such as retail stores (Koerber and Zabara 2017). The level of emotional engagement involved makes a seamless transition from theory to practice complicated, particularly by the fact that frameworks such as IRT are rooted in more formal rhetorical criticism which have traditionally focused on political speakers and speeches (Butterworth 2016). Simultaneously, image repair studies align with public relations scholarship that is more invested in the rhetoric's "instrumental capacities" rather than "its democratic commitments" (Butterworth 2016: 15). In other words, in the process of applying IRT principles to manage sports crises, a bigger question is often ignored – is it even ethical to make allowances for egregious acts committed by athletes such as Lance Armstrong or Ray Rice?

The popularity of sports as a cultural enterprise compels crisis communication scholars to examine it beyond the formal structures and hierarchies of corporate organizations, employees, and stakeholders. As sports comprises both immense financial and emotional stakes, scholars have noted that there is a tendency to turn a blind eye to the transgressions involved, both on the part of the fans (Bird 2002) and journalists, who would rather call attention to sporting appeal than venture into more uneasy considerations of ethics in sports and soil "its sell" (Wenner 2016: 40). But the cultural force that sports has increasingly occupied in the public sphere has been made possible because of what it communicates – about leadership, teamwork, heroism, hard work, and perseverance – and as such, communication scholars need to go beyond merely "fixing" a crisis that has occurred. Wenner's exhortation, therefore, for scholars to find a "'righteous' middle ground" (Wenner 2016: 41) of ethical inquiry within sports thus gains prominence, especially since moral and ethical violations have increasingly become more commonplace in the sporting arena. Most scholarship in sports crisis communication however, tends to avoid confronting the harsh truths of whether IRT or SCCT principles are even moral to consider within the context of often appalling offences committed by prominent sporting personalities – isn't domestic violence, as in the case of Ray Rice, indefensible? How are the transgressions of Harding, Landis, or Armstrong to be reconciled with notions of fair play so often brandished in the sporting world? These, and more such questions in a similar vein, provide grist to the mill of scholarship in sports communication, but empirical approaches often preclude the possibility of making subjective judgements on the nature of morals and ethics.

In addition, it needs to be contended with that a huge portion of sports scholarship is concentrated within the confines of North American sporting culture, a "product both of the influence of the United States on the sporting landscape and the U.S.-centric discipline of rhetorical studies" (Butterworth 2016: 16). Case studies such as those on FIFA by Onwumechili and Bedeau (2017), however, provide refreshing international perspective, and need to become a more staple hallmark of scholarship within the field, more reflective of sports' global reach and impact, as well changing times and milieus.

References

Arai, Akiko, Yong Jae Ko & Stephen Ross. 2014. Branding athletes: Exploration and conceptualization of athlete brand image. *Sport Management Review* 17. 97–106.

Benoit, William L. 1995. *Accounts, excuses, and apologies: A theory of image restoration strategies* (SUNY Series in Speech Communication). Albany: State University of New York Press.

Benoit, William L. 1997a. Image repair discourse and crisis communication. *Public Relations Review* 23. 177–186.

Benoit, William L. 1997b. Hugh Grant's image restoration discourse: An actor apologizes. *Communication Quarterly* 45. 251–267.

Benoit, William L. 2013. Tiger Woods' image repair: Could he hit one out of the rough? In Joseph R. Blaney, Lance R. Lippert & J. Scott Smith (eds.), *Repairing the athlete's image: Studies in sports image restoration*, 89–96. Plymouth, UK: Lexington Books.

Benoit, William L. & Robert S. Hanczor. 1994. The Tonya Harding controversy: An analysis of image restoration strategies. *Communication Quarterly* 42. 416–433.

Benson, James A. 1988. Crisis revisited: An analysis of strategies used by Tylenol in the second tampering episode. *Communication Studies* 39. 49–66.

Bird, Frederick B. 2002. *The muted conscience: Moral silence and the practice of business ethics* (rev. edn.). Westport, CN: Quorum Books.

Branscombe, Nyla R. & Daniel L. Wann. 1994. Collective self-esteem consequences of outgroup derogation when a valued social identity is on trial. *European Journal of Social Psychology* 24. 641–657.

Brazeal, LeAn M. 2008. The image repair strategies of Terrell Owens. *Public Relations Review* 34. 145–150.

Brown, Natalie A. & Andrew C. Billings. 2013. Sports fans as crisis communicators on social media websites. *Public Relations Review* 39. 74–81.

Brown, Natalie A., Kenon A. Brown & Andrew C. Billings. 2015. "May no act of ours bring shame": Fan-enacted crisis communication surrounding the Penn State sex abuse scandal. *Communication & Sport* 3. 288–311.

Brown, Kenon A., Josh Dickhaus & Mia C. Long. 2012. LeBron James and "The Decision": An empirical examination of image repair in sports. *Journal of Sports Media* 7. 149–175.

Brown-Devlin, Natalie & Kenon A. Brown. 2020. When crises change the game: Establishing a typology of sports-related crises. *Journal of International Crisis and Risk Communication Research* 3. 49–70.

Burke, Kenneth. 1961. *Rhetoric of religion*. Berkeley, CA: University of California Press.

Butterworth, Michael L. 2016. Sport as rhetorical artifact. In Andrew C. Billings (ed.), *Defining sport communication*, 11–25. New York, NY: Routledge.

Cheng, Yang. 2018. How social media is changing crisis communication strategies: Evidence from the updated literature. *Journal of Contingencies and Crisis Management* 26. 58–68.

Chewning, Lisa Volk. 2015. Multiple voices and multiple media: Co-constructing BP's crisis response. *Public Relations Review* 41. 72–79.

Compton, Josh & Jordan L. Compton. 2014. College sports, losing seasons, and image repair through open letters to fans. *Communication & Sport* 2. 345–362.

Coombs, W. Timothy. 2004. Impact of past crises on current crisis communication: Insights from situational crisis communication theory. *The Journal of Business Communication* 41. 265–289.

Coombs, W. Timothy. 2006. *Code red in the boardroom: Crisis management as organizational DNA*. Greenwood Publishing Group.

Coombs, W. Timothy. 2007. Protecting organization reputations during a crisis: The development and application of situational crisis communication theory. *Corporate Reputation Review* 10. 163–176.

Coombs, W. Timothy. 2014. *Ongoing crisis communication: Planning, managing, and responding*. Thousand Oaks, CA: Sage Publications.

Coombs, W. Timothy & Sherry J. Holladay. 2002. Helping crisis managers protect reputational assets: Initial tests of the situational crisis communication theory. *Management Communication Quarterly* 16. 165–186.

Ellemers, Naomi, Russell Spears & Bertjan Doosje. 2002. Self and social identity. *Annual Review of Psychology* 53. 161–186.

Evans, Dave. 2010. Social media and customer engagement. In Dave Evans, Jake McKee & Susan Bratton, *Social media marketing: The next generation of business engagement*, 3–21. Indianapolis: Wiley.

Fishman, Donald A. 1999. ValuJet Flight 592: Crisis communication theory blended and extended. *Communication Quarterly* 47. 345–375.

Gilbert, Jeremy. 2011. Scandals challenge sports reporters to look beyond the field of play. *Poynter*, 23 September. https://www.poynter.org/reporting-editing/2011/scandals-challenge-sports-reporters-to-look-beyond-the-field-of-play/ (19 November 2020).

Gledhill, Christine. 1991. *Stardom: Industry of desire*. London, England: Routledge.

Goffman, Erving. 2009. *Relations in public*. Brunswick, NJ: Transaction Publishers.

Hambrick, Marion E., Evan L. Frederick & Jimmy Sanderson. 2015. From yellow to blue: Exploring Lance Armstrong's image repair strategies across traditional and social media. *Communication & Sport* 3. 196–218.

Hearit, Keith M. 1995. "Mistakes were made": Organizations, apologia, and crises of social legitimacy. *Communication Studies* 46. 1–17.

Hughey, S. Morgan. 2015. Social Media, Futbol, and Crisis: An exploratory case study examining the FIFA World Cup addressing player concussions. *Journal of Media Critiques* 1. 51–65.
Koerber, Duncan & Nick Zabara. 2017. Preventing damage: The psychology of crisis communication buffers in organized sports. *Public Relations Review* 43. 193–200.
Kruse, Noreen W. 1981. Apologia in team sport. *Quarterly Journal of Speech* 67. 270–283.
McClearey, Kevin E. 1983. Audience effects of apologia. *Communication Quarterly* 31. 12–20.
Lee, Betty K. 2004. Audience-oriented approach to crisis communication: A study of Hong Kong consumers' evaluation of an organizational crisis. *Communication Research* 31(5). 600–618.
Meadows, Cui Zhang & Charles W. Meadows, III. 2020. He will never walk outside of a prison again: An examination of Twitter users' responses to the Larry Nassar Case. *Communication & Sport* 8. 188–214.
Meng, Juan & Po-Lin Pan. 2013. Revisiting image-restoration strategies: An integrated case study of three athlete sex scandals in sports news. *International Journal of Sport Communication* 6. 87–100.
Onwumechili, Chuka & Koren Bedeau. 2017. Analysis of FIFA's attempt at image repair. *Communication & Sport* 5. 407–427.
Richards Jr., Othello, Christopher Wilson, Kris Boyle & Jordan Mower. 2017. A knockout to the NFL's reputation?: A case study of the NFL's crisis communications strategies in response to the Ray Rice scandal. *Public Relations Review* 43. 615–623.
Sanderson, Jimmy. 2008. Mutual respect, mutual resolve, mutual responsibility: The Prime Minister's apology to Indigenous people and the beginning of a new national framework for Australia. The Shann Memorial Lecture.
Sanderson, Jimmy. 2013. From loving the hero to despising the villain: Sports fans, Facebook, and social identity threats. *Mass Communication and Society* 16. 487–509.
Sanderson, Jimmy & Betsy Emmons. 2014. Extending and withholding forgiveness to Josh Hamilton: Exploring forgiveness within parasocial interaction. *Communication & Sport* 2(1). 24–47.
Sanderson, Jimmy, Katie Barnes, Christine Williamson & Edward T. Kian. 2016. "How could anyone have predicted that #AskJameis would go horribly wrong?" Public relations, social media, and hashtag hijacking. *Public Relations Review* 42. 31–37.
Schönbach, Peter. 1980. A category system for account phases. *European Journal of Social Psychology* 10. 195–200.
Schrotenboer, Brent. 2014. History of leniency: NFL domestic cases under Goodell. *USA Today*, 2 October. http://www.usatoday.com/story/sports/nfl/2014/10/01/nfl-domestic-abuse-history-under-roger-goodell/16566615/ (20 July 2019).
Scott, Marvin B. & Stanford M. Lyman. 1968. Accounts. *American Sociological Review*. 46–62.
Semin, Gün R. & Antony S. Manstead. 1983. *The accountability of conduct: A social psychological analysis*. New York: Academic Press.
Shipley, Brad. A. 1995. Clarence Thomas, sexual harassment, and apologia: An exploration of Thomas's rhetorical strategies of self-defense. *Journal of the Northwest Communication Association* 23. 90–107.
Sisco, H. F. 2012. Nonprofit in crisis: An examination of the applicability of situational crisis communication theory. *Journal of Public Relations Research* 24(1). 1–17.
Smart, Barry. 2005. *The sport star: Modern sport and the cultural economy of sporting celebrity*. London: Sage.
Smith, Lauren Reichart, Ann Pegoraro & Sally Ann Cruikshank. 2019. Tweet, retweet, favorite: The impact of Twitter use on enjoyment and sports viewing. *Journal of Broadcasting & Electronic Media* 63. 94–110.

Tajfel, Henry & John Turner. 1979. An integrative theory of intergroup conflict. In William G. Austin & Stephen Worchel (eds.), *The social psychology of intergroup relations*, 33–37. California: Brooks-Cole.

Tedeschi, James T. & Marc Riess. 1981. Verbal strategies in impression management. In Charles Antaki (ed.), *The psychology of ordinary explanations of social behavior*, 271–309. London: Academic Press.

Walsh, Joseph & Sheila M. McAllister-Spooner. 2011. Analysis of the image repair discourse in the Michael Phelps controversy. *Public Relations Review* 37. 157–162.

Wann, Daniel L. 2006. Understanding the positive social psychological benefits of sport team identification: The team identification-social psychological health model. *Group Dynamics: Theory, Research, and Practice* 10. 272–296.

Ware, B. L. & Wil A. Linkugel. 1973. They spoke in defense of themselves: On the generic criticism of apologia. *Quarterly Journal of Speech* 59. 273–283.

Wenner, Lawrence A. 2016. Sport and the communication of ethics. In Andrew C. Billings (ed.), *Defining sport communication*, 40–58. New York, NY: Routledge.

Zhang, Juyan & William L. Benoit. 2004. Message strategies of Saudi Arabia's image restoration campaign after 9/11. *Public Relations Review* 30. 161–167.

Brody J. Ruihley

33 Communicating fantasy sport

Abstract: Once a pen-and-paper activity and niche hobby, fantasy sport is one industry very thankful for advanced communication activities produced with advent of the Internet. With a pre-Internet estimated consumer base of 500,000, fantasy sport's growth has been steadily increasing to a significant industry size of 59.3 million American and Canadian participants. With this growth and incredible reach within the sport environment, fantasy sport has influenced communication activities in many ways including how much information participants are seeking, what types of information participants are consuming, how people view and use statistics, how mass media outlets cover the activity, and even how sport contests are delivered across communication platforms. Fantasy sport, in the traditional season-long form and contemporary daily/weekly fantasy sport contests, is creating amplified fans desiring amplified information and coverage. This chapter focuses on the rise of fantasy sport and communication in North America.

Keywords: fantasy sport; daily fantasy sport; gaming; uses and gratifications

1 Introduction

Fantasy sport is defined as an "interactive team management activity based on statistics accrued by athletes of real-life professional sport organizations and/or college athletics" (Ruihley and Hardin 2011: 233). Generally speaking, fantasy sport (or fantasy) participants (also known as team managers) select athletes from any real team to be a player on their fantasy team. This takes place in a selection or auction-style draft amongst league participants. Once a team is built, league teams compete against one another, based on real-life athlete statistics, to determine the best team manager. There are many variations to the fantasy game including, but not limited to, draft style, competition format, length of season, and scoring categories. Communication outlets are heavily used in the distribution and consumption of this activity. Examining fantasy sport participation through the lens of Katz, Blumler, and Gurevitch's (1973) uses and gratifications approach reveals just how intertwined the communication industry is with this activity. This approach "represents an attempt to explain something of the way in which individuals use communications, among other resources in their environment, to satisfy their needs and to achieve their goals" (1973: 21). Successful fantasy sport participants are quite aware of their informational environment and how important it is to achieve success. This includes understanding the draft process, player draft value, player performance and statistics, trade value, and in many cases, advanced sport analytics. Participants prepare in a plethora of ways

https://doi.org/10.1515/9783110660883-033

including the purchasing of online and offline draft-preparation materials, listening to fantasy-specific podcasts or other audio programming, watching fantasy-specific television shows, and seeking expert advice and analysis from fantasy sport professionals through a variety of traditional and social media outlets. Enjoying the activity also involves watching and following a fantasy team's performance. The daily or weekly contest has fantasy sport participants consuming *several* different athletic contests in an effort to follow and root on their team, as opposed to a *single* athletic contest featuring a hometown or favorite team.

Once a pen-and-paper type of activity, fantasy sport has evolved into an industry complimented by the technological advancements seen in the communication industry. Thanks in large part to the advent of the Internet, the fantasy sport industry progressed quickly in popularity, prestige, and participant size. While gauging international play is difficult due to widely competing sports gambling practices in Europe (Graham 2016) and a lack of trade association presence outside of the United States (US) and Canada, examining North American play sheds light on the growth of a burgeoning industry. With a pre-Internet estimated consumer base of 500,000, fantasy sport's North American growth continues to trend upwards and as of 2017, is hosting a sizable industry of 59.3 million American and Canadian participants (Industry demographics 2020). This growth and incredible reach influenced sport communication activities in many ways, including how much information participants are seeking, how participants view statistics, how mass media outlets cover the activity, and even how sport contests are delivered across communication platforms (Billings and Ruihley 2013, 2014). This chapter focuses on the rise of fantasy sport and communication in North America.

With each communication advancement mentioned in this chapter, it is apparent how consumers continue to seek out new technologies and ways to gather information to better their experience in fantasy sport. There are major assumptions creating foundation for the uses and gratifications approach and it is important to explore those aspects as it relates to this topic of communicating fantasy sport. The first assumption is that the audience is active in their goal-directed consumption (McQuail, Blumler, and Brown 1972). Fantasy sport, in the traditional season-long form and contemporary daily fantasy sport contests, creates amplified fans desiring very specific information and coverage. A second and third assumption of uses and gratifications claim that audience members are in control of the media while taking initiative in "linking need gratification and media choice" as media outlets contend to fulfill audience needs (Katz, Blumler, and Gurevitch 1973: 511). From web video, social media, and mobile applications to satellite radio, magazine topics, and traditional television consumption, fantasy sport is disseminated in many ways and by many competing providers. The messages being delivered are all-encompassing topics focused on statistical breakdowns, key matchups to consider, weather updates, player profiles, injury status, and scoring outcomes. Fantasy sport users have immense control over their selection between the dozens of competing fantasy sport-specific outlets covering a variety of topics.

Lastly, another assumption of the uses and gratifications approach is that audience members are "self-aware" of their interests, motives, and choices (Katz, Blumler, and Gurevitch 1973: 511). Fantasy sport participants are highly aware of the information needed to better their experience and are presented with information, statistics, analytics, video, and expert analysis to help with decisions. With immense industry-wide growth, fantasy sport alters the way sport is consumed and creating new avenues of communicative efforts from new and existing media outlets. This chapter explores the process of communicating fantasy sport in contemporary times in three sections focusing on (a) communicating with and for the fantasy sport participant, (b) how the fantasy sport industry benefits from mass communication evolution, and (c) how the fantasy sport industry provides content for communication and sport activities. Those reading this chapter will come away with a greater understanding of just how important communication channels are to the fantasy sport industry, how much consumers use technology in their experience, and how important the industry is to the growth of communication-based sport organizations.

2 Communication with and for the fantasy sport participant

In 2010, ESPN's Department of Integrated Media Research (2010) shared a statistic about their users perfectly embodying the information-seeking nature of the fantasy sport participant. They reported their average consumer took in approximately seven hours of ESPN media each week, while the fantasy sport consumer averaged more than three times the amount of media than their non-fantasy sport counterparts (22 hours and 40 minutes). Academic research following this report has backed this claim, though not quite to the same proportion. Billings and Ruihley (2013) examined traditional sport fans and fantasy sport participants and found a near doubling of the average hours per week consuming sport (9.6 hours for traditional fans and 18.0 hours for fantasy sport participants). In *The Fantasy Sport Industry: Games Within Games* (2014), Billings and Ruihley discovered a near 60 percent increase in sport consumption for both male and female fantasy sport participants, compared to the non-fantasy sport participating sport fans. In research collected for Ruihley and Billings (2019), ESPN's Director of Communication, Kevin Ota, was asked about the current consumption difference between the two groups. While he did not provide specific numbers, his answer was telling: "According to the 2017 ESPN Sports Poll, fans who play fantasy sports are more likely to attend games, read sports news, watch sports highlights and spend money on sports compared to fans who aren't fantasy players. Simply put, there are no more engaged and avid sports fans than those who play fantasy" (Ota 2018b).

With this type of emphasis on the information-seeking behaviors of fantasy sport participants, it is important to look deeper into their consumption. Armed with fantasy sport industry data collected from 751 adult fantasy sport participants, Ruihley and colleagues from the Fantasy Sport Writers Association outlined some of the key consumption considerations. The first data point examined why fantasy sport participants sought out fantasy-relevant information. Reasons consisted of the following: 37.2 percent weekly lineup changes, 30.0 percent daily fantasy sport league information, and 25.8 percent for daily lineup changes. When asked about sports of interest, American football, per usual, lead the way with 91.5 percent of respondents having interest. Football was followed by 49.1 percent interest in baseball, 33.3 percent in basketball, and 11.2 percent in hockey. A second data point revealed what communicative outlets were used for fantasy-specific information. The top three outlets were web-based articles, stories, or features (98.1 percent), social media (88.0 percent), and podcasts (51.4 percent). When respondents were asked to choose their primary outlet for information, web articles, stories, or features gained a large majority of the responses (60.2 percent), with the next closest outlet being social media (26.5 percent). A third data point identified characteristics of high-quality fantasy sport information, as identified by respondents. The top results are as follows: information is timely (90.4 percent), opinions, projections, or predictions are explained (82.4 percent), writing is clear (59.9 percent), and the writing or prediction is accurate (56.3 percent). When asked to pick the most important, having opinions, projections, or predictions explained received the top percentage (37.9 percent). Two final data points help highlight the fantasy sport participants' needs for information. The participants identified the most engaging type of information as analytics and statistics (38.3 percent) followed by fantasy strategy (28.2 percent), and player-specific information (26.9 percent). Additionally, when asked how important images, data tables, videos, humor, or usefulness of data each were on a five-point scale, usefulness of data rose to the top with a 4.2/5.0 (indicating very important). The next closest important feature was data tables at 2.9/5.0.

Understanding usage of communication outlets is vital to fantasy sport providers. As outlined further in this chapter, many in the fantasy sport community are broadening their communicative reach to appeal to and attract the fantasy sport participant. In 2017, data from 832 adult fantasy sport participants, Ruihley (2018) shared the frequency of use of many communication outlets and the preferred outlet choice for fantasy sport information (see Table 1). Table 1 illustrates weekly and daily use as very high for social media, television, and website media. Additionally, website media (49.5 percent), social media (25.2 percent), and podcasts (14.9 percent) were the preferred outlets for fantasy sport information. These data points shed light on where consumers put their attention and where they seek out fantasy-specific information. Knowing this, fantasy sport operators can create strategy and communication plans to effectively and efficiently offer their products and information.

Tab. 1: Communication outlet use for fantasy sport information ($n = 832$)

Outlet	Never	Few times per season	Monthly	Weekly	Daily	Percent for best outlet
Print media	60.7 %	26.9 %	1.8 %	7.5 %	3.1 %	1.0 %
Podcasts	32.2 %	17.2 %	5.4 %	20.1 %	25.1 %	14.9 %
Radio trad/sat	43.4 %	21.0 %	6.1 %	16.1 %	13.3 %	2.4 %
Social media	10.8 %	7.3 %	4.9 %	16.9 %	60.0 %	25.2 %
Television	14.3 %	14.2 %	6.5 %	40.4 %	24.6 %	6.1 %
Website media	3.7 %	4.4 %	4.4 %	26.6 %	60.8 %	49.5 %

3 Fantasy sport benefiting from communication advancements

Picture a dining room table or family room surrounded by 10–12 people, each armed with a draft magazine, hand-written notes, highlighters, pens, pencils, and perhaps the latest edition of *Baseball Weekly*. Each person has completed research on just about every athlete that might be drafted in the night's fantasy draft, because time is of the essence when combing through ink and paper. There is no Siri, Alexa, Google, draft podcast, one-click player profile, sortable stats of projections or past statistics, *FantasyPros*' expert consensus percentage, or a 28-hour ESPN fantasy marathon on television to help you prepare and get through your fantasy draft. A team is drafted with the information tangibly in front of you. During the season, imagine tallying and compiling player statistics through information brought to you by a young person flinging the day's newspaper onto your front porch. Standings, transactions, trades, and voting would be handled using the telephone or postal mail throughout the season until a champion was crowned. For those entrenched in contemporary fantasy sport play, this scenario feels archaic for an activity that has become so instant, information-saturated, and dependent on communication tools. Similar to when people cannot imagine a radio soap opera being the entertainment focal point in a home or television without high definition, guided information, or even color, this type of description of pre-Internet fantasy sport play is difficult to grasp. However, this is an important picture to paint, as it illustrates a part of the fantasy sport environment prior to the communication-altering advent of the Internet. Even the earliest of fantasy baseball leagues took place in the 1960s, long before any of the Internet-based technological advancements of today's game. Harvard professor William Gamson is credited with starting the first fantasy baseball league in 1960, called The Baseball Seminar (Billings and Ruihley 2014; Schwartz 2005). Gamson's league drafted players in an auction-style process with US $10 translating to US $100,000 in fantasy sport currency (Walker 2006). In an effort to keep up with their teams and progress in the competition, "the simple act of reading the box scores had become a daily thrill ride" (2006: 62). Describing a newspaper reading as a thrill ride shows the technological times in which this activity began.

Gamson's professorial career and his Baseball Seminar landed him in Ann Arbor, Michigan. One of the team managers of the transported league was Robert Sklar, who advised Daniel Okrent at the University of Michigan. Okrent is well-known for creating the modern version of fantasy baseball called *rotisserie*. Okrent created his version of fantasy baseball in 1979 with a group of friends at a restaurant named *La Rôtisserie Française*. The connection of mass communication and fantasy sport was furthered in 1981 as Major League Baseball had a player/management strike with a long hiatus of games played. Okrent wrote an article for the magazine, *Inside Sports*, outlining the rules of rotisserie baseball and with no *real* sport to cover, this small activity quickly gained attention and momentum. This article sparked an interest in the activity, even creating further communication dependency, as Okrent became the editor for a fantasy-sport specific magazine called *Rotisserie League Baseball*. This was 1984, and few could have anticipated the technological advancements and communication relationships that would propel this activity into a full-fledged industry. Specifically, the fantasy sport industry has had an upward trajectory for over 25 years largely thanks to the accessibility of the Internet, specification of television viewing interests, satellite radio technology, and social media. The following sections discuss each of these areas and how fantasy sport grew as a result of these developments.

3.1 Fantasy sport and the Internet

As one can imagine, the development of the Internet changed the game for many organizations and industries, including sport. As Pedersen, Miloch, and Laucella (2007: 213) state, "the Internet has laid the framework for new and merging media in sport communication, and more than any other medium, the Internet has allowed sport consumers to feed their craving for information regarding their favorite sport products." Feeding the sport information craving was easy, as the World Wide Web provided a fertile environment that was immediate, instantaneous, and complex, with a powerful capacity to share all types of information (Pedersen, Miloch, and Laucella 2007; Peterson and Merino 2003). In the early 2000s, the Internet was classified as New Sport Media (Pedersen, Miloch, and Laucella 2007). McQuail (2002) described new media as "linking information communication technologies with their associated social contexts, bring together three elements: (1) technological artifacts and devices; (2) activities, practices and uses; and (3) social arrangements and organizations forming around the devices and practices (2002: 38). Aspects of new media include interconnectivity, interactivity, accessibility, and multiple usages (Pedersen, Miloch, and Laucella 2007).

Fantasy sport blossomed with the each of the aspects outlined by McQuail and Pedersen, Miloch, and Laucella. Starting with McQuail's areas, fantasy sport is one activity able to link the information associated (player performance, player statistics, and statistical hosting) with the activity to the associated social contexts (i. e., the consumers). Going further, this activity brings together the aforementioned three elements outlined by McQuail. First, fantasy sport could now grow further with its utilization of technological artifacts and devices based on computer-based technology including statistics-based software, online hosting abilities, online written information, and social-based communication applications. Second, the activities, practices, and uses of fantasy sport were still present and able to be enhanced. Third, further social arrangements and organization were taking place around the new technology as geographical or spatial concerns were minimized.

Examining Pedersen and colleagues' (2007) four aspects of new media, fantasy sport benefited tremendously with each playing a large role in the activity's growth. The World Wide Web allowed sports information to be connected with consumers in an instant. News, audio, videos, stories, scores, and player performances travelled faster than ever before. This allowed fantasy sport participants to experience the activity in a new way (for example, instant player statistics and consuming out-of-market player performances) and use this technology in creative ways. The activity was interactive, not only in the way the fantasy sport participants could consume information and play, but also in the way leagues could be formed. No longer was the activity limited to those able to attend an in-person draft, as technology opened up participation for anyone with an Internet connection. In the same way, the activity was accessible for more people to participate and allows those participating to be amplified consumers of information. Lastly, the Internet provided multiple usages for fantasy sport growth. These usages include a place to gather information, an environment to host play, and a hub for a community without geographic restriction. As Billings and Ruihley (2014) state, "Suddenly, many people who loved sports, but did not previously participate in fantasy sport because of the legwork required, opted to join online fantasy sport leagues. Acquiring statistics was easier and so was league upkeep: The Internet provided the needed platform" (2014: 13). Billings, Butterworth, and Turman appropriately summed up the benefit fantasy sport received from the expansion of Internet: "immediacy combined with access" (2012: 298).

3.2 Fantasy sport on television

Turning attention to an older communication device with ever-changing features and updates, television has impacted the fantasy sport industry in many important ways. Fantasy sport has benefited from television's technological and communicative growth and reach, particularly with the expansion of very specific audience interests, creation of niche channels, and 24/7 content needs. There is a mutually beneficial relationship with sports television and fantasy sport. While the next section discusses the benefits of this relationship for television, this section focuses on the advancements in the relationship of television and fantasy sport from a fantasy sport perspective.

Rosenthal's (2019) review of ESPN's 40th anniversary states that "virtually from the start, [ESPN] began altering and accelerating upheaval of not just sports media but sports itself." In his explanation, Rosenthal outlined many aspects on how ESPN had become a "catalyst for widespread change." Included in his reasoning was how ESPN rewrote sport schedules, added a litany of games to television, created a highlight culture, round-the-clock television, and helped support the idea of niche programming. Little did anyone know, in 1979, this station would influence many other sport networks and eventually cover such a vast array of sports not even heard of at the time – including mixed martial arts, Ultimate Fighting Championship, spelling bees, eSports, X Games, and even fantasy sport. The development of ESPN and the move by other networks to increase stations, create more shows, and answer the call for more content, allowed fantasy sport to have a place on the screen. As Stephens (1999) states, the 1980s were a time of new technologies contributing to the growth of television. In particular, videocassette recording and video game technology made the television set more interactive and important within the home. Additionally, in this decade "the number of cable networks grew ... and then exploded in the 1990s as improved cable technology and direct-broadcast satellite television multiplied the channels available to viewers" (1999).

Specifically examining US-based sports, specialized networks now cover all angles with key examples consisting of the NFL Network, NBATV, MLB Network, NHL Network, Golf Channel, the Tennis Channel, and the Olympic Channel. In intercollegiate sports in the US, athletic conferences and even specific universities have even created their own stations and networks. Where does fantasy sport fit in all of this growth and expansion? The relationship took some time to grow due to a perception problem. While the industry was continually growing through the 1990s and early 2000s (Industry demographics 2020), those in charge of programming still considered the activity to be a small hobby. While not always accepted, many in the industry worked hard to pave the way for a fantasy sport presence on television screens. ESPN's Matthew Berry is among those who fought for airtime and helped legitimize fantasy sport to business executives and the sport consumer. Discussing fantasy sport's misperception, Berry told Billings and Ruihley (2014) about the belief people had of fantasy sport being just a game and a small niche activity. As he stated, "In fact, the numbers and studies that we would give when talking to various stakeholders at ESPN would counteract that [opinion]. Once people became aware of the size of the fantasy playing audience, and the amount of our fans that were engaged in it, fantasy became a much bigger part of the conversation" (2014: 78).

When ESPN did embrace fantasy play, they allowed for fantasy sport voices to be heard on airwaves, created shows, hosted fantasy play, and gave it much more attention. While ESPN was providing content to the fantasy sport masses, the industry was benefiting tremendously from the immense exposure ESPN provided to the game.

In a sense, being on ESPN gave fantasy sport a sense of legitimacy and clout. At the same time, other channels followed suit and began providing fantasy sport content, information and analysis.

Fantasy sport also grew as a result of changes in television leading to more games and sporting contests being broadcast nationally. No longer were fantasy sport participants reliant on only the local broadcast; a plethora of games were now available for consumption. Specifically, the DirecTV Sunday Ticket, the NFL RedZone, NBA TV, and MLB.TV all allowed for greater access to their sport, their games, and player performances. As mentioned, part of the allure of fantasy play is watching a constructed team and following their performance against others in the league. Appropriate for the fantasy sport participant, the NFL RedZone (n.d.) touts that fans see "every touchdown from every game Sunday afternoon." The promotion for this channel even describes the station as the "perfect fantasy companion" (n.d.). This channel alone makes the fantasy football experience more enjoyable as fantasy participants can easily follow their team, keep an eye on their opponent's team, and feel a part of the action.

3.3 FNTSY Sports Network

Blending television, streaming, and social media, one television-based advancement greatly assisted the communication reach and growth of fantasy sport. Providing even more evidence of fantasy sport responding to technology and communication advancements, in late 2014, an entire network was built only to offer fantasy sport content. The aptly named FNTSY Sports Network focused on providing fantasy sport content and information for television, video/audio streaming, and radio audiences. FNTSY Sports Network is available on 35 North American cable providers including DISH Network and other streaming services consisting of Apple TV, Xbox, Roku, Amazon Fire TV, Klowd TV, Pluto TV, Fubo TV, and Twitch (FNTSY 2019). Audio streams of the network have been made available on audio platforms iHeartRadio, TuneIn, and the FNTSY Sports Radio Network App. Part of the blessing (and the curse) of having a full network devoted to one topic is having the shows, personalities, information, and content to fill the time. FNTSY has successfully provided content to its consumers in the fantasy and sports gambling environments. While not every on-air personality is in studio, they are still able to provide fantasy sport-specific information to the masses. This type of niche information expansion is made possible by the technological advancements allowing people to have broadcast abilities at the tips of their fingers. With camera and voice-recording capabilities, computers, smartphones, and other portable devices are affordable and give many the ability to produce podcasts, video streams, or even full shows with great ease. At the time of this writing, FNTSY was in the process of merging with SportsGrid, potentially adding more focus to sports betting.

3.4 SiriusXM Fantasy Sports Radio

Another technological advancement aiding the growth of the fantasy sport industry is the creation of satellite radio service. In 2000, the first signal was sent to and from space and appropriately received. Production began for the full release of satellite radio in 2001 (Moran 2000). As Moran (2000) states, this type of services brings to "radio what cable television brought to the TV industry: an abundance of channels, each dedicated to slivers of the national audience ... channels for sports talk; for reggae and merengue; for gospel, salsa and big-band jazz, among many other formats." Unbeknownst to them, a major hobby and budding industry would be one of those slivers of information and the topic of an entire 24-hour-per-day station. In the press release announcing SiriusXM Fantasy Sports Radio station, SiriusXM's President and Chief Content Officer, Scott Greenstein stated:

> We've created a unique destination for fantasy sports fans. Our listeners get live play-by-play from the NFL, MLB, NASCAR, NHL, NBA, PGA, soccer and more that allows them to follow all their fantasy players or teams in real time. Now they have a dedicated fantasy sports channel that they can tune into 24 hours a day that will give them the stats, injury news and expert advice they'll need to dominate their fantasy sports leagues. (Sirius XM 2010)

Listeners responded positively to this new station and quickly accepted it and its premise. In an interview conducted by Billings and Ruihley (2014), SiriusXM's Steve Cohen describes the launch of SiriusXM Fantasy Sports Radio, in summer of 2010, as an immediate hit. He states, "[Almost instantly,] we got more listeners calling our talk shows on our fantasy sports channel than we did on any other SiriusXM produced sports channel. [By December 2011] we had an average of over 28,000 calls a day" (2014: 67). Cohen justified the need for the station, at least in part, by claiming that it reached fans on a "much higher plane in terms of the intellectual level that we discuss sports" (2014: 76). He discussed the need for fans to know strategy and not just player ability. He even mentioned how other sports-talk show hosts do not want to go down the fantasy sport trail because they simply could not "keep up with the knowledge that fantasy fans bring to their talk show" (2014: 78). Another feature of this SiriusXM station is how it is not confined to one particular company, viewpoint, or agenda. With 24 hours in the day and seven days in the week, content needs are robust. The more fantasy voices, from many outlets in the fantasy sport environment, the better and more diverse the end product can be.

3.5 Social media

A final example of fantasy sport growing with and through communication changes revolves around social media. With so much statistical information available to collect, review, analyze, and interpret in fantasy decision-making, it is difficult to keep up with it all. Social media allows fantasy sport personalities, experts, and analysts the perfect platform to provide the much-needed information to fantasy sport participants. Information varies, but fantasy sport social media content largely revolves around draft advice, start/sit recommendations, player performance predictions, injury updates, scoring updates, and overall reaction to fantasy sport performance. With a wide range of topics and interests on social media, audiences seek out topics, people, and organizations from which they want information. With that, fantasy sport content providers do not have to speak in broad terms, placate an uninitiated audience, or water-down any information. The audience is seeking out fantasy sport information and there are social media accounts meeting the need. Facebook and Twitter are particularly popular social media platforms, as they lend themselves nicely to small snippets of information, statistics, and media and provide a portal to further information. Some examples of popular social media Facebook and Twitter accounts include:

- FanDuel with 1,078,000 Facebook followers and 242,300 Twitter followers
- DraftKings with 991,000 Facebook followers and 313,300 Twitter followers
- Matthew Berry of ESPN with 1,000,000 Twitter followers
- ESPN Fantasy Sports with 489,000 Facebook followers and 578,000 Twitter followers
- Adam Rank of NFL Network with 462,000 Twitter followers
- Yahoo! Fantasy Sports with 364,000 Twitter followers
- Stephania Bell of ESPN with 288,000 Twitter followers
- FantasyPros with 280,000 Twitter followers
- Eric Karabell of ESPN with Twitter 160,000 followers
- Brad Evans of SiriusXM with 135,000 Twitter followers

After outlining many of the ways fantasy sport has benefited from changes in the technology and communication industries, the pre-Internet participation story with ink and paper resources is even more difficult to imagine. The amount of information, advice, and access, along with the ease of entry contemporary participants have, is astounding compared to early fantasy sport participants. As advancements continue to be made in the communication industry, so too, will the fantasy sport industry grow and change.

4 Fantasy sport creating communication content

The aforementioned section discussed how fantasy sport benefited from communication and technological growth, but this section flips the script and discusses ways the communication industry benefits and has been able to explore new content avenues thanks to the fantasy sport industry. The quick and immense growth of the fantasy sport industry over three decades (accelerating in the mid-1990s) has allowed for content providers to realize and understand the legitimacy of the industry and explore ways to appease such an information-desperate community. Providing fantasy-based content can come in a myriad of ways including data-rich web articles, podcasts, television shows, and satellite radio content, to social media messages, RedZone-type programming, and live scoring features. This section highlights the areas of television/web-based shows, fantasy sport information providers, and podcasts as ways in which fantasy sport is helping build content in the sport communication landscape.

4.1 Fantasy sport content for television

Fantasy sport provides unique information for television producers to consider. Player performance, while incredibly important to fantasy sport participants, can come across as too statistically based and too "nerdy" for a general viewing audience that may only be concerned about team success. Matthew Berry mentioned conversations about how to do fantasy sport on television would occur frequently at ESPN, prior to their commitment to the activity (Billings and Ruihley 2014). He stated, "How do you make it interesting, informative and fun for a viewer who may or may not be there for fantasy advice" (2014: 66). ESPN has appeared to walk the fine line and provide content for the fantasy sport participant while not alienating their traditional audience. As Ruihley and Billings (2019) note, ESPN has utilized fantasy sport information in three major ways in their television programing. First, thanks to the multiple channel offerings ESPN possesses, ESPN created television content solely for the fantasy football participant as they counter-program *Sunday NFL Countdown* with *Fantasy Football Now.* This show is dedicated to providing fantasy sport participants with as much information as possible for the upcoming slate of National Football League (NFL) games. ESPN's Senior Director of Product Development, John Diver, believed this programming decision advanced fantasy sport further at ESPN because it was now seen as "viable play for content, and just not going around the horn talking about the weather and if the defensive lineman has a hurt foot" (Ruihley, Hardin, and Billings 2015: 229).

Fantasy sport interest and information again provided content for ESPN in 2017 when they added an additional program called *The Fantasy Show with Matthew Berry.* ESPN's Director of Communication, Kevin Ota, states that the show provides consumers "with a mix of news and analysis, as well as special guests and segments, all presented with Berry's smart, irreverent style" (Ruihley and Billings 2019). This show was placed in a prime viewing timeslot at 5:00 p.m. Eastern Time and counter-programmed against two major shows, *Around the Horn* and *Pardon the Interruption* (again, offering content but not disrupting traditional sport viewing habits). A final way fantasy sport assisted with new television programing for ESPN came in an unconventional way. In 2016, ESPN produced and aired a live 28-hour fantasy football marathon on many of their platforms. The marathon brought in many ESPN hosts, analysts, former athletes, and other personalities. This was all done in an effort to sign up one million new fantasy football participants to the ESPN Fantasy Football product. The programming stunt was fruitful as ESPN announced 1.75 million teams drafted as a result of the marathon (Ota 2016). With such success, ESPN conducted another fantasy football marathon in 2017 and 2018, attracting approximately two million teams each year (Ota 2017; 2018a; 2018b).

There are many other examples of fantasy sport-based television programming. These examples all involve the most popular sport in the fantasy sport environment, American professional football and the NFL. The NFL, as an organization, is also capitalizing on the success of fantasy play as the NFL Network's *Fantasy Live* was created to capture some of the fantasy audience. This show's tag line states, "Join our NFL.com experts to discuss all the latest news, injuries, matchups and their impact. Get all the tools you need to dominate your fantasy matchup with the insiders' expertise" (NFL Fantasy Live 2019). In addition to *Fantasy Live*, the NFL produces and airs the aforementioned NFL RedZone Channel. The mutually beneficial relationship between the NFL and the fantasy sport environment has seen the NFL RedZone flourish every Sunday afternoon during the NFL season. As Greene (2017) states, "While [RedZone] started as a sort-of gimmick for fantasy football enthusiasts with short attention spans, it has become the only way to watch the league without losing your mind." This fantasy-minded programming idea became a major component of the NFL experience and allows fans of differing regions to witness great scoring plays from teams all over the league.

Web-based company Yahoo! has solidified its fantasy sport presence as a game host and information provider for many types of fantasy play. Yahoo! provides information through expert analysis, social media presence, and two popular studio-based shows, *Fantasy Football Hour* and *Fantasy Football Live*. Yahoo! answers the same call as ESPN and the NFL Network in the way it provides fantasy sport participants with game-time decisions for their fantasy contests. Broadcast giant, NBC, is also in the fantasy sport production scene as one of their properties is Rotoworld, a fantasy sport information provider. Discussed in the next section, Rotoworld is able to produce video and audio content specific to the fantasy sport community and have access to airtime and streaming space thanks to the resources and reach of their parent company, NBC Sports Group (Rotoworld 2019). In a similar way, CBS is able to produce and air their pre-game show *Fantasy Football Today* with relative ease due to the mass communication experience a broadcast company like CBS has.

A final example of fantasy sport creating content on television is the production of the FXX Television show called *The League*. Airing from 2009 to 2015, IMDB (The League 2019) describes the show as "An ensemble comedy that follows a group of old friends in a fantasy football league who care deeply about one another – so deeply that they use every opportunity to make each other's lives miserable". The comedic elements of the show capitalized on the absurdity of competition in the fantasy sport environment, but highlighted the social, camaraderie, and information-gathering motivations behind the activity (Ruihley and Hardin 2011). As many industry professionals fought for mere seconds of broadcast time when fantasy sport was blossoming in the 1990s (Billings and Ruihley 2014), the fact that a cable network would produce 87 episodes of an original show over seven seasons about the fantasy sport, shows how far the industry has come.

4.2 Information providers and fantasy sport content

Many information providers have created opportunity, content, jobs, and sustainable businesses due to the information-gathering nature of fantasy sport participants. One of those providers is Rotowire. With one of the biggest names in fantasy sport information, Rotowire is a top-tier sport communication company. In the description of their business, you can sense the pride in their accomplishments:

> RotoWire is your premium fantasy sports resource. We pioneered real-time fantasy sports news and Player Notes back in 1997 when the Internet was just taking flight. We've stayed ahead of imitators with the most in-depth analysis, the fastest real-time news and the largest scope of coverage of any fantasy sports site or app. Our quality has won us many industry awards – it's why we have high-profile partners such as ESPN, Yahoo! Sports, Fox Sports, CBS Sports, DraftKings and NBA.com. (About Rotowire 2019)

In their own words, the creators of Rotowire, then RotoNews.com, claimed the demand for real-time fantasy sport information was "beyond their wildest expectations" (2019). The aforementioned NBC property, Rotoworld, followed Rotowire's lead and was created in 1998 by Allstar Stats. Both offering player news and information, these two providers are major leaders in the world of fantasy sport news and information (Ruihley and Billings 2019). Including full list of fantasy sport information providers here would be impractical, but it is fair to say there are many. Notably, however, it is important to note that major sport communication organizations are in the fantasy sport information game. These organizations include ESPN, Fox Sports, NBC Sports, CBS Sports, Yahoo!, *Sporting News*, *USA Today*, *Bleacher Report*, *The Athletic*, *Pro Football Focus*, *FantasyPros*, and even newspaper outlets including the *New York Times*, *The Washington Post*, *New York Post*, and *Denver Post*. In addition to information providers capitalizing off of fantasy sport content, professional sport leagues have dedicated space to fantasy sport news and information. The NFL, MLB, NHL, PGA/LPGA, and MLS are all providing fantasy sport analysis.

4.3 Podcasting fantasy sport

A final example of the communication industry benefiting from the fantasy sport industry comes with a truly unique medium literally meeting the consumer where they are. Podcasts are the ultimate communicative tool. Bertucci (2018) says one of the things attracting people to podcasts is the ability to choose their content on their time. In addition, people like having fresh material automatically available at the touch of a finger. Additionally, Bertucci states, "Podcasts are also a great way for people to listen to content that is of a particular special interest" (2018). Additionally, listening to a podcast is a choice. As stated, fantasy sport participants are in constant need of information. With so much information and only 24 hours in a day, fantasy sport provides great fodder for podcasts hosts and analysts. Many of the organizations previous outlined in this chapter have podcasts to further expand their communicative reach to the fantasy sport community. Fantasy sport communication and information outlets like ESPN, CBS, Rotoworld, Rotowire, and FantasyPros all have podcasts year-round devoted to American football and baseball. Other notable single-sport focused podcasts consist of Fantasy Football Guys, Rotographs Fantasy Baseball, Fantasy Footballers, MLB.com Fantasy Baseball 411, NFL Fantasy Live, and Fantasy Football Weekly. Armed with ever-changing player information, sport personalities, advertisers, and sponsors, podcasts are a perfect example of communication outlets benefiting from the content-rich activity of fantasy sport.

5 Conclusion

This chapter examines the relationship between technological and communication-based developments and the fantasy sport industry. Understanding the mutually beneficial relationship between communication technology and fantasy sport provides information to practitioners and scholars to better understand and explore consumption, motivation, gratifications, and experience in the use of these avenues in fantasy sport play. Three things should be apparent after reading this chapter. First, fantasy sport consumers eagerly, unabashedly, and frequently seek out information and use communication means at double to triple the rates of non-fantasy sport fans. Second, the fantasy sport industry has grown, in large part, due to the technological advancements in the communication industry. These advancements have given fantasy sport the perfect environment to grow and provide the much-needed information participants are seeking. A final takeaway is that sport communication-based organizations are able to benefit from fantasy sport in the way they host play, provide information, or provide access to athletic contests. This is not a one-way street where fantasy sport is taking and never giving, this relationship is mutually beneficial and continuing to grow and thrive. With that, it is important to understand that fantasy sport is powerful activity, game, tool, and resource for communication-based companies. It is not just a hobby or niche activity; it is a powerful industry. Fantasy sport draws in sports fans and converts them into an evolved and information-savvy consumer on the prowl to satisfy their informational needs.

The technological landscape will continue to expand and grow, and sport-based industries intertwined with communication-based organizations will change as well. Take, for instance, a recent example of this evolution of the fantasy sport environment. Just when the sport communication industry had figured out fantasy sport production and information delivery in 2014, the daily fantasy sport surge occurred in 2015 and is still moving to this day. What did the daily fantasy sport surge do? It amplified participation and information-seeking behaviors. Now, instead of drafting once per year and setting a lineup once per week, many participants were adding to their fantasy card and drafting new teams every day, while seeking out updated information at much higher frequencies.

In North America, eSports and sports gambling are two additional ancillary activities gaining acceptance and momentum. Many states in the US are legalizing sports gambling, building eSports arenas, and forging new communication-based relationships with organizations utilizing new technology. While sports gambling is not a new phenomenon, the loosening of legislative holds has opened the door for many to begin offering the activity through a variety of technological means. The eSports community has also seen rapid growth and acceptance within sport culture and in many ways, are leading the push for technological advancements in sport, sponsorship, marketing, and gaming fields. Practitioners and scholars can apply similar examination to eSports and sports gambling as this chapter has to fantasy sport, in an effort to understand relationships between technology, communication, and the activity.

As technology continues to expand, ancillary sport activities gain stronger footholds, and sport fans continue to evolve, it is important that practitioners and scholars continue to examine the relationships between these groups. Information outlets have an expanded need and increased difficulties in trying to adjust their information, programming, and communication strategy to reach those participants desiring very specific information. Times continue to change, and it is up to sport-based companies and communication-focused organizations to work together in mutually beneficial ways to reach, inform, and provide content for users. Growing from a one-league Baseball Seminar in the 1960s to an industry of millions of dedicated users, the fantasy sport industry has set a fine example for sport-based activities charting their course in the ever-changing communicative landscape.

References

About Rotowire. 2019. *Rotowire*. https://www.rotowire.com/about.php (1 August 2019).

Bertucci, Brian. 2018. What is podcasting? Discover the value of making a podcast or tuning in to one. *Lifewire*. https://www.lifewire.com/what-is-podcasting-2722076 (1 August 2019).

Billings, Andrew C. & Brody J. Ruihley. 2013. Why we watch, why we play: The relationship between fantasy sport and fanship motivations. *Mass Communication & Society* 16(1). 5–25.

Billings, Andrew C. & Brody J. Ruihley. 2014. *The fantasy sport industry: Games within games*. London: Routledge.

Billings, Andrew C., Michael L. Butterworth & Paul D. Turman. 2012. *Communication and sport: Surveying the field*. London: Sage.

ESPN Department of Integrated Media Research. 2010. ESPN top ten list for sport research. Paper presented at the Broadcast Education Association Research Symposium, Las Vegas, NV, 15 April.

FNTSY. 2019. *Fantasy Sports Network* (FNTSY). https://fantasysportsnetwork.com/about_us/ (1 August 2019).

Graham, Luke. 2016. Fantasy sports kick off in Europe. *CNBC.com*, 1 July. https://www.cnbc.com/2016/07/01/fantasy-sports-kick-off-in-europe.html (29 June 2020).

Greene, Nick. 2017. RedZone is the cause of and solution to all of the NFL's problems. *Slate*, 17 September. https://slate.com/news-and-politics/2017/09/redzone-is-the-cause-of-and-solution-to-all-of-the-nfl-s-problems.html (1 August 2019).

Industry demographics. 2020. *Fantasy Sports and Gaming Association*. https://thefsga.org/industry-demographics/ (30 June 2020).

Katz, Elihu, Jay G. Blumler & Michael Gurevitch, M. 1973. Uses and gratifications research. *Public Opinion Quarterly* 37(4). 509–523.

McQuail, Denis. (ed.). 2002. *McQuail's reader in mass communication theory*. London: Sage.

McQuail, Denis, Jay G. Blumler & Joseph R. Brown. 1972. The television audience: A revised perspective. In Denis McQuail (ed.), *Sociology of mass communications*, 135–165. Harmondsworth: England.

Moran, Tim. 2000. The space race for satellite radio is picking up speed. *New York Times*, 22 September. https://www.nytimes.com/2000/09/22/automobiles/the-space-race-for-satellite-radio-is-picking-up-speed.html (1 August 2019).

NFL Fantasy Live. 2019. *NFL.com*. http://www.nfl.com/network/shows/nfl-fantasy-live (1 August 2019).

NFL Redzone. n.d. *NFL.com*. https://www.nfl.com/redzone/ (19 November 2020).

Ota, Kevin. 2016. ESPN's fantasy football marathon spurs two days of record sign ups. *ESPN Press Room*, 17 August. http://espnmediazone.com/us/press-releases/2016/08/espns-fantasy-football-marathon-spurs-two-days-record-sign-ups/ (1 August 2019).

Ota, Kevin. 2017. ESPN fantasy football marathon II: More than 2 million teams drafted. *ESPN Press Room*, 17 August. https://espnmediazone.com/us/press-releases/2017/08/espn-fantasy-football-marathon-ii-2-million-teams-drafted/ (1 August 2019).

Ota, Kevin. 2018a. Fans draft nearly 2 million teams during ESPN's fantasy football marathon. *ESPN Press Room*, 15, August. https://espnpressroom.com/us/press-releases/2018/08/fans-draft-nearly-2-million-teams-during-espns-fantasy-football-marathon/ (1 August 2019).

Ota, Kevin. 2018b. Personal communication. 9 April 2018.

Pedersen, Paul M., Kimberly S. Miloch & Pamela C. Laucella. 2007. *Strategic sport communication*. Champaign, IL: Human Kinetics.

Peterson, Robert A. & Maria C. Merino. 2003. Consumer information search behavior and the Internet. *Psychology & Marketing* 20(2). 99–121.

Rotoworld. 2019. *NBC Sports Group*. http://nbcsportsgrouppressbox.com/shows/rotoworld/ (1 August 2019).

Rosenthal, Phil. 2019. How ESPN – now 40 years old – changed the sports world, from your growing cable bill and round-the-clock programming to the glut of bowl games. *Chicago Tribune*, 8 September. https://www.chicagotribune.com/sports/breaking/ct-cb-espn-40th-anniversary-changed-sports-20190906-ogxokpxedjgwdekdlmgudb6myq-story.html (19 November 2020).

Ruihley, Brody J. 2018. Fantasy sport participants: Profile update 2017. Paper presented at the Fantasy Sports Trade Association Winter Conference. Los Angeles, CA, January 23.

Ruihley, Brody J. & Andrew C. Billings. 2019. Ascending as the fantasy giant: ESPN fantasy, mainstreaming fantasy gaming, and the role of Goliath. In Greg Armfield, John McGuire & Adam Earnheardt (eds.), *ESPN and the changing sports media landscape*, 57–68. New York: Peter Lang.

Ruihley, Brody J. & Robin L. Hardin. 2011. Beyond touchdowns, homeruns, and 3-pointers: An examination of fantasy sport participation motivation. *International Journal of Sport Management and Marketing* 10(3/4). 232–256.

Ruihley, Brody J., Robin Hardin & Andrew C. Billings. 2015. ESPN and the fantasy sport experience. In John McGuire, Greg Armfield & Adam Earnheardt (eds.), *The ESPN effect: Academic studies of the worldwide leader in sports*, 225–236. New York: Peter Lang.

Schwartz, Alan. 2005. *The numbers game: Baseball's lifelong fascination with statistics*. New York: St. Martins.

SIRIUS XM to launch "SIRIUS XM fantasy sports radio," 24/7 fantasy sports channel. 2010. *RotoExperts*. https://rotoexperts.com/xnews/sirius-xmtolaunch-sirius-xmfantasy-sports-radio-247-fantasy-sports-channel-available-nationwide/ (19 November 2020).

Stephens, Mitchell. 1999. The history of television. In *Grolier Multimedia Encyclopedia*. https://www.nyu.edu/classes/stephens/History%20of%20Television%20page.htm (1 August 2019).

The League. 2019. *IMDB.com*. https://www.imdb.com/title/tt1480684/ (1 August 2019).

Walker, Sam. 2006. *Fantasyland: A sportswriter's bid to win the world's most ruthless fantasy baseball league*. New York: Penguin.

Norm O'Reilly and Gashaw Z. Abeza

34 The contemporary use of social media in professional sport

Abstract: Social media has become an accepted marketing channel in professional sport. Led by many of the world's elite sporting clubs, including the Dallas Cowboys and Manchester United, in just over a decade, social media has gone from a new initiative to a way to reach as many as 200 million fans and an integral part of marketing communications programs. Concurrently, scholarly research on the topic has similarly evolved and expanded, leading to a diverse body of literature that includes quantitative and qualitative study on topics ranging from evaluation to policy to "how-to" applications. This chapter synthesizes the latest research on the use of social media in the context of professional sport and presents it under the domains of "Other" (professional sport organizations), "I" (professional sport fans), and "We" (social media platforms).

Keywords: leagues; clubs; athletes; agents; owners; platform; influencers; Twitter; Instagram, Facebook

1 Introduction

The use of social media has evolved enormously over the past decade (Li et al. 2019). Indeed, it has become an accepted marketing channel for any industry and in any context where B2B and B2C marketers are seeking to reach particular target groups (Iankova et al. 2019). Professional sport is no different and, in fact, is an area where social media has been deeply embedded and has provided considerable benefit for leagues, clubs, and athletes (Abeza et al. 2017). This was reinforced by the Dallas Cowboys' Director of Content Strategy, who recounted the team's use of its social media platform over the past 10 years:

> We have gone from taking other people's content and repurposing it to creating our own content that fits social [media] and how people consume that content. So, I would say that the biggest thing, especially for us, is going from just repurposing content to becoming content creators and then giving our social channels a personality and injecting some voice and internal personalities into some of that content, as well. (Abeza 2018: 297)

According to the Cowboys' Director of Content Strategy, the club started embracing social media in 2010, spent the first three years experimenting the best use of social media, started generating its own content in 2013, and shifted its attention to influencers and celebrities over the following five-year period (Abeza 2018). A similar pathway can be charted for many of the world's elite sporting clubs, including Manchester

https://doi.org/10.1515/9783110660883-034

United, FC Barcelona, and the New York Yankees. As of October 2019, Barcelona and their La Liga rival Real Madrid, both have in excess of 200 million social media followers (total) on Twitter, Instagram, and Facebook.

Professional sporting clubs have experienced the continual evolution of social media use over the course of its first decade (2009–2019). With this evolving nature of social media, a number of other professional sport organizations, outside of the major ones, are learning and teaching themselves as well as repurposing emerging platforms over the past decade (Abeza, O'Reilly, and Seguin 2019). For instance, clubs in the Canadian Football League (CFL) have provided "gratification" to their fans via Twitter (Gibbs, O'Reilly, and Brunette 2014). Mega-events involving professional athletes are also drivers of social media. The recent 2018 FIFA World Cup, which showcased the world's best professional soccer players in Russia, is a good example. Social media was a key aspect of the event, with reports suggesting that the event generated more than 3 billion Instagram interactions and in excess of 11 million posts (Flamant 2018).

Along with the industry's changing practice and enhanced frequency of social media use, the focus of the academic community's interest and the field's scholarship has concurrently evolved (Billings et al. 2019). The research community conducted a number of research studies on the topic, building a body of literature of significance. The types of research in the area range from the dimensions of social media use to policies of social media use to the issues and impacts of the different platforms on the industry. In their assessment of the social media scholarship in sport management research. Abeza and colleagues (2015) reported that the early age of the scholarship – 2008 to 2010 – studies were typically conducted to gain an understanding of the nature of social media. Then, post 2013, the scholarship output provided more focus to the sport industry regarding the specific "how-to" applications of social media. For example, while the studies advanced our understanding of the intersection of the sport industry and social media, scholars reported that there is a need to synthesize the latest research findings on professional sport organizations use of social media to gain an up-to-date (i. e., post-2017) understanding of its use as a sport marketing communication medium (Abeza 2018). It is important to note that the sport management literature includes a large number of studies on social media that are based on content analyses and theme analyses of social media posts (e. g., Gibbs, O'Reilly, and Brunette 2014), which seek to understand virtual audiences by aggregating posts, tweets, or other social media-based data or impressions. Many of these studies focus on social and cultural issues related to sport (e. g., gender representation), which are not the focus of this chapter.

To accomplish the objective of this chapter, we synthesize the latest research on the use of social media in the context of professional sport. This will be done by first examining the different professional sport domains reported use of social media individually and then by synthesizing the interrelationships between each domain. For this purpose, the chapter is organized in three domains: The "Other" domain (professional sport organizations), the "I" domain (professional sport fans), and the "We" domain (social media platforms). Each of the domains is important and relevant on its own, but more so are they of value to professional sport organizations based on the interactions that happen between the domains. For example, it is much more relevant to a professional sport club, if they can get their content ("Other" domain) to their fans ("I" domain) via a sophisticated and high entertaining medium ("We" domain), than it would be to just post some content on its website without the means to inspire fans (and potential fans) to share it. This approach to the chapter both allows us to (1) gain an understanding of the contemporary use of social media in professional sport, and (2) translate that understanding into actionable findings for organizations in professional sport.

2 Use of social media in professional sport: the "other" domain – sport organizations

The "Other" domain refers to professional sport organizations' use of social media for marketing communication purposes. A few studies have been published recently that focused on sport organizations' use of social media as a marketing communication medium (e.g., Abeza, O'Reilly, and Seguin 2019; Achen et al. 2018; Thompson et al. 2018). According to these studies and others, social media in professional sport today is best understood to be an accepted set of digital tools used by different sport organizations as part of their marketing and communication approach. This would include the many platforms and tactics available via social media to marketers today. The specific purposes of professional sport social media include news delivery, sales, sponsorship, customer service, promotional offers, public relations (Abeza, O'Reilly, and Seguin 2019), enhancing fan loyalty, and building brand equity (Thompson et al. 2018). In addition to these, social media is often used for very custom objectives, such as sponsorship activation, where a unique social media platform can be built to promote a sponsorship. Similarly, 100 percent digital sport properties, such as eSports, provide interesting opportunities for custom social media approaches or tactics.

Today, all major professional sport teams anywhere in the world have a Twitter account and following. The 147 professional sports teams in the five major leagues in the United States (MLB, NHL, NBA, NFL, & MLS), for instance, have a significant presence on Twitter, supported by professional staff and/or agencies. As shown in Figure 1, sport organizations use different social media platforms (e.g., Facebook, Twitter, Instagram) to deliver their content (e.g., texts, videos, pictures, infographics, and audio files) to their audiences and engage in a feedback loop. Social media, for example, can be used as a medium of *customer service*, where a customer can ask the Boston Red Sox professional baseball team (on their Twitter account) "@RedSox could you tell me if/when there would be tickets for the games v Yankees in September?" and @RedSox replied: "might become available to purchase @RedSox replied:

@craignicoll16 Yankees tickets will become available after a drawing for the opportunity to purchase. Likely within the next 2 months."

Similarly, organizations can use different social media platforms for a number of particular practical purposes. First, it can be used to enhance a *sponsorship* (e. g., @chicagobulls: We're at @dunkinchicago at 1500 Larkin Ave in Elgin until 1 pm. Stop by for some donuts and to say hi!) by promoting the corporate partner of a club or athlete (in the example given, this is Dunkin' Donuts). Second, social media can be effective around *public relations* (e. g., @utahjazz:.@rudygobert27 reading with the kids at St. John the Baptist Elementary for the "Be A Team Player – Read!" contest) and the desire to share good news or image-building content with certain communities. Third and fourth, social media platforms are also used to *sell tickets and merchandise* (e. g., @Padres: After Christmas sale at the team store! Store hours are Monday – Saturday 10am to 5pm and Sunday from 11am to 4pm). In the case of ticket sales, social media is ideal for in-venue upgrades or last-minute purchases on the secondary ticket market, or perhaps for a ticket sales promotion that has a special incentive for the social media follower only (e. g., @NHLjets: Season starts in 2 weeks: 10 % discount on Jets single game tickets for home games in Winnipeg for next 24 hours). Finally, for the purpose of *spreading information*, teams use the medium to augment the reach of information by retweeting their stakeholders' messages (e. g., @BlueJays retweeting from player Michael Stroman: "RT @MStroo06: Never had this much fun playing the game I love").

The synthesis of these recently published studies on the topic area informs us that sport organizations use social media for five main general purposes, namely news updates, promotional offers, customer service, brand community hub, and brand personality, but that a broader array of custom benefits and benefits specific to social media are possible. The next few sub-sections discuss each of the general-purpose areas.

2.1 News update

Social Media is used to quickly and efficiently communicate a variety of up-to-date information such as scores, highlights, seat upgrades, and injury report. It is a source for quick and fresh news updates. Particularly, when fans are unable to attend or watch games, social media can become the go-to source to get live play-by-play updates (Li et al. 2019). Social media has the ability to help to provide insider information on issues such as team (e. g., lineup, backstage video, training) and players' status (e. g., trades, free agency, transfers), and players' off-the-field activities (e. g., charity, community, fan meetings). In this regard, Achen and colleagues (2018), in their exploration of the off-season content and interaction on Facebook among US professional sport leagues, found that teams in the National Football League had the most comments, teams in the Major League Baseball had the most shares, and teams in the National Basketball Association had the most likes (passive interaction). According to Kang and colleagues (2019), sport organizations and participants use social media platforms to disseminate an array of information about various sport related issues. Figure 1 outlines the way that professional sport organizations adopt social media for use in their day-to-day activities, outlining the extent (or potential extent) for its use by these clubs.

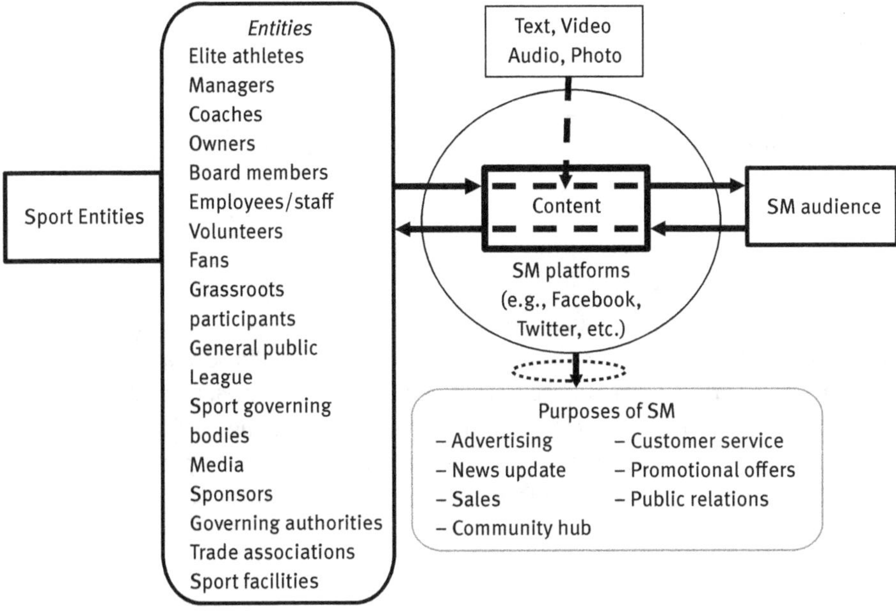

Fig. 1: Sport organizations' use of social media, adapted from Abeza and O'Reilly (2018)

Figure 1 emphasizes the importance of content in social media. It is right at the center of its use, supporting the necessary component of high-quality content (Abeza and O'Reilly 2018) to drive any social media success. From there its purposes, its audience, and its format are the key components that the sport organizations (entities in Figure 1) must consider in applying social media.

2.2 Promotional offers

Social media is often used for the purpose of sales promotions, such as fan reward campaigns which include contests, sweepstakes, giveaways, lotteries, and raffles. Also, social media platforms can serve as a means to provide information about a team's ticket discounts, giveaways, merchandise sales, discounts, and announce contests, prize winners, promotions, and discounts from sponsors. Organizations also use social media platforms to generate sales leads (Kang et al. 2019) and to persuade users to purchase merchandise from the teams' stores and tickets to games, or buy signed jersey, balls, and other memorabilia at auctions (Abeza et al. 2017). Yet, as Achen and colleagues (2018) point out, to be successful here, there is a need for marketers to focus their strategy of encouraging interaction and communication on this player-promotion content instead of on calls to action, polls, or trivia.

2.3 Customer service

Social media enables customers to receive real time and direct customer service support on inquiries on a range of issues. Particularly, as an organization addresses the requests of a particular fan, the question of many other fans with similar concerns can be reached and addressed (i. e., the concept of one-to-many, versus one-to-one), which provides efficiencies for the club from a resourcing perspective. Equally, for the customer, being heard and having their issue being possibly (even, probably) solved could enhance their emotional attachment to the club brand (or league brand, or player brand, depending on the context). Thus, social media serves as a direct line of communication to listen to questions, comments, or concerns, and address them. Organizations also use social media platforms about upcoming products and events through exclusive organization-related content such as videos of products or event highlights, access to a variety of information about the organization, and other types of relevant content.

2.4 Brand community hub

Social media allows for the creation of a hub to a non-geographically bound virtual community (Thompson et al. 2018). As Li and colleagues (2019) reported, social media platforms provide a space where sport fans can interact directly with sport organizations and among themselves. As a hub for customers, it serves as a venue where like-minded customers virtually unite, voice their comments, concerns, questions, and complaints, and possibly bond over the brand or issue. With this kind of interaction happening, customers normally express satisfaction or issue a complaint about a product or a service on social media. In turn, customers (for instance, on Twitter) may use hashtags to initiate and engage in conversation with other like-minded users about the issue, either positive (satisfaction) or negative (complaint). Such interactions can create a hub for a brand online community. The brand benefits can occur as much with a negative complaint as with a positive mention of fan satisfaction, however it can be challenging to get responses in the complaint context. In this regard, O'Hallarn and colleagues (2018: 397) reported that social media users are less drawn to engage in an interaction with other hashtag users and particularly with those who express contrary views. They go on to say that "an open forum with free opinions being shared through a common hashtag evolves organically into conversation threads of common thought."

2.5 Brand personality

Social media has been identified as an important customer-to-customer value-co-creation platform for engaging with sport teams and brands and sharing brand-related content with various stakeholders (Popp, Horbel, and Germelmann 2018). According to these authors, social media enables organizations to humanize their brand in a way that is intimate and personal in nature. This can be done, according to Abeza and colleagues (2019) by helping organizations develop an online personality (e. g., humor and funny pictures), engaging in a friendly tone, and creating a closer relationship through personalization (e. g., fans' personalized birthday wishes). Professional sport organizations have been observed attempting to create brand personality by hosting question and answers with owners, senior executives, and general managers (e. g., online chat with the Chief Marketing Officer), using other informal forms of communications (e. g., GIFs, inside jokes), and creating and sharing emotional content (e. g., pictures of customers' families and friends). Some organizations also use nostalgia (i. e., content that is a throwback to the organization's history) as a tool to activate fan attachment and fan engagement. In this regard, Achen and colleagues (2018) reported that Facebook content related to players and personnel receives the most interaction, more than content related to promotions at the organization (i. e., club or league) level. According to the authors, the NFL does a good job here by focusing on player and personnel promotion that further encourages the connection between fans and their team, thus humanizing the players in a way that is more effective than what other leagues do. In contrast, Li and colleagues (2019) suggest providing more team-related content such as a team's game videos and practice information. It is equally important, as Popp, Horbel, and Germelmann (2018) noted, to carefully handle anti-brand social media communities that may oppose a sport team (or a player or a coach) and communicate negative messages about a brand than a message that is completely different from or even contradictory to the team's (intended) brand communication.

3 Use of social media in professional sport: the "I" domain – sport fans

The "I" domain refers to sport fans who use the different platforms seeking gratifications and uses. Social media platforms, such as Twitter, Instagram, Facebook, and YouTube, are the prime venues where fans today exhibit their allegiance to their favourite team or player outside of the stadium. Sport fans (near or far) are the primary active collaborators on different SM platforms (Billings et al. 2019). While users' participation ranges from passive visitor to committed contributor, fans are today producers, consumers, and distributors of content (Abeza, O'Reilly, and Séguin 2019). As Abeza, O'Reilly, and Séguin (2019) noted, some dedicate substantial time producing and consuming content, while others do not. Relatedly, users/followers of a given SM site (e. g., an NBA team's Facebook account) are not all necessarily fans of the team, and not all offline fans of the team are necessarily users of the team's social media site (Abeza et al. 2015). Taking into consideration the scale and magnitude of social media use by sport fans, scholars (e. g., Abeza, O'Reilly, and Séguin 2019; Billings et al. 2019; Li et al. 2019; Vale and Fernandes 2018; Wakefield and Bennett 2018), in a series of studies, acknowledged the need to understand the underlying dimensions of social media use from the fans' perspective further.

A number of social media studies related to sport fans have been published that have, in turn, made significant contributions to our understanding of fans' use of social media in sport. Wakefield and Bennet (2018), in their study of fans' use of ephemeral social media (e. g., Snapchat), found that sport fans want their social media content to be available for a relatively longer time (i. e., for days and weeks), as opposed to a shorter time period (i. e., for a few minutes or moments). These authors inform us that users prefer to use the self-delete feature when offered, as opposed to following Billings and colleagues' (2017) suggestion that sports fans prefer ephemeral social media (i. e., Snapchat) to other media. The authors concluded that sport fans are less interested in social media platforms that drastically reduce the lifespan of their message, such as Snap Chat, which is at odds with some reports which indicate the popularity of this social media application. Williams, Chinn, and Suleiman (2014) investigated the value of Twitter messages (i. e., Tweets) for sport fans, and explored whether or not there is a relationship between value of Tweets and team identification. After competing their study, they found that team identification influences how much people value specific categories of sports Tweets (i. e., news, opinion, and promotion) and noted that those using Twitter need to be very focused and targeted in their content. Importantly, Twitter allows fans to voice their interests and be heard by the team and other fans. Also, according to Williams and colleagues, Twitter facilitates an exchange of content that can increase "fan involvement, strengthen associations [with certain images of a team or player] and allow closer connections to the team" (2014: 46). They also reported that some fans' Twitter consumption might predominately be visiting but do not Tweet at all themselves. Those who do not Tweet but do follow others are often called "lurkers."

In their research, Vale and Fernandes (2018) investigated why and how sport fans engage with clubs on social media, reported that fans' need for information (e. g., team-related news updates), empowerment (i. e., the inclination to influence others) and brand love (i. e., their passion for their team) drive their social media usage. Specifically, if a fan is getting quality information via social media, they use it more. Relatedly, Meng and colleagues (2015) addressed the enrichment of fan identity through relationship building that is based on communication and interaction, including social media. The results of this study inform us that, first, social media enables fans to be informed (i. e., to access up-to-date information on the team, players, coaches, etc.) and, thereby, be gratified through real-time updates and behind-the-scenes news. Second, social media allows fans to enrich their relationship with their teams through the teams' humanized and personalized communications. Third, social media makes fans feel that they have a say in teams' management, by eliciting feedback and opinions, and teams' commitment to involve fans in dialogue.

Li and colleagues (2019) investigated and explored whether social media users' motivations differed when following a sport organization on two similar microblogging services: Twitter and Weibo. The authors reported that Weibo users have higher motives for obtaining information, entertainment, technical knowledge, passing time, and escaping from their life than Twitter users, while Twitter followers had higher motivations to express team support than their Weibo counterparts. The authors' findings imply the need for platform-based and market-centered strategies to engage sport fans through these mediums. Thus, sport organizations need a specific strategy for each specific platform they use. For their part, Stavros and colleagues (2013), through a content analysis of NBA fans' interaction on Facebook, reported on what motivates fans to engage with sport on social media, and identified four key drivers: passion, hope, esteem, and camaraderie. In their analysis, the authors demonstrated that Facebook provides an avenue for fans to satisfy motives that are not fully met through other forms of sport consumption such as game attendance and/or TV viewership. In summary, these studies outline that social media helps fans connect with other like-minded individuals and carry, extend, and amplify a fresh game experience outside the sport arena.

Abeza, O'Reilly, and Séguin (2019) studied the use of social media as a relationship marketing tool from the perspective of fans. The authors reported that fans require teams to facilitate their social media platforms: (1) as a customer service tool, (2) as a gateway to and present themselves to fans as open and accessible entities, and (3) as a medium that enriches fan identity. The authors also recommended managers to organize their social media content into four: (1) informational content (providing content with resourceful and helpful information directly by a sport team to its audiences on its platforms), (2) entertaining content (providing content that is fun and entertaining to fans), (3) relational content (providing content that enhances the fan relationship to the team, such as belongingness to a fan nation, customer service, staying in touch with other fans, fan personalized messages (e. g., birthday wishes), and (4) remunerative content (providing content that offers a reward such as giveaways).

In reaching fans, a key characteristic of social media and fans is the idea of user generated content (UGC) where the fan (as a user in the context of professional sport) can create their own content (something which is impossible (or very difficult) on most other promotional channels). UGC enables the fan to share their own content with the team, their online communities and other fans, often increasing the interaction among those groups of social media users.

4 Use of social media in professional sport: the "we" domain – platforms

The "We" domain refers to the different social media platforms where we (e. g., sport fans, athletes, coaches, teams, sponsors, sporting events, and sport media) meet online to participate in conversations with each other, listen to each other, and learn from each other. Sharing content with each other is also part of the "We" domain. In this context, it is evident that the emergence and expansion of social media has influenced the everyday lives of people across the globe over the course of its first decade (2009–2019). During this period, the evolution and advancement of the different social media platforms have changed the dynamics of sport marketing faster than ever (Winand et al. 2019). As of October 2019, there are at least 15 major social media platforms, all launched in the past 23 years, since ICQ was the first to marketing in 1996. The two most recent platforms to be launched are Periscope (2015), a video streaming platform, and TikTok (2017) a video sharing one.

The exponential growth of social media has provided different stakeholders in professional sport with a multitude of opportunities (Abeza, O'Reilly, and Seguin 2019) and, at the same time, led these sport organizations to reposition their marketing efforts through these mediums (Thompson et al. 2018). However, social media remains a marketing tactic with limited understanding of its potential and the full extent of the use of the different social media platforms is still being explored (Billings et al. 2019). For example, one area that has received the attention of researchers, as observed in the recent publications in the sport management literature, is purposing the discrete use of the different platforms for marketing communications in the industry. As Billings and colleagues (2019) noted, it is not yet certain if the use of a particular social media platform (e. g., Facebook, Twitter, Instagram, YouTube, Weibo) in sport indicates a desire fulfilled or, rather, a desire sought yet relatively unfulfilled by that given platform (but that could have been fulfilled by another platform). In fact, different social media platforms may function differently in different markets and each type of social media platform can serve a different purpose in different markets or contexts. Further, some social media platforms can be more popular among certain target groups than others (Li et al. 2019). For example, Facebook – in 2019 – has a very large following of older adults, while Snapchat has an audience that is primarily quite young. Hence, management of social media use cannot be underpinned by a one-size-fits-all approach (Thompson et al. 2018) and there is a limited understanding of the important distinctions that various types of social media platforms use (Weinberg and

Pehlivan 2011). This needs to be fully understood. The synthesis of the existing limited scholarship (e. g., Li et al. 2019; Thompson et al. 2018) informs us that most social media platforms have much in common, yet each serves a different purpose, and therefore unique strategies are required to leverage opportunities afforded by each.

With the maturity of the research on the topic area as well the knowledge acquired in the industry over the past ten years, it will be revealing to examine how differently organizations are using various social media platforms for marketing purposes. Over the course of its first decade, a diverse area of sport management has been studied in the context of a specific type of social media platform, typically as Twitter and/or Facebook. Examples of such studies include professional athletes and Twitter (e. g., Hambrick and Mahoney 2011; Pegoraro 2010; Lebel and Danylchuk 2012), journalism and Twitter (e. g., Deprez, Mechant, and Hoebeke 2013; McEnnis 2013; Schultz and Sheffer 2010), motives and constraints of Twitter use (e. g., Witkemper, Lim, and Waldburger 2012), Twitter and its impact on sport teams' communication (e. g., Price, Farrington, and Hall 2013), and Twitter and fans' experience of a major sporting event (e. g., Kassing and Sanderson 2010). Similarly, scholars focused on Facebook to study the motivations to communicate on Facebook (e. g., Stavros et al. 2013), Facebook's attributes and fans (e. g., Pronschinske, Groza, and Walker 2012), Facebook and the creation and maintenance of social capital (e. g., Phua 2012), using Facebook to manage a social identity threat (e. g., Sanderson 2013), and Facebook and customer relationship (e. g., Boehmer and Lacy 2014).

In the context of professional sport, in particular, previous studies have addressed marketing related research questions focusing on a specific type of social media platform (e. g., Twitter, Facebook). In the context of Twitter, some examples include Price, Farrington and Hall's (2013) study that investigated how the arrival and growth of Twitter is shaping the communications activities of football clubs and their relationships with supporters and the traditional sports media, and Gibbs, O'Reilly, and Brunette's (2014) study that explored what motivates and satisfies Twitter followers of professional sport teams in the CFL, measured through the gratifications sought and the fulfillment of these motives through the perceived ratifications obtained. Similarly, in the context of Facebook, examples include the Pronschinske, Groza, and Walker (2012) study that examined the attributes of Facebook that attract the most fans in the four major professional sport leagues in North America, and the work of Achen and colleagues (2018) who explored the off-season content and interaction on Facebook among the same major professional sport leagues.

A close examination of the abovementioned studies finds that these studies investigated either social media as a whole, thereby disregarding the distinct features of each platform, or that they focused on a specific platform without identifying its uniqueness. Hence, there is a need to recognize the distinctive aspects of the different types of social media platforms. This is both a future research challenge and one for implementation in practice. Doing this will help sport organizations to understand how organizations are using various social media sites for marketing communication purposes in a variety of different ways, and to highlight the distinctive values of each platform. In order to accomplish this objective, there is a need to recognize that different social media platforms do not all offer the same services or have the same focus. In fact, a salient feature of social media platforms, including Facebook and Twitter, is that they are distinctly different. This may lead to the thinking that Twitter is more universal than it really is, and that Facebook should not be underestimated, particularly with professional sport leagues/clubs who have fans with high affinity (and, thus, a willingness to share access to their Facebook accounts). Therefore, before synthesizing research reports as to how professional sport organizations are using various social media sites differently seeking to highlight the distinctive values of each platform, it would be informative to first understand the unique features of, at least, the two most studied platforms in sport studies (Abeza et al. 2015), namely Twitter and Facebook.

Since its launch in 2004, Facebook has become increasingly popular, growing from 5.5 million active users in 2005 (Hoffman and Novak 2012) to 2.41 billion monthly active users on Facebook as of June 30, 2019 (Our mission 2019). Facebook users can add friends, update their profiles, and post web links, pictures, and videos. Users can form and join virtual groups as well as develop applications enabling the exchange of messages in real time. Facebook opened its registration process to organizations in 2006, attracting more than 4,000 organizational users within the first two weeks (Waters et al. 2009). In early 2013, the Facebook Company announced that 15 million businesses, companies, and organizations are now using its services (Abeza and O'Reilly 2014).

Twitter has also grown rapidly since 2006. The platform allows users to communicate with "followers" using short messages (i. e., "Tweets") that are a maximum of 280 characters in length (Rosen 2017). Twitter users, whether individuals or organizations, can create an account through personalized home pages and follow other Twitter users (Our company 2019). A user's tweets are broadcast to followers, who can respond by providing commentary or retransmitting (i. e., "retweeting") the message to their own followers. Twitter has 330 million monthly active users generating content (Number of monthly 2019). Many organizations, including professional sport organizations, are using Twitter to share information, communicate, and interact with their stakeholders (Abeza et al. 2017). Table 1 reports on both the similarities and difference of the two popular sites, namely Facebook and Twitter.

With the expansion and advancement of social media platforms, as Thompson and colleagues (2018) pointed out, sport organizations are developing specific strategies to use them. As these authors uncovered in their study, Twitter and Facebook serve different purposes and, thus, require organizations to develop unique strategies to leverage the (potential) opportunities afforded by each. In line with what Thompson and colleagues (2018) claim, Billings and colleagues (2019: 646) argued that "any conclusion about what social media is or is not for sports fans is much more platform-specific than monolithic."

Tab. 1: Features of Facebook and Twitter, adapted from Abeza and O'Reilly (2014)

Features	Facebook	Twitter
Connection	– Users need approval from another user to contact them. Friendship has to be mutually agreed and accepted. – Users cannot view some other users' profile, post, or feeds unless connected.	– Users do not require the same type of approval as Facebook. Users can follow anyone without the permission of the person one follows. – Users can view other users' profile and tweets.
Users' intention of use	– Users connect with friends and members, and other people that they care to keep in touch with. – More on expanding the breadth of the conversation networking and connection.	– Twitter is less about social friendships rather allows users to follow important topics, people, and conversations that are relevant or interesting to them. – It is more of a portal to get fresh and breaking news, to connect with people with whom users have no means of connecting otherwise.

Source: Adapted from Abeza and O'Reilly (2014)

In their study that investigated Europe's ten most valued professional football clubs (e. g., Manchester United, FC Barcelona) and their use of Facebook and Twitter as vehicles to communicate a variety of brand attributes, Maderer and colleagues (2018) reported that fans' interaction rate with their teams on Twitter is lower than on Facebook over the course of three consecutive sport seasons (2013–2016). In a like manner, Billings and colleagues (2019) reported that fans' excitement level(s) towards a professional team seemingly stem from Twitter, while fans find Facebook as a more preferred platform for passing time and for being entertained. Thompson and colleagues (2018), in their study that investigated the use of Facebook and Twitter as a brand management tool in the context of the Grand Slam tennis events, found that different strategies exist in the use of these two platforms. As they concluded, Facebook serves as a site for long-term relationship cultivation through the display of event-related visual imagery and core values, more so than Twitter. In contrast, Twitter serves to provide fans with an opportunity to experience the brand through real-time online text-based communication and interaction. The authors also found that Twitter usage is most often reported to fall into one of three primary purposes: interpersonal (i. e., two-way communication), informational (i. e., information dissemination), and promotional (i. e., relating to upcoming activities as a marketing function). Thompson and colleagues (2018) further reported that Facebook functions as a channel to assist in the development of brand image, with the prolific use of visual imagery offering further opportunities for fans to be subtly exposed to unique brand-related associations. On the other hand, Twitter aids in the facilitation of real-time connections leading to opportunities to develop emotional connections and socialization amongst fans.

The abovementioned findings support the arguments of some of the initial publications in the social media literature, by Abeza and colleagues (2015) and Eagleman (2013), who argued that there is no one-size-fits-all approach in the management of social media and called for the need for platform-specific management approaches. As noted, while most social media platforms have much in common, there are key variances and function in a uniquely different way (Billings et al. 2019). Particularly, Facebook and Twitter serve a different purpose, and therefore unique strategies are required to leverage opportunities afforded by each (Li et al. 2019; Thompson et al. 2018). While the distinct features and values of the different platforms are identified above, different social media platforms have commonly shared opportunities presented to sport marketers and are discussed below.

5 A final word on social media for practitioners in professional sport

This chapter describes and summarizes the considerable body of work that has been carried out on social media in professional sport. Notably, it highlights (1) its growing importance, (2) the vast array of purposes – both general and custom – that it can achieve, (3) its grounding in strong literature, and, perhaps most importantly, (4) the need for a clear focus on platform specific research, practical applications, and learning. In this regard, professional sport managers and marketers working in or with social media are strongly advised to use the "social media platform" as their "unit of analysis" when undertaking market research and building strategy or implementation plans around social media.

References

Abeza, Gashaw. 2018. The past, present, and future of social media in professional sports: Interview with Shannon Gross, Director of Content Strategy, Dallas Cowboys. *International Journal of Sport Communication* 11(3). 295–300.

Abeza, Gashaw & Norm O'Reilly. 2014. Social media platforms use in building stakeholder relationships: The case of national sport organizations. *Journal of Applied Sport Management* 6(3). 103–126.

Abeza, Gashaw & Norm O'Reilly. 2018. Social, digital, and mobile media in sport marketing. In Eric C. Schwarz & Jason D. Hunter (eds.), *Advanced theory and practice in sport marketing*, 3rd edn., 244–267. New York: Routledge.

Abeza, Gashaw, Norm O'Reilly & Benoît Séguin. 2019. The sequential-funnel-based focus group design: Adapting the focus group for research in sport management. *Journal of Global Sport Management*. doi: 10.1080/24704067.2018.1550621 (19 November 2020).

Abeza, Gashaw, Norm O'Reilly, Benoît Séguin & Ornella Nzindukiyimana. 2015. Social media scholarship in sport management research: A critical review. *Journal of Sport Management* 29(6). 601–618.

Abeza, Gashaw, Norm O'Reilly, Benoît Séguin & Ornella Nzindukiyimana. 2017. Social media as a relationship marketing tool in professional sport: A netnographical exploration. *International Journal of Sport Communication* 10(3). 325–358.

Achen, Rebecca M., John Kaczorowski, Trisha Horsmann & Alanda Ketzler. 2018. Exploring off-season content and interaction on Facebook: A comparison of US professional sport leagues. *International Journal of Sport Communication* 11(3). 389–413.

Billings, Andrew C., Ryan M. Broussard, Qingru Xu & Mingming Xu. 2019. Untangling international sport social media use: Contrasting US and Chinese uses and gratifications across four platforms. *Communication & Sport* 7(5). 630–652.

Boehmer, Jan & Stephen Lacy. 2014. Sport news on Facebook: The relationship between interactivity and readers' browsing behavior. *International Journal of Sport Communication* 7(1). 1–15.

Deprez, Annelore, Peter Mechant & Tim Hoebeke. 2013. Social media and Flemish sports reporters: A multimethod analysis of Twitter use as journalistic tool. *International Journal of Sport Communication* 6(2). 107–119.

Eagleman, Andrea N. 2013. Acceptance, motivations, and usage of social media as a marketing communications tool amongst employees of sport national governing bodies. *Sport Management Review* 16(4). 488–497.

Flamant, Albane. 2018. World Cup 2018: Social media stats and insights. *Social Media Today*, 22 May. https://www.socialmediatoday.com/news/world-cup-2018-social-media-stats-and-insights/524003/.

Gibbs, Chris, Norm O'Reilly & Michelle Brunette. 2014. Professional team sport and Twitter: Gratifications sought and obtained by followers. *International Journal of Sport Communication* 7(2). 188–213.

Hambrick, Marion E. & Tara Q. Mahoney. 2011. "It's incredible – trust me": Exploring the role of celebrity athletes as marketers in online social networks. *International Journal of Sport Management and Marketing* 10(3/4). 161–179.

Hoffman, Donna L. & Thomas Novak. 2012. Why do people use social media? Empirical findings and a new theoretical framework for social media goal pursuit. 17 January. https://dx.doi.org/10.2139/ssrn.1989586.

Iankova, Severina, Iain Davies, Christopher Archer-Brown, Ben Marder & Amy Yau. 2019. A comparison of social media marketing between B2B, B2C and mixed business models. *Industrial Marketing Management* 81. 169–179.

Kang, Sun J., Jason A. Rice, Marion E. Hambrick & Chulhwan Choi. 2019. CrossFit across three platforms: Using social media to navigate niche sport challenges. *Physical Culture and Sport. Studies and Research* 81(1). 36–46.

Kassing, Jeffrey W. & Jimmy Sanderson. 2010. Fan–athlete interaction and Twitter tweeting through the Giro: A case study. *International Journal of Sport Communication* 3(1) 113–128.

Lebel, Katie & Karen Danylchuk. 2012. How Tweet it is: A gendered analysis of professional tennis players' self-presentation on Twitter. *International Journal of Sport Communication* 5(4). 461–480.

Li, Bo, Stephen W. Dittmore, Olan K. Scott, Wen-juo Lo & Sarah Stokowski. 2019. Why we follow: Examining motivational differences in following sport organizations on Twitter and Weibo. *Sport Management Review* 22(3). 335–347.

Maderer, Daniel, Petros Parganas & Christos Anagnostopoulos. 2018. Brand-image communication through social media: The case of European professional football clubs. *International Journal of Sport Communication* 11(3). 319–338.
McEnnis, Simon. 2013. Raising our game: Effects of citizen journalism on Twitter for professional identity and working practices of British sport journalists. *International Journal of Sport Communication* 6(4). 423–433.
Meng, Matthew D., Constantino Stavros & Kate Westberg. 2015. Engaging fans through social media: implications for team identification. *Sport, Business and Management: An International Journal* 5(3). 199–217.
Number of monthly active Twitter users worldwide from 1st quarter 2010 to 1st quarter 2019. 2019. *Statista.com*. https://bit.ly/2dt7OI9 (19 November 2020).
O'Hallarn, Brendan, Stephen L. Shapiro, Marion E. Hambrick, D. E. Wittkower, Lynn Ridinger & Craig A. Morehead. 2018. Sport, Twitter hashtags, and the public sphere: A qualitative test of the phenomenon through a Curt Schilling case study. *Journal of Sport Management*. 32(4). 389–400.
Our company. 2019. *Twitter*. https://about.twitter.com/en_us/company.html (19 November 2020).
Our mission. 2019. *Facebook*. https://newsroom.fb.com/company-info/ (19 November 2020).
Pegoraro, Ann. 2010. Look who's talking – Athletes on Twitter: A case study. *International Journal of Sport Communication* 3(4). 501–514.
Phua, Joe. 2012. Use of social networking sites by sports fans: Implications for the creation and maintenance of social capital. *Journal of Sports Media* 7(1). 109–132.
Popp, Bastian, Chris Horbel & Claas Christian Germelmann. 2018. Social-media-based anti-brand communities opposing sport-team sponsors: Insights from two prototypical communities. *International Journal of Sport Communication* 11(3). 339–368.
Price, John, Neil Farrington & Lee Hall. 2013. Changing the game? The impact of Twitter on relationships between football clubs, supporters and the sports media. *Soccer & Society* 14(4). 446–461.
Pronschinske, Mya, Mark D. Groza, & Matthew Walker. 2012. Attracting Facebook "fans": The importance of authenticity and engagement as a social networking strategy for professional sport teams. *Sport Marketing Quarterly* 21(4). 221–231.
Rosen, Aliza. 2017. Tweeting made easier. *Twitter*, 7 November. https://bit.ly/2OJDLzx (19 November 2020).
Sanderson, Jimmy. 2013. From loving the hero to despising the villain: Sports fans, Facebook, and social identity threats. *Mass Communication and Society* 16(4). 487–509.
Schultz, Brad & Mary Lou Sheffer. 2010. An exploratory study of how Twitter is affecting sports journalism. *International Journal of Sport Communication* 3(2). 226–239.
Stavros, Constantino, Matthew D. Meng, Kate Westberg & Francis Farrelly. 2013. Understanding fan motivation for interacting on social media. *Sport Management Review* 17(4). 455–469.
Thompson, Ashleigh-Jane, Andrew J. Martin, Sarah Gee & Andrea N. Geurin. 2018. Building brand and fan relationships through social media. *Sport, Business and Management: An International Journal* 8(3). 235–256.
Vale, Leonor & Teresa Fernandes. 2018. Social media and sports: Driving fan engagement with football clubs on Facebook. *Journal of Strategic Marketing* 26(1). 37–55.
Waters, Richard D., Kimberly A. Burke, Zachary H. Jackson & Jamie D. Buning. 2011. Using stewardship to cultivate fandom online: Comparing how National Football League teams use their web sites and Facebook to engage their fans. *International Journal of Sport Communication* 4. 163–177.
Wakefield, Lane T. & Gregg Bennett. 2018. Sports fan experience: Electronic word-of-mouth in ephemeral social media. *Sport Management Review* 21(2). 147–159.

Weinberg, Bruce D. & Ekin Pehlivan. 2011. Social spending: Managing the social media mix. *Business Horizons* 54(3). 275–282.

Williams, Jo, Susan J. Chinn & James Suleiman. 2014. The value of Twitter for sports fans. *Journal of Direct, Data and Digital Marketing Practice* 16(1). 36–50.

Winand, Mathieu, Matthew Belot, Sebastian Merten & Dimitros Kolyperas. 2019. International sport federations' social media communication: A content analysis of FIFA's Twitter account. *International Journal of Sport Communication* 12(2). 209–233.

Witkemper, Chad, Choong Hoon Lim & Adia Waldburger. 2012. Social media and sports marketing: Examining the motivations and constraints of Twitter users. *Sport Marketing Quarterly* 21(3). 170–183.

Ann Pegoraro and Katie Lebel

35 Social media and sport marketing

Abstract: Social media have fundamentally transformed the sport media landscape. In just a decade, sport marketers have moved from a reliance on traditional, one-way media filtered by PR professionals, to a dynamic two-way dialogue that focuses on authenticity and audience engagement. This chapter will explore the rise of digital platforms and their impact on the marketing of sport. Specifically, the chapter will focus on the influence of social media platforms on digital fandom, sport marketing strategy, and sponsorship opportunities, while also considering the evolving role of social media for athletes and sport organizations. The authors will examine key literature to date related to these topics and offer a glimpse of the future in digital sport marketing.

Keywords: social media; sport marketing; digital platforms; digital fandom; athletes and digital world; digital marketing strategy; sport sponsorship

1 Introduction

Social media (SM) platforms have fundamentally altered consumer behavior and subsequently had a profound impact on marketing communications (Hutter et al. 2013). Within this technological sea change, few industries have been as deeply impacted by social media as the world of sport (Sanderson 2011). Once considered something of a toy, the early adoption and swift integration of social media has spurred the sport industry to become a leader in the social media revolution. Athletes and sport organizations have used social media to enhance their digital branding and build strategic business advantages. Sport managers have used SM platforms to stimulate business innovation, developing SM tools to achieve goals related to ticket sales (Boatwright 2013), fan identification, and engagement (Hopkins 2013). A growing number of scholars have researched the diversified roles of social media (SM) platforms in sport marketing (Filo, Lock, and Karg 2015). This chapter serves to trace the growth of SM in sport and highlight some of the empirical, applied scholarship that has been conducted in this space. The goal is to illustrate how the use of practical, evidence-based research can empower practitioners with a more detailed understanding of sport fans' affinity with brands and athletes (Clavio and Kian 2010; Pegoraro, Scott, and Burch 2017) and inform overall social media strategy in the sport marketing sphere.

https://doi.org/10.1515/9783110660883-035

2 The rise of social media in sport

The contemporary sport fan has the ability to consume sport through a variety of different ways. Social media platforms have augmented these options innumerably over the past decade with the rise of social media. The 2012 London Olympics are generally referred to as the major turning point for social media in sport, with the London Games dubbed the "first social media Olympics." The global scale of the Olympics was able to showcase both the power and scope of social media technology with athletes and fans from around the world gathering to engage with the Olympics via SM platforms (Humphreys 2012). Fast forward to the 2018 World Cup and Twitter activity was found to generate 115 billion Impressions (views on Twitter) during the tournament (Bavishi and Filadelfo 2018). Today, coaches, athletes, fans, and sports media professionals alike maintain accounts and interact with one another on social media (Browning and Sanderson 2012; Sanderson and Kassing 2011). The live nature of sport has leant itself well to the immediacy afforded by social media, resulting in collective successes.

As each new sporting event unfolds, SM platforms consistently generate new record-breaking traffic, fueled by the persistent growth of the SM user base. While the total number of social media users in 2010 was just under one billion, projections suggest there will be over three billion users by 2021 (Number of monthly 2019). The sport industry continues to reflect the mass popularity of social media and it is leveraging SM technologies in increasingly innovative ways.

Tab. 1: Top sport entities on social media by number of followers*

Sport entity	Twitter	Facebook	Instagram
UEFA Champions League	24 Million	67 Million	44.4 Million
NBA	28.3 Million	37 Million	39 Million
Premier League	19.9 Million	42 Million	28.9 Million
UFC	7.10 Million	23 Million	14.6 Million
NFL	24.5 Million	17 Million	14.8 Million
MLB	8.39 Million	7.2 Million	5.6 Million
NHL	6.22 Million	4.5 Million	3.6 Million
MLS	3.26 Million	3.2 Million	1.3 Million
NRL	540,000	1.5 Million	679,000
AFL	715,000	1 Million	706,000
Super Rugby	283,000	596,000	550,000

* number of followers on each platform recorded on July 30, 2019.

3 Digital sport consumers

Sport organizations have broadly employed SM platforms as fan engagement mechanisms since their introduction (e. g., Facebook in 2004 and Twitter in 2007) (Blaszka et al. 2012). SM tools have simultaneously been embraced by fans as channels to display their fandom (Pegoraro, Comeau, and Frederick 2018). Originally SM media platforms were envisioned to operate as virtual communities that allow users to participate in designing, publishing, editing, and sharing in a dynamic environment (van Dijck and Poell 2013). The capacity of SM platforms to foster these kinds of self-expressions among users has provided instantaneous connectivity and helped to break down geographic and communicative boundaries for sport fans allowing them to interact with their favourite athletes and teams with relative ease (Pegoraro 2013). These new opportunities for engagement by fans and sport consumers have drawn significant attention from sport researchers.

The earliest scholarship in communication and sport concerned itself with why fans use SM platforms. Clavio and Kian (2010) investigated the most common reasons fans followed an athlete on Twitter and found that affinity for the athlete and content related to the athlete were deemed the most important factors. Looking at the specific context of US college sport, Clavio and Walsh (2013) found student college sport fans used SM platforms to watch videos, while using traditional media sources or university athletic websites to obtain information. Researchers discovered that student fans were willing to post comments on existing content or upload pictures, but were unwilling to engage in the creation of more substantial content on SM platforms. Haugh and Watkins (2016) found that college sport fans were more likely to use Facebook and Twitter to obtain information about sports, fanship, team support, and entertainment; Instagram was more likely to be used for entertainment purposes, fanship, and to pass time; while Snapchat was the platform of choice for fans looking to pass time, provide entertainment, fanship, and escape. These findings provided important insights around fan consumer behavior and helped to inform platform specific content strategies for practitioners.

In the realm of professional sport, Gibbs, O'Reilly, and Brunette (2014) found Canadian sport fans were drawn to SM platforms for their immediacy of information. This study noted fans' preference to hear about player or roster moves immediately and/or discover information before others. This research also found that fans tended to use SM to follow games they could not watch and specified Twitter use as a means to learn about upcoming games. Billings and colleagues (2019) took this work a step further with an investigation of social media sport fandom from an international lens. This research investigated the differences in uses and gratifications obtained within four different SM platforms: Facebook and Twitter (in the United States) and WeChat and Weibo (in China). It was determined that sport fans viewed each of the platforms in contrasting ways. In the United States, Facebook scored higher than Twitter on every motivational measure in the study and in China, sport fans viewed WeChat as the best means to foster camaraderie, entertainment, habitual use, and maintaining relationships, while Weibo was found to be better for arousal motivations (Billings et al. 2019). These findings again highlight the platform-specific uses of SM platforms for sport fans (Billings et al. 2019) and illustrate the maturation of both SM platforms and users alike. Overall, research has found that individuals participate on SM platforms for entertainment, information, surveillance (i. e., keeping up with others), and the ability to create social connections. Additionally, users have been found to be more likely to engage and interact with SM content when they feel it meets their needs, is easy to use, and offers an emotional connection.

In line with analyses of SM content, the study of SM engagement has emerged as an area of great interest to scholars and practitioners alike. Scholars have investigated how different types of content prompt consumers to engage or interact, moving them from passive consumers on SM platforms to active roles. Thompson and colleagues (2014) found consumers most often interact with content that poses questions and provides behind-the-scenes content opportunities. Boehmer and Tandoc (2015) found retweets of sport news by students were impacted by perceptions of credibility and likability of the source. Respondents were influenced by a tweet's originality, informativeness, and style when deciding what types of content to retweet. Characteristics of the users, including their interest in the tweet's topic, the relevancy of the tweet's topic to the user, similarity in opinion, and impact on the user's followers, all impacted users' decisions on whether they would retweet a post. Engaging with content was also found to be influenced by students' perceptions of their own Twitter followers' interests (Boehmer and Tandoc 2015).

As SM platforms and their user bases have matured, scholars have re-focused their attention to issues beyond *why* people follow and *what* prompts engagement, to studies that investigate the different types of *outcomes* that SM interaction can provide to sport consumers. At the same time, there has been a rise in social television (TV), or second-screen experiences, which involves watching televised events while also engaging on SM platforms. As referenced earlier, each new live sporting event draws increasingly more posts on SM platforms – the 2018 Super Bowl, for example, generated 4.8 billion tweets around the event (Cohen 2018). Cunningham and Eastin (2017) found that 79 percent of participants used second screens for social media interaction while watching sports (e. g., posting and commenting on Facebook or Twitter) and 65 percent looked online for information related to the game or sport while it was being played. Recognizing that sports fans are increasingly turning to Twitter to experience events and receive commentary, Smith, Pegoraro, and Cruikshank (2019) surveyed sports fans to measure how Twitter might influence their enjoyment of viewing live and mediated sporting events. Respondents in this study were found to focus on American football and they primarily reported using Twitter to augment their consumption of sports. This finding confirms what previous scholars had found. When asked about how Twitter use impacted their enjoyment level while consuming live and broadcast sports, heavy Twitter users reported higher enjoyment levels when using the platform to watch sports (Smith, Pegoraro, and Cruikshank 2019). The study findings suggested that the manner in which respondents use Twitter could impact their overall sports viewing enjoyment. The highest levels of enjoyment came from individuals who only posted their own thoughts or replied to other individuals, and individuals who did both of these actions, while also retweeting/favoriting other tweets. Enjoyment levels dropped for individuals who only retweeted/favorited others' content or did not post at all. Practically speaking, this research shows that engagement with content and posting of one's own content can be important drivers of consumer enjoyment on Twitter (Smith, Pegoraro, and Cruikshank 2019).

Considering the impact of watching broadcast sport on traditional sport consumer behavior, Fan and colleagues (2019) investigated BIRGing and CORFing on SM platforms during the 2018 World Cup. BIRGing (Basking In Reflective Glory) has been defined as a tendency to associate with successful others or teams (Cialdini et al. 1976). When fans identify with a losing team, research suggests they often weaken associations to protect their social identity, or CORF (Cut Off Reflective Failure) (Snyder, Lassegard, and Ford 1986). In their study, Fan et al. (2019) analyzed close to 100,000 tweets sent by fans during two of England's games during the 2018 World Cup. Their analysis found that English fans tended to perform Basking in Reflected Glory (BIRG) when England was leading or victorious and tended to engage in Cutting Off Reflected Failure (CORF) when England was trailing or defeated, thereby illustrating that fans were using SM platforms to extend traditional fan behaviors during live sport events (Fan et al. 2019).

More recently, scholars have increasingly connected communicative usages of sport SM platforms to patterns of economic consumption in a more quantitative approach to digital sport consumer behavior (e. g., Watanabe et al. 2015, 2016; Jensen, Ervin, and Dittmore 2014). Specifically, the use of SM platforms as a proxy for consumer interest in sport products has been studied with a focus placed upon analytical modeling of micro-transactions (i. e., Twitter or Facebook Followers/Likes) as indicators of sport consumer behavior. These results reveal that the popularity of sport teams on SM platforms is related to various market characteristics as well as team operations (Perez 2013; Watanabe et al. 2015, 2016). O'Hallarn, Shapiro, and Pegoraro (2018) investigated the relationship between price levels in the secondary ticket market and activity on SM platforms. The study investigated the prices for eight National Football League games adding the use of official team hashtags on Twitter to a multiple regression model, controlling for other price determinants established in previous research. The two models, one to predict prices for tickets sold on StubHub, the second to predict prices for tickets available on StubHub, demonstrated that increased Twitter hashtag use is a significant positive predictor of ticket prices on the secondary market (O'Hallarn, Shapiro, and Pegoraro 2018).

In line with this, researchers have used similar methods to investigate rivalry through SM platforms as rivalries have long been a part of sport consumer behavior. The convenience to engage in expressions of rivalry – to commiserate, celebrate, as well as antagonize by interacting with teams and fans – has reached an unprecedented degree of flexibility and freedom on SM platforms. Watanabe and colleagues (2019) utilized Twitter data measuring the number of posts by individuals about US college football teams to model how often fans create content during game days. After controlling for a number of factors, including the type of rivalry game, results indicated that fans post more during traditional rivalries. Furthermore, newer rivalry games had less impact on the amount of content posted about a team. Previous research on the effect of conference realignment on attendance (Szymanski and Winfree 2018), revealed the loss of rivalries were estimated to only have a negligible impact on attendance at games, sometimes accounting for only half a percent change in attendance demand. Therefore, the study demonstrated that rivalries may play a more substantial role in driving consumer interest for college football teams in the digital realm, compared to actual physical attendance (Watanabe et al. 2019).

Overall, research into sport consumer behavior on SM platforms has evolved alongside the growing sophistication of both SM platforms and their users. New platforms have emerged while others have disappeared; however, there is no doubt that fans have embraced the digital realm as a place to exhibit fan behavior.

One of the key insights that researchers have discovered with respect to digital fan behavior includes the finding that fans appear to derive many types of gratifications from their SM usage. This ranges from information seeking behaviors to pure enjoyment and can be translated into strategic content delivery that prompts engagement by these fans which in turn provides value for teams, leagues, and athletes alike. Fans exhibit offline behavior online, so sport marketers can use the notion of team identification to prompt BIRGing behavior on SM platforms and monitor the same platforms for CORFing. This kind of research can inform sport marketers who might take note of the fact that fans who use SM platforms to follow sport more frequently exhibit high levels of enjoyment when watching both televised sport (social TV) and live sport. Finding ways to engage with these heavy users could provide significant value to sport marketers. Research also demonstrates that rivalries can help to boost the volume of content individuals post about a team, suggesting these types of games provide teams with an opportunity to maximize their engagement with fans and focus on key marketing objectives.

In terms of quantifying digital consumer behavior, research has proven that likes/follows can be a proxy for demand for a team or athlete and therefore indicate popularity, which can be used to inform marketing plans. Research further shows that sport consumer posts on SM platforms can drive up prices in the secondary ticket market, which could provide valuable insights into pricing strategies, specifically dynamic pricing applications. Collectively, over a decade of sport digital consumer behavior research has provided many salient contributions to inform both academic literature and industry practitioners.

4 Impact and opportunity for athletes

The growth for SM platforms in sport has been in some part driven by the novelty of extending to athletes the control to shape their own public image (Pegoraro 2010) through digital channels. Fundamentally, this has positioned SM platforms as a stage for self-presentation for athletes and a catalyst to create relationships not possible through traditional media outlets (Lebel and Danylchuk 2012). Fundamentally, this has inspired a revolution around the ways in which athletes are able to market themselves and interact with fans.

The social media insight platform, Hookit, tracks the social media activity of athletes based upon metrics of influence, engagement, and interactions (likes, comments, shares, re-tweets, and views of videos). As of June 2019, Hookit calculated that the top twenty most followed athletes in the world had a combined 1,726,100,000 total followers on Facebook, Twitter, and Instagram, speaking volumes to the potential reach of social platforms. Table 2 illustrates the social footprint of the most-followed athletes in the world. Engagement was calculated by dividing the total number of interactions by the total number of fans following a particular athlete. Interactions were defined as a combined measurement of the total number of likes, comments, and re-tweets each athlete post received. It should be noted that female athletes are noticeably absent among this top-twenty ranking. The first female appearing on the list is Rhonda Rousey, a Mixed Martial Arts athlete, who was ranked 41st overall. This observation underscores the issue of gender equity in sport and its reflection in the SM context. It has also inspired advocacy through a variety of research traditions designed to more specifically address this issue.

Though the relative novelty of social media's influence on sport remains difficult to quantify, from a revenue generation standpoint, *Forbes* has suggested that professional soccer star Cristiano Ronaldo, currently the second most followed athlete on social media, generated US $500 million in value for Nike through his social media properties in 2016 (Badenhausen 2017). Sponsors have been quick to understand the potential influence of athletes with large SM followings; this has led to lucrative marketing opportunities for athletes that command large audiences. Recent data from Hopper HQ provides the following valuation for an Instagram post by some of the athletes on this list: Cristiano Ronaldo – $975,000; Neymar – $722,000; Lionel Messi – $648,000; David Beckham – $357,000; and LeBron James – $272,000 (Front Office Sports 2019).

From a research standpoint, consideration of athletes' use of social media was among the earliest contributions to scholarship around social media in sport. Two foundational studies by Pegoraro (2010) and Hambrick and colleagues (2010) provided content analyses of athletes' tweets across various sports. They found that interactivity – "direct communication with fellow athletes and fans" (Hambrick et al. 2010: 460) – and information not related to sports were the two most common types of tweets posted by professional athletes, totaling more than 60 percent of the tweets analyzed in each study. Pegoraro (2010: 501) concluded that Twitter is "a powerful

Tab. 2: Athlete rankings on social media (ranked by total followers, June 1–June 30, 2019)*

Rank	Name	Sport	Followers	Twitter	Facebook	Instagram	New followers	Posts	Interactions
1	Lionel Messi	Global Football	221.1M	310.4K	90.0M	124.0M	3.1M	42	72.3M
2	Cristiano Ronaldo	Global Football	208.5M	78.5M	122.3M	–	816.8K	67	12.3M
3	PewDiePie*	Esports	123.2M	17.8M	7.3M	–	830.3K	56	20.5M
4	Neymar da Silva	Global Football	111.6M	43.7M	60.5M	–	819.9K	37	3.6M
5	Ronaldinho Gaúcho	Global Football	99.8M	18.8M	34.4M	46.6M	1.2M	46	12.0M
6	James Rodriguez	Global Football	92.7M	18.3M	32.4M	42.1M	672.6K	29	12.5M
7	Gareth Bale	Global Football	87.9M	18.0M	28.3M	40.2M	284.6K	30	4.0M
8	Sergio Ramos	Global Football	72.7M	16.2M	23.5M	33.0M	969.0K	55	22.1M
9	Marcelo Vieira	Global Football	71.6M	11.6M	19.8M	39.0M	980.9K	36	24.7M
10	Virat Kohli	Cricket	67.5M	30.3M	37.2M	–	636.5K	53	10.5M
11	Lebron James	Basketball	66.1M	43.0M	23.1M	–	251.1K	36	2.7M
12	Karim Benzema	Global Football	61.0M	9.7M	22.7M	28.6M	766.0K	56	15.0M
13	Ricardo Kaka	Global Football	60.4M	29.7M	30.7M	–	–38.8K	6	23.9K
14	David Beckham	Global Football	59.4M	609.8K	52.6M	–	–104.3K	15	99.0K
15	Mesut Özil	Global Football	59.3M	24.1M	31.2M	–	352.6K	19	2.0M
16	Wayne Rooney	Global Football	55.9M	17.1M	24.7M	14.1M	138.2K	36	3.0M
17	Gerard Pique	Global Football	55.3M	19.3M	18.7M	17.3M	110.8K	12	2.8M
18	Paul Pogba	Global Football	54.7M	6.9M	7.4M	35.8M	1.3M	80	24.5M
19	Andrés Iniesta	Global Football	50.8M	24.2M	26.6M	–	26.9K	53	1.0M
20	Conor McGregor	Mixed Martial Arts	46.6M	7.6M	7.9M	31.1M	164.2K	92	22.4M

* the rankings include eSports athletes alongside traditional sport athletes. A debate about the treatment of eSports as sport continues on amongst academics and practitioners alike.

tool for increasing fan–athlete interaction." These two studies became the impetus for much of the body of research on athletes' use of social media that has been produced to date. For example, Browning and Sanderson (2012) examined student athletes' tweets and similarly found interactivity to be a dominant strategy. Their study revealed that student athletes used Twitter for three primary reasons: keeping in contact, communicating with followers, and accessing information.

Once researchers discovered how athletes were using Twitter, they turned their attention to consider how athletes were choosing to present themselves on SM platforms. In research that centered on Goffman's (1978) theory of self-presentation, Lebel and Danylchuk (2012) found that both men and women athletes utilized backstage (i. e., candid) performances more often than frontstage (i. e., calculated) performances on SM. Overall, the authors discovered that men utilized the role of super fan (e. g., informal discussion of sport) most often, while women utilized the brand manager role (e. g., formal, brand conscious acknowledgments) more often than men, indicating a persistence of hegemonic values. This finding provided valuable insight for women athletes looking to grow their personal brands using SM tools.

Further to this, gendered differences were explored relative to how professional athletes present their self-image in profile pictures with an investigation into how this type of digital athlete self-presentation is interpreted by Generation Y audiences (Lebel and Danylchuk 2014b). Strong tendencies were found toward more formal, front stage performances with a distinct preference noted for passive self-presentations by all athletes under examination. Female athletes, however, were found to more often present a glamorized photo of themselves, in a non-sport setting, while male athletes overwhelmingly elected to portray themselves in either a sport setting or a sport context. This research offered evidence to suggest that audiences invested meaning in the various social cues provided through profile photos and concluded profile photos that were in line with an athlete's personality and established "athletic brand" were most effective among Gen Y audiences.

4.1 Women athletes

Social media has afforded athletes the opportunity to build brands capable of turning the table on traditional power structures (Lebel, Pegoraro, and Harman 2018). While traditional media is infamously known to afford dismal coverage to women in sport (Cooky, Messner, and Musto 2015) and portray women athletes in a biased manner that trivializes their place in sport (Bruce 2016), social media is less restrictive and offers a means to create relationships and visibility not otherwise possible in traditional media outlets. This has not only inspired a revolution in sport consumption strategies, it has left advocates of women's sport hopeful that SM platforms might serve to level the playing field for women athletes in particular. Social media is an opportunity for women athletes to craft their own messages and indeed be their own media outlets.

In July 2019, Hookit rankings of SM interactions found two women athletes emerge among the top twenty athletes globally: Alex Morgan from the US Women's National Soccer team was ranked in fifth place and teammate Megan Rapinoe was ranked in twelfth place. This shift illustrates the power of a mega event, the 2019 Women's World Cup, on SM attention for athletes, in particular female athletes. It also illustrates the power social media has afforded athletes to build their own brands and craft narratives that counter traditional media storylines around women athletes. It shows what *could* be possible.

In an innovative study that investigated how women athletes would themselves choose to be portrayed, Krane and colleagues (2010) found that, when given a choice, a majority of college-aged female athletes elected to emphasize their power, strength, and athleticism. The decision of these women athletes to select physical competence as a means of self-presentation contradicts years of research that has suggested an inclination of sportswomen to balance traditional gender identities with athletic selves (e. g., Griffin 1992). Shreffler, Hancock, and Schmidt (2016) investigated how women athletes were choosing to present themselves on Twitter by conducting a review of 206 female athlete avatars on Twitter profiles. The authors found, similar to Krane and colleagues (2010), that female athletes were more likely to present themselves as athletically competent individuals as opposed to depicting themselves as sexualized beings. This type of research offers a glimpse into the taken for granted branding strategies long associated with women's sport and underscores the power of SM to help change traditional, hegemonic narratives for women athletes.

To date, limited sport-specific research has examined Instagram use as it pertains to gender. Geurin-Eagleman and Burch (2015) focused on the self-presentation tactics of athletes and found that women were more likely to share personal photos from private settings, while men posted a variety of photos, which encouraged more engagement among followers. Smith and Sanderson (2015) analyzed the Instagram feeds of both men and women professional athletes. They found that women athletes utilized more active photos than men athletes. This finding ran counter to past research which indicated that women are more likely to be shown in more passive roles (e. g., on the sidelines) thereby demonstrating that women athletes are using social media platforms to counteract traditional media narratives.

Lebel and colleagues (2018) investigated the Instagram accounts of four top women athletes for both self-presentation and fans' responses to the chosen self-presentation strategies. The first set of findings related to athletes' self-presentation strategies and engagement indicated that while fan engagement is notably dependent upon the type of audience each athlete attracts through their presentation of self, it is significant to note that photos depicting athletic competence generated the most likes among this sample of women athletes. Sexually suggestive photos continued to engender significant attention, however, and typically garnered the greatest number of comments among followers (Lebel, Pegoraro, and Harman 2018). The second set of findings investigated the content of fan comments to determine the impact of fan engagement on the athlete's overall brand. A thematic review of comments revealed differing forms of fan engagement. Sexualized images, for example, tended to evoke comments focused on the "beauty" of the athlete, while images depicting athletic competence were linked to inspiration and respect for the athlete. This suggests that increased fan engagement may not necessarily equate to positive brand exposure (Lebel, Pegoraro, and Harman 2018) for women athletes. Self-presentation strategies that feature images of athletic competence may be of significant benefit to women athletes looking to authenticate their brands based upon their athletic accomplishments. Given the rise of Instagram and visual communications, these findings illustrate important implications for the personal branding strategies of women athletes in the construction of their digital brands (Lebel, Pegoraro, and Harman 2018).

5 Sport marketing strategy and sponsorship

Social media have had a substantial impact on marketing communications (Hutter et al. 2013). Current forecasts predict there will be 3.43 billion monthly social network users globally by 2023 and digital ad spending will rise by 20 percent to $452,593 billion (Number of monthly 2019). This marks the first time in history that digital will account for half of the global ad market (Enberg 2019) and is emblematic of the significant behavioral evolution that has turned social media into an such an attractive marketing channel.

In the sport context, research has examined the use of social media as a marketing tool for athletes (Hull 2014; Kassing and Sanderson 2010; Lebel and Danylchuk 2012, 2014a; Pegoraro 2010); professional sport organizations (Gibbs, O'Reilly, and Brunette 2014; Wang and Zhou 2015), and non-profit sport organizations (Pegoraro, Scott, and Burch 2017). This work has generally found promotional tweets to account for a small percentage of overall SM content production and highlighted an opportunity for more strategic growth.

Specific to platform use, Pegoraro, Scott, and Burch (2017) investigated the use of one SM platform, Facebook, by National Olympic Committees in two countries, Australia and Canada, over specific time periods related to three Olympic Games (2010, 2012, and 2014 Games), to determine the types of brand-related post content and communication style utilized as well as the consumer response to these posts. The two organizations generally used Facebook to broadcast product-related brand attributes such as information about athletes and teams. There was a significant difference in Facebook post use and focus by the two organizations indicating some international differences in using Facebook for branding a sport organization.

Social media engagement is yet another emerging area of scholarship related to social media marketing strategy. In an investigation that considered how sport fans view their own social media engagement, a series of exploratory focus groups found that sport consumers are diverse in their understanding of what SM engagement means (Achen et al. 2017). Results suggested that sport-minded social media users embrace a diverse range of social media interaction strategies that go well beyond the basic metrics of likes and comments. The research concluded that more sophisticated engagement metrics should be developed to more fully capture how audiences are interacting with SM content and better inform content strategies.

5.1 Sponsorship

Abeza and colleagues (2015) were among the first to examine sport sponsorship in a social media context. Their work explored the use of Twitter for sponsorship activation by The Olympic Program (TOP) sponsors during the 2014 Sochi Olympic Winter Games. Using NCapture, a total of 7,519 tweets and retweets of all ten TOP sponsors around the Games were captured from January 1 (pre-Olympic) to April 3, 2014 (post-Olympic). Results indicated that there is no regular pattern of Twitter use for activation that was identifiable amongst the TOP sponsors; moreover, all were found to adopt different strategic approaches. Notably, the TOP sponsors differed in terms of the number and types of tweets they produced, retweets they broadcast, hashtags they ran, and the registered growth of their followers from pre-games to post-games. The results also show three possible sponsorship objectives communicated by TOP sponsors, namely promotion (of services, products, and company's image), customer appreciation, and athletes' encouragement.

Delia and Armstrong (2015) built on this work through an examination of sponsorship at the French Open tennis tournament. This research found that of the 300,000 tweets that included the official tournament hashtag, less than 1 percent contained sponsored content, again underscoring the potential of this area in sport.

Social media sponsorship is a budding area of research in the sporting context. What is abundantly clear is that it has become an avenue for brands to obtain more value from a deal. According to Zoomph, a leading digital intelligence company, the 2019 Women's World Cup generated 56.9 billion social media impressions for an estimated engagement value of $16.5 million. These impressive figures draw light to the vast potential of social media marketing and the incredible potential of digital sponsorship in sport.

6 Future of digital sport marketing

So, what is next in the digital world for sport marketing? There are several trends that are affecting the industry, and they are bound to disrupt it yet again and provide future avenues for research. We now review a few of these trends and the potential for future SM research.

6.1. The rise of women's sport

In 2018, Neilson surveyed 1000 individuals in eight of the most commercially active sports markets the United States, the United Kingdom, France, Germany, Italy, Spain, Australia, and New Zealand. The findings were impressive, with 84 percent of all general sport fans showing interest in women's sport and 66 percent reporting they watch at least one women's sport. The report also found that 63 percent of respondents feel that brands should invest in women's sport, 75 percent could recall at least one brand that is involved in women's sport, and one in five said they were more influenced by a brand associated with women's sport than one associated with men's sport. These figures reveal not only the public's interest and appetite for women's sport, but also the presence a huge business opportunity for sports marketers to explore.

According to FIFA (France 2019), the Women's World Cup drew record audiences. In the Netherlands, an average audience of 5.481 million (34.5 percent of the potential TV audience) watched their women's team in their first-ever FIFA Women's World Cup Final versus the United States. In the United States, 15.277 million viewers tuned in to watch the women's team win their fourth title (France 2019). Advertisers also spent a record $100 million on TV ads for the World Cup (Bruell and Bachman 2019).

On the Fox Digital Platforms, the US broadcasting channel, the final had an average audience of 289,000 viewers, a 402 per cent increase on the 2015 final (France 2019). Social media channels for FIFA also saw an increase in viewership with mid tournament numbers reaching a record 433 million views, 83 million video views and 2 million new followers, all before the knockout round began (Women's World Cup 2019). As noted above, individual athletes saw huge increases in followers throughout the month-long tournament.

All of these numbers and growth in interest provide opportunities for digital marketers but also for researchers. Overall, there is a lack of data around women's sport in terms of quantifying the impact on social media channels. Researchers can help bridge that data gap. Studies that can provide insight into return on investment on digital channels, specific digital consumer behavior of women's sport fans, and continuing study of what is working on social media channels for leagues, teams, associations, and athletes at all levels of sport are areas where researchers can play a role.

6.2 The impact of AR and VR

Digital sport marketing is still in the very early days the impact of virtual (VR) and augmented reality (VR) technology. But visual-based social media channels like Instagram and Snapchat are allowing early adopter teams and brands to leverage these platforms to create immersive experiences. These immersive experiences are happening both inside stadiums and on digital channels around the world.

For example, in 2017 FC Bayern Munich used their own team app to create a fun interface where fans could virtually insert themselves into selfies with the team's star players like Arjen Robben (Srivastav 2017). While the feature was available to fans via the team app, fans could also personalize jerseys and then purchase that jersey from club's online store. This immersive experience is reported to have increased the club's revenue (Srivastav 2017). Major League Baseball has also added AR to its At Bat app with the aim of enhancing the game that fans are watching on the field (Newman 2017).

While the use of these technologies is still in its infancy, research opportunities exist to assess the impact in several ways. First researchers can investigate the sharing of these experiences, that happen predominantly in the stadium, across digital channels. Additional questions that researchers could investigate include whether fans truly enjoy these augmented experiences and how they impact their digital fandom; what happens when their favorite athlete uses them, do fans; are fans more likely to engage with teams that use immersive experiences on social media; and do these digital immersive experiences lead to increased attendance or purchases.

6.3 Continued importance of social media channels

Social media is not a fad, and it is not going away. Therefore, it is important that sport entities across the board recognize the continued importance of social media in building fanbases and capitalizing on brand opportunities. As research has illustrated (e. g., Pegoraro, Comeau, and Frederick 2018; Achen, Lebel, and Clavio 2017), social media platforms like Twitter, Instagram, and Facebook present spaces where fan communities can be cultivated and maintained. As these platforms continue to evolve, they provide opportunities for brands, athletes, leagues, and teams to build relationships with fans, regardless of geography. Newer features such as "stories" on Instagram and Facebook, the ability to livestream on Twitter and Facebook, allows athletes and teams to provide their followers what appears to be exclusive, behind-the-scenes access on a 24-hour basis. In addition, athletes often have larger followings on social platforms than the teams, leagues, or organizations they play for or represent. These entities now have the ability to leverage the large social followings of their star athletes to increase engagement with their own SM accounts and content.

The continued importance of social media platforms in sport marketing provides researchers with many opportunities to add to the existing body of evidence. Likewise, SM research can be leveraged by practitioners to refine SM content strategies with evidence-based solutions. For example, researchers could investigate the content in athletes' Instagram stories, determine what are they sharing, how are they constructing their self-presentation, what brand elements are evident, and whether or not they integrate sponsors or teams into the content. Sport communication practitioners could use the results of this research to educate athletes and help them to employ more targeted SM strategies to increase brand awareness and ROI. Other research questions that can be explored include the digital streaming of sport through social media platforms and the reactions of fans, the increased reach and how these new channels can help niche sports reach new audiences. Researchers could also investigate how teams and leagues are leveraging the huge social followings of their star athletes both in-season and out of season to provide some insight into how these athlete and team brands can work together to build value for both.

References

Abeza, Gashaw, Ann Pegoraro, Michael Naraine, Benoît Seguin & Norm O'Reilly. 2015. Activating a global sport sponsorship with social media: An analysis of TOP sponsors, Twitter, and the 2014 Olympic Games. *International Journal of Sport Management and Marketing* 15(3–4). 184–213.

Achen, Rebecca M., Katie Lebel & Galen Clavio. 2017. What customers want: Defining engagement in sport media in sport. *Global Sport Business Journal* 5(3). 1–21.

Badenhausen, Kurt. 2017. Ronaldo beats Messi by 800 % when it comes to return on social media for their brands. *Forbes*, 23 February. https://www.forbes.com/sites/kurtbadenhausen/2017/02/23/ronaldo-beats-messi-by-800-when-it-comes-to-return-on-social-media-for-their-brands/?sh=d9aa5ec401b1.

Bavishi, Jay & Elaine Filadelfo. 2018. Insights into the 2018 #WorldCup conversation on Twitter. *Twitter*, 17 July. https://blog.twitter.com/en_us/topics/events/2018/ 2018-World-Cup-Insights.html (30 July 2019).

Billings, Andrew C., Ryan M. Broussard, Qingru Xu & Mingming Xu. 2019. Untangling international sport social media use: Contrasting US and Chinese uses and gratifications across four platforms. *Communication & Sport* 7(5). 630–652.

Blaszka, Matthew, Lauren Burch, Evan Frederick, Galen Clavio & Patrick Walsh. 2012. #WorldSeries: An empirical examination of a Twitter hashtag during a major sporting event. *International Journal of Sport Communication* 5(4). 435–453.

Boatwright, Brandon. 2013. Interview with Chris Yandle, Assistant Athletic Director of Communications, University of Miami Athletics, *International Journal of Sport Communication* 6(4). 388–390.

Boehmer, Jan & Edson Tandoc. 2015. Why we retweet: Factors influencing intentions to share sport news on Twitter. *International Journal of Spot Communication* 8(2). 212–232.

Browning, Blair & Jimmy Sanderson, J. 2012. The positives and negatives of Twitter. Exploring how student-athletes use Twitter and respond to critical tweets. *International Journal of Sport Communication* 5(4). 503–521.

Bruce, Toni. 2016. New rules for new times: Sportswomen and media representation in the third wave. *Sex Roles* 74(7–8). 361–376.

Bruell, Alexandra & Rachel Bachman. 2019. Women's World Cup drew nearly $100 million in TV ads. *Wall Street Journal*, 15 September. https://www.wsj.com/articles/ womens-world-cup-drew-nearly-100-million-in-tv-ads-11568556000 (16 September 2019).

Cialdini, Robert B., Richard J. Borden, Avril Throne & Marcus R. Walker. 1976. Basking in reflected glory: Three (football) field studies. *Journal of Personality and Social Psychology* 34(3). 366–375.

Clavio, Galen & Ted M. Kian. 2010. Uses and gratifications of a retired female athlete's Twitter followers. *International Journal of Sport Communication* 3(4). 485–500.

Clavio, Galen & Patrick Walsh. 2013. Dimensions of social media utilization among college sport fans. *Communication & Sport* 2(3). 261–281.

Cohen, David. 2018. What drove discussion during super bowl LII on Twitter, Facebook, YouTube? *AdWeek*, 5 February. https://www.adweek.com/digital/super-bowl-lii-wrap-twitter-facebook-youtube/ (19 November 2020).

Cooky, Cheryl, Michael A. Messner & Michela Musto. 2015. "It's dude time!": A quarter century of excluding women's sports in televised news and highlight shows. *Communication & Sport* 3(3). 261–287.

Cunningham, Nicole R. & Matthew S. Eastin. 2017. Second screen and sports: A structural investigation into team identification and efficacy. *Communication & Sport* 5(3). 288–310.

Delia, Elizabeth B. & Cole G. Armstrong. 2015. #Sponsoring the #FrenchOpen: An examination of social media buzz and sentiment. *Journal of Sport Management* 29(2). 184–199.

Enberg, Jasmine. 2019. Global digital ad spending 2019. *Insider Intelligence*, 28 March. https://www.emarketer.com/content/global-digital-ad-spending-2019 (19 November 2020).

Fan, Minghui, Andrew Billings, Xiangyu Zhu & Panfeng Yu. 2019. Twitter-based BIRG-ing: Big data analysis of English national team fans during the 2018 FIFA World Cup. *Communication and Sport* 8(3). 1–29.

Filo, Kevin, Daniel John Lock & Adam Karg. 2015. Sport and social media research: A review. *Sport Management Review* 18. 166–181.

France 2019 Final sets viewing records in participating and neutral territories. 2019. *FIFA.com*, 9 July. https://www.fifa.com/womensworldcup/news/france-2019-final-sets-viewing-records-in-participating-and-neutral-territories (16 September 2019).

Front Office Sports. 2019, New data: Sports organizations are crushing it on Instagram stories. 1 August. https://frontofficesports.com/instagram-stories-conviva-report/.

Geurin-Eagleman, Andrea & Lauren M. Burch. 2015. Communicating via photographs: A gendered analysis of Olympic athletes' visual self-presentation on Instagram. *Sport Management Review*. DOI: 10.1016/j.smr.2015.03.002.

Gibbs, Chris, Norm O'Reilly & Michelle Brunette. 2014. Professional team sport and Twitter: Gratifications sought and obtained by followers. *International Journal of Sport Communication* 7(2). 188–213.

Goffman, Erving. 1978. *The presentation of self in everyday life*. Harmondsworth: Penguin.

Griffin, P. 1992. Changing the game: Homophobia, sexism, and lesbians in sport. *Quest* 44. 251–265.

Hambrick, Marion E., Jason M. Simmons, Greg P. Greenhalgh & T. Christopher Greenwell. 2010. Understanding professional athletes' use of Twitter: A content analysis of athlete tweets. *International Journal of Sport Communication* 3. 454–471.

Haugh, Betsy R. & Brandi Watkins. 2016. Tag me, tweet me if you want to reach me: An investigation into how sports fans use social media. *International Journal of Sport Communication* 9(3). 278–293.

Hopkins, John L. 2013. Engaging Australian Rules Football fans with social media: A case study. *International Journal of Sport Management and Marketing* 13(1). 104–121.

Hull, Kevin. 2014. A hole in one (hundred forty characters): A case study examining PGA Tour golfers' Twitter use during the Masters. *International Journal of Sport Communication* 7(2). 245–260.
Humphreys, Lee. 2012. Social media and the Olympics. *Culture Digitally*, 22 August. https://culturedigitally.org/2012/08/social-media-the-olympics/
Hutter, Katja, Julia Hautz, Severin Dennhardt & Johann Füller. 2013. The impact of user interactions in social media on brand awareness and purchase intention: The case of MINI on Facebook. *Journal of Product & Brand Management* 22. 342–351.
Jensen, Jonathan A., Shaina M. Ervin & Stephen W. Dittmore. 2014. Exploring the factors affecting popularity in social media: A case study of Football Bowl Subdivision head coaches. *International Journal of Sport Communication* 7(2). 261–278.
Kassing, Jeffrey W. & Jimmy Sanderson. 2010. Fan–athlete interaction and Twitter tweeting through the Giro: A case study. *International Journal of Sport Communication* 3(1). 113–128.
Krane, Vikki, Sally R. Ross, Montana Miller, Julie L. Rowse, Kristy Ganoe, Jaclyn A. Andrzejczyk & Cathryn B. Lucas. 2010. Power and focus: Self-representation of female college athletes. *Qualitative Research in Sport and Exercise* 2. 175–195.
Lebel, Katie & Karen Danylchuk. 2012. How Tweet it is: A gendered analysis of professional tennis players' self-presentation on Twitter. *International Journal of Sport Communication* 5(4). 461–480.
Lebel, Katie & Karen Danylchuk. 2014a. An audience interpretation of professional athlete self-presentation on Twitter. *Journal of Applied Sport Management* 6(2). 16–36.
Lebel, Katie & Karen Danylchuk. 2014b. Facing off on Twitter: A Generation Y interpretation of professional athlete profile pictures. *International Journal of Sport Communication* 7(3). 317–336.
Lebel, Katie, Ann Pegoraro & Alanna Harman. 2018. The impact of digital culture on women in sport. In Dian C. Parry, Corey W. Johnson & Simone Fullagar (eds.), *Digital dilemmas: Transforming gender identities and power relations in everyday life*, 163–182. Cham: Palgrave Macmillan.
Newman, Mark. 2017. MLB takes AR to next level for fans at ballpark. *MLB.com*, 10 October. https://www.mlb.com/news/mlb-to-use-augmented-reality-to-enhance-data-c258179374 (16 September 2019).
Number of monthly active Twitter users worldwide from 1st quarter 2010 to 1st quarter 2019. 2019. *Statista.com*. https://bit.ly/2dt7OI9 (19 November 2020).
O'Hallarn, Brendan, Stephen L. Shapiro & Ann Pegoraro. 2018. Hashmoney: Exploring Twitter hashtag use as a secondary ticket market price determinant. *International Journal of Sport Management and Marketing* 18. 199–219.
Pegoraro, Ann. 2010. Look who's talking – athletes on Twitter: A case study. *International Journal of Sport Communication* 3(4). 501–514.
Pegoraro, Ann. 2013. Sport fandom in the digital world. In Paul M. Pedersen (ed.), *Handbook of sport communication*, 248–258. New York: Routledge.
Pegoraro, Ann, Gina S. Comeau & Evan Frederick. 2018. #SheBelieves: Fans' use of social media to frame the US Women's soccer team during #FIFAWWC. *Sport in Society* 21(7). 1063–1077.
Pegoraro, Ann, Olan Scott & Lauren Burch. 2017. Strategic use of Facebook to build brand awareness: A case study of two national sport organizations *International Journal of Public Administration in the Digital Age* 4(1). 69–87.
Pérez, Levi. 2013. What drives the number of new Twitter followers? An economic note and a case study of professional soccer teams. *Economics Bulletin* 33. 1941–1947.
Sanderson, Jimmy. 2011. *It's a whole new ball-game: How social media is changing sports*. New York: Hampton Press.

Sanderson, Jimmy & Jeffrey Kassing. 2011. Tweets and blogs: Transformative, adversarial and integrative developments in sports media. In Andrew C. Billings (ed.), *Sports media: Transformation, integration, consumption*, 114–127. New York: Routledge.
Shreffler, Megan B., Meg Hancock & Samuel H. Schmidt. 2016. Self-presentation of female athletes: A content analysis of athlete avatars. *International Journal of Sport Communication* 9. 460–475.
Smith, Lauren Reichart & Jimmy Sanderson. 2015. I'm going to Instagram it! An analysis of athlete self-presentation on Instagram. *Journal of Broadcasting and Electronic Media* 59(2). 342–358.
Smith, Lauren Reichart, Ann Pegoraro & Sally Ann Cruikshank. 2019. Tweet, retweet, favorite: The impact of Twitter use on enjoyment and sports viewing. *Journal of Electronic and Broadcast Media* 63(1). 94–110.
Snyder, C., M. Lassegard & C. E. Ford. 1986. Distancing after group success and failure: Basking in reflected glory and cutting off reflected failure. *Journal of Personality and Social Psychology* 51(2). 382–388.
Srivastav, Taruka. 2017. FC Bayern Munich rolls out augmented reality feature to offer fans personalised selfies with players. *The Drum*, 18 October. https://www.thedrum.com/news/2017/10/18/fc-bayern-munich-rolls-out-augmented-reality-feature-offer-fans-personalised-selfies.
Szymanski, Stefan & Jason A. Winfree. 2018. On the optimal realignment of a contest: The case of college football. *Economic Inquiry* 56(1). 483–496.
Thompson, Ashleigh-Jane, Andrew M. Martin, Sarah Gee & Andrea N. Geurin. 2014. Examining the development of a social media strategy for a national sport organisation: A case study of Tennis New Zealand. *Journal of Applied Sport Management* 6(2). 42–63.
Van Dijck, José & Thomas Poell. 2013. Understanding social media logic. *Media and Communication* 1(1). 2–14.
Wang, Yuan and Shuhua Zhou 2015. How do sports organizations use social media to build relationship? A content analysis of NBA Clubs' Twitter use. *International Journal of Sport Communication* 8(2). 133–148.
Watanabe, Nicholas M., Ann Pegoraro, Grace Yan & Stephen L. Shapiro. 2019. Does rivalry matter? An analysis of sport consumer interest on social media. *International Journal of Sport Marketing and Sponsorship* 20. 646–665.
Watanabe, Nicholas M., Grace Yan & Brian P. Soebbing. 2015. Major League Baseball and Twitter usage: The economics of social media use. *Journal of Sport Management* 29(6). 619–632.
Watanabe, Nicholas M., Grace Yan & Brian P. Soebbing. 2016. Consumer interest in Major League Baseball: An analytical modeling of Twitter. *Journal of Sport Management* 30(2). 207–220.
Women's World Cup: Record-breaking numbers. 2019. *BBC News*, 8 July. https://www.bbc.com/news/world-48882465#targetText=US%20forward% 20Alex%20Morgan%20has,gained%20another%20two%20million%20followers (16 September 2019).

Galen Clavio and Brian Moritz

36 Sport media, sport journalism, and the digital era

Abstract: The early 2000s have seen the world of sports journalism deal with a tremendous amount of upheaval. The collapse of the print media industry, combined with the influence of social media and the expansion of sport organizations into the business of media content creation and distribution, has created a sport media landscape that looks very different from what existed even a decade ago. This chapter examines the various forces that have led to the reorganization of sport media, including digital distribution, bad business practices, consumer preference, and the wave of subscriber-only sport journalism sites that threaten the remnants of the traditional order.

Keywords: sports journalism; sports media; digital journalism; business models; sports broadcasting; social media

1 Introduction

Sport journalism's transition into the digital age of media has seen a tremendous amount of disruption. The industry's intellectual backbone of print journalism has struggled due to financial and technological pressures causing the broader print media business to collapse. Meanwhile the successful transitions of multimedia companies such as ESPN from the mass media age into the digital age have created a new order of sorts within the field. The convergence of written, aural, and visual content into the social media content streams popular with audiences has compressed the different kinds of sports media into a singular consumption experience. Additionally, social media's growing importance in the delivery of news and information to consumers has caused sport journalism to rethink its approach to content, while facing competition over access to sports stories and the audiences that consume them. Throughout this chapter, we trace the history and development of sport journalism in the United States that led to this point, discuss the present-day circumstances of the industry, and look to the future of sport journalism from both theoretical and practical perspectives.

https://doi.org/10.1515/9783110660883-036

2 The development of sport journalism

In order to understand the forces that have led to the reorganization of sport media, it is important to understand the history of sport journalism. The present is informed by the past, and the story of digital distribution is incomplete without understanding the industry's history.

2.1 Newspaper sport journalism

The history of newspaper sport journalism in the United States dates back to the nation's early days and is intertwined with both the history of newspaper journalism and with the growth of sport as an American cultural institution. As newspaper journalism grew from a highly partisan avocation into a commercialized profession, and as sport grew from a regional pastime to a national industry, so sport journalism developed into a profession with its own norms, values, and routines (Bryant and Holt 2006; Boyle 2006; McChesney 1989).

Sport journalism in the United States began in earnest in the 1820s and 1830s, with specialized magazines covering primarily horse racing and boxing. At the time, newspaper sport coverage was sporadic, and tended to focus on events with greater social context rather than just games themselves, such as a race between horses from the North and the South, or a boxing match between American and British fighters. (Bryant and Holt 2006). By the end of the 19th century, newspapers would become the primary medium covering sport in America (McChensey 1989).

The 19th century saw two major developments in the evolution of American newspaper journalism. The first was the emergence of the Penny Press in the 1830s and 1840s, when newspapers expanded their circulation by dropping the price of an issue in an attempt to appeal to a new demographic of middle-class, urban readers. This was also when newspapers began relying on advertising, rather than circulation, as their primary business model (Bryant and Holt 2006). The second was the Industrial Revolution in the mid to late 19th century, during which urbanization grew in large part to waves of European immigration. This was the era of yellow journalism and sensationalism (McChesney 1989).

Both of these developments influenced sport journalism. The growth of the Penny Press saw publishers looking for content that would appeal to a larger and wider audience. Sport fit that bill perfectly. The *New York Herald*, published by James Gordon Bennett, was one of the first papers to begin showcasing sport coverage, though Bennett apparently expressed regret that he had done so (Bryant and Holt 2006). The profession continued to grow throughout the 19th century.

The Industrial Revolution, with increased urbanization and technological innovations that reduced the cost of gathering and printing news, created conditions in which newspaper circulations soared. "Sport, with its proven capacity to attract readers, became a logical area of emphasis in this era of yellow journalism" (McChesney 1989: 53). Newspaper sport coverage expanded greatly in this era in which the defining feature of many newspapers was exaggerated, sensationalized coverage of stories. The *New York World*, owned by Joseph Pulitzer, became the first American newspaper with its own sport department in 1883. In 1895, the *New York Journal*, owned by William Randolph Hearst, introduced the first distinct sport section.

Sport journalism continued to grow in prominence throughout the end of the 19th and beginning of the 20th century. Schlesinger (1933) reported that in 1880, American newspapers dedicated only 04 percent of their space to sport coverage. By 1920, that total ranged from 12 to 20 percent of a newspaper's total news hole. By the mid-1920s, nearly every newspaper in the country had some kind of sport section. McChesney (1989: 55) wrote that this is when sport journalism emerged as a distinct genre of journalism and became an "indispensable section of the daily newspaper."

Bryant and Holt (2006) defined the growth of the Penny Press and the Industrial Revolution as two of the key eras of evolution for newspaper journalism. They also defined a third era – the Information Age, which includes the present time and is defined by the growth of the internet and digital and social media. One of the defining characteristics of this era is convergence – the combining of previously separate media formats. It is no longer possible to split sport journalism into just print and broadcast, because the growth of digital media has created a new format that combines elements of both. The characteristics of this era, and how this era is influencing sport media, will be discussed later in this chapter.

2.2 Sport magazines

Equally as important to the development of sport journalism and sport media were weekly magazines. In the pre-digital age, sport magazines served the role as a national platform for sports news. *The Sporting News* began publishing in 1886 and was long known as the paper of record for baseball statistics before becoming a general-interest sport magazine in the later 20th century (Zara 2012). *Sports Illustrated* began publishing in 1954 and quickly became the standard for weekly sport coverage as well as long-form feature writing and sport photography. However, the digital age has not been kind to weekly and monthly magazines. In many ways, sport magazines (like many news and general-interest magazines) were perfectly suited for the mass media age, which was defined by informational and technological scarcity (Crosbie 2018).

The digital age, on the other hand, is being defined by informational and technological abundance, meaning that access to news and information is not limited by geography or the physical size of a publication. Magazines such as *Sports Illustrated* and *The Sporting News* were well suited to the era of scarcity but have struggled to find their place in the era of abundance. *The Sporting News* became a digital-only brand in 2013 (Zara 2012), and *Sports Illustrated*, amid falling circulation, was sold from

Time-Warner to the Meredith Corporation, which is licensing the magazine's digital publishing to a third party (Kelly 2019)

2.3 Broadcast sports journalism

The development of radio as a mass medium in the early 20th century had an important impact on sport journalism. Sport coverage on radio became a regular part of the consumer environment, with both collegiate and professional sports utilizing game broadcasts to expand the reach and appeal of their games and athletes. The first live play-by-play broadcast of a game happened during the 1921 World Series, and it was a famed sportswriter, Grantland Rice, who furnished audiences with a verbal account of the game as it happened (Schneider 2017).

Live radio broadcasts of games provided audiences with immediate information and analysis of games, something that newspapers were unable to do. Over time, broadcasts of games became increasingly more specialized, as full-time professional broadcasters who focused on sport became the norm rather than the exception.

As radio matured in the mid-20th century, television was just getting started. With an increasing number of television sets in homes, broadcasting companies and sport entities found themselves in a symbiotic partnership. For leagues such as the National Football League (NFL), televised coverage of games provided an entry point into the culture that they had heretofore struggled to attain. With its low number of games per week and with a pattern of play that was much friendlier to the conventions of television than baseball, the NFL used televised broadcasts to promote the game and increase its popularity, and distributed the revenue for those broadcasts equally across its member franchises (Moore 2015).

Broadcast networks such as NBC and CBS were happy to broadcast NFL games due to the high ratings the games garnered and the positive effect that those ratings had on their other programming. National sport broadcasting crews normally featured a trained broadcaster providing play-by-play of the events of the game, paired with a former player or former coach who would provide analysis and commentary, with both broadcasters approaching the broadcast from a journalistically neutral perspective.

The launch of the cable-only network ESPN in 1979 aimed to bring a national perspective to sport news coverage while combining it with traditional game coverage. While local broadcast journalism coverage of sport had existed for many years prior to ESPN's founding, it was considered second tier to newspapers in terms of quality. However, ESPN made hires that focused specifically on journalistic integrity and quality, first hiring broadcast network veteran Chet Simmons to head up its news and programming operations, and later hiring print media veteran John Walsh, the former editor of *Inside Sports*, first as a consultant and then as managing editor of the network's flagship news program *SportsCenter* (Miller and Shales 2011). ESPN would grow significantly in popularity through the 1980s and 90s, positioning itself as "The Worldwide Leader in Sports" and using its dual revenue streams of advertising and cable subscribers to integrate horizontally into other aspects of media, including the launch of a magazine, the development of a national radio network, and most importantly, the development of a web presence that would eventually become ESPN.com. ESPN's secret weapon in all of this was the high carriage fees that it earned from cable subscribers. In 2017, ESPN received $7.21 from every cable subscriber in the United States just for its flagship network (for comparison, the second most expensive network for cable subscribers charged $1.41 in carriage fees). In all, ESPN received $9 a month from every cable subscriber in the United States (Gaines 2017).

2.4 Digital convergence

In order to understand what is happening to newspaper sport journalism, it is important to see what is going on in the digital space and to see how the profession is practiced online. Digital sport journalism serves as both a complement to and a competitor of newspaper sport journalism.

The digital sport media landscape can actually be broken up into at least two categories – digital news sites and blogs. Digital news sites are often connected with a larger media network, be it a cable TV network (e. g., ESPN.com, Foxsports.com, CBSSports.com), a city's daily newspaper, or an established internet company (Yahoo Sports). Reporters and writers at these sites often appear to work within a more traditional journalistic framework – covering games, interviewing sources, writing stories and columns. Calling the second categories "blogs" is a bit of a misnomer, since these sites can range from personal ones operated by fans as passion projects to corporately owned sites such as SB Nation (owned by Vox Media,) or Bleacher Report (owned by Turner Broadcasting). Regardless of label, the idea is that there was a growth in the number of and the types of sites that cover sports in ways that are different from and unaffiliated with traditional media outlets like newspapers or broadcast stations.

Digital sports journalism began in the mid-1990s, the same time that news journalism began publishing online (Boczkowski 2005). ESPN started its first website in 1995, originally named ESPNSportsZone. It became ESPN.com in 1998 (Bryant and Holt 2006). Other TV networks, such as Fox and CBS, began sports-focused websites during the same time frame (Bryant and Holt 2006). Yahoo, the internet search engine, began a sports-only site in 1997. It was during this era that most newspapers began to publish online editions. At first, these online editions served primarily as complements to the daily print product, a mentality that slowly but gradually changed (as the next section will illustrate).

2.5 The democratization of media production

One of the biggest threats to sport journalism has stemmed from technology's leveling of the playing field when it comes to producing media content that can be accessed and consumed by a large audience. In the mass-media era, content production was generally left in the hands of an elite few media companies who could afford the time and money required to fully staff and equip a television studio, operate a printing press, or distribute a newspaper. This, as stated earlier, led to an age of scarcity. However, the technological advances of social media and mobile technology took away much of that exclusivity from media companies and put the means of production in the hands of any party willing to expend effort and time to learn how media was made. This has created an era of abundance (Crosbie 2018).

The biggest beneficiary of this process has been sport leagues and teams, who have used the democratization of media production to construct direct competition to traditional media. In some cases, this has taken the form of partnerships between traditional media and sport entities, such as ESPN's partnership with the Southeastern Conference over the SEC Network or FOX Sports' partnership with the Big Ten Conference over the Big Ten Network. In other cases, it has involved the sport entities creating entire sport media outlets whole cloth, such as the NFL Network, or the formation of websites such as *The Player's Tribune*, which provides ghostwriting and ghost editing to media pieces created by current and former athletes.

Even in the realm of internet and social media traffic, sport entities are producing media that competes directly with traditional sport journalism on a daily basis. Leagues and teams craft feature stories, videos, and podcasts, all of which are aimed directly at fans, and are crafted in a form that is hard for the untrained consumer to distinguish from more traditional journalistic fare. Of course, this type of media lacks the objectivity that is the hallmark of good journalism, but it often compensates for it by having much greater access to athletes, coaches, and facilities, all things in which audience members are generally interested (Mirer 2019). That access, however, does not necessarily translate to credibility, as fans have viewed independent media reports as more credible than those done by team websites (Mirer, Duncan, and Wagner 2018).

Furthermore, athletes and organizations have begun to view the symbiotic relationship between them and sport journalists with increasing suspicion. Some of the most popular professional athletes in the United States have been openly critical of sports journalists (Curtis 2015), and athletes have increasingly turned to their own social media channels and to announce important news about their careers, rather than going through the established media.

3 Collapse of business models

The late mass media era of the 1990s and early 2000s in the United States was an incredibly profitable time for media organizations, particularly newspapers. Their broadly accepted cultural and societal importance, ubiquity in markets across the country, and lack of competition for advertising services led to a scenario where ownership of a daily newspaper was a highly coveted position due to the opportunities for revenue generation (Kyse and Jordan n.d.). Profit margins and stock prices were high, and newspapers had few reasons to change their models or consider evolving their businesses. The year 2005 saw the newspaper industry hit its high-water mark in terms of total revenue, with nearly $50 billion collected in revenue that year alone (Newspapers fact sheet 2019).

Sport media was a particular beneficiary of this era of largesse. Newspapers of a variety of circulation sizes routinely credentialed and paid for multiple reporters and columnists to cover events across the country. Sport staffs often dedicated multiple reporters to a single beat, particularly for coverage of popular sports teams in high school athletics, major college athletics, and the pros.

3.1 Online news

Initially, the development of the World Wide Web in late 1992 did not appear to be a major problem or obstacle to the continued hegemony of newspapers. While the Web existed, access was limited to those with expensive desktop computers, and that access itself was slow and lacking in infrastructure. Rare was the local news site that had any sort of online presence, and in many markets that online presence was limited to a few posted articles without photos, and no other forms of media beyond the occasional discussion forum.

The early 2000s saw a gradual and significant shift in the way that people used the internet. High-speed internet access, which many consumers across the globe now take for granted, did not even exist in the United Kingdom until 2000 (Youde 2010) and comprised only about 5 percent of home internet access in the United States at the start of 2001 (Horrigan 2006). However, broadband access would rapidly spread over the next several years, with over 40 percent of adult Americans having broadcast internet access at home by mid-2006 (Horrigan 2006). The spread of broadband internet access allowed for much easier transmission of dynamic media forms, such as video, audio, and photography. This allowed for convergence-oriented media companies, such as ESPN in the sports world, to establish themselves as a sort of national "home base" for sports fans.

At the same time, broader access to the internet started to cut the legs out of newspapers' advertising revenue streams. The free online classified advertisement site Craigslist, founded in 1995, along with e-commerce sites like Amazon and eBay, suddenly gave consumers a viable option for buying and selling goods that did not rely on having to place or read an ad in a newspaper.

3.2 Social media

Meanwhile, social media outlets began to grow in importance. Facebook capitalized on consumer mania for social networking in the mid-2000s, leveraging a successful launch among college students into a user base that would eventually comprise nearly 70 percent of all online adults in the United States (Wagner and Molla 2018). Twitter became a trendy addition to journalists' social media activities, thanks to its near-instantaneous news spreading capacity. At one point, the most tweeted-about moment in Twitter's history was a sporting event, during the German national men's soccer team's rout of Brazil in the 2014 World Cup (Chase 2014).

In some cases, the effects of social media on sport journalism have been positive. Social networks have allowed journalists and sports fans to interact around live sporting events, with journalists often serving as opinion leaders and their reporting garnering significant attention through the rapid spread of news.

However, social media introduced plenty of negative aspects to the business of journalism, none more so than Facebook's impact on advertising revenue. The social media giant, along with search engine giant Google, were estimated to have control over nearly 85 percent of the global digital advertising market, along with the likelihood of increasing that number through additional growth (Ingram 2018). This stranglehold on advertising revenue, which was the lifeblood of journalism in the mass-media age, has forced journalistic outlets to chase dollars and consumers through the social media and search giants, with returns that are significantly lower than what these outlets used to generate.

3.3 Traditional sport journalism business struggles

The growth of digital technologies and the internet changed how media do business. Dating back to the era of the Penny Press, newspapers in the United States relied primarily on advertising to cover costs and make money (Bryant and Holt 2006; McChesney 1989; Schudson 1981). This practice continued through the industrial age and throughout much of the 20th century. The reliance on advertising for revenues is one of the reasons sports journalism became such an important part of the newspaper – newspapers needed to capture and hold onto an audience, and that audience's attention could then be sold to advertisers.

However, the growth of digital technologies and the internet changed how media do business. Newspapers were unable to find a consistent way to charge readers to read news online, and so for many years news organizations posted their content online for free (Ingram 2013). The availability of free news online – both local and national news – led to a drop of print circulation for virtually all newspapers (Wihbey 2013). The falling circulation led to consistent drops in advertising revenue – and the recession of 2008 exacerbated the situation, as did the growth of digital media giants such as Craigslist (which replaced what was journalism's cash cow, the daily classified ads), Google, and Facebook (which, as stated earlier, began dominating online advertising).

The numbers paint a stark picture of an industry in crisis. Daily print circulation at newspapers has decreased every year since 1987 and overall has fallen nearly 55 percent to an estimated total of 28 million (Newspapers fact sheet 2019). Advertising revenue, the economic engine of newspapers for decades, has been hit even harder, plummeting more than 70 percent since 2005 (Newspapers fact sheet 2019). And while digital circulation and revenues are growing, particularly at larger newspapers like *The New York Times* and the *Washington Post*, that has not yet translated to local or regional papers. One of the primary side effects of these issues has been a reduction in workforce. Overall newsroom employment is down 47 percent from 2004. In all, four out of every 10 newsroom jobs disappeared in the 2000s. Neither the Associated Press Sports Editors nor the National Sports Journalism Institute at Indiana University was able to report any specific number of sports journalists who had lost their jobs. However, no area of the newsroom was untouched.

There is a mindset among some print journalists and media observers that the rise in digital media and the internet caught newspapers off guard – that the industry failed to understand the new technology, did not recognize its revolutionary potential, or was caught off guard by the sudden change in the media environment (Brock 2013; Ingram 2013; Shirky 2009). However, Boczkowski (2005) wrote that this was not the case. Newspapers neither ignored nor fully embraced the Web when the technology emerged in the early and mid-1990s. Instead, the culture of innovation within news organizations was marked by a combination of what Boczkowski called reactive, defensive, and pragmatic traits. Reactive traits, he wrote, were demonstrated by the fact that newspapers followed technology and social trends rather than leading them. They reacted to change, instead of being proactive in changing. Defensive traits were illustrated by how newspapers were focused on maintaining their print territory rather than offensively trying to expand into new areas. Pragmatic traits, Boczkowksi defined, as newspapers focusing on protecting the short-term well-being of their core business.

4 Paywalls and subscription models

Many newspapers experimented with paywalls throughout the early stages of the 21st century, with generally poor results. In one extreme example, the publishing site *Newsday* launched a paywall, and three months later had amassed a grand total of

35 subscribers (Masnick 2010). As of 2017, many major publications had some form of subscription service, but the paywalls were often semi-permeable, allowing audiences to access a decent number of articles for free without actually requiring a subscription (Stulberg 2017). For most sites, a hard paywall made little sense, because audiences unable to access any content were unlikely to subscribe in the first place, impacting both the chances of generating subscriptions and the ability to earn money from advertising.

There were no major sport journalism sites that required a subscription for access through the first several years of the social media era. Newspaper sites either required whole-site subscriptions to access sports stories or provided content for free. Some sites made the decision to bombard users with pop-up advertisements and auto-play videos upon accessing a story, decisions which generally made reading stories unpleasant and made consumers angry (Chen 2018).

But on July 23, 2014, a new era in American sport journalism began. That day, the sports news site, DK on Pittsburgh Sports launched (Kalaf 2018). It was a new source for Pittsburgh sports news and commentary, led by Dejan Kovacevic, a long-time sportswriter for the city's *Post-Gazette*. The innovation offered by Kovacevic's site was that it was a subscription-based site. Unlike most news sites at that time, which were either free to read or had a paywall reached after a certain number of articles, in order to read DK Pittsburgh Sports (as it was soon renamed), one had to pay for a subscription.

Nearly 18 months after DK Sports debuted, a site with a similar business model, dubbed *The Athletic*, debuted in Chicago.

4.1 *The Athletic*

The emergence of *The Athletic* became one of the dominant stories in sports journalism at the end of the 2010s. At a time when newspapers, online news sites, and even cable networks are cutting jobs, *The Athletic* has consistently expanded since its debut in 2016 and has hired some of the sport journalism industry's biggest stars (Fang 2017).

While *The Athletic* is not the only site to offer unbundled subscription sports journalism – along with DK Sports in Pittsburgh, the *Boston Sports Journal* began, under the direction of veteran sports writer Greg Bedard (Bedard 2017) – those sites are focused exclusively on their local markets. *The Athletic*, on the other hand, has grown to an almost national voice. *The Athletic* can be understood largely as a federation of sites in individual markets under one umbrella.

The Athletic began in 2016 as the brainchild of Alex Mather and Adam Hansmann, two entrepreneurs who worked together on the fitness-tracking app Strava (Draper 2017). In 2016, they pitched the idea for *The Athletic* at Y Combinators, a well-known conference for entrepreneurs and venture capitalists (Tepper 2016). *The Athletic* debuted in January 2016 with a site focused solely on Chicago-area professional sports.

Sites focusing on sport in Cleveland and Toronto, respectively, soon followed, and the site has continued expansion ever since. In 2017, the site received more than $8 million in venture capital funding (Draper 2017), and then a subsequent $20 million in March 2018 and $40 million in October 2018, marking some of the largest venture capital investments in sport media history (Bucholtz 2018).

The Athletic's defining feature has been its reliance on subscriptions and a total absence of advertising. Mather and Hansmann have said that their motivation for creating the site was their own "frustration at the difficulty of finding high-quality sportswriting that wasn't bogged down by pop-up ads" (Draper 2017). To access *The Athletic*, users must subscribe – with only a limited number of exceptions for special stories, all content is behind the subscriber wall. A subscription costs $9.99 a month or just under $60 when paid for annually, although the site regularly offers discounts of 50 percent or more for new subscribers. With that subscription, users get access to all of *The Athletic*'s coverage of sports. The site has no advertising – it is entirely funded through subscriptions and venture funding.

The Athletic became known for its aggressive expansion – at the time of this writing, a little more than three years after the site debuted, there are sites in 40 US cities and seven Canadian markets – as well as its combative attitude toward newspaper sports sections that has been called "pillaging" (Draper 2017) and "exterminating" (Redford 2017). Mather, the site's cofounder, told *The New York Times*, "We will wait every local paper out and let them continuously bleed until we are the last ones standing. We will suck them dry of their best talent at every moment. We will make business extremely difficult for them" (Draper 2017).

4.2 Growth and expansion of subscription models

While many media observers reacted with understandable negativity at the tone of Mather's content, the results through the end of the decade indicated that *The Athletic*'s approach was on to something. As of the summer of 2019, *The Athletic* had exceeded 500,000 subscribers, with significant gains expected by their founders over the following year (Boudway 2019).

Even in light of the site's surging subscription numbers, *The Athletic* showed little sign of slowing down, with a consistent expansion of content and coverage into other areas. This included the launching of numerous podcasts available only behind the subscription paywall of the site (Khalid 2019) and expanding their coverage to include writers in the United Kingdom writing about English Premier League soccer (Koster 2018) with a focus on serving both the US and UK markets (Rigdon 2019). *The Athletic*'s approach created, according to one UK-based writer, "the biggest shake-up in sports journalism [in the United Kingdom] since the digital era ... there has probably been more movement in the last four months [since the entry of *The Athletic*] than in the last 15 years" (Burrell 2019).

One of the main questions facing sports journalism heading into the 2020s is whether *The Athletic*'s success with the subscription model will be a template for other sports news organizations to follow or an anomaly. The growth of subscription models in news, entertainment, and software – especially the explosion of streaming television platforms – could potentially lead to subscription fatigue (Moritz 2018).

However, business decisions in the immediate aftermath of *The Athletic*'s success seemed to indicate that the early market for subscriptions to sport content may still be open to more services, as other sports media entities made the move towards subscription-based content as well. In addition to the aforementioned *DK Pittsburgh Sports* and *The Athletic*, *Boston Sports Journal* launched a service catering to that marketplace, and the *Austin American-Statesman* launched a Texas sports-focused subscription site (Willens 2019). ESPN launched its own subscription-based streaming service, titled ESPN+, which charged $5 a month at launch but featured access to a wide variety of domestic and international live sporting events, plus ESPN's library of documentary films, as well as original programming (Perry 2020). In less than a year, ESPN+ had more than two million subscribers (Welch 2019).

5 Evolution of routines

In looking at sport media and sport journalism in the digital age, it is natural to focus on the business side, the distribution channels, and the economic models. And while those are important, they are not the only aspect of sport media worth examining. One other important area to look at is the work routines of sport journalists.

Traditionally, the routines of sport journalists have echoed those of news journalists, which have been widely studied in the field of media sociology. Rowe (2007) found that sport journalists tend to use star athletes, coaches, and administrators as sources in stories, and Lowes (1999) wrote that sportswriters are reliant upon access to athletes, which leads to a culture that promotes more positive than critical coverage. These findings are consistent with literature on sources from political news, where journalists are reliant on official government sources (e. g., Gans 1979; Sigal 1973).

Shultz and Sheffer (2007) have extensively studied how sport reporters and editors use blogs as a part of their coverage, finding that the act of blogging does not change how sports journalists conceptualize their roles. Schultz and Sheffer (2010) found that sport reporters use Twitter primarily as a way to enhance, rather than to transform, their journalistic work – a finding that reflects similar findings among news reporters that journalists are normalizing Twitter (Lasorsa, Lewis, and Holton 2011). Benigni, Porter, and Wood (2009) wrote that the online communities of college football fans are beginning to influence the kinds of stories journalists write and the kind of coverage fans expect, in terms of tone (how positive or negative it is toward the team) and content (more multimedia content). Because fans can get content from any number of online sources, they can be more discerning, which creates more pressure on news organizations to provide unique content for their readers. Sanderson and Hambrick (2012) studied how journalists used Twitter during the Penn State football scandal in 2012 and noted that reporters were likely to use Twitter to step outside of professional norms and practices by engaging with fans with opinionated posts that deviated from the journalistic norm of objectivity. Sanderson and Hambrick also found that sport journalists used Twitter to promote their competitors by linking to stories in publications other than their own, and that the speed of Twitter creates a dialectic in breaking-news coverage of trying to be first with a story while also maintaining professional levels of accuracy.

It is easy to think that digital media has forever and radically changed sport journalists' routines. After all, publishing news online, both to websites and social media platforms, seems so fundamentally different than a newspaper job. However, the research reveals a more subtle, nuanced picture. In fact, the interview data suggest that the primary dichotomy for sport journalists is not "print vs. online" but is, as Moritz (2015) called it, the "story vs. the stream." The story represents the traditional notions of sport journalism, many of which remain unchanged in the digital era. For instance, sport journalism tends to revolve around game coverage, and the norms and values of sport reporters such as story ideation and source identification are similar in 2019 to what they were in 1999. The stream refers to the "constant flow of information, including interaction with readers, in which news is reported as it happens" (Moritz 2015: 408) that is inherent in social media. This is the sport version of Robinson's (2011) paradigm of journalism as process, and it is an evolution that marks a dramatic change from previous generations of sport journalism (Lowes 1999; Boyle 2006; Vecsey 1989; Walsh 2006; Wilstein 2002).

That tension between the desire to tell a good story and the need to keep up with the stream is central to sport journalism routines, and makes for a useful conceptual model for understanding the profession.

6 The future of sport journalism

The world of sport journalism has been in a state of near-constant flux since the dawn of the 21st century, with technology disrupting many of the traditional aspects of the business. This chapter has sought to trace the history of sport media and to examine the causes and effects of this state of flux.

Despite the tumultuous nature of the business, there are certain trends within the new order of sports journalism that highlight a path towards how the industry will operate in the future. The final section of this chapter will identify those trends and apply them to potential pedagogical and research agendas.

6.1 Training and pedagogy

Journalists entering the field will need to be trained and prepared as multimedia specialists, comfortable with creating and promoting their work on a number of different platforms. The sum effect of the many changes discussed within this chapter led to the reality that the media landscape has in essence become flattened, with no real difference in delivery systems between written content, visual content, and audio content. For an increasingly large number of users, all of those content types are interconnected and do not require typological distinguishing, because they all arrive via the same delivery system – the user's smartphone.

In a marketplace where name recognition and audience trust help to distinguish a journalist's work from others, successful sport journalists will have to be entrepreneurial in how they approach their work. The successful writer will have to be effective on video and in podcasting, just as the successful video journalist will need to be effective in writing. Additionally, journalists will regularly have to consider their own positioning in the market and leverage the changing business and journalistic fortunes of media outlets to best position themselves within that market. Effective utilization of social media for professional brand-building and distribution of content has become a regular part of the profession for most sports journalists. Employers often require that journalists be active on social media and interact with potential audience members, but journalists should cultivate that level of activity regardless of whether their current employer requires it or not, because the ability to do so consistently and effectively is often a prerequisite for being hired by a larger and more prestigious media outlet.

Journalism programs at universities will need to ensure that they provide aspiring journalism students with the skills courses, experiential education, and other tools necessary to help develop skills in the various areas of media creation and promotion. Media outlets hiring those journalists will need to have a clear understanding of how a multimedia journalist's output can be best utilized to cover a story and garner audience attention.

6.2 Theoretical considerations

There are a variety of important scholarly issues worthy of examination in light of the digital transition of sport journalism, and it will be important for scholars to examine further these areas in the coming years. The impact of subscription services on the agendas of sport journalism institutions will be worthy of continued monitoring, particularly with those institutions having to compete with sport industry media for audience and advertising numbers. Will the agenda setting function of journalistic media be significantly altered from its historical focus? Will sport journalism continue to move away from the traditional game story and towards a more analytical approach to sport coverage? Will there be a continued politicization of sport coverage, with social issues continuing to be brought to the fore?

Functionally speaking, it will be worth monitoring the uses and gratifications of sport audiences in the coming years, as successive generations of consumers become more adapted to the digital environment. Much as 20th-century consumers adapted their habits as they became comfortable with various forms of broadcast journalism, 21st-century consumers will adapt their habits as they become more firmly ensconced in the digital media era.

The changing role of the sport journalist is another area worthy of future theoretical evaluation. As mentioned earlier in this chapter, the industry's converged media landscape has increased the number of content areas that journalists must be able to use effectively and has also caused journalists to act as public figures on social media, promoting their own work and interacting directly with audiences. These represent significant shifts from the traditional role of sport journalists and may have an effect on the self-selection process for the career path, the level of satisfaction journalists feel with their careers, and the impact that this new breed of sport journalist has on audience perceptions of the journalism being published.

References

Bedard, Greg A. 2017. Welcome to Boston Sports Journal. *Boston Sports Journal*, July 24. https://www.bostonsportsjournal.com/2017/07/24/boston-sports-journal/ (20 November 2020).

Benigni, Vince, Lance Porter & Chris Wood. 2009. The rant: How online fan culture is revolutionizing college football. *The Electronic Journal of Communication* 19(3).

Boczkowski, Pablo J. 2005. *Digitizing the news: Innovation in online newspapers*. Cambridge: MIT Press.

Boudway, Ira. 2019. The Athletic sports news site has 500,000 subscribers. *Bloomberg*, 29 July. https://www.bloomberg.com/news/articles/2019-07-29/the-athletic-sports-news-site-hits-500-000-subscribers (20 November 2020).

Boyle, Raymond. 2006. *Sports journalism: Context and issues*. London: Sage.

Brock, George. 2013. *Out of print: Newspapers, journalism and the business of news in the digital age*. London: Kogan.

Bryant, Jennings & Andrea M. Holt. 2006. A historical overview of sports and media in the United States. In Arthur A. Raney & Jennings Bryant (eds.), *Handbook of sports and media*, 22–45. New York: Routledge.

Bucholtz, Andrew. 2018. The Athletic brings in another $40 million in one of the largest sports media funding rounds ever. *Awful Announcing*, 30 October. https://awful announcing.com/athletic/the-athletic-brings-in-another-40-million.html.

Burrell, Ian. 2019. How the Athletic is spending millions of pounds to shake up sports journalism. *iNews*, 21 July. https://inews.co.uk/opinion/columnists/how-the-athletic-is-hoping-to-shake-up-the-world-of-sports-journalism/ (20 November 2020).

Chase, Chris. 2014. Germany's World Cup rout of Brazil was the most tweeted event in history. *USA Today*, 9 July. Retrieved from https://ftw.usatoday.com/2014/07/germany-brazil-most-tweeted-event-history-miley-cyrus (20 November 2020).

Chen, Brian X. 2018. Autoplay videos are not going away. Here's how to fight them. *The New York Times*, 1 August. https://www.nytimes.com/2018/08/01/technology/personaltech/autoplay-video-fight-them.html (20 November 2020).
Crosbie, Vin. 2018. The rise of individuated media. Paper presented at the Rethinking Theories and Concepts of Mediated Communications Conference, Barcelona, Spain, 13–14 September.
Curtis, Bryan. 2015. Distant thunder: What did Oklahoma City's media do to piss off Russell Westbrook and Kevin Durant? *Grantland*, 20 March. https://grantland.com/the-triangle/nba-russell-westbrook-kevin-durant-oklahoma-city-thunder-sports-media/ (20 November 2020).
Draper, Kevin. 2017. Why The Athletic wants to pillage newspapers. *New York Times*, 23 October. Retrieved from https://www.nytimes.com/2017/10/23/sports/the-athletic-newspapers.html (20 November 2020).
Fang, Ken. 2017. More writers are flocking to The Athletic. *Awful Announcing*, 31 July. http://awfulannouncing.com/culture/media/writers-flocking-athletic.html.
Gaines, Cork. 2017. Cable and satellite TV customers pay more than $9.00 per month for ESPN networks whether they watch them or not. *Business Insider*, 7 March. https://www.businessinsider.com/cable-satellite-tv-sub-fees-espn-networks-2017-3 (31 July 2019).
Gans, Herbert J. 1979. *Deciding what's news: A study of CBS evening news, NBC nightly news, Newsweek, and Time*. Evanston, IL: Northwestern University Press.
Horrigan, John B. 2006. Part 1. Broadband adoption in the United States. *Pew Research Center*, 28 May. https://www.pewinternet.org/2006/05/28/part-1-broadband-adoption-in-the-united-states/ (20 November 2020).
Ingram, Mathew. 2013. Newspapers may be dying, but the internet didn't kill them. *Gigaom*, 6 September. https://gigaom.com/2013/09/06/newspapers-may-be-dying-but-the-internet-didnt-kill-them-and-journalism-is-doing-just-fine/ (20 November 2020).
Ingram, Mathew. 2018. The Facebook Armageddon. *Columbia Journalism Review*, Winter. https://www.cjr.org/special_report/facebook-media-buzzfeed.php (20 November 2020).
Kalaf, Samer. 2018. Pittsburgh's cutting-edge sports site is a meat grinder of a workplace. *Deadspin*, 25 January. https://deadspin.com/pittsburghs-cutting-edge-sports-site-is-a-meat-grinder-1821797940 (20 November 2020).
Kelly, Keith J. 2019. Sports Illustrated's media ops are getting a new operator. *New York Post*, 17 June. https://nypost.com/2019/06/17/sports-illustrateds-media-operations-just-got-sold-again/ (31 July 2019).
Khalid, Amrita. 2019. The Athletic expands its sports news subscription with over 20 podcasts. *Engadget*, 9 April. https://www.engadget.com/2019/04/09/the-athletic-sports-news-subscription-podcasts/ (20 November 2020).
Koster, Kyle. 2018. The Athletic going for world domination with Premier League coverage. *The Big Lead*, 9 August. Retrieved from https://thebiglead.com/2018/08/09/the-athletic-premier-league/ (20 November 2020).
Kyse, Bruce & Allegra Jordan. n.d. The debate over the change in media ownership and the public's interest. *Newspaper Ownership*. http://newspaperownership.com/additional-material/newspaper-ownership-debate/ (20 November 2020).
Lasorsa, Dominic L., Seth C. Lewis & Avery E. Holton. 2012. NORMALIZING TWITTER: Journalism practice in an emerging communication space. *Journalism Studies* 13(1). 19–36.
Lowes, Mark Douglas. 1999. *Inside the sports pages: Work routines, professional ideologies, and the manufacture of sports news*. Toronto: University of Toronto Press.
Masnick, Mike. 2010. After three months, Newsday's grand paywall experiment has 35 customers. Yes, 35. *TechDirt*, 27 January. https://www.techdirt.com/articles/20100126/1515217905.shtml (20 November 2020).

McChesney, Robert W. 1989. Media made sport: A history of sports coverage in the United States. In Lawrence A. Wenner (ed.), *Media, sports, & society*, 49–69. Newbury Park, CA: Sage.
Miller, James Andrew & Tom Shales. 2011. *Those guys have all the fun: Inside the world of ESPN*. New York: Little, Brown & Company.
Mirer, Michael. 2019. Playing the right way: In-house sports reporters and media ethics as boundary work. *Journal of Media Ethics* 34. 1–14.
Mirer, Michael, Megan A. Duncan & Michael W. Wagner. 2018. Taking it from the team: Assessments of bias and credibility in team-operated sports media. *Newspaper Research Journal* 39(4). 481–495.
Moore, Jack. 2015. Throwback Thursday: The TV deal that created modern sports. *Vice.com*, 11 June. https://www.vice.com/en_us/article/qkq7xq/throwback-thursday-the-tv-deal-that-created-modern-sports (20 November 2020).
Moritz, Brian. 2015. The story versus the stream: Digital media's influence on newspaper sports journalism. *International Journal of Sport Communication* 8(4). 397–410.
Moritz, Brian. 2018. The subscription-pocalypse is about to hit. *Nieman Lab*. http://www.niemanlab.org/2018/12/the-subscription-pocalypse-is-about-to-hit/ (20 November 2020).
Newspapers fact sheet. 2019. *Pew Research Center*, 9 July. https://www.journalism.org/fact-sheet/newspapers/ (20 November 2020).
Perry, Nick. 2020. ESPN+: Everything you need to know. *Digital Trends*, 18 November. https://www.digitaltrends.com/movies/what-is-espn-plus/ (20 November 2020).
Redford, Patrick. 2017. What is the Athletic's plan beyond exterminating newspapers? *Deadspin*, 23 October. https://deadspin.com/what-is-the-athletics-plan-beyond-exterminating-newspap-1819776358 (20 November 2020).
Rigdon, Jay. 2019. The Athletic reportedly planning a UK expansion focusing on the Premier League, will include 50–55 writers. *Awful Announcing*, 7 June. https://awfulannouncing.com/athletic/the-athletic-reportedly-planning-a-uk-expansion-focusing-on-the-premier-league-will-include-50-55-writers.html (20 November 2020).
Robinson, Sue. 2011. "Journalism as process": The organizational implications of participatory online news. *Journalism & Communication Monographs* 13(3). 137–210.
Rowe, David. 2007. Sports journalism: Still the 'toy department' of the news media?. *Journalism* 8(4). 385–405.
Sanderson, Jimmy & Marion E. Hambrick. 2012. Covering the scandal in 140 characters: A case study of Twitter's role in coverage of the Penn State Saga. *International Journal of Sport Communication* 5(3). 384–402.
Schlesinger, Arthur M. 1933. *The rise of the city*. New York: Macmillan.
Schneider, John. 2017. The beginnings of sports broadcasting and radio's first sportscasters. *The Radio Historian*, December. http://www.theradiohistorian.org/sports/sports.html (20 November 2020).
Schudson, Michael. 1981. *Discovering the news: A social history of American newspapers*. New York: Basic Books.
Schultz, Brad & Mary Lou Sheffer. 2007. Sports journalists who blog cling to traditional values. *Newspaper Research Journal* 28(4). 62–76.
Schultz, Brad & Mary Lou Sheffer. 2010. An exploratory study of how Twitter is affecting sports journalism. *International Journal of Sport Communication* 3(2). 226–239.
Shirky, Clay. 2009. Newspapers and thinking the unthinkable. *Gale Academic Onefile*, May. http://www.shirky.com/weblog/2009/03/newspapers-and-thinking-the-unthinkable (20 November 2020).
Sigal, Leon V. 1973. *Reporters and officials: The organization and politics of newsmaking*. Washington, DC: D. C. Heath.

Stulberg, Ariel. 2017. In paywall age, free content remains king for newspaper sites. *Columbia Journalism Review*, 22 September. https://www.cjr.org/united_states_project/newspaper-paywalls.php (20 November 2020).

Tepper, Fitz. 2016. The Athletic is bringing subscription-based local sports coverage to a city near you. *Tech Crunch*, 8 July. http://social.techcrunch.com/2016/07/08/the-athletic-is-bringing-subscription-based-local-sports-coverage-to-a-city-near-you/ (20 November 2020).

Vecsey, George. 1989. *A year in the sun*. New York: Crown.

Wagner, Kurt & Rani Molla. 2018. Facebook is not getting any bigger in the United States. *Vox*, 1 March. https://www.vox.com/2018/3/1/17063208/facebook-us-growth-pew-research-users (20 November 2020).

Walsh, Christopher J. 2006. *No time outs: What it's really like to be a sportswriter today*. Lanham, MD: Taylor Pub.

Welch, Chris. 2019. ESPN+ passes 2 million subscribers in under a year. *The Verge*, 5 February. https://www.theverge.com/2019/2/5/18212699/espn-plus-subscribers-2-million-ufc-disney-sports-streaming (31 July 2019).

Wihbey, John. 2013. State of the news media 2013: Pew Research Center's project for excellence in journalism. *Journalist's Resource*, 18 March. https://journalistsresource.org/studies/society/news-media/news-media-2013-pew-research-center/ (20 November 2020).

Willens, Max. 2018. Why subscription sports sites have scored early wins. *Digiday*, 12 March. https://digiday.com/media/subscription-sports-sites-scored-early-wins/ (20 November 2020).

Wilstein, Steve. 2002. *Associated Press sports writing handbook*. New York: McGraw-Hill.

Youde, Kate. 2010. Broadband: The first decade. *The Independent*, 28 March. https://www.independent.co.uk/life-style/gadgets-and-tech/news/broadband-the-first-decade-1929515.html (20 November 2020).

Zara, Christopher. 2012. In memoriam: Magazines we lost in 2012. International *Business Times*, 22 December. https://www.ibtimes.com/memoriam-magazines-we-lost-2012-956388_ (20 November 2020).

Haim Hagay and Alina Bernstein

37 The male and female sports journalists divide on the Twittersphere

Abstract: Scholarly studies of journalists' Twitter activities have steadily been on the rise as more journalists take to this platform as a means of disseminating news stories. These studies suggest that Twitter has in fact overhauled journalistic notions of objectivity, readership interactions, transparency, and fact verification. With these shifts in mind, this current study explores whether the gendered sports journalism discourse, which remains predominantly patriarchal in traditional media, has in fact changed owing to journalists' migration to the Twittersphere. To that end, tweets by prominent Israeli sports journalists were sampled between 2014 and 2016. The findings point to major differences in four main areas, in the tweeting of male and female journalists: interaction, personal life, sports fandom, and professional commentary. With that, two prevalent types of Twitter users emerge in the Israeli context: the professional tweeter – common amongst male journalists and the all-around players – and versatile tweeters whose tweets are also personal prevalent amongst female tweeters for whom Twitter is both a social and professional arena.

Keywords: sports journalists; Twitter; gender, sports coverage; social media

1 Introduction

This chapter examines the different ways in which male and female sports journalists use Twitter. The rationale behind this study is the assumption that social networks offer women journalists a way to challenge the masculine culture prevailing in the sports field. The Israeli Twittersphere offers examples that allegedly support this assumption. On August 9, 2016, for example, Daniela Samari, a sports journalist, asked the Israeli Professional Football League (IPFL) on Twitter, regarding an event she wasn't invited to, "Why didn't you invite women journalists to this event? Is football just for men?" (Samari 2016c). On February 5, 2013, Maayan Efrat, a former sports journalist tweeted sarcastically, "Should women journalists cover women's sports only because they are women? Surely we have made progress" (Erfat 2013). But besides anecdotal examples, do women journalists use Twitter to criticize the masculine culture prevalent in the sports field? Rooted in the literature related to gender, media, and sport in general and gender, sports journalism, and Twitter, in particular, we investigate how prominent female and male Israeli sports journalists use Twitter in an attempt to find the major points of difference and the types of Twitter users specifically focused in the Israeli context.

https://doi.org/10.1515/9783110660883-037

2 Literature review

2.1 Gender, media and sport

Over the past decades, hundreds of studies have shown sports media generally provide greater emphasis to male athletes regardless of the type of sport, level or age of competitors, form of medium, or host country of the media outlet (see Bernstein and Kian 2013; Fink 2015). Despite record numbers of female-athlete participation in sporting events, the media continues to valorize elite, able-bodied, heterosexual, and professional sports*men* (Bernstein and Kian 2013; Cooky, Messner, and Musto 2015; Tamir, Yarchi, and Galily 2017). Early academic research in internet sports journalism suggested that attitude may be different online and that online sportswriters may subvert the gender-bias in sports media coverage, which has regularly appeared in traditional media (Kian, Mondello, and Vincent 2009). However, to date, there is more evidence that many new media channels do not provide greater coverage of women's sport (Kian and Clavio 2011; Lisec and McDonald 2012). Despite the hope and transformative potential digital media provide for challenging male hegemony and traditional gender ideologies in sports media, most of the research that exists to date does not look promising. Indeed, it seems that old patterns of media representations of women's sport and female athletes are being reproduced in "new" media (Creedon 2014).

2.2 Sports media as a gendered institution

A possible reason for media importance placed upon men's sports is a hegemonic masculine cultural and organizational structure that permeates not only most sports organizations and franchises but is also prevalent within the overall ranks and hierarchy of the sport media outlets that determine which athletes and sports are worthy of coverage (Bernstein and Kian 2013; Knoppers and Elling 2004). An assumption from this is that only men truly comprehend sport; and thus only masculine, heterosexual men are qualified to work in sports media (Hardin 2005; Abisaid and Li 2020).

In the early 1970s, The Associated Press estimated that only about 25 women were employed as sportswriters in US newspapers (Creedon 1994). Recent research suggests that not much has changed over the years. Studies in numerous Western countries have consistently shown that men author most sports media content, irrespective of medium (Bernstein and Kian 2013; The status of women 2019) and in all mediums, the percentage of female employees generally drops at the higher ranks of sports journalism meaning that a *glass-ceiling* effect is present for women trying to advance within sports journalism (Hardin 2005; Pfister 2010).

However, it is important to emphasize that contending with just hiring more female journalists or editors may not deliver greater and/or better coverage of women's sports. Some researchers found evidence that many female sports journalists adopt masculine practices and tend to imitate their male colleagues' attitudes toward the importance of specific men's and women's sports, making them less likely to facilitate any change in the sports field (Hardin and Shain 2005; Tamir and Bernstein 2013). Furthermore, as Tamir, Yarchi, and Galily (2017) concluded in their study of Israeli female sports journalists and their impact on the coverage of women's sports that a growing female presence in sports media does not necessarily guarantee any form of change.

Recently scholars have suggested that social media can open up cultural spaces where women's sport can be discussed and promoted (Sanderson and Gramlich 2016). So can female journalists use social media in a way that will challenge the hegemonic masculine culture? In the next section, we will discuss the changes that have taken place in the journalism field with the advent of social networking and the differences in the way male and female journalists use social media.

2.3 Journalism and Twitter

Scholarly studies of journalists' Twitter activities suggest that Twitter has overhauled journalistic notions of objectivity (Lasorsa, Lewis, and Holton 2012), readership interactions, and sourcing (Kim et al. 2015; Hermida, Lewis, and Zamith 2014) and transparency (Hedman & Djerf-Pierre 2013).

2.3.1 Objectivity

Schudson (2001) argued that objectivity is the chief occupational value in American journalism. According to the objectivity norm, journalists are supposed to separate facts from values and do not let their personal preferences influence their coverage. This norm has become the marker of good journalism (Van Zoonen 1998; Berkowitz 2000) and still seems to be the default for most journalists (Ryfe 2012; Muñoz-Torres 2007; Schudson and Anderson 2009), although in the Israeli context journalists question their ability to mirror reality as it is (Tsfati, Meyers, and Peri 2006).

The nature of online media and social networks have brought new challenges to the objective model of journalism. Scholars found that journalists on Twitter offer a considerable amount of opinion in a way that deviates from the objective convention (Lasorsa, Lewis, and Holton 2012). However, the level of objectivity on Twitter was not affected by gender – male and female journalists expressed their opinions at the same level (Lasorsa 2012).

2.3.2 Interaction

A common claim against journalists before the digital age was that they acted in a closed professional field in which their fellow journalists affected their coverage more than their readers (Rosen 1991). This is why one of the main questions researchers have been trying to answer regarding journalistic use of Twitter is how this new tool affected the interaction between journalists and their audiences.

Overall, previous studies have found that despite the emergence of the ethic of participation (Lewis 2012) and organizational pressure that requires journalists to engage with their audiences (Holton and Molyneux 2015), they interact mainly with other journalists and exclude the public (Molyneux and Mourão 2019; Lawrence et al. 2014; Hedman 2016). Regarding the issue of gender, Usher, Holcomb, and Littman (2018) found asymmetry in the way the journalists interact with each other – male journalists engage with male peers almost exclusively leaving women out of the picture, while female journalists tend to engage most with each other.

2.3.3 Transparency

In the current era, when journalistic content is always subject to dispute and news organizations are losing public trust (Willnat, Weaver, and Wilhoit 2019), transparency has become one of the most important professional ideals (Chadha and Koliska 2015). Three types of journalistic transparency have been defined in the literature (Karlsson 2010; Hedman 2016): disclosure transparency in which the journalists explain the process of making the news to the audience; participatory transparency invites the audience to interact with the journalists and take part in the process of making the news; personal transparency includes personal opinions and details from journalists' private life.

Twitter offers an opportunity for journalists to be more transparent, but findings of previous research suggest that journalists show a limited level of transparency on Twitter (Hedman 2016; Lasorsa, Lewis, and Holton 2012). Regarding the degree of personal transparency journalists allow themselves on Twitter, scholars have found differences in several variables: elite journalists tweet less about their personal life (Lasorsa, Lewis, and Holton 2012); TV journalists tweet more about their personal life than radio or tabloids journalists (Hedman 2016); freelance journalists are more personal than employed journalists (Brems et al. 2017); and the longer journalists have been active on Twitter, the more personal and private they become (Hedman 2016).

However, despite these findings, there seems to be a consensus among scholars regarding the significant role of gender in understanding these differences. Researchers have found that female journalists tweet significantly more about their personal life and everyday activities than their male colleagues. Hedman (2016), for example, found among Swedish journalists that women's tweets are almost twice as personal or private to those of men. Lasorsa (2012) speculated that the difference may be the result of the type of stories male and female cover – male journalists cover more hard news topics and therefore need to guard themselves against challenges to their work resulting from revealing their personal life. His remark raises the question of whether sports journalists behave similarly even though they are covering soft news stories?

2.4 Sports journalism and Twitter

Social media has changed the ways in which sports clubs, leagues, federations, and athletes interact with their supporters by enabling a direct connection between them (Abeza, O'Reilly, and Seguin 2017; Thompson et al. 2018). This direct connection between sports organizations and their fans has also affected the way sports journalists cover sports events and interact with their audiences (Kian and Murray 2014; Sheffer and Schultz 2010).

One of the most popular social platforms used by journalists is Twitter. In the US nearly all sports journalists have an active Twitter account (Abisaid and Li 2020). The digital presence of sports journalists on Twitter stems from both an external pressure by their managers who expect them to market their stories online and engage continuously with their readers (Daum and Scherer 2017), and internal pressure to establish their distinctiveness by using Twitter as a personal branding tool (Roberts and Emmons 2016).

Like journalists in other fields, sports journalists use Twitter to research and monitor the news, source, report stories, express opinion, and interact with followers (Bowman and Cranmer 2014; Sherwood and Nicholson 2012; Schultz and Sheffer 2010). However, Sheffer and Schultz (2010) found that sports journalists used Twitter primarily for opinion and commentary and much less for breaking news, promotion, and interaction with audiences. Regarding interaction, research among sports journalists provided mixed results: while sports journalists claimed that they use Twitter to interact with their readers (English 2016; Sherwood and Nicholson 2012), Emmons and Butler (2013) claimed that sports journalists are less likely to engage with fans than bloggers.

2.5 Gender, sports journalism, and Twitter

As already mentioned, much academic attention has been paid over the years to gender in the context of media and sports but much less to the context of journalism, gender, and social media (Schmidt 2013) or Twitter in particular. Yet, the small number of studies that do exist raise some interesting findings. It seems that male and female sports journalists tweet at statistically the same rate (Abisaid and Li 2020), but when examining the content of the tweets a few differences emerge. The most consistent finding is that male journalists' tweets are focused on commentary and analysis of sports events whereas the female journalists' tweets offer a far more personal angle (Abisaid and Li 2020; Weathers et al. 2014). Another finding which suggests that traditional gender roles are replicated in the Twittersphere is that female journalists, more than male journalists, use what are considered traditional feminine language features in computer-mediated communication (CMC) like exclamation points, puzzled punctuation, emoticons, and photos (Kaiser 2016).

With regard to the type of sports being discussed on Twitter, findings are mixed. While some scholars claim that female journalists tweet more about female sports (Kaiser 2016; Abisaid and Li 2020), Hull (2017) found that local male sports broadcasters were more likely to tweet about women's sports than were local female sports broadcasters. Findings are also mixed regarding the language male and female sports journalists use. While Kaiser (2016) found no differences between male and female journalists' use of aggressive language, Abisaid and Li's (2020) findings suggest that male sports journalists use assertive language in their tweets more than female sports journalists.

3 Research questions and methodology

The current study explores whether the sports journalism discourse, which remains predominantly patriarchal in traditional media, has in fact changed owing to journalists' migration to the increasingly influential Twittersphere. The research question, therefore, is what are the differences between the way male and female sports journalists use Twitter?

The study's sample was assembled to reflect the way Israeli male and female sports journalists use Twitter. Our first step in the sampling process was to identify prominent Israeli sports journalists who are active Twitter users. To that end, we examined all the daily Israeli newspapers and sports sites' lists of employees and searched for journalists who hold active Twitter accounts. Whenever we found a new journalist, we searched his list of "followers" and "following" for more journalists who hold an active Twitter account. Following Tsfati and Meyers (2012) we have defined a journalist as a person who works for a media organization and makes decisions that have a direct effect on news content. Therefore, we have included in our list editors, reporters, columnists, and anchorwomen but excluded photographers, graphic editors, and so on. We did not limit our sample to journalists in a specific medium and therefore included journalists working for newspapers, online sports news sites, sports TV channels, and radio. We ended up with a list of 56 male and 14 female sports journalists, which reflects the fact that there are much fewer female journalists in sports media in Israel. We then selected all female journalists and 14 of the male journalists based on their number of followers and number of tweets. We have checked those journalists' bios on Twitter to make sure that they all identified themselves as sports journalists and link themselves to a news organization.

In the next stage, we used Mozdeh to collect the last 3,200 tweets and retweets for each journalist's account from the day of data collection (January 31, 2017), backward.[1] The earliest tweet we sampled was published on January 13, 2014. We decided to exclude retweets and analyze only tweets written by the journalists themselves. Overall, the study population was comprised of 42,871 tweets by male journalists and 23,361 tweets by female journalists, of which we randomly sampled 500 tweets by male sports journalists and 500 tweets by their female peers.

The analysis of the corpus was generally based on the principles of grounded theory (Glaser and Strauss 1967), but not in its purist version (Dunne 2011). While the original version of grounded theory explicitly advises ignoring prior research, we conducted a very limited literature review in order to identify the central issues in the field of journalists' use of Twitter. The issues we identified included objectivity, interactivity, and transparency. However, we deliberately avoided imposing these specific concepts on the analysis of our sample at the outset. Instead, we followed an inductive approach and used these issues as general optional lines of inquiry. So, for example, even though a central concept in the study of gender, Twitter, and journalism was interactivity between male and female journalists, our analysis suggested that the interaction between journalists and their followers was much more meaningful in our sample. We used ATLAS.ti software to systemize the analysis process.

4 Findings

The findings point to major differences in four main areas in the tweeting of male and female journalists: personal life, interaction with fans, Fandom, and professional commentary.

4.1 Personal life

As mentioned above, previous research found that male journalists tweet less about their private life than their female colleagues (Hedman 2016; Lasorsa 2012; Weathers et al. 2014). Our findings are consistent with these findings. Unlike the majority of the male sports journalists who share almost no details about their personal lives, their female peers frequently tweet about several aspects of their private life. These aspects refer mainly to topics that are perceived as feminine and include:

1 For more on Mozdeh, visit: http://mozdeh.wlv.ac.uk. Twitter's API limits the ability to collect tweets to 3,200 per user.

4.1.1 Weddings

The social perception of gender roles regarding wedding ceremonies is that females should be obsessed with wedding decisions, and males should be uninterested in wedding details (Pepin et al. 2008). Israeli journalists in our sample have tweeted in a way that complies with these gender stereotypes. When Daniela Samari, a TV journalist, posted an invitation to her wedding, Yael Shahrur, a print and online journalist, tweeted, “I'll rest in the grave. ... My zinger after another morning that started at 6:30 AM #Wedding Preparation” (Shahrur 2016), and Tamar Rippel, a print and online journalist, tweeted to Yael's husband, “I'll even see your wife before you will on your wedding day,” after he tweeted that he is insulted by the fact that Tamar got an invitation to the wedding before he did. This last tweet demonstrates how they both play their gender roles – he seems uninterested in the wedding and she is delighted even though it's not her wedding.

4.1.2 Pregnancy and kids

Female sports journalists in our sample mentioned pregnancy and children in their tweets while male journalists didn't tweet about their own kids at all. Maya Ronen, a TV journalist, tweeted, “The Signs of Maternity Leave, Before Maternity: I began reading the material for an embryology course, the second year. My nerdiest to date” (Ronen 2016b). Shirley bar Dayan, a TV reporter, wrote, “Who said jet lag is bad? At 8:30 my girl begged to keep on sleeping!” (Bar-Dayan 2016). Daniella Samari even mentioned unborn kids when she wrote, “My consolation from all the pictures of children flooding the net: My girls will no longer know who Elsa is” (Samari 2016a). Men, on the other hand, mentioned “kid” in their tweets only to refer to young athletes (Ackerman 2016b). Lachover (2005) found that female journalists attribute maternal stereotypes to their female colleagues because they perceive it as positive. This may explain the reason they tweet about it more than male journalists.

4.1.3 Expressing emotions

Goldshmidt and Weller (2000) found that Israeli women use expressions of emotions more than men do in a variety of settings. Lindsey (2015) claimed that men are less likely to share personal feelings on Facebook. Concurring with these findings, female journalists in our sample shared their emotions on Twitter while men did not reveal publicly any sign of vulnerability. Female journalists share their feeling regarding sports events, “Tori Pilenowski finishes the World championship in tears after failing to get the ticket to Rio. A shattered dream. I Admit I cried with her #rgwc” (Nevo 2015d). But they also share their emotions regarding personal life events. These personal events include self-exposure on different levels. The low level of self-exposure includes daily events like crying because of being sentimental, "I'm Sitting in front of 'The Voice,' one of the contestants sang our wedding song. I'm Crying like a girl" (Samari 2017). The medium level of self-exposure includes real concern for the health of family and friends. Oshrat Eni, for example, wrote about her Dad, "Dad had a motorcycle accident three weeks ago, broke the collarbone in several places so that it stood out and he remained conscious but vague," and she ended the thread by tweeting, "That's it, I had to unburden" (Eni 2017). The high level of self-exposure includes sharing feelings regarding tragic events like when Maya Ronen shared her heartbreaking experience with abortion, "The experience I had in the pregnancy termination committee was more painful and hurtful than anything else in the tragedy I went through when I decided to say goodbye to a fetus in my abdomen that was infected with CMV. Get out of our womb. Get out" (Ronen 2017). Miri Nevo shared her feelings regarding the death of a friend, "I'm crying and crying over the death of a dear man and a dear friend. Motti ... I'll miss you" (Nevo 2015e). These tweets serve as good examples of the claim that women express vulnerability much more easily in public than men. Men journalists, on the other hand, did not share their feelings or reveal vulnerabilities in the sample we analyzed.

4.1.4 Friendship

Friendship is a relationship marked by traits like openness, altruism, and need for belonging, and this is the reason men often perceive friendship as feminine emotional labor and refrain from talking about it (Butera 2006). This might be the reason we did not find any tweet by a male journalist that reveals something about his social life. Female sports journalists, on the other hand, have no trouble telling their followers about their social life in a variety of contexts. Most of the time, these tweets reveal the positive and humorous aspects of friendship. Daniela Samari, for example, wrote, "Sometimes I don't understand why my girlfriends stay my friends" (Samari 2015b), and added a screen capture of an amusing WhatsApp conversation with her friends. However, sometimes the tweets reveal the negative aspects of friendship, like when Rebecca Griffin tweeted, "I used to think that I get along better with boys/men just because I love sports. The truth is rather simpler, I attracted manipulative psychotic girls and women" (Griffin 2017).

4.1.5 Vacations

Previous studies found that females post more photos than males on social network sites (Rui and Stefanone 2013; Stefanone and Lackaff 2009). In concordance with these findings, female journalists in our sample shared more photos from their vacations, links to their Instagram pages, and posted texts regarding their everyday life experiences during vacations. Lee Nof, for example, posted links to pictures on her Instagram page showing her running in Barcelona and traveling to London (Nof 2016a).

Men talk about the benefits of social networks in terms of functionality and efficiency (Tufekci, cited in Lindsey 2015). This is perhaps the reason that male journalists, unlike females, tweet about their private life only when they have a specific target with practical implications. So, for example, when Tal Shorer, a TV sports reporter, was looking for an apartment, he tweeted, "The negotiations exploded, returning to the apartment search. # Bummer" (Shorer 2016a), and Asaf Ackerman, a TV reporter who branded himself as an Italian football expert, tweeted, "Looking for a good Italian teacher. Do you have anything interesting to offer?" (Ackerman 2016a). In fact, these are the only two examples found in our sample for a male tweet about his private life. This finding echoes Lindsey's claim (2015) that men talk about their use of SNS in more goal-oriented terms.

Tweeting about one's personal life may blur the boundaries between the professional and private sphere. However, transparency may have a positive effect when it promotes credibility in an age of hostile public (Plaisance 2007). Based on our small sample it seems that Israeli female journalists limit their transparency on Twitter to the personal one and don't try to reveal t the journalistic backstage process by using disclosure or participatory transparency (Hedman 2016), thus don't promote their professional credibility.

4.2 Interaction

Previous research (Usher, Holcomb, and Littman 2018) found asymmetry in the way male and female journalists interact with each other. Our findings suggest that gender asymmetry exists not only in the way journalists interact with each other but with the way they interact with their audiences. Male journalists maintained more frequent fan interactions than their female peers in several ways. According to our sample, fans feel free to initiate an interaction with male journalists with professional questions on three topics: basic information, tactics, and future speculations.

4.2.1 Basic information

Followers often ask male journalists for information regarding statistics and laws, viewing them as professional authority figures and therefore assuming that they have the knowledge. Some of the questions request basic information such as the number of medals that are awarded in the Olympics (Shorer 2016b), statistics of a specific player in a specific game (Cooper 2016b), or information regarding competition laws (Hoffman 2015). On other occasions, the tone is more critical and the male journalist's authority is challenged, @Iraqinator82: "How do you write that Naimi [a basketball player] may be loaned to Galil? Haven't you heard about the law that forbids a player over the age of 24 to be loaned to another team in Israel" and Roei Gladstone, a basketball reporter, answered, "Great question. There is a way around. You simply make a triple purchase contract for one season, between the player and the two teams" (Gladstone 2013)

4.2.2 Tactics

The professional questions regarding tactics are often directed at the male commentators, who reply with short and polite answers and don't start a long Q&A session. So, when Ori Cooper was asked, "Wouldn't it make more sense that Rikan will play as a midfielder and Zehavi will play as a winger?" he answered, "Makes sense but we haven't seen it to date" (Cooper 2015).

4.2.3 Future speculations

This category of professional questions relates to fans asking the male journalists to speculate about future events, based on their inside information. Ido Gur, for example, was asked, "Will Farmer return to Yad Eliyahu? And Mekel will join Lior Eliyahu in the Arena? @idogur what is your assessment?" He answered, "Chances are that Farmer will sign in the next few days, don't know yet what that means about Mekel except that he probably won't play for Maccabi Tel Aviv" (Gur 2015a).

It is important to note that fans often ask male journalists professional questions even when it's not the journalist's main field of expertise. During the 2016 Olympic Games, for example, @Oyel asked Eran Soroka, who defines himself in his Twitter bio as a basketball journalist and NBA analyst, questions regarding rhythmic gymnastics, "It was a great performance and the score is a bit low, don't you think?" Soroka answered, "They were not as good as yesterday in both exercises (even with yesterday's scores there probably wasn't a medal). Some small mistakes, but this profession is based on accuracy" (Soroka 2016b). Soroka was indeed a reporter covering the Olympics, but the user who asked him this question could have asked Miri Nevo who was also covering the Olympics and was a rhythmic gymnast in her youth. However, we did not find this kind of professional question addressed to female journalists in our sample.

4.3 Transparency

Karlsson (2010) differentiated between disclosure transparency and participatory transparency. The interaction between the audience and male journalists in our sample mixed these categories because it required the journalists to be open about how news is being produced as part of a dialogue and interaction with the audience and not just communicating standards to the audience.

On some occasions, the male journalist's followers ask mundane questions regarding the journalist's working conditions but sometimes they challenge their professional decisions. An example of the first category we found when just before the Olympic games began, Ben Mittelman, a TV sports journalist, when asked, @eran65: "Are the journalists supposed to stay in the Olympic village with the athletes or do they rent rooms in Rio hotels?" he answered, "Not in the village. Hotels – private or rents by the IOC" (Mittelman 2016). This is an example of disclosure transparency that explains to the audience not only the journalist's working conditions but also something about the journalist's funding sources. But sometimes the journalists are criticized by their followers for their professional decisions and answer in a way that reveals the backstage of the editing process. Ido Gur, for example, was criticized for starting his television show "Open Court" with European football and not with the coming Eurobasket (European Basketball Championship), and answered, "It's because we had an interview with the agent. We aligned with his schedule" (Gur 2015b), and thus revealed the practical considerations behind the lineup for his show. Some of the interactions were initiated by the male journalists, such as when they created Twitter polls to start a dialogue. Oren Josipovich, for example, asked his followers, "How many Israeli football teams will get to the group stage in the European league?" (Josipovich 2016).

The interaction between female journalists and the audience was different in several aspects. First, since female journalists tweeted more about their personal life the dialogue between them and their followers was focused more on personal issues. Daniela Samari, for example, reminded her followers that she was getting married and got several "Mazal tov" wishes. Another example of an interaction that is based on personal issues involves early acquaintance in real life. A user labeled @happy_idrissou, for instance, tweeted, "Just met @TaliasTalia in person. I more pretty," and she reacted, "Your secret is safe with me" (Salant 2013).

On the few occasions in which fans approached female journalists with a professional question, it dealt mainly with women's sports. So for example, Oshrat Eni, a TV football commentator and an active player, was asked, "When was the Women's football league rebranded as the Women's premier league?" she answered, "From the moment they decided that the mama league will be the national league" (Eni 2016c). However, we did not find another woman journalist who was asked a direct professional question by her followers, so Eni's perceived authority to answer such questions might be derived from her being an active football player and not from her journalistic role.

Female journalists in our sample did not discuss professional issues regarding male sports almost at all. On the few occasions in which they did, the interaction was initiated by them and dealt with minor professional issues like the correct pronunciation of a player name. The only example we found in our sample of female journalists interacting with fans regarding male sports was when a user asked a general question to his feed about the rules of Judo and a male journalist asked Maya Ronen to answer him (Ronen 2016a). This interaction can be understood as one where male authority allows the female journalist to share her knowledge in the public space.

The last kind of interaction between female journalists and sports fans we found in our sample was when female journalists supported their female colleagues who were criticized by male fans. When Karin Shavit, for example, was criticized by Hapoel Beer Sheva fans for what they thought was unprofessional coverage, Daniela Samari answered one of them, "She is one of the great and talented writers and moreover – the most objective – I know. Comments like the ones she got are far from being legitimate" (Samari 2016b). Rui and Stefanone (2013) claim that females are more vulnerable to criticism on social media and therefore are more likely to react protectively to unwanted comments. The last example suggests that female journalists may react protectively to criticism directed at their female colleagues as well.

Our last note regarding the kind of interaction female journalists have is that they admit their mistakes more freely. When a user named @HaiTanami asked Maya Ronen, "I saw the pregame for the game against Italy a little late. Did you accidentally say something like 'Erez team's specialty is in the third quarter?'" she replied, "Thanks for your effort in checking! I was wrong, Happens. Thanks and have a great day" (Ronen 2015c). Samari apologized to one of her followers for a tweet that was similar to his tweet, "I'm shocked! I apologize if it looks like plagiarism. But you've earned a follower to make sure it won't happen again" (Samari 2015a). These fast apologetic replies echo Bryans (1999) claim that women often blame themselves for mistakes while men find someone else to blame.

4.4 Objectivity and sports fandom

Objectivity and journalistic impartiality have always been a problematic area among sports journalists who are often depicted as "fans with typewriters" (Boyle 2006). Rowe (2005) argues that sports journalists are expected both to cover sport "objectively" as a news item but often they are supposed to celebrate particular teams as partisan fans. In the Israeli context, Hagay (2015) found that sports journalists are abandoning their commitment to a neutral-objectivist model and the boundary between PR work and journalism has become increasingly obscure.

Unlike Lasorsa (2012) who found that gender made little difference regarding objectivity, our findings reveal a big difference between male and female sports journalists with regard to this topic. While Israeli female sports journalists publicly pledge support for their favorite sports team, their male peers attempt to maintain the appearance of professional objectivity and refrain from posting similar tweets.

Tweets supporting a local sports team by male journalists were rare in our sample. Female journalists, on the other hand, expressed their fandom much more freely. They tweeted their support for tennis players: “Now that Federer and Dudi [Sela – an Israeli tennis player] are out I’m with Nadal” (Nevo 2015a); for football players, “I’m a Ronaldo fan. I will follow him everywhere. My love” (Shavit 2016a); for Spanish football clubs, “To see Juventus–Real when you are a Milan and a Barca fan from childhood ... Interesting # can they both lose?” (Rippel 2015); English football clubs, “cfc# and his back!!! #diegooo #cfc” (Shahrur 2017); and national teams other than Israel, “Every time David Luiz touches the ball my heart beats faster #copaamerica” (Nevo 2015b). In a way that moves further away from the objective model, some of the female journalists in our sample identified as fans of first-tier league clubs in Israel. They did so in implicit ways, as when Shahrur tweeted her disappointment from her favorite team’s performance in Israel and abroad, “In the measure of which defense is more embarrassing I find it difficult to choose between Chelsea and Maccabi Tel Aviv #Desperate” (Shahrur 2015); and in explicit ways, “I’m a Bnei Yehuda fan and my partner is a Haifa fan. We couldn’t decide which stand we’ll sit in, so we decided to watch the game on TV” (Samari 2015c). Lee Nof even shattered the illusion of her colleagues’ objectivity when she wrote, “I’m letting you know in advance – I’m the only Maccabi Fan on the desk today. I’m not responsible for what will happen if they choose to bother me” (Nof 2016b). When asked directly by their followers regarding their favorite team they have no trouble answering, “Of course I’m a Bnei Yehuda fan ...” (Samari 2014a).

Overall, it seems that female journalists consider Twitter to be a different private arena in which they are not confined to the norms of objectivity. This type of behavior echoes the depiction of sports journalists in the literature as cheerleaders, fans, and biased journalists (Boyle, Rowe, and Whannel 2010). Male journalists, on the other hand, use social media in a way that is closely connected to the objective model of journalism and therefore provide further evidence for the shifts that are taking place within the professional ideology of sports journalism towards the objective model, as several studies suggested (McEnnis 2016; English 2017).

4.5 Commentary and analysis

Previous research has found that journalists used Twitter primarily for opinion and commentary (Sheffer and Schultz 2010). Regarding gender differences, Weathers et al. (2014) studied a small test case of two sports broadcasters and found that the male journalists provided more commentary and analysis. Our findings are consistent with theirs. Israeli male sports journalists are prone to commentating about events in their field of coverage whereas their female colleagues will offer more recap of events and less commentary.

Male journalists offer their commentary regarding various aspects of the game. During the game, they offer their followers statistical information – "Curry needs only 6 more points to get to an average of 30 points per game" (Soroka 2016a); criticism regarding a player – "Toni Kroos kicking from the 16 is as precise as Stephen Curry in free throws" (Hoffman 2016b); or a coach – "Pochettino thinks, changes, responds, replaces. He is living the game. Wenger is tired" (Hoffman 2016a); future predictions – "Moussa Dembele will get to one of the best teams in the world and will be legendary in it" (Daskal 2016); and video clips that explain their analysis (Cooper 2016a).

Female journalists, on the other hand, offer far less analysis and critical comments. The only female journalist in our sample who often tweeted analysis is Oshrat Eni who, as mentioned, is also an active football player so her authority to provide analysis might be based on her professional experience. Eni uses professional jargon as she comments on live games, "Kjartansson is the first for the rebound after a fast break by Haifa. Two goals from a trailer of a fast break can teach us something about commitment among Maccabi Tel Aviv players" (Eni 2016b). However, when other female journalists shared professional comments a few patterns could be identified:

4.5.1 General and vague statements

Some of the comments the female journalists share are general and vague impressions that do not relate to tactics or criticism. Samari, for example, tweeted, "A very cute kids team they gathered in Hapoel. I'm not being cynical" (Samari 2014b)

4.5.2 Emotional comments

Emotional comments include those that are focused on the mental and emotional aspects of the players, such as, "The players of Beer Sheva should wipe their tears, raise their heads and proudly embark on the European road that awaits them. There is no reason for them not to go far in this arena" (Samari 2016d); and fans' feelings, "there is something sad in the situation in which two Israeli athletes meet and one of them represents Britain" (Nevo 2015c).

4.5.3 Deriving the authority from a male commentator

In some instances, it seems as though the female journalists feel that they need a male voice that would justify their claims. Maya Ronen, for example, tweeted, "Memorizing what Erez says – small things win big games. Haifa does everything right but fails in the small things" (Ronen 2015b).

4.5.4 Apologetic tone

When female journalists do offer their analysis, they use rhetorical strategies that pre-empt criticism authority by self-reducing their authority and understanding. Maya Ronen, for example, tweeted, “Nadal must win this set. The way he looks right now he won’t make it to the fifth set. On the other hand, I thought he would lose so many times. I have no idea” (Ronen 2015a). Eni tweeted, “Lol. Alaves did nothing for 38 minutes and then ... a goal. Now they have upset Barcelona. The final score will be between 4 and 6 to 1. Or not. I have no idea” (Eni 2016a). This rhetoric resembles the “help me” tactic that Israeli female journalists use with their sources in which the journalist allows herself to look stupid to enhance the power of the male source (Lachover 2005). However, since we found no interaction between sources and reporters in our sample, this rhetoric might be explained by the different roles men and women play within the field of sports journalism. While male journalists act as commentators and senior reporters, female journalists often play the role of sideline reporters and anchorwomen. Yet, male reporters feel free to comment on topics that are not their area of coverage while female journalists provide analysis only when they have a history as an athlete in the field and are thus regarded as experts.

5 Conclusion

Women who try to enter the sports field, whether they are athletes, coaches, or journalists, still do not enjoy complete legitimacy in the Israeli social environment (Galily, Kaufman, and Tamir 2015). Despite a dramatic increase in labor force participation (Mandel and Birgier 2016), the sports field in Israel is still perceived as a male-only environment. Therefore, female journalists who wish to be part of the sports desk must adopt, or at least appear to adopt, male perception and embrace masculine values (Tamir and Galily 2010; Tamir and Bernstein 2013). Further to these findings, the purpose of our study was to compare the way male and female sports journalists use Twitter in order to understand if social media has given female journalists the opportunity to break the old constraints imposed on them by the male hegemony in traditional media. However, our findings suggest that even though female journalists declare that they reject classic femininity (Tamir and Bernstein 2013), they act according to traditional gender roles in social media.

Two prevalent types of Twitter users emerge in the Israeli context:

(1) The professional Tweeter: Chiefly common amongst male journalists whose tweets predominantly relate to professional issues, who interact with colleagues and fans alike but who limit, or altogether refrain, from personal tweets. These journalists view Twitter as a professional platform by which they brand themselves as authority figures while maintaining the appearance of professional objectivity.

(2) The all-around Tweeter: Versatile tweeters who blur the boundaries between professional and personal, who limit their professional comments, and who publicly pledge support for their favorite teams. This type is prevalent amongst female tweeters for whom Twitter is both a social and professional arena where they showcase the human face behind the voice (Lasorsa, Lewis, and Holton 2012).

The aforementioned differences seem to contradict previous findings regarding the way female sports journalists adopt masculine values. However, they can be explained by several factors rooted in the field of gender, social media, and journalism. First, previous research found that males and females use social media in a way that mirrors traditional gender roles – while men talk about social media in terms of functionality and efficiency (Tufekci, cited in Lindsey 2015), women say that social media allow them to talk about their feelings more openly (Lindsey 2015). On Twitter, research has found that females disclose more private information while men feel more need to manage their professional image and limit the disclosure (Walton and Rice 2013). These findings may explain the differences in the way male and female journalists perceive social media – while men regard it as a professional arena only, women use it as a private and professional space, as Karin Shavit tweeted, “Before everything I'm a human being and I have the right to tweet beyond my job” (Shavit 2016b).

Another factor that might explain the way female journalists use Twitter is related to the perception of gender roles. Mandel and Birgier (2016) claim that even though Israel has experienced a gender revolution in recent decades, there have been no major changes in attitude to gender roles over the years. Men and women alike still perceive women as responsible for childcare and house duties. Moreover, female journalists attribute maternal stereotypes to other female journalists and perceive this stereotype as positive (Lachover 2005). These findings may explain why female journalists feel more comfortable sharing their personal life on Twitter – they are influenced by stereotypic norms which they don't find harmful.

Lastly, the fact that female journalists limit their analysis and critical comments on Twitter might be explained by their, still, inferior place in the field of sports journalism (Tamir and Bernstein 2013). Although in the Israeli context a few female journalists have gained access to senior editorial positions, the field is still dominated by men. Therefore, it seems that women feel less authoritative and tend to present less analysis for fear of being mocked by chauvinist fans.

These findings offer insight into the conservative nature of sports discourse. While in traditional media female journalists tend to identify with their profession more than with their gender (Tamir and Bernstein 2013), they do the opposite in social media. Thus, despite Twitter's potential to offer female journalists a more egalitarian playing field, the discourse's patriarchal overtones persist online. Determining the reason behind this kind of behavior is beyond the scope of our study. We believe that the structural constraints imposed on women sports journalists limit their agency and lead them to this kind of behavior, but further research is needed to confirm this belief.

Therefore, we suggest two possible inquiries for future research: (1) Media production study in which women sports journalists who use Twitter will be interviewed; (2) Interaction – in our study, we sampled only the journalists' tweets. Future research should focus on the interaction between fans and sports journalists to examine the differences between the responses women and men journalists get from fans and followers.

References

Abeza, Gashaw, Norm O'Reilly & Benoît Seguin. 2017. Social media in relationship marketing: The perspective of professional sport managers in the MLB, NBA, NFL, and NHL. *Communication & Sport* 7(1). 80–109.

Abisaid, Joseph L. & Bo Li. 2020. He said, she said: An exploration of male and female print sports journalist tweets, sports coverage, and language style. *Communication & Sport* 8(6). 757–781.

Ackerman, Asaf. 2016a. *Twitter*, 12 September. https://twitter.com/AckermanAsaf/status/775279785824124928 (20 November 2020).

Ackerman, Asaf. 2016b. *Twitter*, 17 Decmeber. https://twitter.com/AckermanAsaf/status/810058909360721920 (20 November 2020).

Bar-Dayan, Shirley. 2016. *Twitter*, 13 December. https://twitter.com/shirlybardayan/status/808596419561029633 (20 November 2020).

Berkowitz, Dan. 2000. Doing double duty: Paradigm repair and the Princess Diana what-a-story. *Journalism* 1(2). 125–143.

Bernstein, Alina & Edward M Kian. 2013. Gender and sexualities in sport media. In Paul Pedersen (ed.), *Routledge handbook of sport communication*, 319–327. London: Routledge.

Bowman, Nicholas David & Gregory A. Cranmer. 2014. SocialMediaSport: The fan as a (mediated) participant in spectator sports. In Andrew C. Billings & Marie Hardin (eds.), *Routledge handbook of sport and new media*, 213–224. New York: Routledge.

Boyle, Raymond. 2006. *Sports journalism: Context and issues*. London: Sage.

Boyle, Raymond, David Rowe & Garry Whannel. 2010. "Delight in trivial controversy"? Questions for sports journalism. In Stuart Allan (ed.), *The Routledge companion to news and journalism*, 245–255. New York: Routledge.

Brems, Cara, Martina Temmerman, Todd Graham & Marcel Broersma. 2017. Personal branding on Twitter. *Digital Journalism* 5(4). 443–459.

Bryans, Patricia. 1999. What do professional men and women learn from making mistakes at work? *Research in Post-Compulsory Education* 4(2). 183–194.

Butera, Karina J. 2006. Manhunt: The challenge of enticing men to participate in a study on friendship. *Qualitative Inquiry* 12(6). 1262–1282.

Chadha, Kalyani & Michael Koliska. 2015. Newsrooms and transparency in the digital age. *Journalism Practice* 9(2). 215–229.

Cooky, Cheryl, Michael A. Messner & Michela Musto. 2015. "It's dude time!": A quarter century of excluding women's sports in televised news and highlight shows. *Communication & Sport* 3(3). 261–287.

Cooper, Ori. 2015. *Twitter*, 19 August. https://twitter.com/CoopSport/status/634060089045839872 (20 November 2020).

Cooper, Ori. 2016a. *Twitter*, 30 August. https://twitter.com/CoopSport/status/770579954941751297 (20 November 2020).

Cooper, Ori. 2016b. *Twitter*, 7 December. https://twitter.com/CoopSport/status/806388614074667008 (20 November 2020).

Creedon, Pam. 1994. Women in toyland: a look at women in American newspaper sports journalism. In Pam Creedon (ed.), *Women, media and sport: Challenging gender values*, 67–108. Thousand Oaks, CA: Sage.

Creedon, Pam. 2014. Women, social media, and sport: Global digital communication weaves a web. *Television & New Media* 15(8). 711–716.

Daskal, Ouriel. 2016. *Twitter*, 31 December. https://twitter.com/odaskal/status/815197998456119296 (20 November 2020).

Daum, Evan & Jay Scherer. 2017. Changing work routines and labour practices of sports journalists in the digital era: a case study of Postmedia. *Media, Culture & Society* 40(4). 551–566.

Dunne, Ciarán. 2011. The place of the literature review in grounded theory research. *International Journal of Social Research Methodology* 14(2). 111–124.

Efrat, Maayan. 2013. *Twitter*, 5 February. https://twitter.com/maayanef/status/298844981014171648 (20 November 2020).

Emmons, Betsy & Sim Butler. 2013. Institutional constraints and changing routines: Sports journalists tweet the Daytona 500. *Journal of Sports Media* 8(1). 163–187.

English, Peter. 2016. Twitter's diffusion in sports journalism: Role models, laggards and followers of the social media innovation. *New Media & Society* 18(3). 484–501.

English, Peter. 2017. Cheerleaders or critics? *Digital Journalism* 5(5). 532–548.

Eni, Oshrat. 2016a. *Twitter*, 10 September. https://twitter.com/osh15eni/status/774686942474694656 (20 November 2020).

Eni, Oshrat. 2016b. *Twitter*, 24 October. https://twitter.com/osh15eni/status/790639715129196548 (20 November 2020).

Eni, Oshrat. 2016c. *Twitter*, 31 October. https://twitter.com/osh15eni/status/793155318138212352 (20 November 2020).

Eni, Oshrat. 2017. *Twitter*, 27 October. https://twitter.com/osh15eni/status/791642529263419392 (20 November 2020).

Fink, Janet S. 2015. Female athletes, women's sport, and the sport media commercial complex: Have we really "come a long way, baby"? *Sport Management Review* 18(3). 331–342.

Galily, Yair, Haim Kaufman & Ilan Tamir. 2015. She got game?! Women, sport and society from an Israeli perspective. *Israel Affairs* 21(4). 559–584.

Gladstone, Roey. 2013. *Twitter*, 21 August. https://twitter.com/RoeyGladstone/status/370256555528441856 (20 November 2020).

Glaser, Barney G. & Anselm L. Strauss. 1967. *The discovery of grounded theory*. Chicago: Aldine Publishing.

Goldshmidt, Orly Turgeman & Leonard Weller. 2000. "Talking emotions": Gender differences in a variety of conversational contexts. *Symbolic Interaction* 23(2). 117–134.

Griffin, Rebecca. 2017. *Twitter*, 16 January. https://twitter.com/dorothyofisrael/status/820984780867194880 (20 November 2020).

Gur, Ido. 2015a. *Twitter*, 5 July. https://twitter.com/idogur/status/617779353007472640 (20 November 2020).

Gur, Ido. 2015b. *Twitter*, 1 September. https://twitter.com/idogur/status/638711856387874816 (20 November 2020).

Hagay, Haim. 2015. *"The content is important, but traffic is more important ..." An ethnography of sports journalism in Israel*. Haifa, Israel: University of Haifa Ph.D. Thesis.

Hardin, Marie. 2005. Stopped at the gate: Women's sports, "reader interest," and decision making by editors. *Journalism & Mass Communication Quarterly* 82(1). 62–77.

Hardin, Marie & Stacie Shain. 2005. Strength in numbers? The experiences and attitudes of women in sports media careers. *Journalism & Mass Communication Quarterly* 82(4). 804–819.
Hedman, Ulrika. 2016. When journalists tweet: Disclosure, participatory, and personal transparency. *Social Media + Society* 2(1). 1–13.
Hedman, Ulrika & Monika Djerf-Pierre. 2013. The social journalist. *Digital Journalism* 1(3). 368–385.
Hermida, Alfred, Seth C. Lewis & Rodrigo Zamith. 2014. Sourcing the Arab Spring: A case study of Andy Carvin's sources on Twitter during the Tunisian and Egyptian revolutions. *Journal of Computer-Mediated Communication* 19(3). 479–499.
Hoffman, Dor. 2015. *Twitter*, 2 December. https://twitter.com/dorhoffman/status/672172758588104704 (20 November 2020).
Hoffman, Dor. 2016a. *Twitter*, 5 March. https://twitter.com/dorhoffman/status/706121110878883840 (20 November 2020).
Hoffman, Dor. 2016b. *Twitter*, 27 August. https://twitter.com/dorhoffman/status/769624941515931648 (20 November 2020).
Holton, Avery E. & Logan Molyneux. 2015. Identity lost? The personal impact of brand journalism. *Journalism* 18(2). 195–210.
Hull, Kevin. 2017. An examination of women's sports coverage on the Twitter accounts of local television sports broadcasters. *Communication & Sport* 5(4). 471–491.
Josipovich, Oren. 2016. *Twitter*, 5 August. https://twitter.com/Josifoon/status/761522908820897792 (20 November 2020).
Kaiser, Kent. 2016. Sports reporters in the Twittersphere. *Online Information Review* 40(6). 761–784.
Karlsson, Michael. 2010. Rituals of transparency. *Journalism Studies* 11(4). 535–545.
Kian, Edward M. & Galen Clavio. 2011. A comparison of online media and traditional newspaper coverage of the men's and women's U.S. Open Tennis Tournaments. *Journal of Sports Media* 6(1). 55–84.
Kian, Edward M. & Ray Murray. 2014. Curmudgeons but yet adapters: Impact of Web 2.0 and Twitter on newspaper sports journalists' jobs, responsibilities, and routines. *#ISOJ* 4(1). 61–77.
Kian, Edward Ted M., Michael Mondello & John Vincent. 2009. ESPN – The women's sports network? A content analysis of internet coverage of March Madness. *Journal of Broadcasting & Electronic Media* 53(3). 477–495.
Kim, Yonghwan, Youngju Kim, Joong Suk Lee, Jeyoung Oh & Na Yeon Lee. 2015. Tweeting the public: journalists' Twitter use, attitudes toward the public's tweets, and the relationship with the public. *Information, Communication & Society* 18(4). 443–458.
Knoppers, Annelies & Agnes Elling. 2004. "We do not engage in promotional journalism": Discursive strategies used by sport journalists to describe the selection process. *International Review for the Sociology of Sport* 39. 57–73.
Lachover, E. 2005. The gendered and sexualized relationship between Israeli women journalists and their male news sources. *Journalism* 6(3). 291–311.
Lasorsa, Dominic. 2012. Transparency and other journalistic norms on Twitter. *Journalism Studies* 13(3). 402–417.
Lasorsa, Dominic L., Seth C. Lewis & Avery E. Holton. 2012. Normalizing Twitter. *Journalism Studies* 13(1). 19–36.
Lawrence, Regina G., Logan Molyneux, Mark Coddington & Avery Holton. 2014. Tweeting conventions. *Journalism Studies* 15(6). 789–806.
Lewis, Seth C. 2012. The tension between professional control and open participation. *Information, Communication & Society* 15(6). 836–866.
Lindsey, Linda L. 2015. *Gender roles: A sociological perspective*. New York: Routledge.
Lisec, John & Mary G. McDonald. 2012. Gender inequality in the new millennium: An analysis of WNBA representations in sport blogs. *Journal of Sports Media* 7(2). 153–178.

Mandel, Hadas & Debora P. Birgier. 2016. The gender revolution in Israel: Progress and stagnation. In Nabil Khattab, Sami Miaari & Haya Stier (eds.), *Inequality in Israel*, 153–184. New York: Palgrave.
McEnnis, Simon. 2016. Following the action. *Journalism Practice* 10(8). 967–982.
Mittelman, Ben. 2016. *Twitter*, 26 July. https://twitter.com/BenMittelman/status/757883587387650048 (20 November 2020).
Molyneux, Logan & Rachel R. Mourão. 2019. Political journalists' normalization of Twitter. *Journalism Studies* 20(2). 248–266.
Muñoz-Torres, Juan Ramón. 2007. Underlying epistemological conceptions in journalism. *Journalism Studies* 8(2). 224–247.
Nevo, Miri. 2015a. *Twitter*, 23 January. https://twitter.com/MiriNevo/status/558590549398020096 (20 November 2020).
Nevo, Miri. 2015b. *Twitter*, 21 June. https://twitter.com/MiriNevo/status/612758443707904000 (20 November 2020).
Nevo, Miri. 2015c. *Twitter*, 18 July. https://twitter.com/MiriNevo/status/622326768880369665 (20 November 2020).
Nevo, Miri. 2015d. *Twitter*, 11 September. https://twitter.com/MiriNevo/status/642441996179668992 (20 November 2020).
Nevo, Miri. 2015e. *Twitter*, 25 September. https://twitter.com/MiriNevo/status/647327656166293504 (20 November 2020).
Nof, Lee. 2016a. *Twitter*, 12 February. https://twitter.com/leenof/status/698073556937285632 (20 November 2020).
Nof, Lee. 2016b. *Twitter*, 2 May. https://twitter.com/leenof/status/727177838114291712 (20 November 2020).
Pepin, Joanna, Toni Schindler Zimmerman, Christine A. Fruhauf & James H. Banning. 2008. An analysis of wedding books for grooms: A feminist perspective. *Journal of Feminist Family Therapy* 20(4). 328–356.
Pfister, Gertrud. 2010. Women in sport – gender relations and future perspectives. *Sport in Society* 13(2). 234–248.
Plaisance, Patrick Lee. 2007. Transparency: An assessment of the Kantian roots of a key element in media ethics practice. *Journal of Mass Media Ethics* 22(2–3). 187–207.
Rippel, Tamar. 2015. *Twitter*, 5 May. https://twitter.com/tamaripel/status/595671691067531265 (20 November 2020).
Roberts, Chris & Betsy Emmons. 2016. Twitter in the press box: How a new technology affects game-day routines of print-focused sports journalists. *International Journal of Sport Communication* 9(1). 97–115.
Ronen, Maya. 2015a. *Twitter*, 21 January. https://twitter.com/maya_ronen/status/557849646845157376 (20 November 2020).
Ronen, Maya. 2015b. *Twitter*, 16 February. https://twitter.com/maya_ronen/status/567411150489280513 (20 November 2020).
Ronen, Maya. 2015c. *Twitter*, 15 September. https://twitter.com/maya_ronen/status/643719836510457856 (20 November 2020).
Ronen, Maya. 2016a. *Twitter*, 7 August. https://twitter.com/maya_ronen/status/762378901133922304 (20 November 2020).
Ronen, Maya. 2016b. *Twitter*, 19 September. https://twitter.com/maya_ronen/status/777898845279776768 (20 November 2020).
Ronen, Maya. 2017. *Twitter*, 2 January. https://twitter.com/maya_ronen/status/815912395839340544 (20 November 2020).
Rosen, Jay. 1991. Making journalism more public. *Communication* 12(4). 267–284.

Rowe, David. 2005. Fourth estate or fan club? Sports journalism engages the popular. In Stuart Allan (ed.), *Journalism: Critical issues*, 125–136. Maidenhead, England: Open University Press.
Rui, Jian & Michael A Stefanone. 2013. Strategic self-presentation online: A cross-cultural study. *Computers in Human Behavior* 29(1). 110–118.
Ryfe, David. 2012. Why has news production in the United States remained stable in a time of great change? In Vicki Mayer (ed.), *The international encyclopedia of media studies. Volume II: Media production*, 325–344. Hoboken, NJ: Wiley-Blackwell.
Salant, Talia. 2013. *Twitter*, 18 July. https://twitter.com/TaliasTalia/status/357924505911427073 (20 November 2020).
Samari, Daniela. 2014a. *Twitter*, 31 August. https://twitter.com/DanielaSamari/status/506147705890942976 (20 November 2020).
Samari, Daniela. 2014b. *Twitter*, 31 August. https://twitter.com/DanielaSamari/status/506156976674336770 (20 November 2020).
Samari, Daniela. 2015a. *Twitter*, 12 April. https://twitter.com/DanielaSamari/status/587301358279139328 (20 November 2020).
Samari, Daniela. 2015b. *Twitter*, 21 July. https://twitter.com/DanielaSamari/status/623600575419060224 (20 November 2020).
Samari, Daniela. 2015c. *Twitter*, 12 December. https://twitter.com/DanielaSamari/status/675689033910124544 (20 November 2020).
Samari, Daniela. 2016a. *Twitter*, 22 March. https://twitter.com/DanielaSamari/status/712173998264729600 (20 November 2020).
Samari, Daniela. 2016b. *Twitter*, 19 July. https://twitter.com/DanielaSamari/status/755495316263231488 (20 November 2020).
Samari, Daniela. 2016c. *Twitter*, 9 August. https://twitter.com/DanielaSamari/status/762947200972386305 (20 November 2020).
Samari, Daniela. 2016d. *Twitter*, 24 August. https://twitter.com/DanielaSamari/status/768192519049912320 (20 November 2020).
Samari, Daniela. 2017. *Twitter*, 28 January. https://twitter.com/DanielaSamari/status/825423197843632128 (20 November 2020).
Sanderson, Jimmy & Kelly Gramlich. 2016. "You go girl!": Twitter and conversations about sport culture and gender. *Sociology of Sport Journal* 33(2). 113–123.
Schmidt, Hans C. 2013. Women, sports, and journalism: Examining the limited role of women in student newspaper sports eporting. *Communication & Sport* 1(3). 246–268.
Schudson, Michael. 2001. The objectivity norm in American journalism. *Journalism* 2(2). 149–170.
Schudson, Michael & Chris Anderson. 2009. Objectivity, professionalism, and truth seeking in journalism. In Karin Wahl-Jorgensen & Thomas Hanitzsch (eds.), *The handbook of journalism studies*, 88–101. New York: Routledge.
Schultz, Brad & Mary Lou Sheffer. 2010. An exploratory study of how Twitter is affecting sports journalism. *International Journal of Sport Communication* 3(2). 226–239.
Shahrur, Yael. 2015. *Twitter*, 24 October. https://twitter.com/YaelShahrur/status/657924141497131008 (20 November 2020).
Shahrur, Yael. 2016. *Twitter*, 19 February. https://twitter.com/YaelShahrur/status/700574795717595136 (20 November 2020).
Shahrur, Yael. 2017. *Twitter*, 22 January. https://twitter.com/YaelShahrur/status/823219571486232576 (20 November 2020).
Shavit, Karin. 2016a. *Twitter*, 10 July. https://twitter.com/karin_shavit/status/752219579250769920 (20 November 2020).
Shavit, Karin. 2016b. *Twitter*, 22 August. https://twitter.com/karin_shavit/status/767690052096974849 (20 November 2020).

Sheffer, Mary Lou & Brad Schultz. 2010. Paradigm shift or passing fad? Twitter and sports journalism. *International Journal of Sport Communication* 3(4). 472–484.
Sherwood, Merryn & Matthew Nicholson. 2012. Web 2.0 platforms and the work of newspaper sport journalists. *Journalism* 14(7). 942–959.
Shorer, Tal. 2016a. *Twitter*, 22 June. https://twitter.com/TalShorrer/status/745536929316233216 (20 November 2020).
Shorer, Tal. 2016b. *Twitter*, 11 August. https://twitter.com/TalShorrer/status/763610060241108992 (20 November 2020).
Soroka, Eran. 2016a. *Twitter*, 13 April. https://twitter.com/sorokman/status/720464824120041474 (20 November 2020).
Soroka, Eran. 2016b. *Twitter*, 21 August. https://twitter.com/sorokman/status/767376913534967808 (20 November 2020).
Stefanone, Michael A. & Derek Lackaff. 2009. Reality television as a model for online behavior: Blogging, photo, and video sharing. *Journal of Computer-Mediated Communication* 14(4). 964–987.
Tamir, Ilan & Alina Bernstein. 2013. Battlefield sport: Female sports journalists in Israel. *Kesher* 44. 20–28.
Tamir, Ilan & Yair Galily. 2010. Women's sports coverage in Israel: Perception versus reality. *International Journal of Sport Communication* 3(1). 92–112.
Tamir, Ilan, Moran Yarchi & Yair Galily. 2017. Women, sport and the media: Key elements at play in the shaping of the practice of women in sports journalism in Israel. *Communications* 42(4). 441–464.
The status of women in the U.S. Media. 2019. *Womens Media Center*, 21 February. https://www.womensmediacenter.com/reports/the-status-of-women-in-u-s-media-2019 (20 November 2020).
Thompson, Ashleigh-Jane, Martin Andrew, Sarah Gee & Andrea Geurin. 2018. Building brand and fan relationships through social media. *Sport, Business and Management* 8(3). 235–256.
Tsfati, Yariv & Oren Meyers. 2012. Journalists in Israel. In David H. Weaver & Lars Willnat (eds.), *The global journalist in the 21st century*, 443–457. New York: Routledge.
Tsfati, Yariv, Oren Meyers & Yoram Peri. 2006. What is good journalism? Comparing Israeli public and journalists' perspectives. *Journalism* 7(2). 152–173.
Usher, Nikki, Jesse Holcomb & Justin Littman. 2018. Twitter makes it worse: Political journalists, gendered echo chambers, and the amplification of gender bias. *The International Journal of Press/Politics* 23(3). 324–344.
Van Zoonen, Liesbet. 1998. A professional, unreliable, heroic marionette (M/F): Structure, agency and subjectivity in contemporary journalisms. *European Journal of Cultural Studies* 1(1). 123–143.
Walton, Courtney & Ronald Rice. 2013. Mediated disclosure on Twitter: The roles of gender and identity in boundary impermeability, valence, disclosure, and stage. *Computers in Human Behavior* 29(4). 1465–1474.
Weathers, Melinda, Jimmy Sanderson, Pauline Matthey, Alexia Grevious, Samantha Warren & Maggie Tehan. 2014. The tweet life of Erin and Kirk. *Journal of Sports Media* 9(2). 1–24.
Willnat, Lars, David H. Weaver & G. Cleveland Wilhoit. 2019. The American journalist in the digital age. *Journalism Studies* 20(3). 423–441.

Thomas Horky and Robin Meyer

38 #Rio2016 and #WorldCup2018: social media meets journalism

Abstract: Social networks like Facebook, Twitter, and Instagram have continuously impacted sports and sports journalism. The methods of communication in sports have changed through social media in many ways and it has influenced several actors in the field with its characteristics of information, participation, and interaction. In this chapter, particularly the development of sport mega-events will be used to illustrate the ongoing process of change through the impact of modern media technology and digital forms of social conversation. Additionally, some limitations of this process will be described. The transition will be explained by looking at major sports events like the Olympic Games and football tournaments such as the World Cup and the European Championships. Demonstrating the function and general impact of social networks on sports journalism, the particular characteristics of (social) communication at major sports events will be discussed and explained with a special focus on the 2016 Olympic Games and the 2018 FIFA World Cup.

Keywords: sports journalism; social media; sports mega-events; Olympic Games; FIFA World Cup

1 Introduction

Since their emergence in the first decade of the 21st century, social networks have continuously impacted sports and sports journalism. The methods of communication have changed, for clubs, associations, federations, events and, not least, individual athletes (Sanderson 2011). Particularly, the development of mega-events in different sports illustrates the ongoing process of change through media coverage and the influence of modern media technology (Wenner and Billings 2017). Digital forms of social conversation like social media seem to have a huge impact and with that lead the way for new means of sports communication. The transition becomes most apparent when we look at major sports events such as the Olympic Games or large-scale football tournaments like the World Cup and the European Championships (Horky 2013). This chapter focuses on the changes in sports communication through the rise of social media. Demonstrating the general impact of social networks on sports journalism, we will describe particular characteristics of communication at major sports events by focusing on the 2016 Olympic Games and the 2018 FIFA World Cup.

https://doi.org/10.1515/9783110660883-038

2 Emergence of social media

Which features can be identified as distinctive and new about the phenomena of social media and web 2.0? Particularly compared to traditional media such as newspapers, radio, and television, the most crucial characteristic of social networks and web 2.0 websites are their participatory potential and user generated content. The development from web 1.0 to web 2.0 is characterized by the blurring of boundaries between the producers and the consumers of media content, which has led to the rise of the so-called prosumers. Actually, this has introduced a transition, from a hitherto one-to-many communication to a many-to-many form of communication. With regard to the rise of social media, two developments in particular have pioneered the way: firstly, the democratization of the means of production in the form of mobile end devices such as smartphones, digital cameras, blogs, and so forth, and secondly, the democratization of the means of publication – i. e., no longer do we need a carrier.

These two essential trends, then, enabled all users to participate in the production of web 2.0 content, and paved the way for the rise of social networks. The most essential forms of social media are social networks (Facebook, Twitter, Instagram); social video platforms (YouTube, Pinterest); blogs; web TV (livestreaming); video and photo sharing websites (Flickr), and microblogging services (Twitter).

The interconnection between these different types of services can be seen as rather diverse. Certain events, such as major sports, often appear in various social media outlets in a variety of ways and intensities. After the 2006 FIFA World Cup Final, Zinedine Zidane's header caused an initial stir as it was broadcast countless times by the then still new video platform YouTube. During the 2010 Winter Olympics in Vancouver, the American alpine skier Julia Mancuso offered lots of information to her followers on Twitter, while neglecting press conferences and television interviews (Horky 2013). This caused a first round of intense discussions about the impact of social media on sports, particularly on sports journalism and the allocation of broadcasting rights.

3 Characteristics and functions of social media

Social media outlets have broadened the possibilities of communication and have altered communication patterns. There has always been a great emotional connection between athletes and fans, or teams and clubs, respectively. Yet, any communication between these groups has long been dominated by the rather passive consumption of traditional media content, except for the occasional visit to the stadium or training ground. However, as users of social media, fans are now able to contribute to the emergence of "media reality" by generating their own content. The most important characteristics of this form of exchange are the three features of information, participation, and interaction (Burk and Grimmer 2016; Sanderson 2011):

> *Information:* Athletes, clubs, associations, and leagues are able to distribute information directly to certain external reference groups via social media outlets. This may entail releasing images and information about former matches and events, announcing upcoming events or a presale date, advertising competitions or charity schemes, or even publishing details about certain athletes' private lives. There really is no limit to what can be done with regards to content (Clavio and Frederick 2014; Hambrick et al. 2010; Whiteside 2014). Such a comprehensive scope of information can be both curse and blessing, particularly for sports journalists. On the plus side, it offers a range of additional possibilities for research. Quite often, journalists discover quotable statements on social media profiles of athletes and clubs; however, such statements are accessible to everyone, thus lacking exclusiveness and autonomy (Nölleke, Grimmer, and Horky 2017).
> *Participation*: The development from web 1.0 to web 2.0 has led to the rise of the so-called prosumers. A direct exchange has now become possible, and the former role of the traditional mass media as gatekeepers and facilitators of discussion has decreased in importance. Involving users with regard to subject matter, content, and themes promotes a mutual bond between fans and sports organizations. Hence, such active involvement in the production of content, the so-called user generated content, is an effect largely desired and intended (Williams and Chinn 2010).
> *Interaction*: Ultimately, web 2.0 media content offers the possibility to participate actively in the entire process of communication. Users can like, favor, share, pass on, and comment on the content of other users, they can take part in discussions, start or moderate a debate, and offer their opinions to a wider public, even to the world (with maybe a few restrictions). In using mobile devices, audiences can network, communicate, and interact in a variety of ways (Clavio and Walsh 2014; Frederick et al. 2012; Gibbs, O'Reilly, and Brunette 2014; Wallace, Wilson, and Miloch 2011).

When we talk about social media, in Western countries we often use the term as a synonym for Facebook, Twitter, and, increasingly, Instagram (Chaffey 2020). Indeed, these are the three top platforms for worldwide sports communication (Smith and Sanderson 2015). Yet, apart from these leading channels, a large number of additional platforms exist in different regions, offering many added opportunities to digital sports communication. Important examples are WeChat in China and VK in Russia; however, for reasons of time and space we will not discuss these in detail in this text.

4 Social media and sports journalism

The traditional role and function of sports journalism as a facilitator and moderator of themes for the public debate about sports has changed enormously by the rise of social media (Nölleke, Grimmer, and Horky 2017). The gatekeeper function has dissolved, as social networks are being employed by sports journalists in various ways. The most important changes can be summarized as follows:

Research: Social media have become increasingly important as tools for journalistic research, in particular in view of the growing distance between journalists and sports associations, clubs, and officials. Effectively, journalists are able to contact athletes directly, rather than going through their officials. Moreover, social media represent sources for additional information, and provide further issues for coverage. There is also a growing trend to using statements from tweets or other posts within social media and incorporating them into the coverage of the traditional media (Horky 2013; Wigley and Meirick 2008).

Collegiality: Social media networks provide a space for cooperative exchange. Working on major sports events in particular, journalists can access additional bits of information and share important issues for coverage through social media networks. Providing opportunities for journalists to connect with their colleagues and compare their work, social media networks can help re-examining research findings, reviewing one's own classification of themes, and checking facts (Hambrick et al. 2010).

Audience structure: Popular sports organizations are not the only ones using social media feeds to cater to their audiences. In order to distribute news and generate themes, niche sports likewise deploy channels such as, for instance, WebTV (livestreaming); thereby targeting a wider public. In the course of general trends like internationalization and commercialization, many professional sports clubs and major sports events have turned to setting up various accounts and profiles in social media networks (for instance, on Facebook) in different languages to engage with a larger audience. In similar ways, sports journalists can also increase their popularity and develop a distinctive brand identity for themselves by using such profiles (Hambrick 2012; Hambrick and Sanderson 2013).

Marketing: Social media are being employed as a space for issues of self-marketing, advertising, sponsoring, and product placement by the organizers of major sports events, by athletes, sports clubs, unions, and journalists alike. Aside from creating a specific image and maintaining a certain reputation, other goals of using social media include the monetization of communication, as sponsors in particular can gain access to specific target groups through social media channels (Pegoraro 2010; Williams and Chinn 2010).

Intimacy: The private and, in the case of some sports personalities, rather authentic form of communication with fans through social media outlets establishes a rare sense of intimacy and connectedness. This does not, or only rarely, apply to the more traditional forms of sports communication such as press conferences, for instance, which are usually characterized by cool professionalism and a certain personal restraint. In major sports events, the feature of intimacy can be used as a new form of communication. Seemingly more intimate and exclusive, sports journalism becomes more relevant by appearing even closer to the sport itself (Schultz and Sheffer 2010; Sheffer and Schultz 2010; Williams and Chinn 2010).

5 Historical overview of the use of social media in sports mega-events

5.1 FIFA World Cup

In 2010, the FIFA World Cup was the first major sports event worldwide to be recognized through social media on a grand scale. It was also the first event in which the new media was used deliberately as an innovative method of communication. The World Cup still featured hugely in traditional media outlets; however, the world's largest platform for social networks, Facebook, and the microblogging service Twitter were clearly at the forefront of media engagement with the event. Robin Sloan, then responsible for media partnerships at Twitter, claimed, "The World Cup will surpass anything we have seen before." Indeed, Twitter set up a distinctive theme page for the World Cup, containing a range of new features. Users were supplied with specific hashtags using World Cup graphs ("flag tags") for their communication; they were offered individual live feeds for the games and presented with lists containing top tweets about specific issues relating to the World Cup. Facebook, likewise, saw an overwhelming growth of the number of pages relating to the World Cup, and it seemed impossible at that time to gauge the implications (for instance, in terms of the number of fans reached). Graves (2010), indeed, noted a sharp rise in user frequency during the World Cup.

"Fans can unite via social media, and communicate in various ways," Matt Stone proclaimed, at that time Head of New Media at FIFA, the world football association (quoted in Horowitz 2010). FIFA itself launched its own World Cup club on their website which saw about five million members at the start of the tournament. Impressively, there were 250 million visits of about 150 million unique users and approximately seven billion page views on fifa.com during the entire World Cup (FIFA.com attracts 2010). Hence, the 2010 FIFA World Cup can be seen as the first social media World Cup in history (Horky 2013).

In contrast to Facebook with its strong emphasis on community, the key focus of Twitter as a social media tool lies on information. Indeed, Twitter experienced a massive growth of users in just a few years. During the World Cup of 2006, Twitter users amounted to only a few thousand; however, only four years later in 2010 there were already about 190 million people tweeting about 65 million times per day. Indeed, the 2010 World Cup made tweeting a worldwide phenomenon for the first time, as only 35 percent of users of the microblogging service were American citizens (Siegler 2010).

Twitter saw record numbers during the 2010 World Cup, which consolidated its position as the most important social media channel during major sports events. The US-based news channel CNN counted 300,000 tweets relating to the World Cup during the opening match between the national teams of South Africa and Mexico. There were some 150,000 tweets sent out per hour. Even more so, the number of tweets peaked to about 3,000 per second during the group stage whenever goals were scored, only surpassed by the NBA Finals taking place at the same time as the World Cup that year. On average, Twitter resumed to about 750 tweets per second (The World Cup 2010). For the first time, the hashtag #WorldCup made it on the list of the most used hashtags on Twitter worldwide, holding this position during the entire tournament.

Twitter is also of crucial importance when it comes to the distribution of information during major sports events, suggested by the large number of followers of the official account of the World Championships' Organizing Committee, the international football association FIFA. Josef (Sepp) Blatter was the first FIFA President to set up his own official Twitter account shortly before the start of the World Cup in 2010. Only a few days had passed when he already counted more than 50,000 followers. However, Blatter's tweets were rare and only focused on particular themes or events; moreover, they appeared as little more than public relations. He also did not respond to requests and left questions and discussions unanswered. FIFA launched a special World Cup 2010 service (@FIFAWorldCupTM) which quickly had about 130,000 followers; however, the different accounts' followers overlapped to a large extent.

The 2014 World Cup finals generated further evidence of the historical significance of Twitter to communication during major sports events. Scoring 618,725 tweets, the moment of the final whistle in the match between Germany and Argentina (1:0 after overtime) marked the most-commented-on moment in the history of Twitter in Germany (Horky and Grimmer 2014). New records were also set by Facebook at that time, as 350 million people provided for three billion interactions, equaling about 11 percent of the world's television viewers (FIFA Fussball-WM 2015).

5.2 Olympic Games

With regard to the Olympics, London 2012 marks the historical starting point of social media. "These games will be the first Social Media Olympics – the 'Socialympics,' they called it," Pfanner (2012) stated. By that time, the biggest social media platforms had been around for several previous Olympics, including the Beijing Summer Games of 2008 and the Vancouver Winter Games of 2010. But for the first time they were used in an official way by the International Olympic Committee (IOC).

In 2012, four years after the Beijing Games, use of social media platforms had spread widely. Since that time, Facebook went from about 100 million active users to about 900 million, and Twitter from six million to about 150 million. The use of smartphones and mobile communication possibilities rose to a higher level, so people increasingly reacted immediately to something they had seen in a stadium, arena, court, pool, ring, or velodrome. Clearly, the London Games were tweeted, tagged, liked, blogged, mashed, and rehashed like no previous Olympics (Pfanner 2012).

This development created new opportunities for the Olympic organizers, sponsors, participants, and spectators, most of all from a marketing point of view. At the Beijing Games, the IOC did not even have a coordinated social media presence. In 2012, it started for the first time the "Olympic Athletes' Hub," to help fans find and follow competitors' Twitter feeds and Facebook pages. The IOC also started its own Twitter account and Facebook page, as well as separate areas for the public and the news media. "We are at a dawn of a new age of sharing and connecting, and London 2012 will ignite the first conversational Olympic Games, thanks to social media platforms and technology," Alex Huot, the IOC's head of social media, said via e-mail (cited by Pfanner 2012).

During the London 2012 Games, Olympic sponsors began to communicate actively on social media too. Procter & Gamble unleashed a far-ranging social media initiative, as part of a broader marketing campaign called "Thank You, Mom," which highlights the behind-the-scenes roles that mothers play in the lives of Olympic athletes – and in the lives of lesser mortals (Pfanner 2012). This campaign debuted originally during the 2010 Winter Olympics in Canada and was refreshed for the 2014 Sochi and 2016 Rio Olympic Games. "Thank you, Mom" has been the most successful campaign in P&G's 175-year history. In 2012, the campaign was distributed on social, digital, and mobile via television spots, documentary-style films, by a mobile app, and, most of all, social networks like Facebook, Twitter, and YouTube (Medaling in media 2017; Procter & Gamble 2012).

5.3 The limitations of social media at sports mega-events

From the very beginning, the organizers of sports mega-events had strong reservations about social media, as did the unions, clubs, and associations. At first, the IOC and FIFA tried to regulate athletes', associations', and clubs' use of social networks, not least as a measure of protection of license holders' television broadcasting rights. Yet, in terms of the Olympics, this did not seem to be an issue of concern after the 2008 Olympic Games were granted to Beijing. "When the 2008 games took place in China, a country known for internet restrictions, YouTube, Twitter, and Facebook were still in their infancy," explained Wardle (2012: 1). In fact, for the 2010 Olympics in Vancouver the IOC set up so-called blogging guidelines for the first time (IOC Blogging 2009). Although these rules regulating the publication of photos, videos, and also news-like texts are updated regularly, any infringement of rules has rarely been severely dealt with. Many national Olympic associations, such as the German Olympic Sports Confederation DOSB, also hand out their own guidelines to accredited athletes.

FIFA issues similar guidelines each year, regulating the digital marketing of protected content. With regard to the 2018 final tournament in Russia, FIFA's media and marketing guidelines even entailed rather precise instructions about the correct use of digital media by teams and athletes (Media and marketing 2018).

In fact, such restrictions concerning the use of social media at major sports events are similar to the regulations in effect for two of the major professional sports leagues in the United States, the National Football League (NFL) and the National Basketball Association (NBA), as well as other sports leagues and sports events. For years now, participants have abided by the rules designed for the use of social media using mobile phones and other communication devices (Bowman and Cranmer 2014; Clavio et al. 2013; Martens 2011).

6 The current position of social media in sports mega-events

6.1 The 2016 Olympics in Rio de Janeiro

In light of the fundamental changes following the increasing digitalization of the media, it was not surprising that changes in viewing patterns also applied to the Olympics. London 2012 had already been pronounced the "first social Olympics" (Lee 2012, quoted from Li, Scott, and Dittmore 2018: 377) since communication through social networks had been a vital part of the Games. However, the 2016 Olympics in Rio de Janeiro exceeded this by reaching a higher range than ever before and as a result they were called the "most social Olympics" (Tang and Cooper 2018). In total, social media posts issued by the official channels of the IOC during the 2016 Olympics generated more than four billion visits (IOC Marketing 2017: 17). On the day of the closing ceremony in Rio, more than 50 million people followed the official channels of the IOC throughout all social networks, in particular Twitter, Facebook, Instagram, YouTube, and Google+ (Quirling, Kainz, and Haupt 2017: 168). Compared to 4.7 million followers by the end of London 2012, this represented a rise of 963 percent (London 2012 Facts 2012).

Even though Twitter's social media reach did not increase as much as that of other social networks, it still remains the most frequented social media platform during the Olympic Games. During the 2012 London Olympics, there were about 150 million tweets (Fitzgerald 2012). Four years later, more than 187 million tweets containing the official hashtag #Rio2016 were posted, generating 75 billion hits during the 16 contest days (Filadelfo 2016; Quirling, Kainz, and Haupt 2017; Hutchinson 2016, quoted in Li, Scott and, Dittmore 2018: 377). For the first time in the history of the Olympic Games, the 2016 hashtag became an official symbol of the Olympics and was registered a trademark – only eight years after the first hashtag for #Beijing2008 was introduced by fans (Barkho 2016).

Instagram, in particular, saw an enormous boom during the Olympics compared to 2012, which was clearly in line with the social network's general success worldwide. Previously, Instagram had played a minor role in official communication via social networks. During the 2016 Olympics, however, interactions to IOC posts on Instagram peaked to 913 million from 131 million users (Quirling, Kainz, and Haupt 2017: 168). Facebook saw a comparable increase as access numbers doubled compared to four years prior. 277 million Facebook users were active about 1.5 billion times during the 2016 Olympics (Quirling, Kainz, and Haupt 2017: 167).

Such enormous growth can, in part, be attributed to the fact that Rio 2016 established new ways of social interaction with recipients, outside of sporting competitions. The IOC established special fan profiles for symbols such as the Olympic Flame or the mascot of the games (IOC Marketing 2017: 129). Moreover, 15.2 million users embraced a new feature on Facebook and placed a specifically designed frame for the 2016 Olympics around their profile picture (Quirling, Kainz, and Haupt 2017: 167). Last but not least, it should be mentioned that the social networks offer an excellent platform for advertising services and sponsoring. During the 2016 Olympics, the IOC started a social media collaboration with the worldwide leading beverage producer Coca-Cola, thereby providing a space for athletes and fans to celebrate gold medals and other moments of happiness together. Indeed, the hashtag #ThatsGold generated about 500 million social media views and interactions, supported by Coca-Cola advertisements in print and television, and pushed by global influencers (IOC Marketing 2017: 46–49).

Social media has also increasingly impacted the moving image and broadcasting industry during the Olympic Games. Aside from 584 linear broadcasting stations, 270 online platforms as well as hundreds of officially licensed social media outlets covered the 2016 Olympics in Rio. In total, they supplied their audiences with more than 243,000 hours of digital and about 120,000 hours of linear moving image material. Indeed, the amount of digital coverage was about three times as high as during the 2012 Olympics in London, while the number of online users doubled. In total, videos officially produced for the 2016 Olympics were viewed about seven billion times throughout all social media networks (IOC Marketing 2017: 24).

Aiming at an even wider audience, the IOC attempted to expand their range of services with every Olympics. During the 2016 Games, the US broadcaster NBC shared its material with other media partners for the first time, thus multiplying its reach. Snapchat, an instant messaging service based on pictures, sought a contractual guarantee from NBC in order to exclusively post video compilations comprised of NBC material (Frier 2016; IOC Marketing 2017: 33). Similar arrangements were made by other media partners. For instance, the media company BuzzFeed was allowed to integrate NBC video material such as short sports videos and behind the scenes coverage to feed their own *Discover Channel* (Frier 2016). Through these new ways of communication viewers watched about 230 million minutes of video material and generated about 2.2 million additional views during the 2016 Olympics in Rio (IOC Marketing 2017: 33).

Contrary to widespread concerns, Tang and Cooper's research findings (2018) suggest that the extensive use of social networks complemented the more traditional forms of sports reporting and consumption around the Olympic Games, rather than replacing them. Drawing on this, managing director at the Olympic Broadcasting Services (OBS) Yiannis Exarchos is certain that "Rio has paved the way for the future of Olympic broadcasting" (IOC Marketing 2017: 28). Indeed, almost half of the entire world population viewed at least one video relating to the 2016 Olympics, thanks to the large variety of broadcasting via traditional media, internet, and social networks. This made Rio 2016 the most consumed Olympics of all times according to the IOC (2017: 23).

6.2 The 2018 FIFA World Cup in Russia

Similarly, the FIFA World Cup has seen an enormous rise in attention throughout social networks, culminating in the most recent World Cup in 2018. The International Federation of Association Football (FIFA) counted more than 580 million interactions and 7.5 billion views during the four-week tournament in Russia in 2018 (Russia 2018 most 2018) across all social networks. FIFA mainly focuses on the market-leading social networks Facebook, Instagram, and Twitter, yet some official profiles for the World Cup have also been set up and updated regularly on the Russian communication network VK and the Chinese providers Weibo or WeChat (Russia 2018 most 2018).

In total, the number of followers across rose up to the 10 million mark during the World Cup (Fans drive record 2018) and reached more than 120 million (FIFA.com 2018). FIFA also provided a Smartphone App in 2018 as an additional tool for interaction, which achieved number one status in terms of their download charts worldwide (Fans drive record 2018). FIFA called their historic reach during the 2018 World Cup groundbreaking in terms of the attention they received from their fans in the online world (Russia 2018 most 2018).

While Twitter mainly represented a tool for the exchange of opinions and served as a space for discussion about sports competitions, audiences on Facebook and Instagram focused on other topics. During the 2018 World Cup, Facebook users mainly shared their thoughts about individual matches and players and celebrated any victories of their favorite national teams (How the world 2018). Facebook also commissioned a study (2018) which found that 94 percent of the sports fans using Instagram sought to discover a more personal side of certain athletes (How the world 2018).

Similar to the 2016 Olympics, Twitter saw the most interactions between users during the FIFA World Cup 2018; hence, the platform remains the most important tool for digital communication. In 2018, Twitter's hashtag #WorldCup generated 115 million interactions linked to events around the tournament, all of which were issued directly before, during, or after the relevant event (Bavishi and Filadelfo 2018). On Facebook, 383 million football fans interacted during the four weeks of the tournament, and on Instagram, 272 million users posted content such as stories relating to the competition (How the world 2018).

Aside from connecting with fans via social networks, FIFA also established a range of concepts and innovations to aid social interaction during the World Cup in Russia. In order to communicate throughout all of the social networks in a timely manner at any time, individual online journalists for each of the 32 teams were assigned to cover official social media interaction by exclusively presenting FIFA content relating to the relevant teams they covered (Russia 2018 most 2018). A Community Manager for social media also assisted FIFA in answering more than 100,000 questions from fans directly (Fans drive record 2018).

However, there were further novelties outside of FIFA, too. Facebook launched a new "text delight" feature in celebration of the World Cup. Writing the word for "goal" as a text post or as a comment in any language, a little football appeared, racing across the screen accompanied by fireworks and applause. The animation was used 583 million times in total in posts and comments linked to the World Cup, despite the fact that it was only active during tournament days (Kortikar and Blair 2018).

Clearly both the traditional broadcasting sector and sports journalism were affected by these innovations and the enormous increase in social media reach during the 2018 World Cup. FIFA produced a wide range of videos including sports highlights, statistics, and behind-the-scenes coverage which were published via the official FIFA social media channels, reaching a total of 1.25 billion viewers and generating four million additional followers for the official YouTube channel (Russia 2018 most 2018). Representing the general development of broadcasting at the 2018 FIFA World Cup, the rights-holder and official broadcasting partner Fox Sports published every single goal scored in the tournament via the social networks in real time (Bavishi and Filadelfo 2018). Fox Sports also produced a live television show for the FIFA World Cup which took place on the Red Square in Moscow and was broadcast exclusively on Twitter. Indeed, the platform generated about 7.1 million viewers through this show (Bavishi and Filadelfo 2018). After the tournament, FIFA claimed that the large variety of social networks presence could be seen as the result of a number of digital initiatives launched before the competition, all of which aiming to intensify fans' engagement and sense of connectedness (Fans drive record 2018).

7 Conclusion

Sports communication during major sports events has been revolutionized by the rise of social media in many ways. Crucially, IOC and FIFA's own contents aid the associations' commercialization, help with sponsoring, and extend and stabilize an increasingly fragmented public. Sports mega-events are highlights of sports communication, illustrating the change of media technology and with that sports communication. The enormous growth of information, of comments, and conversational talks in the permanent flow on diverse social media platforms demonstrate some new ways for transmitting a major sports event to a broader public. It seems not the future of broadcasting, TV is still the biggest media channel for sports including the option for financing with marketing of licensing rights. But it is something like a permanent conversation or communication about sports which helps associations to faster and better distribute their own content, and as well marketing messages. Emphazising this, social media has changed sports communication not only during major sports events.

In recent years, the work of sports journalists has changed enormously through social media (Nölleke, Grimmer, and Horky 2017), and it seems difficult to predict where the development towards an increasing digitalization is taking us. Representing the growing importance of self-production and distribution of content via social media by the organizers of major sports events, the IOC launched their own Olympic Channel directly after the 2016 Olympics in Rio, sporting the slogan "Where the Games never end" (www.olympicchannel.com). A new, continuous Olympic media outlet, this self-operated online portal from both IOC and television rights' holders' issues livestream videos, photos, and texts, thus combining the work of the editorial office in Madrid (Spain) with a range of social media accounts on Facebook, Twitter, and Instagram (Spangler 2016).

This seems just one more initial step in the direction of what can be called the *socialization of sports communication* at major sports events. On the one hand, sports communication is tracing back to the public by individual commenting on social media called "second screening," and individual streaming via platforms like Twitch. On the other hand, new media technology like AR, VR, and 360-degree replay heads sports communication towards a virtualization and social experience of major events. This difference of individual and virtual sports communication can be combined on social media platforms (Hebbel-Seeger and Horky 2019).

Summarizing these developments, social media at sports mega-events still needs to be researched, in the future adding new topics and emphasizing new questions: What social messages get the most attention and most of all the most credibility? How are themes in a broader understanding influenced by the social conversation during major sports events? What is the impact of new social platforms and ways of communicating on major sports events, athletes, associations, and sports journalists? We believe, with the development of social media at major sports events, sports communication has first entered a digital era, and now changed again into a virtual communication for individual experiences.

References

Barkho, Gabriela. 2016. How social media changed the Olympics, and what it means for #Rio2016. *Later*, 11 August. https://later.com/blog/how-social-media-changed-the-olympics-and-rio-2016/ (28 August 2019).

Bavishi, Jay & Elaine Filadelfo. Insights into the 2018 #WorldCup conversation on Twitter. *Twitter*, 17 July. https://blog.twitter.com/en_us/topics/events/2018/2018-World-Cup-Insights.html (29 August 2019).

Bowman, Nicholas D. & Cranmer, Gregory. A. 2014. SocialMediaSport: The fan as a (mediated) participant in spectator sports. In Andrew C. Billings & Marie Hardin (eds.), *Routledge handbook of sport and new media*, 213–224. New York: Routledge.

Burk, Verena & Christoph G. Grimmer. 2016. Die Fußball-WM 2014 im fokus der sozialen medien – information, partizipation, interaktion. In Holger Ihle, Michael Meyen, Jürgen Mittag & Jörg-Uwe Nieland (eds.), Die WM *2014 in Brasilien im Blickfeld der kommunikations- und politikwissenschaftlichen Forschung*, 83–106. Wiesbaden: Springer VS.

Chaffey, Dave. 2020. Global social media research summary 2020. *Smart Insights*, 17 April. https://www.smartinsights.com/social-media-marketing/social-media-strategy/new-global-social-media-research/ (17 April 2020).

Clavio, Galen, Joshua Bowles, Ryan Vooris & Paul Pedersen. 2013. The integration of social media and sport: Perspectives and examples from the United States. In Andreas. Hebbel-Seeger & Thomas Horky (eds.), *Crossmediale Kommunikation und Verwertung von Sportveranstaltungen*, 59–72. Aachen: Meyer & Meyer.

Clavio, Galen & Evan Frederick. 2014. Sharing is caring: An exploration of motivations for social sharing and locational social media usage among sport fans. *Journal of Applied Sport Management* 6(2). 70–85.

Clavio, Galen & Patrick Walsh. 2014. Dimensions of social media utilization among college sport fans. *Communication & Sport* 2(3). 261–281.

Fans drive record digital interest in FIFA World Cup. 2018. *FIFA.com*, 29 June. https://www.fifa.com/worldcup/news/fans-drive-record-digital-interest-in-fifa-world-cup (30 August 2019).

FIFA.com attracts over a quarter of a billion visits as the world engages online with the 2010 FIFA World Cup. 2010. *FIFA.com*, 13 July. http://www.fifa.com/worldcup/organisation/media/newsid=1273696/index.html#fifa+attracts+over+quarter+billion+visits+world+engages+online+with+2010+cup (22 November 2020).

FIFA Fussball-WM 2014™: 3,2 Milliarden Zuschauer, 1 Milliarde beim Finale. 2015. FIFA.com, 16 December. http://de.fifa.com/worldcup/news/y=2015/m=12/news=fifa-fussball-wm-2014tm-3-2-milliarden-zuschauer-1-milliarde-beim-fina-2745551.html (3 October 2017).

Filadelfo, Elaine. 2016 The #Rio2016 Twitter data recap. *Twitter*, 22 August. https://blog.twitter.com/official/en_us/a/2016/the-rio2016-twitter-data-recap.html (27 August 2019).

Fitzgerald, Andrew. 2012. Olympic (and Twitter) records. *Twitter*, 13 August. https://blog.twitter.com/official/en_us/a/2012/olympic-and-twitter-records.html (28 August 2019).

Frederick, Evan, Choonghoon Lim, Galen Clavio & Patrick Walsh. 2012. Why we follow: An examination of parasocial interaction and fan motivations for following athlete archetypes on Twitter. *International Journal of Sport Communication* 5(4). 481–502.

Frier, Sarah. 2016. Snapchat scores unique deal with NBC to showcase Olympics. *Bloomberg*, 29 April. https://www.bloomberg.com/news/articles/2016-04-29/snapchat-scores-unprecedented-deal-with-nbc-to-showcase-olympics (28 August 2019).

Gibbs, Chris, Norm O'Reilly & Michelle Brunette. 2014. Professional team sport and Twitter: Gratifications sought and obtained by followers. *International Journal of Sport Communication* 7(2). 188–213.

Graves, Matt. 2010. The 2010 World Cup: A global conversation. *Twitter*, 15 July. http://blog.twitter.com/2010/07/2010-world-cup-global-conversation.html (22 November 2020).

Hambrick, Marion E. 2012. Six degrees of information: Using social network analysis to explore the spread of information within sport social networks. *International Journal of Sport Communication* 5(1). 16–34.

Hambrick, Marion E. & Jimmy Sanderson. 2013. Gaining primacy in the digital network: Using social network analysis to examine sports journalists' coverage of the Penn State football scandal via Twitter. *Journal of Sports Media* 8(1). 1–18.

Hambrick, Marion E., Jason M. Simmons, Greg Greenhalgh & Chris Greenwell. 2010. Understanding professional athletes' use of Twitter: A content analysis of athlete tweets. *International Journal of Sport Communication* 3(4). 454–471.

Hebbel-Seeger, Andreas & Thomas Horky. 2019. Patterns, trends, and crystal-ball gazing. In John McGuire, Greg G. Armfield & Adam Earnheardt (eds.), *ESPN and the changing sports media landscape*, 337–356. New York: Peter Lang.

Horky, Thomas. 2013. Sportveranstaltungen und social media – chancen, risiken, regelungen und crossmediale thematisierung: Die Fußball-Weltmeisterschaft und die Olympischen Spiele in den neuen medien. In Andreas Hebbel-Seeger & Thomas Horky (eds.), *Crossmediale kommunikation und verwertung von sportveranstaltungen*, 134–159. Aachen: Meyer & Meyer.

Horky, Thomas & Christoph G. Grimmer. 2014. The football World Cup 2010 in the German media: Presenting and constructing a major sporting event. In Tendai Chari & Nhamo A. Mhiripiri (eds.), *African football, identity politics and global media narratives. The legacy of the FIFA 2010 World Cup*, 207–230. Houndmills: Palgrave Macmillan.

Horowitz, Etan. 2010. South Africa's World Cup to drive record social media traffic. *CNN.com*, 4 May. http://edition.cnn.com/2010/SPORT/football/04/26/football.world.cup.social/index.html (22 November 2020).

How the world cheered football's finest on Facebook and Instagram. 2018. *Facebook*, 16 July. https://www.facebook.com/business/news/insights/how-the-world-cheered-footballs-finest-on-facebook-and-instagram (30 August 2019).

IOC Blogging Guidelines. 2009. International *Olympic Committee*. http://www.olympic.org/Documents/Reports/EN/en_report_1433.pdf (22 November 2020).

IOC Marketing Report Rio 2016. 2017. International *Olympic Committee*, 9 February. https://stillmed.olympic.org/media/Document%20Library/OlympicOrg/Games/Summer-Games/Games-Rio-2016-Olympic-Games/Media-Guide-for-Rio-2016/IOC-Marketing-Report-Rio-2016.pdf (20 September 2019).

Kortikar, Rujuta & Nick Blair. GOOOOOOAL! How Fans Came Together to Celebrate on Facebook. *Facebook*, 18 July. https://newsroom.fb.com/news/2018/07/insidefeed-soccer-text-animations/ (30 August 2019).

Li, Bo, Olan K. Scott & Stephen W. Dittmore. 2018. Twitter and Olympics. *International Journal of Sport Marketing and Sponsorship* 19(4). 370–383.

London 2012 Facts and Figures. 2012. *World Archery*, 23 November. https://worldarchery.org/news/101308/london-2012-facts-and-figures (27 August 2019).

Martens, René. 2011. Social Sport? Wie sich Berichterstattung und Rechtelage im Zeitalter von Twitter, Flickr und Smartphones verändert haben. In Dietrich Leder & Hans-Ulrich Wagner (eds.), *Sport und medien. Eine deutsch-deutsche geschichte*, 204–220. Köln: Halem.

Medaling in media: P&G proud sponsor of mom. 2017. *ANA Educational Foundation*, February. https://www.aef.com/wp-content/uploads/2017/02/award-2013chiat-pg-olympic-sponsor-case.pdf (11 June 2020).

Media and marketing regulations for the 2018 FIFA World Cup Russia. 2018. *FIFA.com*. https://resources.fifa.com/image/upload/media-and-marketing-regulations-for-the-2018-fifa-world-cup-2922838.pdf?cloudid=dbibgs0syrpkdbzbgbxr (15 September 2019).

Nölleke, Daniel, Christoph G. Grimmer & Thomas Horky. 2017. News sources and follow-up communication: Facets of complementarity between sports journalism and social media. *Journalism Practice* 11(4). 509–526.

Pegoraro, Ann. 2010. Look who's talking – athletes on Twitter: A case study. *International Journal of Sport Communication 3*(4). 501–514.

Pfanner, Eric. 2012. Social media is the message for Olympics. *New York Times*, 1 July. https://www.nytimes.com/2012/07/02/technology/social-media-is-the-message-for-olympics.html (13 September 2019).

Procter & Gamble launches global "Thank you Mom" campaign in celebration of 100 days to go until the London 2012 Olympic Games. 2012. *Business Wire*, 17 April. https://www.businesswire.com/news/home/20120417006777/en/Procter-Gamble-Launches-Global-%E2%80%98Thank-You-Mom%E2%80%99-Campaign-in-Celebration-of-100-days-to-go-until-the-London-2012-Olympic-Games (22 November 2020).

Quirling, Christian, Florian Kainz & Tobias Haupt. 2017. Vermarktung und kommunikation. In Christian Quirling, Florian Kainz & Tobias Haupt (eds.), *Sportmanagement: Ein anwendungsorientiertes lehrbuch mit praxisbeispielen und fallstudien*, 167–174. München: Vahlen.

Russia 2018 most engaging FIFA World Cup ever. 2018. *FIFA.com*, 20 July. https://www.fifa.com/worldcup/news/russia-2018-most-engaging-fifa-world-cup-ever (29 August 2019).
Sanderson, Jimmy. 2011. *It's a whole new ball game: How social media is changing sports.* New York: Hampton Press.
Schultz, Brad & Mary Lou Sheffer. 2010. An exploratory study of how Twitter is affecting sports journalism. *International Journal of Sport Communication 3*(2). 226–239.
Sheffer, Mary Lou & Brad Schultz. 2010. Paradigm shift or passing fad? Twitter and sports journalism. *International Journal of Sport Communication 3*(4). 472–484.
Siegler, M. G. Tweeeeeeeeeeeeeet! Twitter has a way to show off your World Cup allegiances. *Tech Crunch*, 10 June. http://techcrunch.com/2010/06/10/twitter-world-cup/ (22 November 2020).
Smith, Lauren Reichart & Jimmy Sanderson. 2015. I'm going to Instagram it! An analysis of athlete self-presentation on Instagram. *Journal of Broadcasting & Electronic Media* 59(2). 342–358.
Spangler, Todd. 2016. IOC sets post-Rio launch for Olympic Channel free over-the-top video service. *Variety*, 27 July. https://variety.com/2016/digital/news/ioc-launch-olympics-channel-ott-1201824707/ (19 September 2019).
Tang, Tang & Roger Cooper. 2018. The most social games: Predictors of social media uses during the 2016 Rio Olympics. *Communication & Sport* 6(3). 308–330.
The World Cup was huge on Twitter. 2010. *Mashable*, 14 July. http://mashable.com/2010/07/13/world-cup-twitter-chart/ (22 November 2020).
Wallace, Laci, Jacquelyn Wilson & Kimberly Miloch. 2011. Sporting Facebook: A content analysis of NCAA organizational sport pages and Big 12 Conference athletic department pages. *International Journal of Sport Communication* 4(4). 422–444.
Wardle, Claire. 2012. Social media, newsgathering and the Olympics. *JOMEC Journal* 2. 1–13.
Wenner, Lawrence A. & Andrew C. Billings (eds.). 2017. *Sport, media and mega-events.* New York: Routledge.
Whiteside, Erin. A. 2014. New media and the changing role of sports information. In Andrew C. Billings & Marie Hardin (eds.), *Routledge handbook of sport and new media*, 143–152. New York: Routledge.
Wigley, Shelley & Patrick C. Meirick. 2008. Interactive media and sports journalists: The impact of interactive media on sports journalists. *Journal of Sports Media 3*(1). 1–25.
Williams, Jo & Susan J. Chinn. 2010. Meeting relationship-marketing goals through social media: A conceptual model for sport marketers. *International Journal of Sport Communication 3*(4). 422–437.

Amber Roessner

39 Ghosted gods: commodifying celebrities, decrying wraiths, and contesting graven images

Abstract: Contemporary athletes have turned to social media and digital sites such as the *Players' Tribune* in ways that have revived the practice of ghostwriting, raising questions about journalism ethics and the potential of (un)filtered material to offer critical insights into problematic behind-the-scenes conditions in professional baseball. This study analyzes archival materials and ancillary primary sources related to ghosted material in the first half of the 20th century in top-circulating US sports magazines, newspaper sports sections, and the industry trade press. It explores the evolution of ghostwriting in baseball journalism and autobiographies throughout the course of the 20th century and focuses special attention on three interrelated developments – the commodification of celebrity images through ghostwriting; the debate over the ethics of ghostwriting in sports journalism amid industry professionalization and credibility crises; and the practice of deploying ghostwriting to contest dominant narratives in sports journalism and to critique problematic behind-the-scenes conditions in Major League baseball. While ethical considerations should remain at the center of the century-long debate over ghostwriting in journalism, collaborations between star ballplayers and sports journalists that once offered symbiotic financial gain to newspaper publishers, sportswriters, and celebrity-athletes remain a productive means to contest dominant narratives in sports journalism and to expose problematic conditions in professional baseball.

Keywords: ghostwriting; baseball; heroes; journalism; ethics, professionalization; advocacy

1 Introduction: his words, his very own?

"Who is writing Yaz' stuff?" columnist Victor O. Jones, referring to Boston Red Sox leftfielder Carl Yastrzemski, asked sports editor Fran Rosa in passing one late summer morning at the *Globe*'s headquarters on Morrissey Boulevard (Jones 1967: 61). "Vic, you probably won't believe this, but Yaz is writing it all by himself, with no more editorial assistance than Clif Keane or you get from the copy desk."

Earlier that summer, Jones, still a sportswriter at heart, watched in shock as the team, which had been perennial cellar-dwellers when he was hired on at the *Globe* in 1929 and had finished in the bottom half of the American League for the prior eight years, fired off ten consecutive victories after the break, behind the phenom-

https://doi.org/10.1515/9783110660883-039

enal performance of Yastrzemski, their team captain, to ignite the Red Sox Nation (Victor O. Jones 1970; Moskowitz 2017). Though the world around him was transforming before his eyes, one thing had not changed, or at least so Jones thought. Based upon the common-sense logic that the American public still craved dope on celebrity athletes, newspaper publishers paired star players, such as Yastrzemski, who was on the way to his best season in baseball, featuring Golden Glove and Major League Player of the Year honors (Swartz 2008), with ghostwriters to collaborate on behind-the-scenes stories (Carvalho, Chung, and Koliska 2018; Roessner 2014). Not dissimilar to the process *Players' Tribune* editorial director Gary Hoenig confessed to sportswriters nearly five decades later (Bucholtz 2015), Rosa's disclosure that Yaz dictated to a tape-recorder, the contents of which were later transcribed word-for-word and lightly copyedited, shocked Jones. And he determined that the anomalous revelation of authentic player authorship warranted space, alongside a brief amateur history of the practice of ghostwriting in sports journalism, in his popular "Notes from the Back of an Envelope" column (Jones 1967).

Within his regular ten-inch contribution, Jones (1967) cursorily acknowledged the symbiotic financial motives that prompted the rise of ghostwriting in baseball reporting to fulfill the perceived public demand for behind-the-scenes glimpses into the lives of celebrity sports stars in the early 20th century and the advancement of the ethics in ghostwriting underway amid the emergence of another credibility crisis in professional journalism (Pressman 2018). But he neglected to consider the discourse over labor and economic competition underlying prior debates centered on the ethics of ghostwriting in sports journalism and the new wave of ghosted material that critiqued behind-the-scenes conditions in Major League baseball.

However, these omissions were hardly shocking. Jones's writing reflected a long tradition of commemorations of ghostwriting by gee-whiz sports journalists (Mandell 1984; Roessner 2010; Roessner 2014), who offered historical context about origins of the practice while simultaneously mythologizing baseball's ghosts (i. e., Dyer 1960; King and Spink 1958; McGeehan 1929; Menke 1938; Povich 1946, 1950, 1955; Rice 1940; Spink 1931, 1942, 1944; Walsh 1938a, 1938b, 1938c; Wheeler 1934, 1947, 1949, 1958). Aside from these amateur histories and ancillary scholarship in book history on the origins of ghostwriting (Freeman 2010; Johanningsmeier 2002; Lavin 2016), the widespread practice in sports journalism has received scant treatment, with the locus of attention concentrated on discourse over ethical implications involved in acts that transpired in the Jazz Age and the age of social media (Carvalho 2007; Carvalho, Chung, and Koliska 2018).

In the last decade, celebrity athletes, such as former New York Yankees shortstop Derek Jeter, following in the tradition of Yastrzemski, as well as others such as New York Giants pitcher Christy Mathewson and Brooklyn Dodgers infielder Jackie Robinson, have sought to connect directly to their fans, in their own words, through social media and digital sites, such as the *Players' Tribune*, and the practice of ghostwriting has once again become the focal point of media industry discourse surrounding journalism ethics and the potential of (un)filtered material to offer critical insights into problematic behind-the-scenes conditions in professional baseball (Carvalho, Chung, and Koliska 2018). This study analyzes archival materials and ancillary primary sources related to two major sports news syndicates that dealt in ghosted material in the first half of the 20th century and more than 450 articles in top-circulating US sports magazines, newspaper sports sections, and the industry trade press. After briefly situating ghostwriting in the tradition of hack writing that corresponded with the disembedding of American authorship in the last half of the 19th century (Jackson 2008; Lavin 2016), this chapter explores the evolution of ghostwriting in baseball journalism and autobiographies throughout the course of the 20th century. This chapter focuses special attention on three interrelated developments – the commodification of celebrity images through ghostwriting; the debate over the ethics of ghostwriting in sports journalism amid industry professionalization and credibility crises; and the practice of deploying ghostwriting to contest dominant narratives in sports journalism and problematic behind-the-scenes conditions in Major League baseball.[1] In the end, this chapter contends that, while ethical considerations should remain at the center of the century-long debate over ghostwriting in journalism, collaborations between star ballplayers and sports journalists that once offered symbiotic financial gain to newspaper publishers, sportswriters, and celebrity-athletes remain a productive means to contest dominant narratives in sports journalism and to expose problematic conditions in professional baseball.

2 Shrouded in mystery: exposing hack-writing wraiths, unveiling specter-specializing syndicates

Referred to as the second oldest profession, ghostwriting – or compensation for material written without primary credit on behalf of another – has been traced to ancient times, when illiterate and semiliterate members of the poorer working classes paid public scriveners to prepare official manuscripts (Lavin 2016). This practice, later referred to as "wordsmithing," which included the penning of first-person letters and speeches, continued unabated in public communication through the age of crafts-

1 This chapter involves analysis of primary source and archival materials related to John Wheeler and Christy Walsh's syndicates, housed at Columbia University and the National Baseball Hall of Fame Library, alongside more than 450 articles in top-circulating baseball magazines (n=159), such as the *Sporting Life* (1883–1917, 1922–1924); the *Sporting News* (1886–present), the longest continuously published sports magazine; and *Baseball Magazine* (1908–1957); top-circulating newspapers (n=302), such as the *Atlanta Constitution*, the *Baltimore Sun*, the *Boston Globe*, the *Chicago Tribune*, the *Hartford Courant*, the *New York Times*, the *Los Angeles Times*, and the *Washington Post*; and industry trade publications (n=12), such as *Editor & Publisher* and the *Columbia Journalism Review*.

men's literacy that characterized the 16th through the 18th centuries (Carvalho, Chung, and Koliska. 2018; Lavin 2016).

However, modern ghostwriting – or "ghostwriting in the context of modern authorial individualism," as Lavin (2016: 237) described it – accompanied the rise of authorial professionalization in the 19th century and increasingly occurred through an unspecified market-dominant exchange between professional freelance and hack writers and individuals possessing narrative material in public demand. Since both parties benefited from the opacity involved in the practice and thus had a vested interest in keeping these symbiotic relationships obscure, the origins of the profession of ghostwriting have been challenging to pinpoint. However, Lavin (2016) traced the emergence of the profession to the 1880s when the term "ghost" evolved to refer to "one who secretly does artistic or literary work for another person, the latter taking the credit" (237). As Lavin (2016) contends, accounts from aging ghosts appearing in the popular press in the 1930s (Hartt 1933) attested to a burgeoning profession in the 1890s. Moreover, by the dawn of the Jazz Age, due largely to publisher demand for autobiographical accounts that they believed audiences craved, ghostwriting had become "one of the most profitable fields for the free lancer and hack writer" in the book publishing, journalistic, and ancillary public communication industries (Lavin 2106: 238). Within these related industries, savvy entrepreneurs established syndicates and agencies that specialized in the production and distribution of ghosted material (Bormann 1956; Boyle 1959; Carvalho, Chung, and Koliska 2018; Hudson and Boyajy 2009; Roessner 2014).

Although the presence of ghostwriting in the world of sport media was well-acknowledged by the early 20th century, dean of sportswriters Grantland Rice yearned to learn the identity of the first ghost writer in sports journalism (Rice 1940). As one of the leading – and thus, one of the best paid – New York-based sports journalists throughout much of his four-decade career, Rice did not entertain a gig as a ghostwriter, but he encountered professional ghosts – mostly low-paid, green sports reporters, many of whom he considered to be chums, looking for extra income through the side hustle – on a regular basis in the nation's press boxes, especially during World Series time (Roessner 2014; Smythe 1980). Moreover, in the prior decade, he witnessed a surge of aging ghosts, such as "America's foremost sports writer" Frank G. Menke and syndicate owners John N. Wheeler and Christy Walsh, coming forward to divulge their spectral careers and to otherwise reminisce about their roles in mythologizing star ballplayers (i. e., Menke 1938; Walsh 1938a, 1938b, 1938c; Wheeler 1934). Nevertheless, he was still left with one nagging question: "who was the first ghost writer in sport" (Rice 1940: 2B).

As one might suspect, the answer to Rice's question is not simple, nor is it precise. The emergence of professional ghostwriters surrounding baseball accompanied the rise in popularity of the professional game and publisher demands for first-person stories about its top athletes based on perceived public interest. By the mid-1880s, professional baseball boasted one such superstar: Chicago White Stocking outfielder Mike

"King" Kelly was "as a drawing card ... the greatest of his time," acknowledged one of baseball's first historians MacLean Kennedy (Appel 1996: 45). Nor did his popularity wane after his trade to the Boston Beaneaters in 1887. And, interested in cashing in on his success, he enlisted his pal, *Boston Globe* sports reporter John J. Drohan, to help him "prepare" *Play Ball: Stories of the Diamond Field* to be sold to local book publishing house Emory & Hughes, which published the volume designed to appeal to boys and young men for 25 cents per copy in 1888 (Cullen and Taylor 1889: 316; Riess 1999; Rosenberg 2004). By the following decade, both ghosted and authentic athlete-bylined (or, as it was commonly referred to in the era, player-author) material were regular features in newspaper sports pages and in specialty sports magazines (Carvalho 2014; Roessner 2014). Moreover, by the dawn of the 20th century, professional ghostwriters – with identities only destined to be divulged through reporting around labor controversies and collective memories of their acts – dotted the press boxes of baseball grounds.

3 Wordsmiths cash in on the craze for spooked player-author material and debate the specter of phantoms in sports journalism

In the early 20th century, publisher demands for player-author material, which many attributed to an uptick in circulation, were vast (Peet 1913), but the presence of star ballplayers, such as Cleveland sportswriter-ace Adrian "Addie" Joss, with the interest and ability to churn out copy was an anomaly. Thus, amid the continued demand for content similar to the material the Naps hurler churned out for the *Cleveland Press* during the 1907–1909 World Series and offseasons, publishers often turned to ghostwriters – primarily underpaid sportswriters on their existing payrolls who were eager to make a few extra bucks – to supply in demand copy (Roessner 2014).

In 1910, for instance, after finishing third in the American League pennant race behind the Philadelphia Athletics and the New York Highlanders, Detroit Tigers star centerfielder Ty Cobb and pitcher George Mullin teamed up with two ghosts – Joe S. Jackson of the *Detroit Free Press* and William James MacBeth of the *New York American*, respectively – to offer their expert analysis to Detroit and New York newspaper readers. In a later moment of commemorative mythmaking, *New York Herald-Tribune* sports columnist W. O. McGeehan described the typical collaborative approach common in the era: an informal session about the athlete's take, if the star could be found. When, as occurred on this occasion, the star athlete arrived late, he might find his copy already sent to the desk editor without his consent. And, in such cases, he might soon discover this was the process for "how prophets are made" – as did Mullin when true to MacBeth's account he accurately predicted the underdog Athletics would win the series (McGeehan 1929: 24).

By the opener of the following season's World Series between the Athletics and the New York Giants, the press box at the Polo Grounds was littered with star athletes and managers, such as Cobb and Detroit manager Hugh Jennings, and their ghosts. Among them was the *New York Herald*'s baseball beat writer John N. Wheeler, who, at the request of publisher Frank Gordon Bennett, Jr., signed on famed hurler Christy Mathewson after the Giants clinched the National League championship in Cincinnati to "cover" the series for $500 – a sizeable sum to be accrued while playing professional baseball for an annual salary of $10,000 (Roessner 2014). Mathewson agreed. Over the next three weeks, Wheeler collaborated with Mathewson to deliver daily columns about the 1905 World Series rematch. "Big Six supplied all the material, and I ran it through the typewriter, and it made a hit," Wheeler recalled, acknowledging that their copy ran in newspapers across the nation (Gerrity 1973; Philips 1973: 40; Wheeler 1961: 11–13). Though some writers simply signed their names below columns of ghosted material, Mathewson almost always shared his ideas, "even if he did none of the actual writing," Wheeler divulged, reaffirming Mathewson's moral and ethical compass, in a moment when, amid a Depression-induced downturn in the profession, ghostwriters began to "tell all" (Wheeler 1934: B3).

In the ensuing two decades, however, media publishers and syndicates, such as McClure's, which sold material to publishers, were eager to profit from perceived consumer demand for human-interest journalism, most notably behind-the-scenes, first-person narratives that appeared under celebrity bylines (Ponce de Leon 2002). In the offseason, Wheeler and Mathewson capitalized on the plum financial opportunity by engaging in a collaboration that involved the exchange of symbolic and economic capital for a weekly first-person series of "Inside Baseball" columns for McClure's Newspaper Syndicate that successfully commodified Mathewson's image as a Christian Gentleman (Lavin 2016; Roessner 2014). Recognizing the popularity of the series, which was published inside of *Sporting News* and on the sports pages of major national newspapers, Wheeler compiled and edited the columns into a memoir that combined inside baseball tidbits with his version of the mythic narrative of a hero's journey that seemed to be lifted straight from a Frank Merriwell dime novel. Moreover, amid the financial reorganization of the McClure Publishing Company, he sold *Pitching in a Pinch* to the New York-based G. P. Putnam's Sons, who released the volume with a cover price of one dollar in spring 1912.

In a move typical of the era, Wheeler's role in ghosting the volume remained concealed (Lavin 2016), but he did everything in his power to ensure the book's success – crafting an effusive introduction for the "breezy" account that likened Mathewson to the nation's first hero, George Washington, and penning a gushing review for the *New York Herald*'s book editor James Ford, thereby crossing every ethical line by today's standards (Roessner 2014: 129). Based upon the book's popularity, Putnam's Sons released two subsequent editions of the memoir under subsidiary publishing houses – Grossett & Dunlap's children's division and the Boy Scouts of America's Every Boy's Library. Thereafter, Wheeler confirmed plans to ghost World Series material for eight baseball stars and to engage in a work of image repair for Cobb, who sought to circumvent adversarial sportswriters by going public – a practice that continued throughout the 20th century until the present moment (Jeter 2014; Littwin 1980; Roessner 2014).

Through the process, Wheeler recognized that huge sums stood to be made from non-fiction material about celebrity athletes, but as the ghost, he had seen little of the profit (Roessner 2014; Spink 1942; Wheeler 1934). Thus, when his managers at the *New York Herald* refused his request for a basic raise in 1913, he embarked on a new venture, later acknowledging, "Early in my life, I decided I could make a bigger profit by selling other men's brains than my own, and so far I don't think I have ever found myself wrong" (Philips 1973: 40). With aid from two financial backers, he established Wheeler Syndicate, initially specializing in sports features, material provided by sports journalists and celebrities based upon a gentleman's agreement (a handshake or a nod). However, the syndicate soon expanded to become a comprehensive news clearinghouse, featuring the work of pioneering cartoonists Bud Fisher and Fontaine Fox, among others (Gerrity 1973; Philips 1973; Wheeler 1961).

In the midst of brewing wars overseas and at home in the Major Leagues, Wheeler selected an opportune time to expand his syndicate's offerings. As celebrity athletes such as Mathewson and Cobb advocated for more professional autonomy and personal profits from their talents (Roessner 2014; Wiggins 2008; Wilbert 2007), league magnates balked. When, for instance, New York Yankees owner Frank Farrell complained about the controversial player-author practice that served to dupe readers and create clubhouse strife in early 1913, American League President Ban Johnson publicly condemned the practice, involving the acceptance of "soft money" in the *Sporting Life*, one of the nation's oldest specialty sports magazines, and forbade American League players from further engaging in the act (Farrell 1913; Johnson 1913: 8; Peet, 1913: 8). Moreover, after a *Sporting Life*'s investigative exposé that revealed many athletes and sportswriters were engaged in the transgression and amid muckraking calls for greater industry professionalization after waves of sensationalism and propaganda (Creech and Roessner 2018; Nord 2008), two New York-based chapters of the Base Ball Writers' Association of America denounced ghostwriters for ethical misconduct that served to "deceive the Base ball reading public [and] to lower the tone and dignity of the sport" (Herrmann 1913: 14).

Nevertheless, a great paradox remained: many of those who denounced ghostwritten accounts engaged in or otherwise profited from the practice of expert-bylined content. Moreover, recognizing the hypocrisy of these prominent individuals in the industry and a discourse around ethics in sports journalism that masked fears over economic disruption from competition in labor that played out with the establishment of the Baseball Players' Fraternity and the rival Federal League (1913–1915), many star athletes and their ghosts continued with the practice, only temporarily heeding the National Commission's edict forbidding World Series participants from engaging in the act (Roessner 2014).

Recognizing this new volatility surrounding "the ghosting business" in baseball, Wheeler focused on distributing news, columns, features, and comic strips produced by national icons, such as Theodore Roosevelt, and celebrity-journalists, such as Richard Harding Davis, with Wheeler Syndicate. And, when amid an internal dispute between Wheeler and his partners McClure's Newspaper Syndicate absorbed the competing entity in 1916, the news entrepreneur immediately established the rival Bell Syndicate. Thereafter, over the course of the next half century, Bell Syndicate was absorbed – alongside McClure's – into the North American Newspaper Alliance, where Wheeler served as an executive until he retired at the age of 78 in 1965 (Spink 1942: 9; Philips 1973). "As things progressed, thinking it was bad journalism and bordering on faking, we got away from ghostwritten stuff in the syndicate business," Wheeler (1934: B3) later divulged. "When a man didn't do the job himself, we carried the line 'as told to.' But we probably made a mistake because ghostwriting seems to be more prevalent today than ever – not only among ball players, prize fighters, and other athletes, but also among politicians, bankers, actors and so on."

Wheeler's momentary regret was triggered by the recognition that another shrewd entrepreneur had cashed in on the demand for ghostwritten material. After international conflict subsided, former advertising agent Christy Walsh recognized a vibrant market still existed for ghostwritten material, and he "picked [the ghosting syndicate business] up for a big revival, with New York Yankees slugger Babe Ruth, [New York Giants manager John] McGraw, Cobb ... and other heroes," Wheeler (1942: 8) recalled.[2] Recognized by Carvalho and colleagues as establishing the "first agency of its kind, syndicating ghostwritten sports articles" (2018: 4), Walsh in fact stepped in where Wheeler left off by establishing the Christy Walsh Syndicate after securing Babe Ruth as his first client (with a case of beer) in 1921.[3] Walsh ultimately boasted netting approximately $100,000 for the thirty-four ghosts on his payroll during his 16-year career as a syndicator.

Nevertheless, amid a second wave of controversy surrounding player-author material surrounding the World Series in the mid-1920s, he encountered vigorous industry debate over ghostwriting similar in tenor to the discourse that prompted Wheeler to move away from the practice a decade prior (Carvalho 2008; Carvalho, Chung, and Koliska 2018; Roessner 2014). For his part, however, he responded to organizational rebukes from the *Washington Post* and the Base Ball Writers' Association of America over ethical improprieties involved in ghostwriting by asking those who had not

2 After a five-year stint with the International News Service, Wheeler's rival ghost, "Six-Man Menke," also recognized a vibrant market still existed for ghostwritten material, and into a competitive vacuum he strode, briefly establishing his own syndicate in 1917, which was quickly dissolved amidst the outbreak of World War I, before engaging in a lengthy career as journalist and wraith for King Syndicate Features and other outlets (Brands 1954; Menke 1938; Spink 1944).

3 A masterful mythologizer of his own place in sports journalism, Walsh (1938a, 1938b, 1938c) contributed to his later memorialization as the "Father of Ghost Writing" (1956: 22).

engaged in the practice to cast the first stone, and due in part to advocates, such as Walsh, the American Society of Newspaper Editors left the topic unaddressed in its reports on the ethics of sports journalism in the late 1920s (Carvalho 2008; Carvalho, Chung, and Koliska 2018; Roessner 2014). In the end, however, amid a reported 50 percent decrease in the demand for ghostwritten material in 1931, Walsh decided it might behoove him to dissolve his syndicate (Spink 1931). Though the practice of ghostwriting temporarily receded, it remained a constant presence in the world of sport.

4 Unmasking the real ghouls of the game

As *Baseball Digest* correspondent Harold Rosenthal suggested in October 1960, "ghost-writing in baseball goes in cycles" (Rosenthal 1960: 48; Roessner 2014). Thus, though the excesses of exuberant ghostwriting temporarily receded from sports journalism during the height of the Great Depression amid complaints from double-crossed celebrity-athletes and duped readers, industry criticism over the unethical practice, and publisher cost-cutting measures that limited the purchase of ghosted material, demand for behind-the-scenes, player-author accounts resumed in postwar America.

As *Washington Post* sports columnist Shirley Povich (1946, 1955) observed, newspaper publishers not only permitted and profited from a more transparent brand of ghosted material, especially during the World Series, that involved authentic collaborations between moonlighting sportswriters, such as Hy Hurwitz, and star players, such as Boston Red Sox leftfielder Ted Williams. Although sports editors did not adopt uniform standards for disclosing authorship, many incorporated collaborative bylines that featured disclosure statements, such as *with* or *as told by*. Moreover, they otherwise revealed the collaborative practice in news stories (Jones 1967; Orr 1951) that described the transcription of tape-recorded, post-game sessions; the editing process; and the procedure for final player approval. Nonetheless, some detractors in the profession remained and decried the disingenuous practice for limiting material for competing sportswriters (King 1955; Orr 1951; Reporter Yastrzemski 1967). Moreover, even sports reporters, who were uncritical of the practice, admitted that in most cases it contributed to a glut of "gee-whiz" material (Povich 1946).

Breezy ghostwritten accounts never disappeared from sports journalism, but as the decade of change approached, activist athletes and ghostwriters transformed the tone and character of ghostwritten accounts. Robinson, the courageous African American athlete who bravely defied Jim Crow to integrate professional baseball, first signaled this shift when he turned to Roger Kahn, a sympathetic 25-year-old Dodgers beat reporter at the *New York Herald Tribune*, to help expose the brutal racism that he encountered on a daily basis. Shortly after they met in spring 1952, Robinson confessed "this racist stuff is terrible" (Curtis 2014; Kahn 2014). When Kahn agreed that it was indeed abhorrent, the Major League All-Star, commencing his sixth season in the National League, responded, "Then fucking write it" (Curtis 2014).

On several occasions that spring, Kahn attempted to do just that. But each time, editors censored his content, spurning his efforts to expose racism in professional baseball, and insisted that Kahn "WRITE BASEBALL – NOT RACE RELATIONS!" (Kahn 2014: 174). Persistent in his attempts to "smoke out" the bigots, Kahn cunningly divulged racial divisions amongst the team, writing "remarks passed by some Dodgers in the clubhouse and at their hotel indicate the problem of Negroes has still to be finally resolved" in paragraph eight of an otherwise routine column about clubhouse discord (Curtis 2014). Kahn, however, was shocked three days later when the *New York Journal-American* included a ghostwritten column under Robinson's byline, asserting "by no means do we have a racial problem" (Curtis 2014).

Robinson long before recognized that the press box "was by far the most acutely bigoted" arena that he visited (Kahn 2014: 173). And, after the incident of "guerilla ghostwriting" (Curtis 2014), he entreated Kahn to team up with him on *Our Sports*, a specialty monthly magazine featuring player-generated material designed to reach primarily African American audiences with content that the white-owned, mainstream press refused to deliver (Carroll 2019; Kahn 2014; Rampersad 2011). For $150 each issue, Kahn agreed to assist in the editing process, to collaborate on Robinson's regular column, and to pen a piece of his own for the niche magazine designed to attract advertisements from white-owned, mainstream corporations, such as General Motors, with thought-provoking articles about hot-button issues facing African American athletes (Kahn 2014: 180–181). Despite addressing provocative topics, such as race relations and the glass ceiling in the Major League, major white-owned national corporations refused to advertise in the specialty sports magazine geared toward African American audiences, and white male sportswriters at white-owned, mass-circulating newspapers ignored pressing concerns, such as racial inequality, that *Our Sports* exposed. When white sportswriters did engage with a controversial issue, such as Robinson's accusation of salary containment, they focused on exonerating Dodger management and exposing Robinson in misleading readers. Amid this racist milieu, *Our Sports* folded after five issues. However, in the final analysis, Robinson's magazine served as a model for an activist brand of ghostwriting that came into fashion in the coming years and a precursor to celebrity athlete-owned ventures featuring collaboratively produced, player-generated content.

Despite its short-lived existence, *Our Sports* reflected a shift in the tone and character of sports reporting after mid-century propelled by the arrival of a new generation of college-educated athletes and reporters, who rejected the mythologizing involved in the promotional, gee-whiz brand of sports writing that predominated US journalism in the century prior and sought to offer more probing accounts to compete with live broadcast coverage of baseball (Armour 2006; Riess 2015; Roessner 2014; Voigt 1984). Though well-respected veterans, such as New York-based journalist Jimmy Cannon, scorned this new breed of sports journalists, members of the so-called "chipmunk" school, including Dick Young (*New York Daily News*), Leonard Shecter (*New York Post*), Stan Isaacs (*Newsday*), and Larry Merchant (*Philadelphia Daily News*), sought out more hard-hitting news angles, asked tough questions, and interpreted actions along the base paths and in the dugouts and clubhouses against the grain of the national tumult over civil rights and the Vietnam War (Voigt 1984).

Amid this more cynical milieu, Major League pitcher Jim Brosnan harnessed the lingering craze for first-person narratives and exploited the journalistic diary feature format to expose the farce of chummy player-management relationships to *Sports Illustrated* readers in July 1958 after his trade from the Chicago Cubs to the St. Louis Cardinals. Bolstered by the popular demand for tell-all, confessional books, he returned to the trope for Harper & Brothers Publishers the following year to offer a behind-the-scenes look at a professional baseball player's day-to-day life, which included allusions to the pervasive boozing and womanizing that often accompanied road trips (Armour n.d.; Mullins 2013). The critical acclaim that greeted Brosnan's *The Long Season* (1960) coincided with a resurgence in the book publishing industry's demand for first-person, nonfiction narratives about the private lives of prominent individuals in sports, entertainment, and politics. In the coming years, ghostwriters once again teamed up with sports personalities to exploit this new craze for confessional, insider accounts. Moreover, inspired by these alternatives to the once pervasive promotional narratives involving the mythologizing of sports heroes, one unlikely pair of collaborators offered a controversial, behind-the-scenes account of the lives of professional baseball players that accompanied a credibility crisis in American culture and contributed to the transformation of sports journalism (Armour n.d.; Riess 2015).

Still intrigued with Brosnan's day-in-the-life diary, Jim Bouton was warned not to get too chummy with so-called chipmunk sports journalists when he arrived at spring training with the New York Yankees in 1962. But, like so many of his predecessors (Roessner 2014), he warmed up to like-minded reporters, and subsequently, he openly shared his liberal opinions on civil rights and the Vietnam War, a refreshing development for sportswriters searching for good copy on deadline that contributed to their high regard for the rookie (Armour 2011). After Bouton's 1963 breakout season, Shecter reflected this admiration in a flattering profile for *Sport* magazine, praising his pal as a "decent young man in a game which does not recognize decency as valuable" and assuring readers that no matter his fate in baseball he would "make the world a better place" (Armour 2011; Shecter 1964: 73). But the rising star's heyday was short-lived. Still suffering from a nagging bicep injury suffered in 1964, his final season of athletic grandeur, the washed-up hurler struggled to maintain his place on the New York club's roster in 1967 and supplemented his meager baseball salary by documenting, in his first-person narrative for *Sport*, life in the minor leagues during his stint that summer with the club's triple-A affiliate (Bouton 1968).

Likewise recognizing continued demand for insider accounts after the bestselling release of Green Bay Packers' offensive lineman Jerry Kramer's *Instant Replay* (written with Dick Schaap), Shecter, with some assistance from Bouton in spring 1968, offered *Life* magazine readers a candid glimpse inside the American League's 1967 pennant-winning Boston Red Sox clubhouse, exposing the grim reality behind the façade of America's national pastime (Armour 2006; Shecter 1968). In the powerful piece, Shecter contended that during an average season professional athletes endured "an emotional roller coaster – high highs, low lows; the life of the paranoid" (Shecter 1968: 49), but in the final analysis, he observed, "the talk always comes back to what the game is all about – money" and moneymaking potential rooted in identities of players, such as Yastrzemski, who banked on advertising endorsements that doubled their baseball salaries (Shecter 1968: 58).

Several months later, Shecter approached Bouton to exploit his identity as a struggling Major League star to offer readers more of what they were said to crave – a frank, insider's look at the daily lives of professional baseball players designed "to illuminate the game as it never had been before" (Shecter 1970: x). But, as Shecter explained in his enthusiastic introduction to the autobiography, "as usual [Bouton] was ahead of me. 'Funny you should mention that,' he said when I first brought it up. 'I've been keeping notes'" (1970: ix). Over the next season, spent mostly with the Major League expansion club, the Seattle Pilots, Bouton recorded his thoughts and took notes about his day-to-day life in professional baseball. After the tapes were transcribed by typist Elisabeth Rehm, Bouton and Shecter engaged in a collaborative production process, involving long days of "cutting, editing, correcting, [and] polishing" the 1,500 pages of copy down to 520 manuscript pages of material that was ultimately released by World Publishing Company in spring 1970 (Shecter 1970: x).

With the release of the first excerpts of the volume in *Look* magazine's May edition, coming on the heels of Detroit catcher Bill Freehan's *Behind the Mask* (with Steve Gelman and Dick Schaap), *Ball Four – My Life and Hard Times Throwing the Knuckleball in the Big Leagues* unleashed a firestorm of controversy with its revelations of pervasive fornication, adultery, and drug usage in professional baseball. By 1970, ghostwriting had "become a respectable occupation" (Steward 1970: 69), and well-respected book critics, such as Rex Lardner, Jr., Roger Angell, and David Halberstam, praised Bouton for his courageous act and lauded the "book deep in the American vein" as a "welcome" intervention in American life for its work in exposing professional baseball's façade with its narrative of survival in an "ultimately unforgiving business" (Armour 2006: 112). Nevertheless, prominent sports journalists, such as dean of New York sportswriters Dick Young and *New York Journal-American* sports reporter Jimmy Cannon, frustrated over the assault by these competitors to their popular mythological narrative, denigrated the collaborators as "social leper[s]" who sought revenge and denounced their unethical, disingenuous ghostwriting process, lamenting that "one has to speculate where Bouton stops and the ghost begins" (Armour 2006: 112). Despite this disparagement by well-respected veteran sports journalists, the collaborative account offered an authentic, inside look into problematic behind-the-scenes conditions in the national pastime and struck a chord with millions of American readers cynical over disingenuous accounts that they had been offered about national institutions and icons, thereby contributing to the trend toward more investigative reporting in sports journalism moving forward (Armour 2006; Mullins 2013; Riess 2015). These more transparent collaborations between athletes and ghostwriters from the 1950s to the 1970s (a moment that reflected greater reflexivity in response to the credibility crisis in American journalism (Lerner 2019; Pressman 2018)), resulted in alternative accounts on the news stands that contested dominant narratives and exposed systemic racism, sexism, and corruption in Major League baseball (Bouton 1970; Curtis 2014).

6 The menace of ghostwriting's lingering shadow in sports journalism

Despite the decades-long establishment of ethical standards for ghostwriting in sports journalism, more opaque ghostwriting relationships resumed in the 1990s amid trends toward undisclosed, nontransparent ghostwriting arrangements in the book publishing world's genre of nonfiction/autobiography (Baruch 2002; Gietschier 1992; Kakutcad 1979) that predated the disruption to legacy sports outlets by the rise of digital media platforms (Carvalho, Chung, and Koliska 2018). However, amid the disruption to legacy sports outlets by the rise of digital media platforms in the first decade of the 21st century (Carvalho, Chung, and Koliska 2018), the controversial practice of ghostwriting again made headlines within the digital sphere among circles of those involved in the communication industry.

As some leading scholars recently contended, ghostwriting has "adapted to changes in media technology," but "the ethical setting in which it is practiced has undergone considerable transformation, which in turn casts doubt on ghostwriting as a legitimate practice – not only within the field of sports journalism but also increasingly in public relations" (Carvalho, Chung, and Koliska 2018: 2). Though situated in modern professional terms of transparency and credibility, the debate surrounding the legitimacy of ghostwriting in sports journalism and public relations share similar thematic overtones as those negotiated a century prior – as the discourse around the controversy continues to center on the degree of collaboration, message integrity, and audience awareness of the practice.

Moreover, though the ethics of ghosting in journalism and public relations were well established after emerging unevenly over the previous century, communication practitioners wrote column inch after column inch, debating the controversial practices of ghost blogging and tweeting for celebrity athletes in the first two decades of the 21st century. "You'll ... see all manner of buzzwords flying through the discussion: ethics, transparency, integrity, continuity and disclosure, among others," freelance writer Justin P. Lambert (2018) first wrote in a 2011 blog post, warning that the "battle lines have been drawn." Lambert's analysis was apt: in the two decades prior, two sides had emerged, echoing those from a century prior – the staunch critics of ghostwriting, particularly of content for social media, digital spaces that promised more authenticity and transparency, and the proponents of ghostwriting who vehemently defended the practice regardless of the medium.

Nonetheless, amid the glut of ghosted content produced for celebrity athletes, aside of a stray piece of media commentary critiquing the "outrageous" practice in sports journalism (Gietschier 1992: 55) and other fields (Baruch 2002), many journalists and scholars – a segment of whom continued to profit from the practice (Kindred 1991; Seymour Mills 2002) – remained silent about the ethics of ghostwriting in sports journalism until the establishment of competing independent digital sites peddling (primarily ghostwritten) player-generated content.

For instance, soon after Derek Jeter (2014) announced the launch of the *Players' Tribune*, "a new media company that provides athletes with a platform to connect directly with their fans, in their own words" (para 6), the media industry debate around the ethics of ghostwriting in sports journalism returned with a vengeance unseen since the Jazz Age (Carvalho, Chung, and Koliska 2018). For instance, former sportswriter Richard Sandomir (2015) of the *New York Times* revisited the familiar topics of ghostwriting and authorship (Sandomir 1990) in his examination of the athletes who found their voice through the *Players' Tribune* and exposed the disingenuous, undisclosed process behind the first-person accounts featured on the site:

> Like nearly every post on the site, the [Boston Red Sox star David] Ortiz essay [on drug testing in baseball] was not written directly by its bylined athlete but instead crafted from a recorded interview with a *Tribune* staff producer. [Editorial director Gary] Hoenig said these interviews are less traditional question-and-answer sessions than monologues with questions to nudge the conversation along. Editing is minimal, he added, and the athletes get the final approval. The staff producers who talk to them do not get bylines.

Though some industry commentators, such as Sandomir (2015), and scholars, such as Schmittel and Hull (2015), admitted that the site might offer agency to athletes, who hope to share their side of a controversial story, unfiltered by sports journalists, or to uncover problematic conditions in sport (as media outlets, such as *Our Sports*, had in the previous century), many cultural observers focused on the site's ethical lapses (Boudway 2016; Bucholz 2015; Moskovitz 2014), in particular, the lack of candor related to authorship and the collaborative process involved in production of player-generated material.

Moreover, as Carvalho and colleagues (2018) acknowledged, despite the counter-hegemonic promise of such sites for the empowerment of athletes, the lack of transparency exhibited by the *Players' Tribune* and in other ghosted material have broader consequences than duping unsuspecting audiences. In a cultural moment rife with fake news and alternative facts, opaque ghostwritten material might further delegitimize the credibility of both the public relations and journalism industries, contributing to the continued erosion in the health of the US democracy (Carlson and Lewis 2015; Kovach and Rosenstiel 2007).

In the last instance, it is worth remembering a *New York Times* headline, which appeared during the height of the me-decade and still remains true today – "it pays [well] to be a ghost" (Kakutcad 1979), and in spite of similar moments of media industry debate over ethical implications involved in the practice, ghostwriting has continued unabated in sports journalism; in book publishing, particularly in the genre of nonfiction/autobiography; and unrelated areas, such as corporate communications and medical writing, for more than a century. Moreover, it would be naïve to suggest the profitable practice, which has proven effective at offering athletes agency in image negotiation and as a means to expose problematic conditions in sport, might recede in the future. Instead, as Carvalho and colleagues (2018) suggest, in this cultural moment, it would behoove journalists and other communicators to engage in the unfinished act undertaken in the Jazz Age – to establish uniform ethical standards for ghostwriting that emphasize transparency in the collaborative process and honest disclosure of collaborative authorship.

7 Unmasking the secret ghosts: a call for future studies

As Lavin (2016) suggests, the breach by ghostwriters of what theorist Philippe Lejeune referred to as "the autobiographical pact" – the presumption of authenticity entailed by an author's signature – has contributed to the challenge in book history of reconstructing a comprehensive narrative of ghostwriting. Moreover, journalism historians are further prone to avoid this chapter of the past due to the controversial practice's violation of the journalistic promise of trustworthy reporting and the related norm of ethical transparency that emerged in the 20th century (Creech and Roessner 2018). Though case studies on ghostwriting abound in book history, only scant treatments (Carvalho 2007; Carvalho and Ankney 2008; Carvalho, Chung, and Koliska 2018) exist in media history. Therefore, the author recommends future studies that examine the evolving practice of ghostwriting in journalism and book publishing, including ones that consider the agency it offered well-known celebrities and lesser-known journalists, amid the perceived public craze for tell-all, behind-the-scenes accounts in the areas of sports, entertainment, and politics throughout the course of the 20th and 21st centuries.

References

Appel, Marty. 1996. *Slide, Kelly, slide: The wild life and times of Mike "King" Kelly, baseball's first superstar*. Lanham, MD: Scarecrow Press.

Armour, Mark. n.d. Jim Brosnan. *Society for American Baseball Research*. https://sabr.org/bioproj/person/b15e9d74 (18 June 2019).

Armour, Mark. 2006. *Rain check: Baseball in the Pacific Northwest*. Lincoln, NE: University of Nebraska Press.

Armour, Mark. 2011. Jim Bouton. *Society for American Baseball Research*. https://sabr.org/bioproj/person/75723b1f (18 June 2019).

Baruch, Gregory. 2002. Artful Deception. *Washington Post*, 31 March. B1.

Bormann, Ernest G. 1956. Ghostwriting agencies. *Today's Speech* 4(3). 20–30.

Boudway, Ira. 2016. How Derek Jeter got pro athletes into personal essays. *Bloomberg Businessweek*, 23 March. https://www.bloomberg.com/news/articles/2016-03-23/how-derek-jeter-got-pro-athletes-into-personal-essays (18 June 2019).

Bouton, Jim 1968. Returning to the minors. *Sport*, April. 30.

Bouton, Jim & Leonard Shecter (ed.).1970. *Ball four: My life and hard times throwing the knuckleball in the big leagues*. New York: Sports & Recreation.

Boyle, Harold. 1959. Stable of authors: Ghosts write for live clients. *Los Angeles Times*, 6 December. D23.

Brands, Edgar G. 1954. Frank G. Menke. *Sporting News*, 19 May. 30.

Brosnan, Jim. 1960. *The long season*. New York: Harper and Brothers Publishing.

Bucholtz, Andrew. 2015. Players' Tribune articles aren't written by the players, which creates a host of issues. *Awful Announcing*, 30 March. https://awfulannouncing.com/2015/players-tribune-articles-arent-written-by-the-players-which-creates-a-host-of-issues.html (18 June 2019).

Carlson, Matt & Seth C. Lewis. 2015. *Boundaries of journalism: Professionalism, practices and participation*. New York: Routledge.

Carroll, Brian. 2019. "Jackie Robinson says": Robinson's surprising, multifaceted career in journalism. In William M. Simons (ed.), *The Cooperstown Symposium on Baseball and American Culture*, 150–170. New York: McFarland.

Carvalho, John. 2007. The banning of Bill Tilden: Amateur tennis and professional journalism in Jazz-Age America. *Journalism and Mass Communication Quarterly* 84. 122–136.

Carvalho, John. 2014. Journal's sports innovations evolve slowly over time. *Newspaper Research Journal* 35. 40–51.

Carvalho, John & Raymond Ankney. 2008. Haunted by the Babe: Baseball Commissioner Ford Frick's columns about Babe Ruth. *American Journalism* 25. 65–82.

Carvalho, John, Angie Chung & Michael Koliska. 2018. Defying transparency: Ghostwriting for the Jazz Age to social media. *Journalism*. 1–17. doi:10.1177/1464884918804700.

Creech, Brian & Amber Roessner. 2018. Declaring the value of truth. *Journalism Practice* 13(3). 263–279.

Cullen, James Bernard & William Taylor. 1889. *The story of the Irish in Boston*. Boston: J. B. Cullen & Company.

Curtis, Bryan. 2014. Jackie's ghost: Roger Kahn and Jackie Robinson. *Grantland*, 24 October. http://grantland.com/the-triangle/jackies-ghost-roger-kahn-and-jackie-robinson/ (18 June 2019).

Dyer, Braven. 1960. Sports parade. *Los Angeles Times*, 10 October. C2.

Farrell, Frank. 1913. Farrell facts. *Sporting Life*, 1 February. 11.

Father of ghost writing, Christy Walsh dies at 64. *Sporting News*, 11 January. 22.

Freeman, Janet Ing. 2010. "Poor Ralph": The precarious career of a regency hack. *Library* 11. 197–226.

Gerrity, Edward J. 1973. This is my town. John N. Wheeler Player File, National Baseball Hall of Fame Library, Cooperstown, New York.
Gietschier, Steven. 1992. Ghostwriting reaches the point of outrageous. *Sporting News*, 20 January. 55.
Hartt, Rollin L. 1933. Ghost writing. *The Bookman*, March. 22.
Herrmann, August. 1913. Player-scribe. *Sporting Life*, 29 March. 14.
Hudson, Berkley & Karen Boyajy. 2009. The rise and fall of an ethnic advocate and American huckster. *Media History* 15. 287–302.
Jackson, Leon. 2008. *The business of letters: Authorial economies in Antebellum America*. Palo Alto: Stanford University Press.
Jeter, Derek. 2014. The start of something new. *The Players' Tribune*, 1 October. https://www.theplayerstribune.com/en-us/articles/introducing-derek-jeter (18 June 2019).
Johanningsmeier, Charles. 2002. *Fiction and the American literary marketplace: The role of newspaper syndicates in America, 1860–1900*. Cambridge: Cambridge University Press.
Johnson, Ban. 1913. Johnson jolt. *Sporting Life*, 15 March. 8.
Jones, Victor O. 1967. Notes for envelope. *Boston Globe*, 10 September. 61.
Kahn, Roger. 2014. *Rickey and Robinson: The true, untold story of the integration of baseball*. New York: Rodale.
Kakutcad, Michiko. 1979. It pays to be a ghost. *New York Times*, 18 March. https://www.nytimes.com/1979/03/18/archives/it-pays-to-be-aghost-more-and-more-writers-are-ghosting.html (18 June 2019).
Kindred, Dave. 1991. As series go, '91 is one to remember. *Sporting News*, 4 November. 6.
King, Joe 1955. Clouting 'em. *Sporting News*, 19 October. 12.
King, Joe & John George Taylor Spink. 1958. Revelations of a ghost writer. *Sporting News*, 22 October. 5.
Kovach, Bill & Tom Rosenstiel. 2007. *The elements of journalism: What newspeople should know and the public should expect*. New York: Crown.
Lavin, Matthew J. 2016. Reciprocity and the "real" author: Willa Cather as S. S. McClure's ghostwriter. *Auto/Biography Studies* 31. 233–260.
Lampert, Justin P. 2018. That ain't right! ... or is it? Ghostwritten blogposts. *Medium*, 1 September. https://medium.com/@justin_plambert/that-aint-right-or-is-it-ghostwritten-blog-posts-ec9536311c67 (8 April 2020).
Lerner, Kevin. 2019. *Provoking the press: [More] magazine and the crisis of confidence in American journalism*. Columbia: University of Missouri Press.
Littwin, Mike. 1980. Author! Author! *Sporting News*, 14 May. E1.
McGeehan, William O'Connell. 1929. Down the line. *Atlanta Constitution*, 24 September. 24.
Mandell, Richard D. 1984. *Sport: A cultural history*. New York: Columbia University Press.
Menke, Frank G. 1938. "I, too, was a ghost," asserts Menke. *Sporting News*, 10 February. 5.
Moskovitz, Diana. 2014. The Players Tribune says nothing – and that's the point. *Deadspin*, 16 October. https://deadspin.com/the-players-tribune-says-nothing-and-thats-the-point-1644419157 (18 June 2019).
Moskowitz, Eric. 2017. The 10-game winning streak that ignited the Red Sox nation. *Boston Globe*, 21 July. https://www3.bostonglobe.com/metro/2017/07/21/dream/dMzSMBJ36AilLH-WRgeA0FN/story.html?arc404=true (18 June 2019).
Mullins, Bill. 2013. *Becoming big league: Seattle, the Pilots, and stadium politics*. Seattle: University of Washington Press.
Nord, David Paul. 2008. Accuracy or fair play? Complaining about the newspaper in early twentieth-century New York. In Philip Goldstein & James L. Machor (eds.), *New directions in American reception study*, 233–254. New York: Oxford University Press.

Orr, James. 1951. Ghosts have busy series. *Sporting News*, 17 October. 12.
Peet, William. 1913. The public exploitation of expert reputation. *Sporting Life*, 15 March. 8.
Philips, McCandlish. 1973. John N. Wheeler is dead at 87. *New York Times*, 15 October. 40.
Ponce de Leon, Charles. 2002. *Self-exposure: Human-interest journalism and the emergence of celebrity in America, 1890–1940*. Chapel Hill: University of North Carolina Press.
Povich, Shirley. 1946. This morning. *The Washington Post*, 12 September. 10.
Povich, Shirley. 1950. This morning. *The Washington Post*, 24 May. 17.
Povich, Shirley. 1955. This morning. *The Washington Post*, 28 September. 49.
Pressman, Matthew. 2018. *On press: The liberal values that shaped the news*. Boston: Harvard University Press.
Rampersad, Arnold. 2011. *Jackie Robinson: A biography*. New York: Random House Publishing Group.
Reporter Yastrzemski holds back for scoop. 1967. *New York Times*, 6 October. 44.
Rice, Grantland. 1940. The sportlight. *Atlanta Constitution*, 4 August. 2B.
Riess, Steven A. 1999. *Touching base: Professional baseball and American culture in the progressive era*. Chicago: University of Illinois Press.
Riess, Steven A. 2015. *Sports in America from colonial times to the twenty-first century*. New York: Routledge.
Roessner, Lori A. 2010. Remembering the "Georgia Peach": Popular press, public memory and the shifting legacy of an (anti-)hero. *Journalism History* 36. 83–95.
Roessner, Lori A. 2014. *Inventing baseball heroes: Ty Cobb, Christy Mathewson, and the sporting press in America*. Baton Rouge, LA: Louisiana State University Press.
Rosenberg, Howard. 2004. *Cap Anson 2: The theatrical and kingly Mike Kelly: U.S. team sport's first media sensation and baseball's original Casey at the Bat*. New York: Title Books.
Rosenthal, Harold. 1960. Ghosts find World Series their happy hunting grounds. *Baseball Digest*, October. 48.
Sandomir, Richard. 1990. Ghost stories: Author finds success by getting inside the skin and becoming the voice of his collaborators. *Los Angeles Times*, 11 May. https://www.latimes.com/archives/la-xpm-1990-05-11-vw-1140-story.html (18 June 2019).
Sandomir, Richard. 2015. Athletes finding their voice in Derek Jeter's digital venture. *New York Times*, 29 March. https://www.nytimes.com/2015/03/29/sports/athletes-finding-their-voice-in-derek-jeters-digital-venture.html?smid=nytcore-iphone-share&smprod=nytcore-iphone&_r=0 (18 June 2019).
Schmittel, Annelie & Kevin Hull. 2015. "Shit got cray cray #MYBAD": An examination of the image-repair discourse of Richie Incognito during the Miami Dolphins' bullying scandal. *Journal of Sports Media* 10. 115–137.
Seymour Mills, Dorothy Jane. 2002. Ghost writing for baseball historian Harold Seymour. *Nine* 11. 49–58.
Shecter, Leonard. 1964. Jim Bouton – everything in its place. *Sport*, March. 71–73.
Shecter, Leonard. 1968. Baseball: great American myth. *Life*, 9 August. 48–58.
Shecter, Leonard. 1970. Introduction, *Ball four*. New York: World Publishing.
Smythe, Ted Curtis. 1980. The reporter, 1880–1900: Working conditions and their influence on the news. *Journalism History* 7(1). 1–10.
Spink, John George Taylor. 1931. Casual comment. *Sporting News*, 15 October. 4.
Spink, John George Taylor. 1942. Three and One. *Sporting News*, 12 February. 4, 9.
Spink, John George Taylor. 1944. Three and One. *Sporting News*, 19 October. 11.
Steward, Hal D. 1970. *The successful writer's guide*. New York: Parker.
Swartz, Cody. 2008. The great forgotten season: Carl Yastrzemski, 1967. *Bleacher Report*. https://bleacherreport.com/articles/73398-the-great-forgotten-season-carl-yastrzemski-1967 (23 November 2020).

Victor O. Jones, 64, Boston columnist 1970. *New York Times*, 22 April. https://www.nytimes.com/1970/04/22/archives/victor-o-jones-64-boston-columnist.html (18 June 2019).
Voigt, David Q. 1984. From Chadwick to the chipmunks. *Journal of American Culture* 7. 31–37.
Walsh, Christy. 1938a. Adios to ghosts! *Sporting News*, 06 January. 5.
Walsh, Christy. 1938b. Adios to ghosts! *Sporting News*, 13 January. 5.
Walsh, Christy. 1938c. Adios to ghosts! *Sporting News*, 20 January. 5.
Wheeler, John N. 1934. Ghost writer tells all! *Boston Globe*, 7 October. B3.
Wheeler, John N. 1947. I was ghost writer for six great stars. *Boston Globe*, 5 October. A9.
Wheeler, John N. 1949. Baseball memories. *Boston Globe*, 6 April. 20.
Wheeler, John N. 1958. How I got my first job. *Boston Globe*, 13 July. A46.
Wheeler, John N. 1961. *I've got news for you*. New York: E. P. Dutton.
Wiggins, Robert Peyton. 2008. *The Federal League of Base Ball Clubs: The history of an outlaw major league, 1914–1915*. New York: McFarland.
Wilbert, Warren N. 2007. *The arrival of the American League: Ban Johnson and the 1901 challenge to the National League monopoly*. New York: McFarland.

Contributors to this volume

Gashaw Abeza (Ph.D., University of Ottawa) is an Assistant Professor at Towson University. Dr. Abeza has a long-standing and on-going research program studying the impact of social media on the sport industry and its implications for society at large. He has written extensively on the topic of social media in sport, publishing over 45 journal articles and book chapters. He is the co-author of two books: one, on e-sport and a second, on sport marketing. His co-edited book, *Social Media in Sport*, is in press. Abeza serves on the editorial boards of seven different academic journals, and as an ad hoc reviewer for a few.

Pablo Alabarces (Ph.D., University of Brighton) is Professor in Popular Culture in the Faculty of Social Sciences at the Universidad de Buenos Aires (Argentina), where he chaired its Doctoral Program; he is also Superior Researcher at CONICET (National Council for Scientific Research). He is known as one of the founders of Sociology of Sport in Latin America. Among his published books are *Fútbol y Patria* (2002); *Hinchadas* (2005), *Héroes, machos y patriotas. El fútbol entre la violencia y los medios* (2014) and *Historia Mínima del Fútbol en América Latina* (2018).

Mahfoud Amara (Ph.D., Loughborough University) is Associate Professor in Sport Social Sciences & Management at Qatar University. He has published extensively on sport business, culture, and politics in Arab and Muslim contexts. He has conducted research for international organizations and delivered lectures and workshops on his work in the Middle East and North African region and debates about sport and multiculturalism in Europe. He is the author of *Sport, Politics and Society in the Arab World*, editor of *The Olympic Movement and the Middle East and North Africa Region*, and co-editor of *Sport in the African World* and *Sport in Islam and in Muslim Communities*.

David L. Andrews (Ph.D., University of Illinois) is Professor of Physical Cultural Studies in the Department of Kinesiology at the University of Maryland, College Park. His research contextualizes sport and physical culture in relation to the intersecting cultural, political, economic, and technological forces shaping contemporary society. His recent books include: *Making Sport Great Again?: The Uber-Sport Assemblage, Neoliberalism, and the Trump Conjuncture* (2019, Palgrave): *The Routledge Handbook of Physical Cultural Studies* (edited with Michael Silk and Holly Thorpe, 2017, Routledge); and, *Sport, Physical Culture, and the Moving Body: Materialisms, Technologies, Ecologies* (edited with Josh Newman and Holly Thorpe, 2020, Rutgers University Press).

Alina Bernstein (Ph.D., University of Leicester) is a Senior Lecturer at the School of Communications, College of Management, and lectures at the Steve Tisch School of Film and Television, Tel Aviv University. Her main area of research is media and sport, in which she has published extensively. Among her publications are Sport, Media, Culture: Global and Local Dimensions (Frank Cass, 2003, co-edited with Neil Blain) and Bodies of Discourse: Sport Stars, Mass Media and the Global Public (Peter Lang, 2012, co-edited with Cornel Sandvoss and Michael Real). She co-heads the media, communication and sport section at the International Association for Mass Communication Research (IAMCR).

Andrew C. Billings (Ph.D., Indiana University) is the Executive Director of the Alabama Program in Sports Communication and Ronald Reagan Chair of Broadcasting in the Department of Journalism and Creative Media at the University of Alabama. His research interests lie in the intersection of sport, mass media, consumption habits, and identity-laden content. Recent books include *The Rise and Fall of Mass Communication* (with William L. Benoit, Peter Lang, 2020) and *Mascot Nation: The Controversy Over Native American Representations in Sports* (with Jason Edward Black, University of Illinois Press, 2018).

https://doi.org/10.1515/9783110660883-040

Kim Bissell (Ph.D., Syracuse University) is the Southern Progress Endowed Professor in Magazine Journalism and Associate Dean for Research in the College of Communication and Information Sciences at the University of Alabama. She is also the Director of the college's research institute, the Institute for Communication and Information Research. She has done research in health and sports communication for more than 20 years and has received external funding for her work in health disparities and children. Much of her research examines the social effects of media specific to health outcomes in children.

Michael L. Butterworth (Ph.D., Indiana University) is the Governor Ann W. Richards Chair for the Texas Program in Sports and Media, Professor in the Department of Communication Studies, and Director of the Center for Sports Communication & Media at The University of Texas at Austin. His research focuses on rhetoric, democracy, and sport, with particular interests in national identity, militarism, and public memory. He is an author or editor of *Baseball and Rhetorics of Purity*, *Communication and Sport: Surveying the Field*, *Sport and Militarism: Contemporary Global Perspectives*, *Sport, Rhetoric, and Political Struggle*, and *Rhetorics of Democracy in the Americas*.

Younghan Cho (Ph.D., University of North Carolina) is Professor of Korean Studies at the Graduate School of International and Area Studies in Hankuk University of Foreign Studies. He has published widely on global sports and fandom, the Korean Wave and East Asian pop culture, and nationalism and modernity in modern Korea and East Asian society. His monographs include "Global Sports Fandom in South Korea: American Major League Baseball and its Fans in the Online Community" (Palgrave, 2020) and "The Yellow Pacific: Multiple Modernities and East Asia" (SNU Press, 2020, in Korean). He is a founding editor of Palgrave Series of *Sport in Asia*.

Galen Clavio (Ph.D., Indiana University) is an associate professor of sports media at Indiana University, where he also serves as the Director of the National Sports Journalism Center. Clavio has authored over fifty peer-reviewed articles that explore a variety of current areas in sports media and technology. He also is the author of *Social Media and Sports*, a textbook focused on the development of students looking to work in the sports social media industry.

Danielle Sarver Coombs (Ph.D., Louisiana State University) is a professor in the School of Media and Journalism at Kent State University. She is an author, media commentator, and consultant on areas related to sports, politics, and politics of sport. Prior to joining Kent State, Danielle was a consumer insights researcher and brand consultant in New York and Cleveland. Danielle is the author and editor of a number of books and articles, including a textbook on consumer insights research methods (Rowman & Littlefield, 2021) and the forthcoming *Routledge Handbook of Sport Fans and Fandom*.

Courtney M. Cox (Ph.D., University of Southern California) is an assistant professor in the Indigenous, Race, and Ethnic Studies department at the University of Oregon. Her research examines issues related to identity, globalization, and labor within sport. She previously worked for ESPN in Bristol, Connecticut and Longhorn Network in Austin, Texas and has also spent time at NPR-affiliate KPCC in Pasadena, California and with the WNBA's Los Angeles Sparks.

Gregory A. Cranmer (Ph.D., West Virginia University) is an Assistant Professor of Sport Communication at Clemson University and fellow at the Robert H. Brooks Sports Science Institute. His research focuses on optimizing the functioning of sports teams via highlighting the underlying social dynamics associated with athletic coaching and athlete experience. He has authored over 50 works of scholarship, including the 2020 Sue DeWine Distinguished Book: *Athletic Coaching: A Communication Perspective*. He has received early career awards from the National and International Communication Associations for his contributions to Sport Communication.

Natalie Brown-Devlin (Ph.D., University of Alabama) is an Assistant Professor in the Stan Richards School of Advertising & Public Relations and the Associate Director for Research for the Center for Sports Communication & Media at the University of Texas at Austin. Her primary research interests include social identity, crisis communication, and digital media, primarily in the context of sport.

Tyana Ellis (MSPH, Campbell University) is a doctoral student studying Health Communication in the College of Communication and Information Sciences at the University of Alabama. As a Graduate Research Assistant she has done research on various health disparities including mental health and food insecurity, and she has presented at both regional and national conferences. Additionally, as a Graduate Teaching Assistant she has taught courses on Organizational Communication, Small Group Communication, and Public Speaking. Much of her research focuses on health disparities experienced by college students, community health initiatives, and health discourse on social media.

Beth Fielding-Lloyd (Ph.D., Manchester Metropolitan University) is a Principal Lecturer in the Academy of Sport and Physical Activity at Sheffield Hallam University. Her research interests are in the fields of equity policies and media representations of gender and nation in sport. Her work appears in journals such as *Communication & Sport*, the *International Review for the Sociology of* Sport, *Sex Roles*, and *Soccer and Society*.

Walter Gantz (Ph.D., Michigan State University) is professor and associate dean of the Media School at Indiana University. He has been on the faculty at IU since 1979 and has been studying mediated sports fans for about as long.

Daniel A. Grano (Ph.D., Louisiana State University) is a Professor in the Department of Communication Studies at the University of North Carolina at Charlotte. His work focuses on intersections between sport and politics, with particular emphasis on health, the body, race, religion, and public memory. His work appears in the *Quarterly Journal of Speech*, *Rhetoric & Public Affairs*, *Critical Studies in Media Communication*, and *Rhetoric Society Quarterly*. He is the author of *The Eternal Present of Sport: Rethinking Sport and Religion* and co-editor of *Sport, Rhetoric, and Political Struggle*.

Haim Hagay (Ph.D., University of Haifa) is a lecturer at The Department of Communication Studies, Kinneret Academic College and a lecturer at the School of Communication, Netanya Academic College. His research interests include: the intersection of sports media and nationalism, sports media and gender; sports Journalism and Media Production studies.

Kamal Hamidou (Ph.D., University of Paris) is Associate Professor and Head of Mass Communication at Qatar University. His primary research interests are in inter-corporate communication and the sociology of and uses of legacy media and social media. His interests in media and smart devices are within the scope of studying the influence of communication content, processes, and systems on social and socio-cultural change, as well as on perception and cognition processes. He has published in three languages (Arabic, English, and French), and he is a member of the Association for Education in Journalism and Mass Communication and the French Society of Information & Communication Sciences.

Richard Haynes (Ph.D., University of Strathclyde) is Professor of Media Sport and Associate Dean of Research in the Faculty of Arts and Humanities, at the University of Stirling. He is author of several books on communications and sport, including the award winning media history *BBC Sport in Black and White* (Palgrave, 2016).

Brett Hutchins (Ph.D., University of Queensland) is Professor of Media and Communications Studies and Head of the School of Media, Film and Journalism at Monash University, Australia. He has published extensively on sport, media, and environmental conflict. His latest publications appear in *International Journal of Communication, Media, Culture & Society* and *Telematics & Informatics.*

Hatsuko Itaya (M.A., University of Nottingham) is Professor at Hokkaido Musashi Women's Junior College in Japan. As a lifelong learner herself, her research centers on the role languages play in different arenas of life, including sports, education, and international communication. Her current work applies the Economics of Happiness to determine happiness outcomes in different contexts. Her scholarship appears in *Studies in Sports and Language* and *Interpreting and Translation* Studies.

Daniel Jackson (Ph.D., Bournemouth University) is Associate Professor of Media and Communication at Bournemouth University. His research broadly explores the intersections of media, power and social change, including news coverage of politics, political communication, the mediation of sport and the dynamics of civic culture in online environments. He has edited five books and is co-editor of the election analysis reports, published within ten days of major electoral events. Daniel is former convenor of the Political Studies Association's Media and Politics Group and International Liaison for the ICA Sports Communication Special Interest Group.

Jeffrey W. Kassing (Ph.D., Kent State University) is Professor of Communication Studies in the School of Social & Behavioral Sciences at Arizona State University. His research interests include sport and identity, sports media, and soccer. He is the co-director of the Sport, Media, and Culture Research Group at Arizona State University and the co-editor of *Perspectives on the U.S.-Mexico Soccer Rivalry: Passion and Politics in Red, White, Blue and Green.*

John Kelly (Ph.D., University of Loughborough) is the programme director for the Sport and Recreation Management degree at the University of Edinburgh where he is a founding member of the Edinburgh Critical Studies in Sport (ECSS) research group. His research interests are varied and his articles have looked at "sectarianism", sociology of rugby union, symbolic self-representations of ballet dancers, sport and militarism and schoolchildren's virtual idealized body image. He has authored or edited books including the *Routledge Handbook of Sport and Politics, Bigotry, Football and Scotland,* and *Sport and Social Theory: An Introduction.*

Abraham I. Khan (Ph.D., University of Minnesota) is a rhetorical scholar who specializes in research on civic engagement and race, with a particular emphasis on Black athletes and the history of sports in the United States. His book, *Curt Flood in the Media: Baseball, Race, and the Demise of the Activist Athlete*, examines the competing models of public address at work in Black political culture in the late 1960s and 1970s. Other examples of Khan's scholarship link our regard for contemporary Black athletes such as Richard Sherman and Michael Sam to historical public figures such as Jackie Robinson and Muhammad Ali.

Katie Lebel (Ph.D., University of Western Ontario) is an Assistant Professor in the Ted Rogers School of Management at Ryerson University in Toronto, Canada. Her research agenda is grounded in gender equity and investigates the evolution of sport business in the digital era.

Jung Woo Lee (Ph.D., Loughborough University) is the Programme Director of MSc Sport Policy, Management and International Development at the University of Edinburgh, UK. Dr. Lee is a Guest Editor of an annual Asia Pacific Sport and Social Science special issue *of Sport in Society*. He is also an editorial board member of the *Journal of Global Sport Management* and the *Asian Journal of Sport History and Culture*. His research interests lie in sport, diplomacy and international relations. He is currently writing a book, *Sport and Nationalism in Korea* (Palgrave).

Libby Lester (Ph.D., University of Melbourne) is Director of the Institute for Social Change and Professor of Media at the University of Tasmania, Australia. Her research investigates who contributes to public debate and decision-making and how, with a focus on environmental communication. Her latest book is *Global Trade and Mediatised Environmental Protest: The View from Here.*

Katie Lever (M.A., Western Kentucky University) is a doctoral candidate in the Department of Communication Studies at The University of Texas at Austin, where she studies NCAA discourse. She is also a freelance sportswriter who educates audiences about the realities of college sports. She writes primarily for LRTsports.com and has also been published in Tropics of Meta, Extra Points, and Fansided. As a former Division 1 athlete and current member of the Drake Group, Katie is passionate about reforming collegiate athletics.

Nicky Lewis (Ph.D., Indiana University) is an assistant professor in the Department of Communication at the University of Kentucky. Her research interests center on the social psychological processing and effects of mass media, especially as they relate to the consumption of sports and entertainment content. Her research has been published in *Communication & Sport*, *Journalism & Mass Communication Quarterly*, and *Journal of Media Psychology.*

Jennifer McClearen (Ph.D., University of Washington) is a feminist media scholar whose research examines the cultural production of difference in popular media with a focus on sports and consumer culture. She is an assistant professor of media studies in the Department of Radio-Television-Film at The University of Texas at Austin where she is also affiliated faculty with the Center for Sports Communication & Media. Her research can be found in *Communication & Sport*, *Feminist Media Studies*, and the *International Journal of Communication*, among others. Dr. McClearen published her first monograph, *Fighting Visibility: Sports Media and Female Athletes in the UFC*, in 2021.

Lindsey Meân (Ph.D., University of Sheffield) is an Associate Professor in the School of Social and Behavioral Sciences in the New College of Interdisciplinary Arts and Sciences at Arizona State University and an affiliated faculty member with the Global Sport Institute. Her research focuses on the intersection of identities, sport, gender and sexuality, ideology and culture, discourses, language, and representational practices across multiple sites and levels of enactment. Her work appears in journals such as the *American Behavioral Scientist*, *Communication & Sport*, the *Journal of Language and Social Psychology*, and *Soccer and Society.*

Toby Miller (Ph.D., Murdoch University) is Stuart Hall Professor of Cultural Studies, Universidad Autónoma Metropolitana—Cuajimalpa and Sir Walter Murdoch Distinguished Collaborator, Murdoch University. The author and editor of over fifty books, his work has been translated into Spanish, Chinese, Portuguese, Japanese, Turkish, German, Italian, Farsi, French, Urdu, and Swedish. His most recent volumes are *Violence*, *The Persistence of Violence: Colombian Popular Culture*, *How Green is Your Smartphone?*, *El trabajo cultural*, *Greenwashing Culture*, *Greenwashing Sport*, *The Routledge Companion to Global Cultural Policy*, *Global Media Studies*, *The Routledge Companion to Global Popular Culture*, *Greening the Media*, and *Blow Up the Humanities*. *A COVID Charter, a Better Future* is in press.

Brian Moritz (Ph.D., Syracuse University) is an associate professor and the Journalism MA programs director at St. Bonaventure University. A former award-winning sports reporter and columnist, Moritz previously taught at SUNY-Oswego, has had research published in the *International Journal of Communication and Sport* and *Communication & Sport*, and served as president of the AEJMC Sports Communication Interest Group. Moritz is the author of the Sports Media Guy blog, and received his graduate degrees from Syracuse University and his undergraduate degree from St. Bonaventure.

Chuka Onwumechili (Ph.D., Howard University) is Professor of Strategic, Legal, and Management Communications at Howard University in Washington, DC. Onwumechili serves as Editor-In-Chief of the *Howard Journal of Communications*. He has authored and co-authored more than 10 books and several peer-reviewed journal articles. Among his recent books are *Africa's Elite Football: Structure, Politics, and Every Day Challenges; Sport Communication: An International Approach*; and *Identity and Nation in African Football: Fans, Community and Clubs*. His recent journal articles appear in the *International Review of the Sociology of Sports, Soccer & Society, Sport in Society,* and the *International Journal of Communication*.

Norm O'Reilly (Ph.D., Carleton University) is Professor and Founding Director of the International Institute for Sport Business & Leadership in the Gordon S. Lang School of Business & Economics at the University of Guelph, and is recognized as one of the leading scholars in the business of sports. He has authored 15 books, and more than 140 journal articles. He was awarded the Career Achievement Award by the American Marketing Association's Sport Marketing Special Interest Group and is a Fellow of the North American Society for Sport Management. He was Deputy Chef for the Canadian Team at the 2016 Paralympic Games.

Ann Pegoraro (Ph.D., University of Nebraska) is the Lang Chair in Sport Management in the Gordon S. Lang School of Business and Economics at the University of Guelph and is also the co-Director of E-Alliance, the Research Hub for Gender Equity in Canadian Sport. Dr. Pegoraro's research focuses on sport consumers, marketing and communication, including how different forms of media are used to establish connections with consumers of sport. Her recent work in digital media is focused on analytics, gender and diversity.

Emma Pullen (Ph.D., Loughborough University) is a lecturer in the sociology of sport and sport management at Loughborough University, UK. Her research focuses on Parasport media and broadcast, gender (feminisms) at the intersection of disability, and social inclusion. Emma has published several articles on these topics in journals such as *Media, Culture & Society, Cultural Studies* and, *European Journal of Communication*. She can be found at @DrEmmaPullen.

Lori Amber Roessner (Ph.D., University of Georgia), an associate professor at the University of Tennessee's School of Journalism & Electronic Media, teaches and studies media history and its relationship to cultural phenomena and practices, including the operation of politics, the negotiation of public images and collective memories, and the construction of race, gender, and class. She is the author of *Inventing Baseball Heroes: Ty Cobb, Christy Mathewson and the Sporting Press in America*, and *Jimmy Carter and the Birth of the Marathon Media Campaign*, and co-editor of *Political Pioneer of the Press: Ida B. Wells-Barnett and Her Transnational Crusade for Social Justice*.

David Rowe (Ph.D., University of Essex, FAHA, FASSA) is Emeritus Professor of Cultural Research, Institute for Culture and Society, Western Sydney University; Honorary Professor, Faculty of Humanities and Social Sciences, University of Bath; and Research Associate, Centre for International Studies and Diplomacy, SOAS University of London. His books include *Global Media Sport* (2011); *Sport Beyond*

Television (2012); *Sport, Public Broadcasting, and Cultural Citizenship* (2014), and *Making Culture* (2018). A frequent commentator in (inter)national media, he received the Australian Sociological Association Distinguished Service to Sociology Award in 2018 and the International Communication Association's Sport Communication Interest Group Legacy Award for lifetime scholarly achievement in 2020.

Brody J. Ruihley (Ph.D., University of Tennessee) is an Associate Professor of Sport Leadership & Management and Assistant Chair of the Department of Sport Leadership & Management at Miami University in Oxford, Ohio (USA). Ruihley's educational background consists of a bachelor's degree in Communication from the University of Kentucky (2005), a master's degree in Sport Administration from the University of Louisville (2006), and a doctorate degree in Sport Studies from the University of Tennessee (2010). Ruihley's primary research interests lie in the areas of fantasy sport, sport marketing, and public relations in sport.

Alfredo Sabbagh Fajardo (M.A., Universidad del Norte) is a professor in the School of Social Communication and Journalism at the Universidad del Norte in Barranquilla, Colombia, where he has served as Director of the School and the Media Production Center. He combines teaching with media production, broadcast journalism, and a newspaper column.

Jimmy Sanderson (Ph.D., Arizona State University) is an Assistant Professor in the Department of Kinesiology and Sport Management at Texas Tech University. His research centers on social media and its intersections in sport along with family communication in sport. His work has appeared in outlets such as *Communication & Sport, International Journal of Sport Communication, and Western Journal of Communication.*

Karsten Senkbeil (Ph.D., University of Heidelberg) is an assistant professor at the University of Hildesheim, Germany, in the Department of Intercultural Communication. He has researched and published on sports cultures worldwide, and particularly on transcultural exchange processes between North America and Europe through sports and in other areas of popular culture. His current research combines methodologies from cognitive linguistics, applied linguistics, intercultural pragmatics, and discourse analysis to explore the impact of digital technology on inter- and transcultural communication.

Brett Siegel (M.A., University of Southern California) is a Ph.D. Candidate and Assistant Instructor in Media Studies in the Department of Radio-Television-Film at the University of Texas-Austin's Moody College of Communication. His research focuses on power, ideology, and identity in sports and sports media. He has published articles in the *Journal of Sport and Social Issues* and the *Journal of Emerging Sport Studies*, and he has an article forthcoming in *The International Journal of the History of Sport.*

Michael Silk (Ph.D., University of Otago) is a Professor and Deputy Dean (Research & Professional Practice) in the Bournemouth University Business School. He is Director of the Bournemouth University Sport & Physical Activity Research Centre (SPARC) and former Managing Editor of *Leisure Studies.* His research and scholarship is interdisciplinary; he has published over 150 articles, chapters and books on the various relationships between sport & physical activity (physical culture), mediated spectacle, and inequality.

Markus Stauff (Ph.D., Utrecht University) is Associate Professor at the University of Amsterdam's (UvA) Media Studies department of (UvA). His main research interests are television and digital media, governmentality, and the visual culture of media sports. Recent publications on sports are: "A Culture of Competition: Sport's Historical Contribution to Datafication." TMG – Journal for Media History 21.2 (2018); "Formatting Cross-Media Circulation: On the Epistemology and Economy of Sports Highlights." In Format Matters. Standards, Practices, and Politics in Media Cultures, edited by Marek Jancovic, Axel Volmar, and Alexandra Schneider, meson press 2020. Accessible at: http://www.uva.nl/profiel/s/t/m.stauff/m.stauff.html.

Sabitha Sudarshan (M.A., Mudra Institute of Communications) is a Ph.D. candidate in the Stan Richards School of Advertising & Public Relations at the University of Texas at Austin. Her dissertation investigates the nature of social capital of social media influencers, and the personality facets that influence their relationship with their followers. For the past 3 years, her research interests have primarily spanned across Human-Computer Interaction (HCI), in such varied contexts as anti-smoking websites, recommendation systems and 360-degree videos.

Ilan Tamir (Ph.D., Bar-Ilan University) is Head of the School of Communication at Ariel University. His research focuses on the connection between sports, society, and the media. He has served as a visiting researcher at Harvard University and serves as a research fellow at the Center for Sports Research at Northeastern University in Boston. He is rated as one of 12 inspiring lecturers by the National Union of Israeli Students.

Lee Thompson (Ph.D., Osaka University) is Professor in the Faculty of Sport Sciences, Waseda University, Japan, researching the relationship between sport and the media in Japan, with a focus on sumo. He has published in the *International Review for the Sociology of Sport*, *Sport in Society*, and the *International Journal of the History of Sport*, as well as a range of Japanese publications, and is coauthor of *Japanese Sports: A History*. He is past president of the Japan Society of Sport Sociology, and a commentator on the live sumo broadcasts of the Japan Broadcasting Corporation (NHK).

Irene I. van Driel (Ph.D., Indiana University) is a postdoctoral researcher at the Amsterdam School of Communication Research (ASCoR) and the Center for research on Children, Adolescents, and the Media (CcaM). She is broadly interested in the intersection of media and socioemotional wellbeing across the lifespan, such as emotion-regulation and changes in sports fanship with age.

Travis Vogan (Ph.D., Indiana University) is Associate Professor in the School of Journalism and Mass Communication and the Department of American Studies at the University of Iowa. His most recent book is *The Boxing Film: A Cultural and Transmedia History* (Rutgers University Press).

Lawrence A. Wenner (Ph.D., University of Iowa) is Von der Ahe Professor of Communication and Ethics at Loyola Marymount University in Los Angeles. He is founding Editor of the bi-monthly research journal *Communication & Sport*, and former editor of the *International Review for the Sociology of Sport* and the *Journal of Sport & Social Issues*. With ten books and over 140 scholarly journal articles and book chapters, his work focuses on sport, media, gender, and commodity culture. His recent books include *Sport, Media, and Mega-Events* (with Andrew Billings). An upcoming work, the *Oxford Handbook of Sport and Society*, will be published in 2022.

Elisabetta Zengaro (M.A., Delta State University) is a Ph.D. candidate at The University of Alabama in Communication and Information Sciences researching mental health communication and stigma in college sports. Her research and teaching interests include sport and health communication. She earned her Bachelor's degree in journalism and Master's degree in Sport and Human Performance from Delta State University where she worked in sports media as a graduate assistant for Delta State Athletics.

Index

https://doi.org/10.1515/9783110660883-041

www.ingramcontent.com/pod-product-compliance
Lightning Source LLC
Chambersburg PA
CBHW080116020526
44112CB00037B/2751

* 9 7 8 3 1 1 1 2 5 7 8 3 9 *